Rare and threatened
Bryophytes *of* IRELAND

First published 2012

ISBN 978 1 905989 35 5
National Museums Northern Ireland Publication No. 028

Published by
National Museums Northern Ireland
153 Bangor Road
Cultra
Holywood
County Down
BT18 0EU
Northern Ireland
www.nmni.com

Printed by Nicholson & Bass Ltd

Rare and threatened Bryophytes *of* IRELAND

Sphagnum skyense and *Polytrichum commune*, Mweelrea, Co. Mayo.

Neil Lockhart   Nick Hodgetts   David Holyoak

Sruhauncullinmore River, Mweelrea, Co. Mayo.

Ministerial Foreword

BRYOPHYTES ARE ALL AROUND US. To a great extent they are overlooked yet they are a vitally important component of the vegetation in many parts of the world and constitute a major part of both the biomass and the biodiversity in forest, wetland and mountain ecosystems. Their capacity to retain water facilitates gradual release of water into watercourses, thus regulating flash floods, erosion and landslides downstream. They are important in stabilising soils through their ability to colonise exposed ground, and are a major constituent of peat bogs and therefore contribute to carbon sequestration.

Ireland's temperate and humid climate provides suitable conditions for a particularly rich bryophyte flora, with 835 taxa, representing nearly 48% of the entire European flora. Ireland has a particular responsibility for the conservation of those bryophyte species and habitats that are rare on a global scale, such as the Atlantic communities of large liverworts in wet heath in the hills, the remaining stands of Atlantic woodland, the remnants of the midland bogs, the dune slack and machair communities of the west coast and the unique bryophyte assemblages to be found in the Dartry Mountains.

This volume gives a detailed review of the distribution, status, ecology, threats and conservation of those liverworts and mosses that are rare or declining in Ireland. IUCN criteria are used to assess status, on the basis of distribution, population sizes and any evidence of decline, so that the book provides the first Red List for the bryophytes of all of Ireland. For each species the status of populations in Ireland is also compared to that in Europe as a whole. Hence this study establishes an agenda for the conservation of the most threatened species by ranking them in order of priority, identifying the most important areas in which they occur and outlining practical concerns in managing their populations and habitats.

This book results from a collaborative programme of research by National Parks and Wildlife Service in the Republic of Ireland and Northern Ireland Environment Agency (formerly EHS). These studies have involved fieldwork annually from 1999–2010, during which almost all previously known sites for rare bryophytes in Ireland have been revisited, in all the counties. This intensive field research has also resulted in many finds of rare species at new localities, including 22 species previously unknown in Ireland. This work is not just a testament to cross-border co-operation but also to the painstaking dedication of the authors in producing such a comprehensive, valuable and visually pleasing book.

Jimmy Deenihan, TD
Minister for Arts, Heritage and the Gaeltacht

Alex Attwood, MLA
Minister, Department of the Environment

Contents

List of tables

Preface

I AM DELIGHTED to have been invited to write the preface to *Rare and Threatened Bryophytes of Ireland*. This work is the product of over ten years' research and survey. At its inception, I recall being asked by Neil Lockhart to lend my support, as then Director of the National Botanic Gardens, Glasnevin, and to become external supervisor to the project as it evolved. So it is with interest that I have kept a watching brief on its progress over the years, and wonderful to see the results of all this labour come to fruition in this magnificent book.

When I started as a bryologist in the 1960s, Ireland was a good place for the beginner. The richness of the Irish flora had been demonstrated by the early collectors such as Hutchins and Taylor and further expanded by the early twentieth-century workers that included Waddell and Lett. However, from the census catalogues of the British Bryological Society (BBS), it was clear that recording in Ireland had fallen behind. Bryologists were thin on the ground.

Mrs A.L. Kathleen King was then the resident star. She lost no opportunity to find new vice-county records, either with the Dublin Naturalists' Field Club or the forestry society which went to places beyond the reach of public transport. A foresters' meeting at Ravensdale led to the discovery of *Ptilidium pulcherrimum*, still the only Irish record. Prompted by T.A. Barry of Bord na Móna she had found *Tomentypnum nitens* and *Meesia triquetra*, new to Ireland, at Bellacorick in Mayo. A later find of *Tomentypnum* at Scragh Bog near Mullingar coaxed her to join me for a memorable day out to refind it, regrettably one of the few occasions when we joined forces in the field.

Analysing peat profiles for the same T.A. Barry created an awareness of changes in the bryophyte cover over time. The great fens with *Paludella*, *Meesia* and *Tomentypnum* were eventually overcome by lawns of *Sphagnum fuscum* and *S. austinii* and these in turn by *Sphagnum capillifolium* and *S. papillosum*. This was natural succession, sometimes aided by climatic change. The discovery of a living population of *Paludella* in Mayo was as unexpected as it was welcome, another remarkable relict of a disappearing flora. When Neil Lockhart told me of the *Paludella* find, I could not hide my astonishment and recall saying that a more exciting find would hardly ever be made in Ireland.

Change, however, was now happening all around aided by building developments, drainage, pollution, overgrazing and peat erosion. A growing unease led to the establishment of An Foras Forbartha where the first official steps towards conservation of what was good and desirable in the countryside were taken.

The BBS continued to use the census catalogues to encourage bryological recording in the poorly worked vice-counties, but also began work for an atlas of bryophyte distribution. My early bryology was of the lucky dip kind – sketchy and not well focused and based on a belief that all but the largest species should be checked under the microscope. A first meeting with the BBS was something of a revelation. It was based at Clonmel where the participants included such luminaries as Jean Paton, Jean and Bob Fitzgerald, Joan Appleyard, Jeff Duckett and George Argent. Most came armed with desiderata lists for the adjacent vice-counties. No opportunity to record was missed: car parks, town walls, hotel steps and old motor cars were searched before breakfast and after dinner, while normal working hours were reserved for the designated targets of mountains, wooded valleys, bogs and fens and stubble fields. The recently described *Fissidens celticus* was actively sought and duly found in a number of places. The confident identification of bryophyte specimens in the field using the ×20 lens was impressive and inspirational.

This dedication to recording was amusingly demonstrated by Bob Fitzgerald on the drive up the forest track to Galtymore. A fallen Sitka Spruce blocked the way. The more robust members lifted the trunk and heaved it off the road. Bob was on the downhill side and tumbled into a deep ditch. After an anxious silence he emerged unscathed and announced '*Ditrichum heteromallum*' for the day's record card!

The BBS holds a field meeting in Ireland about every four years, usually based at two different locations. I have been privileged to join the meetings held at Clonmel, Sligo, Arklow, Limerick, Glengarriff, Killorglin, Kenmare, Derry, Donegal, Westport, Achill and Clifden. The Achill meeting resulted in a bryophyte flora of the island and a day spent on Clare Island has made an important contribution to the New Survey of the island. Most visits resulted in additions to the Irish flora and large numbers of vice-county records as well as well-marked cards for the mapping schemes. Younger Irish botanists who joined in were encouraged to study bryophytes and given much ongoing help from experienced members of the Society.

Recording for the bryophyte atlas led me to concentrate on the underworked Midlands in a swathe that took in Meath, Westmeath, Longford, Roscommon and parts of Mayo, making useful, if not spectacular, discoveries in the process but leaving much still to be done there and elsewhere in the country. It is hardly surprising that in these limestone areas *Neckera complanata* was the only constant on the dozens of 10 km grid cards returned to Tony Smith, the Mapping Secretary.

The National Parks and Wildlife Service, and the Northern Ireland Environment Agency, have been working systematically on the various gaps in the coverage of the country as well as on the conservation of the rarer species. The records of generations of bryologists from Ireland, Great Britain and further afield have been assembled and provide a basis for the work. However, very significant additional contributions have been made by the authors of this book. Thanks to their dedicated work in the field, at the microscope and in the office, we know much more than when they first proposed it. It is a major aid to Irish bryology and an important reference for conservation and planning for the future.

Donal Synnott
14th February 2012

Richard Lewington 2011

Campylostelium saxicola, Luke's Bridge, Benbulbin, Co. Sligo.

Acknowledgements

MUCH OF THE recent research on bryophytes in Ireland and the work preparing this book has been funded jointly by the National Parks and Wildlife Service and the Northern Ireland Environment Agency. This funding is gratefully acknowledged, along with the hard work of colleagues in both agencies in sustaining the project over the past decade. Particular thanks are due to Dr Tom Curtis, for his encouragement at the inception of this project, to Dr Colmán Ó Críodáin, Dr Andy Bleasdale and Dr Ciaran O'Keeffe for their sustained support at NPWS, and to Richard Weyl for promoting bryophyte conservation in Northern Ireland throughout this period. The assistance of the many NPWS and NIEA field staff in facilitating access to lands is also gratefully acknowledged.

Our work has been underpinned by loans of herbarium specimens from BBSUK, BEL, DBN, E and NMW for which the respective curators are thanked, as are those at Truro Museum for assistance in receiving some loans. We have also received much help during visits to study material at BM and S. Recorders of the British Bryological Society have checked many specimens resulting from fieldwork in Ireland carried out over the past decade, principally Tim Blackstock and Gordon Rothero, but also their successors Sam Bosanquet and Tom Blockeel. Access to data from the Biological Records Centre and CEDaR has also been fundamental to our studies. Nick Stewart provided the detailed notes he prepared during earlier work for a Red Data Book covering Irish bryophytes. Donal Synnott allowed use of his detailed typescript catalogue of Irish liverwort records.

We are indebted to Dr Damian McFerran, at CEDaR, Marianne McKeown, at NMNI and to Robert Thompson, natural history photographer, for their invaluable contributions to the editing, design and publication of this book. Particular thanks are due to Mel Conway, GIS Technician at NPWS, for analysis of record data and the design and compilation of all the maps. Maps are reproduced under Ordnance Survey Ireland Licence Number EN 0059208, © Ordnance Survey Ireland/Government of Ireland. Met Éireann, UK Met Office and Geological Survey of Ireland are acknowledged for granting permission to use their data for the rainfall and solid geology maps. Many bryologists very generously allowed us to reproduce their photographs, with major contributions from Dr Michael Lüth and Dr Des Callaghan, but also from Prof. John Birks, Sam Bosanquet, Dr Joanne Denyer, Prof. Jan-Peter Frahm, Dr Tomas Hallingbäck, Rory Hodd, Richard Lansdown, Dr David Long, Graham Motley, Alan Orange, Dr Caroline Pannell, Ron Porley, Gordon Rothero, Dr Norbert Schnyder, Dr Jonathan Sleath, Robert Thompson and Prof. David Wagner. Thanks are also due to Alexandra Caccamo, Librarian at the National Botanic Gardens, Dublin; Kenneth James, National Museums Northern Ireland, and the archives of the British Bryological Society for assistance with providing images of bryologists and past bryological meetings. Dr Charles Nelson kindly gave permission to use the image of a portrait of Walter Wade, reproduced from *The Brightest Jewel* (Nelson & McCracken 1987).

Help is acknowledged from many individuals with specimens, provision of information and comments on drafts of the text, especially: John Blackburn, Tom Blockeel, Sam Bosanquet, Dr Agneta Burton, Muiris de Buitléir, Christina Campbell, Dr Linda Coote, Dr John Cross, Caitríona Douglas, Prof. Jeff Duckett, Len Ellis, Dr Catherine Farrell, Richard Fisk, Howard Fox, Dr Karen Gaynor, Mary Ghullam, Paul Hackney, Clare Heardman, Dr Lars Hedenäs, Dr Mark Hill, Rory Hodd, Geraldine Holyoak, Dr Matthew Jebb, Dr Daniel Kelly, Dr Naomi Kingston, Heribert Köckinger, Dr Jan Kučera, Willem Labeij, Richard Lansdown, Dr David Long, Howard Matcham, Dr Caroline Mhic Daeid, Rosaline Murphy, Dr Angela Newton, Dr Fionnuala O'Neill, Jean Paton MBE, Dr Niklas Pedersen, Dr Philip Perrin, Roy Perry, Dr Peter Pitkin, Ron Porley, Dr Chris Preston, Patrick Reilly, Dr Fred Rumsey, Jim Ryan, Dr David Rycroft, Prof. Mark Seaward, Dr Noeleen Smyth, Dr Philip Stanley, Dr Georgina Thurgate, Prof. Jiri Váňa, Sally Whyman, Jo Wilbraham, Edwin Wymer, Dr Michael Wyse Jackson and Mark Wright.

Abbreviations

ASSI	Area of Special Scientific Interest (in Northern Ireland)
auct.	of authors
b.	born
BBS	British Bryological Society
BBSUK	Herbarium of British Bryological Society, at National Museum and Gallery of Wales, Cardiff
BEL	Herbarium of Ulster Museum, Belfast
BFNA	Bryophyte Flora of North America (online web site)
BFT	Herbarium of Department of Botany, The Queen's University, Belfast
BM	Herbarium of Department of Botany, The Natural History Museum, London
BRC	Biological Records Centre (UK)
C.	central
c.	*circa* (approximately)
CBD	Convention on Biological Diversity
CEDaR	Centre for Environmental Data and Recording (Northern Ireland)
CC	*Census Catalogue* of MEC or BBS
cf.	compare with
Co.	County
Cos	Counties
CR	Critically Endangered
d.	died
DBN	Herbarium of National Botanic Gardens, Glasnevin, Dublin
DD	Data Deficient
E	Herbarium of Royal Botanic Garden, Edinburgh, Scotland
E.	east
e.g.	for example
EN	Endangered
ESE	east-south-east
et al.	and others
etc.	and so forth
EU	European Union
EW	Extinct in the Wild
EX	Extinct
f.	form
FNA	Flora of North America
GPS	Global Positioning System
IBrA	Important Bryophyte Area
in litt.	*in litteris* (in correspondence)
INJ	*Irish Naturalists' Journal*
IPA	Important Plant Area
IUCN	International Union for Conservation of Nature
leg.	collected by
LGM	Last Glacial Maximum (c. 26,000 years ago)

Ma	Megaannum, one million years
MEC	Moss Exchange Club
MS.	Manuscript
MSS	Manuscripts
N.	north
NBDC	National Biodiversity Data Centre (Republic of Ireland)
NBN	National Biodiversity Network
NE	north-east (direction) and Not Evaluated (IUCN threat status)
NGO	non-governmental organisation
NHA	Natural Heritage Area (Republic of Ireland)
NIEA	Northern Ireland Environment Agency (formerly Environment and Heritage Service of Department of Environment)
NNE	north-north-east
NNR	National Nature Reserve (in Northern Ireland)
NNW	north-north-west
No.	number
nom. illeg.	illegitimate name
NPWS	National Parks and Wildlife Service
NT	Near Threatened
NVC	National Vegetation Classification
NW	north-west
pNHA	proposed Natural Heritage Area (Republic of Ireland)
pp.	pages
p.p.	*pro parte* (in part)
q.v.	*quod vide* (which see)
RE	Regionally Extinct
S	Herbarium of Swedish Museum of Natural History, Stockholm, Sweden
S.	south
SAC	Special Area of Conservation (protected under European law)
SE	south-east
s.l.	*sensu lato* (in the wider sense)
s.str.	*sensu stricto* (in the narrow sense)
subsp.	subspecies
SW	south-west
syn.	synonym(s)
TCD	Herbarium of Trinity College, Dublin
U	Herbarium of Institute for Systematic Botany, Utrecht, the Netherlands
μm	micron
var.	variety
Vol.	volume
VU	Vulnerable
W.	west

Torc waterfall, Co. Kerry.

Maps

Map 1. Relief, drainage and main towns.

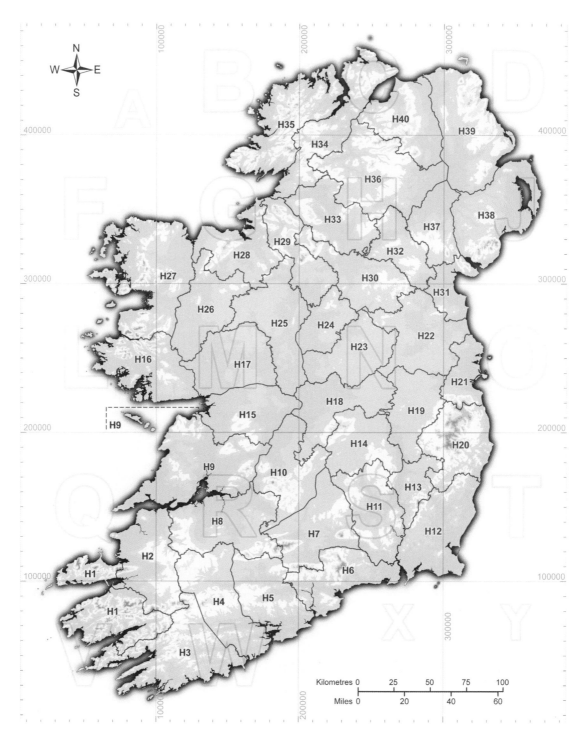

Map 2. Vice-counties, 100 km Irish Grid co-ordinates and sub-zone letters.

1. South Kerry	9. Clare	17. North-east Galway	25. Roscommon	33. Fermanagh
2. North Kerry	10. North Tipperary	18. Offaly	26. East Mayo	34. East Donegal
3. West Cork	11. Kilkenny	19. Kildare	27. West Mayo	35. West Donegal
4. Mid Cork	12. Wexford	20. Wicklow	28. Sligo	36. Tyrone
5. East Cork	13. Carlow	21. Dublin	29. Leitrim	37. Armagh
6. Waterford	14. Laois	22. Meath	30. Cavan	38. Down
7. South Tipperary	15. South-east Galway	23. Westmeath	31. Louth	39. Antrim
8. Limerick	16. West Galway	24. Longford	32. Monaghan	40. Londonderry

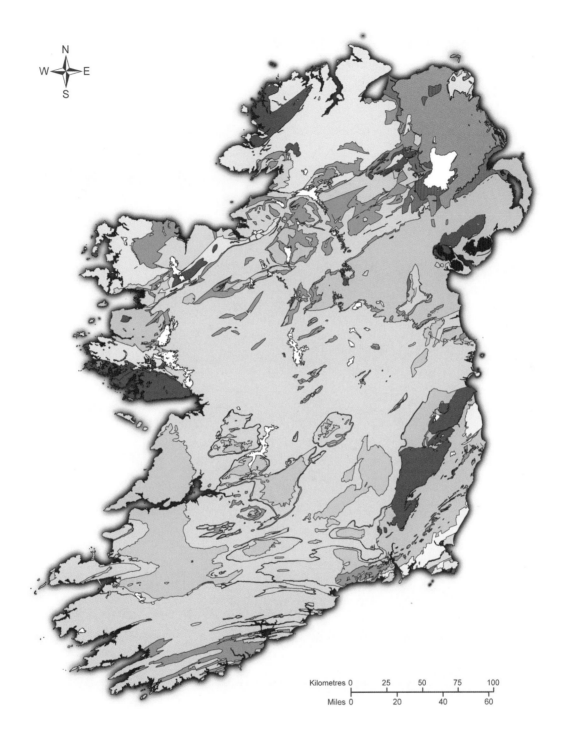

Map 3. Bedrock geology.

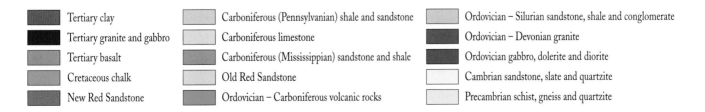

Tertiary clay	Carboniferous (Pennsylvanian) shale and sandstone	Ordovician – Silurian sandstone, shale and conglomerate
Tertiary granite and gabbro	Carboniferous limestone	Ordovician – Devonian granite
Tertiary basalt	Carboniferous (Mississippian) sandstone and shale	Ordovician gabbro, dolerite and diorite
Cretaceous chalk	Old Red Sandstone	Cambrian sandstone, slate and quartzite
New Red Sandstone	Ordovician – Carboniferous volcanic rocks	Precambrian schist, gneiss and quartzite

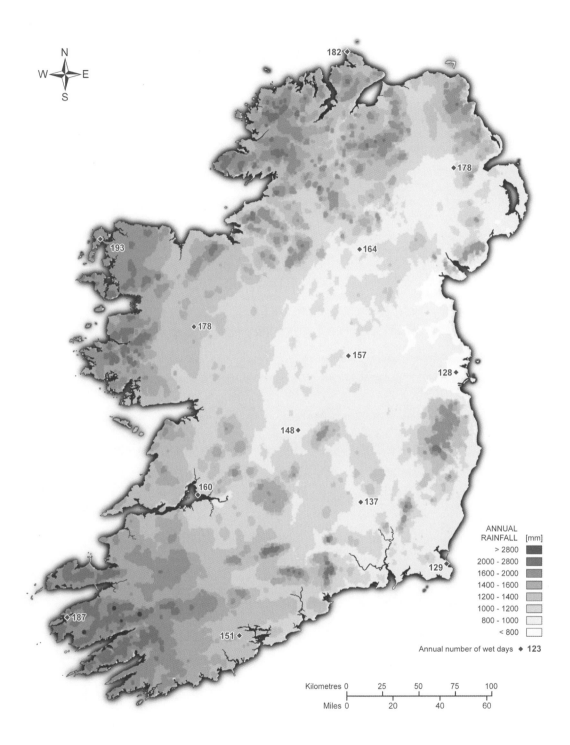

Map 4. Mean annual rainfall and number of wet days (days with ≥ 1 mm rainfall) 1961–1990.

CHAPTER ONE

Introduction

Dumortiera hirsuta, Killarney, Co. Kerry.

Aims

THIS BOOK aims to fill a gap in the knowledge of the Irish flora by reviewing and updating information on the status of Ireland's bryophytes (mosses and liverworts). It presents the results of a critical reappraisal of the literature and herbarium records for over 300 taxa (over one-third of the known flora) and incorporates the findings of 10 years' field research into the distribution, ecology and conservation status of the rarest and most threatened of the Irish bryophytes. It is not intended as an introduction to the structure and biology of bryophytes, these large subjects being covered in several other works including an introduction by Watson (1971) and more detailed accounts from varying points of view by Schuster (ed., 1983, 1984), Schofield (1985), Crum (2001) and Goffinet & Shaw (2009). Nor is it intended as a diagnostic flora for the identification of species, for which the reader is directed to the standard floras of Ireland and Britain, for hornworts and liverworts by Paton (1999) and mosses by Smith (2004), and the introductory field guide by Atherton *et al.* (2009).

Introductory chapters on the origins of the bryophyte flora, important bryophyte habitats and the history of bryophyte recording in Ireland are followed by chapters on the application of IUCN threat assessment criteria, for the derivation of a bryophyte Red List, and the evaluation of Important Bryophyte Areas. The bulk of this book then describes in detail the identification features, distribution, ecology and conservation status of 251 taxa, with shorter accounts for a further 146 taxa. Scientific names for bryophytes follow the *Census Catalogue* of the British Bryological Society (Hill *et al.* 2008) with a very few minor modifications. English and scientific names of vascular plants follow Stace (2010).

1

Flora and distribution

With about 835 taxa (species, subspecies and varieties), Ireland has a rich bryophyte flora and supports nearly 48% of the total European flora (Porley *et al.* 2008). Bryophytes form a large and conspicuous part of the vegetation in some regions of Ireland, competing effectively with vascular plants to cover large areas of bog, sand dune and mountain slope. Besides their beauty and rich biodiversity, plant communities dominated by bryophytes play an important role in environmental economics in storing both water resources and carbon (Crum 1992, O'Neill in Goffinet & Shaw 2009).

The majority of Irish bryophyte species have widespread ranges in Europe and elsewhere. Extensive comparative analyses by Hill & Preston (1998) and Preston & Hill (1999) reaffirm the conclusions of Herzog (1926) that bryophytes tend to have much more extensive global ranges than vascular plant species. This difference is increasingly interpreted as being attributable to the frequent wide dispersal of wind-blown spores rather than to the great antiquity of bryophyte species distribution (e.g. Muñoz *et al.* 2004, cf. R.M. Schuster in Schuster 1983). Bryophytes from a surprisingly wide diversity of distributional elements are represented in Ireland, from a Boreo-arctic Montane element to a Mediterranean-Atlantic element (Hill & Preston 1998).

The cloudiness, year-round high rainfall and mild winters of Ireland provide conditions that favour a group of bryophyte species confined in Europe to the Atlantic coastal fringes and islands. Although recognised by Herzog (1926), the first detailed analysis of these 'Atlantic Bryophytes' was by Ratcliffe (1968), who classified the Atlantic species into six distributional elements, all of which are present in Ireland. These include a Northern Atlantic element (shared with western Scotland and parts of SW Norway), Widespread Atlantic, Southern Atlantic (often shared with NW Spain, Portugal and such Atlantic islands as the Azores, Madeira and the western Canary Islands) and Mediterranean Atlantic elements (the last comprising plants of southern distribution that extend to the Mediterranean). Ratcliffe's analyses revealed that climatic factors are often more important than rock or soil types in determining the distribution of Atlantic

Slievemore, Doogort, Achill Island, Co. Mayo, a site for *Adelanthus lindenbergianus*.

bryophytes. The most critical climatic factor appears to be the number of 'wet days' each year, defined as days with at least 1 mm of rainfall. The richest areas for Atlantic bryophytes are those with 200 or more 'wet days', not necessarily those with the highest total rainfall. Parts of the west coast of Ireland in counties Kerry, Galway, Mayo and Donegal thus rank alongside the western coast and islands of Scotland as the richest areas in all of Europe for Atlantic bryophytes.

There are no endemic species of bryophyte in Ireland. Some of the Atlantic liverworts were initially thought to be endemic when they were first discovered, including *Adelanthus dugortiensis* from Achill Island, which is now known to be the same as *A. lindenbergianus*, a species widespread in the tropics. Similarly, *Cephalozia hibernica* was initially regarded as an Irish endemic, then found in Macaronesia, and is now regarded as synonymous with *C. crassifolia*, which occurs in the Caribbean and C. and S. America. Several moss species recognised more recently have also been regarded as possible Irish endemics, including *Didymodon maximus* and *Ephemerum hibernicum*. However, subsequent taxonomic and floristic studies have revealed that the former species also occurs in Alaska, arctic Canada, NE Siberia and Mongolia, and that the latter also occurs (as *E. crassinervium* subsp. *rutheanum* (Schimp.) Holyoak) in S. Wales, France and W. Poland. It seems that Britain is similar in having very few, if any, truly endemic bryophytes, since of the 10 species recently listed as British or Irish endemics (Porley & Hodgetts 2005), two are now known from continental Europe, two more appear from molecular data to be unworthy of species rank (Olsson *et al.* 2009) and most of the others are poorly known plants likely to be overlooked elsewhere or taxonomically dubious. Ireland also lacks any really distinctive endemic vascular plants, the few true endemics apparently being microspecies that are likely to have evolved recently in critical genera such as *Hieracium*.

Cloontyprughlish (Glenade), Co. Leitrim, one of several sites for *Didymodon maximus* in the Dartry Mountains.

3

Bryophyte colonisation

This lack of endemic bryophytes is at first sight surprising. The oldest rocks in Ireland are Precambrian and around 700 million years old (Ma) and large parts of the island are underlain by limestones and other Carboniferous sediments that were exposed to the air around 300 Ma (Holland 1981, Feehan 1997). Bryophytes are also very ancient, with fossils indicating the divergence of the main groups of bryophytes before 280 Ma, whereas the earliest flowering plants appeared only at around 135 Ma. Phylogenetic analyses of molecular data now substantially extend evidence from fossils in our understanding of the early radiations of land plants. Thus the ancestral land plants were apparently algae related to the Charophyceae and the origins of a land flora are now dated to as far back as the Upper Ordovician-Lower Silurian boundary at about 440 Ma. The hornworts may have been the first group to diverge, with liverworts and mosses also arising from relatively early branches (Goffinet in Shaw & Goffinet 2000).

Despite the great age of both Irish rocks and of bryophyte evolution, the lack of endemic Irish bryophytes is no paradox. It is readily explained by the much more recent climatic and geological history of north-western Europe, with the same explanation accounting for the great paucity of other endemic plants and of endemic animals in Ireland. Geologists established long ago that landforms resulting from glacial ice cover extend over all parts of Ireland and that these were formed during several different cold stages during the Middle and Late Pleistocene (Mitchell 1976, McCabe 1987). During the latest (Midlandian) cold stage, the maximum ice-cover (the Last Glacial Maximum or LGM) was attained between 28,000 and 15,000 years ago during the Glenavy Stadial, which coincided with one of the largest expansions of glacial conditions across the northern hemisphere. Traditionally, ice was assumed to have lain over all of the island at the LGM apart from in southernmost Ireland, but the extent of end moraines on the continental shelf (King *et al.* 1998) and more recent cosmogenic dating have suggested that only small areas in the south-west may have remained ice-free (Coxon 2008). These small ice-free areas are deduced to have had periglacial climates maintaining permafrost and hence to have supported only cold-tolerant vegetation similar in character to tundra (cf. West 2000). They are therefore unlikely to have supported any but the more cold-tolerant bryophytes and vascular plants (cf. Dickson 1973). All or almost all of the bryophytes of Ireland must

therefore have arrived as colonists within the past 20,000 years, a timescale apparently too short for evolution of distinctive endemic species.

Biogeographers have argued for decades about the pathways by which postglacial recolonisation of the Irish flora and fauna occurred (e.g. Devoy 1985, Davenport *et al.* 2008). In particular, the role of land bridges linking Ireland and Britain has been much discussed. It is clear that at the LGM global sea levels were 120 m lower than at present, exposing portions of the modern sea floor around north-western Europe and joining Ireland to Britain and the rest of the European continent. These land bridges were drowned by rising sea levels as ice sheets melted. The details and timing of relative sea level rise are nevertheless very difficult to calculate because of the complicated interplay between rising of the land surface as the ice load was removed, the input of water into the shallow seas and oceans and the thermal expansion of the water. A recent review and modelling data suggest Ireland was separated from Britain by c. 16,000 years ago, at which time the climate was still cold and local ice caps persisted in parts of the country (Edwards & Brooks 2008). Thus, no support was found for the idea that a Littletonian (Holocene) land bridge was instrumental in the migration of temperate flora or fauna into Ireland.

Most bryophytes produce small spores that are readily dispersed by the wind (van Zanten & Pócs 1981, Schofield 1985), so there is little difficulty in explaining their arrival in late-glacial or postglacial Ireland by overseas dispersal. The explanation is less clear for bryophytes with large spores, such as the liverwort genera *Fossombronia* or *Riccia* or mosses such as *Andreaea megistospora*, although accidental carriage in or on migratory birds is likely. Dispersal of species that do not produce spores also seems problematical, although some may have produced spores under different climatic conditions in the past, or there may be other propagules such as bulbils, gemmae, tubers or detached leaves that have aided dispersal. Schuster (in Schuster (ed.) 1983: 476) has drawn attention to the remarkable power and potential efficacy of wind dispersal, noting that in 'South Greenland, I have witnessed föhn winds so strong that they 'dispersed' empty 55-gallon oil drums for considerable distances. It is absurd to think such winds could not disperse Marchantioid spores.'

Among the few fossiliferous assemblages providing direct evidence of the early recolonisation of Ireland by bryophytes, that from Drumurcher, Co. Monaghan, has 20 moss species from shortly before 10,000 years ago, during

Female receptacles of *Marchantia polymorpha* subsp. *polymorpha*.

a brief substage with renewed cold at the end of the Midlandian (Dickson 1973). All the plant remains indicate open habitats at that time. Among taxa recorded are *Hypnum bambergeri*, *H. revolutum*, *Pseudocalliergon turgescens*, and perhaps *Sciuro-hypnum glaciale*, all northern species that are no longer part of the Irish flora. In addition, the cold-tolerant *Abietinella abietina*, *Bartramia ithyphylla*, *Plagiopus oederianus*, *Polytrichastrum alpinum* and *Timmia* sp. no longer occur at low elevations in Co. Monaghan. Some of the moss species represented are calcicoles that would nowadays be unexpected in that region.

The postglacial development of Irish vegetation has been well documented from studies of pollen as well as plant macrofossils (Godwin 1975, F. Mitchell 1976, F.J.G. Mitchell 2006, Overland & O'Connell 2008, Feeser & O'Connell 2009). Birch (*Betula* spp.) pollen dominated from about 10,000 to 9250 years ago, after which both Hazel (*Corylus avellana*) and Scots Pine (*Pinus sylvestris*) take over from c. 9250–8000 years ago. Mitchell (1976) envisaged that a 'visitor to Ireland at that time would have seen endless sheets of trees interrupted only by the water of lakes and river-channels', which if correct, would imply that shade-intolerant bryophytes would have been by then restricted to small open areas, perhaps on the mountain tops, coasts and riverbanks. Oak (*Quercus* spp.), elm (*Ulmus* spp.) and Alder (*Alnus glutinosa*) had reached Ireland by about 9000 years ago, but did not fully replace the Pine-Hazel assemblage in the lowlands until c. 8000 years ago. Then, 8000–7000 years ago a Hazel-Pine-oak-elm assemblage dominated the lowlands, to be replaced by the 'climax-phase' woodland of Hazel-Alder-oak-elm on low ground for a long period from 7000–5500 years ago, with birch and Pine probably still holding their own in the

uplands. There are few assemblages of fossil bryophytes from Ireland dating from these millennia of forest dominance, but Jessen (1949) reported mosses extracted from 'lagoon silt and peat' at Cushendun, Co. Antrim in the Pine-Hazel zone that were identified by Hesselbo as: *Eurhynchium* sp., *Hylocomium* sp., *Neckera complanata*, *Thamnobryum alopecurum* and *Thuidium tamariscinum*, none of which would be surprising in woodland in Co. Antrim at the present day.

Raised bogs had begun to form by building up highly humified *Sphagnum* peat both in the midlands and the north of Ireland by 7000 years ago, with rather slow peat accumulation continuing up to c. 5000 years ago. Subsequently peat growth extended widely in the lowlands, with expanding bogs replacing forest cover over large areas by 4000 years ago. Moss peat in a hollow between drumlins at Fallahogy in Co. Londonderry (Smith 1958) dating from the Pine-Hazel pollen-zone has fossils of *Paludella squarrosa*, *Tomentypnum nitens* and *Warnstorfia fluitans*, implying that both basic and oligotrophic fen occurred. Above the lower boundary of the Hazel-Pine-oak-elm pollen-assemblage zone it was succeeded by a 4 m thickness of peat from ombrogenous bog, in which only *Sphagnum imbricatum* (i.e., *S. affine* or *S. austinii*) and *S. papillosum* occur, reflecting an obvious change to acidic ground conditions and probably higher regional rainfall.

Other fossil records of rare fen bryophytes from Ireland are mainly poorly dated, but many of them may be from deposits antedating the widespread increase in bog development at c. 5000 years ago. Among the latter are records from Coolearagh townland in Co. Kildare of *Meesia triquetra*, *Paludella squarrosa*, *Pseudocalliergon trifarium* and *Tomentypnum nitens* (Barry & Synnott 1970), all of them species with very restricted modern records from Ireland. More surprising perhaps is the report from Littleton Bog, Co. Tipperary of *Meesia longiseta* Hedw. from c. 4500–5000 years ago (Barry & Synnott 1973); this mainly boreal species has never been found living in Ireland or Britain.

Humans first became firmly established in Ireland by around 8150 years ago, during the period of forest dominance. Evidence of these Mesolithic hunter-gatherer cultures during the period c. 8000–5000 years ago comes mainly from the north-eastern half of Ireland. Neolithic farmers arrived in Ireland about 5500 years ago, beginning a process of forest clearance for agriculture that continued progressively as axes and ploughs improved over several millennia (Mitchell 1976, Caulfield *et al.*

Lejeunea hibernica habitat, Kylemore, Co. Galway.

Paludella squarrosa and *Tomentypnum nitens*, with *Sphagnum contortum* and *Campylium stellatum*, in a fen in north Mayo, 2010.

1998). Initially, small tillage patches probably reflected a pattern of shifting agriculture in a largely forested landscape, but the increases in human population that could be sustained from better farming practices led to larger permanent settlements, larger numbers of domestic livestock and much more forest clearance. The woodlands in Ireland had almost all been destroyed by the early 19th century.

There are few detailed reports of subfossil bryophytes of the Littletonian (postglacial) in Ireland other than those from bogs or fen peat noted above. However, a medieval assemblage from Winetavern Street, Dublin, had 13 bryophyte species (Dickson 1973), none of which would be surprising in the same county today, and excavations from a medieval mill site in Co. Roscommon yielded several typical woodland mosses (Overland & O'Connell in press).

The paucity of fossil records makes it difficult, if not impossible, to establish whether many bryophyte species are long-standing natives in Ireland or more recent immigrants that have arrived accidentally due to human activity. Any finer analysis into native, 'archaeophyte' (introduced before 1500 A.D.) and 'neophyte' taxa (as for vascular plants which have many more fossil records, cf. Dines *et al.* in Preston *et al.* 2002, Preston *et al.* 2004) would therefore only complicate a largely futile task. Certain bryophyte habitats such as arable land (tillage), garden soil, mortared-walls, mud-capped walls, reservoir inundation zones, metalliferous mine spoil, conifer trunks and tree fern 'trunks' exist in Ireland only because of human activities. Many of the bryophytes of these places are certainly colonists from adjacent natural or semi-natural habitats, but it is uncertain that they all are.

The long-vanished rarities of mud-capped walls (*Pterygoneurum lamellatum*, *P. ovatum*) might have been accidental introductions to Ireland, as might other rare species of walls such as *Atrichum angustatum*, *Grimmia crinita* and *Leptobarbula berica*, or they might equally well have been natural colonists arriving as wind-blown spores from overseas. Much the same applies to *Ephemerum spinulosum*, *Physcomitrium sphaericum* and *Riccia huebeneriana* known only or mainly on reservoir margins, for which migrant waterfowl or mobile anglers are among the likely vectors. Similarly, several species known only from tillage, such as *Didymodon tomaculosus*, could have arrived as tubers attached to soil on birds' feet, or more prosaically on tyres of vehicles. *Atrichum crispum* is normally regarded as introduced to Europe from North America because it has a restricted and peculiarly patchy distribution and is represented here only by male plants, but recent natural spread could produce the same pattern. *Hennediella stanfordensis* and *Didymodon umbrosus* have been regarded as introductions because they are known in Ireland and Britain only from rather altered or artificial habitats, but the true native range of both species seems very poorly understood (both were dubbed 'mundivagant' taxa by R.H. Zander in FNA 2007). Several bryophytes restricted to metalliferous mine spoil are strongly suspected of having been dispersed accidentally in Ireland by past mining activity or more recent visitors (Holyoak & Lockhart 2009a). Scattered occurrences of such rare epiphytes as *Leptodon smithii*, *Orthotrichum pallens*, *Ptilidium pulcherrimum*, or of *Aongstroemia longipes* (in one old sandpit), of *Sematophyllum substrumulosum* and *Bryum creberrimum* (found once on wood in a park and once in a plant pot) are usually assumed to result from natural spore dispersal, but there is apparently no way of knowing whether some or all of these occurrences result from accidental transport by human activities.

With just 13 species, the number of instances of bryophytes being established as probable aliens in the Irish flora is in fact surprisingly small. This is possibly because dispersal of spores is so frequent and widespread that it has allowed most species likely to survive in Ireland to reach the island unaided. Whatever the explanation, the small number of alien bryophytes in Ireland contrasts sharply with the situation for vascular plants where a recent review recorded 920 alien taxa, nearly as many as there are native (Reynolds 2002); among the alien species are some that now form an important part of the vegetation such as Sycamore (*Acer pseudoplatanus*) and Montbretia (*Crocosmia* spp.). Among the alien bryophytes, only two mosses have become widespread (*Campylopus introflexus* and *Orthodontium lineare*) and only the first of these is a really common plant. Another moss, *Atrichum crispum*, is more locally established (but as noted above, not securely confirmed as an introduction). Three liverworts have become established very locally in semi-natural habitats (*Lophocolea bispinosa*, *L. semiteres*, *Riccia rhenana*), as have three more mosses (*Calyptrochaeta apiculata*, *Didymodon umbrosus*, *Hennediella stanfordensis*). Four bryophytes closely associated with tree ferns likewise remain highly localised (the liverwort *Heteroscyphus fissistipus*; the mosses *Calomnion complanatum*, *Dicranoloma menziesii*, *Leptotheca gaudichaudii*).

The clearest examples of bryophyte species being of alien origin in Ireland, or elsewhere in western Europe, are with taxa from the southern hemisphere, especially where recent rapid spread has been well documented (for *Campylopus introflexus* by Richards & Smith 1975; for *Orthodontium lineare* by Margadant & Meijer 1950, Hedenäs *et al.* 1989; for *Lophocolea semiteres* by Stieperaere 1994, Paton 1999). Since it is much harder to judge whether species that are native nearer at hand are present in Irish localities as a result of accidental introductions, it has usually been tacitly assumed they are not. Nevertheless, some should not be above suspicion, such as *Grimmia orbicularis* or *Schistidium elegantulum* on bridge walls, *Fissidens fontanus* in lake edges visited by anglers, or *Racomitrium canescens* beside paths in dunes. Pearman (2007) used a series of 10 criteria to judge whether vascular plant species are likely to be native or alien, but these criteria are not all useful with bryophytes

(which are not cultivated, and mainly lack subfossil records from archaeological sites). Greater reliance is therefore needed on evidence of patterns and rates of spread, which must be judged from patchy recording activity. 'Presence in semi-natural habitats' seems a poor criterion since some of the bryophytes known to be aliens have colonised the remotest and least altered natural habitats in Ireland, especially *Campylopus introflexus* (although this is a feature also of New Zealand Willowherb *Epilobium brunnescens*). It is thus often impossible to judge from the conditions in which a bryophyte is found whether it arrived from nearby or far away, aided or unaided.

None of the alien bryophytes established in Ireland appears to pose any general threat to native species at present, although *Campylopus introflexus* can cover so much bared peat or sand that it is presumably excluding other species at least locally, and *Lophocolea semiteres*, known from a single locality at Murlough Dunes, Co. Down, may be expected to spread in Ireland in the future.

Uncertainties over native and 'alien' status of bryophytes notwithstanding, they are all treated in this book, although little detail is given on some obviously recent arrivals. To exclude a few known aliens as unworthy of consideration while ignoring the doubts attaching to the claims to native status of a larger number of other taxa would be arbitrary and unscientific. Furthermore, at least one established bryophyte that is undoubtedly an alien (*Calomnion complanatum* on tree fern 'trunks') merits attention from conservationists because it is regarded as a threatened species in its native Australian range.

Tree ferns (*Dicksonia* spp.) with the Endangered Australian moss *Calomnion camplanatum*, at the woodland garden on Garinish Island, Co. Kerry.

CHAPTER TWO

Bryophyte habitats in Ireland

Herbertus aduncus and *Polytrichum commune*, Mweelrea, Co. Mayo.

IRELAND IS a very diverse country for its size with a wide range of habitats, some of them rich in bryophytes, several of them of international importance and listed on the EU Habitats Directive, but many of them threatened in some way. This chapter presents a brief overview of these habitats and their bryological importance. It is not always easy to define habitats with regard to bryophytes because mosses and liverworts tend to occur in microhabitats rather than conventional macrohabitats such as woodland, grassland, etc. A woodland bryophyte, for example, is usually one that thrives in conditions of shelter, damp and shade, and therefore can grow equally well *outside* woodland wherever these conditions prevail, such as in rock crevices and ravines. Bryophytes are small and very efficient at dispersal, so they tend to come and go as conditions fluctuate, not necessarily being tied to a particular macrohabitat. Nonetheless, it is still useful to examine bryophytes within macrohabitats, as these are at a scale that we can relate to more easily.

Relatively little phytosociological work has been carried out on bryophytes in Ireland and Britain by comparison to the studies in continental Europe (Bardat & Hauguel 2002, Marstaller 1993). Nevertheless, a considerable number of vegetation studies have included bryophytes in their classification of Irish vascular plant communities (White 1982). Pioneering work by Braun-Blanquet & Tüxen (1952), who visited Ireland for the second International Phytosociological Excursion in 1949, provided a stimulus for Irish researchers and several studies in the subsequent decades have featured communities that are defined, at least in part, by their bryophyte component, including: grasslands (O'Sullivan 1965); bogs (Moore 1968, Mhic Daeid 1976, Doyle & Moore 1980, Doyle 1982, O'Connor 2000); fens (O'Connell 1981, Lockhart, 1991, Ó Críodáin & Doyle 1994, 1997); woodlands (Kelly 1975, Kelly & Iremonger 1997, Perrin *et al.* 2006, 2008); heaths (Kirkpatrick 1988, Bleasdale 1995, McKee 2000, Hodd & Sheehy Skeffington 2011) and sand dunes (Gaynor 2006, 2008).

Visiting botanists from Britain and continental Europe have also made significant contributions to the knowledge of bryophyte communities and the habitats in which they occur (Osvald 1949, Bellamy & Bellamy 1966, Ivimey-Cook & Proctor 1966, Rubers 1975, van Groenendael *et al.* 1979, Dierssen 1982, Schouten 1984, 1990, 2002). Surveys of habitats and sites of conservation interest undertaken by the National Parks and Wildlife Service (NPWS), in the Republic of Ireland, and the Northern Ireland Environment Agency (NIEA) in Northern Ireland, as well as research by universities, environmental consultancies and NGOs, also include descriptions of bryophyte communities in Ireland.

While the plant communities of Ireland and Britain are quite similar, owing to similarities in geography, geology and climate, there are also clearly many differences (White & Doyle 1982). The National Vegetation Classification (NVC) (Rodwell 1991–2000, Rodwell 2006) is sometimes used by field ecologists in Ireland, but it was designed to cover Britain only. Ireland certainly contains communities that are not described in the NVC, notably in the south-west, where the climate is more Mediterranean-Atlantic than anywhere in Britain and therefore supports species and communities not found there. Turloughs are almost unique to Ireland, and the limestone pavement of the Burren, Co. Clare, is more extensive than anything found in Britain, as well as subtly different. There are also differences arising from historical land management, such as the paucity of woodland in Ireland, and the extensive river callows that have been virtually eliminated from Britain. The NVC also tends to be of less value in Ireland because of the absence from Ireland of many of the species present in Britain.

At a more general level, the habitats of Ireland have been classified into a hierarchical framework (Fossitt 2000) (Table 1) and links established to European habitat classification schemes (CORINE, EUNIS) via the habitat lists on Annex I of the EU Habitats Directive. However, bryophytes tend not to form an important element in such systems, except where they are the major component of the flora, such as *Cratoneurion* for Petrifying Springs or metallophyte bryophytes in Calaminarian Grassland. In the descriptions that follow, the habitat categories only loosely adhere to those described by Fossitt (*op. cit.*), but where similarities occur these are indicated by listing the equivalent Fossitt codes in parentheses. Most emphasis is placed on those habitats and landforms that are especially important for bryophytes (e.g. mountains).

Woodland and epiphytes
Records suggest that much of the native ancient woodland in Ireland had been felled by the early 17th century and that this was part of a more or less continuous process since the Bronze Age, largely as a result of pastoral farming (Cross 2006). Most woodland that survived until the 19th century was probably grubbed up to make room for farming during the population explosion that culminated in the Great Famine in the 1840s. Present-day Ireland is indeed one of the least wooded areas in Europe. In the Republic of Ireland, about 10% of the surface is covered by forest and only 2% (20% of forest estate) is native woodland (Forest Service 2007). Similar figures pertain to Northern Ireland, where the total cover of forest is estimated to be 6% (Forest Service of Northern Ireland). Extensive research on native woodlands in the Republic of Ireland (National Survey of Native Woodlands, Perrin *et al.* 2008) has shown that much of what remains is located in valleys, on hillsides, lowlands, along rivers and beside lakes. While the historical loss of woodland must have had a dramatic effect on the abundance of bryophytes in Ireland as a whole, it probably resulted in few or no bryophyte extinctions. Unlike the lichens, in which there is a group of ancient woodland indicators, there are very few bryophytes that are strictly confined to woodland. Thus many of the semi-natural and mixed woodland stands in Ireland support communities of common species that take advantage of the increase in shelter, shade and humidity to grow in greater luxuriance within woodlands than they do in other habitats.

The owners of large country demesnes planted woodland in the 18th and 19th centuries to try to reverse woodland decline and for the purpose of landscape enhancement, and in the latter half of the 20th century there was very extensive afforestation in the uplands, with the planting of thousands of hectares of conifers, principally Sitka Spruce (*Picea sitchensis*) and Lodgepole Pine (*Pinus contorta*). The planting of native woodlands has been encouraged in more recent years through grant-aided programmes such as the Native Woodland Scheme. Considerable progress has also been made on managing existing native woodland on the NPWS and Forest Service of Northern Ireland estates, principally by removal of conifers, invasive aliens and grazing control, and under the Native Woodland Scheme on private and Coillte-owned lands. Expansion of native woodland is now also occurring in parts of Ireland due to land abandonment and natural regeneration on cutaway bogs.

Table 1. Hierarchical classification of habitats in Ireland (Fossitt 2000)

Code	Description	Code	Description
F	*Freshwater*	WD1	(Mixed) broadleaved woodland
FL1	Dystrophic lakes	WD2	Mixed broadleaved/conifer woodland
FL2	Acid oligotrophic lakes	WD3	(Mixed) conifer woodland
FL3	Limestone/marl lakes	WD4	Conifer plantation
FL4	Mesotrophic lakes	WD5	Scattered trees and parkland
FL5	Eutrophic lakes	WS1	Scrub
FL6	Turloughs	WS2	Immature woodland
FL7	Reservoirs	WS3	Ornamental/non-native shrub
FL8	Other artificial lakes and ponds	WS4	Short rotation coppice
FW1	Eroding/upland rivers	WS5	Recently-felled woodland
FW2	Depositing/lowland rivers	WL1	Hedgerows
FW3	Canals	WL2	Treelines
FW4	Drainage ditches	*E*	*Exposed rock and disturbed ground*
FP1	Calcareous springs	ER1	Exposed siliceous rock
FP2	Non-calcareous springs	ER2	Exposed calcareous rock
FS1	Reed and large sedge swamps	ER3	Siliceous scree and loose rock
FS2	Tall herb swamps	ER4	Calcareous scree and loose rock
G	*Grassland and Marsh*	EU1	Non-marine caves
GA1	Improved agricultural grassland	EU2	Artificial underground habitats
GA2	Amenity grassland (improved)	ED1	Exposed sand, gravel or till
GS1	Dry calcareous and neutral grassland	ED2	Spoil and bare ground
GS2	Dry meadows and grassy verges	ED3	Recolonising bare ground
GS3	Dry-humid acid grassland	ED4	Active quarries and mines
GS4	Wet grassland	ED5	Refuse and other waste
GM1	Marsh	*B*	*Cultivated and built land*
H	*Heath and dense bracken*	BC1	Arable crops
HH1	Dry siliceous heath	BC2	Horticultural land
HH2	Dry calcareous heath	BC3	Tilled land
HH3	Wet heath	BC4	Flower beds and borders
HH4	Montane heath	BL1	Stone walls and other stonework
HD1	Dense bracken	BL2	Earth banks
P	*Peatlands*	BL3	Buildings and artificial surfaces
PB1	Raised bogs	*C*	*Coastland*
PB2	Upland blanket bog	CS1	Rocky sea cliffs
PB3	Lowland blanket bog	CS2	Sea stacks and islets
PB4	Cutover bog	CS3	Sedimentary sea cliffs
PB5	Eroding blanket bog	CW1	Lagoons and saline lakes
PF1	Rich fen and flush	CW2	Tidal rivers
PF2	Poor fen and flush	CM1	Lower salt marsh
PF3	Transition mire and quaking bog	CM2	Upper salt marsh
W	*Woodland and scrub*	CB1	Shingle and gravel banks
WN1	Oak-birch-holly woodland	CD1	Embryonic dunes
WN2	Oak-ash-hazel woodland	CD2	Marram dunes
WN3	Yew woodland	CD3	Fixed dunes
WN4	Wet pedunculate oak-ash woodland	CD4	Dune scrub and woodland
WN5	Riparian woodland	CD5	Dune slacks
WN6	Wet willow-alder-ash woodland	CD6	Machair
WN7	Bog woodland	CC1	Sea walls, piers and jetties
		CC2	Fish cages and rafts

In semi-natural and mixed broadleaf woodlands on acid or base-poor soils (WN1), including more modified and non-native woodland (WD1 and WD2), the pleurocarpous mosses *Kindbergia praelonga* and *Brachythecium rutabulum* are the most ubiquitous bryophytes and can dominate the ground flora, forming untidy wefts on the woodland floor and over dead wood and litter. *Fissidens* spp., *Polytrichastrum formosum*, *Atrichum undulatum* and several small pleurocarps may be much in evidence wherever there is bare ground, such as on shady banks and track sides. Tree trunks and bases are often completely covered with a layer of bryophytes, with a few common pleurocarps such as *Brachythecium rutabulum*, *Kindbergia praelonga*, *Hypnum cupressiforme* and *Isothecium myosuroides* again the most frequent species. Tufts of *Mnium hornum* often cover the ground at the extreme bases of trees, with *Hypnum cupressiforme* and *H. andoi* further up the trunks, frequently mixed with smaller mosses such as *Zygodon viridissimus* and liverworts such as *Lophocolea bidentata* and *Metzgeria furcata*. Epiphytes can be abundant on branches and twigs, taking full advantage of the usually clean air and oceanic climate found in Ireland. Smaller branches and twigs can support a community of cushion-forming mosses and leafy liverworts, with species of *Ulota* and *Frullania* frequent, and *Orthotrichum* species less so. Woodland bryophyte diversity is always increased by the presence of rock exposures, flushes and streams, the different substrates providing niches for species unable to compete elsewhere.

Oak-birch-holly woodlands (WN1 and Old Oak Woodlands on Annex I of the EU Habitats Directive) are perhaps the most important woodlands for bryophytes, especially where they occur in high rainfall areas in the west. Even small and isolated examples can contain a rich variety of bryophytes many of which are restricted or absent from mainland Europe. Typical species include *Dicranum majus*, *Plagiochila spinulosa* and *Scapania gracilis*.

The most well-known examples of these oak woodlands are found at Killarney, Glengarriff and Uragh, in the south-west, but excellent examples also occur further to the north, such as at Old Head and Brackloon, in Co. Mayo, Lough Gill, Co. Sligo, and at Glenveagh, Co. Donegal. The Killarney oakwoods are the most extensive in Ireland and are particularly important for their bryophytes because the mild climate and more or less constant high humidity favour the growth of an assemblage of oceanic (or Atlantic) species that are very rare or absent elsewhere in the country (Richards 1938,

Oak woodland on the south slopes of Torc Mountain, near Killarney, Co. Kerry.

Kelly 1975, 1981, Kelly & Moore 1975, Mitchell & Averis 1988). Although probably a genuine wilderness prior to about 1580 (Watts 1984), the Killarney woods were heavily exploited up to about 1815 (charcoal burning and clear felling). Since then, they have gradually regenerated and now have the feel of ancient woodland again, in spite of the fact that much of the timber is less than 200 years old. The bryophytes have certainly recolonised effectively, presumably from small undisturbed refugia, and form an important component of the biota, both in terms of vegetation cover and in species diversity. Small, rare oceanic liverworts such as *Cephalozia crassifolia*, *Lejeunea flava* subsp. *moorei*, *L. eckloniana*, *L. hibernica*, *L. mandonii*, *Radula carringtonii*, *R. voluta*, etc., and a few rare mosses such as *Daltonia splachnoides* are relatively frequent. Even larger mosses

Hypnum uncinulatum on sandstone boulders in oak woodland, east of Brickeen, Co. Kerry.

Uragh Wood, on the shore of Inchiquin Lough, Co. Kerry.

such as *Hypnum uncinulatum*, unknown in the rest of Ireland, occur here. All but the oldest records of this mainly Macaronesian species in Ireland were until recently regarded with scepticism, but examination of herbarium specimens showed that its occurrence was genuine, and several sites for it in the Killarney area have been discovered recently. Like several of the local specialities, including the Strawberry-tree (*Arbutus unedo*), this plant is restricted to the extreme south-west of Ireland and does not occur in Britain.

Semi-natural and mixed broadleaf woodlands on calcareous soils (WN2), and more modified woodland (WD1 and WD2), support a particularly distinctive bryophyte flora (Kelly & Kirby 1982, Cross, 1992). *Eurhynchium striatum*, *Plagiomnium undulatum*, *Rhytidiadelphus triquetrus* and *Thamnobryum alopecurum* are often the dominant mosses on the ground, the latter forming miniature forests with its dendroid growth form. Colonies of *Cirriphyllum piliferum*, distinctive with its leaves ending in a hair-point, and of the large leafy liverwort *Plagiochila asplenioides*, can also occur.

Isothecium alopecuroides may largely replace *I. myosuroides* as the dominant epiphyte on trees, and other epiphytes are generally more diverse and more abundant than they are in less base-rich environments. Ash (*Fraxinus excelsior*) trees are usually prominent in the woodland landscape on calcareous soils, and these are particularly rich in epiphytes, having rough-textured bark with a relatively high pH. While *Hypnum* is still usually abundant, it may be joined, or even replaced, by species of *Neckera*, beautiful mosses that form flattened brackets peeling away from the bark. Liverworts can also be abundant, with the purplish-brown *Frullania dilatata* forming spreading, often more or less circular, patches and often accompanied by the bright yellowish-green *Radula complanata* and tiny shoots of *Lejeunea* spp. Tufts of *Zygodon* need to be examined microscopically to check whether they are the common *Z. viridissimus* or the rarer *Z. conoideus* or *Z. rupestris*; the three are easily differentiated by the structure of their axillary gemmae, but these can only be observed under the microscope.

Hazel woodland, Poulacarra, The Burren, Co. Clare.

The scrubby Hazel woodland (included in WS1) that develops over thin limestone soils, and especially on limestone pavement, is a significant and extensive habitat in Ireland (Kelly & Kirby 1982). This supports roughly the same bryophyte flora as other limestone woodlands but with the species assemblage even more restricted to strongly calcicolous species. Huge brackets of *Neckera crispa* can be very prominent, hanging off the trunks of the trees, with cushions of *Ulota* all over the branches and twigs. *Ulota calvescens*, a considerably rarer species than either *U. crispa* or *U. bruchii*, is particularly associated with this habitat. Large cushions of *Tortella tortuosa* and *Scapania aspera* are often found growing directly on the limestone clints on the woodland floor. Smaller and rarer calcicoles may also be found on damp limestone rocks, including tiny bristle-like species of *Seligeria*, in shaded crevices, and the extremely small pleurocarpous moss *Amblystegium confervoides*, on damp sloping limestone screes and rock faces.

Woodlands on alluvial soils (WN4, WN5 and WN6, some of which are referable to Alluvial Woodland on Annex I of the EU Habitats Directive) are found around the margins of lakes, along rivers and in fens and more widely on heavily gleyed soils (White 1985, Kelly & Iremonger 1997, Cross & Kelly 2003). Bryophytes are often very abundant in these habitats, although not necessarily very habitat-specific. The constant humidity and high water table are favourable to luxuriant stands of species sensitive to dehydration, such as *Hookeria lucens*, and mosses such as *Climacium dendroides*, *Calliergonella cuspidata* and *Calliergon cordifolium* are commonly found on the woodland floor. Epiphytes can be abundant, especially on willows (*Salix* spp.), with the common *Metzgeria furcata* joined by bright green masses of *M. violacea*, *M. consanguinea*, or both. *Frullania dilatata* and *Radula complanata* are usually abundant too, often with smaller leafy liverworts of the Lejeuneaceae. The rare *Orthotrichum sprucei* occupies a distinctive habitat as an epiphyte on trunks of trees within the regularly inundated flood zone beside lowland rivers, often on bark that is silt-encrusted. Plants that are more restricted to wetland woods such as *Oxyrrhynchium speciosum* and *Plagiomnium affine* may be locally common, especially on wooded lakesides. Some of the best examples of alluvial woodlands

Alluvial woodland, Glengarriff, Co. Cork.

are found in the Killarney valley, Co. Kerry and along the Glengarriff River and in The Gearagh, Co. Cork.

Birch woodlands on peat soils (WN7 and including Bog Woodland on Annex I of the EU Habitats Directive) can support calcifuge bryophyte communities dominated by carpets of *Sphagnum* and *Polytrichum* spp. This is the habitat for the subterranean liverwort *Aneura mirabilis* (until recently much more evocatively named *Cryptothallus mirabilis*), usually associated with *Sphagnum palustre* and *S. fimbriatum*. *A. mirabilis* has a white thallus, entirely without chlorophyll, and parasitizes birch roots through a basidiomycete ectomycorrhizal fungus. *A. mirabilis* is always difficult to find, as peeling away layers of *Sphagnum* is required to reveal it, and this is of course harmful to the habitat. High humidity levels in wet birch woodland can allow a rich epiphytic flora to develop on any willows that may be present. Dry birch woodland is usually less rich in bryophytes, the ground flora often taken over by Bracken (*Pteridium aquilinum*) and Bramble (*Rubus fruticosus* agg.). Birch trees themselves are poor substrates for epiphytes, with their acidic and easily-peeling bark.

Epiphytes may grow wherever there are trees, particularly if the air quality is good, as it is over most of Ireland. The country remained largely unaffected by the intense sulphur dioxide pollution that smothered the English Midlands until the Clean Air Acts came into force last century, so escaped a widespread elimination of pollution-sensitive epiphytic bryophytes. Scattered trees in parkland (WD5), or well-illuminated trees in hedgerows (WL1 and WL2), can sometimes support colonies of uncommon mosses such as *Leucodon sciuroides*, *Orthotrichum stramineum* and *Pterogonium gracile*. The bark of Elder (*Sambucus nigra*) is especially ideal for epiphytes, being base-rich, rough-textured, spongy and water-retentive, and mature trees often support an assemblage of species that are less frequent or absent elsewhere, including *Orthotrichum* spp., *Ulota* spp., *Zygodon* spp., *Metzgeria* spp., etc.

Conifer plantations are generally very poor habitats for bryophytes (WD4). The combination of dense shade and thick carpets of acid needles is usually inimical to the development of a ground flora, except perhaps a few patches of very common species such as *Kindbergia praelonga*, *Hypnum jutlandicum* and *Plagiothecium undulatum*. Conifer plantations may not be entirely without interest, however. Recent records of *Daltonia splachnoides* and *Plagiothecium laetum* (L. Coote, *in litt.*) hint that rare bryophytes may sometimes be overlooked in Sitka Spruce stands. A mature plantation in Glenmalur, in the Wicklow Mountains, is notable for its abundance of *Sphagnum girgensohnii*. Forestry tracks through conifer plantations may contain quite a diverse bryophyte flora, with many species taking advantage of the newly-exposed soils. Rich ruderal communities can sometimes develop on the tracks themselves, the diversity often enhanced by surfacing with gravels imported from elsewhere, especially of limestone in otherwise acidic sites. Peaty banks and ditches to the side of tracks can support extensive *Sphagnum* hummocks and a variety of liverworts. One rare species, *Diplophyllum obtusifolium*, appears to be particularly associated with conifer plantations in Ireland, growing on recently disturbed acid soil. Individual colonies of this species often do not last long, disappearing as natural succession progresses, but new colonies turn up regularly on track sides and banks.

Sam Bosanquet leading a field course for the Dublin Naturalists' Field Club, in conifer woodland, Raven's Glen, Co. Wicklow.

Many of the woodland bryophytes are able colonists, appearing wherever conditions are suitably humid and shady, but some can certainly be regarded as threatened. This is primarily because of the threats to their habitat as a whole. Obviously, clear-felling is detrimental, whether purely for clearance or for replacement by conifers, but other threats to woodlands include overgrazing and the spread of invasive alien plants. Rhododendron (*Rhododendron ponticum*) has been especially problematic in some woodlands, notably at Killarney and Glenveagh, and much effort has been put into its removal. However, although the heavy shade of Rhododendron is unsuitable for most bryophytes, it nevertheless provides optimal habitat for the small liverworts *Cephalozia crassifolia* and *Telaranea europaea*.

Peatland

Peatlands can be divided into two main categories; bogs and fens (Fossitt 2000). Bogs are ombrotrophic peatlands, fed largely by rainwater, where acid oligotrophic peat deposits accumulate. Fens are minerotrophic peatlands, fed by groundwater as well as rainwater, are more nutrient-rich than bogs and can be either acid or base-rich. Both bogs and fens are very important habitats for bryophytes, the different species assemblages reflecting the many variations in environmental conditions found in the range of peatland types across Ireland.

Raised bogs (PB1) develop in depressions or former lake basins and are found mostly in the midlands. Unfortunately, many raised bogs have been destroyed in Ireland by domestic and commercial peat-cutting, and even those that still have uncut surfaces are to varying extents hydrologically degraded. About 50,000 ha of uncut raised bog are estimated to occur in the Republic of Ireland (16% of the original area), of which only 1945 ha is still considered peat forming (Active Raised Bog on Annex I of the EU Habitats Directive) (Douglas *et al.* 2008). In Northern Ireland, the *Northern Ireland Peatland Survey*, completed by The Queen's University of Belfast (Cruickshank & Tomlinson 1988), estimated that the original lowland raised bog resource was 25,196 ha and that only 2270 ha (9% of original area) was uncut. Nevertheless, the wetter uncut raised bogs still support specialised bryophyte communities, notably those dominated by the *Sphagnum* bog-mosses. The most prominent are the cushion-forming species: *Sphagnum papillosum*, *S. capillifolium*, *S. austinii* and *S. fuscum*; but lawns and pools are also dominated by Sphagna, with the

Uncut raised bog surface, rich in *Sphagnum* hummocks, Kilcarren Bog, Co. Tipperary.

deeply wine-red carpets of *S. magellanicum* covering wide areas on parts of the wettest sites, and typically *S. inundatum*, *S. denticulatum* and *S. cuspidatum* in the lawns and pools. The golden carpets of *S. pulchrum* occur in some of the western raised bogs, such as at Cloonmoylan Bog, Co. Galway and Bellanagare Bog, Co. Roscommon (Douglas 1987), and several sites in Northern Ireland, including Ballynahone Bog, Co. Londonderry and Garry Bog, Co. Antrim (Leach & Corbett 1987). Wet areas with pool systems are the best places to search for tiny leafy liverworts creeping through the *Sphagnum*; the most frequent ones which are found in most bogs are *Cephalozia connivens*, *Kurzia pauciflora*, *Mylia anomala* and *Odontoschisma sphagni*. *Calypogeia sphagnicola* and *Cephalozia macrostachya* are rarer but can usually be found wherever *Sphagnum austinii* hummocks are seen. Rarer still are *Cephalozia loitlesbergeri*, *Cephaloziella elachista* and *C. spinigera*, apparently confined to the wettest, most intact parts of raised bogs. Another microhabitat often associated with bogs is the decaying remains of animal bones and dung, which when kept moist by high water table levels can support necrophilous and coprophilous mosses such as *Tetraplodon mnioides*, *Splachnum sphaericum* and *S. ampullaceum*. The rare *Tetraplodon angustatus* was found once in Ireland on a raised bog at Clara Bog, Co. Offaly, amongst *Sphagnum magellanicum*. These plants appear to have evolved in partnership with insects, which are the main agents in spore dispersal (Goffinet *et al.* 2004). As well as being enticed by the dung itself, flies are attracted by the rather large and brightly coloured capsules and the aromatic compounds that the capsules produce (Koponen 1990, Marino 1997).

Cutover bog (PB4) and drained bog tend to have fewer bryophyte species, with drier peat surfaces often colonised by heath communities dominated by *Campylopus* and *Polytrichum* spp. Wetter peat banks can sometimes hold more interest though, with small leafy liverworts such as *Lophozia* spp., *Kurzia* spp. and *Cephalozia* spp., until Heather (*Calluna vulgaris*) and other larger plants replace the early successional bryophyte communities. Nevertheless, at least one specialised raised bog bryophyte, recorded at a few sites in the midlands, has now disappeared from Ireland. *Dicranum undulatum* was first recorded in 1957 by Donald Pigott, in Pollagh Bog in Co. Offaly (Warburg 1958a), with a few more records from the same area in 1960 by David Bellamy, but the raised bogs where it grew have now all been destroyed or seriously damaged by industrial-scale peat extraction. It has not been refound,

Industrial-scale peat extraction, raised bog west of Tullycross, Co. Westmeath.

in spite of intensive searching, and is now presumed to be extinct in Ireland. Pollagh Bog was also the only Irish locality for the Rannoch-rush (*Scheuchzeria palustris*) (Moore 1955), which despite efforts to transplant it to nearby Clara Bog (Moore 1959), has not been refound in Ireland (Crushell *et al.* 2006).

Blanket bogs (Blanket Bog on Annex I of the EU Habitats Directive) can be subdivided into upland (i.e. above 150 m elevation, PB2) and lowland (i.e. below 150 m elevation, PB3) types, the latter also known as Atlantic or oceanic blanket bog. Upland blanket bog is extensively developed on flat or gently sloping ground on hills and mountains throughout Ireland. Lowland blanket bog is more restricted in its distribution and is largely confined to wetter regions along the western seaboard where

Upland blanket bog on Garron Plateau, Co. Antrim.

annual rainfall exceeds 1250 mm (Fossitt 2000). Both types are characterised by a mosaic of herbaceous vegetation, typically of Purple Moor-grass (*Molinia caerulea*), Deergrass (*Trichophorum germanicum*) and Cottongrasses (*Eriophorum* spp.) with dwarf ericoid shrubs (*Calluna vulgaris, Erica* spp.) and Black Bog-rush (*Schoenus nigricans*) in the lowlands, and often intergrading with shallower peat areas of heath, acid grassland and exposed rock. *Sphagnum* mosses can play an important role in the wettest and most intact areas of blanket bog, where a species assemblage similar to that of raised bogs can occur. Additional species that appear to be confined to blanket bogs include the uncommon *S. platyphyllum* and *S. strictum*, both occasionally found in the lowland blanket bogs in the west, especially in Connemara, Co. Galway. The large leafy liverwort *Pleurozia purpurea* and the black patches of the moss *Campylopus atrovirens* are often prominent in blanket bogs, as are the occasional hummocks of *Racomitrium lanuginosum* and *Leucobryum glaucum*. Where heathers dominate the drier slopes and banks within blanket bog, the heath species can come to the fore, such as *Hypnum jutlandicum, Hylocomium splendens, Pleurozium schreberi* and *Rhytidiadelphus loreus*.

Although considerable areas of blanket bog still remain in Ireland, much has been planted with conifers (196,800 ha in the Republic of Ireland according to the National Forest Inventory), cut for turf (6833 ha for electricity generation), seriously impacted by overstocking (at least 38,000 ha) or remain threatened by infrastructural developments such as wind farms (Douglas *et al.* 2008). A similar situation occurs in Northern Ireland (Northern Ireland Blanket Bog Habitat Action Plan – NIEA web site http://www.nienviron-ment.gov.uk). All these activities have no doubt had their impact on bryophyte communities, not just within blanket bogs themselves, but also in habitats and vegetation closely associated or hydrologically linked to them. Industrial-scale peat extraction of lowland blanket bog at Oweninny in Co. Mayo undoubtedly caused the extinction of *Meesia triquetra* from its only known site in Ireland at the Bellacorick Iron Flush (King 1958, King & Scannell 1960). Even though restoration of degraded peatland habitats is underway here (Farrell 2008), it is unlikely that boreal relict species such as *Meesia triquetra* will ever return by natural means.

Rich fens (PF1, Alkaline Fens and Calcareous Fens with *Cladium mariscus* on Annex I of the EU Habitats

Oweninny peat-fuelled power station, Co. Mayo (decommissioned).

Rich fen vegetation, near Crossmolina, Co. Mayo.

Directive), poor fens (PF2) and transition mires (PF3, Transition Mires and Quaking Bogs on Annex I of the EU Habitats Directive) often occur in close association with bogs, especially in the uplands and west of the country where they can occur as flushes amongst blanket bog vegetation. Further east, fens can also occur in spring-fed topogenous depressions and on slopes and valley sides in association with woodland and other habitat types. Typically, instead of *Sphagnum*, there is a carpet of so-called brown mosses underneath and amongst the herbaceous vegetation. The type of fen that develops varies according to base status. A little enrichment leads to poor fen, in which species such as *Sarmentypnum exannulatum* and *Warnstorfia fluitans* appear and the most characteristic bog Sphagna, such as *S. capillifolium* and *S. papillosum*, disappear, while *S. fallax* and *S. subnitens* assume greater importance. This is the habitat for the rare species *Hamatocaulis vernicosus* in Ireland (listed on Annex II of the EU Habitats Directive). This moss occurs in very wet blanket bog flushes in upland areas such as Meentygrannagh, Co. Donegal, Largan More, Co. Mayo and in the Comeragh Mountains, Co. Waterford. It can also occur in slightly more base-rich intermediate fen, or transition mire, such as at Owenbrin (Lough Mask) and near Gortachalla Lough in Co. Galway and at Scragh Bog, Co. Westmeath. The basiphilous *Sphagnum contortum* can become prominent in this vegetation, along with *Scorpidium revolvens* and *Campylium stellatum*, and there are usually flush species such as *Philonotis fontana* and *Bryum pseudotriquetrum* present. Rich fen develops in strongly base-rich conditions, and here *Sphagnum contortum* may again be abundant, sometimes joined by

the rarer species *S. teres* and *S. warnstorfii*, all of which are strictly confined to base-rich conditions. Other rich-fen species commonly include *Scorpidium cossonii*, *Philonotis calcarea* and *Palustriella commutata*, but this habitat also holds much rarer species such as *Rhizomnium pseudopunctatum*, *Cinclidium stygium* and *Tomentypnum nitens*. The rich fens and flushes that occur in association with the lowland blanket bogs in north Co. Mayo are perhaps the best examples of this habitat left in Ireland and support some of the rarest bryophytes, such as *Leiocolea rutheana* (Lockhart 1989b) and *Paludella squarrosa* (Lockhart 1999).

The transition between acid bog and rich fen is, of course, continuous, and it is not uncommon to find the whole range at a single locality. One of the main threats to fenland, and indeed mires in general, is nutrient enrichment (eutrophication), primarily in the form of nitrogen input. A small amount of nutrient enrichment, as might occur in natural conditions, encourages the growth of a different assemblage of brown mosses, including *Calliergonella cuspidata*, *Calliergon cordifolium*, *C. giganteum* and *Drepanocladus aduncus*. However, an excessively high level of nitrogen leads to the whole delicate gradation of species being disrupted. In these conditions, the common moss *Calliergonella cuspidata* tends to take over at the expense of the more ecologically demanding species (Kooijman 1993). It is, indeed, often almost the only bryophyte present in wet meadows and mires where there has been excessive nutrient input from livestock, fertiliser or agricultural run-off. *Hamatocaulis vernicosus* is particularly vulnerable to this sort of damage, especially because in Ireland it is confined to just a small handful of scattered sites.

Lowland grassland, rock and heath

Modern improved agricultural grassland (GA1) is bryologically dull, being a highly artificial, nutrient-rich environment in which species such as Ryegrass (*Lolium* spp.) thrive at the expense of other plants. However, species-rich grassland still exists in some quantity in Ireland, especially in limestone areas. Grassland becomes more interesting for bryophytes where the soil is thin, nutrient inputs are low and where the grazing regime maintains an open sward. This can result in a species-rich vegetation in which the bryophyte component develops more naturally beneath the vascular plants. Bare skeletal soil in calcareous grassland is particularly rich, offering a habitat in which small and uncompetitive species can complete their life cycle before coarser vegetation encroaches.

Where these conditions prevail, such as on esker ridges in the midlands and in limestone areas of the Burren and Aran Islands, dry calcareous grassland (GS1 and sometimes Semi-natural Dry grasslands and Scrubland facies on Calcareous Substrates on Annex I of the EU Habitats Directive) can support a wide variety of mosses and liverworts. Some large pleurocarpous mosses dominate on north-facing slopes, where the growth of grass is thicker: ubiquitous plants such as *Calliergonella cuspidata*, *Pseudoscleropodium purum* and *Rhytidiadelphus squarrosus* are usually abundant, often with the liverwort *Frullania tamarisci*, but there may also be calcicoles such as *Ctenidium molluscum*, *Homalothecium lutescens* and *Hypnum cupressiforme* var. *lacunosum*. The generalist species tend to decrease on more skeletal soils on south-facing slopes, where the larger calcicoles occur in less luxuriance and are joined by a diverse group of smaller acrocarpous mosses on more open ground, including *Fissidens dubius* and *Dicranella varia*. Tufts of uncommon pleurocarpous calcicoles such as *Entodon concinnus* and *Thuidium assimile* develop amongst the grasses, with much smaller acrocarpous species on bare patches: *Trichostomum brachydontium*, *T. crispulum*, *Encalypta streptocarpa*, *Didymodon* spp., *Weissia* spp., etc. Really good-quality turf supports *Tortella tortuosa* (usually a plant of limestone rock outcrops), and the liverworts *Reboulia hemisphaerica* and *Scapania aspera*.

Other kinds of lowland grassland tend to be less rich in bryophytes, except for those on the coast (see section on Coastland). Hay meadows (GS2 and Lowland Hay Meadows on Annex I of the EU Habitats Directive) may be almost devoid of bryophyte cover, although very rich in flowering plants. Neutral or acid grasslands (GS3) normally support a small number of common species, only becoming interesting for bryophytes where there is very little nutrient input (in which case it is more likely that heath will develop), or where it becomes wetter (when *Sphagnum* appears and the habitat becomes something approaching mire). Wet grassland on poorly-drained mineral or organic soils (GS4 and sometimes *Molinia* Meadows on Calcareous, Peaty or Clayey-silt-laden Soils in the EU Habitats Directive) is a very widespread habitat in Ireland, and although usually relatively dull for bryophytes, can sometimes hold more interest. There are occasionally sparse colonies of *Sphagnum* that may support small liverworts, and *Cephalozia pleniceps* occurs in this habitat. The rare *Sphagnum subsecundum* was once recorded (1986) from this type of wet grassland on the Shannon callows at Clonmacnoise, Co. Offaly but has not been found there since. The very rare liverwort *Pallavicinia lyellii* tends to favour the shaded bases of *Molinia* tussocks and was found as recently as 2009 in this habitat at Shronowen Bog in Co. Kerry.

Calcareous grasslands on skeletal soils often occur with scattered exposures of limestone rock (ER2 including Limestone Pavements and Calcareous Rocky Slopes with Chasmophytic Vegetation in the EU Habitats Directive) and these normally support a good variety of bryophytes. *Tortella tortuosa* is often one of the most frequent species, much more common on rock than in turf, and is easily recognised by its bright green tufts and leaves twisted when dry. It is often joined by a rich assemblage of plants including *Encalypta streptocarpa*, *Anomodon viticulosus*, *Eurhynchium striatum*, *Ctenidium molluscum*, *Homalothecium sericeum*, and the dendroid shoots of *Thamnobryum alopecurum*. Less often, especially where the rock is shaded by Holly (*Ilex aquifolium*) or some other vegetation, there may be *Plasteurhynchium striatulum*, looking like a small form of *E. striatum*, and extensive colonies of the liverwort *Marchesinia mackaii*. Where this occurs, there is usually a smaller, greener liverwort, *Cololejeunea calcarea*, forming tiny grass-green mats on rock surfaces, or overgrowing other bryophytes. It is occasionally joined by the rarer *C. rossettiana*, distinguishable with certainty only under the microscope.

The Burren in Co. Clare is undoubtedly Ireland's most famous limestone area, but, spectacular as it is for flowering plants, the bryophyte flora is relatively mundane. It is rather dry for the most part, and limestone pavement in any case supports a relatively small range of specialist calcicole bryophytes, although often in great

Lough Gealain, The Burren, Co. Clare.

quantity. Thus, while *Tortella tortuosa*, *Hypnum cupressiforme* var. *lacunosum*, *Ctenidium molluscum*, *Scapania aspera* and other common calcicoles are abundant, rarities are few. There is one site for *Orthothecium rufescens*, and *Tortella densa* is locally frequent in places. Limestone pavement occurs in many other parts of Ireland too but is threatened in most places by changes in agricultural practices, especially changes to grazing regimes which have led to the extensive encroachment of Hazel scrub, notably in the Burren. Other threats, including quarrying and removal of stone for rockeries, although important, are by comparison relatively minor.

The hard chalk of Cos Antrim and Down is one of the lesser-known Irish habitats, but there are many very interesting records, including rare species. The chalk specialist *Seligeria calycina*, for example, is known only from this area of Ireland, although it has not been seen since 1964. It is a rare European endemic, relatively frequent only on the chalk of south-eastern England. *Seligeria calcarea* and *Metzgeria pubescens* also have their only Irish localities on this rock type. Sallagh Braes in Co. Antrim is a classic chalk site.

Lowland heath is widespread in Ireland, especially in the west. Dry heath (listed on Annex I of the EU Habitats Directive) occurs on nutrient-poor acid soils (HH1) or on leached soils overlying limestone (HH2) and tends to be dominated, below the ericaceous shrubs, by lichens. Wet heath (HH3 and listed on Annex I of the EU Habitats Directive) develops on shallow peat (15–50 cm) with a fluctuating water table, but intergrades with blanket bog on deeper (> 50 cm), waterlogged peat. While wet heath is bryologically richer, heathland in general is often overwhelmingly dominated in the bryophyte layer by three large pleurocarps: *Hypnum jutlandicum*, *Hylocomium splendens* and *Pleurozium schreberi*. *Plagiothecium undulatum* and *Dicranum scoparium* are also usually frequent or abundant, and wetter areas support *Sphagnum*, with *S. compactum* perhaps the most characteristic species of short heavily grazed heath. Varying amounts of leafy liverworts creep through the mosses, including *Barbilophozia floerkei*, *Lophozia ventricosa*, *Diplophyllum albicans* and (rarely) *Ptilidium ciliare*. However, many areas of heath have been degraded by overstocking with grazing livestock or subjected to burning in order to encourage new heather and grass growth, and this tends to destroy, or at least badly damage, the bryophytes. Thus, recently burned areas support fewer species than those that have not been burned for a long time. Patches of bare, dry peat are

Sallagh Braes, Co. Antrim.

usually colonised by *Ceratodon purpureus*, *Pohlia nutans* and species of *Campylopus*, and these, particularly the invasive alien *Campylopus introflexus*, tend to be encouraged by burning. *C. introflexus*, a native of the southern hemisphere, was first recorded in Britain in 1941 and in Ireland in 1942, and is now recorded from every Irish vice-county. Like some other species of *Campylopus*, *C. introflexus* is very efficient at dispersal by fragmentation and from spores. It often occurs in huge quantity on bare peat, seemingly occupying the niche that should naturally be filled by native species of *Campylopus*. Lowland heath is threatened by reclamation for agriculture, afforestation, infrastructural developments, excessive burning, overstocking and bracken invasion.

Bare peaty banks can support a variety of leafy liverworts, whether in lowland heath or on blanket peat at higher altitudes. *Calypogeia fissa* and *C. muelleriana* are usually prominent, less often with *C. arguta*, and species of *Cephalozia*, *Kurzia* and *Lophozia* are usually abundant too, along with common acidophiles such as *Diplophyllum albicans* and *Nardia scalaris*. *Cephalozia catenulata* is a specialist of this kind of habitat and *Cladopodiella francisci*, although rare, can be very locally abundant on some wet peaty banks.

Montane

Montane habitats often occur in complex mosaics and elements of several of the habitat categories described by Fossitt (2000) are considered together here (notably HH4, ER1, ER2, ER3 and ER4). Many montane habitats in Ireland are also listed on Annex I of the EU Habitats Directive: Alpine and Boreal Heath, Wet Heath, Dry Heath, Species-rich *Nardus* Upland Grassland, *Molinia* Meadows, Blanket Bog, Rhynchosporion, Alkaline Fen, Transition Mires, Petrifying Springs, Siliceous Scree, Calcareous Scree,

Calcareous Rocky Slopes, Siliceous Rocky Slopes, Dystrophic Lakes and (Upland) Oligotrophic Lakes.

Mountains are places where bryophytes can really come into their own: places where the climate is harsh and there is reduced competition from vascular plants. The highest Irish mountain ranges are arranged more or less in a coastal ring around the central lowlands, with some inland mountain massifs rising directly and dramatically from the plain. While most of the Irish mountains have base-poor geology, there are some significantly base-rich outcrops in most of them, and the Dartry Mountains are composed largely of Carboniferous Limestone. Many of the Irish mountains are capped with blanket bog peat, where the slope and local topography permits, and cloaked on their flanks by wet and dry heaths. Whilst these are of bryological interest in their own right, the greatest bryophyte diversity lies in the ravines, gullies, corries and cliffs, especially those that occur at higher altitudes with north-facing aspects.

What might be termed a typical Irish mountain bryophyte flora can be found on the predominantly siliceous rocks of many of the ranges. The ground is often dominated by heather and other dwarf shrubs in the Ericaceae, with Bilberry (*Vaccinium myrtillus*) on higher ground, beneath which there is a carpet of bryophytes. As in the lowlands, the most common of these are *Hypnum jutlandicum*, *Hylocomium splendens* and *Pleurozium schreberi*, all big pleurocarps that form extensive untidy mats. *Dicranum scoparium*, *Plagiothecium undulatum*, *Racomitrium lanuginosum* and *Rhytidiadelphus loreus* are almost as widespread, and common species of *Sphagnum*, *Polytrichum commune* and leafy liverworts such as *Diplophyllum albicans*, *Lophozia ventricosa*, *Anastrophyllum minutum* and *Scapania gracilis* occur where the ground is wetter, or on sheltered north-facing slopes.

Rock exposure often increases with steepness and altitude, and different bryophytes begin to appear. Where the geology is a rather unproductive granite or quartzite, as it often is in the Irish hills, the saxicolous flora is composed of a rather limited and predictable suite of species. The most prominent on acid rocks are species of *Racomitrium* and *Andreaea*, especially *R. heterostichum*, *R. fasciculare*, *A. rothii* and *A. rupestris*, as well as *Dicranum scoparium*, *Campylopus* spp. and a number of common leafy liverworts such as *Diplophyllum albicans*. While these plants are usually the dominant bryophytes, there are sometimes other species present in smaller quantity. *Andreaea* was a poorly understood genus in Ireland and

Britain until the work of Murray (1988), when a number of additional species were added to the flora. Most of these are rare high-altitude plants absent from Ireland, but one that does occur is *A. megistospora*, distinguished from the common *A. rothii* by its relatively large spores. It is still under-recorded, but appears to be fairly widely scattered in the Irish mountains. Of the two subspecies of *A. rothii*, the more frequent seems to be subsp. *falcata*, with subsp. *rothii* more sparsely distributed. However, there appears to be less of a distinction between the two taxa in Ireland than there is in some parts of Britain, and it is often not at all easy to differentiate them. *Kiaeria blyttii* is a small montane acrocarp with long narrow leaves, looking superficially very like a *Dicranum* or a *Campylopus*. Until recently, this was thought to be a very rare species in Ireland, but it must have been widely overlooked, because fieldwork has shown it to be widespread, albeit uncommon, on the higher rocks of most of the Irish ranges.

Crevices among the rocks support a slightly different community, although some of the same species that grow directly on the rocks are still present: *Dicranum scoparium*, *Campylopus* spp. and *Diplophyllum albicans*. Small members of the Polytrichaceae are frequent, including *Polytrichastrum alpinum*, *Pogonatum aloides*, *P. urnigerum* and *Oligotrichum hercynicum*, all plants that find a second home on banks in coniferous plantations in the uplands. *Dicranella heteromalla* is more frequent in crevices than it is on rock surfaces. Small plants like *Blindia acuta* and *Anomobryum julaceum* are usually to be found where there is seepage. Rarer species can occasionally be found, but are not necessarily very predictable in their occurrence. *Oedipodium griffithianum*, for example, grows in acid montane screes and rock crevices, but its only known recent site is on Mweelrea in Co. Mayo.

Mountain summits can sometimes be capped by blanket bog dominated by ericaceous shrubs, sedges and rushes, beneath which are common species of *Sphagnum* and a limited range of other bryophytes. The peat is often eroded into bare channels between vegetated hags or remnants of the former bog, and the underlying bedrock or sand and gravel may be exposed in places. Summit ridges that are not capped with peat, or where rock exposures protrude through the peat, can be of some bryophyte interest, although usually limited. There can sometimes be a development of *Racomitrium* heath, where *R. lanuginosum* is dominant. This community is, however, seriously damaged by overgrazing and so has been lost from some sites. *Racomitrium* and *Andreaea* are again usually prominent on the rocks, sometimes

Oedipodium griffithianum habitat in acid montane scree, west of Lough Bellawaum, Mweelrea, Co. Mayo.

accompanied by smaller quantities of other species, including *Dicranum fuscescens*, *Kiaeria blyttii* and *Gymnomitrion* spp. The other bryologically significant aspect of summit vegetation consists of apparently vegetation-free peaty, stony hollows and flushes. Sometimes these are indeed almost devoid of plants, but occasionally close inspection will reveal a biotic crust of bryophytes and lichens, usually dark in colour and scarcely distinguishable from the peat without a hand lens. Very small liverworts such as *Cephaloziella* spp., *Anthelia juratzkana* and montane species of *Marsupella*, notably *M. sphacelata*, grow here.

The Wicklow Mountains have a relatively low diversity of bryophytes, partly because of the granite lithology and partly because of their management history. They are not particularly Atlantic in character, and the rock has little basic enrichment, giving rise to predominantly acid substrates with relatively little variety.

Although there are some extensive areas of intact blanket bog, such as Liffey Head Bog, many of the mountain tops and plateaux consist mainly of hagged and often burned peat and are particularly poor for bryophytes. Corries, streams and ravines provide some variety, but finding interesting bryophytes can be hard work, particularly in the rain; these hills have a wet climate, in spite of their eastern position. At higher altitudes the montane rocks typically support a bryophyte flora dominated by common species of *Racomitrium* and *Andreaea*, often accompanied by the alien species *Campylopus introflexus* in the rock crevices, although the rare *Ditrichum zonatum* occurs on the dripping north-facing rocks of North Prison, near the summit of Lugnaquilla, with *Kiaeria blyttii* nearby. The latter species occurs in abundance on boulders in the north corrie of Mullaghcleevaun, the second-highest Wicklow peak. The blanket peat, having been subjected to much

Lugnaquilla North Prison, Co. Wicklow.

disturbance, is species-poor, and dominated by common pleurocarps such as *Hypnum jutlandicum*, common species of *Sphagnum*, *Racomitrium lanuginosum* and *Campylopus introflexus*. At lower altitudes, in corries and ravines, the rock appears to be a little more minerotrophic, and therefore supports a rather more varied bryophyte flora. This is best seen at Glendalough and Powerscourt Waterfall, where *Cynodontium bruntonii* and *Rhabdoweisia fugax* are locally frequent on rock exposures, although this probably has more to do with the water-retentive properties of the rock than its mineral content. *R. fugax* is a particularly rare plant in Ireland. Interesting species of *Grimmia* also occur occasionally on these lower rocks, such as *G. decipiens* and *G. torquata*, although the latter has not been seen in Wicklow for over a century. *Sphagnum russowii* is occasional on steep heathy banks, sometimes growing with *S. girgensohnii*.

The Blue Stack Mountains in Co. Donegal, formed mainly of slaty rocks and granite, were thought to be botanically poor, and the standard montane flora described above does indeed predominate. However, recent survey work has revealed some unexpected interest. *Kiaeria blyttii* is there, and *Gymnomitrion concinnatum*, a rare liverwort in Ireland, is locally frequent. *Cynodontium jenneri* and *Philonotis tomentella* were both discovered there, new to Ireland, on previously unexplored crags (Rothero 2003), along with *Rhabdoweisia fugax*. An unexpected recent discovery, also new to Ireland, was a small tuft of *Kiaeria falcata*, found growing on an outcrop near one of the Blue Stack summits. This species is most characteristic of areas of late-lying snow in the Scottish Highlands.

The montane flora can improve dramatically with changes in the geology and topography. The Galty Mountains, for example, are considerably more varied

The Blue Stack Mountains, Co. Donegal, currently the only known site in Ireland for *Cynodontium jenneri* and *Kiaeria falcata*.

North crags of Carrignabinnia, habitat for *Bartramia ithyphylla*, Galty Mountains, Co. Limerick.

Temple Hill pinnacle, Galty Mountains, Co. Limerick, currently the only site in Ireland for *Encalypta ciliata*.

than either the Wicklow Mountains or the Blue Stacks. They are composed of Old Red Sandstone, conglomerates and slates, with many places where mineral enrichment leads to a richer bryophyte flora. They also have a series of north-facing corries with lakes and extensive crags, ideal bryophyte territory. These cliffs and crags are covered with a rich montane flora amongst which the bryophytes are prominent: plants like *Amphidium mougeotii* growing in large, dark green, swelling cushions; *Grimmia torquata*, forming much smaller cushions on dry rocks with contorted leaves and small white hair-points; *Bartramia ithyphylla*, forming small tufts of spiky, glaucous-green leaves in inaccessible crevices, and all against a rich backdrop of smaller creeping mosses and liverworts. The Galty Mountains are of additional interest because of the outcrops of Carboniferous Limestone further down the slopes, on one of which is the only currently known Irish locality for *Encalypta ciliata*.

Similarly, the Comeragh Mountains support many base-rich outcrops (ER2) and are very rich for their size. *Sphagnum skyense* and *Tortella bambergeri*, both recently added to the Irish flora, grow there in at least two sites each. The Comeraghs are particularly good for another aspect of the montane bryophyte flora—lake shores. Boulders surrounding corrie lakes in the hills can be rich in bryophytes, probably because of a combination of geology and humidity, and the Comeragh lakes seem to meet the requirements for a really good bryophyte flora. Most of them have abundant mosses such as *Racomitrium* spp., *Grimmia lisae*, *G. ramondii* and *Schistidium strictum*, and several have good populations of the rare *Antitrichia curtipendula*, a large and handsome moss, although the best population of this species in the area is not on a lake shore at all, but on an extensive boulder scree in the north-facing corrie of Farbreaga. One of the Sgilloge Loughs has the only known Irish population of *Hedwigia ciliata* var. *ciliata*, another

Lakeside boulders with *Hedwigia ciliata* and *Antitrichia curtipendula*, Sgilloge Loughs, Comeragh Mountains, Co. Waterford.

strikingly beautiful moss that grows in abundance at this one site, and Coumshingaun Lough has a population of the rare *Plagiothecium platyphyllum*. Other lakeside rarities in the area include *Hedwigia integrifolia*, *Grimmia funalis* and *Grimmia muehlenbeckii*. The nearby Knockmealdown Mountains are also notable for the considerable bryophyte diversity in the north-east corrie. Here, significant base-rich exposures hold more *Tortella bambergeri* and the rocks around the small lakes support an interesting bryophyte community which again includes *Antitrichia curtipendula*, with *Plagiothecium platyphyllum* at the second of its three known Irish localities.

Montane flushes can occur below cliffs and often support fen vegetation. The bryophytes of base-poor flushes usually include plants such as *Dichodontium palustre*, *Philonotis fontana* and *Sphagnum denticulatum*, but in base-rich conditions diversity increases dramatically, and species such as *Sphagnum contortum*, *Campylium stellatum*, *Philonotis calcarea*, *Scorpidium cossonii*, *S. revolvens* and *S. scorpioides* occur. There are

often intricate patterns of water movement over the hillside, with different flushes supporting slightly different floras according to base status, so a whole range of communities may be present. Sometimes rare species may be found, as in the Comeragh Mountains, where *Hamatocaulis vernicosus* grows in extensive flush systems along with *Sphagnum teres* and *Sarmentypnum exannulatum*.

In general, bryophyte cover and diversity in the uplands both increase westwards. Sometimes, however, diversity may remain rather low even in areas of extreme oceanicity. On Slieve Tooey in Co. Donegal, for example, north-facing slopes are entirely clothed in a colourful bryophyte-dominated rock garden composed of a relatively small number of species, with huge swelling hummocks of *Sphagnum*, especially the bright red *S. capillifolium* and the red-and-green *S. quinquefarium*, interspersed with the pale greens, oranges and browns of various large and locally common leafy liverworts such as *Diplophyllum albicans*, *Lophozia ventricosa*, *L. incisa* and *Herbertus aduncus* subsp. *hutchinsiae*. In some circumstances, the extreme climate seems to favour just a few species, which proliferate luxuriantly, suppressing, rather than promoting, diversity.

On the other hand, western hills can support an extremely beautiful and diverse bryophyte flora, often centred on the 'Northern Atlantic hepatic mat', a community of oceanic montane heath first described by Ratcliffe (1968). This community develops in extremely specific conditions of topography and climate, and is seen to its best advantage on north- to east-facing hillsides at medium to high altitudes in areas with at least 1500 mm of rainfall annually and (more importantly) with at least 200 wet days (i.e. days on which there is at least 1 mm of rainfall). The community is dominated by medium-sized to large leafy liverworts of which the most frequent (in approximately descending order of frequency) are *Mylia taylorii*, *Scapania gracilis*, *Bazzania tricrenata*, *Pleurozia purpurea*, *Plagiochila spinulosa*, *Herbertus aduncus* subsp. *hutchinsiae* and *Anastrepta orcadensis*. The richest sites support rarities: *Bazzania pearsonii*, *Mastigophora woodsii* and *Scapania ornithopodioides*, and even the extremely rare plants *Adelanthus lindenbergianus*, *Plagiochila carringtonii* and *Scapania nimbosa*. Many of these liverworts have a fascinating phytogeography, exhibiting widely-disjunct global patterns of distribution. Thus, *Adelanthus lindenbergianus* has its only European sites in the west of Ireland and Scotland (where there is a single site for it), but is widespread in the tropics on isolated mountain

Plagiochila carringtonii and *Herbertus aduncus*, Mweelrea, Co. Mayo.

ranges. *Scapania ornithopodioides* occurs elsewhere in Scotland, the Faeroe Islands and Norway, with disjunct populations in the Himalaya, China, Japan, Taiwan, the Philippines and Hawaii. Perhaps the most extreme example is *Plagiochila carringtonii*, with populations in

Scotland and the Faeroes, but outside Europe it is known only from Nepal, where it is represented by a different subspecies. Ireland is thus of great international importance for this community. Classic sites for the Northern Atlantic hepatic mat in Ireland are found in the corries of Brandon Mountain and Macgillycuddy's Reeks in Co. Kerry, the Twelve Bens of Connemara in Co. Galway, Slievemore and Corraun in Co. Mayo and Slieve League and Errigal in Co. Donegal.

Unfortunately the habitat for the Northern Atlantic hepatic mat in Ireland has been seriously damaged. The Twelve Bens of Connemara used to be one of the best sites, but impacts from overstocking have virtually destroyed it. Although quoted by Porley & Hodgetts (2005), the following extract from the account of the 1994 British Bryological Society (BBS) meeting in Connemara (Blockeel 1995a) is well worth repeating here:

> The problems of overgrazing were evident during our ascent (of Benbreen): in one

The Twelve Bens, Co. Galway.

small area of block scree the heather was badly damaged but we were still able to find a little *Bazzania pearsonii* and *Adelanthus lindenbergianus* among the more plentiful *Herbertus aduncus*. We were scarcely prepared, however, for the devastation which awaited us in the northern corrie. Here, on the stony north-facing slope, a few broken fragments of heather and the dead remains of large *Herbertus* tussocks bore sombre witness to the destruction of the dwarf shrub heath which once clothed these slopes. We could find only small and sorry pieces of *A. lindenbergianus*, with a little *Bazzania tricrenata* and *B. pearsonii*. *Herbertus aduncus* had fared slightly better. The *Adelanthus* must have been plentiful here only a few years ago. Several people observed that the overstocking with sheep has been precipitated and encouraged by EEC subsidies.

A single small colony of *A. lindenbergianus* was found recently on the north slope of Bengower, on a steep rocky slope with patchy heather and Crowberry (*Empetrum nigrum*) cover (Long 2010). Long comments, 'This could be literally the last survivor in the Bens of a formerly widespread species'.

Many of the oceanic mountains of the west have corrie lakes which support interesting bryophytes amongst the boulders strewn along their shores. Most of the same species that grow in similar habitat in the Comeragh Mountains are abundant here, but are joined

North-east slope of Bengower, an area where Northern Atlantic hepatic mat has been lost, Co. Galway.

Lough Cruttia, below Brandon Mountain, Co. Kerry.

by many oceanic species growing in the crevices among the boulders. Around the lakes below Brandon Mountain, for instance, there is an excellent development of a community of rare small liverworts. Normally a community found in wooded ravines, here it grows in dark shady hollows in block scree near to the lakes: many species of *Lejeunea*, including the rare *L. eckloniana*, *L. flava*, *L. hibernica* and *L. mandonii*, with *Radula carringtonii*, *R. holtii*, *R. voluta*, *Metzgeria leptoneura* and the elusive *Acrobolbus wilsonii* are all found here. The western mountains also support many other oceanic species that are rare or absent elsewhere in Ireland, including the large and spectacular mosses *Campylopus setifolius* and *C. shawii*, the latter found in acid flushes and confined to the extreme south-west, the related *Dicranodontium uncinatum*, in block screes in west Galway and Mayo, and the beautiful *Paraleptodontium recurvifolium*, occasionally found in local abundance among rocks by streams and waterfalls in the south-west and in west Mayo.

The Macgillycuddy's Reeks are Ireland's highest mountains and are of bryological interest mainly for their Northern Atlantic hepatic mat communities, which include the very rare liverwort *Scapania nimbosa*, refound on Carrauntoohil at 830 m in 2009 by R.L. Hodd. Other rarities include the mosses *Amphidium lapponicum*, discovered above Lough Cummeenoughter on Carrauntoohil in 2007, and *Arctoa fulvella*, reported from Beenkeragh-Carrauntoohil in 1983.

The mountains of the Dingle Peninsula in Co. Kerry are more geologically varied and therefore support a

North-east face of Carrauntoohil, Co. Kerry.

David Long, en route to Brandon Mountain during BBS field meeting, 2009.

Grimmia muehlenbeckii on knife-edge slab, Brandon Mountain, Co. Kerry.

richer flora than the Macgillycuddy's Reeks. Brandon Mountain, and the Slieve Mish range, host excellent examples of Northern Atlantic hepatic mat communities, with *Adelanthus lindenbergianus* discovered at An Loch Dubh in 2008 and *Scapania nimbosa* seen at one locality in 2009 in the upper corrie below Brandon, but with much *Scapania ornithopodioides*, *Bazzania pearsonii* and *Mastigophora woodsii* found there during the BBS summer field meeting in 2009. Other montane rarities include *Amphidium lapponicum* and *Plagiothecium cavifolium*. *Tortella bambergeri* and *Grimmia muehlenbeckii* are both frequent here, and the rare *Scapania gymnostomophila* was found recently on base-rich rocks in a north-east-facing corrie.

Slieve League in Co. Donegal is likewise of additional interest because of the base-rich exposures in its northern corrie, with a very rich mixture of oceanic and calcicolous

bryophytes present. The rare arctic-alpine *Arctoa fulvella* also occurs there. Also in Donegal, Muckish Mountain has Northern Atlantic hepatic mat vegetation, with *Scapania ornithopodioides* and *Adelanthus lindenbergianus* recently refound there. Bulbin Mountain is of exceptional bryological interest and holds the only known surviving Irish population of *Gymnomitrion corallioides* along with several other very rare species.

Mweelrea in Co. Mayo is extremely rich in both oceanic and montane bryophytes, including species of the Northern Atlantic hepatic mat and associated communities such as *Bazzania pearsonii*, *Scapania ornithopodioides*, *S. nimbosa* (which was last seen there

Northern Atlantic hepatic mat vegetation, under *Calluna*, north slopes of Muckish Mountain, Co. Donegal.

in 1987), *Dicranodontium uncinatum*, *Paraleptodontium recurvifolium*, *Mastigophora woodsii* and the very rare *Plagiochila carringtonii*, the latter at one of its two known localities in Ireland (the other last seen at Benbaun, Co. Galway in 1984). *Amphidium lapponicum* was found new to Ireland on Mweelrea in 2003 (Rothero 2004) and other plants of great rarity and interest on this mountain include *Bryum riparium*, *Ditrichum zonatum*, *Hygrohypnum duriusculum*, *Marsupella sprucei*, *Oedipodium griffithianum*, *Philonotis cernua*, *P. tomentella*, *Ptilium crista-castrensis*, *Racomitrium macounii* subsp. *alpinum* and *Sphagnum skyense*. It represents the only Irish locality for *Ptilium* and the only recent locality for *H. duriusculum*; for the very rare moss *P. cernua*, it represents the most recent record (1987) in either Ireland or Britain.

Other mountain ranges in Ireland all contain some bryophyte interest, albeit often rather limited. The

North-west of the summit of Bulbin Mountain, Co. Donegal, habitat for the only known surviving population of *Gymnomitrion corallioides* in Ireland.

Northern Atlantic hepatic mat vegetation, with *Mastigophora woodsii*, *Herbertus aduncus*, *Pleurozia purpurea* and *Sphagnum skyense*, Mweelrea, Co. Mayo.

Blackstairs Mountains in Cos Carlow and Wexford have a little *Kiaeria blyttii* and a very depauperate variant of the Northern Atlantic hepatic mat, with only the most common species present, high in the east corrie of Mount Leinster. The Ox Mountains of Co. Sligo are fairly low in elevation, but have extensive, intact areas of blanket bog, rich in Sphagna, and with some crags and lakes on the lower ground. There are many interesting old records from the Mourne Mountains of Co. Down, notably from Slieve Donard, but some of them are unsubstantiated and not refound in recent years. However, although they are composed mainly of granites and slates, they certainly retain some interest as *Kiaeria blyttii*, *Grimmia decipiens* and *G. funalis* still grow there, the area beneath the Black Stairs on Slieve Donard being particularly rich. The considerably lower Sperrin Mountains of Cos Londonderry and Tyrone are less diverse but support

Kiaeria blyttii, *Marsupella sprucei* and *Campylopus subulatus*. The basalt hill of Benbradagh in Co. Londonderry is bryologically very interesting, with populations of *Grimmia funalis*, *G. muehlenbeckii*, *Myurella julacea* and also *Encalypta rhaptocarpa* at its only recent Irish site. In addition, this is the only site in Ireland where *Eurhynchiastrum pulchellum* and *Tayloria tenuis* have ever been recorded, the former last seen for certain in 1964, and the latter in 1884.

One mountain range deserving special mention is the Dartry Mountains in Cos Sligo and Leitrim, centred on the famous Benbulbin. The extraordinary and dramatic karst landscape of peaks, cliffs and gullies is characteristic of the Carboniferous Limestone of which they are composed, and harbours a unique bryophyte flora. As well as all the usual lowland calcicolous species and many of the more common montane species, there are plants

Crumbling basalt of the west slopes of Benbradagh, Co. Londonderry, currently the only locality in Ireland for *Encalypta rhaptocarpa*.

here that are either very rare or not found anywhere else in Ireland. Not only that, but some of these are quite abundant in this very limited area. One of the country's most spectacular species, the red-coloured *Orthothecium rufescens*, is abundant in these hills but very rare in Ireland as a whole, occurring elsewhere only as small populations in the Burren, Co. Clare, on Slieve League, Co. Donegal and near Glencreawan Lough in Co. Fermanagh. Similarly, the liverwort *Pedinophyllum interruptum* is confined to these hills, the Burren and the Co. Fermanagh limestone. *Seligeria oelandica* is a plant of very specialised ecology, growing on cliff faces in more or less vertical, north-east-facing spongy tufa that is kept permanently moist by constant seepage, or less often on wet stones in flushes. Until recently it was thought to occur elsewhere only in Scandinavia or north-west North America, but during the past two decades it has been discovered in Co. Fermanagh, S. Wales, C. Europe and

Quebec. *Didymodon maximus* is found nowhere else in Ireland, or indeed Europe: the next nearest localities are in Alaska, arctic Canada, the Russian Far East and Mongolia, but there are many luxuriant colonies of this large and attractive species here in the Benbulbin range and outliers on the nearby Aghadunvane. *Seligeria patula*, *Timmia norvegica* and *Hymenostylium recurvirostrum* var. *insigne* are all plants that have their main Irish stations in this area; the *Timmia* is particularly conspicuous, as a large species of rock outcrops. *Schistidium robustum* was discovered new to Ireland a few years ago on Benwiskin (Rothero 2005). The best and most famous site for the special bryophyte flora of this area is probably Annacoona in Gleniff. The spectacular cliffs here are extraordinarily rich, supporting virtually all the local rarities. Unfortunately the glen has been overstocked with sheep in recent years, severely impacting the vascular plant flora and making the steep slopes dangerous

South side of Benbulbin, Co. Sligo.

Cliffs of Annacoona, Gleniff, Co. Sligo.

Soil erosion at Lettereeragh, Co. Mayo.

through boulders dislodged by sheep, but most of the rare bryophytes are relatively safe, occurring in sheltered crevices in vertical cliffs.

Overstocking and afforestation are probably the greatest threats to the bryophyte flora of the Irish mountains, although the impacts of climate change are clearly likely to become evident on the montane flora too. Overstocking has caused widespread damage to native vegetation in the uplands in recent years through overgrazing, trampling, eutrophication and soil erosion. Now that overstocking with sheep is no longer as profitable as it once was, and grazing pressure has to some extent eased in many areas, there is hope that vegetation can to some extent recover, although it may already be too late for the Northern Atlantic hepatic mat communities in parts of Connemara, Co. Galway, where both vegetation and soil cover has been lost (Long 2010). Afforestation with conifers has also caused widespread

habitat loss for montane bryophytes, especially on the slopes of the larger upland massifs and on many of the smaller hills that occupy the central Irish plain. Other significant threats include the spread of invasive aliens, particularly Rhododendron, pollution of watercourses, water abstraction from upland lakes, quarrying, erosion and burning. Infrastructural developments for wind farms and for hydroelectricity schemes also pose threats to bryophytes in upland areas.

Coastland

As an island at the edge of the Atlantic Ocean, Ireland is clearly profoundly influenced by the sea, and the many kilometres of coastline have a distinctive maritime vegetation in which bryophytes play their part. Most of the Irish coastline is hard, composed of rocky cliffs, although much is soft, with sand dunes, mud flats, shingle, lagoons, estuarine habitats and saltmarsh. Only

Rocky sea cliffs, south-east from Coastguard Hill, Co. Donegal, habitat for *Acrobolbus wilsonii*.

a very limited number of bryophyte species have physiological adaptations that allow them to tolerate salt spray, and are therefore able to grow in maritime conditions. The most maritime moss is *Schistidium maritimum*, which is widespread on (and almost confined to) coastal rocks, growing from just above the high water mark to several metres up the cliff, virtually throughout the length of the Irish coast. It is often accompanied on rocky coasts by *Ulota phyllantha*, *Ptychomitrium polyphyllum*, *Tortella flavovirens* and the liverwort *Frullania tamarisci*, with *U. hutchinsiae* rather less frequent, although none of these occurs quite so close to the high water mark as does *S. maritimum*. A much greater range of species can colonise further away from the most severe effects of salt spray, and a pseudo-woodland flora develops in shaded ravines and gullies in sea cliffs away from the immediate impact of the sea. The variety is, of course, greater in the west, not only because

the proportion of hard rock is greater but also because of the oceanic climate. Oceanic specialists such as *Glyphomitrium daviesii*, an attractive cushion-forming moss, may be very locally frequent, especially on basalt. The rare *Cyclodictyon laetevirens* can grow on wet shaded rocks in caves and ravines by the sea in the south-west.

The upper lip of sea cliffs (CS1, CS3 and Vegetated Sea Cliffs on Annex I of the EU Habitats Directive), where rocks become interspersed with a short maritime turf over thin soil, can be a rich habitat for small ephemeral bryophytes. Many of these are southern species with their main centre of distribution in Portugal, Spain and the Mediterranean region, reaching their northern limit on the southern coasts of Ireland, Wales and England. They are often small plants in the Pottiaceae, winter annuals completing their life cycle by the early spring, shrivelling or disappearing completely in the summer when the soil becomes desiccated. Two of

Maritime turf with *Tortula atrovirens*, *T. viridifolia* and *T. canescens*, near Ballycotton, Co. Cork.

the most frequent are *Tortula atrovirens* and *T. viridifolia*, once regarded as very rare in Ireland but now known to be much more widespread on southern coasts. *Weissia perssonii* is occasional but scattered on open soil or in rock crevices. *Tortula canescens* is a much rarer plant, discovered recently new to Ireland at two sites on the Cork coast. There are now several sites on the south coast for *Scleropodium touretii*, a larger perennial moss of trampled turf among cliff rocks.

The most important coastal habitats for bryophytes in Ireland are probably the extensive dune systems and machair, the latter of which is scattered along western and northern coasts (Gaynor 2006, 2008). Dry and newly

Machair at Dooaghtry, Co. Mayo.

stabilising coastal dunes (CD1, CD2) are usually devoid of bryophytes, but *Syntrichia ruralis* var. *ruraliformis*, the chief moss capable of colonising such unstable substrates, can occur in great abundance in more fixed dunes (CD3). Further species can colonise with a little more stability, including species such as *Tortella flavovirens*, *Ditrichum gracile* and the much less common *Rhynchostegium megapolitanum*. With increasing age and stabilisation, dunes can support quite a wide range of other bryophytes, eventually supporting large and sometimes extensive mats of big pleurocarpous mosses such as *Brachythecium albicans*, *Homalothecium lutescens*, *Rhytidiadelphus triquetrus*, *Hypnum cupressiforme* var. *lacunosum* and *Pseudoscleropodium purum*. The handsome pleurocarp *Rhytidium rugosum* occurs in such fixed dunes, and at the dry edges of dune slacks at Magilligan in Co. Londonderry.

Dune heath (Decalcified Dune Heath on Annex I of the EU Habitats Directive) appears to be a comparatively rare habitat in Ireland, but may be of considerable interest for bryophytes. Dune heath at Maghera Strand in Co. Donegal supports a population of the rare leafy liverwort *Scapania cuspiduligera* and Murlough Dunes in Co. Down holds the largest Irish populations of the mosses *Racomitrium canescens* and the very rare *Tortella inclinata*.

If sand is significantly base-rich, particularly if composed of shell fragments, the short, tight turf that develops in damp or seasonally flooded dune slacks (CD5 and Humid Dune Slacks on Annex I of the EU Habitats Directive) and machair (CD6 and listed on Annex I of the EU Habitats Directive) can be very rich in bryophytes, supporting not only small acrocarpous mosses such as species of *Didymodon*, but also much rarer, fen plants including the thallose liverwort *Moerckia flotoviana* and the mosses *Amblyodon dealbatus*, *Catoscopium nigritum*, *Distichium inclinatum* and *Meesia uliginosa*. The rare leafy liverworts *Leiocolea gillmanii* and *Scapania cuspiduligera* are both exclusively confined to coastal dune slacks and machair in Ireland, but are also known in Britain from base-rich rock ledges, flushes and among rocks by streams in montane areas, suggesting that they might be worth looking out for in these upland habitats in Ireland. *Scapania gymnostomophila* also demonstrates a similar and unusual distribution, with records from Malin Beg, a small south-facing bay in Co. Donegal, where it occurs on damp shell sand at the back of the beach, and known elsewhere in Ireland only from base-rich rock crevices in the mountains and on limestone pavement.

Magilligan Point, Co. Londonderry.

Dune heath at Murlough, Co. Down.

Dune slacks are also the main habitat for some exclusively coastal species of *Bryum*, a group of rare plants that have become better understood with recent fieldwork in Ireland. This includes *Bryum warneum*, seen recently at just four sites: North Bull, Co. Dublin, Garter Hill, Co. Mayo and Fahan and Catherine's Isle in Co. Donegal; *Bryum calophyllum*, also seen recently at four sites: Dooaghtry and two localities on Achill Island in Co. Mayo, with a single record near Ballyconneely in Co. Galway; and the recently described *Bryum dyffrynense*, scattered in the north and west. Several other rare species of *Bryum* also occur in dune slacks, notably *B. uliginosum* and *B. intermedium*, both of which are found on North Bull, but these species are also known from other calcareous habitats inland.

David Holyoak, with (from left to right) Christina Campbell, Deirdre Lynn and Noeleen Smyth, examining *Bryum uliginosum* at North Bull, Co. Dublin.

Abietinella abietina is a calcareous grassland moss that tends to occur at the junction between the damp dune slacks and the drier sand dunes above. It occurs as two varieties, var. *abietina* and var. *hystricosa*. The latter appears to be widespread in calcareous dune grassland in the north and west of Ireland, while the former is very rare and occurs only in the dune systems at Magilligan in Co. Londonderry, with old records from Malahide in Co. Dublin. Curiously, neither occurs in inland calcareous grassland, their main habitat in Britain.

If there is one species that can be regarded as a flagship for western Irish dune slacks and machair, it is *Petalophyllum ralfsii*. Formerly regarded as rare and threatened on an international scale, it was included on

Annex II of the EU Habitats Directive, but knowledge of this species in Ireland was very incomplete up until the late 1990s. Survey work, fuelled by the plant's inclusion on the international list, has since revealed several sites of surpassing importance for this attractive and unusual species. It now appears that Ireland may be the global headquarters for it, with some populations running into hundreds of thousands, or even millions of individuals, notably those at machair sites at Slyne Head, Co. Galway and Dooaghtry and Garter Hill in Co. Mayo, and the dune slacks at Inch, Co. Kerry. *P. ralfsii* has an odd distribution globally, with two disjunct clusters of records; one in Ireland and Britain, the other in the Mediterranean basin and southern Portugal (Porley *et al.* 2008). There are apparently no connecting populations in France or mainland Spain. This distribution raises an interesting question about whether there could be any genetic differences between the two populations.

Saltmarshes and estuaries are of relatively little importance for bryophytes because of their high salinity, but a few species can just tolerate the mildly saline conditions at the upper edges of saltmarsh (CM2), notably *Amblystegium serpens* var. *salinum* and *Hennediella heimii*. The rare *Bryum marratii* is another halophyte that tends to grow in brackish coastal habitats, usually on open muddy ground where there is at least a trickle of fresh water, especially at the upper edges of saltmarshes. This species has recently been found to be more widespread in north-western Ireland than was previously realised, but is thought to have been lost from its only locality in Northern Ireland (Portstewart) due to undergrazing. *Bryum salinum* is even rarer, with just one recent locality seen on upper saltmarsh near Derrymore Island, Co. Kerry in 2005. This species is probably an obligate halophyte restricted to regions where the summer rainfall is sufficient to prevent excess concentration of salt building up in the soil.

Coastal habitats are often under intense pressure from human activities. The main threats to both dune slacks and machair are inappropriate grazing regimes (both overgrazing and undergrazing), water abstraction and drainage, housing and leisure developments, recreation (including golf courses), forestry, coastal protection works and over-stabilisation. *Petalophyllum ralfsii* is a pioneer dune slack/machair species that needs open patches of ground and naturally fluctuating groundwater tables. Water abstraction, drainage, over-stabilisation and undergrazing (which can lead to scrub encroachment) are therefore particular threats to its conservation status.

Machair at Garter Hill, Co. Mayo, holds a large population of *Petalophyllum ralfsii*.

Dune slacks at Inch, Co. Kerry, an important habitat for *Petalophyllum ralfsii*.

Another threat that affects machair is the restructuring of agricultural holdings, with open commonage areas being divided and fenced and then subject to a range of different management practices. Many saltmarsh edges are now ungrazed or undergrazed, whereas some dune systems are overgrazed, with poaching a significant threat to at least one rich dune slack complex on the Dingle Peninsula. Holiday and leisure developments such as hotels and golf courses and widespread building of holiday accommodation have more or less ruined many areas, and threaten many others. Sand dunes in particular are often threatened by plans for golf links, leisure complexes and parking facilities. The special coastal bryophytes need undisturbed natural coasts with natural processes of erosion and deposition operating if they are to survive. Unfortunately, even wild and remote areas are often subject to tourist pressure, and excessive trampling by tourists and nutrient input from dog excrement can have a very destructive effect on the fragile skeletal soils that support species-rich clifftop grassland.

Golf course on machair at Keel, Achill Island, Co. Mayo.

Freshwater

There are very few *strictly* aquatic bryophytes, but there are many that grow on rocks in and by streams, where it is always humid, or where water splashes up to keep the mosses moist. The characteristic bryophyte flora of upland lakeside rocks, for example, is really a saxicolous flora of humid places rather than a flora that is strictly confined to lakesides, and has been discussed under montane communities. Beneath the surface of upland or lowland lakes, there is often only a single species of moss—*Fontinalis antipyretica*, a true aquatic with long, flexuose shoots and keeled leaves that is capable of reaching a metre or more in length. This plant grows from some metres below the surface to periodically inundated ground at or just above it. *F. antipyretica* is an aquatic generalist, however, and also grows in ponds and canals, and in fast-flowing streams and sluggish lowland rivers. The closely related *F. squamosa* is more restricted to upland streams.

Several leafy liverworts can also grow submerged in upland lakes (FL2) and streams, most notably *Nardia compressa*. There is a wide range of leafy liverworts associated with upland streams (FW1), including *Scapania undulata*, *Marsupella emarginata*, *Jungermannia exsertifolia* subsp. *cordifolia* and *Chiloscyphus polyanthos*. None of these is strictly aquatic, since they also occur in flushes and on wet dripping rocks. The large pleurocarpous moss *Platyhypnidium ripariodes* is perhaps the most common moss that can be regarded as aquatic, or nearly so. It is often abundant on riverine rocks, especially in small waterfalls, and appears to be resistant to a considerable amount of eutrophication and pollution. It is sometimes the only bryophyte present in polluted watercourses. Its close relative, *P. lusitanicum*, occupies a similar niche in clean water in oceanic areas. Emergent rocks usually support common mosses in the genera *Hygrohypnum* and *Hygroamblystegium*, with *Sciuro-hypnum plumosum* just above them, grading into a more varied and less specialist flora at the tops of the boulders. The rare *Hygrohypnum duriusculum* occurs on rocks in fast-flowing water in an upland stream at just one currently known locality in Ireland, below Lough Bellawaum, Mweelrea, Co. Mayo.

There are many more species that grow only in conditions of extreme moisture, while not actually submerged, and these are best seen on banks and rocks at the margins of upland streams, especially in and near the spray zone of waterfalls. There is often a characteristic zonation of bryophytes, with the pleurocarpous moss *Hyocomium armoricum* forming a conspicuous golden band on soil at and just above the water level, with liverworts such as *Pellia epiphylla* and *Cephalozia bicuspidata* forming another band on the bank just above it. *Thamnobryum alopecurum* is usually abundant (and forms a zone at water level) on base-rich rocks, and thallose liverworts such as *Conocephalum conicum* are also often frequent in this habitat. A wide range of leafy liverworts occur on wet rocks by streams, becoming even

Hygrohypnum duriusculum in an upland stream at its only known current location in Ireland, south-east of Lough Bellawaum, Mweelrea, Co. Mayo.

more varied and abundant in oceanic areas, where a rich community occurs on shaded, humid rock faces in ravines. This includes tiny plants in the Lejeuneaceae: *Aphanolejeunea microscopica*, *Colura calyptrifolia*, *Drepanolejeunea hamatifolia*, *Harpalejeunea molleri* and *Lejeunea* spp., and larger species such as *Jubula hutchinsiae* and *Dumortiera hirsuta*.

Fissidens fontanus is a strictly aquatic moss of still or slow-flowing water in the lowlands (FW2). It is very rare in Ireland, with populations recorded only from rocks in shallow water at the margins of lakes (Carrickaport Lough in Co. Leitrim, Lough Leane, Co. Kerry and Lough Donoghmeave in Co. Galway) and recently from the River Blackwater in Co. Cork. In Britain, it grows in a number of canals, and this habitat should perhaps be investigated more closely in Ireland. There are several other members of the genus *Fissidens* that are closely associated with water, usually growing on the banks of lowland rivers where they are regularly inundated, but scarcely aquatic in a true sense. All are rare plants in Ireland, but may be under-recorded: *F. monguillonii*, *F. polyphyllus*, *F. rivularis*, *F. rufulus* and *F. serrulatus*. Another plant of still or slow-moving lowland water is *Ricciocarpos natans*, a thallose liverwort that either floats free on the surface of the water or temporarily colonises muddy stream banks. It too is rare, appearing unpredictably at scattered sites throughout the central part of Ireland. *Riccia fluitans*, another rare thallose liverwort, is a little more frequent and may turn up almost anywhere amongst emergent vegetation at the side of streams and ditches in the lowlands, individual populations usually not persisting for very long.

There is a characteristic community of species that grow on silt-encrusted rocks, tree trunks and exposed roots on the banks of lowland rivers. This habitat is restricted in extent because many lowland rivers have been canalised, or otherwise disturbed. The pleurocarpous moss *Leskea polycarpa* is perhaps the most frequent member of this group, often forming extensive dark green mats covered with sporophytes, and sometimes accompanied by *Hygroamblystegium* spp., *Cirriphyllum crassinervium* and *Cinclidotus fontinaloides*. Rarer members of the community include *Syntrichia latifolia*, an acrocarpous moss with very wide leaves, *Didymodon nicholsonii*, *Orthotrichum rivulare*, *O. sprucei* and *Scleropodium cespitans*. Some of these plants can be very locally abundant, given available substrate. A concrete retaining wall by the River Lee in Cork city has an extraordinary amount of *S. cespitans* growing on it.

One tantalising record from a lowland river is of *Cinclidotus riparius* in the River Fergus near Ennis, Co. Clare, where it was found in 1884 by S.A. Stewart. This plant has hopped in and out of the Irish and British checklists over the years, and until recently it was thought that old records were errors. However, recent work on herbarium specimens (Blockeel 1998) showed that the species is indeed part of the flora. It was subsequently found to persist in the River Teme in central England, but has not yet been refound in the River Fergus. So far, the water level has been too high during all visits to have a chance of locating it, and it remains a target for future fieldwork.

The margins of lowland reservoirs, pools and riversides can sometimes support a highly specialised community of ephemeral plants that complete their life cycle within a few months, or even weeks, taking advantage of bare mud that might appear at the end of a dry summer, most conspicuously in the draw-down zone of reservoirs (FL7). A spore bank can survive in the mud for years, even decades in some cases, waiting for a dry spell to expose it, at which point it can explode into growth producing millions of plants very quickly, all of them rushing to spore production. This ephemeral flora consists mainly of small acrocarps such as *Aphanorrhegma patens* and *Tortula truncata*, sometimes with the thallose liverwort *Riccia cavernosa*, but there are some very rare species that are more or less restricted to this habitat. *Physcomitrium sphaericum*, *Weissia rostellata*, *Ephemerum cohaerens*, *E. crassinervium* subsp. *rutheanum*, *E. crassinervium* subsp. *sessile* and *E. spinulosum* are all known only from a handful of sites in Ireland. *Riccia huebeneriana* is a particularly beautiful liverwort, its thallus often tinged with violet as it matures, and is known only from Vartry Reservoir in Co. Wicklow. This is a rare habitat in Ireland, as many waterbodies are either too peaty, or too calcareous, or do not have the seasonal water level fluctuations that suit this community of plants.

Turloughs (FL6 and listed on Annex I of the EU Habitats Directive) are temporary lakes, usually filling and emptying through swallow holes, confined to limestone areas mostly in the western half of Ireland. The seasonal change in water level is often dramatic, and the blackish summer exposure of *Cinclidotus fontinaloides*, forming a continuous zone on the bushes and rocks, can be very striking. The large pleurocarps *Pseudocalliergon lycopodioides* and *Drepanocladus sendtneri* are both rare plants but may be locally abundant in turloughs, and both can sometimes be found washed up at the margins of larger turloughs. Turloughs are often associated with rich fen vegetation, as in the Burren in Co. Clare, where some of the best sites (notably Mullagh More) support a good

Margin of Cloon River, Co. Mayo, habitat for *Ephemerum crassinervium* subsp. *rutheanum* and *E. spinulosum*.

Garryland Turlough, Co. Galway.

population of the worm-like moss *Pseudocalliergon trifarium*. Other base-rich lakes on the limestone (FL3 and Hard Water Lakes on Annex I of the EU Habitats Directive) can be rich in many of the same species. Garryland Wood, near Coole in Co. Galway, has developed next to a turlough. The trees are sometimes flooded to a depth of several metres in winter, leading, if visited in summer, to the unusual sight of the semi-aquatic mosses *Cinclidotus fontinaloides* and *Leskea polycarpa* growing well up the tree trunks, apparently well away from any water!

Bryophytes can be an important component of spring vegetation. Calcareous springs (FP1 and Petrifying Springs on Annex I of the EU Habitats directive) can often be dominated by mosses, particularly *Palustriella commutata* and *Cratoneuron filicinum*, which can be abundant in tufa-forming communities. Calcareous springs and seepage areas can also provide niches for a wide variety of other calcicole bryophytes, including the thallose liverwort *Preissia quadrata*, the leafy liverwort *Leiocolea turbinata* and mosses such as *Bryum pseudotriquetrum*, *Eucladium verticillatum*, *Gymnostomum* spp., *Philonotis* spp. and *Didymodon tophaceus*. The very rare leafy liverwort *Southbya tophacea* was recorded on tufa on a dripping limestone wall in Knocknarea Glen, Co. Sligo in 1963. This species has only ever been recorded twice from Ireland, but last seen in 1988 at its other locality in Glenmalur, Co. Wicklow.

Non-calcareous springs (FP2) are widespread, particularly in the uplands, and are also important habitats for bryophytes. *Sphagnum denticulatum* is often the most common moss, forming swelling mounds at the upper headwaters of streams where water seeps from hillsides. Other species can include *Sarmentypnum exannulatum*, *Warnstorfia fluitans*, *Calliergonella cuspidata* and *Dichodontium palustre*, amongst others. This is also the habitat for some upland populations of the rare *Hamatocaulis vernicosus*, notably at Largan More in Co. Mayo.

Aquatic habitats are highly vulnerable to water pollution, and particularly from eutrophication, primarily from agricultural run-off. This has the effect of promoting the growth of a few species of nutrient-demanding algae at the expense of the richer bryophyte and vascular plant communities, and in severe cases the algae can be so dense that almost nothing else can survive. Canalisation and general tidying-up of riverbanks can also be a significant threat, especially in the lowlands, with the large-scale removal of big trees and rocks and complete loss of the riverside habitat.

Spring vegetation, Glenamoy, Co. Mayo.

Loss of bank-side habitat, north shore of Annaghmore Lough, Co. Roscommon, former locality for *Bryum uliginosum*.

Fortunately many areas of more or less intact lowland riverbank remain in Ireland, notably the seasonally flooded callows of rivers such as the Shannon and the Suck. Another important potential threat to freshwater habitats is the introduction of invasive alien plants. Some of these, presumably tipped out into ponds and lakes from home aquaria, thrive in Europe at the expense of the native vegetation. One of the worst offenders is Pigmyweed (*Crassula helmsii*), a plant from New Zealand that is not yet widespread in Ireland; experience in Britain shows it can blanket ponds and reservoirs completely, smothering nearly everything else.

Anthropogenic habitats

While nearly all habitats are anthropogenic to some extent, those more obviously influenced by human intervention can be differentiated from the semi-natural habitats such as woodland and grassland. Urban parks, buildings, walls, gardens, arable fields, mine-spoil tips and quarries are all examples of anthropogenic habitats that may support a significant bryophyte flora. Furthermore, this flora can be regarded as semi-natural in that it has colonised without any human assistance.

Car Moss, Toberroe, Co. Galway.

There is a characteristic urban bryophyte flora that tends to crop up wherever there are buildings or roads. The most conspicuous elements of this flora are the wall-top mosses *Tortula muralis* and *Grimmia pulvinata*. Both have leaves with long, white (hyaline) hair-points, an adaptation to growing in drought conditions. Many other large, common, pleurocarpous species grow on bricks and mortar; *Hypnum cupressiforme*, *Homalothecium sericeum*, *Brachythecium rutabulum* and *Kindbergia praelonga* to name but a few; and a wide range of small acrocarpous mosses such as *Bryum capillare*, *Didymodon* spp. and *Barbula* spp. The genus *Schistidium* is usually present on concrete and mortar, most often represented by *S. crassipilum*, the most common species of a difficult and only recently-understood species complex. Old stone

walls (BL1), particularly those of limestone, are an important substrate for some rare species. *Grimmia orbicularis* and *Schistidium elegantulum* have their only habitat in Ireland on old walls, sometimes as part of a rich bryophyte assemblage that may also include *Orthotrichum cupulatum*, *Porella platyphylla* and *Zygodon viridissimus*. The rare *Leptobarbula berica* was until recently, when it turned up at two sites in Kilkenny, only known in Ireland from the stonework of Letterdife House, Roundstone, Co. Galway.

Tarmac (BL3) is usually a less interesting substrate, with *Bryum argenteum*, *B. dichotomum* and *Ceratodon purpureus* the main species, although old crumbling tarmac (ED3) may be richer, with *Didymodon* spp., *Syntrichia* spp. and other mosses. *Syntrichia virescens* was found recently (2009) new to Ireland on tarmac outside the Montrose Hotel in Dublin and *Didymodon nicholsonii* seems to be particularly frequent on old tarmac in wetter sites, sometimes covering many square metres, but was overlooked until recently in this habitat.

Disturbed soil supports a characteristic ruderal flora, and this is best seen in arable fields (BC1). Stubble that is left unploughed until the spring, or arable fields left uncultivated for a year, are the optimum habitats for these species. Most of the plants are small ephemeral acrocarps, many of them reproducing both by spores and vegetative means. Many of this group of plants have tubers, which are small vegetative propagules produced on the rhizoids below the soil surface. Several small *Bryum* species typify this flora, including *B. rubens*, *B. subapiculatum*, *B. klinggraeffii*, *B. violaceum* and *B. ruderale*. *Tortula truncata*, *Dicranella staphylina*, *D. schreberiana*, *D. varia* and *Trichodon cylindricus* are also typical members of this assemblage. Even smaller and shorter-lived are the tiny plants of *Ephemerum minutissimum*. Thallose liverworts are sometimes interspersed between the mosses, mainly rosette-forming species of *Riccia*, the most frequent of which are *R. glauca* and *R. sorocarpa*. Hornworts (*Anthoceros* and *Phaeoceros* spp.) may also be found occasionally on damp acid soils.

A similar, if less varied, flora can be found in municipal flower beds (BC4), and *Hennediella stanfordensis*, a presumed introduction, has its only known Irish sites in the Phoenix Park, the National Botanic Gardens, Glasnevin and St Stephen's Green, all in central Dublin. There is also a small group of very obviously introduced species that have been imported from the southern hemisphere with garden plants, particularly on the trunks (erect rhizomes) of tree ferns.

This includes *Heteroscyphus fissistipus*, *Calomnion complanatum*, *Dicranoloma menziesii* and *Leptotheca gaudichaudii*, all of which find a home on tree ferns planted in gardens in the south-west, where the mild oceanic climate clearly suits them.

Several parts of Ireland have richly metalliferous veins running through the rock, which have been mined for copper, lead, zinc and other heavy metals for centuries. The metal-rich spoil (ED1, ED2 and Calaminarian Grassland on Annex I of the EU Habitats Directive) from disused mines forms the habitat for a specialist bryophyte flora that is able to tolerate a soil that is poisonous to most plants, exploiting a niche available to few others. Several of these were unknown in Ireland until very recently, when targeted survey work revealed their presence. Apparently bare heaps of metal-rich soil in spoil and on track sides can, on close inspection, yield tiny plants such as blackish leafy liverworts in the genus *Cephaloziella*. *C. stellulifera* may be dominant over wide areas. *C. integerrima*, *C. massalongi* and *C. nicholsonii* are very much rarer. Mosses are usually sparse, but tiny narrow-leaved acrocarps, such as *Ceratodon purpureus*, *Ditrichum* spp. and *Dicranella* spp., predominate. The mine-spoil specialists *Ditrichum plumbicola* and *D. cornubicum* are very rare. Until very recently, the latter species was thought to be endemic to Cornwall in south-west England, but it then turned up at Allihies copper mine in Co. Cork where it might be a recent accidental introduction (Holyoak & Lockhart 2009a). Allihies is indeed probably the richest Irish locality for the metallophyte bryophytes, with most of the rare species present. All the strict metallophyte bryophytes tend to grow mainly on acidic rather than base-rich substrates.

Quarries have a less specialised bryophyte flora but are often very valuable in providing substrates such as rock exposures in areas where they may be otherwise rare or absent. Gravel and limestone quarries usually have extensive spoil heaps (ED1) where a rich ruderal calcicole bryophyte flora can develop, including species of *Didymodon*, *Tortula*, *Aloina* and many others. The artificial rock ledges and cliffs at the sides of recently disused quarries can also be of great interest, providing newly-exposed crevices that can be colonised by tiny species of *Seligeria*. Scrabo Quarry in Co. Down has sandstone boulders which provide one of the very few sites in Ireland for the minute moss *Brachydontium trichodes*. An old sand quarry near Pollranny in Co. Mayo is the only known site in Ireland for another diminutive moss, *Aongstroemia longipes*.

Cephaloziella nicholsonii on mine spoil at Mountain Mine, Allihies, Co. Cork.

Paradoxically, many anthropogenic sites are under potential or actual threat. Mud-capped walls were formerly important for bryophytes, with old records of rarities such as *Pterygoneurum ovatum* and *P. lamellatum* from this habitat in and around Dublin. The practice of capping walls with mud ceased in the mid-20th century, so the habitat disappeared and these species were driven to extinction in Ireland. Whether or not this is important is largely a matter of opinion—after all, the habitat was artificial and the species may well have been introduced in the first place—but it is surely a cause for some regret, especially as the same thing has happened almost throughout Europe, although both species remain locally common in the Mediterranean region. Old mines and quarries are often regarded as eyesores, ripe for infilling with domestic waste and rehabilitation through landscaping. Yet, left to themselves, they can become places of great beauty and value, with nesting birds, carpets of wild flowers and, of course, luxuriant bryophytes during the early- and mid-successional stages. Some habitats depend on specific practices, such as leaving fields through the winter to develop a bryophyte community rather than ploughing them as soon as the autumn harvest has been taken in. Small changes in agricultural practice may have unforeseen consequences for the bryophyte flora. Other anthropogenic habitats tend to support ruderal species that are more than capable of looking after themselves, colonising new sites as quickly as they disappear from old sites.

The supreme efficiency of bryophytes as colonists is certainly a reason to be optimistic about their future as a group. However, if they are to survive at their greatest diversity, we have to ask ourselves whether it is sufficient to leave them to get on with it, common species simply occupying new niches as we make them available, or whether we want to see them in a more natural context, with rarer species allowed to thrive in the woodlands, grasslands, bogs and mountains in which they have evolved in partnership with all the other elements of our natural heritage.

Sand pit, near Pollranny, Co. Mayo supports the only known population of *Aongstroemia longipes* in Ireland.

CHAPTER THREE

Bryophyte recording in Ireland

Scapania ornithopodioides, Mweelrea, Co. Mayo.

THIS IS THE first of two chapters that describe the origins and sources of the data used in the rest of this book. An understanding of the history of bryophyte collecting and recording in Ireland is essential in judging the varying accuracy and completeness of past records and the precision (or otherwise) of recorded localities. The validity of any evidence for decline of particular species is of course largely dependent on the completeness and quality of the older records. The present chapter covers the three centuries up to about 1999, when the targeted field recording described in the next chapter was begun. More details of some of the history of bryophyte recording in Ireland are to be found in Stewart & Corry (1888) and Lett (1915). The account that follows is based largely on information assembled and reviewed by Holyoak (2003a). It is presented in a more or less chronological order, giving notes on the main recording activities in Ireland and notable additions to the bryophyte flora. As well as the contributions made by individuals, special mention is made of the collective contribution made by members of the British Bryological Society. The BBS held their first meeting in Ireland in 1928 and have continued to visit Ireland to this day, with a summer meeting held usually every fourth year, the most recent being in 2009. Acronyms for major herbaria used in the text follow *Index Herbariorum* (Thiers 2010). Dates of births and deaths are cited from Desmond (1994).

Early bryophyte recorders

The Rev. John Ray (1627–1705) of Black Notley, in Essex was the first botanist to describe any bryophytes found in Ireland. His *Synopsis Methodica Stirpium Britannicarum* (London 1690; 3rd ed., 1724) describes eight mosses from Ireland, of which only one has a locality specified. These mosses were probably all collected in Co. Down by William Sherard of Oxford.

Caleb Threlkeld (1676–1728) gave early descriptions of eleven Irish bryophytes in his *Synopsis Stirpium Hibernicarum* (Threlkeld 1726). It is difficult to relate his polynomials to modern names in the absence of preserved specimens, but two of his descriptions are quoted here in full as unique gems of early Irish bryological history and recorded human usage of mosses:

'MUSCUS INNATUS CRANIO HUMANO, Seu Usnea, Hypnum repens trichoides terrestre viridus Capitulis Cernuis minus tumidis, *Moss growing on a Dead Mans Skull*. Frequent in *Ireland*, where the poor People who are naturally hospitable, being misled by restless Companions, run into War, foolishly thinking to throw off the Blessings of the *English* Government. I took some from Skulls upon the *Custom-house-key* imported in large Butts from *Aughrim*.

The *Unguentum Armarium*, or *Weapon-salve* is compounded of this; the Vanity of which is plain from one Instance of a *Charlatan Jew* recited by *Luther*: This Juggler offered to impart this infallible Art of healing to *Albert* Duke of *Saxony*; well quoth the Duke, that I may be sure of it, I will make the Tryal first upon thee; so drew his Sword, and hacked the Fellow, insomuch that neither by the *Shemhamphorasch*, nor by the hanging of the *Kamea*, (which is a Parchment wherein the sacred Names were written) could he be cured: One experiment overthrew all the vaunting of the Pretender to that incommunicable Attribute of the Deity, I mean perfect Infallibility.

Merret tells us like an honest Man, that he could not distinguish the *Moss* growing on the Jaw of a Sheep, from that which grows on human Skulls; therefore Mr. *Ray* calls it, *Terrestris minor omnium vulgatissimus*. Growing in dry Pastures, and at Roots of Trees, as also upon rotten Bones, which cannot be distinguished either in Colour, or Figure from the other'.

'MUSCUS TRICHOIDES LANUGINOSIS ALPINUS, Bryum trichoides erectis Capitulis, Languinosum, *A Tough Thready Moss*, called in the *North*, *Old Wives Tow*. Mr. *King* who takes Notice of this, says, that *Ireland* doth abound with *Moss* more than any other Kingdom'.

Walter Wade.

Walter Wade (1750–1825) was Professor to the Dublin Society and instigated the establishment of their Botanic Gardens at Glasnevin. In his *Plantae rariores in Hibernia inventae* (Wade 1804) he gives names and localities for 27 mosses. Although few, these include the remarkable records of *Microbryum curvicollum* (as *Phascum curvicollum*), *Buxbaumia aphylla* and *Pylaisia polyantha* (as *Stereodon polyanthos*). Despite the apparent lack of voucher specimens, Lett (1915) accepted the first and second of these, although *M. curvicollum* is rejected here as the 'Benlettery' locality seems wildly inappropriate for a lowland calcicole that is extremely rare in Ireland. Wade's report of *Buxbaumia* from Purple Mountain remains its only accepted Irish record, but it too seems questionable.

Dawson Turner (1775–1858) wrote the first book devoted to Irish bryophytes, with detailed descriptions and fine coloured illustrations. His *Muscologiae Hibernicae Spicilegium* (Turner 1804) is a rare book that has recently been reprinted (as a Facsimile edition by Presses universitaires de Namur, Belgium in 1998). Although he apparently never visited Ireland, Turner corresponded with Robert Scott MD., Professor of Botany in Trinity

College, Dublin, and Whitley Stokes, Fellow of Trinity College, Dublin, where he was Lecturer in Natural History, and both contributed specimens to him. Turner dedicated his *Muscologiae Hibernicae Spicilegium* to Robert Scott and also named *Dicranum scottianum*, described by Scott from Co. Cavan, in his honour (Nelson 1998).

Ellen Hutchins (1785–1815) of Ballylickey, near Bantry, Co. Cork, was a remarkable botanist who contributed many significant new bryophyte records from Ireland. Sadly, she died at the young age of 30 and is commemorated in the names of the liverwort *Jubula hutchinsiae* (Hook.) Dumort., which she described as 'in gloomy caverns by the banks of mountain rivulets', and the moss *Ulota hutchinsiae* (Sm.) Hammar. Hutchins corresponded with Dawson Turner between 1807 and 1814 and the publication of a selection of their letters (edited by Mitchell 1999) provides an interesting insight into her bryophyte collecting activities. Not many detailed localities were attached to most of her bryophyte specimens, the 'near Bantry' that is often repeated in later literature apparently being added by others based on the domicile of the collector rather than any written evidence. The wide variety of bryophyte habitats represented by her specimens makes it clear that localities at least as far from Bantry as Glengarriff were involved, and Gougane Barra is mentioned once.

John Templeton (1766–1825) lived at Cranmore, Belfast and produced the manuscript for a 'Hibernian Flora' alluded to by Turner (1804), some of which still survives in the library of the Royal Irish Academy. Two of his MSS describe 258 mosses found in Ireland, some of which were new records.

Isaac Carroll (1828–1880) collected bryophytes mainly around Cork. He added several moss species to the Irish list, including some small acrocarps, and left an important herbarium that is at the **BM**. Subsequent attempts to assign some of Carroll's gatherings from 'Cork' or 'near Cork' to vice-counties H4 or H5, or to assign them to hectads, appear to be largely guesswork, although a few specimens have more exact localities.

Jubula hutchinsiae, Kylemore, Co. Galway.

Isaac Carroll.

Thomas Taylor.

David Moore.

Thomas Taylor (1786–1848) lived at Dunkerron, near Kenmare in Co. Kerry. He contributed the mosses to Mackay's *Flora Hibernica* (Part II, 1836). A series of notable bryophyte records made by Taylor have all been listed or mapped by subsequent authors as 'near Dunkerron' but recent surveys in that unremarkable region make it apparent that they were collected from a much wider catchment.

David Moore (1808–1879) was probably the most productive and important of all Irish bryologists during the 19th century. He was successively assistant to J.T. Mackay, the Director of Trinity College Botanic Garden; field botanist with the Ordnance Survey of Ireland, during which time he collected mosses in many of the counties of Ireland; and lastly, Director of the Royal Dublin Society's Botanic Gardens at Glasnevin. Lett (1915) lists 67 mosses that Moore added to the Irish flora and gives a full bibliography (including a detailed review of Irish mosses: Moore 1872). He published county lists of mosses (Moore 1878a) and liverworts (Moore 1878b) for Dublin and Wicklow. Moore's herbarium (at **DBN**) is notable for the high standard of accuracy of many of the determinations, tricky species such as *Ulota drummondii* mainly being correctly named. Localities written alongside Moore's specimens are often rather vague and sometimes completely absent.

David Orr (1818–1890) was an assistant to Dr Moore in Glasnevin Gardens. He collected and studied mosses in Cos Antrim, Dublin and Wicklow and assembled numerous herbarium specimens that are now mainly in **BM** and **DBN**. Lett (1915) notes that 'Much doubt exists as to some of Orr's discoveries, which prevents reliance being placed upon his work unless it is corroborated by other botanists'. More recent study of some of Orr's specimens labelled as from Ireland has revealed admixtures of continental European taxa, so that at least some of his localities seem fraudulent rather than merely careless. As a precaution, none of Orr's records have been accepted during compilation of the Red List, although many of them seem plausible.

Samuel Alexander Stewart (1826–1910) of Belfast began to study mosses in 1862. *A flora of the north-east of Ireland* (Stewart & Corry 1888) gives a detailed account of the bryophytes of Cos Antrim, Down and Londonderry, with large numbers of new records and detailed localities.

Lett (1915) should be consulted for a more detailed account of the great progress made in the study of bryophytes in Ireland through the 19th century. Lett's own correspondents included several active Irish

Samuel Alexander Stewart.

bryologists, particularly W.N. Tetley, James Glover, William Porter (of Balmoral near Belfast) and James Dick Houston. British bryologists visiting Ireland were also productive in the closing years of the 19th century and start of the 20th, including C.H. Binstead (1894, 1900, in Cos Cork and Kerry), and D.A. Jones, J.C. Wilson, J.B. Duncan and J. Owen (in Cos Mayo, Kerry and Cork).

Moss Exchange Club (MEC) and British Bryological Society (BBS)

In late 1895 and early 1896 C.H. Waddell of Saintfield Vicarage, Co. Down proposed by advertisement that a Moss Exchange Club (MEC) should be formed, in letters to *Science Gossip*, *Journal of Botany* and the *Irish Naturalist*. The MEC thus owes its origins to a worker in Ireland, although the already successful Botanical Exchange Club for exchange of vascular plant specimens doubtless provided a model for the Rev. Waddell. *A short account of the Moss Exchange Club and the British Bryological Society* by Eleonora Armitage (1944; 2nd ed., 1956) gives a useful account of salient points in the subsequent history of the

MEC and earlier years of the BBS that has been used in preparing the notes given here.

Twenty-three MEC members were enrolled in 1896, after which the membership rose gradually to 45 then fell again until the functions of the Club were taken over by the BBS when it was formed in 1923. More than 3000 packets (specimens) were distributed to the members in some years (with tens to hundreds from Ireland) and a system of expert referees was established to check determinations. An annual *Report* and *Census Catalogues* were published (bibliographical notes on the MEC publications are given by Holyoak 2003a). Bryologists from the north of Ireland contributed prominently to the MEC, with four Irish members among the founders: J. Hunter (of Londonderry), H.W. Lett (Loughbrickland, Co. Down) and J.B. Parker (Culmore, Co. Londonderry) in addition to Waddell (of Saintfield, Co. Down, later of Grey Abbey, Co. Down). In later years they were joined by J.D. Houston (of Kilrea, Co. Londonderry, then Lurgan, Co. Armagh, finally of Elphin, Co. Roscommon) but J.B. Parker left Ireland to live in Sheffield. Eleonora Armitage was the only woman member throughout the history of the MEC.

In 1901, a 'Beginner's Section' was formed that became The Moss Exchange Club Section II. Many of the members of Section II soon outgrew their status as 'beginners' but conflicting personalities kept the two sections of the MEC separate. Section II therefore continued to function as an independent exchange club for many years until it effectively merged with Section I to create the BBS in 1923. Section II issued its own Reports (see Holyoak 2003a for bibliographical notes) from 1903 onwards. There were 30 members by 1903 (none in Ireland), the total having risen to 48 by 1921. Like the senior section, the exchange in Section II distributed thousands of packets of bryophytes annually for many years, sometimes with a hundred or two from Ireland. Activity was somewhat reduced during the 1914–1918 war, but 1400 packets were circulated even in 1916. As in Section I, the material was checked by a panel of expert referees. In the later years there were several active contributors in Ireland, especially James Glover (of Kirkcubbin, Co. Down; see Megaw 1925 for obituary), J.D. Houston (see above) and W.N. Tetley (of Portora, Enniskillen, Co. Fermanagh). It is remarkable that J.D. Houston was a member of both Sections I and II of the MEC.

A system of vice-counties in Great Britain was devised by H.C. Watson (1852) and used to record the distribution of British vascular plants in *Topographical Botany* (Watson 1883). An adaptation of the scheme for publication of Irish botanical records was proposed by C.C. Babington (1859) and modified by R.L. Praeger for his influential *Irish Topographical Botany* (1901). There was some delay before bryologists fully adopted vice-counties for Irish records, in that *A list of Irish Hepaticae* (McArdle 1904) continued usage of 12 Botanical Districts in Ireland (following the tradition maintained in the 2nd edition of *Cybele Hibernica* by Colgan & Scully 1898). However, the *MEC Report* for 1898 gives a 'New County Record' for *Mnium cuspidatum* in Co. Down (anon. 1899: 17), the *Report* for 1900 gives vice-county numbers for some of the British records, and the earliest *Census Catalogues* issued by the MEC (Hepatics: Macvicar 1905; Mosses: Barker *et al.* 1907) used only vice-counties for Ireland and Britain. It was noteworthy that the 1908 *MEC Report* contained 'new V.C. records' (p. 270) and in the *Report* for the following year H.H. Knight stated that 'new county records are indicated by placing an asterisk to the V.C. number', a practice maintained until about 1938, after which the new vice-county records were listed separately. The important *Census Report on the Mosses of Ireland* (Lett 1915) presented data by vice-counties.

Recording in the 20th century

Cosslett Herbert Waddell (1858–1919) and Henry William Lett (1838–1920) were both clergymen of the Church of Ireland and both were among the most active and influential of bryologists in Ireland during the early years of the 20th century. The various parishes in Cos Armagh and Down in which they officiated were within 20 miles of their respective birthplaces, Magheralin and Hillsborough. Waddell's first appointment, a curacy at Lurgan, was in 1880, a time when Lett was rector of Ardmore, only four miles away. Fitzgerald & Fitzgerald (1961) give an account of several Waddell MSS housed at **BFT**, including the manuscript notebooks of the MEC for 1897–1901. Lett reported on the mosses and liverworts of Clare Island, Co. Mayo as part of an extraordinarily complete investigation of the flora and fauna of the island undertaken from 1901–1911 (Lett 1912). Synnott (1978) gives an account of Lett's main herbarium in **DBN**; Parnell (1982) reports additional material at **TCD**. Many specimens in Lett's herbarium at **DBN** have been redetermined during studies over the past decade, making it clear that he was somewhat careless by contemporary standards. Indeed, sufficient

Cosslett Herbert Waddell.

Henry William Lett.

Clare Island, Co. Mayo.

errors are apparent that published records from the long lists by Lett (1915) should not be uncritically accepted and mapped as distributional records.

William Rutledge Megaw (1885–1953) was born at Carrowdore, Co. Down, son of a Presbyterian minister (Chase 1954). He was ordained in Trinity Church, Ahoghill in 1910 where he ministered until 1919, when he became minister of Newtownbreda where he remained up to his retirement in 1950, after which he went to live at Portstewart. Megaw was local secretary for the BBS meeting at Belfast in 1928 and remained for many years the leading bryologist in the north-east of Ireland. He published a series of lists of significant bryophyte records (Megaw 1926a, 1926b, 1929a, 1929b, 1930, 1936, 1937), a fuller review of new records (Megaw 1929c) and compiled the authoritative account of bryophytes in the 2nd edition of the *Flora of the North East of Ireland* (Megaw 1938). His herbarium is at **BFT**.

The first field meeting of the BBS to be held in Ireland was based in Belfast from 25th August to 1st September 1928. Excursions were made to the Giant's Causeway and Portrush, Colin Mountain, Fair Head and Glenariff, all in Co. Antrim. One day was spent in Co. Down on Slieve Donard. A further excursion was

William Rutledge Megaw.

55

BBS 1928 meeting, Belfast. Left to right, front row: Mrs Sherrin, Miss I.M. Roper, Mrs Milsom, Miss K.E. Smith, Rev. C.H. Binstead, Miss D. Hilary, Mrs A.S. Bacon, Miss C.A. Cooper back row: Miss A.M. Saunders, H.H. Knight, Rev. W.R. Megaw, W.R. Sherrin, J.B. Duncan, I. Helsby, A. Sutton, D.A. Jones, D.B. Bradshaw, unknown, F.E. Milsom.

undertaken by some members to Co. Sligo, when Benbulbin was visited, and to part of Co. Leitrim (Duncan 1928, 1929a, Armitage 1956). Numerous interesting and new records were obtained, among the best of the novelties being *Timmia norvegica* new to Ireland from Gleniff in Co. Sligo.

The second BBS field meeting in Ireland was held from 10th to 17th August 1935 at Muckross, Killarney, Co. Kerry (Watson 1936, 1937, Armitage 1956); 25

BBS 1935 meeting, Killarney. Left to right: J.B. Duncan, W.C.R. Watson, D.A. Jones, Dr Walter Watson, F.E. Milsom, Miss A.J. Cottis, Mrs A.S. Bacon.

members attended, and after the meeting 15 members and friends went on to Dingle, Slea Head and Brandon Mountain. It is recorded that 'Help was rendered by Irish friends, Messrs. Bradshaw, Cronin and Lloyd Praeger in the excursions' and that the 'rare flowering plants were also sought after' (Armitage 1956).

The BBS was evidently much impressed by Irish bryophytes, since a third field meeting was arranged soon after the second, from 19th to 26th June 1937, based at Bundoran in Co. Donegal. About 20 members and friends attended and excursions were made into Co. Leitrim, Co. Sligo and Co. Fermanagh, mainly to explore the bryological riches of the Dartry Mountains in Glenade and Gleniff. Thirteen members went on to Achill Island (Co. Mayo) for a second week (Armitage 1938, 1956). After 1937 there was a long wait before the next BBS meeting in Ireland (1951), with not only the Second World War intervening, but also a large decline in bryological activity in Ireland and Britain throughout the 1940s.

At a time when there was little bryological activity in Britain, Jane Smithson Thomson was associated with a steady flow of new records obtained by The Moss Group, Dublin Naturalists' Field Club (DNFC), from widely

BBS 1937 meeting, Bundoran. Left to right, front row: Miss Jackson, Miss M. Weightman, J.B. Duncan, Rev. C.H. Binstead, Miss G. Wigglesworth back row: Miss E.M. Lobley, Miss A.M. Irwin, Miss E. Armitage, Mrs Watson, Dr Walter Watson, H.N. Dixon, Miss A.M. Saunders, C.V.B. Marquand, Miss M. Knox.

Jane Smithson Thomson (1943).

scattered localities in Ireland, from 1944 until the early 1950s. An article in the *Irish Naturalists' Journal* (*INJ*) (by The Moss Group, DNFC 1951) lists J.S. Thomson as Secretary of the DNFC and notes that 'though never having more than five members, [it] has done a great deal of work in filling up gaps in the Irish Moss Census'. Indeed, the article reports 223 new vice-county records for species and an additional 21 for varieties obtained 1945–50, all of them verified by BBS referees.

The 1951 BBS Meeting was held in Co. Kerry, the first week based at Glenbeigh, the second week based at Waterville (R.D. Fitzgerald 1952a, Richards 1952, R.D. Fitzgerald & J.W. Fitzgerald 1952, Wallace 1952). Nearly 30 members attended and the new finds included at least five species new to Ireland that are still regarded as valid taxa (*Eremonotus myriocarpus*, *Kurzia sylvatica*, *Didymodon nicholsonii*, *Fissidens curvatus*, *Isopterygiopsis muelleriana*). E.C. Wallace's (1952) account of the meeting notes that Mr and Mrs Fitzgerald 'were of the party and contributed greatly to the success of the meeting in using their car (as did other members with cars) for local transport'. A.C. Crundwell (1952) spent an additional week on the Dingle Peninsula and published an account in the *INJ* of the bryophytes he found.

BBS 1951 meeting, Kerry. Left to right: Mme V. Allorge, E.F. Warburg, P.W. Richards.

From 1947 to 1977 A.L. Kathleen King of Mount Merrion, Dublin made a collection of about 4000 well-documented bryophyte specimens that is now housed at **DBN** (Scannell 1977). Over many years A.L.K. King was methodical in working previously unexplored and often rather unexciting lowland localities, including State Forest plantations and Bord na Móna bogs. Although numerous new vice-county records were obtained (e.g. King 1950, 1953a, 1953b, 1954b, 1956, 1966a, 1966b, 1967a, 1967b,

1970), there were few rarities, except that her finds of *Meesia triquetra* (at a flush in an area of peat workings in Co. Mayo, sadly drained long ago: King 1958, King & Scannell 1960) and *Ptilidium pulcherrimum* (on Scots Pine in a forestry plantation in Co. Louth: King 1954a) provided spectacular additions to the known Irish flora. A small parcel of bryophytes collected in October 1966 by N. Chuter 'while on holiday in Donegal and the West' was passed to her and yielded *Nardia geoscyphus* new to Ireland from Kinnagoe Bay in E. Donegal.

From 1948 to 1958 (with a brief resumption in 1971) the late A.P. Fanning collected bryophytes mainly in Co. Kerry and Co. Offaly. Among his finds were new localities for *Fissidens curvatus* and *Petalophyllum ralfsii*, while his material of *Brachythecium mildeanum*, *Plathypnidium lusitanicum* and *Hageniella micans* appears to have been correctly identified by the collector (Synnott 1984, with notes on his herbarium which is now at **DBN**).

During 1950 to 1969, knowledge of bryophytes mainly in the northern half of Ireland was greatly enriched by the work of R.D. (Bob) Fitzgerald and J.W. (Jean) Fitzgerald (for obituaries see Perry 1990, 1991, Kertland 1991). Both spent their early years in Belfast, where they were married in 1940. They published numerous papers and notes reporting new records (e.g. J.W. Fitzgerald 1950, 1951, 1958, 1960, 1962, 1969,

A.L. Kathleen King.

Bob Fitzgerald (1962).

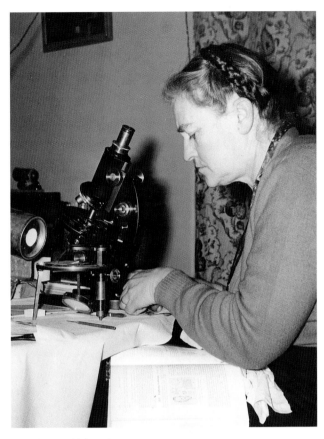

Jean Fitzgerald (1963).

The BBS meeting for 1957 was held in Co. Galway and northern Co. Clare (Lobley 1958, Parker 1958). About 15 members attended the meeting, which was organised by R.E. Parker. Three members 'most fortunately had cars, which solved the great difficulty of transport' (Lobley 1958). Many new vice-county records were obtained, including *Bryum salinum* new to Ireland. Immediately after the meeting A.C. Crundwell (1959) spent a week based at Belcoo, obtaining numerous new records from Co. Cavan and Co. Fermanagh.

Publication of *An outline of the bryophytes of County Laois (Queen's County)* by A.A. Cridland (1958) provided the first modern county bryoflora for any county in the Republic of Ireland. Fieldwork in Ireland by D.A. Ratcliffe in September 1961 resulted in the discovery of *Plagiochila carringtonii* in Co. Mayo and a detailed account of the habitat of *Adelanthus lindenbergianus* on Achill Island in the same county (Ratcliffe 1962). E.M. Lobley also reported observations from holiday visits to Ireland (mainly the north) in 1952, 1953, 1961 and 1962, which were reported in a series of papers and notes in the *INJ* (Lobley 1954, 1955, 1962, 1963). In addition, she attended the 1957 BBS Meeting in Co. Galway and

Fitzgerald & Fitzgerald 1960a, 1966a, 1966b, 1967, 1968a, 1968b, 1969, R.D. Fitzgerald 1950, 1952b, 1952c, 1952d) and a detailed bryophyte flora for Co. Tyrone (Fitzgerald & Fitzgerald 1960b). Many species were added to the Irish list by them, including *Calypogeia suecica, Cephalozia macrostachya, Discelium nudum, Eurhynchiastrum pulchellum, Lejeunea mandonii, Lophozia opacifolia, Pohlia proligera s.str., Seligeria calycina* and *Southbya tophacea*. Another important contribution involving J.W. Fitzgerald was the extensive revision of specimens of *Sphagnum* from the north-east of Ireland (vice-counties H38–40: Lobley & Fitzgerald 1970). Their very large collection of Irish bryophytes is mainly in **NMW**, but with the vouchers for Co. Tyrone in **BEL**. Unfortunately, the fieldwork by the Fitzgeralds antedated use of grid references to record their localities, which often seem rather imprecise.

In September 1952, E.W. Jones (1954) 'spent a short and pleasant holiday collecting bryophytes in NE Ireland, principally in the county of Antrim' but with short visits also to Co. Londonderry and Co. Down. New vice-county records were obtained for several mosses and liverworts.

Evelyn Lobley (1942).

wrote the detailed account of it in the *INJ* (Lobley 1958) and contributed substantially to a revision of Sphagna from the north-east of Ireland (Lobley & Fitzgerald 1970).

The 1962 BBS meeting was based at Dunfanaghy, Co. Donegal (Wallace 1963) for a fortnight in early September; eleven members attended. Numerous new vice-county records were made, among the most notable finds being of *Adelanthus lindenbergianus* on Errigal and Muckish Mountains by E.F. Warburg and others, and *Bryum marratii* found on the coast near Dunfanaghy by A.C. Crundwell 'on before-breakfast forays'. Immediately before this meeting E.F. Warburg spent a fortnight on Achill Island, Co. Mayo, resulting in several additions to the known flora of this well-studied island and a published list (Warburg 1963b).

A. Roy Perry began bryological work as a student at Oxford, encouraged by Dr Warburg. He accompanied the Fitzgeralds on some of their visits to Ireland (e.g. in 1963 when *Herbertus aduncus* was rediscovered at Fair Head in Co. Antrim: Fitzgerald & Perry 1964) and also searched independently in later years, during holidays from his post in charge of the Cryptogamic Herbarium at **NMW**. Work was carried out for several field seasons on a projected bryophyte flora for Connemara and the Burren, but through lack of funding that was reduced to a chapter in the *Flora of Connemara and the Burren* by

D.A. Webb and M.J.P. Scannell (Perry 1983). His many new vice-county records include that of *Leiocolea gillmanii* new to Ireland from Achill Island (W. Mayo).

The 1966 BBS meeting was based at Clonmel, Co. Tipperary (Synnott 1967a, 1967c). Two liverworts were discovered new to Ireland (*Cephaloziella integerrima* and *Fossombronia incurva*) and one moss, *Fissidens celticus*, which was found at three localities (Little 1967).

Much bryological fieldwork in Ireland was carried out during the 1960s and 1970s by Donal M. Synnott, resulting in a stream of new vice-county records. He also published critical reviews of all the records from Cos Meath, Westmeath and Louth (Synnott 1964, 1967b, 1982) and contributed many important revisions of specimens in **DBN** for the *Census Catalogue* (*CC*). During the 1970s he prepared a distributional checklist of the liverworts of Ireland (Synnott MS., 1977), providing details of the earliest vice-county record for all but the most common species. Unfortunately this work was never published, but he has kindly made a copy available during the present work, for which it has proved valuable in checking for missing records and erroneous details.

Roy Perry (with Jean Paton, 1974).

Donal Synnott, with (left to right) Matthew Jebb, Noeleen Smyth, Deirdre Lynn and Naomi Kingston at Bull Island, Co. Dublin, 2008.

A visit to Ireland by H.J.B. Birks, H.H. Birks and D.A. Ratcliffe in autumn 1967 produced significant records including *Geocalyx graveolens* new to Ireland in Co. Kerry (H.H. Birks, H.J.B. Birks & Ratcliffe 1969) and a short paper on the mountain plants of Slieve League in Co. Donegal (H.J.B. Birks, H.H. Birks & Ratcliffe 1969). In 1968, extensive phytosociological studies were carried out in central Ireland by W.V. Rubers, J. Klein and P. Hessel from Utrecht, the Netherlands, which included some bryophyte collecting in the area between Roosky and Athlone and along the Shannon and Lough Ree (specimens at **U**). An account of bryophyte habitats was published (Rubers 1975) and several interesting bryophyte records were made, most notably of *Bryum uliginosum* in Co. Roscommon.

In May and June 1968 and May 1969, Jean A. Paton visited Ireland to study liverworts with grant in aid from the Royal Society. Among the most notable of her many new records were four liverwort species new to Ireland found in 1968 (*Riccardia incurvata*, *Fossombronia 'husnotii'*, *Marsupella adusta* and *Cephalozia pleniceps*: Paton 1969) and four more found in 1969, *Gymnomitrion corallioides* (although an old Irish record of this species was also reported), *Solenostoma subellipticum* and *Scapania gymnostomophila* (all on Bulbin Mountain, Co. Donegal:

Paton 1971) and *Leiocolea heterocolpos* in Co. Antrim (Paton 1972). Paton's records are noteworthy not only for the large number of new discoveries but also the meticulous collection and labelling of voucher specimens (now mainly at **BBSUK** and **E**).

The 1970 BBS meeting was based at Sligo, with field excursions in Co. Sligo, Co. Leitrim and less extensively in east Co. Mayo and Co. Cavan (Appleyard 1971). The number attending was low, averaging six at any one time. New vice-county records were made of 29 liverworts and 34 mosses, amongst which was a new Irish record from the Benbulbin range of *Bryum elegans* (found by J.A. Paton). The 1975 BBS meeting was based at Arklow, Co. Wicklow for two weeks (Synnott 1976a, 1976b). Although only six people attended, scores of new vice-county records were obtained, mainly from Co. Wicklow but with some from Co. Carlow (cf. Synnott 1979).

The BBS meeting in 1979 spent the first week based at Limerick (with excursions into Co. Clare, Co. Limerick and Co. Tipperary) and the second week at Glengarriff in Co. Cork, with excursions also into Co. Kerry (Crundwell 1980). Over 150 new vice-county records were made, including *Atrichum tenellum* and *Pohlia lescuriana* both new to Ireland. Following the BBS meeting, N. Kirby, N. Lockhart and D. Synnott visited Gleniff in Co. Sligo and published notes on the bryophytes found there (Kirby *et al.* 1980).

Jean Paton (1972).

BBS 1979 meeting, Glengarriff. Left to right: N. Kirby, M.V. Fletcher, A.C. Crundwell (behind), Fletcher junior, N. Lockhart (in front), A.J.E. Smith, Mrs R. Fletcher, Mrs J.A. Paton (behind), Fletcher junior, Fletcher junior, unknown (behind), unknown (removing sweater), D.M. Synnott, E.C. Wallace (behind), P. Goyvaerts (in front), G. Bloom, F. Bentley.

A series of national habitat inventories and river catchment surveys by the Forest and Wildlife Service (now National Parks and Wildlife Service) in the Republic of Ireland between the late 1970s and the mid-1990s produced many new vice-county records. Research into the ecology of raised bogs, in particular, gave rise to a better understanding of the distribution of several scarce species, such as *Sphagnum pulchrum* (Douglas 1987), and turned up *Tetraplodon angustatus* (found by N. Lockhart) and *Sphagnum subsecundum* (found by C. Douglas, H. Grogan and J. Cross) new to Ireland.

The 1983 BBS meeting was held in Co. Kerry, the first week based at Killorglin (Kelly 1984, Lockhart 1984) and the second week based at Kenmare (Rothero 1984). It was noted that 15 people attended the second week, when the total number of species seen was 343, with nine confirmed new vice-county records. D.G. Long found *Fissidens rivularis* new to Ireland during the second week (Long 1984a) and also published a list of the sparse bryoflora on the very exposed island of Skellig Michael (Long 1984b).

BBS 1983 meeting, Kerry. Gordon Rothero and Neil Lockhart, Macgillycuddy's Reeks, Co. Kerry.

J. White (1985) published an account of the woodland flora at the Gearagh in Co. Cork, with a list of bryophytes (p. 393) mainly found by N. Lockhart that included several new records for W. Cork.

The 1987 BBS meeting was held in Co. Mayo, the first week on Achill Island, the second week based at Westport (Rothero 1988, Rothero & Synnott 1988, Synnott 1988). About 21 people attended, of whom 10 remained until the end of the second week. The group had an international flavour with bryologists from Alaska, Canada, Germany and the Netherlands added to a strong British contingent. Numerous new vice-county records were obtained, including *Scapania curta* and *Leiocolea gillmanii* new to Ireland on the previously 'well-worked' Achill Island and *Ptilium crista-castrensis* new to Ireland on Mweelrea.

The BBS meeting in 1990 was based in the north of Ireland, the first week in Co. Antrim and Co. Londonderry (Lewis 1991), the second week in Co. Donegal (Blockeel 1991a). The meeting was not well attended, with just six members present during the first week in Northern Ireland. Nevertheless, the party made several significant discoveries, including *Grimmia atrata* new to Ireland from a mist-shrouded ridge near Lough Feeane, Co. Donegal.

In 1990 *Glasra*, the journal of the National Botanic Gardens, Glasnevin, Dublin, published three papers that together form a bryophyte flora of Achill Island (Co. Mayo) (Long 1990, Smith 1990b, Synnott 1990a) along with an account of the bryophytes of Lambay Island (Co. Dublin) (Synnott 1990b). Around the same time, research on the floristic composition of calcareous mires by N. Lockhart (1987, 1988, 1989a, 1989b, 1991, 1999) yielded a series of important bryophyte records, including finds of *Tomentypnum nitens* at new localities, then of *Leiocolea rutheana* and *Paludella squarrosa* which were both new to Ireland.

Two days of fieldwork during a visit to Co. Fermanagh in February 1993 by the European Committee for the Conservation of Bryophytes generated many records, although *Orthodontium gracile* in the Lough Navar Forest was the only one of several taxa reported new to Ireland (Hodgetts & Hallingbäck 1994) for which the identification is still accepted. A series of visits to Foynes Island and the adjacent mainland of Co. Limerick resulted in a published bryophyte list (Wiltshire 1995) with four mosses as new vice-county records, including *Tortula atrovirens* and *Weissia rutilans*.

BBS 1994 meeting, Clare Island. Left to right: S. Drangard, Miss K. Long, D.G. Long. D.M. Synnott, D.L. Kelly.

The BBS field meeting in 1994 spent the first week in The Burren, Co. Clare (Whitehouse 1995) and the second week based at Clifden (Blockeel 1995a). Clare Island (Co. Mayo) was also visited. About 12 bryologists attended the first week and 17 the second, which was a joint meeting with the Nordic Bryological Society. Some of the areas visited in Co. Clare and Co. Galway (and also Clare Island) were already well known bryologically, so they produced few new records, but a visit to the Slieve Aughty Mountains in SE Galway was more productive. As on several previous meetings in Ireland, much of the preparatory work and organisation was carried out by D.M. Synnott.

Extensive national surveys of *Petalophyllum ralfsii* and *Hamatocaulis vernicosus*, both listed on Annex II of the EU Habitats Directive, were undertaken in 1998–1999 by N. Lockhart. This work resulted in the discovery of the enormous populations of *P. ralfsii* on some of the machairs in western Ireland, the largest yet known in the world.

A short visit to Lough Navar Forest in Co. Fermanagh by R.D. Porley in 7–11 June 1999 was unsuccessful in refinding *Orthodontium gracile* at its only Irish station, but he obtained eight new county records including *Mnium thomsonii* and a remarkable inland record of *Geocalyx graveolens* (Porley 2001).

The 1999 BBS meeting was based at Dungarvan for the first week and New Ross for the second week (Fox *et al.* 2001). A total of 15 people participated in at least part of the meeting. The excursions for the first week were mainly in Co. Waterford, with an incursion into E. Cork; those for the second week were largely in Co. Wexford. Highlights during the first week included *Barbilophozia atlantica*, *Fissidens rivularis* and *Telaranea europaea* new to Co. Waterford. In the second week some bryologically rather unpromising country was surveyed, which nevertheless produced several new county records. A.R. Perry and P.E. Stanley visited Co. Kerry and refound the adventives *Calomnion complanatum* and *Leptotheca gaudichaudii* on the 'trunks' of tree ferns, presumably at Derreen Garden where they were discovered a year earlier by W. Labeij who lodged his specimens at **DBN** (Holyoak & Lockhart 2009b).

Census Catalogues and atlas recording

The BBS *Census Catalogues* (*CC*) have provided convenient checklists of the bryophytes of Ireland and Britain for many years, with the distribution of each species (or subspecies, or variety) in all vice-counties listed using the vice-county numbers. *CC* for liverworts were issued as follows: Macvicar (1905) [1st edition,

MEC]; Ingham (1913) 2nd edition, MEC; Wilson (1930) 3rd edition, BBS (Supplement by Wilson 1935); Paton (1965) 4th edition, BBS. *CC* for mosses were issued as follows: Barker *et al.* (1907) [1st edition, MEC]; Duncan (1926) 2nd edition, BBS (Supplement by Duncan 1929b, BBS) (2nd Supplement by Duncan 1935, BBS); Warburg (1963a) 3rd edition, BBS. All three editions of the moss *CC* included *Sphagnum*, but separate publications for this genus were also issued as follows: Sherrin (1937) [1st edition, BBS]; Sherrin, revised by Thompson (1946) [2nd edition, BBS]. In recent decades the separate *CC* have been replaced by a single publication covering all groups of bryophytes (co-authored for the BBS by successive Recorders of Hepatics and Recorders of Mosses): Corley & Hill (1981); Blockeel & Long (1998); Hill *et al.* (2008).

Before about 1960 very few of the deletions made from the *CC* were explained in any published account, and in the early years records frequently come and go from successive *CC* without any explanation. Most records that were omitted in the early years were doubtless excluded for good reasons, but in the absence of any published explanation it is sometimes unclear whether particular records were excluded or merely overlooked (Holyoak 2003a). In the past few decades the BBS recorders have usually been meticulous in publishing details of additions and deletions to the *CC* in the annual Recorders' Reports (published in *BBS Reports* 1923–1948, *Transactions of the BBS* 1949–1972, *Journal of Bryology* 1972–1974, *Bulletin of the British Bryological Society* 1975–2003, *Field Bryology* 2004–2009). The content of each recent *CC* can therefore mainly be predicted (and checked) from work already published. However, a considerable number of vice-county records were 'updated' in 2008 for a new *Census Catalogue* (Hill *et al.* 2008) on the basis of records in the UK Biological Records Centre (BRC) database that are not supported by voucher specimens, although few of those are for Red Listed species. Almost all of the BRC records are open for inspection on the internet, as the database is posted on the National Biodiversity Network (NBN) Gateway and on the National Biodiversity Data Centre (NBDC) web site. However, many records lack details other than a hectad and an approximate date.

Much of the bryological fieldwork in Ireland from the 1960s up to 1990 was devoted to collecting distributional data for *The Atlas of the Bryophytes of Britain and Ireland* (Hill *et al.* 1991–1994). This work followed the lead of vascular plant recording in adopting 10-kilometre grid squares (hectads) rather than vice-counties as the units for recording distributional information. Whereas mapping for the *Atlas of the British Flora* (Perring & Walters 1962) had used an extension of the British Ordnance Survey National Grid to cover Ireland, because no gridded maps were then available, the bryophyte *Atlas* was able to utilise the Irish National Grid that had become available on new Ordnance Survey Ireland maps. Coverage for bryophytes at the scale of 10-kilometre squares was nevertheless generally poor in Ireland, although the species-rich western counties of Kerry, Galway, Mayo, Sligo and Donegal were relatively well recorded because these areas had attracted the attention of visiting bryologists. Elsewhere, well-worked areas include Fermanagh, Meath, Tyrone and Wicklow (Hill *et al.* 1991: 31). Overall, it might be estimated that only about 10% of the approximately 1000 hectads in Ireland were thoroughly covered for bryophytes by the early 1990s and the situation was little better by 1999 when active work was commenced on a Red List of Irish bryophytes.

CHAPTER FOUR

Data collection and analysis

Grimmia anomala, Easky, Co. Sligo.

THIS CHAPTER describes fieldwork and other studies carried out since 1998. The aim of much of the work during 1999–2010 has been to produce a reliable Red List of Irish bryophytes, and to collect detailed information on the threatened species. This contrasts with earlier fieldwork described in the last chapter which had a variety of aims: largely specimen-collecting in the early years, replaced in the past few decades mainly by collection of distributional data covering all bryophyte species to be mapped alongside that for Britain (Hill *et al.* 1991–1994).

By the 1990s, it was already clear that compared to Britain, current knowledge of Irish bryophytes and their distribution was much less complete. The *Atlas of the Bryophytes of Britain and Ireland* (Hill *et al.* 1991–1994), as discussed in Chapter 3, achieved really good coverage of bryophytes in only about 10% of the hectads of the Irish grid, whereas better coverage was obtained for much of Britain. Knowledge of Irish bryophytes at county level

was better (Holyoak 2003a), but still demonstrably incomplete since active fieldwork added up to 100 new vice-county records annually over a six-year period (Blackstock 2000–2005; Rothero 2000–2005).

Preparatory work for a *Red Data Book* of bryophytes for Britain and Ireland was carried out during the early 1990s, with much of the data for Ireland being assembled from herbaria and literature by N.F. Stewart. It became apparent as this work progressed that the data from Ireland on rare species were much less complete than those from Britain, so that Ireland was eventually excluded from the published book (Church *et al.* 2001). The evident need for a better inventory of rare and threatened bryophyte species in Ireland thus led to collaborative research during 1999–2010 by the National Parks and Wildlife Service (NPWS) in the Republic of Ireland and the Northern Ireland Environment Agency (NIEA) in Northern Ireland. Extensive field surveys of bryophytes during 1999–2009 and considerable research

David Holyoak and Nick Hodgetts, Killarney, Co. Kerry.

BBS 2009 meeting, Chris Preston (and Gordon Rothero), Brandon, Co. Kerry.

on herbarium material were undertaken, with the aim of preparing the present book by 2012. Two of the present authors (DTH and NGH) were commissioned to undertake the field surveys, with the third author (NL) co-ordinating much of the research. DTH has worked at this annually from 1999–2009, NGH annually from 2001–2009. Each has spent a substantial part of each year (up to four months, generally between April and October) on bryological fieldwork in Ireland followed by determination and curation of specimens. DTH has also carried out extensive additional research on herbarium material and literature in some years; in the meantime NGH has contributed to development of a database of Irish bryophyte records using Recorder software at NPWS.

Other significant contributions have been made by British bryologists on visits to Ireland over the past decade, notably by D.G. Long (e.g. Blackstock & Long 2002; Holyoak & Long 2005), S.D.S. Bosanquet and C.D. Preston. In 2005, a BBS field meeting based at Derrygonnelly in Co. Fermanagh was organised by DTH, with fieldwork in Cos Fermanagh, Leitrim and Cavan (Holyoak 2006a). Several interesting new finds during the meeting included two of *Schistidium trichodon* new to Ireland. In 2009 a further BBS field meeting (organised by S.D.S. Bosanquet and C.D. Preston) visited parts of Co. Cork and Co. Kerry, again resulting in numerous new records, including *Grimmia anomala* new to Ireland (Bosanquet & Preston 2010). J. Denyer and the Dublin Naturalists' Field Club have run a

number of bryophyte field outings and identification workshops during 2010, led by invited British bryologists including G.P. Rothero, D. Chamberlain, N.G. Hodgetts and S.D.S. Bosanquet, and these too have added new records and stimulated interest in bryophyte recording in Ireland. The need for further recording in Ireland, and evidence that much still remains to be discovered, is clearly demonstrated by the recent finds of *Entosthodon pulchellus* (by S.D.S. Bosanquet at Holycross Abbey, S. Tipperary) and *Dialytrichia mucronata* (by T. Blockeel at Lough Derg, N. Tipperary), both new to Ireland, in early February 2011 (S.D.S. Bosanquet, pers. comm.), and the discovery of *Encalypta ciliata*, *Pogonatum nanum* and *Hamatocaulis vernicosus* (by NGH at Sallagh Braes, Antrim, September 2011) and *Southbya tophacea* (by NL at Island Lake, E. Mayo, October 2011) whilst this book was still in press.

Dublin Naturalists' Field Club outing to Skerries, Co. Dublin, 2010. Left to right: Maurice Eakin, Nick Hodgetts, Melinda Lyons, Con Breen, Gerry Sharkey and Daniel Kelly.

In 1998, a draft list of species likely to be included in a Red Data List of Irish bryophytes was assembled by NL, based on hectad counts in the *Atlas* by Hill *et al.* 1991–1994. This generally comprised those with 12 or fewer modern (post-1950) hectads, initially 295 taxa, but later increased to 325 taxa. This list was then published as the Provisional Red List (Holyoak 2006b). It was of course realised that this was only a provisional assessment, but some targeting of fieldwork was undoubtedly necessary since seeking all Irish bryophyte species in all counties would inevitably dilute the time and effort available for tracking down the rarest species. Fieldwork by 2005 had done much to modify the original list: no fewer than 53 taxa were excluded because they had been under-recorded; 24 others were added as additions to the Irish flora; six more were added as newly recognised taxa; and another six were deleted as misidentifications following herbarium research. Thus 27% of the original list had been changed after six years of work (Holyoak 2006b). During the early years of fieldwork a great deal of time and effort was devoted to finding and recording numerous populations of some of the species, only to result in their eventual exclusion from the Red List. Nonetheless, their exclusion based on detailed evidence was important in clarifying the agenda for future action to protect Irish bryophytes. The experience also demonstrated the risks that would be inherent in preparing a Red List based on insufficient data.

Evidence of extensive recent losses of Northern Atlantic hepatic mat habitat (see Chapter 2) had suggested by 2005 that some other species which had more than 12 modern (post-1950) hectad records in 1998 may have become seriously threatened, especially *Bazzania pearsonii*, *Mastigophora woodsii*, *Paraleptodontium recurvifolium* and *Scapania ornithopodioides*. It was apparent that these might qualify as additions to the Red List since they might by then have had fewer than 12 hectad records in Ireland and those populations that remained might be especially vulnerable. They were therefore added to the list of species that were targeted.

All Irish counties were visited during the fieldwork from 1999–2009, the amount of time spent in each of them being approximately in proportion to their richness in uncommon bryophytes. The timetable of fieldwork was as follows:

1999	DTH	Surveys of *Petalophyllum ralfsii* in Cos Donegal, Galway, Mayo and Sligo; fuller bryophyte surveys in Cos Antrim and Londonderry;
2000	DTH	Cos Fermanagh and Leitrim;
2001	NGH	Co. Donegal (S. part);
2001	DTH	Cos Leitrim (mainly) and Cavan;
2002	NGH	Co. Roscommon;
2002	DTH	Co. Donegal (N. part);
2003	NGH	Co. Sligo;
2003	DTH	Cos Antrim, Armagh, Down, Mayo and Tyrone;
2004	NGH	Cos Clare and Waterford;
2004	DTH	Co. Galway;
2005	NGH	Cos Limerick and Tipperary (N. part);
2005	DTH	Co. Kerry (N. part); also Cos Carlow, Dublin, Kildare, Kilkenny, Laois and Offaly;
2006	NGH	Co. Kerry (Dingle Peninsula);
2006	NGH	Co. Cork (Mid and East);
2006	DTH	Cos Cork (West) and Kerry (S. part);
2007	NGH	Brief supplementary visit to Co. Cork (E. Cork coast);
2007	NGH	Cos Dublin, Wicklow, Waterford, Wexford and Tipperary (upland parts);
2007	DTH	Cos Dublin, Longford, Louth, Meath, Monaghan, Waterford, Westmeath and Wexford (lowland parts);
2008	NGH	Brief visits to Cos Dublin, Wicklow, Wexford, Carlow, Waterford, Sligo, Donegal and Kerry;
2008	DTH	Brief visits to Cos Cork (West), Donegal (West), Kerry (South), Louth, Mayo (West); wide-ranging survey of metalliferous mine sites; Cos Antrim, Down and Londonderry;
2009	NGH	Brief visits to Cos Offaly, Laois and Tipperary;
2009	DTH	Brief visits to Cos Cork, Galway, Wexford and metalliferous mine-sites elsewhere.

In some years the weather hindered fieldwork. Particularly wet weather led to wasted days in summer 2002 in Co. Donegal and in 2007 in Co. Wicklow. The summer and autumn of 2003 spent in Co. Mayo were drier than average allowing completion of almost all of the fieldwork that had been planned, although even then eight full days and several half-days were lost to sustained rain, and low cloud prevented work on high ground in the mountains on numerous other days. Fieldwork in Co. Galway during 2004 was unusual because prolonged dry weather through May and early June was very encouraging initially, but soon became problematical as the ground and bryophytes became increasingly desiccated. May 2006 in S. Kerry was notable for record high rainfall.

Access to land usually presented no problems anywhere in Ireland, with permission readily being granted whenever an owner could be found. However, 'Private, No Access' signs were met with occasionally, although some of them seemed unwarranted. Lack of parking places near a few lakes and an occasional height-barrier on an access road sometimes also impeded access.

Much of the time in the field was devoted to attempts to refind old records of target species at known localities, with about a quarter to a third of the time used for 'exploration' to seek additional localities. Success in refinding old records varied widely. A very encouraging start was made in 2000 and 2001 in Cos Leitrim and Cavan when a high proportion of old records was refound (54% of 106 records). In contrast, results were poorer in Cos Donegal, Mayo and Galway (being worst of all at 25.6% of 133 records in Co. Galway in 2004).

The higher success rate in Co. Leitrim may partly reflect better data for many of the old records because a high proportion were on well-defined sites such as the bases of large limestone crags. Furthermore, a high proportion of the Leitrim records were based on relatively recent fieldwork by observers who recorded localities carefully. There may also have been a lower proportion of losses of populations from the crag habitats (or perhaps of additional populations being found in the same general area!).

The low proportion of records refound in some other counties had several likely explanations (exemplified here from the report on work in Co. Galway):

(1) In addition to 'discounted' records, some others were known at the outset to be poorly localised (several were given only as hectads; at worst, the locality was given merely as 'Connemara').

(2) Many other records undoubtedly had very poor locality data, including not only the old records by H.W. Lett and others, but also at least some of the more recent records from BBS excursions. The frequently poor quality of locality data became apparent through instances such as *Campylophyllum calcareum* 'near Cong', but some modern records were little better. Voucher specimens exist to confirm the identification of most of the records, but the locality details are often too scanty to offer much hope of rediscovering the plants. The then unique Irish record of *Bryum salinum* from east of Galway city is particularly unsatisfactory as the locality is very vague. The proportion of more modern records refound was generally higher than that for old records, especially those from a few bryologists such as D.G. Long and H.L.K. Whitehouse, who are known to have carefully recorded locality data.

(3) Some old records which have been accepted are now known to be based on errors of identification. In particular, the *Amblystegium confervoides* specimen from near Cong at **DBN** was misidentified. Many others are suspect because much of the old herbarium material is misdetermined (e.g. most old records of *Bryum caespiticium* and *Brachytheciastrum velutinum*).

(4) Some old records have localities which are so unlikely that an error is surely involved, notably *Microbryum curvicollum* and *Abietinella abietina* from 'Benlettery, 1804, W. Wade'. These are lowland calcicoles and Benlettery is a quartzite mountain, so both records should be rejected.

(5) Some sites have been lost. In particular, rare bryophytes of the Northern Atlantic hepatic mat community have gone from the montane slopes of the Twelve Bens, including nearly all the populations of *Adelanthus lindenbergianus* and *Plagiochila carringtonii*. Where D.A. Ratcliffe recorded the height of the *Calluna* canopy in the 1960s, we now found open scree slopes with little or no trace of *Calluna* or bryophytes, all as a result of overgrazing by sheep due to excessive stocking levels. Other losses recorded were from former fen habitats in the lowlands where grazing has ceased and reed swamp has grown up (e.g. roadside at Menlough; Ballindooly Castle Fen).

Methodology of fieldwork in the Republic of Ireland from 2000–2009 followed a standard format, with results for each year being presented in an unpublished report to NPWS.

Well in advance of the field surveys, the details of all records from the survey areas from the NPWS database were collated. Fuller information on these was sought by: (1) checking them against the then current vice-county census (Blockeel & Long 1998) and where problems were apparent, a full set of older *CC*; (2) checking original publication details of vice-county records by means of a comprehensive search in *British Bryological Society Bulletins, Transactions of the BBS, Reports of the BBS* and *MEC Reports* and later, a published summary of Irish vice-county records (Holyoak 2003a); (3) checking meeting reports, taxonomic papers and all other relevant publications; (4) checking a set of photocopies of the 'pink cards' on which N.F. Stewart compiled *Red Data Book* information for Irish bryophytes. A few errors were uncovered through this checking, a few extra records, and numerous scraps of extra information that sometimes proved valuable in relocating the plants.

Since the draft Red List was assembled in 1998, it had become apparent that some bryophyte species which are difficult or time-consuming to identify had been under-recorded in Ireland. Later fieldwork therefore spent little or no time seeking out old records for these when those records had poor data; also, only a minimum of basic information was recorded (along with a voucher specimen) for most new finds of those species. This allowed significantly more time to be devoted to searches for genuinely rare and threatened taxa. Not even the basic information was recorded for *Amblyodon dealbatus, Anomobryum concinnatum, Distichium inclinatum, Jungermannia exsertifolia* and *Pohlia drummondii*, so that the absence of data on these relatively frequent species had considerably reduced the bulk of the paper records of work by 2004 and allowed efforts to be more closely focused on rarer species.

Little attention was given to refinding old records of several other species that have usually been misidentified by recent visitors to Ireland (notably *Brachytheciastrum velutinum, Bryum caespiticium* and *Tortula marginata*), all of which are so common in SE England that visiting English bryologists have often recorded them in a careless manner because their significance in Ireland was not appreciated. There are no voucher specimens for most of their records.

Recording of information was as far as possible carried out according to a standard format, using an A4 species-site data sheet along with marked copies of 1:50,000 and 1:10,560 maps and an aerial photograph, all of which are archived at the NPWS offices in Dublin. Various minor snags were found: the 1:10,560 maps became almost useless above the 1000-foot contour because portrayal of topographic detail ceased at that level; also drawing of crags on these maps was sometimes artistic but inaccurate; usefulness of aerial photographs of the mountains was often restricted by cloud or by dark shadows over crags, elsewhere they were very helpful (and would have been even more valuable if used as stereo-pairs). Photography of sites was carried out from 2004 onwards using only a small digital camera (mainly Nikon Coolpix), which proved easier to use in wet or showery weather than the 35 mm SLR used in previous years. In addition to much photography to document locations and habitats of rare bryophytes, numerous digital photographs of rare bryophytes and their habitats were taken, mainly using a Nikon Coolpix.

Where a target species was found at several or numerous closely adjacent locations, the closely associated plants were normally listed in the field for a representative location (or two), accompanied by limited sampling to check determinations microscopically for key associates. A question that often arose during the fieldwork was whether two more or less closely adjacent populations should be treated as a single site or two, respectively requiring one or two data sheets. No hard and fast rule was followed since the spatial distribution of populations is endlessly variable. However, sites 1 km or more apart were generally treated separately, unless they were linked by a chain of intervening populations.

A frequent problem with bryophyte studies is that a proportion of small and rather nondescript plants cannot be determined in the field (e.g. small *Bryum, Cephalozia, Cephaloziella, Didymodon, Grimmia* and *Philonotis* spp.). Checking these is time-consuming and a large proportion of the gatherings eventually turn out to be common species. Hence, rather than ignore them, it was decided to collect a good representation of samples from scattered localities, each with sound basic data such as are needed for labelling a herbarium packet. A consequence of this approach is that when a rarity such as *Philonotis caespitosa* or *Cephalozia macrostachya* is eventually recognised, only the basic details (and no site photographs or marked aerial photographs) will be available. Limited information will also be available on the rare occasions when an unrecognised rarity turns up unexpectedly among 'associates' being checked microscopically.

Improvements in accuracy of hand-held GPS in the early years of the surveys greatly assisted in location of sites in open country. A Garmin GPS12 was therefore used throughout the fieldwork from 2003 onwards. Frequent checks at known locations suggested that, with care and patience, sites were located by the GPS to within 10 m horizontally (but only to within c. 50 m in terms of altitude above sea level). Hence the data record grid references to 10 m accuracy (e.g. M1237/3701), except occasionally on steep crags or in woodland or deep ravines where the GPS could not be used effectively.

Herbarium specimens were collected as vouchers for almost all records, the few exceptions being with small populations unable to withstand collecting of the distinctive species *Petalophyllum ralfsii*. However, the material collected was scanty for a few other species at sites where the populations of the plants were small (the material for species named in the Flora (Protection) Order 1999 was collected under a licence from NPWS). Microscopic checking of vouchers revealed a few errors in field identification (especially with *Drepanocladus* spp., *Hamatocaulis vernicosus*, *Sphagnum platyphyllum*), so record sheets associated with these were revised or discarded. All new or updated vice-county records have been checked by the then BBS Recorder of Hepatics (T.H. Blackstock) or Recorder of Mosses (G.P. Rothero), with small (usually duplicate) specimens being passed to the BBS Herbarium in Cardiff (**BBSUK**). All curated vouchers from the fieldwork in Northern Ireland have been passed to the Herbarium of the Ulster Museum (**BEL**) and those from the Republic of Ireland have been passed to the Glasnevin herbarium (**DBN**), except for a few represented only at **BBSUK**.

The methodology of fieldwork in Northern Ireland (1999, 2000, 2003, 2008) was essentially similar to that in the Republic of Ireland. The list of species targeted was slightly larger because it was based on the lists of Northern Ireland Species of Conservation Concern, but it included all of those sought in the Republic. Detailed species-site sheets were not completed, although similar basic data were recorded for all finds. Results are described in unpublished reports on the work for each year that are lodged with NIEA. At most sites, full lists of bryophyte species were recorded. All of the data is held in digital form at the Centre for Environmental Data and Recording (CEDaR, the Northern Ireland Biological Records Centre). As in the Republic of Ireland, almost all old records of target species with reasonably precise data had been sought by the end of the fieldwork in 2008.

The few gaps in this coverage were mostly in Co. Armagh or around Belfast.

Literature records of most rare Irish bryophytes were reviewed during the compilation of a detailed list of the vice-county records (Holyoak 2003a). These were later assembled on to an Excel spreadsheet listing 323 taxa, forming the basis of a fuller listing of data that underlies this book. At this stage, decisions were made regarding which records were accepted or rejected as correct identifications, and which were accepted as sufficiently precisely localised to be assigned to a hectad for mapping. As far as possible, old records that might have been from more than one hectad were assigned to the most likely hectad when no better information was available (e.g. 'Dublin' was assigned to O13, whereas 'near Dublin' and 'Co. Dublin' were not mapped).

Examination of a range of herbarium specimens made it clear that significant numbers were misidentified, particularly of mosses. Systematic efforts were therefore made to check as many Irish specimens as possible of taxa likely to be at high risk of misidentification, with large loans of specimens studied from **BBSUK**, **BEL**, **DBN** and **NMW**, smaller loans from **E** and **TCD** and study visits to **BM** and **S**. Errors proved to be particularly frequent with *Abietinella abietina* var. *abietina*, *Brachytheciastrum velutinum*, *Bryum bornholmense*, *B. caespiticium*, *B. intermedium*, *B. tenuisetum*, *B. torquescens*, *B. uliginosum*, *Pogonatum nanum* (especially non-fertile gatherings) and *Ulota drummondii*. Irish material of many other species was also checked or revised, including *Campylopus schimperi*, *Fossombronia caespitiformis*, *Seligeria* 'trifaria agg.', *Weissia condensa* and *W. controversa* var. *crispata*. The only Irish records of *Fontinalis squamosa* var. *dixonii*, *Tortella fragilis* and *Timmia austriaca* were found to be erroneous and all material checked for *Campylophyllum calcareum*, *Conardia compacta* and *Pylaisia polyantha* has so far proved to be misidentified. Notes on the taxa that have been erroneously reported from Ireland are given in Appendix I. It is clear that old literature reports such as those from Lett (1915) cannot be accepted uncritically as reliable records.

One unintended consequence of the targeted recording of 325 taxa since 1999 has become apparent from subsequent analyses. This is the under-recording of certain taxa that were not on the original list. Most relatively common species were found repeatedly during 1999–2009 and the finds were listed so that records accumulated. On the other hand, very few or no records accumulated for some more localised species that were not sought after or which require troublesome microscopy for reliable identification. Thus the absence or scarcity of recent records of *Dicranella cerviculata*, *Douinia ovata*, *Lejeunea flava* subsp. *moorei*, *Metzgeria leptoneura*, *Scapania subalpina*, *Solenostoma sphaerocarpum*, *S. paroicum* and *S. obovatum*, among others, can be attributed to the fact that little or no effort was made to refind them at their old localities, or to deliberately seek them out in appropriate habitats. Hence, 'evidence' of a recent decline in these species is almost certainly an artefact of their exclusion from the list of species being targeted.

Certain habitats and taxonomic groups were also relatively under-recorded. Habitats known to be rich in rare bryophytes were generally well recorded, particularly: basic montane crags and ledges, montane summits, deep ravines, large waterfalls, old native woodlands, inundation zones of lakes and reservoirs, riverbanks, sunny south-facing sea-cliff slopes and dune slacks. Rich fens were particularly thoroughly covered during research by NL through the 1990s as well as by other fieldwork since 1999. Dune slacks and machair received special attention in the late 1990s through research on *Petalophyllum ralfsii* as well as subsequently. Old copper

David Holyoak receives thanks from Daniel Kelly, Christina Campbell and Noeleen Smyth following his 'heavy metal' tour of old mine sites in 2009.

and lead mines were deliberately sought out in the early years, then made the subject of a special survey in 2008 and some repeat visits in 2009 (Holyoak & Lockhart 2009a). On the other hand, tillage was relatively neglected in proportion to its extent, partly because the best conditions on stubble fields occur outside the main

Petalophyllum ralfsii with sporophytes, Truska Machair, Co. Galway.

71

fieldwork seasons in late winter. Some relatively dull and species-poor habitats were also greatly under-recorded in proportion to their extent (e.g. pastures and other grasslands, stands of *Juncus effusus*, coniferous plantations, cutover bogs, blanket bog, roadsides, roofs of houses and gardens).

Besides favouring of certain habitats over others, biases in recording also undoubtedly arose through personal preferences for particular taxonomic groups. DTH has developed particular enthusiasms for the genera *Bryum* and *Ephemerum*, and also for *Cephaloziella* and *Ditrichum* on metalliferous substrata, so has undoubtedly generated proportionately more new records for these than for say *Schistidium*, *Sphagnum*, or small liverworts of bog habitats. On the other hand, NGH has shown much more enthusiasm for tracking down small liverworts and Sphagna and consequently spent less time scouring dune slacks or reservoir inundation zones and more in bogs and on montane slopes. Various kinds of recording biases undoubtedly limit the scope for any detailed quantitative analyses of population trends with Irish bryophytes. Thus any apparently 'objective' evidence of declines or increases needs very careful scrutiny, given the patchy nature of past and recent recording, the different seasonal patterns of activity of recorders in different time periods and the differing habitat preferences of individual recorders.

Taxonomic changes affecting the Irish bryophyte flora have quickened in pace over the past decade and seem likely to influence work over the next decade. This is partly because more bryologists have become involved in studies of bryophytes worldwide than at any time in the past, but also because traditional taxonomic techniques of study based on morphology and distribution are being supplemented by data derived from molecular analyses. In particular, data from DNA sequences are increasingly showing that some of the existing taxonomy of mosses and liverworts is poorly founded or misleading (e.g. Goffinet *et al.* 2004). Recent changes to understanding of Irish bryophytes resulting from combined molecular and morphological studies include: that *Aneura pinguis* consists of several cryptic species in Ireland (D.G. Long

pers. comm., cf. Bączkiewicz & Buczkowska 2005, Buczkowska *et al.* 2006, Bączkiewicz *et al.* 2008); *Amblystegium fluviatile* and *A. tenax* are merely phenotypes of the morphologically plastic *A. varium*, from which *A. humile* is scarcely separable, and all belong in a segregate genus *Hygroamblystegium* (Vanderpoorten 2004, Vanderpoorten & Hedenäs 2009); realisation that *Bryum 'neodamense'* is an inconstantly produced phenotype of *B. pseudotriquetrum* (Holyoak & Hedenäs 2006), which anyway belongs in the segregate genus *Ptychostomum* (Holyoak & Pedersen 2007); European *Hamatocaulis vernicosus* consists of two cryptic species showing no morphological differentiation (Hedenäs & Eldenäs 2007), as does *Antitrichia curtipendula* (Hedenäs 2008); *Polytrichum commune* consists of two widespread European species, of which the small forms var. *humile* and var. *perigoniale* should probably retain the familiar name *P. commune*, whereas the tall common plants of mires should become *P. uliginosum* (Schriebl 1991, Van der Velde & Bijlsma 2000, Hyvönen & Bell in Hill *et al.* 2006, N. Bell *in litt.*). Notes on taxa reduced to synonymy with more common species, and therefore excluded from consideration in this book, are given in Appendix I.

These new data have had some influence on the latest Irish and British checklist (Hill *et al.* 2008) that we follow in this book. However, not all of the new results are expressed in the latest taxonomy, many genera have still not been subjected to combined molecular and morphological studies, and others are as yet only very incompletely investigated. Irish specimens recently sent to active researchers are already pointing to the need for radical taxonomic changes affecting *Didymodon* (J. Kučera *in litt.*) and *Oxystegus* (Köckinger *et al.* 2010). Thus the next few years are almost certain to result in numerous further taxonomic revisions and the need for reconsideration of Irish distributions, population sizes and hence conservation status of some of the taxa that will be redefined. Thus, against a background of quickening habitat change and likely effects of climate change there is little doubt that much remains to be done to limit population losses and make the most of future opportunities for bryophyte conservation in Ireland.

CHAPTER FIVE

Threat levels and conservation priorities

Leiocolea rutheana var. *rutheana*, near Crossmolina, Co. Mayo.

Introduction

THIS CHAPTER presents the results of an assessment of the current status of the Irish bryophyte flora and identifies which taxa (species, subspecies and varieties) are considered to be under threat. A Red List of threatened bryophytes, based on the criteria developed by the International Union for Conservation of Nature (IUCN 2001) is given for the entire Irish bryophyte flora for the first time. The Red List was compiled by NGH, with comments and inputs from DTH and NL. The completed list was then circulated for consideration and acceptance to Richard Weyl (NIEA) and to the Conservation and Recording Committee of the BBS.

The IUCN system for allocating threat status was originally designed to be applied to large animals on a global scale, but more recently has been developed so that it is applicable to any organism at any geographical scale, if interpreted sensibly. The previously approved IUCN

threat categories (*Extinct*, *Endangered*, *Vulnerable* and *Rare*) were replaced in 1994 by a revised system (World Conservation Union 1994) that abandoned the *Rare* category (as it was an expression of frequency rather than of threat), and introduced the category of *Critically Endangered*. The sub-Red List category of *Near Threatened* was also established, and the category of *Extinct in the Wild* was distinguished from *Extinct*. The IUCN categories and criteria for allocating species to each category were further refined over a period of several years, with version 3.1 published in 2001. This is the current version, and the one used here.

To accompany the IUCN categories and criteria, a series of guidelines has been produced to assist with their interpretation and use (IUCN 2006, 2008). One of the main innovations in the guidelines is a more realistic approach to extent of occurrence, using the so-called α-hull method. This is a system for establishing the range (extent of occurrence) of a taxon while excluding aberrant occurrences well outside its normal range and is explained more fully elsewhere (IUCN 2006). The latest versions of the criteria (IUCN 2008, 2010) differ only in minor details and points of clarification from the 2006 version.

The IUCN has also produced *Guidelines for Application of IUCN Red List Criteria at Regional Levels* (IUCN 2003). This established a *Regionally Extinct* category for use in regional Red Lists (as distinct from *Extinct*, which is global and final), and this category has been used for the Irish bryophytes. It also introduced the possibility of changing the threat status of a taxon on the basis of its status in neighbouring territories: taxa can be downgraded (or upgraded) depending on conditions outside the region covered and whether or not the population can be rescued from extra-regional populations. However, this has not been used for the Irish bryophyte Red List, as the concept of populations being rescued from elsewhere seems more appropriate for large animals than for small plants.

The Red List for bryophytes is for the whole island of Ireland, a single list for the biogeographic unit being considered the most practical approach for the application of IUCN criteria. Separate lists of species of conservation concern, or species requiring conservation actions, can be compiled from the all-island Red List by the relevant authorities as necessary, taking into account policy factors that may operate differently within the two jurisdictions.

In applying the IUCN criteria, 1970 has been chosen as the cut-off date to represent the threshold between old and recent records. This was essentially a compromise decision. There were strong arguments for having a 1960 threshold (much fieldwork was done in the 1960s, especially in the north, and should therefore be taken into account); or a 1980 threshold (the data would be more current and the landscape of Ireland has changed a great deal since the 1960s, presumably resulting in changes in the bryophyte flora). Using 1970 resulted in a reasonably large all-island data set of recent records to which the IUCN criteria could be applied.

The main data sources used for the compilation of the Red List are described in some detail in Chapters 3 and 4. In summary, these were: NPWS database, CEDaR database, National Biodiversity Data Centre (NBDC), Biological Records Centre (BRC), herbarium material, field records collected during the course of targeted fieldwork from 1999–2009, mainly by DTH and NGH, and recent field records from Chris Preston, Sam Bosanquet and others.

The IUCN criteria have been applied to all bryophyte taxa reported to occur in Ireland according to the latest checklist (Hill *et al.* 2008). This includes species and infraspecific taxa. The exceptions, which are not included in the evaluation process, are taxa that have been incorrectly reported from Ireland, or with uncertain status in Ireland, invalid or synonymised taxa and those that are thought to be introductions. These are listed in Table 7.

Application of IUCN criteria

The Red List consists of taxa in the categories *Extinct* (or *Regionally Extinct* in the case of the Irish bryophyte flora), *Critically Endangered*, *Endangered* and *Vulnerable*. For each of the main threat categories (*Critically Endangered*, *Endangered* and *Vulnerable*) there is a set of five main criteria A–E, any one of which qualifies a taxon for listing at that level of threat. The qualifying thresholds within the criteria A–E differ between threat categories.

Criterion A considers percentage decline, regardless of current range or abundance, and has been used very sparingly. For bryophytes, it is often difficult to decide what constitutes a mature individual, or even if an individual can be defined, and so estimates of the size of bryophyte populations are rarely available. It is also difficult to measure the rate of decline of bryophyte taxa from the available data that do exist, because records have so often been made at different times, in different areas, and there has been little systematic monitoring of populations over time. When considering population decline, the use of generation time is a useful concept for bryophytes as it enables decline over a longer time period than 10 years to be used. Hallingbäck *et al.* (1995) advise using a *maximum* of 25 years for one generation (for species that are not known to reproduce sexually), with a sliding scale of 11–25 years for species that reproduce sexually only infrequently, down to 1–5 years for short-lived ephemeral colonists that reproduce frequently with small, highly mobile spores. In other words, a system of life strategies, such as that devised by During (1992), needs to be adopted in order to obtain a broad estimate of generation time.

Subcriterion A1 has not been used, as there are no taxa for which there is certainty about whether their decline is reversible, understood and ceased. However, subcriteria A2 and A3 allow inferred or suspected decline, and the inference or suspicion can be based on a decline in habitat. This can sometimes be seen only too clearly. Thus, the very specific oceanic wet heath habitat of *Adelanthus lindenbergianus* and *Scapania ornithopodioides* has clearly declined in some areas, so subcriterion A2c can be used to contribute towards their assessment. *Tomentypnum nitens*, although occurring in too many populations to qualify as *Vulnerable* under other criteria, is known to have been destroyed at several of its localities, so A2c is also appropriate here. Subcriterion A3c has been used for *Aongstroemia longipes* and *Pohlia filum*, as it seems clear that their habitat will deteriorate in the future through natural succession. Subcriterion A4 has not been used, as it requires decline in both the past and the future, a level of detail too specific for bryophytes at our current state of knowledge.

Criterion B is used to categorise taxa that have a restricted distribution and are also declining. Extent of occurrence was at first used sparingly to determine threat category, but the advent of the α-hull method (IUCN 2006) allowed it to be used more extensively. If this shows a significant reduction in extent of occurrence (i.e. range), when old records (pre-1970) were compared with recent records (1970–2010), then clearly the concept is a useful one for determining threat category. However, bryophytes tend naturally to have very wide ranges, often with wide disjunctions between populations, so the concept of extent of occurrence may be less relevant to them as it is to many other species groups. Consequently, subcriteria B1a and B1b (extent of occurrence) have been used infrequently and with caution. Subcriterion B1c has not been used at all.

Area of occupancy also presents problems of interpretation. It should be measured, according to the IUCN Guidelines, on grid squares 'which are sufficiently small', and which are of appropriate size for the biological aspects of the taxon. This criterion is perhaps more applicable to a mobile animal holding a territory or a home range that can be measured. For a plant, it is either much more difficult to determine the area needed for its survival, or the area might be tiny in comparison. For simplicity, the area of occupancy of the bryophytes considered in this book has been interpreted in terms of hectads, which is the finest resolution attainable with the existing data. Subcriteria B2a and B2b (area of occupancy) have been used extensively.

The concepts of extreme fluctuation and fragmentation are listed as additional risk factors by IUCN, but these are seldom applicable to most bryophytes, as many species can fluctuate considerably as part of their natural population dynamics, and their distribution naturally appears to be fragmented. The only exception to this generalisation is found in the specialised bryophyte flora that grows in the draw-down zone of reservoirs and similar habitats. Subcriterion B2c has been used for two reservoir species, *Ephemerum cohaerens* and *E. spinulosum*, where their populations could be at risk and subject to extreme fluctuation if water levels are kept artificially high for too long.

Criterion C requires detailed data on both population size and decline, and has not been used at all, since this level of information is not available for Irish bryophytes.

Criterion D identifies very small or restricted populations and is an expression of rarity, inferring that a taxon is threatened by human activities or stochastic events simply because it is rare, without necessarily having declined. Criterion D has been used very sparingly for assigning taxa to the *Critically Endangered* or *Endangered* categories, as there is usually no detailed information on population size. However, it has been used in a few cases where it can reasonably be inferred that a population consists of fewer than 50 mature individuals or fewer than 250 mature individuals (depending, of course, on the interpretation of 'an individual'). Subcriterion D2 has been used more extensively for assigning taxa with less than 5 localities to the *Vulnerable* category.

Criterion E uses quantitative analyses to consider the probability of extinction in the wild. This has not been used at all, as there have been no population viability analyses published on bryophytes in Ireland.

Red Data List categories

Extinct (EX). A taxon is *Extinct* when there is no reasonable doubt that the last individual has died. There are no taxa in this category in the Irish bryophyte flora.

Extinct in the Wild (EW). A taxon is *Extinct in the Wild* when it is known to survive only in cultivation or as a naturalised population well outside the past range. There are no taxa in this category in the Irish bryophyte flora.

Regionally Extinct (RE). A taxon is regarded as *Regionally Extinct* in Ireland if there are no recent (1970–2010) records and all known localities have been visited and surveyed without success. Failure to refind older records may sometimes just reflect the imprecision of the original locality data, or adverse weather conditions during recent survey visits, or simply that certain taxa occur sporadically and are inherently difficult to find. It is possible therefore that some *Regionally Extinct* taxa may persist in Ireland, albeit at a relatively low frequency, and might yet turn up at some future date. An effort has been made, however, to distinguish between taxa that have probably genuinely disappeared and those that may still occur, the latter being placed in the *Data Deficient* category.

Critically Endangered (CR). A taxon is *Critically Endangered* when it is facing an extremely high risk of regional extinction in the wild in the immediate future, as detailed by any of the criteria A, B or D.

Endangered (EN). A taxon is *Endangered* when it is not *Critically Endangered* but is facing a very high risk of regional extinction in the wild in the near future, as defined by any of the criteria A, B or D.

Vulnerable (VU). A taxon is *Vulnerable* when it is not *Critically Endangered* or *Endangered* but is facing a high risk of regional extinction in the wild in the medium-term future, as defined by any of the criteria A, B or D.

Near Threatened (NT). A taxon is *Near Threatened* when it has been evaluated against the criteria but does not qualify for *Critically Endangered*, *Endangered* or *Vulnerable*, but is close to qualifying for a threatened category in the future. A taxon is regarded as close to qualifying for a threatened category in Ireland if it occurs in 6–12 hectads (1970–2010) but has not declined; or < 20 hectads (1970–2010) and has declined.

Data Deficient (DD). A taxon is *Data Deficient* when there is inadequate information to make a direct or indirect assessment of its risk of extinction based on its distribution and population status. A taxon is regarded as *Data Deficient* in Ireland if it is thought likely that future research will show that a threatened classification is appropriate and that it will be included in the Red List at some stage.

Least Concern (LC). A taxon is regarded as *Least Concern* in Ireland if it occurs in > 20 hectads (1970–2010); or 13–19 hectads (1970–2010) and shows no decline.

Not Evaluated (NE). A taxon is *Not Evaluated* when it has not been assessed against the criteria. A taxon is regarded as *Not Evaluated* in Ireland if it has not been confirmed in the Irish list; if it is treated as a synonym in the latest checklist (Hill *et al.* 2008); or if it is considered to be a recent introduction and therefore not part of the native Irish flora.

Summary of the IUCN criteria and categories as interpreted for the Irish bryophyte flora

Fulfilling *any one* of these criteria leads to the application of a threat category at the appropriate level.

Criterion A. Rapid decline. A2c used for a small number of taxa, on the basis of a decline in habitat quality; A3c used for a small number of taxa, on the basis of a predicted decline and loss of habitat. > 80% decline (CR); > 50% decline (EN); > 30% decline (VU).

Criterion B. Small range; fragmented, declining or fluctuating. Fragmented and extreme fluctuations only used for specialist reservoir species, as both phenomena are common natural features of bryophyte populations.

1. Extent of occurrence (estimated using α-hull method, where $\alpha = 2$): < 100 km² (CR); < 5000 km² (EN); < 20,000 km² (VU) AND both a and b:

   (a) single location (CR); 5 locations or fewer (EN); 10 locations or fewer (VU).

   (b) continuing decline observed, inferred or projected, in any of the following:
       (i)   extent of occurrence
       (ii) area of occupancy
       (iii) area, extent and/or quality of habitat
       (iv) number of locations or subpopulations
       (v)   number of mature individuals

2. Area of occupancy: < 10 km², using 1 hectad (CR); < 500 km², using 5 hectads (EN); < 2000 km², using 20 hectads (VU) AND at least two of a–c:

   (a) single location (CR); 5 locations or fewer (EN); 10 locations or fewer (VU).

   (b) continuing decline observed, inferred or projected, in any of the following:
       (i)   extent of occurrence
       (ii) area of occupancy
       (iii) area, extent and/or quality of habitat
       (iv) number of locations or subpopulations
       (v)   number of mature individuals

   (c) Extreme fluctuations in any of the following (but only used for reservoir species):
       (i)   extent of occurrence
       (ii) area of occupancy
       (iii) number of locations or subpopulations
       (iv) number of mature individuals

Criterion D/D1. Very small population. Used very sparingly, and only if there is no reasonable doubt: < 50 individuals estimated (CR); < 250 individuals estimated (EN); < 1000 individuals estimated (VU).

Criterion D2. Very small range. Used extensively to assign taxa to VU: 5 or fewer locations.

The Red List

The number of taxa in each threat category is summarised in Table 2. Red List, *Near Threatened* and

76

Data Deficient taxa are listed by category in Tables 3–6. Not Evaluated taxa are shown in Table 7, with an explanation of why they fall into this category. Finally, the complete Irish bryophyte flora, with the status of each taxon, is listed alphabetically for hornworts, liverworts and mosses in Table 8.

Table 2. Summary of the number of taxa in each threat category in Ireland

	RE	CR	EN	VU	NT	DD	LC	NE	**Total**
Hornworts and liverworts	5	4	13	25	28	9	151	4	**239**
Mosses	35	19	30	64	69	28	344	7	**596**
Total	**40**	**23**	**43**	**89**	**97**	**37**	**495**	**11**	835

Table 3. The Irish Bryophyte Red List: *Regionally Extinct* taxa

Name of taxon	Threat category	Last Irish record
Liverworts		
Anastrophyllum hellerianum	RE	1964
Barbilophozia kunzeana	RE	1880
Calypogeia suecica	RE	1967
Ptilidium pulcherrimum	RE	1953
Targionia hypophylla	RE	1902
Mosses		
Acaulon muticum	RE	1951
Aloina rigida	RE	1969
Atrichum angustatum	RE	1957
Bartramia halleriana	RE	1967
Bryum turbinatum	RE	1937
Buxbaumia aphylla	RE	1804
Campylopus schimperi	RE	1969
Conardia compacta	RE	1928
Ctenidium molluscum var. *robustum*	RE	1917
Dicranum undulatum	RE	1960
Didymodon icmadophilus	RE	1880
Entosthodon muhlenbergii	RE	1915
Eurhynchiastrum pulchellum var. *diversifolium*	RE	1964
Fissidens curvatus	RE	1951
Grimmia crinita	RE	1950
Grimmia laevigata	RE	1956
Grimmia longirostris	RE	1951
Meesia triquetra	RE	1958
Microbryum curvicollum	RE	1950
Microbryum starckeanum	RE	1950
Myurium hochstetteri	RE	1969
Pohlia proligera	RE	1965

Table 3. The Irish Bryophyte Red List: *Regionally Extinct* **taxa (continued)**

Name of taxon	Threat category	Last Irish record
Pohlia wahlenbergii var. *glacialis*	RE	1963
Pterigynandrum filiforme	RE	1926
Pterygoneurum lamellatum	RE	1875
Pterygoneurum ovatum	RE	1873
Rhynchostegiella curviseta	RE	1965
Rhytidiadelphus subpinnatus	RE	1966
Seligeria calycina	RE	1964
Syntrichia princeps	RE	1962
Tayloria tenuis	RE	1884
Tortula protobryoides	RE	1904
Tortula vahliana	RE	1949
Tortula wilsonii	RE	1934
Ulota drummondii	RE	1966

Table 4. The Irish Bryophyte Red List: *Critically Endangered, Endangered* **and** *Vulnerable* **taxa**

Name of taxon	Threat category	Criteria sub-heads
Critically Endangered		
Hornworts and liverworts		
Barbilophozia barbata	CR	B1a, bi, ii, iv, B2a, bi, ii, iv
Gymnomitrion corallioides	CR	B1a, bi, ii, iv, B2a, bi, ii, iv
Leiocolea heterocolpos	CR	B2a, biii
Southbya tophacea	CR	B1a, bii, iv, B2a, bii, iv
Mosses		
Aongstroemia longipes	CR	A3c
Bryum moravicum	CR	B1a, bii, iv, 2a, bii, iv
Bryum salinum	CR	B1a, bi, ii, iv, B2a, bi, ii, iv, D
Ditrichum cornubicum	CR	D
Ditrichum lineare	CR	B1a, bi, ii, iv, B2a, bi, ii, iv
Encalypta ciliata	CR	B1a, bi, ii, iv, B2a, bi, ii, iv
Encalypta rhaptocarpa	CR	B1a, bi, ii, iv, B2a, bi, ii, iv
Hygrohypnum duriusculum	CR	B1a, bi, ii, iv, B2a, bi, ii, iv
Kiaeria falcata	CR	D
Oedipodium griffithianum	CR	B1a, bi, ii, iv, B2a, bi, ii, iv
Orthodontium gracile	CR	B2a, biii
Oxyrrhynchium schleicheri	CR	B2a, biii
Paludella squarrosa	CR	B2a, biii, D
Philonotis cernua	CR	B1a, bi, ii, iii, iv, B2a, bi, ii, iii, iv
Plagiopus oederianus	CR	B1a, bi, ii, iv, B2a, bi, ii, iv
Ptilium crista-castrensis	CR	B2a, biii, D
Tortula cuneifolia	CR	B1a, bi, ii, iv, B2a, bi, ii, iv
Tortula lanceola	CR	B1a, bi, ii, iii, iv, B2a, bi, ii, iii, iv
Ulota coarctata	CR	D

Table 4. The Irish Bryophyte Red List: *Critically Endangered, Endangered* and *Vulnerable* **taxa** (continued)

Name of taxon	Threat category	Criteria sub-heads
Endangered		
Hornworts and liverworts		
Barbilophozia atlantica	EN	B2a, bii, iv, v
Calypogeia integristipula	EN	B1a, bi, ii, iv, B2a, bi, ii, iv
Cephalozia crassifolia	EN	B2a, bii, iv
Geocalyx graveolens	EN	D
Gymnomitrion concinnatum	EN	B1a, bi, ii, iv, B2a, bi, ii, iv
Leiocolea rutheana var. *rutheana*	EN	B2a, biii, D
Lejeunea mandonii	EN	B2a, bii, iv
Marchantia polymorpha subsp. *montivagans*	EN	D
Pallavicinia lyellii	EN	B1a, bi, ii, iv, B2a, bi, ii, iv
Plagiochila carringtonii	EN	B2a, biii
Plagiochila heterophylla	EN	B2a, bii, iv
Riccia crozalsii	EN	D
Scapania nimbosa	EN	B2a, bii, iii, iv
Mosses		
Abietinella abietina var. *abietina*	EN	B2a, biii, iv
Aloina ambigua	EN	B1a, bi, ii, iv, B2a, bi, ii, iv, D
Brachydontium trichodes	EN	B2a, bi, ii, iv
Brachytheciastrum velutinum	EN	B2a, bi, ii, iv
Bryum calophyllum	EN	B2a, biii
Bryum intermedium	EN	B2a, bii, iv
Bryum knowltonii	EN	D
Bryum riparium	EN	B2a, bii, iv
Bryum uliginosum	EN	B2a, bii, iv
Bryum warneum	EN	B2a, bii, iii, iv
Campylostelium saxicola	EN	B1a, bi, ii, iv, B2a, bi, ii, iv
Dicranella crispa	EN	B1a, bi, ii, iv, B2a, bi, ii, iv
Didymodon acutus	EN	B2a, bii, iii, iv
Ditrichum plumbicola	EN	D
Ditrichum zonatum	EN	B2a, bii, iv
Ephemerum spinulosum	EN	B2a, ciii, iv
Fissidens rufulus	EN	B1a, bi, ii, iii, iv, B2a, bi, ii, iii, iv
Grimmia anomala	EN	D
Grimmia atrata	EN	D
Hygroamblystegium humile	EN	B1a, bi, ii, iv, B2a, bi, ii, iv
Leptodon smithii	EN	B1a, bi, ii, iv, B2a, bi, ii, iv
Meesia uliginosa	EN	D
Myurella julacea	EN	B2a, bii, iv
Orthotrichum pallens	EN	B1a, bi, ii, iv, B2a, bi, ii, iv
Philonotis arnellii	EN	B1a, bi, ii, iv, B2a, bi, ii, biv
Pogonatum nanum	EN	B1a, bi, ii, iv, B2a, bi, ii, iv
Pohlia andalusica	EN	B1a, biii, B2a, biii
Pohlia elongata var. *greenii*	EN	B1a, bi, ii, iv, B2a, bi, ii, iv
Scleropodium touretii	EN	B1a, bi, ii, iii, iv, B2a, bi, ii, iii, iv
Tortella inclinata	EN	B2a, bii, iv

Table 4. The Irish Bryophyte Red List: *Critically Endangered, Endangered* and *Vulnerable* taxa (continued)

Name of taxon	Threat category	Criteria sub-heads
Vulnerable		
Hornworts and liverworts		
Acrobolbus wilsonii	VU	D1
Adelanthus lindenbergianus	VU	A2c, B2a, biii, iv
Aneura mirabilis	VU	B2a, bii, iii, iv
Anthoceros agrestis	VU	D2
Bazzania pearsonii	VU	B2a, bii, iii, iv
Cephalozia loitlesbergeri	VU	B2a, biii
Cephalozia pleniceps	VU	B2a, bii, iv
Cephaloziella integerrima	VU	D2
Cephaloziella massalongi	VU	D2
Cephaloziella nicholsonii	VU	B2a, biii
Cephaloziella rubella	VU	D2
Cephaloziella turneri	VU	D2
Cladopodiella francisci	VU	D2
Fossombronia fimbriata	VU	D2
Leiocolea gillmanii	VU	D2
Lejeunea flava subsp. *moorei*	VU	B2a, bii. Iv
Lophozia opacifolia	VU	D2
Marsupella sphacelata	VU	B1a, bi, ii, iv, B2a, bi, ii, iv
Marsupella sprucei	VU	B2a, bii, biv
Metzgeria pubescens	VU	D2
Scapania curta	VU	D2
Scapania cuspiduligera	VU	D2
Scapania gymnostomophila	VU	D2
Scapania ornithopodioides	VU	A2c
Tritomaria exsecta	VU	B2a, bii, iv
Mosses		
Amphidium lapponicum	VU	D2
Andreaea megistospora	VU	B1a, bi, ii, iv, B2a, bi, ii, iv
Arctoa fulvella	VU	B2a, bii, iv, D2
Aulacomnium androgynum	VU	B2a, bii, iv
Bartramia ithyphylla	VU	B2a, bii, iv
Bryum caespiticium	VU	D2
Bryum elegans	VU	D2
Bryum gemmiparum	VU	D2
Bryum torquescens	VU	B2a, bi, ii, iv
Campylopus subulatus	VU	B2a, bii, iv
Cinclidium stygium	VU	B2a, biii
Cynodontium jenneri	VU	D2
Dicranodontium asperulum	VU	D2
Dicranodontium uncinatum	VU	B1a, bi, ii, iii, iv, B2a, bi, ii, iii, iv
Didymodon tomaculosus	VU	D2
Didymodon umbrosus	VU	D2
Encalypta alpina	VU	D2
Ephemerum cohaerens	VU	B2a, ciii, iv

Table 4. The Irish Bryophyte Red List: *Critically Endangered, Endangered* **and** *Vulnerable* **taxa** (continued)

Name of taxon	Threat category	Criteria sub-heads
Fissidens exilis	VU	B2a, bii, iv
Fissidens fontanus	VU	D2
Fissidens polyphyllus	VU	D2
Fissidens rivularis	VU	D2
Fissidens serrulatus	VU	D2
Grimmia dissimulata	VU	D2
Grimmia orbicularis	VU	B2a, bii, iv
Hedwigia ciliata var. *ciliata*	VU	D2
Hedwigia integrifolia	VU	B2a, bii, iv
Isopterygiopsis muelleriana	VU	D2
Leptobarbula berica	VU	D2
Molendoa warburgii	VU	D2
Orthotrichum sprucei	VU	B2a, biii
Orthotrichum stramineum	VU	B2a, bii, iv
Philonotis rigida	VU	B2a, bii, iv
Philonotis tomentella	VU	D2
Physcomitrium sphaericum	VU	D2
Plagiothecium cavifolium	VU	D2
Plagiothecium curvifolium	VU	D2
Plagiothecium laetum	VU	D2
Plagiothecium latebricola	VU	D2
Plagiothecium platyphyllum	VU	D2
Pohlia filum	VU	A3c, D1
Pseudocalliergon lycopodioides	VU	A2c
Pseudocalliergon trifarium	VU	D2
Racomitrium canescens	VU	D2
Racomitrium elongatum	VU	D2
Racomitrium macounii subsp. *alpinum*	VU	D2
Rhabdoweisia fugax	VU	B1a, bi, ii, iv, B2a, bi, ii, iv
Rhytidium rugosum	VU	D2
Schistidium agassizii	VU	D2
Schistidium platyphyllum	VU	B2a, bii, iii, iv
Schistidium trichodon	VU	D2
Scopelophila cataractae	VU	D2
Seligeria calcarea	VU	B2a, bii, iv
Seligeria oelandica	VU	D1
Sematophyllum substrumulosum	VU	D2
Sphagnum affine	VU	D2
Sphagnum flexuosum	VU	D2
Sphagnum warnstorfii	VU	B2a, bii, iv
Thuidium recognitum	VU	B2a, bii, iv
Timmia norvegica	VU	D1
Tomentypnum nitens	VU	A3c
Tortula modica	VU	B2a, bii, iv
Weissia longifolia var. *angustifolia*	VU	B1a, bii, iv, B2a, bii, iv
Weissia rutilans	VU	B2a, bii, iv

Table 5. *Near Threatened* taxa

Name of taxon	Threat category	Name of taxon	Threat category
Liverworts		*Ephemerum crassinervium* subsp. *sessile*	NT
Anthelia juratzkana	NT	*Fissidens monguillonii*	NT
Cephaloziella stellulifera	NT	*Fontinalis antipyretica* var. *gracilis*	NT
Diplophyllum obtusifolium	NT	*Grimmia decipiens*	NT
Douinia ovata	NT	*Grimmia donniana*	NT
Dumortiera hirsuta	NT	*Grimmia funalis*	NT
Eremonotus myriocarpus	NT	*Grimmia ramondii*	NT
Fossombronia maritima	NT	*Grimmia torquata*	NT
Gymnomitrion obtusum	NT	*Hageniella micans*	NT
Kurzia sylvatica	NT	*Hamatocaulis vernicosus*	NT
Leiocolea bantriensis	NT	*Heterocladium wulfsbergii*	NT
Leiocolea fitzgeraldiae	NT	*Hygroamblystegium fluviatile*	NT
Lejeunea eckloniana	NT	*Hygroamblystegium varium*	NT
Lejeunea hibernica	NT	*Hylocomiastrum umbratum*	NT
Marsupella adusta	NT	*Hymenostylium recurvirostrum* var. *insigne*	NT
Marsupella funckii	NT	*Hypnum callichroum*	NT
Mastigophora woodsii	NT	*Hypnum uncinulatum*	NT
Metzgeria leptoneura	NT	*Leptodontium flexifolium*	NT
Nardia geoscyphus	NT	*Mnium thomsonii*	NT
Odontoschisma elongatum	NT	*Orthothecium rufescens*	NT
Porella cordaeana	NT	*Orthotrichum rivulare*	NT
Radula carringtonii	NT	*Oxyrrhynchium speciosum*	NT
Radula holtii	NT	*Paraleptodontium recurvifolium*	NT
Ricciocarpos natans	NT	*Philonotis caespitosa*	NT
Solenostoma paroicum	NT	*Plagiobryum zieri*	NT
Solenostoma sphaerocarpum	NT	*Plagiomnium cuspidatum*	NT
Solenostoma subellipticum	NT	*Plagiothecium denticulatum* var. *obtusifolium*	NT
Sphenolobopsis pearsonii	NT	*Plasteurhynchium striatulum*	NT
Telaranea europaea	NT	*Platydictya jungermannioides*	NT
		Platyhypnidium lusitanicum	NT
Mosses		*Pleurochaete squarrosa*	NT
Abietinella abietina var. *hystricosa*	NT	*Pohlia elongata* var. *elongata*	NT
Amblystegium confervoides	NT	*Rhabdoweisia crispata*	NT
Antitrichia curtipendula	NT	*Rhizomnium pseudopunctatum*	NT
Atrichum tenellum	NT	*Rhodobryum roseum*	NT
Bryum bornholmense	NT	*Rhynchostegium megapolitanum*	NT
Bryum dyffrynense	NT	*Schistidium strictum*	NT
Campyliadelphus elodes	NT	*Scleropodium cespitans*	NT
Campylopus atrovirens var. *falcatus*	NT	*Seligeria patula*	NT
Campylopus shawii	NT	*Sematophyllum demissum*	NT
Catoscopium nigritum	NT	*Sphagnum girgensohnii*	NT
Cyclodictyon laetevirens	NT	*Sphagnum platyphyllum*	NT
Dicranella cerviculata	NT	*Sphagnum russowii*	NT
Dicranella grevilleana	NT	*Sphagnum subsecundum*	NT
Didymodon maximus	NT	*Sphagnum teres*	NT
Discelium nudum	NT	*Tetrodontium brownianum*	NT
Drepanocladus sendtneri	NT	*Tortella densa*	NT
Encalypta vulgaris	NT	*Tortula atrovirens*	NT
Entosthodon fascicularis	NT	*Tortula marginata*	NT
Ephemerum crassinervium subsp. *rutheanum*	NT	*Weissia rostellata*	NT

Table 6. *Data Deficient* **taxa**

Name of taxon	Threat category
Liverworts	
Cephalozia macrostachya var. *spiniflora*	DD
Cephaloziella elachista	DD
Cephaloziella spinigera	DD
Fossombronia caespitiformis subsp. *multispira*	DD
Lophozia wenzelii	DD
Moerckia hibernica	DD
Riccia huebeneriana	DD
Scapania lingulata	DD
Scapania subalpina	DD
Mosses	
Bryum creberrimum	DD
Bryum tenuisetum	DD
Cinclidotus riparius	DD
Ditrichum flexicaule	DD
Ditrichum pusillum	DD
Ephemerum recurvifolium	DD
Fissidens crispus	DD
Fontinalis antipyretica var. *cymbifolia*	DD
Grimmia muehlenbeckii	DD
Phascum cuspidatum var. *papillosum*	DD
Phascum cuspidatum var. *piliferum*	DD
Pohlia lescuriana	DD
Pohlia wahlenbergii var. *calcarea*	DD
Polytrichum commune var. *perigoniale*	DD
Schistidium confertum	DD
Schistidium elegantulum subsp. *elegantulum*	DD
Schistidium elegantulum subsp. *wilsonii*	DD
Schistidium pruinosum	DD
Schistidium robustum	DD
Sphagnum capillifolium subsp. *capillifolium*	DD
Sphagnum skyense	DD
Sphagnum strictum	DD
Syntrichia virescens	DD
Tetraplodon angustatus	DD
Tortula canescens	DD
Weissia brachycarpa var. *brachycarpa*	DD
Weissia condensa	DD
Weissia controversa var. *crispata*	DD

Table 7. *Not Evaluated* taxa

Name of taxon	Explanation
Liverworts	
Heteroscyphus fissistipus	Alien introduction
Jungermannia borealis	Not correctly reported from Ireland
Lophocolea bispinosa	Alien introduction
Lophocolea semiteres	Alien introduction
Lophozia longiflora	Not correctly reported from Ireland
Riccia rhenana	Probable alien introduction
Scapania uliginosa	Not correctly reported from Ireland
Mosses	
Atrichum crispum	Probable alien introduction
Bryum dunense	Synonymised with *Bryum dichotomum*
Bryum neodamense	Synonymised with *Bryum pseudotriquetrum*
Bryum weigelii	Not confirmed from Ireland
Calomnion complanatum	Alien introduction
Calyptrochaeta apiculata	Alien introduction
Campylophyllum calcareum	Not confirmed from Ireland
Ctenidium molluscum var. *fastigiatum*	Synonymised with *Ctenidium molluscum*
Dicranoloma menziesii	Alien introduction
Ephemerum stellatum	Synonymised with *Ephemerum serratum*
Fontinalis squamosa var. *dixonii*	Synonymised with *Fontinalis squamosa*
Hennediella stanfordensis	Alien introduction
Homomallium incurvatum	Not correctly reported from Ireland
Hypopterygium immigrans	Alien introduction (indoors only)
Leptotheca gaudichaudii var. *gaudichaudii*	Alien introduction
Orthotrichum cupulatum var. *riparium*	Synonymised with *Orthotrichum cupulatum*
Palustriella commutata var. *virescens*	Synonymised with *Palustriella commutata*
Pylaisia polyantha	Not confirmed from Ireland
Timmia austriaca	Not correctly reported from Ireland
Tortella fragilis	Not correctly reported from Ireland

Table 8. Complete list of Irish bryophytes with threat category

Only taxa with confirmed records from Ireland have been included. Nomenclature follows Hill *et al.* (2008), except for the following additions: *Dicranoloma menziesii* (Taylor) Renauld, *Ephemerum crassinervium* (Schwägr.) Hampe, *Grimmia anomala* Hampe ex Schimp. and *Hypopterygium immigrans* Lett.

Name of taxon	Threat category	Name of taxon	Threat category
Hornworts and liverworts		*Cephalozia macrostachya*	
Acrobolbus wilsonii	Vulnerable	var. *spiniflora*	Data Deficient
Adelanthus decipiens	Least Concern	*Cephalozia pleniceps*	Vulnerable
Adelanthus lindenbergianus	Vulnerable	*Cephaloziella divaricata*	Least Concern
Anastrepta orcadensis	Least Concern	*Cephaloziella elachista*	Data Deficient
Anastrophyllum hellerianum	Regionally Extinct	*Cephaloziella hampeana*	Least Concern
Anastrophyllum minutum	Least Concern	*Cephaloziella integerrima*	Vulnerable
Aneura mirabilis	Vulnerable	*Cephaloziella massalongi*	Vulnerable
Aneura pinguis	Least Concern	*Cephaloziella nicholsonii*	Vulnerable
Anthelia julacea	Least Concern	*Cephaloziella rubella*	Vulnerable
Anthelia juratzkana	Near Threatened	*Cephaloziella spinigera*	Data Deficient
Anthoceros agrestis	Vulnerable	*Cephaloziella stellulifera*	Near Threatened
Anthoceros punctatus	Least Concern	*Cephaloziella turneri*	Vulnerable
Aphanolejeunea microscopica	Least Concern	*Chiloscyphus pallescens*	Least Concern
Barbilophozia atlantica	Endangered	*Chiloscyphus polyanthos*	Least Concern
Barbilophozia attenuata	Least Concern	*Cladopodiella fluitans*	Least Concern
Barbilophozia barbata	Critically Endangered	*Cladopodiella francisci*	Vulnerable
Barbilophozia floerkei	Least Concern	*Cololejeunea calcarea*	Least Concern
Barbilophozia kunzeana	Regionally Extinct	*Cololejeunea minutissima*	Least Concern
Bazzania pearsonii	Vulnerable	*Cololejeunea rossettiana*	Least Concern
Bazzania tricrenata	Least Concern	*Colura calyptrifolia*	Least Concern
Bazzania trilobata	Least Concern	*Conocephalum conicum*	Least Concern
Blasia pusilla	Least Concern	*Conocephalum salebrosum*	Least Concern
Blepharostoma trichophyllum	Least Concern	*Diplophyllum albicans*	Least Concern
Calypogeia arguta	Least Concern	*Diplophyllum obtusifolium*	Near Threatened
Calypogeia azurea	Least Concern	*Douinia ovata*	Near Threatened
Calypogeia fissa	Least Concern	*Drepanolejeunea*	
Calypogeia integristipula	Endangered	*hamatifolia*	Least Concern
Calypogeia muelleriana	Least Concern	*Dumortiera hirsuta*	Near Threatened
Calypogeia neesiana	Least Concern	*Eremonotus myriocarpus*	Near Threatened
Calypogeia sphagnicola	Least Concern	*Fossombronia angulosa*	Least Concern
Calypogeia suecica	Regionally Extinct	*Fossombronia caespitiformis*	
Cephalozia bicuspidata	Least Concern	subsp. *multispira*	Data Deficient
Cephalozia catenulata	Least Concern	*Fossombronia fimbriata*	Vulnerable
Cephalozia connivens	Least Concern	*Fossombronia foveolata*	Least Concern
Cephalozia crassifolia	Endangered	*Fossombronia incurva*	Least Concern
Cephalozia leucantha	Least Concern	*Fossombronia maritima*	Near Threatened
Cephalozia loitlesbergeri	Vulnerable	*Fossombronia pusilla*	Least Concern
Cephalozia lunulifolia	Least Concern	*Fossombronia wondraczekii*	Least Concern
Cephalozia macrostachya		*Frullania dilatata*	Least Concern
var. *macrostachya*	Least Concern	*Frullania fragilifolia*	Least Concern

Table 8. Complete list of Irish bryophytes with threat category (continued)

Name of taxon	Threat category	Name of taxon	Threat category
Frullania microphylla		*Lophocolea bispinosa*	Not Evaluated
var. *microphylla*	Least Concern	*Lophocolea fragrans*	Least Concern
Frullania tamarisci	Least Concern	*Lophocolea heterophylla*	Least Concern
Frullania teneriffae	Least Concern	*Lophocolea semiteres*	Not Evaluated
Geocalyx graveolens	Endangered	*Lophozia bicrenata*	Least Concern
Gymnocolea inflata	Least Concern	*Lophozia excisa*	Least Concern
Gymnomitrion concinnatum	Endangered	*Lophozia incisa*	Least Concern
Gymnomitrion corallioides	Critically Endangered	*Lophozia opacifolia*	Vulnerable
Gymnomitrion crenulatum	Least Concern	*Lophozia sudetica*	Least Concern
Gymnomitrion obtusum	Near Threatened	*Lophozia ventricosa*	Least Concern
Haplomitrium hookeri	Least Concern	*Lophozia wenzelii*	Data Deficient
Harpalejeunea molleri	Least Concern	*Lunularia cruciata*	Least Concern
Harpanthus scutatus	Least Concern	*Marchantia polymorpha*	
Herbertus aduncus		subsp. *montivagans*	Endangered
subsp. *hutchinsiae*	Least Concern	*Marchantia polymorpha*	
Heteroscyphus fissistipus	Not Evaluated	subsp. *polymorpha*	Least Concern
Hygrobiella laxifolia	Least Concern	*Marchantia polymorpha*	
Jubula hutchinsiae		subsp. *ruderalis*	Least Concern
subsp. *hutchinsiae*	Least Concern	*Marchesinia mackaii*	Least Concern
Jungermannia atrovirens	Least Concern	*Marsupella adusta*	Near Threatened
Jungermannia exsertifolia		*Marsupella emarginata*	
subsp. *cordifolia*	Least Concern	var. *aquatica*	Least Concern
Jungermannia pumila	Least Concern	*Marsupella emarginata*	
Kurzia pauciflora	Least Concern	var. *emarginata*	Least Concern
Kurzia sylvatica	Near Threatened	*Marsupella emarginata*	
Kurzia trichoclados	Least Concern	var. *pearsonii*	Least Concern
Leiocolea badensis	Least Concern	*Marsupella funckii*	Near Threatened
Leiocolea bantriensis	Near Threatened	*Marsupella sphacelata*	Vulnerable
Leiocolea collaris	Least Concern	*Marsupella sprucei*	Vulnerable
Leiocolea fitzgeraldiae	Near Threatened	*Mastigophora woodsii*	Near Threatened
Leiocolea gillmanii	Vulnerable	*Metzgeria conjugata*	Least Concern
Leiocolea heterocolpos	Critically Endangered	*Metzgeria consanguinea*	Least Concern
Leiocolea rutheana		*Metzgeria furcata*	Least Concern
var. *rutheana*	Endangered	*Metzgeria leptoneura*	Near Threatened
Leiocolea turbinata	Least Concern	*Metzgeria pubescens*	Vulnerable
Lejeunea cavifolia	Least Concern	*Metzgeria violacea*	Least Concern
Lejeunea eckloniana	Near Threatened	*Microlejeunea ulicina*	Least Concern
Lejeunea flava subsp. *moorei*	Vulnerable	*Moerckia flotoviana*	Least Concern
Lejeunea hibernica	Near Threatened	*Moerckia hibernica*	Data Deficient
Lejeunea lamacerina	Least Concern	*Mylia anomala*	Least Concern
Lejeunea mandonii	Endangered	*Mylia taylorii*	Least Concern
Lejeunea patens	Least Concern	*Nardia compressa*	Least Concern
Lepidozia cupressina	Least Concern	*Nardia geoscyphus*	Near Threatened
Lepidozia pearsonii	Least Concern	*Nardia scalaris*	Least Concern
Lepidozia reptans	Least Concern	*Nowellia curvifolia*	Least Concern
Leptoscyphus cuneifolius	Least Concern	*Odontoschisma denudatum*	Least Concern
Lophocolea bidentata	Least Concern	*Odontoschisma elongatum*	Near Threatened

Table 8. Complete list of Irish bryophytes with threat category (continued)

Name of taxon	Threat category	Name of taxon	Threat category
Odontoschisma sphagni	Least Concern	*Ricciocarpos natans*	Near Threatened
Pallavicinia lyellii	Endangered	*Saccogyna viticulosa*	Least Concern
Pedinophyllum interruptum	Least Concern	*Scapania aequiloba*	Least Concern
Pellia endiviifolia	Least Concern	*Scapania aspera*	Least Concern
Pellia epiphylla	Least Concern	*Scapania compacta*	Least Concern
Pellia neesiana	Least Concern	*Scapania curta*	Vulnerable
Petalophyllum ralfsii	Least Concern	*Scapania cuspiduligera*	Vulnerable
Phaeoceros laevis	Least Concern	*Scapania gracilis*	Least Concern
Plagiochila asplenioides	Least Concern	*Scapania gymnostomophila*	Vulnerable
Plagiochila bifaria	Least Concern	*Scapania irrigua*	Least Concern
Plagiochila britannica	Least Concern	*Scapania lingulata*	Data Deficient
Plagiochila carringtonii	Endangered	*Scapania nemorea*	Least Concern
Plagiochila exigua	Least Concern	*Scapania nimbosa*	Endangered
Plagiochila heterophylla	Endangered	*Scapania ornithopodioides*	Vulnerable
Plagiochila porelloides	Least Concern	*Scapania scandica*	Least Concern
Plagiochila punctata	Least Concern	*Scapania subalpina*	Data Deficient
Plagiochila spinulosa	Least Concern	*Scapania umbrosa*	Least Concern
Pleurozia purpurea	Least Concern	*Scapania undulata*	Least Concern
Porella arboris-vitae	Least Concern	*Solenostoma gracillimum*	Least Concern
Porella cordaeana	Near Threatened	*Solenostoma hyalinum*	Least Concern
Porella obtusata	Least Concern	*Solenostoma obovatum*	Least Concern
Porella pinnata	Least Concern	*Solenostoma paroicum*	Near Threatened
Porella platyphylla	Least Concern	*Solenostoma sphaerocarpum*	Near Threatened
Preissia quadrata	Least Concern	*Solenostoma subellipticum*	Near Threatened
Ptilidium ciliare	Least Concern	*Southbya tophacea*	Critically Endangered
Ptilidium pulcherrimum	Regionally Extinct	*Sphenolobopsis pearsonii*	Near Threatened
Radula aquilegia	Least Concern	*Targionia hypophylla*	Regionally Extinct
Radula carringtonii	Near Threatened	*Telaranea europaea*	Near Threatened
Radula complanata	Least Concern	*Trichocolea tomentella*	Least Concern
Radula holtii	Near Threatened	*Tritomaria exsecta*	Vulnerable
Radula lindenbergiana	Least Concern	*Tritomaria exsectiformis*	Least Concern
Radula voluta	Least Concern	*Tritomaria quinquedentata*	Least Concern
Reboulia hemisphaerica	Least Concern		
Riccardia chamedryfolia	Least Concern	Mosses	
Riccardia incurvata	Least Concern	*Abietinella abietina*	
Riccardia latifrons	Least Concern	var. *abietina*	Endangered
Riccardia multifida	Least Concern	*Abietinella abietina*	
Riccardia palmata	Least Concern	var. *hystricosa*	Near Threatened
Riccia beyrichiana	Least Concern	*Acaulon muticum*	Regionally Extinct
Riccia cavernosa	Least Concern	*Aloina aloides*	Least Concern
Riccia crozalsii	Endangered	*Aloina ambigua*	Endangered
Riccia fluitans	Least Concern	*Aloina rigida*	Regionally Extinct
Riccia glauca	Least Concern	*Amblyodon dealbatus*	Least Concern
Riccia huebeneriana	Data Deficient	*Amblystegium*	
Riccia rhenana	Not Evaluated	*confervoides*	Near Threatened
Riccia sorocarpa	Least Concern	*Amblystegium serpens*	
Riccia subbifurca	Least Concern	var. *salinum*	Least Concern

87

Table 8. Complete list of Irish bryophytes with threat category (continued)

Name of taxon	Threat category	Name of taxon	Threat category
Amblystegium serpens		*Bryum archangelicum*	Least Concern
var. *serpens*	Least Concern	*Bryum argenteum*	Least Concern
Amphidium lapponicum	Vulnerable	*Bryum bornholmense*	Near Threatened
Amphidium mougeotii	Least Concern	*Bryum caespiticium*	Vulnerable
Andreaea alpina	Least Concern	*Bryum calophyllum*	Endangered
Andreaea megistospora	Vulnerable	*Bryum capillare*	Least Concern
Andreaea rothii subsp. *falcata*	Least Concern	*Bryum creberrimum*	Data Deficient
Andreaea rothii subsp. *rothii*	Least Concern	*Bryum dichotomum*	Least Concern
Andreaea rupestris var. *rupestris*	Least Concern	*Bryum donianum*	Least Concern
Anoectangium aestivum	Least Concern	*Bryum dyffrynense*	Near Threatened
Anomobryum concinnatum	Least Concern	*Bryum elegans*	Vulnerable
Anomobryum julaceum	Least Concern	*Bryum gemmiferum*	Least Concern
Anomodon viticulosus	Least Concern	*Bryum gemmiparum*	Vulnerable
Antitrichia curtipendula	Near Threatened	*Bryum intermedium*	Endangered
Aongstroemia longipes	Critically Endangered	*Bryum klinggraeffii*	Least Concern
Aphanorrhegma patens	Least Concern	*Bryum knowltonii*	Endangered
Archidium alternifolium	Least Concern	*Bryum marratii*	Least Concern
Arctoa fulvella	Vulnerable	*Bryum moravicum*	Critically Endangered
Atrichum angustatum	Regionally Extinct	*Bryum pallens*	Least Concern
Atrichum crispum	Not Evaluated	*Bryum pallescens*	Least Concern
Atrichum tenellum	Near Threatened	*Bryum pseudotriquetrum*	
Atrichum undulatum		var. *bimum*	Least Concern
var. *undulatum*	Least Concern	*Bryum pseudotriquetrum*	
Aulacomnium androgynum	Vulnerable	var. *pseudotriquetrum*	Least Concern
Aulacomnium palustre	Least Concern	*Bryum radiculosum*	Least Concern
Barbula convoluta var. *convoluta*	Least Concern	*Bryum riparium*	Endangered
Barbula convoluta var. *sardoa*	Least Concern	*Bryum rubens*	Least Concern
Barbula unguiculata	Least Concern	*Bryum ruderale*	Least Concern
Bartramia halleriana	Regionally Extinct	*Bryum salinum*	Critically Endangered
Bartramia ithyphylla	Vulnerable	*Bryum sauteri*	Least Concern
Bartramia pomiformis	Least Concern	*Bryum subapiculatum*	Least Concern
Blindia acuta	Least Concern	*Bryum tenuisetum*	Data Deficient
Brachydontium trichodes	Endangered	*Bryum torquescens*	Vulnerable
Brachytheciastrum velutinum	Endangered	*Bryum turbinatum*	Regionally Extinct
Brachythecium albicans	Least Concern	*Bryum uliginosum*	Endangered
Brachythecium glareosum	Least Concern	*Bryum violaceum*	Least Concern
Brachythecium mildeanum	Least Concern	*Bryum warneum*	Endangered
Brachythecium rivulare	Least Concern	*Buxbaumia aphylla*	Regionally Extinct
Brachythecium rutabulum	Least Concern	*Calliergon cordifolium*	Least Concern
Breutelia chrysocoma	Least Concern	*Calliergon giganteum*	Least Concern
Bryoerythrophyllum		*Calliergonella cuspidata*	Least Concern
ferruginascens	Least Concern	*Calliergonella lindbergii*	Least Concern
Bryoerythrophyllum		*Calomnion complanatum*	Not Evaluated
recurvirostrum	Least Concern	*Calyptrochaeta apiculata*	Not Evaluated
Bryum algovicum		*Campyliadelphus chrysophyllus*	Least Concern
var. *rutheanum*	Least Concern	*Campyliadelphus elodes*	Near Threatened
Bryum alpinum	Least Concern	*Campylium protensum*	Least Concern

Table 8. Complete list of Irish bryophytes with threat category (continued)

Name of taxon	Threat category	Name of taxon	Threat category
Campylium stellatum	Least Concern	*Dicranella staphylina*	Least Concern
Campylopus atrovirens var. *atrovirens*	Least Concern	*Dicranella subulata*	Least Concern
Campylopus atrovirens var. *falcatus*	Near Threatened	*Dicranella varia*	Least Concern
		Dicranodontium asperulum	Vulnerable
Campylopus brevipilus	Least Concern	*Dicranodontium denudatum*	Least Concern
Campylopus flexuosus	Least Concern	*Dicranodontium uncinatum*	Vulnerable
Campylopus fragilis	Least Concern	*Dicranoloma menziesii*	Not Evaluated
Campylopus gracilis	Least Concern	*Dicranoweisia cirrata*	Least Concern
Campylopus introflexus	Least Concern	*Dicranum bonjeanii*	Least Concern
Campylopus pilifer	Least Concern	*Dicranum fuscescens*	Least Concern
Campylopus pyriformis	Least Concern	*Dicranum majus*	Least Concern
Campylopus schimperi	Regionally Extinct	*Dicranum scoparium*	Least Concern
Campylopus setifolius	Least Concern	*Dicranum scottianum*	Least Concern
Campylopus shawii	Near Threatened	*Dicranum undulatum*	Regionally Extinct
Campylopus subulatus	Vulnerable	*Didymodon acutus*	Endangered
Campylostelium saxicola	Endangered	*Didymodon fallax*	Least Concern
Catoscopium nigritum	Near Threatened	*Didymodon ferrugineus*	Least Concern
Ceratodon purpureus	Least Concern	*Didymodon icmadophilus*	Regionally Extinct
Cinclidium stygium	Vulnerable	*Didymodon insulanus*	Least Concern
Cinclidotus fontinaloides	Least Concern	*Didymodon luridus*	Least Concern
Cinclidotus riparius	Data Deficient	*Didymodon maximus*	Near Threatened
Cirriphyllum crassinervium	Least Concern	*Didymodon nicholsonii*	Least Concern
Cirriphyllum piliferum	Least Concern	*Didymodon rigidulus*	Least Concern
Climacium dendroides	Least Concern	*Didymodon sinuosus*	Least Concern
Conardia compacta	Regionally Extinct	*Didymodon spadiceus*	Least Concern
Cratoneuron filicinum	Least Concern	*Didymodon tomaculosus*	Vulnerable
Cryphaea heteromalla	Least Concern	*Didymodon tophaceus*	Least Concern
Ctenidium molluscum var. *condensatum*	Least Concern	*Didymodon umbrosus*	Vulnerable
		Didymodon vinealis	Least Concern
Ctenidium molluscum var. *molluscum*	Least Concern	*Diphyscium foliosum*	Least Concern
		Discelium nudum	Near Threatened
Ctenidium molluscum var. *robustum*	Regionally Extinct	*Distichium capillaceum*	Least Concern
		Distichium inclinatum	Least Concern
Cyclodictyon laetevirens	Near Threatened	*Ditrichum cornubicum*	Critically Endangered
Cynodontium bruntonii	Least Concern	*Ditrichum flexicaule*	Data Deficient
Cynodontium jenneri	Vulnerable	*Ditrichum gracile*	Least Concern
Daltonia splachnoides	Least Concern	*Ditrichum heteromallum*	Least Concern
Dichodontium flavescens	Least Concern	*Ditrichum lineare*	Critically Endangered
Dichodontium palustre	Least Concern	*Ditrichum plumbicola*	Endangered
Dichodontium pellucidum	Least Concern	*Ditrichum pusillum*	Data Deficient
Dicranella cerviculata	Near Threatened	*Ditrichum zonatum*	Endangered
Dicranella crispa	Endangered	*Drepanocladus aduncus*	Least Concern
Dicranella grevilleana	Near Threatened	*Drepanocladus polygamus*	Least Concern
Dicranella heteromalla	Least Concern	*Drepanocladus sendtneri*	Near Threatened
Dicranella rufescens	Least Concern	*Encalypta alpina*	Vulnerable
Dicranella schreberiana	Least Concern	*Encalypta ciliata*	Critically Endangered
		Encalypta rhaptocarpa	Critically Endangered
		Encalypta streptocarpa	Least Concern

Table 8. Complete list of Irish bryophytes with threat category (continued)

Name of taxon	Threat category	Name of taxon	Threat category
Encalypta vulgaris	Near Threatened	*Fontinalis antipyretica*	
Entodon concinnus	Least Concern	var. *cymbifolia*	Data Deficient
Entosthodon attenuatus	Least Concern	*Fontinalis antipyretica*	
Entosthodon fascicularis	Near Threatened	var. *gracilis*	Near Threatened
Entosthodon muhlenbergii	Regionally Extinct	*Fontinalis squamosa*	
Entosthodon obtusus	Least Concern	var. *squamosa*	Least Concern
Ephemerum cohaerens	Vulnerable	*Funaria hygrometrica*	Least Concern
Ephemerum crassinervium		*Glyphomitrium daviesii*	Least Concern
subsp. *rutheanum*	Near Threatened	*Grimmia anomala*	Endangered
Ephemerum crassinervium		*Grimmia atrata*	Endangered
subsp. *sessile*	Near Threatened	*Grimmia crinita*	Regionally Extinct
Ephemerum minutissimum	Least Concern	*Grimmia decipiens*	Near Threatened
Ephemerum recurvifolium	Data Deficient	*Grimmia dissimulata*	Vulnerable
Ephemerum serratum	Least Concern	*Grimmia donniana*	Near Threatened
Ephemerum spinulosum	Endangered	*Grimmia funalis*	Near Threatened
Epipterygium tozeri	Least Concern	*Grimmia hartmanii*	Least Concern
Eucladium verticillatum	Least Concern	*Grimmia laevigata*	Regionally Extinct
Eurhynchiastrum pulchellum		*Grimmia lisae*	Least Concern
var. *diversifolium*	Regionally Extinct	*Grimmia longirostris*	Regionally Extinct
Eurhynchium striatum	Least Concern	*Grimmia muehlenbeckii*	Data Deficient
Fissidens adianthoides	Least Concern	*Grimmia orbicularis*	Vulnerable
Fissidens bryoides var. *bryoides*	Least Concern	*Grimmia pulvinata*	Least Concern
Fissidens bryoides		*Grimmia ramondii*	Near Threatened
var. *caespitans*	Least Concern	*Grimmia torquata*	Near Threatened
Fissidens celticus	Least Concern	*Grimmia trichophylla*	Least Concern
Fissidens crassipes	Least Concern	*Gymnostomum aeruginosum*	Least Concern
Fissidens crispus	Data Deficient	*Gymnostomum calcareum*	Least Concern
Fissidens curvatus	Regionally Extinct	*Gymnostomum viridulum*	Least Concern
Fissidens dubius	Least Concern	*Gyroweisia tenuis*	Least Concern
Fissidens exilis	Vulnerable	*Hageniella micans*	Near Threatened
Fissidens fontanus	Vulnerable	*Hamatocaulis vernicosus*	Near Threatened
Fissidens gracilifolius	Least Concern	*Hedwigia ciliata* var. *ciliata*	Vulnerable
Fissidens incurvus	Least Concern	*Hedwigia integrifolia*	Vulnerable
Fissidens monguillonii	Near Threatened	*Hedwigia stellata*	Least Concern
Fissidens osmundoides	Least Concern	*Hennediella heimii*	Least Concern
Fissidens polyphyllus	Vulnerable	*Hennediella stanfordensis*	Not Evaluated
Fissidens pusillus	Least Concern	*Heterocladium heteropterum*	
Fissidens rivularis	Vulnerable	var. *flaccidum*	Least Concern
Fissidens rufulus	Endangered	*Heterocladium heteropterum*	
Fissidens serrulatus	Vulnerable	var. *heteropterum*	Least Concern
Fissidens taxifolius		*Heterocladium wulfsbergii*	Near Threatened
var. *pallidicaulis*	Least Concern	*Homalia trichomanoides*	Least Concern
Fissidens taxifolius		*Homalothecium lutescens*	Least Concern
var. *taxifolius*	Least Concern	*Homalothecium sericeum*	Least Concern
Fissidens viridulus	Least Concern	*Hookeria lucens*	Least Concern
Fontinalis antipyretica		*Hygroamblystegium fluviatile*	Near Threatened
var. *antipyretica*	Least Concern	*Hygroamblystegium humile*	Endangered

Table 8. Complete list of Irish bryophytes with threat category (continued)

Name of taxon	Threat category	Name of taxon	Threat category
Hygroamblystegium tenax	Least Concern	*Loeskeobryum brevirostre*	Least Concern
Hygroamblystegium varium	Near Threatened	*Meesia triquetra*	Regionally Extinct
Hygrohypnum duriusculum	Critically Endangered	*Meesia uliginosa*	Endangered
Hygrohypnum eugyrium	Least Concern	*Microbryum curvicollum*	Regionally Extinct
Hygrohypnum luridum	Least Concern	*Microbryum davallianum*	
Hygrohypnum ochraceum	Least Concern	var. *davallianum*	Least Concern
Hylocomiastrum umbratum	Near Threatened	*Microbryum rectum*	Least Concern
Hylocomium splendens	Least Concern	*Microbryum starckeanum*	Regionally Extinct
Hymenostylium recurvirostrum		*Mnium hornum*	Least Concern
var. *insigne*	Near Threatened	*Mnium marginatum*	
Hymenostylium recurvirostrum		var. *marginatum*	Least Concern
var. *recurvirostrum*	Least Concern	*Mnium stellare*	Least Concern
Hyocomium armoricum	Least Concern	*Mnium thomsonii*	Near Threatened
Hypnum andoi	Least Concern	*Molendoa warburgii*	Vulnerable
Hypnum callichroum	Near Threatened	*Myurella julacea*	Endangered
Hypnum cupressiforme		*Myurium hochstetteri*	Regionally Extinct
var. *cupressiforme*	Least Concern	*Neckera complanata*	Least Concern
Hypnum cupressiforme		*Neckera crispa*	Least Concern
var. *lacunosum*	Least Concern	*Neckera pumila*	Least Concern
Hypnum cupressiforme		*Oedipodium griffithianum*	Critically Endangered
var. *resupinatum*	Least Concern	*Oligotrichum hercynicum*	Least Concern
Hypnum jutlandicum	Least Concern	*Orthodontium gracile*	Critically Endangered
Hypnum uncinulatum	Near Threatened	*Orthodontium lineare*	Least Concern
Hypopterygium immigrans	Not Evaluated	*Orthothecium intricatum*	Least Concern
Isopterygiopsis muelleriana	Vulnerable	*Orthothecium rufescens*	Near Threatened
Isopterygiopsis pulchella	Least Concern	*Orthotrichum affine*	Least Concern
Isothecium alopecuroides	Least Concern	*Orthotrichum anomalum*	Least Concern
Isothecium holtii	Least Concern	*Orthotrichum cupulatum*	Least Concern
Isothecium myosuroides		*Orthotrichum diaphanum*	Least Concern
var. *brachythecioides*	Least Concern	*Orthotrichum lyellii*	Least Concern
Isothecium myosuroides		*Orthotrichum pallens*	Endangered
var. *myosuroides*	Least Concern	*Orthotrichum pulchellum*	Least Concern
Kiaeria blyttii	Least Concern	*Orthotrichum rivulare*	Near Threatened
Kiaeria falcata	Critically Endangered	*Orthotrichum rupestre*	Least Concern
Kindbergia praelonga	Least Concern	*Orthotrichum sprucei*	Vulnerable
Leptobarbula berica	Vulnerable	*Orthotrichum stramineum*	Vulnerable
Leptobryum pyriforme	Least Concern	*Orthotrichum striatum*	Least Concern
Leptodictyum riparium	Least Concern	*Orthotrichum tenellum*	Least Concern
Leptodon smithii	Endangered	*Oxyrrhynchium hians*	Least Concern
Leptodontium flexifolium	Near Threatened	*Oxyrrhynchium pumilum*	Least Concern
Leptotheca gaudichaudii		*Oxyrrhynchium schleicheri*	Critically Endangered
var. *gaudichaudii*	Not Evaluated	*Oxyrrhynchium speciosum*	Near Threatened
Leskea polycarpa	Least Concern	*Paludella squarrosa*	Critically Endangered
Leucobryum glaucum	Least Concern	*Palustriella commutata*	Least Concern
Leucobryum juniperoideum	Least Concern	*Palustriella falcata*	Least Concern
Leucodon sciuroides		*Paraleptodontium*	
var. *sciuroides*	Least Concern	*recurvifolium*	Near Threatened

Table 8. Complete list of Irish bryophytes with threat category (continued)

Name of taxon	Threat category	Name of taxon	Threat category
Phascum cuspidatum var. *cuspidatum*	Least Concern	*Pohlia annotina*	Least Concern
		Pohlia bulbifera	Least Concern
Phascum cuspidatum var. *papillosum*	Data Deficient	*Pohlia camptotrachela*	Least Concern
		Pohlia cruda	Least Concern
Phascum cuspidatum var. *piliferum*	Data Deficient	*Pohlia drummondii*	Least Concern
		Pohlia elongata var. *elongata*	Near Threatened
Philonotis arnellii	Endangered	*Pohlia elongata* var. *greenii*	Endangered
Philonotis caespitosa	Near Threatened	*Pohlia filum*	Vulnerable
Philonotis calcarea	Least Concern	*Pohlia flexuosa*	Least Concern
Philonotis cernua	Critically Endangered	*Pohlia lescuriana*	Data Deficient
Philonotis fontana	Least Concern	*Pohlia lutescens*	Least Concern
Philonotis rigida	Vulnerable	*Pohlia melanodon*	Least Concern
Philonotis tomentella	Vulnerable	*Pohlia nutans*	Least Concern
Physcomitrium pyriforme	Least Concern	*Pohlia proligera*	Regionally Extinct
Physcomitrium sphaericum	Vulnerable	*Pohlia wahlenbergii* var. *calcarea*	Data Deficient
Plagiobryum zieri	Near Threatened	*Pohlia wahlenbergii* var. *glacialis*	Regionally Extinct
Plagiomnium affine	Least Concern	*Pohlia wahlenbergii* var. *wahlenbergii*	Least Concern
Plagiomnium cuspidatum	Near Threatened		
Plagiomnium elatum	Least Concern	*Polytrichastrum alpinum*	Least Concern
Plagiomnium ellipticum	Least Concern	*Polytrichastrum formosum*	Least Concern
Plagiomnium rostratum	Least Concern	*Polytrichastrum longisetum*	Least Concern
Plagiomnium undulatum	Least Concern	*Polytrichum commune* var. *commune*	Least Concern
Plagiopus oederianus	Critically Endangered		
Plagiothecium cavifolium	Vulnerable	*Polytrichum commune* var. *perigoniale*	Data Deficient
Plagiothecium curvifolium	Vulnerable		
Plagiothecium denticulatum var. *denticulatum*	Least Concern	*Polytrichum juniperinum*	Least Concern
		Polytrichum piliferum	Least Concern
Plagiothecium denticulatum var. *obtusifolium*	Near Threatened	*Polytrichum strictum*	Least Concern
		Pseudephemerum nitidum	Least Concern
Plagiothecium laetum	Vulnerable	*Pseudocalliergon lycopodioides*	Vulnerable
Plagiothecium latebricola	Vulnerable	*Pseudocalliergon trifarium*	Vulnerable
Plagiothecium nemorale	Least Concern	*Pseudocrossidium hornschuchianum*	Least Concern
Plagiothecium platyphyllum	Vulnerable		
Plagiothecium succulentum	Least Concern	*Pseudocrossidium revolutum*	Least Concern
Plagiothecium undulatum	Least Concern	*Pseudoscleropodium purum*	Least Concern
Plasteurhynchium striatulum	Near Threatened	*Pseudotaxiphyllum elegans*	Least Concern
Platydictya jungermannioides	Near Threatened	*Pterigynandrum filiforme*	Regionally Extinct
Platyhypnidium lusitanicum	Near Threatened	*Pterogonium gracile*	Least Concern
Platyhypnidium riparioides	Least Concern	*Pterygoneurum lamellatum*	Regionally Extinct
Pleuridium acuminatum	Least Concern	*Pterygoneurum ovatum*	Regionally Extinct
Pleuridium subulatum	Least Concern	*Ptilium crista-castrensis*	Critically Endangered
Pleurochaete squarrosa	Near Threatened	*Ptychomitrium polyphyllum*	Least Concern
Pleurozium schreberi	Least Concern	*Racomitrium aciculare*	Least Concern
Pogonatum aloides	Least Concern	*Racomitrium affine*	Least Concern
Pogonatum nanum	Endangered	*Racomitrium aquaticum*	Least Concern
Pogonatum urnigerum	Least Concern	*Racomitrium canescens*	Vulnerable
Pohlia andalusica	Endangered	*Racomitrium ellipticum*	Least Concern

Table 8. Complete list of Irish bryophytes with threat category (continued)

Name of taxon	Threat category	Name of taxon	Threat category
Racomitrium elongatum	Vulnerable	*Scleropodium touretii*	Endangered
Racomitrium ericoides	Least Concern	*Scopelophila cataractae*	Vulnerable
Racomitrium fasciculare	Least Concern	*Scorpidium cossonii*	Least Concern
Racomitrium heterostichum	Least Concern	*Scorpidium revolvens*	Least Concern
Racomitrium lanuginosum	Least Concern	*Scorpidium scorpioides*	Least Concern
Racomitrium macounii		*Scorpiurium circinatum*	Least Concern
subsp. *alpinum*	Vulnerable	*Seligeria acutifolia*	Least Concern
Racomitrium sudeticum	Least Concern	*Seligeria calcarea*	Vulnerable
Rhabdoweisia crenulata	Least Concern	*Seligeria calycina*	Regionally Extinct
Rhabdoweisia crispata	Near Threatened	*Seligeria donniana*	Least Concern
Rhabdoweisia fugax	Vulnerable	*Seligeria oelandica*	Vulnerable
Rhizomnium pseudopunctatum	Near Threatened	*Seligeria patula*	Near Threatened
Rhizomnium punctatum	Least Concern	*Seligeria pusilla*	Least Concern
Rhodobryum roseum	Near Threatened	*Seligeria recurvata*	Least Concern
Rhynchostegiella curviseta	Regionally Extinct	*Sematophyllum demissum*	Near Threatened
Rhynchostegiella tenella	Least Concern	*Sematophyllum substrumulosum*	Vulnerable
Rhynchostegiella teneriffae	Least Concern	*Sphagnum affine*	Vulnerable
Rhynchostegium confertum	Least Concern	*Sphagnum angustifolium*	Least Concern
Rhynchostegium		*Sphagnum austinii*	Least Concern
megapolitanum	Near Threatened	*Sphagnum capillifolium*	
Rhynchostegium murale	Least Concern	subsp. *capillifolium*	Data Deficient
Rhytidiadelphus loreus	Least Concern	*Sphagnum capillifolium*	
Rhytidiadelphus squarrosus	Least Concern	subsp. *rubellum*	Least Concern
Rhytidiadelphus subpinnatus	Regionally Extinct	*Sphagnum compactum*	Least Concern
Rhytidiadelphus triquetrus	Least Concern	*Sphagnum contortum*	Least Concern
Rhytidium rugosum	Vulnerable	*Sphagnum cuspidatum*	Least Concern
Sanionia uncinata	Least Concern	*Sphagnum denticulatum*	Least Concern
Sarmentypnum exannulatum	Least Concern	*Sphagnum fallax*	Least Concern
Sarmentypnum sarmentosum	Least Concern	*Sphagnum fimbriatum*	Least Concern
Schistidium agassizii	Vulnerable	*Sphagnum flexuosum*	Vulnerable
Schistidium apocarpum	Least Concern	*Sphagnum fuscum*	Least Concern
Schistidium confertum	Data Deficient	*Sphagnum girgensohnii*	Near Threatened
Schistidium crassipilum	Least Concern	*Sphagnum inundatum*	Least Concern
Schistidium elegantulum		*Sphagnum magellanicum*	Least Concern
subsp. *elegantulum*	Data Deficient	*Sphagnum molle*	Least Concern
Schistidium elegantulum		*Sphagnum palustre*	
subsp. *wilsonii*	Data Deficient	var. *palustre*	Least Concern
Schistidium maritimum	Least Concern	*Sphagnum papillosum*	Least Concern
Schistidium platyphyllum	Vulnerable	*Sphagnum platyphyllum*	Near Threatened
Schistidium pruinosum	Data Deficient	*Sphagnum pulchrum*	Least Concern
Schistidium rivulare	Least Concern	*Sphagnum quinquefarium*	Least Concern
Schistidium robustum	Data Deficient	*Sphagnum russowii*	Near Threatened
Schistidium strictum	Near Threatened	*Sphagnum skyense*	Data Deficient
Schistidium trichodon	Vulnerable	*Sphagnum squarrosum*	Least Concern
Sciuro-hypnum plumosum	Least Concern	*Sphagnum strictum*	Data Deficient
Sciuro-hypnum populeum	Least Concern	*Sphagnum subnitens*	
Scleropodium cespitans	Near Threatened	var. *ferrugineum*	Least Concern

Table 8. Complete list of Irish bryophytes with threat category (continued)

Name of taxon	Threat category	Name of taxon	Threat category
Sphagnum subnitens		*Tortula muralis*	Least Concern
var. *subnitens*	Least Concern	*Tortula protobryoides*	Regionally Extinct
Sphagnum subsecundum	Near Threatened	*Tortula subulata*	Least Concern
Sphagnum tenellum	Least Concern	*Tortula truncata*	Least Concern
Sphagnum teres	Near Threatened	*Tortula vahliana*	Regionally Extinct
Sphagnum warnstorfii	Vulnerable	*Tortula viridifolia*	Least Concern
Splachnum ampullaceum	Least Concern	*Tortula wilsonii*	Regionally Extinct
Splachnum sphaericum	Least Concern	*Trichodon cylindricus*	Least Concern
Straminergon stramineum	Least Concern	*Trichostomum brachydontium*	Least Concern
Syntrichia laevipila	Least Concern	*Trichostomum crispulum*	Least Concern
Syntrichia latifolia	Least Concern	*Trichostomum hibernicum*	Least Concern
Syntrichia montana	Least Concern	*Trichostomum tenuirostre*	Least Concern
Syntrichia papillosa	Least Concern	*Ulota bruchii*	Least Concern
Syntrichia princeps	Regionally Extinct	*Ulota calvescens*	Least Concern
Syntrichia ruralis		*Ulota coarctata*	Critically Endangered
var. *ruraliformis*	Least Concern	*Ulota crispa*	Least Concern
Syntrichia ruralis var. *ruralis*	Least Concern	*Ulota drummondii*	Regionally Extinct
Syntrichia virescens	Data Deficient	*Ulota hutchinsiae*	Least Concern
Taxiphyllum wissgrillii	Least Concern	*Ulota phyllantha*	Least Concern
Tayloria tenuis	Regionally Extinct	*Warnstorfia fluitans*	Least Concern
Tetraphis pellucida	Least Concern	*Weissia brachycarpa*	
Tetraplodon angustatus	Data Deficient	var. *brachycarpa*	Data Deficient
Tetraplodon mnioides	Least Concern	*Weissia brachycarpa*	
Tetrodontium brownianum	Near Threatened	var. *obliqua*	Least Concern
Thamnobryum alopecurum	Least Concern	*Weissia condensa*	Data Deficient
Thuidium assimile	Least Concern	*Weissia controversa*	
Thuidium delicatulum	Least Concern	var. *controversa*	Least Concern
Thuidium recognitum	Vulnerable	*Weissia controversa*	
Thuidium tamariscinum	Least Concern	var. *crispata*	Data Deficient
Timmia norvegica	Vulnerable	*Weissia controversa*	
Tomentypnum nitens	Vulnerable	var. *densifolia*	Least Concern
Tortella bambergeri	Least Concern	*Weissia longifolia*	
Tortella densa	Near Threatened	var. *angustifolia*	Vulnerable
Tortella flavovirens	Least Concern	*Weissia perssonii*	Least Concern
Tortella inclinata	Endangered	*Weissia rostellata*	Near Threatened
Tortella nitida	Least Concern	*Weissia rutilans*	Vulnerable
Tortella tortuosa	Least Concern	*Zygodon conoideus*	
Tortula atrovirens	Near Threatened	var. *conoideus*	Least Concern
Tortula canescens	Data Deficient	*Zygodon rupestris*	Least Concern
Tortula cuneifolia	Critically Endangered	*Zygodon viridissimus*	
Tortula lanceola	Critically Endangered	var. *stirtonii*	Least Concern
Tortula marginata	Near Threatened	*Zygodon viridissimus*	
Tortula modica	Vulnerable	var. *viridissimus*	Least Concern

Interpretation of the Red List

Regional extinctions

There are a large number of taxa that are considered *Regionally Extinct*; five liverworts and 35 mosses. An effort has been made to distinguish between taxa that have probably genuinely disappeared and those that may still occur, the latter being placed in the *Data Deficient* category. Nevertheless, it is possible that a number of *Regionally Extinct* taxa do still occur in Ireland, perhaps at a very low frequency, but have not been detected because of the generally low level of field recording in Ireland over recent decades.

Some *Regionally Extinct* taxa may have been temporary colonists in Ireland, although in the absence of data this is obviously only a speculative inference. These include: *Grimmia crinita*, a thermophilous species found mainly in Mediterranean countries, where it grows on calcareous sandstone and weathered mortar-covered walls; *Ptilidium pulcherrimum*, a pioneer epiphyte on trees; *Buxbaumia aphylla*, a colonist of soil and rotting wood that is rare and often ephemeral in its occurrence elsewhere in Europe; and *Bryum turbinatum*, a short-lived colonist of damp sandy or gravelly soils. These species may have been transient in Ireland, coming in from outside as spores, establishing themselves on a small patch of suitable habitat, then disappearing possibly without forming a permanent population.

The disappearance of some other taxa is closely linked to the loss of their habitat in Ireland and their listing as *Regionally Extinct* can be made with a greater degree of certainty. The community of mosses that used to grow on mud-capped walls, which includes *Aloina rigida*, *Microbryum curvicollum*, *Pterygoneurum ovatum*, *P. lamellatum* and *Tortula vahliana*, has almost certainly disappeared in Ireland, although some of these could recolonise in chalk or gravel pits from the chance arrival and establishment of spores. The loss of *Dicranum undulatum* from midland raised bogs, and *Meesia triquetra* from its single recorded locality at the Bellacorick Iron Flush, is almost certainly due to damage to their habitat by industrial-scale peat extraction. Species of rotting wood, such as *Anastrophyllum hellerianum* and *Calypogeia suecica*, may have been lost due to a decline in the availability of suitable niches, reflecting changes in woodland management practices, but these species might have been overlooked, despite recent efforts to refind them.

The reasons for the apparent disappearance of other taxa in the *Regionally Extinct* list remain mysterious. They are mostly plants that were always rare in Ireland, and therefore prone to stochastic events such as the destruction of small populations at individual sites or over-collecting by botanists. These include several taxa that have only ever been recorded on a single occasion from Ireland: *Myurium hochstetteri*, *Pohlia proligera*, *Rhytidiadelphus subpinnatus*, *Tortula protobryoides*, and a group from Benbulbin and Gleniff, Cos Sligo and Leitrim: *Barbilophozia kunzeana*, *Conardia compacta* and *Didymodon icmadophilus*. But why should *Bartramia halleriana* or *Targionia hypophylla*, both recorded from several localities and neither of them unique to obviously threatened habitats, have become extinct? Does long-term climate change have a part to play here? And why are there fewer liverworts than would be expected in the *Regionally Extinct* list, compared to the number of mosses? There is much we simply do not know.

Habitats of Red List taxa

Many of the taxa on the Red List are threatened because of changes in habitat conditions. The internationally important Northern Atlantic hepatic mat community of upland corries in the west has been severely affected by the impacts of overstocking with sheep; riverine species have been affected by canalisation of watercourses, channel maintenance and pollution locally, and many of the Irish bogs have been very severely damaged or destroyed by drainage, afforestation and peat extraction. How these changes are reflected in the Red List can be seen by examining the principal habitats and substrates in which the taxa are usually found. Table 9 is a simplified representation, combining both the substrate on which a taxon occurs, such as rock, rotting wood or soil, with the major habitat types, such as dune, fen or woodland. Whereas substrates may be relatively unimportant for most vascular plants, most of which are rooted in soil, they are much more relevant to the ecology of a poikilohydrous group such as the bryophytes. More detail on bryophyte habitats is provided by Hill *et al.* (2007), who list Ellenberg indicator values and EUNIS habitat classes for all bryophyte taxa.

Table 9. Habitats of the Red List taxa

Note that several taxa are characteristic of more than one habitat, so the totals do not correspond with the numbers by threat category listed in Table 2.

Habitat	RE	CR	EN	VU	Total
Non-calcareous rock (upland)	4	5	5	11	25
Calcareous rock (upland)	8	4	2	10	24
Bare ground	4	1	3	10	18
Calcareous rock (other)	3	1	2	9	15
Riverine	2	1	3	7	13
Dunes	0	0	7	4	11
Oceanic peatland/rocks	1	1	3	6	11
Fen	1	1	2	6	10
Calcareous soil/mud wall tops	6	1	1	1	9
Metalliferous	0	2	3	4	9
Woodland	1	1	1	6	9
Epiphytic	2	2	3	1	8
Bog	2	0	0	5	7
Coastal turf	1	2	2	2	7
Non-calcareous rock (other)	1	1	1	4	7
Non-calcareous soil/banks	1	0	1	5	7
Peaty banks	1	1	3	1	6
Arctic-alpine	1	0	1	2	4
Rotting wood	2	0	1	1	4
Reservoir margins	0	0	1	2	3
Wet ground	1	0	1	0	2
Organic detritus	1	0	0	0	1

A high proportion of the Red List taxa are saxicolous, growing directly on rocks. Of these, many are naturally rare montane plants; their potential habitat is very limited in extent, and many of the best places for them are protected through SAC, NHA, ASSI or National Park designations. This does not mean that they are not threatened, however. Some of the populations are so small that they might easily be extirpated by a single event. *Gymnomitrion corallioides*, for example, may already have been eliminated in Kerry by botanical collection; *Encalypta ciliata* and *Cynodontium jenneri* could easily succumb if conifers happened to be planted on their sites (both of which are just outside protected areas); *Leiocolea heterocolpos* could be severely compromised if careless path and boardwalk maintenance work were to dislodge it from its substrate. Many more upland saxicolous plants are placed in the sub-Red List category *Near Threatened*: rare and susceptible, but not really subject to any specific threats (other than, perhaps, climate change), and therefore not appropriately placed in any of the Red List categories.

General physical damage and nutrient enrichment from overstocking is also a significant threat to most of the upland taxa. Those that occur in rock crevices are relatively protected by their sheltered situation, as can be seen at Annacoona, Co. Sligo, but their spread and ultimate viability as healthy populations must be severely restricted by the activities of sheep. Much more serious is the effect that overstocking has had on the non-saxicolous taxa, notably those in the Northern Atlantic

North-east slope of Bengower, an area where hepatic mat has been lost, Co. Galway.

hepatic mat community. Their habitat has been more or less damaged throughout Ireland, but almost completely destroyed in Connemara, where the cover of heather-dominated heath has been removed entirely in many places.

Lowland saxicolous taxa can be even more threatened than those in the uplands, simply because there is more development pressure to contend with, including housing projects and quarrying. Perhaps surprisingly, then, there are relatively few lowland saxicolous taxa on the Red List. A possible explanation is that many of these plants find a secondary habitat on walls and can persist even in the absence of natural rock outcrops. Old walls are now a threatened habitat in their own right and Irish populations of species such as *Grimmia orbicularis* and *Southbya tophacea* are entirely dependent on walls.

A high proportion of the most threatened bryophytes grow in ruderal habitats, but it is not immediately obvious why this should be the case. Firstly, a high proportion of *all* bryophytes grow in ruderal habitats, so it is likely that some of these will be threatened; secondly, it may be that the nature of 'bare ground' has changed, and that most bare ground is no longer suitable for some bryophytes. Thus, formerly widespread bare ground, such as second-year stubble in arable fields or skeletal turf in species-rich limestone grassland, is now relatively rare in Ireland, whereas extremely short-lived bare ground that quickly becomes colonised by vigorous and nutrient-demanding plants is quite common. The latter is widely promoted by a combination of frequent disturbance and nutrient enrichment, both features of the modern countryside, and is usually the substrate for only a small number of common bryophytes, such as *Bryum argenteum*, *B. dichotomum*, *Ceratodon purpureus*, *Funaria hygrometrica* and common species of *Barbula* and *Didymodon*. Rare (or, in Ireland, *Regionally Extinct*) species such as *Acaulon muticum*, *Microbryum curvicollum* and *Tortula protobryoides* are presumably unable to compete successfully against the more vigorous species except in very specific conditions which are, by and large, not yet fully understood.

Several bog bryophytes have declined because their habitat has been destroyed, or severely damaged, through exploitation for agriculture, forestry and energy resources. One of the most beautiful, *Dicranum undulatum*, is apparently extinct, and many of the tiny liverworts (*Cephalozia* spp., *Cephaloziella* spp.) that are confined to the wettest parts of raised bogs are well represented on the Red List. Fen bryophytes are also well represented, with several taxa severely threatened and reduced to just small populations (*Paludella squarrosa*, *Leiocolea rutheana* var. *rutheana*, *Pseudocalliergon trifarium*). Fossil remains of bryophytes preserved in peat show that fen habitat has declined in extent over a long period since the late-glacial in Ireland (Dickson 1973), but the extinction of species such as *Meesia triquetra* in 1958 is testament to the accelerated degradation and loss of fen habitat in recent decades. The last remaining fragments of fen, along

Catherine Farrell and John Cross at Bellacorick Iron Flush, Co. Mayo, the only recorded locality for *Meesia triquetra* in Ireland, last seen here in 1958.

with their specialised bryophytes, are a high priority for conservation.

The prominence of coastal taxa in the Red List reflects both the loss of bryophyte habitat in coastal dune systems, often due to leisure developments (including golf courses), and the ongoing threats posed by

Coastal developments at Murlough Dunes, Co. Down.

inappropriate grazing regimes (both overgrazing and undergrazing), water abstraction and drainage, coastal protection works and over-stabilisation. Several species of *Bryum*, notably *B. calophyllum*, *B. intermedium*, *B. uliginosum* and *B. warneum*, are especially sensitive to changes in habitat conditions and their survival will also depend on the maintenance of dynamic dune and machair systems.

Maritime clifftop grassland was overlooked as an important habitat for bryophytes in Ireland until relatively recently. Extensive survey on southern coasts has revealed that *Tortula viridifolia* is widespread in this habitat, but that a number of others are much rarer and probably in decline, including *T. atrovirens* and *Scleropodium touretii*, and that *Tortula cuneifolia* may even have disappeared. This is a habitat that has become threatened almost without being noticed, as agricultural land has squeezed it into an ever-narrowing band at the top of sea cliffs. The tiny strips that remain are vulnerable to nutrient enrichment, especially from dog faeces, and scrub encroachment through undergrazing. The best sites need to be taken into conservation management, and bryophyte conservation requirements should be integrated into wider conservation plans for the coastline.

The distribution of metallophyte bryophytes in Ireland was also poorly understood until recently, but several old mine workings are now known to be important habitats for several of these globally threatened taxa, notably *Ditrichum cornubicum*, *D. plumbicola*, *Cephaloziella massalongi* and *C. nicholsonii*. The challenge here lies in integrating the bryophyte conservation requirements with the preservation of industrial archaeology at old mine sites. Such sites are important for their social and industrial history, but also as hotspots of biodiversity, and should be presented as such in any future restoration works.

Quite a large number of Red List taxa can be put in a category that can broadly be defined as riverine. A few of these are upland plants of mountain streams (*Hygrohypnum duriusculum*, *Bryum riparium*), but most occur in the lowlands and are under varying degrees of threat from drainage, canalisation, inappropriate riverbank management, pollution and conifer afforestation. Changes to flow regimes, especially by arterial drainage of the main lowland river systems over recent decades, and the subsequent loss of suitable niches and substrates for bryophytes, has undoubtedly had an impact on riverine bryophytes. Species such as

Orthotrichum sprucei, which occur on silt-encrusted tree trunks, roots and rocks, require regular inundation through flooding. Ephemeral bryophytes such as *Ephemerum crassinervium* subsp. *rutheanum* also depend on the availability of temporarily exposed and regularly flooded substrates on riverbanks (and lake shores). Several species of *Fissidens* are represented on the Red List because they require small niches by rivers that can only be provided if the riverbank structure is allowed to develop naturally. Management with minimal intervention is suitable for these plants, allowing a natural riverbank vegetation structure to develop, with tangles of riverside trees and swamp woodland, wet vegetated banks and plenty of rocks.

Although there are few bryophytes in the Red List that are strictly woodland plants, there are several that grow as epiphytes on trees and others that grow mainly on dead, rotting timber. The rare epiphytes are largely plants of woodland edges or isolated trees that require good illumination to thrive, such as *Orthotrichum pallens* and *O. stramineum*. Although most of these plants are capable of dispersing efficiently through the production of spores, they are often very substrate-specific and individual plants are short-lived, so they require a continuity of suitable habitat spread over as large an area as possible. Wayside trees and clumps of elder are good substrates, and these are often removed without a second thought if they obstruct projects such as housing developments or road-widening.

Species of the oceanic west feature in the Red List, but perhaps not as greatly as might be expected. Many of these species, while globally rare, are relatively frequent in parts of western Ireland, and relatively secure in remote ravines or on mountains. This is not always the case, however, and some of the oceanic species, such as *Acrobolbus wilsonii*, *Lejeunea mandonii* and *Plagiochila heterophylla*, are so rare and grow in such small quantity that they have to be regarded as threatened.

Life strategies of Red List taxa

It is important to take the differing life strategies of the Red List taxa into account when considering how to conserve them, although other aspects of population biology (e.g. competition and niche breadth) and habitat characters are also clearly relevant. During (1992) devised a classification system of bryophyte life strategies based on sexual reproductive performance, spore size and longevity of individuals. The categories of bryophyte life strategy he coined are:

- Fugitives: annual taxa producing many small (< 20 μm) spores
- Colonists: short-lived taxa producing many small (< 20 μm) spores
- Perennial stayers: long-lived taxa producing many small (< 20 μm) spores
- Annual shuttles: annual taxa producing few large (> 20 μm) spores
- Short-lived shuttles: short-lived taxa producing few large (> 20 μm) spores
- Long-lived shuttles: long-lived taxa producing few large (> 20 μm) spores
- Dominants: potentially very long-lived taxa producing few large (> 20 μm) spores (only applies to some species of *Sphagnum*)

Fugitives and colonists tend to be highly mobile taxa, coming and going as habitat becomes available in different places. Perennial stayers tend to be competitive, stress-tolerant taxa that nevertheless may have the potential to colonise elsewhere. Shuttle taxa tend to reoccur at or near the same place, as suitable conditions recur regularly (e.g. arable weeds, reservoir bryophytes, etc.).

The system developed by During (1992) provides a convenient framework for analyses, although one of the principal conclusions of Longton (1997) was that 'the strategies should be regarded as noda within a continuous array of reticulate variation rather than as discrete entities'. Using this system, and developing it by adding asexual reproductive performance and size of asexual propagules, all taxa on the Irish bryophyte list have been allocated a life strategy (Table 10). No attempt has been made here to apply statistical analyses to this data set, and the system is still somewhat oversimplified, but it is sufficient to give a crude indication of bryophyte life strategies and their relationships to threat status. The table shows that although a slightly higher proportion of Red List taxa have perennial, colonist and short-lived shuttle strategies, the percentage figures are overall quite similar for Red List taxa and for the flora as a whole, suggesting that there is little correlation between bryophyte life strategy and threat status. The *Regionally Extinct* list contains a higher proportion of colonist and annual shuttle taxa than the flora as a whole, but this might just reflect the relatively high number of taxa with these life strategies that may have been affected by the demise of mud-capped wall habitat in Ireland.

Reproductive characteristics of Red List taxa

Sexual reproduction is also an important feature for bryophyte survival since it produces both diaspores for dispersal in time and space, and genetic variation (Longton 1994, Söderström & During 2005). Although statistical analyses have not yet been applied to the Irish data set, a summary list of the sexual reproductive characteristics of Irish bryophytes (Table 11) suggests that a relatively higher proportion of monoicous taxa may be on the Red List than would otherwise be expected in the flora as a whole. Longton (1992) and Laaka-Lindberg *et al.* (2000) observed a similar trend for monoicous taxa in relation to rarity; a higher proportion of monoicous taxa are rare in the British bryophyte flora compared to dioicous taxa. They also noted that monoicous taxa tend to produce sporophytes more often than dioicous taxa, and that rarity and failure to produce sporophytes are strongly associated, both in Britain (Longton 1992, Laaka Lindberg 2000) and at a world level (Longton & Schuster 1983). These latter traits are also hinted at in Table 11, where the Red List has a slightly higher proportion of taxa that produce sporophytes abundantly, a characteristic that may be linked to the high proportion of monoicous taxa on the Red List, and a higher proportion of taxa that are not known to produce sporophytes at all.

The relationship between threat status and rarity is complex, but the similarity between the reproductive characteristics of Red List taxa and rare taxa is partly to be expected, given that a high proportion of all threatened taxa are also rare. Söderström and During (2005) observed that not all rare species are threatened and that natural rarity should be distinguished from human-induced rarity, with species that are rare for the latter reason being regarded as threatened. They hypothesised that most naturally rare species are habitat limited, but that at least some naturally rare species may be dispersal limited, particularly those characterised by a long-lived bank of large spores or asexual propagules in the soil.

Different life strategies and reproductive behaviour in bryophytes may require different sorts of conservation action. Fugitive and colonist taxa are likely to exist as metapopulations (Gilpin & Hanski 1991), with individual populations short-lived, producing sporophytes and moving on to new habitat elsewhere (Söderström & Herben 1997). Thus, many of these taxa rely on a continual turnover of habitat over the whole, or part, of their potential geographical distribution (or 'extent of

Table 10. Life strategies of Irish bryophytes

Note that many taxa have been allocated more than one life strategy: these taxa are capable of behaving in different ways in different conditions. The total percentages in each column do not always add up to exactly 100 because of the effects of rounding up or down. The raw data for this table were taken from BRYOATT (Hill *et al.* 2007).

Life strategy	Percentage of all taxa on Irish list	Percentage of Red List + NT and DD taxa	Percentage of Red List taxa	RE	CR	EN	VU
Perennial	18.9	22.5	22.6	17.5	21.7	27.9	22.5
Colonist	12.4	14.6	15.4	22.5	8.7	20.9	11.2
Short-lived shuttle	11.4	11.9	13.8	10.0	21.7	18.6	11.2
Long-lived shuttle	10.0	11.6	9.2	12.5	0	7.0	11.2
Colonist/perennial	13.3	10.3	6.2	2.5	8.7	2.3	9.0
Short-lived shuttle/ long-lived shuttle	4.8	6.1	8.7	5.0	13.0	11.6	7.9
Short-lived shuttle/colonist	5.4	5.5	6.2	5.0	8.7	2.3	7.9
Annual shuttle	2.5	4.3	3.6	10.0	0	2.3	2.2
Annual shuttle/short-lived shuttle	4.8	4.0	4.1	2.5	8.7	4.7	3.4
Fugitive/annual shuttle	0.1	0.3	0.5	2.5	0	0	0
Long-lived shuttle/dominant	3.7	3.0	2.6	2.5	0	0	4.5
Long-lived shuttle/perennial	2.5	1.8	3.1	0	8.7	0	4.5
Fugitive/colonist	1.2	1.2	1.0	2.5	0	0	1.1
Short-lived shuttle/long-lived shuttle/colonist	0.5	0.9	1.5	2.5	0	2.3	1.1
Colonist/short-lived shuttle/ perennial	0.5	0.9	0	0	0	0	0
Short-lived shuttle/perennial	0.1	0.3	0.5	0	0	0	1.1
Colonist/long-lived shuttle	3.2	0.3	0	0	0	0	0
Colonist/long-lived shuttle/ perennial	1.0	0.3	0.5	2.5	0	0	0
Fugitive/colonist/annual shuttle/ short-lived shuttle	1.7	0	0	0	0	0	0
Fugitive	0.6	0.6	0.5	0	0	0	1.1

occurrence'). Protected areas may not be the best way to address the conservation of these plants, unless such areas are at a landscape scale.

The ability of bryophytes to colonise through spore dispersal is limited by their diminutive size and even those taxa with relatively small spores tend to deposit many of them close to the parent plant (Miles & Longton 1987, Söderström & Jonsson 1989). Epiphytic species of *Orthotrichum*, for example, form short-lived tufts and produce small spores regularly and are therefore defined as colonists. Many spores, despite their small size, almost certainly land very close to the parent plants and develop into new plants on the same tree; other spores are blown further afield, but have a better chance of establishing new plants if there is a substantial *local* area of suitable substrate (e.g. willows in swamp woodland).

Table 11. Sexual reproductive characteristics of Irish bryophytes

The total percentages do not always add up to exactly 100 because of the effects of rounding up or down. The raw data for this table were taken from BRYOATT (Hill *et al.* 2007).

	Percentage of all taxa on Irish list	Percentage of Red List + NT and DD taxa	Percentage of Red List taxa	RE	CR	EN	VU
Dioicous	58.9	50.5	50.8	52.5	52.2	51.2	49.4
Monoicous	37.1	45.0	46.2	45.0	47.8	41.9	48.3
Monoicous or dioicous	2.8	3.3	2.1	2.5	0	2.3	2.2
Sexuality not known	1.0	1.5	1.0	0	0	4.7	0
Sporophytes abundant	25.1	29.2	30.8	35.0	43.5	27.9	27.0
Sporophytes frequent	19.5	15.8	12.3	15.0	4.3	14.0	12.4
Sporophytes occasional	14.1	7.6	6.7	5.0	8.7	11.6	4.5
Sporophytes rare	25.5	25.8	24.1	17.5	21.7	27.9	25.8
Sporophytes unknown in Ireland	15.6	21.9	26.7	27.5	21.7	18.6	31.5

The further away from the parent plant the spores travel, the less likelihood there is of finding suitable habitat. Taxa that rely almost entirely on long-distance spore dispersal (e.g. *Funaria hygrometrica*) have to produce vast quantities of spores *and* be capable of establishing and growing in habitats that are widespread and common.

Shuttle taxa invest a lot of energy in reproductive effort but a high proportion of their propagules, being relatively large, tend to fall close to the parent plants. These taxa therefore require a constant or reappearing habitat within a small area, and the designation of protected areas may be very suitable for their conservation, provided they are managed in such a way as to ensure continuity of habitat or continuity of the processes that lead to the habitat reappearing regularly.

Arable weed taxa comprise an interesting subset of the flora in that most of them are annual or short-lived, and capable of behaving as annual or short-lived shuttle taxa (reproducing locally through relatively large gemmae, bulbils or rhizoidal tubers), and also producing spores regularly, allowing them to move away and colonise elsewhere. The various reproductive structures produced by these plants are also probably quite long-lived, surviving as diaspore banks in the soil (Bisang 1996, During 1997). On the face of it, therefore, the rare arable weeds would appear to be the best-equipped to survive with little or no targeted conservation effort, and indeed all the plants with this multiple life strategy fall into the *Least Concern* category. On the other hand, their survival depends on the right sort of arable field management. Too little disturbance of the soil and more competitive taxa take over; too much and they cannot complete their life cycles. The ideal management for these plants is the sort of arable farming that permits overwintering stubble, and leaves 'conservation headlands' and uncultivated field margins (Porley 2008).

Perennial stayers and dominants are the taxa most suited to the 'nature reserve treatment', as they require a habitat that is more or less stable, in terms of both its quality and extent. The most obvious examples of these are the large liverworts of the Northern Atlantic hepatic mat community, which seldom, if ever, produce either spores or vegetative propagules and must rely on the relatively inefficient process of fragmentation for their dispersal. Protection and management of the best sites for this internationally important community is highly appropriate. Most of the sites are in remote NE-facing corries in the mountains, so all that might need to be done is to leave them alone and not impose excessive grazing regimes. Many of the sites are now protected for habitat reasons by SAC designations.

Stubble field with *Entosthodon fascicularis* and *Weissia brachycarpa* var. *brachycarpa*, south-east of Tomacurry, Co. Wexford.

Ex situ conservation

The most effective means of conserving the bryophyte flora is *in situ*; retaining and managing areas of habitat so that the populations can survive, breed and disperse. *Ex situ* conservation involves taking plants out of their natural habitat and trying to grow them in garden, greenhouse or laboratory conditions. It is considered a useful adjunct to *in situ* conservation, but in no way an alternative to it. It can include, for example, breeding and 'bulking up' rare taxa for eventual reintroduction, long-term storage of cryogenically frozen plants and spores as a backstop against their disappearance in the wild, and providing a reservoir of genetic material for species that have become extinct in the wild. *Ex situ* conservation undoubtedly raises some profound practical and philosophical questions. What is the point of conserving plants divorced from their natural habitat? Is it possible to preserve in an *ex situ* population the full range of genetic variation that might be required in future? How do you grow bryophytes?

The *ex situ* conservation of rare Irish bryophytes is under investigation at the National Botanic Gardens, Glasnevin, Dublin, in partnership with the Royal Botanic Gardens, Kew, London, where much pioneering work has taken place, and a number of co-workers in continental Europe. It may well prove to be an important tool in the conservation of the Irish bryophyte flora.

Protection status in the Republic of Ireland

A number of bryophytes in Ireland have been afforded legal protection under domestic and European law. Species that are protected in the Republic of Ireland, under the Flora (Protection) Order, 1999, are listed in Table 12.

**Table 12.
Species listed on the Flora (Protection) Order, 1999**

Mosses
Bryum calophyllum
Bryum marratii
Catoscopium nigritum
Hamatocaulis vernicosus (as *Drepanocladus vernicosus*)
Leptobarbula berica
Orthotrichum pallens
Orthotrichum sprucei
Orthotrichum stramineum
Paludella squarrosa
Tortula wilsonii (as *Pottia wilsonii*)
Tetraplodon angustatus
Tortella inclinata
Weissia longifolia
Weissia rostellata

Liverworts
Leiocolea gillmanii
Leiocolea rutheana
Petalophyllum ralfsii
Plagiochila heterophylla (as *P. atlantica*)

Christina Campbell undertaking research into *in vitro* culture techniques with rare Irish bryophytes, Teagasc Laboratory, Kinsealy, Co. Dublin, 2010.

Under the terms of the Wildlife Act, 1976, as amended by the Wildlife (Amendment) Act, 2000 (which also includes vascular plants), it is not allowed, other than with a licence granted by the government, to 'cut, pick, collect, uproot or otherwise take, injure, damage, or destroy any specimen' of these species; to 'purchase, sell, keep for sale, transport for sale or exchange, offer for sale or exchange or be in possession of any such specimen whether alive or dead or the flowers, roots, seeds, spores or any part, product or derivative thereof'; or to 'wilfully alter, damage, destroy or interfere with the habitat or environment' of any of these species.

The list, of course, reflects the state of knowledge of the Irish bryophyte flora as it was in 1999, and might look somewhat different if the exercise were to be repeated today. *Hamatocaulis vernicosus* and *Petalophyllum ralfsii* were included because both were listed in European legislation. As in other parts of Europe, this listing has led to a great deal of targeted fieldwork on these two species, and it is now known that neither is nearly as rare as was once thought. In Ireland, *H. vernicosus* is now considered *Near Threatened*, while there are now so many sites for *P. ralfsii* that it has to be considered *Least Concern*. This is not to minimise their importance, however. *H. vernicosus* is still a rare and very habitat-specific plant in Ireland. Ireland is of global importance for *P. ralfsii*, and some sites support an estimated several million individuals, almost certainly the greatest concentration of large populations of this species in the world. Most of the other species would probably remain on the list, but it is likely that several additional bryophytes now considered *Critically Endangered* will be added when the Flora (Protection) Order, 1999 is reviewed and revised.

Protection status in Northern Ireland

The Wildlife (Northern Ireland) Order 1985 generally protects plants against unauthorised removal from the wild, although bryophytes are specially protected under this legislation. The Conservation (Nature Habitats, etc.) Regulations (Northern Ireland) 1995 offers special protection to species protected at a European level; *H. vernicosus* and *P. ralfsii*, both of which have been recorded in Northern Ireland, although *H. vernicosus* has not been seen there since 1901. These plants cannot be intentionally picked, uprooted or destroyed, or offered for sale.

The pending Northern Ireland Wildlife and Natural Environment Bill proposes to offer protection to a wider group of bryophytes including the mosses *Orthotrichum sprucei*, *Eurhynchiastrum pulchellum* and *Orthodontium gracile* and the liverworts *Leiocolea heterocolpos* and *Petalophyllum ralfsii*.

In addition, the UK Biodiversity Action Plan (UKBAP) contains subsidiary Action Plans for many rare bryophytes in the UK, including some species that occur in Northern Ireland. UKBAP was introduced in 1995, with further species added in 1999. All the species included by that date have UK Action Plans, and conservation action has taken place for them. UKBAP was reviewed in 2007 (Biodiversity Reporting and Information Group 2007), when the bryophyte list was modified extensively and was based on more objective scientific criteria. Species added in 2007 do not yet have individual Action Plans, and individual countries are responsible for any conservation action that they require. UKBAP species that occur (or have occurred) in Northern Ireland are listed in Table 13.

During the preparation of the Northern Ireland Biodiversity Strategy (EHS 2002) an initial list of Northern Ireland Priority Species requiring conservation action was identified. A more comprehensive list of Northern Ireland Priority Species was later published in March 2004. The latest list was published in March 2010 (Table 14) and includes species over and above those which appear on the main UKBAP list. These are species which require conservation action because of their decline, rarity and importance in either an all-Ireland or a UK context, and were arrived at using the draft Irish Red List. The conservation needs for individual species are being addressed through ASSI designation and management, with species requirements met through

Table 13. UKBAP species in Northern Ireland

Mosses
Atrichum angustatum
Bryum marratii
Bryum uliginosum
Ephemerum spinulosum
Eurhynchiastrum pulchellum var. *diversifolium*
Orthodontium gracile
Seligeria oelandica
Tayloria tenuis
Tortula cuneifolia

Liverwort
Petalophyllum ralfsii

more general habitat management and additional survey and research where possible. It is intended that this list will be subject to review on an annual basis.

Selection criteria for Northern Ireland Priority Species bryophyte list are:
1. Listed as a UK Priority Species.
2. Rapid decline (2% per year).
3. Decline (1% year) with Northern Ireland being a stronghold consisting of > 50% Irish population or > 20% UK population/range; or with the Irish or UK population restricted to Northern Ireland.
4. Rare (confined to a small population of one or two sites in Northern Ireland) with Northern Ireland being a stronghold consisting of either > 50% Irish population or > 20% UK population/range; or with the Irish or UK population restricted to Northern Ireland.
5. At least 20% of international population of species or well-recognised subspecies occurring in Northern Ireland.

6. Irish Red Data Book (RDB) species classed as critically endangered (CR), endangered (EN) or vulnerable (VU).

International protection status
The Convention on the Conservation of European Wildlife and Natural Habitats (the Bern Convention) was adopted in Bern, Switzerland in 1979, and came into force in 1982. Both the Republic of Ireland and the UK are signatories. This Convention aims to ensure conservation and protection of wild plant and animal species and their natural habitats (listed in Appendices I and II of the Convention) and imposes legal obligations on contracting parties, protecting over 500 wild plant species and more than 1000 wild animal species across Europe. Twenty-six species of bryophytes were added to the list of 'strictly protected' species (Appendix I) in 1991, the only ones occurring in Ireland being *Hamatocaulis vernicosus* and *Petalophyllum ralfsii*. Signatory states are responsible for protecting these plants through their own domestic legislation.

Table 14. Northern Ireland Priority Species (2010 list)

Hornworts and liverworts	*Daltonia splachnoides*
Anthoceros agrestis	*Dicranodontium asperulum*
Calypogeia integristipula	*Encalypta rhaptocarpa*
Cephalozia pleniceps	*Ephemerum spinulosum*
Cephaloziella rubella	*Eurhynchiastrum pulchellum* var. *diversifolium*
Cladopodiella francisci	*Hedwigia integrifolia*
Dumortiera hirsuta	*Myurella julacea*
Geocalyx graveolens	*Orthodontium gracile*
Gymnomitrion concinnatum	*Orthotrichum sprucei*
Leiocolea heterocolpos	*Philonotis rigida*
Marsupella funckii	*Physcomitrium sphaericum*
Marsupella sprucei	*Pohlia filum*
Metzgeria pubescens	*Pseudocalliergon lycopodioides*
Petalophyllum ralfsii	*Racomitrium canescens*
	Rhabdoweisia fugax
Mosses	*Rhytidium rugosum*
Abietinella abietina	*Schistidium platyphyllum*
Aulacomnium androgynum	*Schistidium trichodon*
Bartramia ithyphylla	*Seligeria calcarea*
Brachydontium trichodes	*Seligeria oelandica*
Bryum intermedium	*Thuidium recognitum*
Bryum torquescens	*Tortella inclinata*
Campylopus subulatus	*Weissia rutilans*
Cinclidium stygium	

Slightly later, the European Community published the Directive on the Conservation of Natural Habitats and of Wild Fauna and Flora (the Habitats Directive), which came into force in 1992. The bryophytes listed in Appendix I of the Bern Convention were more or less copied to Annex IIb of the Habitats Directive: as far as Ireland is concerned the lists are identical, with *H. vernicosus* and *P. ralfsii* again the only two species that occur in Ireland. This Annex requires signatory states to designate Special Areas of Conservation (SACs) for the listed species as part of the Natura 2000 network. The Habitats Directive also provides indirect protection for many bryophytes in Ireland through SAC designation for habitats. In addition, Annex V of the Directive deals with exploitation and taking from the wild of certain species. Thus, signatory states are required to monitor *Sphagnum*, as a genus, and *Leucobryum glaucum*, both taxa that are exploited commercially, and take measures to protect them if necessary. A review of wildlife trade in Ireland (Ferriss *et al.* 2007) found that although some trade in Annex V plants was noted, it appeared to be low-level and, with one exception, did not involve plants collected in Ireland.

Other EU legislation also helps to enforce measures that will benefit bryophyte conservation, notably that relating to river basin management (Water Framework Directive), water pollution (Nitrates Directive) and the requirement for environmental impact assessments for developments (EIA Directive). International agreements such as the Convention on Biological Diversity (CBD) can greatly assist bryophyte conservation through the requirement of member parties to publish and implement action plans for species. The National Biodiversity Plan (DAHGI 2002) for the Republic of Ireland and the Northern Ireland Biodiversity Strategy (EHS 2002) include recommendations to foster all-island species action programmes, including the production of Red Lists, and both were stimulated in response to CBD. Several other international agreements, such as The Convention on Wetlands of International Importance (Ramsar Convention), can also benefit bryophytes.

Conservation priorities

Traditionally, conservation effort has been directed towards species and habitats that are rare and threatened on a country basis. This is perfectly understandable, and in many ways both sensible and effective. The Red List is a tool for determining which species are threatened in a specific geographical area, in this case bryophytes in Ireland. However, it is only one of several tools that can be employed for assessing where most conservation effort should be directed, and should not be used in isolation. While *Barbilophozia barbata* may be *Critically Endangered* in Ireland, there is plenty of it in Britain and continental Europe. To what extent does it actually matter if this species, which is probably at the edge of its range here, becomes *Regionally Extinct* in Ireland? On the other hand, *Campylopus setifolius*, which is *Least Concern* in Ireland, is considered a rare European endemic. As well as conserving species that are rare and threatened in Ireland, there is an international responsibility to conserve those species and habitats which may not be particularly rare or threatened in Ireland, but for which Ireland has a large proportion of the global resource.

We must certainly try to take care of, say, *Paludella squarrosa*, a plant that is relatively common in Scandinavia, because its presence here may have wider phytogeographical significance; it might be genetically distinct from its continental cousins, and it is indicative of, and integral to, a very special and diverse part of Ireland's natural heritage. However, effort and resources should also be put into the conservation of features that are relatively common here but extremely rare globally. These are nearly all habitats and plant communities that occur in Ireland because of its oceanic position and for which Ireland has a special responsibility to conserve: the Atlantic communities of large liverworts in wet heath in the hills; the remaining stands of Atlantic woodland; the now damaged and restricted remnants of the midland bogs; the dune slack and machair communities of the west coast; the unique bryophyte assemblages to be found in the Dartry Mountains. All of these habitats and plant communities are under pressure and threat from human influences.

To summarise, to determine conservation priorities, it is necessary to employ as much information as possible. One source is the domestic Red List; others may include international Red Lists, information about species and habitat distribution globally, and information about global threats and trends to species and habitats. Conservation efforts for bryophytes should aim to address those species that are already declining and scarce, as well as those assemblages of species that are more common but for which Ireland holds a special responsibility.

CHAPTER SIX

Important Bryophyte Areas

Glenveagh, Co. Donegal.

What are Important Bryophyte Areas?

IMPORTANT BRYOPHYTE Areas (IBrA) form part of the Important Plant Area (IPA) programme, a project promoted by Plantlife International to identify and protect a network of the best sites for plant conservation worldwide. Important Plant Areas are seen as a means to fulfil Target 5 of the Convention on Biological Diversity's Global Strategy for Plant Conservation: protection of 50% of the world's most important areas for plant diversity by 2010. Though not a statutory site designation, IPAs can be used to support conservation actions and initiatives.

Anderson (2002) defines an IPA as a site that exhibits exceptional botanical richness and/or supports an outstanding assemblage of rare, threatened and/or endemic plant species and/or vegetation of high botanical value. The selection of sites follows international and regional guidelines to ensure consistency and is based on three main criteria: threatened species, species richness/diversity and threatened habitats. The assessment methodology applies to all plants and fungi.

Important Bryophyte Areas aim to identify areas which are important from a bryological point of view. IPAs that include bryophytes (Anderson *et al.* 2005, Radford & Odé 2009), and IBrAs dealing solely with bryophytes (Papp 2008), have been published for several European countries. In Northern Ireland, IPAs have been identified as part of UK projects for algae (Brodie *et al.* 2007), stoneworts (Stewart 2004), arable plants (Byfield & Wilson 2005) and vascular plants (http://www.plantlife.org.uk/wild_plants/important_plant_areas). In the Republic of Ireland, IPAs have only been identified at a local level for vascular plants in Co. Waterford (Green & Fitzpatrick 2008: http://floraofcountywaterford.biodiversityireland.ie). The criteria used in these works, as well as the Plantlife International criteria (Anderson 2002), have been drawn upon for the selection of IBrAs in Ireland. As in the rest of this book, the island of Ireland has been treated as a single unit for the purposes of IBrA selection.

Background to IBrA selection

Plantlife International give three basic principles, listed as criteria, for IPA identification (Anderson 2002):

Criterion A identifies a site that holds significant populations of one or more species that are of global or European conservation concern.

Criterion B identifies a site that has an exceptionally rich flora in a European context in relation to its biogeographic zone.

Criterion C identifies a site that is an outstanding example of a habitat type of global or European plant conservation and botanical importance.

Stewart (2004) sought to interpret and adapt these principles for the selection of IPAs for stoneworts in Northern Ireland. Sites were chosen if they were exceptionally rich in threatened species, if they were exceptionally species-rich, or if they supported threatened habitats of major significance to stoneworts. These factors were considered at both a national and a European level. Green & Fitzpatrick (2008) approached the task of selecting local IPAs in Co. Waterford by targeting tetrad 'hotspots'. They identified tetrads within Co. Waterford that contained either any legally protected species, ≥ 3 nationally Red Listed species, ≥ 5 nationally scarce species, or > 10 locally rare species. In addition, tetrads that were rich in axiophytes (species 'worthy of conservation'; http://www.bsbi.org.uk/axiophytes.html), and tetrads rich in species indicative of good habitat quality were identified. This built up a picture of where the significant plant sites in Co. Waterford were to be found.

Elements of both these approaches were adopted here to identify bryophyte IBrAs for Ireland. Key considerations taken into account for bryophytes were:

Internationally threatened taxa:-
These are defined as taxa included on the European Red List (ECCB 1995), or updates to this list

(http://www.bio.ntnu.no/users/soder/ECCB/RDBTaxon.php). These are listed in Table 15. All bar eight of these taxa are also listed on the Irish Red List, or as *Near Threatened* or *Data Deficient* in Ireland.

Rare and threatened taxa in Ireland:-
Red List, *Near Threatened* and *Data Deficient* taxa (Tables 4, 5 and 6).

Legally protected taxa:-
Species listed on the Flora (Protection) Order 1999, for the Republic of Ireland (Table 12), the Conservation (Nature Habitats, etc.) Regulations (Northern Ireland) 1995 and on pending legislation in the Northern Ireland Wildlife and Natural Environment Bill.

Internationally significant taxa and assemblages:-
Taxa and assemblages for which Ireland has a special responsibility. These are interpreted here as those ascribed to hyperoceanic or oceanic biogeographical elements, as defined by Hill *et al.* (2007) (Table 16). Most of these are included within the three categories above (i.e. Red Listed in Europe, or Red Listed or protected in Ireland), but several fall outside these categories and are listed as *Least Concern* in Ireland.

Outstanding examples of species-rich assemblages:-
Particularly important species-rich assemblages, such as Northern Atlantic hepatic mat community.

Outstanding examples of bryophyte-rich habitats:-
Habitats containing rich assemblages of bryophytes, such as EU Habitats Directive Annex I priority habitats Active Raised Bog and Machair, amongst others.

Application of criteria for selecting bryophyte IBrAs in Ireland

The selection of IBrAs followed a two-stage approach; an initial selection of hectad 'hotspots' rich in threatened taxa, followed by a more detailed overlay with the recorded plant localities and the protected site boundary layers. Hectad 'hotspots' were defined as: all hectads with legally protected taxa; all hectads with ≥ 3 Red List taxa; and all hectads with ≥ 5 Red List, *Near Threatened* or *Data Deficient* taxa. Only recent (1970–2010) records were considered. Sites selected *solely* because of the presence of a legally protected taxon that has more recently been assigned to *Near Threatened* or *Least Concern* were deleted.

Table 15. Irish taxa threatened in Europe

With the exception of a few species that have been updated more recently (http://www.bio.ntnu.no/users/soder/ECCB/RDBTaxon.php), the European Red List (ECCB 1995) uses the old IUCN categories and criteria (IUCN 1978), in which *Rare* (R) approximately equates to an amalgamation of *Vulnerable* (VU) and *Near Threatened* (NT), and *Insufficiently Known* (K) approximately equates to *Data Deficient* (DD).

	Status in Europe	Status in Ireland		Status in Europe	Status in Ireland
Liverworts			*Campylostelium saxicola*	R	EN
Acrobolbus wilsonii	NT	VU	*Cyclodictyon laetevirens*	R	NT
Adelanthus lindenbergianus	VU	VU	*Daltonia splachnoides*	NT	LC
Anastrophyllum hellerianum	NT	RE	*Dicranodontium asperulum*	K	DD
Bazzania pearsonii	R	VU	*Didymodon maximus*	R	NT
Cephalozia crassifolia	VU	EN	*Didymodon tomaculosus*	K	VU
Cephaloziella elachista	K	DD	*Didymodon umbrosus*	R	VU
Cephaloziella massalongi	R	VU	*Ditrichum cornubicum*	EN	CR
Cephaloziella nicholsonii	R	VU	*Ditrichum plumbicola*	NT	EN
Dumortiera hirsuta	R	NT	*Ephemerum cohaerens*	CR	VU
Fossombronia fimbriata	R	VU	*Ephemerum crassinervium*		
Haplomitrium hookeri	R	LC	subsp. *sessile*	R	NT
Lejeunea flava subsp. *moorei*	R	DD	*Fissidens curvatus*	K	VU
Lejeunea hibernica	R	NT	*Fissidens monguillonii*	R	NT
Lejeunea mandonii	R	EN	*Glyphomitrium daviesii*	R	LC
Mastigophora woodsii	R	NT	*Grimmia atrata*	R	EN
Pallavicinia lyellii	VU	EN	*Grimmia lisae*	R	LC
Petalophyllum ralfsii	VU	LC	*Hamatocaulis vernicosus*	VU	NT
Plagiochila carringtonii	R	EN	*Hedwigia integrifolia*	R	VU
Plagiochila heterophylla	R	EN	*Hymenostylium recurvirostrum*		
Radula carringtonii	R	NT	var. *insigne*	R	NT
Radula holtii	R	NT	*Molendoa warburgii*	R	VU
Radula voluta	R	LC	*Orthodontium gracile*	VU	CR
Riccia huebeneriana	R	DD	*Orthotrichum sprucei*	R	VU
Scapania nimbosa	R	EN	*Paraleptodontium recurvifolium*	R	NT
Solenostoma paroicum	NT	NT	*Philonotis cernua*	R	CR
Sphenolobopsis pearsonii	R	NT	*Physcomitrium sphaericum*	R	VU
Telaranea europaea	R	NT	*Pterygoneurum lamellatum*	VU	RE
			Schistidium pruinosum	K	RE
Mosses			*Schistidium trichodon*	K	DD
Andreaea megistospora	R	VU	*Seligeria oelandica*	K	VU
Brachydontium trichodes	R	EN	*Seligeria patula*	K	VU
Bryum calophyllum	R	EN	*Sematophyllum demissum*	R	NT
Bryum riparium	R	EN	*Sphagnum skyense*	K	NT
Bryum tenuisetum	K	DD	*Syntrichia virescens*	VU	DD
Bryum warneum	R	EN	*Trichostomum hibernicum*	R	LC
Campylopus setifolius	R	LC	*Weissia perssonii*	R	LC
Campylopus shawii	R	NT	*Weissia rostellata*	R	NT

Table 16. Taxa with Hyperoceanic or Oceanic distributions in Europe

Name of taxon	Name of taxon	Name of taxon
Hornworts and liverworts	*Porella obtusata*	*Fissidens serrulatus*
Acrobolbus wilsonii	*Porella pinnata*	*Fissidens taxifolius* var. *pallidicaulis*
Adelanthus decipiens	*Radula aquilegia*	*Glyphomitrium daviesii*
Adelanthus lindenbergianus	*Radula carringtonii*	*Gymnostomum viridulum*
Anthoceros punctatus	*Radula holtii*	*Hageniella micans*
Aphanolejeunea microscopica	*Radula voluta*	*Hedwigia integrifolia*
Bazzania pearsonii	*Riccia crozalsii*	*Heterocladium wulfsbergii*
Cephalozia crassifolia	*Saccogyna viticulosa*	*Hymenostylium recurvirostrum*
Cephaloziella turneri	*Scapania gracilis*	var. *insigne*
Cololejeunea minutissima	*Scapania nimbosa*	*Hyocomium armoricum*
Colura calyptrifolia	*Scapania ornithopodioides*	*Hypnum uncinulatum*
Douinia ovata	*Solenostoma paroicum*	*Isothecium holtii*
Drepanolejeunea hamatifolia	*Southbya tophacea*	*Isothecium myosuroides*
Dumortiera hirsuta	*Telaranea europaea*	var. *brachythecioides*
Fossombronia angulosa		*Leptobarbula berica*
Fossombronia caespitiformis	Mosses	*Leptodon smithii*
subsp. *multispira*	*Andreaea alpina*	*Leptodontium flexifolium*
Fossombronia fimbriata	*Andreaea megistospora*	*Microbryum rectum*
Fossombronia maritima	*Breutelia chrysocoma*	*Molendoa warburgii*
Frullania microphylla	*Bryum donianum*	*Oedipodium griffithianum*
Frullania teneriffae	*Bryum dyffrynense*	*Orthodontium gracile*
Gymnomitrion crenulatum	*Bryum gemmiparum*	*Orthotrichum pulchellum*
Harpalejeunea molleri	*Bryum riparium*	*Orthotrichum sprucei*
Herbertus aduncus subsp. *hutchinsiae*	*Bryum torquescens*	*Paraleptodontium recurvifolium*
Jubula hutchinsiae	*Campylopus atrovirens*	*Philonotis cernua*
Leiocolea fitzgeraldiae	var. *atrovirens*	*Philonotis rigida*
Leiocolea turbinata	*Campylopus atrovirens* var. *falcatus*	*Platyhypnidium lusitanicum*
Lejeunea eckloniana	*Campylopus brevipilus*	*Ptychomitrium polyphyllum*
Lejeunea flava subsp. *moorei*	*Campylopus pilifer*	*Racomitrium ellipticum*
Lejeunea hibernica	*Campylopus setifolius*	*Rhabdoweisia crenulata*
Lejeunea lamacerina	*Campylopus shawii*	*Schistidium maritimum*
Lejeunea mandonii	*Cyclodictyon laetevirens*	*Scleropodium touretii*
Lejeunea patens	*Daltonia splachnoides*	*Scorpiurium circinatum*
Lepidozia cupressina	*Dicranum scottianum*	*Sematophyllum demissum*
Lepidozia pearsonii	*Didymodon maximus*	*Sematophyllum substrumulosum*
Leptoscyphus cuneifolius	*Didymodon umbrosus*	*Sphagnum austinii*
Lophocolea fragrans	*Ditrichum cornubicum*	*Sphagnum skyense*
Marchesinia mackaii	*Ditrichum plumbicola*	*Sphagnum strictum*
Mastigophora woodsii	*Entosthodon attenuatus*	*Sphagnum subnitens* var. *ferrugineum*
Metzgeria leptoneura	*Ephemerum crassinervium*	*Tortella nitida*
Petalophyllum ralfsii	subsp. *rutheanum*	*Tortula canescens*
Phaeoceros laevis	*Ephemerum spinulosum*	*Tortula cuneifolia*
Plagiochila bifaria	*Epipterygium tozeri*	*Tortula marginata*
Plagiochila carringtonii	*Fissidens bryoides* var. *caespitans*	*Tortula viridifolia*
Plagiochila exigua	*Fissidens celticus*	*Trichostomum hibernicum*
Plagiochila heterophylla	*Fissidens crispus*	*Ulota calvescens*
Plagiochila punctata	*Fissidens monguillonii*	*Ulota phyllantha*
Plagiochila spinulosa	*Fissidens polyphyllus*	*Weissia perssonii*
Pleurozia purpurea	*Fissidens rivularis*	*Zygodon conoideus* var. *conoideus*

It was soon evident that sites selected by this method also included most of the internationally threatened taxa, nearly all the internationally significant taxa and assemblages, and many of the outstanding species-rich assemblages and bryophyte-rich habitats. As an experiment, all the Irish records of the common oceanic species *Campylopus atrovirens* were downloaded from the National Biodiversity Network Gateway (http://www.searchnbn.net/index_homepage/index.jsp). This species has been recorded in virtually every hectad that has a significant oceanic bryophyte flora. It was found that selecting potential IBrAs using only Red List, *Near Threatened* and *Data Deficient* taxa also selected many sites with *C. atrovirens*. It is inferred from this that common oceanic taxa, and therefore oceanic assemblages generally, are almost always more than adequately covered by selecting on the basis of threatened taxa alone. As a backstop, in case some sites had slipped through the net, subjectively assessed 'top ten' county lists, produced over the past 10 years, were also examined.

It also became clear that the majority of sites supporting these 'key species' were located within existing protected areas (SACs, NHAs, pNHAs, ASSIs, Nature Reserves, National Parks), and that most of those that occurred on unprotected land could be easily linked to one or more protected areas in order to produce effective, realistic and pragmatic IBrAs. No distinction has been made between IBrAs of international or national importance. Most of them support internationally restricted oceanic bryophyte assemblages, or contain internationally threatened or significant habitats (e.g. bogs, sand dunes), or include taxa listed on international legislation.

Thus, the final criteria for selecting IBrAs for bryophytes in Ireland are as follows:
A. The site holds significant populations of at least one legally protected taxon, OR at least three Red List taxa, OR at least five Red List, *Near Threatened* or *Data Deficient* taxa.
B. The site is exceptionally rich in internationally significant taxa and assemblages.
C. The site is an outstanding example of a habitat type of global or European plant conservation and botanical importance, containing rich assemblages of habitat-specific taxa.

List of bryophyte IBrAs
A total of 47 bryophyte IBrAs have been selected in Ireland. In line with the guidelines published for the selection of sites boundaries, a site is defined so that, as far as possible, it is different in character, or habitat, or botanical significance from the surrounding area and exists as an actual or potential protected area or an area that could be managed for conservation (Anderson 2002). Thus most of the IBrAs in Ireland are defined by the boundaries of protected sites that lie within the 'hotspot' or 'core' hectads. The IBrA is taken to include the full extent of the protected area beyond the 'core' hectads, unless stated otherwise, and also includes the localities of taxa that occur on unprotected land located nearby.

Most IBrAs cover very large areas. Many contain montane taxa that occur in large upland complexes and some lowland sites cover extensive coastal and river systems. An expansive approach to IBrA selection is favoured by most European countries that have undertaken the IPA programme. IPA data for 11 countries in central, eastern and south-eastern Europe (Anderson *et al.* 2005, Radford & Odé 2009) show that most countries have developed a mixture of larger mosaic IPAs to include particular species and habitats and that of 1087 published IPAs: 278 (25%) were 100–1000 ha; 263 (24%) were 1000–10,000 ha and 171 (16%) were 10,000–100,000 ha in extent. Not surprisingly, many of the larger SACs and better known bryophyte localities have been included in the Irish IBrA list, but with additional data and research into bryophyte populations and distribution it is likely that further IBrAs, perhaps smaller in area, will be added to the list in the future. Much of the focus of this round of IBrAs has been on rare and threatened taxa, so it is likely that future efforts will include more sites selected for bryophyte-rich assemblages and sites with habitats important for bryophytes, such as raised bogs, turloughs and fens.

Each IBrA is described under the following headings:-

Location: listed by county.

Core hectads: a list of 'hot spot' hectads with either legally protected taxa; ≥ 3 Red List taxa; or ≥ 5 Red List, *Near Threatened* or *Data Deficient* taxa.

Criteria: IBrA criteria (A, B or C) under which a site qualifies.

Protected sites included: a list of sites designated, or proposed for designation, as SAC, NHA, pNHA, ASSI,

NR and NP included within the IBrA. Internationally protected sites take precedence over national designations in the listings, so that NHA, pNHA, ASSI, NR and NP are only listed separately if they extend outside the boundaries of SACs.

Unprotected sites included: localities and grid references for listed taxa included in the IBrA, but not within protected areas.

Synopsis: a brief description of the IBrA, its important bryophyte taxa, bryophyte habitats and bryophyte assemblages.

Key taxa: a list of Red List, *Near Threatened* and *Data Deficient* taxa, and other taxa given full accounts in the text of this book (e.g. legally protected taxa and some internationally threatened taxa).

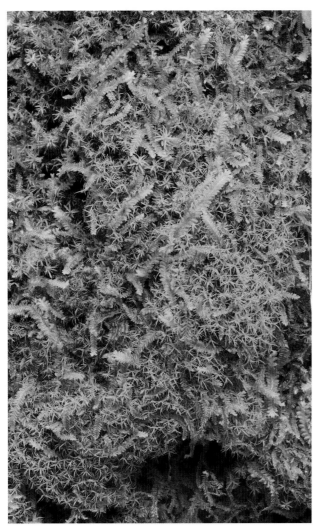

Amphidium mougeotii and *Saccogyna viticulosa*, Killarney, Co. Kerry.

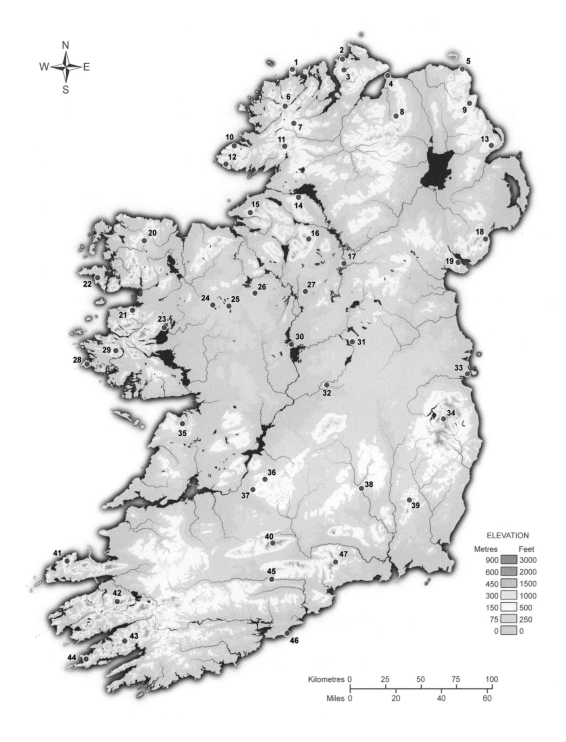

Map 5. Important Bryophyte Areas (IBrA).

Horn Head, Co. Donegal.

1. Horn Head IBrA

Location Co. Donegal

Core hectads B93, C03, C04, C13, C14

Criteria A, B, C

Protected sites included
IE0001090 Ballyness Bay SAC (1236 ha)
IE0000147 Horn Head and Rinclevan SAC (2344 ha)
IE0000164 Lough Nagreany Dunes SAC (221 ha)
IE0001190 Sheephaven SAC (1842 ha)
IE0000194 Tranarossan and Melmore Lough SAC (654 ha)

Unprotected sites included
Rinnafaghla Point (C08824086 – site for *Cephalozia pleniceps*)

Synopsis
Extensive coastal dune systems, maritime heath, boulder cliff slopes and saltmarsh with a distinctive and rich bryophyte flora, including oceanic species and fen and dune-slack specialists. Only known locality in Ireland for *Meesia uliginosa*.

Key taxa
Abietinella abietina var. *hystricosa* (NT), *Acrobolbus wilsonii* (VU), *Bryum dyffrynense* (NT), *Bryum marratii* (LC), *Bryum tenuisetum* (DD), *Bryum warneum* (EN), *Campyliadelphus elodes* (NT), *Catoscopium nigritum* (NT), *Cephalozia pleniceps* (VU), *Cephaloziella turneri* (VU), *Geocalyx graveolens* (EN), *Leiocolea bantriensis* (NT), *Leiocolea gillmanii* (VU), *Meesia uliginosa* (EN), *Petalophyllum ralfsii* (LC), *Platydictya jungermannioides* (NT), *Scapania cuspiduligera* (VU), *Thuidium recognitum* (VU)

Malin Head, Co. Donegal.

2. North Inishowen Coast and Lough Swilly IBrA

Location Co. Donegal

Core hectads C23, C32, C34, C45

Criteria A, B

Protected sites included
IE0002287 Lough Swilly SAC (9262 ha) (small part only)
IE0002012 North Inishowen Coast SAC (7069 ha)

Unprotected sites included
Dunree Head (C286390 – site for *Cephaloziella integerrima* and other metallophytes)

Synopsis
Sandy banks and metal-rich coastal turf, as well as the Urris Hills, which support an oceanic flora. Supports one of only three extant populations of *Bryum uliginosum* known in Ireland. There is a large and important population of *Bryum warneum* in dune slacks N. of Fahan (C3327, C3328).

Key taxa
Bryum torquescens (VU), *Bryum marratii* (LC), *Bryum uliginosum* (EN), *Bryum warneum* (EN), *Cephaloziella integerrima* (VU), *Pohlia wahlenbergii* var. *calcarea* (DD), *Sphagnum strictum* (DD – might be on Mamore Hill, just outside SAC, but record not accurately localised), *Thuidium recognitum* (VU)

Bulbin Mountain, just north-west of summit, Co. Donegal.

3. Bulbin Mountain IBrA

Location Co. Donegal

Core hectad C34

Criteria A, C

Protected sites included
IE0000120 Bulbin Mountain pNHA (423 ha)

Unprotected sites included
None

Synopsis
Mountain with extensive outcropping of base-rich schistose rocks supporting a rich upland calcicole flora. Currently the only known locality in Ireland for *Gymnomitrion corallioides*.

Key taxa
Anthelia juratzkana (NT), *Eremonotus myriocarpus* (NT), *Grimmia funalis* (NT), *Gymnomitrion corallioides* (CR), *Myurella julacea* (EN), *Nardia geoscyphus* (NT), *Philonotis tomentella* (VU), *Plagiobryum zieri* (NT), *Plagiothecium cavifolium* (VU), *Pohlia elongata* var. *elongata* (NT), *Solenostoma subellipticum* (NT)

North-facing cliffs of Binevenagh, Co. Londonderry.

4. Binevenagh and Magilligan IBrA

Location Co. Londonderry

Core hectads C63, C73

Criteria A, B, C

Protected sites included
UK0030089 Binevenagh SAC (90 ha)
UK0016613 Magilligan SAC (1058 ha)
Downhill ASSI (if designated)

Unprotected sites included
None

Synopsis
Coastal sand dunes with a rich specialist flora, and basalt rocks on Binevenagh Mountain and The Umbra. Only known locality in Ireland for *Abietinella abietina* var. *abietina* and *Rhytidium rugosum*. Only locality in Northern Ireland for *Petalophyllum ralfsii*.

Key taxa
Abietinella abietina var. *abietina* (EN), *Abietinella abietina* var. *hystricosa* (NT), *Antitrichia curtipendula* (NT), *Bartramia ithyphylla* (VU), *Bryum torquescens* (VU), *Drepanocladus sendtneri* (NT), *Eremonotus myriocarpus* (NT), *Leiocolea bantriensis* (NT), *Metzgeria pubescens* (VU), *Petalophyllum ralfsii* (LC), *Porella cordaeana* (NT), *Pseudocalliergon lycopodioides* (VU), *Rhodobryum roseum* (NT), *Rhytidium rugosum* (VU), *Thuidium recognitum* (VU)

Coastal cliffs at Fair Head, Co. Antrim.

5. Fair Head and Murlough Bay IBrA

Location Co. Antrim

Core hectads D14

Criteria A

Protected sites included
Fair Head and Murlough Bay ASSI (251 ha)

Unprotected sites included
None

Synopsis
Coastal dolerite cliffs and boulders with a rich bryophyte flora.

Key taxa
Campylopus atrovirens var. *falcatus* (NT), *Dicranella cerviculata* (NT), *Grimmia decipiens* (NT), *Grimmia ramondii* (NT), *Hedwigia integrifolia* (VU), *Marsupella adusta* (NT), *Marsupella sprucei* (VU)

Errigal Mountain and Dunlewy Lough, Co. Donegal.

6. Derryveagh and Muckish Mountains IBrA

Location Co. Donegal

Core hectads B91, B92, C02, C12

Criteria A, B, C

Protected sites included
IE0000116 Ballyarr Wood SAC (30 ha)
IE0002047 Cloghernagore Bog and Glenveagh National Park SAC (33,460 ha)
IE0000140 Fawnboy Bog/Lough Nacung SAC (1105 ha)
IE0001179 Muckish Mountain SAC (1523 ha)

Unprotected sites included
SW of Lough Salt (C1125, C1226 – site for several species)

Synopsis
Large and varied predominantly upland area with good representation of oceanic taxa and also taxa of high-altitude base-rich rocks. It includes the only Irish locality for *Grimmia atrata*, a plant of copper-rich rocks.

Key taxa
Adelanthus lindenbergianus (VU), *Aneura mirabilis* (VU), *Anthelia juratzkana* (NT), *Atrichum tenellum* (NT), *Bazzania pearsonii* (VU), *Brachydontium trichodes* (EN), *Bryum bornholmense* (NT), *Bryum tenuisetum* (DD), *Ditrichum zonatum* (EN), *Grimmia atrata* (EN), *Kurzia sylvatica* (NT), *Lophozia opacifolia* (VU), *Marsupella adusta* (NT), *Marsupella sprucei* (VU), *Nardia geoscyphus* (NT), *Plagiobryum zieri* (NT), *Pohlia filum* (VU), *Scapania ornithopodioides* (VU), *Schistidium agassizii* (VU), *Solenostoma subellipticum* (NT), *Sphagnum girgensohnii* (NT), *Telaranea europaea* (NT), *Tetrodontium brownianum* (NT)

Meentygrannagh Bog, Co. Donegal.

7. Meentygrannagh Bog IBrA

Location Co. Donegal

Core hectad C00

Criteria A, B, C

Protected sites included
IE0000173 Meentygrannagh Bog SAC (530 ha)

Unprotected sites included
None

Synopsis
Large blanket bog and wet heath, with extensive base-rich flushing, supporting a rich fen flora.

Key taxa
Hamatocaulis vernicosus (NT), *Sphagnum subsecundum* (NT), *Sphagnum teres* (NT), *Sphagnum warnstorfii* (VU), *Tomentypnum nitens* (VU)

Benbradagh Mountain, Co. Londonderry.

8. Benbradagh IBrA

Location Co. Londonderry

Core hectads C71

Criteria A, C

Protected sites included
None

Unprotected sites included
Benbradagh

Synopsis
Basalt hill with rich upland calcicole flora, including the only known surviving Irish locality for *Encalypta rhaptocarpa*.

Key taxa
Antitrichia curtipendula (NT), *Bartramia ithyphylla* (VU), *Douinia ovata* (NT), *Encalypta rhaptocarpa* (CR), *Encalypta vulgaris* (NT), *Grimmia funalis* (NT), *Grimmia muehlenbeckii* (DD), *Grimmia ramondii* (NT), *Myurella julacea* (EN), *Plagiobryum zieri* (NT)

Glenariff and Antrim Glens, Co. Antrim.

9. Antrim Hills and Glens IBrA

Location Co. Antrim

Core hectads D21, D22, D30, D31

Criteria A

Protected sites included
UK0016606 Garron Plateau SAC (4650 ha)
Glenariff Glen ASSI (66 ha) (scheduled for declaration 2011)
ASSI323 Little Deer Park ASSI (19 ha)
ASSI161 Straidkilly ASSI (16 ha)
Glenariff NR (8 ha)

Unprotected sites included
SW of Cushendall (D208246 – site for *Seligeria calcarea*)
Carrivemurphy (D259246 – site for *Seligeria calcarea*)
Knock Dhu (D3307, D3406 – site for several rare species)
Sallagh Braes (D353047 – site for *Metzgeria pubescens*)

Synopsis
Basalt and chalk exposures with a rich calcicole flora, including the only known Irish locality for *Leiocolea heterocolpos*.

Key taxa
Anthelia juratzkana (NT), *Bartramia ithyphylla* (VU), *Bryum intermedium* (EN), *Cinclidium stygium* (VU), *Fontinalis antipyretica* var. *gracilis* (NT), *Grimmia donniana* (NT), *Hygroamblystegium fluviatile* (NT), *Leiocolea bantriensis* (NT), *Leiocolea heterocolpos* (CR), *Marsupella funckii* (NT), *Metzgeria pubescens* (VU), *Philonotis rigida* (VU), *Rhizomnium pseudopunctatum* (NT), *Rhodobryum roseum* (NT), *Schistidium pruinosum* (DD), *Schistidium strictum* (NT), *Seligeria calcarea* (VU), *Sphagnum girgensohnii* (NT)

Loughros Beg Bay, Co. Donegal.

10. Slieve Tooey/Sheskinmore IBrA

Location Co. Donegal

Core hectads G69, G79

Criteria A, B, C

Protected sites included
IE0000190 Slieve Tooey/Tormore Island/Loughros Beg Bay SAC (9435 ha)
IE0000197 West of Ardara/Maas Road SAC (6739 ha)

Unprotected sites included
None

Synopsis
The core of this IBrA comprises coastal dune slacks at Sheskinmore, with *Petalophyllum ralfsii*. A number of other key species – *Campylopus subulatus*, *Sphagnum strictum* and *Catoscopium nigritum* – have been recorded from 'Rossbeg', and are probably within the SAC, but the records are not accurately localised. Also included are dune heath at Maghera Strand and the oceanic massif of Slieve Tooey.

Key taxa
Abietinella abietina var. *hystricosa* (NT), *Bryum marratii* (LC), *Lophozia opacifolia* (VU), *Petalophyllum ralfsii* (LC), *Scapania cuspiduligera* (VU)

Lough Nabrackboy and Lough Asgarha, Blue Stack Mountains, Co. Donegal.

11. Blue Stack Mountains IBrA

Location Co. Donegal

Core hectads G98, G99

Criteria A

Protected sites included
IE0001880 Meenaguse Scragh SAC (627 ha)
IE0002301 River Finn SAC (5502 ha)

Unprotected sites included
Binnasruell (G923896 – site for *Cynodontium jenneri* and *Rhabdoweisia fugax*)
Edergole Bridge (G96948689 – site for *Cladopodiella francisci*)
Eglish (G93998810 – site for *Grimmia funalis*)
Lavagh More/Lavagh Beg (site for *Kiaeria falcata*, *Philonotis tomentella* and *Sphagnum russowii*)
Meenaguse (G9089 – site for several key taxa)
Meenavale (G903948 – site for *Sphagnum strictum*)

Synopsis
The Blue Stack Mountains are predominantly acidic and granitic, but they hold important bryophyte communities and populations of rare montane species, including the only known sites in Ireland for *Cynodontium jenneri* and *Kiaeria falcata*. Although two SACs are included in the IBrA, much of it is currently outside any protected area.

Key taxa
Andreaea megistospora (VU), *Cynodontium jenneri* (VU), *Grimmia funalis* (NT), *Gymnomitrion concinnatum* (EN), *Gymnomitrion obtusum* (NT), *Kiaeria falcata* (CR), *Marsupella adusta* (NT), *Marsupella sphacelata* (VU), *Marsupella sprucei* (VU), *Philonotis tomentella* (VU), *Pohlia elongata* var. *elongata* (NT), *Rhabdoweisia crispata* (NT), *Rhabdoweisia fugax* (VU), *Sphagnum russowii* (NT), *Sphagnum strictum* (DD), *Sphagnum subsecundum* (NT)

Slieve League, Co. Donegal.

12. Slieve League IBrA

Location Co. Donegal

Core hectad G57

Criteria A, B

Protected sites included
IE0000189 Slieve League SAC (3926 ha)

Unprotected sites included
Carrick Lower Bridge (G585782 – site for *Heterocladium wulfsbergii*)
Croleavy Lough (G570773 – site for *Rhizomnium pseudopunctatum*)

Synopsis
Hyperoceanic montane vegetation, including a good assemblage of rare, arctic-alpine and oceanic taxa, especially in the north-facing corrie. The site also includes fen vegetation at the nearby Croleavy Lough, rich coastal turf at Trabane, Malin Beg (which is also within the SAC) and riverside rocks at Carrick.

Key taxa
Arctoa fulvella (VU), *Campylopus subulatus* (VU), *Dicranella cerviculata* (NT), *Ditrichum zonatum* (EN), *Gymnomitrion concinnatum* (EN), *Heterocladium wulfsbergii* (NT), *Hylocomiastrum umbratum* (NT), *Marsupella sphacelata* (VU), *Mnium thomsonii* (NT), *Nardia geoscyphus* (NT), *Orthothecium rufescens* (NT), *Philonotis rigida* (VU), *Pohlia elongata* var. *elongata* (NT), *Rhizomnium pseudopunctatum* (NT), *Scapania gymnostomophila* (VU), *Solenostoma subellipticum* (NT), *Tortula atrovirens* (NT)

South Woodburn Reservoir, Co. Antrim.

13. Antrim Reservoirs IBrA

Location Cos Antrim, Down

Core hectads J38, J39, J49

Criteria A

Protected sites included
ASSI345 Copeland Reservoir ASSI (10 ha)
ASSI343 North Woodburn Reservoir ASSI (9 ha)
ASSI344 South Woodburn Reservoir ASSI (78 ha)

Unprotected sites included
None

Synopsis
This site supports very good examples of the ephemeral bryophyte flora that occurs in the draw-down zones of reservoirs. One of only two known sites in Ireland for *Ephemerum spinulosum*.

Key taxa
Ephemerum crassinervium subsp. *sessile* (NT), *Ephemerum spinulosum* (EN), *Physcomitrium sphaericum* (VU), *Weissia rostellata* (NT)

Cliffs of Magho, Lough Navar, Co. Fermanagh.

14. West Fermanagh Uplands IBrA

Location Co. Fermanagh

Core hectads H05, H13

Criteria A, C

Protected sites included
UK0030045 Largalinny SAC (245 ha)
UK0016619 Monawilkin SAC (175 ha)
UK0030300 West Fermanagh Scarplands SAC (2270 ha)
ASSI108 Braade ASSI (3 ha)
ASSI191 Cliffs of Magho ASSI (350 ha)
Lough Navar Scarps and Lakes ASSI (325 ha) (scheduled for declaration 2011)

Unprotected sites included – None

Synopsis
Area of predominantly limestone karst with a rich calcicole flora, and also large sandstone exposures. Only locality in Ireland for *Calypogeia integristipula* and *Orthodontium gracile*.

Key taxa
Amblystegium confervoides (NT), *Aulacomnium androgynum* (VU), *Bryum torquescens* (VU), *Calypogeia integristipula* (EN), *Campyliadelphus elodes* (NT), *Daltonia splachnoides* (LC), *Fissidens rufulus* (EN), *Geocalyx graveolens* (EN), *Hygroamblystegium fluviatile* (NT), *Hypnum callichroum* (NT), *Leiocolea bantriensis* (NT), *Leiocolea fitzgeraldiae* (NT), *Mnium thomsonii* (NT), *Orthodontium gracile* (CR), *Orthothecium rufescens* (NT), *Oxyrrhynchium speciosum* (NT), *Plagiomnium cuspidatum* (NT), *Platydictya jungermannioides* (NT), *Platyhypnidium lusitanicum* (NT), *Rhizomnium pseudopunctatum* (NT), *Schistidium elegantulum* subsp. *elegantulum* (DD), *Schistidium trichodon* (VU), *Scleropodium cespitans* (NT), *Seligeria oelandica* (VU), *Seligeria patula* (NT), *Sphagnum teres* (NT), *Tetrodontium brownianum* (NT), *Thuidium recognitum* (VU)

Cloontyprughlish, Glenade, Co. Leitrim.

15. Dartry Mountains IBrA

Location Cos Leitrim, Sligo

Core hectads G64, G73, G74, G75, G84, G85

Criteria A, B, C

Protected sites included
IE0001403 Arroo Mountain SAC (3926 ha)
IE0000623 Ben Bulben, Gleniff and Glenade Complex SAC (5983 ha)
IE0000625 Bunduff Lough and Machair/Trawalua/Mullaghmore SAC (4389 ha)
IE0001976 Lough Gill SAC (3320 ha)
002435 Crockauns/Keelogyboy Bogs NHA (1315 ha)
001658 Colgagh Lough pNHA (39 ha)

Unprotected sites included
Luke's Bridge (G69934719 – site for *Campylostelium saxicola*)
Lissadell Wood (G630439 – site for *Brachytheciastrum velutinum*)

Synopsis
Large area of Carboniferous Limestone hills in a spectacular karst landscape. Very good representations of the upland calcicolous flora, including rare species. Several local specialities restricted or almost restricted to this area in Ireland – *Didymodon maximus*, *Encalypta alpina*, *Hymenostylium recurvirostrum* var. *insigne*, *Orthothecium rufescens*, *Pedinophyllum interruptum*, *Seligeria oelandica* and *Timmia norvegica*. *Didymodon maximus* is globally rare, found nowhere else in Europe, and is known elsewhere only in Alaska, Canada, the Russian Far East and Mongolia. The IBrA also includes coastal dune systems at Mullaghmore, with *Petalophyllum ralfsii* and other coastal specialists, and Lough Gill, with calcicolous lakeside species.

Gleniff, Co. Sligo.

Key taxa

Abietinella abietina var. *hystricosa* (NT), *Brachytheciastrum velutinum* (EN), *Bryum elegans* (VU), *Campylostelium saxicola* (EN), *Cinclidium stygium* (VU), *Daltonia splachnoides* (LC), *Dicranella grevilleana* (NT), *Didymodon maximus* (NT), *Drepanocladus sendtneri* (NT), *Dumortiera hirsuta* (NT), *Encalypta alpina* (VU), *Fissidens monguillonii* (NT), *Hygroamblystegium varium* (NT), *Hymenostylium recurvirostrum* var. *insigne* (NT), *Leiocolea bantriensis* (NT), *Leiocolea fitzgeraldiae* (NT), *Lejeunea mandonii* (EN), *Marchantia polymorpha* subsp. *montivagans* (EN), *Mnium thomsonii* (NT), *Myurella julacea* (EN), *Orthothecium rufescens* (NT), *Orthotrichum sprucei* (VU), *Oxyrrhynchium speciosum* (NT), *Petalophyllum ralfsii* (LC), *Plagiobryum zieri* (NT), *Plagiomnium cuspidatum* (NT), *Platydictya jungermannioides* (NT), *Rhizomnium pseudopunctatum* (NT), *Scapania cuspiduligera* (VU), *Schistidium robustum* (DD), *Schistidium trichodon* (VU), *Scleropodium cespitans* (NT), *Seligeria oelandica* (VU), *Seligeria patula* (NT), *Solenostoma subellipticum* (NT), *Timmia norvegica* (VU), *Tortella densa* (NT), *Tortula marginata* (NT)

Cuilcagh Mountain, Cos Cavan and Fermanagh.

16. Cuilcagh, Marlbank and Boleybrack IBrA

Location Cos Cavan, Fermanagh, Leitrim

Core hectads H03, H12

Criteria A

Protected sites included
IE0002032 Boleybrack Mountain SAC (4244 ha)
IE0000584 Cuilcagh-Anierin Uplands SAC (9740 ha)
UK0016603 Cuilcagh Mountain SAC (2744 ha)
Crossmurrin NR (96 ha)
Marble Arch NR (24 ha)

Unprotected sites included
Glenfarne (H03 – site for *Solenostoma sphaerocarpum*)
Glengevlin (H12 – poorly localised site for *Orthotrichum rivulare*)
Marlbank

Synopsis
Gritstone hills with rock outcrops, boulder scree, limestone karst and wooded ravine supporting a variety of species, including *Dicranodontium asperulum*, which is restricted in Ireland to this area; also shale banks with *Discelium nudum*.

Key taxa
Antitrichia curtipendula (NT), *Aulacomnium androgynum* (VU), *Daltonia splachnoides* (LC), *Dicranodontium asperulum* (VU), *Discelium nudum* (NT – some colonies may be outside protected sites), *Orthotrichum rivulare* (NT), *Philonotis arnellii* (EN), *Philonotis caespitosa* (NT), *Platydictya jungermannioides* (NT), *Rhizomnium pseudopunctatum* (NT), *Solenostoma sphaerocarpum* (NT), *Sphenolobopsis pearsonii* (NT), *Tetrodontium brownianum* (NT), *Thuidium recognitum* (VU), *Tortella densa* (NT)

Lough Oughter, Co. Cavan.

17. Lough Oughter and Associated Loughs IBrA

Location Co. Cavan

Core hectads H30

Criteria A

Protected sites included
IE0000007 Lough Oughter and Associated Loughs SAC (4758 ha)

Unprotected sites included
None

Synopsis
Lough Oughter supports a good example of the ephemeral bryophyte flora that develops in the inundation zones of lakes and rivers.

Key taxa
Ephemerum crassinervium subsp. *rutheanum* (NT), *Fissidens monguillonii* (NT), *Hygroamblystegium humile* (EN), *Plagiomnium cuspidatum* (NT), *Scleropodium cespitans* (NT), *Weissia rostellata* (NT)

Silent Valley, Mourne Mountains, Co. Down.

18. Mourne Mountains and Murlough IBrA

Location Co. Down

Core hectads J32, J33

Criteria A

Protected sites included
UK0016615 Eastern Mournes SAC (7507 ha)
UK0016612 Murlough SAC (11,902 ha)

Unprotected sites included
West of Dundrum (J39553569 – site for *Phascum cuspidatum* var. *papillosum*)

Synopsis
The Mournes are a large and mainly acidic upland massif supporting a good range of montane taxa; Murlough is a dune system notable chiefly for the presence of *Tortella inclinata* and *Racomitrium canescens*.

Key taxa
Cladopodiella francisci (VU), *Grimmia decipiens* (NT), *Grimmia funalis* (NT), *Grimmia ramondii* (NT), *Kurzia sylvatica* (NT), *Marsupella adusta* (NT), *Marsupella sprucei* (VU), *Phascum cuspidatum* var. *papillosum* (DD), *Racomitrium canescens* (VU), *Tortella inclinata* (EN)

Carlingford Mountain, Co. Louth.

19. Cooley Mountains IBrA

Location Co. Louth

Core hectad J11

Criteria A

Protected sites included
IE0000453 Carlingford Mountain SAC (3101 ha)

Unprotected sites included
None

Synopsis
The Cooley Mountains lie to the south-west of the Mourne Mountains and comprise two acidic upland ridges, with exposures of granites, slates and gabbro. They support a good range of montane bryophytes, including two of the three known populations of *Pogonatum nanum* in Ireland.

Key taxa
Campylopus subulatus (VU), *Grimmia decipiens* (NT), *Grimmia ramondii* (NT), *Hedwigia integrifolia* (VU), *Leiocolea bantriensis* (NT), *Marsupella funckii* (NT), *Pogonatum nanum* (EN)

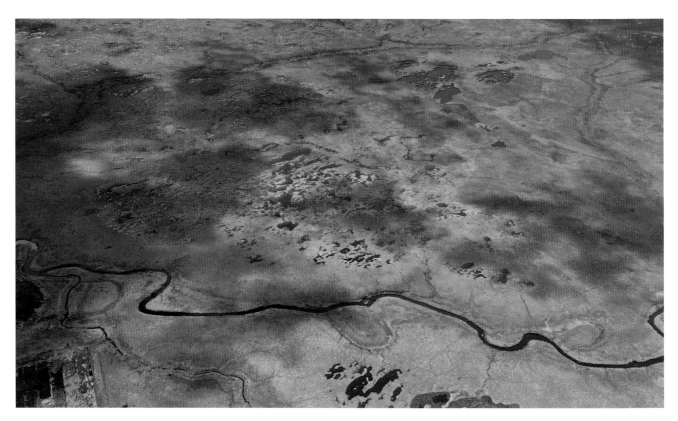

Knockmoyle, Co. Mayo.

20. North Mayo IBrA

Location Co. Mayo

Core hectads F84, F91, F92, G01, G02

Criteria A, B, C

Protected sites included
IE0001922 Bellacorick Bog Complex SAC (9524 ha)
IE0000466 Bellacorick Iron Flush SAC (17 ha)
IE0000476 Carrowmore Lake Complex SAC (3648 ha)
IE0000500 Glenamoy Bog Complex SAC (12,902 ha)
Ballycroy National Park (Lough Nambrackkeagh area only, F943154)

Unprotected sites included
Lough Keeran (F943154 – site for *Tomentypnum nitens*)

Synopsis
Comprising an outstanding series of blanket bogs, fens and lakes, with the only known populations of *Paludella squarrosa* and *Leiocolea rutheana* in Ireland. The IBrA also includes the dune and machair system at Garter Hill, which has an important assemblage of coastal taxa, including large populations of *Petalophyllum ralfsii*.

Key taxa
Abietinella abietina var. *hystricosa* (NT), *Bryum dyffrynense* (NT), *Bryum marratii* (LC), *Bryum warneum* (EN), *Catoscopium nigritum* (NT), *Cephalozia pleniceps* (VU), *Hamatocaulis vernicosus* (NT), *Leiocolea rutheana* var. *rutheana* (EN), *Paludella squarrosa* (CR), *Petalophyllum ralfsii* (LC), *Pseudocalliergon lycopodioides* (VU), *Sphagnum teres* (NT), *Sphagnum warnstorfii* (VU), *Tomentypnum nitens* (VU)

Croagh Patrick, Co. Mayo.

21. Croagh Patrick IBrA

Location Co. Mayo

Core hectad L98

Criteria A, B

Protected sites included
000483 Croagh Patrick pNHA (1667 ha)

Unprotected sites included
None

Synopsis
An isolated mountain north of the main concentration of oceanic bryophytes in Connemara, Croagh Patrick nevertheless supports a good representation of montane oceanic communities, including rare species.

Key taxa
Adelanthus lindenbergianus (VU), *Andreaea megistospora* (VU), *Bazzania pearsonii* (VU), *Dicranodontium uncinatum* (VU), *Eremonotus myriocarpus* (NT), *Grimmia decipiens* (NT), *Hylocomiastrum umbratum* (NT), *Marsupella adusta* (NT), *Nardia geoscyphus* (NT), *Plagiobryum zieri* (NT), *Rhabdoweisia crispata* (NT), *Scapania ornithopodioides* (VU), *Schistidium strictum* (NT)

Shingle beach, Trawmore, south of Dookinelly, Achill Island, Co. Mayo.

22. Achill Island and Corraun Plateau IBrA

Location Co. Mayo

Core hectads F50, F60, F70, L79

Criteria A, B, C

Protected sites included
IE0000485 Corraun Plateau SAC (3887 ha)
IE0001955 Croaghaun/Slievemore SAC (3295 ha)
IE0001497 Doogort Machair/Lough Doo SAC (184 ha)
IE0001513 Keel Machair/Menaun Cliffs SAC (1616 ha)

Unprotected sites included
E. of Doo Lough (F71380943 – site for *Pohlia filum*)
E. of Keel (F6705 – site for *Campylopus subulatus* and *Scapania curta*)
E. of Pollranny (F759007 – site for *Aongstroemia longipes* and *Pohlia filum*)
Sraheens Lough (L7299 – site for *Cephalozia crassifolia* and *Telaranea europaea*)
SE of Killeenabausty (L70549407 – site for *Fossombronia maritima*)
SW of Keel (F61880385 – site for *Cephalozia pleniceps*)
Slievemore deserted village (F624070, F639072 – site for *Atrichum tenellum* and *Nardia geoscyphus*)

Keel Lough, Achill Island, Co. Mayo.

Synopsis

Achill Island is one of the three most important areas in Ireland for oceanic bryophytes, with a huge diversity of species, many of them growing in great abundance. The habitats are relatively undamaged compared with those in Connemara. Corraun Plateau, on the mainland, is a logical extension of this site, with many of the same oceanic taxa. There are also important areas of machair, supporting many coastal rarities, and fen, some of which are outside protected areas. A number of localities, such as old quarries with rare taxa, are included in the site.

Key taxa

Adelanthus lindenbergianus (VU), *Anthelia juratzkana* (NT), *Aongstroemia longipes* (CR), *Atrichum tenellum* (NT), *Bazzania pearsonii* (VU), *Bryum calophyllum* (EN), *Bryum dyffrynense* (NT), *Bryum marratii* (LC), *Bryum riparium* (EN), *Campylopus subulatus* (VU), *Catoscopium nigritum* (NT), *Cephalozia crassifolia* (EN), *Cephalozia pleniceps* (VU), *Cyclodictyon laetevirens* (NT), *Dicranella cerviculata* (NT), *Dicranodontium uncinatum* (VU), *Douinia ovata* (NT), *Fossombronia fimbriata* (VU), *Fossombronia maritima* (NT), *Geocalyx graveolens* (EN), *Grimmia ramondii* (NT), *Hylocomiastrum umbratum* (NT), *Hypnum callichroum* (NT), *Kurzia sylvatica* (NT), *Leiocolea gillmanii* (VU), *Leptodontium flexifolium* (NT), *Marsupella funckii* (NT), *Marsupella sprucei* (VU), *Mastigophora woodsii* (NT), *Metzgeria leptoneura* (NT), *Molendoa warburgii* (VU), *Nardia geoscyphus* (NT), *Odontoschisma elongatum* (NT), *Petalophyllum ralfsii* (LC), *Philonotis rigida* (VU), *Plagiomnium cuspidatum* (NT), *Plagiothecium cavifolium* (VU), *Platyhypnidium lusitanicum* (NT), *Pohlia filum* (VU), *Rhizomnium pseudopunctatum* (NT), *Rhodobryum roseum* (NT), *Scapania curta* (VU), *Scapania cuspiduligera* (VU), *Scapania lingulata* (DD), *Scapania ornithopodioides* (VU), *Solenostoma subellipticum* (NT), *Telaranea europaea* (NT), *Tortella inclinata* (EN), *Tortula marginata* (NT), *Tortula modica* (VU), *Tritomaria exsecta* (VU)

Inishard, Lough Mask, Co. Mayo.

23. Lough Carra and Lough Mask IBrA

Location Cos Galway, Mayo

Core hectads M16, M17

Criteria A, B, C

Protected sites included
IE0001774 Lough Carra/Mask Complex SAC (13,527 ha)

Unprotected sites included
E.of Ballintober (M17 – site for *Orthotrichum pallens*)

Synopsis
An extensive hard-water lake system with associated fens, calcareous grasslands, limestone pavement and rivers. Lake margins support the only known populations of *Bryum gemmiparum* and *B. knowltonii* in Ireland. Large populations of *Hamatocaulis vernicosus* occur on the west shore of Lough Mask. Ephemeral bryophytes occur on the exposed banks in the inundation zone of the Cloon River, including *Ephemerum spinulosum*. Extended to include a site for *Orthotrichum pallens*, epiphytic on Sycamore.

Key taxa
Bryum caespiticium (VU), *Bryum gemmiparum* (VU), *Bryum knowltonii* (EN), *Campyliadelphus elodes* (NT), *Cephalozia pleniceps* (VU – possibly outside protected area but not accurately localised), *Ephemerum crassinervium* subsp. *rutheanum* (NT), *Ephemerum crassinervium* subsp. *sessile* (NT), *Ephemerum spinulosum* (EN), *Hamatocaulis vernicosus* (NT), *Hygroamblystegium varium* (NT – possibly outside protected area but not accurately localised), *Kurzia sylvatica* (NT – possibly outside protected area but not accurately localised), *Orthotrichum pallens* (EN), *Plagiomnium cuspidatum* (NT), *Plasteurhynchium striatulum* (NT), *Pseudocalliergon lycopodioides* (VU), *Scapania gymnostomophila* (VU), *Tortella densa* (NT), *Tortula marginata* (NT), *Weissia rostellata* (NT)

Mannin Lakes, Co. Mayo.

24. Mannin and Island Lakes IBrA

Location Co. Mayo

Core hectad M48

Criteria A

Protected sites included
IE0002298 River Moy SAC (15,396 ha) (Mannin and Island Lakes only)

Unprotected sites included
None

Synopsis
Marl lakes with rare bryophytes growing amongst the emergent marginal vegetation.

Key taxa
Bryum intermedium (EN), *Bryum uliginosum* (EN), *Pseudocalliergon lycopodioides* (VU)

Carrowbehy/Caher Bog, Co. Roscommon.

25. Carrowbehy/Caher Bog IBrA

Location Co. Roscommon

Core hectad M58

Criteria A, C

Protected sites included
IE0000597 Carrowbehy/Caher Bog SAC (344 ha)

Unprotected sites included
None

Synopsis
One of the best west-midland raised bogs, this site also includes a fen, with a number of rare species present. Eighteen species of *Sphagnum* have been recorded, and there is a good representation of bog liverworts.

Key taxa
Cephalozia pleniceps (VU), *Sphagnum flexuosum* (VU), *Sphagnum subsecundum* (NT), *Sphagnum teres* (NT), *Sphagnum warnstorfii* (VU)

Bellanagare Bog, Co. Roscommon.

26. Cloonshanville and Bellanagare Bogs IBrA

Location Co. Roscommon

Core hectads M78, M79

Criteria C

Protected sites included
IE0000592 Bellanagare Bog SAC (1208 ha)
IE0000614 Cloonshanville Bog SAC (226 ha)

Unprotected sites included
None

Synopsis
This IBrA has been selected because these two adjacent raised bogs have large areas of active uncut peat surfaces with a very good structure and an outstanding assemblage of bog *Sphagnum*, with at least 15 species recorded, including abundant *S. pulchrum*.

Key taxa
None

Lough Rinn, Co. Leitrim.

27. Lough Rinn IBrA

Location Co. Leitrim

Core hectad N09

Criteria A

Protected sites included
001417 Lough Rinn pNHA (278 ha)

Unprotected sites included
None

Synopsis
Midland lake with interesting and rare bryophytes growing at its margins, in the inundation zone, including two species of *Ephemerum* that are characteristic specialists of this habitat.

Key taxa
Ephemerum cohaerens (VU), *Ephemerum crassinervium* subsp. *rutheanum* (NT), *Fissidens monguillonii* (NT), *Plagiomnium cuspidatum* (NT), *Scleropodium cespitans* (NT)

Truska Machair, Slyne Head, Co. Galway.

28. West Galway Coast IBrA

Location Co. Galway

Core hectads L54, L55, L63, L64

Criteria A, C

Protected sites included
IE0002129 Murvey Machair SAC (80 ha)
IE0001309 Omey Island Machair SAC (229 ha)
IE0002074 Slyne Head Peninsula SAC (4028 ha)

Unprotected sites included
None

Synopsis
Important and extensive areas of machair on the Galway coast with the largest populations of *Petalophyllum ralfsii* in Ireland (at Slyne Head) and several other coastal taxa.

Key taxa
Bryum calophyllum (EN), *Bryum dyffrynense* (NT), *Campyliadelphus elodes* (NT), *Catoscopium nigritum* (NT), *Petalophyllum ralfsii* (LC), *Thuidium recognitum* (VU)

North corrie, Mweelrea, Co. Mayo.

29. West Galway and South Mayo IBrA

Location Cos Galway, Mayo

Core hectads L63, L64, L74, L75, L76, L84, L86, L94, L96

Criteria A, B, C

Protected sites included
IE0002034 Connemara Bog Complex SAC (49,228 ha)
IE0002008 Maumturk Mountains SAC (13,472 ha)
IE0001932 Mweelrea/Sheeffry/Erriff Complex SAC (20,983 ha)
IE0002031 The Twelve Bens/Garraun Complex SAC (16,170 ha)
001253 Dernasliggaun Wood pNHA (23 ha)
000735 Maumtrasna Mountain Complex pNHA (12,897 ha)

Unprotected sites included
Derrylea Lough (L74 – site for *Pseudocalliergon trifarium*)
Letterdife House (L724415 – site for *Leptobarbula berica* and *Tortula marginata*)
Lough Donoghmeave (L652466 – site for *Fissidens fontanus*)
Ballinaboy (L65054821 – site for *Grimmia funalis*)
Tullyconor Bridge (L86 – site for *Aneura mirabilis* and several riverine taxa)

Synopsis
This vast and mountainous part of west Galway and south Mayo, along with Achill Island and Corraun Plateau IBrA and Killarney IBrA, is one of the three most outstanding areas in Ireland for oceanic taxa, with many rare and restricted species present, including *Plagiochila carringtonii* at its only locality in Ireland, and many other representatives of the Northern Atlantic

144

Pollacappul Lough, Kylemore, Co. Galway, view to south with Benbaun on left.

hepatic mat community. Mweelrea is the only known current locality in Ireland for *Hygrohypnum duriusculum*, *Oedipodium griffithianum*, *Ptilium crista-castrensis* and *Philonotis cernua*. The peatlands are also important, with good areas of fen vegetation, as well as extensive areas of lowland blanket bog rich in *Sphagnum* species. The site includes Dooaghtry, an important coastal machair with large populations of *Petalophyllum ralfsii* and *Catoscopium nigritum*.

Key taxa
Acrobolbus wilsonii (VU), *Adelanthus lindenbergianus* (VU), *Amphidium lapponicum* (VU), *Andreaea megistospora* (VU), *Aneura mirabilis* (VU – possibly outside SAC but not accurately localised), *Arctoa fulvella* (VU), *Atrichum tenellum* (NT – possibly outside SAC but not accurately localised), *Bazzania pearsonii* (VU), *Bryum calophyllum* (EN), *Bryum marratii* (LC), *Bryum riparium* (EN), *Campylopus atrovirens* var. *falcatus* (NT), *Catoscopium nigritum* (NT), *Cephalozia crassifolia* (EN), *Daltonia splachnoides* (LC), *Dicranodontium uncinatum* (VU), *Ditrichum zonatum* (EN), *Douinia ovata* (NT), *Eremonotus myriocarpus* (NT), *Fissidens fontanus* (VU), *Fissidens serrulatus* (VU), *Fontinalis antipyretica* var. *gracilis* (NT), *Fossombronia caespitiformis* subsp. *multispira* (DD), *Fossombronia fimbriata* (VU – possibly outside SAC but not accurately localised), *Grimmia decipiens* (NT), *Grimmia donniana* (NT), *Grimmia funalis* (NT), *Gymnomitrion obtusum* (NT), *Hageniella micans* (NT), *Hamatocaulis vernicosus* (NT), *Hygrohypnum duriusculum* (CR), *Hylocomiastrum umbratum* (NT), *Hypnum callichroum* (NT), *Kurzia sylvatica* (NT), *Leiocolea bantriensis* (NT), *Lejeunea eckloniana* (NT), *Lejeunea flava* subsp. *moorei* (VU), *Lejeunea hibernica* (NT), *Leptobarbula berica* (VU), *Lophozia opacifolia* (VU), *Marsupella adusta* (NT), *Marsupella funckii* (NT), *Marsupella sprucei* (VU), *Mastigophora woodsii* (NT), *Metzgeria leptoneura* (NT), *Mnium thomsonii* (NT), *Oedipodium griffithianum* (CR), *Paraleptodontium recurvifolium* (NT), *Petalophyllum ralfsii* (LC), *Philonotis cernua* (CR), *Philonotis rigida* (VU), *Philonotis tomentella* (VU), *Plagiobryum zieri* (NT), *Plagiochila carringtonii* (EN), *Plagiothecium denticulatum* var. *obtusifolium* (NT), *Platyhypnidium lusitanicum* (NT), *Pogonatum nanum* (EN), *Pohlia elongata* var. *elongata* (NT), *Pohlia elongata* var. *greenii* (EN), *Pseudocalliergon trifarium* (VU), *Ptilium crista-castrensis* (CR), *Racomitrium macounii* subsp. *alpinum* (VU), *Rhabdoweisia crispata* (NT), *Rhizomnium pseudopunctatum* (NT), *Radula holtii* (NT), *Scapania nimbosa* (EN), *Scapania ornithopodioides* (VU), *Scapania subalpina* (DD), *Sematophyllum demissum* (NT), *Solenostoma paroicum* (NT), *Solenostoma subellipticum* (NT), *Sphagnum affine* (VU), *Sphagnum flexuosum* (VU), *Sphagnum platyphyllum* (NT), *Sphagnum skyense* (DD), *Sphagnum strictum* (DD), *Sphagnum subsecundum* (NT), *Sphagnum warnstorfii* (VU), *Sphenolobopsis pearsonii* (NT), *Telaranea europaea* (NT), *Tetrodontium brownianum* (NT), *Tomentypnum nitens* (VU), *Tortula marginata* (NT)

Lough Ree, east shore at Cow Island, Co. Longford.

30. Lough Ree IBrA

Location Cos Longford, Roscommon, Westmeath

Core hectads M95, N04, N05, N06

Criteria A, C

Protected sites included
IE0000448 Fortwilliam Turlough SAC (52 ha)
IE0000440 Lough Ree SAC (14,371 ha)

Unprotected sites included
Doonis Lough (N05 – site for several bog liverworts)
Tully Cross (N0742 – site for *Cephaloziella elachista* and *Dicranella cerviculata*)
W. of Elfeet (N01406013 – site for *Ephemerum cohaerens*)

Synopsis
A large lake in the midlands with a rich bryophyte flora at the margins, in the inundation zone, on emergent rocks and in swampy woodland; the IBrA also includes some good examples of raised bog nearby, which are, however, unprotected.

Key taxa
Campyliadelphus elodes (NT), *Cephalozia pleniceps* (VU), *Cephaloziella elachista* (DD), *Cephaloziella rubella* (VU), *Cephaloziella spinigera* (DD), *Dicranella cerviculata* (NT), *Drepanocladus sendtneri* (NT), *Encalypta vulgaris* (NT), *Ephemerum cohaerens* (VU), *Fontinalis antipyretica* var. *cymbifolia* (DD), *Hygroamblystegium fluviatile* (NT), *Hygroamblystegium humile* (EN), *Hygroamblystegium varium* (NT), *Oxyrrhynchium speciosum* (NT), *Porella cordaeana* (NT – at Killinure Lough, possibly outside protected area), *Pseudocalliergon lycopodioides* (VU), *Tortula marginata* (NT – at Killinure Lough, possibly outside protected area)

Scragh Bog, Co. Westmeath.

31. Scragh Bog IBrA

Location Co. Westmeath

Core hectads N45

Criteria A, B, C

Protected sites included
IE0000692 Scragh Bog SAC (24 ha)

Unprotected sites included
None

Synopsis
A small fen with a rich flora, including an exceptionally large population of *Hamatocaulis vernicosus*. It is also considered important because it is one of the best remaining examples of this habitat in the Irish midlands.

Key taxa
Cinclidium stygium (VU), *Hamatocaulis vernicosus* (NT), *Ricciocarpos natans* (NT), *Tomentypnum nitens* (VU)

Clara Bog, Co. Offaly.

32. Clara Bog IBrA

Location Co. Offaly

Core hectad N23

Criteria A, C

Protected sites included
IE0000572 Clara Bog SAC (837 ha)

Unprotected sites included
None

Synopsis
One of the largest of the remaining raised bogs in Co. Offaly, this site is notable for the record of *Tetraplodon angustatus* at its only site in Ireland, although it has not been seen since its discovery in 1988 and might have been a transient occurrence. The site is selected as an IBrA because of the extent and quality of its bryophyte-rich raised bog habitat, as well as the presence of a protected species.

Key taxa
Cephalozia loitlesbergeri (VU), *Tetraplodon angustatus* (DD)

Bull Island, Co. Dublin.

33. Dublin Bay IBrA

Location Co. Dublin

Core hectads O23

Criteria A, B, C

Protected sites included
IE0000202 Howth Head SAC (375 ha)
IE0000206 North Dublin Bay SAC (1475 ha)

Unprotected sites included
Howth (O23 – site for *Didymodon umbrosus*, probably outside SAC)

Synopsis
North Bull Island holds important dune slack bryophytes that include the only east coast occurrence of *Petalophyllum ralfsii*. Additionally, Howth has some interesting maritime turf on the cliff tops. Numerous other rare species have been recorded from Howth in the past, but most have not been seen for many years.

Key taxa
Bryum bornholmense (NT), *Bryum intermedium* (EN), *Bryum marratii* (LC), *Bryum uliginosum* (EN), *Bryum warneum* (EN), *Didymodon umbrosus* (VU), *Petalophyllum ralfsii* (LC), *Rhynchostegium megapolitanum* (NT)

Scarr Mountain, with Djouce Mountain behind, Co. Wicklow.

34. Wicklow Mountains IBrA

Location Cos Dublin, Wicklow

Core hectads N90, O00, O10, O11, O12, O21, O22, T08, T09, T19

Criteria A, C

Protected sites included
IE0000719 Glen of The Downs SAC (74 ha)
IE0000725 Knocksink Wood SAC (90 ha)
IE0002122 Wicklow Mountains SAC (32,946 ha)
001754 Dargle River Valley pNHA (19 ha)
001769 Great Sugar Loaf pNHA (339 ha)
000731 Poulaphouca Reservoir pNHA (2216 ha)
001767 Powerscourt Waterfall pNHA (83 ha)
001771 Vartry Reservoir pNHA (352 ha)

Unprotected sites included
Ballybarney Bridge (S9790 – site for *Brachytheciastrum velutinum*)
Ballycorus (O2220 – site for several metallophyte species)
Ballycoyle (O1615 – site for *Cephalozia pleniceps* and *Kurzia sylvatica*)
Ballycurragh, S. of Lugnaquilla (T061831 – site for *Plagiothecium laetum*)
Ballyreagh Wood (O11 – site for *Philonotis caespitosa*)
Glencree (O142180 – site for *Solenostoma sphaerocarpum*)
Glendalough, Seven Churches (T12309670 – site *Orthotrichum stramineum*)
Glenmalur (T0694 – site for *Southbya tophacea* and *Sphagnum girgensohnii*; T0892 – site for *Cephaloziella stellulifera* and *Fissidens polyphyllus*)

Glenmacnass Valley, Wicklow Mountains, Co. Wicklow.

Kilmashogue Mountain (O152262346 – site for *Grimmia orbicularis*)
Rathduffmore Bog (T0182 – site for several bog liverworts, including *Pallavicinia lyellii*)
SW slopes of White Hill, N. of Roundwood (O180084 – site for *Plagiothecium laetum*)

Synopsis
The largest mountain massif on the east side of Ireland, the Wicklow Mountains have some significant bryophyte communities and rare species, in spite of the rarity of base-rich rocks. There are important montane communities on the high ground, while localities such as Glendalough and Powerscourt Waterfall are rich and varied in saxicolous and epiphytic species. Oceanic species are also present, although much less so than in the west of Ireland. Peripheral sites hold important bog, metallophyte, epiphyte and riverine communities. Old records suggest that this area was formerly even richer, but land-use change over the past 200 years has contributed to the decline or disappearance of many species.

Key taxa
Aneura mirabilis (VU), *Aulacomnium androgynum* (VU), *Barbilophozia barbata* (CR), *Brachydontium trichodes* (EN), *Brachytheciastrum velutinum* (EN), *Bryum bornholmense* (NT), *Cephalozia macrostachya* var. *spiniflora* (DD), *Cephalozia pleniceps* (VU), *Cephaloziella massalongi* (VU), *Cephaloziella nicholsonii* (VU), *Cephaloziella rubella* (VU), *Cephaloziella spinigera* (DD), *Cephaloziella stellulifera* (NT), *Cephaloziella turneri* (VU), *Diplophyllum obtusifolium* (NT), *Ditrichum plumbicola* (EN), *Ditrichum zonatum* (EN), *Douinia ovata* (NT), *Fissidens polyphyllus* (VU), *Fissidens rufulus* (EN), *Grimmia decipiens* (NT), *Grimmia donniana* (NT), *Grimmia orbicularis* (VU), *Grimmia ramondii* (NT), *Gymnomitrion obtusum* (NT), *Hedwigia integrifolia* (VU), *Heterocladium wulfsbergii* (NT), *Kurzia sylvatica* (NT), *Leptodontium flexifolium* (NT), *Marsupella sphacelata* (VU), *Marsupella funckii* (NT – Upper Lake, possibly outside protected area but not accurately localised), *Marsupella sprucei* (VU), *Orthotrichum stramineum* (VU), *Pallavicinia lyellii* (EN), *Philonotis caespitosa* (NT), *Plagiothecium curvifolium* (VU), *Plagiothecium laetum* (VU), *Plagiothecium denticulatum* var. *obtusifolium* (NT), *Plagiothecium platyphyllum* (VU), *Platyhypnidium lusitanicum* (NT), *Racomitrium elongatum* (VU), *Rhabdoweisia crispata* (NT), *Rhabdoweisia fugax* (VU), *Riccia hueberiana* (DD), *Solenostoma sphaerocarpum* (NT), *Southbya tophacea* (CR), *Sphagnum girgensohnii* (NT), *Sphagnum russowii* (NT), *Tetrodontium brownianum* (NT), *Weissia longifolia* var. *angustifolia* (VU)

The Burren, near Black Head, Co. Clare.

35. The Burren IBrA

Location Cos Clare, Galway

Core hectads M10, M41, R29, R38, R39

Criteria A, C

Protected sites included

IE0000020 Black Head-Poulsallagh Complex SAC (7805 ha)

IE0000242 Castletaylor Complex SAC (146 ha)

IE0000032 Dromore Woods and Loughs SAC (877 ha)

IE0001926 East Burren Complex SAC (18,814 ha)

Unprotected sites included

Addroon Bridge (R358878 – site for *Plasteurhynchium striatulum*)

Ballycorey Bridge, R. Fergus (R347809 – site for *Hygroamblystegium fluviatile*)

Ballyogan Bridge (R335892 – site for *Plasteurhynchium striatulum* and *Schistidium elegantulum* subsp. *elegantulum*)

Killinaboy, R. Fergus (R2691 – site for *Porella cordaeana*)

Nutfield Bridge, R. Fergus (R34298332 – site for *Fontinalis antipyretica* var. *gracilis*)

Synopsis

Famous as the most extensive karst landscape in Ireland, the Carboniferous Limestone of The Burren supports a wide range of calcicolous taxa, many of them in fens, marl lakes and turloughs, and on lake margins and riversides, but also growing directly on rock and walls. Some bog is also included.

Key taxa

Amblystegium confervoides (NT), *Campyliadelphus elodes* (NT), *Cephalozia pleniceps* (VU), *Cephaloziella spinigera* (DD), *Cephaloziella stellulifera* (NT), *Cinclidium stygium* (VU), *Didymodon acutus* (EN), *Drepanocladus sendtneri* (NT), *Fontinalis antipyretica* var. *gracilis* (NT), *Grimmia dissimulata* (VU), *Hygroamblystegium fluviatile* (NT), *Leiocolea bantriensis* (NT), *Leptodon smithii* (EN), *Orthothecium rufescens* (NT), *Petalophyllum ralfsii* (LC), *Plasteurhynchium striatulum* (NT), *Pleurochaete squarrosa* (NT), *Porella cordaeana* (NT), *Pseudocalliergon lycopodioides* (VU), *Pseudocalliergon trifarium* (VU), *Schistidium elegantulum* subsp. *elegantulum* (DD), *Scleropodium cespitans* (NT), *Solenostoma sphaerocarpum* (NT), *Tortella densa* (NT)

Keeper Hill, Co. Tipperary.

36. Keeper Hill and Silvermine Mountains IBrA

Location Co. Tipperary

Core hectads R86, R87

Criteria A, C

Protected sites included
IE0001197 Keeper Hill SAC (414 ha)

Unprotected sites included
Garryard West (R8271 – site for *Bryum torquescens* and *Cephaloziella stellulifera*)
Keeper Hill outside SAC (R86 – possible site for several species)
Shallee (R8071 – site for several metallophyte species)

Synopsis
Several interesting plants have been recorded from Keeper Hill, but unfortunately most of them were not accurately localised, so it is impossible to know whether they were recorded within the SAC. One of these is *Oxyrrhynchium schleicheri* at its only known locality in Ireland, but this may have been eliminated by afforestation. The Silvermine Mountains support some good metallophyte communities, with rare species, but these are just outside the SAC.

Key taxa
Bryum torquescens (VU), *Cephaloziella nicholsonii* (VU), *Cephaloziella stellulifera* (NT), *Daltonia splachnoides* (LC), *Ditrichum plumbicola* (EN), *Douinia ovata* (NT), *Leptodontium flexifolium* (NT), *Oxyrrhynchium schleicheri* (CR – possibly outside protected area but not accurately localised), *Rhabdoweisia crispata* (NT), *Scapania lingulata* (DD – possibly outside protected area but not accurately localised)

Grageen Fen, Cos Limerick, Tipperary.

37. Clare Glen and Grageen Fen IBrA

Location Cos Limerick, Tipperary

Core hectad R75

Criteria A, C

Protected sites included
IE0000930 Clare Glen SAC (25 ha)
002186 Grageen Fen and Bog NHA (48 ha)

Unprotected sites included
None

Synopsis
A wooded river gorge with important Atlantic species and communities, plus a nearby fen.

Key taxa
Dumortiera hirsuta (NT), *Fontinalis antipyretica* var. *gracilis* (NT), *Hygroamblystegium fluviatile* (NT), *Kurzia sylvatica* (NT), *Lejeunea eckloniana* (NT), *Leptodontium flexifolium* (NT – possibly outside protected area but not accurately localised), *Tomentypnum nitens* (VU)

River Nore, south of Thomastown, Co. Kilkenny.

38. River Barrow and River Nore IBrA

Location Cos Carlow, Kildare, Kilkenny, Laois, Offaly, Tipperary, Waterford, Wexford

Core hectads S36, S55, S62, S70, S73, S74, S75

Criteria A

Protected sites included
IE0002162 River Barrow and River Nore SAC (12,373 ha) (in part only)
IE0000849 Spahill and Clomantagh Hill SAC (147 ha)

Unprotected sites included
Kilkenny Castle (S509557 – site for *Leptobarbula berica*)
S. of Graiguenamanagh (S705428 – site for *Orthotrichum stramineum*)
The Pink Point, Bearstown (S684232 – site for *Aulacomnium androgynum*, just outside protected area)
W. of Ballykeenan (S725448 – site for *Orthotrichum pallens* and *O. stramineum*)

Synopsis
This is a very diffuse site for its bryophytes, but the River Barrow and River Nore SAC and some immediately adjacent areas support a good range of bryophytes of various habitats, including some rarities. In addition, *Leptobarbula berica* has recently been found on the walls of Kilkenny Castle.

Key taxa
Aulacomnium androgynum (VU), *Bryum torquescens* (VU), *Cephaloziella turneri* (VU), *Didymodon umbrosus* (VU), *Fissidens exilis* (VU), *Grimmia orbicularis* (VU), *Leptobarbula berica* (VU), *Orthotrichum pallens* (EN), *Orthotrichum stramineum* (VU), *Rhynchostegium megapolitanum* (NT), *Tortula marginata* (NT)

Mount Leinster, Blackstairs Mountains, Cos Carlow and Wexford.

39. Blackstairs Mountains IBrA

Location Cos Carlow, Wexford

Core hectad S74, S84, S85

Criteria A

Protected sites included
IE0000770 Blackstairs Mountains SAC (5053 ha)

Unprotected sites included
River Clody (S85 – site for *Platyhypnidium lusitanicum*)
SW of Caim Cross Roads (S8840 – site for metallophyte species)

Synopsis
This range has some conglomerate rock outcrops with an interesting montane flora, and the corrie on Mount Leinster supports several oceanic species well to the east of their core range. In addition, the old copper-mine site near Caim Cross Roads has some rare metallophytes.

Key taxa
Cephaloziella nicholsonii (VU), *Cephaloziella stellulifera* (NT), *Gymnomitrion obtusum* (NT), *Leptodontium flexifolium* (NT), *Marsupella funckii* (NT – possibly outside protected area but not accurately localised), *Platyhypnidium lusitanicum* (NT), *Scopelophila cataractae* (VU), *Schistidium strictum* (NT), *Sphagnum russowii* (NT)

Galty Mountains, Cos Limerick and Tipperary.

40. Galty Mountains IBrA

Location Cos Limerick, Tipperary

Core hectads R82, R92

Criteria A

Protected sites included
IE0000646 Galtee Mountains SAC (6422 ha)

Unprotected sites included
Temple Hill (R83032153 – site for *Encalypta ciliata* and *Schistidium strictum*)
Clydagh River (R874273 – site for *Dumortiera hirsuta*)

Synopsis
A high mountain range with frequent outcrops of base-rich rock, and supporting significant montane communities, including rare species. The best bryophyte assemblages are centred on the crags above the small mountain lakes in the north-facing corries. *Encalypta ciliata*, perhaps the rarest and most threatened of these, occurs on a prominent rock outcrop that is just outside the SAC. This is the only known site in Ireland for this species.

Key taxa
Bartramia ithyphylla (VU), *Dumortiera hirsuta* (NT), *Encalypta ciliata* (CR), *Grimmia ramondii* (NT), *Grimmia torquata* (NT), *Metzgeria leptoneura* (NT), *Mnium marginatum* var. *marginatum* (NT), *Plagiobryum zieri* (NT), *Plagiothecium denticulatum* var. *obtusifolium* (NT), *Pohlia elongata* var. *elongata* (NT), *Pohlia elongata* var. *greenii* (EN), *Rhabdoweisia crispata* (NT), *Schistidium strictum* (NT), *Solenostoma paroicum* (NT), *Sphagnum russowii* (NT), *Sphenolobopsis pearsonii* (NT)

View from Cloghane towards Brandon, Co. Kerry.

41. Dingle Peninsula IBrA

Location Co. Kerry

Core hectads Q40, Q41, Q50, Q61, Q70, V39

Criteria A, B, C

Protected sites included
IE0000343 Castlemaine Harbour (8687 ha)
IE0000375 Mount Brandon SAC (14,355 ha)
IE0002185 Slieve Mish Mountains SAC (9792 ha)
IE0002070 Tralee Bay and Magharees Peninsula, West to Cloghane SAC (11,632 ha)

Unprotected sites included
Mount Eagle (V3399 – site for oceanic species, including *Radula carringtonii*)

Synopsis
The mountain ranges of the Dingle Peninsula are of great bryological importance and are only slightly less rich in rare and oceanic taxa than the Killarney IBrA to the south. Several species occur here in more abundance than elsewhere in Ireland, especially *Lejeunea* spp. and *Radula carringtonii*, and there are excellent examples of the Northern Atlantic hepatic mat community. Old records indicate that Mount Brandon was once even richer, and species may have disappeared as a result of botanical collecting, climate, or both. The dune systems at Inch, Rossbehy and Magharees Peninsula, each with populations of *Petalophyllum ralfsii*, are also included.

158

Faha Ridge, below Brandon, Co. Kerry.

Key taxa

Acrobolbus wilsonii (VU), *Adelanthus lindenbergianus* (VU), *Amphidium lapponicum* (VU), *Anthelia juratzkana* (NT), *Antitrichia curtipendula* (NT), *Bazzania pearsonii* (VU), *Bryum marratii* (LC), *Campylopus atrovirens* var. *falcatus* (NT), *Campylopus shawii* (NT), *Cyclodictyon laetevirens* (NT), *Daltonia splachnoides* (LC), *Drepanocladus sendtneri* (NT), *Dumortiera hirsuta* (NT), *Grimmia donniana* (NT), *Grimmia funalis* (NT), *Grimmia muehlenbeckii* (DD), *Grimmia ramondii* (NT), *Grimmia torquata* (NT), *Hageniella micans* (NT), *Heterocladium wulfsbergii* (NT), *Hylocomiastrum umbratum* (NT), *Hypnum callichroum* (NT), *Leiocolea bantriensis* (NT), *Lejeunea eckloniana* (NT), *Lejeunea flava* subsp. *moorei* (VU), *Lejeunea hibernica* (NT), *Lejeunea mandonii* (EN), *Mastigophora woodsii* (NT), *Metzgeria leptoneura* (NT), *Moerckia hibernica* (DD), *Paraleptodontium recurvifolium* (NT), *Petalophyllum ralfsii* (LC), *Plagiothecium cavifolium* (VU), *Plagiothecium denticulatum* var. *obtusifolium* (NT), *Platyhypnidium lusitanicum* (NT), *Pohlia elongata* var. *elongata* (NT), *Porella cordaeana* (NT), *Radula carringtonii* (NT), *Radula holtii* (NT), *Rhabdoweisia crispata* (NT), *Scapania gymnostomophila* (VU), *Scapania nimbosa* (EN), *Scapania ornithopodioides* (VU), *Schistidium strictum* (NT), *Sphagnum platyphyllum* (NT), *Sphenolobopsis pearsonii* (NT), *Tritomaria exsecta* (VU)

Torc Mountain from Newfoundland Bay, Killarney, Co. Kerry.

42. Killarney IBrA

Location Cos Cork, Kerry

Core hectads V68, V77, V78, V87, V88, V97, V98

Criteria A, B, C

Protected sites included
IE0000365 Killarney National Park, Macgillycuddy's Reeks and Caragh River Catchment SAC (76,478 ha)
IE0002173 Blackwater River (Kerry) SAC (5903 ha)

Unprotected sites included
Ardtully E. of Cloontoo (V986728 – site for several riverine species)

Synopsis
One of the three most important areas for oceanic bryophytes in Ireland, this very large site also contains Ireland's largest remaining area of semi-natural woodland. This is exceptionally rich in bryophytes, especially at classic localities such as Torc Cascade and O'Sullivan's Cascade. Because of the extreme south-western position of this IBrA, several Macaronesian species, most notably *Hypnum uncinulatum*, have their Irish headquarters here. The Reeks, though not as rich as might be expected, support a range of montane species and good examples of the Northern Atlantic hepatic mat community. There are also some good localities for riverine species and a site for metallophytes within the IBrA.

Key taxa
Acrobolbus wilsonii (VU), *Amphidium lapponicum* (VU), *Andreaea megistospora* (VU), *Aneura mirabilis* (VU), *Antitrichia curtipendula* (NT), *Arctoa fulvella* (VU), *Bazzania pearsonii* (VU), *Campyliadelphus elodes* (NT), *Campylopus shawii* (NT), *Campylostelium saxicola*

160

Lough Erhogh, Co. Kerry.

Carrauntoohil summit, with Beenkeragh behind, Co. Kerry.

(EN), *Cephalozia crassifolia* (EN), *Cephaloziella massalongi* (VU), *Cephaloziella stellulifera* (NT), *Cyclodictyon laetevirens* (NT), *Daltonia splachnoides* (LC), *Douinia ovata* (NT), *Dumortiera hirsuta* (NT), *Eremonotus myriocarpus* (NT), *Fissidens crispus* (DD), *Fissidens fontanus* (VU), *Fissidens polyphyllus* (VU), *Fissidens rivularis* (VU), *Fontinalis antipyretica* var. *cymbifolia* (DD), *Grimmia funalis* (NT), *Grimmia ramondii* (NT), *Grimmia torquata* (NT), *Gymnomitrion obtusum* (NT), *Hageniella micans* (NT), *Heterocladium wulfsbergii* (NT), *Hylocomiastrum umbratum* (NT), *Hypnum callichroum* (NT), *Hypnum uncinulatum* (NT), *Isopterygiopsis muelleriana* (VU), *Leiocolea bantriensis* (NT), *Lejeunea eckloniana* (NT), *Lejeunea flava* subsp. *moorei* (VU), *Lejeunea hibernica* (NT), *Marsupella sprucei* (VU), *Mastigophora woodsii* (NT), *Metzgeria leptoneura* (NT), *Moerckia hibernica* (DD), *Odontoschisma elongatum* (NT), *Orthotrichum rivulare* (NT), *Oxyrrhynchium speciosum* (NT), *Paraleptodontium recurvifolium* (NT), *Philonotis rigida* (VU), *Plagiochila heterophylla* (EN), *Plagiomnium cuspidatum* (NT), *Plagiothecium denticulatum* var. *obtusifolium* (NT), *Plasteurhynchium striatulum* (NT), *Platyhypnidium lusitanicum* (NT), *Pohlia elongata* var. *elongata* (NT), *Radula carringtonii* (NT), *Radula holtii* (NT), *Rhabdoweisia crispata* (NT), *Scapania nimbosa* (EN), *Scapania ornithopodioides* (VU), *Schistidium platyphyllum* (VU), *Schistidium strictum* (NT), *Scleropodium cespitans* (NT), *Sematophyllum demissum* (NT), *Sematophyllum substrumulosum* (VU), *Solenostoma paroicum* (NT), *Sphagnum affine* (VU), *Sphagnum girgensohnii* (NT), *Sphagnum strictum* (DD), *Sphenolobopsis pearsonii* (NT), *Telaranea europaea* (NT), *Tritomaria exsecta* (VU), *Ulota coarctata* (CR)

Magannagan Loughs, Caha Mountains, Co. Cork.

43. Glengarriff IBrA

Location Cos Cork, Kerry

Core hectads V75, V76, V77, V85, V86, V95, V96, W06, W15

Criteria A, B, C

Protected sites included
IE0000093 Caha Mountains SAC (6859 ha)
IE0001342 Cloonee and Inchiquin Loughs, Uragh Wood SAC (1155 ha)
IE0001873 Derryclogher (Knockboy) Bog SAC (1713 ha)
IE0001879 Glanmore Bog SAC (1148 ha)
IE0000090 Glengarriff Harbour and Woodland SAC (1306 ha)

Unprotected sites included
Coomclogherane Lake (V9967 – site for several species)
Derreen Garden (V7659 – site for several oceanic species)
Derrynabrack (V81136507 – site for *Diplophyllum obtusifolium*)
Dromanassig Waterfall on Sheen River SE of Kenmare (V952679 – site for *Racomitrium macounii* subsp. *alpinum*)
E. of Coomroe (W0765 – site for *Andreaea megistospora*, *Hypnum uncinulatum* and *Tritomaria exsecta*)
Glantrasna River at Lauragh Bridge (V7758 – site for several riverine and oceanic species)
Glenbeg Lough (V713527 – site for *Pohlia lescuriana*; V7253 – site for *Paraleptodontium recurvifolium*)
Gougane Barra (W0865 – site for *Campylopus shawii* and *Plagiochila heterophylla*)

Megalithic stone circle overlooking Lough Inchiquin and Uragh Wood, Co. Kerry.

Lough Akinkeen (W0164, W0165 – site for *Metzgeria leptoneura* and *Odontoschisma elongatum*)
Nowen Hill Gully (W1453 – site for several species)
Rossdohan Island (V7162 – site for several oceanic species)

Synopsis
A large and complex IBrA, composed of many protected areas and many additional unprotected ones. It contains a wide variety of bryophyte communities and taxa, including important sites for oceanic species, notably the Macaronesian *Hypnum uncinulatum*. It holds one of the two known Irish populations of *Grimmia anomala* (the other at Easky Lough, Sligo) and is Ireland's only known site for *Bryum moravicum*.

Key taxa
Andreaea megistospora (VU), *Aneura mirabilis* (VU), *Antitrichia curtipendula* (NT), *Atrichum tenellum* (NT), *Bryum moravicum* (CR), *Campylopus shawii* (NT), *Cyclodictyon laetevirens* (NT), *Daltonia splachnoides* (LC), *Diplophyllum obtusifolium* (NT), *Douinia ovata* (NT), *Dumortiera hirsuta* (NT), *Eremonotus myriocarpus* (NT), *Fissidens polyphyllus* (VU), *Fissidens serrulatus* (VU), *Grimmia anomala* (EN), *Grimmia ramondii* (NT), *Grimmia torquata* (NT), *Hedwigia integrifolia* (VU), *Heterocladium wulfsbergii* (NT), *Hylocomiastrum umbratum* (NT), *Hypnum uncinulatum* (NT), *Lejeunea eckloniana* (NT), *Lejeunea flava* subsp. *moorei* (VU), *Lejeunea hibernica* (NT), *Leptodontium flexifolium* (NT), *Marsupella funckii* (NT – possibly outside protected area but not accurately localised), *Metzgeria leptoneura* (NT), *Odontoschisma elongatum* (NT), *Paraleptodontium recurvifolium* (NT), *Plagiochila heterophylla* (EN), *Platydictya jungermannioides* (NT), *Pohlia elongata* var. *elongata* (NT), *Pohlia lescuriana* (DD), *Racomitrium macounii* subsp. *alpinum* (VU), *Radula holtii* (NT), *Rhabdoweisia crispata* (NT), *Sematophyllum demissum* (NT), *Sematophyllum substrumulosum* (VU), *Sphagnum flexuosum* (VU), *Telaranea europaea* (NT), *Tritomaria exsecta* (VU)

Mountain Mine, Allihies, Co. Cork.

44. Allihies IBrA

Location Co. Cork

Core hectad V54

Criteria A, C

Protected sites included
IE0002158 Kenmare River SAC (43,301 ha) (small part in Co. Cork only)

Unprotected sites included
Allihies (V5745, V5845, V5945 – site for metallophytes)

Synopsis
Old copper mine complex near the end of the Beara Peninsula. This is the richest and most extensive such site in Ireland, and supports nearly all the specialist rare and threatened metallophyte species, including *Ditrichum cornubicum* at its only Irish site.

Key taxa
Cephaloziella integerrima (VU), *Cephaloziella massalongi* (VU), *Cephaloziella nicholsonii* (VU), *Cephaloziella stellulifera* (NT), *Ditrichum cornubicum* (CR), *Ditrichum lineare* (CR), *Pohlia andalusica* (EN), *Scopelophila cataractae* (VU)

Knockmealdown Mountains, Cos Cork and Waterford.

45. Blackwater River and Knockmealdown Mountains IBrA

Location Cos Cork, Kerry, Limerick, Tipperary, Waterford

Core hectads S00, S01, W69, W99, X08

Criteria A

Protected sites included
002170 Blackwater River (Cork/Waterford) SAC (10,150 ha)

Unprotected sites included
Knockmealdown (S00 – site for several species)
Lismore, Owenashad R. (S0402 – site for *Solenostoma paroicum*, possibly within protected area)
Toorgarriff (W691921 – site for *Daltonia splachnoides*)

Synopsis
The Blackwater River SAC is a diffuse site comprising a river and its tributaries that, taken together, are important for bryophytes, especially *Orthotrichum sprucei* and other riverine species. The north corrie, and its small corrie lakes, in the Knockmealdown Mountains contain base-rich rocks which support a limited but fairly rich flora, including rare species.

Key taxa
Antitrichia curtipendula (NT), *Daltonia splachnoides* (LC), *Dumortiera hirsuta* (NT), *Fissidens fontanus* (VU), *Orthotrichum rivulare* (NT), *Orthotrichum sprucei* (VU), *Plagiothecium platyphyllum* (NT), *Polytrichum commune* var. *perigoniale* (DD), *Porella cordaeana* (NT), *Schistidium elegantulum* subsp. *elegantulum* (DD), *Solenostoma paroicum* (NT), *Telaranea europaea* (NT), *Tortula marginata* (NT)

Ballycotton Cliffs, Co. Cork.

46. Ballycotton Cliffs IBrA

Location Co. Cork

Core hectad W96

Criteria A

Protected sites included
None

Unprotected sites included
Ballycotton (W9762, W9763, W9963 – site for several maritime cliff species)
St Coleman's Cathedral, Cloyne (W917676 – site for *Entosthodon fascicularis* and *Tortula modica*)

Synopsis
The cliffs at Ballycotton support the best example of the maritime turf bryophyte flora on the south coast. Ballycotton is one of two known sites in Ireland for *Tortula canescens*. Recent records at the nearby cathedral at Cloyne add to the interest of this area.

Key taxa
Entosthodon fascicularis (NT), *Rhynchostegium megapolitanum* (NT), *Scleropodium touretii* (EN), *Tortula atrovirens* (NT), *Tortula canescens* (DD), *Tortula modica* (VU)

Coumshingaun, Co. Waterford.

47. Comeragh Mountains IBrA

Location Co. Waterford

Core hectads S20, S21, S31

Criteria A, B

Protected sites included
IE0001952 Comeragh Mountains SAC (6293 ha)

Unprotected sites included
Knockanaffrin (S284161 – site for *Gymnomitrion obtusum* and *Heterocladium wulfsbergii*)

Synopsis
This mountain range is particularly important for bryophytes, the north-facing crags and lakeside boulders being particularly rich. There are also good flush complexes with large populations of *Hamatocaulis vernicosus* and steep heathy slopes support *Sphagnum skyense*. These are the only hills in Ireland where *Hedwigia ciliata* var. *ciliata* has been found, they contain the only known extant site for *Barbilophozia atlantica*, and *Antitrichia curtipendula* is especially abundant here.

Key taxa
Andreaea megistospora (VU), *Antitrichia curtipendula* (NT), *Barbilophozia atlantica* (EN), *Bartramia ithyphylla* (VU), *Grimmia decipiens* (NT), *Grimmia funalis* (NT), *Grimmia muehlenbeckii* (DD), *Grimmia ramondii* (NT), *Grimmia torquata* (NT), *Gymnomitrion obtusum* (NT), *Hamatocaulis vernicosus* (NT), *Hedwigia ciliata* var. *ciliata* (VU), *Hedwigia integrifolia* (VU), *Heterocladium wulfsbergii* (NT), *Marsupella sphacelata* (VU), *Plagiothecium platyphyllum* (VU), *Schistidium strictum* (NT), *Solenostoma paroicum* (NT), *Sphagnum girgensohnii* (NT), *Sphagnum skyense* (DD), *Sphagnum teres* (NT)

Coumaknock Loughs, below Brandon Mountain, Co. Kerry.

CHAPTER SEVEN

Notes on the species accounts

Sphagnum pulchrum and *Sphagnum magellanicum*, Roundstone Bog, Co. Galway.

THIS CHAPTER explains the arrangement of information in the species accounts that follow, along with various conventions adopted both there and elsewhere in this book. Accounts of the liverwort taxa and early moss families were mainly prepared by NGH, those of later moss families mainly by DTH, with all authors contributing to revision and editing of the accounts. Hectad counts for 317 taxa were derived from an Excel spreadsheet compiled and reviewed by DTH, including all those that receive a fuller treatment in this book. Hectad counts for a further 80 taxa, all with shorter accounts, were obtained from records provided to the National Biodiversity Data Centre, Waterford by the UK Biological Records Centre, Wallingford (formerly at Monks Wood) in July 2009. These data were supplemented and updated by additional records supplied to DTH and NL by C.D. Preston in October 2009, and in April 2010, and by additional records from

C. Campbell (mainly for *Petalophyllum ralfsii* and *Hamatocaulis vernicosus*), G.P. Rothero (*Brachydontium trichodes*), F. O'Neill (February 2010), S.D.S. Bosanquet and J. Denyer (September 2010) and from NGH's database.

Full accounts

Full accounts are given for 251 taxa (species, subspecies or varieties). These include all those placed on the Red List (*Regionally Extinct, Critically Endangered, Endangered* or *Vulnerable*), with the exception of *Pohlia wahlenbergii* var. *glacialis*, a variety of questionable taxonomic status, which receives only a short account. Full accounts are also given for most *Data Deficient* taxa because many of these might appear on the Red List in the future. Several *Near Threatened* or *Least Concern* taxa are treated in full because they are protected by European law (*Hamatocaulis vernicosus, Petalophyllum ralfsii*), or national law (*Catoscopium nigritum*), show strong evidence of decline in some regions of Ireland (e.g. *Drepanocladus sendtneri, Pseudocalliergon lycopodioides*), or because most of the European populations are in Ireland, so there is a special responsibility to protect them (e.g. *Daltonia splachnoides, Bryum marratii, Cyclodictyon laetevirens*).

Short accounts

Short accounts are given for 146 various other taxa. These include a few *Data Deficient* taxa, mostly varieties that are currently under-recorded and unlikely to be Red Listed in the future, or taxa that have only very recently been recognised as valid. Short accounts are given for the majority of *Near Threatened* taxa, but also for a number of *Least Concern* taxa that were included in the Provisional Red List (Holyoak 2006b) but have since been found to have too many localities to qualify for the Red List or as *Near Threatened*. A few non-native aliens also have short accounts and are listed as *Not Evaluated*. Several other taxa that were included in the Provisional Red List (*op. cit.*), but which are no longer regarded as taxonomically valid, or that have been incorrectly reported from Ireland, are assigned a status of *Not Evaluated* and given a brief note in Appendix I.

Heading

The heading gives the valid name of the taxon, synonyms ('syn.') and an English name. The systematic sequence and scientific names adopted follow the *Census Catalogue of the British Bryological Society* (Hill *et al.* 2008) with a very few minor modifications. Scientific names adopted in other modern literature (including Aleffi 2005, Blockeel & Long 1998, Grolle & Long 2000, Hill *et al.* 1991–1994, Konstantinova & Bakalin 2009, Paton 1999, Schumacker & Váňa 2000, 2006, Smith 1978, 1990a, 2004), those from key older works (Dickson 1924, Lett 1915, Macvicar 1926, McArdle 1904) and other important literature are listed as synonyms. Abbreviations for authors' names follow Brummitt & Powell (1992). English names of bryophytes mostly follow Edwards (2003). English and scientific names of vascular plants follow Stace (2010). Full scientific names with authorities are given for the few taxa not covered in these standard works.

The threat status for the taxon is given, based on IUCN criteria (see Chapter 5), as Status in Ireland and Status in Europe (the latter taken from the European *Red Data Book*: ECCB 1995).

All taxa are illustrated by a photograph. Every effort has been made to use photographs of Irish plants, but where this was not possible, either because the taxon has become extinct in Ireland or not refound during survey work, photographs from other countries have been used. Several taxa are exceedingly difficult to photograph in the field, mainly due to their small size (*Cephalozia, Cephaloziella*, etc.), the nature of their habitat (e.g. silt-encrusted semi-aquatics) and not least because several require microscopic confirmation following collection. Of the 397 taxa illustrated, 204 (51%) are of Irish plants, 125 British (31%) and the remainder from elsewhere in Europe, except for *Cephaloziella spinigera*, which was from Oregon, USA. Over half the taxa illustrated (53%) were photographed by the authors. Two field visits were made with natural history photographer Robert Thompson, who captured images of 31 taxa, as well as numerous habitat and landscape photographs. Images of the remaining taxa were generously provided by colleagues, with notable contributions from Michael Lüth and Des Callaghan. Most photographs illustrate living plants, usually taken *in situ*, but 11 taxa are illustrated by photographs of herbarium specimens, many of which were provided by Alan Orange, and one photograph (*Hypopterygium immigrans*) is a reproduction from a drawing. Appendix II lists all the illustrated taxa, with the name of photographer, locality, country and date.

Robert Thompson (centre), Neil Lockhart (left) and Nick Hodgetts (right), Mweelrea, Co. Mayo.

The distribution of records at a hectad scale (ten-kilometre squares of the Irish grid) is shown on a map for all taxa with a full account. The legend to the map states the total number of hectads from which a taxon has been correctly recorded in Ireland, followed by the number of old hectad records (pre-1970) and recent hectad records (1970–2010). The sum of the old and recent hectad records can often exceed the total number of hectads because records can fall into both old and recent categories within the same hectad.

Identification

The identification section aims to give a succinct pen portrait of the plant (including type of bryophyte, size, colour, growth form) and an outline description of gametophyte and sporophyte, allowing an overview of the plant for the general reader with no flora for reference. In addition, there is usually a more detailed commentary on identification characters for the reader working with a standard flora, including critical discussion of any real difficulties in distinguishing similar taxa. The terminology used essentially follows modern botanical usage (Paton 1999, Smith 2004, Malcolm & Malcolm 2006) with its inherent clarity and precision; many terms are defined in the glossary. References are often given to more detailed recent treatments that expand or correct information in standard floras. The end of this section sometimes also comments on taxonomic issues, such as invalidity of varieties or segregate species, nomenclatural confusion, or frequency of misidentification in literature accounts.

Distribution in Ireland

Distribution in Ireland gives information to supplement that in the map. The text gives an overview of occurrence in each vice-county, with more detail for the rarest taxa. Records are always critically appraised. The term 'report' is used for any reference to a taxon, 'record' for a report believed to be correct and 'locality' for an occurrence of a taxon at a named location. Nevertheless, so many old records are vaguely localised that some flexibility in wording is often needed to avoid spurious accuracy while making the most of what is known. 'Records' for which specimens have not been checked often need careful scrutiny.

Whenever there is reason to believe that a taxon is significantly overlooked or under-recorded, it is made clear under this heading. It is also noted if there has been a special effort made to refind old records (e.g.

Petalophyllum ralfsii), a woeful neglect because the taxon was not targeted during recent fieldwork (e.g. *Metzgeria leptoneura*), or if it is likely to be of recent 'alien' origin in Ireland (e.g. *Didymodon umbrosus*).

Ecology and biology

This heading covers data on habitats and life-history characteristics of the plant. The habitats in Ireland are described in some detail for those taxa treated fully here, often making comparisons with the habitats in Britain or adjoining areas of continental Europe. For the conservation worker, it is usually important to understand the habitat preferences and ecological requirements of a threatened or declining plant, since maintenance or enhancement of conditions will usually be the key to sustaining or increasing its populations. Information on the population biology of the plants is also given so far as it is known, since there is an obvious need for the conservationist to understand the longevity and life cycle of the plants, their modes of reproduction and the methods by which new sites are colonised. Data on altitudinal range in Ireland are very incomplete because most old specimens lack information. Hence it is only possible to give reasonably complete and accurate figures for a few of the rarer taxa or those with just modern records.

World distribution

World distribution provides an overview of the global range in order to place Irish occurrences and conservation concerns in a wider context. Such data allows the significance of the Irish populations to be judged, sometimes as part of a wider picture of decline of a threatened taxon, sometimes as mere outposts at the edge of the range for taxa that are common and flourishing elsewhere. Information of this kind can be valuable in deciding conservation priorities within Ireland, since it may be impossible and probably unnecessary to protect every rare or declining taxon in Ireland and hence desirable to concentrate on those that are threatened globally, or at least over wider regions of Europe. The level of detail in describing the range is normally greater for Britain than for the rest of Europe, and greater for Europe than the rest of world. A lot of the global and European range information in standard British sources is now incomplete because it is either out of date or uncritical, especially for mosses. Hence an attempt has been made to search recent literature to provide up-to-date information with a moderate level of detail.

The distribution-type in Europe and beyond is cited from the data on 'European distributions and biogeographic elements' presented in BRYOATT (Hill *et al.* 2007). These generalised categories provide a convenient shorthand for the main patterns of distribution within Europe. When taxa are endemic to restricted areas such as Europe or western Europe or Europe and Macaronesia, this is noted.

Threat categories for Europe as a whole are given beneath the species heading. Those for individual European countries are mentioned in this section, especially for some taxa that are very rare throughout Europe, whereas an overview of the European status is attempted for taxa that are threatened only in some European countries and not others. Information on threat status is derived from the following sources: Austria (Krisai 1999), Bulgaria (Natcheva *et al.* 2006), Czech Republic (Kučera & Váňa 2003), Estonia (Ingerpuu 1998), Luxembourg (Werner 2003), the Netherlands (Siebel *et al.* 2006), Norway (Direktoratet for naturforvalning 1999), Portugal, Spain and Andorra (Sérgio *et al.* 2006), Serbia and Montenegro (Sabovljević *et al.* 2004), Sweden (Gärdenfors 2005), Switzerland (Schnyder *et al.* 2004).

Threats

Threats summarise what is known of the causes of decline of Irish populations or of factors likely to cause future decline. In many cases we simply do not know the cause of apparent loss of populations and this lack of knowledge is stated. Where reasonable inferences of causes of loss can be made this is also noted in general terms, although the usual culprits ('afforestation, overstocking, pollution, land-use change, development'), may turn out to be wrong in some particular cases. Climate change may be an overriding threat in future, but it is mentioned only where the risks seem greatest, such as with high-montane taxa and those coastal taxa most at risk from rising sea levels.

Conservation

Conservation mainly describes measures already taken in Ireland. Sometimes these are directed at individual rare species, as when statutory protection of populations is afforded under the Flora (Protection) Order, 1999 in the Republic of Ireland, listed as a Species of Conservation Concern or a Priority Species in Northern Ireland, or protected under EU legislation. More often, there is only a combination of targeted survey work to report, along with general conservation activities such as those covering designation of protected areas. In the Republic of Ireland these protected areas are mainly sites that are proposed or designated Natural Heritage Areas (pNHA and NHA), Special Areas of Conservation (SAC), Nature Reserves (NR) and National Parks (NP). In Northern Ireland the protected areas are primarily Areas of Special Scientific Interest (ASSI), SACs or NRs.

Following on from consideration of existing conservation efforts, the current need for further work is appraised and if action is needed, its character is discussed. Often the immediate need will only be for further survey work aimed at fuller understanding of the status, location and future prospects of populations. Where the need is already apparent, suggestions are also frequently made for habitat management appropriate to counter known or likely threats. These comments are directed especially towards those responsible for management of protected areas, but similar considerations should apply on other land whether in private or public ownership. Any deliberate habitat management to benefit the taxon is also described, along with evident desiderata for such action, or need for research to ascertain what action is needed. Priorities for conservation in Ireland are identified in this section where the Irish populations are not only threatened but also comprise a significant proportion of the European or global population of the taxon.

A list of protected sites with recent (1970–2010) records is given for each taxon treated with a full account. These sites are thought likely or certainly to contain extant populations. The localities of recent records that lie outside protected areas are also given. Many taxa have older records that may also fall within protected areas, but these have not been identified here. A list of Red List taxa, together with those *Near Threatened* and *Data Deficient* taxa treated with a full account, is given for each protected site in Appendix III.

Literature references are given throughout the text, leading to fuller information in the bibliography. Given the scattered literature on bryophytes and the limited availability of worldwide bryophyte literature in some libraries in Ireland, we believe that ample text references are desirable to aid with leads into the literature as well as in documenting our sources. However, some important standard works have been used so often that they are not referred to repeatedly (especially Hill *et al.* 2008, Dierssen 2001, Hill *et al.* 1991–1994, Hill *et al.* 2007, Holyoak 2003a, Paton 1999, Schumacker & Váňa 2006, Smith 2004).

CHAPTER EIGHT

Hornworts and Liverworts

Anthoceros agrestis Paton

syn. *Anthoceros crispulus* (Mont.) Douin, *A. multifidus* auct., *Anthoceros punctatus* auct. non L.,
Aspiromitus agrestis (Paton) Schljakov, *A. punctatus* (L.) Schljakov subsp. *agrestis* (Paton) R.M.Schust.
Status in Ireland: Vulnerable (D2); **Status in Europe:** Least Concern

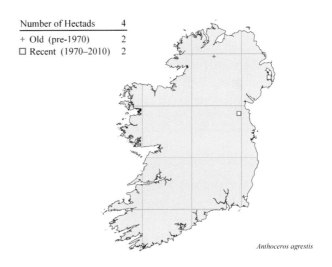

Number of Hectads	4
+ Old (pre-1970)	2
□ Recent (1970–2010)	2

Anthoceros agrestis

Identification

A. agrestis is a hornwort that bears a superficial resemblance to a thallose liverwort. The cells of the thallus contain a single large chloroplast, however, and the structure of the sporophyte is quite different from that of a liverwort. The thalli of *A. agrestis* form small, dark green rosettes up to c. 15 mm in diameter, which are pockmarked with antheridial cavities. The distinctive sporophytes lack a seta and are long, green and cylindrical, turning black when mature, splitting longitudinally into two valves to expose a persistent columella and releasing the black spores. *A. agrestis* can be distinguished from the much more common *A. punctatus* only by microscopic examination of the antheridia, which are significantly smaller in *A. agrestis* (length of antheridial body < 90 μm). *Phaeoceros* has yellow spores and much larger antheridia.

Distribution in Ireland

Accepted records are from four localities in four vice-counties: Louth (Collon, N. of Emerson's Bridge, 2003); W. Donegal (near Doe Castle, 1969); Tyrone (Butterlope Glen, 1957) and Down (near Toy and Kirkland, 2008). Other records, not necessarily confirmed microscopically, must be regarded as at best dubious. These include records from Tyrone (Davagh Forest Park, 1958); Down (Saintfield, 1903) and Antrim (Giant's Causeway, 1991).

Ecology and biology

Growing in the lowlands on moist soil in arable fields, marshy fields and in ditches and field drains, it favours soils that are neither strongly basic nor strongly acidic, and often occurs in association with species of *Riccia* and *Fossombronia*. The large spores suggest that *A. agrestis*

173

may act as a shuttle species, reappearing at or near the same sites whenever conditions allow.

A. agrestis is a monoicous summer annual, maturing between July and December. Fertile plants and sporophytes are common. Specialised organs of vegetative reproduction are unknown.

World distribution

Interestingly, this species is more widespread in Europe than *A. punctatus*, which is much the more frequent of the two species in Ireland. However, it is unclear just how common it is in Europe, because of confusion with *A. punctatus*. It is listed as *Extinct* in Portugal, although Sérgio & Carvalho (2003) say that it is 'almost certainly under-recorded', *Endangered* in Austria and Poland, and *Vulnerable* in Slovakia, but in most countries it is simply listed with no comment on its status, apart from Luxembourg, where it is *Near Threatened*, and Switzerland and the Czech Republic, in both of which it is *Least Concern*. It occurs in the Faeroes, the Canary Islands and the Azores, but has not been recorded from a number of Mediterranean countries, including Spain and most of the Balkan states. It is assigned to a European Temperate floristic element in Europe. *A. agrestis* is also present in Asia, the Caribbean and N. America.

Threats

Complete habitat destruction, through cessation of tillage, afforestation or building developments, is probably the greatest threat; the plant should survive if agricultural practices continue to provide regularly disturbed bare, water-retentive soil.

Conservation

More surveys are needed of bryophytes on arable fields in Ireland. It would be interesting to attempt to raise the plant from soil samples collected at the known sites, to determine whether a spore bank is present. *A. agrestis* is listed as a Northern Ireland Priority Species.

Protected sites with recent records: none; **Unprotected sites with recent records:** Collon, N. of Emerson's Bridge; near Toy and Kirkland.

Marchantia polymorpha L. subsp. *montivagans* Bischl. & Boisselier   Star-headed Liverwort

syn. *Marchantia alpestris* (Nees) Burgeff, *M. polymorpha* var. *alpestris* (Nees) Gottsche *et al.*
Status in Ireland: Endangered (D); **Status in Europe:** Least Concern

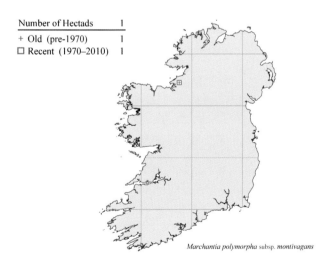

Number of Hectads	1
+ Old (pre-1970)	1
□ Recent (1970–2010)	1

Marchantia polymorpha subsp. *montivagans*

Identification

This is a large, branching, dark green thallose liverwort that forms dense mats. The thalli can grow to c. 10 cm long and 2 cm wide, are covered in conspicuous pores and bear circular gemmae cups. This subspecies is distinguished from the common subsp. *polymorpha* by the absence of a dark median line on the upper surface of the thallus. There are, however, dark lines *between* the thallus lobes; these are absent in other genera. Of other large thallose liverworts, *Lunularia cruciata* has half-moon-shaped gemmae cups; *Conocephalum conicum* has no gemmae cups and is strongly aromatic; *Preissia quadrata* has no gemmae cups and is a smaller plant, usually with some purplish colouration. *Marchantia* has one of the most complex inflorescences of any liverwort: the male receptacle is roughly disc-shaped and borne on an erect stalk up to c. 1.2 cm long; the female receptacle is an umbrella-shaped rayed structure on a stalk up to c. 5.5 cm long, with the sporophytes pendent beneath the rays.

Distribution in Ireland
Known only from a single recent record from Leitrim (Glencar Waterfalls, 2005) and an older specimen from Sligo (Benbulbin), collected by D. Moore in 1871. It is possible that it is genuinely restricted in Ireland to the Dartry Mountains, but it may be under-recorded.

Ecology and biology
The habitat of the only recent Irish record of this plant was on a small rock in a river downstream from a waterfall. Nothing is known of the older record. In Britain, it also occurs in upland flushes and other wet ground, often near late-lying snow, and in dune slacks. Generally lowland to alpine, it grows at c. 100 m in Ireland.

It is dioicous and often fertile, but sporophytes are very rare. Gemmae are usually present.

World distribution
This subspecies is widespread in northern and montane areas of Europe (Fennoscandia, northern Russia, the arctic islands, the Alps, Carpathians and Pyrenees), but much rarer in the lowlands and the south, although it occurs in Madeira and the Canary Islands. It is listed as *Rare* in Slovakia, *Near Threatened* in Bulgaria, and *Data Deficient* in the Czech Republic. It is categorised as a Circumpolar Boreo-arctic montane floristic element in Europe. Elsewhere, it is recorded in Africa, Asia and N. and S. America.

Threats
Water pollution upstream may be a threat to this subspecies at its known site. It is in an area of high sheep-stocking density, and this can lead to green algae becoming dominant in streams at the expense of bryophytes.

Conservation
This plant should be looked for in other upland areas, as it is probably present elsewhere. On the other hand, if it is genuinely restricted to the Dartry Mountains, the known population should be monitored regularly, as a single event could eliminate it.

Protected sites with recent records: Ben Bulben, Gleniff and Glenade Complex SAC; **Unprotected sites with recent records:** none.

Riccia cavernosa Hoffm.   Cavernous Crystalwort

syn. *Riccia crystallina* auct. non L., *R. huebeneriana* Lindenb. var. *cavernosa* (Hoffm.) Ast., *R. montagnei* Steph., *R. tenellii* Gola, *R. terracianoi* Gola, *Ricciella rautanenii* Steph.
Status in Ireland: Least Concern; **Status in Europe:** Least Concern

Widespread but scarce in Ireland in a broad band from Kerry to Antrim, though curiously absent from the south-east, *R. cavernosa* is a small thallose liverwort characteristic of bare mud at the sides of reservoirs, pools and rivers. This species was included in the Provisional Red List (Holyoak 2006b) but fieldwork over the last decade revealed several new records and that it had previously been under-recorded. It has now been reported from 12 vice-counties, with records from 16 hectads (3 old, 13 recent). It is unlikely that it has declined, but its status should be monitored because its habitat is scarce and often threatened.

Riccia huebeneriana Lindenb.

Violet Crystalwort

syn. *Riccia pseudofrostii* Schiffn. ex Müll.Frib., *Ricciella huebeneriana* Dumort.
Status in Ireland: Data Deficient; **Status in Europe:** Rare

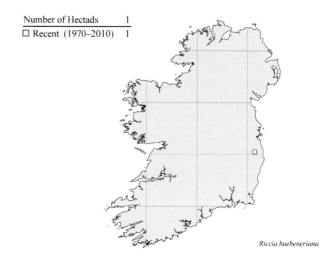

Number of Hectads	1
☐ Recent (1970–2010)	1

Riccia huebeneriana

Identification

This is a small green thallose liverwort, usually tinged with purple or violet, that forms rosettes up to 1 cm across. Like other species of *Riccia*, the indehiscent sporophytes are entirely enclosed within the gametophyte, and the spores are liberated as the thallus disintegrates with age. The older parts have a spongy appearance, becoming areolate with cavities. This, combined with the narrow, channelled thallus and the colour, distinguishes *Riccia huebeneriana* from other Irish species of *Riccia*.

Distribution in Ireland

The only known sites for this plant in Ireland are on the shores of Vartry Reservoir in Wicklow, where it was recorded in 1973, 1975 and 1992. More recent surveys have failed to find the plant because water levels in the reservoir have been consistently too high.

Ecology and biology

It grows on mud exposed in the draw-down zone of a reservoir. This plant survives (potentially for many years) as a spore bank in the mud, only developing when the mud is exposed, whether by drought or by artificial lowering of water levels. The spores are large (up to 80 μm in diameter) and can presumably disperse only over short distances, unless assisted by birds. *R. huebeneriana*

therefore acts as a 'shuttle species', populations reappearing regularly at the same site whenever conditions allow. This is a lowland plant, occurring at c. 210 m in Ireland. Its principal habitat in Britain is also reservoir margins.

This species is monoicous, usually fertile and sporophytes are abundant.

World distribution

Scattered throughout much of Europe, except in the extreme north and the Balkans, but apparently rare throughout its range, *R. huebeneriana* is *Nationally Scarce* in Britain, *Extinct* in Austria, *Endangered* in Switzerland and Luxembourg, *Vulnerable* in Portugal, Spain, Norway, Sweden, Italy and Finland, *Rare* in Belgium and Latvia, 'presumably threatened' in Germany, and *Data Deficient* in the Czech Republic. It is assigned to a European Temperate floristic element in Europe. It is also found in Africa and parts of Asia and N. America, but its full distribution remains poorly known because of confusion with other species.

Threats

The biggest threat to this species arises from the water level being kept artificially high in the reservoir (e.g. to benefit angling or water-sports interests). Water pollution such as by eutrophication could also be a problem, although there is no evidence of this at Vartry Reservoir.

population should be monitored in years when conditions allow it.

Conservation

This plant should survive providing there is some mud exposure at least once every few years. The

Protected sites with recent records: Vartry Reservoir pNHA; **Unprotected sites with recent records:** none.

Riccia rhenana Lorb. ex Müll.Frib.   Pond Crystalwort

syn. *Ricciocarpos natans* var. *decipiens* Schiffn.
Status in Ireland: Not Evaluated; **Status in Europe:** Least Concern

A pale green and slender thallose liverwort, with both floating and terrestrial forms, found on mud or floating at the margins of ponds and lakes, and morphologically very similar to the more common *Riccia fluitans*. It has been recorded once in Ireland; from shallow water with *Lemna minor* at the base of *Equisetum fluviatile* and *Carex rostrata* on the shores of Ballaghdacker Lough in Co. Galway in 2004. It is thought that this species is probably an introduction to both Ireland and Britain, resulting from aquaria being emptied into waterbodies. However, as a central European species that occurs north to Scandinavia and south to Portugal, it is possible that it occurs in Ireland as a result of natural processes.

Riccia subbifurca Warnst. ex Croz.   Least Crystalwort

syn. *Riccia baumgartneri* Schiffn., *R. warnstorfii* auct. non Limpr. ex Warnst.
Status in Ireland: Least Concern; **Status in Europe:** Least Concern

R. subbifurca is a small pale or yellow-green thallose liverwort, often tinged violet or reddish along the thallus margins, with a distinct, shallow, flat-bottomed median groove. It grows in rosettes to 1.5 cm in diameter or in mats on banks, tracks, footpaths, arable fields and reservoir margins. Scattered throughout Ireland, it has been reported from 22 vice-counties, with records from 39 hectads (25 old, 13 recent, 1 undated). It is a more or less ruderal species of thin soils and has probably not declined. Several records, especially from Northern Ireland, are unsubstantiated by specimens.

Riccia crozalsii Levier

Ciliate Crystalwort

Status in Ireland: Endangered (D); **Status in Europe:** Least Concern

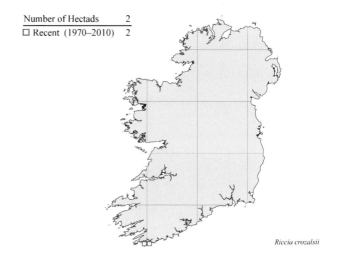

Number of Hectads	2
□ Recent (1970–2010)	2

Riccia crozalsii

Identification

A small rosette-forming thallose liverwort that grows to 1.4 cm in diameter and is typically greyish-green in colour, tinged purple at the sides. As in other species of *Riccia*, the indehiscent sporophytes are entirely enclosed within the gametophyte, so the spores are liberated as the thallus degenerates from the centre. It differs from most other species of *Riccia* by the frequent presence of numerous long marginal cilia curving over the dorsal surface of the thallus. *R. subbifurca* can be similar, but in that species the cilia are straighter, the branches are not as thick at the apex, and their edges form distinct swollen lateral ridges.

Distribution in Ireland

This species is known from two sites in West Cork; a small area around South Harbour on Clear Island, where it was found in 1993 and again in 2008; and Knockomagh Wood Nature Reserve, where it was found in 2009.

Ecology and biology

R. crozalsii was found on Clear Island on soil among rocks in maritime turf and on small ledges of the sandstone rock of a coastal road-cutting. At Knockomagh it occurred in small quantity on a roadside bank. In SW England it is also recorded from tracks and arable ground on the coast.

This species is monoicous, usually fertile and sporophytes are abundant. Gemmae are absent.

World distribution

A common species in much of the Mediterranean area, extending to Macaronesia and northwards along the Atlantic coast, it is *Nationally Scarce* in Britain, *Endangered* in Italy, Sardinia and Sicily, *Vulnerable* in Switzerland, 'susceptible' in the Netherlands, and 'potentially threatened' in Austria. It is absent further north. It is assigned to an Oceanic Mediterranean-Atlantic floristic element in Europe. The species is also found in Africa, SW Asia and Australasia.

Threats

Potentially at risk from widening or other improvement of the coastal road on Clear Island, or the roadside bank at Knockomagh. Spread of coarse vegetation such as grasses could also threaten this plant.

Conservation

The populations should be monitored regularly.

Protected sites with recent records: Knockomagh Wood Nature Reserve; Lough Hyne Nature Reserve and environs SAC; Roaringwater Bay and Islands SAC; **Unprotected sites with recent records:** none.

Ricciocarpos natans (L.) Corda

Fringed Heartwort

syn. *Riccia capillata* Schmidel, *R. natans* L., *R. velutina* Wilson, *Ricciocarpos velutinus* (Wilson ex Hook.) Steph.
Status in Ireland: Near Threatened; **Status in Europe:** Least Concern

R. natans is an aquatic, rosette-forming thallose liverwort, easily identified when floating by the dense growth of violet-coloured ventral scales that protrude beneath the thalli. Found in ditches, ponds, canals and slow-flowing streams, it seems likely that it is transported from site to site by waterbirds, although there is no direct evidence for this, and it probably acts as a metapopulation, with individual populations being impersistent from year to year. It has a scattered distribution throughout the midlands of Ireland, but is absent from the north and north-west, and has been reported from 12 vice-counties, with records from 20 hectads (11 old, 11 recent). Although naturally restricted by its habitat requirements, there is no evidence of any decline.

Targionia hypophylla L.

Orobus-seed Liverwort

syn. *Targionia bifurca* Nees, *T. convoluta* Lindenb. & Gottsche, *T. germanica* Corda, *T. michelii* Raddi
Status in Ireland: Regionally Extinct; **Status in Europe:** Least Concern

Number of Hectads	6
+ Old (pre-1970)	6

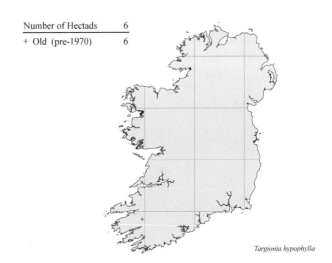

Targionia hypophylla

Identification

This is a strongly aromatic, shiny dark green thallose liverwort, with conspicuous pores on the dorsal surface. The branches are up to 2.5 cm long and 5 mm wide. Dark purple or almost black scales on the underside of the thalli can envelop the plant when its thalli curve inwards as they dry. Thus, while conspicuous when hydrated, its appearance when dry is suggestive of black string. The dark and bulbous female involucres just below the shoot apices are often conspicuous.

Distribution in Ireland

Records are from six localities in four vice-counties, all bar one from the 19th century: S. Kerry (Cahersiveen, 1877; Blackwater Bridge, 1890); N. Kerry (Muckross Abbey, 1890); Mid Cork (Carrigaline, 1852) and Antrim (Little Deer Park, Glenarm, 1834 and 1836; Cave Hill, 1809 and 1902). In spite of persistent searching, it has not been seen in Ireland since 1902.

Ecology and biology

This is a plant of rock crevices, stone walls and base-rich soils, usually exposed to the sun and drying out in summer. Few details exist about the Irish colonies, but one was apparently growing on a bank behind a chapel, another on limestone, another on 'warm basaltic rocks on an exposed bank' and still another on rocks on the north side of a cave (presumably at the entrance).

T. hypophylla is autoicous or sometimes dioicous and sporophytes are frequent, maturing in winter or early spring. Gemmae are unknown.

World distribution

Widespread and common in S. Europe, reaching its northern limit in Scotland, *Targionia* is rare or absent in the north: it has not been found in Fennoscandia or Russia. It is listed as *Nationally Scarce* in Britain, *Extinct* in Luxembourg, *Critically Endangered* in the Czech Republic, *Endangered* in Germany, *Vulnerable* in Switzerland, and *Rare* in Belgium and the Crimea. The species is classified as an Oceanic Mediterranean-Atlantic floristic element in Europe. *T. hypophylla* is widespread generally in warm parts of the world, and is recorded in Africa, Asia, Australasia, Oceania and N. and S. America.

Threats

It is not easy to explain why this species has disappeared from Ireland. Apparently suitable habitats are still present, and climate change would be expected, if anything, to favour such a thermophilous species. It hardly seems possible that collecting by botanists eliminated it, even if it occurred as small isolated populations at the edge of its range.

Conservation

No conservation measures are currently required. Climate change could conceivably result in this species returning to Ireland.

Protected sites with recent records: none; **Unprotected sites with recent records:** none.

Dumortiera hirsuta (Sw.) Nees   Dumortier's Liverwort

syn. *Dumortiera trichocephala* (Hook.) Nees, *Marchantia hirsuta* Sw., *M. irrigua* (Taylor) Wilson, *M. trichocephala* Hook.
Status in Ireland: Near Threatened; **Status in Europe:** Rare

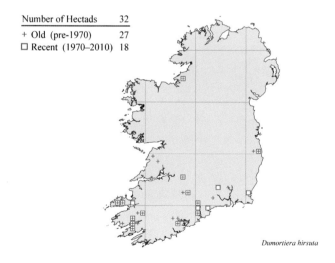

Number of Hectads	32
+ Old (pre-1970)	27
□ Recent (1970–2010)	18

Dumortiera hirsuta

Identification

This large, thallose species is an easy plant to identify. It forms spreading dark green, aromatic patches, with the thallus rather dull and usually with distinct wrinkles running across its surface. Individual branches may be up to 12 cm long and 2 cm wide, so the area covered by a single stand can be considerable. The thallus margins are sparsely hairy. It is related to other large thallose liverworts such as *Conocephalum* and *Targionia*, and thus has pores on the upper surface of the thallus. Unlike these species, however, the pores are very indistinct and *Dumortiera* is more likely to be mistaken for a very large form of *Pellia*. The latter has a more shiny thallus, so the texture looks rather different, and lacks the wrinkles and marginal hairs. The circular male receptacles are more or less unlobed, up to 5 mm in diameter, slightly concave and borne on a very short stalk up to 1 mm long. The female receptacles are larger, up to 9 mm in diameter, lobed, and borne on a stalk up to 5 cm long.

Distribution in Ireland

Records for this plant are concentrated in the southern half of Ireland, with one outlier in Antrim, but it has not been refound at nearly half its known sites since 1970. There are recent records from 17 localities in 10 vice-counties: S. Kerry (Lough Anscaul, 1897–2006; Blackwater Bridge, 1820–1983; Ballaghbeama Gap, 1967–1983; O'Sullivan's Cascade, 1893–1983; Loch an Duin, 2009); N. Kerry (Torc Cascade, 1832–2010; Newfoundland Bay, Upper Lake, 1976); W. Cork (Lackawee, 1967–2006); Waterford (Glendine Wood, 1967–2007; Glendine River at Glendine Bridge, 1967–2007; Lismore, 1966–1999); Limerick (Clare Glen, 1972); N. Tipperary (Clare Glen, 1967–1979); Kilkenny (SW of Kilmaganny, 2010); Wexford (Castlebridge, 1999); Wicklow (Newtownmountkennedy Wood, 1980) and Leitrim (Glencar Waterfalls, 1928–2005). Older records are from a further 20 localities: S. Kerry (Lough an Mhónáin, 1967; An Loch Dubh, 1899; Brandon Mountain, 1829–1963; Ballyduff, 1829–1951; Finglas River, 1967; Mullaghanattin, 1967; Inchiquin Lough, 1967; Cummeenduff Glen, 1967); Mid Cork (Ballinhassig Glen, 1844; 'Cork', 1876); Waterford (Coumshingaun, 1961–1966); S. Tipperary (Galtymore, 1963; Carrignabinnia, 1966); Limerick (Galbally, 1966); Clare (Lough Inchiquin, 1962; Spectacle Bridge, 1968); Kilkenny (Inistioge, 1966); Wicklow (Altidore Glen, 1872–1902; Luggala, 1876) and Antrim (Glenarm Glen, 1952).

Ecology and biology

D. hirsuta grows in dark, damp places in ravines and woodland, typically on dripping, vertical rocks next to splash pools beneath waterfalls, with associates such as *Thamnobryum alopecurum*, *Conocephalum conicum*, *Jubula* *hutchinsiae* and small Lejeuneaceae. It favours base-rich or neutral rocks, and may also occur in caves and rocky recesses. Mainly a plant of low elevations, it has been recorded at 330 m in moist block scree in SW Ireland.

Fertile examples of this species, which may be autoicous or dioicous, are common, although sporophytes are less so. Gemmae are absent, but vegetative reproduction could presumably occur simply through colonies growing new lobes while old parts of the thallus die back.

World distribution

In Europe, it has been recorded from Britain (where it is listed as *Vulnerable* and confined to a few scattered sites in Cornwall, Devon, Sussex, Argyll, Islay, Jura and the Isle of Man), France, Spain, Italy, Portugal, Canary Islands and Madeira. It is classified as an Oceanic Southern-temperate floristic element in Europe. *D. hirsuta* is a common plant throughout the tropics.

Threats

This is a large and conspicuous liverwort, and although not specifically targeted in recent fieldwork, the absence of records during the last decade, especially from some of its well-known sites, suggests that a decline may be genuine. The reasons for decline are not clear, but may reflect deterioration in water quality, water management or even climate change.

Conservation

Further efforts should be made to relocate *D. hirsuta* at some of its old sites, and its best surviving populations require regular monitoring. *D. hirsuta* is listed as a Northern Ireland Priority Species and a UK Biodiversity Action Plan (UKBAP) species.

Protected sites with recent records: Ben Bulben, Gleniff and Glenade Complex SAC; Blackwater River and Estuary pNHA; Blackwater River (Cork/Waterford) SAC; Blackwater River (Kerry) SAC; Clare Glen SAC; Glanmore Bog SAC; Glendine Wood SAC; Killarney National Park; Killarney National Park, Macgillycuddy's Reeks and Caragh River Catchment SAC; Mount Brandon SAC; Slieve Mish Mountains SAC; **Unprotected sites with recent records:** Ballinhassig Glen; Castlebridge; Newtownmountkennedy Wood; SW of Kilmaganny.

Petalophyllum ralfsii (Wils.) Nees & Gottsche

Petalwort

syn. *Codonia ralfsii* (Wils.) Dumort., *Diplolaena lyellii* f. *lamellosa* Nees, *Fossombronia corbulaeformis* Trab., *Jungermannia ralfsii* Wils., *Petalophyllum lamellatum* Lindb.

Status in Ireland: Least Concern; **Status in Europe:** Vulnerable

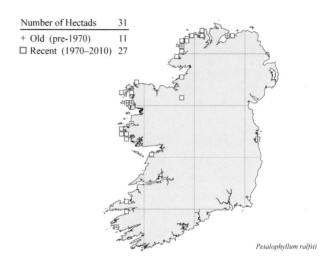

Number of Hectads	31
+ Old (pre-1970)	11
□ Recent (1970–2010)	27

Petalophyllum ralfsii

Identification

P. ralfsii is a small, pale green thallose liverwort with erect lamellae on its upper surface. The green part of the plant grows from a subterranean, rhizome-like axis. Sporophytes develop sheathed in a cylindrical involucre on the upper surface of the female thallus. The orange antheridia occur in clusters on the upper surface of the male plants. *P. ralfsii* may be confused with species of *Fossombronia*, particularly *F. caespitiformis* subsp. *multispira*, in which the rhizoids are usually colourless or pale brown (other species of *Fossombronia* have purple rhizoids). However, close examination will reveal the characteristic lamellae of *Petalophyllum*, unique in our flora.

Distribution in Ireland

P. ralfsii was first recorded in Ireland in 1861 near Malahide, Dublin, by B. Carrington. Subsequently it was recorded on the North Bull in north Dublin Bay by D. Moore in 1874, at Inny Ferry (S. Kerry) by R.W. Scully in 1890, on Achill Island by Rev. H.W. Lett in 1903 and on Clare Island by Rev. H.W. Lett in 1920. A handful of 'new' sites were discovered in the 1950s and 1960s, but fieldwork by N. Lockhart in 1998, following the inclusion of *P. ralfsii* on the Bern Convention and EU Habitats Directive, revealed several hitherto-undiscovered populations, many of them large. It is now known in Ireland from about 30 localities, most of which are on the west coast, in eight vice-counties: S. Kerry (west of Inny Ferry, 1890 and 1998; Inch, 1983–2010; Magherabeg, 1998–2010; Lough Naparka, 1998; Kilshannig, 2002 and north of Rossbehy, 2006); Clare (Fanore, 1994–2010); W. Galway (Omey Island,1998–2006; Aillebrack, 1988–2004; Mannin More, 2004–2006; Truska Machair, 1998–2010; Murvey Machair, 1998–2006); Dublin (North Bull, 1874–2010); W. Mayo (North Inishkea, 1998; Doogort Machair, 1903–2010; Keel Machair, 1962–2006; Doolough 1998–2006; Dooyork, 1998; Garter Hill, 1998–2010; Dooaghtry, 1968–2010); Sligo (Bunduff Machair, 1998–2010); W. Donegal (Keadew Point, 1962–2010; Dooey Point 1999–2002; Derrybeg, 2002–2006; Damph Beg, 1999–2002; Tramore, 2002; Tranarossan, 2002–2010; S. Rosepenna, 1999–2009; Sheskinmore, 1998–2010) and Londonderry (Ballymaclary, 1904–2008). It may have disappeared from some sites: it was found once at Banna, N. Kerry, by A.P. Fanning in 1954 but has not been refound there, in spite of searching; it has almost certainly disappeared from Malahide, where its habitat has largely been destroyed; in Antrim it has gone from Portrush and White Rocks (both 1928 records) following destruction of the habitats. Neither was it refound during recent fieldwork on Clare Island. One anomalous site was an old limestone quarry near Derry, by Lough Arrow, Sligo, where *P. ralfsii* was found by Jean Paton in 1970, but this appears to have been a transient population.

Ecology and biology

This plant is usually found on damp, calcareous sandy turf in dune slacks or machair, often where it is subject to inundation in the winter. *P. ralfsii* seems to favour soil that is bare and somewhat compacted, as at the sides of paths. It does not grow in slacks that are water-filled for long periods or heavily shaded. It has also been recorded in Cornwall growing over metalliferous mine spoil and old masonry. The green part of the plant usually disappears from view when the substrate dries out in the summer, and then it survives as an underground axis. *P. ralfsii* can vary in apparent abundance from year to year, depending on conditions. It is exclusively a lowland plant.

Both sexes of this dioicous species are often fertile. Sporophytes are frequent, and usually mature between March and June. Gemmae are unknown.

World distribution

It is sparsely distributed in Mediterranean and Atlantic parts of Europe, and listed as *Nationally Scarce* in Britain, probably *Extinct* in Italy (including Sicily), *Vulnerable* in Portugal, and also recorded from Sardinia, the Balearic Islands, Malta and Greece (including Crete). The report from Sardinia, previously considered doubtful, has now been confirmed (Aleffi 2005). In Europe, it is categorised as an Oceanic Mediterranean-Atlantic floristic element. Outside Europe, *P. ralfsii* has been recorded from Turkey, Morocco and Algeria. Söderström *et al.* (2007) list it for N. America, but Crandall-Stotler *et al.* (2002) consider American *Petalophyllum* to be specifically distinct from European material and have therefore described it as a different species, *P. americanum* C.H.Ford & Crand.-Stotl.

Threats

Because of the fragility of its habitat and its specialised ecology, *P. ralfsii* is potentially threatened by a large number of factors, including holiday developments, recreational activities, removal of turf, undergrazing and desiccation due to water abstraction.

Conservation

It is possible that Ireland has more *P. ralfsii* than anywhere else in the world, and it certainly appears to have larger populations than any yet found elsewhere: the Truska Machair population runs into millions of thalli. The Irish sites are therefore of international importance and their conservation should be regarded as a priority, even though the status of *P. ralfsii* in Ireland is *Least Concern*. This means protecting dune and machair sites from disturbance and development and monitoring the

Petalophyllum ralfsii, Truska, Co. Galway.

populations. *P. ralfsii* is listed on Appendix 1 of the Bern Convention, protected under the EU Habitats Directive and covered by the Flora (Protection) Order, 1999 in the Republic of Ireland. It is listed as a Northern Ireland Priority Species and a UK Biodiversity Action Plan (UKBAP) species.

Protected sites with recent records: Ballinskelligs Bay and Inny Estuary SAC; Ballymaclary Nature Reserve; Black Head-Poulsallagh Complex SAC; Bull Island Nature Reserve; Bunduff Lough and Machair/ Trawalua/Mullaghmore SAC; Doogort Machair/Lough Doo SAC; Glenamoy Bog Complex SAC; Gweedore Bay and Islands SAC; Horn Head and Rinclevan SAC; Inishkea Islands SAC; Keel Machair/Menaun Cliffs SAC; Magilligan ASSI; Magilligan SAC; Mullet/ Blacksod Bay Complex SAC; Murvey Machair SAC; Mweelrea/Sheeffry/Erriff Complex SAC; North Dublin Bay SAC; Omey Island Machair SAC; Sheephaven SAC; Slyne Head Peninsula SAC; Tralee Bay and Magharees Peninsula, West to Cloghane SAC; Tranarossan and Melmore Lough SAC; West of Ardara/Maas Road SAC; **Unprotected sites with recent records:** near Derry, by Lough Arrow.

Fossombronia foveolata Lindb.

Pitted Frillwort

syn. *Fossombronia dumortieri* Huebener & Genth ex Lindb.
Status in Ireland: Least Concern; **Status in Europe:** Least Concern

Fossombronia foveolata is typical of the genus in its semi-thallose growth form, forming small green cabbage-like rosettes. This plant is a summer annual or a perennial, and grows on ground that floods in winter but dries out in summer. It favours neutral to acid soils, usually with at least some peat, on reservoir, pond and stream margins, wet heath, banks and fields. It has a scattered distribution, mainly in western Ireland, and has been reported from 11 vice-counties with records from 20 hectads (9 old, 13 recent). Although rather rare and probably under-recorded, it does not seem to be threatened and there is no evidence of decline.

Fossombronia caespitiformis De Not. ex Rabenh.

Spanish Frillwort

subsp. *multispira* (Schiffn.) J.R.Bray & Cargill

Husnot's Frillwort

syn. *Fossombronia husnotii* Corb., *F. husnotii* var. *anglica* W.E.Nicholson
Status in Ireland: Data Deficient; **Status in Europe:** Least Concern

Identification

This is a semi-thallose liverwort growing in green to purple, reddish or brownish prostrate to suberect rosettes or mats. Stems are up to 10 mm long and 3.5 mm wide, often branched, with a row of succubous, leaf-like lobes on each side of the costa. These 'leaves' are often closely imbricate, erect and crispate. The gametophyte is almost identical to that of the common *F. pusilla*, except that the rhizoids are often hyaline rather than violet. Young sporophytes are protected by an erect perianth. Spores are (30)32–35(37) μm (perhaps sometimes larger, up to 64 μm) with distinctive ornamentation on the distal surface comprising a dense cover of long flattened spines 4–6 μm long with truncate apices; the spines being

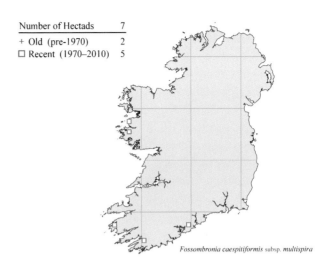

Number of Hectads   7
+ Old (pre-1970)   2
□ Recent (1970–2010)   5

Fossombronia caespitiformis subsp. *multispira*

broadened basally and some having confluent bases, but they do not form a reticulum of lamellae.

F. husnotii has been distinguished from other European *Fossombronia* for many years largely on the basis of its colourless to pale brown rather than violet rhizoids (e.g. Müller 1909, Macvicar 1926, Paton 1999). However, it has become apparent that several different species of the genus can produce forms lacking the usual violet rhizoid colouration (Scott & Pike 1984, H. During *in* Gradstein & van Melick 1996, Perold 1998). Spore characters also vary widely in European plants identified by rhizoid colouration (e.g. Paton 1999). Subsequently, Stotler *et al.* (2003) have ignored rhizoid colouration in distinguishing two subspecies in *F. caespitiformis*, which is identified specifically mainly on the basis of spore ornamentation: subsp. *multispira* (with *F. husnotii* as a synonym) has elaters that are 3–5 spiralled (rarely 2-spiralled); in subsp. *caespitiformis* they are mainly 2-spiralled (rarely 3-spiralled). Schumacker & Váňa (2005) follow this nomenclature but invite confusion by still keying out *F. caespitiformis* subsp. *multispira* on colourless to pale brown rhizoids and variable spore ornamentation, as in the first edition of their guide, without mentioning the elaters.

Distribution in Ireland

Recent records based on redetermined specimens for which spores and elaters have been checked are from five localities in five vice-counties: S. Kerry (N. end of Glanleam Gardens, Valencia Island, 2006); W. Cork (Dromore, 2009); E. Cork (Glenbower Wood, near Killeagh, 2002); W. Galway (E. of Kylemore Castle, 1970) and W. Mayo (Lough Nahatora, S. of Louisburgh, 1970). There are older confirmed records from S. Kerry (Staigue Fort, Castlecove, 1951) and W. Cork (Allihies, 1962).

Specimens of *F. husnotii* with colourless rhizoids but lacking spores have been examined from two additional vice-counties (Clare: near Inagh River W. of Lough Burke, 1979; E. Galway: Dunree Head, 2002). However, as discussed above, rhizoid colouration is an unreliable character for species identification. Hence, simply transferring records of *F. husnotii* to *F. caespitiformis* subsp. *multispira* without checking spores or elaters of specimens (as in Hill *et al.* 2008) is likely to introduce errors.

Ecology and biology

Data from recently redetermined specimens imply that subsp. *multispira* occurs over much of the range of habitats described for *F. husnotii* in the literature (e.g. Paton 1999): on acidic to mildly base-rich soils, predominantly in open sunny sites prone to desiccation and mostly on or near the coast. Irish gatherings are all from coastal counties, mostly from on or near coasts but one was from inland at 55 m elevation. Sites and substrata were noted as thin soil among gravel on track through shrubbery, bare peaty humus by a gravelly path, a track, a damp track, a path among copper mines and a roadside bank near a lake. *F. caespitiformis s.l.* (with violet rhizoids) is also frequent in arable fields in Britain (Paton 1999) and most, if not all, of its records are presumably of subsp. *multispira*. A Belgian specimen of that subsp. was collected from a ditch bank between a wheat field and woodland (Sotiaux *et al.* 2009).

The species is monoicous and often fertile, with spores ripening mainly from late summer or autumn to spring. Plants on coastal paths are often short-lived perennials, but in arable fields they are presumably winter annuals that grow from spores (which are large and perhaps form a long-lived spore bank). Vegetative propagules are apparently lacking.

World distribution

The range of subsp. *multispira* is still rather poorly known because its taxonomy has only recently been elucidated. Both subspp. of *F. caespitiformis* occur in nearly all of the Mediterranean countries and in Madeira and the Canary Islands (Ros *et al.* 2007). Only subsp. *multispira* has been recorded further north in W. Europe, with recent records confirmed by study of elaters from Ireland (see above), SW England (Cornwall and Devon: J. A. Paton pers. comm.) and Belgium (Sotiaux *et al.* 2009). Records of *F. caespitiformis s.l.* from Africa, SW Asia and Australia need to be reassessed to establish which sspp. are involved.

Threats

It apparently requires open, unshaded ground and is therefore likely to disappear if taller vegetation cover develops (e.g. through cessation of grazing at coastal sites). The threat status of subsp. *multispira* in Ireland needs to be established by further research, but if all records of *F. husnotii* really belong with this taxon it will still remain on the Red List (as Vulnerable: B2a, bii, iv).

Conservation

Further research on the status of subsp. *multispira* is needed to establish its precise status in Ireland.

Protected sites with recent records: Mweelrea/ Sheeffry/Erriff Complex SAC; The Twelve Bens/ Garraun Complex SAC; **Unprotected sites with recent records:** Dromore; Glenbower Wood, near Killeagh; N. end of Glanleam Gardens, Valencia Island.

Fossombronia maritima (Paton) Paton   Sea Frillwort

syn. *Fossombronia pusilla* var. *maritima* Paton
Status in Ireland: Near Threatened; **Status in Europe:** Least Concern

Fossombronia maritima is very similar to the common *F. pusilla*, but differs in having a greater number of marginal tubercles on the spores (19–24 rather than 15–19), having a more prominent central axis in its thalli, and being almost exclusively coastal. Stotler *et al.* (2003) consider this species to be synonymous with *F. pusilla*, but European bryologists still regard it as a good species. It is a plant of non-calcareous peaty soil in coastal heathland, disused quarries and dune slacks and has been reported from two vice-counties, with records from six hectads (1 old, 6 recent). While it may still be under-recorded in Ireland, it does seem to be genuinely rare. Its relatively recent taxonomic recognition precludes possible evidence of decline.

Fossombronia fimbriata Paton   Fragile Frillwort

Status in Ireland: Vulnerable (D2); **Status in Europe:** Rare

Identification

Although small, this is a very distinctive semi-thallose liverwort. It forms dense rosettes up to c. 3.5 mm across composed of pale green 'leaves' which are deeply dissected into irregular fimbriate lobes, giving the plant a distinctive fluffy appearance. The rosettes arise from an ascending, subterranean rhizome-like axis, which may act as a perennating structure. Like most other species of *Fossombronia*, it has purple rhizoids. The spores are permanently united in tetrads. *Equisetum* prothalli look rather similar, but lack purple rhizoids.

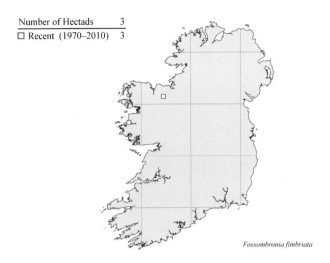

Number of Hectads   3
☐ Recent (1970–2010)   3

Fossombronia fimbriata

Distribution in Ireland

This species was discovered new to science in 1967, and first found in Ireland in 1970, but not described as a species until 1974 (Paton 1974). There are three known Irish localities in two vice-counties: W. Mayo (Bunakee River, 1987 and Trawmore, Achill Island, 1987) and Sligo (near Masshill in the Ox Mountains, 1970).

Ecology and biology

In Ireland, *F. fimbriata* has been found on damp sandy ground in coastal sand dunes, in an old quarry and by a river. More generally, it grows, usually as scattered thalli, on a variety of damp, bare soils, often in association with other species of *Fossombronia*, bulbiliferous species of *Pohlia* and *Haplomitrium hookeri*. It is mainly a lowland plant.

It is often fertile but is dioicous and sporophytes are very rare. The fragile leaves readily fragment and vegetative reproduction occurs by the development of rhizoids and of tuber-like regenerants from the leaf cells (Paton 1999).

World distribution

F. fimbriata is a European endemic, known only from Ireland, Britain, the Netherlands and Germany. It is *Near Threatened* in Britain and *Rare* in Germany. Its distribution pattern, as far as is known from the presumably very incomplete data available, is categorised as Oceanic Temperate.

Threats

No specific threats have been identified, but the sites may be vulnerable to land-use change.

Conservation

This seems to be a colonist species and is almost certainly overlooked. However, because it is currently known from so few sites, these should be maintained in a suitable condition and the plant monitored. At least two of its three sites require new survey work to ascertain whether it is still present. The third site (Trawmore) has been revisited several times in recent years, but *F. fimbriata* has not been refound there.

Protected sites with recent records: Keel Machair/ Menaun Cliffs SAC; **Unprotected sites with recent records:** Bunakee River; near Masshill in the Ox Mountains.

Moerckia hibernica (Hook.) Gottsche

Irish Ruffwort

syn. *Jungermannia hibernica* Hook., *Moerchia hibernica* (Hook.) Gottsche f. *hibernica*, *Pallavicinia hibernica* (Hook.) Gray
Status in Ireland: Data Deficient; **Status in Europe:** Not Evaluated

Identification

A thallose liverwort that grows on wet, open ground. The branched thalli are yellowish-green, pale green, green, or sometimes brownish, shiny, 2–7 mm wide and up to c. 30 mm in length, with a narrow costa and lamina varying from plane and nearly horizontal to undulate and ascending or erect. The strong aroma is a feature of thalli of this species and the closely allied *M. flotoviana* (Nees)

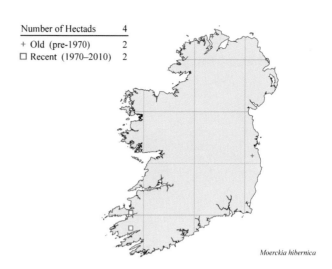

Number of Hectads	4
+ Old (pre-1970)	2
□ Recent (1970–2010)	2

Moerckia hibernica

Schiffn., providing an easy distinction from *Pellia* spp. Both of these *Moerckia* species also have hyaline or pale yellow rhizoids, female thalli possessing an involucre of laciniate lamellae and a cylindrical pseudoperianth (plicate above with mouth contracted and dentate-ciliate). Most of the modern literature treats *M. flotoviana* as a synonym of *M. hibernica* (e.g. Paton 1999) or merely a form of that species (Damsholt 2002), but Crandall-Stotler & Stotler (2007) have demonstrated that they are distinct species. *M. hibernica s.str.* differs from *M. flotoviana* in the elongate, stipitate thalli; frequent formation of ventral branches from the stipe; homogeneous costa that lacks hydrolysed strands; mostly unistratose lamina; transversely inserted, ovate perigonia that are arranged alternately in two rows; single posterior gynoecial scale complex; an inclined pseudoperianth; fairly thick shoot calyptra; bistratose capsule wall and tuberculate spores (Crandall-Stotler & Stotler *op. cit.*). Characters in which *M. hibernica s.str.* was said to differ from *M. flotoviana* by Damsholt (2002) are not diagnostic (including smaller thalli, much less undulate lamina, thinner costa and smaller spores).

Distribution in Ireland

Currently there are confirmed recent reports of *M. hibernica* from two vice-counties (D.G. Long *in litt.*): S. Kerry (Mullaghanattin, 1983) and N. Kerry (head of Gormagh Valley, Slieve Mish Mountains, 2009), with older confirmed records from Wicklow (Lough Bray, 1814, leg. Taylor, [type specimen, **BM**] and 1897, leg. McArdle) and E. Donegal (Bulbin Mountain, 1968). More research is needed to establish the Irish range and status of *M. hibernica s.str.*, although it seems likely to be rare because there are few records of *Moerckia* inland.

Ecology and biology

In Ireland and Britain, *M. flotoviana* appears to be much the more common species, occurring in coastal dune slacks, whereas *M. hibernica* occurs mainly in upland flushes (Hill *et al.* 2008, Blackstock 2009). Crandall-Stotler & Stotler (2007) noted that *M. hibernica s.str.* generally grows intermixed with Sphagna in wet boggy habitats, implying a preference for much more acidic conditions than those favoured by *M. flotoviana*. Reports from Fennoscandia implying *M. hibernica s.str.* occurs in open depressions of rich fens, or their edges, among other calciphiles (Damsholt 2002) therefore need confirmation.

The species is dioicous, but usually fertile, with frequent sporophytes that have mature spores in spring or early summer. Vegetative propagules are lacking, but as in *M. flotoviana* the rhizome-like costae may enable the plants to survive in periods of desiccation (Paton 1999).

World distribution

Information on *M. hibernica s.str.* is incomplete because many authors have not separated it from *M. flotoviana*. Recent reappraisal of British specimens by D.G. Long (in Hill *et al.* 2008) records it only from Scotland (Mid Perthshire, Angus, S. Aberdeenshire, Easterness, Shetland). The aggregate of both species has a wide range in the Pyrenees, Alps, Balkans, Caucasus, N. Asia (Siberia) and northern N. America (Alaska and Ellesmere I. to Washington State and New York State), but it is at present uncertain how much of this is occupied by *M. hibernica s.str.* and how much by *M. flotoviana*. Records confirmed as *M. hibernica s.str.* are as yet only from Ireland, Scotland and the Pacific Northwest of

N. America (Crandall-Stotler & Stotler 2007, D.G. Long in Hill *et al.* 2008). Reports of *M. hibernica s.str.* from Scandinavia (Damsholt 2002) thus need confirmation.

Threats

There is no detailed information, but this rare liverwort is likely to be at risk if conditions change in montane flushes. Excessive trampling or erosion could be harmful, as would increased shade from taller plants if grazing pressure was greatly reduced. Like other montane plants it might also be at risk from long-term climate change.

Conservation

Little information is available on the status and ecology of *M. hibernica s.str.* because it has only recently been recognised as taxonomically distinct from the more common coastal *M. flotoviana*. However, there are so few records of any *Moerckia* from montane habitats in Ireland that it is almost certainly a genuinely rare species that merits targeted surveys.

Protected sites with recent records: Killarney National Park, Macgillycuddy's Reeks and Caragh River Catchment SAC; Slieve Mish Mountains SAC; **Unprotected sites with recent records:** none.

Pallavicinia lyellii (Hook.) Carruth.   Ribbonwort, Veilwort

syn. *Blyttia lyellii* (Hook.) Engl. ex Gottsche, Lindenb. & Nees, *Dilaena lyellii* (Hook.) Dumort., *Diplomitrion lyellii* (Hook.) Corda, *Jungermannia lyellii* Hook., *Sweetzia lyellii* (Hook.) Lehm.
Status in Ireland: Endangered (B1a, bi, ii, iv, B2a, bi, ii, iv); **Status in Europe:** Vulnerable

Number of Hectads	13
+ Old (pre-1970)	9
□ Recent (1970–2010)	4

Pallavicinia lyellii

Identification

This delicate thallose liverwort somewhat resembles a large *Metzgeria* or a species of *Pellia*. It is pale green and grows as patches or scattered thalli; the thallus is simple or occasionally branched, up to 5 cm long and 4 mm wide, unistratose and translucent, with a thicker and well-defined costa. The costa is often ornamented with the frilly inflorescences; the antheridia, which are protected by lobed scales, are in two rows, one on either side of the costa; the perianth is cylindrical, 5–7 mm long, with the lobed involucre at the base. A steroid isolated from *P. lyellii* has been shown to have anti-fungal properties (Subhisha & Subramoniam 2005).

Distribution in Ireland

This species is widely scattered in suitable habitats, but absent from the north. There are four recent records: N. Kerry (Shronowen Bog, 2009); W. Cork (NW of Knocknamaddree, Goleen, 2007); Limerick (Sugar Hill, 1979) and Wicklow (Rathduffmore Bog, 1975). There are also older records from 11 localities in seven vice-counties: S. Kerry (Maghanaboe Glen, 1865; Stradbally Mountain, 1953–1954); N. Kerry ('Killarney woods', 1836); W. Cork (near Bantry, 1850); Kilkenny (Derryfadda, W. of Johnstown, 1966); Kildare (Leixlip railway station, 1890); Wicklow (Lough Bray, 1836–1887) and W. Mayo ('Achill', 1962; Keel, 1962; Corraun,

1965; Purteen, 1968). Sugar Hill, Rathduffmore Bog and all of the older sites have been revisited as part of a recent programme of fieldwork, but without success. A record from Antrim (White Park Bay, 1991) is unconfirmed and must be considered erroneous.

Ecology and biology

Habitat information on this species in Ireland is rather sketchy, but it has been recorded from wet peaty ground in drains, ditches and hollows in bogs, in *Molinia*-dominated acidic mire and on wet rocks by waterfalls in ravines. The most recent record (Shronowen Bog) came from *Molinia* hummocks in a peat cutting on a bog. In Britain, it also grows on wet, shaded sandstone rocks. It is mainly a lowland species.

P. lyellii is dioicous and although fertile male and female plants are both frequent, sporophytes are rare.

World distribution

This plant is widely but very sparsely distributed in Europe. It is recorded but not red-listed in Denmark, France, the Netherlands, Germany, Portugal, Spain, Romania, Greece, Ukraine, the Azores and Madeira. It is listed as *Extinct* in Sweden, Austria, Slovakia and probably in the Czech Republic and Italy, *Endangered* in Poland and Lithuania, *Vulnerable* in Britain and *Rare* in Belgium. In Europe, it is categorised as a Suboceanic Southern-temperate floristic element. *P. lyellii* is very widely distributed outside Europe and is a common plant in some parts of its range. It has been recorded from Africa, Asia, N. and S. America, Oceania and Australasia.

Threats

P. lyellii appears to have declined in Ireland because of habitat degradation. Loss of some of its former sites through drainage of bogs and marshes and afforestation has certainly taken place. The inability of single-sex populations to colonise new sites by spores may be a significant factor in reducing its mobility. The situation in Ireland appears to be part of a Europe-wide decline of this plant.

Conservation

More intensive survey is needed of some of this plant's known sites, although it must have disappeared from others, as the habitat has been destroyed. Strict protection of any sites found is recommended, coupled with appropriate management. *Ex situ* conservation and eventual reintroduction to suitable sites could also be considered.

Protected sites with recent records: none; **Unprotected sites with recent records:** NW of Knocknamaddree, Goleen; Rathduffmore Bog; Shronowen Bog; Sugar Hill.

Metzgeria leptoneura Spruce   Hooked Veilwort

syn. *Metzgeria hamata* Lindb. *nom. illeg.*
Status in Ireland: Near Threatened; **Status in Europe:** Least Concern

Metzgeria leptoneura is a strongly Atlantic species that grows in sheltered, wet places in ravines, especially on rocks in the spray zone of waterfalls, and on other dripping rocks. It can form large patches growing like 'brackets' and is distinguished from other more common species of *Metzgeria* by the many long, hooked hairs, arranged in pairs, which give the downturned margins of the thalli a tubular appearance. It has been reported from 10 vice-counties, with records from 34 hectads (29 old, 13 recent). *M. leptoneura* was not included in the Provisional Red List (Holyoak 2006b) so was not particularly sought during much of the recent fieldwork. It is undoubtedly under-recorded over the past decade rather than showing much evidence of decline.

Metzgeria pubescens (Schrank) Raddi

Hairy Veilwort

syn. *Apometzgeria pubescens* (Schrank) Kuwah., *Echinomitrion furcatum* var. *pubescens* (Schrank) Corda, *Jungermannia pubescens* Schrank

Status in Ireland: Vulnerable (D2); **Status in Europe:** Least Concern

Number of Hectads	7
+ Old (pre-1970)	6
☐ Recent (1970–2010)	4

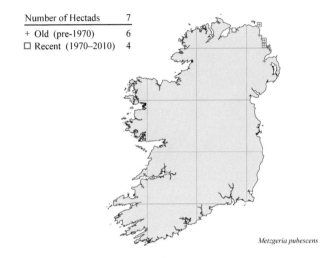

Metzgeria pubescens

Identification

M. pubescens is a green thallose liverwort with a delicate, unistratose thallus and a conspicuous costa. It differs from other members of the genus *Metzgeria* in having the thallus densely covered with short hairs, making it one of the most distinctive and easily identified liverwort species. It also tends to be larger than other *Metzgeria* spp., with thalli up to c. 3.5 cm long and c. 2 mm wide. This species was until recently separated from *Metzgeria* in its own genus, *Apometzgeria*. However, molecular studies (Forrest *et al.* 2006) have shown that it is too closely related to justify this generic placement, so it is now considered to be a member of *Metzgeria*.

Distribution in Ireland

Confined to sites near the coast in Northern Ireland, there are recent records from four localities in two vice-counties: Antrim (Sallagh Braes, 1876–1999; Straidkilly Wood, 1992–2008 and West Torr, 1952–2008) and Londonderry (The Umbra, 1999). There are older records from Antrim (Garron Plateau, 1952; Bellair Hill, 1910; Carr's Glen, Belfast, 1876–1887 and Larne (1888). An additional Antrim report from White Park Bay in 1991 is unconfirmed and must be disregarded.

Ecology and biology

A strict calcicole, *M. pubescens* grows on shaded chalk ('limestone') and (rarely) basalt rocks, associated with other calcicoles such as *Ctenidium molluscum* and *Neckera* spp. It is usually found at low altitudes.

This species is often fertile, with male plants more frequent than female, but sporophytes are unknown in Ireland or Britain. Gemmae are unknown.

World distribution

Widespread in most upland and montane parts of C. and W. Europe, but rare or absent in most northern areas (in spite of its distinctly northern distribution in Ireland and Britain), it is present in Norway, northern Russia, Ukraine and the Caucasus and present but *Endangered* in Sweden and Luxembourg and *Vulnerable* in Poland. It is scattered in Mediterranean and Balkan regions, but absent from several countries. In Europe, it is assigned to a Circumpolar Boreal-montane floristic element. It is widespread in Asia and N. America, and also present in southern S. America.

Threats

No obvious threats have been identified.

Conservation

Several populations are at protected sites. *M. pubescens* is listed as a Northern Ireland Priority Species.

Protected sites with recent records: Downhill ASSI; Straidkilly ASSI; Straidkilly Nature Reserve; **Unprotected sites with recent records:** Knockdu and Sallagh Braes (proposed ASSI); West Torr.

Aneura mirabilis (Malmb.) Wickett & Goffinet

Ghostwort

syn. *Cryptothallus mirabilis* Malmb.
Status in Ireland: Vulnerable (B2a, bii, iii, iv); **Status in Europe:** Least Concern

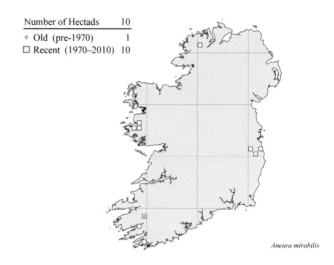

Number of Hectads	10
+ Old (pre-1970)	1
☐ Recent (1970–2010)	10

Aneura mirabilis

Identification

The identification of this thallose liverwort is usually no problem, as it is unique in comprising a pure white thallus, devoid of chlorophyll, resembling a white form of *Aneura pinguis*. Nevertheless, the plant resembles a fungus at first sight, although fertile material demonstrates that it is a liverwort. Finding it is less easy, as searching may necessitate peeling back layers of *Sphagnum*. The thallus grows up to c. 4 cm long and 5 mm wide, and has a very simple structure, without any pores, gemmae or other ornamentation. This species was recently transferred from *Cryptothallus* to *Aneura* on the basis of molecular data (Wickett & Goffinet 2008).

Distribution in Ireland

A. mirabilis appears to be widespread, and must surely be overlooked. There are recent records from 10 localities in six vice-counties: S. Kerry (Uragh Wood, 2006); N. Kerry (Five Mile Bridge, 2005); W. Cork (Mount Gabriel Woods, 2009); W. Galway (Kylemore Castle, 1970; Tullyconor Bridge, 1970 and Derryclare Wood, 1994); Wicklow (Great Sugar Loaf, 1991 and 2007, Kippure House, 1992 and Lough Dan, 1975 and 2007); W. Donegal (Glenveagh, 1991). There is an older record, the first Irish record, from Muckross, 1968 (S. Kerry).

Ecology and biology

This is an underground parasite that relies on a mycorrhizal fungal endophyte to gather nutrients from a host tree (Ligrone *et al.* 1993). It grows principally on wet acid peat underneath *Sphagnum* (particularly *Sphagnum palustre*) in boggy birch woodland. It may also grow beneath other mosses on damp peat, and thalli are occasionally visible on the surface. Other associates in Ireland include *Molinia caerulea*, *Pteridium aquilinum*, *Sphagnum fallax*, *S. fimbriatum*, *S. subnitens*, *Loeskeobryum brevirostre* and *Thuidium tamariscinum*. It is a lowland plant, growing at altitudes up to 230 m in Ireland.

This species is dioicous, usually fertile and sporophytes are frequent. Gemmae are absent.

World distribution

Its European distribution is inevitably poorly known, but seems to be centred in W. Europe and Scandinavia, with only very few records further east. It is *Nationally Scarce* in Britain, *Extinct* in Austria, *Vulnerable* in Finland, *Rare* in Germany, and *Data Deficient* in Sweden and Portugal. The only other European countries where *A. mirabilis* is currently recorded (and either not threatened or with status not mentioned) are Norway, Denmark, France, Belgium and NW Russia. In Europe, it is assigned to a European Boreal-montane floristic element. The species is also known from subarctic N. America.

Threats

Habitat destruction through drainage, afforestation or other land-use change is the main threat to this species. Although admittedly under-recorded, *A. mirabilis* is probably also declining, as it is known that at least two of the populations have been destroyed: Derryclare Wood in W. Galway is now deep-ploughed and afforested with conifers, and the site at Kippure House in Wicklow has also been afforested, except for a narrow marginal strip of birchwood that can probably no longer sustain *A. mirabilis*. Vegetation succession has probably rendered a third site (Muckross) unsuitable for the plant.

Conservation

Areas of wet birch woodland known to support this species should be considered for protection. Other similar areas should be surveyed to determine whether it is present, and so build up a more complete picture of its distribution.

Protected sites with recent records: Cloghernagore Bog and Glenveagh National Park SAC; Cloonee and Inchiquin Loughs, Uragh Wood SAC; Glenveagh National Park; Great Sugar Loaf pNHA; Killarney National Park; Killarney National Park, Macgillycuddy's Reeks and Caragh River Catchment SAC; Wicklow Mountains SAC; Uragh Wood Nature Reserve; **Unprotected sites with recent records:** Derryclare Wood; Kippure House; Kylemore Castle (probably just outside The Twelve Bens/Garraun Complex SAC); Mount Gabriel Woods; Tullyconor Bridge (probably just outside The Twelve Bens/Garraun Complex SAC).

Great Sugar Loaf, Co. Wicklow.

Porella cordaeana (Huebener) Moore

Cliff Scalewort

syn. *Jungermannia cordaeana* Huebener, *Madotheca cordaeana* (Huebener) Dumort., *M. dentata* Mass., *M. rivularis* Nees, *Porella dentata* Lindb.
Status in Ireland: Near Threatened; **Status in Europe:** Least Concern

This leafy liverwort forms dull, dark green patches, or grows through other bryophytes, on rocks and tree bases in wooded ravines, sometimes on rocks beside upland corries, but especially on silt-covered tree bases and rocks in the flood zone of lowland rivers and streams. It is rather rare and scattered in Ireland and has been reported from 20 vice-counties, with records from 27 hectads (20 old, 10 recent). The evidence suggests that it may have declined to some extent, though not significantly.

Porella pinnata L.

Pinnate Scalewort

syn. *Madotheca porella* (Dicks.) Nees
Status in Ireland: Least Concern; **Status in Europe:** Least Concern

This leafy liverwort forms lax, dull green, or olive green patches or tufts on rocks and tree boles subject to flooding. It is essentially an aquatic species of rivers and streams and is fairly widespread in Ireland, especially in the south. It is known from 16 vice-counties, with records from 27 hectads (19 old, 16 recent) and cannot be considered to have declined. However, it may be sensitive to pollution so a watching brief needs to be kept on its presence.

Radula lindenbergiana Gottsche ex C.Hartm.

Lindenberg's Scalewort

syn. *Radula commutata* Gottsche, *R. complanata* subsp. *lindbergiana* (Gottsche ex C.Hartm.) R.M.Schust., *R. germana* Jack, *R. lindbergiana* auct., *R. ovata* Jack
Status in Ireland: Least Concern; **Status in Europe:** Least Concern

Although often confused with the common *R. complanata*, and only reliably distinguished when fertile, this attractive pale yellow-green leafy liverwort appears to be quite widespread in the south and west. It is usually found on rocks, especially in upland areas, and has been reported from 10 vice-counties, with records from 23 hectads (10 old, 15 recent, 1 undated). It was included in the Provisional Red List (Holyoak 2006b) but it is now clear that there is no evidence of decline.

Radula voluta Taylor ex Gottsche *et al.*

Pale Scalewort

Status in Ireland: Least Concern; **Status in Europe:** Rare

This leafy liverwort has a strongly oceanic range and is almost confined to the west, where it occurs on shaded, damp rocks in streams, especially by waterfalls. It has been reported from nine vice-counties, with records from 27 hectads (18 old, 18 recent). It does not appear to have declined significantly, if at all. However, *R. voluta* has a very restricted range in Europe, being otherwise known only from the extreme west of Britain. Elsewhere, it occurs in Africa and the southern Appalachian Mountains in the USA.

Radula holtii Spruce

Status in Ireland: Near Threatened; **Status in Europe:** Rare

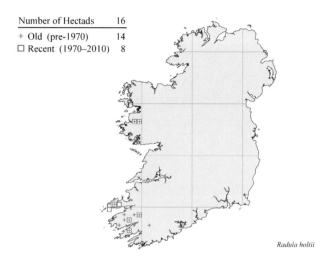

Number of Hectads	16
+ Old (pre-1970)	14
☐ Recent (1970–2010)	8

Radula holtii

Identification

Like all species of *Radula*, *R. holtii* is a rather fleshy leafy liverwort with a rounded leaf lobe much larger than the almost square lobule beneath, and no underleaves. It is yellowish-green in colour and the shoots grow up to c. 2 cm long and 1.8 mm wide. Although superficially similar to the much more common *R. complanata* and *R. lindenbergiana*, the antical leaf margin of *R. holtii* does not cross the stem, and gemmae are very rare, whereas they are very common in the other two species. Furthermore, the perianths are characteristically trumpet-shaped, with a narrow base and a wide mouth; the other two species have oblong perianths. Finally, the cell walls of the stem medulla are thin-walled rather than collenchymatous.

Distribution in Ireland

R. holtii is confined to the extreme west and south-west, with recent records from 11 localities in four vice-counties: S. Kerry (Brandon Mountain, 1961–2008; Lough Anscaul, 2006; Loch an Duin, 2006; An Loch Dubh, Ballysitteragh, 2006; Mount Eagle, 2006; Ballaghbeama Gap, 1967–1983); N. Kerry (Muckross-Ross Island, 1905–1983; Torc Cascade, 1885–2005); W. Cork (Glenbeg Lough and Lackawee, 1955–1979) and W. Mayo (Ben Gorm, 1901–1987; Devil's Mother, 1901–1987). There are older records from a further 11 localities in: S. Kerry (Lough Currane, 1967; Lough Coomeathcun, 1951; Coomasaharn, 1961; Inchiquin

Lough, 1967; Uragh Wood, 1967; Cummeenduff Glen, 1967; O'Sullivan's Cascade, 1912–1935); N. Kerry (Eagle's Nest, 1911–1925; Derrycunihy Wood, 1967); W. Cork (Pass of Keimaneigh, 1967) and W. Mayo (Old Head Wood, 1901–1909). It is not clear whether there has actually been a decline in the species, since *R. holtii* was not on the original list of target species for recent fieldwork and little effort has therefore been made to refind it at old localities. This plant is described as Southern Atlantic by Ratcliffe (1968).

Ecology and biology

R. holtii is a hyperoceanic species that grows in shade, usually deep shade, on wet rocks in ravines, woodland, by lakes, in small caves or under overhangs, usually by streams and waterfalls, especially where permanently wet from spray. It is a lowland plant, recorded in Ireland from near sea level to c. 330 m. Associates include *Jubula hutchinsiae*, *Lejeunea* spp., *Plagiochila exigua*, *Porella pinnata*, other *Radula* spp., *Trichostomum hibernicum* and *Trichomanes speciosum*.

Paroicous and often fertile, sporophytes are frequent in this species. Gemmae are very rare.

World distribution

This plant is recorded from the Azores, Madeira and the Canary Islands, where it is not on any list of rare or threatened species, and also from Spain and Portugal, in both of which it is listed as *Vulnerable*. It is absent from Britain. It is classified as a Hyperoceanic Southern-temperate floristic element and is apparently endemic to Europe and Macaronesia.

Threats

There are probably few real threats to *R. holtii*, but water abstraction for hydroelectric schemes could endanger this species at some sites.

Conservation

This species has a very restricted distribution and the

Irish populations are of global importance for conservation. Efforts should be made to target this species for resurvey, in particular the many localities described from the 1960s. Populations at the more important sites should be monitored.

Protected sites with recent records: Glanmore Bog SAC; Killarney National Park; Killarney National Park, Macgillycuddy's Reeks and Caragh River Catchment SAC; Maumtrasna Mountain Complex pNHA; Mount Brandon SAC; Mweelrea/Sheeffry/Erriff Complex SAC; **Unprotected sites with recent records:** Mount Eagle.

Radula carringtonii J.B.Jack

Carrington's Scalewort

Status in Ireland: Near Threatened; **Status in Europe:** Rare

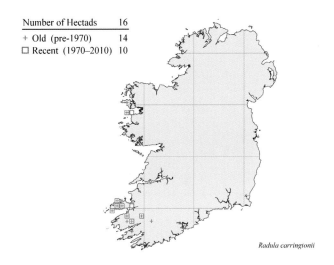

Number of Hectads	16
+ Old (pre-1970)	14
□ Recent (1970–2010)	10

Radula carringtonii

Identification

R. carringtonii is a dull green or sometimes brownish leafy liverwort with shoots up to c. 4 cm long and 2.5 mm wide, loosely appressed to the substratum, forming thin mats or creeping among other bryophytes. Like all species of *Radula*, the rounded leaf lobe is much larger than the almost square lobule lying beneath, there are no underleaves, and the texture is rather fleshy. The marginal cells of the leaf are small and thick-walled. The dull, dark colour is different from the pale yellowish-green of *R. complanata*, *R. lindenbergiana* and *R. voluta*, and *R. carringtonii* lacks gemmae. It may easily be confused with *R. aquilegia*, which is also dark and has small marginal cells, but that species normally has inflated lobules and erecto-patent stem leaves, whereas those of

R. carringtonii are patent. There are also differences in the male bracts.

Distribution in Ireland

R. carringtonii is confined to the extreme west coast of Ireland, centred on Kerry, where it can be locally abundant at some sites on the Dingle Peninsula. There are recent records from 15 localities in three vice-counties: S. Kerry (Ballaghbeama Gap, 1967–2006; below Brandon Mountain, 1899–2009; Coomacullen Lake, 2006; Coomnacronia Lake, 1983; Loch Bhearna na Gaoithe, 2006; Lough Anscaul, 1894–2006; Mount Eagle, 1898–2006; Mullaghanattin, 1983; O'Sullivan's Cascade, 1873–1988); N. Kerry (Brickeen Bridge, 1951–2005; Torc Cascade, 1861–2005; Cahnicaun Wood, 1988; Lough

197

Erhogh-Lough Managh, 1983; Gormagh, 2009) and W. Mayo (Clare Island, 1909–1994). There are older records from several other sites in Kerry, as well as old records from Ballyfinnane Bridge and Lackawee in W. Cork, at both of which it was last seen in 1967, and Bengorm (1901) and Slievemore (1909) in W. Mayo. It is listed as a Southern Atlantic species by Ratcliffe (1968).

Ecology and biology

R. carringtonii grows on shaded, wet or damp, usually base-rich, rocks in ravines and among boulders by streams, waterfalls and lakes. It occasionally grows on drier rocks on more or less open N.- and NE-facing hillsides, especially where shaded amongst boulders, beneath overhangs or in small caves. It is usually associated with other bryophytes, notably *Fissidens dubius*, *Isothecium myosuroides*, *Lejeunea* spp., *Metzgeria* spp., *Plagiochila* spp., *Saccogyna viticulosa*, *Thamnobryum alopecurum* and *Trichostomum hibernicum*. This is a lowland plant, recorded in Ireland from near sea level to c. 500 m.

It is dioicous and often fertile, but sporophytes are very rare. Gemmae are unknown.

World distribution

This plant is confined to the extreme Atlantic fringe of Europe, where it is listed as *Vulnerable* in Britain (occurring at a few scattered sites in W. Scotland), and is also present in the Azores, Madeira and the Canary Islands. A record from Spain has been discounted (Söderström *et al.* 2002). It is highly oceanic in its European distribution, and therefore categorised as a Hyperoceanic Southern-temperate floristic element. Until recently considered a European endemic, *R. carringtonii* has now also been recorded from Costa Rica (Yamada 1995) and Réunion (Arts & Yamada 1998). This rather unusual global range deserves closer study through molecular analyses.

Threats

There are probably few real threats to *R. carringtonii* in its south-western strongholds, but afforestation, overstocking, burning and development pressures are all potential threats. Water abstraction for hydroelectric schemes could endanger this species at some sites.

Conservation

The very restricted distribution of this species and the global importance of the Irish populations mean that conservation measures, if necessary, would be appropriate. Populations at the more important sites should be monitored.

Protected sites with recent records: Clare Island pNHA; Killarney National Park; Killarney National Park, Macgillycuddy's Reeks and Caragh River Catchment SAC; Mount Brandon SAC; Slieve Mish Mountains SAC; **Unprotected sites with recent records:** Mount Eagle.

Cololejeunea rossettiana (C.Massal.) Schiffn.

Rossett's Pouncewort

syn. *Lejeunea rossettiana* C.Massal., *Physcocolea rossettiana* (C.Massal.) Steph.
Status in Ireland: Least Concern; **Status in Europe:** Least Concern

This minute leafy liverwort forms dense yellowish-green patches, often growing epiphytically on bryophytes and lichens, or on thin humus layers on calcareous rock surfaces, in shaded ravines, cliffs and other humid habitats. It was included in the Provisional Red List (Holyoak 2006b) but recent fieldwork has shown it to be widespread in Ireland. It has been reported from 16 vice-counties, with records from at least 22 hectads (13 old, 13 recent). There is no evidence of decline.

Lejeunea flava (Sw.) Nees **subsp.** *moorei* (Lindb.) R.M.Schust.

Yellow Pouncewort

Status in Ireland: Vulnerable (B2a, bii, iv); **Status in Europe:** Rare

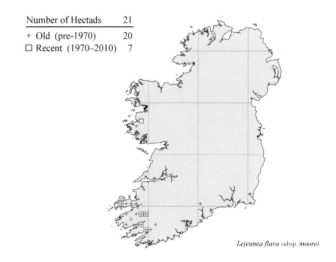

Number of Hectads	21
+ Old (pre-1970)	20
☐ Recent (1970–2010)	7

Lejeunea flava subsp. *moorei*

Identification

L. flava is a small leafy liverwort that forms mats or creeps among other bryophytes, with shoots up to 2 cm long and c. 1.5 mm wide. As in other species of the genus, the leaves are more or less oval with sac-like ventral lobules and the underleaves are bilobed. It differs from other species of *Lejeunea* in its relatively long leaves (oval or ovate rather than suborbicular or ovate), the relatively large, ovate underleaves and its opacity and intense yellow-green colour. Further points of distinction are the finely papillose cuticle, the oil bodies, which are 3–8 (–14) per cell, coarsely granular and disappear rapidly on drying, and the strongly arcuate antical leaf margin, with a relatively short line of insertion. At present, the Irish (and Macaronesian) material is referred to subsp. *moorei*. However, there is some dispute about the validity and relationships of the various subspecies of *L. flava*, as it is a complex and variable species.

Distribution in Ireland

L. flava is an essentially tropical species, just reaching the extreme south-west coast of Ireland, and listed as Southern Atlantic by Ratcliffe (1968). There are recent records from 11 localities in four vice-counties: S. Kerry (Brandon Mountain, 1881–2008; Uragh Wood, 1967–1979; Looscaunagh Wood, 1973; Cahnicaun Wood, 1988; O'Sullivan's Cascade, 1893–1988); N. Kerry (Eagle's Nest, 1906–2005; Derrycunihy Wood, 1906–1988; Five Mile Bridge, 1965–1983; Torc Cascade,

1897–1983); W. Cork (Glengarriff, 1893–1979) and W. Mayo (Ben Gorm, 1987). There are many further older records from S. Kerry (20 localities) and N. Kerry (7 localities), as well as older records from W. Cork (Coomroe, 1967; Pass of Keimaneigh, 1967); Waterford (Lismore, 1967) and W. Galway (Benlettery, 1968; Kylemore, 1950–1968). Although recorded in the past from many localities, little targeted effort was made to refind it during recent fieldwork, but it is thought unlikely to have declined severely.

Ecology and biology

This species grows on the sides of boulders and on more or less vertical rock faces in humid woodland, ravines, lake sides and block scree (and once on a shaded stone wall). It favours neutral to base-rich rocks, and can grow directly on the rock, or creeping over other bryophytes and filmy-fern *Hymenophyllum* fronds. It is strongly oceanic, and is usually associated with other oceanic species, including *Adelanthus decipiens*, *Lejeunea hibernica*, *L. lamacerina*, *L. patens*, *Harpalejeunea molleri*, *Plagiochila bifaria*, *P. exigua*, *Radula* spp. and *Saccogyna viticulosa*. It is a lowland species, growing from sea level up to 300 m.

It is autoicous and often fertile, but sporophytes are rare. Gemmae are absent.

World distribution

It is also present in the Azores, Madeira and the Canary Islands, where it is not considered threatened. Its European distribution is classified as Hyperoceanic Southern-temperate. While subsp. *moorei* is endemic to Europe and Macaronesia, *L. flava* as a species is widespread in the tropics, occurring in Africa, S. and SE Asia, Australasia, Oceania, southern N. America and S. America.

Threats

This species was not initially included on the list of target species for recent fieldwork because there were many records from the 1950s and 1960s. Hence the paucity of more recent records is at least partly due to lack of searching. Possible threats could include shading from Rhododendron, overenthusiastic collecting by botanists, afforestation, overstocking and nutrient enrichment, leading to vigorous growth of green algae.

Conservation

Old localities for this species should be revisited in order to gain a better understanding of its current status.

Protected sites with recent records: Cloonee and Inchiquin Loughs, Uragh Wood SAC; Derrycunihy Wood Nature Reserve; Glengarriff Harbour and Woodland SAC; Glengarriff Wood Nature Reserve; Killarney National Park; Killarney National Park, Macgillycuddy's Reeks and Caragh River Catchment SAC; Mount Brandon SAC; Mweelrea/Sheeffry/Erriff Complex SAC; Uragh Wood Nature Reserve; **Unprotected sites with recent records:** none.

Lejeunea hibernica Bischl. *et al.* ex Grolle

Irish Pouncewort

syn. *Lejeunea diversiloba* auct. non Spruce
Status in Ireland: Near Threatened; **Status in Europe:** Rare

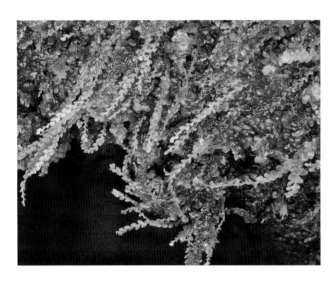

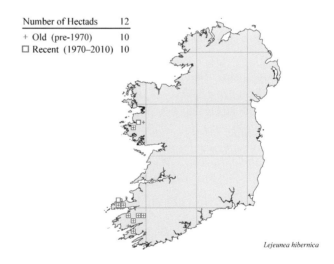

Number of Hectads	12
+ Old (pre-1970)	10
□ Recent (1970–2010)	10

Lejeunea hibernica

Identification

As in other species of the genus, the leaves of *L. hibernica* are more or less oval with sac-like ventral lobules and the underleaves are bilobed. *L. hibernica* is a particularly small species, the pale green, rather rigid shoots reaching only c. 1.5 cm long and 0.6 mm wide. It grows as isolated shoots creeping through other bryophytes or as mats, which can occasionally be extensive. It is characterised by its neat, rigid shoots, and the very variable lobules, which may, on the same shoot, be minute or obsolete to inflated and almost as large as the lobes. The leaf cells are unlike those of other Irish *Lejeunea* species, being uniformly thick-walled. It is most similar to *Microlejeunea ulicina*, but that species has much less variable lobules and lacks the uniformly thick-walled leaf cells.

Distribution in Ireland

This plant has a strongly south-western distribution, with most records from Co. Kerry where it can be locally abundant at some sites. There are recent records from 17 localities in five vice-counties: S. Kerry (Brandon Mountain, 1967–2006; Connor Pass, 1881–2006; An Loch Dubh, 2006; An Loch Geal, 2006; Lough Cummeenoughter, 2006; Lough Anscaul, 1898–2006;

Lough Doon, 2006; Loch Bhearna na Gaoithe, 2006; Maghanaboe Glen, 2006; S. of Coomacullen Lake, 2006; Mullaghanattin, 1972, 1983; Ballaghbeama Gap, 1967–2006; Looscaunagh Wood, 1983); N. Kerry (Torc Cascade, 1842–2005); W. Cork (Lackawee, 1955–2006); W. Galway (Kylemore, 1933–2010) and W. Mayo (Mweelrea, 1987, 2003). There are older records from S. Kerry (Lough Coomeathcun, 1951; Cummeenduff Glen, 1967); N. Kerry (Five Mile Bridge, 1965; Eagle's Nest, 1861–1965; Glena, 1863) and W. Mayo (Devil's Mother, 1901) as well as unconfirmed records from Pontoon (W. Mayo, 1901) and Errisbeg (W. Galway, 1994). Ratcliffe (1968) includes *L. hibernica* in the Southern Atlantic group.

Ecology and biology
A strongly oceanic species, this plant grows with other bryophytes on shaded, moist rocks and boulders, particularly near streams, lakes and waterfalls, in damp recesses, ravines, block scree and under rock overhangs. It tends to grow on mildly base-rich rocks. Typical associates include *Fissidens dubius*, *Heterocladium heteropterum*, *Isothecium myosuroides*, *Jubula hutchinsiae*, other *Lejeunea* spp., *Plagiochila* spp., *Radula* spp., *Saccogyna viticulosa* and *Thamnobryum alopecurum*. Lowland or subalpine, it has been found at altitudes of 50–400 m in Ireland.

This species may be autoicous or dioicous, and is usually fertile although sporophytes are rare. Gemmae and other specialised means of vegetative reproduction are unknown.

World distribution
L. hibernica is known outside Ireland only from Madeira, where it is considered *Rare*, and the Azores. It is assigned to a Hyperoceanic Southern-temperate floristic element in Europe.

Threats
There are no clear threats to this species, as it seems to be relatively frequent in the extreme south-west. Some of the localities may be vulnerable to change through afforestation, overstocking, burning, building, etc.

Conservation
The very restricted distribution of this species and the global importance of the Irish populations mean that conservation measures, if necessary, are appropriate. Its continued presence at the more important sites should be monitored.

Protected sites with recent records: Glanmore Bog SAC; Killarney National Park; Killarney National Park, Macgillycuddy's Reeks and Caragh River Catchment SAC; Mount Brandon SAC; Mweelrea/Sheeffry/Erriff Complex SAC; The Twelve Bens/Garraun Complex SAC; **Unprotected sites with recent records:** none.

Lejeunea eckloniana Lindenb.   Holt's Pouncewort

syn. *Lejeunea holtii* Spruce
Status in Ireland: Near Threatened; **Status in Europe:** Least Concern

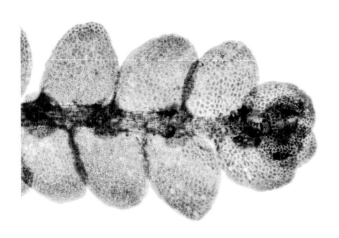

This species has a south-western and strongly oceanic distribution in Ireland and can be locally abundant at some sites. It has been reported from seven vice-counties, with records from 20 hectads (19 old, 10 recent). A rare plant in Europe as a whole, *L. eckloniana* is *Vulnerable* in Britain (where it is known only from sea caves on Islay in W. Scotland), *Rare* in Madeira, *Data Deficient* in Spain and Portugal, and has also been recorded from France, the Azores and the Canary Islands. It is also widely distributed in tropical and southern Africa and on some of the Indian Ocean islands. It grows on damp or wet rocks, especially where base-rich and typical habitats include shaded rocks by streams and waterfalls in ravines or woodlands, often in deep shade. This species was not included in Provisional Red List (Holyoak 2006b) because there were too many records, so it was not targeted for fieldwork and has probably been under-recorded over the past decade rather than showing

evidence of decline. However, the very restricted distribution of this species and the global importance of the Irish populations mean that conservation measures, if necessary, are appropriate. Populations at the more important sites should be monitored.

Lejeunea mandonii (Steph.) Müll.Frib.

Atlantic Pouncewort

syn. *Inflatolejeunea mandonii* (Steph.) Perss., *Lejeunea macvicari* Pearson, *Microlejeunea mandonii* Steph.
Status in Ireland: Endangered (B2a, bii, iv); **Status in Europe:** Rare

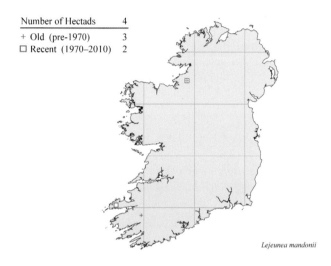

Number of Hectads	4
+ Old (pre-1970)	3
□ Recent (1970–2010)	2

Lejeunea mandonii

Identification

L. mandonii is a very small leafy liverwort forming small mats or creeping among or over other bryophytes, with shoots up to 1.2 cm long and c. 0.6 mm wide. The leaves are more or less oval with sac-like ventral lobules and the underleaves are bilobed. It differs from other species of *Lejeunea* by the relatively long leaves (oval or ovate rather than suborbicular or ovate) and smooth cylindrical perianths. There are c. 8–15 homogeneous to faintly granular and fugacious oil bodies per cell, but this feature has to be observed in fresh material. *L. mandonii* is similar in size and general appearance to *Harpalejeunea molleri*, but that species has a pointed leaf apex and broad, retuse underleaves, whereas in *L. mandonii* the leaf apex is rounded and the underleaves are more or less oval and deeply bilobed.

Distribution in Ireland

A hyperoceanic species confined to the extreme west, and listed as Southern Atlantic by Ratcliffe (1968), *L. mandonii* is very rare. It has recently been recorded from just two localities in two vice-counties: S. Kerry

(Loch an Mhónáin, below Brandon Peak, 2006) and Leitrim (Peakadaw, 1963–2000). There are also older records from S. Kerry (below Brandon Mountain, 1967–1968) and N. Kerry (below Torc Cascade, 1966), where it may persist in small quantity, although recent survey work has failed to refind it.

Ecology and biology

This species is found among base-rich boulders and on crags, in shaded damp crevices with other bryophytes, especially Atlantic species, in oceanic areas. On Brandon Mountain, it was found in a deeply shaded declivity amongst boulders by a mountain stream. At Peakadaw, it grows on small ledges in crevices on a S.-facing limestone crag at the base of, and shaded by, a large N.-facing crag. *L. mandonii* usually occurs in very small quantity. Associates in Ireland include *Cololejeunea rossettiana*, *Fissidens dubius*, *Lejeunea hibernica*, *L. lamacerina*, *L. patens*, *Radula carringtonii* and *Trichomanes speciosum*. In Britain, it also occurs as an epiphyte on Ash, and its normal habitat in Macaronesia is also epiphytic. It is a lowland plant, growing at altitudes up to 275 m in Ireland.

Although this species is autoicous and often fertile, it rarely produces sporophytes. Gemmae are absent.

World distribution
It is also present in England and Scotland (*Endangered* in Britain), Spain and Portugal (*Vulnerable* in both), Madeira and the Canaries. This is a rare species globally, being endemic to Europe and Macaronesia, where its distribution is categorised as Hyperoceanic Southern-temperate.

Threats
The small size of the populations renders them susceptible to damage; only a very small amount was seen during recent fieldwork on Brandon Mountain and only small patches were found at Peakadaw. Potential threats include thoughtless collection of specimens, afforestation, overstocking, desiccation and nutrient enrichment leading to unsuccessful competition with coarser species and algae.

Conservation
Populations should be monitored, and the localities should be protected from afforestation, overstocking and disturbance generally. *L. mandonii* may occur elsewhere on the west coast, and it should be searched for actively by bryologists, as it is very small and easy to overlook.

Protected sites with recent records: Ben Bulben, Gleniff and Glenade Complex SAC; Mount Brandon SAC; **Unprotected sites with recent records:** none.

Ptilidium ciliare (L.) Hampe   Ciliated Fringewort

syn. *Blepharozia ciliaris* (L.) Dumort., *Jungermannia ciliaris* L., *J. hoffmannii* Wallr., *J. leersii* A. Roth
Status in Ireland: Least Concern; **Status in Europe:** Least Concern

A large reddish-brown or greenish leafy liverwort with bilobed and ciliate leaves, forming lax patches or scattered shoots in heathland, bogs, acid grassland and amongst boulders in rocky scree. This species was included in the Provisional Red List (Holyoak 2006b) but has been found to be widely, if rather sparsely, distributed in upland and montane areas. It has been reported from 15 vice-counties, with records from 29 hectads (13 old, 22 recent). It usually occurs in small quantity, but occasionally may be locally frequent.

Ptilidium pulcherrimum (Weber) Vain.   Tree Fringewort

syn. *Blepharozia ciliaris* var. *wallrothiana* Nees, *B. pulcherrima* (G.Weber) Lindb.,
Jungermannia pulcherrima Weber, *Ptilidium ciliare* var. *pulcherrimum* (Weber) Hoffm. ex Pfeiff.
Status in Ireland: Regionally Extinct; **Status in Europe:** Least Concern

Identification
This is essentially a yellowish or reddish-brown leafy liverwort with bilobed leaves and large underleaves, but the structure is often difficult to discern because of the mass of long cilia at the edge of the leaves, which give the plant a fluffy appearance. It is a smaller plant (up to 3 cm long and 2 mm wide) than the much more common *P. ciliare* and is often a paler colour. Furthermore, the leaves are more deeply divided, the leaf lobes of *P. pulcherrimum* are narrower (antical lobe 5–12 cells wide at base) than those of *P. ciliare* (antical lobe 15–25 cells wide at base). *P. pulcherrimum* is usually epiphytic,

Number of Hectads	1
+ Old (pre-1970)	1

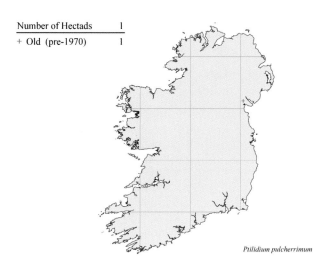

Ptilidium pulcherrimum

growing closely appressed to bark, whereas *P. ciliare* normally occurs in terrestrial heathland habitats.

Distribution in Ireland
It is known from a single site at Ravensdale State Forest in Louth, where it was recorded in 1953 by A.L.K. King. It has not been seen there since, but the original locality was imprecise, so there is little hope of refinding it.

Ecology and biology
The Irish record was from Scots Pine, where it was associated with *Metzgeria furcata*. In Britain, *P. pulcherrimum* is found as an epiphyte on a variety of trees, sometimes on rotten wood and much more rarely on rock. This is a pioneer species, and the Irish record was presumably a transient occurrence (a 'sink population') resulting from long-distance dispersal from British or continental plants (a 'source population'). Although *P. pulcherrimum* spores are relatively large (24–34 μm), and most spores are deposited close to parent colonies (Söderström & Jonsson 1989), it is assumed that at least some spores can be transported for longer distances, perhaps by birds. It is mainly a lowland plant.

Although dioicous, this species is often fertile. Sporophytes have not been recorded in Ireland.

World distribution
This is a widespread and fairly common species in Europe, particularly in boreal forest, but it becomes rarer in the south and is listed as *Endangered* in Spain and *Rare* in Italy. In Europe, it is assigned to a Circumpolar Boreal-montane floristic element. The species is also widespread in northern Asia and N. America.

Threats
None: probably extinct in Ireland.

Conservation
No conservation action is required. It is possible that another colonisation event could occur, resulting in the return of this species.

Protected sites with recent records: none; **Unprotected sites with recent records:** none.

Mastigophora woodsii (Hook.) Nees   Wood's Whipwort

syn. *Jungermannia woodsii* Hook.
Status in Ireland: Near Threatened; **Status in Europe:** Rare

Identification
This is an easily recognised leafy liverwort that forms loose mats with other bryophytes or quite large cushions. It is medium-sized to large, with yellowish-brown, well-branched shoots up to c. 12 cm long and 1.5 mm wide.

The branches tend to become narrow and attenuate at the apices. The leaves are imbricate and essentially bilobed, but the margins are ornamented with long teeth and cilia, so the lobes are difficult to discern. The underleaves are similar to, and only a little smaller than, the lateral leaves.

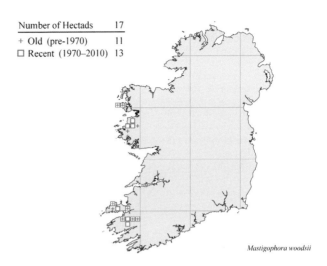

Number of Hectads	17
+ Old (pre-1970)	11
□ Recent (1970–2010)	13

Mastigophora woodsii

M. *woodsii* could be mistaken for *Ptilidium* spp., but *Ptilidium* has even more abundantly ciliate leaves and non-attenuate branches. *Trichocolea* has much more finely divided leaves and a characteristic pale green colour.

Distribution in Ireland

Confined in Ireland to the Atlantic fringe, the distribution of *M. woodsii* is centred on Kerry, with a few populations further north in Galway and Mayo. There are recent records from 17 localities in three vice-counties: S. Kerry (Brandon Mountain, 1829–2009; Connor Pass, 2006–2009; Derrymore Lough, 1950, 2006; Coomacullen Lake, 2006; Ballaghbeama Gap, 1983; Coomloughra, 2007; Coom Callee, 1983; Cloghernoosh, 1972; Lough Googh, 1972–2009; Lough Cummeenoughter, 1983–2009; Lough Cummeenapeasta, 1983); N. Kerry (Coumbrack Lake, 2009; Mangerton Mountain, 1885–2009) and W. Mayo (Croaghaun, 1987; Slievemore, 1951–1999; Mweelrea, 1970–2010; W. of Lough Brawn, Sheeffry Hills, 2010), with a small number of older records from other sites. It may be extinct in W. Galway, having been seen on Benbaun (1957) and Maumtrasna (1963), but not refound, in spite of searching. Ratcliffe (1968) classifies *M. woodsii* as a Northern Atlantic species.

Ecology and biology

M. *woodsii* is one of the group of Northern Atlantic hepatic mat species, confined to N.- and NE-facing slopes in the hills in hyperoceanic areas. It often grows under open cover of heather and in boulder scree, and is normally associated with other oceanic bryophytes such as *Bazzania pearsonii*, *B. tricrenata*, *Breutelia chrysocoma*, *Herbertus aduncus* subsp. *hutchinsiae*, *Mylia taylorii*, *Scapania gracilis* and *S. ornithopodioides*, as well as common species such as *Diplophyllum albicans*, *Lophozia ventricosa* and *Racomitrium lanuginosum*. Its range is subalpine and alpine, recorded at altitudes of 400–940 m in Ireland.

Inflorescences, sporophytes and gemmae are not known to occur, so presumably this species spreads vegetatively by fragmentation.

World distribution

In Europe, it is known only from Ireland, the Faeroe Islands and Scotland, where it is confined to the western highlands (*Nationally Scarce* in Britain). Its European distribution pattern is considered to be Oceanic Boreal-montane. Elsewhere, this is a disjunct species occurring in the Himalaya, Taiwan and the Pacific coast of north-western N. America (Queen Charlotte Islands and Pitt Island). There is also a report from Australasia (He-Nygren *et al.* 2006). Schofield (FNA 2007) considers *M. woodsii* to be relictual in its whole range, but there is evidence now that such disjunct distributions arose from long-distance dispersal rather than representing very ancient relict populations.

Threats

Overstocking in the uplands, afforestation and burning are the main threats. It appears that *M. woodsii* may have disappeared from W. Galway, where its habitat has been hit particularly hard by overstocking with sheep in Connemara.

Conservation

This is a widely disjunct species and the Irish populations are of European and global significance. Populations at the more important sites should be monitored and reinstatement of a less intensive grazing regime at key sites should be a priority.

Protected sites with recent records: Croaghaun/ Slievemore SAC; Killarney National Park,

Macgillycuddy's Reeks and Caragh River Catchment SAC; Mount Brandon SAC; Mweelrea/Sheeffry/ Erriff Complex SAC; Slieve Mish Mountains SAC; **Unprotected sites with recent records:** none.

Bazzania pearsonii Steph.

Arch-leaved Whipwort

syn. *Mastigobryum pearsonii* (Steph.) Steph.
Status in Ireland: Vulnerable (B2a, bii, iii, iv); **Status in Europe:** Rare

Number of Hectads	16
+ Old (pre-1970)	11
☐ Recent (1970–2010)	12

Bazzania pearsonii

Identification

A pale green, more or less erect, turf-forming leafy liverwort with shoots up to c. 9 cm long and 1.5 mm wide. It has incubous leaves tapering from broadly rounded bases, with the antical margin extending well beyond the stem, to narrowly pointed, 2–3-dentate or bidentate apices. The underleaves are large and conspicuous, shortly oblong and not or barely notched at the apex. It differs from the more common *B. tricrenata* in the antical leaf bases widely crossing the stem and the underleaves being longer than wide. Flagella are common.

Distribution in Ireland

B. pearsonii is confined to the extreme west, but is more widespread in Ireland than *Adelanthus lindenbergianus* or *Plagiochila carringtonii*, with recent records from 15 localities in five vice-counties: S. Kerry (Brandon Mountain, 1950–2009; Connor Pass, 2009; Lough Googh, 2009; Derrymore River, 2006; Stradbally Mountain, 2006; Carrauntoohil, 1961–2009); N. Kerry

(Coumbrack Lake, 2009; Lough Erhogh, 2009); W. Galway (Muckanaght, 1957–1994; Benbreen and Bengower, 1994); W. Mayo (Croagh Patrick, 1987; Mweelrea, 1950–2010; Slievemore, 1910–1999) and W. Donegal (Errigal, 1962–2002; Muckish Mountain, 1955–2009). There are older records from S. Kerry (Beenkeragh, 1964 and 1965; Coomasaharn, 1951); N. Kerry (Mangerton Mountain, 1855–1963); W. Galway (Maumtrasna, 1957–1963) and W. Mayo (Skeltia, 1957; Clare Island, 1910). Ratcliffe (1968) places *B. pearsonii* into the Northern Atlantic group.

Ecology and biology

One of the Northern Atlantic hepatic mat species, confined to N.- and NE-facing slopes in the hills in hyperoceanic areas, *B. pearsonii* often grows under open cover of dwarf shrubs on cliff ledges and in boulder scree, and is usually associated with other large oceanic bryophytes such as *Anastrepta orcadensis*, *Bazzania tricrenata*, *Breutelia chrysocoma*, *Herbertus aduncus* subsp. *hutchinsiae*, *Mastigophora woodsii*, *Mylia taylorii*,

Plagiochila spinulosa and *Scapania gracilis*, as well as common species such as *Diplophyllum albicans* and *Lophozia ventricosa*. It is primarily an upland species, but has been recorded at altitudes as low as 100 m in Ireland.

This species is dioicous; female inflorescences are frequent, but male inflorescences, perianths and sporophytes are unknown. Gemmae are also unknown, so fragmentation is likely to play a part in its vegetative propagation.

World distribution

Apart from Ireland, this species is only known in Europe from Scotland, where it is almost confined to the western highlands (*Nationally Scarce* in Britain). Its distribution pattern in Europe is categorised as Oceanic Boreal-montane. Elsewhere, *B. pearsonii* occurs in disjunct populations in E. and SE Asia and the Pacific coast of north-western N. America.

Threats

Overstocking in the uplands, afforestation and burning are the main threats. Sites in W. Galway have been hit particularly hard by overstocking with sheep, and *B. pearsonii* may have been eliminated completely from sites in Connemara.

Conservation

The restricted distribution and global importance of the Irish populations of this species mean that conservation measures to reinstate a less intensive grazing regime at key sites should be a priority. Populations at the more important sites should be monitored.

Protected sites with recent records: Cloghernagore Bog and Glenveagh National Park SAC; Croagh Patrick pNHA; Croaghaun/Slievemore SAC; Killarney National Park, Macgillycuddy's Reeks and Caragh River Catchment SAC; Mount Brandon SAC; Muckish Mountain SAC; Mweelrea/Sheeffry/Erriff Complex SAC; Slieve Mish Mountains SAC; The Twelve Bens/Garraun Complex SAC; **Unprotected sites with recent records:** none.

Kurzia sylvatica (A.Evans) Grolle   Wood Fingerwort

syn. *Kurzia makinoana* (Steph.) Grolle, *Lepidozia sylvatica* A.Evans, *Microlepidozia sylvatica* (A. Evans) Jörg., *Telaranea sylvatica* (A.Evans) K.Müller
Status in Ireland: Near Threatened; **Status in Europe:** Least Concern

A small leafy liverwort related to *Lepidozia*, this plant is apparently uncommon in Ireland but doubtless overlooked due to its similarity to the more common *K. trichoclados*. It has been reported from 15 vice-counties, with records from 23 hectads (9 old, 14 recent). The records suggest that it may have declined in the south-west, but as it was not included in the Provisional Red List (Holyoak 2006b) and therefore not looked for during recent fieldwork, there is no evidence to support this.

Telaranea europaea Engel & G.L.S.Merr.

Irish Threadwort

syn. *Cephalozia nematodes* Austin, *Telaranea nematodes* auct. eur.
Status in Ireland: Near Threatened; **Status in Europe:** Rare

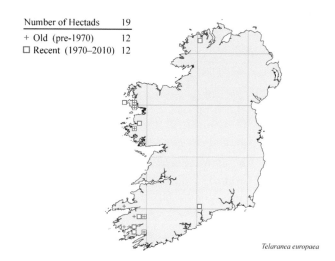

Number of Hectads	19
+ Old (pre-1970)	12
□ Recent (1970–2010)	12

Telaranea europaea

Identification

This is a very small and delicate mat-forming leafy liverwort, with translucent pale green shoots up to c. 1.5 cm long and 1 mm wide. The leaves are very deeply divided (though not quite to the base) into (2–) 3 (–4) very narrow lobes, so that the plant looks rather 'fuzzy', and also has a characteristic glistening appearance. It could be confused with species of *Kurzia*, which are neither translucent nor glistening, and have smaller leaf cells. *Blepharostoma trichophyllum* is even more similar, but in this plant the leaves are divided all the way to the base, and the cells of the leaf lobes are shorter and more numerous. Until recently, this plant was known as *T. nematodes*, but Engel & Merrill (2004) established that the American *T. nematodes* and the European *T. europaea* are distinct taxa.

Distribution in Ireland

T. europaea has been reported from at least 18 localities in seven vice-counties, mainly along the west coast: S. Kerry (Looscaunagh Woods, 1983; Derreen Garden, 2006, 2008; Rossdohan Island, 2008); N. Kerry (Killarney, Upper Lake, 1972–1976, Camillan Wood, 1973; Derrycunihy Wood, 1936–1983; Galway's Bridge, 1983; Torc Cascade, 1951–1983; Muckross, 1983; below Eagle's Nest, 2005); W. Cork (Glengarriff, 1967–1979; Glenbeg Lough and Lackawee, 1979); Waterford (Lismore, 1999); W. Galway (Kylemore, 1957–2010);

W. Mayo (Aasleagh and Delphi, 1970; Lough Nakeeroge and Lough Bunafreva West, Achill Island, 1987; Sraheens Lough on Achill Island, 1962–1987) and W. Donegal (Glenveagh, 2002). There are several older records from other localities within these vice-counties.

Ecology and biology

T. europaea is a calcifuge species of peaty banks, sandy soil, humus and occasionally rotten wood. It grows in humid, shady places, often under Rhododendron, and often forming mats, along with *Calypogeia muelleriana* and *Cephalozia* spp. It is a lowland species confined to extremely oceanic areas, mainly in the south-west.

It is autoicous and often fertile, with sporophytes frequent. It also sometimes produces bulbils, which form a means of vegetative reproduction.

World distribution

This plant is tightly restricted to the Atlantic fringes of Europe, with records from Britain (where it occurs only in Cornwall and is considered *Endangered*), France (only in the Pyrenees), northern Spain (*Vulnerable*), Portugal (*Vulnerable*), the Azores and the Canary Islands. Söderström *et al.* (2002) list it as occurring in western Asia, but this is not mentioned by Engel & Merrill (2004). It is assigned to a Hyperoceanic Southern-temperate floristic element in Europe and is considered endemic to Europe and Macaronesia (Engel & Merrill 2004).

Threats

There is no evidence that this species has declined. It is one of the few bryophytes that is able to thrive under the dense shade of Rhododendron, and no specific threats have been identified.

Conservation

This species was not included in the Provisional Red List (Holyoak 2006b) and so was not specifically targeted during recent fieldwork. It was nevertheless recorded incidentally from four new localities (in S. Kerry, N. Kerry and W. Donegal). Its preference for shaded peaty banks and Rhododendron scrub, widespread and frequent habitats in the south-west, suggests that its status might be 'downgraded' to *Least Concern* at some point in the future.

Protected sites with recent records: Blackwater River (Cork/Waterford) SAC; Cloghernagore Bog and Glenveagh National Park SAC; Croaghaun/Slievemore SAC; Derrycunihy Wood Nature Reserve; Glanmore Bog SAC; Glengarriff Harbour and Woodland SAC; Glengarriff Wood Nature Reserve; Glenveagh National Park; Killarney National Park; Killarney National Park, Macgillycuddy's Reeks and Caragh River Catchment SAC; Mweelrea/Sheeffry/Erriff Complex SAC; The Twelve Bens/Garraun Complex SAC; **Unprotected sites with recent records:** Derreen Garden; Rossdohan Island; Sraheens Lough on Achill Island.

Photographing *Telaranea europaea*, Kylemore, Co. Galway.

Lophocolea bispinosa (Hook.f. & Taylor) Gottsche *et al.* Great Crestwort

syn. *Chiloscyphus bispinosus* (Hook.f. & Taylor) J.J.Engel & R.M.Schust., *Jungermannia bispinosa* Hook.f. & Taylor

Status in Ireland: Not Evaluated; **Status in Europe:** Not Evaluated

A yellowish-green leafy liverwort with bilobed leaves, forming dense mats or low turfs, often with filiform branches, giving the plant a fragile and delicate appearance. *L. bispinosa* is an Australasian species, thought to have been introduced in Europe with exotic garden shrubs and trees, and has so far been found in Ireland at one site on a track in a forestry plantation in Tyrone (near Kelly's Bridge, Ardnamona, 2002). It has spread widely in some areas in Britain, becoming locally abundant in parts of E. Cornwall. It appears to be slightly less invasive than *L. semiteres*.

Lophocolea semiteres (Lehm.) Mitt. Southern Crestwort

syn. *Chiloscyphus semiteres* (Lehm.) Lehm. & Lindenb., *Jungermannia semiteres* Lehm.

Status in Ireland: Not Evaluated; **Status in Europe:** Not Evaluated

This is a pale-green leafy liverwort, distinguished from others of the genus in Ireland by its retuse or only slightly bilobed leaves. An introduction from the southern hemisphere, *L. semiteres* has been recorded in Ireland from damp acidic sand in dune heath at a single site in Down (Murlough Dunes, 2008), where it has become common. It is spreading in Britain and may be expected to do likewise in Ireland in the future.

Heteroscyphus fissistipus (Hook. f. & Taylor) Schiffn.

Square-cut Yokewort

Status in Ireland: Not Evaluated; **Status in Europe:** Not Evaluated

A leafy liverwort that grows on peaty soil, over rocks and as an epiphyte on the bases of tree ferns. It is a native of Australia and New Zealand that was discovered new to the northern hemisphere in the woodland garden on Garinish Island (S. Kerry) in 1999 (Blackstock & Long 2002). In 2008, large populations were still present in and near the garden area (Holyoak & Lockhart 2009b). It has not been reported from any other locality in Europe.

Plagiochila carringtonii (Balf.) Grolle

Carrington's Featherwort

syn. *Adelanthus carringtonii* Balf., *Jamesoniella carringtonii* (Balf.) Schiffn.
Status in Ireland: Endangered (B2a, biii); **Status in Europe:** Rare

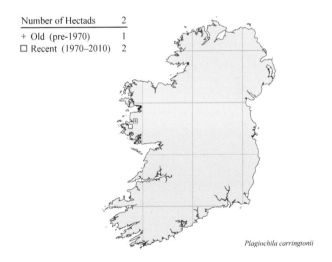

Number of Hectads	2
+ Old (pre-1970)	1
□ Recent (1970–2010)	2

Plagiochila carringtonii

Identification

This is a pale green leafy liverwort that grows in more or less erect turfs, with shoots up to c. 10 cm long and 1.5 mm wide. It is easy to recognise from its unlobed and almost circular leaves, which are vertical and appressed (so that the whole shoot is laterally compressed). The leaves are not or hardly toothed, and have a very long and conspicuously decurrent antical margin. Underleaves are often present, but they are very small and insignificant.

Flagella are frequent. This species is so unlike other species of *Plagiochila* that for a long time it was placed in the genus *Jamesoniella*. Recent molecular work (Renker *et al.* 2002) has confirmed that it belongs in *Plagiochila*.

Distribution in Ireland

Known only from a very confined area on the west coast, this plant has been recorded from two localities in two vice-counties: W. Galway (Benbaun, 1984) and W. Mayo

(Mweelrea, 1961–2010). Ratcliffe (1968) places it into the Northern Atlantic group of species.

Ecology and biology

One of the Northern Atlantic hepatic mat species, *P. carringtonii* is confined to N.- and NE-facing slopes in the hills in hyperoceanic areas, usually growing under very open cover of heather and amongst boulder scree. In Ireland, it has been found in a bryophyte turf amongst boulders on an exposed hillside (Benbaun) and in Northern Atlantic hepatic mat vegetation, shaded amongst boulders, on the steep, N.-facing slope of a corrie (Mweelrea). It is associated with other Northern Atlantic hepatic mat species, such as *Herbertus aduncus* subsp. *hutchinsiae*. Essentially alpine or subalpine, it has been recorded at altitudes of 350–850 m in Ireland.

This is a dioicous species in which male plants are fairly frequent, but female plants and sporophytes are unknown in Europe. Gemmae and caducous leaves are absent.

World distribution

This species is known elsewhere in Europe only from Scotland, where it is much more frequent near the west coast than it is in Ireland (*Nationally Scarce* in Britain), and the Faeroe Islands. In Europe, it is included in the Oceanic Boreal-montane floristic element. European material is subsp. *carringtonii*, which is endemic to Europe. Another taxon, subsp. *lobuchensis* Grolle, occurs in Nepal, where only female plants are known.

Threats

Overstocking in the uplands has affected this plant severely and it is possible that the population at Benbaun has been lost.

Conservation

This attractive species has a very restricted distribution in Ireland and its populations are of European and global importance. Reinstatement of less intensive grazing regimes in the uplands should be a priority and further efforts to relocate its population at Benbaun should be made. Populations should be monitored to document their continued survival.

Protected sites with recent records: Mweelrea/Sheeffry/Erriff Complex SAC; The Twelve Bens/Garraun Complex SAC; **Unprotected sites with recent records:** none.

Plagiochila britannica Paton — British Featherwort

Status in Ireland: Least Concern; **Status in Europe:** Least Concern

Relatively recently described (Paton 1979), this large leafy liverwort is widespread in the north and west of Ireland, occurring mostly on limestone substrates. It has been reported from 14 vice-counties, with records from 24 hectads (3 old, 21 recent). Its inclusion in the Provisional Red List (Holyoak 2006b) is therefore not supported by recent fieldwork. This species is now known from continental Europe and is considered a European endemic.

Plagiochila heterophylla Lindenb. ex Lehm.

Western Featherwort

syn. *Plagiochila ambagiosa* auct. non Mitt., *P. atlantica* F.Rose
Status in Ireland: Endangered (B2a, bii, iv); **Status in Europe:** Rare

Number of Hectads	5
+ Old (pre-1970)	1
□ Recent (1970–2010)	4

Plagiochila heterophylla

Identification

Like most other species of the genus, this leafy liverwort has broad, toothed, unlobed leaves with an obliquely-inserted and longly-decurrent antical margin, and no underleaves. It is a large species, with shoots up to c. 10 cm long and 5.5 mm wide, with coarse and irregular teeth on the leaf margins (making them look something like a very roughly torn edge of paper) and a slightly decurrent postical margin. It is usually a fresh green colour. The leaves are longer in proportion to their breadth than they are in *P. spinulosa* and, when dry, roll up more strongly, giving it a characteristic appearance. Heinrichs (2002) synonymised the European plant previously known as *P. atlantica* (Jones & Rose 1975) with the S. American *P. heterophylla* var. *heterophylla*.

Distribution in Ireland

Recent records are from four localities in three vice-counties, all from the extreme south-west: S. Kerry (Derreen Garden, Lauragh, 1998); N. Kerry (Galway's Bridge, 1983) and W. Cork (Gougane Barra, 2002; Nowen Hill Gully, 2009). There is an older confirmed record from S. Kerry (Lough Coomeathcun, 1951). The west Cork records from 'near Bantry', attributable to Ellen Hutchins (1815 and 1839), are too vaguely localised to assign to a hectad. The recent programme of survey work has failed to refind it at Derreen Garden, Galway's Bridge, Gougane Barra or Lough Coomeathcun, so it is either present in very small quantity or has disappeared from these sites. This is quite unlike the position in Scotland, where it is locally abundant at some localities. Described too late to appear in Ratcliffe's lists of Atlantic species (Ratcliffe 1968), this species is listed as Atlantic by Averis (1991).

Ecology and biology

In Ireland, this species has been found on a rock face on a SE-facing crag; in an open, nearly vertical well-lit rock crevice in the splash zone of a waterfall; and at the base of a holly tree in a glade surrounded by Rhododendron in shady oak woodland by a river, growing with *Isothecium myosuroides*. The most recent record at Nowen Hill reported several patches on a rock face on the south-facing side of a gully. In Britain, it grows on rocks and tree trunks in Atlantic woodland, or occasionally, on more open rocks in strongly oceanic areas. It appears to favour south-facing aspects, particularly on boulders and tree trunks at the lip of ravines and gullies. In Scotland, *P. heterophylla* appears to require a delicate balance of at least moderate (but not excessive) light intensity, relatively warm temperatures and high humidity, and is therefore strongly associated with ancient woodland (B. Averis, unpublished, Scottish Natural Heritage note 121). It is a lowland plant, recorded in Ireland at altitudes of near sea level up to 370 m.

This is a dioicous species: female inflorescences are frequent, but male inflorescences and sporophytes are unknown. Gemmae and caducous leaves are also unknown.

World distribution

In Europe, this plant is confined to the Atlantic fringe, with records from Britain (where it is *Nationally Scarce*) and France (where it is known from a single site in Brittany: Bates & Hodgetts 1995), but nowhere else. It is most abundant in the west of Scotland, with outlying sites in west Wales and the English Lake District. In Europe, it is assigned to a Hyperoceanic Temperate floristic element. The species is also present in C. and S. America and the Caribbean, both as var. *heterophylla* and var. *beauvardii* (Steph.) J.Heinrichs.

Threats

Clear-felling of the woods in which it grows, or afforestation with conifers are probably the chief threats to this species.

Conservation

P. heterophylla is protected in the Republic of Ireland (as *P. atlantica*) by the Flora (Protection) Order, 1999. The unprotected sites where this plant grows should be considered for statutory protection, and populations should be monitored regularly.

Protected sites with recent records: Killarney National Park; Killarney National Park, Macgillycuddy's Reeks and Caragh River Catchment SAC; **Unprotected sites with recent records:** Derreen Garden; Gougane Barra; Nowen Hill Gully.

Adelanthus lindenbergianus (Lehm.) Mitt.

Lindenberg's Featherwort

syn. *Adelanthus dugortiensis* Douin & Lett, *Jungermannia lindenbergiana* Lehm.
Status in Ireland: Vulnerable (A2c, B2a, biii, iv); **Status in Europe:** Vulnerable

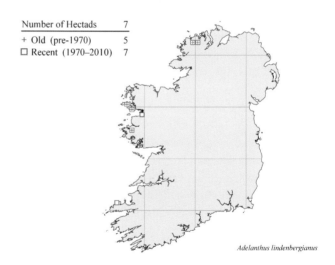

Number of Hectads	7
+ Old (pre-1970)	5
□ Recent (1970–2010)	7

Adelanthus lindenbergianus

Identification

This is a medium-sized to large, reddish or brownish leafy liverwort, forming lax tufts of erect shoots 2–10 cm long. The leaves are curved downwards and are imbricate, ovate and unlobed, with a strongly incurved antical margin (a unique feature) and a toothed postical margin. There are no underleaves. While *A. lindenbergianus* superficially resembles a species of *Plagiochila*, this leaf structure and arrangement makes it an easy plant to identify in the field. It also bears some resemblance to

Anastrepta orcadensis, which has adaxially convex leaves with an edentate postical margin and commonly produces conspicuous red gemmae.

Distribution in Ireland

This plant is confined to the extreme west, with recent records from 10 localities in four vice-counties: S. Kerry (Brandon Mountain, 2008, 2009); W. Galway (Benbreen, 1961–1994; Bengower, 1961–2007; Benbaun, 1984); W. Mayo (Slievemore, 1903–2003; Corraun

Peninsula, 1965–2008; Croagh Patrick, 1987) and W. Donegal (Errigal, 1962–2002; Mackoght, 1962, 2002; Muckish Mountain, 1962–2009). Ratcliffe (1968) places it into the Northern Atlantic group.

Ecology and biology

One of the suite of Northern Atlantic hepatic mat species, *A. lindenbergianus* is confined to N.- and NE-facing slopes in the hills in hyperoceanic areas. It often grows under sparse heather and in boulder scree at medium to fairly high altitudes (300–800 m recorded in Ireland). It is normally associated with other oceanic liverworts such as *Bazzania tricrenata*, *Scapania gracilis*, *Herbertus aduncus*, *Mylia taylorii* and *Pleurozia purpurea*.

Only male plants of this dioicous species are known in Europe (Paton 1999, correcting Hill *et al.* 1991). Gemmae are known to occur, but have not yet been found in European material. Vegetative reproduction by fragmentation probably takes place.

World distribution

Elsewhere in Europe, this species is restricted to a single site on Islay in SW Scotland (listed as *Endangered* in Britain). It is assigned to an Oceanic Boreal-montane floristic element in Europe and is disjunct in montane parts of Africa (the Rift Valley highlands and South Africa (Wigginton & Grolle 1996)), Madagascar, Mauritius, Réunion (Grolle 1995), C. and S. America, Tristan da Cunha, Juan Fernandez and the subantarctic islands.

Threats

Overstocking in the uplands has affected this plant severely, in recent years almost eliminating it from its W. Galway sites (Long 2010). Whereas Ratcliffe (1962) measured the average height of the *Calluna* layer on the north slope of Bengower at '9 inches', more recent visits showed that the *Calluna* had been completely lost, along with virtually all the Northern Atlantic hepatic mat species (Holyoak 2006b). This damage has been repeated throughout the Twelve Bens and, to a lesser extent, elsewhere. Botanical collecting might be a threat at sites where populations are small.

Conservation

This is a disjunct species with a very restricted distribution, so the Irish populations are of global importance. Reinstatement of a less intensive grazing regime at its key sites should be a priority. The system of EU farm subsidies, which has largely been responsible for overstocking of sheep in the uplands over the last few decades, is now changing, and hopefully, this will rescue the habitat before it is all destroyed. Populations require monitoring to document their continued survival.

Protected sites with recent records: Cloghernagore Bog and Glenveagh National Park SAC; Corraun Plateau SAC; Croagh Patrick pNHA; Croaghaun/Slievemore SAC; Glenveagh National Park; Mount Brandon SAC; Muckish Mountain SAC; The Twelve Bens/Garraun Complex SAC; **Unprotected sites with recent records:** none.

Cephalozia macrostachya Kaal. var. *macrostachya*   Bog Pincerwort

Status in Ireland: Least Concern; **Status in Europe:** Least Concern (treated along with var. *spiniflora*)

Widely overlooked in the past and included in the Provisional Red List (Holyoak 2006b), this small and delicate leafy liverwort is now known to be widespread on Irish peatlands, especially in the north-west and in midland bogs. It has been reported from nine vice-counties, with records from 19 hectads (4 old, 15 recent). It appears to be present on most midland bogs, if they have not been too severely damaged or degraded. There are several more records of *C. macrostachya* agg. that have not been identified to variety, as specimens of the plant are often non-fertile, but it appears from fertile gatherings that var. *macrostachya* is more frequent in Ireland than var. *spiniflora*.

Cephalozia macrostachya Kaal. var. *spiniflora* (Schiffn.) Müll.Frib.

Frilly Pincerwort

syn. *Cephalozia spiniflora* Schiffn.

Status in Ireland: Data Deficient; **Status in Europe:** Least Concern (treated along with var. *macrostachya*)

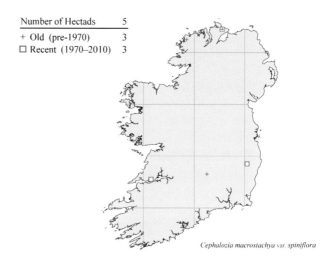

Number of Hectads	5
+ Old (pre-1970)	3
□ Recent (1970–2010)	3

Cephalozia macrostachya var. *spiniflora*

Identification

This small and delicate leafy liverwort has pale green or brownish shoots that grow to c. 3.5 cm long and c. 1 mm wide, with bilobed leaves and no underleaves. The leaves are divided to c.^{1}/$_3$–^{1}/$_2$, with triangular to subulate lobes that terminate in 1–2 apical cells. Care is required not to confuse it with other species of *Cephalozia* that grow in the same habitat. The leaf cells are smaller than those of the much more common *C. connivens* (c. 20 –38 μm wide rather than 28–50 μm wide). *C. loitlesbergeri* is always autoicous and has 2–3 apical cells on the leaf lobes. *C. lunulifolia* normally lacks brownish pigmentation and has hyaline stem medullary cell walls, whereas they are yellowish in *C. macrostachya* (visible in cross section). The two varieties of *C. macrostachya* are only distinguishable when fertile: var. *spiniflora* has crenulate-serrate or even dentate male bract margins (more or less entire in var. *macrostachya*), and the lobes of the female bracts terminating in a row of 2–4 short cells (2–6 narrow, elongate cells in var. *macrostachya*); in addition var. *spiniflora* has larger gemmae and, unlike var. *macrostachya*, is not always dioicous. Unfortunately, it is often difficult to find fertile material of this species.

Distribution in Ireland

C. macrostachya var. *spiniflora* has been recorded recently from three localities in three vice-counties: Clare (N. of Bohyodaun, 2007); Wicklow (Rathduffmore Bog, 1975) and E. Donegal (bog north of Gorey, 1968 and 2002). Older records are from S. Tipperary (Longfordpass Bridge, 1966) and W. Donegal (near Corveen, 1969). It is undoubtedly under-recorded, but does seem to be much rarer than var. *macrostachya*.

Ecology and biology

This is one of a group of small liverworts that are more or less confined to creeping amongst *Sphagnum* in undisturbed or little-disturbed bogs. Populations are usually small and consist of scattered stems. Typically, it occurs in Ireland with species of *Sphagnum* that are also characteristic of relatively undisturbed bogs, such as *Sphagnum austinii*, *S. fuscum* and *S. magellanicum*, although at its Clare locality, it is reported from bog recolonising old cutaway. It is often found growing with other small liverworts amongst the *Sphagnum*, notably *Calypogeia sphagnicola*, *Cephalozia connivens*, *C. macrostachya* var. *macrostachya*, *C. pleniceps*, *Cephaloziella* spp., *Cladopodiella fluitans*, *Kurzia pauciflora*, *Mylia anomala* and *Odontoschisma sphagni*. Essentially a lowland plant, but can also occur at moderate altitudes.

This plant may be dioicous, autoicous, paroicous or synoicous; male inflorescences are common but females less so, and perianths and sporophytes are unknown. Gemmae are occasional.

World distribution

The international distribution of this plant is poorly known, although, as in Ireland, it seems generally much less common than var. *macrostachya*. It is known from Britain, Norway, Germany and Poland. In Europe, it is assigned to a Suboceanic Boreal-montane floristic element. This variety has not yet been reported from outside Europe.

Threats

Remaining sites are potentially threatened by peat-cutting, drainage, afforestation and pollution, notably by nitrates and phosphates, through high stocking levels. Some sites are also at risk of physical damage from overstocking. It is likely that this plant has disappeared from many sites without ever having been recorded, following industrial-scale peat extraction in the midlands.

Conservation

Conservation efforts for this species should focus on retaining suitably wet hydrological conditions for the maintenance of *Sphagnum* growth. Its known remaining sites should be considered for statutory protection and any peat-cutting should cease. Where necessary, remedial work to restore bogland habitats should take place.

Protected sites with recent records: none; **Unprotected sites with recent records:** bog north of Gorey; N. of Bohyodaun; Rathduffmore Bog.

Cephalozia pleniceps (Austin) Lindb.　　　　　Blunt Pincerwort

syn. *Cephalozia bicuspidata* (L.) Dumort. var. *alpicola* Mass. & Carest., *C. macrantha* Kaal. & W.E.Nicholson, *C. symbolica* (Gott.) Breidl. var. *sphagnorum* Mass., *Jungermannia pleniceps* Austin
Status in Ireland: Vulnerable (B2a, bii, iv); **Status in Europe:** Least Concern

Number of Hectads	11
+ Old (pre-1970)	3
☐ Recent (1970–2010)	9

Cephalozia pleniceps

Identification

This is a very small (shoots < 2 cm long and c. 0.5–1.2 mm wide), slender, pale green leafy liverwort with longitudinally inserted, bilobed leaves and no underleaves. The leaves are divided to c.$^1/_3$–$^1/_2$, with the lobes rather shortly triangular, not drawn out to long, narrow points. It is closely related to the common *C. connivens* and other small *Cephalozia* species but, unlike these, the apical cell of the leaf lobes is not thickened at the apex. Supporting characters include the suborbicular leaves with more or less parallel lobes and the crenulate-dentate perianth mouth. Gemmae are rounded and single-celled.

Distribution in Ireland

C. pleniceps is widely scattered in Ireland, with recent records from 11 localities in seven vice-counties: Clare (N. of Rinroe in the Burren, 2004); Wicklow (Ballycoyle, 1975, 2007; Rathduffmore Bog, 1978, 2007); Westmeath (Doonis Lough, 1970); Roscommon (Carrowbehy/ Caher Bog, 2002); E. Mayo (Partry-Cloon River, 1987); W. Mayo (Deel Bridge, 1987; Keel Harbour, 1987-2010;

Keel Lough, 1987; Owenboy, 1987) and W. Donegal (Rinnafaghla Point, 1969–2002). There are older records from S. Kerry (Hog's Head, 1968) and Antrim (Ballintoy, 1969). This species was not recorded in Ireland before 1968, presumably having been overlooked in the past.

Ecology and biology

This is one of a group of species that grow creeping amongst *Sphagnum* in undisturbed bogs, particularly on *S. capillifolium*, *S. papillosum* and *S. subnitens*. It can also grow with *Sphagnum* in flushes, in wet acidic meadows and on damp banks. Other associates in Ireland include *Anagallis tenella*, *Carex* spp., *Molinia caerulea*, *Narthecium ossifragum*, *Calypogeia fissa*, *Cephalozia bicuspidata*, *C. connivens*, *C. leucantha*, *C. macrostachya*, *Cephaloziella hampeana*, *C. spinigera*, *Hypnum jutlandicum* and *Odontoschisma sphagni*. Essentially lowland, *C. pleniceps* ascends to 200 m in Ireland.

It is an autoicous species (rarely paroicous) and fertile plants and sporophytes are frequent. Gemmae are also frequent.

World distribution

This species is widespread and frequent in northern and some of C. and E. Europe, including Fennoscandia, the Baltic States, Poland, Belarus, Ukraine, Russia, the Caucasus, Switzerland, Austria, Slovakia, Slovenia and Romania, but becoming rarer and more confined to montane areas further south. Having previously been thought of as *Rare* in Spain, it is now listed as *Least Concern* in Spain and Andorra. It is *Nationally Scarce* in Britain, *Endangered* in Hungary, *Vulnerable* in Germany and the Czech Republic, *Rare* in Belgium and Italy, and

Data Deficient in Bulgaria. In Europe, it is assigned to a Circumpolar Boreo-arctic montane floristic element. It is also recorded in N. Asia, N. and S. America, northern Oceania and the subantarctic islands.

Threats

Peat-cutting and associated drainage of bogs threaten this species. It may be more secure than some other bog liverworts because it can also grow with *Sphagnum* in other habitats. However, these habitats, particularly those close to Dublin, may be under additional pressures, such as new building and other development projects. Scrub encroachment due to a reduction of grazing in the lowlands may also be a threat at some sites.

Conservation

Conservation efforts for this species should focus on retaining suitably wet hydrological conditions for the maintenance of *Sphagnum* growth. Known sites for this species should be protected from peat-cutting and drainage, as well as from other forms of disturbance (e.g. housing developments, roads). *C. pleniceps* is listed as a Northern Ireland Priority Species.

Protected sites with recent records: Bellacorick Bog Complex SAC; Carrowbehy/Caher Bog SAC; East Burren Complex SAC; Owenboy, Nephin Mor Forest Nature Reserve; **Unprotected sites with recent records:** Ballycoyle (possibly within Glencree Valley pNHA); Doonis Lough; Keel Harbour; Keel Lough (possibly within Keel Machair/Menaun Cliffs SAC); Partry-Cloon River (possibly within Lough Carra/Mask Complex SAC); Rathduffmore Bog; Rinnafaghla Point.

Cephalozia loitlesbergeri Schiffn.   Scissors Pincerwort

Status in Ireland: Vulnerable (B2a, biii); **Status in Europe:** Least Concern

Identification

This is a small, delicate, leafy liverwort with bilobed leaves and no underleaves. The pale green or brownish shoots are up to c. 3 cm long and c. 1 mm wide, with leaves divided to c. $1/3$–$1/2$, and lobes drawn out to long subulate points. Care is required not to confuse it with other species of *Cephalozia* that grow in the same habitat, particularly *C. connivens*. It is distinguished from these by the relatively long apex of the leaf lobes (ending with a uniseriate point 2–3 cells long), and the autoicous inflorescences. The leaf lobes sometimes

cross over in a scissor-like fashion, hence its English name. In addition, the leaf cells are smaller than those of the much more common *C. connivens* and the rare *C. crassifolia* (c. 20–38 μm wide rather than 28–50 μm wide).

Distribution in Ireland

Recent records are from seven localities in four vice-counties: Clare (Creevosheedy Bog, 1979–2004); Laois (Caher Bog, 2009; N. of Clonreher, Portlaoise, 2009); Offaly (Clara Bog, 2009; Ferbane Bog, 2009;

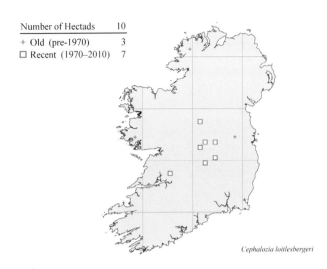

Number of Hectads	10
+ Old (pre-1970)	3
□ Recent (1970–2010)	7

Cephalozia loitlesbergeri

Raheenmore Bog, 2009) and Longford (Mount Jessop, 1986). Older records are from W. Galway (near Tullywee Bridge, 1968); Meath (Agher Bog near Summerhill, 1969) and W. Donegal (Poisoned Glen, 1962). However, undoubtedly, it is overlooked at some sites. Records made in the 1960s from Derreenargan Bog (Roscommon) and Derrylee, E. of Verner's Bridge (Armagh) are erroneous; the specimens are *C. macrostachya*.

Ecology and biology

This is one of several small liverworts that are more or less confined to creeping amongst *Sphagnum* in undisturbed or little-disturbed bogs. Populations are usually small and consist of scattered stems amongst the *Sphagnum*. Typically, it occurs in Ireland with species characteristic of relatively undisturbed bogs, such as *Sphagnum austinii*, *S. fuscum* and *S. magellanicum*. It is often found growing with other small liverworts amongst the *Sphagnum*, notably *Calypogeia sphagnicola*, *Cephalozia connivens*, *C. macrostachya*, *C. pleniceps*, *Cephaloziella* spp., *Cladopodiella fluitans*, *Kurzia pauciflora*, *Mylia anomala* and *Odontoschisma sphagni*. However, it may well be more demanding in its ecology than *C. macrostachya*, in ways not yet understood, since it appears to be so much rarer than that species. It is a lowland plant, not exceeding altitudes of c. 30 m in Ireland.

This species is autoicous and usually fertile. Sporophytes are frequent but gemmae are unknown.

World distribution

This species is fairly frequent in parts of northern and C. Europe but becomes much more scattered and montane southwards and is rare or absent in many southern areas. Thus, it is present and widespread in much of Finland, Norway, Sweden, Poland, Russia, Belarus, Ukraine and Romania, but absent from Iceland, the Faeroes and Denmark. It is *Nationally Scarce* in Britain, *Critically Endangered* in Bulgaria, *Endangered* in Slovakia, *Vulnerable* in Germany, Austria, the Czech Republic and Switzerland, *Rare* in Italy, Estonia and Lithuania, and present (without a published status) in France. It has also been recorded from Spain, where its status is *Data Deficient*. The record from Belgium is erroneous (Söderström *et al.* 2007). Its European distribution is categorised as European Boreal-montane. It also occurs in Siberia, Greenland and eastern N. America.

Threats

Remaining sites are potentially threatened by peat-cutting, drainage and afforestation. Some sites may also be at risk of physical damage from overstocking. It is likely that this plant has disappeared from many sites without ever having been recorded, following industrial-scale peat extraction in the midlands.

Conservation

Conservation efforts for this species should focus on retaining suitably wet hydrological conditions for the maintenance of *Sphagnum* growth. Its known remaining sites should be protected from further drainage and peat-cutting. Where necessary, remedial work to restore bogland habitats should take place.

Protected sites with recent records: Clara Bog Nature Reserve; Clara Bog SAC; Clonreher Bog NHA; Coolrain Bog SAC; Raheenmore Bog Nature Reserve; Raheenmore Bog SAC; **Unprotected sites with recent records:** Creevosheedy Bog; Ferbane Bog; Mount Jessop.

Cephalozia crassifolia (Lindenb. & Gottsche.) Fulford

Irish Pincerwort

syn. *Cephalozia hibernica* Spruce ex Pearson, *Jungermannia crassifolia* Lindenb. & Gottsche
Status in Ireland: Endangered (B2a, bii, iv); **Status in Europe:** Vulnerable

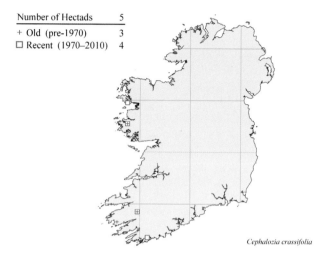

Number of Hectads	5
+ Old (pre-1970)	3
☐ Recent (1970–2010)	4

Cephalozia crassifolia

Identification

A very small, slender, whitish-green leafy liverwort, sometimes glistening, with shoots less than 1.5 cm long and c. 1 mm wide. Like other members of the genus, *C. crassifolia* has bilobed leaves and no underleaves. The leaves are bilobed to c. $^1/_3$–$^1/_2$, and the leaf lobes are long and subulate. It is closely related to *C. connivens* but the leaf lobes terminate in 2 or 3 uniseriate cells rather than 1 or 2. Single-celled, rounded gemmae are produced at the apices of attenuated shoots. The conspecificity of *Cephalozia hibernica* and *C. crassifolia* proposed by Váňa (1988) was accepted by Grolle & Long (2000), but Paton (1999) drew attention to various features of Irish material indicating that *C. hibernica* could be distinct.

More recently, however, it has been realised that Fulford's account of *C. crassifolia* (Fulford 1968) is inadequate, and that there are no significant differences between *C. crassifolia* and *C. hibernica* (D.G. Long, pers. comm.).

Distribution in Ireland

C. crassifolia is an oceanic species, confined to the extreme west, with recent records from four localities in four vice-counties: S. Kerry (O'Sullivan's Cascade, 1893–2006); W. Cork (Castletownshend Wood, 2009); W. Galway (Kylemore, 1968–2004) and W. Mayo (Sraheens Lough, Achill Island, 1987–2003). There are older records from S. Kerry (Lough Currane, 1951; Derrycunihy Wood,

1936–1957) and N. Kerry (various sites in the Killarney area, 1860–1966; Cromaglan, 1889–1938). Ratcliffe (1968) places this species in the Southern Atlantic group.

Ecology and biology

Habitats for this species include humic soil among sandstone rocks shaded by the base of a fallen tree low on the side of a valley in *Quercus petraea–Ilex aquifolium* woodland; very large patches with *C. lunulifolia* and *Telaranea europaea* on shaded ground under Rhododendron; on an old rotting fallen tree trunk in deciduous woodland near a small stream; on the emergent root of a Rhododendron in deep shade in a thicket in woodland; on peat in the deep shade of a Rhododendron thicket; on sloping peat on a low bank, heavily shaded inside Rhododendron scrub. It is a lowland plant, recorded at altitudes up to 45 m in Ireland.

Male inflorescences are rare and female inflorescences are occasional in this dioicous species, but sporophytes are apparently unknown, even in non-European material; Fulford (1968) noted 'sporophyte not seen', and J. Váňa (pers. comm.) has not seen them either. Gemmae are frequent.

World distribution

C. crassifolia is otherwise known in Europe only from Spain, where it is *Endangered*, Madeira (where it is *Vulnerable*) and the Azores. Its European range is categorised as

Hyperoceanic Southern-temperate. It is known elsewhere from C. and S. America and the Caribbean.

Threats

There are no obvious threats to this species, but clear-felling or other destruction of its shady habitat would clearly be detrimental to its continuing survival. It is unlikely that the spread of Rhododendron is a threat to this species as it is to many others: certainly, *C. crassifolia* is capable of growing under Rhododendron, but it is much more tolerant of deep shade than most other oceanic bryophytes.

Conservation

The sites for this species should be monitored to ensure that its populations remain in a favourable condition.

Protected sites with recent records: Castletownshend SAC; Killarney National Park; Killarney National Park, Macgillycuddy's Reeks and Caragh River Catchment SAC; The Twelve Bens/Garraun Complex SAC; **Unprotected sites with recent records:** Sraheens Lough, Achill Island.

Cladopodiella francisci (Hook.) Jörg.

Holt Notchwort

syn. *Cephalozia borealis* Lindb., *C. francisci* (Hook.) Dumort., *Cephaloziella francisci* (Hook.) Dumort., *Cladopus francisci* (Hook.) Meyl., *Jungermannia francisci* Hook., *Trigonanthus francisci* (Hook.) C. Hartm.
Status in Ireland: Vulnerable (D2); **Status in Europe:** Least Concern

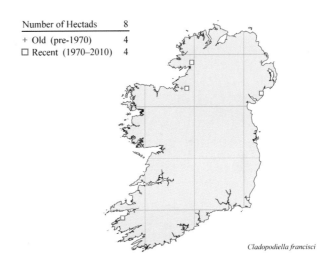

Number of Hectads	8
+ Old (pre-1970)	4
□ Recent (1970–2010)	4

Cladopodiella francisci

Identification

This is a small greenish or reddish weft-forming leafy liverwort with shoots c. 1 cm long and up to 0.8 mm wide. It is distinguished by the almost transversely inserted, concave and shallowly-bilobed leaves with rather blunt lobe apices, the small peg-like underleaves and the presence of flagella. The leaves have a characteristic oval shape, notched to c. 1/4 at the apex, with two small, rounded lobes. The gemmae are greenish or pinkish and more or less angular. Most other small bilobed liverworts have obliquely or longitudinally-inserted leaves, or acute leaf lobes, or smooth rounded gemmae.

Distribution in Ireland

Recent records are from four localities in four vice-counties: S. Kerry (Roads, west of Kells, 1983); Leitrim (Moneyduff, 2000); W. Donegal (Edergole Bridge, near Lough Eske, 2001, 2008) and Down (Silent Valley in the Mourne Mountains, 2002). There are older records from Dublin (Howth, 1892–1894); Leitrim (near Sriff Cottage, 1963, 1965); W. Mayo (Clare Island, 1910) and Antrim (Carnmoney Hill, leg. Templeton, *fide* Megaw 1938; the record leg. Templeton in 1815 from High Town Hill near the Cave Hill and Hightown Road is probably the same). Ellen Hutchins' 1816 record from 'near Bantry' is too inexact to allocate to a hectad. A 1951

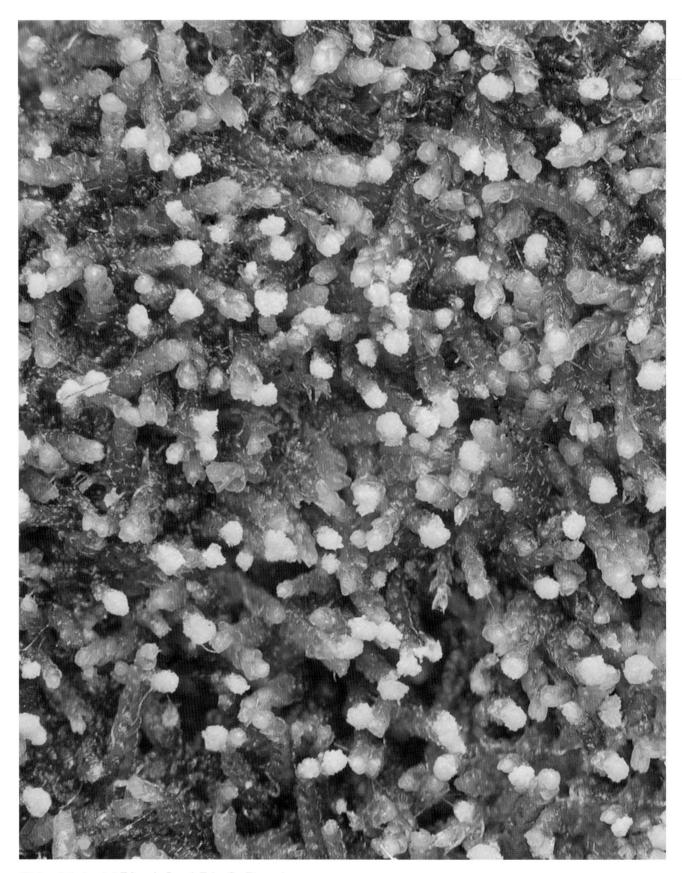

Cladopodiella francisci, Edergole, Lough Eske, Co. Donegal.

record from Cummergorm Glen in S. Kerry is considered erroneous.

Ecology and biology

Wet peaty soil in bogs, moorland and heath is the main habitat of this calcifuge species, usually found on banks and ditch sides, and sometimes as a pioneer on wet peat. One population is described as growing on a clay bank. *Sphagnum tenellum* is recorded as an associate in Ireland. Although individual plants may not last very long, it is likely that *C. francisci* acts as a 'shuttle species', reproducing by gemmae and rapidly recolonising the same site as the parent plant. Persistent flagella in the soil and associations with mycorrhizal fungi may also play a part in growth and vegetative reproduction (Pocock & Duckett 1985). It is lowland species, having been recorded up to c. 200 m in Ireland.

This species is dioicous, often fertile but sporophytes are very rare. Gemmae are frequent or abundant.

World distribution

Mainly montane in N., C. and W. Europe, this plant is rare or absent in the south and east. It is relatively frequent in Fennoscandia (but not the Faeroes) and northern Russia, and also occurs in France, the Netherlands, the Azores and Madeira. It is *Nationally Scarce* in Britain, *Extinct* in Italy, *Critically Endangered* in the Czech Republic, *Endangered* in Germany, Poland, and Slovakia, *Vulnerable* in Austria, Switzerland, Spain and Svalbard, and *Rare* in Belgium. The European distribution is categorised as European Boreal-montane. It also occurs in N. Asia, eastern N. America and Greenland.

Threats

Few threats to this species can be identified, providing that sufficient wet clay banks or peaty areas persist for colonisation. In spite of the abundance of such apparently suitable habitat, this species remains oddly rare in Ireland. There is no evidence of any decline.

Conservation

Populations should be monitored regularly to determine whether this plant persists at the known sites. *C. francisci* is listed as a Northern Ireland Priority Species.

Protected sites with recent records: Eastern Mournes ASSI; Eastern Mournes SAC; **Unprotected sites with recent records:** Edergole Bridge, near Lough Eske; Moneyduff; Roads, west of Kells.

Odontoschisma elongatum (Lindb.) A.Evans

Brown Flapwort

syn. *Odontoschisma denudatum* (Nees) Dumort. subsp. *elongatum* (Lindb.) Potemkin
Status in Ireland: Near Threatened; **Status in Europe:** Least Concern

This dark brown to black leafy liverwort can be found amongst debris and filamentous algae on exposed peaty mud on lake margins, but also in stony flushes in bogs. It has been reported from five vice-counties, with records from seven hectads (1 old, 6 recent). *O. elongatum* is an inconspicuous plant and has probably been overlooked in the past in Ireland, with four of the recent records coming from the BBS summer field meeting in S. Kerry and W. Cork in 2009. Nevertheless, it may be a rare species in Ireland, for although searched for recently at three of its former localities (League Point, Trawmore Strand and Tullywee Bridge), *O. elongatum* has not been refound at any of them.

Cephaloziella spinigera (Lindb.) Warnst.

Spiny Threadwort

syn. *Cephalozia spinigera* Lindb., *C. striatula* C.E.O.Jensen, *Cephaloziella subdentata* Warnst.
Status in Ireland: Data Deficient; **Status in Europe:** Least Concern

Number of Hectads	9
+ Old (pre-1970)	2
□ Recent (1970–2010)	7

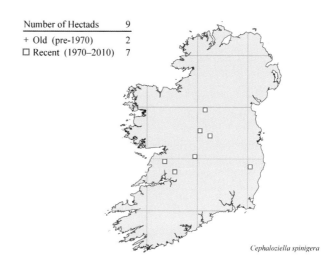

Cephaloziella spinigera

Identification

C. spinigera is one of a pair of exceedingly small and thread-like green or brownish leafy liverworts that are usually found creeping through *Sphagnum*. Its scattered shoots are about 5 mm long and no more than 0.3 mm wide; more occasionally, it forms thin mats. The leaves are distant, deeply bilobed to ²/₃ or more, mostly not or very sparsely toothed, but often with a single spiniform tooth near one or both leaf bases. Small subulate underleaves are usually present. It is often fertile, with more or less straight male bracts and dentate female bracts surrounding the perianth. Its sister species, *C. elachista* (*q.v.*), is larger, with larger and less incrassate stem and leaf cells. It has strongly incurved male bracts and dentate-ciliate female bracts. However, non-fertile material cannot always be confidently assigned to one species or the other.

Distribution in Ireland

This is a more common species than *C. elachista*, but still rare and scattered. Recent records are from seven localities in five vice-counties: Clare (Creevosheedy Bog, 1979, 2004; N. of Rinroe, 2004); N. Tipperary (Kilcarren-Firville Bog, 2005); Wicklow (Rathduffmore Bog, 1975); Westmeath (Ballinderry, 1986, 2007; S. of Doonis Lough, 2007) and Leitrim (Clooncoe Wood, 1980). There are older records from S. Kerry (Reenearagh, 1968) and W. Mayo (Clare Island, 1909; Maum, 1909). Non-fertile

material that might have been either *C. spinigera* or *C. elachista* was found in several bogs in Co. Roscommon during recent fieldwork, and other indeterminate material has been collected from sites in Leitrim and Donegal.

Ecology and biology

This is a calcifuge species, one of a group of small liverworts that are more or less confined to creeping amongst *Sphagnum* in undisturbed or little-disturbed bog and wet heath. Populations are usually small and consist of scattered stems amongst the *Sphagnum*. Typically, it occurs in Ireland with species characteristic of relatively undisturbed bogs, such as *Sphagnum austinii*, *S. fuscum* and *S. magellanicum*, but *S. subnitens* and *S. tenellum* have also been recorded as associates. It is often found growing with other small liverworts, notably *Calypogeia sphagnicola*, *Cephalozia* spp., *Cladopodiella fluitans*, *Kurzia pauciflora*, *Mylia anomala* and *Odontoschisma sphagni*. This is a lowland species and has been recorded in Ireland at altitudes from 20–60 m.

It is autoicous and often fertile. Sporophytes and gemmae are occasional.

World distribution

The European and world distribution of this plant is poorly known, but it appears to be fairly widespread in northern and C. Europe, including Svalbard, Iceland, Fennoscandia, France, Poland, Romania, Latvia, Ukraine and Russia. It is considered *Nationally Scarce* in Britain, *Endangered* in Germany, *Vulnerable* in Switzerland, Austria, the Czech Republic and Slovakia, *Rare* in Lithuania and 'susceptible' in the Netherlands. It is also recorded in Spain according to Söderström *et al.* (2007) and Casas *et al.* (2009), but is not listed by Sérgio *et al.* (2006). In Europe, it is assigned to a Circumpolar Boreo-arctic montane floristic element. Elsewhere, it is known from N. and E. Asia and N. America.

Threats

Remaining sites are potentially threatened by peat-cutting, drainage and afforestation. Some sites may also be at risk of physical damage from overstocking. It is likely that this plant has disappeared from many sites without ever having been recorded, following industrial-scale peat extraction in the midlands.

Conservation

Conservation efforts for this species should focus on retaining suitable hydrological conditions for the maintenance of *Sphagnum* growth.

Protected sites with recent records: Ballynagrenia and Ballinderry Bog NHA; East Burren Complex SAC; Kilcarren-Firville Bog SAC; **Unprotected sites with recent records:** Clooncoe Wood; Creevosheedy Bog; Rathduffmore Bog; S. of Doonis Lough.

Cephaloziella elachista (J.B.Jack ex Gottsche & Rabenh.) Schiffn.   Spurred Threadwort

syn. *Cephalozia elachista* (J.B.Jack.) Lindb., *Jungermannia elachista* J.B.Jack
Status in Ireland: Data Deficient; **Status in Europe:** Insufficiently Known

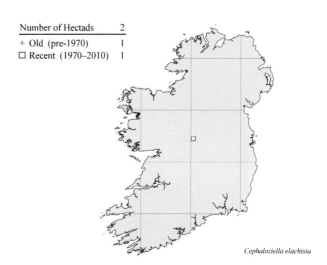

Number of Hectads	2
+ Old (pre-1970)	1
☐ Recent (1970–2010)	1

Cephaloziella elachista

Identification

C. elachista is one of the most attractive *Cephaloziella* species and easily recognised when the leaves are patent or squarrose and bearing 1–2 recurved teeth near the base (Paton 1999). It is one of a pair of exceedingly small and thread-like leafy liverworts that are usually found as scattered shoots creeping through *Sphagnum*. The plants are no more than 12 mm long and 0.4 mm wide and pale green or brown or sometimes darker. Very occasionally, sufficient shoots grow together to form thin mats. The leaves are distant, deeply bilobed to ²/₃ or more, mostly not or very sparsely toothed, but often with a single spiniform tooth near one or both leaf bases. Small subulate underleaves are usually present. It is often fertile, with strongly incurved male bracts and dentate-ciliate female bracts surrounding the perianth. Its sister species, *C. spinigera* (*q.v.*), differs in being even smaller, with smaller and more incrassate stem and leaf cells. It also has straighter male bracts and less strongly dentate female bracts. However, non-fertile material cannot always be confidently assigned to one species or the other.

Distribution in Ireland

There are only two confirmed records in Ireland, perhaps because of the difficulty in separating this species from *C. spinigera*. The most recent record is from Westmeath

(Tully Cross, 1986), with a much older one from Dublin (Hill of Howth, 1892). Non-fertile specimens that might have been of this species were collected in several bogs in Co. Roscommon during recent fieldwork.

Ecology and biology

C. elachista is a calcifuge species, one of a group of small liverworts that are more or less confined to creeping amongst *Sphagnum* in undisturbed or little-disturbed bog and wet heath. Populations are usually small and consist of scattered stems amongst the *Sphagnum*, or sometimes on *Aulacomnium palustre*. Typically, it occurs in Ireland with species characteristic of relatively undisturbed bogs, such as *Sphagnum austinii*, *S. fuscum* and *S. magellanicum* and is usually found in association with a range of other small liverworts including species of *Cephalozia*, *Kurzia*, *Mylia anomala*, *Odontoschisma sphagni* and other *Cephaloziella* spp. Both records from Ireland are from lowland sites.

C. elachista is autoicous and often fertile. Sporophytes and gemmae are occasional.

World distribution

The European and world distribution of this plant are poorly known. In Europe, it is considered *Endangered* in the Netherlands, Germany, Austria and Slovakia, *Vulnerable* in Switzerland, *Rare* in Lithuania and *Data Deficient* in Portugal. It has also been recorded from Britain, Denmark, Sweden, Finland, France, Belgium, Poland, the Czech Republic, Slovenia, Romania, Latvia, Belarus, Ukraine and Russia. It is noted as *Data Deficient* in Spain by Sérgio *et al.* (2006), but has not been correctly reported from Spain in the opinion of Söderström *et al.* (2007). In Europe, it is assigned to a European Boreal-montane floristic element. It is also known from northern and E. Asia and northern N. America.

Threats

The habitat for the species has probably disappeared from the locality at Howth due to urban development. The raised bog at Tully Cross has been destroyed by drainage and mechanised peat-cutting and little or no suitable habitat remains for *C. elachista*.

Conservation

Efforts should be made to survey suitably wet raised bogs, particularly in Co. Roscommon, in an attempt to establish the current status of this species in Ireland.

Protected sites with recent records: none; **Unprotected sites with recent records:** Tully Cross.

Cephaloziella rubella (Nees) Warnst.   Red Threadwort

syn. *Cephalozia bryhnii* Kaal., *C. myriantha* Lindb., *C. raddiana* Mass., *Cephaloziella bifidoides* Douin, *C. pulchella* Douin, *C. raddiana* (Mass.) Schiffn., *C. turfacea* Douin, *Jungermannia raddiana* C.Massal., *J. rubella* Nees, *J. sullivantii* Austin
Status in Ireland: Vulnerable (D2); **Status in Europe:** Least Concern

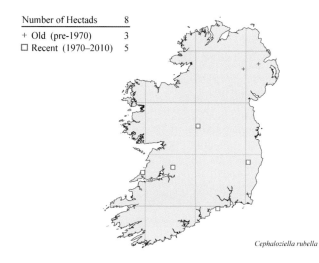

Number of Hectads	8
+ Old (pre-1970)	3
□ Recent (1970–2010)	5

Cephaloziella rubella

226

Identification

This is a very small thread-like reddish leafy liverwort that forms thin mats or grows as isolated shoots. The leaves are deeply bilobed to c. ²/₃. *C. rubella* can be distinguished from other members of this difficult genus only when fertile and by careful microscopic study. Small subulate underleaves are usually absent from non-fertile non-gemmiferous vegetative shoots, or very small, but sometimes present and more obvious. More or less rounded, 2-celled green or reddish gemmae (c. 8–14 × 14–22 μm) are produced on the upper leaves. The paroicous inflorescence distinguishes it from most other species of *Cephaloziella*. The other paroicous species, *C. stellulifera* and *C. nicholsonii*, are usually larger and have underleaves constantly present. Additionally, *C. nicholsonii* usually has toothed leaves and larger gemmae (c. 12–20 × 18–38 μm), and *C. stellulifera* sometimes has squarrose bracts.

Distribution in Ireland

Recent records are from five localities in four vice-counties: Waterford (Knockmahon, 2008); Clare (Creevosheedy Bog, 1979; Tullaher Bog, 2004); Wicklow (Rathduffmore Bog, 1975) and Westmeath (Doonis Lough, 1970). However, it was not refound at Creevosheedy Bog and Rathduffmore Bog during recent fieldwork. There are

Tullaher Bog, Co. Clare.

older records from E. Donegal (Dunree Head, 1968), Armagh (Derrycrow, 1964) and Antrim (Collin Mountain, Belfast, 1952). It is doubtless under-recorded.

Ecology and biology

This species grows on *Sphagnum* or on exposed peat in bogs and wet heath. It is not, however, one of the group of small liverworts indicative of wet undisturbed bogs. On the contrary, it also grows in cutover bogs or on dry, bare peat, or even on compacted, wet soil on tracks, or on stony mine spoil. Recorded associates include *Archidium alternifolium*, *Cephaloziella integerrima*, *Entosthodon obtusus*, *Fossombronia wondraczekii*, *Philonotis fontana*, *Pleuridium* sp., *Pohlia wahlenbergii*, *Riccia sorocarpa*, *Scapania irrigua* and *Sphagnum subnitens*. In Britain, *C. rubella* has also been recorded on sand, gravel and decorticated logs and stumps. In Ireland, this species has been recorded from lowland sites.

It is paroicous (perhaps occasionally autoicous) and sporophytes are common. Gemmae are frequent.

World distribution

Widespread and fairly frequent in most of northern and C. Europe, *C. rubella* is much rarer in the south, although recorded in most regions, including the Azores, Madeira and the Canary Islands. It is listed as *Endangered* in Bulgaria, *Vulnerable* in Serbia, *Rare* (but considered overlooked) in Belgium, and *Data Deficient* in Portugal and Spain. It has not been correctly recorded from the High Arctic islands (Svalbard, Novaya Zemlya, Franz Josef Land), the Balearic Islands, Bosnia-Herzegovina, Macedonia, Albania, Moldova, Greece, Crete, European Turkey or European Kazakhstan. It is assigned to a Circumpolar Boreo-temperate floristic element in Europe and is also known from N. Asia, Greenland and N. America.

Threats

Although some sites are potentially threatened by peat-cutting, drainage and afforestation, this species is a colonist and is probably at less risk than many of the small bog liverworts, which have more exacting ecological requirements.

Conservation

C. rubella is listed as a Northern Ireland Priority Species. **Protected sites with recent records:** Tullaher Lough and Bog SAC; **Unprotected sites with recent records:** Creevosheedy Bog; Doonis Lough; Knockmahon; Rathduffmore Bog.

Cephaloziella stellulifera (Taylor ex Spruce) Schiffn. Heath Threadwort

syn. *Cephalozia limprichtii* Warnst., *C. patula* Steph., *Cephaloziella divaricata* f. *stellulifera* (Taylor) Spruce, *C. gracillima* (Douin) Douin, *C. limprichtii* Warnst., *C. limprichtii* var. *stellulifera* (Taylor) K.Müll., *C. stellulifera* var. *limprichtii* (Warnst.) Macvicar, *Jungermannia stellulifera* Taylor

Status in Ireland: Near Threatened; **Status in Europe:** Least Concern

This is a very small, usually deep green or blackish leafy liverwort that can form extensive patches on damp, open, partly bare ground, typically on mine spoil, less often on metal-rich rocks and sometimes on walls, but also on sandy or heathy ground generally. It has a widely scattered distribution in Ireland and is reported from 11 vice-counties, with records from 20 hectads (7 old, 16 recent). The habitat for this species is probably in decline because some of its localities on lead- and copper-mine spoil are vulnerable to shading by taller vegetation as heavy metal toxicity decreases over time, and many of the old mine sites are themselves prone to redevelopment or other land-use change.

Cephaloziella massalongi (Spruce) Müll.Frib. Lesser Copperwort

syn. *Cephalozia massalongi* Spruce, *Cephaloziella compacta* (Jörg.) Müll.Frib.
Status in Ireland: Vulnerable (D2); **Status in Europe:** Rare

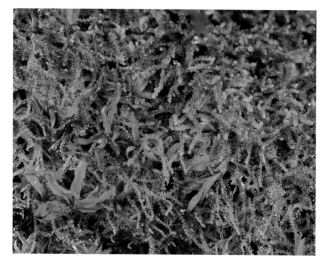

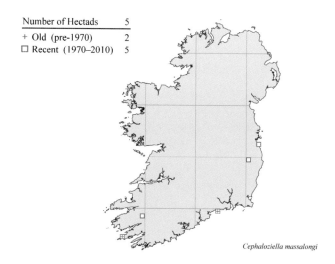

Number of Hectads	5
+ Old (pre-1970)	2
□ Recent (1970–2010)	5

Cephaloziella massalongi

Identification

Although this leafy liverwort has minute stems, it can form quite large patches. It has deep green or blackish (less often yellowish-green or dark reddish-brown) shoots up to c. 6 mm long and 0.3 mm wide, with bilobed, usually toothed leaves, with 2-celled leaf lobe

apices c. 30–48 μm long. However, some populations, notably on Ross Island in N. Kerry, have almost untoothed leaves. The underleaves are conspicuous, and the paired, rounded, symmetrical gemmae are c. 16–28 μm long. This species is very similar to *C. nicholsonii* (*q.v.*), from which it can be separated by the narrower stem cortical cells (c. 8–15 μm) and smaller leaf cells (c. 8–15 × 10–20 μm), which are densely papillose. *C. divaricata* has a shorter leaf apex (c. 16–24 μm) and smaller gemmae (c. 12–22 μm).

Distribution in Ireland

Known in Ireland from six localities in five vice-counties (Holyoak & Lockhart 2009a): N. Kerry (Ross Island, 2005–2009; N. shore of Muckross Lake, 2008); W. Cork (Allihies, 1955–2009); Waterford (E. of Bunmahon, 1966–2009); Wicklow (Vale of Glendasan, 2008–2009) and Dublin (Ballycorus, 2008).

Ecology and biology

C. massalongi is one of several rare bryophyte species that are heavy-metal tolerant; it occurs mainly at old copper mines on substrata rich in this metal, but with small populations also at old lead mines. It usually grows in moist and more or less shaded places, including crevices in walls, mine adits or flushed places on sea cliffs and the banks of pools in old mine workings. It is a lowland plant recorded in Ireland from 3–135 m altitude.

The species is dioicous and rarely fertile: male inflorescences, perianths and sporophytes are unknown in Ireland or Britain. Gemmae are usually abundant and vegetative propagation is also likely to occur from detached stem or leaf fragments.

World distribution

Scattered and rare in W. Europe, *C. massalongi* is listed as *Near Threatened* in Britain, *Extinct* in Germany, *Critically Endangered* in Finland, *Endangered* in Portugal, *Vulnerable* in Italy, *Rare* in Switzerland, Bulgaria and Spain, *Data Deficient* in Norway, 'potentially threatened' in Austria. In Europe, it is assigned to a Suboceanic Boreo-temperate floristic element. The species is also recorded in Asia and N. America.

Threats

Derelict copper and lead mines are usually seen as eyesores and are therefore potentially vulnerable to redevelopment or other land-use changes. If neglected, they are eventually recolonised by taller vegetation, which reduces and eventually eliminates the habitat of the heavy-metal specialists.

Conservation

The old mine sites where it occurs should be monitored and protected from destruction and damage, and managed in such as way as to preserve and promote bare, metal-rich substrates that can be utilised by this species.

Protected sites with recent records: Ballyvoyle Head to Tramore pNHA; Glenealo Valley Nature Reserve; Kenmare River SAC; Killarney National Park; Killarney National Park, Macgillycuddy's Reeks and Caragh River Catchment SAC; Wicklow Mountains National Park; Wicklow Mountains SAC; **Unprotected sites with recent records:** Ballycorus.

Cephaloziella massalongi, Allihies, Co. Cork.

Cephaloziella nicholsonii Douin

Greater Copperwort

syn. *Cephaloziella massalongi* var. *nicholsonii* (Douin) E.W.Jones
Status in Ireland: Vulnerable (B2a, biii); **Status in Europe:** Rare

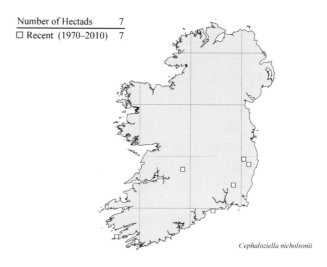

Number of Hectads	7
☐ Recent (1970–2010)	7

Cephaloziella nicholsonii

Identification

A leafy liverwort very similar to *C. massalongi* (*q.v.*), from which it may have evolved by doubling of the chromosome number (Newton in Paton 1999). It differs in being slightly larger, with shoots up to c. 15 mm long and c. 0.5 mm wide, often forming thick and extensive mats. Like *C. massalongi* it is deep green to blackish (or less often yellowish-green or dark reddish-brown), and has bilobed, more or less toothed leaves and fairly conspicuous underleaves. The main differences are its wider stem cortical cells (c. 16–20 μm), the often larger and frequently much more asymmetrical gemmae (c. 12–20 × 18–38 μm) and somewhat larger leaf cells (c. 14–20 × 16–30 μm), which may be smooth or somewhat papillose. Heavily shaded plants can be slender and virtually indistinguishable from *C. massalongi*, even using microscopic characters and measurements.

Distribution in Ireland

Recently discovered in Ireland (Holyoak & Lockhart 2009a), this species is now known from seven sites in five vice-counties: W. Cork (Allihies, 2006–2009; NE of Cappaghglass, 2006–2009); Waterford (Knockmahon, 2008–2009); N. Tipperary (Shallee, 2008–2009); Wexford (SW of Caim Cross Roads, 2008–2009) and Wicklow (Tigroney West, 2008–2009; Vale of Glendasan, 2008).

Ecology and biology

Like *C. massalongi*, this is one of a small number of rare bryophyte species that are tolerant of heavy metals. It occurs in Ireland mainly at old copper mines where substrata are rich in this metal, but also in much smaller amounts at two old lead mines. Its habitats are much like those of *C. massalongi*, mainly in moist rock and wall crevices where it is often somewhat shaded, or on flushed slopes of mine spoil. However, *C. nicholsonii* is not known on sea cliffs and some large populations occur on open banks that are prone to drying. Records in Ireland have come from altitudes between 12–285 m.

In Britain, this paroicous (or sometimes partly autoicous) species is occasionally partly fertile in that it produces perianths, but these fail to develop and sporophytes are unknown. Perianths have not been observed in Irish plants. Gemmae are often abundant and vegetative propagation is also likely to occur from detached stem and leaf fragments.

World distribution

Until recently, *C. nicholsonii* was known only from England, with a few records in Wales, so it was regarded as a British endemic and a Suboceanic Temperate element in the European flora. Since then *C. nicholsonii* has been reported from Germany (Meinunger & Schröder 2007); a report from northern Spain (Ordóñez

& Prieto 2003) was not accepted by subsequent authors (J.A. Paton, *in litt.*).

Threats
Derelict copper mines are usually seen as eyesores and are therefore potentially vulnerable to redevelopment or other land-use changes. If neglected, they are eventually recolonised by coarser vegetation, which eliminates the habitat of the heavy metal specialists.

Conservation
Old copper- and lead-mine sites should be monitored and protected from destruction and damage, and managed in such as way as to preserve and promote the bare, metal-rich substrata that can be utilised by this species.

Protected sites with recent records: Glenealo Valley Nature Reserve; Kenmare River SAC; Wicklow Mountains National Park; Wicklow Mountains SAC; **Unprotected sites with recent records:** Knockmahon; NE of Cappaghglass; Shallee; SW of Caim Cross Roads; Tigroney West.

Cephaloziella turneri (Hook.) Müll.Frib.

Turner's Threadwort

syn. *Anthelia turneri* (Hook.) Dumort., *Cephalozia turneri* (Hook.) Lindb., *Jungermannia turneri* Hook., *Prionolobus turneri* (Hook.) Schiffn.
Status in Ireland: Vulnerable (D2); **Status in Europe:** Least Concern

Number of Hectads	7
+ Old (pre-1970)	3
☐ Recent (1970–2010)	5

Cephaloziella turneri

Identification
This is a minute greenish or brownish leafy liverwort with shoots less than 1 cm long and 0.5 mm wide. The loosely complicate leaves are bilobed to c. ½ and underleaves are absent or obsolete on all shoots. The detailed structure, however, is hardly visible to the naked eye. Under a ×20 hand lens the strongly-toothed bilobed leaves give it a characteristic appearance that distinguishes it from most other *Cephaloziella* spp. It is beautiful under the microscope, with the spinose leaves appearing almost holly-like. It is distinguished from other dentate-leaved species of the genus by the absence of underleaves on non-fertile, non-gemmiferous shoots, by the multiangular greenish or brownish 2-celled gemmae and the autoicous inflorescences.

Distribution in Ireland
This plant has been recorded recently from five localities in four vice-counties: W. Cork (Castletownshend Wood, 2009; Leap, 2009); Kilkenny (The Pink Point, Bearstown, 2010); Wicklow (Glen of the Downs, 1912–1913 and 2007–2008) and W. Donegal (near Duntally Bridge, 2002). There are old records from N. Kerry (Cromaglan Mountain, 1873) and W. Cork (Lough Hyne, undated, but the record was by E.W. Jones, so it must have been in the 20th century). A record by Ellen

Hutchins from near Bantry (1811) is too imprecisely located to assign to a hectad. Ratcliffe (1968) places *C. turneri* in his Mediterranean-Atlantic group.

Ecology and biology

At its recent sites in Ireland, *C. turneri* occurs abundantly on the bank of an estuary; earth on rock ledges of a low cliff immediately above an estuary; on a soil bank by the coast; as scattered shoots and patches on dry, vertical, crumbling soil on a SW-facing bank by a track through oak woodland, often in crevices or beneath overhangs; with mosses on soil in a crevice among low rocks on a hill slope shaded by young deciduous woodland. Associates include *Calypogeia arguta*, *C. fissa*, *Dicranella heteromalla*, *Diplophyllum albicans* and *Isothecium myosuroides*. The old record from 'near Bantry' was described as being 'near a mountain rivulet'. It is a lowland species, growing up to 120 m in Ireland.

This autoicous species is often fertile and sporophytes are frequent. Gemmae are common.

World distribution

C. turneri is widespread in S. Europe, north to Scotland, occurring but not red-listed in France (including Corsica), Portugal (where locally abundant), Spain, Italy (including Sardinia and Sicily), Croatia, Bulgaria, Albania, Greece (including Crete), European Turkey, the Caucasus and Macaronesia. It is considered *Nationally Scarce* in Britain, *Critically Endangered* in Bulgaria and *Vulnerable* in Serbia. It is classified as an Oceanic Mediterranean-Atlantic floristic element in Europe. It also occurs in N. Africa, parts of Asia adjacent to the Mediterranean and in N. America.

Threats

Afforestation or other actions that might shade its habitats or disrupt the dynamic nature of the crumbling banks on which it grows are the main dangers for this species. However, the fact that it survived undetected for nearly 100 years in Wicklow suggests that the populations may be fairly robust.

Conservation

Glen of the Downs is a nature reserve, so the plant should be secure there with sympathetic management. It may still be present at its other sites and elsewhere as it is an easily overlooked species.

Protected sites with recent records: Castletownshend SAC; Glen of the Downs Nature Reserve; Glen of The Downs SAC; River Barrow and River Nore SAC; Sheephaven SAC; **Unprotected sites with recent records:** Leap.

Cephaloziella integerrima (Lindb.) Warnst.   Lobed Threadwort

syn. *Cephalozia integerrima* Lindb., *Cephaloziella piriflora* Douin, *Dichiton integerrimum* (Lindb.) H.Buch, *Lophoziella integerrima* (Lindb.) Douin
Status in Ireland: Vulnerable (D2); **Status in Europe:** Least Concern

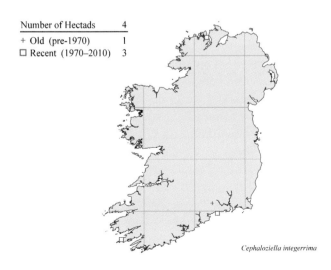

Number of Hectads	4
+ Old (pre-1970)	1
□ Recent (1970–2010)	3

Cephaloziella integerrima

Identification

This is a minute thread-like brownish leafy liverwort, forming short turfs or less often thin mats of shoots, up to 4 mm long and 0.5 mm wide, with rather bluntly-bilobed leaves and lacking underleaves. It can be distinguished from most other members of this difficult genus by the combination of untoothed leaves with shortly pointed or obtuse leaf lobe apices, and distinctive paired multiangular gemmae measuring c. 12–20 × 12–28 μm. *C. calyculata*, which is not known to occur in Ireland, has similar gemmae but differs in its uniquely truncated 'bract tube' surrounding the lower part of the perianth, a feature absent in *C. integerrima*, which instead has distinct but connate toothed bracts around the perianth.

Distribution in Ireland

First recorded from Ireland in 1966 on a roadside bank at the eastern edge of the Comeragh Mountains (Waterford), this plant was refound there in 1968 but not in 2007, by which time the original habitat may have disappeared. It has subsequently been found at three new localities in three vice-counties: W. Cork (Allihies, 2006); Waterford (Knockmahon, 2008–2009) and E. Donegal (Dunree Head, 2002).

Ecology and biology

In Ireland, this plant has been found on an earthy, almost vertical roadside bank; on thin soil among quartzite cobbles receiving drainage from galvanised roofs; on copper mine spoil and on bare ground by a track in an old copper mine. It is a mild calcifuge and a pioneer species and thus a poor competitor. It is presumably tolerant, at least to some extent, of heavy metals, and colonises old mine sites that are contaminated by copper (Holyoak & Lockhart 2009a). It occurs in the lowlands, having been recorded at 10–130 m in Ireland.

This plant is autoicous, and only known fertile, commonly producing sporophytes. Gemmae are apparently always present.

World distribution

Occasional in northern Europe but much rarer or absent further south, this species occurs in Iceland, Denmark, Finland, Norway, Sweden, Poland, northern Russia and Romania. It is listed as *Vulnerable* in Britain (where, oddly, it has a southern distribution, with numerous recent records restricted to Cornwall), Germany and Switzerland, *Rare* in Hungary and Estonia, *Data Deficient* in Spain, and 'potentially threatened' in Austria. In Europe, it is assigned to a Suboceanic Boreal-montane floristic element. Outside Europe, this species is recorded only from subarctic N. America.

Threats

The Allihies site is in a protected area and has no immediate threats. At Dunree Head, it is potentially vulnerable to redevelopment of ground with old military buildings. A housing development may soon destroy the habitat at Knockmahon.

Conservation

The Allihies and Dunree Head sites should be monitored and protected from destruction.

Protected sites with recent records: Kenmare River SAC; **Unprotected sites with recent records:** Dunree Head; Knockmahon.

Barbilophozia kunzeana (Huebener) Müll.Frib.   Bog Pawwort

syn. *Jungermannia kunzeana* Huebener, *J. plicata* C.Hartm., *Lophozia kunzeana* (Huebener) A.Evans, *Orthocaulis kunzeanus* (Huebener) H.Buch, *Schljakovia kunzeana* (Huebener) Konstant. & Vilnet
Status in Ireland: Regionally Extinct; **Status in Europe:** Least Concern

Identification

Often difficult to locate in the field, this leafy liverwort has much the appearance of other species of *Barbilophozia*, but it has bilobed rather than trilobed leaves. The leaves are 1/4–1/2 bilobed and the sinus between the lobes is often rather gibbous or recurved, giving the plants a distinctive appearance. Shoots may reach 5 cm in length and c. 2 mm in width, and creep through other bryophytes either as isolated shoots or as loose mats. The underleaves are fairly conspicuous and deeply bilobed, often with additional lateral teeth, and tend to stick out from the underside of the stem. There are usually clusters of pale yellowish or brownish gemmae at the shoot apex.

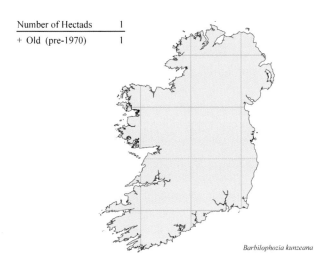

Number of Hectads	1
+ Old (pre-1970)	1

Barbilophozia kunzeana

Distribution in Ireland

B. kunzeana is known from a single record on Benbulbin (Sligo) in 1880. Unfortunately, no specimen is known to exist, but the original record was apparently confirmed by three eminent hepaticologists—R. Spruce, S.M. Macvicar and W.H. Pearson—so it is assumed to be correct.

Ecology and biology

This plant usually occurs as sparse patches or isolated shoots in damp acidic or mildly basic habitats, such as on *Sphagnum* hummocks in bog or wet heath. The only detail known about the Irish plant is that it was growing with *Leiocolea collaris* (*L. alpestris*). Its altitude in Ireland is presumably that of Benbulbin (c. 500 m).

It is dioicous, but often not fertile: sporophytes are unknown in Ireland or Britain. Gemmae are usually present and often abundant.

World distribution

Widespread in northern Europe, occurring throughout Fennoscandia and northern Russia but increasingly scattered and confined to mountain areas further south, *B. kunzeana* is *Extinct* in Latvia and Luxembourg, *Critically Endangered* in the Czech Republic, *Endangered* in Germany, *Vulnerable* in Britain, the Netherlands and Bulgaria, *Rare* in Belgium, Italy, Estonia and Lithuania and *Near Threatened* in Spain and Andorra. It is assigned to a Circumpolar Boreo-arctic montane element in Europe. Also present in Siberia, the Russian Far East, China, Mongolia, N. America and Greenland.

Threats

No threats have been identified. It is possible that it was found in the northern corrie of Benbulbin, which is now substantially cutover for peat.

Conservation

No conservation measures are required unless the plant is refound.

Protected sites with recent records: none; **Unprotected sites with recent records:** none.

Barbilophozia atlantica (Kaal.) Müll.Frib.   Atlantic Pawwort

syn. *Jungermannia atlantica* Kaal., *Lophozia atlantica* (Kaal.) Schiffn., *Orthocaulis atlanticus* (Kaal.) H.Buch
Status in Ireland: Endangered (B2a, bii, iv, v); **Status in Europe:** Least Concern

Identification

A small leafy liverwort, yellowish-green, sometimes tinged reddish, with shoots up to c. 2 mm wide and 3 cm long. It has transversely-inserted 2- or 3-lobed leaves and much smaller bilobed and toothed underleaves. This can be a difficult species to identify, particularly when only

Number of Hectads   2
+ Old (pre-1970)   1
□ Recent (1970–2010) 1

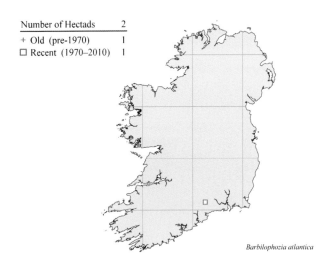

Barbilophozia atlantica

represented by depauperate material. It is distinguished from *B. attenuata* by the lack of specialised attenuate shoots and the larger leaf cells, and from *B. floerkei* by the clusters of red gemmae at the shoot apex, the cilia on the postical leaf base being small or absent and the much smaller underleaves. The gemmae are 1–2-celled and either rounded or angular.

Distribution in Ireland

In spite of its specific name, the distribution of this species in Ireland is certainly not Atlantic. Paton (1999) describes it as a Western British species which is Atlantic only in a European context. The only recent record from Ireland is from Waterford (Lough Coumfea in the Comeragh Mountains, 1999 and 2007). The only other known site is in E. Donegal (Bulbin Mountain) where it was last seen in 1914. An unsupported 1984 record from Crossmurrin (Fermanagh) is probably an error.

Ecology and biology

This is a calcifuge species of boulders, stone walls and thin humus over rocks. In Ireland, it grows in a liverwort crust on and around rocks in glacial moraine on N.-facing slopes, and on peaty humus on a rock in a stream. Associates include *Barbilophozia attenuata*, *B. floerkei*, *Diplophyllum albicans*, *Hypnum jutlandicum*, *Lophozia ventricosa*, *Pleurozium schreberi*, *Rhytidiadelphus loreus*, *R. squarrosus*, *Scapania gracilis*, *Festuca ovina* and *Cladonia* spp. In Ireland, it is recorded from between 400 and 530 m.

Sporophytes are unknown in this dioicous species, but gemmae are usually present.

World distribution

B. atlantica is widespread in northern Europe, occurring in northern Russia and throughout Fennoscandia, including Iceland but excluding the Faeroes, though rare or absent in the south. It also occurs in Britain, where it is locally frequent, and France and Poland, where its status is not known. It is listed as *Endangered* in Slovakia and *Vulnerable* in Spain and Switzerland. In the Czech Republic, its status is *Data Deficient* (*vanished*), indicating that it has not been seen for a long time, but there is enough doubt about its survival not to list it as *Extinct*. In Europe, it is assigned to a Suboceanic Boreal-montane floristic element. It has also been recorded in Siberia, north-eastern N. America and Greenland.

Threats

The principal threats to this species are probably overstocking by sheep, afforestation and burning.

Conservation

The Lough Coumfea site is currently grazed by sheep, but not too heavily.

Protected sites with recent records: Comeragh Mountains SAC; **Unprotected sites with recent records:** none.

Barbilophozia barbata (Schmidel ex Schreb.) Loeske

Bearded Pawwort

syn. *Jungermannia barbata* Schmidel ex Schreb., *J. schreberi* Nees, *Lophozia barbata* (Schmidel ex Schreb.) Dumort., *L. schreberi* (Nees) Boulay

Status in Ireland: Critically Endangered (B1a, bi, ii, iv, B2a, bi, ii, iv); **Status in Europe:** Least Concern

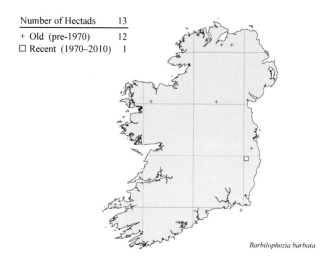

Number of Hectads	13
+ Old (pre-1970)	12
☐ Recent (1970–2010)	1

Barbilophozia barbata

Identification

B. barbata is a rather large yellowish-green or brownish-green leafy liverwort with shoots up to 5 cm long and 4 mm wide. It has rather shallowly and bluntly 3–4-lobed leaves and small, deeply bilobed underleaves. Unlike most other *Barbilophozia* species, the leaves are inserted very obliquely (almost longitudinally) and have no postical cilia. The underleaves are very small and gemmae are absent.

Distribution in Ireland

The most recent record is from Wicklow (Upper Lake, Glendalough, 1975). Older records are from 13 localities in eight vice-counties: S. Kerry (Connor Hill, 1877–1898; An Loch Dubh, 1899; Brandon Mountain, 1881–1898; Lough Anscaul, 1898; Derrymore River, 1898); Wexford (Great Saltee Island, 1913); Wicklow (Djouce Mountain, 1897); Dublin (Howth, 1885); W. Mayo (Nephin, 1901); Cavan (Slieve Glah, 1893); W. Donegal (behind Rathmullan church, 1902) and Londonderry (Ness Glen, 1809; Benbradagh, 1964). Recent surveys have failed to refind it even in the Wicklow Mountains, its most recent locality.

Ecology and biology

The ecology of this plant is very poorly known in Ireland, but it probably grows among predominantly base-poor rocks, since it is a weak calcifuge. On Benbradagh, the habitat is recorded as 'in turf at top of cliff' and 'cliffs and block scree'. In Britain, it grows on drystone walls, scree and natural rock outcrops, usually where there is some shade, but it avoids strongly calcareous substrata. A plant of low to medium altitudes, recorded up to about 550 m in Ireland.

B. barbata is dioicous, but rarely fertile and sporophytes are unknown in Ireland or Britain. Gemmae are not known in this species.

World distribution

A common plant in most of northern Europe, *B. barbata* becomes rarer and more montane southwards. It is *Vulnerable* in Svalbard, Portugal and Latvia; *Rare* in Lithuania, and listed as a Circumpolar Boreal-montane floristic element in Europe. It also occurs in N. Asia, where it is common in part of the Russian Arctic (Konstantinova & Potemkin 1996), Japan, N. America and Greenland.

Threats

The apparent disappearance of this plant in Ireland is a mystery. Since this is a fairly easily identified liverwort, it is probably reasonable to suppose that a large decline has taken place, but the reasons for this decline are unclear. Overstocking in the uplands, afforestation and burning are all possible causes. Disappearance from Saltee Island was doubtless due to loss of open habitats following cessation of grazing. On the other hand, it was always a rare plant in Ireland, compared to its frequency in Britain. It may be that it is naturally at the edge of its range and either that very small-scale environmental changes could have eliminated it, or that the populations are very small and it has been overlooked in recent years.

Conservation
Bryologists should continue to look out for this species in the field.

Protected sites with recent records: Glenealo Valley Nature Reserve; Wicklow Mountains National Park; Wicklow Mountains SAC; **Unprotected sites with recent records:** none.

Sphenolobopsis pearsonii (Spruce) R.M.Schust.   Horsehair Threadwort

syn. *Cephaloziella pearsonii* (Spruce) Douin, *Cephaloziopsis pearsonii* (Spruce) Schiffn., *Jungermannia pearsonii* Spruce, *Sphenolobopsis kitagawae* R.M.Schust., *Sphenolobus pearsonii* (Spruce) Steph.
Status in Ireland: Near Threatened; **Status in Europe:** Rare

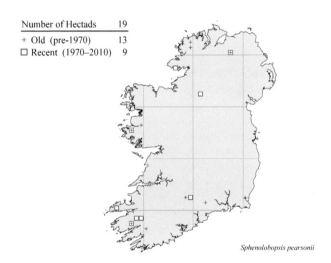

Number of Hectads	19
+ Old (pre-1970)	13
☐ Recent (1970–2010)	9

Sphenolobopsis pearsonii

Identification
This very small leafy liverwort resembles a species of *Cephaloziella*, with tiny thread-like shoots c. 1 cm long and less than 0.5 mm wide forming thin, dark mats. The leaves are deeply bilobed and loosely complicate, with a patent leaf base and more or less erect, acute lobes. Underleaves are absent or extremely small. It can be distinguished from species of *Cephaloziella* by the terminal branching pattern (no intercalary branches), and the postical leaf lobes normally spreading more widely from the stem than the antical lobes. *Eremonotus myriocarpus* is also similar, but is smaller and has more or less imbricate, not spreading, leaves.

Distribution in Ireland
It is scattered in Ireland, with a mainly western distribution. It was not included in the Provisional Red List (Holyoak 2006b) so was not targeted during recent

fieldwork. Nevertheless, there are recent records from 10 localities in seven vice-counties: S. Kerry (Beenkeragh, 1983; Ballaghbeama Gap, 1967, 1983; Connor Hill Pass, 2006); N. Kerry (Mangerton Mountain, 1972); S. Tipperary (Galty Mountains, 1966, 2005); W. Galway (Muckanaght, 1970; Kylemore, 1994); Fermanagh (Cuilcagh Mountain, 2005); W. Donegal (Fintragh Bridge, 2001) and Londonderry (Mullaghmore Mountain, 1965, 1999). There are also older records from W. Cork, Waterford, W. Mayo and Louth.

Ecology and biology
This is a calcifuge species and is strongly oceanic, growing on damp, shaded rock walls in ravines, in crevices in block scree and on humid NE-facing rocks by streams. It is dioicous and sporophytes are unknown. Neither are there any specialised means of asexual reproduction, so fragmentation must play an important part in its dispersal.

World distribution

This species is restricted to Atlantic parts of Europe, being found elsewhere only in Britain (where it is *Nationally Scarce*), Iceland, the Faeroe Islands and Norway, and is assigned to a Suboceanic Boreo-arctic montane floristic element. Elsewhere, there are widely disjunct populations in the Himalaya, Taiwan, British Columbia and the Appalachians.

Threats

There are no obvious threats to this species in Ireland. It is an inconspicuous plant and probably under-recorded, and there is no reason to suppose that it has declined.

Conservation

It should persist in remote oceanic ravines, many of which are in protected areas.

Protected sites with recent records: Connemara National Park; Cuilcagh Mountain ASSI; Cuilcagh Mountain SAC; Galtee Mountains SAC; Killarney National Park, Macgillycuddy's Reeks and Caragh River Catchment SAC; Mount Brandon SAC; The Twelve Bens/Garraun Complex SAC; **Unprotected sites with recent records:** Fintragh Bridge.

Anastrophyllum hellerianum (Nees ex Lindenb.) R.M.Schust.   Heller's Notchwort

syn. *Cephalozia helleri* (Nees) Lindb., *Crossocalyx hellerianus* (Nees ex Lindenb.) Meyl., *Isopaches hellerianus* (Nees ex Lindenb.) H.Buch, *Jungermannia helleriana* Nees ex Lindenb., *Sphenolobus hellerianus* (Nees ex Lindenb.) Steph.
Status in Ireland: Regionally Extinct; **Status in Europe:** Near Threatened

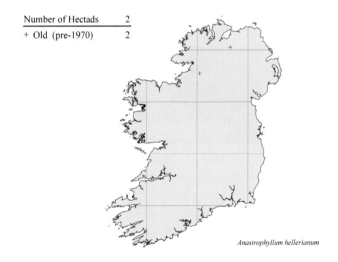

Number of Hectads	2
+ Old (pre-1970)	2

Anastrophyllum hellerianum

Identification

A minute greenish or brownish leafy liverwort with shoots up to only c. 0.6 mm wide and c. 1 cm long, growing in thin mats. The leaves are transversely inserted, bilobed to less than one-half, and underleaves are absent. The shoots creep horizontally and often become gemmiferous at the apices, where they ascend abruptly, becoming stiffly upright, with reduced, irregularly lobed and imbricate leaves. Each of these shoots terminates in a cluster of bright red or purple gemmae, the shoots then resembling clusters of tiny matchsticks. The gemmae are unicellular and angular, unlike the smooth or 2-celled gemmae produced by most other gemmiferous leafy liverworts.

Distribution in Ireland

Known from only two localities in two vice-counties: Fermanagh (Meenameen Scarp in Lough Navar Forest, 1961) and Londonderry (Banagher Glen, 1959 and 1964), but not seen recently, in spite of searching. However, it could well turn up in suitable habitat anywhere in the north. Because of its predominantly western distribution in Ireland and Britain, Ratcliffe (1968) places it into the Western British group.

Ecology and biology

This lowland plant grows on rotting logs and as an epiphyte on tree trunks, usually with *Nowellia curvifolia*. In Ireland, it has been recorded from a rotting Rowan log and a 'large rotting log near the river'. Individual colonies are inevitably transient because the habitat is short-lived, so the species should be considered at a metapopulation level rather than site by site. Revisiting the old sites tends only to confirm the obvious expectation that habitat patches have not persisted in exactly the same place. However, the production of abundant gemmae means that short-distance dispersal within the same sites is likely to be efficient.

It is dioicous but rarely fertile: sporophytes are unknown in Ireland or Britain. Gemmae, however, are always present.

World distribution

Widespread in the mountainous parts of C. and N. Europe, *A. hellerianum* is relatively frequent in Fennoscandia but is considered *Nationally Scarce* in Britain, *Critically Endangered* in the Czech Republic, *Endangered* in Switzerland, Spain and Andorra, *Vulnerable* in Germany, Lichtenstein and Luxembourg, and *Rare* in Italy, Estonia and Lithuania. It has also been recorded in France, Poland, Austria, Slovakia, Slovenia, Serbia, Latvia, Hungary, Romania, Belarus, Ukraine and European Russia, but with no information on status. It has declined in recent decades in Finland because of forestry practices (Pohjamo & Laaka-Lindberg 2003), and is subject to declining habitats and fluctuating populations throughout Europe. In Europe, it is assigned to a European Boreal-montane floristic element. It is scattered outside Europe, and has been reported from Siberia, Bhutan, China (Schill & Long 2002), Japan, N. America and Mexico.

Threats

Habitat destruction, including tidying away dead wood and clear-felling of woodland, are probably the main threats to this species. However, there is no information on the Irish populations.

Conservation

Woodland or plantation areas in the vicinity of the old records should be maintained, with plenty of dead and fallen timber, and further effort should go into survey work to attempt to relocate the species.

Protected sites with recent records: none; **Unprotected sites with recent records:** none.

Tritomaria exsecta (Schmidel) Loeske

Cut Notchwort

syn. *Jungermannia exsecta* Schmidel ex Schrad., *Lophozia exsecta* (Schrad.) Dumort., *Sphenolobus exsectus* (Schmidel) Steph.
Status in Ireland: Vulnerable (B2a, bii, iv); **Status in Europe:** Least Concern

Number of Hectads	13
+ Old (pre-1970)	9
□ Recent (1970–2010)	6

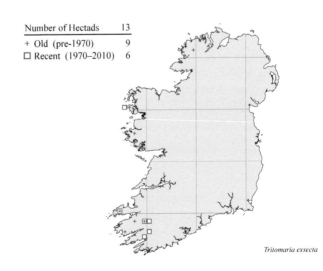

Tritomaria exsecta

239

Identification

This small leafy liverwort (shoots up to 2 cm long and 2 mm wide) is usually interpreted as having trilobed leaves, but it appears bilobed, with the antical lobe reduced to little more than a tooth lying over the much larger, more or less triangular lamina formed by the two postical lobes, which tapers to a narrow, usually slightly notched, apex. In older leaves, the division of this part of the leaf into two discrete lobes is often more obvious. Underleaves are absent. Smooth, relatively small red gemmae (c. 8–12 × 12–18 μm) are produced on leaf tips at the shoot apex, differing from the larger, angular gemmae of the more common *T. exsectiformis* (c. 14–22 × 16–26 μm). The leaf cells of *T. exsecta* are also smaller than those of *T. exsectiformis* (c. 10–14 μm, compared to 19–22 μm wide).

Distribution in Ireland

This plant has a western distribution, and may have declined, although its small patches are easily overlooked unless deliberate efforts are made to seek tiny liverworts. Recent records are from six localities in four vice-counties: S. Kerry (O'Sullivan's Cascade, 2006; Loch an Mhónáin, 2009); N. Kerry (Loo Bridge, 2005); W. Cork (Coomroe, 2006; Glengarriff, 1979) and W. Mayo (Lough Nakeeroge on Achill Island, 1987). There are older records from N. Kerry (Torc Cascade, 1962; Cromaglan, 1829); W. Galway (Kylemore, 1968); W. Mayo (Slievemore, 1911) and W. Donegal (Milford, 1967; The Poisoned Glen, 1967). It is listed as a Western British species by Ratcliffe (1968).

Ecology and biology

T. exsecta grows on damp, mossy rocks and rotting logs in woodland, and rarely on banks outside woodland, creeping among other bryophytes. Specific habitats in Ireland include a fallen, decorticated conifer trunk and the sloping top of a large, damp sandstone boulder. It is essentially a lowland species, but its habitats tend to occur at low altitude in hilly areas.

Both sexes of this dioicous species are occasionally fertile, but sporophytes are unknown in Ireland or Britain.

World distribution

It is widespread in montane regions of Europe, including Madeira and the Canary Islands, but absent from the extreme north. It is *Nationally Scarce* in Britain, *Vulnerable* in Sweden and Bulgaria, *Rare* in Belgium. In Europe, it is assigned to a Circumpolar Boreal-montane floristic element. It also occurs in montane areas of Asia, N. America and Africa.

Threats

Woodland destruction through clear-felling or afforestation is the main threat. Tidying up dead wood may also be a threat. However, it is not clear if this plant has genuinely declined or if it has been widely overlooked in recent years. It may also occur as a metapopulation, no single subpopulation lasting for very long, but readily colonising new sites through gemmae dispersal.

Conservation

Small populations of *T. exsecta* should survive if more or less intact and undisturbed areas of woodland are allowed to remain.

Protected sites with recent records: Croaghaun/ Slievemore SAC; Glengarriff Harbour and Woodland SAC; Glengarriff Wood Nature Reserve; Killarney National Park; Killarney National Park, Macgillycuddy's Reeks and Caragh River Catchment SAC; Mount Brandon SAC; **Unprotected sites with recent records:** Coomroe.

O'Sullivan's Cascade, Co. Kerry.

Lophozia wenzelii (Nees) Steph.

Wenzel's Notchwort

syn. *Jungermannia wenzelii* Nees
Status in Ireland: Data Deficient; **Status in Europe:** Not Evaluated

A taxonomic review by Bakalin (2004) reported *L. wenzelii* var. *wenzelii* from Cavan on the basis of a specimen collected in 1961 by J.W. Fitzgerald (**NMW** C96.17.440). Since *L. wenzelii* has been regarded as a very rare montane species in Britain (Paton 1999) this record was initially thought to be erroneous. However, study by J.A. Paton of the Cavan specimen, and others placed as *L. wenzelii* by Bakalin, has revealed that this identification is correct if judged from characters of the stem section (cf. Meinunger & Schröder 2007, Bd 1: 93–95). An extensive revision of Irish and British material of *Lophozia ventricosa* and allied taxa including *L. wenzelii* is now needed (J.A. Paton, pers. comm.).

Lophozia sudetica (Nees ex Huebener) Grolle

Hill Notchwort

syn. *Jungermannia alpestris* auct. non Schleich. ex F.Weber, *J. sudetica* Nees ex Huebener,
Barbilophozia sudetica (Nees ex Huebener) L. Söderstr., De Roo et Hedd.,
Lophozia alpestris auct. non (Schleich. ex F.Weber) A.Evans,
L. alpestris var. *gelida* (Hook.f. & Taylor) Macvicar,
L. rufescens (Limpr.) M.Howe, *Pseudolophozia sudetica* (Nees ex Huebener) Konstant. & Vilnet
Status in Ireland: Least Concern; **Status in Europe:** Least Concern

A small brownish-green leafy liverwort, with shallowly bilobed leaves and reddish-brown gemmae, found on acidic rocks, boulders and peaty soils in a range of upland habitats. This species has been reported from 18 vice-counties, with records from 33 hectads (20 old, 12 recent, 2 undated). Although included in the Provisional Red List (Holyoak 2006b), it has now been recorded in too many localities for it to be retained. There is no real evidence of decline, and it is probably even more frequent in the uplands than the records indicate.

Lophozia opacifolia Culm. ex Meyl.

Alpine Jagged Notchwort

syn. *Lophozia incisa* subsp. *opacifolia* (Culm. ex Meyl.) R.M.Schust. & Damsh.,
Massula opacifolia (Culm. ex Meyl.) Schljakov, *Massularia opacifolia* (Culm. ex Meyl.) Schljakov,
Schistochilopsis opacifolia (Culm. ex Meyl.) Konstant.
Status in Ireland: Vulnerable (D2); **Status in Europe:** Least Concern

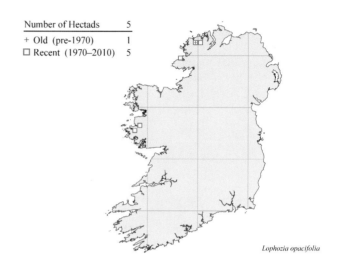

Number of Hectads	5
+ Old (pre-1970)	1
□ Recent (1970–2010)	5

Lophozia opacifolia

Identification

Essentially a bilobed leafy liverwort without underleaves, this species is very similar to the much more common and predominantly lowland *L. incisa*: shoots are up to c. 2 cm long and 3 mm wide, pale green and have a rather thick, succulent texture. Like *L. incisa*, the leaves are irregularly divided up to ½ into 2–4 lobes, which often have further irregular subsidiary teeth. However, *L. opacifolia* has somewhat less strongly and irregularly toothed leaves than *L. incisa*, a thicker, 3–5-stratose leaf base and much shorter teeth on the perianth. Clusters of pale green gemmae occur at the shoot apices.

Distribution in Ireland

Confined to a small number of sites in the north and west, *L. opacifolia* has been found at five localities in three vice-counties: W. Galway (Bengower, 1994, 2004; Muckanaght, 1994); W. Mayo (Mweelrea, 1987) and W. Donegal (Muckish Mountain, 1968–2002; Slieve Tooey, 2001). Other specimens of putative *L. opacifolia* collected from various sites in Kerry, Donegal and Tyrone have all been redetermined as *L. incisa*.

Ecology and biology

This species is found on peaty soil and among rocks on ledges and in crevices at high altitudes, usually on N.-facing slopes. Examples of its habitat in Ireland include wet rocks in a gully on N.-facing cliffs; near-vertical peat exposed at the base of a N.-facing quartzite crag above a corrie; on a mossy slope on an exposed ridge; on damp sandy soil in small quartzite rock ledges and crevices on a small crag high on a N.-facing slope; with grasses in low, patchy Northern Atlantic hepatic mat vegetation on unshaded wet peat on a N.-facing slope. It is an alpine plant, recorded at altitudes of 400–730 m in Ireland.

This dioicous species is often fertile and sporophytes are occasional. Gemmae are frequent.

World distribution

It is a widespread arctic-alpine in northern Europe, including mainly montane parts of Fennoscandia, northern Russia and the arctic islands, but much rarer in the south, occurring sparsely in the C. and W. European mountains (Alps, Carpathians, Pyrenees). It is *Nationally Scarce* in Britain, *Near Threatened* in Spain and Andorra, *Rare* in Italy, Estonia and Slovakia and *Data Deficient* (*vanished*) in the Czech Republic. In Europe, it is assigned to a Circumpolar Arctic-montane floristic element. It is also known from Siberia and the Russian Far East, N. America and Greenland.

Threats

Climate change may be the biggest threat to this species in Ireland, where it is presumably at the southern edge of its range. However, in the absence of older records, it is impossible to determine whether *L. opacifolia* has declined in Ireland. Overstocking in the uplands, afforestation and burning may also be factors threatening this plant.

Conservation
Mountains where this species is known to occur should be protected from the impacts of overstocking and disruptive land-use change. Populations should be monitored regularly.

Protected sites with recent records: Muckish Mountain SAC; Mweelrea/Sheeffry/Erriff Complex SAC; Slieve Tooey/Tormore Island/Loughros Beg Bay SAC; The Twelve Bens/Garraun Complex SAC; **Unprotected sites with recent records:** none.

Diplophyllum obtusifolium (Hook.) Dumort.
Blunt-leaved Earwort

syn. *Diplophylleia obtusifolia* (Hook.) Trevis., *Jungermannia obtusifolia* Hook., *Scapania microscopica* Culm.
Status in Ireland: Near Threatened; **Status in Europe:** Least Concern

D. obtusifolium is a pioneer species of temporarily disturbed base-poor soils on banks and track sides. Recent fieldwork has shown it to be more widespread in Ireland than previously thought and it has now been reported from 10 vice-counties, with records from 19 hectads (10 old, 12 recent). This species is probably not under significant threat, as it is one of the few plants favoured by conifer plantations. Although several sites for *D. obtusifolium* have been revisited recently without success, it continues to turn up at new sites, reinforcing the idea that it behaves as a metapopulation.

Douinia ovata (Dicks.) H.Buch
Waxy Earwort

syn. *Jungermannia ovata* Dicks, *Sphenolobus ovatus* (Dicks.) Schiffn.
Status in Ireland: Near Threatened; **Status in Europe:** Least Concern

This is a *Scapania*-like leafy liverwort that grows on humid rock outcrops and boulders, and sometimes also on trees and peat. Recent fieldwork has shown it to be widely distributed in hilly areas throughout Ireland and it has been reported from 16 vice-counties, with records from 29 hectads (20 old, 11 recent). It often occurs in small, inconspicuous colonies, so may sometimes be overlooked, but is not thought to be in decline.

Scapania gymnostomophila Kaal.

Narrow-lobed Earwort

syn. *Diplophyllum gymnostomophilum* (Kaal.) Kaal.
Status in Ireland: Vulnerable (D2); **Status in Europe:** Least Concern

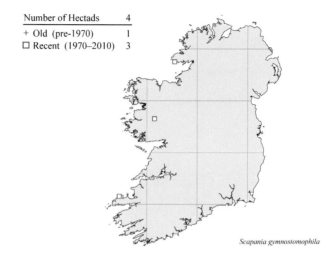

Number of Hectads	4
+ Old (pre-1970)	1
☐ Recent (1970–2010)	3

Scapania gymnostomophila

Identification

This small leafy liverwort (stems to 1.5 cm long with leafy shoots to 2 mm wide) is typical of the genus *Scapania* in its unequally bilobed and keeled leaves, the smaller antical lobe lying folded across the larger postical lobe, and the lack of underleaves. However, the leaf lobes are relatively long and narrow, making it look more like a *Diplophyllum* or a *Tritomaria* rather than a *Scapania*, and their apices can be either rounded or apiculate. It always has clusters of dark brownish gemmae at the shoot apex, and a single large oil body (or occasionally two oil bodies) in each leaf cell, a diagnostic feature.

Distribution in Ireland

Recent records are from four localities in three vice-counties: S. Kerry (Brandon Mountain, 2008); E. Mayo (Keel Bridge, 1987–2004; Inishcoog, 2003) and W. Donegal (Malin Beg, 2001, 2004). The only other Irish record was in E. Donegal (Bulbin Mountain, 1969), where it has not been refound, in spite of recent searching. It may be under-recorded, as it can be very inconspicuous, although its habitat is rather restricted.

Ecology and biology

S. gymnostomophila is a strictly calcicolous plant, growing in Ireland with mosses on thin unshaded damp soil in depressions and crevices in limestone pavement; scattered on very steep, heavily grazed shell-sand turf slopes above a beach, among other bryophytes; on a schistose rock ledge; and in rock crevices in NE-facing base-rich montane cliffs. Associates recorded on Brandon Mountain are *Anoectangium aestivum*, *Ctenidium molluscum*, *Frullania tamarisci*, *Scapania aspera* and *Trichostomum brachydontium*. The colonies in E. Mayo and at Malin Beg are lowland, from 10–20 m altitude, but the Bulbin Mountain record is montane and the Brandon Mountain colony is at 700 m.

This species is dioicous and sporophytes are unknown. Gemmae are very common.

World distribution

S. gymnostomophila is widespread in montane northern Europe, notably Fennoscandia and northern Russia, but becomes very rare and scattered, and more restricted to montane areas, further south. It is absent from many Mediterranean regions. It is *Critically Endangered* in Switzerland, *Endangered* in the Czech Republic, *Vulnerable* in Germany, Svalbard, Spain and Andorra, *Rare* in Poland, Estonia and Slovakia and 'potentially threatened' in Austria. In Europe, it is categorised as a Circumpolar Boreo-arctic montane floristic element. It also occurs in Siberia, the Russian Far East, N. America and Greenland.

Threats

Limestone pavement in some places is under threat from quarrying and other rock removal, as well as from scrub invasion. The coastal site is vulnerable to invasion by coarse vegetation and potentially to leisure and tourist developments.

Conservation

All sites with *S. gymnostomophila* require suitable

grazing regimes to prevent coarse vegetation or scrub invasion.

Protected sites with recent records: Lough Carra/Mask Complex SAC; Mount Brandon SAC; Slieve League SAC; **Unprotected sites with recent records:** none.

Scapania cuspiduligera (Nees) Müll.Frib.   Untidy Earwort

syn. *Jungermannia bartlingii* Hampe, *J. cuspiduligera* Nees, *Martinellius bartlingii* Trevis., *nom. illeg.*,
Scapania bartlingii (Hampe ex Nees) Nees, *S. carestiae* De Not.
Status in Ireland: Vulnerable (D2); **Status in Europe:** Least Concern

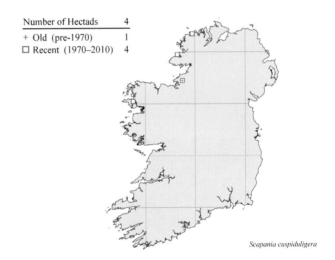

Number of Hectads	4
+ Old (pre-1970)	1
☐ Recent (1970–2010)	4

Scapania cuspiduligera

Identification

This leafy liverwort is essentially similar in structure to other species of *Scapania*, with unequally bilobed leaves, the antical lobe smaller than the postical lobe, and no underleaves. However, this pale greenish or brownish species has a rather different appearance because the leaves are scarcely keeled and the plants are somewhat crispate when dry. Shoots are small, up to c. 1.5 cm long and 2.5 mm wide. There is a sheathing leaf base, and the leaf lobes are subequal, not usually tightly folded together. Clusters of 1- and 2-celled, rounded, brownish gemmae are nearly always present at the shoot apex.

Distribution in Ireland

Recent records for this species are from five localities in three vice-counties: W. Mayo (NW of Lough Doo, Doogort, Achill Island, 2009); Sligo (Gleniff, 1963–2003; Benbulbin, 2003) and W. Donegal (Lurgabrack, 2002; Maghera Strand, 2001).

Ecology and biology

S. cuspiduligera is a strictly calcicolous species that has been found in montane and coastal habitats in Ireland: in rock crevices in limestone cliffs with *Bryum pseudotriquetrum*, *Ctenidium molluscum*, *Distichium inclinatum*, *Neckera crispa*, *Timmia norvegica* and *Trichostomum brachydontium*; on unshaded partly bare soil with low bryophytes and patchy low grasses, sedges and herbs on a rocky N.-facing slope near sand dunes; in short turf in dune heath, with *Ditrichum gracile*; and on sandy mounds in machair with *Leiocolea gillmanii* and *Ditrichum gracile*. It occurs from low to high altitudes, with records in Ireland from 5–500 m.

A dioicous species, it is frequently fertile, but sporophytes are unknown. Gemmae are usually abundant.

World distribution

The species is widespread in northern Europe, but more restricted to the mountains further south; it is *Nationally Scarce* in Britain, *Endangered* in the Czech Republic,

Vulnerable in Luxembourg, and *Data Deficient* in Portugal and Spain. In Europe, it is categorised as a Circumpolar Boreo-arctic montane floristic element. It is also widespread outside Europe, occurring in Africa, Asia, N. and S. America and Greenland. European material is all var. *cuspiduligera*. There is another variety of disputed taxonomic status, var. *diplophyllopsis* R.M. Schust., which grows in Siberia and northern N. America.

Threats
Damage to vegetation and soil erosion, due to overstocking with sheep, is a possible threat, particularly in Gleniff, where sheep density has been very high. The coastal colonies are vulnerable to land-use change such as conversion to golf links or other leisure developments, and possibly also to scrub encroachment.

Conservation
The upland sites are well known as rich bryophyte localities and need to be managed as such. The coastal sites are more vulnerable, and require protection from damaging activities and developments.

Protected sites with recent records: Ben Bulben, Gleniff and Glenade Complex SAC; Doogort Machair/ Lough Doo SAC; Horn Head and Rinclevan SAC; Slieve Tooey/Tormore Island/Loughros Beg Bay SAC; **Unprotected sites with recent records:** none.

Scapania curta (Mart.) Dumort.
Least Earwort

syn. *Jungermannia curta* Mart., *J. rosacea* Corda, *Martinellius curtus* (Mart.) Lindb., *M. rosaceus* (Corda) Lindb., *Scapania rosacea* (Corda) Nees, *S. curta* var. *rosacea* (Corda) Carrington
Status in Ireland: Vulnerable (D2); **Status in Europe:** Least Concern

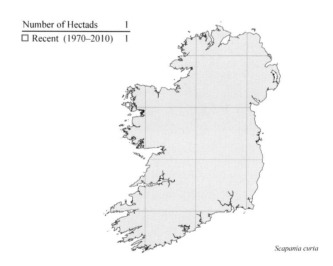

Number of Hectads	1
☐ Recent (1970–2010)	1

Scapania curta

Identification
This leafy liverwort is a small *Scapania* similar to *S. scandica*, with keeled bilobed leaves, the smaller postical lobe folded over the larger antical lobe. There are no underleaves. The shoots are up to c. 1.5 cm long and 2.5 mm wide. It is distinct from related species in having the leaves bordered with several rows of uniformly thick-walled cells, from most of which oil bodies are soon lost. The gemmae are rounded, 2-celled and greenish in colour, borne on the edges of the upper leaves. *S. curta* is a rather difficult species to determine and many older and unsubstantiated records are probably referable to *S. scandica* or other related species.

Distribution in Ireland
The only reliable records of this species from Ireland come from Achill Island in W. Mayo, where it was discovered east of Keel in 1987 and refound in 2003 and 2010. Several old literature records from Northern Ireland are unsubstantiated and unreliable, and must at best be regarded as dubious in the absence of specimens. Commenting on the peculiar distribution pattern in Ireland and Britain (Hill *et al.* 1991), Paton (1999) says 'the curiously disjunct distribution suggests that records are far from complete'.

Ecology and biology

In Ireland, this pioneer calcifuge species grows on unshaded sandy ground with sparse low vegetation in an old roadside sand/gravel quarry. In Britain, it has also been recorded on sandstone rock faces, sandy ground in woodland, peaty soil, a disused china-clay quarry and stream-side detritus. Mainly a lowland species, the most recent Irish record was at an altitude of 39 m.

It is dioicous; male plants are more frequent than female and sporophytes are very rare. Gemmae are usually present.

World distribution

It appears to be widespread in Europe, but its full distribution and abundance is probably not well understood because of confusion with other species. It is currently considered *Endangered* in the Netherlands, Switzerland and Latvia, *Vulnerable* in Luxembourg and Lithuania, and *Data Deficient* in Britain, Portugal, Spain and Svalbard. In Europe, it is categorised as a Circumpolar Boreal-montane floristic element. *S. curta* is also recorded from N. Africa, Asia and N. America.

Three varieties are known, but only var. *curta* has been recorded in Europe; var. *grandiretis* R.M. Schust. has been recorded from N. America and Asia, and var. *isoloba* R.M. Schust. from N. America.

Threats

The main threat to the known colony of this species is that the quarry might be developed or otherwise 'reclaimed'. However, it is not unlikely that *S. curta* may be overlooked elsewhere in Ireland.

Conservation

The only known site should be monitored regularly, and local conservation management workers need to be aware of the presence of *S. curta* there. Specimens of small *Scapania* from the appropriate habitats throughout Ireland need to be examined critically to determine whether this plant is more widespread.

Protected sites with recent records: none; Unprotected sites with recent records: E. of Keel, Achill Island.

Scapania lingulata H.Buch

Tongue Earwort

syn. *Scapania buchii* Müll.Frib., *S. microphylla* Warnst.
Status in Ireland: Data Deficient; **Status in Europe:** Least Concern

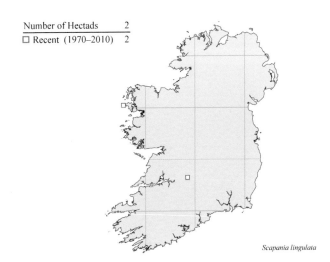

Number of Hectads	2
☐ Recent (1970–2010)	2

Scapania lingulata

Identification

S. lingulata is a small green or brownish bilobed leafy liverwort less than 1 cm long, with the smaller dorsal leaf lobe attached to the larger ventral lobe by a fairly long keel up to ²/₃ the length of the leaf; both leaf lobes are relatively long and narrow. Underleaves are absent. It has

larger leaf cells (c. 20–27 μm wide) and gemmae (c. 12–19 × 23–32 μm) and more numerous oil bodies (c. 6–10 per cell) than related species, notably the much more frequent *S. scandica*. The gemmae are usually greenish in colour. Two varieties have been noted in Europe (var. *lingulata* and var. *microphylla*), but they are not universally recognised and have not been recorded consistently.

Distribution in Ireland

This species has been recorded from two localities in two vice-counties: N. Tipperary (Keeper Hill, 1979) and W. Mayo (Croaghaun on Achill Island, 1987). Both have been revisited recently, but *S. lingulata* was not refound, although the Achill Island site might have been on dangerously steep ground that was not studied. However, this plant is inconspicuous and easily overlooked as *S. scandica*, so it is probably under-recorded.

Ecology and biology

A pioneer species of acid or basic earth banks and rocks, *S. lingulata* has been found in Ireland on a S.-facing slope and on a calcareous boulder on the slope of a deep ravine. It is a lowland to subalpine plant.

This species is dioicous; male plants are occasional but perianths are very rare and sporophytes are unknown. Gemmae are common.

World distribution

It is widespread in northern Europe, particularly Fennoscandia and northern Russia, but very sparsely distributed and montane further south, and absent from many Mediterranean areas. It is *Extinct* in Latvia, *Endangered* in the Czech Republic and Serbia, *Rare* in Hungary and Estonia, and 'potentially threatened' in Austria. In Europe, it is assigned to a European Boreal-montane floristic element. It also grows in Siberia, N. America and Greenland.

Threats

Shading by coarse nutrient-demanding vegetation could become a threat to this species, which requires a supply of bare surfaces to colonise. Thus, undergrazing or cessation of grazing are both possible threats.

Conservation

A suitable grazing regime to limit the growth of coarse vegetation is probably advisable. Repeated survey work to attempt to refind the plant is highly desirable.

Protected sites with recent records: Croaghaun/ Slievemore SAC; **Unprotected sites with recent records:** Keeper Hill (possibly within Keeper Hill SAC).

Scapania subalpina (Nees ex Lindenb.) Dumort.   Northern Earwort

syn. *Jungermannia subalpina* Nees ex Lindenb., *Martinellius subalpinus* (Nees ex Lindenb.) Trevis., *Plagiochila subalpina* (Nees ex Lindenb.) Mont. & Nees, *Scapania franzoniana* De Not.
Status in Ireland: Data Deficient; **Status in Europe:** Least Concern

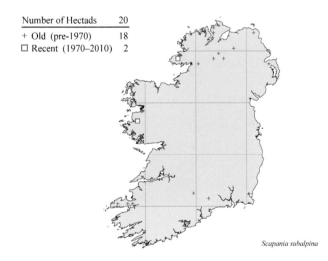

Number of Hectads	20
+ Old (pre-1970)	18
☐ Recent (1970–2010)	2

Scapania subalpina

Identification

Like other species of *Scapania*, *S. subalpina* has bilobed, keeled leaves and no underleaves. In most species of *Scapania*, the antical (upper) lobe is smaller than the postical (lower) lobe, but in *S. subalpina*, the lobes are almost the same size. The shoots are usually up to c. 3 cm long and 3.5 mm wide, green or sometimes brownish, and sometimes tinged with red. *S. compacta*, a more common plant, is similar in that it has subequal leaf lobes. However, the postical lobe in *S. subalpina* is longly decurrent, whereas it is not appreciably decurrent in *S. compacta*. Furthermore, the leaves of *S. subalpina* have a border of 2–3 rows of thick-walled cells that lose their oil bodies, whereas *S. compacta* has no such border. The gemmae are rounded, usually 2-celled, and green or reddish.

Distribution in Ireland

Recent records are from just two localities in two vice-counties: W. Galway (Bunowen River, below Tullyconor Bridge, 1970, 2010) and W. Donegal (Glen River at Meenaneary, 1970). There are many older records, from an additional 11 vice-counties: S. Kerry, N. Kerry, Waterford, S. Tipperary, Wicklow, W. Mayo, E. Donegal, Tyrone, Down, Antrim and Londonderry. This species was not included in the Provisional Red List (Holyoak 2006b) because there were too many post-1950 records, so no effort was made to refind *S. subalpina* at its old sites during recent fieldwork. The absence of records from the past decade certainly does not indicate that a decline has occurred, but rather reflects the lack of survey effort.

Ecology and biology

There is only a little information on the ecology of this species in Ireland: *S. subalpina* has been recorded from sandy detritus and rock crevices by streams and rivers, wet flushed rocks on a NE-facing slope, and a steep earth bank in the side of a stone quarry. It is generally thought of as a plant of gravelly substrates by streams in the uplands, and also grows on lake-shore detritus and soil-capped rocks. *S. subalpina* is well adapted to growing next to icy montane streams: Clausen (1964) found that it was one of the few bryophytes tested that fully tolerated freezing in ice at −40°C for 24–26 hours. It is subalpine to alpine.

Male and female inflorescences and sporophytes are frequent in this dioicous species. Gemmae are very common.

World distribution

This plant is widespread in montane parts of Europe, but rare or absent in the lowlands. It has not been recorded, for example, in Denmark, Belgium, the Netherlands, Hungary, the Baltic states or Belarus. It is listed as *Vulnerable* in Germany and Svalbard, *Rare* in Slovakia and *Near Threatened* in Spain and Portugal. In Europe, it is assigned to a Circumpolar Boreo-arctic montane floristic element. Elsewhere, it is known from North Africa, C. and N. Asia and N. America.

Threats

It is difficult to know what threats have faced this species, because it is doubtful whether a genuine decline has taken place, as discussed above. It is possible that river management operations such as dredging or canalising water channels might have destroyed fragments of its habitat. The effect of water pollution upon this species is not known.

Conservation

The first priority must be for new survey work at, and near, sites where this species has been recorded in the past. Only then will it be clear whether conservation measures are necessary for this plant.

Protected sites with recent records: Mweelrea/Sheeffry/Erriff Complex SAC; **Unprotected sites with recent records:** Glen River at Meenaneary.

Scapania ornithopodioides (With.) Waddell

Bird's-foot Earwort

syn. *Jungermannia ornithopodioides* With.
Status in Ireland: Vulnerable (A2c); **Status in Europe:** Least Concern

Identification

This is a large dark reddish-brown or purple leafy liverwort. Like other species of *Scapania*, it has the leaves divided into two unequal lobes, the slightly smaller antical lobe overlying the postical lobe, and there are no underleaves. It resembles *S. nimbosa* in size (shoots up to c. 10 cm long and 5.5 mm wide) and general appearance, but the leaf lobes are divided all the way to the base, so that there is no keel, and the lobes are bordered with many closely-set teeth, more numerous and shorter than those of *S. nimbosa*.

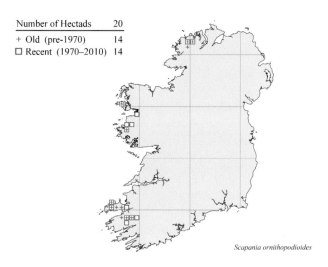

Number of Hectads	20
+ Old (pre-1970)	14
□ Recent (1970–2010)	14

Scapania ornithopodioides

Distribution in Ireland

S. ornithopodioides is confined to the extreme west, with recent records from at least 13 localities in five vice-counties: S. Kerry (Brandon Mountain, 1813–2009; Macgillycuddy's Reeks, 1961–2009; Cummeenduff Glen, 1972; The Pocket, Mullaghanattin, 1972); N. Kerry (Mangerton Mountain, 1972–2009; Gormagh, 2009; Coumbrack Lake, 2009); W. Galway (Muckanaght, 1933–1970); W. Mayo (Croagh Patrick, 1987; Mweelrea, 1970–2010; Slievemore, 1910–1999) and W. Donegal (Errigal, 1962–2002; Muckish Mountain, 1955–2009). There are older records from S. Kerry (Ballysitteragh, 1951; Coomacullen Lake, 1951; Coomasaharn, 1951; Coomanare Lakes, 1898; Mount Eagle Lough, 1898; Stradbally Mountain, 1953); W. Galway (Benbaun, 1957; Bengower, 1950); W. Mayo (Croaghaun, 1951) and W. Donegal (Slieve Snaght, 1962). Ratcliffe (1968) places *S. ornithopodioides* into the Northern Atlantic group.

Ecology and biology

One of the Northern Atlantic hepatic mat species in Ireland, *S. ornithopodioides* is confined to N.- and NE-facing rocky slopes, often in block scree or in patchy heather, at medium to high altitudes in oceanic areas. It is usually associated with other large Atlantic liverworts, including *Herbertus aduncus* subsp. *hutchinsiae*, *Bazzania tricrenata*, *B. pearsonii*, *Mastigophora woodsii*, *Pleurozia purpurea* and *Mylia taylorii*, and the moss *Breutelia chrysocoma*. At Stumpa Barr na hAbhainn, Beenkeragh, Macgillycuddy's Reeks (S. Kerry) it occurs in numerous large patches across an area of c. 5 × 10 m, among large overhanging rocks/boulders, in association with other hepatics and grasses, mainly *Festuca vivipara* and *Agrostis*

capillaris; at Muckish Mountain (W. Donegal) it is found in large patches across a slope, within an area of c. 100 × 50 m, under an open canopy of *Calluna*, in association with *Herbertus aduncus* subsp. *hutchinsiae* and *Pleurozia purpurea* (R.L. Hodd, pers. comm.). It is alpine to subalpine, recorded at 400–1035 m in Ireland.

It is dioicous; female inflorescences are rare and male inflorescences and sporophytes are unknown. Gemmae are also rare.

World distribution

This plant is restricted to the north-western fringe of Europe, occurring in the Faeroes, Scotland (*Nationally Scarce* in Britain) and Norway. In Europe, it is classified as an Oceanic Boreal-montane floristic element. Outside Europe, it occurs in disjunct populations in the Himalaya, China, Japan, Taiwan, the Philippines and Hawaii.

Threats

Overstocking with sheep has damaged the habitat at some sites, particularly in the Connemara area of W. Galway, where this species was not refound during recent fieldwork. Burning is also a potential threat. Climate change may also affect this species.

Conservation

It is difficult to recommend any conservation measures to counter climate change, but the now very restricted stands of Northern Atlantic hepatic mat vegetation should not be subjected to any more overstocking or burning. The system of EU farm subsidies, which has largely been responsible for overstocking with sheep in the uplands over the last few decades, is now changing, and hopefully the habitat will recover. Populations require monitoring to ensure their continued survival.

Protected sites with recent records: Cloghernagore Bog and Glenveagh National Park SAC; Croagh Patrick pNHA; Croaghaun/Slievemore SAC; Killarney National Park, Macgillycuddy's Reeks and Caragh River Catchment SAC; Mount Brandon SAC; Muckish Mountain SAC; Mweelrea/Sheeffry/Erriff Complex SAC; Slieve Mish Mountains SAC; The Twelve Bens/Garraun Complex SAC; **Unprotected sites with recent records:** none.

Scapania nimbosa Taylor ex Lehm.

Cloud Earwort

Status in Ireland: Endangered (B2a, bii, iii, iv); **Status in Europe:** Rare

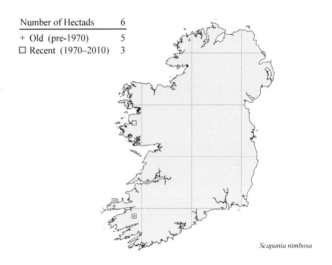

Number of Hectads	6
+ Old (pre-1970)	5
□ Recent (1970–2010)	3

Scapania nimbosa

Identification

This is a large and very distinctive leafy liverwort, usually dark reddish-brown or purple in colour, with shoots up to c. 7 cm long and c. 4 mm wide. As in other species of *Scapania*, the leaves are bilobed and divided into two unequal lobes attached by a keel, the slightly smaller antical lobe overlying the postical lobe, and there are no underleaves. The keel is very short in *S. nimbosa*, and the leaves have long ciliate teeth on the margins: these teeth are longer, more widely spaced and fewer in number than in *S. ornithopodioides*.

Distribution in Ireland

S. nimbosa is known from a few sites in the extreme west: the most recent records are from S. Kerry (Brother O'Shea's Gully, Lough Cummeenoughter, 2009; near the summit of Carrauntoohil, 1983; Brandon Mountain, 1813–2009) and W. Mayo (NE corrie of Mweelrea, 1987). There are older records from S. Kerry (Beenkeragh, 1964, 1965); W. Mayo (Slievemore, 1911) and W. Donegal (Errigal, 1962), but searching has failed to refind it in these places. Ratcliffe (1968) places it into the Northern Atlantic species group.

Ecology and biology

One of the rarest of the Northern Atlantic hepatic mat species in Ireland, *S. nimbosa* is confined to N.- and NE-facing rocky slopes, often in block scree or in heather, at relatively high altitudes. Its habitat is similar to that of *S. ornithopodioides*, although it tends to occur at even higher altitudes and usually in smaller quantities than that species. It is normally associated with other Atlantic liverworts such as *Anastrepta orcadensis*, *Bazzania tricrenata*, *B. pearsonii*, *Herbertus aduncus*, *Mylia taylorii* and *Scapania ornithopodioides*. On Brandon Mountain it was found recently in two patches, one 5 × 3 cm, in association with other hepatics, including *Scapania ornithopodioides*, *S. gracilis* and *Anastrepta orcadensis*, as well as *Poa pratensis*, the second patch 15 m to west, 7 × 15 cm, with numerous stems, both patches on the near-vertical edge of small rocks; at Brother O'Shea's Gully it occurs in at least three patches, c. 10 × 10 cm, on a steep, grassy, hepatic-rich slope, beside an increasingly eroded path, in association with *Festuca vivipara*, *Agrostis capillaris*, *Saxifraga spathularis*, *Scapania ornithopodioides* and *Scapania gracilis* (R.L. Hodd, pers. comm.). The occurrences are subalpine and alpine, at altitudes of 700–1010 m in Ireland.

Fertile plants and sporophytes are unknown anywhere. Gemmae are produced on the leaf margins but are very rare. Vegetative reproduction by fragmentation probably takes place to some extent.

World distribution

This plant is only recorded elsewhere in Europe from Scotland (*Nationally Scarce* in Britain) and Norway (where it is considered *Critically Endangered*). In Europe, it is categorised as an Oceanic Boreal-montane floristic element. Elsewhere, there are disjunct populations in the Himalaya and China.

Threats

Climate change may be the most serious threat to this species, as it is one of the most northern of the Northern Atlantic hepatic mat plants. Overstocking with sheep has damaged the habitat in most areas, and botanical collecting may have contributed to the disappearance of

some populations. It seems likely that more material has been removed from some localities than can easily be replenished, in a plant that is apparently so reproductively inefficient.

Conservation

It is difficult to recommend any conservation measures to counter climate change, but the very special places where this plant has been recorded should at least be protected from the impacts of overstocking. It may still occur at some of its older sites, perhaps in places inaccessible to botanists and sheep. Hopefully, the system of EU subsidies that has encouraged destructively high stocking levels in the uplands is now changing, and sheep numbers should decline as a consequence.

Protected sites with recent records: Killarney National Park, Macgillycuddy's Reeks and Caragh River Catchment SAC; Mount Brandon SAC; Mweelrea/Sheeffry/Erriff Complex SAC; **Unprotected sites with recent records:** none.

Acrobolbus wilsonii Nees

Wilson's Pouchwort

Status in Ireland: Vulnerable (D1); **Status in Europe:** Near Threatened

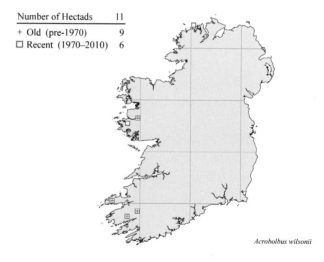

Number of Hectads	11
+ Old (pre-1970)	9
☐ Recent (1970–2010)	6

Acrobolbus wilsonii

Identification

This is a small bilobed leafy liverwort that grows as isolated shoots or in thin mats, with shoots up to 2.5 cm long and 3 mm wide. The leaves are almost longitudinally inserted and bilobed 1/3–1/2, occasionally with small irregular subsidiary lobes. The underleaves are very small,

consisting of only a few cells, or more rarely up to 8 cells long and lanceolate. *A. wilsonii* is superficially rather similar to small plants of *Leiocolea collaris*, but with more distant, more deeply bilobed leaves with longer, more tapering lobes and underleaves smaller or almost absent. It has a characteristically opaque, pale green, fleshy appearance and fragile texture, differentiating it from the delicate, translucent, not particularly fragile (and very common) *Lophocolea bidentata*. Furthermore, unlike *Lophocolea* and *Leiocolea*, *A. wilsonii* is not aromatic and produces female inflorescences in marsupia rather than perianths. Specimens collected below Brandon Mountain are particularly difficult, since they have relatively large, lanceolate underleaves, and could easily be taken for diminutive *L. collaris*. They were eventually assigned to *Acrobolbus* on the basis of habitat and lack of aroma.

Distribution in Ireland

This species is confined to the extreme west, with recent records from seven localities in five vice-counties: S. Kerry (Mullaghanattin, 1983; Ballaghbeama Gap, 1967, 1983; Brandon Mountain, 1961–2006); N. Kerry (Torc Cascade, 1841–1983); W. Galway (Bengower, 1994); W. Mayo (Devil's Mother, 1901–2003) and W. Donegal (Horn Head, 1991 and 2002). Older records are known from N. Kerry (Galway's Bridge, 1936; Cromaglan, 1829–1955; Derrymore River, 1950); W. Cork (Lackawee, 1968; Glengarriff, 1869, 1876) and W. Mayo

Devil's Mother, ravine on north-west slope, Co. Mayo.

(Croaghaun, 1925). Ellen Hutchins' (1812) record from 'near Bantry' in Cork is too vague to assign to a hectad. There is no real evidence of decline. Ratcliffe (1968) places *A. wilsonii* into the Southern Atlantic group.

Ecology and biology

It grows among other Atlantic bryophytes on damp shaded rocks, in ravines or in crevices between boulders on N.-facing slopes in oceanic areas, often where there is some base-rich influence. Recorded associates in Ireland include *Bryum pseudotriquetrum*, *Ctenidium molluscum*, *Dumortiera hirsuta*, *Fissidens adianthoides*, *Hyocomium armoricum*, *Jubula hutchinsiae*, *Pellia epiphylla*, *P. neesiana*, *Rhizomnium punctatum* and *Trichostomum hibernicum*. It is essentially a lowland plant, although the highest recorded altitude for this species in Ireland is 490 m.

This is an autoicous species; female inflorescences are frequent, but male inflorescences and sporophytes are rare. Gemmae are unknown.

World distribution

It is known elsewhere in Europe and Macaronesia only from Scotland (it is listed as *Nationally Scarce* in Britain), the Faeroes (where only a single locality is known), the Azores (c. 6 sites on 4 islands, *Endangered*), and Madeira (single known site, *Endangered*). Ros *et al.* (2007) mention a doubtful old (pre-1962) record from Spain, but this is rejected by Söderström *et al.* (2002, 2007). In Europe, it is assigned to a Hyperoceanic Southern-temperate floristic element. Outside Europe, *A. wilsonii* has been reported from C. and S. America (Söderström *et al.* 2002), but Paton (1999) does not list localities outside Europe and Macaronesia, and the European *Red Data Book* (ECCB 1995) considers it to be endemic to Europe.

Threats

Although there are no obvious threats to this species, it always occurs in small amounts, so populations could potentially be destroyed very easily. By the same token, it may be overlooked, so there is probably more of it in Ireland than records suggest.

Conservation

A. wilsonii should survive if its habitats are allowed to remain more or less undisturbed.

Protected sites with recent records: Horn Head and Rinclevan SAC; Killarney National Park; Killarney National Park, Macgillycuddy's Reeks and Caragh River Catchment SAC; Maumtrasna Mountain Complex pNHA; Mount Brandon SAC; The Twelve Bens/ Garraun Complex SAC; **Unprotected sites with recent records:** none.

Southbya tophacea (Spruce) Spruce   Green Blackwort

syn. *Coleochila stillicidiorum* (De Not.) Dumort., *Jungermannia alicularia* De Not., *J. stillicidiorum* De Not., *J. tophacea* Spruce, *Southbya alicularia* C. Massal., *S. stillicidiorum* (Raddi) Lindb.
Status in Ireland: Critically Endangered (B1a, bii, iv, B2a, bii, iv); **Status in Europe:** Least Concern

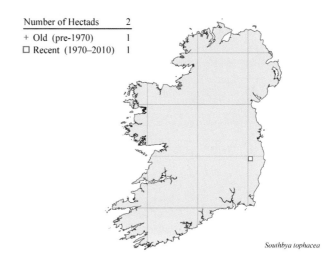

Number of Hectads	2
+ Old (pre-1970)	1
□ Recent (1970–2010)	1

Southbya tophacea

Identification

This is a small and bright green entire-leaved leafy liverwort without underleaves. The shoots are less than 1 cm long and the leaves are usually longer than wide and closely imbricate. Unusually among liverworts, the leaves are opposite rather than alternate, and are inserted almost transversely, easily distinguishing it from *Jungermannia* and most other entire-leaved genera. The other European species of the genus, *S. nigrella*, differs in its darker colouration and having leaves wider than long, but this species is not known to occur in Ireland.

Distribution in Ireland

The only recent record for this species in Ireland is at Glenmalur in Wicklow (1988). There is also an older record from Sligo (Knocknarea Glen, 1963). Both sites were revisited during recent fieldwork but *S. tophacea* was not refound. It is listed as a Mediterranean-Atlantic species by Ratcliffe (1968).

Ecology and biology

In Ireland, this species grows (or grew) on the limy mortar of a damp shady wall in an old conifer plantation in Glenmalur, and over *Eucladium* with *Leiocolea turbinata* on tufa on a dripping limestone wall in Knocknarea Glen. In Britain, it has also been found in other calcareous habitats, including dune slacks with scattered mine spoil areas and marl pits. It is a lowland plant, recorded at 60 m and 160 m in Ireland.

Dioicous and often fertile, sporophytes are frequent in *S. tophacea*. Gemmae are absent and asexual reproduction is unknown.

World distribution

In Europe, this species is frequent in the Mediterranean area but becomes very rare or absent further north. It occurs in Britain (where it is *Vulnerable*), France (including Corsica), Portugal, Spain (including the Balearic Islands), Italy (including Sicily), Hungary, Montenegro, Albania, Greece (including Crete), N. Caucasus, Madeira and the Canary Islands. In Europe, it is categorised as an Oceanic Mediterranean-Atlantic floristic element. Elsewhere, it is confined to the Mediterranean parts of N. Africa and W. Asia. The Sligo site is the northernmost locality in the world for this species.

Threats

The Wicklow locality is becoming shaded by plantation conifers, but it still supports a fairly rich bryophyte flora. There does not seem to be any particular threat at its Sligo site, although parts of it are becoming overgrown with coarse vegetation.

Conservation

Conifers should be removed from the close vicinity of the old wall at the Wicklow site. Further survey work should take place at both sites to try to refind this species. It may survive in small quantity; its small size and habit of growing amongst other bryophytes make it an easy plant to overlook. Similarly, it may occur in suitable habitat elsewhere in Ireland.

Protected sites with recent records: none; **Unprotected sites with recent records:** Glenmalur.

Knocknarea Glen, Co. Sligo.

Calypogeia integristipula Steph.

Meylan's Pouchwort

syn. *Calypogeia meylanii* H.Buch, *C. neesiana* auct. non (C.Massal. & Carest.) Müll.Frib.,
C. neesiana var. *meylanii* (H.Buch.) R.M.Schust.
Status in Ireland: Endangered (B1a, bi, ii, iv, B2a, bi, ii, iv); **Status in Europe:** Least Concern

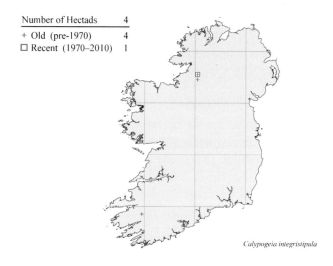

Number of Hectads	4
+ Old (pre-1970)	4
☐ Recent (1970–2010)	1

Calypogeia integristipula

Identification

This leafy liverwort, like other species of *Calypogeia*, has more or less oval, incubously-arranged leaves and produces pale green gemmae on slightly attenuated shoot apices. The lateral leaves are entire, and distinctly longer than wide; the underleaves are large, entire or retuse. The whole plant has a characteristic dull green colour and opaque appearance and is relatively large for the genus, with shoots up to 3 cm long and 3 mm wide. It is closely related to *C. neesiana*, which differs in its more distinct leaf border, composed of elongate cells, the decurrent underleaves and the lack of oil bodies in the stem cells.

Distribution in Ireland

C. integristipula has been seen recently at several sites in Fermanagh, all in the same hectad: Correl Glen (2000–2005), Derryvahon (2000) and Meenameen Scarp (1999–2000), with several strong populations. There are older records from N. Kerry (Mangerton Mountain, 1902); Fermanagh (Reyfad, 1961) and Antrim (Murlough Bay, 1969).

Ecology and biology

This plant has usually been found growing on damp, shaded sandstone rocks, and under overhangs, on predominantly N.-facing crags; often in deciduous woodland, or at least shaded by shrubs and saplings; also on dry soil on sandstone rock ledges. Associates include *Kurzia sylvatica*, *Calypogeia muelleriana* and *Lepidozia cupressina*. In Britain, *C. integristipula* is also found on peat, banks and rotting logs. It is a lowland plant, recorded up to 250 m in Ireland.

Sporophytes are very rare in this species, which may be either autoicous or paroicous, but gemmae are common.

World distribution

It is widespread in Europe, particularly in central and northern areas, including Fennoscandia, the Baltic States, northern Russia, the Netherlands, France, Luxembourg, Germany, Switzerland, Poland, Austria, the Czech Republic, Slovakia, Romania, Italy, Belarus, Ukraine, the Caucasus and the Azores, and listed as *Nationally Scarce* in Britain, *Endangered* in Hungary and Serbia, *Vulnerable* in Spain and Andorra and *Rare* in Belgium. It is categorised as a Circumpolar Boreo-temperate floristic element in Europe, and is also present in Siberia, E. Asia, N. America and Greenland.

Threats

Possible threats may arise from growth of planted conifers close to the sandstone crags, but these have now been removed from some of its sites in Lough Navar

Forest. However, growth of scrub and other vegetation on ledges of the crags may also cause excessive shading now that grazing stock are no longer present.

Conservation

Populations on sandstone scarps in Fermanagh seem unlikely to be threatened, except perhaps by increased shade now that grazing of the ledges is carried out only by feral goats. Monitoring of the populations is desirable

to document their locations and continued survival. *C. integristipula* is listed as a Northern Ireland Priority Species.

Protected sites with recent records: Correl Glen Forest Nature Reserve; Largalinny ASSI; Largalinny SAC; Lough Navar Scarps and Lakes ASSI (scheduled for declaration 2011); **Unprotected sites with recent records:** none.

Calypogeia suecica (Arnell & J.Perss.) Müll.Frib.

Swedish Pouchwort

syn. *Calypogeia trichomanis* var. *suecica* Meyl., *Cincinnulus suecicus* (Arnell & J.Perss.), *Kantius suecicus* Arnell & J.Perss.
Status in Ireland: Regionally Extinct; **Status in Europe:** Least Concern

Number of Hectads	4
+ Old (pre-1970)	4

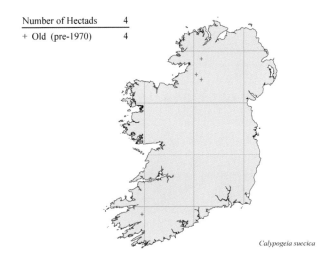

Calypogeia suecica

Identification

This is a small pale yellowish-green or brownish-green leafy liverwort with shoots up to 1.5 cm long and 2 mm wide. The leaves are ovate or oval, unlobed or occasionally slightly notched, and arranged incubously. The underleaves are suborbicular and 1/3–3/4 bifid. Pale green, rounded, 2-celled gemmae are produced at the shoot apex. It is distinguished from other *Calypogeia* species by its small size, habitat and the entire and more or less truncate leaf apex. It also has smaller leaf cells and gemmae, and the oil bodies are simple or 2–6-segmented.

Distribution in Ireland

C. suecica has been recorded from four localities in three vice-counties: S. Kerry (O'Sullivan's Cascade, 1967); Fermanagh (Aghahoorin, 1959; Little Dog [Knockmore

Cliff], 1951) and Tyrone (Sheskinawaddy, 1957–1958). All these sites have been visited during the recent programme of fieldwork, and *C. suecica* has been searched for without success.

Ecology and biology

A specialised calcifuge pioneer species of moist rotten logs in humid woodland, particularly decorticated coniferous logs, *C. suecica* is also recorded from bare exposed peat at two sites in Ireland. The peat had been burned the previous year at one site; at the other it was on a W.-facing slope. Associates recorded in Ireland include *Riccardia palmata*, *Tritomaria exsectiformis*, *Cephalozia catenulata*, *C. lunulifolia*, *Scapania umbrosa* and *Lophozia incisa*. *C. suecica* is considered an old forest indicator in the native spruce forests of northern Fennoscandia and Russia (Maksimov *et al.* 2001), but this is not the case in Ireland. It is a lowland plant that has been recorded up to 185 m in Ireland.

C. suecica is often fertile but rarely has sporophytes and may be dioicous or autoicous. Gemmae, however, are frequent.

World distribution

Widespread but not common in C. and northern Europe, it is listed as *Nationally Scarce* in Britain, *Extinct* in Luxembourg, *Endangered* in Portugal, Spain and Serbia, *Vulnerable* in Sweden, Finland and Germany, *Near Threatened* in the Czech Republic, *Rare* in Lithuania, *Rare* (but considered overlooked) in Belgium and *Data Deficient* in Norway. It is also recorded in Poland, Estonia, Latvia, Switzerland, Italy, Hungary, Slovakia, Slovenia, Croatia, Bosnia-Herzegovina, Romania, Bulgaria, Ukraine, Russia, the Caucasus, the Azores and the Canary Islands. In Europe, it is assigned to a European Boreal-montane floristic element.

Elsewhere, it occurs in N. America and Siberia.

Threats

This species may have been eliminated from some sites by habitat destruction, including tidying away dead wood and clear-felling woodland, but O'Sullivan's Cascade remains in very good condition. Alternatively, as it is a very inconspicuous plant of short-lived habitats, it may have been overlooked, despite recent efforts to refind it.

Conservation

Woodland areas in the vicinity of the old records should be maintained with plenty of fallen and rotting timber, and further effort should go into survey work, to attempt to relocate the species.

Protected sites with recent records: none; **Unprotected sites with recent records:** none.

Leiocolea rutheana (Limpr.) Müll.Frib. **var.** *rutheana*   Lesser Fen Notchwort

syn. *Jungermannia rutheana* Limpr., *J. schultzii* Nees, *Lophozia rutheana* (Limpr.) M.Howe, *L. schultzii* (Nees) Schiffn.
Status in Ireland: Endangered (B2a, biii, D); **Status in Europe:** Least Concern

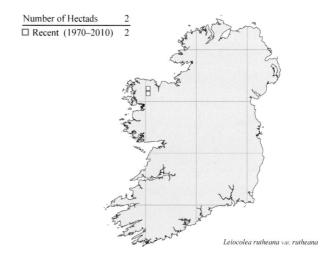

Number of Hectads	2
☐ Recent (1970–2010)	2

Leiocolea rutheana var. *rutheana*

Identification

This is a fairly large olive green to purple-brown leafy liverwort growing among other plants or forming tufts or thin mats with ascending, unbranched shoots up to 6 cm long and 5 mm wide. The blunt, shallowly two-lobed leaves (divided to < ¼) and relatively conspicuous underleaves are typical of *Leiocolea*. The postical leaf insertion is distinctly decurrent, and the underleaves

are large and multiciliate, unlike related species. *L. gillmanii* is somewhat similar but is usually a pale green and generally smaller plant, has slightly smaller leaf cells and much smaller underleaves. *L. bantriensis* and *L. collaris* also resemble *L. rutheana*, but are dioicous rather than paroicous. *L. rutheana* has two varieties, var. *laxa* and var. *rutheana*, but only the latter occurs in Ireland.

Distribution in Ireland

First discovered in Ireland in 1987 (Lockhart 1989b), this plant is now known from three sites all close to one another in W. Mayo: Brackloon Lough (1987–2010), Doobehy (1998 and 2010) and near Formoyle (1998–2010).

Ecology and biology

L. rutheana var. *rutheana* is an obligate calcicole and occurs in calcareous fens, where it grows intermixed with other bryophytes in wet hollows and lawns, usually in open places unshaded by herbaceous vegetation. It often grows more or less at water level or even submerged. Frequent associates include *Campylium stellatum*, *Ctenidium molluscum*, *Sphagnum contortum*, *S. warnstorfii*, *Aulacomnium palustre* and *Tomentypnum nitens*, with *Schoenus nigricans* and *Molinia caerulea*. Hydrological and phytogeographical studies of the sites are described by Lockhart (1989b, 1991). Always lowland, it grows at 65–75 m in Ireland.

It is paroicous and occasionally fertile; sporophytes were recorded in Ireland for the first time in 2010 (C. Campbell, pers. comm.). Gemmae are absent.

World distribution

L. rutheana var. *rutheana* is among a group of species, including *Tomentypnum nitens*, *Paludella squarrosa* and *Meesia triquetra*, which are considered to have postglacial relictual distribution in Ireland. Elsewhere, this species is scattered and rare in most of northern Europe, and absent in the south, but more frequent in Fennoscandia and northern Russia. Listed as *Critically Endangered* in Germany, *Endangered* in Britain, Poland, Latvia and Lithuania, *Vulnerable* in Svalbard, *Rare* in Estonia. In Europe, it is assigned to a Circumpolar Boreo-arctic montane floristic element. It also occurs in Siberia, the Russian Far East, N. America and Greenland.

Threats

The habitat of this species is very rare and fragile in Ireland. The main threats are probably reduction in grazing levels, which could lead to coarse vegetation and scrub development, and agricultural improvement through drainage and lowering of the water table.

Conservation

The small area where this species is known to occur should be treated as a conservation priority and managed for the preservation and promotion of the fen habitat. As the habitat is so fragile, great care should be taken to avoid damage while conducting survey and monitoring work. *L. rutheana* is protected in the Republic of Ireland by the Flora (Protection) Order, 1999.

Protected sites with recent records: Bellacorick Bog Complex SAC; **Unprotected sites with recent records:** none.

Leiocolea gillmanii (Austin) A.Evans

Gillman's Notchwort

syn. *Jungermannia gillmanii* Austin, *J. kaurinii* Limpr., *Leiocolea kaurinii* (Limpr.) Jörg., *Lophozia gillmanii* (Austin) R.M.Schust., *L. kaurinii* (Limpr.) Steph.
Status in Ireland: Vulnerable (D2); **Status in Europe:** Least Concern

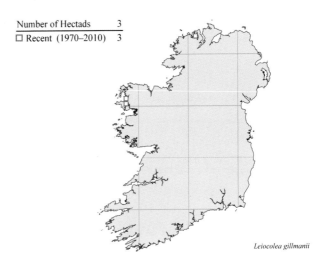

Number of Hectads	3
☐ Recent (1970–2010)	3

Leiocolea gillmanii

Leiocolea gillmanii, Lough Doo, Achill Island, Co. Mayo.

Identification

This is a yellowish-green or brownish leafy liverwort that grows in thin mats or creeps amongst other bryophytes. The shoots are up to c. 2 cm long and 3 mm wide. It has rather shallowly bilobed (to ⅙–⅓) leaves and small but distinct underleaves, which are more or less subulate, and often have small additional lobes or teeth. It differs from the much more common *L. bantriensis* in being paroicous rather than dioicous and the male bracts below the perianth more or less clearly inflated basally. *L. rutheana* is a larger plant, the var. *rutheana* with much more prominent underleaves, the var. *laxa* (which is not known in Ireland) with an arcuate and slightly decurrent postical leaf insertion. In *L. gillmanii*, the postical leaf insertion is scarcely arcuate and not decurrent.

Distribution in Ireland

This species has been recorded from two localities in Ireland: W. Mayo (Lough Doo on Achill Island, where it was discovered in 1987 and was still present in abundance in 2010) and W. Donegal (small population SE of Rosepenna, Rosguill, 2009).

Ecology and biology

At Lough Doo, *L. gillmanii* is found growing with other bryophytes and low-growing grasses, sedges and herbs on damp sand, where it appears to favour tightly-grazed low mounds within a machair plain. It occurs in similar calcareous coastal fen habitat at Rosepenna, but in much less quantity, and with *Schoenus nigricans*. At both localities, it is associated with *Catoscopium nigritum*, and at the latter with the only known population in Ireland of *Meesia uliginosa*. In Britain, as well as growing in dune slacks, it has also been recorded on mossy, irrigated, base-rich rock ledges, in flushes and among rocks by streams in montane areas. It is exclusively lowland in Ireland, recorded at c. 10 m.

A paroicous species, it is only known fertile. Gemmae are unknown.

World distribution

Found mainly in the mountains of C. and northern Europe, this plant is rare or absent further south. It is recorded but not red-listed in Iceland, Norway, Sweden, Finland, France, Romania, Belarus and Russia (including Novaya Zemlya and Franz Josef Land). It is listed as *Near Threatened* in Britain, *Vulnerable* in Switzerland and Svalbard, *Rare* in Germany, Italy and the Czech Republic, and 'potentially threatened' in Austria. In Europe, it is assigned to a Circumpolar Boreo-arctic montane floristic element. *L. gillmanii* is also recorded in N. Asia, N. America and Greenland.

Threats

Any land-use change, such as change in grazing regime through fencing off commonage, could potentially affect this plant. It occurs in very small quantity at the Rosepenna site.

Conservation

Maintenance of the current grazing regimes at these open, unfenced commonages is essential for the survival of this species. Alteration of management practices, particularly attempts to enclose the open machair and fencing off portions of commonage, should be avoided. *L. gillmanii* is protected in the Republic of Ireland by the Flora (Protection) Order, 1999.

Protected sites with recent records: Doogort Machair/ Lough Doo SAC; Sheephaven SAC; **Unprotected sites with recent records:** none.

Lough Doo, Achill Island, Co. Mayo.

Leiocolea bantriensis (Hook.) Jörg.   Bantry Notchwort

syn. *Jungermannia bantriensis* Hook., *Lophozia bantriensis* (Hook.) Steph.
Status in Ireland: Near Threatened; **Status in Europe:** Least Concern

This is a widespread species of fens and flushes, with scattered records in areas near the north and west coasts. It was not included in the Provisional Red List (Holyoak 2006b) so was not especially looked for during recent fieldwork. It has been reported from 19 vice-counties, with records from 40 hectads (29 old, 17 recent, 1 undated) and is thought to have declined and contracted in range somewhat due to loss of habitat. It is still too widespread to be included in the Red List, but its situation should be monitored for any further decline.

Leiocolea fitzgeraldiae Paton & A.R.Perry   Fitzgerald's Notchwort

syn. *Lophozia muelleri* (Nees) Dumort. var. *libertae* auct. non (Huebener) Schiffn.
Status in Ireland: Near Threatened; **Status in Europe:** Near Threatened

This species was first collected in Gleniff (Co. Sligo) by H.H. Knight in 1928, and several times subsequently, especially by J.W. Fitzgerald, but was not described as a new species until 1995 (Paton & Perry 1995). *L. fitzgeraldiae* is a strictly calcicole leafy liverwort, found on N.-facing limestone cliffs, rock ledges, amongst rocks and boulders, and in limestone turf. It has been reported from five vice-counties, with records from eight hectads (3 old, 8 recent). Although restricted in its distribution and almost confined to the Dartry Mountains, it occurs at numerous sites, including along many kilometres of limestone crags in Glenade (Co. Leitrim). It is not thought to be in decline, nor particularly threatened, but as this species is thought to be endemic to Ireland and Britain, populations should be monitored periodically to ensure their continuing health.

Leiocolea heterocolpos (Thed. ex C.Hartm.) H.Buch

Ragged Notchwort

syn. *Jungermannia heterocolpos* Thed. ex C.Hartm., *Lophozia heterocolpos* (Thed. ex C.Hartm.) M.Howe
Status in Ireland: Critically Endangered (B2a, biii); **Status in Europe:** Least Concern

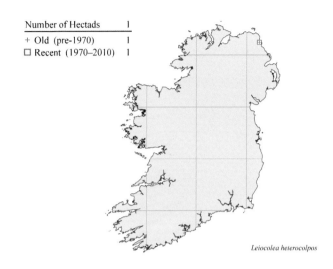

Number of Hectads	1
+ Old (pre-1970)	1
□ Recent (1970–2010)	1

Leiocolea heterocolpos

Identification

A pale green leafy liverwort with shoots up to 2 cm long, forming loose mats or creeping among mosses. The leaves are bilobed up to ¹/3, and often appear rather misshapen, sometimes with one lobe larger than the other and with irregular blunt marginal teeth. The underleaves are small, but fairly conspicuous. It is the only member of the genus to produce gemmae. These are greenish or brownish, smooth, mostly 2-celled and produced on modified, erect, attenuate shoots with reduced and even more irregularly-shaped leaves. *L. heterocolpos* is usually easily recognised by its untidy appearance and the combination of erect gemmiferous shoots, bilobed leaves, underleaves and greenish or brownish gemmae. Irish material is referable to var. *heterocolpos*.

Distribution in Ireland

L. heterocolpos is known in Ireland only from a single locality in Antrim (two small populations in Glenariff) where it was first recorded in 1969 and was still present in 2008.

Ecology in Ireland

In Ireland, it grows on thin soil and mixed with other bryophytes on steep to vertical wet basalt above a river near a waterfall, within the spray zone, partly shaded by deciduous trees. More generally, it is a plant of damp calcareous rocks. Indifferent as to altitude, it grows at c. 130–140 m altitude in Ireland.

This dioicous species is occasionally fertile, but male inflorescences and sporophytes are unknown in Ireland and Britain. Gemmae are abundant.

World distribution

This species is found in montane areas in most of Europe, but becomes more common further north. It is widespread in Fennoscandia, N. Russia (including Novaya Zemlya and Franz Josef Land), and the C. and W. European mountains (Alps, Carpathians, Pyrenees) and also present in Bulgaria, Greece, Latvia, Madeira and the Canary Islands. It is considered *Nationally Scarce* in Britain, *Critically Endangered* in the Czech Republic, *Endangered* in Luxembourg, *Vulnerable* in Serbia and Montenegro, and *Rare* in Belgium, Estonia and Hungary. In Europe, it is assigned to a Circumpolar Boreo-arctic montane floristic element. It is also present in Asia, N. America and Greenland. Some specimens from the Arctic have been named var. *arctica* (S.W. Arnell) R.M. Schust. & Damsh. and var. *harpanthoides* (Bryhn & Kaal.) R.M. Schust.

Threats

The small size of the populations makes them very vulnerable to mishaps, such as patches of bryophyte mat being dislodged or peeling off the rock. Work on the boardwalks at this tourist site could easily threaten the populations, but site managers have been informed of the need for care.

Conservation

Those maintaining the boardwalk are aware of the existence and rarity of this plant so that appropriate management can avoid damage to the population. The population should be regularly monitored and remedial action taken if it, or its habitat, is found to be declining.

L. heterocolpos is listed as a Northern Ireland Priority Species.

Protected sites with recent records: Glenariff Glen ASSI (scheduled for declaration 2011); Glenariff Nature Reserve; **Unprotected sites with recent records:** none.

Eremonotus myriocarpus (Carrington) Pearson — Clubwort

syn. *Anastrophyllum myriocarpum* (Carrington) R.M.Schust. ex Váňa, *Anomomarsupella cephalozielloides* R.M. Schust., *Cephalozia myriocarpa* (Carrington) Lindb., *Hygrobiella myriocarpa* (Carrington) Spruce, *Jungermannia myriocarpa* Carrington

Status in Ireland: Near Threatened; **Status in Europe:** Least Concern

E. myriocarpus is a very small, usually dark brown leafy liverwort that forms small mats or cushions on base-rich, and often flushed, rocks on ledges, cliffs and boulders in ravines. This is an arctic-alpine species, confined to upland areas near the west and north coasts, but recorded at altitudes of 140–490 m in Ireland. It has been reported from six vice-counties, with records from 10 hectads (4 old, 9 recent). There is no real evidence of decline, and despite being difficult to spot in the field, it was refound at several of its older localities during recent survey work.

Jungermannia exsertifolia Steph. **subsp.** *cordifolia* (Dumort.) Váňa — Cordate Flapwort

syn. *Aplozia cordifolia* Dumort., *Haplozia cordifolia* (Dumort.) Müll.Frib., *Jungermannia eucordifolia* Schljakov, *Solenostoma cordifolium* (Dumort.) Steph.

Status in Ireland: Least Concern; **Status in Europe:** Least Concern

A large dark green to blackish-purple leafy liverwort with cordate leaves forming tufts, patches or swollen mounds in springs and flushes. This subspecies was included in the Provisional Red List (Holyoak 2006b) but it is now clear that this plant is reasonably well scattered, though rather scarce, in upland areas, particularly in the north and west. It has been reported from 14 vice-counties, with records from 29 hectads (14 old, 17 recent) and cannot be considered threatened.

Nardia geoscyphus (De Not.) Lindb.

Earth-cup Flapwort

syn. *Alicularia geoscyphus* De Not., *A. minor* (Nees) Limpr., *A. scalaris* var. *minor* Nees, *Jungermannia scalaris* var. *minor* Nees, *Nardia haematosticta* Lindb.
Status in Ireland: Near Threatened; **Status in Europe:** Least Concern

N. geoscyphus is a pale green to brown leafy liverwort that can form dense mats on damp, sandy or gravelly soil on steep banks by streams, track sides, disused quarries, and on thin soil in rock crevices amongst limestone rocks and crags. Mainly north-western in its Irish distribution, this plant has been reported from six vice-counties, with records from 13 hectads (5 old, 10 recent). Recent fieldwork refound it at five of its known localities and discovered four new populations, so there is no convincing evidence of any decline.

Solenostoma sphaerocarpum (Hook.) Steph.

Round-fruited Flapwort

syn. *Aplozia amplexicaulis* (Dumort.) Dumort., *A. lurida* (Dumort.) Dumort., *A. nana* (Nees) Breidl., *A. sphaerocarpa* (Hook.) Dumort., *A. tersa* (Nees) Bernet, *Haplozia amplexicaulis* (Dumort.) Dumort., *H. lurida* Dumort., *H. sphaerocarpa* (Hook.) Müll.Frib., *H. sphaerocarpa* var. *nana* (Nees) Müll.Frib., *Jungermannia amplexicaulis* Dumort., *J. lurida* Dumort., *J. nana* Nees, *J. sphaerocarpa* Hook., *J. tersa* Nees,, *Solenostoma amplexicaule* (Dumort.) Steph.
Status in Ireland: Near Threatened; **Status in Europe:** Least Concern

This leafy liverwort is usually subalpine, occurring on and among acid to weakly base-rich rocks in damp places, often by streams, but also on cliffs and banks. Records of this species are scattered in upland areas and it has been reported from 17 vice-counties, with records from 35 hectads (23 old, 11 recent). *S. sphaerocarpum* was not included in the Provisional Red List (Holyoak 2006b) and its known sites were not revisited, so it is unclear if there has been any significant decline. Recent work (2007) in the Wicklow Mountains revealed four new localities, which suggests that this species has been under-recorded in Ireland.

Solenostoma paroicum (Schiffn.) R.M.Schust.

Shining Flapwort

syn. *Jungermannia paroica* (Schiffn.) Grolle
Status in Ireland: Near Threatened; **Status in Europe:** Near Threatened

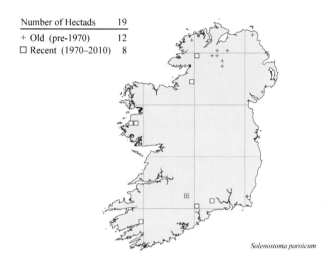

Number of Hectads	19
+ Old (pre-1970)	12
☐ Recent (1970–2010)	8

Solenostoma paroicum

Identification

Like other species of the genus, *S. paroicum* is a leafy liverwort with entire, rounded leaves and no underleaves. It is one of a group of four species that have a well-developed perigynium (a sheath that envelopes the archegonia and raises the perianth) and often some violet colouration, particularly on the rhizoids. It is very similar to *S. hyalinum*, but is a relatively large species, with shoots up to c. 2 cm long and 4 mm wide, and large leaf cells, averaging 36–50 μm wide (22–38 μm in *S. hyalinum*). The normally paroicous inflorescence is another point of distinction. It can be distinguished from *S. obovatum* and *S. subellipticum* by the large cells, the asymmetrical, widely and obliquely inserted leaves, and the perianth, which may be exserted up to halfway, whereas in the other two species it is not or hardly exserted.

Distribution in Ireland

Records of this species are widely scattered, but mainly concentrated in the north. There are recent records from nine localities in seven vice-counties: S. Kerry (Roughty River, 1979); Waterford (Lismore, 1972; Coumshingaun Lough, 2007); Limerick (Galty Mountains, 1966, 2005); W. Galway (Bunowen River, Tullyconor Bridge, 1970, 1994; Benchoona, 1994); W. Mayo (Mweelrea, 1987); Leitrim (Dough Mountain, 2005) and E. Donegal (River Finn at Cloghan More, 2001). Older records are from S. Kerry (Blackwater Bridge, undated, but

post-1950 and pre-1989); W. Donegal (Errigal Mountain, 1969; Fintragh Bay, 1969); Tyrone and Down (a cluster of unlocalised records made by J.W. and R.D. Fitzgerald, around 1950); Antrim (Ardagh, 1964; Glendun, 1969) and Londonderry (Banagher Glen, 1961).

Ecology and biology

Mainly growing in the lowlands, *S. paroicum* is a plant of wet, acid, or moderately basic turf and rocks, on banks and ledges, often where base-rich water seeps through. In Ireland, it is usually found among rocks by the sides of streams and lakes, sometimes where covered with detritus. Associated species in Ireland are little-recorded, but at Coumshingaun Lough other bryophytes growing close by included *Plagiochila spinulosa*, *Scapania compacta* and *Trichostomum tenuirostre*.

S. paroicum is paroicous and always found fertile. Sporophytes are frequent. Gemmae are unknown.

World distribution

This species is relatively frequent in Scotland, northern England and Wales, but is rare on a global scale. It is listed as *Extinct* in Belgium, 'extremely rare' in Germany and *Data Deficient* in Spain. It has also been recorded from the Faeroe Islands and France. It is endemic to Europe and is assigned to an Oceanic Temperate floristic element.

Threats
There are very few obvious threats to this species in Ireland, but it may be susceptible to climate change as its narrow global range suggests that its climatic requirements might be quite specific.

Conservation
As a globally rare species with a very restricted geographical range, the Irish populations require some attention and should be monitored. The Tyrone records in particular need to be followed up, but all populations should be checked, as *S. paroicum* was not targeted for recent fieldwork.

Protected sites with recent records: Comeragh Mountains SAC; Dough/Thur Mountains NHA; Mweelrea/Sheeffry/Erriff Complex SAC; Roughty River Estuary pNHA; The Twelve Bens/Garraun Complex SAC; **Unprotected sites with recent records:** Bunowen River, Tullyconor Bridge; Galty Mountains (but outside Galtee Mountains SAC); Lismore; River Finn at Cloghan More.

Solenostoma subellipticum (Lindb. ex Kaal.) R.M.Schust.

Two-lipped Flapwort

syn. *Eucalyx subellipticus* (Lindb. ex Kaal.) Breidl., *Haplozia subelliptica* (Lindb. ex Kaal.) Cas.-Gil, *Jungermannia subelliptica* (Lindb. ex Kaal.) Levier, *Nardia obovata* Lindb. var. *minor* Carrington, *N. subelliptica* Lindb. ex Heeg., *Plectocolea subelliptica* (Lindb. ex Heeg.) A.Evans
Status in Ireland: Near Threatened; **Status in Europe:** Least Concern

S. subellipticum is principally a plant of rocks by streams, sometimes where periodically inundated, and rock crevices in cliffs, gullies, etc. It has a strongly north-western distribution in Ireland, with none of its sites far from the coast, and appears to be fairly frequent in this restricted area. It has been reported from seven vice-counties, with records from 15 hectads (3 old, 14 recent), but because it was not recorded in Ireland until 1969, there can be no evidence of decline. As an essentially northern species, it may be threatened by climate change.

Geocalyx graveolens (Schrad.) Nees

Turps Pouchwort

syn. *Jungermannia graveolens* Schrad., *Saccogyna graveolens* (Schrad.) Lindb.
Status in Ireland: Endangered (D); **Status in Europe:** Least Concern

Identification
This bilobed leafy liverwort is reminiscent of *Lophocolea* spp., but is less translucent, characteristically appearing opaque, with a dull green colour. Shoots are up to c. 4 cm long and 3 mm wide and form loose wefts and mats. The leaves are bilobed to c. 1/6–1/3, and the leaf lobes are shorter and less attenuate than in *Lophocolea*. The underleaves also differ from those of *Lophocolea*, being deeply bifid and narrower than the stem, with nearly parallel lobes and no subsidiary teeth. Furthermore, the sporophyte is produced in a pouch-like marsupium rather than a perianth, and the turpentine-like smell of *Geocalyx* is different from the aroma of *Lophocolea*. The underleaves of *Leiocolea* spp. are either not bilobed, or completely absent. *Harpanthus* has unlobed underleaves. *Acrobolbus* has only rudimentary underleaves and differently-shaped leaves.

Lough Nakeeroge (east), Achill Island, Co. Mayo.

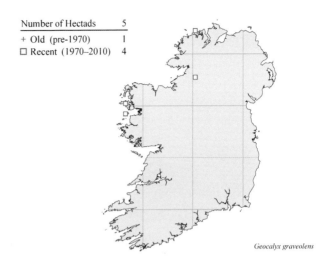

Number of Hectads	5
+ Old (pre-1970)	1
☐ Recent (1970–2010)	4

Geocalyx graveolens

Distribution in Ireland

Recent records are from five sites in three vice-counties; W. Mayo (Lough Nakeeroge, 1987; Tower Hill, 1987; Clare Island, 1994); Fermanagh (Lough Navar Forest, 1999) and W. Donegal (Horn Head, 1991). There is also an older record from Hog's Head, S. Kerry (1967). Its western distribution in Ireland and Britain is noteworthy because it is not considered an oceanic species elsewhere. It is listed as Western British by Ratcliffe (1968).

Ecology and biology

G. graveolens is a lowland plant of damp peaty banks near the coast, often growing with a variety of other liverworts. It is recorded in Ireland on a heather-shaded, N.-facing peaty bank; on peaty soil in a declivity on a damp rocky slope; growing around the base of *Mnium thomsonii* on peaty humus on a base-rich rock ledge on a N.-facing sandstone escarpment; and growing on a shady boulder on a steep bank high on a sea cliff with tall heather.

G. graveolens is autoicous and often fertile; sporophytes are frequent. Gemmae are unknown.

World distribution

Although widespread over much of northern Europe, including Fennoscandia, the Baltic States, Russia, Belarus and Ukraine, *G. graveolens* becomes rather thinly scattered southwards. It is listed as *Extinct* in Slovakia and possibly also in Italy, *Critically Endangered* in Switzerland, *Endangered* in Luxembourg and the Czech Republic, *Vulnerable* in Britain, Germany, Poland, and Austria, *Rare* in Estonia and *Data Deficient* in Spain. There are also records from France, Romania and the Azores. In Europe, it is assigned to a European Boreal-montane floristic element. It is also widespread in Asia, Oceania and N. America (where it is a common plant).

Threats

No particular threats have been identified, but the small size of the populations makes them vulnerable to mishaps. Any actions that might disrupt or destroy the bryophyte-rich banks where it grows are to be avoided.

Conservation

Populations, and potentially suitable habitat nearby, should be monitored. This is a naturally rare species in Ireland, but it remains a mystery why it is not more frequent, considering there is plenty of apparently suitable habitat. *G. graveolens* is listed as a Northern Ireland Priority Species.

Protected sites with recent records: Croaghaun/ Slievemore SAC; Horn Head and Rinclevan SAC; Lough Navar Scarps and Lakes ASSI (scheduled for declaration 2011); **Unprotected sites with recent records:** Clare Island (possibly within Clare Island Cliffs SAC).

Anthelia juratzkana (Limpr.) Trevis.

Scarce Silverwort

syn. *Anthelia andina* Herzog, *A. julacea* var. *gracilis* (Hook.) Nees,
A. julacea (L.) Dumort. subsp. *juratzkana* (Limpr.) Meyl., *A. nivalis* (Sw.) Lindb.,
Jungermannia julacea L. var. *clavuligera* Nees, *J. juratzkana* Limpr.
Status in Ireland: Near Threatened; **Status in Europe:** Least Concern

This small leafy liverwort forms whitish, silvery-grey or pale grey-green mats in rock crevices, mainly on N.- or NE-facing crags and in ravines in the uplands. It has a mainly north-western distribution in Ireland and has been reported from six vice-counties, with records from 11 hectads (3 old, 10 recent). There is no evidence of any decline and recent fieldwork has revealed eight new localities, so this species has probably been under-recorded in Ireland.

Gymnomitrion concinnatum (Lightf.) Corda

Braided Frostwort

syn. *Acolea concinnata* (Lightf.) Dumort., *Cesia concinnata* (Lightf.) Lindb.,
Gymnomitrion concinnatum var. *intermedium* Limpr., *Jungermannia concinnata* Lightf.
Status in Ireland: Endangered (B1a, bi, ii, iv, B2a, bi, ii, iv); **Status in Europe:** Least Concern

Number of Hectads	8
+ Old (pre-1970)	6
☐ Recent (1970–2010)	3

Gymnomitrion concinnatum

Identification

This is a small cushion-forming, pale yellowish-green leafy liverwort, with the individual shoots up to 2 cm long and 0.5 mm wide. The leaves are transversely inserted, more or less oval, densely imbricate and notched (divided to c. ¹/10–¹/3), forming almost terete shoots in which individual leaves are often difficult to distinguish. The leaf lobes are acute, unlike the rounded leaf lobes of *G. obtusum*, a plant that can normally also be distinguished by its whitish colour. The cuticle is densely papillose.

270

Distribution in Ireland

Recent records are confined to four localities in W. Donegal: the summit ridge of the Lavagh Beg–Binnacally massif, Binnasruell and Meenaguse in the Blue Stack Mountains (2001, 2008) and Slieve League (1970). It apparently used to be more widespread, but has either been somewhat overlooked during recent fieldwork, or its range may have contracted. Accepted older records are from W. Galway (Muckanaght, 1933); E. Donegal (Bulbin Mountain, 1968); W. Donegal (Slieve Snaght, 1962; Glenveagh, 1962) and Antrim (Fair Head, 1951, 1964). Old records from Down (Slieve Donard, 1884–1928; Slieve Commedagh, 1884) are regarded as suspect until confirmed by checking voucher specimens.

Ecology and biology

This is a plant of exposed mountain rocks and peaty crusts among rocks, often on mountain summits and ridges, avoiding strongly base-rich substrata, but recorded on basalt at Fair Head. Associates in Ireland include *Gymnomitrion obtusum*, *Kiaeria blyttii*, *Marsupella adusta*, *M. sphacelata* and *M. sprucei*. Essentially upland, it is normally recorded at altitudes from c. 500–600 m in Ireland, with one record (Fair Head) from below 100 m.

Although dioicous, it is usually fertile and sporophytes are frequent. Gemmae are absent.

World distribution

In Europe, *G. concinnatum* is frequent in montane areas, but much more common in the north than in the south, being widespread in Fennoscandia (except Denmark), northern Russia (including Novaya Zemlya and Franz Josef Land), montane parts of C. and W. Europe (Alps, Carpathians, Pyrenees) and the Caucasus. It is *Near Threatened* in the Czech Republic. It is assigned to a Circumpolar Arctic-montane floristic element in Europe. Elsewhere, it has been recorded in Asia, N. and S. America and Greenland.

Threats

Climate change is perhaps the main threat to this species in Ireland: its range may have contracted northwards, and this will possibly continue. Overstocking in the uplands may also be a potential threat.

Conservation

Populations should be monitored. *G. concinnatum* is listed as a Northern Ireland Priority Species.

Protected sites with recent records: Meenaguse Scragh SAC; Slieve League SAC; **Unprotected sites with recent records:** Meenaguse.

Gymnomitrion obtusum Lindb.

White Frostwort

syn. *Acolea obtusa* (Lindb.) Stephani, *Cesius obtusus* Lindb., *Gymnomitrion obtusatum* (Lindb.) Pearson
Status in Ireland: Near Threatened; **Status in Europe:** Least Concern

G. obtusum is a small whitish cushion-forming leafy liverwort with closely imbricate leaves, superficially resembling a lichen at first sight. This is an alpine and subalpine species that grows on exposed, generally neutral to acid rocks in the mountains. In Ireland, it occurs typically as tiny cushions growing directly on exposed vertical faces of granitic or conglomerate rocks, often on N.-facing cliffs, boulder faces or summit ridges. It has been reported from nine vice-counties, with records from 15 hectads (8 old, 9 recent). Although included in the Provisional Red List (Holyoak 2006b), it was not especially looked for during recent fieldwork because it was thought to be under-recorded. Nevertheless, at least six new localities were found in the last decade. Further survey work is needed to check whether it is still present at many of the old sites.

Gymnomitrion corallioides Nees

Coral Frostwort

syn. *Acolea corallioides* (Nees) Dumort., *Calypogeia corallioides* (Nees) Carruth., *Cesius corallioides* (Nees) Carruth.
Status in Ireland: Critically Endangered (B1a, bi, ii, iv, B2a, bi, ii, iv); **Status in Europe:** Least Concern

Number of Hectads	2
+ Old (pre-1970)	2
□ Recent (1970–2010)	1

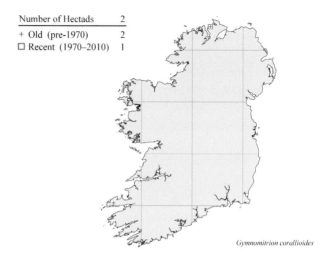

Gymnomitrion corallioides

Identification

Although a leafy liverwort, this plant looks more like a lichen at first sight. The leaves are so densely imbricate that individual leaves cannot easily be discerned, and the shoots form small whitish club-like structures up to 15 mm long, which are usually densely packed in a cushion. The shoots are slightly compressed, whereas the similarly pale shoots of *G. obtusum* are terete. The leaves are shallowly divided, to <1/6, and the leaf lobes are obtuse and broadly rounded. Further differences in the leaves from those of *G. obtusum* and *G. concinnatum* are the thin-walled marginal cells and the smooth cuticle.

Distribution in Ireland

The only recent record of this species is from Bulbin Mountain in E. Donegal (1969 and 2002). In the past it has also been recorded from S. Kerry (Brandon Mountain, 1840 and Connor Hill, 1881) in the Dingle Peninsula, but has not been refound at either of these localities, despite recent searches.

Ecology and biology

At its only recent site, *G. corallioides* was growing on firm soil in small crevices of steep schist rock of a NNW-facing crag just below the hill summit. There is no information on its habitat in Dingle, but in Britain, it grows on exposed base-rich rocks in the mountains, often in crevices and on thin overlying soils, normally at high altitudes. *G. corallioides* is well adapted to its montane environment: Clausen (1964) found that it was one of the few bryophytes tested that fully tolerated freezing in ice at −40°C for 24–26 hours. It is a montane plant, growing at 485 m on Bulbin Mountain.

Sporophytes are occasional in this dioicous species, but they have not been seen in Irish material. Gemmae are absent.

World distribution

This species is abundant in arctic and subarctic Europe, becoming more scattered and confined to mountain areas further south. It is widespread in Fennoscandia (except Denmark), the W. and C. European mountains (Alps, Carpathians, Pyrenees) and northern Russia. It is listed as *Near Threatened* in Britain, *Endangered* in the Czech Republic, *Vulnerable* in Bulgaria, *Near Threatened* in Switzerland and *Rare* in Slovakia. In Europe, it is assigned to a Circumpolar Arctic-montane floristic element. It has a similar distribution pattern in N. Asia and N. America.

Threats

Climate change is possibly a threat to this species in Ireland, as it has a northern, montane distribution. It is possible that botanical collecting may have led to its demise in Kerry, where it was in any case at the edge of its range and possibly present in very small amounts.

Conservation

The Bulbin Mountain colony should be monitored regularly. Further survey work might reveal that this species survives somewhere on relatively inaccessible rocks on Brandon Mountain or elsewhere.

Protected sites with recent records: Bulbin Mountain pNHA; **Unprotected sites with recent records:** none.

Marsupella sphacelata (Gieseke ex Lindenb.) Dumort.   Speckled Rustwort

syn. *Jungermannia sphacelata* Gieseke ex Lindenb., *Marsupella erythrorhiza* Schiffn., *M. joergensenii* Schiffn., *M. sphacelata* var. *media* (Gottsche) E.W.Jones, *M. sullivantii* (De Not.) A.Evans, *Nardia sphacelata* (Gieseke ex Lindenb.) Carrington, *Sarcoscyphos sphacelatus* (Gieseke ex Lindenb) Nees, *S. sullivantii* De Not.

Status in Ireland: Vulnerable (B1a, bi, ii, iv, B2a, bi, ii, iv); **Status in Europe:** Least Concern

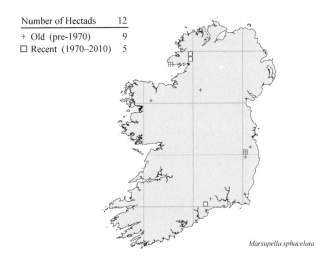

Number of Hectads	12
+ Old (pre-1970)	9
□ Recent (1970–2010)	5

Marsupella sphacelata

Identification

This is a bilobed leafy liverwort that forms loose turfs or mats, with shoots up to c. 5 cm long and 3 mm wide, and leaves divided to ¼–½. Although a rather variable species, *M. sphacelata* can often be recognised in the field by its more or less transversely inserted leaves, obtuse leaf lobes with a narrow sinus between them and the clasping leaf base. There are no underleaves. The colour is also variable, but it is usually very dark purple and often virtually black. The combination of dioicous inflorescences, a conspicuous hyalodermis and rounded leaf lobes differentiate it from most other species of *Marsupella*. The much more common *M. emarginata* usually has at least some leaves with partially recurved margins.

Distribution in Ireland

M. sphacelata is scattered in the mountains, with recent records from six localities in three vice-counties: Waterford (Coumtay, in the Comeragh Mountains,

2007); Wicklow (Lough Ouler, in the Wicklow Mountains, 1975, 2007) and W. Donegal (Slieve League, 1902–2008 and Meenaguse, Binnacally and Binnasruell in the Blue Stack Mountains, 2001–2008). There are older records from Waterford (Coumshingaun, 1966); Wicklow (Glenreemore Brook, 1964; Liffey Head Bridge, 1929; Lough Bray, 1869, 1898; Glenmalur, 1896); W. Mayo (Slievemore, 1909; Nephin, 1901; Ben Gorm, 1901) and Fermanagh (Cuilcagh, 1959). A 1979 record from Keeper Hill (N. Tipperary) is an error; the specimen is *M. emarginata*; and old records from Slieve Donard in the Mourne Mountains (Down) are unsubstantiated and must be disregarded.

Ecology and biology

It is found on boulders around upland lakes and streams, and on peaty soil and rocks on summit ridges, usually where there is some seasonal accumulation of water. It also occurs on wet rocks in cliffs. Associates in Ireland include *Hedwigia stellata*, *Hypnum cupressiforme*, *Racomitrium aciculare*, *Rhytidiadelphus squarrosus*, *Cephalozia bicuspidata*, *Diplophyllum albicans* and *Tetrodontium brownianum*. It is a subalpine and alpine plant, with most modern Irish records at altitudes of 500–600 m.

This species is dioicous and often fertile. Sporophytes are occasional. Gemmae are absent.

World distribution

This species is sparsely distributed in the European mountains, with records from Norway, Sweden, France (including Corsica), Poland, Switzerland, Austria, the Czech Republic, Slovakia, Portugal, Spain, Andorra, Romania, Bulgaria, Greece, Ukraine, Russia and the Azores. It is *Nationally Scarce* in Britain, *Vulnerable* in Finland and Germany, *Rare* in Belgium and Italy. It is assigned to a European Boreo-arctic montane floristic element in Europe. Elsewhere, it occurs in N. and E. Asia, N. America and Greenland.

Threats

Climate change may be the most significant threat to this species in Ireland. Some upland lakes, such as those in the Comeragh Mountains, appeared, during fieldwork in 2007, to be drying out, but it is not known if this is a significant long-term trend. Afforestation and nutrient enrichment due to overstocking are also threats.

Conservation

Populations should be protected from afforestation and the impacts of overstocking, and regular monitoring should take place.

Protected sites with recent records: Comeragh Mountains SAC; Meenaguse Scragh SAC; Slieve League SAC; Wicklow Mountains National Park; Wicklow Mountains SAC; **Unprotected sites with recent records:** Binnasruell; Meenaguse.

Marsupella funckii (F.Weber & D.Mohr) Dumort. — Funck's Rustwort

syn. *Jungermannia funckii* F.Weber & D.Mohr, *Marsupella badensis* Schiffn., *M. hungarica* Boros et Vajda, *M. pygmaea* (Limpr.) Steph., *M. ramosa* Müll.Frib., *Nardia funckii* (F.Weber & D.Mohr) Carrington, *Sarcoscyphus funckii* (F.Weber & D.Mohr) Nees, *S. muelleri* Nees, *S. pygmaeus* Limpr.

Status in Ireland: Near Threatened; **Status in Europe:** Least Concern

M. funckii is a small yellowish, brownish or blackish bilobed leafy liverwort, typical of this difficult genus in the transverse leaf insertion and absence of underleaves. It forms dense turfs of erect or suberect shoots and is distinguished by its non-decurrent leaves with a deep, narrow sinus between the lobes, the small leaf cells (c. 12–17 μm wide) and the dioicous inflorescence. Unlike *M. emarginata*, the leaf margins are not recurved, and the stem lacks a hyalodermis. A colonist species, *M. funckii* grows in upland areas but not at very high altitudes, and is completely absent from the high mountains. It is found on sandy ground and heathy banks, less often on rocks and its habitats in Ireland include loamy soil on a path, sandy ground by a road, a heathy bank, a stone wall, the floor of a disused quarry and crumbling basalt on a low crag on a NE-facing grassy slope. It has been reported from 12 vice-counties, with records from 18 hectads (10 old, 10 recent). It was not included in the Provisional Red List (Holyoak 2006b) and so was not sought during recent fieldwork. There is no evidence of decline, but as many of the most recent records are from the 1970s, its situation should be monitored.

Marsupella sprucei (Limpr.) Bernet

Spruce's Rustwort

syn. *Marsupella gracilis* (C.Massal. & Carest.) C.Massal., *M. neglecta* (Limpr.) Steph.,
M. ustulata Spruce non (Huebener) Spruce ex Pearson, *M. ustulata* var. *neglecta* (Limpr.) K.M.,
M. ustulata var. *sprucei* (Limpr.) R.M.Schust., *Nardia gracilis* C. Massal. et Carest., *N. sprucei* Limpr.,
Sarcoscyphus neglectus Limpr., *S. sprucei* Limpr. *S. ustulatus* auct.
Status in Ireland: Vulnerable (B2a, bii, iv); **Status in Europe:** Least Concern

Number of Hectads	11
+ Old (pre-1970)	3
□ Recent (1970–2010)	9

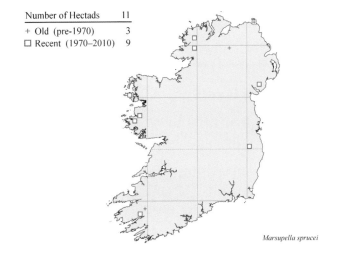

Marsupella sprucei

Identification

M. sprucei is a reddish-brown (less often yellowish) leafy liverwort that forms small tufts or dense or open turfs. It is typical of this difficult genus in the transverse leaf insertion and the absence of underleaves. It has bilobed leaves divided to c. 1/4–1/3, with acute or sometimes obtuse or rounded lobe apices, and is distinguished from *M. funckii* by its non-decurrent leaves with a slightly shallower sinus, slightly larger leaf cells (c. 12–20 μm wide), and the paroicous inflorescence. Like *M. funckii* but unlike *M. emarginata*, the leaf margins are not recurved, and the stem lacks a hyalodermis.

Distribution in Ireland

This species is scattered in upland areas, with recent records from ten localities in seven vice-counties: S. Kerry (Boughil, 1973); W. Galway (Benbaun, 1970; Muckanaght, 1970, 1994); Wicklow (Lough Ouler, 1975); W. Mayo (Slievemore, 1987; NE corrie of Mweelrea, 2003); W. Donegal (Binnacally, 2001; Moylenanav, 2002); Down (Meelbeg, 2004) and Antrim (Fair Head, 1952–1999). There are older records from N. Kerry (Mangerton Mountain, 1925) and Tyrone (Dart Mountain, 1957–59).

Ecology and biology

This species grows on rocks and stones, or on thin soil among rocks, in upland areas. Habitats recorded in Ireland include a wet siliceous rock face, soft 'calcareous' blocks in scree, sandstone in quartzite scree, soft rock on a slope, thin soil over rock, on peat among rocks on a summit ridge with *M. adusta* and *M. sphacelata*, on unshaded thin soil in a near-horizontal crevice on an exposed granitic rock on a hilltop, on thin unshaded peaty soil over dolerite on a slope at the base of crags, and on the flat inclined surface of a very large block with abundant *Andreaea*. Although more montane in continental Europe, this species seems indifferent to altitude in Ireland, having been recorded from near sea level to over 600 m.

It is paroicous (or rarely synoicous), usually fertile, and sporophytes are frequent. Gemmae are absent, as in all species of *Marsupella*.

World distribution

A widespread plant in montane parts of Europe, *M. sprucei* is recorded but not red-listed in Iceland, Faeroes, Norway, Sweden, Britain, France, Poland, Switzerland, Austria, Slovakia, Portugal, Spain, Andorra, Italy, Slovenia, Romania, Bulgaria, Ukraine, Russia and Madeira. It is listed as *Critically Endangered* in the Czech Republic, *Endangered* in Germany, *Vulnerable* in Finland and *Rare* in Belgium. In Europe, it is assigned to a

Circumpolar Boreo-arctic montane floristic element. Elsewhere, it occurs in northern Asia, N. and S. America, New Zealand and the subantarctic islands.

Threats
No particular threats have been identified.

Conservation
No action is currently required. *M. sprucei* is listed as a Northern Ireland Priority Species.

Protected sites with recent records: Cloghernagore Bog and Glenveagh National Park SAC; Connemara National Park; Croaghaun/Slievemore SAC; Eastern Mournes ASSI; Eastern Mournes SAC; Fair Head and Murlough Bay ASSI (scheduled for declaration 2011); Killarney National Park, Macgillycuddy's Reeks and Caragh River Catchment SAC; Meenaguse Scragh SAC; Mweelrea/Sheeffry/Erriff Complex SAC; The Twelve Bens/Garraun Complex SAC; Wicklow Mountains National Park; Wicklow Mountains SAC; **Unprotected sites with recent records:** none.

Marsupella adusta (Nees emend. Limpr.) Spruce

Scorched Rustwort

syn. *Acolea adusta* (Nees) Trevis., *Cesius adustus* (Nees) Lindb., *Gymnomitrion adustum* Nees, *Marsupella obscura* Spruce
Status in Ireland: Near Threatened; **Status in Europe:** Least Concern

Predominantly a montane species of small crevices in low granitic rocks or hepatic crusts over rocks or peat, this leafy liverwort was overlooked until recently in Ireland. It has been reported from seven vice-counties, with records from nine hectads (2 old, 8 recent) but with six of these resulting from recent survey work. It has a northerly distribution, and is undoubtedly a rare plant in Ireland, but there is no evidence of decline.

CHAPTER NINE

Mosses

Sphagnum affine Renauld & Cardot

Imbricate Bog-moss

syn. *Sphagnum imbricatum* subsp. *affine* (Renauld & Cardot) Flatberg
Status in Ireland: Vulnerable (D2); **Status in Europe:** Least Concern

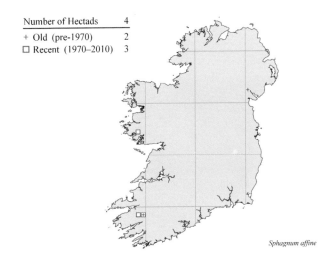

Number of Hectads	4
+ Old (pre-1970)	2
□ Recent (1970–2010)	3

Sphagnum affine

Identification

Sphagnum is an easy genus to identify, absorbing water like a sponge and having a unique branching pattern of a single main shoot with branches arranged in fascicles. *S. affine* is fairly clearly closely related to *S. palustre* and *S. papillosum*, with similar large size, swollen appearance, hooded branch leaves and wide stem cortex. It tends to form loose tussocks or lawns of greenish or yellowish-brown shoots up to 15 cm long, or not infrequently in Ireland forming compact raised hummocks. It is very closely related to *S. austinii*, which almost always grows as large, compact hummocks in undisturbed bogs, but *S. affine* has two pendent branches per fascicle, whereas *S. austinii* has only one. This pair of species is easily identified under the microscope by the presence of 'comb-fibrils' in the cells of the branch leaves. *S. affine*, however, lacks them in the stem leaves.

Distribution in Ireland

Recent records are from three localities in three vice-counties: S. Kerry (Looscaunagh-Derrycunihy Woods, 1983); N. Kerry (Cromaglan Bridge, 1959–2005) and W. Galway (south end of Derryclare Lough, 2003–

2004). There is an old record from Armagh (Camlough Mountain, 1898). This species has always been rare in Ireland, but may be overlooked.

Ecology and biology

In Ireland, it has been recorded from the edge of a small pool with *Rhynchospora fusca*, in a cutover bog at the edge of a spruce plantation by a lake and forming hummocks in an open bog, the latter a more typical habitat for the closely related *S. austinii*. In Britain, this is normally a plant of mires where there is some mineral enrichment, including poor fens, slightly base-rich seepages, ditches and stream banks, often in very wet places, at low to medium altitudes.

This is a dioicous species in which sporophytes are rare. *Sphagnum* does not produce vegetative propagules, but the shoots do fragment fairly readily when dry.

World distribution

S. affine is widespread in N. and C. Europe south to the Alps and also in the Azores. It is listed as *Nationally Scarce* in Britain, *Endangered* in Germany, *Vulnerable* in Finland, Switzerland and the Czech Republic and 'very rare and critical' in the Netherlands. In Europe, it is classified as a Suboceanic Boreal-montane floristic element. Outside Europe, it is known only from Asian Russia and eastern N. America, where it is frequent.

Threats
Afforestation is probably the major threat to this plant at Derryclare Lough, although there is no danger of it being shaded out by existing conifers. Drainage of peatland is clearly a threat to all sites for this species.

Conservation
The known populations should be monitored and protected from afforestation and drainage.

Protected sites with recent records: Killarney National Park; Killarney National Park, Macgillycuddy's Reeks and Caragh River Catchment SAC; The Twelve Bens/Garraun Complex SAC; **Unprotected sites with recent records:** none.

Sphagnum teres (Schimp.) Ångstr.

Rigid Bog-moss

Status in Ireland: Near Threatened; **Status in Europe:** Least Concern

This is a species of base-rich mires and flushes, widely distributed in Ireland and locally frequent in blanket bog flushes in parts of north Mayo. It has been reported from 18 vice-counties, with records from 19 hectads (7 old, 11 recent, 1 undated). Although there is no evidence of decline, substantial areas of suitable habitat for this species must have been lost in recent times due to drainage and reclamation of fens. Its conservation status should therefore be monitored.

Sphagnum girgensohnii Russow

Girgensohn's Bog-moss

Status in Ireland: Near Threatened; **Status in Europe:** Least Concern

This is a green species of *Sphagnum* that forms carpets or hummocks on damp woodland banks, amongst rocks by streams and lakes, in poor fens and on N.-facing hill slopes. Until recently, it was regarded as very rare in Ireland and was included in the Provisional Red List (Holyoak 2006b). Additional populations have been found over the past decade and have shown it to be more common, while still rather scattered and infrequent. It has been reported from 12 vice-counties, with records from 21 hectads (10 old, 13 recent). There is no evidence of any decline.

Sphagnum russowii Warnst.

Status in Ireland: Near Threatened; **Status in Europe:** Least Concern

This species is found in various habitats, but is particularly characteristic of heathy N.-facing slopes, growing under heather and other ericaceous shrubs. It may have declined somewhat, but may equally well have been overlooked in recent years. It has been reported from 19 vice-counties, with records from 24 hectads (15 old, 9 recent, 2 undated). Although originally included in the Provisional Red List (Holyoak 2006b), it was not particularly looked for during recent fieldwork when it became apparent that it was probably under-recorded in Ireland, and hence not especially threatened.

Sphagnum warnstorfii Russow

Status in Ireland: Vulnerable (B2a, bii, iv); **Status in Europe:** Least Concern

Number of Hectads	10
+ Old (pre-1970)	4
□ Recent (1970–2010)	6

Sphagnum warnstorfii

Identification

This medium-sized, vividly crimson species is one of the 'red Sphagna' in the Section *Acutifolia*, with more or less erect stem leaves. In the field, it can be distinguished from the closely related *S. capillifolium* by the straighter branches and branch leaves, and by the noticeably five-ranked branch leaf arrangement. The basic habitat, where it usually forms small but conspicuous colonies, is also a good clue as to its identity. However, it is always necessary to check it microscopically, when the small, thick-ringed pores (usually 2–6 μm in diameter) on the abaxial side near the apex of the branch leaves are distinctive (usually 8–13 μm in *S. capillifolium*).

Distribution in Ireland

This plant has a distinctly north-western distribution in Ireland, with recent records from six localities in five vice-counties: W. Galway (Errisbeg, on the NE side of Lough Nalawney, 2000); Roscommon (Carrowbehy/ Caher Bog, 2002); W. Mayo (Coolturk, Brackloon Lough, 1987–2003; Formoyle, 1998); Monaghan (Lisarilly, 1980) and W. Donegal (Meentygrannagh, 1998). In addition, there are older records from Laois (Clonaslee, 1966); W. Mayo (Knappagh, 1961; Slievemore, 1909) and Londonderry (Glenshane Pass, 1936).

Ecology and biology

S. warnstorfii occurs in basic habitats: fens, base-rich mires and flushes along with other base-demanding Sphagna such as *S. contortum* and *S. teres*, other mosses such as *Scorpidium scorpioides*, *S. cossonii* and *Campylium stellatum*, and often beneath open stands of *Phragmites australis*, *Carex* spp., *Cladium mariscus*, *Schoenus nigricans* or *Juncus acutiflorus*. It can grow at a wide range of altitudes, but Irish records with altitude information are from c. 40–100 m.

This is a dioicous species. Sporophytes have not been recorded in Ireland or Britain but are known from elsewhere. Vegetative dispersal is presumably by fragmentation.

World distribution

Reasonably common in N. Europe and in the C. European mountains, *S. warnstorfii* is *Extinct* in Hungary, *Critically Endangered* in Luxembourg, *Vulnerable* in Austria and Serbia and *Near Threatened* in the Czech Republic. In Europe, it is categorised as a Circumpolar Boreo-arctic montane floristic element. Elsewhere, it is widespread in N. Asia and N. America and is known also from Greenland.

Threats

Many rich fen sites are potentially threatened by land reclamation and resultant drainage and eutrophication. The site at Lisarilly is known to have been lost to arterial drainage in the 1980s.

Conservation

Protection from damage caused by drainage and associated reclamation or afforestation should be a priority for all the remaining sites where *S. warnstorfii* grows in Ireland.

Protected sites with recent records: Bellacorick Bog Complex SAC; Carrowbehy/Caher Bog SAC; Connemara Bog Complex SAC; Meentygrannagh Bog SAC; **Unprotected sites with recent records:** Lisarilly.

Sphagnum capillifolium (Ehrh.) Hedw. subsp. *capillifolium*　　　　　Acute-leaved Bog-moss

Status in Ireland: Data Deficient; **Status in Europe:** Least Concern

Although undoubtedly less frequent than subsp. *rubellum*, this plant must be greatly under-recorded in Ireland. The two subspecies are only subtly different and known to intergrade in Ireland and Britain (although they are more distinct in continental Europe) so subsp. *capillifolium* has been largely overlooked or ignored. So far it has been recorded only from Clare (Cloonybreen, 2007), Wicklow (Ballysmuttan, 2003) and Tyrone (Bessy Bell, 2009).

Sphagnum subnitens

Russow & Warnst. **var.** *ferrugineum* (Flatberg) M.O.Hill

syn. *S. subnitens* subsp. *ferrugineum* Flatberg
Status in Ireland: Least Concern; **Status in Europe:** Not Evaluated

A scarce variety that nevertheless turns up reasonably frequently in western mires and on montane slopes, this plant is now known from 10 vice-counties and 17 hectads (all recent). Included in the Provisional Red List (Holyoak 2006b), there are now too many records to retain this variety on the Irish Red List. It is reported to occur at one locality in Scotland, from oceanic parts of central and southern Norway (Thingsgaard 2003) and in N. America.

Sphagnum skyense Flatberg

Status in Ireland: Data Deficient; **Status in Europe:** Insufficiently Known

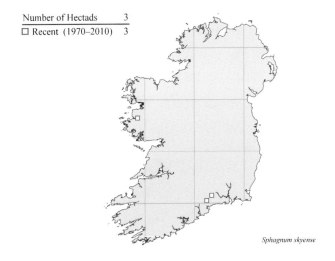

Number of Hectads	3
☐ Recent (1970–2010)	3

Sphagnum skyense

Identification

This species resembles a very large form of *S. subnitens*. It forms loose cushions or tussocks of shoots up to 3.5 cm in diameter, and is highly pigmented with a vivid pinkish-red colour, often greener at the centre of the capitulum. It has the more or less erect stem leaves of *S. subnitens*, *S. capillifolium* and related species, but is characterised by having two pendent and two spreading branches (*S. subnitens* nearly always has but one pendent branch) and very widely triangular stem leaves. *S. capillifolium* is much smaller and has blunter, fibrillose stem leaves. *S. quinquefarium* has three spreading branches and is usually much less highly pigmented. It was discovered on the Isle of Skye new to science in 1987 (Flatberg 1988), when it was suggested that it may be a hybrid between *S. subnitens* and *S. quinquefarium*. Daniels

& Eddy (1990) subsequently suggested it may be conspecific with *S. junghuhnianum* Dozy & Molk., a mainly Asian plant that also occurs on the west coast of N. America. However, Shaw *et al.* (2005) present molecular data supporting a hybrid origin involving *S. warnstorfii* and *S. subnitens*, although involvement of *S. quinquefarium* was not excluded.

Distribution in Ireland

This species is so far known only from two sites in Ireland: the Comeragh Mountains in Waterford, where it grows on the slopes above Lough Coumshingaun (2007–2008) and Lough Coumfea (2007), and the north corrie of Mweelrea, W. Mayo (2010), where it is found amongst steep boulder scree. It may well prove to be more widespread.

Ecology and biology

S. skyense grows mainly on steep, N.-facing heathy slopes below cliffs and crags in areas with high rainfall, often under patchy heather. It is not a bog plant. In Ireland, it grows between 400–540 m altitude, with *Bazzania tricrenata*, *Calluna vulgaris*, *Deschampsia flexuosa*, *Diplophyllum albicans*, *Festuca ovina*, *Galium saxatile*, *Hymenophyllum wilsonii*, *Hypnum jutlandicum*, *Polytrichastrum alpinum*, *Polytrichum commune*, *Racomitrium lanuginosum*, *Rhytidiadelphus loreus*, *Scapania gracilis*, *Thuidium tamariscinum* and *Vaccinium myrtillus*. At Mweelrea, it occurs amongst hepatic mat community in boulder scree, with *Herbertus aduncus* subsp.

hutchinsiae, *Pleurozia purpurea* and rarities such as *Scapania ornithopodioides*, *Bazzania pearsonii* and *Plagiochila carringtonii*.

The sexuality of *S. skyense* is unknown, as it has never been observed with sporophytes or gametangia. Vegetative propagules do not occur.

World distribution

As far as is known, this species is endemic to Ireland and Britain, but it is likely to be found elsewhere eventually. It is considered *Near Threatened* in Britain, where it has been found at several sites in the west of Scotland and one in Wales. It is categorised as a Hyperoceanic Temperate floristic element.

Threats

There are no obvious threats to any of the known populations at present, but damage to the vegetation on steep turf could quite easily occur if sheep stocking levels were to increase.

Conservation

Bryologists should look out for this moss elsewhere in Ireland in suitable habitats. Meanwhile, the existing populations should be monitored occasionally.

Protected sites with recent records: Comeragh Mountains SAC; Mweelrea/Sheeffry/Erriff Complex SAC; **Unprotected sites with recent records:** none.

Sphagnum strictum Sull.

Pale Bog-moss

Status in Ireland: Data Deficient; **Status in Europe:** Least Concern

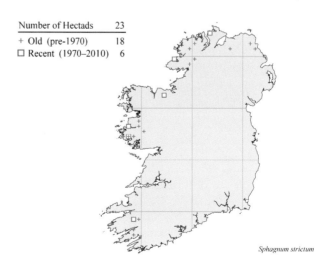

Number of Hectads	23
+ Old (pre-1970)	18
□ Recent (1970–2010)	6

Sphagnum strictum

Identification

This is a medium-sized plant with the shoots up to 15 cm long (but usually much shorter), and is closely related to the common *S. compactum*, forming dense cushions, sharing the compact habit and very small stem leaves of that species. However, it is uniformly pale green in colour, with a pale rather than a dark stem, and the branch leaves are squarrose (like *S. squarrosum*), so it is an easy plant to recognise. At first sight, it can often look something like *Leucobryum glaucum* rather than a species of *Sphagnum*.

Distribution in Ireland

Rare and scattered in the west of the country, there are recent records from six localities in five vice-counties: S. Kerry (Brassel Mountain, 1982); W. Galway (Killary Harbour-Lough Fee, 1976; Errisbeg, 1994); Sligo (Cloonacool in the Ox Mountains, 2008); E. Donegal (Gap of Marmore, 1976) and W. Donegal (Portnoo and Rossbeg, 1970). There are older records from a further five vice-counties: N. Kerry, W. Cork, W. Mayo, Antrim and Londonderry, all from the 1950s and 1960s. The species was not included in the Provisional Red List (Holyoak 2006b), so was not targeted for survey, but the preponderance of old records and the loss of its habitat to afforestation and reclamation in recent decades suggests that a considerable decline may have taken place.

Ecology and biology

This is a species of blanket peat and wet heath in highly oceanic areas, growing especially on N.- to E.-facing slopes under heather and other ericaceous shrubs, in wet flushes and with *Molinia caerulea*. It does not occur on raised bogs. It grows at low to medium altitudes, and has not been recorded above 550 m in Ireland or Britain.

Capsules are frequent in this autoicous species. *Sphagnum* does not produce vegetative propagules, but fragmentation of dry material probably plays a part in its dispersal.

World distribution

S. strictum is considered a species complex (Daniels & Eddy 1990) with its main area of distribution in warm regions of the world. European plants belong to subsp. *strictum* and are confined to north-western coastal areas. Séneca & Söderström (2009) list subsp. *strictum* as occurring in Ireland, Britain (where it is confined to the west), Iceland, Norway, Sweden, Denmark and Germany (where it is considered *Extinct*). In Europe, it is assigned to a Hyperoceanic Temperate floristic element.

Elsewhere, subsp. *strictum* occurs in eastern North America, from Newfoundland to Florida and Mexico. A different subspecies (subsp. *pappeanum* (Müll. Hal.) A. Eddy) is widespread in the tropics, southern Africa and Antarctica.

Threats

S. strictum can grow on thin blanket peat, wet heath and wet *Molinia*-dominated moorland, often in areas considered of more marginal interest than deeper-peat blanket bogs. Its localities may therefore be more at risk from afforestation, drainage, peat-cutting and reclamation for agriculture. For the same reason, it is possible that it has been overlooked in recent survey work, though it was not especially looked for, so further evidence is needed before it can definitely be assigned to one of the Red List categories. It may also be threatened by climate change.

Conservation

Further survey work is required to clarify the status of *S. strictum* in Ireland and to identify its best sites for conservation.

Protected sites with recent records: Connemara Bog Complex SAC; Killarney National Park, Macgillycuddy's Reeks and Caragh River Catchment SAC; North Inishowen Coast SAC (probably within SAC); Ox Mountains Bogs SAC; West of Ardara/Maas Road SAC (probably within SAC); **Unprotected sites with recent records:** none.

Cashel Hill, Roundstone Bog, Connemara, Co. Galway.

Sphagnum subsecundum Nees

Lesser Cow-horn Bog-moss

Status in Ireland: Near Threatened; **Status in Europe:** Least Concern

This species was confirmed as an Irish plant as recently as 1985, and it is now known from five vice-counties and eight hectads. Although there are no old records, *S. subsecundum* has probably declined in Ireland as it is confined to base-rich mires or base-rich flushes in moorland, a habitat that has certainly diminished in extent. A large group of records from Northern Ireland are either erroneous or unconfirmed.

Sphagnum platyphyllum (Lindb. ex Braithw.) Warnst.

Flat-leaved Bog-moss

Status in Ireland: Near Threatened; **Status in Europe:** Least Concern

This is very much a western species in Ireland, found in intermediate fens, poor flushes and swamps, particularly in blanket bogs in Connemara, W. Galway. It has been reported from four vice-counties, with records from nine hectads (1 old, 8 recent). Although undoubtedly rare, there is no evidence that it has declined and it is probably somewhat overlooked because of its resemblance to forms of the much more common *S. denticulatum*.

Sphagnum flexuosum Dozy & Molk.

Flexuous Bog-moss

syn. *Sphagnum recurvum* var. *amblyphyllum* (Russow) Warnst.
Status in Ireland: Vulnerable (D2); **Status in Europe:** Least Concern

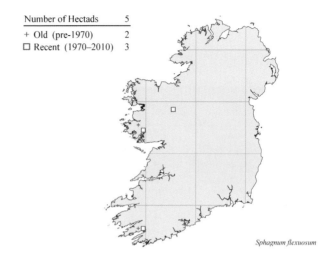

Number of Hectads	5
+ Old (pre-1970)	2
☐ Recent (1970–2010)	3

Sphagnum flexuosum

Identification

S. flexuosum is in the *Cuspidata* Section of the genus *Sphagnum*, close to *S. fallax*. Thus, it has hanging stem leaves and the green cells of the branch leaves more exposed on the convex side of the leaf. It is rather large, green, never reddish or brownish, occasionally with a faint yellow tinge, and forms loose carpets. It differs from *S. fallax* in the rounded and usually slightly tattered apices to the stem leaves (acute and inrolled in *S. fallax*). *S. angustifolium* is also similar, but has the pendent branches longer than the spreading branches (shorter or equal in *S. flexuosum*), shorter, non-tattered stem leaves, and some reddish pigmentation at the branch bases.

Distribution in Ireland

Apparently rare and with a western distribution in Ireland, this plant must surely be under-recorded and widely overlooked as *S. fallax*. Recent records are from three localities in three vice-counties: W. Cork (Glengarriff, 2002); W. Galway (Orrid Lough, 1987) and Roscommon (Carrowbehy/Caher Bog, 2002). There are older records from W. Cork (Sugarloaf Mountain, 1934) and W. Galway (Lough Inagh, 1957).

Ecology and biology

This is a 'poor fen' species, preferring slightly more mineral-rich sites than *S. fallax*, typically occurring in boggy open woodland or at the edge of bogs, often in extensive carpets and with other Sphagna. It generally grows at low altitudes and has not been recorded above 500 m in Ireland or Britain.

Capsules are rare in this dioicous species, and have not been seen in Irish or British material. *Sphagnum* does not produce vegetative propagules, but fragmentation of dry plants probably plays a part in its dispersal.

World distribution

This moss is widely distributed in N. Europe, becoming more montane to the south. It is considered *Vulnerable* in Austria and Serbia, *Data Deficient* in Luxembourg, 'declining' in Germany and 'rare' in the Netherlands. In Europe, it is categorised as a European Boreo-temperate floristic element. Elsewhere, its distribution is incompletely known, but it has been recorded in China, Japan and N. America.

Threats

The mineral-rich edges of bogs where *S. flexuosum* is usually found are vulnerable to disturbance, land-use change, dumping, pollution and eutrophication. Boggy woodland may also be threatened from land-use change, such as for building development or agriculture.

Conservation

While this species is almost certainly under-recorded, the sites where it is part of a more or less intact semi-natural habitat (such as at Carrowbehy/Caher Bog) should continue to be protected. New sites should be sought during bryological fieldwork.

Protected sites with recent records: Carrowbehy/Caher Bog SAC; Connemara Bog Complex SAC; Glengarriff Harbour and Woodland SAC; Glengarriff Wood Nature Reserve; **Unprotected sites with recent records:** none.

Sphagnum angustifolium (C.E.O.Jensen ex Russow) C.E.O.Jensen   Fine Bog-moss

syn. *Sphagnum recurvum* var. *tenue* H.Klinggr.
Status in Ireland: Least Concern; **Status in Europe:** Least Concern

This species forms loose carpets of slender green or yellowish shoots in minerotrophic flushes on blanket and raised bogs, or in woodland. Formerly under-recorded or just ignored as a mere variety of *S. recurvum*, it has only recently become clear that this species is reasonably widespread in scattered localities across Ireland. It is now known from 15 vice-counties, with records from 16 hectads (all recent). There is certainly no evidence of a decline.

Andreaea megistospora B.M.Murray   Big-spored Rock-moss

Status in Ireland: Vulnerable (B1a, bi, ii, iv, B2a, bi, ii, iv); **Status in Europe:** Rare

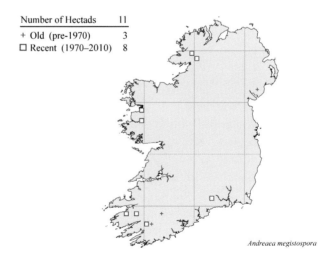

Number of Hectads	11
+ Old (pre-1970)	3
□ Recent (1970–2010)	8

Andreaea megistospora

Identification

This is a small saxicolous moss that forms tight dark reddish to brownish cushions less than 1 cm tall which tend to crumble when removed from the rock, as with

other species of the genus. The capsules of *Andreaea* are unique in that they dehisce with four longitudinal slits rather than with the usual apical peristome. *A. megistospora* is closely related to the common *A. rothii*, and like that species has a strong costa. It differs from that species in its larger spores, c. 50–90 μm in diameter, and having the leaf lamina cells distinct all the way to the leaf apex, rather than having the apex almost entirely consisting of costa tissue. In the field, the wider leaf apices of *A. megistospora* give it a less densely black appearance than *A. rothii*. This species was described new to science as recently as 1987 (Murray 1987), so has doubtless been overlooked. The old records are based on a revision of herbarium specimens. Some Irish material is to some extent intermediate in spore size between 'good' *A. megistospora* and *A. rothii*.

Distribution in Ireland

This strongly oceanic species is mainly found near the western seaboard, with a handful of older records from further east. Recent records are from eight localities in six vice-counties: S. Kerry (Coomeeneragh Lake, 2006; Lough Gouragh, 2006); W. Cork (E. of Coomroe, 2006); Waterford (Comeragh Mountains, 2010); W. Galway (Maumtrasna, 2003); W. Mayo (Croagh Patrick, 1987) and E. Donegal (Barnesmore Gap, 2001; Cronloughan, 2008). Older records are from W. Cork (Coomataggart Mountain, 1953); Mid Cork (Musheragh Mountain, 1851) and Down (Rocky Mountain, near Hilltown, 1923).

Ecology and biology

Like other *Andreaea* spp., it grows on exposed acidic rocks and boulders, typically granite, sandstone or quartzite, and usually in upland areas. Irish records with altitudinal information are from 100–380 m. In Britain, it has been recorded from sea level to c. 700 m.

This is an autoicous species which usually has sporophytes (being unidentifiable without mature spores), which mature in the summer. *Andreaea* does not produce gemmae or other specialised vegetative propagules, but fragmentation probably plays a part in its dispersal.

World distribution

Elsewhere in Europe, *A. megistospora* is recorded only from Britain (where it is *Nationally Scarce*), Norway, Spain and Portugal. It is categorised as a Hyperoceanic Temperate floristic element. Elsewhere, it is only recorded from the Pacific coast of N. America (Alaska, British Columbia and Washington State).

Threats

Planting of conifers is probably the most serious threat to this species, as many of the colonies are on otherwise rather undistinguished rocks on shallow slopes. Unknown numbers of colonies have probably been shaded out and lost through conifer afforestation over the last few decades.

Conservation

No specific measures are necessary for the conservation of this moss.

Protected sites with recent records: Comeragh Mountains SAC; Croagh Patrick pNHA; Killarney National Park, Macgillycuddy's Reeks and Caragh River Catchment SAC; Maumtrasna Mountain Complex pNHA; River Finn SAC; **Unprotected sites with recent records:** Barnesmore Gap (possibly within Barnesmore Bog NHA); E. of Coomroe.

Lough Gouragh, Co. Kerry.

Oedipodium griffithianum (Dicks.) Schwägr.

Gouty-moss

Status in Ireland: Critically Endangered (B1a, bi, ii, iv, B2a, bi, ii, iv); **Status in Europe:** Least Concern

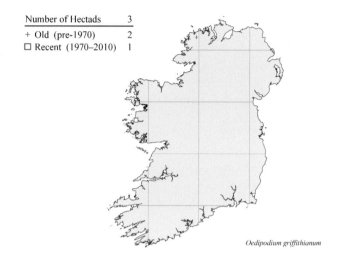

Number of Hectads	3
+ Old (pre-1970)	2
□ Recent (1970–2010)	1

Oedipodium griffithianum

Identification

An acrocarpous moss that grows as scattered plants or loose pale green tufts up to about 10 mm tall. The leaves are obovate-spathulate to almost orbicular with a long narrow ciliate base and soft succulent texture, becoming shrivelled when dry. The leaf apex is rounded, the margins plane and entire and the costa ends well below the leaf apex. Leaf cells are hexagonal, smooth, large and rather lax. Stalked discoid or oval multicellular gemmae are often present in the leaf axils or scattered on the leaves after they become detached. The capsules are shortly ellipsoid, with a long fleshy neck, gymnostomous and exserted on a succulent seta.

Molecular studies have revealed that the traditional classification of *Oedipodium* among the Splachnales or Funariales is incorrect and that this monotypic family occupies an isolated position among much more primitive groups of mosses.

Distribution in Ireland

The only modern record is from the NE slope of Mweelrea in W. Mayo, where it was discovered by D.G. Long in 2003. There are two old records, from S. Kerry (Brandon Mountain, 1836) and W. Donegal (Errigal, 1890). Despite the distinctive appearance of the species, an old report from N. Kerry (near Loo Bridge) must be rejected because it seems unlikely to occur in this lowland locality and no voucher specimen has been traced.

Ecology and biology

The only recent record was from loose, partly bare, fine soil on a slope of unshaded fine scree of Mweelrea Grit, facing east at 530 m altitude. The old record 'near summit of Errigal' was presumably somewhere just below 751 m altitude. In Britain, it grows on moist humus-rich or peaty soil in more or less shaded rock crevices or block screes or in mountain regions, mainly at moderate to high altitudes (A.C. Crundwell in Hill *et al.* 1994). In Norway, it is also known beside tree roots and on earth at the edge of grassy turf on rocks and boulders (Störmer 1969).

Individual plants are probably short-lived, but no details are available. The species is autoicous or synoicous and (in Britain) it frequently produces capsules that ripen in summer. Tubers are unknown but vegetative propagation presumably occurs from the discoid foliar gemmae.

World distribution

In Europe, it is known in Norway, Sweden (where it is listed as *Near Threatened*) and the extreme NW of Finland, mainly in the mountains (Störmer 1969). It is assigned to an Oceanic Boreal-montane floristic element in Europe. Elsewhere, there are records from the Russian Far East, Japan, Alaska, Washington State, Canada, Greenland, Tierra del Fuego and the Falkland Islands.

Threats

O. griffithianum is apparently extinct around the summit

of Errigal, where intense pressure from human visitors has eutrophicated and littered potential habitat. Mweelrea has the only population known to survive and, although in a remote location, it occurs only in small quantity there and potentially is at risk from disturbance of the scree by sheep or botanists and from thoughtless collection of specimens.

Conservation

The Mweelrea site and the two localities with old records are all on protected land.

Protected sites with recent records: Mweelrea/Sheeffry/Erriff Complex SAC; **Unprotected sites with recent records:** none.

Atrichum crispum (James) Sull.

Fountain Smoothcap

Status in Ireland: Not Evaluated; **Status in Europe:** Not Evaluated

This species is usually assumed to be an old, accidental introduction from N. America and is therefore not included in the Red List evaluation process. It grows mainly on soil by upland streams and occurs in two clusters of localities in Ireland: Wicklow (eight localities) and on the border of Roscommon and Leitrim (five localities). All the plants found so far in Ireland and Britain are non-fertile or male.

Atrichum tenellum (Röhl.) Bruch & Schimp.

Slender Smoothcap

Status in Ireland: Near Threatened; **Status in Europe:** Least Concern

This species forms dull green patches on gravelly soil in acidic open habitats and has been recorded in Ireland from stream banks, river margins, lake edges and from earthy crevices among conglomerate blocks on N.-facing hillsides. Recorded new to Ireland as recently as 1979, this species has since been shown to be rare and scattered, but apparently not threatened, in upland areas in the west and north-east. It has been reported from seven vice-counties, with records from eight hectads.

Atrichum angustatum (Brid.) Bruch & Schimp.

Lesser Smoothcap

syn. *A. angustatum* var. *rhystophyllum* auct. non (Müll.Hal.) P.W.Richards & E.C.Wallace,
Catharinea angustata (Brid.) Brid., *C. angustata* var. *rhizophylla* (Müll.Hal.) Dixon
Status in Ireland: Regionally Extinct; **Status in Europe:** Least Concern

Number of Hectads	2
+ Old (pre-1970)	2

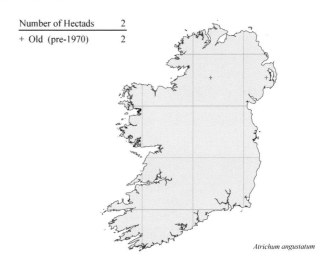

Atrichum angustatum

Identification

A. angustatum is a robust moss that grows in turfs up to about 3 cm high. As with other species of *Atrichum*, this is an erect acrocarpous moss with strongly toothed leaf margins, costa extending to the leaf apex with teeth on its upper dorsal surface and distinctive raised lamellae along the ventral surface of the costa. In *A. angustatum* the rather stiff leaves are typically narrower than in the very common *A. undulatum*, narrowly lingulate to lingulate-lanceolate, the costal lamellae are rather broad and the isodiametric mid-leaf cells are consistently smaller (mostly 12–18 μm). Capsules (unknown in Ireland) are narrowly cylindrical, erect and almost straight to inclined and curved, exserted on a long yellowish to purple seta.

Distribution in Ireland

Confirmed records are from two localities; Tyrone (Trillick, 1957) and Down ('Mr Armitage Moore's garden near Saintfield', also given as 'S. of Saintfield demesne', 1908–1910). Both areas have been searched for the species without success in the past decade, although the Saintfield garden was not relocated. Megaw (1938) reports finding it at a second locality in Down (Rowallane), but this is unconfirmed.

Ecology and biology

The Saintfield records were from a garden on a 'mud-capped wall' or 'sods on top wall', that from Trillick was

in an 'old sand pit'. In SE England the species occurs on damp non-calcareous loamy rides and paths in ancient woodland, although older records were on heaths and commons. Nyholm (1971) reports it from fairly dry habitats, on sandy or loamy open soil, on fallow fields, beside roads, on walls, etc.

The plants are probably short-lived perennials, but details are unknown. The species is dioicous and sporophytes are rare (in Britain), with spores maturing in winter. Rhizoidal tubers have been reported from Austria (Suanjak 1999) but not from Ireland or Britain (Preston 2004).

World distribution

Widespread in Europe from Denmark, S. Sweden and Estonia southwards to S. Portugal and the Caucasus; also reported from Iceland. It is listed as *Critically Endangered* in Britain, *Endangered* in Sweden, *Vulnerable* in Germany, *Data Deficient* in Bulgaria and the Czech Republic, 'very rare' in Estonia and 'very rare and susceptible' in the Netherlands. It is assigned to a European Temperate floristic element in Europe. Elsewhere, it is known from the Azores, Madeira, Canary Islands, N. America, mountains of C. America, Jamaica and Haiti. Reports from E. Asia are now attributed to *A. rhystophyllum* (Müll.Hal.) Paris which Nyholm (1971) treats as a distinct species.

Threats

No information, except that the sand pit at Trillick had

been considerably enlarged by 2000 and the species was not refound there.

Conservation

No action has been taken other than attempts to relocate populations. Further efforts to relocate the Saintfield garden might nevertheless prove worthwhile.

Protected sites with recent records: none; **Unprotected sites with recent records:** none.

Pogonatum nanum (Hedw.) P.Beauv.

Dwarf Haircap

syn. *Polytrichum nanum* Hedw.
Status in Ireland: Endangered (B1a, bi, ii, iv, B2a, bi, ii, iv); **Status in Europe:** Least Concern

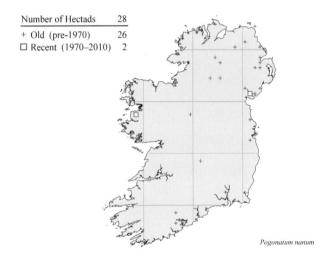

Number of Hectads	28
+ Old (pre-1970)	26
☐ Recent (1970–2010)	2

Pogonatum nanum

Identification

A small dark green member of the Polytrichaceae, this acrocarpous moss has thick-textured leaves with longitudinal lamellae, capsules with an epiphragm uniting the peristome teeth, and a prominent hairy calyptra. The shoots of *Pogonatum* are much smaller than those of most members of the genus *Polytrichum*, less than 1 cm tall, and arise from a persistent alga-like protonemal mat. The leaves are up to c. 5 mm long. *P. nanum* differs from the common *P. aloides* in the shape of the capsule, which is short and more or less spherical rather than shortly cylindrical. Furthermore, the exothecial cells of the capsule are finely papillose rather than coarsely mamillose and the spores are larger. The two species can be reliably separated only when fertile. *P. urnigerum* has distinctive papillose apical cells on the leaf lamellae and its leaves are usually glaucous-green.

Distribution in Ireland

The true distribution of this moss in Ireland is not well known, but it certainly appears to be very rare. Many older specimens have been reidentified as *P. aloides*, or else they lack capsules and thus cannot be identified. However, there are enough old records to suggest that *P. nanum* may have declined. There are only three confirmed recent records: W. Mayo (by Lough Brawn in the Sheeffry Hills, 2008) and Louth (Two-Mile River, Carlingford, 1999; Windy Gap, Carlingford, 2010). The older records that are correct, or probably correct, are from: Mid Cork (Ballinhassig Glen, 1845); E. Cork (Templemichael, 1851); N. Tipperary (Roscrea, 1911); Wexford (Strokestown, 1907); Wicklow (Kilcock Mountain, 1908); Dublin (Howth, 1861; Ticknock, 1969); Meath (between Stamullen and Bellewstown, 1967); Roscommon (Slieve Bawn, 1968); W. Mayo (Clare Island, 1910); Sligo (Knocknarea Glen, 1904); Monaghan (Eskmore, 1910); Fermanagh (Topped Mountain, 1905); Tyrone (Glen Curry Bridge, 1956; Newtownstewart, 1958); Armagh (Carrifkeeny, 1913; Slieve Gullion, 1964); Down (Slieve Donard, 1884; Manyburn Glen, undated; Slieve Commedagh, 1908; Sydenham near Belfast, 1871; Rostrevor, 1928); Antrim (Glarryford, 1920; Torr Head, undated; Derriaghy, 1874; Cranmore, undated; Slievetrue, 1871; Sallagh Braes, 1874) and Londonderry (Maghera, 1879).

Ecology and biology

This is a colonist of bare acidic soil, such as on the side of forestry tracks, ditches, vehicle ruts, etc. The minimal information on its ecology in Ireland suggests that it favours sandstone and sandy substrates. Habitats include a damp sandy hollow by a forest road, a loamy bank in a sandstone pit, on mineral soil on a rocky outcrop by a stream (Two-Mile River, Carlingford), on dry heath in block scree on a montane slope (Lough Brawn) and with *P. aloides* on a roadside bank (the most recent record, from Windy Gap, Carlingford). *P. nanum* might prefer more recently disturbed soil than *P. aloides*, and therefore have a more ruderal lifestyle, but they often occur together in Britain. It probably exists as a metapopulation, the individual colonies being transient. It grows in the lowlands or at moderate altitudes (the recent Irish records are from 300 m and c. 560 m).

Although dioicous, capsules are abundant, at least in winter and early spring, tending to be produced earlier in the year than those of *P. aloides*. No specialised vegetative reproductive structures are known.

World distribution

This species is widespread on acidic substrata throughout lowland Europe, including the Faeroes, Iceland and Macaronesia. It is *Critically Endangered* in Switzerland, *Vulnerable* in Germany and the Netherlands, *Data Deficient* in the Czech Republic, 'potentially threatened' in Austria and 'very rare' in Estonia. In Europe, it is categorised as a European Temperate floristic element. Elsewhere, it is recorded only from N. Africa.

Threats

Although afforestation must have destroyed much suitable habitat for this species, it has probably also created it, along forestry tracks, and it is difficult to see why this species should have declined. The alternative explanation is that it may be widely overlooked, perhaps because there has been very little recent bryological fieldwork in Ireland during the early months of the year, when the capsules are ripe. This seems unlikely because the tough capsules persist into the summer. However, if the species is a mobile colonist it may never have had very many Irish populations at any one time.

Conservation

It is difficult to make conservation recommendations for this ruderal species. Suitable ground, such as forestry tracks in areas where *P. nanum* has been recorded previously, should be examined during winter and spring.

Protected sites with recent records: Carlingford Mountain SAC; Mweelrea/Sheeffry/Erriff Complex SAC; **Unprotected sites with recent records:** none.

Polytrichum commune Hedw. **var.** *perigoniale* (Michx.) Hampe Dense Haircap

Status in Ireland: Data Deficient; **Status in Europe:** Not Evaluated

Recent culture experiments (Schriebl 1991) and molecular studies (Van der Velde & Bijlsma 2000, Hyvönen & Bell in Hill *et al.* 2006, N. Bell unpublished) have established that *P. commune* consists of two widespread species in W. Europe. It seems likely that small forms (known as *P. commune* var. *perigoniale* and *P. commune* var. *humile* Sw.) should be synonymised under the name *P. commune*, whereas the familiar large plant of moorland and acidic mires should be known as *P. uliginosum* (Wallr.) Schriebl. Hill *et al.* (2008) do not adopt this nomenclature pending further research, maintaining past usage of the (illegitimate) name *P. commune* var. *perigoniale* for the smaller plants. This taxon has been recorded from six Irish localities, all since 2007, and the plant is undoubtedly under-recorded. As it tends to occur on the sides of tracks in conifer plantations and on rocky slopes in quarries, it is probably not a rare plant.

Tetrodontium brownianum (Dicks.) Schwägr.

Status in Ireland: Near Threatened; **Status in Europe:** Least Concern

This is a small and often inconspicuous species that grows mainly under rock overhangs. It has been reported from 10 vice-counties, with records from 22 hectads (15 old, 7 recent, 2 undated). It was included in the Provisional Red List (Holyoak 2006b) but was not especially looked for when recent fieldwork showed it to have too many records to merit further survey. Always rather rare in Ireland, it is debatable whether this species has actually declined.

Buxbaumia aphylla Hedw.

Status in Ireland: Regionally Extinct; **Status in Europe:** Regionally Threatened

Number of Hectads	1
+ Old (pre-1970)	1

Buxbaumia aphylla

Identification

This bizarre-looking acrocarpous moss essentially consists of a relatively enormous sporophyte that appears to emerge directly out of the substratum, with no obvious gametophyte, leading to its American name of 'bug-on-a-stick'. In fact, the gametophyte is extremely reduced, consisting only of a brownish protonemal mat that produces female shoots with tiny perichaetial leaves, which are ciliate and become filamentous with age, making them difficult to distinguish from the protonema. The even smaller male shoots grow on the side of the female shoots. The seta is c. 1 cm long and papillose, and the strange, glossy brown, asymmetrical capsule is c. 6 mm long, obliquely ovoid, has a flattened upper surface and tapers to a narrow operculum. It contains about five million small spores.

Distribution in Ireland

There is a single Irish record of this species, made by W. Wade on Purple Mountain, S. Kerry in 1804. The rarity of this plant is curious, considering its prodigious production of small spores, but it is also rare in Britain. It is conceivable but unproven that it occurs undetected at other sites as a protonemal mat, fruiting only rarely.

Ecology and biology

B. aphylla is a colonist that is often ephemeral in occurrence, and grows on humus-rich sandy soil, rotten wood and (in Britain) colliery slag in the lowlands. On the only occasion this species has been seen in Ireland, it was recorded 'on decayed leaves, impacted with earth, in a shady situation'. Presumably, the very numerous small spores are capable of dispersal over considerable distances.

This dioicous plant is only ever recorded fertile. Vegetative propagules are unknown.

World distribution

B. aphylla is widely distributed in Europe, but generally rare. It is most widespread in Fennoscandia, becoming less frequent southwards, and is *Nationally Scarce* in Britain (Preston 2006), possibly *Extinct* in Italy, *Critically Endangered* in the Netherlands, *Endangered* in Spain, Switzerland, Bulgaria and Montenegro, *Vulnerable* in the Czech Republic and Austria, *Near Threatened* in Luxembourg, and 'rather rare' in Estonia. It remains unrecorded in a few countries, including Greece, Portugal and Iceland. In Europe, it is categorised as a Circumpolar Boreal-montane floristic element. Elsewhere, it occurs in N. Asia, N. America, New Zealand and Tasmania.

Threats

There are no obvious threats to the habitat of this plant, and potentially it could turn up, unpredictably, almost anywhere.

Conservation

Bryologists should bear this plant in mind when recording in suitable habitats. If it is rediscovered, some site protection measures may be necessary.

Protected sites with recent records: none; **Unprotected sites with recent records:** none.

Timmia norvegica J.E.Zetterst.

Norway Timmia

Status in Ireland: Vulnerable (D1); **Status in Europe:** Least Concern

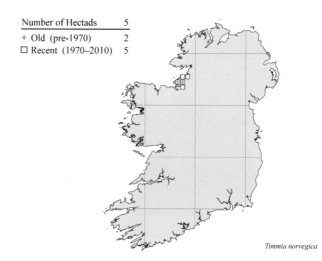

Number of Hectads	5
+ Old (pre-1970)	2
□ Recent (1970–2010)	5

Timmia norvegica

Identification

A robust acrocarpous moss that grows as green to yellowish-green tufts or as scattered shoots among other plants, with erect stems 2–8 cm high. The leaves are longer (6–8 mm) towards the shoot tips than below (3–5 mm), patent when moist and show a weak spiral arrangement. The leaf shape is narrowly lanceolate, with a somewhat sheathing base and an acute apex. The leaf margin is plane, coarsely toothed above; the costa is stout, reddish-brown in older leaves, percurrent and papillose basally on the dorsal surface. Mid-leaf cells are hexagonal or quadrate-hexagonal, mamillose on the ventral surface, smooth dorsally; basal cells are narrowly rectangular to linear. Capsules (unknown in Ireland or Britain) are cylindrical to ovoid, horizontal and exserted on a reddish-brown seta 15–20 mm long.

Timmia norvegica, Gleniff, Co. Sligo.

Distribution in Ireland

Records are from about 13 localities in two vice-counties: Sligo (Benbulbin, 1928–1970, with records in 2003 from sites in summit area, on E. cliffs of E. corrie, W. cliffs of E. corrie; Gleniff, 1937–1970, with records in 2003 from E. corrie and Annacoona; Kings Mountain, 1970–2003; Cormac Reagh's Hole, 2003; Keelogyboy Mountain, 2003) and Leitrim (Cloontyprughlish, 2000–2005; Drumnagran, 2001; S. and SE of Aghadunvane, 2000–2005; S. of Crumpaun, 2001; NE slope of Crockauns, 2000).

Ecology and biology

T. norvegica is a montane moss restricted to Carboniferous Limestone country, mainly in the Dartry Mountains. Records are from c. 250–550 m altitude, mostly on NW-, N.- or E.-facing slopes, but with a few from S.-facing slopes that are sheltered or shaded by large crags. It grows on dry to damp or sometimes wet soil or thin soil amongst rock fragments, mainly on ledges of crags in gullies or ravines, in crevices, or on rocky slopes, usually amongst other bryophytes and low phanerogams. There are also single records of large patches on a grassy slope at the edge of a flush and of small patches in short sheep-grazed grassland below a crag. In Britain, it occurs mainly at higher altitudes (from 550–1170 m) over calcareous schist, less often limestone or calcareous basalt (H.J.B. Birks in Hill *et al.* 1994).

The plants are perennial. It is a dioicous species in which capsules are unknown in Ireland or Britain (very uncommon in Scandinavia; extremely rare in N. America). Gemmae, bulbils and tubers are absent. Plants observed at Drumnagran, Glenade in August 2001 had the large upper leaves caducous; these presumably function as vegetative propagules.

World distribution

T. norvegica has a northern and montane range in Europe, found in Spitsbergen, Iceland, Scotland, Norway, mountains of Sweden and arctic Russia, southwards in mountain regions to the Pyrenees, Alps, Apennines (Prov. Abruzzo: Cortini Pedrotti 2001) and Caucasus. It is listed as *Critically Endangered* in Bulgaria, *Endangered* in Finland and Spain, *Vulnerable* in Switzerland and *Near Threatened* in Britain. It is assigned to a Circumpolar Boreo-arctic montane floristic element in Europe. The range elsewhere includes SW Asia (Turkey; Georgia and Kazakhstan: Ignatov *et al.* 2007), N. and C. Asia, N. America (from Alaska and Quebec southwards in mountains to Colorado), Greenland and New Zealand.

Threats

It occurs mainly as small, scattered populations, but few immediate threats were apparent at sites visited over the past decade. Overstocking with sheep, causing erosion, is a potential threat that may now be reduced as stocking levels are tending to decline. Some individual patches are likely to be at risk from rockfalls and other natural events, but these doubtless also create new habitat for the species.

Conservation

All populations are on protected land.

Protected sites with recent records: Arroo Mountain SAC; Ben Bulben, Gleniff and Glenade Complex SAC; Crockauns/Keelogyboy Bogs NHA; **Unprotected sites with recent records:** none.

Gleniff, Co. Sligo.

Encalypta alpina Sm.

syn. *Encalypta commutata* Nees & Hornsch.
Status in Ireland: Vulnerable (D2); **Status in Europe:** Least Concern

Number of Hectads	2
+ Old (pre-1970)	2
□ Recent (1970–2010)	2

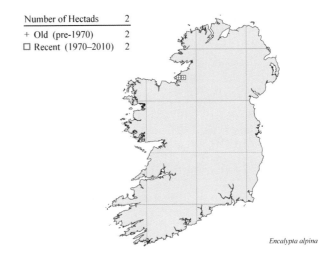

Encalypta alpina

Identification

This is a pale green acrocarpous moss with rather wide leaves that taper gradually to a short, usually hyaline hair-point. It is often fertile, and its cylindrical capsules are covered with very large calyptrae, characteristic of the genus. Also like other species of *Encalypta*, the leaves have a distinctive matt, opaque appearance caused by the large dense papillae on the cells. It is distinct from other members of the genus in the gradually tapering leaves with small cells (8–10 μm as against 10–20 μm), the smooth (not ribbed) capsules, and the base of the calyptra lacking a fringe of cilia.

Distribution in Ireland

All the Irish records of *E. alpina* come from two famous botanical localities in Sligo: Benbulbin and Gleniff (1928–2003 at both). It is not clear how many separate colonies have been recorded altogether, but fieldwork in 2003 located two on Benbulbin and one in Gleniff (on the cliffs of Annacoona). All were small, measuring just a few centimetres in diameter.

Ecology and biology

A strong calcicole, all the Irish records are from limestone, the recent ones on boulders and in crevices at the base of N.- or NE-facing cliffs at about 450–500 m, and associated with other montane calcicoles including *Distichium* sp., *Gymnostomum aeruginosum*, *Orthothecium rufescens*, *Trichostomum brachydontium*, *T. crispulum* and *Timmia norvegica*. In Britain, *E. alpina* grows in crevices among limestone rocks, calcareous schist and basalt, at medium to high altitudes.

Capsules are frequent on this autoicous species but no specialised means of vegetative reproduction are known.

World distribution

E. alpina is generally distributed in upland parts of N. Europe as far as the High Arctic, becoming more montane further south, and occurring even in Spain, Italy and Sardinia. It is generally not threatened in European countries, but is listed as *Nationally Scarce* in Britain and *Near Threatened* in Finland. In Europe, it is assigned to a Circumpolar Arctic-montane floristic element. Elsewhere, it grows in Turkey, N. Asia and N. America.

Threats

There are few direct threats, although overstocking with sheep at Annacoona may ultimately be detrimental. Afforestation of the ground below the cliffs would clearly be a disaster for this (and many other) species.

Conservation

All sites for this species are on protected land but should be monitored periodically. A reduction in sheep-grazing at Annacoona would probably be beneficial, but a complete cessation would not.

Protected sites with recent records: Ben Bulben, Gleniff and Glenade Complex SAC; **Unprotected sites with recent records:** none.

Encalypta rhaptocarpa Schwägr.

Ribbed Extinguisher-moss

syn. *Encalypta rhabdocarpa* Schwägr.

Status in Ireland: Critically Endangered (B1a, bi, ii, iv, B2a, bi, ii, iv); **Status in Europe:** Least Concern

Number of Hectads	5
+ Old (pre-1970)	4
☐ Recent (1970–2010)	1

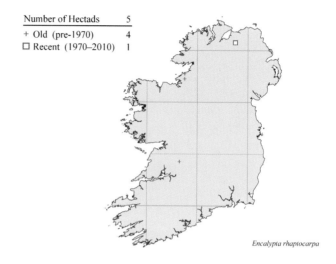

Encalypta rhaptocarpa

Identification

The broad (more or less lingulate-spathulate), opaque green leaves and the large calyptra, covering the entire capsule, immediately identify this acrocarp as a species of *Encalypta*. Shoots can grow up to about 2 cm tall, usually much less; the leaves are up to 2.5 mm long and the excurrent costa sometimes develops into a hyaline hair-point. The capsules are characteristically longitudinally ribbed when moist, with a calyptra that is papillose at the apex, but not fringed at the base (unlike *E. ciliata*).

Distribution in Ireland

There is currently only a single site for this species in Ireland, near the summit of Benbradagh, Londonderry (1999–2008). It has been recorded elsewhere in the past, but the locational details are imprecise: Clare (Scarriff, 1909); W. Mayo (Mallaranny, 1909); Sligo (Benbulbin and Gleniff, 1817–1963) and Leitrim (Largydonnell, 1909). Records from Antrim are unconfirmed.

Ecology and biology

E. rhaptocarpa is a species of base-rich rock crevices at moderate to high altitudes and of calcareous dune slacks. At its only known current site in Ireland, *E. rhaptocarpa* grows on crumbling near-horizontal basalt rock on an open slope near the summit of a hill, at 450 m altitude.

This is an autoicous species in which capsules are produced in abundance. Specialised vegetative reproductive organs are unknown.

World distribution

This species is widespread in N. Europe, particularly in arctic regions, and in montane areas further south. It is listed as *Nationally Scarce* in Britain, *Endangered* in the Czech Republic, *Vulnerable* in Germany and 'sporadic' in Estonia. There are only old records from Albania. In Europe, this species is assigned to a Circumpolar Boreo-arctic montane floristic element. It has a similar distribution in N. America and Asia, and also occurs in the mountains of Morocco and Ethiopia.

Threats

While the site on Benbradagh is probably relatively secure, the small populations must be vulnerable to competition and shading from other plants, or erosion if grazing pressure increases. Most of the dunes at Mallaranny have been developed for a golf course, and *E. rhaptocarpa* has probably been eliminated from this site.

Conservation

E. rhaptocarpa is listed as a Northern Ireland Priority Species. It could not be refound during recent survey work at other sites where it has been recorded previously, but it is possible that it might yet be refound, especially in the extensive limestone outcrops of the Dartry Mountains.

Protected sites with recent records: none; **Unprotected sites with recent records:** Benbradagh (proposed ASSI).

Encalypta vulgaris Hedw.

Status in Ireland: Near Threatened; **Status in Europe:** Least Concern

This lowland calcareous moss is very widely distributed in Ireland and has been reported from 25 vice-counties, with records from 36 hectads (24 old, 9 recent, 3 undated). Although it was not included in the Provisional Red List (Holyoak 2006b), and therefore not sought during recent fieldwork, it may have declined due to habitat loss by removal of old walls and encroachment of coarse vegetation on bare soil due to general nutrient enrichment.

Encalypta ciliata Hedw.

Status in Ireland: Critically Endangered (B1a, bi, ii, iv, B2a, bi, ii, iv); **Status in Europe:** Least Concern

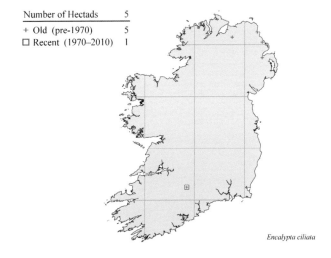

Number of Hectads	5
+ Old (pre-1970)	5
☐ Recent (1970–2010)	1

Encalypta ciliata

Identification

E. ciliata is an acrocarpous moss with broad (lingulate-spathulate), opaque green leaves and a calyptra that covers the entire capsule, a characteristic of the genus. Shoots grow up to 5 cm tall but are usually much less; the leaves are up to 3.5 mm long and lack a hyaline hair-point. The capsules are smooth when moist, not ribbed, and the spores are smooth or ridged, but not papillose. The main feature that distinguishes *E. ciliata* from other species of the genus in Ireland is the fringed base to the calyptra, and (less importantly) its smooth apex.

Distribution in Ireland

This is a very rare species in Ireland, currently known to occur at only one site, on Temple Hill in the Galty Mountains, Limerick, where it was discovered in 1945 and was still present in 2005. Older records are from Antrim (Lurigethan, pre-1879; Agnew's Hill, pre-1879;

Sallagh Braes, 1873–1938; Cave Hill, pre-1825; Squire's Hill, 1895) and Londonderry (Benbradagh, 1834–1950). Of these, only the record from Sallagh Braes is supported by a specimen, although the species is unlikely to be misidentified.

Ecology and biology

This is a moss of base-rich rock crevices at moderate to high altitudes. At its only currently known site in Ireland, *E. ciliata* grows as a patch of scattered shoots in an area of about 8 × 4 cm in a relatively sheltered declivity in a prominent exposed rock pinnacle on mid-altitude slopes (640 m). Associated species include *Ctenidium molluscum*, *Tortella tortuosa*, *Isothecium myosuroides* var. *brachythecioides*, *Bryum capillare*, *Schistidium strictum*, *Anomobryum concinnatum* and *Lejeunea lamacerina*.

Capsules are produced in abundance in this autoicous species. Specialised vegetative reproductive organs are unknown.

World distribution

E. ciliata is frequent in northern parts of Europe, including Fennoscandia and arctic Russia, becoming rarer in the lowlands further south but remaining generally frequent in the mountains. It is listed as *Nationally Scarce* in Britain, *Critically Endangered* in Luxembourg, *Endangered* in Germany, *Vulnerable* in Serbia and Montenegro, *Near Threatened* in the Czech Republic and 'very rare' in Estonia. In Europe, it is assigned to a Circumpolar Boreal-montane floristic element. It has a northern and montane distribution pattern in Asia and N. America and also occurs in Mexico, the West Indies, S. America, Papua New Guinea and the African mountains; it is also reported in Australia (Victoria: Streimann & Klazenga 2002) and New Zealand (Hill *et al.* 1992).

Threats

The single site for this plant in Ireland is on a rock pinnacle that is relatively prominent in the landscape, on steep sheep-grazed slopes. Although apparently fairly secure, it does not currently receive any form of protection (it is just outside the Galtee Mountains SAC), so may be vulnerable to afforestation of the hillside. Any significant nutrient enrichment might encourage the growth of rank vegetation.

Conservation

The site should be monitored regularly to ensure that the rock pinnacle remains more or less undisturbed. Consideration should be given to extending the boundary of the Galtee Mountains SAC, specifically to include the habitat for this species. Particular vigilance will be necessary to be on the alert for any forestry proposals.

Protected sites with recent records: none; **Unprotected sites with recent records:** Temple Hill, Galty Mountains (just outside Galtee Mountains SAC).

Entosthodon muhlenbergii (Turner) Fife　　　　　　Muhlenberg's Cord-moss

syn. *Funaria muhlenbergii* Turner, *F. calcarea* Wahlenb., *F. hibernica* Hook. in Curtis, *F. mediterranea* Lindb.
Status in Ireland: Regionally Extinct; **Status in Europe:** Least Concern

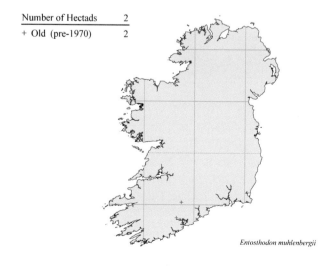

Number of Hectads	2
+ Old (pre-1970)	2

Entosthodon muhlenbergii

Identification

An acrocarpous moss that grows as small yellowish-green patches or tufts, with stems up to 5 mm high. Leaves are obovate to oblanceolate, abruptly narrowed to long fine apices, with the costa ending in or near apex, and bluntly dentate margins. Leaf cells are large and lax as in other Funariaceae. The capsules are exserted on a seta 7–11 mm long, inclined, pyriform, gibbous and asymmetrical with an oblique mouth.

It differs from the common *Funaria hygrometrica* in having the seta straight when moist (not arcuate) and the capsule smooth when dry and empty (not sulcate). *Entosthodon pulchellus* is a much more similar species that occurs in Britain but is unrecorded in Ireland, differing in having entire leaf margins and spores that are more finely papillose.

Distribution in Ireland

The only confirmed records are from two sites and very old: Mid Cork (Blarney, leg. T. Drummond, pre-1836) and E. Cork (Glanworth near Fermoy, leg. I. Carroll, 1852). Three other old records have not been checked because no specimens have been located, but they are likely to have been of *E. muhlenbergii* or *E. pulchellus*: W. Cork (unlocalised) and Antrim (at Belfast Deerpark, leg. Moore and at Carrick-a-rede, leg. Dixon, both reported by Megaw 1938). There are two other reports which were based on misidentified specimens from Londonderry (Magilligan, 1904; Macosquin near Coleraine, 1950).

Ecology and biology

A specimen from near Blarney grew 'on chalky soil'. In Britain, it is a lowland calcicole that occurs on mainly bare, free-draining soil in open sites among rocks, in turf, on anthills, or on thinly earth-covered rocks.

The plants are short-lived, apparently growing from spores each year as annuals. The species is autoicous and capsules are common, maturing in May. Tubers and gemmae are unknown.

World distribution

Scarce in England and Wales (extinct in C. Scotland) and scattered in Europe from S. Scandinavia southwards to the Mediterranean and eastwards to Hungary. It is listed as *Extinct* in Norway, *Critically Endangered* in the Czech Republic and Switzerland, *Endangered* in Germany, *Vulnerable* in Spain and *Near Threatened* in Sweden. It is assigned to a Suboceanic Mediterranean-Atlantic floristic element in Europe. Elsewhere, it is reported from Macaronesia, N. Africa, SW Asia, Caucasus, western N. America (Alaska to California and Texas), Mexico and C. America.

Threats

Reasons for the apparent extinction of the species in Ireland are unknown.

Conservation

No action is proposed.

Protected sites with recent records: none; **Unprotected sites with recent records:** none.

Entosthodon muhlenbergii, Humphrey Head, Cumbria, England.

Entosthodon fascicularis (Hedw.) Müll.Hal.

Hasselquist's Hyssop

syn. *Funaria fascicularis* (Hedw.) Lindb.
Status in Ireland: Near Threatened; **Status in Europe:** Least Concern

This acrocarpous moss is characteristic of lowland tillage (arable) fields, especially of wheat and barley stubbles on rather damp circumneutral to somewhat acidic loamy soils. It has been reported from 17 vice-counties, with records from 42 hectads (24 old, 20 recent). *E. fascicularis* has undoubtedly declined greatly since the 19th century in western counties of Ireland, as tillage has been abandoned over large areas. Nevertheless, the species still appears to be locally frequent in the districts of eastern Ireland with extensive tillage; individual stubble fields can support large populations. It has been somewhat under-recorded in recent decades, partly because it is only identifiable in a short season when capsules approach maturity (mainly March to May) and partly because study of bryophytes in tillage fields has been somewhat neglected compared to other habitats. The 14 records of it made from 2004–2009 reflect deliberate efforts to record bryophytes on arable fields.

Physcomitrium sphaericum (C.F.Ludw. ex Schkuhr) Brid.

Dwarf Bladder-moss

Status in Ireland: Vulnerable (D2); **Status in Europe:** Rare

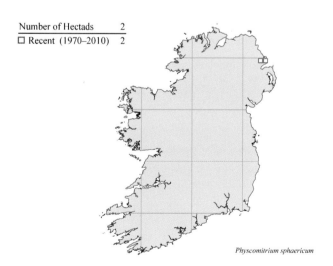

Number of Hectads	2
☐ Recent (1970–2010)	2

Physcomitrium sphaericum

Identification

P. sphaericum is a small acrocarpous moss that grows as scattered plants or small tufts, or forms rather sparse green turfs, with stems up to 5 mm high. Leaves are erecto-patent to patent, concave, ovate to ovate-lanceolate and acute to obtuse. The leaf margin is plane and entire or slightly crenulate above, the costa weak and evanescent. As in other Funariaceae, the leaf cells are smooth and rather large and lax, those in mid-leaf being quadrate to isodiametric, 12–30 *μ*m wide, narrower and rectangular at margins; lower leaf cells are rectangular. The capsule is globose, often turbinate when empty, with a mamillate operculum, held erect on a reddish seta that is usually 1–2 mm long.

Distribution in Ireland

There are two records, both from Antrim in August 1999, at Copeland Reservoir and North Woodburn Reservoir. It was not found on margins of several other reservoirs in Northern Ireland during the same month or on surveys in subsequent years.

Ecology and biology

In Antrim, it was found in the inundation zones of two reservoirs, on damp mud exposed by low water levels. Both populations grew among sparse herbs (*Juncus bufonius, Rorippa palustris, Persicaria maculosa, P. hydropiper, Gnaphalium uliginosum*) on open, humic silty-clay in a zone towards the lower edge of the phanerogam cover. *Riccia cavernosa* was also present. In Britain, the species occurs in similar habitats, on mud exposed on the margins of lakes and reservoirs and on the beds of dried-up ponds.

Observations in Britain show the plants are annual and that they can develop only after periods of drought or when the water has been artificially drained, surviving meanwhile as spores in the submerged mud (Furness & Hall 1981). It is an autoicous species that produces abundant capsules, maturing in autumn and winter. Gemmae, bulbils and tubers are unknown.

World distribution

P. sphaericum occurs in Europe from C. Scotland, S. Sweden (formerly rare, now apparently extinct), Denmark and S. Finland (rare) southwards to France, Switzerland, Austria and the Ukraine (reports from Spain are erroneous). It is listed as *Extinct* in Finland, Sweden and Switzerland, *Vulnerable* in the Czech Republic, Germany, Luxembourg and Serbia, *Near Threatened* in Britain, *Data Deficient* in Spain and 'very rare' in the Netherlands. It is assigned to a Eurasian Temperate floristic element in Europe. Elsewhere, it is known in SW Asia (Georgia, Azerbaijan and Kyrgyzstan: Ignatov *et al.* 2007), NW, NE and C. Asia (W. and S. Siberia and Russian Far East: Ignatov *et al.* 2007), India, China (Gao Chien *et al.* 2003) and Japan.

Threats

Survival of the species depends directly on low water levels that expose substantial areas of mud for periods of at least several months. Although such exposure need not be annual, it probably must occur at least every few years. The main threat is therefore from maintenance of high water levels in reservoirs (e.g. to benefit angling or water-sport interests or for water supply purposes). It might also be at risk if reservoir water becomes eutrophic or other pollution occurs.

Conservation

Both populations are on protected land. Other rare bryophytes, including *Ephemerum spinulosum*, occur at both localities and need similar habitat conditions. *P. sphaericum* is listed as a Northern Ireland Priority Species.

Protected sites with recent records: Copeland Reservoir ASSI; North Woodburn Reservoir ASSI; **Unprotected sites with recent records:** none.

Physcomitrium sphaericum, Earnsdale Reservoir, Lancashire, England.

Aphanorrhegma patens (Hedw.) Lindb.

syn. *Aphanorhegma patens* auct., *Physcomitrella patens* (Hedw.) Bruch & Schimp.,
Physcomitrium patens (Hedw.) Mitt.
Status in Ireland: Least Concern; **Status in Europe:** Least Concern

A small acrocarpous moss with cleistocarpous capsules that grows on drying mud of pools, river edges, turloughs and lakes. It was included in the Provisional Red List (Holyoak 2006b), but numerous additional localities have been found over the past decade. It has now been reported from 22 vice-counties, with records from 38 hectads (9 old, 32 recent). There is very little evidence that the species has declined.

Discelium nudum (Dicks.) Brid.

syn. *Grimmia nuda* (Dicks.) Turner
Status in Ireland: Near Threatened; **Status in Europe:** Regionally Threatened

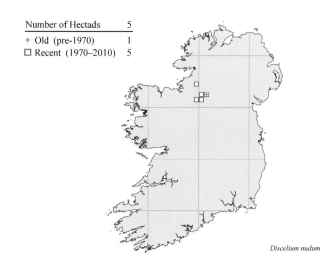

Number of Hectads	5
+ Old (pre-1970)	1
□ Recent (1970–2010)	5

Discelium nudum

Identification

A peculiar acrocarpous moss that is inconspicuous except when sporophytes develop. Its persistent protonema forms very low green mats that are often pure and sometimes extend over several square metres. The female gametophores which arise from it are minute (< 1 mm) and bud-like, with ovate to lanceolate, acute leaves that mainly lack chlorophyll, with costa almost absent and large lax, rhomboid-hexagonal cells, narrower at leaf margins. Capsules are subglobose, almost horizontal, long-exserted on a seta typically 15–25 mm long that becomes pale red as the capsules mature. The whitish remains of the calyptra often persist on the seta beneath the capsule like a small flag. Male gametophores consist of a pinhead-sized cluster of orange-red to red antheridia surrounded by 3–6 tiny leaves.

Distribution in Ireland

Known from nine localities in three vice-counties: Leitrim (E. slope of Bencroy, 2001; NW slope of Slieve Anierin, 2001; W. slope of Slieve Anierin, 2001; SE of Slievenakilla, 2001; S. shore of Lough Allen at Bellantra Bridge, 2001; Dough Mountain, 2005), Cavan (W. of Bellavally Gap, 1961–2001; W. slope of Cuilcagh, 2001) and Fermanagh (Altscraghy on NE slope of Cuilcagh, 2002). A record from near Belfast by R. Brown, presumably from the closing years of the 18th century, was regarded as dubious by Lett (1915).

Ecology and biology

This species is apparently restricted to a hilly district in north-western central Ireland where Carboniferous clays and shales outcrop. All records are from steep to vertical banks of clay or shaly clay, mainly incised stream banks, but also a ditch bank and beside a lake, at c. 57–480 m altitude. It grows in a damp zone rather low on the banks, mainly below the *Pogonatum aloides* usually present nearby, and only c. 30 cm above water level at the edge of Lough Allen. Most British records are from similar habitats, but others include clayey banks of china-clay spoil, clay in a brickworks and dried up reservoir margins.

The long-lived protonemata are apparently perennial (as stated by W.B. Schofield in FNA 2007), persisting as long as the clay surfaces on which they grow remain intact. However, the British study by Duckett & Pressel (2003) argued that '*Discelium* is most abundant where there is annual exfoliation of the surface layer of clay due to frost action in the winter months'; this process seems unlikely to occur regularly at the Irish localities. The species is pseudo-dioicous (male and female gametophores arise from the same protonema) and capsules are abundant, maturing in spring. The protonema produces a sward of unicellular, colourless, starch-filled rhizoidal tubers c. 1 cm below the clay surface. Duckett & Pressel (*op. cit.*) argue that these short-lived and desiccation-intolerant diaspores are exposed on new clay surfaces following winter exfoliation of the original substratum. Other propagules such as bulbils and protonemal gemmae are lacking.

World distribution

Widespread in N. Europe from N. Norway, N. Sweden, N. Finland and N. Russia southwards to N. France, C. and SE Germany and Poland; locally frequent in NW England, C. and N. Sweden and S. Finland but mainly rare elsewhere, and listed as *Critically Endangered* in the Czech Republic, *Endangered* in Luxembourg, *Vulnerable* in Germany, *Data Deficient* in Spain, 'very rare' in Estonia and 'declining' in Norway. It is assigned to a Circumpolar Boreal-montane floristic element in Europe. Elsewhere, it is known in Siberia (widespread: Ignatov *et al.* 2007) and N. America (in east from Quebec to Illinois; in west from the Northwest Territories to California).

Threats

No immediate threats were apparent at the Irish sites. The periodic collapse of a section of stream bank doubtless leads to loss of plants, but simultaneously creates new habitat for recolonisation. Several of its sites are in areas grazed by sheep, which tend to prevent vegetation succession that might shade the plants, as do the rather low nutrient content of the substrata and stream action. Deliberate afforestation should be avoided around the known localities.

Conservation

Several sites are on protected land.

Protected sites with recent records: Cuilcagh-Anierin Uplands SAC; Dough/Thur Mountains NHA; **Unprotected sites with recent records:** Altscraghy on NE slope of Cuilcagh; S. shore of Lough Allen at Bellantra Bridge; SE of Slievenakilla.

Altscraghy, Cuilcagh, Co. Fermanagh.

Schistidium platyphyllum, Ardtully Bridge, Co. Kerry.

Schistidium platyphyllum (Mitt.) H.Perss.

Broadleaf Grimmia

syn. *Grimmia apocarpa* var. *alpicola* auct. non (Hedw.) Röhl., *S. alpicola* auct. non (Hedw.) Limpr.,
S. latifolium (J.E.Zetterst.) Weim., *S. rivulare* subsp. *latifolium* (J.E.Zetterst.), B.Bremer
Status in Ireland: Vulnerable (B2a, bii, iii, iv); **Status in Europe:** Least Concern

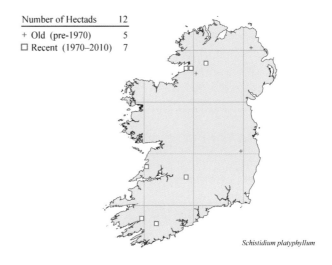

Number of Hectads	12
+ Old (pre-1970)	5
☐ Recent (1970–2010)	7

Schistidium platyphyllum

Identification

This is an acrocarpous moss that grows in dark green tufts or cushions with rather sparsely branched stems 5–40 mm long. The leaves are broadly ovate to ovate-lanceolate, acute to subobtuse, with costa evanescent to percurrent and margins recurved and entire or bluntly toothed towards the apex. Mid-leaf cells are quadrate, not or scarcely sinuose, bistratose towards the apex and at the leaf margins. Capsules are immersed, subglobose, hemispherical when empty, with thin-walled exothecial cells and bright red exostome teeth. Spores measure 16–20 μm. *S. platyphyllum* has often been confused with the more common *S. rivulare* by British workers prior to the revision by Orange (1995), who treated them as subspecies. *S. platyphyllum* differs in usually growing in shorter tufts rather than trailing as wefts, having broader, non-secund leaves, often with a weaker costa, the perichaetial bracts not or scarcely overtopping the capsule and the thin-walled exothecial cells.

Distribution in Ireland

Recent records are from seven localities in six vice-counties: S. Kerry (Ardtully E. of Cloontoo, 2006; also somewhere in same region in 1979); W. Cork (Lough Allua east, 2009); Limerick (Bilboa River, 1991); Clare (Annageeragh Bridge, 2008); E. Donegal (Assaroe Lake near Ballyshannon, 2005; Raheen, 2005) and Tyrone

(Carrickaness Bridge W. of Drumquin, 2002). Five older records are based on specimens that have been checked: Kildare (below Ballymore Eustace, 1957); Sligo (Dromore West, undated but probably during 1960s); Fermanagh (Correl Glen, 1960); Antrim (near Broughshane, 1887) and Londonderry (Downhill, 1939).

Ecology and biology

It grows on limestone rock near water, usually where it is unshaded or lightly shaded and within the inundation zone beside rivers (and a lake) in the lowlands. In Britain, it appears to be restricted to rivers which have base-rich water and is locally frequent growing on calcareous rock in some limestone areas.

Tufts of the species are likely to live for several years, but details are unknown. The plants are autoicous and capsules are common, maturing in spring. Gemmae and tubers are unknown.

World distribution

Recorded in N. and C. Europe, in Svalbard, Fennoscandia, Britain, NW Germany (Meinunger & Schröder 2007) and the Alps. It is listed as *Data Deficient* in Germany and Switzerland. In Europe, it is assigned to a Circumpolar Boreo-arctic montane floristic element. Elsewhere, it is recorded from Siberia, Altai, Tien Shan, Dzhungarskiy Alatau, northern N. America and

Greenland by H.H. Blom (in Nyholm 1998). However, T.T. McIntosh (in FNA 2007) treats N. American material as synonymous with *S. rivulare* because he found morphological differences to be inconsistent.

Threats
The population below Ballymore Eustace (Kildare) has probably been lost due to regulation of river flows following construction of a large reservoir just upstream. The population at Correl Glen (Fermanagh) may have been lost due to increased shading of the river from adjoining woodland. Potential threats to other populations may arise from alteration of flow regimes, eutrophication or other water pollution or afforestation.

Conservation
S. platyphyllum is listed as a Northern Ireland Priority Species.

Protected sites with recent records: Lough Allua pNHA; Lower River Shannon SAC; **Unprotected sites with recent records:** Annageeragh Bridge; Ardtully E. of Cloontoo; Assaroe Lake near Ballyshannon; Carrickaness Bridge W. of Drumquin; Raheen.

Schistidium agassizii Sull. & Lesq.   Water Grimmia

syn. *Grimmia agassizii* (Sull. & Lesq.) A.Jaeger
Status in Ireland: Vulnerable (D2); **Status in Europe:** Least Concern

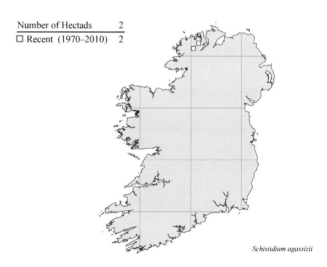

Number of Hectads	2
☐ Recent (1970–2010)	2

Schistidium agassizii

Identification
One of several aquatic *Schistidium* species, *S. agassizii* is an acrocarpous moss that forms small brownish cushions or trailing tufts less than 5 cm high. The leaves are more or less parallel-sided and rather bluntly pointed, with a plane margin, and the capsule, which, like all capsules of *Schistidium*, is immersed and has a characteristic shape when dry and empty, being narrow at the base and very wide-mouthed. *S. rivulare* and *S. platyphyllum*, both also aquatic, have hemispherical capsules and recurved leaf margins, and tend to be dark green rather than brownish with wider leaves.

Distribution in Ireland
There are only two known sites for this species in Ireland, both in W. Donegal: by the Lackagh River near Glen Lough (1998–2002) and at the north end of Gartan Lough (2002). It is possible that it may be more widespread but overlooked.

Ecology and biology
This plant grows on rocks that are more or less submerged or subject to flooding in fast-flowing rivers and streams at medium altitudes, often but not always on base-rich substrata. In Scotland, it has also been recorded on boulders in seasonally-flooded hollows at high altitude. It is, however, a lowland plant in Ireland, where it has been found at altitudes between 18–70 m, on unshaded granitic rocks 5–20 cm above the water level at the edge of a fast-flowing river; with *Racomitrium aciculare* and the lichens *Ephebe lanata* and *Dermatocarpon intestiniforme*; and also on the sloping surface of a

schistose boulder at the edge of a lake, c. 1 m above the water level.

An autoicous species, sporophytes are fairly frequent on *S. agassizii* but there is no specialised form of vegetative reproduction.

World distribution

This plant is widespread in N., W. and C. Europe. Until recently considered *Near Threatened* in Britain, *S. agassizii* has recently been 'downgraded' to *Nationally Scarce*, because of additional recent records and the realisation that it had been substantially overlooked in the past. It is listed as *Vulnerable* in Switzerland, Austria and Montenegro, and 'very rare' in Estonia. In Europe, it is classified as a European Boreal-montane floristic element. Elsewhere, it occurs in N. Asia, N. America and Greenland.

Threats

As with other aquatic species, the main potential threats are water pollution, water abstraction, changes to river channels and inappropriate riverbank management.

Conservation

The two known populations of this moss should be monitored, and local river managers made aware of its presence. Survey work in other river systems and lake shores nearby might reveal further populations.

Protected sites with recent records: Cloghernagore Bog and Glenveagh National Park SAC; Leannan River SAC; **Unprotected sites with recent records:** none.

Schistidium trichodon (Brid.) Poelt

Stook Grimmia

syn. *Grimmia trichodon* Brid.
Status in Ireland: Vulnerable (D2); **Status in Europe:** Insufficiently Known

Number of Hectads	2
☐ Recent (1970–2010)	2

Schistidium trichodon

Identification

An acrocarpous moss that forms tufts or more extensive smooth mats that are characteristically black or blackish, sometimes with green shoot tips, the rather sparsely branched stems being 2–8 cm long, rarely 12 cm. The leaves are imbricate, somewhat recurved, sharply keeled, ovate-lanceolate, acuminate and sometimes ending in a very short hair-point (up to 0.18 mm) that is spinulose-denticulate, the overall leaf length being mostly 1.7–2.6 mm. Leaf margins are irregularly denticulate near the apex, bistratose for one cell row and narrowly recurved over much of the leaf length; the costa is rather weak and percurrent to shortly excurrent. Mid-leaf cells are unistratose, smooth, rounded or shortly oblong and 8–10 µm wide; basal cells are larger and rectangular. The capsule is cylindric to short cylindric, small, reddish, with peristome teeth forming a characteristic dome above the urn mouth and a persistent columella; the capsules are erect and shallowly immersed to emergent, on a seta 0.25–0.6 mm long. *S. trichodon* differs from other members of the taxonomically difficult *Schistidium apocarpum* complex in the domed peristome and persistent columella. It is much harder to detect and identify when fresh mature capsules are lacking, since blackish gametophytes with short hair-points also occur in the more common species of the group. Irish plants of *S. trichodon* are referable to var. *trichodon*.

Distribution in Ireland
There are two records from two vice-counties: Leitrim (S. of Aghadunvane, 2005) and Fermanagh (near Glencreawan Lough, 2005). Both sites were discovered by S.D.S. Bosanquet during a BBS Meeting. The species is likely to have been overlooked among other members of the *S. apocarpum* complex elsewhere in limestone regions, particularly in the Dartry Mountains.

Ecology and biology
At Glencreawan Lough, a few patches were found on open, flat, horizontal limestone outcrops close to a lake shore. South of Aghadunvane, it grew on sloping surfaces of a few limestone blocks in grassland below a N.-facing crag at c. 400 m altitude. In Scandinavia (Blom 1996), it grows on calcareous rocks, most often limestone and dolomite, but also schists, phyllites and greenstones, also occurring locally and in small amounts on wall tops in coastal areas of Norway. Scandinavian plants were characterised as shade-tolerant mesophytes, typical of partly moss-covered boulders and outcrops in closed or open forests.

The plants are perennial. It is an autoicous species in which capsules are common, varying from abundant to sparse on individual patches, apparently maturing in summer in Ireland ('winter' in Smith 1978 may be erroneous; McIntosh in FNA 2007 gives late spring to early summer). Gemmae, bulbils and tubers are absent.

World distribution
In Europe, *S. trichodon* var. *trichodon* is widespread in Norway and the Alps, more local in Sweden, Finland, Scotland, NW England, the Ardennes, Carpathians and Crimea. It is listed as *Critically Endangered* in Luxembourg and *Data Deficient* in Germany. The species as a whole is assigned to a European Boreal-montane floristic element in Europe. Elsewhere, var. *trichodon* occurs in SW Asia (Armenia, Georgia, Kyrgyzstan), NW India, China (Xinjiang, Yunnan, Taiwan: Gao Chien *et al.* 2003), Japan and N. America (Alaska and Newfoundland southwards to Colorado). Var. *nutans* H.H. Blom occurs in Fennoscandia, C. Europe, the Crimea, SW, C. and E. Asia and N. America; it is scarcer than var. *trichodon* over much of this range (Blom 1996).

Threats
No threats were apparent at either locality in 2005. Both populations were rather small and hence potentially vulnerable to shading by other bryophytes or accidental damage.

Conservation
Both sites are on protected land. *S. trichodon* is listed as a Northern Ireland Priority Species.

Protected sites with recent records: Arroo Mountain SAC; Cliffs of Magho ASSI; **Unprotected sites with recent records:** none.

Schistidium pruinosum (Wilson ex Schimp.) G.Roth
Mealy Grimmia

syn. *Grimmia conferta* var. *pruinosa* (Wilson) Braithw.
Status in Ireland: Data Deficient; **Status in Europe:** Insufficiently Known

Identification
An acrocarpous moss that forms dense, dull rather than glossy, olive green to rust-coloured tufts or cushions with branched stems mainly 15–30 mm long, sometimes 45 mm. The leaves are erect, imbricate, oblong, ovate-triangular or elliptical, keeled, acute, with a coarse, toothed hair-point 0.2–1.25 mm long, the overall leaf length being mainly in the range 2.1–2.9 mm. The leaf margins are smooth and usually recurved almost throughout the length of the leaf; the costa is stout, excurrent, its dorsal side only slightly convex and densely papillose. Mid-leaf cells are irregularly bistratose or unistratose with bistratose patches, oval to rounded or shortly oblong, 6–9 μm wide, densely papillose with low broad papillae. Basal cells are larger, oblong, 7–11 μm wide. The perichaetial bracts are large and conspicuously broader than the stem leaves. The capsule is broadly oblong, dark red to red-brown with a characteristic

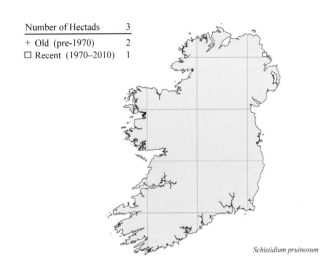

Number of Hectads	3
+ Old (pre-1970)	2
□ Recent (1970–2010)	1

Schistidium pruinosum

'mother-of-pearl shine', erect, deeply immersed among the perichaetial bracts on a seta mainly 0.2–0.4 mm long. *S. pruinosum* differs from *S. strictum* and other *Schistidium* species having a papillose leaf lamina in the small lamina cells that are irregularly bistratose.

Distribution in Ireland

Records are accepted from four localities, all in Antrim: Cave Hill, Belfast, 1890–1953; Collinwood (or Collinward?), 1923; Bellevue Gardens, Belfast, 1928; Knock Dhu, 2008. Two other old reports from Antrim remain unconfirmed. Lett (1915) listed *Grimmia conferta* var. *pruinosa* also for Clare, Down and Londonderry, but the original specimens need to be reidentified. Although *S. pruinosum* has only one recent record, studies of this difficult genus in Northern Ireland have been very incomplete and the species is therefore likely still to occur within its former range.

Ecology and biology

At Knock Dhu, it grows on near-vertical basalt at the base of a low NNE-facing crag at c. 305 m altitude. Records from Cave Hill were from 'basalt cliffs' and 'the weathered basalt surfaces on the hillside'. At Collinwood, it was collected from 'rotten rock'. In Scandinavia, the species grows on both calcareous and siliceous rocks, typically in warm sunny cliff and boulder sites but occasionally in open woodland or on coastal cliffs; it also seems to be common in the basalt areas of Scotland (Blom 1996).

The plants are perennial. It is an autoicous species in which capsules are commonly present, usually abundant, apparently maturing in late spring or summer. Gemmae, bulbils and tubers are absent.

World distribution

S. pruinosum is widespread but generally rather rare and patchily distributed in Europe from Scotland, C. Norway and C. Sweden southwards to N. Spain (in the Pyrenees and Basque Mountains), N. Italy, Bulgaria (Rila Mountains) and the Russian Caucasus, with an isolated record from the S. Urals (Blom 1996, Casas *et al.* 2006, Ignatov *et al.* 2007). It is listed as *Endangered* in Luxembourg, *Near Threatened* in Britain and the Czech Republic and *Data Deficient* in Andorra. It is assigned to a European Temperate floristic element in Europe. Elsewhere, it occurs only in SW Asia (Turkey, Georgia and Armenia: Blom 1996, Ignatov *et al.* 2007).

Threats

No information is available.

Conservation

The old localities near Belfast should be searched thoroughly for this species, preferably in late spring or early summer when its capsules should be in good condition.

Protected sites with recent records: none; **Unprotected sites with recent records:** Knock Dhu (proposed ASSI).

Schistidium strictum (Turner) Loeske ex Mårtensson — Upright Brown Grimmia

Status in Ireland: Near Threatened; **Status in Europe:** Least Concern

This is a rather straggling rusty-orange coloured moss of base-rich rocks and is scattered more or less throughout Ireland, mostly in upland areas. It has been reported from 15 vice-counties, with records from 29 hectads (14 old, 16 recent). Although it was not included in the Provisional Red List (Holyoak 2006b), and therefore not especially looked for during recent survey work, several new populations have been found since 2006. However, its distribution is rather patchy and in some areas, such as the Dartry Mountains, it has not been seen since the 1960s.

Schistidium robustum (Nees & Hornsch.) H.H.Blom — Robust Grimmia

syn. *Grimmia apocarpa* var. *homodictyon* (Dixon) Crundw., *G. homodictyon* Dixon, *S. apocarpum* var. *homodictyon* (Dixon) Crundw. & Nyholm

Status in Ireland: Data Deficient; **Status in Europe:** Not Evaluated

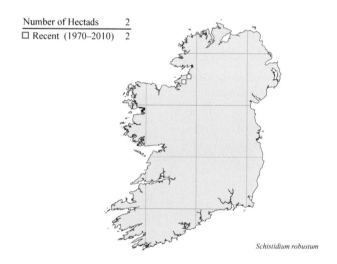

Number of Hectads	2
□ Recent (1970–2010)	2

Schistidium robustum

Identification

An acrocarpous moss that grows as olivaceous to light brown tufts (cushions) with nearly unbranched to much-branched stems 10–30 mm long, occasionally 50 mm. The leaves are erect to erecto-patent, imbricate, sharply keeled above, ovate-lanceolate to ovate-triangular, acute, terminating in a coarse and mostly conspicuous decurrent hair-point typically 0.4–0.8 mm long, the overall leaf length mostly being 1.9–2.5 mm. Leaf margins are narrowly and strongly recurved over much of the leaf length; the costa is smooth and usually excurrent. The mid-leaf cells are usually unistratose, with a mixture of shortly oblong and isodiametric, thick-walled cells that are mainly 9–11 μm wide. In central and lower parts of the leaf, the cell walls are conspicuously sinuose and white or pale yellowish; basal cells are larger and rectangular. Perichaetial bracts are long and narrow. The capsule is narrowly oblong, usually light brown, erect and immersed, on a seta usually 0.4–0.6 mm long. Although *S. robustum* has been known for many years in Britain (as *S. apocarpum* var. *homodictyon*) it was often misidentified until the taxonomic revision by Blom (1996) described several related species of the taxonomically difficult *Schistidium apocarpum* complex. Distinction from other taxa in this group requires careful microscopic study of leaf and capsule characters (Blom 1996, Blom in Nyholm 1998).

Distribution in Ireland

There are two recent records from two vice-counties: Sligo (Benwiskin, 2003) and Leitrim (S. of Aghadunvane, 2005). Since the taxonomic revision by Blom (1996), the *Schistidium apocarpum* group has remained under-recorded in Ireland. Hence, further fieldwork may well produce more records of *S. robustum*, especially in the Dartry Mountains.

Ecology and biology

The Benwiskin record was from a boulder in well-vegetated limestone boulder scree on a steep NW-facing slope at c. 250 m altitude. In Leitrim, it was also on limestone scree and blocks below mainly N.-facing crags at c. 400 m altitude. In Scandinavia, it is a pioneer species on dry or periodically moist calcareous rocks and walls, with most records from limestone and dolomite but some from phyllite, greenstone and conglomerate; it grows both on exposed rocks, including sea cliffs, and semi-shaded in forests (Blom 1996).

The plants are perennial. It is an autoicous species in which capsules are very common, apparently maturing late spring to early summer (as in N. America: McIntosh in FNA 2007). Gemmae, bulbils and tubers are lacking.

World distribution

Widespread in W. and C. Europe, from N. Norway, N. Sweden and C. Finland southwards to the mountains of N. Spain, N. Italy, Croatia, Greece (Mount Olympus), the Crimea and the Russian Caucasus (listed as *Critically Endangered* in Luxembourg). It is assigned to a European Boreal-montane floristic element in Europe. Elsewhere, it is known in SW Asia (Georgia) and northern N. America (Yukon and Newfoundland southwards to S. Dakota: McIntosh in FNA 2007).

Threats

Neither population appears to be threatened.

Conservation

Both localities are on protected land. It is likely that more populations will be found in Ireland.

Protected sites with recent records: Arroo Mountain SAC; Ben Bulben, Gleniff and Glenade Complex SAC; **Unprotected sites with recent records:** none.

Schistidium confertum (Funck) Bruch & Schimp.   Compact Grimmia

syn. *Grimmia conferta* Funck, *S. apocarpum* var. *confertum* (Funck) H.Möller, *S. canariense* H.Winter
Status in Ireland: Data Deficient; **Status in Europe:** Least Concern

Identification

A small acrocarpous moss that grows as small tight tufts (cushions) of a characteristic olivaceous colour (sometimes greenish or yellowish-brown) with a greasy lustre, the branched stems being 3–15 mm long, rarely 20 mm. The leaves are erect and closely imbricate, shortly ovate-lanceolate to ovate or triangular, acute, sharply keeled above and obtusely keeled below, 1.0–1.8 mm long, with a short hair-point that is flattened and sharply and strongly spinulose-denticulate. The leaf margins are smooth, narrowly recurved on much of one side of the leaf but plane to shortly recurved on the other side. The costa is smooth, very strongly convex in the upper half of the leaf and evanescent to excurrent. The lamina in the upper part of the leaf is unistratose to irregularly bistratose, composed of smooth isodiametric cells 5.5–8.5 μm wide. The basal marginal cells form a rectangular alar group of 2–8 rows of square to shortly rectangular cells with thickened cross walls. The capsule is ovoid, obovoid or oblong, erect, immersed among the perichaetial bracts on a seta 0.1–0.3 mm long. *S. confertum* is a member of the taxonomically difficult

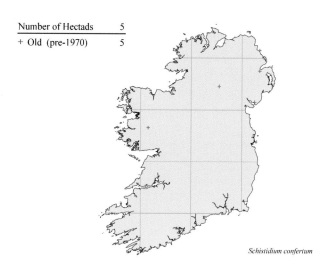

Schistidium confertum

Schistidium apocarpum complex, in which identification requires critical appraisal of several leaf characters (see above) and sporophyte characters (which include its capsule shape, thick-walled exothecial cells and strongly perforated peristome teeth).

Distribution in Ireland
Records are accepted from five localities in four vice-counties: E. Mayo (near Lough Mask, 1910); Louth (Greenore, 1912); Monaghan ('Eskmore', 1910) and Antrim (Bellair Hill, Carnlough, 1910; Cave Hill, Belfast, 1928). The Bellair Hill record has hitherto been assigned to Down in error (there are no confirmed records from H38). Several other reports from Northern Ireland remain unconfirmed.

Ecology and biology
Two Irish specimens confirmed by H.H. Blom were collected from basalt and limestone rocks (i.e. hard chalk), the latter apparently being unusual for this species. Blom (1996) describes it as a moss of dry, more or less exposed, siliceous rocks; granite being the most common substratum both in Europe and N. America, but others frequently recorded were diabase, basalt, gneiss and schist, with American records also from sandstone and quartzite.

The plants are perennial. It is an autoicous species in which capsules are common or abundant, probably maturing in late spring to early summer (as in N. America: T.T. McIntosh in FNA 2007; 'winter' noted by Smith 1978 is probably incorrect or at least atypical). Gemmae, bulbils and tubers are absent.

World distribution
The European range extends from Iceland, Scotland, S. Norway and S. Sweden to C. and S. Spain (including Sierra Nevada), Sicily and the Crimea (Blom 1996, Casas *et al.* 2006, Ignatov *et al.* 2007), and it is listed as *Vulnerable* in the Czech Republic and Luxembourg, *Near Threatened* in Bulgaria, *Data Deficient* in Switzerland and 'declining' in Norway. It is assigned to a European Temperate floristic element in Europe. Elsewhere, the species is known in Cyprus, SW Asia (Turkey to Azerbaijan), Kashmir, Tibet, N. America (Alaska to California and Colorado; also Michigan: T.T. McIntosh in FNA 2007) and S. Greenland. Reports from N. Asia (Siberia, Yakutia, Russian Far East) are regarded as doubtful (Ignatov *et al.* 2007).

Threats
S. confertum was last collected in Ireland in 1928 and has not been refound on visits to several of its (imprecisely localised) sites over the past decade. Much of the possible habitat at Bellair Hill was found to be shaded by scrub when surveyed in 2008. Nevertheless, more attention to this taxonomically critical genus is likely to result in the species being refound in Ireland.

Conservation
No action is proposed.

Protected sites with recent records: none; **Unprotected sites with recent records:** none.

Schistidium elegantulum H.H.Blom **subsp.** *elegantulum*

Status in Ireland: Data Deficient; **Status in Europe:** Not Evaluated

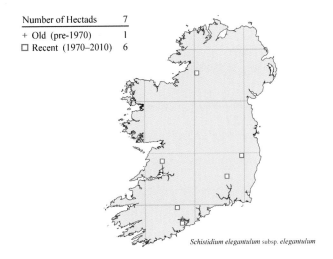

Number of Hectads	7
+ Old (pre-1970)	1
☐ Recent (1970–2010)	6

Schistidium elegantulum subsp. *elegantulum*

Identification

A medium-sized acrocarpous moss that grows as olivaceous or occasionally blackish mats or decumbent tufts, with irregularly branched stems mainly 15–31 mm long. The leaves are erect and densely imbricate, sharply keeled, ovate-lanceolate, acuminate with a fine, narrow, terete, spinulose hair-point, the overall leaf length being 2.25–3.0 mm. The leaf margins are smooth, usually narrowly recurved in lower half of leaf length on one side of leaf and less recurved on the other side; the costa is smooth and excurrent or percurrent, 3-stratose in upper part of leaf, 4–5 stratose in lower part. Cells in mid-leaf are unistratose with bistratose patches or streaks, predominantly isodiametric and 8–10 μm wide. Basal leaf cells are larger, rectangular and 11–16 μm wide. The capsule is oblong, straw-yellow, light orange or light orange-brown, with predominantly oblong exothecial cells, 6–8 stomata on each urn, an orange or orange-red peristome, held erect and immersed among the perichaetial bracts on a seta 0.25–0.5 mm long. *S. elegantulum* is a member of the taxonomically difficult *Schistidium apocarpum* complex. Distinction from other taxa in this group requires careful microscopic study of leaf and capsule characters (Blom 1996, Blom in Nyholm 1998).

Distribution in Ireland

Recent records are from seven localities in six vice-counties: Mid Cork (Carrigaline, 2006; Ringaskiddy, 2006); E. Cork (Bridgetown Priory, 2006); Clare (Ballyogan Bridge, 2007); Kilkenny (Catholic church at Goresbridge, 2006); Wicklow

(Donard, Hell Kettle Bridge, 2007) and Fermanagh (Monawilkin, 2005). There is an older record from E. Cork (Little Island, 19th century). This taxon was named new to science by Blom (1996). It is almost certainly still under-recorded in Ireland since seven records were accumulated during 2005–2007 when bryologists interested in the genus carried out fieldwork.

Ecology and biology

Most of the Irish records are from old walls, including stonework of an old bridge. At Monawilkin, a single tuft was found on a dry shaded limestone rock face at the upper edge of a Hazel wood at c. 150 m altitude. At Ballyogan Bridge, several patches occur on limestone pavement. In Scandinavia, it grows on relatively dry calcareous rocks, especially in woodland, but it is also common on wall tops beside roads.

The plants are perennial. It is an autoicous species in which capsules are very frequent, varying from sparse to abundant on different patches. Gemmae, bulbils and tubers are absent.

World distribution

This is a widespread taxon in Europe from Scotland, S. Norway and S. Sweden southwards to N. Spain, Mallorca, C. Italy, Albania, Macedonia and the Caucasus (Blom 1996, Blom in Nyholm 1998, Casas *et al.* 2006, Ignatov *et al.* 2007). It is listed as *Data Deficient* in the Czech Republic, and *S. elegantulum s.l.* is described as 'very rare' in the Netherlands and Estonia. It is assigned to a Eurasian Temperate floristic element in Europe. Elsewhere, subsp. *elegantulum* is recorded in SW Asia (Turkey, Georgia, Azerbaijan, Iran), C. Asia (S. Siberia), Pakistan, China, NE Asia (S. Russian Far East), Japan and Mexico (Blom 1996, Ignatov *et al.* 2007).

Threats
At some sites it is potentially vulnerable to removal or renovation of old walls.

Conservation
No action is proposed. The taxon is almost certainly under-recorded.

Protected sites with recent records: Blackwater River (Cork/Waterford) SAC; Monawilkin ASSI; Monawilkin SAC; **Unprotected sites with recent records:** Ballyogan Bridge; Carrigaline; Catholic church at Goresbridge; Donard, Hell Kettle Bridge; Ringaskiddy.

Schistidium elegantulum H.H.Blom subsp. *wilsonii*

Wilson's Grimmia

Status in Ireland: Data Deficient; **Status in Europe:** Not Evaluated (Endemic)

Number of Hectads	4
+ Old (pre-1970)	3
□ Recent (1970–2010)	1

Schistidium elegantulum subsp. *wilsonii*

Identification
This moss is very similar to *S. elegantulum* subsp. *elegantulum*, which is described in the preceding account. Subspecies *wilsonii* shows the following differences: it is somewhat more robust than subsp. *elegantulum*, forming rather dense tufts with stems mainly 13–50 mm long. The costa is thicker (4–5 stratose in upper part of leaf, 5–7 stratose in lower part). The hair-point is broader and coarser, less translucent, with shorter, denser spinulae. The capsules are oblong-cylindrical rather than oblong, with 8-16 stomata on each urn (cf. 6–8) and the peristome is red rather than orange to orange-red and straight rather than curved (Blom 1996).

The definitive monograph of the group (Blom 1996) recognised and named subsp. *wilsonii* as a valid taxon that occurs widely in continental Europe. However, Hill *et al.* (2008) discontinued recognition of subsp. *wilsonii* because it is indistinctly differentiated from subsp. *elegantulum* in Ireland and Britain. Nevertheless, a fuller analysis of character variation in continental specimens is desirable to decide whether subsp. *wilsonii* should be recognised, since subspecies may intergrade in some parts of their global range.

Distribution in Ireland
Records are from four localities in four vice-counties, only one of them recent: Clare (summit of Corkscrew Hill, 1962); W. Galway (Connemara, *Cum Vari prope* Renvyle, 1831); Longford (by Royal Canal just S. of Archies Bridge, 2007); E. Mayo ('Cony' = Cong, 1906; the specimen might have been from W. Galway). It was described new to science by Blom (1996) and is almost certainly still under-recorded in Ireland.

Ecology and biology
The only habitat details recorded for Irish specimens are 'on limestone rock' (at summit of Corkscrew Hill) and a wall near the Royal Canal. In Scandinavia, it

is a plant of dry calcareous rocks, sometimes in shade, sometimes on open limestone outcrops; most Norwegian specimens were collected from walls (Blom 1996).

The plants are perennial. It is an autoicous taxon in which capsules are present in about 80% of specimens, being abundant to sparse (Blom 1996); capsules on an Irish specimen were mature in late spring or early summer. Gemmae, bulbils and tubers are absent.

World distribution

Subspecies *wilsonii* is known only in S. and W. Europe, from the Faeroes, Scotland and SW Norway southwards to C. Portugal, N. Spain, Mallorca, C. Italy and Croatia

(Blom 1996, Casas *et al.* 2006). It is assigned to a Suboceanic Temperate floristic element.

Threats

At the Longford site, it would be vulnerable to removal or renovation of old walls near the Royal Canal.

Conservation

No action is proposed. The taxon is almost certainly under-recorded.

Protected sites with recent records: none; **Unprotected sites with recent records:** by Royal Canal just S. of Archies Bridge.

Grimmia crinita Brid.

Hedgehog Grimmia

Status in Ireland: Regionally Extinct; **Status in Europe:** Least Concern

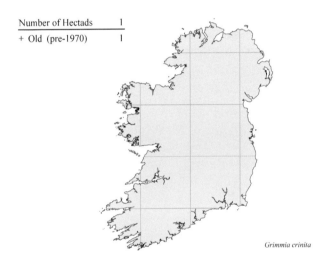

Number of Hectads	1
+ Old (pre-1970)	1

Grimmia crinita

Identification

This is an acrocarpous moss that forms flat, white, hoary patches or small cushions with stems up to 10 mm high. Leaves are usually homomallous, ovate-lanceolate to obovate with plane margins and a long white hair-point that is broadly flattened below, smooth and terete above. Mid-leaf cells are unistratose, quadrate, with slightly incrassate and sinuose walls; basal marginal cells are quadrate with firm walls. Capsules are usually present, immersed, ovoid on a short, slightly arcuate seta. Although careful attention to details of leaf structure is necessary for reliable identification, the richly fruiting plants growing in small hoary patches with homomallous hair-points attract attention when growing among the more common calcicolous *Grimmia* such as *G. pulvinata*.

Distribution in Ireland

The only record from Ireland is based on a specimen in the **TCD** Herbarium labelled 'Dublin, city wall, 1950', collected by S.W. Greene. The precise locality is unknown and it is possible that the species was only a temporary colonist, as appears to have been the case with a recent British record (E. Cornwall, 1999).

Ecology and biology

Its habitat in Ireland is unknown, except that the only Irish specimen was labelled 'Dublin, city wall'. In Europe, it is a thermophilous species found mainly in Mediterranean countries, where it grows on calcareous sandstone and weathered mortar-covered stone walls around vineyards and gardens (Greven 2003).

A recent British record was from weathered vertical concrete.

It grows in cushions or patches that probably persist from year to year. The plants are autoicous and produce abundant capsules. Gemmae and tubers are unknown.

World distribution

In Europe, it is most common in the Mediterranean countries, but extends north to England (recorded in Warwickshire 1872–1888; E. Cornwall, 1999), Belgium, Poland and the former Russian Baltic. It is listed as *Critically Endangered* in Britain and the Czech Republic, *Endangered* in Germany, Luxembourg and Switzerland, *Vulnerable* in Bulgaria, 'very rare' in Estonia and 'very rare and susceptible' in the Netherlands. In Europe, it is assigned to a Suboceanic Mediterranean-Atlantic floristic element. Elsewhere, it is known from Tenerife, N. Africa, the Caucasus, the Near East and Middle East.

Threats

The status of the only Irish record is unclear because the locality is imprecise. It may have been only a temporary colonist.

Conservation

No action is proposed.

Protected sites with recent records: none; **Unprotected sites with recent records:** none.

Grimmia laevigata (Brid.) Brid.   Hoary Grimmia

syn. *Grimmia campestris* Burchell ex Hook., *G. leucophaea* Grev.; *Guembelia laevigata* (Brid.) Ochyra & Żarnowiec
Status in Ireland: Regionally Extinct; **Status in Europe:** Least Concern

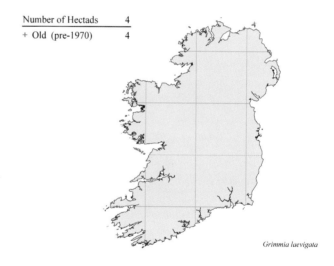

Number of Hectads	4
+ Old (pre-1970)	4

Grimmia laevigata

Identification

An acrocarpous moss that forms cushions, tufts or patches 5–15 mm high that are hoary-greyish when dry and prone to disintegrate, if disturbed. Leaves are patent to spreading when moist, triangular to oblong-lanceolate with a broad base, concave above and abruptly narrowed into a (typically) long, decurrent, slightly denticulate hair-point. The costa is weak and evanescent and leaf margins are plane below, erect to slightly incurved above. Mid-leaf cells are bistratose, irregularly rounded-quadrate, basal juxtacostal cells are rectangular with thin walls and the distinctive basal marginal cells are oblate with incrassate walls. Capsules (unknown in Ireland) are ovoid to oblong-cylindric, smooth and exserted on a short straight seta.

Distribution in Ireland

Four old records from three vice-counties are accepted: W. Cork (Dursey Island, 1894); E. Cork (Youghal, 1956) and Antrim (Giant's Causeway, 1837; S. side of Rathlin Island, c. 1837). Two other reports from Antrim are known to be errors (Cave Hill, 1847; Glenarm, undated).

Ecology and biology

The older records from the north of Ireland are from basaltic rocks (Stewart & Corry 1888) or 'dry basaltic rocks in dry situations' (Megaw 1938). The specimen from Youghal obtained in 1956 was from the stone of a bridge parapet. In Britain, it grows on exposed acidic to slightly basic rocks of varied lithologies, on crags, outcrops, boulders, roofing slates and tiles, often near the coast. Elsewhere in the world, the species occurs in some very arid regions and it has been shown to be remarkably tolerant of both desiccation and heat; remaining alive in herbarium packets for at least 10 years (Keever 1957) and dry plants surviving for 24 hours at up to 80°C (Alpert 1988).

The plants are perennial. It is a dioicous species in which capsules are unknown in Ireland; they are rare in Britain (frequent in Canary Islands: Greven 1995), maturing in spring. Gemmae, bulbils and tubers are absent, but vegetative propagation may occur from detached leaf or stem fragments.

World distribution
G. laevigata is widespread in Europe from C. Scotland, S. Norway, S. Sweden and NW Russia southwards to Spain and Portugal (where locally very abundant), Italy and the Caucasus. However, it is listed as *Vulnerable* in Germany and Luxembourg, *Near Threatened* in Sweden, 'very rare and susceptible' in the Netherlands and 'declining' in Norway. It is assigned to a Circumpolar Southern-temperate floristic element in Europe.

Elsewhere it has a very wide range comprising Macaronesia, N., E. and S. Africa, much of Asia, N., C. and S. America, Hawaii, Indian Ocean islands, Australia and New Zealand. Genetic studies have recently disclosed that its populations within California constitute two distinct geographically overlapping cryptic species (Fernandez *et al.* 2006). Similar studies are needed to investigate whether similar situations occur within other parts of the near-cosmopolitan range of *G. laevigata s.l.*

Threats
Not found or refound at any of the old Irish localities in recent decades, although it may still persist on Dursey Island (briefly searched) or Rathlin Island (no recent surveys). The species has decreased in Britain since the 19th century (A.J.E. Smith in Hill *et al.* 1992) and apparently also in E. and C. Germany (Meinunger & Schröder 2007), possibly due to acid precipitation, nitrogen enrichment of its substrata, or both.

Conservation
No action is proposed other than a bryophyte survey of Rathlin Island, which should deliberately seek to refind this species.

Protected sites with recent records: none; **Unprotected sites with recent records:** none.

Grimmia donniana Sm.   Donn's Grimmia

Status in Ireland: Near Threatened; **Status in Europe:** Least Concern

Scattered in most of the hilly parts of Ireland, this dainty cushion-forming species of acid rocks sometimes forms extensive colonies. It has been reported from 14 vice-counties, with records from at least 27 hectads (19 old, 8 recent, 4 undated). It was not included in the Provisional Red List (Holyoak 2006b), so was not targeted for survey, but it is very doubtful whether it has actually declined.

Grimmia longirostris Hook.

North Grimmia

syn. *Grimmia affinis* Hornsch., *G. ovata* Schwägr., *Guembelia longirostris* (Hook.) Ochyra & Żarnowiec
Status in Ireland: Regionally Extinct; **Status in Europe:** Least Concern

Number of Hectads	5
+ Old (pre-1970)	5

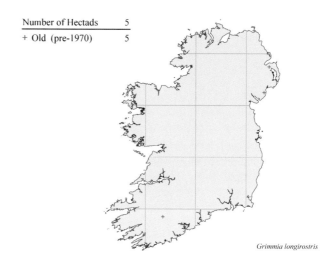

Grimmia longirostris

Identification

An acrocarpous moss that grows in compact, usually rounded cushions that are dull yellowish-green to blackish-green and usually up to about 15 mm high, occasionally 30 mm. The leaves are straight and appressed when dry, erecto-patent when moist, keeled above, lanceolate to narrowly lanceolate from a broad base, tapering to a long, slightly denticulate hair-point. The leaf margin is usually recurved on one or both sides. Cells in the upper part of the leaf are irregularly quadrate, bistratose and opaque; mid-leaf cells are shortly rectangular with incrassate, sinuose walls; basal marginal cells are shortly rectangular with thickened transverse walls. Capsules are obloid to cylindric, smooth and yellowish, exserted on a straight seta. Identification requires careful attention to details of leaf structure, including the areolation.

Distribution in Ireland

Five old records from four vice-counties are accepted: S. Kerry (by Lough Cruttia, Brandon Mountain, 1951); Mid Cork (Musheragh Mountain, leg. I. Carroll in 19th century); Down (Black Stairs, Slieve Donard, 1887; not refound in 2008) and Antrim (Slemish Mountain, 1893; Fair Head, 1898). Vague unconfirmed reports or misidentified specimens exist from four vice-counties: Waterford, W. Galway, Dublin and Down (Scrabo).

Ecology and biology

The only note on the habitat in Ireland appears to be A.C. Crundwell's 'boulders' for the find on Brandon Mountain. Although Megaw (1938) records 'siliceous rocks on mountains', he was merely quoting Dixon (1924). In Britain, it grows on dry exposed acidic to ultrabasic rock, on cliffs, in scree and on rocks by lakes, or rarely by the sea, at 0–550 m altitude. In the Scandes Mountains in Scandinavia, it is common on dry, sun-exposed, siliceous cliffs and boulders, but in S. Sweden, it prefers less dry and exposed sites (Hallingbäck *et al.* 2006).

The cushions are perennial. The species is autoicous and capsules are frequent, maturing in winter. Gemmae, bulbils and tubers are unknown, but vegetative propagation is likely to occur from detached leaves and stem fragments.

World distribution

Widespread in N. Europe from N. Iceland, N. Fennoscandia and arctic Russia southwards; more local and mainly montane in S. Europe, reaching N. Spain, Italy and the Caucasus. It is listed as *Vulnerable* in Bulgaria, Germany and Luxembourg. It is assigned to a Circumpolar Boreo-temperate floristic element in Europe. Elsewhere, it has a very wide range in Asia, N., C. and S. America, Greenland, Africa, Australia and New Zealand (Muñoz & Pando 2000).

Threats
Not found or refound in Ireland since 1951, despite visits to the old localities. It has apparently declined since the 19th century in Britain (A.J.E. Smith in Hill *et al.* 1992) and in at least lowland regions of Germany (Meinunger & Schröder 2007).

Conservation
No action is proposed. Two of the old localities are on land that is now protected.

Protected sites with recent records: none; **Unprotected sites with recent records:** none.

Grimmia atrata Miel. ex Hornsch.

Copper Grimmia

syn. *Streptocolea atrata* (Miel. ex Hornsch.) Ochyra & Żarnowiec
Status in Ireland: Endangered (D); **Status in Europe:** Rare

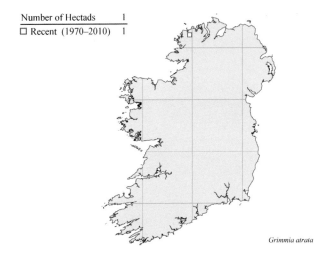

Number of Hectads	1
☐ Recent (1970–2010)	1

Grimmia atrata

Identification
G. atrata is a rather nondescript acrocarpous moss that grows on rocks in dark green to black tufts or patches that are typically 1–4 cm high. Leaves are erect to erecto-patent when moist, flexuose to somewhat crisped when dry, lanceolate to ligulate, tapering to a blunt cucullate apex. The strong costa disappears in the leaf apex and leaf margins are somewhat recurved below and incurved above. Cells in mid-leaf are unistratose with bistratose ridges or entirely bistratose, rectangular, with nearly smooth to sinuosely incrassate walls; basal marginal cells are quadrate and hyaline with thickened transverse cell walls; basal juxtacostal cells are rectangular with smooth to slightly sinuose walls. Capsules are obloid to cylindric, smooth and longly exserted on a straight seta.

Identification of non-fertile plants requires careful microscopic study of leaf characters, although the presence of sinuose cell walls points to them being members of the Grimmiaceae.

Distribution in Ireland
Known from a single locality, on a ridge of Aghla More, south of Lough Feeane in W. Donegal, where it was discovered in 1990 and refound in 2002.

Ecology and biology
In W. Donegal, it occurs in small crevices of schist outcrops and boulders, sometimes on crumbling, flaky rock, on both N.- and S.-facing slopes at 440–460 m altitude. It is likely that the rock at this locality has a high copper content. Elsewhere in Europe, the species grows on the surfaces and in crevices of moist, sheltered or exposed rocks that contain heavy metals, particularly copper, on cliffs and other outcrops, boulders in scree and rocks beside lakes, mainly in hill and mountain regions (A.J.E. Smith in Hill *et al.* 1992, Greven 2003).

G. atrata grows in patches that apparently persist for at least several years. The species is dioicous and capsules are occasional in Britain (unknown in Ireland), maturing in autumn. Gemmae and tubers are unknown.

World distribution

This species is rare in Europe, in N. and W. Britain (N. Scotland to C. Wales) and from Norway and arctic Sweden south to Spain, Italy and Romania. It is listed as *Vulnerable* in the Czech Republic, Sweden and Switzerland. In Europe, it is assigned to a Suboceanic Boreal-montane floristic element. The species is recorded elsewhere in India, Taiwan, Japan, Canada (Labrador) and Bolivia (Muñoz & Pando 2000).

Threats

The population in W. Donegal is small and sparsely scattered over several rock outcrops, within an overall radius of several hundred metres. The greatest potential threat is from thoughtless collection of specimens.

Conservation

The only Irish site is on protected land.

Protected sites with recent records: Cloghernagore Bog and Glenveagh National Park SAC; **Unprotected sites with recent records:** none.

Grimmia orbicularis Bruch ex Wilson   Round-fruited Grimmia

Status in Ireland: Vulnerable (B2a, bii, iv); **Status in Europe:** Least Concern

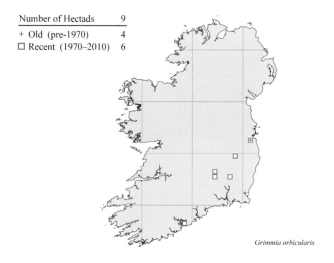

Number of Hectads	9
+ Old (pre-1970)	4
☐ Recent (1970–2010)	6

Grimmia orbicularis

Identification

An acrocarpous moss that grows as lax, readily disintegrating cushions or patches, greenish-black above, blackish below, hoary when dry, with stems up to about 40 mm high. The leaves are broadly lanceolate, abruptly contracted at the apex with a short to long hair-point that is smooth to denticulate. Leaf margins are recurved in the middle of the leaf on one or both sides. Mid-leaf cells are unistratose and subquadrate with thickened transverse walls; basal marginal cells are rectangular with thickened transverse walls. Capsules are ovoid, smooth, exserted, but bent back down into the cushion by the arcuate setae.

Fertile plants are distinct from the common *G. pulvinata* by the shorter ovoid rather than obloid capsules with orange rather than dark red peristome teeth and usually also by the mamillate rather than rostrate operculum. Non-fertile plants can usually be separated by the longer basal juxtacostal cells, which are 8–10 times as long as wide compared to 2–6 times as long in *G. pulvinata*.

Distribution in Ireland

There are recent records from six localities in four vice-counties: E. Cork (W. of Saleen, 2006); Kilkenny (Ballyteigelia Bridge, 2004 and 2005; Robertshill, Kilcreene Lodge, 2010; Freshford, 2010), Wicklow (River Slaney, south of Stratford, 2010) and Dublin (Kilmashogue Mountain, 2007). There are older records from a further five localities: Mid Cork (Carrigaline,

322

1851; Cork or near Cork, 1858–1872); E. Cork (Cove, 1865; Youghal, 1920) and Dublin (Stillorgan, 1859 and 1900). A report from Down (Spelga Mountain, 1886) was erroneous.

Ecology and biology

G. orbicularis is a calciphile that grows on hard surfaces of stone or mortar, although it may be less strongly calciphilous in Ireland than in Britain. Old records were from walls or wall tops. Similarly, recent finds are from an E.-facing wall of an old bridge, vertical masonry of a N.-facing mortared-stone wall of a bridge; a S.-facing old wall and gate pillar and old walls (Robertshill and Freshford). Elsewhere in Europe, it occurs on limestone rocks and walls, masonry and old concrete, usually in sunny places.

Cushions persist for at least several years. The species is autoicous and capsules are common, maturing in spring. Tubers and gemmae are unknown.

World distribution

This species is widespread in Europe from Scotland, the Netherlands, Germany and Poland southwards to the Mediterranean countries, but listed as *Vulnerable* in Germany, *Near Threatened* in Luxembourg and 'rare' in the Netherlands. In Europe, it is assigned to a Suboceanic Mediterranean-Atlantic floristic element. Elsewhere, it is known from the Canary Islands, N. Africa, Near East, Middle East, N., C. and S. America and Australasia.

Threats

Potentially at risk from removal, renovation or cleaning of the walls on which it grows, which include bridge walls beside busy roads. Causes of the apparent long-term decrease in both Ireland and Britain are unknown, although it has been suggested that it is susceptible to atmospheric pollution (A.J.E. Smith in Hill *et al.* 1992).

Conservation

It would be worthwhile to notify owners of walls and the road authorities of populations that might be at risk if walls or bridges are renovated or cleaned.

Protected sites with recent records: River Barrow and River Nore SAC; Rostellan Lough, Aghada Shore and Poulnabibe Inlet pNHA; Slaney River Valley SAC; **Unprotected sites with recent records:** Freshford; Kilmashogue Mountain; Robertshill, Kilcreene Lodge.

Grimmia torquata Drumm.

Twisted Grimmia

syn. *Dryptodon torquatus* (Drumm.) Brid.
Status in Ireland: Near Threatened; **Status in Europe:** Least Concern

G. torquata grows mainly on steep to vertical rock faces or sides of boulders of varied siliceous lithologies that are at least slightly basic, including schists, granitic rocks, other metamorphic lithologies and conglomerate (but not limestone). Most records are from hill or mountain regions, especially on N.- or E.-facing crags and slopes in corries, sometimes beside streams and also on the highest ground. It has been reported from 11 vice-counties, with records from 18 hectads (12 old, 11 recent). There is only slight evidence that more than a very few of the populations represented by old records may have disappeared, whereas numerous new finds in the past decade demonstrate that there are strong regional populations extant (e.g. in the Galty and Comeragh Mountains).

Grimmia funalis (Schwägr.) Bruch & Schimp.

Status in Ireland: Near Threatened; **Status in Europe:** Least Concern

This is an attractive acrocarpous moss that forms neat grey-green cushions in rock ledges and crevices on a range of rock types, including sandstone, schist, basalt and limestone, but usually indicating at least some base-richness. Recent fieldwork has shown it to be widespread but scattered in montane areas in Ireland, found mainly in clusters centred on Cork, Kerry, Galway and Waterford, but also in Donegal and Londonderry. It has been reported from 14 vice-counties, with records from 33 hectads (23 old, 19 recent), but populations are usually small and it may have declined in the east.

Grimmia lisae De Not.

syn. *G. retracta* Stirt.
Status in Ireland: Least Concern; **Status in Europe:** Rare

G. lisae is an acrocarpous moss that grows in cushions or patches on siliceous rocks. It was widely confused with *G. trichophylla* until Maier (2002) pointed out reliable identification characters, particularly those from sections of the leaf costa. It has been reported from 11 vice-counties, with records from 20 hectads (2 old, 19 recent) mostly obtained since 2002. The species is widespread in Ireland and locally common in Kerry, where there are very large populations. *G. retracta* was previously regarded as an uncommon species (placed on the Provisional Red List: Holyoak 2006b) that is found mainly in inundation zones of rivers, but it is now placed as a synonym of *G. lisae* (Hill *et al.* 2008). As reported also by Long (2008), the recent Irish records show that *G. lisae* occurs over a much wider range of habitats, often well away from rivers or lakes.

Grimmia funalis, Errisbeg, Co. Galway.

Grimmia dissimulata E.Maier

Limestone Hair-pointed Grimmia

Status in Ireland: Vulnerable (D2); **Status in Europe:** Least Concern

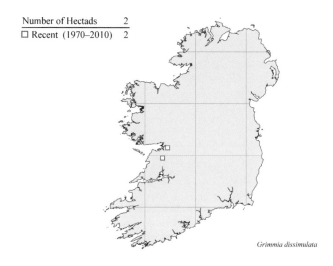

Number of Hectads	2
☐ Recent (1970–2010)	2

Grimmia dissimulata

Identification

An acrocarpous moss that grows as compact cushions, tufts or more extensive mats, which are yellow-green when wet, darker when dry, with stems up to 30 mm high. Leaves are loosely appressed to erecto-patent when moist, somewhat flexuose when dry, the upper leaves mainly 1.9–2.5 mm long, keeled, lanceolate from an ovate base, tapering to acuminate apex, muticous, or with costa excurrent as a weakly denticulate hair-point. Leaf margins are typically recurved on one side only, bistratose in the upper part of the leaf. The upper part of the lamina has unistratose isodiametric cells; the lower part has elongate-rectangular cells with nodulose cell walls. Capsules (unknown in Ireland or Britain) are ellipsoid, pendulous, exserted on a short arcuate seta up to 5 mm long.

Differences from *G. trichophylla* and *G. lisae* are slight and very subtle, so that until it was described by Maier (2002) it was overlooked as a distinct species (cf. Muñoz & Pando 2000, Greven 2003). The most important diagnostic characters are in the cross section of the costa near the leaf base: *G. lisae* has six guide cells, *G. dissimulata* and *G. trichophylla* have four; *G. dissimulata* has guide cells in one layer, *G. trichophylla* has them in two layers (those of dorsal row fewer and smaller). In addition, basal marginal cells of *G. dissimulata* are shortly-rectangular whereas those of *G. trichophylla* are elongate-rectangular.

Distribution in Ireland

There are two records from two vice-counties: Clare (Aughrim Lough near Travaun Lough, 2004) and SE Galway (Caranavoodaun, 2004). It may well be under-recorded in Ireland because it is a recently described species. Nevertheless, there is little doubt that it is uncommon and local since there are no older records of *G. trichophylla* agg. from limestone substrata in Ireland.

Ecology and biology

The Irish records are from limestone substrata in the lowlands (20–23 m altitude). One find was on a large block of limestone pavement in the Burren. The other was from the upper parts of the inundation zone of a turlough in neighbouring SE Galway, on the fully insolated top of a boulder and on another boulder in a limestone wall that was partly shaded by bushes. British records are mainly from limestone walls of churches and churchyards, with a few from natural limestone outcrops (Porley 2004). For continental Europe and Cyprus, Maier (2002) reported it from altitudes up to 1300 m, with nearly 70% of specimens from limestone or dolomite, others being from basic conglomerate, andesite and volcanic rock, sometimes in places subject to occasional seepage or in shady areas.

The plants are perennial. The species is dioicous and capsules are unknown in Ireland or Britain, but known from continental Europe. In continental plants, gemmae occasionally develop on the dorsal surface of the costa (Maier 2002); bulbils and tubers are unknown, but vegetative propagation might also occur from detached leaves or stem fragments.

World distribution

G. dissimulata is widespread in Europe from N. Scotland (Porley 2004) to Germany and southwards to Spain, Mallorca, Sicily and Crete (Maier 2002). It is listed as *Vulnerable* in Luxembourg and *Data Deficient* in Spain and Switzerland. It is assigned to a European Southern-temperate floristic element in Europe. Records outside Europe are from Morocco, Turkey, Cyprus and Syria (Maier 2002).

Threats

No immediate threats were apparent at the two known localities. It may be vulnerable to shading if scrub or saplings encroach on its sites.

Conservation

Both localities are on protected land.

Protected sites with recent records: Burren National Park; Castletaylor Complex SAC; East Burren Complex SAC; **Unprotected sites with recent records:** none.

Grimmia muehlenbeckii Schimp.

Muehlenbeck's Grimmia

Status in Ireland: Data Deficient; **Status in Europe:** Least Concern

Number of Hectads	5
+ Old (pre-1970)	1
□ Recent (1970–2010)	5

Grimmia muehlenbeckii

Identification

This is a grey-green, densely cushion-forming acrocarpous moss with long hyaline hair-points on the leaves, giving the cushions, which can grow up to c. 5 cm in diameter, a hoary appearance. It is very similar to several other species of *Grimmia*, and only recently has been recognised as part of the Irish flora (Porley & Maier 2007). The leaves are lanceolate, c. 2 mm long, and taper gradually into the hair-point. The capsules are produced on a short curved seta, so that they appear to burrow back into the cushion when moist. *G. muehlenbeckii* is most similar to *G. decipiens*, but that species has a more strongly toothed hair-point and less widely spreading leaves. A particularly distinctive feature of *G. muehlenbeckii* is that the costa is angled or even slightly winged in cross section, unlike the rounded cross section found in most allied species.

Distribution in Ireland

The status of this moss in Ireland and Britain has been clarified only recently (Porley & Maier 2007). The earliest known Irish record is from Benbradagh in Londonderry, where it was originally identified as *G. decipiens* 'var. *robusta*' in 1968, and refound in 1999 and 2008. More recent survey work has found it in a further five localities in another two vice-counties: S. Kerry (An

Loch Iochtarach, 2008; Com na Cailli on Brandon Mountain, 2008; E. of Beennaman, 2008; shore of Loch Meáin in the Coomanare Lakes, 2008) and Waterford (Coumshingaun Lough, 2007).

Ecology and biology

This species grows directly on exposed rock faces, often with a S.-facing aspect but sometimes N.-facing, where there is some mineral enrichment, such as on cliffs and outcrops composed of basalt and other basic igneous rocks. In Ireland, it also occurs on boulders on the shores of mountain lakes. Irish records are from altitudes of 240–450 m. Typically it is associated with other bryophytes, most notably including *Amphidium mougeotii*, *Frullania tamarisci*, *F. fragilifolia*, *Grimmia lisae*, *G. funalis*, *Plagiochila bifaria*, *Porella obtusata*, *Schistidium strictum*, *Racomitrium ellipticum* and *Ulota hutchinsiae*.

It is dioicous, and capsules have not been observed in Irish and British plants. Specialised vegetative propagules are not known to occur.

World distribution

The distribution of this species is imperfectly known, but it has been recorded from several sites in Scotland, mainly in the west (it is considered *Data Deficient* in Britain). It is frequent in Scandinavia and also occurs in Germany, Austria, Switzerland, the Czech Republic, Hungary and most of the countries bordering the Mediterranean. It is listed as *Vulnerable* in Spain, Portugal, Luxembourg and Bulgaria. Outside Europe, it is reported from Morocco, Turkey, Siberia, Japan and N. America; other reports from Africa are unsubstantiated.

Threats

No immediate threats have been identified, but afforestation, overstocking and water abstraction are all potential threats.

Conservation

Some populations are on protected land. More survey work will probably discover further colonies of this moss. Meanwhile, no specific conservation work is necessary and periodic monitoring of the known localities should be delayed until it becomes clear that the species is rare or threatened.

Protected sites with recent records: Comeragh Mountains SAC; Mount Brandon SAC; **Unprotected sites with recent records:** Benbradagh (proposed ASSI).

Grimmia hartmanii Schimp.

Hartman's Grimmia

Status in Ireland: Least Concern; **Status in Europe:** Least Concern

This species forms green or yellowish-green patches and tufts, distinguished from most other species of the genus in Ireland by the clusters of brownish gemmae that are usually found at the tips of the upper leaves (*G. anomala*, discovered in Ireland in 2009, has yellowish clusters of gemmae). It grows on humid basic or acidic rocks by water, typically in wooded ravines or by lakes. Although it was included in the Provisional Red List (Holyoak 2006b), recent fieldwork has shown it to be more frequent and widely distributed in the uplands than previously thought. It has been reported from 14 vice-counties, with records from 23 hectads (13 old, 12 recent). However, the very recent discovery of *G. anomala* in Ireland, and its confusion with *G. hartmanii*, may mean that the latter is less frequent than this. Irish specimens of *G. hartmanii* are currently awaiting revision (Ron Porley, pers. comm.)

Grimmia anomala Hampe ex Schimp.

syn. *Dryptodon anomalus* (Hampe ex Schimp.) Loeske,
Grimmia hartmanii var. *anomala* (Hampe ex Schimp.) Mönk.
Status in Ireland: Endangered (D); **Status in Europe:** Least Concern

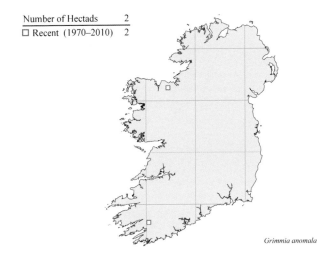

Number of Hectads	2
☐ Recent (1970–2010)	2

Grimmia anomala

Identification

This is a dull to dark green acrocarpous moss that grows in loose patches or dense tufts c. 2–3 cm high. The leaves are 2–2.5 mm long, erect when moist, irregularly imbricate when dry. Their shape is oblong-lanceolate, gradually narrowed towards the apex, which ends in an acuminate, chlorophyllose point or occasionally a short, blunt, hyaline awn. The leaf margins are recurved on one or both sides and the costa is distinctly angular in cross section. The lamina cells are mainly unistratose, but partly bistratose in the upper leaf, 5–7 µm wide in mid-leaf, with slightly sinuose cell walls. The leaf surface has distinct and prominent longitudinal ridges which resemble papillae when seen in cross section. The upper leaf tips have clusters of globular, multicellular gemmae that are yellowish-green to orange. It resembles *G. hartmanii* in the presence of these gemmae, but usually differs from that species in the leaf shape and orientation, the shorter hair-points, the strongly striate-papillose leaves and in having gemmae of a brighter yellow to orange colour rather than brown. Capsules are oblong, erect, exserted, smooth, with a rostrate lid, but they are unknown in Ireland.

Distribution in Ireland

The first record of this moss was made in 2009 during the meeting of the British Bryological Society when it was found at Lough Nambrackderg in West Cork by Niklas Lönnell and others (Bosanquet & Preston 2010). However, there is at least one other Irish record, at Easky Lough in Sligo, where it was found in quantity in 2003 but misidentified as *G. hartmanii*. There may well be other localities for *G. anomala* in Ireland, but the full picture is awaiting revision of herbarium specimens currently labelled as *G. hartmanii* (Ron Porley, pers. comm.).

Ecology and biology

At the West Cork site the moss was found in several small patches on a large, gently sloping rock (a metre or more across) on the western margin of a lake below steep but broken crags of Old Red Sandstone. In Sligo, there are an estimated several hundred cushions and patches on rocks at the lake margin, where it grows with *Racomitrium* spp., *Andreaea rothii* and *Hedwigia stellata*. Both sites would be subject to periodic irrigation and probably frequent wave action. In Europe, it grows on damp, siliceous, often shaded rocks in montane to alpine areas (Greven 1995).

The species forms perennial patches. It is dioicous and capsules are very rare, observed only in Norway and western North America (Greven 1995). The gemmae that are normally present on the leaf tips doubtless serve as vegetative propagules; they were abundant on the Irish material.

World distribution

This is a local species in N., C. and E. Europe, known from N. Iceland, Scotland (Rothero pers. comm.), N. Scandinavia and the Alps southwards to N. Spain and Corsica and eastwards to the S. Urals and Caucasus (Ignatov *et al.* 2007). Greven (1995) commented that the 'rarity of *G. anomala* in its entire distribution area is remarkable'; he noted that it has a boreal-montane range with a disrupted circumpolar-montane distribution. Outside Europe, it is known in Georgia, S. Siberia, the Russian Far East, Kashmir, Japan and North America (widespread in west from California to Alaska; also Ontario to Labrador; Greenland) (Muñoz & Pando 2000, Ignatov *et al.* 2007, R.I. Hastings & F.C. Greven in F.N.A. 2007).

Threats

No immediate threats were apparent at the West Cork locality. A car park has been constructed at the Sligo locality, which must have destroyed some cushions, but there are plenty remaining.

Conservation

Although discovered only recently in Ireland, this species bears a superficial resemblance to *Grimmia hartmanii*, which has been sought during recent fieldwork. Hence, it is undoubtedly rare rather than overlooked, justifying the *Endangered* threat status assigned, rather than being regarded as merely *Data Deficient*. At the West Cork locality it was absent from other rocks in the immediate vicinity and was not seen elsewhere on the lake margin, although only about 40% of the area was searched (G.P. Rothero *in litt.*). At the Sligo locality it was abundant over at least 100 m, but not found elsewhere on the lake shore. However, further survey in the area is desirable.

Protected sites with recent records: Derryclogher (Knockboy) Bog SAC; Ox Mountains Bogs SAC; **Unprotected sites with recent records:** none.

Grimmia decipiens (Schultz) Lindb.

Great Grimmia

Status in Ireland: Near Threatened; **Status in Europe:** Least Concern

This is a large, hoary moss that forms dark green cushions on base-rich or acidic rocks and boulders. It is known in Ireland from scattered localities in several upland areas, including sightings over the last decade from Errisbeg, Wicklow Mountains, Carlingford Mountain and the Mourne Mountains. It has been reported from seven vice-counties, with records from 21 hectads (14 old, 11 recent). Its inclusion in the Provisional Red List (Holyoak 2006b) is therefore not supported by recent fieldwork. It may have declined slightly, but the evidence for this is unconvincing.

Grimmia ramondii (Lam. & DC.) Margad.

syn. *G. curvata* (Brid.) De Sloover; *Dryptodon patens* (Hedw.) Brid.
Status in Ireland: Near Threatened; **Status in Europe:** Least Concern

This large moss forms patches on rock faces and boulders, especially by lakes, and is widespread in hilly parts of Ireland. It has been reported from 15 vice-counties, with records from 43 hectads (33 old, 18 recent, 2 undated). Although not included in the Provisional Red List (Holyoak 2006b), and therefore not targeted for survey work, a slight decline is suggested. However, several new populations have been discovered during fieldwork in upland areas over the last decade, so its status should be kept under review.

Racomitrium macounii Kindb. **subsp.** *alpinum* (E.Lawton) Frisvoll

syn. *Bucklandiella macounii* (Kindb.) Bednarek-Ochyra & Ochyra,
B. macounii subsp. *alpina* (E.Lawton) Bednarek-Ochyra & Ochyra
Status in Ireland: Vulnerable (D2); **Status in Europe:** Least Concern

Number of Hectads	3
☐ Recent (1970–2010)	3

Racomitrium macounii subsp. *alpinum*

Identification

A moss that forms brown or reddish-brown cushions, tufts or mats on rock, with sparsely branched or unbranched stems up to about 5.5 cm long, sometimes 8 cm. The leaves are erect to erect-spreading, ovate-lanceolate, tapered to an acuminate apex with a short hair-point, their total length being up to 2.4–3.0 mm. The leaf margin is usually recurved on much of one side of the leaf, but plane on the other side; the costa is strong and disappears in the leaf apex. Mid-leaf cells are smooth and shortly rectangular to quadrate; alar cells are slightly differentiated, with c. 10–20 pellucid cells in a marginal row. Capsules (perhaps unknown in Ireland) are ovate, erect and exserted on a seta 4.0–5.5 mm long. The sparsely branched stems give a different appearance to that of most other plants of the *Racomitrium heterostichum* species group, but identification should be confirmed by microscopic characters including the leaf-margin that is regularly bistratose for 2–4 cell rows and the costa in the lower part of the leaf that is strongly dorsally convex and mainly 4-stratose.

Distribution in Ireland

There are three records, all recent, in three vice-counties: S. Kerry (Dromanassig Waterfall on Sheen River SE of Kenmare, 1998); W. Cork (Cummeendarrig River in Borlin Valley 13 km NE of Glengarriff, 1998) and W. Mayo (above Lough Bellawaum on Mweelrea, 2003).

Ecology and biology

R. macounii was found new to Ireland by Alan Orange at surprisingly low elevations for what is normally regarded as a montane moss: in S. Kerry at only 40 m altitude on unshaded rocks by a river with *Racomitrium aciculare*, *Sciuro-hypnum plumosum* and *Parmelia conspersa*, and in W. Cork on an unshaded boulder in a river at 225 m. The third record, made by David Long, was in W. Mayo at c. 533 m on a rock slab in a gully on a N.-facing montane slope. In Britain, it is mainly a montane species, recorded at 400–1160 m altitude, growing on flat or steep, moist rocks, often by mountain streams or where there is seepage of water across the rock. Frisvoll (1988) notes that unlike closely related species, it seems to tolerate or prefer less acid or slightly calciferous rocks.

The plants are perennial. It is a dioicous species in which capsules are rare in Britain. Gemmae, bulbils and tubers are absent, but vegetative propagation is likely to occur from detached leaf or stem fragments.

World distribution

R. macounii subsp. *alpinum* has a northern and montane distribution in Europe, in Iceland, Faeroes, W. Ireland, Scotland, N. Wales (*Near Threatened* in Britain), Norway (widespread), N. and C. Sweden, N. Finland, Pyrenees, N. Portugal, N. Spain, Corsica, the Alps and other mountains of C. Europe and the Caucasus. It has become *Extinct* in Germany. In Europe, the species as a whole is assigned to a European Boreal-montane floristic element. Subspecies *alpinum* occurs elsewhere in Japan, north-western N. America (from Attu Island and the Alaskan mainland to Colorado) and in S. Greenland. The nominate subspecies also has a wide range, in NW Iceland, C., S. and E. Europe and western N. America.

Threats

Little information is available. The main potential threat is probably to riverine populations from alterations to the flow regime which would result from water abstraction or storage (e.g. for electricity generation or water storage). Other potential threats could arise from shading of its sites (e.g. by afforestation) or eutrophication of the water.

Conservation

Two populations are on protected land.

Protected sites with recent records: Derryclogher (Knockboy) Bog SAC; Mweelrea/Sheeffry/Erriff Complex SAC; **Unprotected sites with recent records:** Dromanassig Waterfall on Sheen River SE of Kenmare.

Lough Bellawaum, Co. Mayo.

Racomitrium sudeticum (Funck) Bruch & Schimp

Slender Fringe-moss

syn. *Bucklandiella sudetica* (Funck) Bednarek-Ochyra & Ochyra, *R. affine* sensu A.J.E.Sm. 1978,
R. heterostichum var. *sudeticum* (Funck) E.Bauer, *Rhacomitrium sudeticum* auct.
Status in Ireland: Least Concern; **Status in Europe:** Least Concern

This species forms yellowish-green cushions or loose patches on acidic montane rocks. It was poorly understood in Ireland and Britain until the taxonomic revision by Frisvoll (1988) and included in the Provisional Red List for Ireland (Holyoak 2006b). Fieldwork over the past decade has shown that it was previously under-recorded, so that there are currently records from 21 vice-counties and 27 hectads (10 old, 23 recent). It is locally common in some montane regions in W. Donegal and W. Mayo.

Racomitrium affine (F.Weber & D.Mohr) Lindb.

Lesser Fringe-moss

syn. *Bucklandiella affinis* (F.Weber & D.Mohr) Bednarek-Ochyra & Ochyra,
R. heterostichum var. *affine* (F.Weber & D.Mohr) Lesq., *Rhacomitrium affine* auct.
Status in Ireland: Least Concern; **Status in Europe:** Least Concern

R. affine is one of several allied species that were separated from *R. heterostichum* in a taxonomic review by Frisvoll (1988). Records from Ireland and Britain mainly date from the publication by Blockeel (1991b) and subsequent work. It was included in the Provisional Red List for Ireland (Holyoak 2006b), but is somewhat under-recorded in Ireland because of its recent separation, as well as the close similarity to the more common *R. heterostichum* leading to it being overlooked in the field. It has been reported from 15 vice-counties, with records from at least 17 hectads (4 old, 13 recent) with 5 records resulting from fieldwork in 2008.

Racomitrium elongatum Ehrh. ex Frisvoll

Long Fringe-moss

syn. *Niphotrichum elongatum* (Frisvoll) Bednarek-Ochyra & Ochyra,
R. canescens var. *intermedium* Venturi & Bott., *Rhacomitrium elongatum* auct.
Status in Ireland: Vulnerable (D2); **Status in Europe:** Least Concern

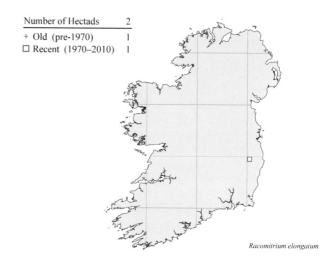

Number of Hectads	2
+ Old (pre-1970)	1
□ Recent (1970–2010)	1

Racomitrium elongatum

Identification

A moss that forms yellowish-green (sometimes hoary) tufts or mats with rather sparsely branched stems 3–6 cm long, sometimes 13 cm. Leaves are recurved when moist, keeled, ovate-lanceolate and tapering rather gradually to an apex that usually has a rather long, whitish hair-point; leaf length is up to 3.2 mm overall. The leaf margin is broadly recurved throughout; the costa reaches to near the leaf apex and is usually unbranched. Cells in mid-leaf are subquadrate to rectangular and distinctly papillose; alar cells are wider and thin-walled. Capsules (unknown in Ireland) are long-cylindric, erect and exserted. Separation from the rather similar *R. canescens* is based on the longer, mostly unbranched costa and strongly, rather than obtusely, keeled leaves. *R. ericoides* is more similar, differing in having its supra-alar marginal cells elongate and thin-walled (not short and thick-walled) and the hair-point non-decurrent and not or faintly denticulate and papillose (whereas in *R. elongatum* it is decurrent, strongly denticulate and spinulose, and papillose below).

The taxonomic revision by Frisvoll (1983) recognised several species within the *Racomitrium canescens* group of which three occur in Ireland. Consistent separation of the segregate species in Ireland and Britain mainly dates from the publication by Hill (1984).

Distribution in Ireland

There are two records from two vice-counties: Wicklow (by Upper Lake, Glendalough, 1975–2007) and Antrim (Sallagh Braes, 1910). It may be somewhat under-recorded since it was not recognised as a distinct taxon in Ireland and Britain until about 1984. It is very locally abundant at Glendalough.

Ecology and biology

At Glendalough it grows on 'heathy bare ground at side of track'. In Britain, it occurs on open sandy or gritty soils, on acidic substrata and sometimes over limestone, from near sea level to 1175 m altitude in the mountains. In Fenno-scandia, it is usually found on exposed, sandy and nutrient-poor soil, typically where it is dry and acidic, but sometimes also on boulders and cliffs (Hallingbäck *et al.* 2006).

The plants are perennial. It is a dioicous species in which capsules have not been found in Ireland or Britain (they are very rare in Fennoscandia and N. America). Gemmae, bulbils and tubers are absent, but vegetative propagation presumably occurs from detached leaf or stem fragments.

World distribution

R. elongatum is widespread in Europe from Iceland, N. Norway, C. Sweden and C. Finland southwards to

C. Portugal, C. Spain, Montenegro (where it is considered *Data Deficient*), the Crimea and the Caucasus (Frisvoll 1983). It is listed as 'very rare' in Estonia and 'declining' in Germany. In Europe, it is assigned to a Suboceanic Boreo-temperate floristic element. Elsewhere, the range includes Madeira, N. America (Alaska and Newfoundland southwards to California) and S. and E. Greenland.

Threats
No immediate threats were apparent at the Glendalough

locality in 2007. There has been no comprehensive search made for the species at Sallagh Braes in recent decades.

Conservation
Both of the localities are on protected land, or land proposed for designation.

Protected sites with recent records: Glenealo Valley Nature Reserve; Wicklow Mountains National Park; Wicklow Mountains SAC; **Unprotected sites with recent records:** none.

Racomitrium canescens (Hedw.) Brid.

Hoary Fringe-moss

syn. *Niphotrichum canescens* (Hedw.) Bednarek-Ochyra & Ochyra, *Racomitrium canescens* var. *canescens*, *Rhacomitrium canescens* auct.
Status in Ireland: Vulnerable (D2); **Status in Europe:** Least Concern

Number of Hectads	4
+ Old (pre-1970)	3
☐ Recent (1970–2010)	3

Racomitrium canescens

Identification
A medium-sized moss that forms yellowish-green tufts that are often whitish when dry, with irregularly and often rather sparsely branched stems up to 8 cm or more long. Leaves are slightly to distinctly falcate, ovate to broadly ovate-lanceolate, tapering rather abruptly to a whitish hair-point and up to 2.8 mm long overall. The leaf margin is broadly recurved from base to apex; the costa reaches 50–75% of leaf length and is broad and mostly forked or branched. Cells in mid-leaf are short-rectangular and rectangular with tall papillae; alar cells are wider and thin-walled. Capsules (unknown in Ireland) are narrowly ellipsoid to cylindric, erect and exserted on a seta 5–25 mm long. Separation from the rather similar *R. elongatum* and *R. ericoides* should be

based on the mostly forked or branched costa and obtusely rather than strongly keeled leaves.

A taxonomic revision by Frisvoll (1983) recognised several species within the *Racomitrium canescens* group of which three occur in Ireland. Consistent separation of the segregate species in Ireland and Britain mainly dates from the publication by Hill (1984). Irish plants of *R. canescens* are referable to subsp. *canescens*.

Distribution in Ireland
Records are accepted from five localities in three vice-counties: Dublin (Donabate, 1979–2006); Meath (Mornington, 1968); Down (Dundrum sandhills, 1961; D.I. Harbour Estate, Belfast, 2008, leg. R. Weyl; Murlough N.N.R., 1992–2002, records from Newcastle

Beach, 1908–1921 doubtless also being from Murlough dunes). There are also numerous unconfirmed records from Northern Ireland that are likely to refer mainly to *R. ericoides*.

Ecology and biology

Irish records are restricted to unshaded sites in coastal sand dune areas on the east coast. Substantial populations at Murlough National Nature Reserve grow in dune grassland and dune heath on slightly acidic sand and sandy-shingle, with very short vegetation forming an incomplete cover that is rich in mosses and lichens and heavily grazed by rabbits. *R. ericoides* grows with it, dry patches of *R. canescens* being conspicuously different because of their hoary whitish appearance. The record from Mornington was of a very small amount on 'calcareous sand dunes'. At Belfast Harbour it grows on stony basalt infill with scattered bryophytes and vascular plants. In Britain, it is a lowland moss of sandy heaths, short dune grassland and stony soil over basic rock in rather dry places and it seems to be exclusively, though rather weakly, calcicolous (M.C.F. Proctor & M.O. Hill in Hill *et al.* 1992). In other parts of the range it occurs on acidic or calcareous substrata, in the mountains (up to 4200 m altitude in N. America) as well as lowlands (Ochyra & Bednarek-Ochyra in FNA 2007).

The plants are perennial. It is a dioicous species in which capsules are rare (unknown in Ireland; found once in Britain). Gemmae, bulbils and tubers are absent, but vegetative propagation presumably occurs from detached leaf or stem fragments.

World distribution

R. canescens subsp. *canescens* is widespread in Europe from C. Norway, N. Sweden and N. Finland southwards to N. Spain, the S. Alps and the Caucasus. It is listed as 'declining' in Germany. *R. canescens s.l.* is listed as *Vulnerable* in the Netherlands, with var. *canescens* 'rare' (although more common than *R. ericoides*). The species as a whole is assigned to a Circumpolar Boreo-arctic montane floristic element in Europe. Elsewhere, subsp. *canescens* is known in the Urals, W. Siberia and N. America (Alaska and Labrador southwards to Utah and Colorado: Ochyra & Bednarek-Ochyra in FNA 2007). *R. canescens* subsp. *latifolium* (C.E.O.Jensen) Frisvoll is mainly an arctic and boreal-montane plant.

Threats

It was not refound at Mornington in 2007, where only a small patch was recorded in 1968. The extent of its sand-dune habitat at Donabate may have been reduced by golf course development. Murlough National Nature Reserve supported a large population in 2002 that was not immediately threatened. In some small areas, the habitat was being damaged by eutrophication resulting from dog dung being deposited alongside footpaths. The short vegetation in the areas where it grows at Murlough is dependent on intensive grazing by rabbits and hence potentially vulnerable if they are affected by epidemic diseases, as has occurred repeatedly in some English sand-dune systems.

Conservation

R. canescens is listed as a Northern Ireland Priority Species.

Protected sites with recent records: Inner Belfast Lough ASSI; Malahide Estuary SAC; Murlough Nature Reserve; Murlough SAC; **Unprotected sites with recent records:** none.

Campylostelium saxicola (F.Weber & D.Mohr) Bruch & Schimp.   Bent-moss

Status in Ireland: Endangered (B1a, bi, ii, iv, B2a, bi, ii, iv); **Status in Europe:** Rare

Identification

C. saxicola is a tiny gregarious acrocarpous moss that grows on rock surfaces. The stems are only 1–2 mm high and bear linear to linear-lanceolate leaves. The costa in each leaf ends just below the apex and mid-leaf cells are rounded-quadrate and partly bistratose. The ellipsoidal capsule is held up on an arcuate seta 3–5 mm long. The calyptra is mitriform and peristome teeth are bifid. The arcuate seta provides a quick distinction from most other tiny mosses that grow on rock surfaces, except the more common *Seligeria recurvata*. That species differs in having the costa of the leaf excurrent and longer cells in the upper part of the leaf lamina.

Campylostelium saxicola

Distribution in Ireland

Recent records are from three localities in three vice-counties: S. Kerry (N. of Coomacullen Lake, 2006); Sligo (Benbulbin, 1937 and 2003) and Leitrim (Glenade, 1963 and 1970). Older records are from a further 12 localities: S. Kerry (Lough Cruttia, 1935; Coomeeneragh, 1951; Lough Coomeathcun, 1951); N. Kerry (Loo Bridge, 1905–1912; Torc Mountain, 1906); Wicklow (Lough Bray, 1836); Dublin ('Dublin Mountains', 1817; Kelly's Glen, 1872); Leitrim (Truskmore, 1909; Glencar Waterfalls, 1963) and Londonderry (Inishgore, 1937; Banagher Glen, 1959). *C. saxicola* is very small and inconspicuous and typically exists as small localised populations, so it may still occur at some of the old sites and be somewhat under-recorded elsewhere, although it is undoubtedly rare.

Ecology and biology

Its habitat is on moderately acidic rock surfaces in more or less shaded, damp or humid places, often on north-facing slopes or near streams. Most records are from sandstone blocks and boulders, although it was on mica schist rock at Banagher Glen and doubtless occurs on other lithologies elsewhere in Ireland (in Europe, it is reported from slate, shale, gneiss and granite).

The biology of the species is poorly understood. The plants can probably be found in all months of the year, growing as pure patches or with other small rupestral bryophytes. They are autoicous and capsules are apparently common (with spores maturing from about July to October in Britain). Tubers and gemmae are unknown, so if vegetative reproduction occurs it is likely to be only from stem and leaf fragments.

World distribution

The species is very sparsely distributed in Britain, where it ranges from S. England to W. Scotland. It occurs in W. and C. Europe (Scotland to Poland and southwards to N. Spain and Romania; absent from Fennoscandia). It is listed as *Endangered* in Switzerland, *Vulnerable* in Germany, Spain and Portugal and *Near Threatened* in the Czech Republic. Elsewhere, it is known from E. China (Jilin and Taiwan: Cao Tong *et al.* in Li Xing-jiang *et al.* 2001), Japan and in N. America (where mainly in east from Quebec to Alabama; also Washington State). In Europe, it is assigned to a Suboceanic Temperate floristic element.

Threats

Threats to the species are poorly understood but may include shading of rock surfaces if scrub or saplings grow up when grazing ceases. Eutrophication of stream water has also been suggested as a cause of decline in Britain (Birks in Hill *et al.* 1992). It grows on nutrient-poor rock surfaces, so is likely to be vulnerable to atmospheric nitrogen pollution.

Conservation

Conservation should aim to maintain a number of viable populations through appropriate habitat management. This will require further survey and assessment of threats. One of the known locations is on protected land.

Protected sites with recent records: Killarney National Park, Macgillycuddy's Reeks and Caragh River Catchment SAC; **Unprotected sites with recent records:** Benbulbin (outside Ben Bulben, Gleniff and Glenade Complex SAC); Glenade.

Brachydontium trichodes (F.Weber) Milde

Bristle-leaf

syn. *Brachyodus trichodes* (F.Weber) Nees & Hornsch.
Status in Ireland: Endangered (B2a, bi, bii, iv); **Status in Europe:** Rare

Number of Hectads	8
+ Old (pre-1970)	6
☐ Recent (1970–2010)	4

Brachydontium trichodes

Identification

B. trichodes is a minute olive green to yellowish-green or brownish acrocarpous moss that grows in small colonies on sheltered rock surfaces. The erect plants are only 1–2 mm high and grow in open patches (low turfs). The leaves are few in number and bristle-like, comprising an ovate-lanceolate basal part from which the costa extends in a long subula. Capsules are borne on an erect seta 2–3 mm tall. They are ovate to obloid, striate when mature and furrowed when dry and empty. Several species of *Seligeria* that occur mainly on more basic rocks are similar in general appearance to *B. trichodes*, as is *Campylostelium saxicola*. However, none of these other tiny rock mosses has the striate or furrowed capsule of *B. trichodes*. The young capsule of *B. trichodes* is covered by a calyptra that is erect with several basal splits (mitrate); in *Seligeria* the calyptra sits more obliquely on the capsule and has only a single basal split (cucullate). Plants lacking capsules are probably unidentifiable.

Distribution in Ireland

Recent records are from four scattered localities in three vice-counties: Wicklow (River Liffey, NW of Sally Gap, 2010); Leitrim (Dough Mountain above Killea, 2005); W. Donegal (N. slope of Muckish, 2002) and Down (Scrabo Hill quarry, 1933–2002). Old records in areas where it has not been refound recently are from a further five localities: Wicklow (Lough Bray area, 1835 and 1878; Kelly's Glen, 1863); Dublin ('Dublin', 1817); Sligo (Benbulbin, 1879–1937) and Londonderry (Inishgore, W. of Draperstown, 1937).

Ecology and biology

The species grows on steep to vertical or slightly overhanging surfaces of soft to hard siliceous rocks of neutral to strongly acidic reaction. It apparently prefers rather humid or sheltered places, occurring in unshaded sites only on N.-facing slopes. Its substrata have been recorded as sandstone, quartzite, granite and decomposing chert, on boulders, natural outcrops and quarried rocks, over an altitudinal range of at least 100–590 m. The species is reported to occur also on calcareous rock in Britain (Corley in Hill *et al.* 1992) and Norway (Lönnell in Hallingbäck *et al.* 2006), but it has apparently never been found on limestone or chalk in Ireland.

It is a perennial that can be seen in all months of the year. Both sexes occur on the same plant, the female inflorescences at the stem tip, the male inflorescences on short branches (autoicous). Capsules are common, with spores maturing in autumn and early winter. There are no reports of gemmae or tubers.

World distribution

The species occurs widely but rather sparsely in Europe, mainly in mountain regions, from SW Norway and Poland southwards to Portugal and east to the Caucasus.

It is listed as *Critically Endangered* in Switzerland, *Endangered* in Spain and Portugal, *Vulnerable* in Bulgaria and 'declining' in Germany and Norway. Distribution maps showing it is locally frequent in Germany (Meinunger & Schröder 2007) suggest that its treatment as 'Rare' in the *Red List* for Europe as a whole may be unnecessary. It is classified as a Suboceanic Temperate floristic element in Europe. Elsewhere, it is recorded from N. America (New Hampshire, North Carolina, Tennessee and Washington State) and Colombia (Vitt & Spence in FNA 2007). Reports from Australia (Vitt & Spence *loc. cit.*) may be based on *B. intermedium* I.G.Stone (cf. Streimann & Klazenga 2002).

Threats

Threats to the species are poorly understood, but at Scrabo Hill quarry it is clearly at risk from shading of boulders on the quarry floor by growth of scrub and saplings. More generally, its occurrence on predominantly acidic, nutrient-poor substrata may imply that it is vulnerable to eutrophication.

Conservation

The preponderance of old records may suggest *B. trichodes* has declined in Ireland, but it is tiny and easily overlooked, so further bryological surveys may rediscover some of the old sites or disclose additional populations. Scrabo Hill quarry is a protected site where maintaining a viable population of *B. trichodes* will depend on appropriate habitat management, especially cutting scrub and saplings around the boulders on which it grows. *B. trichodes* is listed as a Northern Ireland Priority Species.

Protected sites with recent records: Dough/Thur Mountains NHA; Muckish Mountain SAC; Scrabo ASSI; Wicklow Mountains SAC; **Unprotected sites with recent records:** none.

River Liffey, south-west of Sally Gap, Co. Wicklow.

Seligeria pusilla (Hedw.) Bruch & Schimp.

Dwarf Rock-bristle

Status in Ireland: Least Concern; **Status in Europe:** Least Concern

A tiny acrocarpous moss that grows on basic rock in humid sites, usually on limestones (including chalk in Northern Ireland). It was included in the Provisional Red List (Holyoak 2006b) but extensive searches for *Seligeria* over the past decade have revealed additional localities. It has been reported from five vice-counties, with records from 16 hectads (9 old, 12 recent), those from the past decade being from at least 15 localities. The species is probably still somewhat under-recorded and it is not threatened.

Seligeria acutifolia Lindb.

Sharp Rock-bristle

syn. *S. acutifolia* var. *longiseta* (Lindb.) Schimp.
Status in Ireland: Least Concern; **Status in Europe:** Least Concern

A tiny acrocarpous moss that grows on sheltered limestone rocks. It was formerly under-recorded in Ireland, with no records at all shown by Hill *et al.* (1992), and was included in the Provisional Red List (Holyoak 2006b). However reidentification of old specimens along with deliberate efforts to locate *Seligeria* over the past decade has resulted in more than 20 localities being found. It is now known from 10 vice-counties, with records from 16 hectads (3 old, 14 recent). The species appears to be locally common in some limestone areas in Fermanagh, where numerous small populations doubtless still await discovery.

Seligeria calycina Mitt. ex Lindb.

English Rock-bristle

syn. *S. paucifolia* auct. non (With.) Carruth.
Status in Ireland: Regionally Extinct; **Status in Europe:** Least Concern

Number of Hectads	3
+ Old (pre-1970)	3

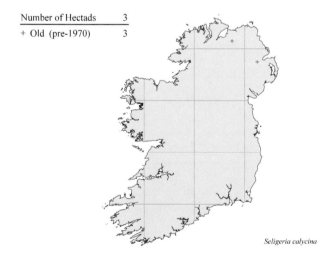

Seligeria calycina

Identification

S. calycina is a tiny acrocarpous moss that grows on rock as sparsely scattered stems or diminutive green turfs, the shoots being less than 2 mm tall. The leaves are erect to erect-spreading, ovate to narrowly lanceolate, acuminate into a long subula that is composed mainly of costa and has an acute tip. The leaf margins are plane and entire. Cells in mid-lamina are smooth and rectangular; those

towards the base of the leaf are rectangular to linear. The capsule is ovoid to ellipsoid with a long neck, narrowed at the mouth when empty, with well-developed peristome, exserted on a straight seta up to 2 mm long. The spores measure 9–12 μm. *S. calycina* differs from other Irish *Seligeria* species in the subulate, entire leaves combined with an exserted, peristomate capsule having a long neck and narrowed mouth.

Distribution in Ireland

Records are from three localities in two vice-counties: Antrim (Black Mountain, 1873–1887; White Park Bay, 1936) and Londonderry (Benbradagh, 1964). It was not refound at White Park Bay or Benbradagh in 1999–2008, despite much time spent searching for *Seligeria*. However, the plants are tiny and hard to find when present on scattered chalk rocks in small amounts, so the species may still persist somewhere.

Ecology and biology

Irish records are all from chalk ('limestone') rocks, including chips of rock in grassland and blocks on a hillside at c. 310 m elevation. In Britain, it is found on fragments of chalk of various sizes, normally on the ground in woodland but also in chalk pits and rarely in grassland (M.F.V. Corley in Hill *et al.* 1992).

The plants are perennial, with shoots arising from a persistent protonema. It is an autoicous species in which capsules are usually present, ripening in summer. Gemmae, bulbils and tubers are absent.

World distribution

Endemic to Europe, where it is mainly known in S. and E. England, with other records from NE Ireland, Belgium and France, along with widely isolated recent records from C. Portugal (where it is listed as *Data Deficient*), Serbia (where it is regarded as *Vulnerable*; Sabovljević *et al.* 2004) and Crete (Gos & Ochyra 1994). Reports from Italy are cited in much of the literature but they are no longer accepted (Gos & Ochyra 1994, Cortini Pedrotti 2001). The species is assigned to a Suboceanic Temperate floristic element.

Threats

No information is available.

Conservation

Some of the old sites are almost certainly on land that is now protected. Further searches for this elusive species in Northern Ireland may well be successful.

Protected sites with recent records: none; **Unprotected sites with recent records:** none.

Seligeria calcarea (Hedw.) Bruch & Schimp.   Chalk Rock-bristle

Status in Ireland: Vulnerable (B2a, bii, iv); **Status in Europe:** Least Concern

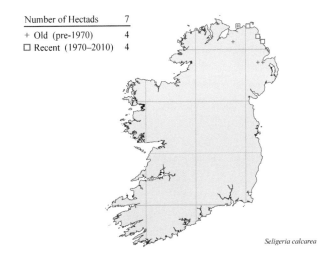

Number of Hectads	7
+ Old (pre-1970)	4
□ Recent (1970–2010)	4

Seligeria calcarea

Identification

A tiny acrocarpous moss that grows on rock as scattered plants or forms diminutive green or olive green turfs, the shoots being up to 2 mm high. The leaves are erect, ovate to ovate-lanceolate or narrowly lanceolate, ending in a rather broad, blunt subula composed entirely of costa. The leaf margins are plane and entire. Cells in the upper leaf lamina are smooth and quadrate, those in the lower part of the leaf are rectangular. The capsule is ovate to hemispherical, as wide as long, widest at the mouth only when old and empty, with well-developed peristome, erect and exserted on a straight seta 1–2 mm long. The spores measure 14–18 *μ*m. *S. calcarea* is distinct from other *Seligeria* in Ireland in its combination of short, blunt-tipped, entire leaves and peristomate capsules that are not much longer than wide.

Distribution in Ireland

Recent records are from seven localities, all from Antrim (White Park Bay, 1936–1999; White Rocks, pre-1938 and 1999; Carrivemurphy, 1999; Park Head, 1999; SE of Whitebay Point, 1999; Straidkilly Point, 1999 and 2008; SW of Cushendall, 1999). Older records are from a further three localities in Antrim (Black Mountain, 1873–1934; Colin Glen, 1875; Carr's Glen, Belfast, 1897–1910) and another from Londonderry (Benbradagh, pre-1938 and 1964). Seven records in 1999 resulted from sustained efforts to locate *Seligeria* spp. during bryophyte surveys in Northern Ireland; almost all of the populations found were small and it was not refound at Benbradagh.

Ecology and biology

In Northern Ireland, *S. calcarea* grows only on hard chalk ('limestone') in humid, sheltered, lowland sites that are not heavily shaded. Most records were from stones on N.-facing grassland slopes, often beneath crags, in old quarries or on coastal slopes. It was also found on the steep sides of a boulder at the base of a sea cliff, on the bottom of a quarry face and in 'scree' on the floor of a quarry. In Britain, it is also mainly a plant of chalk or oolite, avoiding harder limestone, with most occurrences in disused chalk pits and rare records from masonry (M.F.V. Corley in Hill *et al.* 1992).

The plants are short-lived perennials with persistent protonema. It is an autoicous species in which capsules are common, maturing in summer. Gemmae, bulbils and tubers are absent.

World distribution

The European distribution extends from N. Ireland, S. and E. England, Denmark, S. Sweden, C. Finland and Estonia southwards to N. and E. Spain, C. Italy and the Crimea. It is listed as *Critically Endangered* in Finland, *Endangered* in the Czech Republic, *Vulnerable* in Spain, Sweden and Switzerland, 'very rare and susceptible' in the Netherlands and 'declining' in Germany. It is assigned to a European Temperate floristic element in Europe. Elsewhere, it occurs in N. America (from Northwest Territories and Quebec southwards to Arkansas: D.H. Vitt in FNA 2007).

Threats

Most populations of *S. calcarea* are small and some of them are potentially vulnerable to shading if scrub or saplings become established.

Conservation

Several of the sites are on protected land. *S. calcarea* is listed as a Northern Ireland Priority Species.

Protected sites with recent records: Little Deer Park ASSI; North Antrim Coast SAC; White Rocks ASSI; White Park Bay ASSI; **Unprotected sites with recent records:** Carrivemurphy; Straidkilly Point; SW of Cushendall.

Seligeria donniana (Sm.) Müll.Hal.

Donn's Rock-bristle

syn. *S. doniana* auct., *S. donnii* Lindb. *nom. illeg.*
Status in Ireland: Least Concern; **Status in Europe:** Least Concern

A tiny acrocarpous moss that grows on calcareous rocks, mainly limestone in sheltered places. It was included in the Provisional Red List (Holyoak 2006b), but like other *Seligeria*, it was under-recorded in Ireland prior to intensive efforts being made to locate the genus over the past decade. It has been reported from nine vice-counties, with records from 19 hectads (9 old, 13 recent), and is currently known from more than 20 localities. The plants are minute and doubtless still somewhat under-recorded.

Seligeria patula (Lindb.) I.Hagen

syn. *S. alpestris* T.Schauer, *S. patula* var. *alpestris* (T.Schauer) Gos & Ochyra,
S. trifaria auct. non. (Brid.) Lindb., *S. tristichoides* var. *patula* (Lindb.) Broth.
Status in Ireland: Near Threatened; **Status in Europe:** Insufficiently Known

A tiny acrocarpous moss that grows on flushed surfaces of limestone crags, often on tufa. Records of all *Seligeria* from Ireland and Britain with three-ranked leaves were attributed to *S. trifaria* (Brid.) Lindb. (or its synonym *S. tristicha* (Brid.) Bruch & Schimp.) until a new key to the genus was published by Blockeel *et al.* (2000). This key placed plants with small spores (< 23 μm) as *S. patula* and those with larger spores as *S. trifaria*. Subsequent study of plants from Ireland with mature spores revealed only *S. patula* to be present (identification based only on leaf characters apparently being unreliable). The confirmed records, all recent, are from nine localities, confined to five hectads in three vice-counties (Sligo, Leitrim, Fermanagh), with non-fertile specimens from several additional localities. Some of the populations of *S. patula* are large and extensive and the species is not currently threatened. This species is endemic to Europe.

Seligeria oelandica C.E.O.Jensen & Medelius

Status in Ireland: Vulnerable (D1); **Status in Europe:** Insufficiently Known

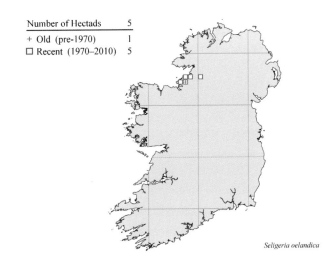

Number of Hectads	5
+ Old (pre-1970)	1
□ Recent (1970–2010)	5

Seligeria oelandica

Identification

A small acrocarpous moss that grows on rock as scattered stems, sparse turfs or small blackish, blackish-green or dark brown tufts, often partly encrusted with tufa, with stems 5–15 mm long, rarely 20 mm. The leaves are erect to erecto-patent, with an oblong or ovate base that tapers abruptly to a stout subula that is mainly filled by the costa, with a narrowly obtuse apex. The leaf margins are plane and entire. Upper leaf cells are shortly rectangular, the basal cells longer. Capsules are almost hemispherical when young, becoming wide-mouthed and turbinate when empty, with a well-developed peristome, exserted on a stout, erect seta up to 2.5 mm long. The columella is attached to the operculum and falls with it. Spores measure 20–30 μm. The species is distinct from other Irish *Seligeria* in its larger size and strikingly turbinate empty capsules; *S. patula* also differs in its three-ranked leaves.

Distribution in Ireland

Records are from 10 localities in three vice-counties: Sligo (Gleniff, 1963–1999; Benbulbin, on E. cliffs of E. corrie, 1962–2003; Benwiskin, 2003; Cormac Reagh's Hole, 2003; Annacoona, 2003); Leitrim (Ballinlig and nearby, Glenade, 1963–1999; Larganavaddoge, 2000; S. or SE of Aghadunvane, 2000–2005) and Fermanagh (N. of Glencreawan Lough, 2000–2005; also nearby, at Cliffs of Magho, 2000).

Ecology and biology

Most populations are on steep, vertical or overhanging tufaceous films on crags of Carboniferous Limestone or the underlying calcareous shales, in places that are flushed with water or receive spray for much of the time, at c. 175–450 m altitude. The sites are often at the base of N.- or E.-facing crags and commonly also close to intermittent waterfalls. Immediate associates are few other than *Seligeria patula* and algal films, but other bryophytes and *Saxifraga aizoides* are often close by. At Larganavaddoge, it extends onto limestone boulders and smaller rocks just below the crags. However, two populations are much further from crags, respectively above and below them on rocks or stones in open flush habitats. In Scandinavia, it grows on periodically flushed limestone and schist, in the Scandes mountains in small dried-up brooks, on sloping flat rocks and at shores of lakes and streams, on Öland and Gotland on coastal cliffs and along streams (Hallingbäck *et al.* 2006).

The plants are perennial. It is an autoicous species in which capsules seem to be frequent rather than plentiful in Ireland, maturing in summer. Gemmae, bulbils and tubers are absent.

World distribution

The range is remarkably disjunct, with small, widely isolated groups of populations. In Europe, it is known in Spitsbergen, N. and SW Norway (where it is 'declining'), S. Sweden (*Vulnerable*), NW Ireland, S. Wales (one locality), Switzerland (*Vulnerable*) and in the W.

Carpathians in Slovakia (Ochyra 1991, Frahm in Frey *et al.* 2006, Hallingbäck *et al.* 2006). Hence it is classified as a European Boreo-arctic montane floristic element in Europe. Elsewhere, it is known in NE Asia (arctic part of Russian Far East: Ignatov *et al.* 2007) and northern N. America (Alaska, Yukon, Northwest Territories and Quebec: D.H. Vitt in FNA 2007).

Threats

There were no immediate threats apparent at most localities visited in the past decade, although small populations in flushes are very vulnerable to disturbance by stock or walkers, or to shading if surrounding vegetation grows taller. Larger populations on crags are potentially vulnerable to hydrological changes or eutrophication of the water.

Conservation

All populations are on protected land. *S. oelandica* is listed as a Northern Ireland Priority Species and a UK Biodiversity Action Plan (UKBAP) species.

Protected sites with recent records: Arroo Mountain SAC; Ben Bulben, Gleniff and Glenade Complex SAC; Cliffs of Magho ASSI; **Unprotected sites with recent records:** none.

Gleniff, Co. Sligo.

Fissidens crispus Mont.

Herzog's Pocket-moss

syn. *Fissidens limbatus* Sull.
Status in Ireland: Data Deficient; **Status in Europe:** Least Concern

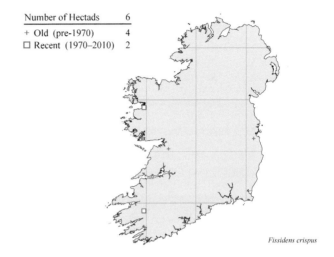

Number of Hectads	6
+ Old (pre-1970)	4
□ Recent (1970–2010)	2

Fissidens crispus

Identification

Like all species of *Fissidens*, *F. crispus* has its leaves arranged in two opposing ranks, each leaf with a sheathing lamina and a strong costa. This plant is part of a difficult complex of small species which have their leaves bordered by long, narrow cells. Plants are no more than 7 mm high, usually considerably less, with up to 15 pairs of leaves about 0.5 mm long. As in some other species of *Fissidens*, the perichaetial bracts are longer and narrower than the stem leaves. The only distinctive features of *F. crispus* are the long cells of the leaf border which do not join those of the costa at the leaf apex, and the small leaf cells (4–8 μm wide) which are bulging in cross section (thicker than wide). Sporophytes are produced at the ends of the shoots, with an erect capsule exserted on a red seta.

Distribution in Ireland

There are only two recent records in Ireland, both in the west of the country: N. Kerry (Ross Island, 1983) and W. Mayo ('near Rose Cottage', NW of Westport, 1987). Older records are from S. Kerry (near Waterville, 1951); W. Cork (Glengarriff, 1966); SE Galway (Punch Bowl, Gort, 1968) and Dublin (Kilmashogue Mountain, 1958). It is almost certainly under-recorded because careful microscopic study and measurements are needed to distinguish it from the more common *F. viridulus* (Sw. ex anon.) Wahlenb. and no consistent effort has been made during recent fieldwork to check all finds of that species.

Ecology and biology

All the Irish records are from earthy banks in the lowlands. In Britain, it is a colonist of sheltered, thin or compacted, circumneutral to basic soils, usually on banks in woodland, at track sides, on sea cliffs or at stream sides. It occasionally grows on limestone rocks and mortar. It has not been recorded above 175 m in Ireland or Britain.

F. crispus may be synoicous, autoicous or dioicous and sporophytes are produced abundantly. It is not known to produce any vegetative propagules.

World distribution

This species is recorded from W. and S. Europe but its distribution is incompletely known. It is listed as *Nationally Scarce* in Britain, *Endangered* in the Czech Republic and *Near Threatened* in Luxembourg, and also occurs in Sweden, Italy, (including Sardinia: Frahm *et al.* 2008a), Greece, Spain, Portugal, Malta (Frahm & Lüth 2008) and Croatia (Sabovljević 2006). Hill *et al.* (1992) list it for Switzerland, the Azores and the Canary Islands, but it is omitted from these territories by Schnyder *et al.* (2004), Gabriel *et al.* (2005) and Dirkse *et al.* (1993) respectively. In Europe, it is assigned to an Oceanic Mediterranean-Atlantic floristic element. Elsewhere, its distribution is also confused. Hill *et al.* (1992) list it as occurring in Turkey, Israel and Iran, but Akhani & Kürschner (2004) do not list it for Iran. It is widely distributed in N. and S. America (FNA 2007).

Threats

There is no real evidence of decline and it is therefore difficult to identify any real threats to this species. It is easily overlooked and must surely be more widespread in Ireland than the records suggest. Individual colonies on bare soil must inevitably be outcompeted by coarser vegetation, but this is a natural process and *F. crispus* presumably colonises new bare areas.

Conservation

No conservation measures are necessary beyond consciously looking for this species during fieldwork. It has not been recorded since 1987, so almost certainly has been overlooked during the surveys over the last decade.

Protected sites with recent records: Killarney National Park; Killarney National Park, Macgillycuddy's Reeks and Caragh River Catchment SAC; **Unprotected sites with recent records:** NW of Westport.

Fissidens gracilifolius Brugg.-Nann. & Nyholm

Narrow-leaved Pocket-moss

syn. *Fissidens pusillus* var. *tenuifolius* (Boulay) Podp., *F. viridulus* var. *tenuifolius* (Boulay) A.J.E.Sm.
Status in Ireland: Least Concern; **Status in Europe:** Least Concern

This is a minute, dark green *Fissidens* with bordered leaves that grows on dry limestone and sandstone rocks in a range of calcareous habitats. This species was probably overlooked in the past, partly because of confusion with other small species of *Fissidens*, particularly with *F. pusillus*, from which it differs in its longer perichaetial bracts. It was included in the Provisional Red List (Holyoak 2006b), but it now appears to be fairly widespread on base-rich rocks in Ireland. It has been reported from 12 vice-counties, with records from 19 hectads (7 old, 15 recent, 1 undated).

Fissidens incurvus Starke ex Röhl.

Short-leaved Pocket-moss

Status in Ireland: Least Concern; **Status in Europe:** Least Concern

A medium-sized *Fissidens*, with bordered leaves and inclined capsules. It was included in the Provisional Red List (Holyoak 2006b), but it is now clear that it is relatively widespread on calcareous soils in lowland areas throughout Ireland. It has been reported from 18 vice-counties, with records from 30 hectads (17 old, 14 recent). It is a common plant in S. Britain and over much of Europe. In the European checklist (Hill *et al.* 2006), this species is relegated to a variety of *F. bryoides*, but this has not been followed by Hill *et al.* (2008). It is also treated as a variety of *F. viridulus* in some European lists.

Fissidens rivularis (Spruce) Schimp.

Water Pocket-moss

Status in Ireland: Vulnerable (D2); **Status in Europe:** Least Concern

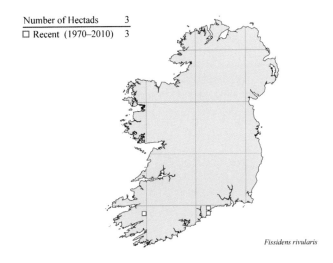

Number of Hectads	3
☐ Recent (1970–2010)	3

Fissidens rivularis

Identification

This is a small to medium-sized dark green plant with shoots 5–20 mm long. It has the typical *Fissidens* growth form of two opposite ranks of leaves with a sheathing lamina, but the leaves of *F. rivularis* have a very thick yellowish border composed of long narrow cells, which joins with the excurrent costa to form a stout mucro. In this respect, it differs from *F. crassipes* and *F. rufulus*, in which the border and costa are not confluent. The rare *F. monguillonii* has distinctive narrow perichaetial bracts, a thinner colourless border and wider leaf cells.

Distribution in Ireland

This species was first recorded in Ireland in 1983 and there are now records from three localities in two vice-counties: N. Kerry (Lough Leane, near Ross Castle and Muckross, 1983–2005) and Waterford (Ballymacart River at Ballymacart Bridge, 1999; Glendine River, near Gorteen, 2008).

Ecology and biology

This is an aquatic species, found on stones, rocks and exposed tree roots in lowland streams, rivers and lakes, and occasionally on firm soil. Its shoots are often encrusted with diatoms and detritus. In Ireland, it has been recorded on damp, shady limestone fragments and tree roots under trees on a lake shore; on firm soil and roots at the base of a tussock of *Osmunda regalis* on a lake shore, slightly shaded by *Alnus glutinosa*; on a firm, steep to vertical, unshaded soil bank 5–20 cm above the water level of a lake; on boulders in a stream; and on damp sloping rock in a part-shaded hollow in a bank above a waterfall in a small river in open deciduous woodland. The Irish sites are at altitudes of up to 70 m.

This is an autoicous species which produces sporophytes occasionally (not recorded in Ireland), but is not known to produce vegetative propagules.

World distribution

This species is widely distributed but rather rare in Europe, with a mainly southern distribution, extending eastwards to Crete, the Balkans and the Caucasus. It is absent from many countries, particularly in the north, *Nationally Scarce* in Britain (where it is almost restricted to the south-west), *Vulnerable* in Bulgaria and Switzerland and *Data Deficient* in Germany. In Europe, it is categorised as an Oceanic Mediterranean-Atlantic floristic element. Elsewhere, it occurs in Macaronesia, Turkey and Iran (Akhani & Kürschner 2004). Although it was listed for Africa by Hill *et al.* (1992), it was excluded by O'Shea (2006), because no confirmed records could be found.

Threats

The greatest threat to this species in Ireland is probably inappropriate lakeside and riverside management, including leisure developments and 'tidying up' operations. It is said (Hill *et al.* 1992) to be at least somewhat tolerant of aquatic pollution.

Conservation

The sites where this species grows should be monitored and protected from development pressures. Local river management authorities need to be aware of its presence.

Protected sites with recent records: Glendine Wood SAC; Killarney National Park; Killarney National Park, Macgillycuddy's Reeks and Caragh River Catchment SAC; **Unprotected sites with recent records:** Ballymacart River at Ballymacart Bridge (possibly within Glenanna Wood pNHA).

Fissidens monguillonii Thér.

Atlantic Pocket-moss

Status in Ireland: Near Threatened; **Status in Europe:** Rare

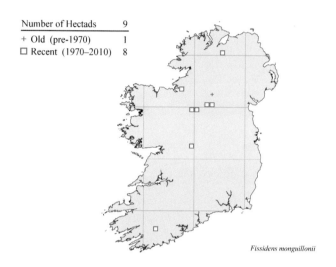

Number of Hectads	9
+ Old (pre-1970)	1
□ Recent (1970–2010)	8

Fissidens monguillonii

Identification

An acrocarpous moss that forms dull or dark green tufts or larger patches 5–25 mm high; the plants sometimes become silt-encrusted. As with other *Fissidens*, the leaves are alternate and distichous, arranged complanately on the stem, with a basal sheathing lamina. In *F. monguillonii*, the leaves are oblong to lingulate-lanceolate, acute to obtuse, often mucronate, with a well-developed 2–3 stratose border that is confluent with the percurrent costa. The isodiametric mid-leaf cells are larger than in several related species, mainly 10–18 μm wide, often with brownish cell walls. Antheridia are on short lateral or terminal branches. Archegonia and capsules are terminal on the stem or sometimes on a side branch, at the base of distinctive linear-lanceolate perichaetial bracts which are markedly longer and narrower than the stem leaves. Capsules are ellipsoid, inclined, exserted on a long seta. Species identification in *Fissidens* is often difficult, but *F. monguillonii* can be determined by the combination of leaves with a 2–3 stratose border reaching the apex, large leaf cells, arrangement of gametangia, and the long, narrow perichaetial bracts.

Distribution in Ireland

Recent records are from nine localities in five vice-counties: W. Cork (Manch Bridge, 2009, 2010); Roscommon (near Devenish Island, 2007); Leitrim (bank of R. Shannon at Carrick-on-Shannon, 2000; by Bonet River near Lough Gill, 2000; N. end of Rinn Lough, 2000; Cavan (Glasshouse Lake, 2005; shore of Lough Oughter at Inishconnell, 2005; shore of Lough Oughter near Gartnanoul Point, 2001) and Londonderry (River Faughan, 2008). There is an older record from Fermanagh (Kilturk Lough, 1959).

Ecology and biology

F. monguillonii grows in a well-defined habitat in the upper part of regularly inundated zones beside lowland rivers and lakes, on substrata of circumneutral to somewhat basic mud or soil, sometimes extending onto exposed *Alnus glutinosa* roots and dead wood. Its sites are lightly to moderately shaded, such as at the base of a stand of tall *Phragmites*, at the upper edge of a reed swamp (beneath *Phragmites*, *Filipendula ulmaria* and *Calystegia*), in edge of *Salix cinerea* carr, or shaded by *Alnus* trees.

The plants are perennial. It is an autoicous species that occasionally produces capsules which mature in winter. Gemmae, bulbils and tubers are unknown. Vegetative propagation might occur from detached plants or stem fragments being carried by water.

World distribution

In Europe, it is known only from Ireland, W. Britain (N. Wales southwards to Devon and E. Cornwall; listed as *Near Threatened* in Britain), Belgium, France, Luxembourg (where it is listed as *Vulnerable*) and N. Spain (*Data Deficient*). It is assigned to an Oceanic Southern-temperate floristic element in Europe. Elsewhere, it occurs in N. and C. Africa. Reports from Macaronesia (Azores, Canary Islands) appear to be based on other *Fissidens* species.

Threats

It is potentially at risk from alterations to the flooding regimes of rivers and lakes. Modern management of water levels along parts of the River Shannon probably precludes its occurrence. It could also be at risk if reed swamp or carr beside rivers or lakes is removed or damaged (e.g. for waterside developments such as construction of jetties or marinas).

Conservation

Several populations are in protected areas.

Protected sites with recent records: Glasshouse Lake pNHA; Lough Gill SAC; Lough Oughter and Associated Loughs SAC; Lough Rinn pNHA; River Faughan and Tributaries ASSI; River Faughan and Tributaries SAC; River Shannon Callows SAC; **Unprotected sites with recent records:** bank of R. Shannon at Carrick-on-Shannon; Manch Bridge.

Fissidens rufulus Bruch & Schimp.   Beck Pocket-moss

Status in Ireland: Endangered (B1a, bi, ii, iii, iv, B2a, bi, ii, iii, iv); **Status in Europe:** Least Concern

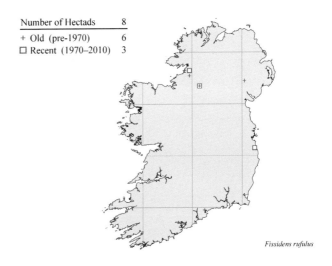

Number of Hectads	8
+ Old (pre-1970)	6
☐ Recent (1970–2010)	3

Fissidens rufulus

Identification

F. rufulus, in common with all species of the genus, has its leaves arranged in two opposing ranks, each leaf with a sheathing lamina and a strong costa. Like some of the other aquatic species of *Fissidens*, the leaves have a strongly thickened border, composed of several layers of long, thin cells. The border does not, however, join with the costa at the leaf apex, as in *F. crassipes*. Sporophytes are produced at the ends of the shoots, with erect or inclined capsules exserted on a red seta. *F. rufulus* can usually be distinguished from *F. crassipes* by the smaller leaf cells (6–10 μm), and fertile material has shorter archegonia and peristome teeth. However, they are very close, and some Irish material is indeed intermediate between the two species.

Fissidens rufulus, Ederamone, Ballyshannon, Co. Donegal.

Distribution in Ireland

With a slightly northern distribution in Ireland, the three recent records of this species are from Wicklow (Glencullin River near Enniskerry, 1975); Fermanagh (Cladagh River at Marble Arch, 1957–2005) and E. Donegal (tributary of the River Erne near Ederamone, Ballyshannon, 1937–2001). There are older records from Waterford (Deelish, near Dungarvan, 1956); Fermanagh (River Erne near Belleek, 1937); E. Donegal (Crana River near Buncrana, 1967) and Down (Knocknagore, 1909).

Ecology and biology

F. rufulus is one of the aquatic members of the genus, growing on rocks in clean, fast-flowing streams and rivers, at or below the water level. It tends to favour limestone and other base-rich rocks, but is also capable of growing on neutral or acid rocks. It is a lowland species that has not been recorded above 365 m in Ireland or Britain.

Although dioicous, capsules are produced occasionally in the winter. There are no known specialised vegetative means of propagation.

World distribution

Nearly endemic to Europe, *F. rufulus* is an uncommon plant, listed as *Nationally Scarce* in Britain, *Endangered* in Switzerland and Luxembourg, *Vulnerable* in Austria, *Near Threatened* in the Czech Republic, *Data Deficient* in Sweden, Germany and Spain, 'very rare and susceptible' in the Netherlands. It is also known from France, Italy (including Sardinia), Croatia, Greece and Russia (Ignatov *et al.* 2007). In Europe, it is categorised as a European Temperate floristic element. Outside Europe, it is known only from Turkey.

Threats

This species has probably been eliminated from the lower River Erne by the hydroelectric scheme engineering works, although it still persists near Belleek. Water pollution is another obvious threat, as it is likely to be eliminated by excessive turbidity, and probably also by eutrophication. Overenthusiastic waterway maintenance is another real threat, as removal of the rocks where it grows is clearly damaging. It was not refound in the Glencullin River during recent fieldwork.

Conservation

The stretches of river where *F. rufulus* is known to occur should be made known to the authorities involved in river management.

Protected sites with recent records: Dargle River Valley pNHA; Knocksink Wood Nature Reserve; Knocksink Wood SAC; **Unprotected sites with recent records:** Cladagh River at Marble Arch (proposed ASSI); tributary of the River Erne near Ederamone, Ballyshannon.

Fissidens exilis Hedw.   Slender Pocket-moss

Status in Ireland: Vulnerable (B2a, bii, iv); **Status in Europe:** Least Concern

Identification

Like all species of *Fissidens*, *F. exilis* has its leaves arranged in two opposing ranks, each leaf with a sheathing lamina and a strong costa. This is one of the smallest species of the genus and is characterised by the leaves lacking a border of long narrow cells, with crenulate or crenulate-serrulate margin, evanescent costa, and the shoots, which are less than 3 mm long, having only 2–4 pairs of leaves. Sporophytes are produced at the ends of the shoots, with an erect capsule exserted on a red seta.

Distribution in Ireland

Recent records are from eight localities in five vice-counties: Mid Cork (Fountainstown, 2007); Limerick (Barrigone, 1979; Foyne's Island, 1992; Rathcahill East, 1992); Kilkenny (Kyleadohir Wood, 2010; Spahill, 2010); Meath (Somerville, 1978) and Monaghan (Hilton Lough, 2007). Older confirmed records are from: Limerick (Ballydonohoe House, 1966); Kildare (Curragh, 1861); Dublin (Mount Merrion Wood, 1969); Monaghan (near Cavanagarvan, 1965) and Londonderry (Kilrea, 1912). Reports from Down, Armagh and Antrim are not supported by specimens and it is not clear whether any of them are reliable.

Ecology and biology

Usually a winter annual, occasionally persisting longer, this plant grows as scattered shoots or small patches on neutral to acidic soils, typically on sheltered and shaded

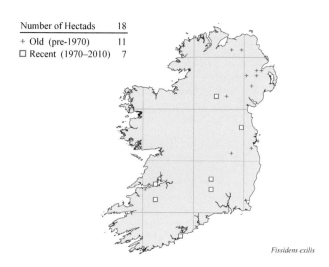

Number of Hectads	18
+ Old (pre-1970)	11
☐ Recent (1970–2010)	7

Fissidens exilis

banks in woodlands or on stream sides. It can also grow on damp soil (and molehills in Britain) in grassland. In Ireland, it has been recorded on earthy banks in woodland and plantations, sometimes by streams or country lanes, with other species colonising partly bare soil, including *Atrichum undulatum*, *Brachythecium rutabulum*, *Dicranella heteromalla*, other *Fissidens* spp. It is confined to the lowlands and has not been recorded above 290 m in Ireland or Britain.

This plant may be dioicous or autoicous, and capsules are produced abundantly in the winter months. No specialised forms of vegetative reproduction are known.

World distribution

F. exilis is widespread but apparently rather rare in Europe as a whole, although it must be overlooked because of its small size. It occurs throughout most of Europe except for the extreme south and north, including Macaronesia, and is currently considered *Vulnerable* in Austria, *Near Threatened* in Switzerland, *Data Deficient* in Portugal, Spain, Bulgaria and Montenegro, 'rare' in the Netherlands, 'rather rare' in Estonia and 'declining' in Norway and Germany. In Europe, it is categorised as a European Temperate floristic element. It also occurs in N. Africa, N. Asia, China (Wu Peng-cheng *et al.* 2002), Turkey, Iran (Akhani & Kürschner 2004), Japan and eastern N. America.

Threats

It is difficult to identify any real threats to this species, even though it appears to be rare in Ireland. Individual colonies are probably transient and eventually shaded out by larger plants, but this is a natural process and can

scarcely be regarded as a threat. It has almost certainly not really declined in Ireland.

Conservation

So long as there is bare, non-calcareous soil available for colonisation on woodland and roadside banks, this species should be secure. It is doubtless under-recorded and should be looked for by bryologists working in these habitats.

Protected sites with recent records: Kyleadohir Nature Reserve; River Barrow and River Nore SAC; Spahill and Clomantagh Hill SAC; **Unprotected sites with recent records:** Barrigone; Fountainstown; Foyne's Island; Hilton Lough; Rathcahill East; Somerville.

Spahill, Co. Kilkenny.

Fissidens curvatus Hornsch.

Portuguese Pocket-moss

syn. *Fissidens algarvicus* Solms
Status in Ireland: Regionally Extinct; **Status in Europe:** Insufficiently Known

Number of Hectads	2
+ Old (pre-1970)	2

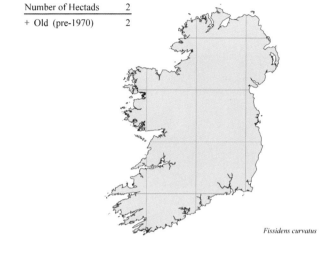

Fissidens curvatus

Identification

As with other species of *Fissidens*, the leaves of *F. curvatus* are alternate and distichous, arranged complanately on the stem, with a basal sheathing lamina. The shoots are small, only up to 3 mm long, with 3–6 (10) pairs of leaves. The leaves are linear-lanceolate, bordered with narrow elongated cells, and characteristically taper gradually to an acuminate apex. Other *Fissidens* species with bordered leaves differ by having more or less parallel-sided leaves, contracted abruptly to shortly pointed apices. The leaf cells are papillose, longer than wide in the upper part of the leaf. The capsules are erect and ovoid, exserted on a red seta.

Distribution in Ireland

This plant was recorded from two sites in S. Kerry in 1951 (west of Glenbeigh and below ruined chapel, West Cove) but has not been recorded elsewhere in Ireland. It has not been refound at the Kerry sites, in spite of searching.

Ecology and biology

F. curvatus grows on clayey soil on shaded banks in lowland areas. Recorded habitats in Ireland are from an earthy roadside bank and a south-facing earth/stone wall.

Although dioicous, sporophytes are produced occasionally in winter and spring. No specialised means of vegetative reproduction are known.

World distribution

This is a plant of south-western and Mediterranean regions in Europe, occurring from Macaronesia and the Iberian Peninsula north to Britain (where it is *Endangered*) and east through Italy (old records only), Croatia, Montenegro (where it is *Data Deficient*) and Hungary to Bulgaria and Greece. In Europe, it is assigned to an Oceanic Mediterranean-Atlantic floristic element. Elsewhere, it appears to be widely distributed, occurring in Iran (Akhani & Kürschner 2004), Turkey (Kürschner & Erdağ 2005), China, India, Japan, N. Africa (Cano *et al.* 2002), sub-Saharan Africa (O'Shea 2006) and C. and S. America (Pursell 1994a & b, He 1998).

Threats

Growth of coarse vegetation over the bare soil habitat might have led to the disappearance of this plant. Road-widening may have caused its loss from the site west of Glenbeigh, but the original location was imprecisely recorded.

Conservation

The habitat of *F. curvatus* does not appear to be particularly exacting, and earthy banks in the south-west should be examined to attempt to refind this plant. However, it is elusive in its occurrence at British sites, perhaps because it is often a short-lived colonist, or varies widely in abundance from year to year. No conservation measures are needed at present.

Fissidens serrulatus Brid.

Large Atlantic Pocket-moss

syn. *Fissidens luisieri* P.de la Varde
Status in Ireland: Vulnerable (D2); **Status in Europe:** Least Concern

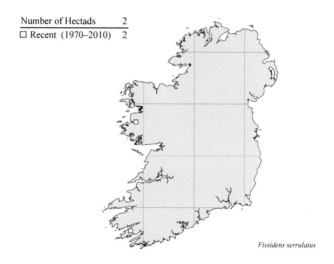

Number of Hectads	2
☐ Recent (1970–2010)	2

Fissidens serrulatus

Identification

This large green semi-aquatic *Fissidens* has shoots up to 7.5 cm long, with alternate, distichous leaves, arranged complanately on the stem. The leaves have the characteristic sheathing lamina of the genus and are up to c. 1 cm long, c. 3–4 times longer than wide, broader than those of *F. polyphyllus*. They are irregularly toothed towards the apex, unbordered but with the smooth marginal cells forming a pale band. *F. serrulatus* resembles large forms of *F. adianthoides* but differs in the more elongated and somewhat more parallel-sided leaves, and in having the leaf cells strongly mamillose.

Distribution in Ireland

This species is known from only two sites in Ireland: Ben Gorm, W. Mayo (1970, but not refound during a search in 2003) and a strong population along the Glantrasna River at Lauragh Bridge, S. Kerry (1992–2008).

Ecology and biology

F. serrulatus is a lowland moss that grows on rocks, tree roots, soil and alluvium just above the normal water level of rivers and streams, but within the periodically inundated zone. Irish plants grow on steep, shaded soil among rocks and Beech roots on a riverbank, sometimes well above the water level, and in a ravine on the south slope of a hill.

It is dioicous, with only non-fertile or male plants known in Ireland and Britain. It produces rhizoidal tubers.

World distribution

F. serrulatus is sparsely scattered in S. and W. Europe, having been recorded from Wales southwards to France, Corsica, Portugal, Spain, Italy, Croatia, Greece (Rhodes) and Macaronesia (Werner *et al.* 2009). The report from Luxembourg is presumably incorrect, as it is omitted by Werner (2003). It is considered *Vulnerable* in Britain, where it is confined to a few sites in Devon, Cornwall and Merioneth. In Europe, it is assigned to an Oceanic Mediterranean-Atlantic floristic element. It is also known from N. Africa (Tunisia and Algeria).

Threats

The greatest potential threats to this species in Ireland are probably from water pollution, alteration of flow (e.g. for hydroelectric schemes), inappropriate riverbank management, such as canalisation, removal of riverbank trees, overenthusiastic 'tidying', or creation of facilities for anglers.

Conservation

The known populations of *F. serrulatus* and the water quality of the streams and rivers should be monitored periodically. Local river management authorities need to be aware of its presence.

Protected sites with recent records: Mweelrea/ Sheeffry/Erriff Complex SAC; **Unprotected sites with recent records:** Glantrasna River at Lauragh Bridge.

Fissidens polyphyllus Wilson ex Bruch & Schimp.   Many-leaved Pocket-moss

Status in Ireland: Vulnerable (D2); **Status in Europe:** Least Concern

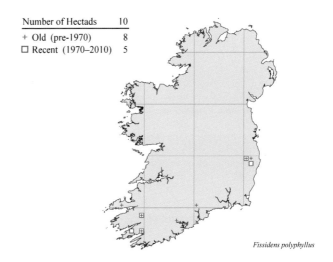

Number of Hectads	10
+ Old (pre-1970)	8
□ Recent (1970–2010)	5

Fissidens polyphyllus

Identification

This is a large and handsome species of *Fissidens* with dark green shoots c. 3.5–6.5 mm wide and up to about 20 cm long (but usually considerably less, sometimes only 1–2 cm). The leaves are longer and narrower than those of most species of the genus (4.5–6 times longer than wide), but it is instantly recognisable as a *Fissidens* by the two opposite ranks of leaves which have a strong costa and a sheathing lamina. There is no border or pale marginal band to the leaf, and the leaf margin is no more than finely and regularly denticulate. The leaf cells are smooth and c. 8–14 μm wide. *F. osmundoides* is a smaller, less aquatic plant, with wider leaves and larger cells.

Distribution in Ireland

This rare species has a mainly southern distribution in Ireland, with recent records from five localities in four vice-counties: S. Kerry (Glantrasna River at Lauragh Bridge, 2006–2008); N. Kerry (Cromaglan, 1900–2005); W. Cork (Glengarriff, 1861–2006) and Wicklow (Carrawaystick Brook, Glenmalur, 1962–2007; Greenan Bridge, 1975–2007). There are additional old records from S. Kerry (Lough Anscaul, 1898); Mid Cork

(Blarney, 1915); Waterford (Lismore, 1967); Wicklow (Drumgoff Bridge, 1942) and Sligo (Benbulbin, 1856). Specimens from Down have been redetermined as *F. taxifolius*.

Ecology and biology

This is a semi-aquatic plant growing on shaded rocks and soil on riverbanks and stream sides in the lowlands, usually somewhat above the mean water levels but subject to periodic inundation. Many of the Irish records are from more or less vertical soil banks or rocks at the edge of rivers, at altitudes from 10–130 m, sometimes growing with *Pellia epiphylla*, *Heterocladium wulfsbergii* or *Thamnobryum alopecurum*. It has also been found at Glengarriff on soil banks and earthy path sides near streams in woodland, but away from open water.

F. polyphyllus is dioicous or autoicous. Sporophytes are unknown in Ireland or Britain, where only non-fertile or male plants have been found. Rhizoidal tubers occur but have not yet been found in Irish material.

World distribution

This species has a southern and western distribution in

Europe, recorded from SW Norway ('declining') and Britain (*Nationally Scarce*) to France, Portugal, Spain and Italy. In Macaronesia, it occurs in the Canary Islands and Madeira (but not the Azores according to Sjögren 2001, cf. Hill *et al.* 1992). In Europe, the species is assigned to a Hyperoceanic Southern-temperate floristic element. Papp & Sabovljević (2003) have recently and unexpectedly recorded this species in Turkish Thrace. Records from China are unconfirmed.

Threats
The greatest threats to this species in Ireland are probably from water pollution, alteration of flow regimes (e.g. for hydroelectric schemes), and inappropriate riverbank management, such as canalisation or overenthusiastic 'tidying'.

Conservation
Large populations at Glengarriff are on protected land. The known populations of *F. polyphyllus* and the water quality of the streams and rivers should be monitored periodically. Local river management authorities need to be aware of its presence.

Protected sites with recent records: Glengarriff Harbour and Woodland SAC; Glengarriff Wood Nature Reserve; Killarney National Park; Killarney National Park, Macgillycuddy's Reeks and Caragh River Catchment SAC; **Unprotected sites with recent records:** Carrawaystick Brook, Glenmalur; Glantrasna River at Lauragh Bridge; Greenan Bridge.

Fissidens fontanus (Bach.Pyl.) Steud.

Fountain Pocket-moss

syn. *Octodiceras fontanum* (Bach.Pyl.) Lindb., *O. julianum* Brid.
Status in Ireland: Vulnerable (D2); **Status in Europe:** Least Concern

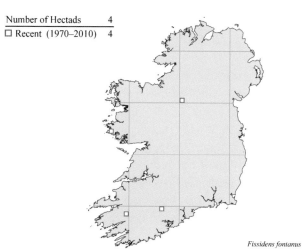

Number of Hectads	4
☐ Recent (1970–2010)	4

Fissidens fontanus

Identification
Formerly treated in a genus of its own (*Octodiceras*), this is a highly distinctive species with all the usual features of *Fissidens*; leaves in two ranks, sheathing lamina, strong costa; but the leaves are very long and narrow (c. 10 times longer than wide), distant, with the sheathing lamina extending only to less than ⅓ the total length. The rather flaccid shoots may be up to c. 3 cm long, with the leaves up to c. 5 mm, dull green and with the costa ending below the apex. Plant surfaces are often colonised by aquatic algae.

Distribution in Ireland
This species has been recorded from four localities in Ireland: N. Kerry (Castlelough Bay, SE shore of Lough Leane, 1997; not refound in 2002); E. Cork (Killavullen Bridge, R. Blackwater, 2009); W. Galway (Lough Donoghmeave, 1999–2000; not refound in 2004) and Leitrim (Carrickaport Lough, 1978; not refound in 2000).

Ecology and biology
Strictly aquatic, *F. fontanus* normally grows in the still or sluggish water of lowland rivers and canals, using rocks,

wood or just about anything as a substratum. The most recent record is from the base of a bridge on the River Blackwater. The older records, however, are from lakes, having been found on rocks at the margin of a lake, in a reed swamp and adherent to emergent rooted vascular water plants, also fixed to sandy bottom and to jetsam, between 0 and 10 cm depth.

It is autoicous, but sporophytes have not been observed in Irish or British material. C. European plants are reported to propagate vegetatively by deciduous branches (Hill *et al.* 1992).

World distribution

This is a widespread moss, growing in most parts of Europe, including Macaronesia, but becoming rare or absent in the far north. It is listed as *Nationally Scarce* in Britain, *Critically Endangered* in Bulgaria, *Vulnerable* in Luxembourg, *Near Threatened* in the Czech Republic and Finland, 'very rare' in Estonia, 'potentially threatened' in Austria and 'sparse' in the Netherlands. In Europe, it is assigned to a European Temperate floristic element. Elsewhere, it occurs in Africa, N. and S. America and Australasia.

Threats

Although known to be able to grow in moderately polluted water, it may be that *F. fontanus* is more sensitive than is generally thought. Hill *et al.* (1992) speculate that it may have disappeared from some localities because of pollution, and also perhaps because of grazing by freshwater snails; Lohammar (1954) found that it was eaten by them in preference to some other aquatic bryophytes, and that it was absent from localities where snails were abundant. Other potential threats might include colonisation of habitats by invasive alien plants.

Conservation

The lakes where this species has been recorded should be searched again for the continued presence of *F. fontanus*, preferably by snorkelling or diving.

Protected sites with recent records: Blackwater River (Cork/Waterford) SAC; Carrickaport Lough pNHA; Killarney National Park, Macgillycuddy's Reeks and Caragh River Catchment SAC; **Unprotected sites with recent records:** Lough Donoghmeave.

Pleuridium subulatum (Hedw.) Rabenh.

Awl-leaved Earth-moss

Status in Ireland: Least Concern; **Status in Europe:** Least Concern

This is a small acrocarpous moss with capsules immersed among longly-acuminate perichaetial bracts. It differs from the more common *P. acuminatum* by the antheridia borne on persistent dwarf axillary branches. It forms green or yellowish-green patches and is a colonist of partly bare circumneutral soils in stubble fields, quarries, ditches and banks. It was included in the Provisional Red List (Holyoak 2006b) but has since been found to be far more frequent in Ireland than previously realised. It has been reported from 19 vice-counties, with records from 44 hectads (17 old, 27 recent).

Ditrichum pusillum (Hedw.) Hampe

Brown Ditrichum

syn. *Ditrichum tortile* (Schrad.) Brockm., *D. tortile* var. *pusillum* Bruch & Schimp.
Status in Ireland: Data Deficient; **Status in Europe:** Least Concern

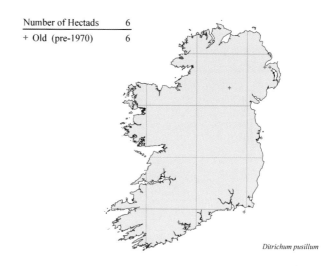

Number of Hectads	6
+ Old (pre-1970)	6

Ditrichum pusillum

Identification

This is a small acrocarpous moss that grows as green or dull green tufts 2–12 mm high. Leaves are ovate, narrowed to a channelled subula, up to c. 3.5 mm long, erecto-patent and slightly secund. The margin is recurved around mid-leaf and denticulate, the costa stout and percurrent to excurrent. Leaf cells are rectangular, those in the lower part of the leaf narrowly rectangular and 10–12 μm wide, narrower at margin. Rhizoidal tubers are often present, these being pyriform, yellowish to pale orange-brown and measuring approximately 100–150 × 75–100 μm. Capsules are ovoid to cylindrical, erect, exserted on a seta that is 0.5–1.5 cm long, reddish-brown below, pale above.

Distribution in Ireland

Eight records are accepted from six vice-counties: E. Cork (Dodge's Glen, 1845–1880); Wexford (Great Saltee Island, 1913); Monaghan (Rossmore Park, 1912); W. Donegal (Rossnowlagh, 1908); Down (Scrabo Hill quarry, 1908) and Antrim (near Belfast, leg. J. Templeton [who died in 1825]; fields beyond the Botanic Garden, Belfast, leg. T. Drummond [c. 1828–29], in Stewart & Corry 1888; in the late Mr Templeton's garden at Cranmore, Malone, *fide* D. Moore [1872] cited by Stewart & Corry 1888). The last record was thus in 1913. It has not been refound during recent fieldwork, despite revisiting several sites, but it is an inconspicuous plant when non-fertile, so perhaps overlooked.

Ecology and biology

Little was recorded for the old Irish localities, other than a habitat on sandy banks and quarries and that it was very rare (Stewart & Corry 1888, Megaw 1938). British records show it is a rather rare lowland moss; they include a number from non-calcareous arable fields, particularly in Scotland, where small non-fruiting plants were very inconspicuous (Whitehouse 1976). In Scandinavia, it is also a calcifuge, growing on moist clay and sand along roadsides and ditches, in screes and arable fields (Hallingbäck *et al.* 2006).

The species is perennial at most sites, but doubtless annual when growing in arable fields. It is dioicous and capsules are frequent in undisturbed sites, maturing in late autumn or winter (but April to June in N. America according to Seppelt *et al.* in FNA 2007). Rhizoidal tubers are frequent; protonemal gemmae are also produced in cultures (Whitehouse 1976, Arts 1994).

World distribution

D. pusillum is widespread in Europe from Iceland and N. Fennoscandia southwards to N. Spain (where it is montane), Ukraine and Caucasus. It is listed as *Endangered* in Switzerland, *Vulnerable* in Luxembourg, the Netherlands and Spain and 'declining' in Germany. It is assigned to a Circumpolar Boreo-temperate floristic element in Europe. Elsewhere, it occurs in Algeria, SW and N. Asia (widespread in Siberia), India and N. America (Quebec southwards to Texas and Florida).

Threats

No information is available from Irish localities. Occurrence on open sandy ground may imply that it is often lost from old sites as they become shaded by taller vegetation, but open ground persists at Scrabo Hill quarry.

Conservation

No action is proposed.

Protected sites with recent records: none; **Unprotected sites with recent records:** none.

Ditrichum cornubicum Paton

Cornish Path-moss

Status in Ireland: Critically Endangered (D); **Status in Europe:** Endangered

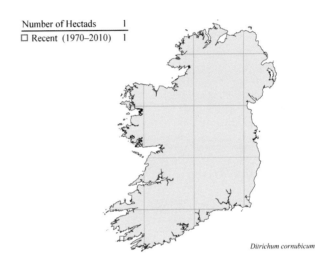

Number of Hectads	1
☐ Recent (1970–2010)	1

Ditrichum cornubicum

Identification

A tiny dull green or dark green acrocarpous moss that grows as scattered stems or small tufts, 1–4 mm high (in Cornwall, occasionally forming low turfs with stems up to 10 mm). The leaves are 0.4–0.9 mm long, erecto-patent, lanceolate, concave, with a strong costa ending just below the apex and plane margin that is entire or with slight denticulation near the apex. Leaf cells are rectangular and mainly 7–10 μm wide, narrower near the costa and at margin. The rhizoidal gemmae provide the most important distinction from small plants of *D. lineare*, these being spherical to ovoid, 80–160 μm long (rather than uniseriate). Only male plants are known.

Distribution in Ireland

Known only from one small population at Allihies, W. Cork, where it was discovered in 2006 and still present in 2009. There is a strong likelihood that the plants were accidentally introduced from Cornwall to W. Cork. This might have occurred with a well-documented immigration of Cornish miners and their equipment in the 19th century. However, it is more likely to have been during 2002–2003, when specialist stonemasons from

Cornwall repaired the closely adjacent mine engine-house at Allihies after working at Cornish sites where *D. cornubicum* occurs (Holyoak & Lockhart 2009a).

Ecology and biology

Restricted to one small area of an old gravelly track at a disused copper mine at c. 145 m altitude. It grows there in small amounts in a few damp, unshaded hollows, close to very sparse *Cephaloziella stellulifera*, *Solenostoma gracillimum*, *Pohlia andalusica* and *Agrostis capillaris*. In Cornwall, it is also known only from sites with spoil from old copper mines, in places which have sparse open vegetation comprised mainly of acidophilous, copper-tolerant plants (Holyoak *et al.* 2000). Chemical analyses of its substrata there show it consistently tolerates high levels of available copper (151–3220 μg/g dry weight), whereas levels of lead and zinc were low to rather high (Holyoak *et al.* 2000, Walsh 2001).

In Cornwall, its patches persist in the same places year after year, so long as open, unshaded substrata remain available. The leafy shoots die down or are very inconspicuous in summer, becoming most obvious after mild, damp weather in late winter or spring. Only male plants are known. Vegetative dispersal is likely to occur from protonemal gemmae (described by Arts 1994), rhizoidal tubers, as well as from stem and leaf fragments.

World distribution

Known elsewhere only from Cornwall, and listed as *Endangered* in Britain. It was discovered at Lanner in W. Cornwall on a roadside lay-by from which it soon disappeared, then refound near Minions in E. Cornwall (Paton 1976, Holyoak *et al.* 2000). Over the past decade, two groups of populations have been closely monitored by English Nature/Natural England, protected respectively by the Phoenix United Mine SSSI and Crow's Nest SSSI. Endemic in Europe.

Threats

The tiny population at Allihies is potentially vulnerable to accidental damage from vehicles, tipping, thoughtless collection of specimens, or disturbance by sheep. In Cornwall, its patches often disappear as taller vegetation cover develops. Eutrophication of its sites from dung of sheep that rest on tracks has been a problem at Phoenix United Mine SSSI, now resolved by fenced exclosures excluding the sheep along with periodic scarification of the soil surface.

Conservation

The site at Allihies is on protected land. Cultures of Cornish plants are cryopreserved at the Royal Botanic Gardens at Kew. Living cultures of the Irish plants are held at **DBN**.

Protected sites with recent records: Kenmare River SAC; **Unprotected sites with recent records:** none.

Ditrichum lineare (Sw.) Lindb.

Dark Ditrichum

syn. *D. vaginans* (Sull.) Hampe
Status in Ireland: Critically Endangered (B1a, bi, ii, iv, B2a, bi, ii, iv); **Status in Europe:** Least Concern

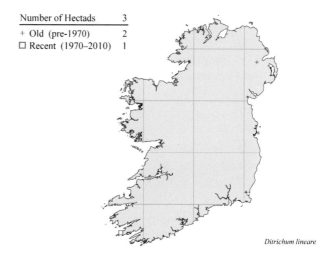

Number of Hectads	3
+ Old (pre-1970)	2
☐ Recent (1970–2010)	1

Ditrichum lineare

Identification

A small or very small acrocarpous moss that grows in dense green or yellow-green tufts or patches, 3–15 mm high. The leaves are loosely appressed, erect, lanceolate to ovate-lanceolate, 0.6–1.4 mm long, tapering to a blunt point. The leaf margin is often narrowly recurved and usually partly bistratose above, the costa strong and percurrent to slightly excurrent. Cells in the upper part of the leaf are rectangular to quadrate and thick-walled. Rhizoidal tubers are usually scarce, uniseriate, becoming spirally coiled as they lengthen. Capsules (unknown in Ireland) are ellipsoid to cylindrical, erect, exserted on a seta 1–2 cm high that is red below and yellow above.

Distribution in Ireland

There are three records from three vice-counties: W. Cork (Allihies, 1999); Sligo (details unknown, found by C.A. Cooper during BBS Meeting in 1928) and Antrim (Collin Mountain, 1901–1952). The Collin Mountain locality is near Belfast (hectad J27, not the other mountain of the same name in Antrim in D21 mapped by Hill *et al.* 1992). A long search for the plant there was unsuccessful in 2002 (as was a search at the other Collin Mountain). Attempts to refind it at Allihies in 2006 and 2008 have also been unsuccessful, although the species can be very inconspicuous and easily missed.

Ecology and biology

Numerous specimens were collected at the Collin Mountain locality in the past, some of them annotated as being from close to the summit on bare peaty or turfy ground. At Allihies (Mountain Mine) it was collected from an open gravelly area amongst mine spoil at the old copper mine. In Britain, it grows on partly bare, often disturbed, free-draining, acidic, nutrient-poor, mineral soils from the lowlands to montane ridges and the proximity of late-lying snow beds at up to 1040 m elevation.

The plants are perennial, sometimes annual. It is a dioicous species for which most records in Ireland and Britain are only of female plants (Smith 1978). However, male plants occur at Allihies, in Cornwall and in S. Wales, apparently associated with metalliferous substrata (Holyoak & Lockhart 2009a). Capsules are known in Britain only from S. Wales, but they are common in Scandinavia (Hallingbäck *et al.* 2006) and known in N. America (maturing April–May: Seppelt *et al.* in FNA 2007).

Rhizoidal tubers are known in British, European and Asian plants and protonemal gemmae also occur (Arts 1994).

World distribution

Widespread in Europe from Iceland, N. Sweden, N. Finland and N. Urals southwards to E. Cornwall, NW Spain and the Alps, but listed as *Extinct* in Luxembourg, *Endangered* in Spain, *Vulnerable* in Bulgaria and Switzerland, 'presumably threatened' in Germany, 'very rare' in Estonia and 'rare' in the Netherlands. It is assigned to a European Boreal-montane floristic element in Europe. Elsewhere, the species is known in NE Asia (Russian Far East: Ignatov *et al.* 2007), Japan and eastern N. America (where the range extends surprisingly far to the south, from Labrador to Alabama, Georgia and Florida: Seppelt *et al.* in FNA 2007).

Threats

No information.

Conservation

The copper mine at Allihies is on protected land. The species is apparently no longer present at Collin Mountain, but there is plenty of potentially suitable habitat and another search might be worthwhile.

Protected sites with recent records: Kenmare River SAC; **Unprotected sites with recent records:** none.

Ditrichum plumbicola Crundw.

Lead-moss

syn. *Ditrichum lineare* (Sw.) Kindb. var. *plumbicola* (Crundw.) J.-P.Frahm *et al.*
(2008; new combination invalid because direct reference to basionym lacking, cf. ICBN Art. 33.2 and 33.3)
Status in Ireland: Endangered (D); **Status in Europe:** Near Threatened

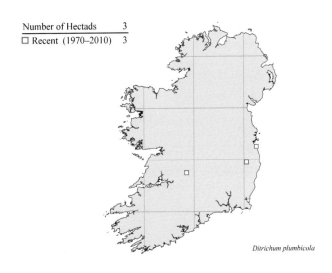

Number of Hectads	3
☐ Recent (1970–2010)	3

Ditrichum plumbicola

Identification

A tiny to small acrocarpous moss that grows as scattered stems or forms pale yellowish-green, somewhat glossy patches, 5–15 mm high. The shoots are very slender with closely appressed, erect leaves that are ovate to ovate-lanceolate, concave and taper to a blunt apex. The costa is strong and percurrent, the leaf margins plane or somewhat incurved above, entire or with slight denticulations near the apex. The upper leaf cells are rectangular, 5–9 μm wide, with incrassate cell walls. Rhizoidal tubers are dark reddish-brown, uniseriate, of 5–8 swollen cells, spirally twisted into a subspherical helix 150–200 μm in diameter (Arts 1994). Capsules are unknown. The tiny, cylindrical, julaceous shoots and close association with lead-mine spoil are distinctive even in the field.

Data recently published on chloroplast DNA sequences of German populations were interpreted as implying that *D. plumbicola* should be regarded as a variety of *D. lineare* (Frahm *et al.* 2008b). However, fuller study of more populations is desirable since an alternative interpretation of the same data would be that German *D. lineare* itself consists of more than one cryptic species.

Distribution in Ireland

Recorded from three localities in different vice-counties: N. Tipperary (Shallee, 2008–2009); Wicklow (Vale of Glendasan, 2009) and Dublin (Ballycorus, 2008). The populations at Ballycorus and the Vale of Glendasan were very small (both occurring over total areas of much less than 1 square metre) but at Shallee it was found in three sites, in larger amounts, growing sparsely over at least several square metres.

Ecology and biology

Known only from spoil of old lead mines, growing on sparsely vegetated, slightly damp surfaces in places that vary from open but sheltered to shaded by *Calluna* or *Ulex europaeus*, at 95–220 m altitude. Other associated plants recorded were algal films, sparse *Diplophyllum albicans* and *Solenostoma gracillimum* and a few stems of *Agrostis*. In Britain, it is also restricted to acidic soils (pH 4.5–6.5: Hill 1988) with a high lead content. The species appears to be unique among metallophyte bryophytes in tolerating high lead concentrations while avoiding copper-rich substrata.

The plants are perennial or sometimes annual. Gametangia and sporophytes are unknown. Tubers are produced on the rhizoids and (in cultures) on protonema (caulonemata) (Arts 1994), these doubtless functioning as propagules, as might broken stem fragments.

World distribution

A European endemic species, known mainly in Ireland, Isle of Man and Britain (SW Scotland, N. England, N. and C. Wales, Somerset, W. Cornwall; listed as *Near Threatened* in Britain). Elsewhere, it is known only from about nine localities in SW Germany (Solga & Frahm 2002, Meinunger & Schröder 2007) ('*rare*').

Threats

The small populations known in Ireland are potentially at risk from 'tidying' or restoration work at disused mine sites, as well as from illegal tipping, disturbance by off-road vehicles, erosion of slopes, or shading due to natural vegetation succession. At Ballycorus there is currently a threat from erosion and disturbance of mine spoil by off-road motorcycling. At Shallee, there is some risk from shading as scrub and heathland vegetation cover increases.

Conservation

Two of the three populations were discovered by a survey during 2008 by NPWS intended to assess the extent of metallophyte bryophyte vegetation in Ireland in order to inform measures for its conservation. Both of those localities are thus among those being considered for protection as NHA. The third site (Vale of Glendasan) is already on protected land.

Protected sites with recent records: Glenealo Valley Nature Reserve; Wicklow Mountains National Park; Wicklow Mountains SAC; **Unprotected sites with recent records:** Ballycorus; Shallee (some colonies may be within Silvermines Mountains West SAC).

Vale of Glendasan, Co. Wicklow.

Ditrichum zonatum (Brid.) Kindb.

Alpine Ditrichum

syn. *D. heteromallum* var. *zonatum* (Brid.) Podp., *D. zonatum* var. *scabrifolium* Dixon
Status in Ireland: Endangered (B2a, bii, iv); **Status in Europe:** Least Concern

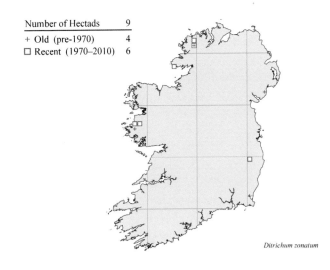

Number of Hectads	9
+ Old (pre-1970)	4
☐ Recent (1970–2010)	6

Ditrichum zonatum

Identification

A small acrocarpous moss that grows as rather dense tufts, cushions or sometimes more extensive patches, 5–50 mm high, occasionally 70 mm, glossy and yellow-green to dark green above, reddish-brown below. Leaves are erecto-patent, with an ovate or ovate-lanceolate base tapering into a short channelled acumen. The costa is stout and percurrent, the leaf margin plane or slightly incurved above, entire or slightly denticulate near the apex. Cells in lower part of the leaf are rectangular and mainly 6–8 μm wide, narrower at leaf margins; those in upper part of leaf are partly bistratose and shortly rectangular to quadrate. Cells in upper part of leaf and on dorsal surface of costa are smooth or (in 'var. *scabrifolium*') scabrous with conical papillae. Rhizoidal tubers are uniseriate, of a few swollen cells, twisted into a helix (Arts 1994). Capsules are apparently unknown.

Treated as a variety of *D. heteromallum* in some older European literature and as a synonym of that species in the recent North American *Flora* (Seppelt *et al.* in FNA 2007), but maintained as a distinct species in the European list (Hill *et al.* 2006). However, *D. zonatum* apparently differs from *D. heteromallum* only in its smaller size, shorter leaves, percurrent rather than excurrent costa, shorter basal cells of the leaf and tendency to develop bistratose upper leaf cells that are sometimes papillose, so its standing as a distinct species should be reviewed. Var. *scabrifolium* has been regarded as a valid taxon in recent British literature,

with possible habitat differences (R.D. Porley in Hill *et al.* 1992), but intermediate plants occur and it is not recognised by Smith (2004) or Hill *et al.* (2006).

Distribution in Ireland

Recent records are accepted from seven localities in three vice-counties: Wicklow (Lugnaquilla, North Prison, 2007); W. Mayo (NE corrie of Mweelrea, two sites, 2003; W. of Lough Bellawaum on Mweelrea, 2003) and W. Donegal (Slieve Snaght, 1962–2002; Moylenanav, 2002; Dooish, 2002; Slieve League, 2008). Older records are from W. Galway (Muckanaght, 1968) and Antrim (Ballycastle, leg. H.N. Dixon, in Lett 1915, Megaw 1938). There is also an unconfirmed report from Down (Slieve Donard, 1928).

Ecology and biology

Recorded from montane rocks at 255–710 m elevation, on predominantly acidic, metamorphic lithologies (granitic, Mweelrea Grit, etc.), in nutrient-poor sites. Most records are from N.-facing slopes, from small ledges or in unshaded crevices of damp or wet rock or on thin overlying soil or detritus, sometimes associated with patches of liverworts, including *Marsupella emarginata*. In Britain, it is reported at 800–1335 m elevation on varied acidic and occasionally basic rock types and overlying skeletal soils, at sites that include exposed ridges and relatively sheltered hepatic mat communities associated with late-lying snow beds.

A perennial moss; when it forms tall tufts they sometimes show annual growth zones. The species is dioicous and capsules are apparently unknown (although 'very rare' according to R.D. Porley in Hill *et al.* 1992). Vegetative propagation occurs from caducous apices of the leafy shoots (Hallingbäck *et al.* 2006). Rhizoidal tubers are present in a small proportion of British specimens (Arts 1994).

World distribution

Widely but rather sparsely distributed in Europe (predominantly in mountains), from N. Iceland, N. Fennoscandia and NW Russia southwards to the French Pyrenees, Harz Mountains and Alps. It is listed as *Endangered* in the Czech Republic, *Vulnerable* in Bulgaria and *Near Threatened* in Finland and Switzerland and *Data Deficient* in Germany. It is assigned to a European Arctic-montane floristic element in Europe. The species is known elsewhere in Japan (Honshu: Iwatsuki 1991) and western N. America.

Threats

No immediate threats were apparent at several sites in W. Mayo and W. Donegal visited over the past decade, although populations are usually small and potentially vulnerable to accidental losses from rockfalls, erosion (which might be worsened by overgrazing) or shading by taller plants (which could increase if grazing pressure declines). Despite unsuccessful searches, absence of recent records from some of the old localities may not represent real evidence of decline, since the plants grow as rather inconspicuous small patches.

Conservation

All the known localities are on protected land.

Protected sites with recent records: Cloghernagore Bog and Glenveagh National Park SAC; Glenveagh National Park; Mweelrea/Sheeffry/Erriff Complex SAC; Slieve League SAC; Wicklow Mountains SAC; **Unprotected sites with recent records:** none.

Ditrichum flexicaule (Schwägr.) Hampe

Bendy Ditrichum

syn. *D. flexicaule* var. *densum* (Bruch & Schimp.) Braithw.
Status in Ireland: Data Deficient; **Status in Europe:** Not Evaluated

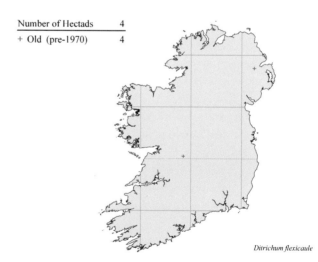

Number of Hectads	4
+ Old (pre-1970)	4

Ditrichum flexicaule

Identification

An acrocarpous moss with narrow leaves that grows as dense or very dense (rarely lax) tufts or patches that are bright green to dark green (less often brownish or yellowish) and 1–5 cm high (rarely 10 cm). The stems are fragile and usually densely tomentose below. Leaves are 1.0–3.5 mm long, stiff to flexuose, with a sheathing basal part forming about one-third to one-half of leaf length, that abruptly tapers to an entire, channelled subula composed largely of the costa, which fills the leaf apex. Cells in the leaf base are variable in shape, those near the costa being rectangular or shortly rectangular. Cells higher in the leaf are quadrate or shortly rectangular and strongly incrassate, the marginal cells around halfway up the leaf lamina being quadrate to oval with thick walls (not hyaline). Capsules (unknown in Ireland or Britain) are cylindrical, erect and exserted on a seta 1.5–3 cm high that is dark red basally, yellow in the upper part.

Prior to a taxonomic review by Frisvoll (1985), this species was more broadly conceived, including the more common *D. gracile* (syn. *D. crispatissimum*). The latter is typically a larger plant forming laxer, glossy tufts. Its leaf bases are more gradually tapered to a longer subula, upper leaf cells tend to be longer and the widest part of the leaf has a narrow border of long, narrow, hyaline cells (Smith 1993). Some specimens are difficult to allocate to the segregate species and R.D. Seppelt *et al.* (in FNA 2007) point out the need for a detailed molecular analysis of the taxonomy.

Distribution in Ireland

Four records from four vice-counties are accepted: N. Tipperary (E. bank of R. Shannon near Portumna, 1957); W. Mayo (near Louisburgh, 1910); E. Donegal (Rossnowlagh, 1916) and Antrim (Divis, 1882). Smith (1993) also accepted a record from Down (Kirkiston = Kirkestown, 1931) but the specimen has been reidentified as *D. gracile*. This species is easily overlooked as small plants of *D. gracile* so that the absence of records from recent fieldwork may not be significant as evidence of decline.

Ecology and biology

Only scanty information was recorded for Irish specimens, which were from a wall on the bank of the R. Shannon and from peat at Divis. British records show the plant is a calciphile of dry, open habitats from sea level to 1200 m altitude, found among limestone rocks, in short chalk grassland and in quarries, less often on walls, cliff ledges or coastal dunes.

The species is apparently a perennial that can be found in all months of the year. It is dioicous and capsules are unknown in Ireland or Britain. In N. America it is more commonly found with sporophytes than *D. gracile*, the capsules maturing in summer (R.D. Seppelt *et al.* in FNA 2007). Microphyllous flagelliform shoots are often present in the tufts and these and caducous shoot apices presumably serve as propagules; other gemmae and tubers are apparently absent.

World distribution

D. flexicaule is widespread in Europe from Spitsbergen, Iceland and N. Fennoscandia southwards to NE Spain, Mallorca, Romania and the Caucasus. It is listed as *Vulnerable* in the Netherlands, *Data Deficient* in Spain and 'declining' in Germany. It is assigned to a Circumpolar Wide-temperate floristic element in Europe. Elsewhere, the segregate species is known from N. and SW Asia, N. America (widespread), Greenland, Guatemala, New Guinea and New Zealand.

Threats

No information is available.

Conservation

Bryologists should remain alert for this species, which is still likely to occur somewhere in Ireland.

Protected sites with recent records: none; **Unprotected sites with recent records:** none.

Distichium inclinatum (Hedw.) Bruch & Schimp.

Inclined Distichium

Status in Ireland: Least Concern; **Status in Europe:** Least Concern

This small acrocarpous moss, with its distinctive distichous spreading leaves and inclined capsules, grows as compact dull green tufts or patches, usually in coastal machair and dune slacks. It has a western and northern distribution in Ireland and was included in the Provisional Red List (Holyoak 2006b) because it had few records from before 1998. However, recent fieldwork has recorded it from many new localities, so that it has now been reported from nine vice-counties and 30 hectads (8 old, 27 recent), sometimes as large populations. It is therefore clear that it was previously under-recorded and that the species is not threatened.

Amphidium lapponicum (Hedw.) Schimp.

Lapland Yoke-moss

syn. *Zygodon lapponicus* (Hedw.) Bruch & Schimp.
Status in Ireland: Vulnerable (D2); **Status in Europe:** Least Concern

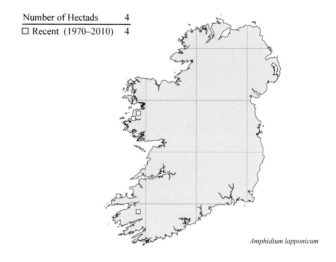

Number of Hectads	4
☐ Recent (1970–2010)	4

Amphidium lapponicum

Identification

An acrocarpous moss that grows in dense dark green tufts, reddish below, up to 5 cm high but often much smaller. It is easily identified when capsules are present because they are only shortly exserted, on a seta 1.5–2.5 mm long, erect, pyriform, gymnostomous, and plicate when dry and empty. Leaves are crisped when dry, patent when moist, ligulate to linear, acute or acuminate with margins recurved below and mid-leaf cells rounded-hexagonal and papillose. Non-fertile plants are distinct from the more common *Amphidium mougeotii* in the more strongly papillose cells in the upper part of the leaf and the thin-walled basal cells.

Distribution in Ireland

Known only by four recent records: S. Kerry (a few tufts, above Lough Cummeenoughter on Carrauntoohil, leg. T.L. Blockeel, 2007; S. corrie, Brandon Mountain, 2009) and W. Mayo (NE slope of Mweelrea, leg. D.G. Long, 2003; NE slopes above Lugaloughaun, Sheeffry Hills, leg. P. Perrin, 2010). An old report from Antrim ('Rosstreva', 1894) was based on misidentified *A. mougeotii*.

Ecology and biology

Recorded in Ireland from a cliff crevice (on Mweelrea Grit) at 510 m altitude, on a vertical rock face cleft at 574 m, on vertical sandstone of a crag by a gully at 950 m and on a damp cliff at 645 m. In Britain and elsewhere in Europe, the species occurs on moist base-rich montane cliffs and crags, on exposed rocks and in gullies, appearing indifferent to lithology provided there is sufficient base present.

The plants grow as perennial tufts. They are autoicous and capsules are common, maturing in summer. Tubers and gemmae are unknown.

World distribution

Widespread in Europe, from Iceland, Svalbard and Scandinavia southwards to the mountains of Spain and Bulgaria and the Caucasus. It is listed as *Critically Endangered* in Germany, *Vulnerable* in Bulgaria and the Czech Republic and *Data Deficient* in Serbia. In Europe, it is assigned to a Circumpolar Boreo-arctic montane floristic element. Elsewhere, it is reported from the Canary Islands, N. Africa, S. Africa (mountains of Natal and Lesotho), E. Asia, N. America, Chile, Hawaii and New Zealand.

Threats

All of the known populations are very small and grow in crevices of steep montane crags. The greatest potential threat may be from thoughtless collection of specimens. However, such small populations could easily be outcompeted by other plants or destroyed by accidents such as rockfalls.

Conservation

All populations are on protected land.

Protected sites with recent records: Killarney National Park, Macgillycuddy's Reeks and Caragh River Catchment SAC; Mount Brandon SAC; Mweelrea/ Sheeffry/Erriff Complex SAC; **Unprotected sites with recent records:** none.

Rhabdoweisia fugax (Hedw.) Bruch & Schimp.

Dwarf Streak-moss

Status in Ireland: Vulnerable (B1a, bi, ii, iv, B2a, bi, ii, iv); **Status in Europe:** Least Concern

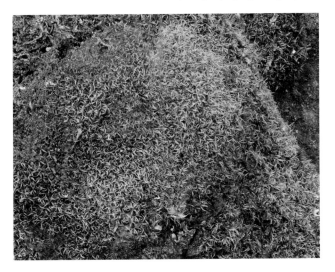

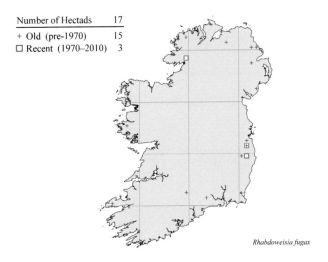

Number of Hectads	17
+ Old (pre-1970)	15
□ Recent (1970–2010)	3

Rhabdoweisia fugax

Identification

This is a small, tuft-forming, bright green acrocarpous moss up to c. 1 cm tall, with narrowly ligulate or linear-lanceolate, entire or denticulate leaves up to c. 3 mm long that become crisped when dry. Small erect, ovoid capsules are exserted on short setae. There are two other Irish species: *R. crenulata* has much broader leaves with irregularly dentate upper margins, while *R. crispata* is to some extent intermediate, with wider and more strongly toothed leaves than *R. fugax*. Sometimes microscopic examination is necessary to separate the latter two species: *R. fugax* has the lamina mostly 3–4 cells wide on either side of the costa at 220 µm below the leaf apex, whereas *R. crispata* has it mostly 5–7 cells wide.

Distribution in Ireland

Records of this species are distributed generally in mountainous areas, but the only recent records are from Wicklow, where it grows in abundance on the rocks in the vicinity of Powerscourt Waterfall and Glendalough (2007), and from W. Donegal (Meenaguse, 2001; Binnasruell, 2008) in the Blue Stack Mountains, where it occurs in much smaller quantity. Older records are from about 12 localities in 11 vice-counties: S. Kerry (Connor Hill Pass, 1915); Waterford (Coumshingaun in the Comeragh Mountains, 1966); S. Tipperary (two sites in the Galty Mountains, 1902); W. Galway (Muckanaght,

1957); Wicklow (Glenmalur, 1878); Dublin ('Dublin Mountains', 1848); Louth (Carlingford Mountain, 1890); W. Donegal (Errigal, 1891); Down (Mourne Mountains, undated); Antrim (Belfast Mountains, undated) and Londonderry (Binevenagh, undated).

Ecology and biology

This is a plant of sheltered, rather dry clefts and crevices in acid rocks, often in woodland and frequently on boulders near lakes or rocks near waterfalls. Typical associates include *Amphidium mougeotii*, *Bartramia pomiformis*, *Cynodontium bruntonii*, *Dicranella heteromalla*, *Dicranum* spp., *Diplophyllum albicans*, *Isothecium myosuroides*, *Mnium hornum*, *Pseudotaxiphyllum elegans*, *Racomitrium* spp. and *Scapania gracilis*. It grows at low or medium altitudes, with recent records ranging from 140–400 m.

This is an autoicous species in which capsules are produced abundantly. No specialised vegetative reproductive structures are known.

World distribution

R. fugax is widespread and not threatened in most of N. Europe, becoming rarer and more montane to the south, including Macaronesia. Although not on any European Red Lists, it is described as 'declining' in Germany (Ludwig *et al.* 1996) and is apparently absent from a few countries. In Europe, it is categorised as a European Boreal-montane floristic element. Elsewhere, it has been recorded in tropical and southern Africa and C. and S. America.

Threats
No immediate threats have been identified, and it is unclear why the range of this species in Ireland should have contracted so markedly. It is all the more puzzling since it grows in such abundance at its Wicklow sites.

Conservation
This species should be monitored at regular intervals in the Wicklow and Blue Stack Mountains. Further efforts need to be made to refind it at other old sites. Two of the colonies at Powerscourt Waterfall are outside both the SAC and the pNHA. *R. fugax* is listed as a Northern Ireland Priority Species.

Protected sites with recent records: Glendalough Nature Reserve; Glenealo Valley Nature Reserve; Powerscourt Waterfall pNHA; Wicklow Mountains National Park; Wicklow Mountains SAC; **Unprotected sites with recent records:** Binnasruell; Meenaguse.

Rhabdoweisia crispata (Dicks.) Lindb.

Toothed Streak-moss

Status in Ireland: Near Threatened; **Status in Europe:** Least Concern

This is a fairly widespread but infrequent moss of rock crevices on dry crags. It has been reported from 21 vice-counties, with records from 31 hectads (17 old, 11 recent, 3 undated). It was not included in the Provisional Red List (Holyoak 2006b) because there were too many records, and was not specifically looked for during recent fieldwork. There is some evidence of a possible decline in the north, where there are no recent records, and its situation needs to be monitored.

Cynodontium bruntonii (Sm.) Bruch & Schimp.

Brunton's Dog-tooth

syn. *Oreoweisia bruntonii* (Sm.) Milde
Status in Ireland: Least Concern; **Status in Europe:** Least Concern

This acrocarpous moss forms dense, dark to mid-green cushions in dry rock crevices on usually more or less sheltered N.-facing crags and other rock exposures, in Ireland mostly on sandstone, mica schist and conglomerate. It is widespread but rather scarce in southern upland areas, with fewer records from further north. It was included in the Provisional Red List (Holyoak 2006b) but fieldwork over the last decade has shown it to be locally frequent at some locations, notably in the Wicklow Mountains and the Comeragh Mountains. It has been reported from 13 vice-counties, with records from 24 hectad records (14 old, 16 recent) and there is no real evidence of decline.

Cynodontium jenneri (Schimp.) Stirt.

Jenner's Dog-tooth

Status in Ireland: Vulnerable (D2); **Status in Europe:** Least Concern

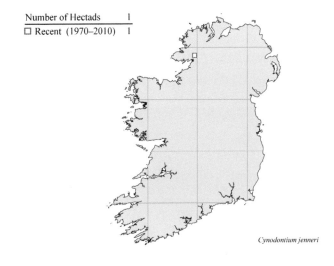

Number of Hectads	1
□ Recent (1970–2010)	1

Cynodontium jenneri

Identification

This is a small green tuft-forming acrocarpous moss up to 4 cm high but usually much less, with leaves about 2–3 mm long that are erect to spreading when moist and crisped when dry. The leaves, while narrow, are not nearly so long and narrow as those of a *Dicranum* or a *Campylopus*. The costa is narrow and ends just below the leaf apex, and the leaf margin is recurved and often toothed above. The leaf cells are larger than those of other *Cynodontium* species (c. 11–22 μm), smooth and unistratose (usually mamillose and at least partly bistratose in other species). The capsule is exserted, erect and striate, with the peristome teeth shorter on one side of the capsule than the other. Irish specimens are depauperate in comparison with most British material. American material is described as 'tall and luxuriant' (FNA 2007).

Distribution in Ireland

Discovered in Ireland as recently as 2001, this species is known only from the Blue Stack Mountains in W. Donegal, where it occurs as small tufts on the crags and cliffs of Meenaguse (2001) and Binnasruell (2008).

Ecology and biology

In Ireland, *C. jenneri* grows sparsely on S.-facing granitic rocks on crags at an altitude of about 400 m, with *Andreaea rothii*, *Bartramia pomiformis*, *Gymnomitrion*

spp., *Kiaeria blyttii* and *Rhabdoweisia* spp. as its most prominent associates. In Britain, it grows from low altitudes to 730 m on moderately sheltered acidic rocks, usually on crags and other exposures, but also sometimes on stone walls and sandy soils in woodland.

It is autoicous. Capsules are normally frequent to abundant. No specialised means of vegetative reproduction are known.

World distribution

C. jenneri is listed as *Nationally Scarce* in Britain and is also rather rare and restricted to western and northern parts of continental Europe, where it is listed as *Extinct* in Finland and Germany, *Critically Endangered* in Portugal, *Near Threatened* in Sweden, and also recorded from Norway, Denmark, Iceland and the Faeroe Islands. In Europe, it is classified as a Suboceanic Boreal-montane floristic element. This plant is also very rare outside Europe, with records only from Turkey (Kürschner & Erdağ 2005) and N. America (Pacific northwest and Newfoundland).

Threats

There are no direct or obvious threats to this species in the Blue Stack Mountains at present. The global distribution and status of this moss suggests however that climate change and an increase in temperature might be damaging.

Conservation

A more comprehensive survey of the S.-facing cliffs on the Blue Stack Mountains might result in further colonies being discovered. Meanwhile, the crags should remain relatively undisturbed and free from new conifer plantations. All the colonies of *C. jenneri* found to date are on unprotected land.

Protected sites with recent records: none; **Unprotected sites with recent records:** Binnasruell; Meenaguse.

Dichodontium flavescens (Dicks.) Lindb.

Yellowish Fork-moss

Status in Ireland: Least Concern; **Status in Europe:** Least Concern

D. flavescens was included in the Provisional Red List (Holyoak 2006b) because there were relatively few records from Ireland. It was formerly thought that this species could only be reliably distinguished from the more frequent *D. pellucidum* when fertile, which it rarely is. Recent work by Werner (2002) has shown that the two can indeed be identified without capsules and this has resulted in many new records for *D. flavescens*, although some specimens examined appear to show a mixture of the gametophytic characters of the two taxa. There are now reports from 13 vice-counties, with records from 23 hectads (6 old, 18 recent), mainly from stream sides in upland areas. Several further records from the north are unsubstantiated, though at least some of them are probably correct.

Arctoa fulvella (Dicks.) Bruch & Schimp.

Arctic Fork-moss

syn. *Dicranum fulvellum* (Dicks.) Sm.
Status in Ireland: Vulnerable (B2a, bii, iv, D2); **Status in Europe:** Least Concern

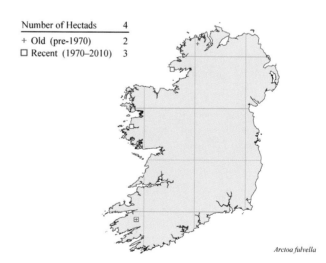

Number of Hectads	4
+ Old (pre-1970)	2
☐ Recent (1970–2010)	3

Arctoa fulvella

Identification

This small yellowish-green to brownish acrocarpous moss forms small tufts or cushions, with long narrow leaves that all tend to point in one direction (secund), although not strongly so. The shoots are less than 3 cm tall, the leaves up to c. 4 mm long. The leaves taper, often rather abruptly from a wider basal part, to a very long, fine apex that is composed almost entirely of costa. The distinctive capsules, which are held erect on a short (2–4 mm) seta, are wide-mouthed with the peristome teeth spreading conspicuously when dry. The combination of the distinctive capsules and very long silky leaf apices serve to differentiate it from other members of the Dicranales in the field.

Distribution in Ireland

There are only three recent localities for this moss, all in the west: S. Kerry (Beenkeragh-Carrauntoohil in Macgillycuddy's Reeks, 1836–1983); W. Galway (Benchoona, 2004) and W. Donegal (Slieve League, 1970). There is one older record from W. Donegal (Muckish Mountain, 1962).

Ecology and biology

This is predominantly an arctic-alpine plant of N.- or NE-facing mountain rocks and rock crevices at high altitudes, although the only Irish record for which there is altitudinal data was at the relatively low elevation of 320 m. It can grow on a wide variety of rocks, but avoids limestone. In Ireland, it has been recorded from small ledges on an E.-facing unshaded crag of slaty rock, and on rocks in a corrie.

Capsules are produced frequently on this autoicous species, but it is not known to produce any vegetative propagules.

World distribution

Widespread in nearly all the mountain regions of Europe, but becoming rarer southwards, *A. fulvella* is listed as *Nationally Scarce* in Britain, *Extinct* in the Czech Republic and *Vulnerable* in Switzerland, Spain and Andorra. Surprisingly, it is apparently absent from Germany. In Europe, it is classified as a European Arctic-montane floristic element. Elsewhere, there are records from C., N. and E. Asia, N. America and Greenland.

Threats

The major threat to this species in Ireland may be climate change. It has not been refound on Slieve League since 1970, in spite of searching, and may have disappeared.

Conservation

All populations are on protected land. Known colonies should be monitored, and any proposals for schemes likely to disturb them, such as forestry, should be resisted.

Protected sites with recent records: Killarney National Park, Macgillycuddy's Reeks and Caragh River Catchment SAC; Slieve League SAC; The Twelve Bens/Garraun Complex SAC; **Unprotected sites with recent records:** none.

Kiaeria falcata (Hedw.) I.Hagen

Sickle-leaved Fork-moss

syn. *Dicranum falcatum* Hedw.

Status in Ireland: Critically Endangered (D); **Status in Europe:** Least Concern

Number of Hectads	1
☐ Recent (1970–2010)	1

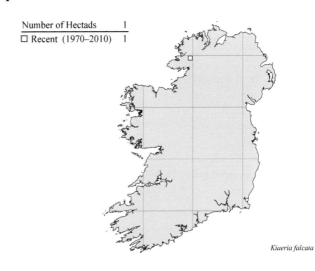

Kiaeria falcata

371

Identification

This attractive acrocarpous moss forms neat yellow-green tufts up to 4 cm high. Its strongly falcato-secund leaves are c. 4 mm long, narrow and tapering, remaining almost unchanged when dry. The more frequent *K. blyttii* is darker in colour and has crisped leaves when dry. The capsules are exserted, inclined and slightly swollen at the base. *Arctoa fulvella* has even longer leaves with a broad base contracting abruptly to a slender, silky apex, more distinct alar cells and an erect capsule which, when dry and empty, has a wide mouth and spreading peristome teeth. Species of *Dicranum* are often larger and usually without such neatly and regularly curved leaves. On the small Irish specimen 'the male inflorescences are unusually large and a long way down the stem' (G.P. Rothero, *in litt.*).

Distribution in Ireland

Found new to Ireland in 2001 on Binnacally, an offshoot of Lavagh Beg in the Blue Stack Mountains, W. Donegal.

Ecology and biology

The single small tuft was found on a NE-facing granitic 'tor' on a hillside at c. 500 m altitude, with *Andreaea* and *Racomitrium* spp., significantly lower than most British records.

K. falcata is autoicous and sporophytes are generally frequent, although they were absent from the Irish specimen.

World distribution

K. falcata occurs in mountainous areas from the Pyrenees, Alps and Carpathians north to the Arctic. It is *Nationally Scarce* in Britain, *Critically Endangered* in the Czech Republic, *Vulnerable* in Finland and Montenegro, *Data Deficient* in Bulgaria and 'extremely rare' in Germany. In Europe, it is assigned to a European Arctic-montane floristic element. Elsewhere, it grows in N. Asia and N. America.

Threats

The very small size of the known population means that it is at risk from accidental damage. The only other potential threat to this species in Ireland may be climate change.

Conservation

The single population of this species is on land that is currently unprotected. Survey work needs to be undertaken in the Blue Stack Mountains to establish if further populations exist. The Blue Stack Mountains should be considered for site protection.

Protected sites with recent records: none; **Unprotected sites with recent records:** Binnacally, Lavagh Beg.

Kiaeria blyttii (Bruch & Schimp.) Broth.

Blytt's Fork-moss

Status in Ireland: Least Concern; **Status in Europe:** Least Concern

Once considered a great rarity in Ireland and therefore included in the Provisional Red List (Holyoak 2006b), recent fieldwork has demonstrated that this plant is actually quite widespread, if infrequent, in upland areas, growing on acid rocks at higher altitudes. There are reports from nine vice-counties, with records from 16 hectads (4 old, 16 recent) and it is not considered threatened or even *Near Threatened*. However, as a montane species near the edge of its range, it could potentially be sensitive to climate change. It might be wise to monitor at least the best of the populations periodically.

Glyphomitrium daviesii (Dicks.) Brid.

Black-tufted Moss

Status in Ireland: Least Concern; **Status in Europe:** Rare

An attractive acrocarpous moss that grows as small dark tufts or cushions on the surfaces of hard rocks. It was included in the Provisional Red List (Holyoak 2006b) and although a rare moss over most of Ireland, it is locally common in parts of W. Galway (Roundstone area) and 'locally abundant' (Megaw 1938) in places on the basalt of Antrim and Londonderry, where many large populations were still present over the last decade. It has been reported from nine vice-counties, with records from 33 hectads (27 old, 11 recent). There is no evidence that it has declined or that it currently faces any widespread threats. This species is endemic to Europe.

Aongstroemia longipes (Sommerf.) Bruch & Schimp.

Sprig-moss

Status in Ireland: Critically Endangered (A3c); **Status in Europe:** Least Concern

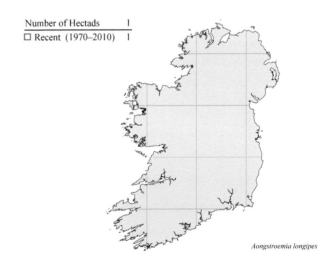

Number of Hectads	1
☐ Recent (1970–2010)	1

Aongstroemia longipes

Identification

A small and slender acrocarpous moss, with shoots mainly less than 12 mm tall, scattered, or forming lax, pale green, slightly glossy tufts or small patches. The leaves are erect and appressed, ovate-oblong, obtuse and difficult to detach from the fragile stems. The terete, julaceous, unbranched or sparsely branched stems with appressed leaves are suggestive of slender plants of *Anomobryum julaceum*, but microscopic differences include the stronger costa and thick-walled, rectangular mid-leaf cells. Perichaetia and perigonia are swollen and their bracts are longer than the leaves, so fertile shoots are clavate. Sporophytes (unknown in Ireland) have a long seta (10–15 mm) and a short, erect, ovoid capsule with a wide mouth and rostrate operculum.

Distribution in Ireland

A. longipes is known from a single record from W. Mayo, where it was found E. of Pollranny in 2003, the southernmost locality in W. Europe.

Ecology and biology

The only Irish record was from unshaded, partly bare sand of disturbed ground in an old sand quarry, in the lowlands (20 m altitude), with sparse low herbs and grasses. Sand nearby appeared to be acidic to somewhat basic, with other low bryophytes including *Bryum dichotomum*, *B. argenteum*, *B. pallens*, *Pohlia annotina* and *P. filum*. In Scotland, the species is known from open communities on damp, slightly basic sandy and gravelly soils, below dams, in quarries, gravel pits, shingle beds and on a moorland track. In Scandinavia, it is found along tracks and streams in the Scandes mountains, but in lowland areas it occurs in strongly disturbed habitats (e.g. in gravel pits and ditches), and along shores of regulated waters. In these lowland sites it may temporarily occupy large areas in moist and disturbed habitats, but disappears as soon as other vegetation establishes (Hallingbäck *et al.* 2006).

The small plants may be rather short-lived, but details of the life cycle are unknown. The species is dioicous and capsules are unknown in Ireland, reported from one locality in Scotland and 'fairly rare' in Fennoscandia (Hallingbäck *et al.* 2006); spores mature in late summer. Bulbils and tubers are unknown; Crundwell (in Hill *et al.* 1992) noted that vegetative propagation by means of fragile stems sometimes results in populations of one sex only.

World distribution

Mainly a boreal and arctic species, *A. longipes* is rather common in Iceland and Norway, rare in Scotland, Sweden, Finland and the Alps (Switzerland, Austria, S. Germany). It is listed as *Vulnerable* in Finland and Switzerland, *Near Threatened* in Britain and 'extremely rare' in Germany. In Europe, it is assigned to a Circumpolar Boreal-montane floristic element. Elsewhere, it is known from Spitsbergen, widely in Siberia, in northern N. America (in west, from Alaska and Northwest Territories south to Washington State; in east, in Newfoundland and Labrador) and Greenland.

Threats

At its locality in an old sandpit near Pollranny in W. Mayo, the exposed sand is being colonised by taller plants such as *Juncus effusus* and *Trifolium repens* that will doubtless soon create too much shade for *A. longipes* to persist, unless there is renewed disturbance. The large, invasive, alien herb *Gunnera tinctoria* was also present within 5 m of it in 2003.

Conservation

The only known locality is not on protected land. It will probably need deliberate management intervention if the habitat is to remain sufficiently open for persistence of *A. longipes*. Further surveys may reveal that this diminutive moss has been overlooked at a few other sites, or possibly imply that it was only of casual occurrence in W. Mayo.

Protected sites with recent records: none; **Unprotected sites with recent records:** E. of Pollranny.

Dicranella grevilleana (Brid.) Schimp.

Greville's Forklet-moss

syn. *Anisothecium grevilleanum* (Brid.) H.Arnell & C.E.O.Jensen
Status in Ireland: Near Threatened; **Status in Europe:** Least Concern

D. grevilleana is a small yellowish-green acrocarpous moss that grows in tufts on disturbed, base-rich soil on rock ledges, below crags, in upland grassland and in quarries. This is a montane species, recorded in Ireland from altitudes between 250 m and 460 m, and restricted to the Dartry Mountains in Sligo and Leitrim, where there are three hectad records (3 old, 3 recent). *D. grevilleana* is a colonist of bare disturbed soil and at several sites in the Dartry Mountains it benefits from recurrent soil disturbance caused by boulders falling from crags above. Although restricted in its distribution in Ireland, it is probably not particularly threatened.

Dicranella crispa (Hedw.) Schimp.

Curl-leaved Forklet-moss

syn. *Anisothecium vaginale* (Dicks.) Loeske

Status in Ireland: Endangered (B1a, bi, ii, iv, B2a, bi, ii, iv); **Status in Europe:** Least Concern

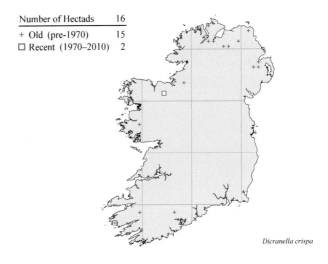

Number of Hectads	16
+ Old (pre-1970)	15
□ Recent (1970–2010)	2

Dicranella crispa

Identification

An acrocarpous moss that grows as yellowish-green to green tufts or patches up to 10 mm high, with conspicuous reddish-brown sporophytes. Separation of *D. crispa* from other species of *Dicranella* requires careful attention to details of structure of both leaves and capsules. All leaves, including perichaetial bracts, have oblong sheathing bases, abruptly narrowed to a long, channelled, linear-subulate limb that is squarrose-flexuose (not secund) when moist, loosely crisped when dry. The costa is thin, percurrent to excurrent, the leaf margin plane or somewhat inflexed above and either entire throughout or denticulate towards the apex. Leaf cells are linear and very narrow, only 4–6 μm wide in mid-leaf. Capsules are ellipsoid or obovoid, erect, striate (furrowed) when dry, exserted on a long red-brown seta. The striate, erect capsules provide a useful field character, but *D. subulata* sometimes also has its striate capsules erect rather than inclined; leaves of that species are somewhat secund and only the perichaetial bracts have sheathing bases.

Distribution in Ireland

Confirmed records are from 10 vice-counties and at least 15 localities, but with only one population refound in the past decade: S. Kerry (Rinneen, 1951–2006); N. Kerry (Killarney, 1827); E. Cork (Dunbulloge Glen, 1842); W. Galway (near Maam Hotel, 1854); Sligo (near Masshill in the Ox Mountains, 1970); Leitrim (Boggaun, 1963); E. Donegal (Grianan Hill, 1902; SE of Clonmany River, 1969); Down (Minnowburn, 1801; Ravarnet, pre-1909; Cregagh Glen, pre-1910; all *fide* Megaw 1938); Antrim (lane from Stranmillis Road leading towards Botanic Garden, 1881; Brean Mountain, 1882; near Lisburn, 1900) and Londonderry (Glenshane Pass, 1937). Megaw (1938) listed several other records from Antrim and Londonderry. The only site known to be extant (Rinneen) had several strong patches in 2006.

Ecology and biology

D. crispa grows on disturbed, open and sparsely vegetated soils that may be sandy, gravelly or of clay, usually damp, and apparently not markedly acidic or strongly basic. Habitat details are known for only a few Irish sites, but these include low sea cliffs (of periglacial head deposits), a roadside quarry, near a stream and wet sandy ground, all mainly in the lowlands. Other habitats recorded occasionally in Britain include rocks, especially vertical sandstone, dune slacks and once an arable field. In Fennoscandia, it is relatively common and typically found along roadsides, in screes and on bare soil at the base of wind-thrown trees.

The open habitat suggests the species may often be a colonist that needs to reach new substrata as old sites

375

develop taller vegetation cover. Indeed, in Scandinavia, it is described as 'a weak competitor and hence dependent on disturbance of the ground' (Hallingbäck *et al.* 2006). However, the Rinneen locality evidently maintained suitable habitats for it over a 25-year period on eroding cliffs, with several large patches that presumably persist from year to year. The plants are dioicous or autoicous (i.e. male inflorescence occurring on a separate branch or a separate plant: Williams 1913) and sporophytes are common, with capsules reportedly maturing in autumn and winter in Britain (but spring and summer in N. America: Crum 2007). Tubers are unknown (unlike most species of the genus) and there are no reports of gemmae.

World distribution

It is widespread in Europe from the Arctic in Spitsbergen, N. Iceland and N. Fennoscandia southwards to the French Pyrenees, Alps and Caucasus. It is listed as *Extinct* in the Netherlands, *Vulnerable* in Germany and *Data Deficient* in the Czech Republic and Switzerland. It is assigned to a Circumpolar Boreo-arctic montane floristic element in Europe. Elsewhere, it is known in N. Asia (widespread in Siberia: Ignatov *et al.* 2007), N. America (Alaska and Nunavut southwards to California and Colorado) and Greenland.

Threats

Causes of the apparent decline of this species in Ireland and in Britain are rather puzzling. The suggestions that in Britain it may have previously been recorded in error, or it may currently be overlooked (Porley in Hill *et al.* 1992) are unconvincing, since many old specimens are correctly identified and those bryologists who know the plant rarely find it. A more likely explanation may be that the species has occurred mainly as a short-lived colonist for the past two centuries, with very few populations in any one year. The 'old' records amassed over many years thus inevitably seem more numerous than those from just the past few decades. The survival of the population at Rinneen will depend on persistence of open cliff-slope habitat, so that development or more extensive disturbance around the jetty should be prevented.

Conservation

The only population known to be extant is not on protected land and some of it is potentially at risk from activity associated with a jetty, (e.g. stacking of materials against part of the cliff slope).

Protected sites with recent records: none; **Unprotected sites with recent records:** near Masshill in the Ox Mountains; Rinneen.

Dicranella subulata (Hedw.) Schimp.

Awl-leaved Forklet-moss

Status in Ireland: Least Concern; **Status in Europe:** Least Concern

A widely distributed moss of sandy or gravelly banks, screes and quarries, mainly in upland and coastal areas in the west. This species was included in the Provisional Red List (Holyoak 2006b), but recent fieldwork has shown it to be more frequent than previously thought. It has been reported from 16 vice-counties, with records from 28 hectads (11 old, 17 recent) and is not considered threatened.

Dicranella cerviculata (Hedw.) Schimp.

Red-neck Forklet-moss

Status in Ireland: Near threatened; **Status in Europe:** Least Concern

This moss is widespread in Ireland on peaty substrata and has been reported from 29 vice-counties, with records from 40 hectads (29 old, 6 recent, 5 undated). It was not included in the Provisional Red List (Holyoak 2006b) and so was not sought during recent fieldwork. The relative scarcity of modern records is probably more a reflection of lack of targeted search effort rather than any actual decline.

Dicranum undulatum Schrad. ex Brid.

Waved Fork-moss

syn. *D. affine* Funck, *D. bergeri* Blandow
Status in Ireland: Regionally Extinct; **Status in Europe:** Least Concern

Number of Hectads	3
+ Old (pre-1970)	3

Dicranum undulatum

Identification

A large acrocarpous moss that grows as yellowish, brownish or dull green tufts, up to 15 cm high, occasionally 20 cm. Like several other species of *Dicranum* it has long leaves (4–7 mm) that are straight to subsecund, lanceolate to ovate lanceolate, tapering to an acute to obtuse apex, with percurrent costa, leaf margins that are plane and usually denticulate to dentate, and large brownish angular cells forming well-defined groups. Distinctive features of this species are the conspicuously transversely undulate and rugose leaves, the predominantly quadrate or rectangular upper leaf cells and the more or less blunt leaf apex. Capsules are rare, narrowly ellipsoid, curved and exserted on a long seta.

Distribution in Ireland

D. undulatum is known only from four sites in Offaly (Pollagh Bog, 1957; Ferbane, 1960; Endrum Hill, 1960; Banagher, 1960). The first record was made by C.D. Pigott, all the others by D.J. Bellamy. These four localities were revisited in 2005 and searched unsuccessfully for the species, albeit that most were rather vaguely localised. A more extensive search of raised bogs in Offaly was made in 2009, but once again was unsuccessful, so *D. undulatum* is probably extinct in Ireland.

Ecology and biology

All of the Irish records were from acidic mires with deep peat, apparently all of them on raised bogs, the original find being associated with hummocks of *Sphagnum*. Similarly, in Britain it is confined to oligotrophic mires, almost all of which are raised bogs. The species is much more common in Fennoscandia, growing among peat mosses in bogs or poor fens, but in the northern regions also on pine heaths (Hallingbäck *et al.* 2006).

The female plants are perennial, growing in patches that persist for some years; male plants are probably annual. The species is dioicous, with dwarf male shoots occurring among the larger female shoots. Capsules are rare in Britain and Scandinavia (apparently unknown in Ireland), maturing in spring or summer. Gemmae, bulbils and tubers are unknown, but vegetative propagation may occur from detached leaves or stem fragments.

World distribution

Mainly a boreal species in Europe, widespread over much of Norway, Sweden and Finland, sparse in Britain (from C. Wales northwards; known further south and south-east only as mid- to late-Flandrian fossil: Dickson 1973), occurring southwards locally to E. Pyrenees, Alps, Ukraine and Caucasus. It is listed as *Endangered* in Bulgaria, Germany and the Netherlands, *Vulnerable* in Britain, *Near Threatened* in Switzerland and *Data Deficient* in Serbia. It is assigned to a Circumpolar Boreo-arctic montane floristic element in Europe. Elsewhere, the species is known in Armenia, N. Asia (widespread in Siberia; also NE China), Sichuan (Gao Chien *et al.* 1999), N. America (Alaska and Nunavut southwards to Washington State and North Carolina; introduced in California) and Greenland.

Threats

Extensive removal of raised bog peat by Bord na Móna has almost certainly caused the extinction of the species in Ireland. The remnants of bog that have been left around the Offaly localities have all suffered damage from lowering of the water table. Elsewhere, populations have also been lost due to destruction of bog habitats in Britain and over much of Germany away from the Alps and Black Forest (Meinunger & Schröder 2007).

Conservation

No action is proposed. Reintroduction of the species to its former range in Offaly would serve no useful purpose because good examples of its wet, raised bog habitat no longer exist there.

Protected sites with recent records: none; **Unprotected sites with recent records:** none.

Dicranoloma menziesii (Taylor) Renauld

Status in Ireland: Not Evaluated; **Status in Europe:** Not Evaluated

A large and handsome acrocarpous epiphyte, with leaves tapering to a long fragile subula. Scott & Stone (1976) give a detailed description. Its native range is restricted to the southern hemisphere, in eastern Australia, Tasmania, New Zealand (and neighbouring islands) and Chile. The only record from the northern hemisphere is from Garinish Island (S. Kerry), where it was found to be well established in the woodland garden in 2008, growing on 'trunks' of several *Dicksonia* tree ferns (Holyoak & Lockhart 2009b).

Dicranodontium uncinatum (Harv.) A.Jaeger

Curve-leaved Bow-moss

syn. *Dicranum uncinatum* (Harv.) Sm.
Status in Ireland: Vulnerable (B1a, bi, ii, iii, iv, B2a, bi, ii, iii, iv); **Status in Europe:** Least Concern

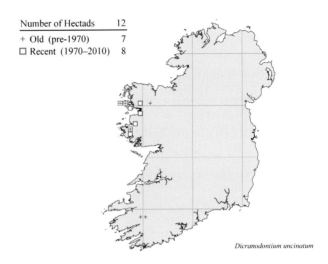

Number of Hectads	12
+ Old (pre-1970)	7
□ Recent (1970–2010)	8

Dicranodontium uncinatum

Identification

This acrocarpous moss is very like a large *Dicranum* or *Campylopus*, forming glossy green tufts up to 12 cm tall, and having narrow falcato-secund leaves that may be nearly 2 cm long and hardly altered when dry. The leaves have a sheathing base and a wide costa, and the alar cells are inflated and brownish or hyaline. The leaf margin is denticulate only in the upper half, and the leaf apex is only faintly toothed. The costa is very wide, similar to that of a *Campylopus*, but rather poorly defined. *Campylopus* species differ in having only one band of stereids visible in sections of the costa, on the abaxial side, whereas *Dicranodontium* species have both abaxial and adaxial bands.

Distribution in Ireland

Recent records are from nine localities in two vice-counties: W. Galway (Benlettery, 1983; Bengower, 1957–2004; Benbreen, undated but recent, leg. D.G. Long) and W. Mayo (Slievemore, 1901–2003; Croaghaun, 1919–1987; Corraun, 1982–2003; Corryloughaphuill, 1982; Croagh Patrick, 1987; Mweelrea, 1987, 2010). There are additional older records from N. Kerry (Eagle's Nest, 1935; Crohane, 1937), W. Galway (Bencollaghduff, 1957) and W. Mayo (Nephin, 1901). There is also an old record from Wicklow (near Arklow, 1867), which seems extraordinary on grounds of both altitude and geography, but is supported by a specimen.

Ecology and biology

Often associated with large oceanic liverworts in the Northern Atlantic hepatic mat community, *D. uncinatum* grows on N.- to E.-facing slopes in montane parts of the Atlantic seaboard, often in block scree, on cliff ledges or under patchy heather, on non-basic substrata. Recent records in Ireland are from 220–600 m altitude. It can also grow at lower altitudes on irrigated vertical rock faces in wooded ravines.

A dioicous species, sporophytes have not been observed in Ireland or Britain, and neither does it produce specialised vegetative propagules or deciduous leaves.

World distribution

This plant has a restricted European distribution, occurring in Britain (fairly widely in the west of Scotland and the Cairngorms plus a few sites in the English Lake District; *Nationally Scarce* in Britain). It also grows in Norway, Spain (*Vulnerable*), the Alps and the Tatra Mountains (*Critically Endangered* in Switzerland, 'potentially threatened' in Austria and *Endangered* in the Czech Republic). In Europe, it is classified as a Suboceanic Boreal-montane floristic element. Its world distribution mimics that of some of the Northern Atlantic hepatic mat liverworts, being widely disjunct in the Himalaya, China, SE Asia, Japan and W. Canada (British Columbia).

379

Threats

The major threat to this species could be climate change, but other threats are probably slight. Its rocky habitat protects it to some extent from the problems on adjoining mountain slopes, including the potential threats from overstocking and burning.

Conservation

All of the localities for this species are on protected land, but periodic monitoring is required.

Protected sites with recent records: Ballycroy National Park; Corraun Plateau SAC; Croagh Patrick pNHA; Croaghaun/Slievemore SAC; Mweelrea/Sheeffry/Erriff Complex SAC; Owenduff/Nephin Complex SAC; The Twelve Bens/Garraun Complex SAC; **Unprotected sites with recent records:** none.

Dicranodontium asperulum (Mitt.) Broth.

Orange Bow-moss

syn. *Dicranum asperulum* Mitt.

Status in Ireland: Vulnerable (D2); **Status in Europe:** Insufficiently Known

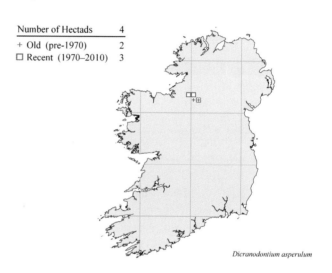

Number of Hectads	4
+ Old (pre-1970)	2
□ Recent (1970–2010)	3

Dicranodontium asperulum

Identification

This acrocarpous moss is much like a large *Campylopus*, forming yellowish-green, silky tufts up to 7.5 cm tall, and having very long, narrow, often secund leaves that may be over 1 cm long. The leaves have a sheathing base and a wide costa, and the alar cells are inflated and brownish or hyaline. The distinctive features of this species are that the leaf margins are toothed almost from base to apex, and the leaf tip is very fine and spinosely denticulate. *Campylopus* species differ in having only one band of stereids in the costa, on the abaxial side, whereas *Dicranodontium* have two bands, both abaxial and adaxial.

Distribution in Ireland

Recent records are from three localities, restricted to a small cluster of hills in neighbouring vice-counties:

Leitrim (Bronagh, 1970–2000); Cavan (S. of Englishman's House, 1965–2001; Cuilcagh, 1909–2001) and Fermanagh (Cuilcagh, 1909–2005). There is also an older record from Tiltinbane, Co. Cavan (1957).

Ecology and biology

Like *D. uncinatum*, this species favours sheltered, moist N.- to E.-facing slopes. It grows in Ireland mainly among gritstone blocks and boulders where sheltered and partly shaded, often on thin very acidic soil, more rarely on peaty humus over sandstone, at altitudes of c. 300–650 m. Common associates include such shade-tolerant acidophiles as *Diplophyllum albicans* and *Pseudotaxiphyllum elegans*.

It is a dioicous species; sporophytes have not been observed in Ireland or Britain. According to Hill *et al.* (1992) and Smith (2004) the leaves are sometimes deciduous (and may act as vegetative propagules), but no mention is made of this in Hill *et al.* (2007). However, a herbarium specimen from Co. Fermanagh (Holyoak 00-172) has many intact deciduous leaves loose in the packet.

World distribution

Elsewhere in Europe, this moss has been recorded from Britain (where it is *Nationally Scarce* and restricted to northern and western areas), Norway, Spain (*Data Deficient*) and the C. European mountains, where it is listed as *Critically Endangered* in Switzerland and 'extremely rare' in Germany. In Europe, it is classified as a Suboceanic Boreal-montane floristic element. It is also known from eastern Russia, China, Japan, Taiwan and N. America.

Threats

There are apparently few threats to this species in Ireland, in spite of its restricted distribution. Its habitat in block- and boulder-screes and at crag bases ensures that the localities are unlikely to be afforested or badly affected by the impacts of overstocking. In the long term, climate change may be the only significant threat.

Conservation

Dicranodontium asperulum is listed as a Northern Ireland Priority Species.

Protected sites with recent records: Boleybrack Mountain SAC; Cuilcagh Mountain ASSI; Cuilcagh Mountain SAC; Cuilcagh-Anierin Uplands SAC; **Unprotected sites with recent records:** none.

Campylopus subulatus Schimp. ex Milde

Awl-leaved Swan-neck Moss

Status in Ireland: Vulnerable (B2a, bii, iv); **Status in Europe:** Least Concern

Number of Hectads	17
+ Old (pre-1970)	9
□ Recent (1970–2010)	9

Campylopus subulatus

Identification

This is a rather nondescript yellowish-green acrocarpous moss that is difficult to spot in the field because it is easily overlooked as *C. flexuosus* or *Dicranella heteromalla*. Like other *Campylopus*, it has long, narrow leaves with a very broad costa. It forms rather loose, uneven patches up to 3 cm high but usually less, with leaves up to 4 mm long. The leaves are more or less straight with the lower part parallel-sided and the upper part tapering to a point, but lacking a hair-point. The stems lack a tomentum. Deciduous branchlets lying loose on the plants often provide a clue to its identity in the field, but microscopical examination is required to confirm that stereid cells are absent from the costa in cross section, and that the base of the leaves lack strong auricles.

Distribution in Ireland

This species has a mainly western distribution in Ireland, as it has in Britain, with recent records from nine localities in six vice-counties: W. Cork (Lough Nambrackderg, 2009; Gurteen, 2009; Dromore, 2009); Laois (Cappard, 2010); W. Mayo (near Keel, Achill Island, 1911–2003); Louth (Windy Gap, 2010); W. Donegal (Slieve League, 1970–2008; Portnoo-Rossbeg,

1970) and Tyrone (Dart Mountain, 1999). There are older records from S. Kerry (Derrymore River, 1949); N. Kerry (Cromaglan, 1865); W. Cork (Glengarriff, 1900); W. Mayo (Doogort, 1911); Leitrim (Truskmore, 1909–1912); E. Donegal (Buncrana, 1903); W. Donegal (Doochary Bridge, 1890); Tyrone (Trillick River, 1901) and Antrim (Cave Hill, Belfast, 1952).

Ecology and biology
This is a plant of bare ground in sandy or gravelly places such as track sides and river margins. More rarely it occurs on and among rocks. In Ireland, it has been found on a damp sandy track in an old quarry with *Fossombronia caespitiformis* subsp. *multispira*, *Riccia subbifurca* and *Pohlia andalusica*, on a forestry track, in an old quarry, on sandy ground among rocks, on thin gravelly soil on an unshaded roadside, on sandy detritus on a boulder, on a steep earthy bank near a stream in a N.-facing mountain corrie, and amongst gravel on rock ledges at the base of basalt outcrops.

This species is dioicous, but virtually always non-fertile (capsules found once in Britain, unknown in Ireland). Like several other species of *Campylopus*, *C. subulatus* propagates vegetatively by deciduous shoot tips.

World distribution
Generally, but sparsely, distributed in W. Europe eastwards to C. Europe, Sweden and the Balkans, *C. subulatus* is listed as *Nationally Scarce* in Britain, *Extinct* in Luxembourg. *Endangered* in Switzerland, *Vulnerable* in Germany, Austria and Sweden, *Data Deficient* (*vanished*) in the Czech Republic, and 'very rare and susceptible' in the Netherlands. In Europe, it is categorised as a Suboceanic Temperate floristic element. Its range in the rest of the world is uncertain because of confusion with other species, but it appears to be known from Turkey, Bhutan, W. China and three sites in the USA (California and Oregon).

Threats
No particular threats have been identified. The species requires open habitats and will disappear when taller plants shade the ground.

Conservation
No specific conservation measures are recommended for this species. It is somewhat under-recorded and apparently grows as an opportunist in habitats that may otherwise be of little conservation interest. However, known sites should be monitored to check that they are not threatened by destructive developments. *C. subulatus* is listed as a Northern Ireland Priority Species.

Protected sites with recent records: Carlingford Mountain SAC; Slieve Bloom Mountains SAC; Slieve League SAC; **Unprotected sites with recent records:** Dart Mountain; Dromore; Gurteen; Lough Nambrackderg; near Keel, Achill Island; Portnoo-Rossbeg (possibly within West of Ardara/Maas Road SAC).

Campylopus schimperi Milde
Schimper's Swan-neck Moss

syn. *Campylopus subulatus* var. *schimperi* (Milde) Husn.
Status in Ireland: Regionally Extinct; **Status in Europe:** Least Concern

Number of Hectads	3
+ Old (pre-1970)	3

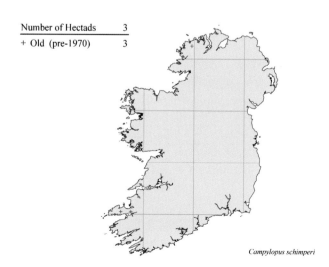

Campylopus schimperi

Identification

This is a medium-sized to fairly large acrocarpous moss (2.5–8 cm high) with narrow leaves 2.5–7.5 mm long, tapering to a long, drawn-out apex. As in other species of *Campylopus*, the costa is extremely broad, occupying c. ⅔ of the width of the leaf base. There are no stereid cells in the costa (cross section), the leaves are not toothed, or minutely toothed near the apex only, and auricles are usually absent from the leaf base. The often dense tufts and the usually dense reddish tomentum matting the lower parts of the stems further distinguish *C. schimperi* from related species including *C. subulatus*.

Distribution in Ireland

This species has been recorded from three localities in two vice-counties: S. Kerry (Stradbally Mountain, 1954; Derrymore River, 1899) and W. Donegal (Muckish Mountain, 1969). Despite recent searching, it has not been seen at any of these sites since. Further old records from Wicklow and Antrim are unreliable and must be disregarded.

Ecology and biology

C. schimperi is essentially an arctic-alpine species of acid turf or rock crevices on cliffs, on steep N.- to NE-facing slopes in montane areas. There is little information on its habitat in Ireland, but one record was from a rocky stream bank.

Sporophytes are not known in Ireland or Britain; the species is dioicous. It propagates vegetatively by fragile leaf tips and sometimes by deciduous leaves and shoot tips.

World distribution

C. schimperi is relatively widespread in Fennoscandia and Arctic areas, the Alps and the Carpathians, but rare or absent elsewhere in Europe. It is *Nationally Scarce* in Britain (Preston 2006), *Vulnerable* in Sweden and Spain, and *Data Deficient* in Switzerland. In Europe, it is assigned to a Circumpolar Arctic-montane floristic element. It is known elsewhere in N. and C. Asia, N. America and Greenland, and also in Japan and the Himalaya (Hill *et al.* 1992).

Threats

Climate change might have had a negative effect on the Irish populations of this species. It is at the southern edge of its European range in Ireland, and even small stresses may have eliminated colonies, although it might simply have remained overlooked around its old sites. Over-stocking and afforestation might also have played a part in the apparent disappearance of *C. schimperi* in Ireland.

Conservation

No conservation measures are currently necessary, but bryologists should look out for this plant in the mountains.

Protected sites with recent records: none; **Unprotected sites with recent records:** none.

Campylopus shawii Wilson

Shaw's Swan-neck Moss

Status in Ireland: Near Threatened; **Status in Europe:** Rare

Identification

This is a handsome acrocarpous moss, growing in yellowish-green turfs up to 15 cm deep (although often much smaller), with elegant, elongated, curved leaves that may be over 1 cm long. The stems are more or less matted below with red-brown rhizoids forming a tomentum. Like other species of the genus, the costa is disproportionately large, filling most of the width of the narrow leaf, but the impression in the field is nevertheless of a broader-leaved plant than with many congeners, more similar to a large *Dicranum*. The alar cells form conspicuous hyaline or orange auricles. It is, however, necessary to confirm the identification microscopically: the leaves are almost entire (toothed in *C. setifolius*), and in cross section, the single row of adaxial cells are very large, occupying more than half the thickness of the costa.

Distribution in Ireland

This is a highly oceanic species with a strongly south-western distribution in Ireland. Recent records are from 13 localities in two vice-counties: S. Kerry (Brandon Mountain, 1967–2009; Coomanare Lakes, Dingle, 2008; Lough Googh, 2009; Lough Currane, NE of Lough Dreenaun, 1951–2006; NW of Uragh Wood, 2006; S. of Cloonaghlin Lough, 2006; Knockowen, 1983; Lough Coomeathcun, 1951–2006; N. of Liss, 2006; Boughil, 2006; Claddaghgarriff, 2006) and W. Cork (Gougane

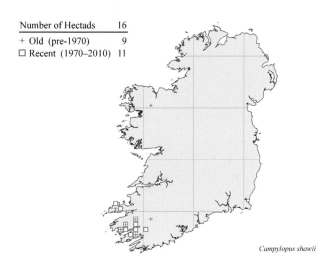

Campylopus shawii

Barra, 1979; Knockowen, 1983–2006). Older records are: S. Kerry (Connor Hill Pass, 1936; Caherdaniel, 1951; Coad Mountain, 1951; Cummeenduff Glen, 1967; Derriana Lough, 1951); N. Kerry (The Paps, 1967); W. Cork (Adrigole, 1896–1925; Glengarriff, 1912) and W. Mayo (Nephin, 1920).

Ecology and biology

This plant grows on wet acidic ground, such as in blanket bog and wet heath, often where there is some flushing, from sea level up to 600 m. Recorded habitats in Ireland include open, gently sloping peaty mire and blanket bog, a wet hollow in heathland, and sloping flushed areas, sometimes extending over low sandstone rocks. Typical associates include *Sphagnum cuspidatum*, *S. palustre*, *S. denticulatum*, *Campylopus atrovirens*, *Pleurozia purpurea*, *Molinia caerulea*, *Nardus stricta* and *Carex* spp.

C. shawii is dioicous, and capsules are unknown in Ireland and Britain. However, it probably propagates vegetatively from fragile leaf tips and caducous leaves.

World distribution

In Europe, this species is known only from Ireland, Scotland (*Nationally Scarce* in Britain) and the Azores. Its European distribution is classified as Hyperoceanic Southern-temperate. Elsewhere, it has been recorded only from the Caribbean, so it is an Atlantic species in a very literal sense.

Threats

Overstocking and inappropriate forestry planting are probably the major threats to this species, particularly as it often grows in otherwise rather species-poor bogland and on acidic montane slopes. Desiccation could also be

a problem if there is a lowering of the water table or significant climate change.

Conservation

Many of the best sites for this species are within protected areas.

Protected sites with recent records: Caha Mountains SAC; Cloonee and Inchiquin Loughs, Uragh Wood SAC; Killarney National Park, Macgillycuddy's Reeks and Caragh River Catchment SAC; Mount Brandon SAC; **Unprotected sites with recent records:** Gougane Barra (possibly within Gouganebarra Lake pNHA); N. of Liss; S. of Cloonaghlin Lough.

Knockowen, Co. Cork.

Campylopus atrovirens De Not. **var.** *falcatus* Braithw.

Status in Ireland: Near Threatened; **Status in Europe:** Not Evaluated

This is a rare variety of a strongly oceanic moss, found on peat and wet rocks in western, usually montane parts of Ireland. There are reports from seven vice-counties, with records from 11 hectads (7 old, 6 recent). There is, however, no evidence of decline. Often subsumed as a synonym of *C. atrovirens*, as in Hill *et al.* (2006), var. *falcatus* is nevertheless recognised as a taxon by Hill *et al.* (2008) in spite of the fact that intermediates between the variety and the type are by no means uncommon.

Leucobryum juniperoideum (Brid.) Müll.Hal.

Smaller White-moss

Status in Ireland: Least Concern; **Status in Europe:** Least Concern

This species was first recorded in Ireland at Torc Cascade, N. Kerry, in 1975, and is now known from seven vice-counties and 15 hectads. Although it was included in the Provisional Red List (Holyoak 2006b), fieldwork over the last decade has shown it to be more frequent that previously thought. Its similarity to the relatively common *L. glaucum* almost certainly led to it being overlooked in the past.

Scopelophila cataractae (Mitt.) Broth.

Tongue-leaf Copper-moss

Status in Ireland: Vulnerable (D2); **Status in Europe:** Not Evaluated

Identification

A small acrocarpous moss that grows as scattered stems or forms dull or deep green cushions (brown basally, or in moribund plants) that may become thick and dense, with branched stems 2–30 mm high. The leaves are erect-spreading when moist, contorted when dry, 1.5–2.5 mm long, keeled, lingulate with a shortly acute apex. The leaf margin is plane and the costa is percurrent within a short mucro or occasionally shortly excurrent. The costa has two layers of parenchymatous cells adaxial to the

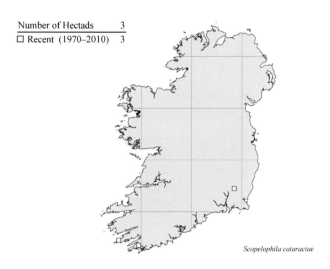

Number of Hectads   3
☐ Recent (1970–2010)   3

Scopelophila cataractae

stereid band, the ventral cells being somewhat enlarged and forming two rows in the lower part of the leaf. Mid-leaf cells are smooth, rounded-quadrate, 8–13 μm wide with thick cell walls; basal cells are wider and shortly-rectangular. Capsules are unknown in Europe. The plants are superficially similar to *Barbula convoluta*, but differ in being darker green, with smooth leaf cells, two rows of enlarged cells on ventral surface of costa and in growing on metalliferous substrata.

Distribution in Ireland

It is known from three localities in two vice-counties: W. Cork (Allihies, 2006–2009; NE of Cappaghglass, 2006–2009) and Wexford (SW of Caim Cross Roads, 2008–2009). The species was apparently overlooked in Ireland until recently: its populations in W. Cork are small and inconspicuous and the mine site in Wexford was first surveyed for bryophytes in 2008.

Ecology and biology

All three Irish sites are at disused lowland copper mines on substrata that are acidic, low in nutrients and which almost certainly have high metal levels. It grows in humid, sheltered and often shaded and damp places on banks or level surfaces of fine-grained mine spoil, occasionally on rock (e.g. in the entrance to a mine adit). Some records are of sparse populations growing from mats of *Cephaloziella massalongi* or *C. nicholsonii*, but others grow on mainly bare surfaces and the Wexford plants form thick, pure mats on vertical mine spoil. Its habitats in Britain and elsewhere in Europe are mostly similar. *S. cataractae* is well known as a colonist of copper-rich substrata on which few other plants can grow (Shaw 1987, 1993, Satake *et al.* 1988). Fletcher (1993) found

that in cultivation it is resistant to applications of a strong copper sulphate solution. In Europe, it has been found mainly on substrata with a high copper content (Corley & Perry 1985, Sotiaux *et al.* 1987, Schumacker & Brugués, 1991) but also occasionally where zinc occurs at high concentrations (van Melick 1986).

The plants are perennial, but small patches sometimes persist as protonemata that do not give rise to leafy shoots in all years (D.T. Holyoak, unpublished data from Cornwall). The species is dioicous and only non-fertile and male plants are known in Europe; both sexes occur in N. America; capsules are known only from Asia. Abundant protonemal gemmae are produced by cultures and known in wild European plants (Arts 1988); rhizoidal tubers are known in Britain and Europe; bulbils are unknown. Regeneration can occur even from small fragments of leaf tissue.

World distribution

First recorded in Europe in 1967, since when it has been found in Ireland, Isle of Man, England, Wales (*Vulnerable* in Britain), France, Belgium, the Netherlands ('very rare'), Germany ('extremely rare'), Italy and N. and S. Spain (*Vulnerable*) (Frahm in Frey *et al.* 2006, Casas *et al.* 2006). Although first found in Britain near a smelting works at Swansea in S. Wales in 1967 it was not identified until 1982 (Corley & Perry 1985). Numerous subsequent British records are from N. and S. Wales, Devon and Cornwall (c. 16 localities in latter county: D.T. Holyoak unpublished). It is assigned to a Circumpolar Southern-temperate floristic element in Europe. Elsewhere, the species is known in N. America (Massachusetts to California and Texas), Mexico, C. America, western S. America, tropical and E. Asia (northwards to Korea and Japan) and C. Africa (including Republic of Congo: Townsend in Blockeel *et al.* 2005a).

The species has been presumed to be an accidental introduction in Europe because some of the earliest European records were at or near smelting works. However, numerous subsequent records from remote disused mine sites increase the likelihood of it being an overlooked native species in Europe (Holyoak & Lockhart 2009a).

Threats

S. cataractae is restricted to a few disused copper mine sites where the extent of suitable habitat is declining. At Cappaghglass, building development is continuing to encroach on to the mine-spoil areas. Illegal tipping at Allihies destroyed one small patch of *S. cataractae* in 2006; some tipping was still occurring there in 2008. All of the localities are at some risk from shading, through natural vegetation succession as scrub and saplings eventually become established on adjoining land.

Conservation

The site at Allihies is on protected land, but the population at Cappaghglass, and the large population near Caim Cross Roads, are currently unprotected.

Protected sites with recent records: Kenmare River SAC; **Unprotected sites with recent records:** NE of Cappaghglass; SW of Caim Cross Roads.

Weissia controversa Hedw. **var.** *crispata* (Nees & Hornsch.) Nyholm Crisped Stubble-moss

Status in Ireland: Data Deficient; **Status in Europe:** Not Evaluated

This is a variety of the common *W. controversa*, differentiated by its stout reddish costa (60–100 μm wide near leaf base), typically found on mortar of bridges and walls. Surveys in 2007 and 2010 by S.D.S. Bosanquet and C.D. Preston have recorded it from 13 hectads in four vice-counties (Clare, S. Tipperary, Kilkenny and Wicklow) and an older record has also been revealed by study of a specimen at **BBSUK** (Offaly: in Wood of Birr, 1949). There is little doubt that this taxon has been overlooked until recently and that it will prove to have additional localities in Ireland, so it is unlikely to be red-listed. Var. *crispata* often appears to be little more than an extreme form of var. *controversa*, with a stout costa and no other characters. However, molecular data show that *W. controversa* is likely to be a complex of allied forms (Werner *et al.* 2004, 2005) and there is evidence of interspecific hybridization in the genus.

Kilcommon Bridge, Tinahely, Co. Wicklow, site for *Weissia controversa* var. *crispata*.

Weissia controversa Hedw. **var.** *densifolia* (Bruch & Schimp.) Wilson   Thick-leaved Earth-moss

Status in Ireland: Least Concern; **Status in Europe:** Not Evaluated

One of several varieties of *W. controversa*, this plant is characteristic of soils rich in heavy metals, such as at old lead or copper mines and beneath galvanised-iron roofs and crash barriers. It was included in the Provisional Red List (Holyoak 2006b) but survey work over the last decade has shown it to be widespread on suitable substrates, and it is now known from 10 vice-counties, with records from 14 hectads (2 old, 13 recent). Duckett *et al.* (2006) found that var. *densifolia* 'stands apart from all the other taxa [of British *Weissia*] in the presence of very deeply pigmented caulonemata with a prominent cuticle. ... These striking differences in the protonemata suggest that var. *densifolia* could well merit elevation to specific status. However, protonemal morphology in intermediate forms from Cornish mining sites has still to be investigated.'

Weissia perssonii Kindb.   Persson's Stubble-moss

Status in Ireland: Least Concern; **Status in Europe:** Rare

This is a small acrocarpous moss that grows in dull green patches in coastal turf and banks. It is distinguished from the common *W. controversa* by its wider costa with elongate adaxial cells. It was included in the Provisional Red List (Holyoak 2006b), but has turned out to be much more common than previously thought. It is now known from 14 vice-counties, with records from 25 hectads (7 old, 21 recent). It seems to be absent from the east coast.

Weissia rutilans (Hedw.) Lindb.   Pointed-leaved Stubble-moss

syn. *Mollia rutilans* (Hedw.) Lindb., *Weissia mucronata* Bruch & Schimp.
Status in Ireland: Vulnerable (B2a, bii, iv); **Status in Europe:** Least Concern

Identification

A small acrocarpous moss that grows in green or yellow-green patches 3–10 mm high. As with several other species of *Weissia*, it has oblong-lanceolate leaves with the stout costa excurrent as a mucro, upper leaf cells that are

subquadrate, obscure because they are papillose, and basal cells that are rectangular and hyaline. The capsule is ovate-ellipsoid to ellipsoid, more or less furrowed when dry, erect and exserted on a yellowish seta 5–10 mm tall. Distinctive features of this species are the somewhat

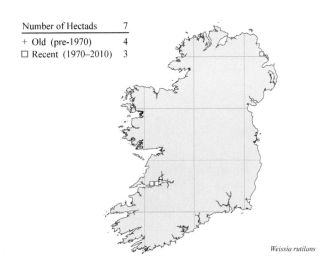

Number of Hectads	7
+ Old (pre-1970)	4
☐ Recent (1970–2010)	3

Weissia rutilans

narrowly-incurved leaf margins combined with short or rudimentary peristome teeth and relatively large spores (21–30 μm).

Distribution in Ireland

Recent records are from three localities in three vice-counties: Limerick (Foynes Island, 1993); Clare (NE of Aughaloge Bridge, 2007) and Antrim (Knock Dhu, 1999). Older records are: W. Donegal (Rathmullan, 1865); Down (Warrenpoint, before 1919); Antrim (Lurigethan, 1952) and Londonderry (Downhill, 1952). This species is difficult to identify without microscopical study of capsules and spores, which are mature mainly from autumn to spring, so it is probably under-recorded. Hence the pattern of distribution in Ireland, with a prevalence of northern records and two in the south-west, might result from incomplete recording, since the species is widespread across S. England.

Ecology and biology

Five Irish records have habitat notes, all of them apparently from exposed soil, at 5–277 m elevation. Three were from hilly areas, on basalt cliffs, on steep soil on a grassy slope below N.-facing basalt crags, and from a bare clay slip in a valley side. The other two were from a flushed roadside verge and an old pasture near an estuary shore in an area ploughed for forestry two years earlier. British localities are on non-calcareous and calcareous soil and clay, on banks, in thin grassland, marshy meadows, damp tracks and woodland rides, occasionally also in arable fields, among rocks, in old quarries, on cliff slopes, on roadsides or in upland flushes. In Scandinavia, it is apparently the only *Weissia* preferring moderately shaded habitats (Hallingbäck *et al.* 2008).

The plants are short-lived perennials, or presumably sometimes annuals when growing on arable land. The species is autoicous and commonly produces capsules, with spores maturing from autumn to spring. Gemmae, tubers or other vegetative propagules are unknown.

World distribution

The species is widespread in Europe from SW Iceland, Faeroes, S. Norway and S. Sweden southwards to N. Spain, Italy and the former Yugoslavia; eastwards it is known in the Ukraine and S. Urals (Ignatov *et al.* 2007). In Europe, it is assigned to a European Temperate floristic element. Elsewhere, it is known from SW Asia (Georgia and Tajikistan: Ignatov *et al.* 2007), E. Asia (Russian Far East; Japan), N. Africa, Ethiopia and Australia (Western Australia, South Australia, Victoria: Streimann & Klazenga 2002). Although sometimes listed for Canada, it is excluded from the taxa treated for N. America by R.H. Zander (in FNA 2007).

Threats

Little is known of threats to populations in Ireland. Those at some sites may be short-lived on temporarily bare areas of soil. On slopes around basalt crags it may perhaps persist longer by recolonising soil on rock ledges or temporary slips. Vegetation succession or afforestation could therefore reduce habitats available to it.

Conservation

W. rutilans is listed as a Northern Ireland Priority Species.

Protected sites with recent records: none; **Unprotected sites with recent records:** Aughaloge Bridge; Foynes Island; Knock Dhu (proposed ASSI).

Weissia condensa (Voit) Lindb.

Curly Beardless-moss

syn. *Hymenostomum tortile* (Schwägr.) Bruch & Schimp., *Weissia tortilis* (Schwägr.) Müll.Hal.
Status in Ireland: Data Deficient; **Status in Europe:** Least Concern

Number of Hectads   1
☐ Recent (1970–2010)   1

Weissia condensa

Identification

This small acrocarpous moss displays the typical leaf characteristics of *Weissia*, these being long, narrow, green, opaque, crisped when dry, with inrolled leaf margins. The shoots are less than 15 mm tall and form loose patches that can sometimes be readily detached from the substrata. It can be distinguished from other species of *Weissia* by the combination of an ellipsoid capsule, which is exserted on a seta 2–4 mm long, the lack of a peristome, the stout costa that is c. 60–120 μm wide near the base, and the small spores (c. 14–20 μm). *W. condensa* has often been confused with forms of *W. controversa*, and only specimens with plenty of good fresh capsules that clearly lack any peristome should be identified as the rarer species.

Distribution in Ireland

The only accepted record is based on a specimen gathered in 2006 at Nutgrove quarry, near Glanworth, E. Cork. There are also a number of unidentifiable specimens that might be *W. condensa*, collected in recent years from Cork and Clare, which may simply be forms of *W. controversa* from which the peristome has been lost. The first report for Ireland, and the basis for the listing of Fermanagh in Hill *et al.* (2008), was of a specimen (collected 8 August 2005 from Monawilkin, Fermanagh) that apparently lacked a peristome. When a fresher gathering made at the same

spot on 21 May 2008 was found to have a short peristome on many of the capsules, renewed study of the original specimen revealed one capsule with peristome rudiments. This record should therefore be rejected and the E. Cork specimen should be critically re-examined.

Ecology and biology

This lowland species grows on open, dry, calcareous soil, such as thin skeletal soil among limestone rocks, often on S.-facing slopes. In E. Cork it has been found on the floor of a disused limestone quarry at 60 m altitude, with *Syntrichia montana* and *Schistidium crassipilum*.

W. condensa is autoicous and produces sporophytes fairly frequently in the late winter and spring. There are no gemmae or other vegetative propagules.

World distribution

It is widespread in S. Europe and Macaronesia but becomes increasingly rare to the north. It is *Nationally Scarce* in Britain, where it is almost confined to the southern coastal counties of England, *Endangered* in Luxembourg and *Vulnerable* in Germany, Austria and Switzerland. The species is categorised as a Suboceanic Mediterranean-Atlantic floristic element in Europe. Elsewhere, it extends into SW Asia (Turkey and Iran) and Russian Asia and has also been found in N. Africa, the Cape Verde Islands and Socotra.

Threats

The quarry where this moss has been found in E. Cork is potentially vulnerable to land-use change, especially because it is something of a local eyesore.

Conservation

The identity of the specimen from E. Cork should be reconfirmed before any conservation action is taken. Any land restoration or potentially destructive management should make allowance for this species. Therefore the appropriate authorities need to be aware of its presence and rarity in Ireland.

Protected sites with recent records: none; **Unprotected sites with recent records:** Nutgrove quarry, near Glanworth.

Weissia brachycarpa (Nees & Hornsch.) Müll.Hal. **var. *brachycarpa***   Small-mouthed Beardless-moss

syn. *Weissia microstoma* var. *brachycarpa* (Nees & Hornsch.) Müll.Hal.
Status in Ireland: Data Deficient; **Status in Europe:** Not Evaluated

Number of Hectads	2
☐ Recent (1970–2010)	2

Weissia brachycarpa var. *brachycarpa*

Identification

This is a small, dark green patch-forming acrocarpous moss less than 1 cm tall, with long, narrowly lanceolate leaves that are crisped when dry, and ovoid to ellipsoid capsules exserted on a yellow seta. The genus *Weissia* has a distinctive appearance because of the narrow leaves, made opaque by the small papillose cells. While the much more common var. *obliqua* has inrolled leaf margins, typical of the genus, var. *brachycarpa* is distinctive because it has plane leaf margins. However, it does share the overall appearance of the other variety. The capsules of *W. brachycarpa* are characterised by their unusually small mouth, which lacks any peristome teeth and the spores that are larger than in most other species of the genus (20–34 μm).

Distribution in Ireland

This moss was first found in Ireland in 2000, on a path edge by Upper Lough Erne in Fermanagh, and then in 2008 at a second site, SE of Tomacurry in Wexford.

Ecology and biology

In Ireland, it has been found growing on patches of unshaded loamy soil in a cereal stubble field near a river, and on steep soil at the edge of a path through scrub near a lake. In Britain, this is a plant of non-calcareous, rather wet soils, typically growing in fields and on earthy banks in the lowlands. (In contrast, var. *obliqua* favours lighter, calcareous soils).

It is autoicous, with capsules produced abundantly in late winter and spring. There are no specialised vegetative propagules.

World distribution

The distribution of this taxon is poorly known because the varieties of the species have not always been differentiated. However, it appears to be widespread in Europe including Macaronesia. *W. brachycarpa s.l.* is listed as *Vulnerable* in the Netherlands, *Near Threatened* in Finland and 'declining' in Germany. Var. *brachycarpa* is assigned to a Circumpolar Southern-temperate floristic element in Europe. It also occurs in N. Asia, N. Africa and N. America.

Threats
No real threats to this moss have been identified, but the trend towards autumn ploughing is unlikely to be favourable if stubble fields are an important habitat.

Conservation
This variety has doubtless been overlooked in Ireland until recently, and is probably more widespread than the records indicate. Further survey work in stubble fields might be expected to reveal further populations, although arable land is not its main habitat in England. Arable management that promotes overwintering stubble should be encouraged, for this species and the bryophyte flora of tillage in general.

Protected sites with recent records: Slaney River Valley SAC; Upper Lough Erne SAC; Upper Lough Erne Trannish ASSI; **Unprotected sites with recent records:** none.

Weissia rostellata (Brid.) Lindb.

Beaked Beardless-moss

syn. *Astomum rostellatum* (Brid.) Bruch & Schimp.; *Hymenostomum rostellatum* Brid.) Schimp.
Status in Ireland: Near Threatened; **Status in Europe:** Rare

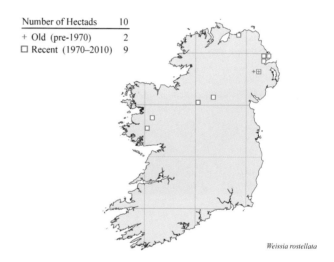

Number of Hectads	10
+ Old (pre-1970)	2
□ Recent (1970–2010)	9

Weissia rostellata

Identification
This is a small, bright green acrocarpous moss that forms ephemeral lax patches about 5 mm tall. The leaves are typical of the genus, being linear-lanceolate with plane to narrowly incurved margins and with a strong costa (c. 50 μm wide near the base), excurrent to 75–150 μm. The shortly cylindrical to ovoid capsules are produced on a short yellow-green seta up to 1.5 mm long, and are half-hidden among the long perichaetial bracts. The lids are not dehiscent, but break down to release the large spores (22–27 μm).

Distribution in Ireland
This species has been found exclusively in the northern half of Ireland, with recent records from nine localities in six vice-counties: W. Galway (S. shore of Lough Mask, N. of Clonbur, 2003); E. Mayo (E. bank of Cloon River, near Partry, 1987); Leitrim (Carrickaport Lough,

2000); Cavan (by the River Erne, 2001); Antrim (Bonner's Reservoir, 2002; Copeland Reservoir, 1999; South Woodburn Reservoir, 1999; North Woodburn Reservoir, 1999) and Londonderry (in a field at Lower Quilley, by A2 W. of Coleraine, 2008). There are older records from two further localities in Antrim (Ballinderry, 1906–1909; Ballymacash, Lisburn, 1902).

Ecology and biology
Most typically, *W. rostellata* grows on the partly bare mud exposed at the sides of reservoirs during draw-down at the end of dry summers. It can also occur by other waterbodies and on mud in ditches, and can be part of the arable field flora, growing in stubble fields. In Ireland, it has been found on unshaded silty clay among herbs and grasses on a riverbank; on silty and clayey mud among limestone fragments c. 15–30 cm above water on

a riverbank; on partly bare mud exposed among patchy low herbs high in the inundation zone beside a reservoir; at the extreme edge of a reservoir on partly dried mud, with sparse low herbs; on exposed mud at the edge of a reservoir, with patchy herbaceous vegetation (common under low *Eleocharis palustris*); on mud exposed at the edge of a reservoir, beneath incomplete cover of *Alopecurus geniculatus*. It appears to be a lowland plant in Ireland, with records from 15–95 m altitude.

This species is autoicous, with capsules produced abundantly in the autumn. There are no specialised vegetative propagules.

World distribution

A rare plant, this species is apparently endemic to Europe and has been recorded from Britain, where it is *Nationally Scarce*, and most central and western European countries. It is listed as *Extinct* in Austria, *Vulnerable* in Luxembourg, Germany and Switzerland, and *Data Deficient* in the Czech Republic. It is also recorded from Italy, Norway, Sweden, the Netherlands, Hungary, Russia, Poland and Finland, petering out both to the north and the south. It is assigned to a European Temperate floristic element.

Threats

This moss requires the regular exposure of suitable temporary habitat, such as mud by reservoirs, riverbanks and overwintered stubble fields. It is potentially at risk from alteration of the flooding regimes of lakes and reservoirs (e.g. for water supply, electricity generation, or recreational uses such as angling or water sports), alteration of their banks (e.g. by development or afforestation) and perhaps also from eutrophication.

Conservation

W. rostellata is protected in the Republic of Ireland by the Flora (Protection) Order, 1999. Several of its sites are on protected land.

Protected sites with recent records: Carrickaport Lough pNHA; Copeland Reservoir ASSI; Lough Carra/Mask Complex SAC; Lough Oughter and Associated Loughs SAC; North Woodburn Reservoir ASSI; South Woodburn Reservoir ASSI; **Unprotected sites with recent records:** Bonner's Reservoir; Lower Quilley, by A2 W. of Coleraine.

Weissia longifolia Mitt. **var.** *angustifolia*
(Baumgartner) Crundw. & Nyholm

Narrow-leaved Beardless-moss

syn. *Astomum crispum* auct., *Weissia crispa* auct.
Status in Ireland: Vulnerable (B1a, bii, iv, B2a, bii, iv); **Status in Europe:** Not Evaluated

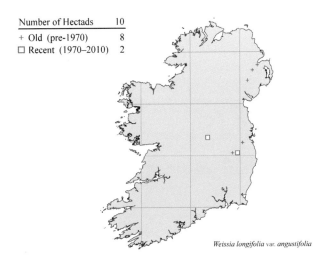

Number of Hectads	10
+ Old (pre-1970)	8
□ Recent (1970–2010)	2

Weissia longifolia var. *angustifolia*

Identification

Like many other species of *Weissia*, this acrocarpous moss forms rather dull green patches up to c. 1 cm tall, with long, narrow leaves that are spreading when moist, strongly curled when dry, of a characteristic opaque appearance because of the small papillose cells, and with an inrolled leaf margin. Unlike the common *Weissia* spp., *W. longifolia* has the ovoid, indehiscent capsule on a very short seta so that it is immersed among the leaves. The perichaetial bracts are somewhat longer than the stem leaves, c. 2.5–3.7 mm long. The other variety of this species, var. *longifolia*, has even longer perichaetial bracts c. 3–6 mm long, with less strongly inrolled margins, but it is not known to occur in Ireland. Non-fertile material cannot be identified with confidence.

Distribution in Ireland

Ireland is clearly at the edge of this plant's range, and there are just a few records, mostly scattered on the eastern side of the country. Recent records are from two localities: Kildare (Pollaphuca Lake at Ballymore Eustace, 2005) and Westmeath (Killavalley Torque near Kilbeggan, 1980). Older records are from nine localities in six vice-counties: Kilkenny (Dysart Castle near Thomastown, 1966); Kildare (Kilcullen Bridge, 1915); Dublin (Dalkey, 1946; Tallaght, 1953); W. Donegal (Melmore, 1910); Down (Lough-brickland, 1888; Lenaderg, undated; Lisburn, 1909) and Antrim (Cave Hill, undated).

Ecology and biology

In Ireland, where details are available, it has been recorded in an old sandpit; on calcareous soil on a grassy bank at the edge of a lake at 180 m altitude; on a dry bank near the sea; and in a crevice in a roadside limestone wall. In Britain, this plant grows on disturbed calcareous soils in the lowlands, usually on skeletal soils over chalk or limestone, in grassland, old quarries, path edges, etc.

This is an autoicous species that produces sporophytes in abundance in late winter and early spring. No specialised vegetative propagules are known.

World distribution

W. longifolia var. *angustifolia* is widespread and frequent in S. Europe, including in the Canary Islands, becoming more scarce further north. The two varieties are less distinct in continental Europe than they are in Ireland and Britain, and have usually not been recorded separately. Only var. *longiflora* has been recorded in Germany (Ludwig *et al.* 1996). *W. longifolia* var. *angustifolia* is *Endangered* in Norway, *Near Threatened* in Switzerland, and 'sparse' in the Netherlands. In Europe, var. *angustifolia* is categorised as a European Temperate floristic element. Elsewhere, it is known only from N. Africa, Turkey and S. Siberia.

Threats

There is no information on threats to *W. longifolia* in Ireland. Although the two recently known populations may disappear, it is likely that new ones will be discovered as colonists of open soil patches.

Conservation

W. longifolia is protected in the Republic of Ireland by the Flora (Protection) Order, 1999. The Irish populations of this plant might be transient, although detailed information is lacking. Periodic monitoring may be appropriate, but there seems little point in allocating resources to their conservation.

Protected sites with recent records: none; **Unprotected sites with recent records:** Killavalley Torque near Kilbeggan; Pollaphuca Lake at Ballymore Eustace.

Tortella bambergeri (Schimp.) Broth.

Bamberger's Crisp-moss

syn. *Tortella tortuosa* var. *bambergeri* (Schimp.) Düll
Status in Ireland: Least Concern; **Status in Europe:** Least Concern

This cushion-forming plant resembles a small *T. tortuosa* and has only recently been recognised as an Irish and British plant (Bosanquet 2006a). It was not especially sought during recent fieldwork, but initial information suggests that it may be fairly widespread in montane parts of Ireland with several populations seen on Brandon Mountain, and in the Comeragh and Dartry Mountains. There are now records from at least 22 localities in 14 hectads and six vice-counties discovered since 2000. There is an additional record from 1965 (identified from herbarium material).

Tortella densa (Lorentz & Molendo) Crundw. & Nyholm

Clint Crisp-moss

syn. *Tortella inclinata* var. *densa* (Lorentz & Molendo) Limpr.
Status in Ireland: Near Threatened; **Status in Europe:** Least Concern

T. densa is an uncommon plant of limestone rocks, where it forms tufts and patches in rock crevices and on shallow soils. Recent fieldwork has found it to be particularly frequent in The Burren and around Lough Conn and Lough Corrib. It has now been reported from eight vice-counties, with records from 11 hectads (5 old, 8 recent). There is no evidence of decline, nor are its habitats particularly threatened at present.

Tortella inclinata (R.Hedw.) Limpr.

Bent Crisp-moss

syn. *Trichostomum inclinatum* (R.Hedw.) Dixon
Status in Ireland: Endangered (B2a, bii, iv); **Status in Europe:** Least Concern

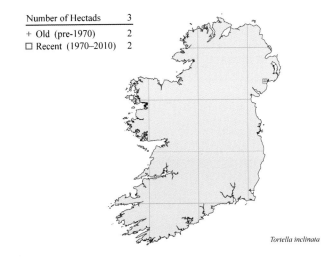

Number of Hectads	3
+ Old (pre-1970)	2
□ Recent (1970–2010)	2

Tortella inclinata

Identification

This is a yellowish-green, tuft- or cushion-forming acrocarpous moss about 1 cm high, with linear-lanceolate leaves c. 2 mm long, which are curled when dry, spreading when wet, tapering rather abruptly to a short, not very sharply pointed apex. Like other species of *Tortella*, it is characterised by the hyaline basal cells extending up the leaf margins, forming a sharp V-shaped transition to the smaller green cells above. It differs from *T. tortuosa* by the shorter leaves that are not crisped to the same extent when dry, and from both *T. tortuosa* and the even more similar *T. flavovirens* by the upper surface of the costa lacking quadrate cells.

Distribution in Ireland

There are only two recent records of this moss, which has always been a great rarity in Ireland, and these are on opposite sides of the island: W. Mayo (Keel Machair on

395

Achill Island, 1987) and Down (Murlough National Nature Reserve, 1952–2008). There is another accepted older record from Cloghmore on Achill Island (1962), but other Irish records are based on misidentifications of *Tortella flavovirens*, *T. tortuosa* and *Trichostomum brachydontium*.

Ecology and biology

One of the recent Irish records (Murlough) is from unshaded, apparently acidic sandy shingle in dune heath, growing with other mosses and lichens in very short vegetation grazed by rabbits and intermittently also by domestic stock. In Britain, *T. inclinata* is regarded as a strict calcicole that grows on thin soil over limestone and chalk, and in sand dunes. It is a lowland plant, growing just above sea level in Ireland and not above 500 m in Britain.

Capsules are very rare indeed in this dioicous species (unknown in Ireland), but it sometimes produces small propaguliferous shoots at the stem apex.

World distribution

This species is distributed throughout most of Europe, but is apparently rarer in Mediterranean regions, and listed as *Nationally Scarce* in Britain, *Near Threatened* in Finland and Luxembourg, 'declining' in Germany and 'very rare and susceptible' in the Netherlands. In Europe, it is assigned to a Circumpolar Temperate floristic element. It is also known from N. Africa, N. and W. Asia, N. America and (according to FNA 2007) S. America and Australia.

Threats

Many coastal dune sites are potentially threatened by development pressures for leisure purposes such as golf links, or hotel and holiday complexes. More general threats often include lowering of the water table, scrub encroachment and inappropriate grazing regimes.

Conservation

The habitat at Murlough was in good condition in 2008, with fenced compounds to ensure that grazing pressure can be maintained. *T. inclinata* was not refound on a recent visit to the site at Keel Machair. Management of these sites should take full account of the presence of this species, especially by maintaining areas of very short, patchy vegetation. Its populations should be monitored regularly. *T. inclinata* is protected in the Republic of Ireland by the Flora (Protection) Order, 1999 and is listed as a Northern Ireland Priority Species.

Protected sites with recent records: Keel Machair/ Menaun Cliffs SAC; Murlough ASSI; Murlough Nature Reserve; Murlough SAC; **Unprotected sites with recent records:** none.

Pleurochaete squarrosa (Brid.) Lindb.

Side-fruited Crisp-moss

Status in Ireland: Near Threatened; **Status in Europe:** Least Concern

P. squarrosa is a distinctive and attractive acrocarpous moss, resembling species of *Tortella*, which forms tufts or extensive turfs, usually on calcareous sand dunes. Recent fieldwork has shown that it occurs in two clusters in Ireland: one on the west coast in Clare, including Inishmore in the Aran Islands, the other on the east coast in Louth, Meath and Dublin. It has been reported from six vice-counties, with records from eight hectads (4 old, 7 recent). There is no evidence of decline, but its habitat is often threatened by development pressures and changes in grazing regimes.

Hymenostylium recurvirostrum (Hedw.)
Dixon **var.** *insigne* (Dixon) E.B.Bartram

Robust Tufa-moss

syn. *Gymnostomum insigne* (Dixon) A.J.E.Sm., *H. insigne* (Dixon) Podp., *Weisia curvirostris* var. *insignis* auct.,
Weissia curvirostris var. *insignis* (Dixon) H.Schmidt
Status in Ireland: Near Threatened; **Status in Europe:** Rare

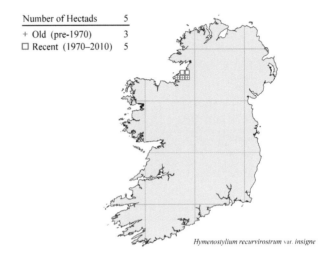

Number of Hectads	5
+ Old (pre-1970)	3
☐ Recent (1970–2010)	5

Hymenostylium recurvirostrum var. *insigne*

Identification

A rather robust acrocarpous moss that forms compact tufts, deep cushions or more extensive patches (sometimes 50 cm across) that are dark green to brownish, with stems 4–12 cm long. Leaves are 1.6–2.4 mm long, ovate-lanceolate, with an erect and almost sheathing leaf base from which the limb is patent to spreading when moist, tapering to an acuminate apex. The costa is evanescent to percurrent, the leaf margin entire and recurved below. Upper leaf cells are irregularly rhomboidal to subquadrate and smooth; basal cells are rectangular to narrowly rectangular with incrassate walls, the transverse walls being more or less oblique and thinner than the longitudinal walls which are often porose. Capsules are ellipsoid, erect and exserted.

Irish specimens appear distinct from the smaller var. *recurvirostrum* but intermediate plants occur in Scotland (G.P. Rothero pers. comm.), implying that treatment of *insigne* as a variety rather than at species rank is appropriate. P.M. Eckel (in FNA 2007) comments that 'Variety *insigne* is an example of gigantism common in the moss flora of hyperoceanic British Columbia', but that characters intermediate with those of var. *recurvirostrum* can be demonstrated in some specimens.

Distribution in Ireland

Restricted to the limestone of the Dartry Mountains, where it is locally frequent with about 17 localities in two vice-counties: Sligo (Benbulbin, including E. cliffs of E. corrie, W. cliffs of E. corrie and Cartronwilliamoge, 1928–2003; Gleniff, including Annacoona and E. corrie, 1928–2003; Benwiskin, 1979–2003; Cormac Reagh's Hole, 2003) and Leitrim (Glenade, 1937–1970; Peakadaw, 1969–2000; E. slope of Truskmore, 2000; Cloontyprughlish, 2000–2008; Eagles Rock, 2000; W. of Glencar Waterfall, 2000–2005; N. of Glencar Lough, 2000; NE slope of Crockauns, 2000; Larganavaddoge, 2000; Aghadunvane, 1970–2005). A report from Fermanagh (Sruh Croppa River at Marble Arch, 1950) was based on misidentified var. *recurvirostrum*.

Ecology and biology

This species grows on ledges and steep rock, often amongst other vegetation, on limestone and calcareous shale crags, extending onto tufa layers or thin soil on ledges, in places that are moist to wet because of flushing from above or spray from waterfalls, at 140–500 m elevation. Frequent associates include *Didymodon maximus*, *Orthothecium rufescens*, *Palustriella commutata* and *Saxifraga aizoides*. Its localities are on both N.- and

397

S.-facing rocks, fully insolated to partly shaded. In Scotland, it is also restricted to wet calcareous montane areas with high rainfall, occurring up to 680 m elevation, but with some lowland sites in ravines.

The plants are perennial. It is a dioicous taxon and capsules are very rare. Gemmae, bulbils and tubers are unknown. Vegetative propagation presumably occurs from detached plants or fragments; whole cushions are sometimes dislodged by torrents of water or falling rocks.

World distribution

In Europe, var. *insigne* is known only from NW Scotland (W. Perthshire to W. Sutherland; listed as *Near Threatened* in Britain), NW Ireland and NW and NE Spain (Asturias and Tarragona Provinces: J. Guerra in Guerra *et al.* 2006) (not evaluated). It is assigned to an Oceanic Boreal-montane floristic element in Europe. Although formerly regarded as endemic to Ireland and Britain (Smith 1978) or in W. Europe, it is now known elsewhere at widely disjunct localities in western N. America (British Columbia), S. America (Peru) and China (P.M. Eckel in FNA 2007).

Threats

The status of var. *insigne* seems secure in the Dartry Mountains, where there are large populations at several localities and no immediate threats are apparent. It also has numerous localities in NW Scotland, but apparently few in Spain.

Conservation

All the Irish localities are on protected land.

Protected sites with recent records: Arroo Mountain SAC; Ben Bulben, Gleniff and Glenade Complex SAC; Crockauns/Keelogyboy Bogs NHA; **Unprotected sites with recent records:** none.

Gymnostomum viridulum Brid.   Luisier's Tufa-moss

syn. *Mollia calcarea* var. *mutica sensu* Lett 1915
Status in Ireland: Least Concern; **Status in Europe:** Least Concern

A very small, bright green acrocarpous moss that grows on limestone rocks and mortar of old walls. It was included in the Provisional Red List (Holyoak 2006b), but has now been reported from 14 vice-counties, with records from 29 hectads (8 old, 23 recent), with little evidence of any decline. It is likely that *G. viridulum* is still somewhat under-recorded, partly because of its small size and partly because it was not usually distinguished from *G. calcareum* until the study by Whitehouse & Crundwell (1991, 1992).

Molendoa warburgii (Crundw. & M.O.Hill) R.H.Zander   Warburg's Moss

syn. *Anoectangium warburgii* Crundw. & M.O.Hill
Status in Ireland: Vulnerable (D2); **Status in Europe:** Rare

Identification

A very small and slender acrocarpous moss that grows as scattered stems, loose tufts or yellowish-green patches, with stems up to 10 mm high. Upper leaves are erecto-patent to patent, ovate to lanceolate, with a rounded apex. The leaf margins are plane and papillose-crenulate, the

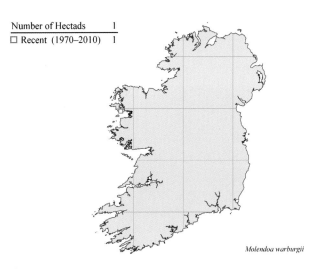

Molendoa warburgii

costa strong but ending well below the leaf apex. Cells in the upper part of the leaf are quadrate or subquadrate, about 8 μm wide and obscure with papillae; the extreme base of the leaf has shortly-rectangular cells; lamina cells extend over the ventral surface of the costa in the upper part of the leaf. Capsules (unknown in Ireland) are ovoid, gymnostomous, erect, exserted on a seta that arises laterally from the stem. This species was confused with *Gymnostomum calcareum* for many years, but that species forms denser bright green tufts, has less strongly papillose leaves, with markedly longer basal cells and it grows in drier places (Crundwell & Hill 1977).

Distribution in Ireland
M. warburgii is known only from two adjacent corries on the N. side of Corraun Hill in W. Mayo (S. of Knockacorraun Lough, 1982–2003; corrie to east of Lough Cullydoo, 1982) (Synnott 1983a).

Ecology and biology
The habitat in W. Mayo is on steep, soft, damp schist and thin soil overlying it on the almost unshaded bases of N.-facing crags, at 290–370 m altitude. In Britain, it is mainly a montane species, recorded at 0–1070 m altitude, growing on wet rocks that are usually base-rich, including mica schist, limestone, basalt and volcanic tuff, extending onto base-poor rock where there is basic flushing. Most sites are in natural habitats near streams and waterfalls or where rocks are kept moist by seepage but it is also known in a highland quarry.

The plants are perennial. It is a dioicous species in which capsules are very rare in Britain (not recorded in Ireland), maturing in spring and early summer; most Scottish plants are female but the Welsh population is

entirely male (T.L. Blockeel in Hill *et al.* 1992). Gemmae occur frequently in the axils of lower leaves and these presumably function as vegetative propagules; bulbils and tubers are absent.

World distribution
It is widespread in Scotland (from Arran north to Sutherland), local in W. Ireland and N. Wales (Snowdonia), S. Iceland, Faeroes and SW Norway (Söderström 1996) (*Endangered*). The species is assigned to an Oceanic Boreal-montane floristic element in Europe, where it is endemic.

Threats
No immediate threats were apparent at the Corraun Hill localities in 2003.

Conservation
Both of the localities are on protected land.

Protected sites with recent records: Corraun Plateau SAC; **Unprotected sites with recent records:** none.

Molendoa warburgii, south of Knockacorraun Lough, Co. Mayo.

Leptobarbula berica (De Not.) Schimp.

Beric Beard-moss

Status in Ireland: Vulnerable (D2); **Status in Europe:** Least Concern

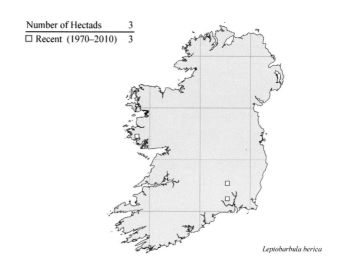

Number of Hectads	3
☐ Recent (1970–2010)	3

Leptobarbula berica

Identification

L. berica is a very small, bright green acrocarpous moss less than 2 mm tall, with narrowly lanceolate, obtuse leaves that are erecto-patent both wet and dry. It strongly resembles *Gyroweisia tenuis* and small plants of *Gymnostomum calcareum*. *Gyroweisia tenuis* differs in having usually abundant capsules without a peristome and less differentiated perichaetial bracts. *Gymnostomum calcareum* is often a larger plant with wider leaves and with shorter basal cells, and it also lacks a peristome (although capsules are rare). *L. berica* is most easily distinguished when fertile, as it has strongly differentiated perichaetial and perigonial bracts, which are much longer and more acute than the stem leaves, with an inflated sheathing base. The erect cylindrical capsules are borne on a long seta and have long, twisted peristome teeth.

Distribution in Ireland

This species is known from three localities in Ireland: Kilkenny (Poulanassy Waterfall, 2010; Kilkenny Castle, 2010) and W. Galway (Letterdife House, 1986). The latter was not refound when the BBS visited Letterdife House in 1994, in spite of having the expertise of the late Harold Whitehouse in the party.

Ecology and biology

The recorded habitats in Ireland are on a wall by a river, on damp mortar of a castle wall and on the moist wall of a house (Letterdife House). In Britain, *L. berica* grows in natural habitats on shaded limestone rocks and stones,

mainly in woodland, but more often it is found on shaded damp masonry on old buildings.

Although perichaetial and perigonial bracts are frequent, capsules are very rare in this dioicous species and unknown in Ireland. *L. berica* is capable of producing gemmae on the aerial filaments of chloronemata in culture on agar (Appleyard *et al.* 1985) and similar gemmae have since been observed in specimens collected in the wild from several European countries (Whitehouse & During 1987, Guerra *in* Guerra *et al.* 2006).

World distribution

This is a southern species in Europe, occurring widely in the Mediterranean basin and reaching north as far as Britain (where it is *Nationally Scarce*) and Ireland, Belgium, Luxembourg (where it is *Vulnerable*), the Netherlands (rare) and Germany (declining), and also found in Madeira and the Azores. In Europe, it is categorised as an Oceanic Mediterranean-Atlantic floristic element. Outside Europe, it is also known only as a Mediterranean plant, having been recorded in N. Africa, Turkey, Lebanon and Palestine.

Threats

Cleaning of stonework might be a possible threat.

Conservation

L. berica is protected in the Republic of Ireland by the Flora (Protection) Order, 1999. This species should be searched for again at Letterdife House, and should also be borne in mind when other old mortared walls, houses or churches are examined for bryophytes.

Protected sites with recent records: none; **Unprotected sites with recent records:** Kilkenny Castle; Letterdife House; Poulanassy Waterfall.

Ephemerum recurvifolium (Dicks.) Boulay

Strap-leaved Earth-moss

syn. *Ephemerella recurvifolia* (Dicks.) Schimp.
Status in Ireland: Data Deficient; **Status in Europe:** Rare

Number of Hectads   1
☐ Recent (1970–2010)   1

Ephemerum recurvifolium

Identification

A tiny acrocarpous moss with scattered gametophores up to 2.2 mm high arising from persistent greenish protonemata that form small inconspicuous mats. The abundantly branched protonema (chloronemata) has branches arising at wide angles, pointed apical cells and fragile ultimate branches; swollen, multicellular, thick-walled tubers with transverse cell walls commonly develop on its lower parts (Pressel *et al.* 2005). Female gametophores have a few leaves up to about 1.75 mm long, the largest being erecto-patent, commonly recurved, narrowly oblong (strap-shaped), with the costa narrow, well-defined and excurrent in a prominent mucro. The leaf margins are plane, usually with a few strong teeth and several small teeth near the apex of the lamina. Cells in the upper part of the leaf lamina are short and rather firm-walled for an *Ephemerum*, smooth, and arranged in rows parallel to the costa. Unlike the normal situation in the genus, *E. recurvifolium* has the calyptra cucullate rather than mitrate, and inflorescences with paraphyses. The capsule is immersed, nearly globose, with an oblique apical projection and a few stomata that are restricted to the base of the urn; the spores are smaller

than in some related species (40-55 μm), smooth-surfaced or very finely papillose, and liberated by breakdown of the capsule wall. Male gametophores are minute (<0.5 mm), with 2-4 leaves surrounding the antheridia.

Handbooks in the 19th century separated *E. recurvifolium* from the other *Ephemerum* in the monotypic genus *Ephemerella*. This was based on its cucullate calyptra and the presence of a few paraphyses in the inflorescences. Douin (1907) subsequently recorded rare and probably atypical instances of other *Ephemerum* species possessing a cucullate calyptra and paraphyses and modern lists have ceased to recognise *Ephemerella* as a separate genus. However, distinct features of *E. recurvifolium* in the protonemata (fragile ultimate branches of chloronemata) and tubers (storing starch rather than lipids) (Pressel *et al.* 2005) suggest its status should be re-evaluated, preferably using molecular data in addition to morphology.

Distribution in Ireland

A single recent record, made by S.D.S. Bosanquet in Co. Wicklow (Ballywaltrim Lane, SW Bray, on 25 September, 2010).

401

Ecology and biology

The recent find in Co. Wicklow was of two small patches, on a sparsely vegetated area of a gently sloping road verge on the eastern side of a lane at 60 m altitude. Several other basiphilous bryophytes were recorded close to it, including *Microbryum davallianum*. In England, it grows on calcareous clay and bare patches of moist soil over chalk and limestone, in the lowlands on woodland rides, in Beech woods, in arable fields and bare patches in grassland (e.g. on anthills).

The gametophores (and probably also protonemata) are annual, apparently maturing within a few months. The species is pseudo-dioicous (male and female gametophores arising from the same protonema) and capsules are common, maturing in autumn and winter. The tubers contain reserves of starch and regenerate rapidly (Pressel *et al.* 2005).

World distribution

Widespread in Europe from N. Wales (Anglesey), N. England (old record in Co. Durham) and S. Scandinavia (Åland; two localities in SE Sweden) southwards, and eastwards to Ukraine. In C. and S. England, it is widespread in calcareous districts (*Least Concern*). It is assigned to a European Southern-temperate floristic element in Europe. Also recorded in N. Africa, Turkey and Israel. Reports from north-western South America (Herrnstadt & Heyn 2004) and N. America appear to be errors.

Threats

No information.

Conservation

Targeted searches in autumn, winter or early spring are needed to establish the status of this inconspicuous species in eastern Ireland.

Protected sites with recent records: none; **Unprotected sites with recent records:** Ballywaltrim Lane, SW Bray.

Ephemerum crassinervium (Schwägr.) Hampe subsp. *sessile* (Bruch) Holyoak

Sessile Earth-moss

syn. *Ephemerum sessile* (Bruch) Müll.Hal.; [Basionym: *Phascum sessile* Bruch, Jahresber. Pollichia 2 (Verz.): 49. 1844]
Status in Ireland: Near Threatened; **Status in Europe:** Rare

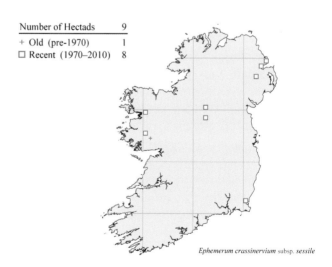

Number of Hectads	9
+ Old (pre-1970)	1
□ Recent (1970–2010)	8

Ephemerum crassinervium subsp. *sessile*

Identification

A tiny acrocarpous moss with scattered gametophores up to about 2 mm high arising from persistent protonemata that form green or yellow-green mats, which are usually rather thin and only a few centimetres across, occasionally up to 10 cm in diameter. The abundantly branched protonema (chloronemata) has branches arising at wide angles and pointed apical cells; swollen, multicellular, thick-walled, branched tubers with oblique cell walls commonly develop on its lower parts (Pressel *et al.* 2005). Female gametophores have a few leaves up to about 1.5 mm long, the largest being erecto-patent, straight, lanceolate or narrowly lanceolate with a narrow acumen ending in the excurrent costa. The leaf margins are plane and denticulate, less often entire. Leaf cells are rather lax and mostly rectangular to elongate-rectangular, much as in other *Ephemerum*, usually smooth, and arranged in rows parallel to the costa. The capsule is immersed, nearly globose, with a straight apical projection and a few stomata scattered over the whole surface; the large spores (60–80 μm) are liberated by breakdown of the capsule wall. Male gametophores are minute (< 0.5 mm), with 2–4 leaves surrounding the antheridia. The taxonomic treatment adopted here follows Holyoak (2010).

Distribution in Ireland

Recorded recently from eight localities in six vice-counties: Wexford (Coolree Reservoir, N. of Newbay, 2000); W. Galway (just S. of Ferry Bridge, 2003); Longford (Lough Gowna, shore W. of Dring, 2001); W. Mayo (SE edge of Beltra Lough, 2003); Cavan (Glasshouse Lough, 2005) and Antrim (Copeland Reservoir, 1999; S. Woodburn Reservoir, 1999; Bonner's Reservoir near Lisburn, 2002). There is also an older record from W. Galway (N. of Oughterard, 1965). The first report of *E. crassinervium* subsp. *sessile* from Ireland (W. Donegal; path to Mevagh Church, Rosguill Peninsula, leg. E.F. Warburg, 1962) has been redetermined as *E. serratum* agg. and a report from Leitrim (Lough Rinn, 2000) was based on misidentified *E. crassinervium* subsp. *rutheanum*. The preponderance of records from the last decade reflects an intensive effort to record *Ephemerum* spp. This work tends to confirm that *E. crassinervium* subsp. *sessile* is rare in Ireland, at least on lake and reservoir edges.

Ecology and biology

Most records are from sediments or soil in the upper part of the inundation zone of lakes (four) and reservoirs (four), although an older record was from a cart rut in a field. It occurs in the lowlands, on circumneutral to slightly acidic substrata, often in damp places, where there are bare patches among scattered or patchy low plants. Associated species sometimes include *E. serratum* and occasionally *E. cohaerens* (the only record of *E.*

crassinervium subsp. *rutheanum* as an associate is from S. Wales). In Britain, it is often recorded on reservoir edges, but also found at times on exposed soil in old pastures, on woodland rides, on heathland tracks and on sea cliffs.

The gametophores (and probably also protonemata) are annual, apparently maturing within a few months. The species is pseudo-dioicous (male and female gametophores arising from the same protonema) and capsules are common, maturing in autumn and winter. The tubers contain reserves of lipids and regenerate slowly (Pressel *et al.* 2005), presumably allowing the plants to persist through periods when the substrata are submerged.

World distribution

Widespread in Europe from N. Ireland, S. Scotland and S. Sweden southwards to SW Portugal, C. Spain, Corsica, Montenegro (where it is listed as *Vulnerable*) and Ukraine. It is considered *Extinct* in Finland, *Data Deficient* in Sweden and 'presumably threatened' in Germany. It is assigned to a European Southern-temperate floristic element in Europe. Elsewhere, the range extends to Morocco, Turkey and Israel (Herrnstadt & Hein 2004).

Threats

There is no real evidence of decline in Ireland despite failure to refind the locality from the 1960s. Elsewhere, the species is potentially at risk from alteration of the flooding regimes of lakes and reservoirs (e.g. for water supply, electricity generation, or recreational uses such as angling or water sports), alteration of their banks (e.g. by development or afforestation) and perhaps also from eutrophication.

Conservation

Most sites are on protected land.

Protected sites with recent records: Copeland Reservoir ASSI; Glasshouse Lake pNHA; Lough Carra/Mask Complex SAC; Lough Gowna pNHA; Newport River SAC; South Woodburn Reservoir ASSI; **Unprotected sites with recent records:** Bonner's Reservoir near Lisburn; Coolree Reservoir, N. of Newbay.

Ephemerum crassinervium (Schwägr.) Hampe **subsp. *rutheanum*** (Schimp. in Ruthe) Holyoak

Irish Earth-moss

syn. *Ephemerum hibernicum* Holyoak & V.S.Bryan; *E. rutheanum* Schimp. in Ruthe, replacement name for *E. longifolium* Schimp. in Ruthe
Status in Ireland: Near Threatened; **Status in Europe:** Not Evaluated

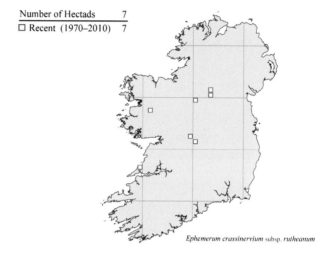

Number of Hectads	7
☐ Recent (1970–2010)	7

Ephemerum crassinervium subsp. *rutheanum*

Identification

A tiny acrocarpous moss with scattered gametophores up to 2.2 mm high arising from persistent protonemata that form dense mats, sometimes up to 50 cm in diameter, which are green above, brown basally. The abundantly branched protonema (chloronemata) has branches arising at wide angles and pointed apical cells; swollen, multicellular, thick-walled, branched tubers with transverse cell walls often develop on its lower parts (Pressel *et al.* 2005). Female gametophores have a few leaves up to 2.0 mm long, the largest being erect to erecto-patent, straight to secund, lanceolate with a narrow acumen but the lamina usually well defined almost to the leaf apex, with the costa varying from percurrent to shortly excurrent. Some leaves have a wider, narrowly oval basal part. The leaf margins are plane and vary from entire to irregularly serrate or spinose above the proximal third, some of the leaves often have one or two strong marginal spines. Leaf cells are rather lax and mostly rectangular to elongate-rectangular, much as in other *Ephemerum*, arranged in rows parallel to costa; the upper cells are often slightly papillose because of prorate cell ends. The capsule is immersed, nearly globose, with an apical projection and a few stomata scattered over the surface; the large spores (61–69 μm) are liberated by breakdown of the capsule wall. Male gametophores are minute (0.44–0.47 mm), with 2–4 leaves surrounding the antheridia.

Distribution in Ireland

Known from 10 localities in seven vice-counties: Clare (Tullaher Bog, 2004); Offaly (by R. Shannon W. of Shannon Harbour, 2005); Roscommon (by R. Shannon at Devenish Island, 2007); E. Mayo (E. bank of Cloon River W. of Partry, 2003); W. Mayo (W. bank of Cloon River W. of Partry, 2003); Leitrim (Rinn Lough, 2000–2005) and Cavan (by R. Erne at Carratraw Bridge, 2001; by R. Erne S. of Baker's Bridge, 2001; by Lough Oughter at, and W. of, Inishconnell, 2001–2005; Lough Oughter, near Gartnanoul Point, 2001). The taxon was discovered new to science during field surveys for NPWS and described as a new species: *Ephemerum hibernicum* (Holyoak & Bryan 2005), but subsequent taxonomic revision assigns it as a subspecies of *E. crassinervium* (Holyoak 2010). Intensive efforts to locate more *Ephemerum* populations have demonstrated that *E. crassinervium* subsp. *rutheanum* is a rather rare and localised subspecies in Ireland.

Ecology and biology

Almost all records are from sediments in the inundation zones of lowland rivers and lakes that are exposed by

404

water levels which fall in summer. It has been recorded on substrata of silty mud, sandy mud, clay and firm soil among limestone rocks, apparently of circumneutral to somewhat basic reaction, often in damp places with sparse vegetation, sometimes fully insolated, more often partly to rather heavily shaded (usually by *Salix cinerea*). An atypical record from Clare was on compacted wet soil on a track between areas of bog. A record from S. Wales was from sediment of a turlough.

Gametophores are short-lived, developing within a few months following subaerial exposure. It is unknown whether the protonemata develop or persist when submerged. The plants are pseudo-dioicous (male and female gametophores growing from the same protonema) and capsules are frequent, maturing in autumn. The tubers contain reserves of lipids and regenerate slowly (Pressel *et al.* 2005), presumably allowing the plants to persist through periods with high water levels.

World distribution
A European endemic, known outside Ireland only from two records from Wales (Monmouthshire and Carmarthenshire: Hill *et al.* 2008) and a few sites in Germany and the Netherlands, with old records from France and W. Poland (Holyoak 2010).

Threats
Potentially at risk from alteration of the flooding regimes of lakes and rivers, alteration of their banks (e.g. by development or afforestation) and perhaps also from eutrophication.

Conservation
All populations are on protected land. *E. crassinervium* subsp. *rutheanum* has strong populations at some Irish localities (covering tens of square metres) and small populations at others. However, only a few waterbodies provide virtually all of the localities (three rivers, the Erne, Shannon and Cloon River; plus two lakes that are both joined to rivers in which it occurs, Rinn Lough being joined to the Shannon, Lough Oughter to the Erne).

Protected sites with recent records: Lough Carra/Mask Complex SAC; Lough Oughter and Associated Loughs SAC; Lough Rinn pNHA; River Shannon Callows SAC; Tullaher Lough and Bog SAC; **Unprotected sites with recent records:** none.

Ephemerum cohaerens (Hedw.) Hampe
Clustered Earth-moss

Status in Ireland: Vulnerable (B2a, ciii, iv); **Status in Europe:** Critically Endangered

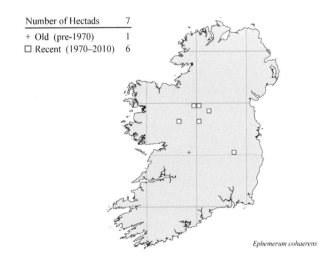

Number of Hectads	7
+ Old (pre-1970)	1
□ Recent (1970–2010)	6

Ephemerum cohaerens

Identification
E. cohaerens is a tiny acrocarpous moss with scattered gametophores less than 2.5 mm high growing from patches of persistent felt-like green protonema that may be a few centimetres to tens of centimetres across. The abundantly branched protonema (chloronemata) shows a fastigiate branching pattern (ultimate ramifications growing parallel to each other) and pointed apical cells;

swollen, multicellular, thick-walled, branched tubers with transverse cell walls often develop on its lower parts (Pressel *et al.* 2005). Female gametophores have a few leaves up to 2.2 mm long which are oblong or oblong-lanceolate and rather abruptly tapered to a recurved acumen, frequently giving an asymmetrically 'shouldered' outline to the largest leaves. The thin costa is percurrent or shortly excurrent, indistinct at the leaf base. The plane leaf margins are dentate, often with larger teeth at the 'shoulders'. Leaf cells are rather lax and oblong-hexagonal as in other *Ephemerum*, a distinctive feature of the present species being the somewhat diagonal rows of cells towards the middle of the leaf, diverging from the costa towards the 'shoulders'. Capsules are ovoid and apiculate, with stomata scattered over the whole capsule, immersed, the large spores (47–95 μm) eventually being liberated by breakdown of the capsule wall. Male gametophores are tiny with a few leaves surrounding the antheridia.

Distribution in Ireland

Accepted recent records are from seven localities in four vice-counties: NE Galway (E. of Glennamaddy, 2004); Kildare (Kingsbog or Common, 2005); Longford (S. shore of Lough Gowna, 2001; Fortwilliam Turlough, 2007; W. of Elfeet, 2007) and Leitrim (bank of R. Shannon N. of Jamestown, 2000; Rinn Lough, 2000–2005). There is an older record from SE Galway (Portumna, 1865). Two unconfirmed reports also exist from Clare (Lough Gash, 1992) and E. Mayo (Ballyglass turlough, 1992), which antedate naming of *E. crassinervium* subsp. *rutheanum* so they might have been based on that species or *E. cohaerens*. The preponderance of recent records reflects intensive efforts to locate *Ephemerum* populations over the past decade. This fieldwork demonstrates that *E. cohaerens* is a rare species in Ireland.

Ecology and biology

It is mainly a moss of drying sediments in the periodically inundated zones beside lowland lakes, turloughs and the River Shannon. It occurs on firm mud and soil, sometimes where sandy or calcareous, typically among sparse patchy vegetation (e.g. of *Carex nigra* and *Potentilla anserina*), fully insolated or partly shaded (e.g. by *Salix cinerea* and *Alnus glutinosa*). An atypical small patch at the edge of a grave in a cemetery, on almost bare damp loamy soil treated with herbicide, probably represented temporary colonisation, perhaps following dispersal on footwear. British records are from inundation zones of reservoirs. In N. America, it is known on wet soil, particularly along streams, also in pastures, meadows and marshes (Crum & Anderson 1981).

The gametophores are annual, maturing within a few months of the onset of subaerial exposure. It is unknown whether protonemata persist when sites are inundated. The species is apparently pseudo-dioicous (male and female gametophores arising from the same protonema) and capsules are sometimes frequent, with spores sometimes maturing in autumn (but maturing all year in N. America: V.S. Bryan in FNA 2007). The tubers contain reserves of lipids and regenerate slowly (Pressel *et al.* 2005), presumably allowing the plants to persist through periods with high water levels.

World distribution

Sparsely distributed in Europe from C. Ireland, S. and C. England, France (Hugonnot *et al.* 2007), Germany and Poland south to N. Spain (Prov. Alava: Infante & Heras 2005), Sardinia and the former N. Yugoslavia (Istria). It is listed as *Critically Endangered* in Switzerland, *Endangered* in Britain and *Vulnerable* in Germany, *Data Deficient* in the Czech Republic and Spain and 'very rare' in the Netherlands. It is assigned to a European Temperate floristic element in Europe. Elsewhere, it is known from the Azores (Crundwell *et al.* 1994), China, Japan and eastern N. America (Quebec to Florida and Texas) (V.S. Bryan in FNA 2007).

Threats

This species is at risk from alteration of seasonal flooding regimes of rivers and lakes. The modern maintenance of high water levels on part of the R. Shannon has probably caused the loss of a population recorded near Portumna in 1865. It is also potentially at risk from drainage of pools or changes to waterside banks (e.g. development, afforestation) and possibly from eutrophication of waterbodies.

Conservation

Several sites are within protected areas.

Protected sites with recent records: Fortwilliam Turlough SAC; Lough Gowna pNHA; Lough Lurgeen Bog/Glenamaddy Turlough SAC; Lough Rinn pNHA; **Unprotected sites with recent records:** Bank of R. Shannon N. of Jamestown; Kingsbog or Common; W. of Elfeet.

Ephemerum spinulosum Bruch & Schimp. ex Schimp.

Prickly Earth-moss

Status in Ireland: Endangered (B2a, ciii, iv); **Status in Europe:** Not Evaluated

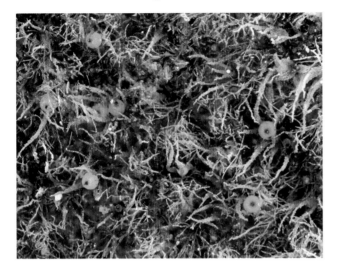

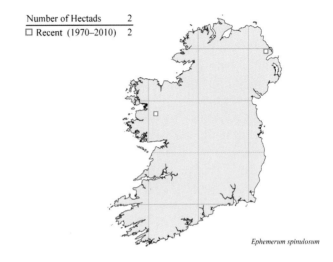

Number of Hectads	2
☐ Recent (1970–2010)	2

Ephemerum spinulosum

Identification

This is a tiny moss with sharply toothed leaves, known in Europe only from the inundation zones of a few reservoirs and lakes. Like several other species of *Ephemerum*, *E. spinulosum* has minute shoots that grow from a mat of protonemata which resembles a patch of a filamentous alga. In *E. spinulosum*, the protonemata are more conspicuous and extensive than the leafy shoots. The leafy shoots are tiny; female shoots up to 2.2 mm high, each with a few leaves up to 0.7 mm long; the male shoots only 0.5 mm high, with the largest leaf-like bracts 0.3 mm long. The larger leaves on female shoots are lanceolate, with a wide but weak costa, conspicuously-toothed margins and tall papillae on the costa and lamina, consisting of the projecting (prorate) ends of cells. There is almost no stem, the ovoid capsule growing immersed among the rosette of leaves.

Several other species of *Ephemerum* grow on sediments in the inundation zones of reservoirs and lakes, *E. serratum* being the most common. *E. spinulosum* differs from *E. serratum* in having a costa in the larger leaves, the presence of tubers and in the papillose leaf lamina. Some other scarce species of *Ephemerum* also have a costa in the leaf, but none of them has such conspicuously papillose leaf cells or such strong, even teeth on the leaf margins.

Distribution in Ireland

E. spinulosum is known in Ireland at only two sites. It was discovered new to Europe at North Woodburn Reservoir (Antrim) in 1999 (Holyoak 2001b), when a single patch

was located that covered several square metres. Surveys at neighbouring reservoirs in Antrim in the same year did not reveal its presence. In 2003, it was found in small quantity on the eastern bank of the Cloon River W. of Partry, close to Lough Mask (E. Mayo). *E. spinulosum* is a tiny and inconspicuous plant so easily overlooked, but extensive surveys of Irish and British reservoirs since 1999 have failed to reveal any other populations.

Ecology and biology

The habitat at North Woodburn Reservoir is on exposed damp silty mud in the inundation zone of a reservoir. It was located close to a small inlet stream, a few metres outside and slightly lower than the lowest cover of patchy herbaceous vegetation. This habitat is exposed to the air only in those years when reservoir water level is low. In E. Mayo, it was found in small amounts on unshaded partly bare mud at the base of sparse low *Carex* and *Agrostis stolonifera* in the inundation zone beside the Cloon River near to the point where it enters Lough Mask. Although regularly flooded, this habitat is exposed for most of each year.

Although all four European records are from inundation zones of lakes or reservoirs, in N. America, the species also occurs on moist or drying soil in various habitats and in Japan, it grows on moist soil in fields (Bryan in FNA 2007, Noguchi 1988).

The biology of this plant is poorly known, but it seems clear that its leafy shoots only grow after prolonged exposure to the air. It is unclear whether the protonemal mats grow and persist underwater or merely survive temporary flooding. However, it is known that the species is autoicous, with male shoots arising from the same protonemal mat as female shoots, and that capsules produced in late summer produce spores. Irregular tubers occur on the rhizoids and these presumably enable the species to persist when flooded and also serve for asexual reproduction (Pressel *et al.* 2005).

World distribution

In other parts of Europe *E. spinulosum* is known only by recent reports from single localities in N. Spain (reservoir in Prov. Alava: Infante & Heras 2005) (*Data Deficient*) and Germany (beside Sorpersee in Sauerland: Meinunger & Schröder 2007) (not evaluated). The species is much better known in N. America, where it is widespread in the eastern states, reaching western limits in Saskatchewan and Texas. Elsewhere, it is recorded from Cuba, Honduras, Brazil, China, Taiwan and Japan (V.S. Bryan in FNA 2007).

Threats

Potential threats to the species are most likely to arise from changes in water-level management: it would be catastrophic if water levels were kept permanently high, (e.g. to benefit water sports or angling interests). Threats could also arise from eutrophication, spread of alien plants such as *Crassula helmsii*, or disturbance on exposed reservoir banks.

Conservation

Conservation priorities should aim to maintain the number of viable populations of the species through appropriate habitat management. *E. spinulosum* is listed as a Northern Ireland Priority Species and a UK Biodiversity Action Plan (UKBAP) species. Very little was found at the E. Mayo locality, so Northern Ireland is therefore its Irish stronghold.

Protected sites with recent records: Lough Carra/Mask Complex SAC; North Woodburn Reservoir ASSI; **Unprotected sites with recent records:** none.

Paraleptodontium recurvifolium (Taylor) D.G.Long — Drooping-leaved Beard-moss

syn. *Bryoerythrophyllum recurvifolium* (Taylor) R.H.Zander, *Leptodontium recurvifolium* (Taylor) Lindb., *Trichostomum recurvifolium* (Taylor) R.H.Zander
Status in Ireland: Near Threatened; **Status in Europe:** Rare

Number of Hectads	16
+ Old (pre-1970)	9
□ Recent (1970–2010)	10

Paraleptodontium recurvifolium

Identification

This green or yellowish-green acrocarpous moss can grow in loose tufts, denser turfs or as individual shoots growing through or amongst other bryophytes. Shoots can be up to 10 cm tall but are usually much less (2–4 cm), and the leaves, which are rather broad, are strongly recurved or even squarrose, but strongly crisped when dry. Individual leaves are ovate to lanceolate, strongly toothed above, with a distinct pale border formed by smooth cells. The rest of the leaf cells are strongly papillose. *Dichodontium pellucidum* can be superficially similar, but lacks the pale border and differs in numerous microscopic characters.

Distribution in Ireland

P. recurvifolium is a plant of the far west, with all records coming from a band running along the west coast. Recent records are from 13 localities in four vice-counties: S. Kerry (Derrymore River in the Slieve Mish, 2006; Coomacullen Lake, 1983; Lough Coomasaharn, 1983; Ballaghbeama Gap, 1983; Cloghernoosh, 1972; Connor Pass, 1896–2009); N. Kerry (Lough Erhogh-Lough Managh, 1983; Mangerton Mountain, 1972); W. Cork (Glenbeg Lough and Lackawee, 1979) and W. Mayo (Corslieve, 1982; Mweelrea, 1950–2010; Ben Gorm, 2008; Caheraspic, 1987). There are additional older records from S. Kerry (Brandon Mountain, 1905–1967; Coomanare Lakes, 1898; Dunkerron, 1842); N. Kerry (Torc Cascade, 1911–1912); W. Galway (Benchoona, 1950–1957; Muckanaght, 1950–1957); W. Mayo (Sheeffry Hills, 1965) and W. Donegal (Slieve League, 1967).

Ecology and biology

This strongly oceanic species is characteristic of wet rock ledges and steep banks with a northerly aspect, usually where water is dripping, or in the spray zone of waterfalls. Sometimes it forms turfs in wet flushed grass underneath dripping cliff faces. It grows with a wide range of associates, usually at medium altitudes, between c. 100–700 m.

This moss is dioicous, and sporophytes are completely unknown. Neither is it known to produce vegetative propagules, so it must presumably reproduce and disperse by fragmentation.

World distribution

Confined in Europe to the west coasts of Britain (where it is *Nationally Scarce*) and Ireland. It is categorised as an Oceanic Boreal-montane floristic element. Like many of the Northern Atlantic hepatic mat liverworts, it has a widely disjunct world distribution, occurring elsewhere in Nepal, British Columbia and Alaska.

Threats

There appear to be few actual threats to this plant, although afforestation and water pollution could be potentially damaging, and burning and overstocking may also be a threat in some areas. It is significant that there are no recent records from W. Galway, where overstocking of the uplands has caused loss of vegetation and much erosion. Climate change may also prove to be a threat.

Conservation

All of the records of this species are within protected areas, with the possible exception of one from W. Cork.

Protected sites with recent records: Ballycroy National Park; Glanmore Bog SAC; Killarney National Park, Macgillycuddy's Reeks and Caragh River Catchment SAC; Mount Brandon SAC; Mweelrea/Sheeffry/Erriff Complex SAC; Owenduff/Nephin Complex SAC; Slieve Mish Mountains SAC; **Unprotected sites with recent records:** none.

Leptodontium flexifolium (Dicks.) Hampe

Bent-leaved Beard-moss

Status in Ireland: Near Threatened; **Status in Europe:** Least Concern

A somewhat weedy species of acid soils, especially below bracken or in bare patches in heathland, or on rock ledges, *L. flexifolium* is recorded occasionally in Ireland, with scattered records from 15 vice-counties and 21 hectads (10 old, 10 recent, 1 undated). It was not included in the Provisional Red List (Holyoak 2006b), so was not sought during recent fieldwork, but there is no real evidence of decline.

Didymodon acutus (Brid.) K.Saito

Pointed Beard-moss

syn. *Barbula acuta* (Brid.) Brid., *Didymodon rigidulus* Hedw. var. *gracilis* (Hook. & Grev.) R.H.Zander
Status in Ireland: Endangered (B2a, bii, iii, iv); **Status in Europe:** Least Concern

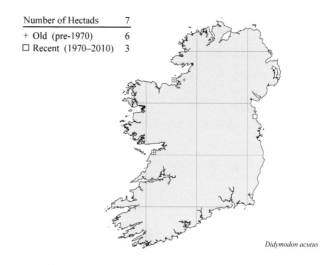

Number of Hectads	7
+ Old (pre-1970)	6
☐ Recent (1970–2010)	3

Didymodon acutus

Identification

Like many other species of *Didymodon*, this is a small (3–20 mm tall) green or brownish acrocarpous moss with lanceolate leaves tapering to an acute apex. Distinctive features of *D. acutus* are its narrowly linear-lanceolate leaves with a long, sharp apex formed by the excurrent costa, the isodiametric adaxial cells over the costa, and the smooth, clear, rounded leaf cells (usually papillose in other species of *Didymodon*). It may be mistaken in the field for *Ceratodon purpureus*, but the cell structure and ecology of that species are quite different. The sporophyte is not particularly helpful in identification, being ellipsoid with spirally curled peristome teeth. There may still be some work to do in elucidating the relationships between this plant, *D. rigidulus* and *D. icmadophilus* (see 'World distribution', below).

Distribution in Ireland

The distribution of *D. acutus* is scattered and concentrated on the coast, but with only three recent records: Clare (Fanore, Murroogh Dunes, 1959–2004); Sligo (Yellow Strand, north of Raghly, 1965–2008) and Louth (dunes near Baltray, 2007). There are additional older records from: Waterford (Bunmahon, 1966); Limerick (Adare, 1902); Sligo (Glencar Lough, 1928) and Louth (Castlecoo Hill, 1968). A number of other old records are errors based on misidentifications of *D. fallax*, *D. luridus* or *D. rigidulus*.

Ecology and biology

This is a calcicolous species of bare patches and thin turf, chiefly on dry limestone banks and in calcareous sand dunes. Most of the Irish records, and all three of the recent ones, are from sand dunes: one on the almost unshaded dry sand of a dune slope at the edge of a golf course, one on thin soil in a stabilised sand dune over limestone and the other on loose soil at the entrance to a rabbit burrow on a low hummock in a dune slack. There is also one record from a quarry and two others from among limestone rocks. Recorded associates in the dune habitat include other *Didymodon* spp., *Ditrichum gracile*, *Pleurochaete squarrosa*, *Trichostomum crispulum* and *Thymus polytrichus*. It is mainly lowland: recent records were at c. 5 m.

Capsules are rare in this dioicous species (unknown in Ireland). Specialised vegetative reproductive organs are not known to occur: reports of axillary gemmae may refer to small plants of *D. rigidulus*.

World distribution

D. acutus is more common in S. Europe and Macaronesia, although forms from N. and C. Europe have sometimes been named *D. validus* Limpr. (Hill *et al.* 1992). It is *Nationally Scarce* in Britain, *Extinct* in the Netherlands, *Vulnerable* in Austria, Germany and Luxembourg, *Near Threatened* in the Czech Republic and *Data Deficient* in Sweden. The European distribution of this plant is categorised as Circumpolar Southern-temperate. FNA (2007) gives its wider distribution as N. America (including Arctic areas and Mexico), C. America, S. America, Asia (Siberia), Africa and Iceland. Some authors treat it as *D. rigidulus* var. *gracilis* (Zander 1993, O'Shea 2006, R.H. Zander in FNA 2007).

Threats

Potential threats to this plant include expansion of a caravan site at Fanore, and perhaps other leisure developments, including golf courses. The colony at Yellow Strand could easily be destroyed by a change in the grazing regime or some other land-use change. At Baltray, it may be placed at risk by shading from tall grasses now that the dunes beside the golf course are ungrazed.

Conservation

The three current sites for this species should be monitored and protected from any developments or habitat changes that are likely to encroach upon the dune habitat.

Protected sites with recent records: Black Head-Poulsallagh Complex SAC; Cummeen Strand/Drumcliff Bay (Sligo Bay) SAC; **Unprotected sites with recent records:** near Baltray.

Didymodon icmadophilus (Schimp. ex Müll.Hal.) K.Saito

Slender Beard-moss

syn. *Barbula acuta* var. *icmadophila* (Schimp. ex Müll.Hal.) H.A.Crum,
Barbula icmadophila Schimp. ex Müll.Hal., *Didymodon acutus* var. *icmadophilus* (Schimp. ex Müll.Hal.) R.H.Zander,
D. rigidulus var. *icmadophilus* (Schimp. ex Müll.Hal.) R.H.Zander
Status in Ireland: Regionally Extinct; **Status in Europe:** Least Concern

Number of Hectads	1
+ Old (pre-1970)	1

Didymodon icmadophilus

Identification

A very slender acrocarpous moss that grows as brownish-green tufts or patches up to 2 cm high, rarely 6 cm. The leaves are appressed when dry, patent when moist, lanceolate and tapering to a long subulate apex. The costa is strong and excurrent, often long-excurrent, the leaf margin entire and narrowly recurved below. Capsules (unknown in Ireland or Britain) are narrowly ellipsoid, erect, exserted on a long seta. *D. icmadophilus* differs from most European *Didymodon* species in the tall, slender shoots and long-excurrent costa, but some forms of *D. acutus* share these characters. However, the mid-leaf cells are quadrate with somewhat angular lumens and often somewhat papillose in *D. icmadophilus*, more incrassate with rounded lumens and smooth in *D. acutus*.

It was treated as a variety of *D. acutus* by Kučera (2000), as a mere form of that species by Meinunger & Schröder (2007), as a variety of *D. rigidulus* by Zander (in FNA 2007), but regarded as a distinct species in other recent literature (including Hill *et al.* 2006, 2008). Molecular data are desirable to establish its affinities.

Distribution in Ireland

The only Irish specimen was collected at Ben Bulben (i.e. Benbulbin, Sligo) by D. McArdle in 1880 and remained overlooked amongst a gathering of *Schistidium apocarpum*

411

agg. until it was noticed in the **DBN** herbarium by D.M. Synnott (1983b). Recent fieldwork in Sligo and Leitrim has failed to detect the species.

Ecology and biology
Nothing is recorded of the habitat of the only Irish specimen, but its occurrence as an admixture with *Schistidium apocarpum* agg. on Benbulbin presumably implies that it grew on the surface of limestone rock. In Britain, the species grows in base-rich montane habitats at 60–600 m altitude, on crags and in gullies, usually on crumbling rock (often of basalt) or in short turf.

The plants are probably short-lived perennials, but details are unknown. The species is dioicous and capsules are unknown in Ireland or Britain, but recorded in Europe (rarely) and N. America, maturing in summer to autumn. Tubers and gemmae are unknown in Ireland or Britain (gemmae are very rare in N. America: Zander in FNA 2007).

World distribution
In Europe, from Iceland, N. Norway, N. Sweden and N. Finland southwards to Faeroes, Britain (rare: Cumbria, Skye, C. Scotland), Alps and Caucasus. It is listed as *Vulnerable* in Switzerland, *Near Threatened* in Britain and *Data Deficient* in Germany. It is assigned to a Circumpolar Boreo-arctic montane floristic element in Europe. Known elsewhere in SW Asia (Georgia to Kyrgyzstan: Ignatov *et al.* 2007), N. Asia (widespread in Siberia: Ignatov *et al.* 2007), Kashmir, N. America (widespread from Alaska and Nunavut southwards to California and Texas) and Greenland. According to Zander (in FNA 2007), it also occurs in Mexico, C. and S. America.

Threats
No information. The species might yet be rediscovered somewhere on Benbulbin, but the lack of precise locality details hinders the search.

Conservation
No action is proposed. Most of Benbulbin is on protected land.

Protected sites with recent records: none; **Unprotected sites with recent records:** none.

Didymodon nicholsonii Culm.

Nicholson's Beard-moss

syn. *Barbula nicholsonii* Culm.
Status in Ireland: Least Concern; **Status in Europe:** Least Concern

A rather nondescript acrocarpous moss that most often grows on damp old concrete or tarmac. It was included in the Provisional Red List (Holyoak 2006b) because it had few records in 1998. However, subsequent fieldwork has found more, so that it has now been recorded from 18 vice-counties and 50 hectads (4 old, 46 recent). There is no evidence of decline and the species is doubtless still under-recorded.

Didymodon umbrosus (Müll.Hal.) R.H.Zander

Shady Beard-moss

syn. *D. australasiae* var. *umbrosus* (Müll.Hal.) R.H.Zander, *D. trivialis* (Müll.Hal.) J.Guerra, *Trichostomopsis trivialis* (Müll.Hal.) H.Rob., *Trichostomopsis umbrosa* (Müll.Hal.) H.Rob.
Status in Ireland: Vulnerable (D2); **Status in Europe:** Rare

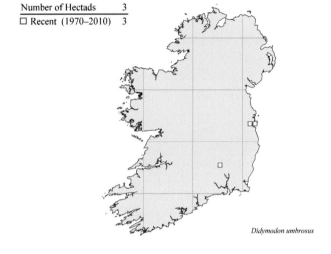

| Number of Hectads | 3 |
| Recent (1970–2010) | 3 |

Didymodon umbrosus

Identification

A small or very small acrocarpous moss that grows as small tufts or more extensive light green to blackish-green patches (turfs) 2–10 mm high, occasionally 15 mm. Leaves vary from lanceolate to linear lanceolate or oblong-lanceolate with acute or acuminate apices, evanescent to percurrent costa and margins that are plane throughout or somewhat incurved to give a hooded apex. The combination of several microscopic characters provides a distinction from other *Didymodon* species: margin bistratose at upper part of leaf, isodiametric mid-leaf cells smooth to papillose, leaf basal cells enlarged, elongate and hyaline, the basal marginal cells often narrower and forming a well-defined band, transverse section of costa with enlarged ventral cells, small rhizoidal tubers often present. Capsules (unknown in Europe) are shortly cylindrical, erect, exserted on a long seta.

Kučera (2000) treated this plant as *D. australasiae* var. *umbrosus*. Since then, a review by Jiménez *et al.* (2005a) kept *D. australasiae* and *D. umbrosus* as separate species and recent molecular data has confirmed they are distinct. The main differences between them are that *D. umbrosus* has stems with hyalodermis, leaves long-lanceolate and marginal basal cells clearly differentiated, whereas *D. australasiae* lacks a hyalodermis (or has only occasional patches of it), has shorter often oblong-lanceolate leaves and basal marginal cells not or weakly differentiated

(Jiménez 2006a, 2006b). However, somewhat intermediate plants were described from N. America by Eckel (1986); the populations in Cornwall also appear intermediate as does the Irish population from North Bull (J. Kučera & D.T. Holyoak, unpublished).

Distribution in Ireland

There are six records: Dublin (Howth, Glasnevin and Ballsbridge, all in 1988; Phoenix Park, 1988–1993; S. end of North Bull, 2004) and Kilkenny (River Nore below Lavistown House, 2010). Illustrations published by Synnott & Robinson (1990) clearly show the leaf characters of the plants found in 1988 are those of *D. umbrosus* rather than *D. australasiae*. However, the plants found in 2004 are much more similar to *D. australasiae* and may well be referable to that species (J. Kučera & D.T. Holyoak, unpublished). Both taxa seem likely to have arrived in Ireland recently.

Ecology and biology

The plants found at Howth, Glasnevin and Ballsbridge were on clay and gritty soil, bricks and mortar, in disturbed places in gardens and near buildings, under trees or in the open, mainly in places treated with the herbicide simazine (Synnott & Robinson 1989, 1990). Plants found in Phoenix Park were on bare loam (Kelly & Synnott, 1993); on North Bull they grew in a patch on unshaded, partly bare, sandy soil on a trackway in short grassland near the coast. In Kilkenny, the plants grew on the mortar of a ruined building. British records of *D. umbrosus* are mostly from bases of calcareous walls, but some are from shaded soil (e.g. in chalk quarries). In S. Europe, *D. australasiae* grows in varied open sites as a colonist on basic soil.

Some patches of *D. umbrosus* apparently persist for several years, whereas others are probably short-lived. Only female plants of *D. umbrosus* are known in Europe, so capsules are unknown; its sporophytes are known in N. America. Both sexes of *D. australasiae* and capsules are known in S. Europe and the Canary Islands. Rhizoidal tubers occur in both species (R.H. Zander in FNA 2007).

World distribution

D. umbrosus is likely to be a relatively recent arrival in Europe (cf. H.L.K. Whitehouse in Hill *et al.* 1992, Kučera 2000), where it is known in Ireland, England, Spain, Portugal (Lisbon), Germany and the Czech Republic. It is assigned to an Oceanic Southern-temperate floristic element in Europe. Its range elsewhere includes the USA (California, New Mexico, Texas, New York State), Mexico and S. America (R.H.

Zander in FNA 2007). *D. australasiae s.str.* has a wider range that includes S. Europe, SW and C. Asia, Canary Islands, N. and S. Africa, N. America (in W. and SW of USA), C. and S. America, New Zealand and Australia. It is quite likely that it is native only in parts of this range, but very uncertain which parts.

Threats

No detailed information is available. The open, artificial, habitats of *D. umbrosus* described by Synnott & Robinson (1990) were apparently maintained in part by regular herbicide applications.

Conservation

No action is proposed. Both *D. umbrosus* and *D. australasiae s.str.* appear to be weedy colonists of disturbed habitats that are spreading widely around the world (dubbed 'mundivagant taxa' by Eckel 1986) and hence they are in no need of conservation efforts.

Protected sites with recent records: North Dublin Bay SAC; River Barrow and River Nore SAC; **Unprotected sites with recent records:** Ballsbridge; Glasnevin; Howth (possibly within Howth Head SAC); Phoenix Park.

Didymodon tomaculosus (Blockeel) M.F.V.Corley

Sausage Beard-moss

syn. *Barbula tomaculosa* Blockeel
Status in Ireland: Vulnerable (D2); **Status in Europe:** Insufficiently Known

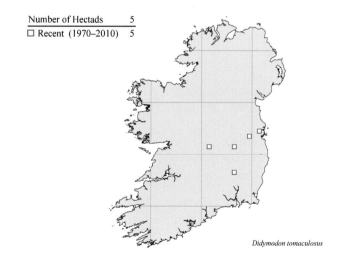

| Number of Hectads | 5 |
| Recent (1970–2010) | 5 |

Didymodon tomaculosus

Identification

Described new to science relatively recently (Blockeel 1981), this small and inconspicuous dark green to

brownish acrocarpous moss forms small patches or grows as scattered shoots up to c. 6 mm tall. It is similar to many other species of *Didymodon*, having widely spreading, occasionally even squarrose, narrowly triangular leaves that taper to a long, pointed apex, and small, mamillose, isodiametric leaf cells. *D. tomaculosus* has an entire leaf margin, elongate cells on the adaxial surface of the costa, and produces brownish sausage-shaped rhizoidal tubers consisting of a single row of cells.

Distribution in Ireland

This species has been found at five localities in four vice-counties in the east midlands: Carlow (Bagenalstown, 2004); Offaly (Derrybrat, 1987); Kildare (Rathangan, 1987) and Dublin (near Hazelhatch station, 2002; Tonlegee, 2003).

Ecology and biology

This moss is one of a group of species that grow principally in lowland arable fields, although there are also English records from bare soil in a pasture and a reservoir margin. *D. tomaculosus* favours heavy clay soils, especially amongst overwintered wheat stubble with species such as *Pohlia melanodon* and *Pseudephemerum nitidum* (Porley 2008). In Ireland, it has been recorded from wheat stubble, with *Bryum klinggraeffii*, *B. rubens*, *Dicranella schreberiana* and *D. staphylina*, and barley stubble, below 100 m altitude. At least some Irish material is rather depauperate and apparently comes from more friable soil than British material (Hill *et al.* 1992).

Only female and non-fertile plants are known in this dioicous species, and sporophytes have never been seen. The distinctive rhizoidal tubers are usually produced in abundance.

World distribution

Until recently considered endemic to Ireland and Britain, this species has now also been found in Germany, and may been overlooked elsewhere in continental Europe. Its centre of distribution in Britain (where it is *Nationally Scarce*) appears to be in the South Yorkshire/ Nottinghamshire area, extending south-westwards to Cornwall and Pembrokeshire. It is assigned to a Suboceanic Temperate floristic element in Europe.

Threats

Cessation of tillage in its field at Derrybrat by 2005 led to loss of the species there. Elsewhere, a change to autumn ploughing could prevent this moss completing its life cycle, as it requires overwintered stubble. However, it is likely to survive as tubers in the soil for at least several years.

Conservation

Arable field management in the areas where this plant has been recorded should include at least some provision of overwintered stubble. This need not always be in exactly the same fields, as it is likely that the tubers may be transported from place to place (e.g. on tractor wheels). Further survey work targeting this very inconspicuous moss would doubtless reveal many additional sites, as in Britain, but it does seem to be rather local.

Protected sites with recent records: none; **Unprotected sites with recent records:** Bagenalstown; Derrybrat; near Rathangan; near Hazelhatch station; Tonlegee.

Didymodon maximus (Syed & Crundw.) M.O.Hill

Irish Beard-moss

syn. *Barbula maxima* Syed & Crundw.
Status in Ireland: Near Threatened; **Status in Europe:** Rare

Identification

D. maximus is unusually large for a *Didymodon*, with shoots reaching up to 9 cm tall. It forms tufts or more extensive patches, yellowish-green tinged rusty-brown in colour. Otherwise typical of the genus, its leaves are 2–4 mm long, lanceolate, broad at the base, tapering to a sharply pointed apex, and strongly recurved or even squarrose when moist, strongly flexuose when dry.

It is much like a giant form of *D. ferrugineus*, but the leaves are narrower and more longly tapering, and the leaf cells thicker-walled and the cell lumina often angular rather than rounded (Syed & Crundwell 1973). Despite an earlier suggestion that *D. maximus* might be synonymous with the continental *D. giganteus* (Funck) Jur., it is now regarded as a distinct species (J. Kučera pers. comm.).

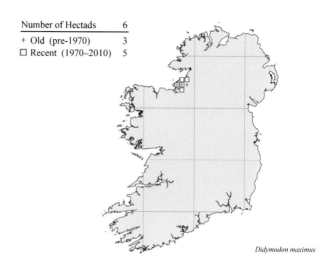

Number of Hectads	6
+ Old (pre-1970)	3
☐ Recent (1970–2010)	5

Didymodon maximus

Distribution in Ireland

One of a small number of species restricted to the Dartry Mountains, *D. maximus* has been recorded recently from at least 14 localities in two vice-counties: Sligo (Benbulbin, 1858–2003; Gleniff, 1928–2003; Benwiskin, 2003; Copes Mountain, 2003; Cormac Reagh's Hole, 2003; Keelogyboy Mountain, 2003; Kings Mountain, 2003) and Leitrim (Aghadunvane, 1970–2005; Cloontyprughlish, 2000–2005; Eagles Rock, Glenade, 2000; Larganavaddoge, 2000; N. of Glencar Lough, 2001; S. of Crumpaun, 2001; Truskmore, 2000). There are also several additional older and poorly localised records from Leitrim (Glenade, 1937–1963).

Ecology and biology

This moss is confined to rock crevices and ledges on limestone cliffs, often where flushed or seasonally irrigated, or in turf beneath the cliffs. Associated species prominently include sedges and grasses, together with *Saxifraga aizoides*, *Epilobium brunnescens*, *Thymus polytrichus*, *Pedinophyllum interruptum*, *Breutelia chrysocoma*, *Ctenidium molluscum*, *Hymenostylium recurvirostrum* var. *insigne*, *Mnium marginatum*, *Plagiochila porelloides*, *Cratoneuron filicinum*, *Fissidens adianthoides*, *Orthothecium rufescens*, *Palustriella commutata*, *Timmia norvegica* and *Trichostomum* spp.

This moss is probably dioicous but fertile material has never been found, and neither is it known to produce any vegetative propagules. A report of capsules by Jiménez *et al.* (2005b) in an Irish specimen (Long 14626) is based on misidentification of *D. spadiceus*.

World distribution

This species is only known in Europe from Ireland. Elsewhere, it has been found in Alaska, arctic Canada (Nunavut) (R.H. Zander in FNA 2007), Wrangel Island in the Russian Far East (Belikovich *et al.* 2006, Ignatov *et al.* 2007) and Mongolia (Müller 2009). In Europe, it is classified as a Hyperoceanic Temperate floristic element, but its climatic affinities are evidently radically different elsewhere in the world.

Threats

It occurs as scattered patches or tufts, but few immediate threats were apparent at sites visited over the past decade. Overstocking with sheep, causing erosion, is a potential threat that may now be reduced as stocking levels are tending to decline. Some individual patches are likely to be at risk from rockfalls and other natural events, but these doubtless also create new habitat for the species. Collecting by botanists may also be a threat, as Ireland is its only location in Europe.

Conservation

All localities are on protected land, but suitable low-intensity management and light grazing levels are appropriate. Ireland has an international responsibility for the conservation of this globally rare species.

Protected sites with recent records: Arroo Mountain SAC; Ben Bulben, Gleniff and Glenade Complex SAC; Crockauns/Keelogyboy Bogs NHA; **Unprotected sites with recent records:** none.

Pterygoneurum ovatum (Hedw.) Dixon

Oval-leaved Pottia

syn. *Tortula pusilla* Mitt.

Status in Ireland: Regionally Extinct; **Status in Europe:** Least Concern

Number of Hectads	2
+ Old (pre-1970)	2

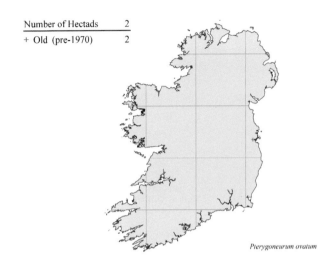

Pterygoneurum ovatum

Identification

This is a small acrocarpous moss up to 2 mm high, the shoots often clustered together in small patches or turfs. Most characteristically, all species of *Pterygoneurum* have 2–4 conspicuous green lamellae on the adaxial (upper) surface of the costa. The leaves have a relatively long, often hyaline hair-point up to 0.6 mm long: in the closely related *P. lamellatum* it is often shorter, up to 0.4 mm. *P. ovatum* is further distinguished from *P. lamellatum* (*q.v.*) by having a shorter seta (2–3 mm), ovoid or ovate-ellipsoid capsules and (diagnostically) the cells of the capsule lid arranged in straight rows.

Distribution in Ireland

P. ovatum is known in Ireland only from old records, with a cluster in and around Dublin city (1815–1915) and another cluster in and around Cork city (1836, 1845). It must now be presumed to have become extinct in Ireland.

Ecology and biology

The only records of its habitat in Ireland are of 'in waste grounds etc.' and 'on the tops of mud walls, very common'. In Britain, *P. ovatum* is a plant of open calcareous soils in the lowlands, as in bare patches in calcareous grassland, chalk and limestone quarries, and on the tops of mud-capped limestone walls, the latter a habitat that has now disappeared. More rarely, it has been recorded from stubble fields and pond sides. Although a strict calcicole, it seems to be somewhat less exacting in its habitat requirements than *P. lamellatum*.

Capsules are common in this autoicous species and produced in the winter months. It is not known to produce specialised vegetative propagules.

World distribution

This species is more common than *P. lamellatum*, and is generally distributed throughout most of Europe, north to S. Fennoscandia. It is common in the Mediterranean region but *Nationally Scarce* in Britain, *Critically Endangered* in the Netherlands, *Vulnerable* in Switzerland, Austria and Serbia, *Near Threatened* in Luxembourg and 'declining' in Norway. In Europe, it is assigned to a Circumpolar Southern-temperate floristic element. It is also present in N. Africa, western-central and N. Asia, N. America, southern S. America and Australia (Hill *et al.* 1992).

Threats

The disappearance of mud-capped walls as a habitat certainly contributed to the extinction of this species in Ireland.

Conservation

It is possible that some of the records of *P. ovatum*, where the habitat is not recorded, came from limestone quarries, particularly in the Cork area, and these should be

417

explored periodically, as it could conceivably return. No other measures are necessary at present.

Protected sites with recent records: none; **Unprotected sites with recent records:** none.

Pterygoneurum lamellatum (Lindb.) Jur.

Spiral Chalk-moss

syn. *Tortula lamellata* Lindb.

Status in Ireland: Regionally Extinct; **Status in Europe:** Vulnerable

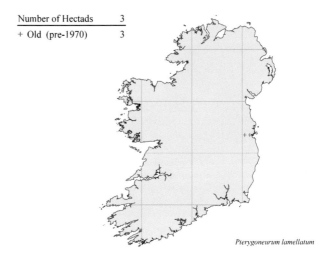

Number of Hectads	3
+ Old (pre-1970)	3

Pterygoneurum lamellatum

Identification

This is a small acrocarpous moss up to 2 mm high, the shoots often clustered together in small patches or turfs. All species of *Pterygoneurum* have 2–4 conspicuous green lamellae on the adaxial (upper) surface of the costa. The leaves have a relatively short, often hyaline hair-point up to 0.4 mm long: it is often longer, up to 0.6 mm, in the closely related *P. ovatum*. *P. lamellatum* is further distinguished from *P. ovatum* (*q.v.*) by having a longer seta (3–6 mm), ellipsoid capsules and (diagnostically) the cells of the capsule lid arranged in spiral rows.

Distribution in Ireland

P. lamellatum is known in Ireland only from old records, with a cluster in and around Dublin city (1830–1875) and one further record from near Donaghadee, Down (1870). It must now be presumed to have become extinct in Ireland.

Ecology and biology

P. lamellatum was most characteristically a plant of mud-capped stone walls, a habitat that has now disappeared. This is its only recorded habitat in Ireland. It can also grow in other bare, calcareous habitats, such as chalk and limestone quarries and calcareous roadside soil, always in the lowlands.

This is an autoicous species and capsules are common in autumn and winter. It is not known to produce specialised vegetative propagules.

World distribution

This species is widespread in W., C. and E. Europe, but has declined in many places. It is listed as *Extinct* in Britain and the Netherlands, *Critically Endangered* in Switzerland, Austria and Serbia and *Endangered* in the Czech Republic. In Europe, it is assigned to a Circumpolar Southern-temperate floristic element. Elsewhere, it is recorded from C. Asia and N. America (in the Arctic and in California, Nevada, Utah and Arizona in the southern USA).

Threats

The disappearance of mud-capped walls as a habitat almost certainly led to the extinction of this species in Ireland, as it did in Britain.

Conservation

No conservation measures are applicable.

Protected sites with recent records: none; **Unprotected sites with recent records:** none.

Aloina rigida (Hedw.) Limpr.

Rigid Aloe-moss

syn. *Tortula rigida* (Hedw.) Schrad. ex Turner
Status in Ireland: Regionally Extinct; **Status in Europe:** Least Concern

Number of Hectads	10
+ Old (pre-1970)	10

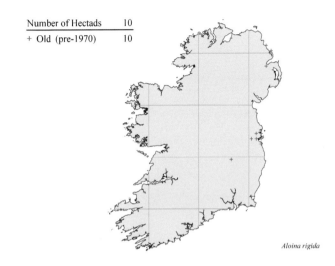

Aloina rigida

Identification

This is a small acrocarpous moss with thick, rigid, leathery dark green leaves, with strongly incurved margins. The leaves form a small rosette on a very short stem. The characteristic texture of the leaves is due to a thick growth of chlorophyllose filaments on the adaxial surface of the broad costa. The more or less cylindrical capsule is borne on a long seta, and has long, spirally coiled, filiform peristome teeth. *A. rigida* differs from the much more common *A. aloides* and the equally rare *A. ambigua* in the leaves having the border at the basal margins of the leaf formed of elongate, thin-walled hyaline cells, forming a border, and the annulus being composed of fugacious cells, which easily separate from the top of the capsule. The rather similar *A. brevirostris* (which has not been recorded in Ireland) has shorter leaves and larger spores (> 17 μm).

Distribution in Ireland

Records of *A. rigida* are concentrated in two clusters, one in the Dublin area and the other on the Antrim coast. The most recent record is from a sandpit at Geraldine House, near Athy in Kildare (1969). Other older records are from: Dublin (Balgriffin, 1833; Cardiff's Bridge, 1855; Chapelizod, 1878; Coolock, 1855; Dublin, 1832; Finglas, 1855; Scalp, undated); Down (Cregagh Glen, 1877) and Antrim (Glenarm, 1928, 1929; near Larne, 1928; Glenariff, 1888). It has not been seen recently and is presumed to have disappeared from Ireland.

Ecology and biology

This is a strict calcicole, occurring on mainly bare, base-rich soils, especially on chalk and limestone, for example in old quarries, and sometimes on other substrates: it used to occur on mud-capped walls, but this habitat has disappeared. Habitat information on the Irish sites is limited, but it has been recorded from a sandpit, in damp debris among slate rocks, on a mud-capped sea wall, and on earth-capped walls, always in the lowlands.

Sporophytes are common, although the plants are dioicous, and usually produced in the winter months. Gemmae and other forms of vegetative reproduction are unknown.

World distribution

This species is widespread in Europe, including Macaronesia, but does not reach the Arctic. It is *Nationally Scarce* in Britain (Preston 2006), *Near Threatened* in Luxembourg and Switzerland, *Vulnerable* in Austria, *Data Deficient* in Bulgaria, 'very rare' in Estonia and 'susceptible' in the Netherlands. It is assigned to a European Boreal-montane floristic element in Europe. Elsewhere, *A. rigida* is widespread in Asia, N. Africa, extending south to Chad, the Cape Verde Islands, Djibouti and Kenya (O'Shea 2006), and N. America, extending south to C. and S. America (Bolivia and Peru—Hill *et al.* 1992). It is also recorded from Australia, where it may be introduced (Smith 2004).

Threats

The disappearance of mud-capped walls presumably had an impact on this species in Ireland, just as it did in Britain, and its disappearance from the Dublin area is perhaps a consequence. It is less clear why it has disappeared from other habitats, and why it has apparently never been recorded in Ireland from limestone quarries, a favourite habitat in Britain.

Conservation

Field bryologists working in Ireland should be aware of the possibility of finding this species as a new colonist in limestone quarries. No conservation action is required at present.

Protected sites with recent records: none; **Unprotected sites with recent records:** none.

Aloina ambigua (Schultz) Mont.   Tall Aloe-moss

syn. *Aloina aloides* var. *ambigua* (Bruch & Schimp.) E.J.Craig, *Tortula ambigua* (Bruch & Schimp.) Ångstr.
Status in Ireland: Endangered (B1a, bi, ii, iv, B2a, bi, ii, iv, D); **Status in Europe:** Least Concern

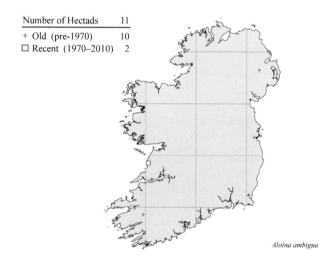

Number of Hectads	11
+ Old (pre-1970)	10
☐ Recent (1970–2010)	2

Aloina ambigua

Identification

Aloina is an easily recognisable genus of small acrocarpous mosses with thick, fleshy leaves, resulting from a dense mass of branched chlorophyllose filaments on the upper surface. The overall impression recalls that of *Polytrichum*, which differs structurally in having raised lamellae. The capsules are long and more or less cylindrical, with long, spirally coiled peristome teeth. *A. ambigua* is similar to the much more common *A. aloides*, with quadrate or rectangular hyaline cells along the margin of the leaf base and a persistent annulus at the mouth of the capsule. It differs in having the basal membrane of the peristome teeth clearly projecting above the mouth of the capsule and in the smaller spores (12–16 μm versus 18–25 μm). However, intermediate plants occur in SW Britain. Another rare species, *A. rigida* (*q.v.*), differs in the elongate and hyaline thin-walled marginal cells at the leaf base.

Distribution in Ireland

A. ambigua has been seen recently at two localities: E. Cork (Youghal Strand, 1956, 2006) and Clare (O'Brien's Bridge, Lehinch, 2007). Of the older records, the following are regarded as reliable: N. Kerry (Cromaglan, 1873); Waterford (Clonea, 1956; Dungarvan Harbour, 1956); Clare (Black Head, 1961); Dublin ('Dublin', 1848–1874; Glasnevin, 1851–1860; S. Dublin, near College botanic garden, 1848); Louth (Carlingford quarry, 1883); Down (Greyabbey, 1914) and Antrim (Derriaghy, Lisburn, 1874, 1924; Carrickfergus, 1877). Several other records, particularly from the north, are unsubstantiated and regarded as unreliable because this species and *A. aloina* were often confused in the past.

Ecology and biology

This lowland species colonises bare base-rich soil, particularly on chalk and limestone but also base-rich

420

sandstone, typically on the floor of quarries and on spoil heaps, but also on banks, in sand dunes and formerly on mud-capped walls. The two recent Irish records have been from sand on a bridge wall (O'Brien's Bridge) and on bare earth banks on top of an old stabilised coastal sand dune, where *A. ambigua* grows with *Bryum dichotomum* (Youghal Strand).

Although dioicous, capsules are produced in abundance, with spores maturing in winter or spring. Specialised vegetative reproductive organs are not known to occur.

World distribution

This moss is distributed widely in Europe north to Fennoscandia and also occurs in Macaronesia. It is *Nationally Scarce* in Britain (where it has a distinctly southern distribution), *Endangered* in Austria, Sweden and the Czech Republic, *Near Threatened* in Luxembourg and Bulgaria, 'sparse' in the Netherlands, 'declining' in Germany, and with only a pre-1950 record from Albania. It is assigned to a European Southern-temperate floristic element in Europe. Elsewhere, *A. ambigua* is recorded from N. Africa, W. and C. Asia (India, Iran, Israel, Jordan, Lebanon, Turkey), southwest USA (Arizona, California), Mexico and Australia (where it may be an introduced species).

Threats

Continuing stabilisation of the dunes and the spread of coarse grasses, encouraged by fertilisation with dog faeces, threaten this plant at Youghal. The situation at the Clare site is not known, but the population is presumably small.

Conservation

Although this species is extremely rare in Ireland, and may have declined, it is a potentially mobile colonist (small spores) and could appear in suitable bare calcareous habitat such as in limestone quarries, where it should be looked for.

Protected sites with recent records: Ballyvergan Marsh pNHA; **Unprotected sites with recent records:** O'Brien's Bridge, Lehinch (possibly within Inagh River Estuary SAC).

Tortula cuneifolia (Dicks.) Turner

Wedge-leaved Screw-moss

Status in Ireland: Critically Endangered (B1a, bi, ii, iv, B2a, bi, ii, iv); **Status in Europe:** Least Concern

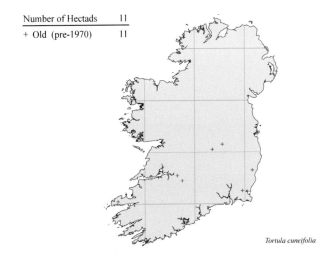

Number of Hectads	11
+ Old (pre-1970)	11

Tortula cuneifolia

Identification

A small acrocarpous moss less than 5 mm high with leaves up to 5 mm long, *T. cuneifolia* has concave, broadly spathulate leaves that are abruptly contracted to an acute apex, where the costa may be percurrent or excurrent, sometimes in a long yellowish or hyaline hair-point. The leaf margins are unbordered, plane and entire, and the leaf cells are c. 16–24 μm wide and smooth, distinguishing it from some other rare *Tortula*, which have smaller, papillose cells. The cylindrical capsules have a longly rostrate lid and long, twisted peristome teeth, and are exserted on a reddish seta up to 3.5 cm long.

Distribution in Ireland

All the Irish records of this species are old, and most of them poorly localised: S. Kerry (Dingle, 1896); W. Cork (Whiddy Island, 1966); E. Cork (Great Island, 1851; 'Cork', 1830–1841), Limerick (Pallas Green, 1966; Plassey, 1832); Wexford (Inch, 1954; Sion House, 1790); Laois (Ballyfin, 1879; Portarlington, 1862); Dublin (Howth, 1839–1860) and Down (Ards Peninsula, 1929). In Britain, this species has decreased markedly and is no longer known from inland habitats and has vanished from many coastal sites (Smith 2004).

Ecology and biology

There is little information about this plant in Ireland, but it has been found on banks by the sea, 'on a wall', 'by a road' and 'on a clay mound'. In Britain, it is a southern and lowland species of thin, bare sandy or loamy soils and rock crevices by paths, in old quarries, on coastal cliff tops, etc.

T. cuneifolia is autoicous and produces capsules frequently in the spring. No vegetative propagules are reported.

World distribution

This species is widespread in S. Europe, including Spain, Portugal, France, Italy (including Sardinia), Greece, Croatia and Albania, and extending north as far as Ireland, Britain and Germany and west into Macaronesia. It is listed as *Critically Endangered* in Germany, *Endangered* in Britain, and *Vulnerable* in Bulgaria. The report from Hungary is now regarded as erroneous (Erzberger & Papp 2004). It is categorised as an Oceanic Mediterranean-Atlantic floristic element in Europe. Elsewhere, it is well known in N. Africa, the Cape Verde Islands and SW Asia, but recently reported also from C. Asia (Tian-Shan Mountains), subarctic E. Siberia (Fedosov 2009) and arctic Canada (Cornwallis Island in Nunavut, as *Tortula cuneifolia* var. *blissii* R.H.Zander: Zander in FNA 2007).

Threats

The reasons for the apparent decline of this species in Ireland are not known. Suitable habitat would appear to be still widely available. Pollution may have played a part, or nutrient enrichment, leading to an increase in coarse vegetation. A similar decline in Britain also remains largely unexplained.

Conservation

Repeated searching for this species has failed to refind any of the old populations or to discover new ones, and it may be that *T. cuneifolia* is now extinct in Ireland. However, Whiddy Island needs revisiting, and it cannot safely be considered extinct before this is done. Experience in Britain shows that the plants are very hard to find except when the tall seta becomes evident in April and May. *T. cuneifolia* is listed as a UK Biodiversity Action Plan (UKBAP) species.

Protected sites with recent records: none; **Unprotected sites with recent records:** none.

Tortula marginata (Bruch & Schimp.) Spruce   Bordered Screw-moss

Status in Ireland: Near Threatened; **Status in Europe:** Least Concern

T. marginata grows on limestone and sandstone rocks and walls, especially on old buildings. At some Irish sites it appears to behave as an opportunist species that comes and goes unpredictably, but it has proved to be persistent for many years at two of its sites. It has been reported from 12 vice-counties, with records from 14 hectads (8 old, 7 recent), well scattered throughout Ireland. There is no evidence to suggest real decline.

Tortula vahliana (Schultz) Mont.

Chalk Screw-moss

Status in Ireland: Regionally Extinct; **Status in Europe:** Least Concern

Number of Hectads	2
+ Old (pre-1970)	2

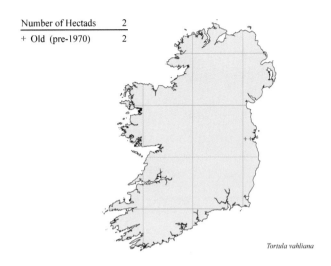

Tortula vahliana

Identification

This small bright green acrocarpous moss grows as patches or scattered plants up to c. 5 mm high. Leaves are narrowly lingulate to spathulate with rounded apices. The costa is more or less excurrent up to c. 220 μm in a hair-point which is greenish at the tip, not hyaline as in several related species. The leaf margins are recurved only in the middle (as opposed to almost throughout their length in muticous forms of *T. muralis*), and 1–2 marginal rows of cells are less papillose, and therefore clearer, than the others, forming a poorly-defined border.

Distribution in Ireland

The only reliable records from Ireland are from Dublin, where it grew at locations in Dublin city (1829–1878), Blanchardstown (1860–1908), Glasnevin ('near the Botanic Garden', 1860–1878) and Whitehall (1949). It must now be regarded as extinct in Ireland. There are a number of other old records, from Bray in Wicklow and Larne in Antrim, but these are unsubstantiated and should be regarded as unreliable because *T. vahliana* was often confused in the past with forms of *T. muralis*.

Ecology and biology

In England, this species is primarily a colonist of bare chalky soil in the lowlands, but the only information on its habitat in Ireland is that it occurred 'on a mud wall', where it perhaps occurred in the same type of open vegetation community as *Pterygoneurum ovatum* and *P. lamellatum*.

This is an autoicous species in which capsules are occasional, maturing in spring. Specialised vegetative reproductive organs are not known to occur.

World distribution

T. vahliana has a Mediterranean distribution in Europe, occurring in France, Spain, Belgium (Andriessen *et al.* 2002), Portugal, Italy, Sardinia, the Balearic Islands, Bulgaria, Crete and Cyprus, extending north to Ireland and Britain along the Atlantic coast; it also occurs in Macaronesia. It is listed as *Vulnerable* in Britain and *Extinct* in the Netherlands. In Europe, it is assigned to an Oceanic Mediterranean-Atlantic floristic element. Elsewhere, it is found in N. Africa and Turkey. Records from Chile actually refer to *T. platyphylla* Mitt., but *T. vahliana* has now been reported correctly from S. America (Cano & Gallego 2008).

Threats

The disappearance of mud-capped walls as a habitat almost certainly contributed to the extinction of this species in Ireland.

Conservation

No measures are necessary at present. It is conceivable that *T. vahliana* could be rediscovered in limestone quarries or other calcareous habitats.

Protected sites with recent records: none; **Unprotected sites with recent records:** none.

Tortula canescens Mont.

Dog Screw-moss

Status in Ireland: Data Deficient; **Status in Europe:** Least Concern

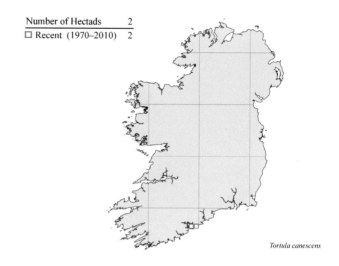

Number of Hectads	2
☐ Recent (1970–2010)	2

Tortula canescens

Identification

A small turf- or patch-forming acrocarpous moss, this species is very like the extremely common *T. muralis*. Shoots grow up to 5 mm tall, and the blunt lingulate leaves terminate in a long, smooth hyaline hair-point. Upon drying, the plants turn from a bright green colour to a more greyish hue, with the hair-points making them hoary. The erect cylindrical capsules are long-exserted and have long, twisted peristome teeth. It differs from *T. muralis* in having the leaf margins plane or only slightly recurved in the middle of the leaf (whereas *T. muralis* has them strongly recurved from base to apex) and in the peristome teeth being united into a tube for about ⅓ their length, becoming free above (whereas they are completely free in *T. muralis*). The habitat difference is also significant, although *T. muralis*, normally a plant of walls and rocks, may occasionally grow on compacted soil.

Distribution in Ireland

This species has a short but interesting history in Ireland. Material suspected of being *T. canescens* was collected at two localities in E. Cork in 2006, but unfortunately the only sporophytes that could be found had been eaten away. Visits in 2007 merely produced the same results, but those in early 2009 finally succeeded in finding intact capsules. Confirmed records are from sea cliffs near Ballycotton (2006–2009), and others almost certainly of this species are from Crosshavenhill (2006–2007), although intact capsules have not yet been seen at the latter site.

Ecology and biology

At its Irish sites, it grows on bare, crumbly soil on S.-facing rocky ledges on sea cliffs at altitudes of 10–15 m. Recorded associates include *Bryum dichotomum*, *Campylopus introflexus*, *Cephaloziella* sp., *Frullania tamarisci*, *Lophozia excisa*, *Hypnum cupressiforme* var. *lacunosum*, *Trichostomum brachydontium*, *Tortella flavovirens*, and *Weissia brachycarpa* var. *obliqua*. In Britain, this species has a southern distribution and grows on soil, mainly on S.-facing slopes near the sea.

An autoicous species, *T. canescens* produces sporophytes abundantly in late winter and early spring, but has no known specialised means of vegetative reproduction. While it may have been present undetected on the south coast of Ireland for some time, it might also be a recent colonist that has been favoured by climate change.

World distribution

The distribution of this species is strongly Mediterranean, occurring in S., W. and C. Europe. It is considered *Nationally Scarce* in Britain, where it is almost restricted to the SW peninsula of England, with a few outlying records from mid-Wales and even one from SW Scotland. It is listed as *Critically Endangered* in Switzerland, *Endangered* in Germany and Bulgaria, *Vulnerable* in Luxembourg, and occurs without red-listing in Italy, Greece, Albania, Croatia, Spain and Portugal. A record from Hungary is of a non-fertile specimen and therefore cannot be relied upon (Erzberger & Papp

2004). In Europe, it is assigned to an Oceanic Mediterranean-Atlantic floristic element. *T. canescens* is restricted globally to Europe and the Mediterranean area, with records outside Europe from the Canary Islands, the Azores, the Cape Verde Islands, N. Africa and W. Asia (Turkey and Iran).

Threats

The main threats are probably nutrient enrichment leading to competition from coarser vegetation. The Ballycotton site had been burned when visited in 2007, but the plant managed to survive and was seen there again in 2009.

Conservation

T. canescens is apparently relatively abundant over a small area at Ballycotton, but much more restricted at Crosshavenhill. The populations should be monitored regularly, and other sites on the south coast should be examined periodically to examine whether climate change might be linked to its spread.

Protected sites with recent records: none; **Unprotected sites with recent records:** Ballycotton; Crosshavenhill.

Tortula atrovirens (Sm.) Lindb.

Rib-leaf Moss

syn. *Desmatodon convolutus* (Brid.) Grout
Status in Ireland: Near Threatened; **Status in Europe:** Least Concern

Until recently thought to be very rare in Ireland, this small acrocarpous moss was recorded at nine new sites during recent fieldwork. It grows in thin turf on coastal cliffs, on bare places on cliff ledges or on coastal wall tops, mainly on the south coast in Cork, Waterford and Wexford. There are now records from 11 vice-counties and 23 hectads (11 old, 13 recent). It is possible that it may have declined in the Dublin area because of building on the coast.

Tortula lanceola R.H.Zander

Lance-leaved Pottia

syn. *Pottia lanceolata* (Hedw.) Müll.Hal.
Status in Ireland: Critically Endangered (B1a, bi, ii, iii, iv, B2a, bi, ii, iii, iv); **Status in Europe:** Least Concern

Identification

T. lanceola is a small, patch- or turf-forming acrocarpous moss up to 5 mm tall, with bright green, ovate-lanceolate, pointed leaves c. 2 mm long, with an excurrent costa and recurved margins. It can be distinguished from similar species that grow on soil by the exserted, rather elongated, red-brown elliptical capsules with longly pointed (rostrate) lids and long, well-developed, peristome teeth. A microscopic character shared with several related species is the presence of inflated, mamillose ventral cells over the costa (visible in a cross section of the leaf).

Distribution in Ireland

Always a rare plant in Ireland, and with a distinctly south-eastern distribution, the most recent record of

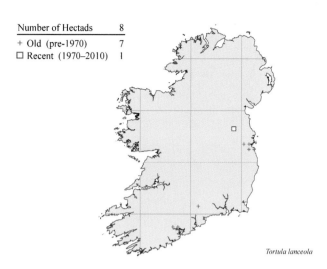

Number of Hectads	8
+ Old (pre-1970)	7
□ Recent (1970–2010)	1

Tortula lanceola

T. lanceola is from Meath (path by the River Boyne 'below Navan', 1978). Apart from that, all other records are old and often poorly localised: Mid Cork ('Cork', 1845); E. Cork (Glanmire, 1845); Waterford (Kilmanahan Bridge, 1956); Kildare (Leixlip, 1952) and Dublin (Mount Merrion Wood, 1967, 'Dublin', 1835; Dun Laoghaire, undated; Glasnevin Botanic Gardens, 1872; Killiney, 1845, 1860).

Ecology and biology

There is little specific information on the ecology of this species in Ireland, but it has been recorded from a sandy bank by a canal, a riverside path and a wall top. Indeed, many of the old records from the Dublin area were probably from mud-capped walls, a habitat that has now vanished from the landscape. In Britain, this is a colonist (or perhaps more accurately a shuttle species, given its rather large spores) of open, disturbed, calcareous soil, most often over chalk, limestone or calcareous clay. Typical habitats include bare patches in limestone grassland, banks near the sea and quarries, but less often it can occur in stubble fields, allotments, etc.

Capsules are produced in abundance by this autoicous species in late winter and early spring. *T. lanceola* is also known to produce rhizoidal tubers, but these have not yet been observed in Irish or British material (Hill *et al.* 2007).

World distribution

T. lanceola is generally distributed in S. and C. Europe northwards to S. Scandinavia, and also occurs in Macaronesia. It is *Endangered* in the Netherlands and Norway, *Vulnerable* in Switzerland, Austria and Bulgaria, 'very rare' in Estonia and 'declining' in Germany. In Europe, it is classified as a Circumpolar Southern-temperate floristic element. It is also recorded from N. Africa, SW, C. and E. Asia and a few southern states of the USA.

Threats

Although this moss was always rare in Ireland, it appears to have declined and contracted in range. One reason for its decline is probably the disappearance of mud-capped walls. Coarse vegetation invading thin calcareous soils, possibly due to increased nitrogen input in the environment generally, may also have reduced the potential habitat for this species. Its disappearance from the path by the R. Boyne below Navan may well have resulted from the virtual disappearance of open soil as the path sides there are now eutrophicated with luxuriant vegetation.

Conservation

It is not possible to recommend meaningful conservation measures for this species with no localities currently known in Ireland. It should be looked for in suitable habitats in calcareous areas, particularly in the vicinity of old records, such as gravel pits near Cork.

Protected sites with recent records: River Boyne and River Blackwater SAC; **Unprotected sites with recent records:** none.

Tortula wilsonii (Hook.) R.H.Zander

Wilson's Pottia

syn. *Pottia wilsonii* (Hook.) Bruch & Schimp.
Status in Ireland: Regionally Extinct; **Status in Europe:** Least Concern

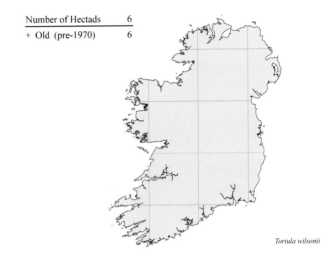

Number of Hectads	6
+ Old (pre-1970)	6

Tortula wilsonii

Identification

T. wilsonii is a small bright green acrocarpous moss up to 5 mm tall with obovate-lanceolate leaves up to 2 mm long, with a recurved margin and a longly excurrent costa. The capsule is produced on a short seta and the peristome is very poorly developed or absent. The small (13–17 μm) and relatively strongly papillose leaf cells distinguish *T. wilsonii* from the much more frequent *T. viridifolia* – the costa in that species is often (though not always) a longer hyaline hair-point. The smaller spores of *T. wilsonii* (mainly < 25 μm) than of *T. viridifolia* are also an important character. The even more common *T. truncata* has a plane leaf margin, smooth cells and a characteristically turbinate capsule.

Distribution in Ireland

The few records of this species are all old, with accepted records from seven localities in four vice-counties: W. Cork (Sherkin Island, 1934); E. Cork (Youghal, 1856; Great and Little Islands, 1872); Wicklow (Bray Head, 1872) and Dublin (Howth, 1856–1877; Killiney, 1872). A number of other records, especially from the north, are unsubstantiated and should be disregarded.

Ecology and biology

This is a lowland species of well-drained soils near the coast, typically growing in skeletal turf, earthy hedge banks or path sides. There is no detailed information about its ecology in Ireland, except that the last sighting of the plant in Ireland (1934) was from earth on walls on Sherkin Island.

Sporophytes are common in this paroicous species, maturing in spring. Tubers and other specialised vegetative means of reproduction are unknown.

World distribution

This southern species reaches its northern limit in Ireland and Britain. It is considered *Endangered* in Britain, where it has declined and its range contracted southwards. Elsewhere, it is known from Mediterranean region, with records from Spain, Portugal, Italy, Greece and Romania. In Europe, it is assigned to an Oceanic Mediterranean-Atlantic floristic element. Elsewhere, it occurs in North Africa and SW Asia. A report from British Columbia was based on misidentified *Pterygoneurum* (R.H. Zander & P.M. Eckel in FNA 2007).

Threats

The reasons for the decline and apparent disappearance of this species from Ireland are not known. It is possible that it might still be overlooked and that some of its former habitat has been lost to rank grasses and other coarse vegetation through nutrient enrichment of coastal grasslands.

Conservation

No conservation measures can be applied at present other than managing coastal cliff sites in such a way as to keep the turf thin and open with a low nutrient input. Rather a critical species, it is difficult to find and identify in the field, but it is possible that it could reappear. *T. wilsonii* is protected (as *Pottia wilsonii*) in the Republic of Ireland by the Flora (Protection) Order, 1999.

Protected sites with recent records: none; **Unprotected sites with recent records:** none.

Tortula viridifolia (Mitt.) Blockeel & A.J.E.Sm.

Bristly Pottia

syn. *Pottia crinita* Bruch & Schimp.
Status in Ireland: Least Concern; **Status in Europe:** Least Concern

Ecologically similar to *T. atrovirens*, this moss grows on thin drought-prone soil near the sea, usually on banks or maritime cliffs. It was included in the Provisional Red List (Holyoak 2006b) but it is now clear that it was under-recorded in Ireland. Recent fieldwork has found it to be fairly frequent on southern coasts from Dublin round to Clare. It is now reported from 14 vice-counties, with records from 35 hectads (14 old, 26 recent).

Tortula modica R.H.Zander

Blunt-fruited Pottia

syn. *Pottia intermedia* (Turner) Fürnr., *P. littoralis* Mitt., *P. truncata* var. *major* (F.Weber & D.Mohr) Bruch & Schimp.
Status in Ireland: Vulnerable (B2a, bii, iv); **Status in Europe:** Least Concern

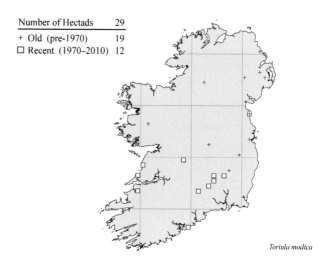

Number of Hectads	29
+ Old (pre-1970)	19
☐ Recent (1970–2010)	12

Tortula modica

Identification

This small dull green acrocarp grows as scattered shoots or small patches up to 15 mm tall. Leaves are rather broad, c. 2.0–2.5 mm long, parallel-sided with recurved margins, tapering abruptly above to a sharp point with an excurrent costa. The leaf cells are large (c. 17–24 μm)

428

and smooth or only slightly papillose, giving them a translucent appearance. It can be distinguished from related species when fertile by the cylindrical capsules, which are longer than wide, with the peristome absent or rudimentary. The spores are large, c. 27–34 μm. *T. truncata* has plane leaf margins and a shorter, wide-mouthed capsule. *T. viridifolia* has more strongly papillose leaf cells and the costa longly excurrent, usually in a hyaline hair-point. *T. modica* may have originated from hybridization between *T. truncata* and *T. lanceola* (Smith 2004); plants intermediate between *T. modica* and *T. truncata* are frequent and might be backcrosses.

Distribution in Ireland

There are records scattered throughout Ireland, with recent ones from 12 localities in nine vice-counties: N. Kerry (River Feale, Listowel, 2009); E. Cork (St Coleman's Cathedral, Cloyne, 2009); S. Tipperary (Rosegreen, 2004); Clare (Ballard, 2004; Liscannor, 2004); N. Tipperary (Luska, 1987); Kilkenny (Westcourt North, NW of Callan, 2010; Robertshill, 2010; Ardaloo, 2010); Carlow (W. of Bagenalstown, 2004); W. Mayo (Trawmore on Achill Island, 1904–2003) and Louth (Clogher Head, 1965–2007). Older records are from S. Kerry (Glenbeigh, 1951); Mid Cork ('Cork', unlocalised, 1848); Carlow (Browne's Hill, 1867); W. Galway (Maumeen Lough, 1969); Offaly (Charleville Castle, 1957); Wicklow (Ballyknockan-Valleymount, 1950); Dublin ('Dublin', unlocalised, 1830); E. Mayo (Ballinrobe, 1910); Fermanagh (Portora, 1917) and Armagh (near Lurgan, 1883). There are a number of other old or very old records from Down and Antrim, but these must be considered unconfirmed in the absence of specimens. It may be under-recorded.

Ecology and biology

This is a plant of disturbed soil in lowland fields, flower beds, earthy banks, anthills, waste ground, etc. Although often on calcareous soils, it can also grow on neutral to somewhat acidic substrates. It grows with a wide range of associates. Some older Irish records are from earth-capped walls, and it is also capable of growing in the upper reaches of saltmarshes.

It is an autoicous species that produces sporophytes frequently in the winter months. Essentially a winter annual or sometimes a perennial shuttle species, the large spores of *T. modica* may form a bank that can regenerate year after year, or that can be dispersed by birds and other animals. Rhizoidal tubers have been found in Belgian material.

World distribution

This is a widespread and frequent species in Europe, including the Canary Islands, with no reports of it being rare or threatened anywhere, except in Ireland. In Europe, it is assigned to a Circumpolar Temperate floristic element. It is also present in N. Africa, non-tropical Asia and N. America, where it is uncommon, and Australia.

Threats

Existing knowledge is inadequate to reveal the factors limiting populations of this rather uncommon plant. It is doubtful whether it has really declined in Ireland. As a plant of disturbed soils, it must colonise new sites as the old ones become shaded by larger plants.

Conservation

No conservation measures are recommended.

Protected sites with recent records: Clogher Head SAC; Keel Machair/Menaun Cliffs SAC; **Unprotected sites with recent records:** Ardaloo; Ballard; Liscannor; Luska; River Feale, Listowel (possibly within Lower River Shannon SAC); Robertshill; Rosegreen; St Coleman's Cathedral, Cloyne; W. of Bagenalstown; Westcourt North, NW of Callan.

Tortula protobryoides R.H.Zander

Tall Pottia

syn. *Pottia bryoides* (Dicks.) Mitt., *Protobryum bryoides* (Dicks.) J.Guerra & M.J.Cano
Status in Ireland: Regionally Extinct; **Status in Europe:** Least Concern

Identification

T. protobryoides is a small acrocarpous moss up to 5 mm high growing as isolated shoots or in small patches. The leaves are broad, the upper leaves longer than the lower, and their large cells are smooth or slightly papillose, resulting in a rather shiny, translucent appearance. The ellipsoid capsules are cleistocarpous, often somewhat inclined, and exserted on a seta up to c. 5.5 mm long. The

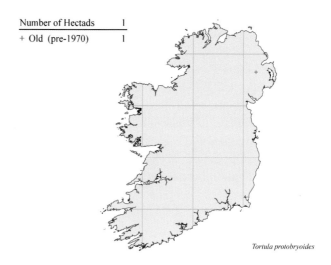

Number of Hectads	1
+ Old (pre-1970)	1

Tortula protobryoides

combination of broad leaves and a cleistocarpous capsule on a relatively long seta is unique in Irish mosses.

Distribution in Ireland

Recorded once, around 1900, by J. Davies near Lisburn (Antrim), this species is otherwise unknown in Ireland. There is another record, from Howth (Dublin) by D. Orr in 1872, but this must be considered unreliable.

Ecology and biology

Nothing is known of the habitat for this species in Ireland. In Britain, it is an ephemeral winter annual that grows on open, freely draining basic soil, often in arable field communities or allotments, or on otherwise rather bare patches in calcareous grassland, usually in the lowlands.

Capsules are abundant in this autoicous species. Tubers are known, but have not yet been found in Ireland or Britain.

World distribution

T. protobryoides is widespread in SE England and most other W., C. and E. European countries, but becomes much rarer in the north and south of Europe. However, it does occur in Hungary, Croatia, Greece, Spain, Portugal, Italy and Macaronesia. It is considered *Critically Endangered* in Switzerland, *Endangered* in Bulgaria, *Vulnerable* in Austria, *Near Threatened* in Sweden, 'very rare' in Estonia and 'declining' in Germany. In Europe, it is categorised as a European-temperate floristic element. It also occurs in Turkey and western N. America.

Threats

No information: the single record of this species was possibly no more than a transient colony, but no population details were recorded.

Conservation

No conservation measures can be recommended. However, this inconspicuous plant might still be overlooked in Ireland.

Protected sites with recent records: none; **Unprotected sites with recent records:** none.

Phascum cuspidatum Hedw. **var.** *piliferum* (Hedw.) Hook. & Taylor   Bearded Earth-moss

syn. *Tortula acaulon* var. *pilifera* (Hedw.) R.H.Zander
Status in Ireland: Data Deficient; **Status in Europe:** Not Evaluated

Identification

Phascum cuspidatum var. *piliferum* is a small acrocarpous moss with bud-like shoots growing as scattered plants or forming greenish tufts up to about 5 mm tall. It has ovate-lanceolate leaves with recurved margins and a strong, excurrent, whitish costa. The capsules are subglobose with a small apiculus, cleistocarpous and borne on a very short seta, so that they are immersed among the erect to imbricate upper leaves. Var. *piliferum* differs from the other varieties of the species in having

430

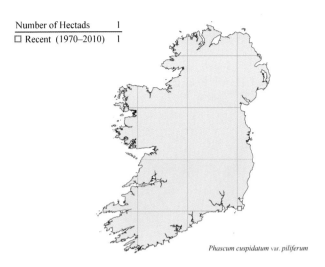

Phascum cuspidatum var. *piliferum*

the excurrent costa forming a flexuose hyaline point up to 1.4 mm long.

Distribution in Ireland

This plant has been found once in Ireland, at Tacumshin Lake, Wexford, in 2006.

Ecology and biology

This is a plant of bare earth in the lowlands. It favours open, base-rich soil on cliffs and banks, in dune slacks and grassland, and at path edges. At Tacumshin Lake it was found on gravelly sand with sparse low grasses and herbs on the unshaded shore of a brackish lagoon on the landward side of sand dunes at c. 5 m altitude. Almost all British sites for this taxon are coastal (Hill *et al.* 1992) and Oesau (2008) reports it as a salt-tolerant ecotype from Germany. Duckett *et al.* (2006) note that coastal specimens of var. *piliferum* 'maintain their diagnostic characters when cultured from both spores and gametophore fragments alongside typical *P. cuspidatum*, [which] makes this variety an obvious candidate for specific recognition'. However, Zander (in FNA 2007) claims that intergrades appear to be common.

It is a short-lived plant, autoicous, with abundant sporophytes that usually mature in spring. Vegetative means of reproduction are not known.

World distribution

This variety is widespread in Europe north to southern Scandinavia. It is listed as *Near Threatened* in Luxembourg and *Data Deficient* in Germany. In Europe, it is assigned to a European Southern-temperate floristic element. Elsewhere, it is known from the Caucasus, Turkey, Iran, North Africa and North America.

Threats

No threats have been identified.

Conservation

No conservation measures are necessary but new populations of this poorly-recorded variety should be looked out for by bryologists.

Protected sites with recent records: Tacumshin Lake SAC; **Unprotected sites with recent records:** none.

Brackish lagoon, Tacumshin Lake, Co. Wexford.

Phascum cuspidatum Hedw. var. *papillosum* (Lindb.) G.Roth　　Rough Earth-moss

Syn. *Tortula acaulon* (Dicks.) H.Buch var. *papillosa* (Lindb.) R.H.Zander
Status in Ireland: Data Deficient; **Status in Europe:** Not Evaluated

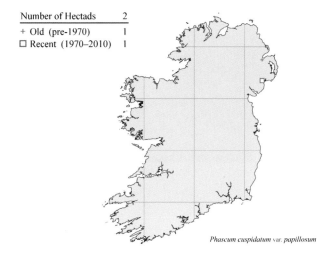

Number of Hectads	2
+ Old (pre-1970)	1
☐ Recent (1970–2010)	1

Phascum cuspidatum var. *papillosum*

Identification

Phascum cuspidatum var. *papillosum* is a small acrocarpous moss with bud-like shoots growing as scattered plants or in small greenish tufts up to about 5 mm tall. It has ovate-lanceolate leaves with recurved margins and a strong costa excurrent in a short yellowish point. The capsules are subglobose with a small apiculus, cleistocarpous and borne on a very short seta, so that they are immersed among the erect to imbricate upper leaves. Var. *papillosum* differs from var. *cuspidatum* in having smaller upper leaf lamina cells (9–15 × 11–20 μm cf. 10–21 × 21–31 μm), with more prominent papillae, spores spinulose (with small rounded papillae in var. *cuspidatum*) and quadrate or shortly rectangular cells over the adaxial side of the upper part of the costa (rectangular in var. *cuspidatum*) (Guerra *et al.* 1991, Blockeel 1995b). Var. *piliferum* resembles var. *cuspidatum* in these characters, but differs in having the costa excurrent in a longer hyaline awn.

Distribution in Ireland

This variety has been found twice in Ireland: Antrim (Belfast, late 19th or early 20th century) and Down (west of Dundrum, 2002). Although clearly much rarer than var. *cuspidatum*, var. *papillosum* must surely be under-recorded. Although rarely recorded in Britain, it is common in W. Cornwall, as are plants intermediate between var. *papillosum* and var. *cuspidatum* (Holyoak 2009), which show little correlation of spore and leaf characters.

Ecology and biology

This is a plant of bare earth in lowland areas, growing especially on disturbed soil in fields. At its recent locality (near Dundrum, Co. Down) it was found on stony soil on disturbed ground by an estuarine bay, part-shaded by long grasses at c. 5 m altitude.

It may be autoicous or paroicous, and sporophytes are very common. Vegetative means of reproduction are not known.

World distribution

This plant appears to be widespread in Europe, with records from Britain, Belgium, Denmark, France, Germany (where it is 'declining'), Italy, the Netherlands, Portugal, Spain and Sweden. It is assigned to a Suboceanic Southern-temperate floristic element in Europe, and has not been recorded elsewhere.

Threats

No threats have been identified.

Conservation

Clarification of the taxonomic status of var. *papillosum*, and the extent of its occurrence and ecology in Ireland, is needed before conservation actions can be recommended. It should be looked out for in suitable habitats.

Protected sites with recent records: none; **Unprotected sites with recent records:** west of Dundrum.

Microbryum starckeanum (Hedw.) R.H.Zander

Starke's Pottia

syn. *Pottia starckeana* (Hedw.) Müll.Hal.; *P. starckeana* var. *brachyodus* (Bruch & Schimp.) Müll.Hal.; *P. starkeana* auct.
Status in Ireland: Regionally Extinct; **Status in Europe:** Least Concern

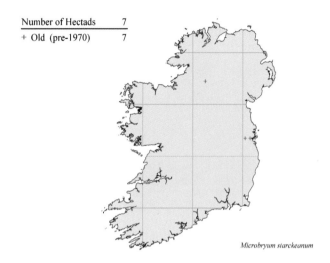

Number of Hectads	7
+ Old (pre-1970)	7

Microbryum starckeanum

Identification

This is a very small acrocarpous moss with shoots up to 3 mm tall growing as scattered stems or small patches. It has ovate-lanceolate leaves forming a small rosette, with exserted sporophytes. The capsule is ellipsoid, erect and exserted on a seta 1–4 mm long. The capsule has a deciduous lid and the peristome teeth vary from absent to well-developed. *M. starckeanum* is one of a pair of species whose identification depends on examination of mature spores. The spores of *M. starckeanum* are very irregular in outline, with coarse warts and ridges, whereas those of the considerably more common *M. davallianum* are rounded and densely covered with tiny papillae or spines.

Distribution in Ireland

Confirmed records for this species are from E. Cork (Youghal, 1851) and Dublin (Killiney Hill, 1830). There are five other old records that have been accepted: Dublin (W. of Chapelizod, 1830; Clontarf, undated; Howth, 1860; Corballis, 1950) and Fermanagh (Portora, 1912) but specimens need to be located and checked before these can be regarded as reliable.

Ecology and biology

This is an ephemeral, annual moss of bare calcareous soil in the lowlands. The ecology of this plant in Ireland is unknown, but typical habitats in Britain are cliff tops, path sides, wall tops, skeletal soil among rocks, in quarries, chalk and limestone grassland and stubble fields. An autoicous species, this plant can only be recorded reliably with sporophytes, which are common, with spores maturing mainly in winter and spring. Gemmae and other vegetative means of reproduction are unknown.

World distribution

The distribution of this plant is imperfectly known because of confusion with related species, but it seems to be widespread in Europe from the Mediterranean north as far as S. Sweden. It is listed as *Nationally Scarce* in Britain, *Extinct* in Sweden, Austria and the Netherlands, *Critically Endangered* in Luxembourg, *Endangered* in Bulgaria, and *Data Deficient* (*vanished*) in the Czech Republic. In Europe, it is assigned to a Suboceanic Mediterranean-Atlantic floristic element. It also occurs in Turkey (Kürschner & Erdağ 2005), N. Africa, China (Inner Mongolia: Zhao *et al.* 2009), western USA (Arizona and California: R. H. Zander in FNA 2007) and Australia (Streimann & Klazenga 2002).

Threats

This might have been one of the plants adversely affected by the disappearance of mud-capped walls.

Conservation

No measures are currently required, but *M. starckeanum* should be looked for in limestone quarries and other potentially suitable short-grassland habitats.

Protected sites with recent records: none; **Unprotected sites with recent records:** none.

Microbryum rectum (With.) R.H.Zander

Upright Pottia

syn. *Pottia recta* (With.) Mitt.
Status in Ireland: Least Concern; **Status in Europe:** Least Concern

A very small ephemeral acrocarpous moss that colonises bare calcareous soils, such as in quarries or limestone grassland. *M. rectum* was formerly considered rare in Ireland and included in the Provisional Red List (Holyoak 2006b), but recent fieldwork has shown that it had previously been under-recorded. It has a scattered distribution in the south of Ireland, largely absent from the north, and is now known from 20 vice-counties, with records from 33 hectads (17 old, 17 recent). There is no evidence of any decline.

Microbryum curvicollum (Hedw.) R.H.Zander

Swan-necked Earth-moss

syn. *Phascum curvicollum* Hedw.
Status in Ireland: Regionally Extinct; **Status in Europe:** Least Concern

Number of Hectads	2
+ Old (pre-1970)	2

Microbryum curvicollum

Identification

Although very small, this acrocarpous moss is easily recognised by its cygneous seta when fertile. The greenish or brownish shoots, which may grow as scattered plants or as extensive colonies, are not more than 3 mm tall, and consist of a rosette of more or less lanceolate leaves, about 1 mm long. The lower leaves are patent, upper and perichaetial leaves are erecto-patent; margins recurved, usually entire with the costa strong above and excurrent in a cuspidate point. The cleistocarpous, ovoid capsule is shortly exserted and borne horizontally on a cygneous seta c. 1 mm long.

Distribution in Ireland

M. curvicollum has only been found twice in Ireland, both times in Dublin ('near Dublin' in 1836 by T. Taylor and

434

at Corballis, Donabate in 1950 by J.P. Brunker). W. Wade's 1804 record from Benlettery in W. Galway is unsupported by a specimen and should be disregarded; the locality is a quartzite mountain, and clearly unsuitable for this species.

Ecology and biology

The ecology of the Irish specimens is unknown. In Britain, this is an annual ephemeral moss of bare calcareous soils in the lowlands, typically in chalk or limestone grassland, especially in old quarries. It also grows in stubble fields and used to grow on mud-capped walls.

Paroicous or synoicous, this species is almost always found with sporophytes, which mature from autumn to spring. Specialised vegetative means of reproduction are unknown.

World distribution

This species is widespread in C. and S. Europe north to Fennoscandia. It is listed as *Endangered* in Norway, the Netherlands and Switzerland, *Vulnerable* in Luxembourg, Austria and the Czech Republic, *Near Threatened* in Sweden and *Data Deficient* in Bulgaria. In Europe, it is assigned to a Suboceanic Mediterranean-Atlantic floristic element. It also occurs in N. Africa and SW Asia.

Threats

The loss of mud-capped walls is a possible explanation for the extinction of this species in the Dublin area.

Conservation

No action is required. However, bryologists should continue to watch for this plant in possible habitats such as in limestone quarries.

Protected sites with recent records: none; **Unprotected sites with recent records:** none.

Hennediella stanfordensis (Steere) Blockeel   Stanford Screw-moss

syn. *Hyophila stanfordensis* (Steere) A.J.E.Sm. & H.Whitehouse, *Tortula stanfordensis* Steere
Status in Ireland: Not Evaluated; **Status in Europe:** Not Evaluated

This is a small green acrocarpous moss with lingulate to spathulate leaves that form rosettes in open patches or as scattered plants. Otherwise known from California, Mexico and Australia, this species is presumed to be an introduction in Europe and is therefore not evaluated as part of the Red List process. In Ireland, it is known only from soil banks and flower beds in Dublin, including banks beside paths at St Stephen's Green, the Phoenix Park and the National Botanic Gardens, Glasnevin.

435

Hennediella heimii (Hedw.) R.H.Zander

Heim's Pottia

syn. *Desmatodon heimii* (Hedw.) Mitt., *Pottia heimii* (Hedw.) Hampe
Status in Ireland: Least Concern; **Status in Europe:** Least Concern

An ephemeral acrocarpous moss that grows in saline coastal localities such as saltmarsh edges and earthy crevices in rocks. It was included in the Provisional Red List (Holyoak 2006b), but recent fieldwork has shown that it is widespread in Ireland and was previously under-recorded. There are now reports from 22 vice-counties, with records from 53 hectads (20 old, 35 recent, 2 undated), including some large populations.

Acaulon muticum (Hedw.) Müll.Hal.

Rounded Pygmy-moss

syn. *Acaulon minus* (Hook. & Taylor) A.Jaeger
Status in Ireland: Regionally Extinct; **Status in Europe:** Least Concern

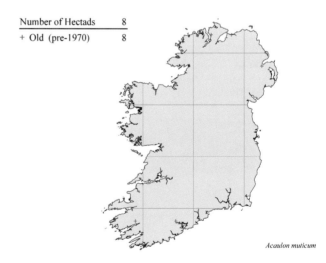

Number of Hectads	8
+ Old (pre-1970)	8

Acaulon muticum

Identification

The tiny, almost stemless, bud-like shoots of this very small acrocarpous moss are no more than c. 2 mm tall, but may grow as small patches. The leaves are ovate and strongly concave, with a costa and a reflexed apiculus, completely enveloping the cleistocarpous capsule, which is perfectly globose or sometimes has a very small blunt apiculus. The perichaetial bracts are usually toothed near the apex. Most of the other small mosses with an immersed cleistocarpous capsule have entire, more longly pointed bracts, which do not enclose the capsule so closely, and a distinct beak at the apex of the capsule. In addition, *Phascum cuspidatum* is a much larger plant. *Ephemerum* spp. are even smaller than *Acaulon*, have a persistent protonema and a quite different leaf shape.

In *A. muticum*, the spores have a finely granulose surface. *A. mediterraneum*, which is otherwise very similar, differs in having a spiculose sporoderm; it was formerly treated as *A. muticum* var. *mediterraneum*, but separated as a distinct species by Hill *et al.* (2006, 2008).

Distribution in Ireland

There are scattered records of this species, mostly from near the coast and often very old and poorly localised, from seven localities in five vice-counties: S. Kerry (Derrynane, 1951, 1957; Hog's Head, 1951; Dunkerron, 1836); W. Cork ('Cork', 1845); Dublin ('Dublin', 1830); E. Donegal (Buncrana, 1902) and Londonderry (Portstewart, 1922). A very old record from Belfast is unsubstantiated and must be regarded as dubious. Study of the sporoderm to confirm that *A. muticum s.str.* rather than *A. mediterraneum* is involved has only been possible with the plants from Portstewart. Other Irish records, particularly from the southern counties, might be of *A. mediterraneum* since the latter accounts for about half of the *Acaulon* records from Cornwall (Holyoak 2003c).

Ecology and biology

This is an ephemeral annual plant of neutral to acid, often well-drained sandy soils, typically occurring in stubble fields, anthills and earthy banks, always in the lowlands. There is no further information on its habitat in Ireland.

A. muticum is monoicous and nearly always recorded fertile. Sporophytes are common, with capsules mainly maturing from autumn to spring. Gemmae or other means of asexual reproduction are unknown.

World distribution

A. muticum is widespread in Europe and is recorded from most countries but rare in the north. It is listed as *Critically Endangered* in Switzerland and Serbia and Montenegro, *Endangered* in the Netherlands and Austria, *Vulnerable* in Norway and the Czech Republic and *Near Threatened* in Luxembourg. It is assigned to a European Southern-temperate floristic element in Europe. It is also recorded in N. Africa, W. and C. Asia and the USA. Old records from Australia are now referred to other species (Stone 1988).

Threats

It is not known if this species has really disappeared from Ireland since the old localities were too imprecise to allow detailed searches. According to Schnyder *et al.* (2004), its decline in Switzerland is due to the effects of intensive agriculture.

Conservation

It is possible that this species will recolonise, or perhaps re-emerge from a spore bank, as its spores are large and possibly long-lived. Further survey work at and near its previous localities might conceivably result in *A. muticum* being refound.

Protected sites with recent records: none; **Unprotected sites with recent records:** none.

Syntrichia princeps (De Not.) Mitt.

Brown Screw-moss

syn. *Tortula princeps* De Not.
Status in Ireland: Regionally Extinct; **Status in Europe:** Least Concern

Identification

This acrocarpous moss is medium-sized to rather large, with shoots 1–4 cm tall forming dense tufts or patches, with the leaves sometimes in interrupted groups on the stems. It is very similar to the common *S. montana*, with long, ovate-spathulate leaves that are constricted in the middle, and a long, denticulate hyaline hair-point protruding abruptly from the broad leaf apex. It differs from *S. montana* in the relatively large size of its leaf cells: they are about 12–20 μm wide, as opposed to about 8–10 μm wide. However, the most important identification character is that *S. princeps* is synoicous, whereas *S. montana* is dioicous.

Distribution in Ireland

S. princeps had a northern distribution in Ireland, but is known only from old records from six localities in three vice-counties: Sligo (Bricklieve Mountains, 1962; Benbulbin, 1872); Antrim (Knock Dhu, 1925; Glenarm, 1866) and Londonderry (Binevenagh, 1914; Downhill, 1913). Recent efforts to refind it at the old localities and elsewhere on the basalt scarps of Antrim and

Number of Hectads	6
+ Old (pre-1970)	6

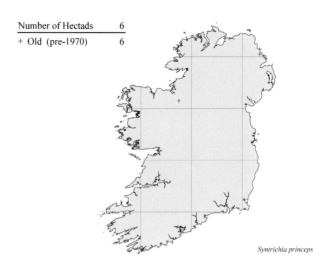

Syntrichia princeps

Londonderry have been unsuccessful, but the potentially suitable habitat extends for many tens of kilometres.

Ecology and biology

This is a plant of dry, base-rich insolated rocks, particularly base-rich sandstones, limestone and basalt. The only habitat information for the Irish records is that it grew on basalt in Antrim and Londonderry, although the Sligo colonies must presumably have been on limestone. It usually grows on cliffs and rock outcrops, but has been recorded (in Britain) on walls and even on trees. It is a lowland plant in terms of altitude, but can also occur in the uplands. There is no information available on its altitude in Ireland, but it has not been recorded above 500 m in Britain.

It is synoicous and capsules are frequent, with spores maturing in autumn. Specialised means of vegetative reproduction are not known.

World distribution

S. princeps is fairly widespread in W. and S. Europe, including Macaronesia, although apparently absent from Albania, Croatia and the Czech Republic. It is *Nationally Scarce* in Britain, *Endangered* in Luxembourg, *Vulnerable* in Bulgaria, *Near Threatened* in Sweden (the northernmost records in Europe) and 'extremely rare' in Germany. In Europe, it is classified as a European Temperate floristic element. Elsewhere, it is known from N. Africa, Asia and western N. America, and it is widespread in temperate and Antarctic regions of the southern hemisphere.

Threats

The reasons for the decline of this species are not known. Overstocking with sheep and afforestation in the uplands may have had some impact, but most of its sites were on rocks and mainly in areas that still have no plantations.

Conservation

No conservation measures are required at present, but *S. princeps* should be looked for in suitable habitat.

Protected sites with recent records: none; **Unprotected sites with recent records:** none.

Syntrichia virescens (De Not.) Ochyra

Lesser Screw-moss

syn. *Tortula virescens* (De Not.) De Not.
Status in Ireland: Data Deficient; **Status in Europe:** Vulnerable

Identification

An acrocarpous moss that grows in dense dull green, grey-green or olive green tufts or turfs (2)5–25(30) mm high. The leaves are oblong-spathulate, usually with an obtuse or rounded apex, red-brown costa excurrent in a hyaline denticulate awn up to one-third as long as the lamina, and margins that are plane or recurved only in the lower part of the leaf. The mid-leaf cells are quadrate-

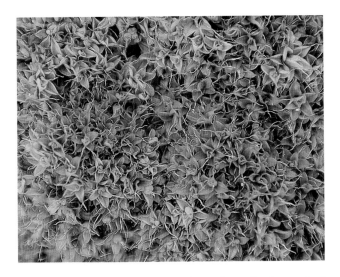

Number of Hectads	1
☐ Recent (1970–2010)	1

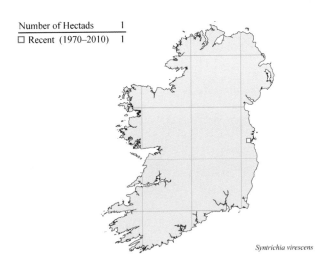

Syntrichia virescens

hexagonal, 12–16 μm wide and papillose, leaf-marginal cells are similar, the basal leaf cells rectangular, hyaline and 20–40(83) μm long. Capsules are erect, narrowly cylindrical, 1.6–2.6 mm long, exserted on a reddish seta c. 15 mm tall; spores are 8–15 μm in diameter. Careful attention to microscopic characters is necessary for reliable separation from other *Syntrichia* species. *S. laevipila* has the awns smooth not denticulate; *S. montana* and *S. ruralis* are often larger, with longer leaf basal cells, but characters of the transverse section of the costa are of greater diagnostic importance: a thinner band of stereids (1 or 2 rows of ventral stereids (rarely 3) in *S. virescens* vs. 3 or more rows in the other species) and lack of hydroids (M.T. Gallego in Guerra *et al.* 2006).

Distribution in Ireland

There is a single report from Ireland, at the entrance to the Montrose Hotel and in the campus of University College Dublin, where J.G. Duckett collected it in May 2009. The species is almost certainly uncommon in E. Ireland as numerous other collections made from similar substrata have been identified only as *S. ruralis* or *S. montana*.

Ecology and biology

The recent collections from Dublin were of plants growing on old tarmac; it was locally abundant in the campus of University College (J.G. Duckett, pers. comm.). In Britain, it grows on tree bark, stones, walls, concrete and tarmac, rarely on thatched roofs, normally in open places and only in the lowlands. In SW Europe, it is also recorded mainly as an epiphyte, but sometimes also on rock (especially in fissures), and rarely on soil (M.T. Gallego in Guerra *et al.* 2006).

The species is dioicous; capsules are unknown in Ireland and in Scandinavia, rare in S. Europe and they have been found only once in Britain. Gemmae, tubers or other vegetative propagules are unknown in Ireland or Britain. However, multicellular rounded or ovate gemmae are reported to occur on the leaf costa in Iberian specimens (M.T. Gallego in Guerra *et al.* 2006).

World distribution

In Britain, found mainly in S. and E. England, but sparsely northwards to NE Scotland. Elsewhere in Europe, it is widespread from S. Scandinavia (one locality in W. Norway) and Estonia southwards to N. Portugal, S. Spain, Sardinia, Sicily and the Caucasus. In Europe, it is assigned to a Temperate European floristic element. It is known elsewhere from the Canary Is., NW Africa (Morocco and Algeria: Ros *et al.* 1999), SW Asia (Turkey; also Georgia to Kazakhstan, Kyrgyzstan and Tajikistan: Ignatov *et al.* 2007) and Kashmir. Reports from N. America (e.g. in Smith 2004) are erroneous (cf. FNA 2007).

Threats

Not immediately threatened at the Dublin sites, but possibly at risk from resurfacing of old tarmac.

Conservation

Fuller surveys are needed to establish its status in and around Dublin.

Protected sites with recent records: none; **Unprotected sites with recent records:** entrance to Montrose Hotel; campus of University College Dublin.

Syntrichia latifolia (Bruch ex Hartm.) Huebener

Water Screw-moss

syn. *Tortula latifolia* Bruch ex Hartm.
Status in Ireland: Least Concern; **Status in Europe:** Least Concern

An acrocarpous moss with broadly spathulate leaves, rounded at the apex and with a brownish costa ending below the apex to percurrent. It can form extensive dull green or brownish, silt-encrusted patches on periodically flooded tree trunks, exposed roots, rocks and walls by lowland rivers, particularly along the large southern rivers (Barrow, Nore, Suir and Blackwater). It was included in the Provisional Red List (Holyoak 2006b), but recent survey work has shown it to be widespread and frequent in Ireland. It has now been reported from 21 vice-counties, with records from 38 hectads (14 old, 28 recent).

Cinclidotus riparius (Host ex Brid.) Arn.

Fountain Lattice-moss

Status in Ireland: Data Deficient; **Status in Europe:** Least Concern

Number of Hectads	1
+ Old (pre-1970)	1

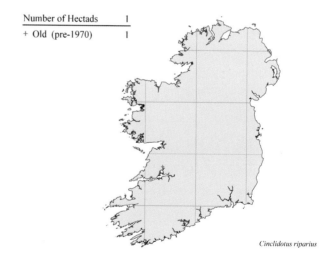

Cinclidotus riparius

Identification

This is a dark green, aquatic pleurocarpous moss that forms tufts up to c. 5 cm tall, with the leaves up to c. 1 mm long. Like the much more common *C. fontinaloides*, the leaves have a dark multistratose border, clearly visible in the field. However, the habit of *C. riparius* is more compact, the leaves are more spreading and relatively short and broad, and the cells of the border are more or less uniform throughout in cross section, whereas the border of *C. fontinaloides* has a central strand of small, thick-walled cells. Furthermore, the capsule of *C. fontinaloides* is immersed, while that of *C. riparius* is exserted. For many years the presence of *C. riparius* in the Irish and British flora was disputed, but the discovery that it was possible to distinguish these two species of *Cinclidotus* vegetatively led to its reinstatement on the list (Blockeel 1998).

Distribution in Ireland

This plant has only been recorded once in Ireland from the River Fergus, in or near Ennis, Clare, where it was found in 1884 by S.A. Stewart. It has not been collected there since, but survey work to detect this species relies on low water levels. The water level was high when the river was visited in 2004 and 2009, and there was abundant *C. fontinaloides* on the upper parts of the riverbank, growing on walls and rocks. It is not unlikely that *C. riparius* still occurs there.

Ecology and biology

In Britain, this is an aquatic species, growing on rocks, stonework and tree roots submerged c. 15–25 cm below the water level, or occasionally higher up, in fairly fast-flowing lowland rivers. It tends to grow in deeper water than *C. fontinaloides*, which is often exposed. All that is known of its Irish habitat is that it was on stones in the river.

Sporophytes have not been found in Irish or British material of this dioicous species, and specialised means of vegetative propagation are unknown.

World distribution

C. riparius has a southern distribution in Europe, being widespread in Mediterranean countries, and extending north to Germany, the Netherlands and Poland, with one locality in Brittany, but it does not occur in Fennoscandia (Blockeel 1998). It is now known from several sites along a short stretch of the River Teme in the English West Midlands, and is listed as *Vulnerable* in Britain, *Critically Endangered* in the Czech Republic and 'sparse' in the Netherlands. In Europe, it is assigned to a Eurosiberian Temperate floristic element. Elsewhere, it occurs in Turkey and N. Africa.

Threats

The most obvious potential threat to this species, if it still occurs, is water pollution. Populations may also be at risk from river maintenance and construction activities.

Conservation

A bryophyte survey of the River Fergus at Ennis, when water levels are low, should be a priority.

Protected sites with recent records: none (but would be within Lower River Shannon SAC if still present); **Unprotected sites with recent records:** none.

Tayloria tenuis (Dicks.) Schimp.

Slender Gland-moss

syn. *T. longicollis* (Dicks.) Dixon, *T. serrata* var. *tenuis* (Dicks.) Bruch & Schimp.
Status in Ireland: Regionally Extinct; **Status in Europe:** Least Concern

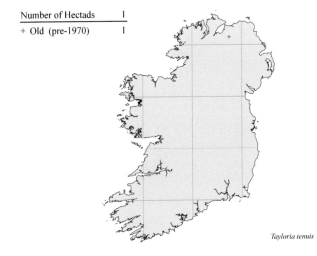

Number of Hectads	1
+ Old (pre-1970)	1

Tayloria tenuis

Identification

This is an acrocarpous moss that grows as dense green or dark green tufts with stems up to 20 mm high. The leaves are erecto-patent, obovate-spathulate to lanceolate-spathulate and shortly acute or with an acuminate apiculus. The leaf-margin is plane and coarsely serrate in the upper part of the leaf; the costa ends just below the leaf apex. Mid-leaf cells are large and lax, hexagonal and 20–40 μm wide; the basal cells are longer and rectangular. Capsules have an ellipsoid theca that tapers into a long narrow apophysis and peristome teeth reflexed when dry; capsules are held erect on a slender, flexuose, deep red seta up to 25 mm long. Fertile plants look superficially similar to *Tetraplodon mnioides*, differing in the much broader, serrate, shortly acute leaves. Non-fertile plants are more like *Splachnum* spp., but differ in the very short leaf point.

Distribution in Ireland

Known from a single Irish locality, on Benbradagh in Londonderry where it was collected in 1868 and 1884.

Ecology and biology

The Irish specimens were recorded as growing 'on old cowdung in mountain bogs' and 'wet peaty and heathy pastures on the top of Benbradagh Mountain' at altitude of 'about 1300 to 1400 feet' [c. 415 m] (Stewart & Corry 1888). In Scotland it grows on damp, decaying vegetable matter and soil in the uplands, where it is usually montane, but found at c. 100 m altitude in Caithness. In continental Europe it is also found mainly on damp, decaying organic matter, but occasionally also on rotten wood.

The plants are reported to be perennial. It is an autoicous or synoicous species in which capsules are frequent; on Benbradagh they were mature in mid-June and early July. Gemmae, bulbils and tubers are unknown.

World distribution

T. tenuis is widespread in N. and C. Europe from N. Fennoscandia and arctic Russia southwards to N. Spain (Pyrenees), N. Italy (Alps) and the Crimea. It is listed as *Critically Endangered* in Britain, *Endangered* in the Czech Republic, *Vulnerable* in Spain, *Near Threatened* in Finland and Sweden, *Data Deficient* in Switzerland and 'very rare' in Estonia. It is assigned to a Circumpolar Boreal-montane floristic element in Europe. Elsewhere, it occurs in SW, C., N. and NE Asia (Kazakhstan, Kyrgyzstan, S. and E. Siberia, arctic parts of Yakutia and Russian Far East: Ignatov *et al.* 2007), northern N. America (British Columbia and Montana to Newfoundland) and Greenland.

Threats

Attempts to refind *T. tenuis* on Benbradagh in 1999 were unsuccessful, but there seems some slight hope that it persists in the region as potentially suitable habitats are still present, with other species of Splachnaceae. However, the species appears to have declined 'catastrophically' in Scotland where it is regarded as *Critically Endangered* (Hill *et al.* 1994, Church *et al.* 2001).

Conservation

Much of the high ground on Benbradagh is protected as an ASSI. *T. tenuis* is listed as a UK Biodiversity Action Plan (UKBAP) species.

Protected sites with recent records: none; **Unprotected sites with recent records:** none.

Tetraplodon angustatus (Hedw.) Bruch & Schimp.   Narrow Cruet-moss

Status in Ireland: Data Deficient; **Status in Europe:** Least Concern

Identification

This is a handsome acrocarpous moss that grows in pale green or light green tufts that may reach over 60 mm high, but are usually much shorter. The leaves are lanceolate to oblanceolate, tapering to a long flexuose acumen, with percurrent costa and margins sharply dentate in the upper part of the leaf. As in other Splachnaceae, the leaf cells are rectangular and rather large and lax. Capsules are barely exserted beyond the leaves (on a seta up to 5 mm long), erect, cylindrical, with apophysis forming half or more of length of capsule and

slightly wider than theca. It can be distinguished from the more common *T. mnioides* mainly by the very short seta. Hybrid sporophytes are known in Norway, but the species usually remain distinct in mixed stands (Frisvoll 1978).

Distribution in Ireland

Known from a single record, from Clara Bog Nature Reserve in Offaly, where it was found in June 1988 by N. Lockhart. It has not been refound on more recent visits to the site.

Number of Hectads | 1
☐ Recent (1970–2010) | 1

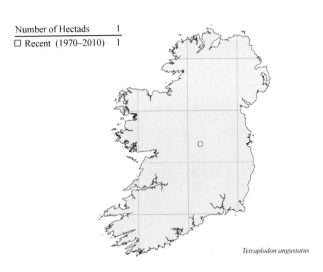

Tetraplodon angustatus

Ecology and biology

Found only once in Ireland, on dung amongst *Sphagnum magellanicum* on a raised bog. In Scotland, it grows on decaying bones of deer and sheep, less frequently on dung, in wet places, especially along tracks at altitudes of up to 910 m in the mountains (A.C. Crundwell in Hill *et al.* 1994).

Tufts of the species on dung probably only persist for one or two years, although decaying bones may provide more persistent habitats. The species is autoicous and capsules are common, maturing in late spring or summer. Gemmae and tubers are unknown. A study in Canada by Marino (1991) found that both this species and *T. mnioides* often colonised dung, with no apparent difference in their habitat requirements, although capsules of *T. angustatus* matured earlier (in May, a month earlier than those of *T. mnioides*). Investigations of the ecology of Splachnaceae that grow on dung (summarised by Koponen 1990 and Marino 1997) have shown that a strong odour from their ripe capsules attracts dung flies, resulting in dispersal of the sticky spores to the widely scattered patches of dung.

World distribution

Widespread in N. and C. Europe from the Arctic in Fennoscandia southwards mainly in the mountains to Scotland (formerly N. Wales), France, Germany, the Alps and N. Italy, but listed as *Endangered* in Switzerland and *Vulnerable* in the Czech Republic and Germany. In Europe, it is assigned to a Circumpolar Boreal-montane floristic element. Elsewhere, the species is known in Siberia, China, Japan, northern N. America and Greenland.

Threats

Disappearance of a closely related dung-moss *Splachnum ampullaceum* from most of its former range in SE England over the past century has been attributed to habitat destruction through drainage (A.C. Crundwell in Hill *et al.* 1994), coupled perhaps with a decline in the grazing of stock on common land and village greens (Cox 1999). However, these factors seem unlikely to be responsible for its recent loss from many areas such as Bodmin Moor and Dartmoor, which still have extensive mires and high stocking levels. Instead, it is feared that loss of *S. ampullaceum* may be an indirect result of the widespread use since the 1980s of ivermectin (an avermectin; used as an endectocide) to remove helminths and other gastrointestinal parasites from domestic stock. Very low concentrations of these drugs kill dung flies, and it is now established that ivermectin usage has caused large and widespread declines of these and other coprophilous insects (Cox 1999). Loss of the community of insects responsible for breakdown of herbivore dung has resulted in longer persistence of the dung, which might have been beneficial for Splachnaceae were it not for the concomitant loss of the dung flies that disperse the moss spores. It is highly likely that similar factors threaten Splachnaceae in Ireland, especially in the lowlands.

Conservation

T. angustatus is protected in the Republic of Ireland by the Flora (Protection) Order, 1999. Its only site is on protected land.

Protected sites with recent records: Clara Bog Nature Reserve; Clara Bog SAC; **Unprotected sites with recent records:** none.

Paludella squarrosa (Hedw.) Brid.

Tufted Fen-moss

Status in Ireland: Critically Endangered (B2a, biii, D); **Status in Europe:** Least Concern

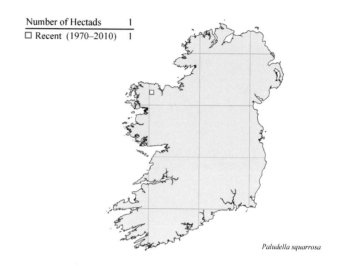

Number of Hectads	1
☐ Recent (1970–2010)	1

Paludella squarrosa

Identification

This is a very distinctive light green acrocarpous moss that grows as dense matted tufts up to 150 mm high, or as scattered stems among other bryophytes. The leaves are strongly squarrose-recurved, five-ranked, ovate, acute, decurrent at the base, sharply toothed above, with costa ending below the apex. Cells in mid-leaf are rounded-hexagonal, coarsely mamillose, with incrassate cell walls. Capsules are erect but curved, ellipsoid and long-exserted on a seta up to 100 mm high. The squarrose-recurved leaves are suggestive of *Meesia triquetra*, but that species has narrower leaves in three ranks with smooth cells.

Distribution in Ireland

Known only in a small area of W. Mayo in part of the Bellacorick Bog Complex near Crossmolina, where it was discovered in 1998 (Lockhart 1999) and is now known at two closely adjoining localities. The species had previously been reported from Ireland only as a Littletonian (postglacial) fossil, in Londonderry (Smith 1958) and Kildare (Barry & Synnott 1984, 1987).

Ecology and biology

It is restricted to small areas in the wettest parts of a rich fen within an extensive area of blanket bog. The largest population occurs beside a pool system amongst a very wet and quaking moss lawn dominated by *Tomentypnum nitens*, *Sphagnum contortum* and *Aulacomnium palustre*, with some *Schoenus nigricans*, *Molinia caerulea*, *Vaccinium*

oxycoccos and stunted *Betula pubescens*. Surface water pH at the sites ranges from 6.50 to 7.67 and the pools are heavily iron-stained (Lockhart 1999). Elsewhere in Europe, *P. squarrosa* is reported from fens, marshes and spring bogs which have some base but are not highly calcareous. Mårtensson (1956) noted that in the Torneträsk area of N. Sweden, it is a characteristic species of the intermediate and richer types of fen but does not occur in extremely poor fens.

Tufts of the species probably live for several years, but details are unknown. The species is dioicous and infrequently produces capsules (which are unknown in Ireland; recorded once in Britain). Tubers and gemmae are unknown, so propagation and dispersal are most likely to occur from shoot or leaf fragments.

World distribution

In Europe, it is widespread in arctic and boreal regions of Svalbard, Iceland and Fennoscandia, occurring much more sparsely southwards to the Alps and Carpathians. In Britain, it was formerly known at three localities in N. England but was last recorded in 1916 and is now considered to be *Extinct*. However, it was much more widespread in Britain and locally abundant as a Flandrian (postglacial) fossil (Dickson 1973). *P. squarrosa* is listed as *Extinct* in the Netherlands, *Critically Endangered* in the Czech Republic and Germany and *Vulnerable* in Switzerland. It is assigned to a Circumpolar Boreo-arctic montane floristic element in Europe. Elsewhere, the species occurs in Asia (Arctic south to Kazakhstan, Mongolia and Japan), N. America (south to northern USA) and Greenland.

Threats
Survival of the small relic populations that have remained in Ireland depends on maintenance of rather precise hydrological and chemical conditions. Drainage, water pollution, overgrazing, undergrazing or afforestation could all pose threats. However, the greatest risk is probably from botanists and bryologists since the wet fen habitat is very fragile and at risk from damage due to

trampling. The populations of *P. squarrosa* are also too small to withstand thoughtless (and illegal) specimen collecting.

Conservation
P. squarrosa is protected in the Republic of Ireland by the Flora (Protection) Order, 1999. Its populations are all on protected land.

Protected sites with recent records: Bellacorick Bog Complex SAC; **Unprotected sites with recent records:** none.

Meesia uliginosa Hedw.

Broad-nerved Hump-moss

syn. *M. trichodes* Spruce
Status in Ireland: Endangered (D); **Status in Europe:** Least Concern

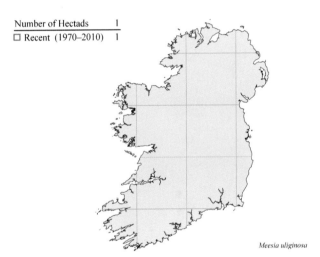

Number of Hectads	1
☐ Recent (1970–2010)	1

Meesia uliginosa

Identification
A moss that grows in dark green tufts 10–50 mm high, or scattered among other bryophytes. The leaves are lingulate to linear-lanceolate with obtuse to rounded apex and a very stout costa that occupies at least half of the width of the leaf base but ends below the apex. Leaf margins are entire and recurved below. Leaf cells are smooth, rectangular above, narrowly rectangular towards the leaf base. Capsules are erect but somewhat curved and asymmetrical, narrowly pyriform, exserted on a thin seta 10–40 mm high. In the field, the capsules recall those of *Amblyodon dealbatus*, but the narrow, blunt leaves with a broad strong costa are very different.

Distribution in Ireland
A small population was discovered in 2002 in sand dunes SE of Rosepenna in West Donegal.

Ecology and biology
Known only from a small area of unshaded, wet, calcareous dune slack, where it grows with other bryophytes and low sedges and herbs in short open vegetation on humic sand. In Britain and Scandinavia, the species grows in calcareous dune slacks and machair near the coasts, but also in the mountains in basic fens, flushes and rock crevices.

Patches of *M. uliginosa* are apparently perennial. The plants are autoicous or synoicous and commonly produce capsules which mature in late spring or summer. Gemmae and tubers are unknown.

World distribution
This species is widespread in Europe from the Arctic in Iceland, Svalbard and Fennoscandia southwards to N. Wales, the Pyrenees, Alps and Carpathians. It is listed as

445

Extinct in the Netherlands, *Critically Endangered* in the Czech Republic and Spain, *Vulnerable* in Bulgaria, Germany and Serbia and Montenegro and 'rare' in Estonia. In Europe, it is assigned to a Circumpolar Boreo-arctic montane floristic element. Elsewhere, it is known in Asia (from the Arctic southwards to the Caucasus, Himalaya, Mongolia and China), Greenland, N. America (from Arctic south to California and New York State), Tierra del Fuego and Antarctica.

Threats
The small population in W. Donegal is vulnerable to disturbance of the wet dune slack in which it grows, such as might arise from hydrological changes, damage from off-road vehicles, overgrazing and excessive poaching by stock. However, some grazing and disturbance is probably necessary to prevent a closed cover of herbaceous vegetation developing that would shade the open niches needed by *M. uliginosa*.

Conservation
The site in W. Donegal is on protected land.

Protected sites with recent records: Sheephaven SAC; **Unprotected sites with recent records:** none.

Meesia triquetra (A.Richter) Ångstr.

Three-ranked Hump-moss

syn. *M. trifaria* H.A.Crum *et al.*, *M. tristicha* Bruch
Status in Ireland: Regionally Extinct; **Status in Europe:** Least Concern

Number of Hectads	1
+ Old (pre-1970)	1

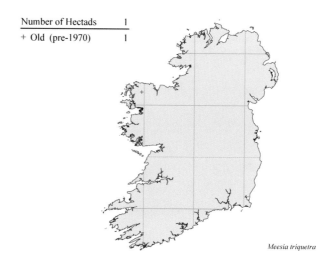

Meesia triquetra

Identification
This is a handsome moss that grows in large lax bright green patches with stems up to 5 cm high. The leaves are trifarious, squarrose, with an erect sheathing basal part, narrowly triangular lamina and a strong costa. Leaf margins are plane, sharply serrate almost from the base. The leaf cells are smooth, pellucid, shortly rectangular in the upper part of the leaf and rectangular near leaf base. Capsules are narrowly pyriform, asymmetrical, erect but curved and exserted on a long thin seta. It somewhat resembles *Dichodontium palustre* or *D. pellucidum* in the field, but differs from both in the trifarious leaves. Other differences are that the former species has untoothed leaf margins; the latter has papillose upper leaf cells.

Distribution in Ireland
Discovered in 1957 by A.L.K. King in W. Mayo in 'T.A.E. Bog stretching N. of the road between Dooleeg and Bellacorick' where a stream called Sruffaunnamuingabatia is deflected by a low gravel ridge. It was seen there again in 1958. Although the immediate vicinity of the site has been protected, the blanket peat was subsequently removed from surrounding areas by Bord na Móna. Despite repeated searches the population has not been refound since 1958 and by 2003 the flushed ground had become drier, so the population is almost certainly extinct. The species is also known in Ireland as a Littletonian (postglacial) fossil in Kildare (Barry & Synnott 1970).

Ecology and biology

M. triquetra formerly grew in a calcareous flush that was rich in iron on very gently sloping peaty ground within an extensive area of blanket bog. It occurred in five almost pure patches with some *Sphagnum denticulatum* growing through them. The site was near small areas of open water in the wettest and richest part of the flush, close to patches of luxuriant growth of *Rhizomnium pseudopunctatum* (Warburg 1958a, King & Scannell 1960). In Fennoscandia 'it is not generally common in the Scandes but must be considered as a normal component of subalpine and low-alpine rich fens' (Mårtensson 1956).

The species grows as perennial patches. It is dioicous and capsules (unrecorded in Ireland) mature in summer. Gemmae and tubers are unknown.

World distribution

Widespread in N. and C. Europe from Iceland, Svalbard and Fennoscandia southwards, but only on mountains further south, including Pyrenees, Spanish Central Ranges and Caucasus. It is listed as *Extinct* in the Netherlands, *Critically Endangered* in the Czech Republic and Germany, Serbia and Spain, and *Near Threatened* in Switzerland. In Europe, it is assigned to a Circumpolar Boreo-arctic montane floristic element. Elsewhere, it is recorded in N. Africa, N. Asia, China, Greenland, N. America and SE Australia.

Threats

There can be little doubt that *M. triquetra* became extinct in Ireland due to drying of the flush where it grew as a consequence of large-scale mechanised extraction of peat from surrounding areas of blanket bog.

Conservation

Peat extraction by Bord na Móna has ceased in the Bellacorick area and ecological restoration of the areas involved has commenced. It is possible that surveys to find this plant may yet be successful, as apparently suitable habitat remains in some neighbouring, intact blanket bog flushes.

Protected sites with recent records: none; **Unprotected sites with recent records:** none.

Amblyodon dealbatus (Hedw.) Bruch & Schimp.   Short-tooth Hump-moss

Status in Ireland: Least Concern; **Status in Europe:** Least Concern

An acrocarpous moss that grows in dune slacks, damp hollows in machair, open basic fens and on ledges of limestone and sandstone crags. It was included in the Provisional Red List (Holyoak 2006b) but recent fieldwork has shown it to be widespread in the western machairs, with some large populations. There are now reports from 17 vice-counties, with records from 31 hectads (15 old, 21 recent, 2 undated). There is evidence of decline from some coastal sand-dune areas (e.g. Dublin, Down, Antrim), due mainly to loss of dune-slack habitats.

Zygodon rupestris Schimp. ex Lorentz   Park Yoke-moss

syn. *Z. baumgartneri* Malta, *Z. viridissimus* var. *rupestris* C.Hartm., *Z. viridissimus* var. *vulgaris* Malta, *Z. vulgaris* Nyholm
Status in Ireland: Least Concern; **Status in Europe:** Least Concern

An acrocarpous moss that grows mainly as an epiphyte on tree trunks, less often on rocks. It was included in the Provisional Red List (Holyoak 2006b), but fieldwork over the past decade has shown that it was previously under-recorded. It is now reported from 11 vice-counties, with records from 14 hectads (4 old, 12 recent). In the past decade it has been found at 12 localities in Kerry, where it appears to be locally frequent on oak trunks.

Orthotrichum rivulare Turner   River Bristle-moss

Status in Ireland: Near Threatened; **Status in Europe:** Least Concern

An acrocarpous moss that grows in the periodically inundated zone beside rivers (or less often lakes), usually on rock or bark. Fieldwork over the past decade has found numerous additional populations and there are now reports from 17 vice-counties, with records from 43 hectads (28 old, 15 recent, 1 undated). There is no evidence of any widespread or substantial decline and the species is probably still under-recorded.

Orthotrichum sprucei Mont.

Spruce's Bristle-moss

Status in Ireland: Vulnerable (B2a, biii); **Status in Europe:** Rare

Number of Hectads	8
+ Old (pre-1970)	2
□ Recent (1970–2010)	7

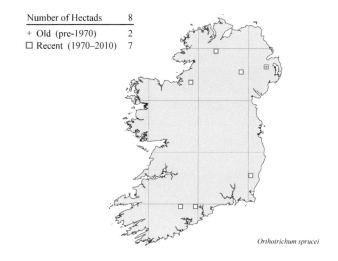

Orthotrichum sprucei

Identification

A rather small acrocarpous moss that grows as scattered plants or small dull or dark green tufts, often encrusted with silt, with stems 5–10 mm high. The leaves are erecto-patent, lingulate, lanceolate or oblanceolate with a rounded apex (often with a small mucro). The costa is evanescent and the leaf margin is recurved. Cells in mid-leaf are isodiametric, large for the genus (16–24 μm across), with thick walls. The capsule is erect, ovate-ellipsoid, striate when mature, with immersed stomata, peristome teeth reflexed when dry, emergent on a short seta. The calyptra is glabrous. *O. rivulare* is a more common species of river flood zones which also has blunt leaves, but it is a larger plant with smaller cells in the upper part of the leaf (mainly 10–14 μm).

Distribution in Ireland

There are recent records from 10 localities in seven vice-counties: E. Cork (R. Bride at Little Grace, 1999; Killavullen Bridge, 2009); Waterford (Tallowbridge, 1999; N. of Ballynerroon East, 2007); Wexford (Camolin, 1975–2000); Leitrim (2 km SW of Manorhamilton, 2000; below Gortgarriganbridge, 2000); Tyrone (River Finn at Carricklee, 2009); Armagh (The Argory, 2004) and Down (Drum Bridge, 1878–2002). There are older records from Waterford (Dromore, 1877; Lismore, 1877); Down (by Lagan Canal near Belfast, 1924; bye-wash on Lagan, 1924) and Antrim (Drum Bridge, 1879). A report from N. Kerry (Ross's Bay, 1861) is unconfirmed.

Ecology and biology

O. sprucei occupies a distinctive habitat as an epiphyte on trunks of trees within the regularly inundated flood zone beside lowland rivers, often on bark that is silt-encrusted. Irish records of phorophytes are of Alder (6), willows (3), Grey Willow (2) and Ash (2), at typical heights of 0.5–1.7 m above summer water levels. Associated species often include *Leskea polycarpa*, *Orthotrichum affine*, *O. diaphanum* and *Syntrichia latifolia*. Its habitats in Britain and continental Europe are very similar, although there are also occasional records from flood-zone rocks, exposed roots and wooden palings.

The plants are perennial. It is an autoicous species on which capsules are usually present, maturing in summer. Gemmae occur occasionally on the leaves and they are produced on the protonema in culture; tubers and bulbils are absent.

World distribution

Mainly in W. Europe, in Britain (S. Scotland southwards to S. England), Ireland, Netherlands (recorded in 1878 but described in the Dutch checklist as 'very rare and susceptible'), Belgium, France, N. and C. Spain (Lara *et al.* 2000) (listed as *Data Deficient*) and N. Portugal (*Data Deficient*); recently found once along the Lower Rhine in Germany ('extremely rare') and once in Hungary (Erzberger & Papp 2000, Frey *et al.* 2006). It is assigned to a Temperate Oceanic floristic element in Europe. The species has been regarded as endemic to Europe, but it has recently been reported from Turkey (Erdağ & Kürschner 2000) and Kazakhstan (Goffinet 2002). An old record from N. America was shown to represent misidentified *O. rivulare* by Vitt (1973).

Threats

It is not immediately threatened at any of the Irish localities that have been visited in the past decade. The main potential threat is from removal of waterside trees, but it would also be at risk if river flooding regimes are altered, afforestation occurs on riverbanks, or possibly if river water becomes eutrophicated or polluted (e.g. with sewage).

Conservation

This species is protected under the Flora (Protection) Order, 1999 in the Republic of Ireland and is listed as a

Northern Ireland Priority Species. Several Irish populations are on protected land. It is treated as a Priority Species within the UK BAP, but little action has resulted from this because strong populations still occur along some British rivers and there is scanty evidence of declines.

Protected sites with recent records: Blackwater River (Cork/Waterford) SAC; Lough Gill SAC; River Foyle and Tributaries SAC; Slaney River Valley SAC; **Unprotected sites with recent records:** Drum Bridge; The Argory (but owned by the National Trust).

Orthotrichum stramineum Hornsch. ex Brid.

Straw Bristle-moss

Status in Ireland: Vulnerable (B2a, bii, iv); **Status in Europe:** Least Concern

Number of Hectads	17
+ Old (pre-1970)	13
□ Recent (1970–2010)	7

Orthotrichum stramineum

Identification

An acrocarpous moss that grows as light green or yellowish-green tufts, 5–10 mm high. As in most *Orthotrichum* species, the leaves are lanceolate, acute, little altered when dry, with recurved margins and a costa ending just below the apex. Cells in mid-leaf are rounded and papillose. The capsules are emergent on a short seta, ellipsoid when moist, very narrow and constricted below the mouth when dry and empty, orange-brown, with eight ribs at maturity. Several other characters of the capsule are important for identification, including the immersed

stomata (largely obscured by exothecial cells), the exostome of eight pairs of finely papillose yellowish teeth (reflexed when dry) and the endostome formed of eight smooth processes. The calyptra is plicate and glabrous or sparsely hairy with a dark or blackish tip that often provides a useful field character. The vaginula has numerous long hairs that are a distinctive feature of this species.

Distribution in Ireland

There are recent records from nine localities in six vice-counties: N. Kerry (Knockeennahone Bridge, 2009);

Kilkenny (S. of Graiguenamanagh, 2005); Wexford (S. of Clonough Bridge, 1975); Carlow (W. of Ballykeenan, 2005); Wicklow (Trooperstown Wood, 1988; Glendalough, Seven Churches, 1872–2007; Kilmacurragh Arboretum, Westaston, 2007; near Powerscourt Waterfall, 2009) and Louth (near Marble Bridge in Ravensdale Park, 2007). There are old records from at least 10 other localities: N. Kerry (Ross Bay, 1863; Muckross, 1872); N. Tipperary (near Roscrea, 1911); Kilkenny (Graiguenamanagh, 1907); Wexford (Strokestown, 1907); Wicklow (Rathdrum, 1878; Woodenbridge, 1878); Down (Tollymore Park, 1885 and 1926; Rostrevor Wood, 1928) and Antrim (Fair Head, before 1880). A recent record from Fermanagh and several additional old records from Down remain unconfirmed.

Ecology and biology

An epiphyte on bark of trees or less often bushes, with recent records from Ash (twice), Beech, Elder and Sycamore and old records from at least Beech and willows. Several of the sites are near streams or rivers or at edges of woodland. Elsewhere in Europe, it is recorded from a wider range of trees and shrubs and rarely also on rock (Lewinsky-Haapasaari 1995).

Tufts probably persist for several years. The species is autoicous and produces abundant capsules (although unidentifiable without sporophytes) that mature in summer. Tubers and gemmae are unknown.

World distribution

Widespread in Europe from Iceland and Norway southwards to Portugal, Spain and the Caucasus, but listed as *Vulnerable* in Finland and Germany and 'very rare' in Estonia. It is assigned to a European Temperate floristic element in Europe. Elsewhere, the species is recorded in N. Africa, Turkey, Cyprus, China and Newfoundland (where possibly introduced).

Threats

Like most epiphytes, *O. stramineum* is potentially vulnerable to loss of the trees on which it grows and to atmospheric pollutants that include sulphur dioxide and nitrogen compounds. Clearance of Elder scrub is a particular threat at some sites.

Conservation

This species is protected under the Flora (Protection) Order, 1999 in the Republic of Ireland. Few of the sites with recent records are on protected land.

Protected sites with recent records: Powerscourt Waterfall pNHA; Ravensdale Plantation pNHA; **Unprotected sites with recent records:** Glendalough, Seven Churches; Kilmacurragh Arboretum, Westaston; Knockeennahone Bridge; S. of Clonough Bridge; S. of Graiguenamanagh; Trooperstown Wood (possibly within Wicklow Mountains SAC); W. of Ballykeenan.

Orthotrichum pallens Bruch ex Brid.

Pale Bristle-moss

Status in Ireland: Endangered (B1a, bi, ii, iv, B2a, bi, ii, iv); **Status in Europe:** Least Concern

Identification

An acrocarpous moss that grows as small green tufts, 5–10 mm high. As in most other *Orthotrichum* species, the leaves are lanceolate, more or less acute, little altered when dry, with recurved margins and a costa ending just below the apex. Cells in mid-leaf are rounded and papillose. The capsules are emergent on a short seta, ellipsoid, pale yellowish-brown, with eight ribs at maturity. Other characters of the capsule that are important for identification include the immersed stomata (hardly obscured by exothecial cells), the exostome of eight pairs of finely papillose yellowish to pale orange teeth (reflexed when dry) and the endostome

formed of eight smooth processes. The calyptra is plicate and glabrous; the vaginula also lacks hairs.

Distribution in Ireland

There are two recent records, from Carlow (W. of Ballykeenan, 2005) and E. Mayo (E. of Ballintober, 1970). Four old records also appear to be correct: Mid Cork (Cork, 1872) and Wicklow (Rathdrum, 1872; Westaston, undated in 19th century; Seven Churches, 1915). Other old reports are unacceptable because they include known errors (W. Galway: near Galway, 1856; Dublin: between Baldoyle and Malahide, 1871), no specimen has been traced (NE Galway) or

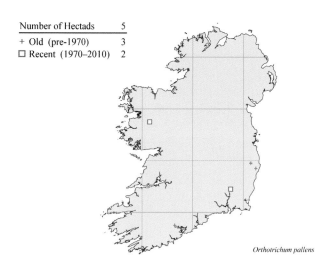

Number of Hectads	5
+ Old (pre-1970)	3
☐ Recent (1970–2010)	2

Orthotrichum pallens

they might be fraudulent (Dublin: Dunsink, 1867 and 1871).

Ecology and biology
Both recent records are from the bark of Sycamore trees. The Carlow record is from a trunk at the edge of a track in mixed deciduous and coniferous woodland. British records are from the bark of Alder, Ash, Elder, Hazel, Holly, Sycamore, willow and Wych Elm, often in rather open but humid sites such as riversides (C.D. Preston in Hill *et al.* 1994, Hodgetts 2003); it has also been found on dead wood and on a wooden fence. In continental Europe, it is recorded from a wider range of tree genera and also occasionally on rock (Lewinsky-Haapasaari 1995).

Tufts of the species appear to be short-lived, although the plants recolonise readily (Hodgetts 2003). *O. pallens* is autoicous and appears to commonly produce sporophytes. Tubers are unknown; foliar gemmae have been reported from American plants (Vitt 1973).

World distribution
Widespread in Europe from Svalbard and Scandinavia southwards to E. Spain, Corsica (Sotiaux *et al.* 2007), Italy and the Caucasus. In Britain, it is very rare and known only from a few localities in E. Scotland and N. England (Bosanquet 2009). It is listed as *Endangered* in Britain and Germany, *Near Threatened* in Luxembourg and 'rare' in the Netherlands. The species is assigned to a European Boreo-temperate floristic element in Europe. Elsewhere, it is known in Morocco (Draper *et al.* 2006), Turkey, Greenland, N. America, Mexico and Venezuela.

Threats
The population discovered in Carlow in 2005 was part of a single small tuft, the remainder of which consisted of *O. stramineum*. The species could not be refound at the locality in E. Mayo in 2003, nor in any of the Wicklow sites when searched in 2007. It therefore seems likely that these records resulted from temporary colonisation following long-distance dispersal. C.D. Preston (in Hill *et al.* 1994) commented that 'at most of its British and Irish sites it is known only from a single collection', but the species is now known from many trees in at least six sites in Weardale, Co. Durham (Hodgetts 2003), where the population appears to be resilient, and was recently refound at one of its Yorkshire sites (Rothero 2006).

Conservation
This species is protected under the Flora (Protection) Order, 1999 in the Republic of Ireland. No other conservation action is proposed unless an established population of the species is discovered (or rediscovered).

Protected sites with recent records: none; **Unprotected sites with recent records:** E. of Ballintober; W. of Ballykeenan.

452

Ulota coarctata (P.Beauv.) Hammar

Club Pincushion

syn. *U. ludwigii* Brid.
Status in Ireland: Critically Endangered (D); **Status in Europe:** Regionally Threatened

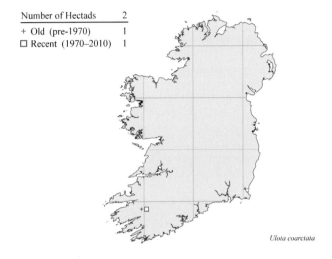

Number of Hectads	2
+ Old (pre-1970)	1
□ Recent (1970–2010)	1

Ulota coarctata

Identification

This is an acrocarpous moss that grows in small green or dull green tufts up to 10 mm high. The leaves are only slightly twisted when dry. They are lanceolate above a wider and concave basal part, with evanescent costa and plane or recurved entire margins. Cells in mid-leaf are oval or rounded, slightly papillose, with incrassate cell walls; marginal cells are quadrate-rectangular; basal cells are narrowly rectangular to linear. Capsules are exserted on a seta 4.0–4.5 mm long, erect, narrowly pyriform, smooth except just below the very narrow mouth, pale brown, becoming whitish and inflated when dry and empty. Calyptrae are hairy. The most important distinction from other species of *Ulota* is in the form and colour of the capsules.

Distribution in Ireland

Found recently only at two adjacent sites NW of Loo Bridge (N. Kerry) in 2005. There was a poorly localised record from the Killarney region in 1967. All the other old records, also from the Killarney area, were from 1861: Glena (S. Kerry) and Torc Wood (N. Kerry); another 'Killarney' record from 1861 may be the same as these.

Ecology and biology

Recent records have been of tufts growing on bark of branches of Grey Willow and a moribund Hazel, 1–2.5 m above the ground, inside open scrub and at the edge of scrub on the base of a rocky (sandstone) slope. In Scotland, it grows as an epiphyte on birch, oak, willow and other trees and bushes in sheltered humid places; a few records from S. England were on Elder and hybrid black poplars.

Tufts of *U. coarctata* probably persist for several years but details are unknown. The species is autoicous and frequently produces capsules which mature in autumn. Tubers and gemmae are unknown.

World distribution

It occurs in W. and C. Europe from about the Arctic Circle in Norway southwards through Scotland, Scandinavia and Estonia to N. and NW Spain, the Alps and Caucasus. The species has shown a marked decline in Germany north of the Alps (Meinunger & Schröder 2007), and is listed as *Critically Endangered* in the Czech Republic and Switzerland, *Endangered* in Germany and Luxembourg, *Vulnerable* in Sweden, *Data Deficient* in Spain and 'very rare' in Estonia and 'very rare and susceptible' in the Netherlands. It is assigned to a Suboceanic Boreal-montane floristic element in Europe. Elsewhere, it is widespread in eastern N. America (Newfoundland to Wisconsin and Michigan, south to North Carolina, Georgia and Tennessee; also Idaho: Crum & Anderson 1981).

Threats
Potentially at risk from scrub clearance, from shading if scrub turns into woodland or becomes heavily infested with Rhododendron, or from atmospheric pollution.

Conservation
Much of the native woodland in the Killarney region is on protected land.

Protected sites with recent records: Killarney National Park, Macgillycuddy's Reeks and Caragh River Catchment SAC; **Unprotected sites with recent records:** none.

Ulota drummondii (Hook. & Grev.) Brid.

syn. *Weissia drummondii* (Hook. & Grev.) Lindb.
Status in Ireland: Regionally Extinct; **Status in Europe:** Least Concern

Drummond's Pincushion

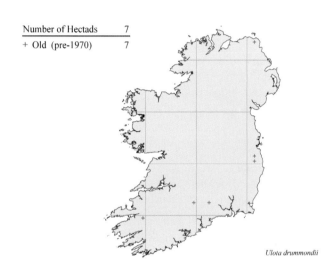

Number of Hectads	7
+ Old (pre-1970)	7

Ulota drummondii

Identification
An attractive acrocarpous moss that grows epiphytically in tufts or small spreading patches. Its stems are 5–10 mm high, with lanceolate to narrowly lanceolate leaves, wider basally, acute or acuminate at the apex, with margins plane or recurved below and costa ending below the apex. Mid-leaf cells are rhomboidal to rounded and papillose. The pale brown capsules are ovoid to ellipsoid, erect, exserted on a seta 3–5 mm long, narrowed at the mouth and furrowed when dry; covered by a hairy calyptra when young.

Careful study of both leaf and peristome characters is necessary to avoid confusion with forms of the variable and much more common *U. bruchii* and *U. crispa*. In *U. drummondii* the leaves are curved (not crisped) when dry, marginal branches of tufts are often procumbent, exostome teeth (when dry and in good condition) are whitish, flexuose and erect to spreading, and the endostome is at most rudimentary and often absent. The

number of stomata on the capsule has been shown to be an unreliable character (Erzberger 2003). Mistakes in identification often arise because fresh exostome teeth in the common species can occasionally be whitish or erect or spreading, and they often become whitish in really old capsules. Some *U. bruchii* also have leaves that are merely curved when dry.

Distribution in Ireland
Records recently confirmed from voucher specimens are from (at least) 10 sites in six vice-counties, the most recent in 1966: N. Kerry (Turk Mountain, 1829; Lusk, Killarney, 1857; Killarney, undated); Waterford (Gurteen Wood, 1852); S. Tipperary (plantation N. of Lough Muskry, Galty Mountains, 1966); Wicklow (Powerscourt Waterfall, 1859; Seven Churches, undated; between Roundwood and [?] Annamoe, Seven Churches, undated; 'Luggielaw', undated); W. Donegal (near Mid Town, Mulroy Bay, 1962); Antrim (Breen, Glenshesk,

1957). Reports from 10 other vice-counties include known misidentifications and records based on specimens too poor to allow reliable identification (S. Kerry, N. Tipperary, W. Galway, W. Mayo, Dublin, Sligo, Fermanagh, E. Donegal, Tyrone, Down).

It was only realised during 2009 that many Irish records of this species are erroneous and that so few reliable records exist. The complete absence of recent records is therefore likely to result mainly from lack of attempts to refind the species at its old sites during the fieldwork of the past decade. However, visits to five of the rather poorly localised old sites in September 2009 (in S. Tipperary, Waterford and Wicklow) failed to refind it. Hence it is by no means certain it is now *Regionally Extinct*, but the absence of new finds leaves no doubt that the species is at least rare in Ireland.

Ecology and biology

U. drummondii is an epiphyte that grows on trunks, branches and twigs of trees and shrubs. Reliable information on its habitats in Ireland is scanty, including records from an Ash bole (S. Tipperary), a young larch (Waterford), trees including 'Grey Birches' (Wicklow), trees in a wood (W. Donegal) and on trees in several places in oak and birch woods (Antrim). In Britain, its phorophytes include birch, Hazel, Rowan, Alder, Juniper and willow and it grows most commonly in wet upland areas, at up to 620 m elevation (M.C.F. Proctor in Hill *et al.* 1994). Scandinavian accounts mention occurrence on smooth bark of such deciduous trees as Hazel, Aspen, oaks and willows and very rarely also on stones (Hallingbäck *et al.* 2008).

The species is autoicous and sporophytes are common, with spores maturing in autumn. There are no reports of gemmae, bulbils, or tubers, but vegetative propagation possibly occurs from detached leaves or stem fragments.

World distribution

U. drummondii is a northern species in Europe, occurring in N. Scotland, N. Wales, Norway (where it reaches the Arctic), C. and S. Sweden, the Åland Islands, Latvia and Estonia. It has or had outlying localities further south in the Vosges, Tatra and Carpathians (including Ukraine), and formerly in N., C. and S. Germany (where it became extinct more than a century ago: Meinunger & Schröder 2007). It is assigned to a Suboceanic Boreal-montane floristic element in Europe. Elsewhere, it is known in the Russian Far East (Ignatov *et al.* 2007), Japan and northern N. America (British Columbia north to the Aleutians; Quebec and Newfoundland; D.H. Vitt in BFNA online web site, 2003).

Threats

There is no recent information on populations in Ireland. A decline is clearly apparent from the southern edge of its range in Germany, but apparently not in Wales (Hill *et al.* 1994).

Conservation

There is an urgent need for a targeted survey seeking the species at the sites in Ireland with old records, especially those in S. Tipperary, W. Donegal and Antrim. This would be best carried out in early autumn, when capsules should have the intact peristomes needed for accurate identification.

Protected sites with recent records: none; **Unprotected sites with recent records:** none.

Hedwigia ciliata (Hedw.) P.Beauv. var. *ciliata*

Fringed Hoar-moss

syn. *H. albicans* auct. pro parte
Status in Ireland: Vulnerable (D2); **Status in Europe:** Least Concern

Identification

A trailing or prostrate moss of rock surfaces that grows as green or brownish-green patches (rough mats) that are greyish-green when dry, with irregularly branched stems up to 10 cm long. Stem leaves are 1.7–2.3 mm long, erecto-patent to spreading when moist, erect when dry, slightly homomallous or falcate when moist, ovate, tapering to an acuminate, spinosely toothed hyaline apex. The leaves are ecostate with margin recurved below. Mid-leaf cells are quadrate to rectangular, incrassate to strongly incrassate, with 1–3 papillae on both adaxial and abaxial surfaces. Capsules are obloid or shortly obovoid, with operculum almost flat to low-conical, subsessile among the narrow perichaetial leaves which have ciliate

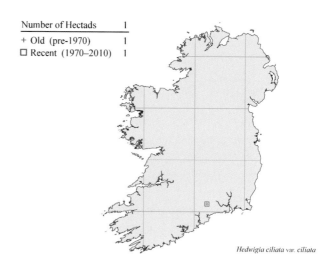

Number of Hectads	1
+ Old (pre-1970)	1
□ Recent (1970–2010)	1

Hedwigia ciliata var. ciliata

margins. Studies by Hedenäs (1994) revealed that *H. ciliata* consists of three taxa in Europe, of which Crundwell (1995) found mainly the newly described *H. stellata* amongst specimens from Ireland, with only one locality for *H. ciliata* var. *ciliata*. The most obvious differences between them are that *H. stellata* has mid-leaf cells mainly unipapillose (not 1–4 papillose) and the apex of the hair-point usually pointed (not truncate and crowned with 2–5 papillae). *H. ciliata* consists of two varieties, var. *leucophaea* (unknown in Ireland) having a longer hair-point that is more strongly papillose.

Distribution in Ireland

Known only from Sgilloge Loughs (Waterford). Specimens collected in 1966 were identified as the segregate species by Crundwell (1995). In 2007, it was present in five locations around Sgilloge Loughs, in some abundance locally.

Ecology and biology

At the only known Irish locality it grows on boulders by a lake shore at around 385 m elevation. In Britain, it grows on non-calcareous rocks in a wide range of habitats, also on walls and on tiled or stone roofs, most of the rather few records from natural habitats being from the shores of lakes (Crundwell 1995). Based mainly on Swedish data, Hedenäs (1994) reported this taxon from rocks and boulders in both exposed and more protected habitats (e.g. open forests), on siliceous substrata or in slightly base-rich habitats; occasionally, also on tree trunks or rotten wood.

The plants are perennial. It is an autoicous species in which capsules are frequent (in Sweden at least),

maturing in spring. Gemmae, bulbils and tubers are unknown, but vegetative propagation presumably occurs from detached leaf and stem fragments.

World distribution

Distributional data for *H. ciliata* var. *ciliata* from prior to 1994 are confused because *H. stellata* and *H. ciliata* var. *leucophaea* were not separated. Var. *ciliata* is now known to occur throughout Fennoscandia, locally in Britain (from N. Scotland to S. England; listed as *Near Threatened* in Britain) and over much of W. Europe southwards to Portugal and Spain. *H. ciliata* is listed as *Vulnerable* in the Netherlands and 'presumably threatened' in Germany. It is assigned to a Circumpolar Boreo-temperate floristic element in Europe. Elsewhere, the segregate is known in N. America, but it is unclear how much of the rest of the near-cosmopolitan range of the aggregate species is attributable to this taxon.

Threats

No immediate threats to the species were apparent at Sgilloge Loughs in 2007. It is potentially vulnerable to shading, (e.g. from afforestation), which is unlikely to occur in that area.

Conservation

The locality at Sgilloge Loughs is on protected land.

Protected sites with recent records: Comeragh Mountains SAC; **Unprotected sites with recent records:** none.

Hedwigia integrifolia P.Beauv.

Green Hoar-moss

syn. *H. imberbis* (Sm.) Spruce, *Hedwigidium integrifolium* (P.Beauv.) Dixon
Status in Ireland: Vulnerable (B2a, bii, iv); **Status in Europe:** Rare

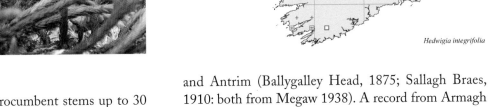

Number of Hectads	14
+ Old (pre-1970)	12
□ Recent (1970–2010)	7

Hedwigia integrifolia

Identification

An acrocarpous moss with procumbent stems up to 30 mm long, forming tufts or patches that are yellowish-green above and brownish below. Leaves are imbricate when dry, erecto-patent when moist, ovate, acute or acuminate, concave, with recurved margins and lacking a costa. Leaf cells are narrowly rectangular at the base and extending up the middle of the leaf, rounded-quadrate or quadrate-rectangular and pluripapillose in the upper part of the leaf and towards the margins. Capsules are obloid, scarcely emergent, on a seta about 1 mm long.

H. integrifolia lacks the white hair-points of the more common *H. stellata*, but resembles that species in general appearance, growth habit and the character of the leaf cells and sporophytes.

Distribution in Ireland

Recent records are from eight localities in six vice-counties: S. Kerry (Derrynane House, 2 km west of Caherdaniel, 1951–2007); W. Cork (Glengarriff, 1829–2006; Mount Gunnery, 2009); Waterford (Coumshingaun, 1966–2007); Wicklow (Glendalough, 1981); Louth (Carlingford Mountain, 2010; Windy Gap, 2010) and Antrim (Fair Head, 1879–1999). There are old records from nine additional localities: S. Kerry (Kenmare, undated; by Cloonaghlin Lough, 1951; Brandon Mountain, 1872); W. Cork (Bantry, 1912; Adrigole, 1963); Wicklow (Lugnaquilla, 1872; Luggala, undated)

and Antrim (Ballygalley Head, 1875; Sallagh Braes, 1910: both from Megaw 1938). A record from Armagh (Slieve Gullion, 1967, leg. R.E. Parker) requires confirmation.

Ecology and biology

It grows on unshaded or lightly shaded surfaces of sloping, mildly acidic rocks of crags, outcrops and boulders, including sandstone, dolerite and varied metamorphic lithologies, from near sea level to 460 m altitude.

Patches of the species live for at least several years. It is autoicous and occasionally produces capsules, which mature in early summer. Gemmae and tubers are unknown.

World distribution

It occurs in W. Europe from SW Norway to N. Spain and eastwards to C. and E. France and N. Italy and is listed as *Near Threatened* in Spain and 'declining' in Norway. It is assigned to an Oceanic Temperate floristic element in Europe. Elsewhere, it is known from E. and S. Africa, Caucasus, Sri Lanka, Réunion, C. America, northern S. America and Australasia.

Threats

Reasons for the apparent decline in Ireland are unknown; no comparable decline is evident in Britain. Some populations of *H. integrifolia* are probably vulnerable to shading if scrub or saplings grow up near to rocks.

Conservation

Several populations are on protected land. *H. integrifolia* is listed as a Northern Ireland Priority Species.

Protected sites with recent records: Carlingford Mountain SAC; Comeragh Mountains SAC; Fair Head

and Murlough Bay ASSI (scheduled for declaration 2011); Glenealo Valley Nature Reserve; Glengarriff Harbour and Woodland SAC; Glengarriff Wood Nature Reserve; Wicklow Mountains National Park; Wicklow Mountains SAC; **Unprotected sites with recent records:** Derrynane House, 2 km west of Caherdaniel (possibly within Kenmare River SAC); Mount Gunnery.

Catoscopium nigritum (Hedw.) Brid.

Down-looking Moss

Status in Ireland: Near Threatened; **Status in Europe:** Least Concern

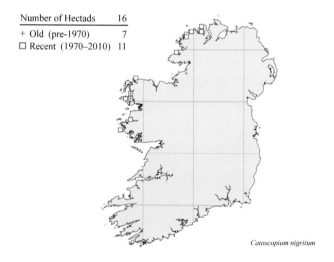

Number of Hectads	16
+ Old (pre-1970)	7
☐ Recent (1970–2010)	11

Catoscopium nigritum

Identification

An acrocarpous moss that typically forms rather dense rounded green cushions up to 4 cm (occasionally 7 cm) high or grows less conspicuously as scattered stems or tufts among other bryophytes. The leaves are lanceolate, tapering gradually to an acuminate apex, with plane, entire margins recurved below and a stout evanescent costa. Mid-leaf cells are quadrate-rectangular, narrower basally and near costa, smooth, with rather thick cell walls throughout. At first sight the leaf characters are reminiscent of those of the common *Ceratodon purpureus*, but that species has the costa percurrent to excurrent and teeth are usually present near the leaf apex. Sporophytes are distinctive, with a small globose capsule (c. 1 mm long), blackish when mature, cernuous and exserted on a slender, rigid seta up to 10 mm in length.

Distribution in Ireland

Recent records are from 13 localities in three vice-counties: W. Galway (W. of Aillebrack, 2004); W. Mayo

(Keel, Achill Island, 1987–2003; near Lough Doo, Achill Island, 1965–2009; near Ridge Point, Achill Island, 1987; Dooaghtry, 2003–2009; Garter Hill, 2003–2009) and W. Donegal (Rossbeg, NW of Ardara, 1970; W. of Dunfanaghy, 1990; N. of Lough Nagreany, 2002; NW of Carrick, 2002; NW of Derrybeg, 2002–2009; south of Glashagh Lower, 2002; SE of Rosepenna, 2002–2009). Older records are from a further five localities in a further three vice-counties: E. Donegal (Bundoran, 1937); Antrim (Portrush, 1925–1928) and Londonderry (Magilligan, 1900–1944; SE of Castlerock, 1944; Portstewart, 1947). Several new finds in the last decade imply the species had previously been somewhat overlooked, at least where it occurs only as small non-fertile populations. Particularly close attention was also given to surveying dune-slack habitats in this recent fieldwork. Failure to refind populations near Bundoran and at all localities in Antrim and Londonderry over the same period points to local extinctions.

Ecology and biology

Most Irish populations grow in dune slacks or damp hollows in machair, in moist, basic places, prone to shallow flooding, with short, species-rich, open vegetation on calcareous, nutrient-poor sand. It has also been found on the bank of a small stream on a machair slope and in rather muddy fen in a dune slack. In Britain and elsewhere in Europe, it also grows in the mountains in flushes and around calcareous springs, often on semi-open rocky ground.

The plants are perennial with at least the large cushions persisting for several years. The species is dioicous but capsules are frequent, with spores maturing in autumn. Tubers, gemmae and bulbils are unknown, although some vegetative propagation might occur from dispersal of leaf or stem fragments.

World distribution

Mainly an Arctic and northern species, occurring in Europe from Iceland, Spitsbergen and N. Fennoscandia southwards to southern limits on high ground in the Pyrenees, Alps, Caucasus and Georgia. It is considered *Extinct* in the Netherlands, *Endangered* in Germany and Spain and *Vulnerable* in Switzerland. It is assigned to a Circumpolar Boreo-arctic montane floristic element in Europe. Elsewhere, it is widespread in N. and C. Asia (southwards to Sayan Mountains), N. America (southwards to British Columbia and the Great Lakes) and in Greenland.

Threats

Loss of populations from coastal dunes in Northern Ireland can be attributed to development of golf courses (Castlerock; Portstewart) and perhaps to cessation or reduction of grazing and other disturbance associated with establishment and use of a large military training camp (Magilligan). Coastal development and disturbance may also have caused the loss of the Bundoran population. Threats to extant populations are now most likely to arise from changes in grazing intensity on machair and dune systems, severe overgrazing resulting in erosion obviously being deleterious, but probably less harmful than cessation of grazing would be in allowing development of tall vegetation cover.

Conservation

Most of the larger populations are on protected land. The species is protected by the Flora (Protection) Order, 1999 in the Republic of Ireland.

Protected sites with recent records: Broadhaven Bay SAC; Doogort Machair/Lough Doo SAC; Glenamoy Bog Complex SAC; Gweedore Bay and Islands SAC; Horn Head and Rinclevan SAC; Keel Machair/Menaun Cliffs SAC; Lough Nagreany Dunes SAC; Mweelrea/Sheeffry/Erriff Complex SAC; Sheephaven SAC; Slyne Head Peninsula SAC; **Unprotected sites with recent records:** Rossbeg, NW of Ardara (possibly within West of Ardara/Maas Road SAC).

Plagiopus oederianus (Sw.) H.A.Crum & L.E.Anderson — Oeder's Apple-moss

syn. *Bartramia oederi* Brid., *Plagiopus oederi* (Brid.) Limpr.
Status in Ireland: Critically Endangered (B1a, bi, ii, iv, B2a, bi, ii, iv); **Status in Europe:** Least Concern

Identification

This is an acrocarpous moss that grows in green tufts up to 60 mm high. The leaves are narrowly lanceolate with an acuminate apex, flexuose or crisped when dry, with costa percurrent or excurrent and margins that are recurved below and toothed above. Cells in mid-leaf are rectangular and minutely verruculose-striate; cells in the lower part of the leaf are longer with similar striae. Capsules are almost globose, asymmetrical, with an oblique mouth, striate, suberect and exserted on a seta 5–15 mm long. *P. oederianus* is similar at first sight to some *Bartramia* species, but differs in the shorter leaves with shorter points, lack of sheathing leaf bases, smaller capsules and minutely striate rather than papillose leaf cells.

Distribution in Ireland

The only recent records are from Peakadaw in Glenade (Leitrim) where it was collected in 1963 and reported again in 1970. Difficulties in obtaining access to the site have prevented a really thorough search there over the last decade. Reliable old records exist from four sites: S. Kerry (Brandon Mountain, 1872); Leitrim (Truskmore, 1909) and Antrim (Sallagh Braes, 1924; Glenarm, 1879). Reports known to be based on misidentified specimens exist from W. Cork or Mid Cork (near Iniscarra, 1891); Down (Slieve Donard, 1870) and Antrim (Colin Glen, 1831; Glenariff, 1889); unconfirmed reports exist from Fermanagh (Marble Arch, 1978) and Antrim (Colin Glen, 1862 and 1879), those from the latter

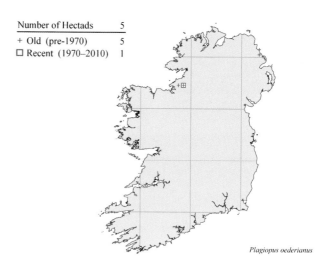

Number of Hectads	5
+ Old (pre-1970)	5
□ Recent (1970–2010)	1

Plagiopus oederianus

locality presumably being incorrect in view of the 1831 record.

Ecology and biology

Specimens from Glenade were collected from limestone or wet limestone at c. 246 m altitude and an old record from Sallagh Braes was from a rock ledge at the foot of the crags. In Britain, it occurs on basic rock ledges and in crevices, mostly on hard calcareous rock, in rocky woods, ravines and on crags, mainly in upland regions (T.L. Blockeel in Hill *et al.* 1994).

Tufts of the species live for at least several years. It is synoicous and capsules are common, maturing in spring and summer. Tubers and gemmae are unknown.

World distribution

P. oederianus is widespread in Europe from Iceland and Svalbard southwards to S. Spain, Italy and the Balkans. It is listed as *Extinct* in the Netherlands, *Endangered* in the Czech Republic, 'rare' in Estonia and 'declining' in Germany. It is assigned to a Circumpolar Boreo-arctic montane floristic element in Europe. Elsewhere, it is known in Turkey, Iran, N. and C. Asia, China, Japan, S. Africa, Hawaii, N. America and Greenland.

Threats

Reasons for the apparent decline of this species in Ireland are unknown. There does not appear to be evidence of any comparable decline in Britain (cf. Hill *et al.* 1994) or Germany (cf. Meinunger & Schröder 2007). Rock-ledge sites on large crags such as those at Peakadaw (Glenade) and Sallagh Braes seem unlikely to have changed much since it was recorded there.

Conservation

Further efforts should be made to obtain permission for access to Peakadaw in order to make a thorough search. The records are very poorly localised and it is not known whether *P. oederianus* occurred on protected land.

Protected sites with recent records: none; **Unprotected sites with recent records:** Peakadaw in Glenade (possibly within Ben Bulben, Gleniff and Glenade Complex, SAC).

Bartramia halleriana Hedw.

Haller's Apple-moss

syn. *Bartramia norvegica* Gunnerus ex Lindb.
Status in Ireland: Regionally Extinct; **Status in Europe:** Least Concern

Identification

This is a large, handsome, tufted, acrocarpous moss with leafy stems up to 150 mm high. It has closely set long-subulate leaves which are erect at the base but spreading and often subsecund above. The leaves are crisped when dry. The capsule is inclined, globose and striate when moist (sulcate when dry), held among the leaves on a curved seta only 2–3 mm long. Two other large species of Bartramiaceae that occur in Ireland could be confused with *B. halleriana*. The common *Bartramia pomiformis* has a much longer seta and somewhat glaucous leaves that are less strongly crisped when dry. The rare *Plagiopus oederianus* also has a longer seta but differs in being a smaller plant with shorter leaves that lack sheathing bases.

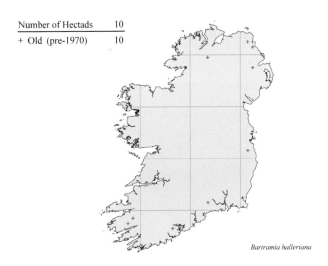

| Number of Hectads | 10 |
| + Old (pre-1970) | 10 |

Bartramia halleriana

Distribution in Ireland

There are old records from 10 localities in six vice-counties: S. Kerry (Purple Mountain, 1904; Ballaghbeama Gap, 1967); Mid Cork (Ballinhassig Glen, 1845); Waterford (Coumshingaun, 1902); Wicklow (Lough Bray, 1804); Tyrone (Strabane Glen, 1914) and Antrim (Carnlough/Glenarm, 1842; Colin Glen, 1879; Glenariff, 1887–1928; Parkmore, 1909). Specimens have been seen only from Glenariff, so some doubt may exist over identification of early records, although the short seta should be distinctive of this species. Attempts to refind it in the past decade have been unsuccessful, although there is some hope that it might still persist in small quantity on a rock ledge. The species has thus shown a long-term decline in Ireland and may now be extinct.

Ecology and biology

The Irish records were from shaded calcareous rock ledges, usually in ravines or on crags. Megaw (1938) described it as occurring on 'damp shady rocks, near water, very rare'. In Britain, it usually grows in dry crevices of moderately calcareous rocks and under overhangs, in wooded ravines, from the lowlands to the mountains. Elsewhere, it is regarded as indifferent to the reaction of the rocks (Augier 1966) or weakly acidophilous (Boros 1968).

The plants are perennial and grow in long-persistent patches. The species is autoicous or synoicous and commonly produces capsules, with spores maturing in summer. Gemmae and tubers are unknown, so vegetative reproduction is likely to occur only from stem fragments or detached leaves.

World distribution

B. halleriana has always been very local in Ireland, but more common in N. and W. Britain from N. Scotland southwards to S. Wales. It has a wide range in Europe from Fennoscandia and N. Russia (Kola Peninsula) southwards to N. Spain, Corsica and the Caucasus, and is listed as *Critically Endangered* in Luxembourg and *Vulnerable* in Germany. In Europe, it is assigned to a European Boreal-montane floristic element. Elsewhere, it is known in Asia (Caucasus, Himalaya, S. China, Japan), along with a few widely isolated localities in N. America (Canadian Rockies), C. America and tropical Africa. Reports from southern S. America, New Guinea, Australasia and Hawaii are referred to *B. mossmaniana* Müll.Hal. in the taxonomic revision by Fransén (2004b).

Threats

Causes of the long-term decline of *B. halleriana* are unknown, since most of its habitats are likely to have changed little since the 19th century. Specimen-collecting during the Victorian era may have destroyed some populations. Since it is a northern and montane species that is presumably at its climatic limits in Ireland, it may now be vulnerable to effects of climate change.

Conservation

Bryophyte surveys in Antrim by NIEA during 1999 failed to rediscover this species at Glenariff or Glenarm, but its other old localities including Colin Glen were not searched. *B. halleriana* should be sought at all of its historic sites and if it is refound appropriate conservation action undertaken.

Protected sites with recent records: none; **Unprotected sites with recent records:** none.

Bartramia ithyphylla Brid.

Straight-leaved Apple-moss

syn. *Bartramia ithyphylla* var. *strigosa* (Wahlenb.) Hartm.
Status in Ireland: Vulnerable (B2a, bii, iv); **Status in Europe:** Least Concern

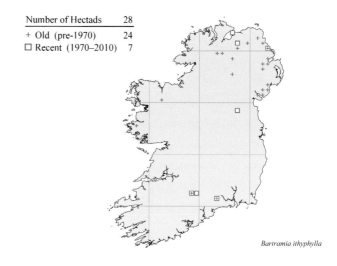

Number of Hectads	28
+ Old (pre-1970)	24
☐ Recent (1970–2010)	7

Bartramia ithyphylla

Identification

An acrocarpous moss that grows as tufts or low turfs 5–40 mm high. The leaves are narrowly lanceolate, glaucous green, spreading as a subula from an erect, white or hyaline, sheathing base. The costa is shortly excurrent and the leaf margins are plane and serrulate. Cells in the upper part of the leaf are narrowly rectangular, opaque and mamillose. *B. ithyphylla* is distinct from other *Bartramia* species in the white, sheathing leaf bases and narrow, mainly bistratose upper leaf cells. The capsule is inclined, globose, striate, with an oblique mouth, exserted on a seta 1–3 cm long.

Distribution in Ireland

Confirmed recent records are from nine localities in six vice-counties: Waterford (Coum Iarthar, 2007); S. Tipperary (Lough Muskry, 2005); Limerick (Carrignabinnia, 1944–2005; Temple Hill, 1966–2005; Knockateriff, Blackrock Glen, 2005); Meath (4 miles NE of Moynalty, 1978); Antrim (N. of Knock Dhu, 1999) and Londonderry (Binevenagh, 1999; Benbradagh, 1986). Older confirmed records are from Waterford (Coumshingaun, 1902); S. Tipperary (Lough Curra, 1966); W. Galway (Kylemore, 1951); W. Mayo (Pontoon, 1903); Louth (Carlingford Mountain, 1890) and W. Donegal (Slieve League, 1903). There are numerous other unconfirmed reports, particularly from Tyrone, Down, Antrim and Londonderry.

Ecology and biology

It is mainly montane in Ireland, but with some records from the lowlands. Most sites are in rock crevices on crags or thin soil over rock, often of mildly basic lithologies such as basalt, and often on N.- or NE-facing slopes in corries. However, it has been found on a roadside wall in Meath and on soil at the edge of rock on a slope below crags in Londonderry. In Britain, it is also predominantly montane (recorded up to 1170 m altitude), typically found in shaded crevices of montane crags, but with some old lowland records from hedge banks in SE England.

The plants are perennial and can be seen in all months of the year. The species is synoicous and frequently produces capsules, which mature in summer. Gemmae and tubers are unknown, but vegetative reproduction might occur from detached leaf or stem fragments.

World distribution

The species is widespread in the Arctic and N. Europe, occurring in Iceland, Spitsbergen, over most of Fennoscandia and widely in N. and W. Britain. In S. Europe, it is mainly montane, reaching Portugal, Spain and the Caucasus, and is listed as *Extinct* in the Netherlands, *Near Threatened* in Luxembourg, 'declining' in Germany and 'very rare' in Estonia. It is assigned to a Circumpolar Boreo-arctic montane floristic element in Europe. Elsewhere, it occurs in N. Africa, widely in

N. and C. Asia, Himalaya, Taiwan, Japan, N. America and Greenland. Following the taxonomic revision by Fransén (2004a), reports from southern S. America are now referred to *B. ithyphylla* subsp. *patens* (Brid.) Fransén and those from S. and E. Africa and Australia are attributed to other species of the genus (cf. Bell 2006).

Threats

Many of the populations of this species are within protected areas. None of the populations reported over the past decade appears to be immediately threatened, although several are small. Overstocking in the uplands and afforestation must both be considered potential threats. The *Vulnerable* threat status is based partly on evidence of decline, but this may be misleading if the species tends to form small, impersistent colonies. Indeed, there have been more new localities recorded over the past decade than failed attempts to refind it at old sites which were accurately described.

Conservation

Several populations are on protected land. *B. ithyphylla* is listed as a Northern Ireland Priority Species.

Protected sites with recent records: Binevenagh ASSI; Binevenagh Nature Reserve; Binevenagh SAC; Comeragh Mountains SAC; Galtee Mountains SAC; **Unprotected sites with recent records:** Benbradagh (proposed ASSI); 4 miles NE of Moynalty; N. of Knock Dhu (proposed ASSI).

Philonotis rigida Brid.

Rigid Apple-moss

Status in Ireland: Vulnerable (B2a, bii, iv); **Status in Europe:** Least Concern

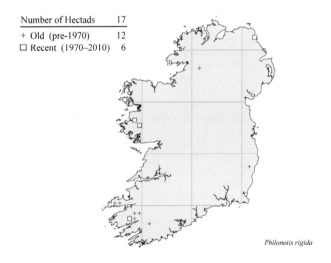

Number of Hectads	17
+ Old (pre-1970)	12
☐ Recent (1970–2010)	6

Philonotis rigida

Identification

This is an acrocarpous moss that grows as rather dense light green to green tufts, cushions or larger patches, with stems up to 15 mm high. The leaves are erect to erecto-patent, crowded, rather stiff, lanceolate with an acuminate apex. The leaf margin is plane or narrowly recurved, dentate (with single teeth); the costa is strong and shortly excurrent. Cells in mid-leaf are narrowly rectangular, 5–8 μm wide, with mamillae on the distal ends of the cells (appearing to be on the end walls); basal cells are shorter and wider, rectangular. Unlike other *Philonotis* species, it is autoicous, with bud-like androecia beneath the perichaetia. Capsules are globose, asymmetrical, striate, inclined and exserted on a reddish seta about 2 cm long. The stiff leaves and rather dense tufts give a different appearance to that of other *Philonotis*, but identification is best confirmed also by the autoicous sexuality and position of the mamillae on the mid- and upper-leaf cells.

Distribution in Ireland

Recent accepted records are from seven localities in five vice-counties: S. Kerry (Blackwater River near Old Dromore House, 1983); W. Galway (N. side of Benbeg, 1970); W. Mayo (near Aasleagh, 1970; Ben Gorm, 1970; Dookinelly, Achill Island, 1987); W. Donegal (Trabane, Malin Beg, 1963–2004) and Antrim (Glenariff, 2008). Older records are accepted from a further 13 localities:

S. Kerry (Maghanaboe Glen, Brandon Mountain, 1829–1865; near Dunkerron, 1848; Looscaunagh, 1863; Connor Hill, 1865; Rossbehy, 1951); N. Kerry (Cromaglan, 1861–1885; Glena, Killarney, 1885; below Torc Cascade, 1885); W. Cork (Bantry region, 1815; Pass of Keimaneigh, 1846; Glengarriff, 1896–1900); Wicklow (Woodenbridge, 1867–1868) and Fermanagh (Stonefort near Boa Island, 1961).

Ecology and biology

Where the habitat was described, Irish records were all associated with rocks, from the bases of sea cliffs to montane slopes, on crags, stream sides and in a ravine. Two of the records mention wet rocks and a third was in a small stream on a cliff. Varied siliceous lithologies account for most of them, that at Stonefort being atypical, in cracks of limestone. In Britain, it is a lowland species occurring on seeping cliffs, undercliffs, coastal slumps and riverbanks, growing on soil and in rock crevices, mainly in natural coastal habitats but sometimes also in quarries; the substratum is typically non-calcareous but with flushing by moderately basic water (M.O. Hill in Hill *et al.* 1994). In W. Cornwall it prefers steep, flushed bases of N.-facing sea cliffs.

The species is perennial, with large patches persisting for several years at some sites. It is autoicous and capsules are frequent, maturing in spring and summer. Deciduous branchlets are frequently produced in leaf axils and these presumably serve as propagules; gemmae and tubers are unknown.

World distribution

P. rigida has a western and southern distribution in Europe from Scotland, Ireland and N. France (Normandy) southwards to Portugal and S. Spain, eastwards to the Alps, Italy, Sicily and the Caucasus (Raeymaekers 1983). It is listed as *Vulnerable* in Bulgaria and Montenegro. It is assigned to an Oceanic Mediterranean-Atlantic floristic element in Europe. Elsewhere, it occurs in Macaronesia (Azores, Madeira, Canary Islands), N. Africa (Algeria) and SW Asia (Georgia: Ignatov *et al.* 2007).

Threats

The species may have declined in Ireland, since the 20 recorded localities include only seven where it has been found since 1970, only two of which were post-2000. It has also apparently disappeared from several accurately recorded localities which have been revisited. At some well-known and frequently searched bryophyte localities it seems to have made a brief appearance in the past but not to have persisted (e.g. Torc Cascade, Glengarriff). Hence, the preponderance of old records might result merely from the species being a short-lived colonist at many of its sites (producing about one record in Ireland each decade). Potentially suitable habitat is still present at several of the sites from which it seems to have disappeared, such as at Dookinelly, where recent spread of *Gunnera tinctoria* on the cliffs nevertheless still leaves plenty of open habitat.

Conservation

Several localities (or former localities) are on protected land. *P. rigida* is listed as a Northern Ireland Priority Species.

Protected sites with recent records: Blackwater River (Kerry) SAC; Glenariff Glen ASSI (scheduled for declaration 2011); Glenariff Nature Reserve; Keel Machair/Menaun Cliffs SAC; Maumtrasna Mountain Complex pNHA; Mweelrea/Sheeffry/Erriff Complex SAC; Slieve League SAC; **Unprotected sites with recent records:** near Aasleagh (possibly within Mweelrea/Sheeffry/Erriff Complex SAC).

Philonotis arnellii Husn.

Arnell's Apple-moss

syn. *Philonotis capillaris* auct. non Lindb.
Status in Ireland: Endangered (B1a, bi, ii, iv, B2a, bi, ii, iv); **Status in Europe:** Least Concern

Identification

This is a slender green or light green acrocarpous moss that grows in small tufts or patches or as scattered stems 5–10 mm high. The leaves are lanceolate, acuminate or long-acuminate, with shortly excurrent costa and margins that are toothed and plane or narrowly recurved. Cells in the upper part of the leaf are narrowly rectangular, with low distal mamillae or smooth; cells in the lower part of the leaf are rectangular and smooth. Capsules are inclined, globose, asymmetrical, striate and exserted. *P. arnellii* is superficially very similar to small plants of other *Philonotis* species or a small *Pohlia*. Identification relies

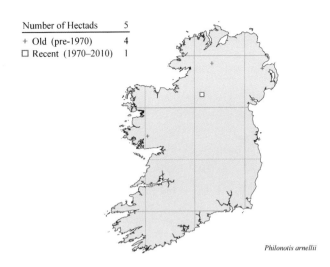

Number of Hectads   5
+ Old (pre-1970)   4
☐ Recent (1970–2010)   1

Philonotis arnellii

on careful study of microscopic characters of the leaves, particularly the presence of distal (not proximal) mamillae on some of the upper leaf cells and smooth lower leaf cells.

The correct name for this species should almost certainly be *P. capillaris* Lindb. ex Hartm. as adopted by Ordóñez (2007), rather than *P. arnellii* as used by Hill *et al.* (2006, 2008).

Distribution in Ireland

Found recently in Ireland at only one site: Cavan (on W. slope of Cuilcagh, 2001). Older records based on correctly identified specimens are from: W. Galway (near Farravaun, 1969); Tyrone (by Mourne River at Lisnatunny, 1931); Down (below Cloghmore, Rostrevor, 1929) and Antrim (woods on Cave Hill, 1954). Nine other old records are rejected as known errors or remain as unconfirmed: W. Mayo, W. Donegal (three records), Down (three records) and Antrim (two records).

The species is small, inconspicuous and troublesome to identify so that it is almost certainly under-recorded in Ireland.

Ecology and biology

The only recent record was from near-vertical damp shale of a slightly shaded bank about 1.5 m above the water of a stream at c. 458 m altitude. Older records are from a moist shaded vertical bank at the side of a track, a clay path on a steep slope, wet sand among rocks and on a shady ledge of rocks. In Britain, it occurs on slightly acid to slightly basic non-calcareous soil and in rock crevices in situations that are not permanently wet but where it would be intermittently flushed or flooded or where the ground is kept open by slippage (e.g. on woodland rides, earthy banks, stream sides, floors of quarries and basic montane cliffs) (M.O. Hill in Hill *et al.* 1994).

Longevity of the small plants is unrecorded but it is unlikely they persist for more than one or two years and they are evidently short-lived colonists in some sites. The species is dioicous and capsules are very rare (unrecorded in Ireland). Tubers are unknown but caducous filamentous flagelliform shoots are frequently produced in the leaf axils.

World distribution

P. arnellii is widespread in Europe, from Iceland and N. Scandinavia southwards to Portugal, Spain, Italy and the Caucasus, but is listed as *Extinct* in the Netherlands, *Vulnerable* in Switzerland, *Near Threatened* in Luxembourg and *Data Deficient* in Germany and Serbia and Montenegro. In Europe, it is assigned to a European Temperate floristic element. Elsewhere, there are records from Turkey, western and eastern N. America and Greenland.

Threats

The population on Cuilcagh is on an extensive shale bank and unlikely to be at any immediate risk, although afforestation or other changes could be harmful. British populations are often on patches of open soil that become unsuitable as vegetation succession progresses.

Conservation

The locality on Cuilcagh is on protected land.

Protected sites with recent records: Cuilcagh-Anierin Uplands SAC; **Unprotected sites with recent records:** none.

465

Philonotis caespitosa Jur.   Tufted Apple-moss

Status in Ireland: Near Threatened; **Status in Europe:** Least Concern

This is an acrocarpous moss that grows in open, damp places, often on lake edges. There are reports from 15 vice-counties, with records from 18 hectads (8 old, 10 recent). Morphological distinctions between *P. caespitosa* and *P. fontana* are troublesome and sometimes seem rather arbitrary in the usual absence of male inflorescences. These difficulties arise partly because *P. fontana* is very variable (cf. Buryová & Shaw 2005) but partly because there are intermediate populations that are likely to have resulted from hybridization (Buryová 2004). Hence *P. caespitosa* is probably under-recorded.

Philonotis tomentella Molendo   Woolly Apple-moss

syn. *P. fontana* var. *pumila* (Turner) Brid., *P. fontana* var. *tomentella* (Molendo) Dixon
Status in Ireland: Vulnerable (D2); **Status in Europe:** Least Concern

Number of Hectads	4
☐ Recent (1970–2010)	4

Philonotis tomentella

Identification

An acrocarpous moss that grows as straggling shoots, tufts or light green patches, with stems to 5 cm (occasionally 9 cm) long that are usually matted below with brownish tomentum. The leaves are erecto-patent, often subsecund, 0.5–1.5 mm long, narrowly lanceolate to ovate-lanceolate and tapering to an acuminate to subulate apex. The leaf margin is plane or narrowly recurved, sharply dentate (with single or double teeth); the costa is narrow, excurrent in a fine, usually long, denticulate point. Cells in mid-leaf are narrowly rectangular with a mamilla at the proximal end of each cell (also sometimes with another mamilla at distal end); cells in the lower part of the leaf are larger and relatively wider, rectangular. Capsules (unknown in Ireland and Britain) are almost globose, asymmetrical, near-horizontal and exserted on a tall seta. *P. tomentella* is rather similar to the more common and variable

P. fontana, differing mainly in its narrower leaves with excurrent costa and the acute (not obtuse) tips to the inner perigonial bracts. However, Nyholm (1998) notes that there are intermediate plants which are difficult to assign to either species. Hence subspecific rank within *P. fontana* might be more appropriate for *P. tomentella*.

Distribution in Ireland

Records are accepted from four localities in three vice-counties: W. Mayo (NE corrie of Mweelrea, 2003–2008); E. Donegal (NW slope of Bulbin Mountain, 2002) and W. Donegal (Lavagh More, 2001; Binnasruell, 2008). It was apparently listed in error for Louth and W. Donegal by Smith (1978). A report for W. Galway (N. side of Benbeg, 1970) was based on a specimen that has been reidentified as *P. fontana*.

Ecology and biology

A montane species, found at 250–550 m elevation on a few rocky north-facing slopes with acidic to mildly basic schist or Mweelrea Grit bedrock. It grows on rock surfaces or thin overlying soil, often amongst other bryophytes, in damp or wet places on steep sides of gullies or on crags. In Britain, it occurs mainly on wet, basic cliffs and rocky slopes on mountains, with occasional records also from sandy ground beside a river and flushed, open, basic ground beside a lake, mostly at 400–1100 m elevation (rarely at 80 m, in Shetland). In Scandinavia, it is regarded as an arctic-alpine plant found from the subalpine belt to the lower part of the high alpine belt, beside streams and springs and in fens with moving water, on wet rocks, etc. (Nyholm 1998).

The plants are perennial. It is a dioicous species for which capsules are unknown in Ireland or Britain (but known in Fennoscandia). Gemmae, bulbils and tubers are lacking, but vegetative propagation probably occurs from detached stem and leaf fragments.

World distribution

Widespread in N. Europe from Spitsbergen, N. Iceland, N. Fennoscandia and arctic Russia southwards; montane in C. and S. Europe, extending southwards to Portugal, S. Spain (Sierra Nevada), Austria, Romania and Bulgaria and eastwards to the Caucasus. It is listed as *Vulnerable* in the Czech Republic and *Data Deficient* in Germany. It is assigned to a Circumpolar Arctic-montane floristic element in Europe. Elsewhere, it occurs in N. Asia (widespread from the N. Urals and W. Siberia to the Russian Far East: Ignatov *et al.* 2007), SW and C. Asia, N. America and Greenland; also reported from mountains of SE Africa.

Threats

No immediate threats were apparent when the four Irish localities were visited from 2001–2008. There is a potential risk to some patches of the plant from erosion if sheep-stocking levels remain very high on Mweelrea.

Conservation

All but one of the localities is on protected land.

Protected sites with recent records: Bulbin Mountain pNHA; Meenaguse Scragh SAC; Mweelrea/Sheeffry/Erriff Complex SAC; **Unprotected sites with recent records:** Lavagh More (just outside Meenaguse Scragh SAC).

Philonotis cernua (Wilson) D.G.Griffin & W.R.Buck   Swan-necked Apple-moss

syn. *Bartramidula cernua* (Wilson) Lindb., *B. wilsonii* Bruch & Schimp., *Philonotis wilsonii* (Bruch & Schimp.) Mitt.
Status in Ireland: Critically Endangered (B1a, bi, ii, iii, iv, B2a, bi, ii, iii, iv); **Status in Europe:** Rare

Identification

A small and slender acrocarpous moss that grows as scattered plants, tufts or more extensive pale green patches with stems 2–5 mm high (occasionally up to 10 mm or more), remaining inconspicuous until capsules develop. Leaves are erecto-patent, sometimes subsecund, 0.6–1.0 mm long, lanceolate to narrowly lanceolate with an acuminate apex. The leaf margin is plane and serrate to below the middle, the costa evanescent to almost percurrent, papillose above on its dorsal surface. Mid-leaf cells are narrowly rectangular, about 8 μm wide, smooth or weakly mamillose; basal cells are rectangular. The capsule is globose with a very short neck, inclined to pendulous, gymnostomous, exserted on a seta that is arcuate when moist, flexuose when dry. The leaf characters are rather similar to those of other small *Philonotis* species, but it is distinct from them in having an arcuate seta.

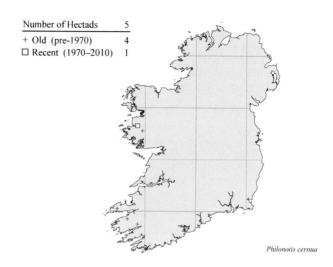

Philonotis cernua

Distribution in Ireland

There is only one recent record for this species in Ireland: W. Mayo (NE corrie of Mweelrea, 1987). Older records from five localities in a further two vice-counties are accepted: S. Kerry (Connor Hill Pass, 1829; Knock-avohila near Dunkerron, 1846; above Coomasaharn Lake, 1951; Coomeeneragh Lake, 1951) and W. Galway (near Maam, 1868).

Ecology and biology

Above Coomasaharn Lake, it was found on peat in burned *Callunetum* at about 245 m altitude. The Mweelrea record was from soil on a gravelly N.-facing scree slope beneath crags at about 450 m altitude. British records are usually on damp, bare, previously burnt acidic peat on heathy montane slopes, from near sea level to 500 m elevation (F.J. Rumsey in Hill *et al.* 1994).

The plants are probably short-lived perennials that sometimes form large patches. The species has a reputation for appearing sporadically in Britain, presumably because of the infrequent appearance of burnt peat and the resulting habitat becoming shaded again and unsuitable for *P. cernua* within a few years. The species is synoicous and produces capsules in abundance, maturing from summer to late autumn. Its spores are very large (28–40 μm) implying limited dispersal ability, but that they may be long-lived, allowing populations to reappear when conditions become suitable. Gemmae, bulbils and tubers are unknown.

World distribution

Known in Europe only from a few localities in N. Scotland, N. Wales (Gwynedd: last recorded in 1931) and W. Ireland; it is therefore assigned to a Hyperoceanic Temperate floristic element in Europe. It is listed as *Critically Endangered* in Britain, but has not been seen since 1961 and may have vanished. Elsewhere, it has a disjunct range in China (Yunnan, Hainan, Taiwan: Li Xing-jiang *et al.* 2007), eastern N. America (mountains of North Carolina and Tennessee), Mexico, Costa Rica, Brazil, Peru (Delgadillo *et al.* 1995) and W. Africa (Bioko).

Threats

It has not been refound at any of the old localities in the past decade, despite close searches on Mweelrea and in S. Kerry. The scree habitat on Mweelrea appeared to still exist undamaged in 2008. However, the burnt *Callunetum* habitat recorded in S. Kerry in 1951 was not encountered on recent visits to those localities. Over the past two decades the extent of *Calluna*-dominated vegetation has declined greatly in the Kerry hills and elsewhere in W. Ireland as a consequence of overstocking with sheep. Habitat potentially available for *P. cernua* on burnt *Callunetum* must therefore have decreased.

Conservation

Several sites (or former sites) are on protected land. This is one of a number of rare bryophyte species that would be expected to benefit from reduction of sheep-stocking levels on Irish mountains. It is similarly categorised as *Critically Endangered* in Britain (Church *et al.* 2001); the 'Rare' status afforded it in Europe as a whole therefore needs to be reassessed since it is regarded as *Critically Endangered* in both of the European countries where it occurs.

Protected sites with recent records: Mweelrea/Sheeffry/Erriff Complex SAC; **Unprotected sites with recent records:** none.

468

Plagiobryum zieri (Hedw.) Lindb.

Zierian Hump-moss

syn. *Bryum zieri* Hedw., *Plagiobryum zierii* auct. (orthogr. err.), *Ptychostomum zieri* (Hedw.) Holyoak & N.Pedersen
Status in Ireland: Near Threatened; **Status in Europe:** Least Concern

An acrocarpous moss that forms silvery or whitish tufts growing on soil among basic montane rocks, usually on ledges or in crevices. There are reports from 11 vice-counties, with records from 20 hectads (9 old, 14 recent, 1 undated). The species often grows as a colonist on small patches of bare soil and most of its populations are very small. However, there is no evidence that it has declined.

Anomobryum concinnatum (Spruce) Lindb.

Neat Silver-moss

syn. *Anomobryum filiforme* subsp. *concinnatum* (Spruce) J.J.Amann, *A. filiforme* var. *concinnatum* (Spruce) Loeske, *A. julaceum* var. *concinnatum* (Spruce) J.E.Zetterst., *A. leptostomoides* Schimp., *Bryum concinnatum* Spruce, *B. filiforme* var. *concinnatum* (Spruce) Boulay, *B. julaceum* var. *concinnatum* (Spruce) Wilson
Status in Ireland: Least Concern; **Status in Europe:** Least Concern

A small, slender acrocarpous moss that grows as tufts or scattered shoots on open, basic substrata on rocky coastal slopes, machair slopes and montane crags. It differs from the more common *A. julaceum* in its less julaceous shoots, leaves only slightly concave and the costa reaching the leaf apex. Although placed on the Provisional Red List (Holyoak 2006b), fieldwork over the past decade has found many additional populations, including new vice-county records for West Cork, Waterford, West Mayo, Leitrim, Fermanagh, East Donegal and Antrim. There are now reports from 14 vice-counties, with records from 21 hectads (5 old, 18 recent). There is no evidence of decline.

Bryum marratii Hook.f. & Wilson

Baltic Bryum

Status in Ireland: Least Concern; **Status in Europe:** Regionally Threatened

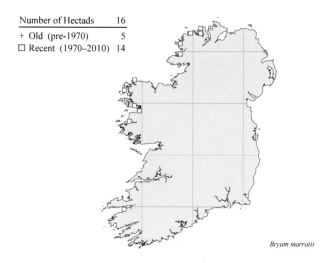

Number of Hectads	16
+ Old (pre-1970)	5
☐ Recent (1970–2010)	14

Bryum marratii

Identification

An acrocarpous moss of coastal sites that grows as scattered stems or small loose tufts, typically bright or deep green and up to about 10 mm tall. Like other species of *Bryum*, it has the cells in mid-leaf irregularly rectangular or rhomboid to rhomboid-hexagonal, but this is one of a few Irish species combining a blunt to rounded leaf apex, evanescent costa and lack of red cells at the leaf base. These characters are shared with *B. calophyllum*, from which well-grown non-fertile plants (at least 5 mm tall) can usually be distinguished by careful appraisal of a combination of characters: upper leaves longer and relatively narrower in *B. marratii* (normally with length: breadth > 2:1); leaves with a blunt to broadly rounded rather than acute to blunt apex; leaf border of narrow cells absent or only weakly developed; leaf margin not or less recurved below; costa ending further below leaf apex. Capsules are cernuous to pendulous, on a long seta, distinctive in being almost spherical with a shortly rostellate operculum (very different to the shortly ovoid capsule with a conical operculum of *B. calophyllum*).

Distribution in Ireland

Recent records are accepted from 16 localities in five vice-counties: S. Kerry (Rossbehy Creek, 1983–2000); Dublin (North Bull, 1873–2007); W. Mayo (near Keel, Achill Island, 1987; Garter Hill, 2003; E. of Rosmoney, 2003; Elly Harbour, 2003; S. of Mallaranny, 2003; SE of Dooaghtry, 2003); E. Donegal (Binnion, NW of Clonmany, 1969–2002) and W. Donegal (near Black Rock, 2002; near Gortnalughoge Bay, 1999; S. of Rosepenna, 1999; SE of Sheskinmore Lough, 1999; W. of Tawny, 2002; SW of Kincaslough, 2002; W. of Lough Nagreany, 2002). Older accepted records are from two further localities: W. Donegal (near Dunfanaghy, 1962) and Londonderry (Bann Estuary near Portstewart, 1936). Numerous new records from the past decade reflect intensive efforts to find the species.

Ecology and biology

A halophyte, characteristic of a narrowly defined habitat on unshaded damp mud or sand exposed at the top edge of saltmarshes, typically in sheltered bays or inlets and in places where there is some flushing with fresh water from the landward side. Associated plants commonly include *Agrostis stolonifera*, *Glaux maritima* and *Juncus gerardii*. It does not usually occur in dune slacks or on machair. In Europe, its rare inland localities in Germany (Westfalen) and Slovakia are known to be in saline habitats.

The species is a short-lived perennial. Most Irish populations are very small, commonly occupying much less than a square metre, so it is likely that it repeatedly colonises small patches of open habitat. The plants are usually autoicous, producing sporophytes occasionally with spores ripening in summer or autumn in Europe (late October recorded from Ireland). Gemmae and tubers are lacking, but the leafy tips of the fragile stems commonly break off and these doubtless function as vegetative propagules.

World distribution

Mainly known from NW Europe, from Iceland and N. Norway southwards to SW Ireland, Wales, NW France (Normandy), Baltic coasts and Slovakia, it is listed as *Endangered* in Britain and Germany, *Vulnerable* in Finland and the Netherlands, *Data Deficient* in Sweden and 'rare' in Estonia. It is classified as a European Boreal-montane floristic element in Europe by Hill *et al.* (2007), although there are no montane records. Elsewhere, it is reported from NC Asia (Altai Mountains: Zolotov 2006) and known very locally in N. America (coast of N. Newfoundland; inland at one locality each in Alberta and North Dakota). A report from Yemen (Kürschner 1996, 2000) is so widely divergent from its known range and presumed climatic tolerance that further investigation appears to be needed.

Threats

B. marratii appears to have been lost from its only locality in Northern Ireland (Portstewart) because of cessation of grazing at the saltmarsh edges, perhaps as a consequence of development of a golf course inland. Lack of grazing leading to dense grass cover at saltmarsh edges currently threatens several other Irish populations. Some are evidently also vulnerable to accidents because of their small extent, with obvious risks from burial beneath tideline debris and anthropogenic disturbance.

Conservation

Most populations are on protected land. The species is protected by the Flora (Protection) Order, 1999 in the Republic of Ireland.

The species may be correctly treated as of *Least Concern* in Ireland because of the numerous recent records and slight evidence of decline, but nearly all of its Irish populations are small and some are vulnerable. However, the species anyway merits special attention because of its relatively restricted global range and the evidence that it has declined greatly around its southern range limits in NW Europe. Thus, following long-term declines, it is now known in England and Wales from only two localities in each country (Holyoak 2002a, 2002b). It was always rare in Germany and is now absent from numerous former localities (Düll 1994, Meinunger & Schröder 2007). Furthermore, there are apparently few records from numerous other countries in its range (Iceland, Norway, Denmark, Finland, Estonia, Latvia, Poland, Slovakia, Canada, USA).

Protected sites with recent records: Ballyness Bay SAC; Bull Island Nature Reserve; Castlemaine Harbour SAC; Clew Bay Complex SAC; Glenamoy Bog Complex SAC; Gweedore Bay and Islands SAC; Keel Machair/Menaun Cliffs SAC; Lough Nagreany Dunes SAC; Mullet/Blacksod Bay Complex SAC; Mweelrea/Sheeffry/Erriff Complex SAC; North Dublin Bay SAC; North Inishowen Coast SAC; Sheephaven SAC; Tranarossan and Melmore Lough SAC; West of Ardara/Maas Road SAC; **Unprotected sites with recent records:** S. of Mallaranny (possibly within Clew Bay Complex SAC); W. of Tawny (possibly within Mulroy Bay SAC).

Bryum warneum (Röhl.) Brid.

Warne's Thread-moss

syn. *B. mamillatum* Lindb., *Ptychostomum warneum* (Röhl.) J.R.Spence
Status in Ireland: Endangered (B2a, bii, iii, iv); **Status in Europe:** Rare

Identification

An acrocarpous moss that grows in tufts or low turfs, typically light olive green to slightly pinkish in colour, with stems 5–10 mm high. It becomes conspicuous when fruiting because of the long setae (30–60 mm), each bearing a pendent capsule. Mature or nearly mature capsules are needed for identification, when typical plants of *B. warneum* are distinctive in combining broadly pyriform capsules with narrow mouth, presence of at least

a few vertical or oblique cross walls joining lamellae of exostome, narrow perforations of the endostome processes, spores usually > 40 μm, and lack of red at (most) leaf bases. Additional characters are the (usually) autoicous sexuality, long seta, high conical operculum and short cilia. However, occasional populations have short ovoid capsules with a wide mouth and low operculum (formerly separated as '*B. mamillatum*'), synoicous sexuality, a short seta, or lack oblique cross walls.

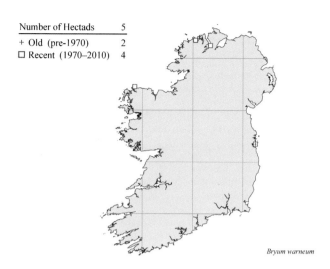

Number of Hectads	5
+ Old (pre-1970)	2
□ Recent (1970–2010)	4

Bryum warneum

Distribution in Ireland

There are recent records from four localities: Dublin (North Bull, 1856–1857 and probably later; unconfirmed reports also from 1975, leg. P.H. Pitkin and a large population present in a foredune slack 2007, though at a different site to the occurrences reported in 1975); W. Mayo (strong population SW of Garter Hill, 2003); E. Donegal (strong populations N. of Fahan, 2002) and W. Donegal (small population at Catherine's Isle, 2002). Old records are all from the coast of Dublin: Portmarnock (pre-1823, and almost certainly again in 1908), Malahide Sands (pre-1823 to 1870) but surveys in 2007 revealed that no suitable habitat survives at either of these areas.

Ecology and biology

Restricted to sandy coastal sites with unshaded, partly bare, damp, calcareous sand exposed, such as in foredune slacks, near dune slack pools or near small streams. *B. warneum* often forms part of a low carpet of bryophytes that may include *Aneura pinguis*, *Pellia endiviifolia* and other *Bryum* species, often among sparse or patchy cover of low grasses, sedges and herbs. A few of the localities in Britain are on edges of gravel pits just inland of the coast and in C. Europe it occurs more extensively inland on river and lake margins.

In Britain, the individual plants mature in their second year of growth but patches tend to persist as if they are short-lived perennials. The species is usually autoicous, less often synoicous, producing abundant capsules in which spores mainly mature from September to November. Gemmae and tubers are unknown.

World distribution

Widespread in N. and C. Europe, from Iceland and arctic Norway southwards to N. France, the Netherlands and Hungary, occurring mainly on coasts in western and northern parts of its range, but frequently also inland in parts of C. Europe (e.g. Germany: Meinunger & Schröder 2007). It is listed as *Extinct* in Finland, *Vulnerable* in Britain and the Netherlands, *Data Deficient* in Germany and Sweden and 'rare' in Estonia. Reports from Svalbard and Sardinia are probably errors. In Europe, it is assigned to a European Boreal-montane floristic element. Elsewhere, it is known from Asia (Altai and Baikal: Savicz-Ljubitzkaja & Smirnova 1970; Himalaya) and Canada (Quebec). Reports from Alaska and Greenland have been discounted (H. Ochi, unpublished MS.).

Threats

Restriction of *B. warneum* to early-successional vegetation that is colonising damp sand limits its occurrence to coastal sites where active erosion and accretion of sand still occur above beach level. Coastal defence works and coastal developments (of golf courses, roads and houses) over the past century have destroyed all such habitats in the Portmarnock and Malahide areas leading to loss of the species. Local extinctions have occurred for similar reasons around the British coasts (Church *et al.* 2001, Holyoak 2002a, 2002b). The greatest risk to the surviving populations is from loss of habitat to shading as vegetation succession proceeds, coupled with scarcity or lack of open habitat nearby for colonisation. Future sea-level rise may worsen this problem. The species is also intolerant of trampling and quickly lost if sites become eutrophicated (e.g. from fertiliser inputs on golf courses).

Conservation
Most of the populations that still exist are on protected land. These populations require open habitats on bare, damp, calcareous sand to be recreated every few years for recolonisation as older habitats nearby become shaded and unsuitable. Where such habitats cease to reappear

through natural processes they should be produced artificially by scraping vegetation from small areas.

Protected sites with recent records: Bull Island Nature Reserve; Glenamoy Bog Complex SAC; Lough Swilly SAC; North Dublin Bay SAC; **Unprotected sites with recent records:** Catherine's Isle (possibly within Horn Head and Rinclevan SAC).

Bryum calophyllum R.Br.   Blunt Bryum

syn. *B. acutiforme* Limpr., *B. acutum* Lindb., *B. axel-blyttii* Kaurin ex H.Philib., *Ptychostomum calophyllum* (R.Br.) J.R.Spence
Status in Ireland: Endangered (B2a, biii); **Status in Europe:** Rare

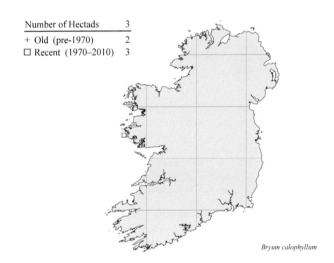

Number of Hectads	3
+ Old (pre-1970)	2
☐ Recent (1970–2010)	3

Bryum calophyllum

Identification
An acrocarpous moss of sandy coastal sites that grows as scattered stems or in short, very open turfs, usually 5–15 mm tall. Fertile *B. calophyllum* can usually be identified in the field by the combination of a pendent, shortly ovoid capsule on a rather long seta with wide concave leaves having shortly acute to blunt apices. Other characters that aid detection of non-fertile plants in the field include the leaves that are rather evenly spaced along the stem and patent to spreading, with leaves and stems typically light olive to tan or pinkish. *B. marratii* resembles *B. calophyllum* in having wide concave leaves with rather blunt apices, but plants of that species with mature capsules are easily separated by their rostellate operculum and almost globular capsules. Non-fertile *B. marratii* is normally green in colour, with the upper leaves longer and relatively narrower (often with length: breadth

> 2:1), leaf apex typically blunt to broadly rounded rather than shortly acute, leaf border of narrow cells usually less developed, leaf margin less often recurved below, costa extending less far towards leaf apex. However, the temptation to name small non-fertile plants (< 5 mm) on the basis of these differences should be resisted.

Distribution in Ireland
There are recent records from four localities in two vice-counties: W. Galway (west of Doon Hill, near Ballyconneelly, 1982; not refound in 2004) and W. Mayo (Dooaghtry, 1968 and 2003; Trawmore, near Keel on Achill Island, 1962 and 2003; SE of Barnynagappul Strand on Achill Island, 2003). In 2003, strong populations were recorded at Dooaghtry and SE of Barnynagappul Strand, but only a few small plants at Trawmore. There are unconfirmed old records from

Dublin (Malahide, 1860; North Bull, 1860 and 1915) which are most likely errors or fraudulent, and an erroneous record from Londonderry (Magilligan, 1936).

Ecology and biology

B. calophyllum is a colonist of unshaded, damp, calcareous sand at coastal sites and is known in Ireland from hollows in dunes, sandy stream edges near beaches, sandy hollows just inland of a ridge of beach shingle and open sand areas with sparse vegetation on machair. It grows on partly bare sand surfaces with other low bryophytes, short grasses, sedges, rushes or herbs.

Individual stems probably live only for one or two years, but patches persist in the same areas for at least several years. The plants are autoicous and frequently produce capsules, with spores maturing from late summer to early winter. Gemmae and tubers are absent.

World distribution

Widespread in N. Europe, from Iceland and Svalbard southwards to England, the Netherlands ('very rare and susceptible'), Germany (*Endangered*) and Romania, but it has decreased greatly in the southern part of this range and is now rare or extinct at the southernmost localities (one small population now known in Wales: Holyoak 2002a; extinct in England: Holyoak 2002b; extinct in Germany: Meinunger & Schröder 2007, cf. Düll 1994). Even in Norway it is listed as 'declining', and it is listed as *Endangered* in Britain and 'very rare' in Estonia. A report from Sardinia needs confirmation as the species is otherwise unknown in the Mediterranean region. In Europe, it is assigned to a Circumpolar Boreo-arctic montane phytogeographical element. Elsewhere, it is widespread in arctic and subarctic regions in Asia, N.

America and Greenland, and recorded further south in the Rocky Mountains and Tibet. Reports for C. Africa (e.g. Smith 1978) are almost certainly erroneous and probably based on *B. afro-calophyllum* P. de la Varde from Kenya (cf. Ochi 1972, O'Shea 2006).

Threats

Occurs only at coastal localities where early-successional vegetation is colonising damp sand, so it is restricted to coastal sites where active erosion and accretion of sand still occur above beach level. Coastal defence works and coastal developments (e.g. of roads, houses, or golf courses) often destroy these habitats and losses due to these causes have occurred at some British localities (Church *et al.* 2001, Holyoak 2002a, 2002b). Future sea-level rise may also threaten the sites.

Conservation

B. calophyllum is protected in the Republic of Ireland by the Flora (Protection) Order, 1999 and all known populations are on protected land. Future survival of the species will depend on maintaining the dynamic coastal processes at its sites so that open sandy habitats continually become available for recolonisation every few years. If such habitats cease to reappear through natural processes they should be produced artificially by scraping vegetation from small areas.

Protected sites with recent records: Doogort Machair/ Lough Doo SAC; Keel Machair/Menaun Cliffs SAC; Mweelrea/Sheeffry/Erriff Complex SAC; Slyne Head Peninsula SAC; **Unprotected sites with recent records:** none.

Bryum uliginosum (Brid.) Bruch & Schimp.

Cernuous Thread-moss

Syn. *Bryum cernuum* (Hedw.) Lindb., *Ptychostomum cernuum* (Hedw.) Hornsch.
Status in Ireland: Endangered (B2a, bii, iv); **Status in Europe:** Regionally Threatened

Identification

Bryum uliginosum is a large, handsome acrocarpous moss that grows in tufts. Like many other species of *Bryum*, it has ovate to ovate-lanceolate leaves with a shortly excurrent costa and border of narrow cells. It is larger than many species of the genus with leafy stems up to 30 mm tall and a long seta, which may be 45 mm high. It has long capsules that are narrowly ellipsoid, slightly

curved with an oblique mouth, and cernuous to pendulous. A combination of several microscopic characters needs to be carefully checked for reliable identification, including autoicous sexuality (both sexes on same plant: female inflorescences at shoot tip; male inflorescences on branch apices), lack of red bases to leaves, capsule shape, inner peristome structure (cilia rudimentary) and large spores (22–30 μm). Other *Bryum*

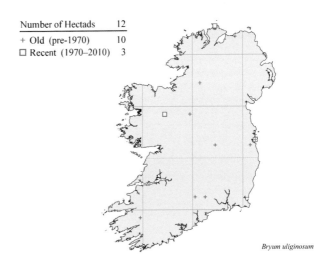

Number of Hectads 12
+ Old (pre-1970) 10
□ Recent (1970–2010) 3

Bryum uliginosum

species can be easily mistaken for *B. uliginosum*, although few of its more common relatives are as large with curved capsules having an oblique mouth. Large plants of the much more common *B. pallens* can look very similar but they have dioicous rather than autoicous inflorescences and may have appendiculate cilia. *B. pseudotriquetrum* occurs in similar habitats and can also be tall and handsome, but it has red leaf bases, dioicous or synoicous sexuality, appendiculate cilia and smaller spores.

Distribution in Ireland

Three recent records are accepted: Dublin (small population at North Bull, 2007–2008); E. Mayo (strong population at Island Lake, 2003–2009) and E. Donegal (strong population NW of Malin, 2002–2009). Old records which appear to be correct include those from N. Kerry (Ross Bay, 1861), S. Tipperary (Kedsah Bog near Clonmel, 1852), Dublin (Glen near Killakee, 19th century) and Antrim (Portrush, 1914), although some of the historic specimens involved are too small to confirm that the plants are autoicous. Study of herbarium specimens has shown that many of the older records are errors of identification or suspected errors, including those from: Kildare (1864); Dublin (several of the 19th-century records); W. Mayo (Clare Island, 1909); Leitrim (Lough Allen, 1883); Monaghan (1910); W. Donegal (Melmore and Rosepenna, 1910) and Londonderry (Magilligan, 1904; Benbradagh, 1938). Other old records that have not been checked may well include further errors: S. Tipperary (Caher, 1870); Offaly (Geashill, 1915); Dublin (Malahide, 1860; North Bull, 1858, the latter probably correct) and Fermanagh (Monea, 1905). A record from Roscommon (Annaghmore Lough, 1968)

was confirmed by the BBS Recorder of Mosses but the species could not be refound there in 2001 or 2002.

Ecology and biology

The habitat is in moist, open, calcareous sites such as dune slacks, stream banks or on lake shores. The recent Irish records are from damp calcareous sand in a foredune slack, soil patches exposed on the steep bank of a small stream near the coast (with soils derived from blown sand), and banks of a drainage ditch/stream dug into the edge of a dried marl lake. All three sites have nutrient-poor soils and short, species-rich vegetation, which includes *Bryum intermedium* at or close to two of the sites and *B. warneum* at one of them.

B. uliginosum is a perennial moss with both sexes on the same plant (autoicous). Capsules are produced freely and spores ripen in late summer and early autumn. It is therefore likely that dispersal of the species occurs mainly or entirely from spores. Gemmae and tubers are unknown.

World distribution

There are widespread correctly identified records in Europe, from Iceland and Fennoscandia south to the Pyrenees, Alps and Balkans, but *B. uliginosum* has often been misidentified. It is assigned to a Circumpolar Boreal-montane floristic element in Europe. The species now appears to be very rare or extinct over most of the lowlands of W. and C. Europe. For example, in Britain, there has been a large decline over the past 100 years and although Church *et al.* (2001) list it as *Critically Endangered*, it may now be extinct since there has been no confirmed record since before 1950. It has also declined greatly and either disappeared or become very rare in the Netherlands (*Extinct*) (Touw & Rubers 1989), Germany (*Vulnerable*) (Meinunger & Schröder 2007) and the Czech Republic (*Endangered*) (Kučera & Váňa 2003), and *Near Threatened* in Finland. It is listed as *Data Deficient* in Spain. Elsewhere, the species has a wide geographical range with confirmed records from scattered locations in Asia, Greenland, N. America, S. America (Chile, Argentina, S. Georgia) and New Zealand. Reports from Mexico and Africa (Düll 1985) are probably errors.

Threats

There are no detailed data on causes of its decline in Ireland, but drainage has undoubtedly played a part and eutrophication and 'tidying' of farmland areas may also be significant. Reasons for the widespread historic decline of the species elsewhere in Europe are also poorly understood, but include drainage, destruction of coastal dune slacks and development or other alteration of river and stream banks and lake margins. Eutrophication or other pollution of farmland habitats must now limit the scope for its occurrence in many lowland regions. However, the magnitude of its decline in Ireland, Britain and some other countries has probably been somewhat exaggerated by numerous misidentifications in the past, so there may be no need to conclude that it has decreased

'much more than would be expected from normal human activities' (A.C. Crundwell in Hill *et al.* 1994: 87). Suggestions that it may be producing capsules less frequently so that it may be more often overlooked now than in the past are speculation that is not supported by observations at the three populations known in Ireland, which produce abundant viable capsules.

Conservation

The three populations of *B. uliginosum* extant in Ireland should be a high conservation priority because they are among the very few populations left in temperate W. Europe. *Ex-situ* cultivation experiments and research into its genetic variation and ecology in Ireland are being undertaken by NPWS, the National Botanic Gardens, Glasnevin and Trinity College, Dublin. Conservation management of the Irish populations should seek to ensure that the plants do not become shaded as vegetation succession proceeds. Regular intervention may be needed to ensure that patches of open soil are available for the species to colonise.

Protected sites with recent records: Bull Island Nature Reserve; North Dublin Bay SAC; North Inishowen Coast SAC; River Moy SAC; **Unprotected sites with recent records:** none.

Bryum turbinatum (Hedw.) Turner — Topshape Thread-moss

Status in Ireland: Regionally Extinct; **Status in Europe:** Least Concern

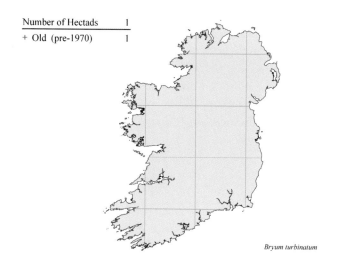

Number of Hectads	1
+ Old (pre-1970)	1

Bryum turbinatum

Identification

Like other species of *Bryum*, this is a tufted acrocarpous moss with pendent capsules. Plants with mature

sporophytes attract attention because the capsule is strikingly turbinate (i.e. short, wide-mouthed and markedly contracted below the mouth when dry).

476

However, considerable care is needed in identification because capsules with the mouth conspicuously wider than the theca occur in several common species of the genus. Additional characters of *B. turbinatum* that should be checked are the dioicous inflorescences, appendiculate cilia, small spores (16–20 μm), concolorous leaves (lacking red at base), with plane margins and poorly developed unistratose border. Non-fertile gatherings cannot be reliably identified because much the same combination of gametophytic characters occurs in odd forms of *B. pallens* (which normally has recurved leaf margins and often a bistratose border) and possibly in poorly developed material of other species lacking a red leaf base.

Distribution in Ireland

Reliably known only from a specimen collected at 'L. Gaul' (i.e. Lough Gall), near Valley, Achill Island (W. Mayo) in 1937 by A. Holderness and G.H. Allison. The identification of the specimen (which is perhaps housed at the Lincoln Museum, UK) has been confirmed by A.J.E. Smith. The species was not refound at Lough Gall in 2003. Old records from Dublin and Down were listed by Lett (1915) but lack of specimens or supporting detail has led to their exclusion from the modern *Census Catalogues* (cf. Holyoak 2003a). Dawson Turner (1804) also listed the species for Ireland but without any locality other than '*in palustribus*' in his *Muscologiae Hibernicae Spicilegium*, the first book to be published on Irish bryophytes. This account by Turner validated the combination *Bryum turbinatum* (Hedw.) Turner based on *Mnium turbinatum* Hedw. However, it is unlikely that Turner's own description based on Irish material was from the correct species, especially since Wilson (1855: 229, 233) noted that misidentified material named *B. turbinatum* was sent to Turner by Hedwig.

Ecology and biology

Nothing was recorded of the habitat in Ireland. British records were from thinly-vegetated, damp sandy or gravelly soils, such as in dune slacks and old peat and gravel pits. It was once locally abundant in Oxfordshire, but probably transient at most sites (Smith 1978, Jones 1991, Church *et al.* 2001). Elsewhere, it is recorded from a wider range of habitats; in Ukraine and Crimea sporadically on moist sandy soil and peaty soil in forests, boggy meadows, along shores of rivers and lakes, in a ditch and on moist cliffs (Lazarenko 1955); in Urals on wet tundras of montane forest, subalpine and alpine (montane tundra) belts (Dyachenko 1999).

European data show the species is a short-lived perennial, dioicous, with capsules frequent or common and maturing spring to early summer; tubers and gemmae are unknown.

World distribution

Now *Extinct* in Britain, where formerly rare and local in England with isolated records also in Wales and W. Scotland, but unrecorded since 1947. Reported from numerous other European countries from Scandinavia southwards to N. Spain, Italy and the Balkans, but there are few modern records in W. Europe, and it is listed as *Extinct* in the Netherlands, *Endangered* in the Czech Republic, *Near Threatened* in Finland, *Data Deficient* in Sweden, 'presumably threatened' in Germany, 'very rare' in Estonia and 'declining' in Norway. In Europe, it is classed as a Eurasian Boreal-montane floristic element. It is known elsewhere in N. Africa, Middle East, Ethiopia, South Africa, C. and E. Asia (southwards to Kashmir and Sikkim and east to Japan), S. Alaska, Argentina and Chile. Reports from elsewhere in the USA, the mountains of Peru and Ecuador, and from Iceland appear to be erroneous.

Threats

The cause of extinction in W. Mayo is unknown, as is the reason for loss of the species from Britain before the mid-20th century. However, there is some evidence to suggest that it was only a short-lived colonist at many sites.

Conservation

The need to protect this species in Ireland will only arise if a population is rediscovered.

Protected sites with recent records: none; **Unprotected sites with recent records:** none.

Lough Gall, Valley, Achill Island, Co. Mayo.

Bryum salinum I.Hagen ex Limpr.

Saltmarsh Thread-moss

syn. *Ptychostomum salinum* (I.Hagen ex Limpr.) J.R.Spence
Status in Ireland: Critically Endangered (B1a, bi, ii, iv, B2a, bi, ii, iv, D); **Status in Europe:** Least Concern

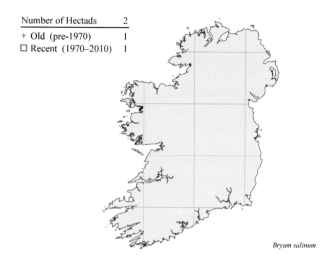

Number of Hectads	2
+ Old (pre-1970)	1
□ Recent (1970–2010)	1

Bryum salinum

Identification

This is an acrocarpous moss that forms bright to rather dull green tufts or low turfs up to about 10 mm tall and has pendent capsules much like those of several other *Bryum* species. Reliable separation from more common species of the genus depends on characters of the mature capsule, the main differences from *B. archangelicum* (syn. *B. inclinatum* auct.) being the red rather than yellowish to orange colour of the capsule mouth, exostome teeth straw colour (not yellow above and reddish below), exostome teeth often perforated along the midline, endostome processes with fine uniform papillae (not more strongly papillose down middle than at edges), larger exothecial cells, and neck of capsule gradually rather than abruptly tapered into seta; *B. archangelicum* also has less porose leaf cells. Forms of *B. algovicum* are sufficiently similar to these two species to be virtually inseparable from them in the field, and they all have very similar leaves, but its exostome is quite different with numerous vertical and oblique lines ('cross walls') joining the trabeculae on the lower part of the inner surface; it also differs in having the endostome strongly adherent to the exostome.

B. salinum was generally ignored by bryologists prior to the study by Nyholm & Crundwell (1958) and it may still be somewhat overlooked since careful study of material with ripe capsules is necessary for identification. Non-fertile and apparently unidentifiable *Bryum* that

might be this species or one of its more common relatives are frequently encountered at upper edges of saltmarshes.

Distribution in Ireland

There are two records from Ireland, from S. Kerry (SW of Derrymore Island, late May 2005, in small quantity) and NE Galway (by the sea on E. side of Galway City, where discovered in July 1957; not refound in 2004).

Ecology and biology

Found 'on tussocks in drainage channel in field by the sea' in NE Galway in 1957, apparently at the upper limit of tidal saltwater influence in a coastal pasture. In Kerry, it was found on a cattle-poached saltmarsh edge growing on damp, partly bare clay soil on a low hummock, with patchy and sparse low grasses. Similar hummocks close by had both *B. archangelicum* and *B. pseudotriquetrum*. In Britain, it grows in the upper parts of saltmarshes and on damp sandy ground where there is some saline influence, where it is usually present only in small quantity and often on ground grazed by cattle, 'who do not improve the quality of the material' (A.C. Crundwell in Hill *et al.* 1994). The same author suggests it is probably an obligate halophyte restricted to regions where the summer rainfall is sufficient to prevent excess concentration of salt from building up in the soil. Strong populations recently discovered in Cumbria were in very short, heavily grazed grassland at the upper edge of a saltmarsh, at and not far below extreme high-water level of spring tides (EHWST), while a small population in the same region was also near EHWST level on grassy hummocks in cattle-poached muddy ground beside an estuary (Holyoak 2002b).

Observations in Britain suggest the species is a short-lived perennial. It is synoicous and frequently produces capsules in which spores ripen in spring and summer. Gemmae and tubers have not been recorded.

World distribution

It is found on the coasts of N. Europe from SW England, Denmark and Poland north to Iceland and Spitsbergen. It is listed as *Endangered* in Britain and 'very rare' in Estonia. It is assigned to a European Boreo-arctic montane floristic element in Europe. Elsewhere, it is reported from Alaska, Canada and Greenland. The extent of its range in the former USSR outside the Baltic area seems uncertain because a lack of data is noted by Savicz-Ljubitzkaja & Smirnova (1970); recent records from SE European Russia (Orenburg Prov.: Spirina &

Zolotov 2004) and N. Asia (W. Taimyr: Zolotov 2006) may therefore hint at more extensive occurrence.

Threats

The most obvious threats to Irish populations arise from the likelihood of drainage or other agricultural improvement such as fertiliser inputs destroying their habitat at the saltmarsh-grassland transition. Abandonment or reduction of grazing would also be catastrophic as the bare patches needed by *B. salinum* would soon become shaded by grasses and herbs. In Britain, the species has apparently been lost from its southernmost site in S. Somerset as a result of land-use changes (Holyoak 2002b).

Conservation

Neither of the Irish sites appears to be on protected land, although the precise location of the Galway locality is uncertain.

Protected sites with recent records: none; **Unprotected sites with recent records:** SW of Derrymore Island.

Bryum knowltonii Barnes

Knowlton's Thread-moss

syn. *B. lacustre* (F.Weber & D.Mohr) Blandow non Brid., *Ptychostomum knowltonii* (Barnes) J.R.Spence
Status in Ireland: Endangered (D); **Status in Europe:** Least Concern

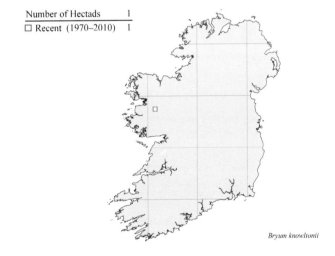

Number of Hectads	1
☐ Recent (1970–2010)	1

Bryum knowltonii

Identification

An acrocarpous moss that grows as green to reddish-brown tufts or low turfs, resembling other *Bryum* species in having a pendent capsule. In the field *B. knowltonii* resembles *B. warneum* in the leaves with short costa (evanescent to at most slightly excurrent) and the long

seta, but differs in the ellipsoid rather than (usually) pyriform capsules and smaller leaves with red bases. Microscopic differences include smaller spores (all < 44 μm, often much less: Holyoak 2004), perforations in endostome processes oval rather than narrow and 'cross walls' on the inner surface of exostome teeth absent or

479

few. Several more common *Bryum* species share the rosulate, red-based leaves of *B. knowltonii*, but all of these usually differ in having the costa longer excurrent. However, identification is best confirmed by microscopic checking of the following additional characters: plants synoicous; upper leaves ± bordered; mid-leaf cells 14–24 μm wide; 'cross walls' on the inner surface of exostome teeth usually lacking, rarely a few present; cilia rudimentary. Distinction from *B. archangelicum* (syn. *B. inclinatum* auct.) requires particular care and is best based on that species having a more longly excurrent costa, better defined leaf border and a longer capsule with longer neck.

Distribution in Ireland
The only confirmed record is from the shore of Lough Carra in E. Mayo, where fertile plants were found in 2003. Unconfirmed records based on plants lacking sporophytes were made at two other localities in E. Mayo in 2003 (near Keel Bridge; shore of Lough Mask) and one in SE Galway in 2004 (Cloghballymore Lough).

Ecology and biology
The confirmed records are from unshaded, highly calcareous substrata on limestone boulders in the inundation zone of the edge of Lough Carra, a marl lake. Here the plants grew with other mosses 10–40 cm above summer water level on thin calcareous marl, thin soil or thin sand. Several unconfirmed records are also from unshaded, moist, calcareous sites in small hollows in limestone pavement or with other mosses on flat limestone rocks near shores of a turlough and a lake. In Britain, it is a rare species that grows on damp basic sand or soil, with recent records from open foredune slacks, the sandy uppermost edges of saltmarshes, gravel/sand pits and railway ballast.

The plants are short-lived perennials. They are synoicous and frequently produce capsules which mature from late spring through to autumn. Gemmae and tubers are unknown.

World distribution
In Britain, there are historic records from a wide scatter of mainly coastal localities from West Ross to Dorset, but there are fewer recent records (Church *et al.* 2001, Holyoak 2002a, 2002b). The species is widespread in Europe from Iceland, Svalbard and Fennoscandia southwards to S. England, N. France, Switzerland, Germany and Ukraine, but listed as *Endangered* in Germany and the Netherlands, *Vulnerable* in Britain and Switzerland, *Near Threatened* in Finland and 'very rare' in Estonia. In Europe, it is classified as a European Boreal-montane floristic element. Elsewhere, it is reported from Siberia, the Russian Far East, Himalaya, Greenland, Alaska and Canada.

Threats
Irish populations are potentially vulnerable to disturbance on lake shores such as might result from building jetties or increased amenity use, from shading (e.g. by trees), from changes in water-level regimes, or from eutrophication or other pollution of lake water.

Conservation
The only confirmed record for this species is on protected land. The rare *B. gemmiparum* occurs near to it.

Protected sites with recent records: Lough Carra/Mask Complex SAC; **Unprotected sites with recent records:** none.

Bryum intermedium (Brid.) Blandow
Many-seasoned Thread-moss

syn. *Bryum nitidulum* Lindb., *Ptychostomum intermedium* (Brid.) J.R.Spence
Status in Ireland: Endangered (B2a, bii, iv); **Status in Europe:** Least Concern

Identification
Bryum intermedium is a tufted acrocarpous moss with pendent capsules. It often differs from other species of *Bryum* in having capsules at differing stages of development on the same tuft. As in numerous other species of the genus, it has ovate-lanceolate leaves with red basal cells. The costa is shortly excurrent and the leaf border is strongly recurved. Both sexes occur on the same plant in the same inflorescences (synoicous). Mature capsules are needed for reliable identification, allowing the nodulose (and often also appendiculate) cilia of the inner peristome to be seen, along with the spore size of

Number of Hectads 13
+ Old (pre-1970) 10
□ Recent (1970–2010) 4

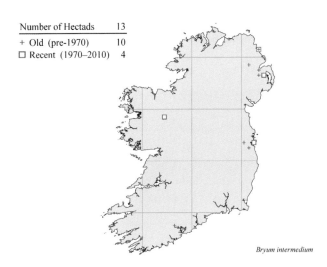

Bryum intermedium

18–24 µm and a usually somewhat asymmetrical capsule shape with a slightly oblique mouth. The genus *Bryum* is taxonomically difficult because there are numerous superficially similar species and careful attention to combinations of microscopic characters is necessary for reliable identification.

Distribution in Ireland

Recent records are from five localities in four vice-counties: Dublin (North Bull, large population, 2007); E. Mayo (Island Lake, 2003); Down (Castle Espie, 2008) and Antrim (just E. of Glenarm Village, 2008; Whitebay Point, 2008). It was recorded in the past from about twenty localities, but re-examination of specimens shows that some of the records were based on misidentification of other *Bryum* species or material too poor to determine. Only three old records have been confirmed as correct: Down (Drumbo Glen, 1870) and Antrim (People's Park near Belfast, 1869; opposite Madman's Window, 1928). Known or suspected errors are from: Wexford (1913); Dublin (Malahide, 1860); W. Mayo (Clare Island, 1910); Down (Ormeau Park, 1871; Ballymaghan, 1871 and 1910; Portano, 1884; etc.) and Armagh (Lough Neagh, 1870). Old records for which specimens have not been checked and which presumably include some errors are from: Mid Cork ('Cork', unlocalised, 1856); Dublin (Killakee, 1854, Abbotstown, 1857); E. Donegal (Bridge End, 1902) and Londonderry (Bann Estuary at Portstewart, 1931, 1938).

Ecology and biology

Its habitats are on unshaded, open, moist, basic soil in varied places such as on roadsides, stream banks, rock ledges or among sand dunes. Recent records are from marl heaps at the edge of a pool dug into the bed of a dried lake (E. Mayo), sand on top of a mortared-stone wall (Down), disturbed areas on chalk near the coast (Antrim) and on damp sand with sparse low vegetation in a foredune slack (North Bull in Dublin). All of these locations have nutrient-poor soils. At two of the sites the vegetation nearby supports *Bryum uliginosum*, and *B. warneum* occurs with it at North Bull. At many sites elsewhere in Europe, the species appears to be a colonist of exposed calcareous soil that does not persist as taller vegetation becomes established.

Although the plants are perennial, they can only be identified when mature capsules are present. Capsules are freely produced over a long season from early summer to autumn, so that reproduction doubtless occurs from spores. Gemmae and tubers have not been reported.

World distribution

The species is widespread in N. and C. Europe from the Arctic south to the Pyrenees and Alps. It is listed as *Endangered* in Luxembourg, *Vulnerable* in Bulgaria, the Netherlands and Switzerland, and *Data Deficient* in the Czech Republic, Germany and Spain. In Europe, it is assigned to a Eurasian Temperate floristic element. Elsewhere, it is known in Siberia, Greenland and Canada (Alberta). Reports from Morocco (Jelenc 1955, Ros *et al.* 1999) probably need confirmation; those from Australia are errors (cf. Spence & Ramsay 2006: 326).

Threats

The impression of decline of this species in Ireland is much reduced when account is taken of the large proportion of old records that were based on misidentifications. It should also be remembered that many of the open habitats it occupies are present only in early stages of vegetation succession, so the species needs to colonise new sites as old sites become unsuitable; this colonist life-strategy inevitably leads to a preponderance of old over recent records. Nevertheless, suitable habitats have doubtless declined, due to drainage, eutrophication and agricultural 'improvement'.

Conservation

B. intermedium is undoubtedly rare in Ireland and presumably severely threatened. The five populations currently known should be maintained through appropriate habitat management, which is likely to involve periodic recreation of open substrata. *B. intermedium* is a listed as a Northern Ireland Priority Species.

Protected sites with recent records: Bull Island Nature Reserve; Little Deer Park ASSI; North Dublin Bay SAC; River Moy SAC; Strangford Lough Part 3 ASSI; Strangford Lough SAC; **Unprotected sites with recent records:** just E. of Glenarm Village.

Bryum donianum Grev.

Don's Thread-moss

syn. *B. donii* Grev. ex Kindb. *orthogr. pro B. donianum*, *B. obovatum* Mitt., *B. pachyloma* Cardot
Status in Ireland: Least Concern; **Status in Europe:** Least Concern

A small green acrocarpous moss, with leaves, often widest above the middle, with a stout, thickened, yellowish border, that forms tufts on soil or in crevices, usually on walls, banks, or cliff slopes. It was included in the Provisional Red List (Holyoak 2006b), but recent fieldwork has revealed it to be relatively widespread in Ireland, with a scattered distribution in southern counties, though absent from the north. There are now reports from 16 vice-counties, with records from 43 hectads (10 old, 36 recent). There is little evidence of decline.

Bryum elegans Nees in Brid.

Blushing Bryum

syn. *B. capillare* var. *elegans* (Nees) Husn., *B. capillare* var. *ferchelii* (Funck) Bruch & Schimp., *B. stirtonii* Schimp., *Rosulabryum elegans* (Nees) Ochyra
Status in Ireland: Vulnerable (D2); **Status in Europe:** Least Concern

Identification

An acrocarpous moss that grows in loose to rather dense tufts, typically 10–40 mm high, green or green tinged with red, usually with long slender julaceous branches. *B. elegans* is a member of the group of species related to *B. capillare*, with bordered leaves widest at or above the middle, entire, mucronate to cuspidate or awned at the apex. Typical forms of *B. elegans* are distinctive in the julaceous shoots with broad, concave leaves combined with porose mid-leaf cells and very coarsely papillose rhizoids. Occasional gatherings of *B. capillare* from very humid sites may have concave and imbricate leaves with a shorter piliferous point than usual for that species, but these differ from *B. elegans* in having leaf cells less porose and rhizoids less coarsely papillose.

Distribution in Ireland

Known only from the Dartry Mountains, in Sligo (in and above Gleniff, 1970 and 1987, with more detailed localities recorded as: E. of Benbulbin, 1970; below

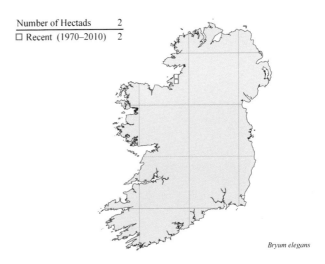

Bryum elegans

Cormac Reagh's Hole, 1970; Clogh, 1987; Annacoona, 2003) and Leitrim (Cloontyprughlish, 2005).

Ecology and biology

All records are from among limestone rocks at 300–500 m altitude, where noted as growing on boulders or rocks at base of high crags and on rocky slopes. The Leitrim record was from ledges with low vegetation on the base of a steep, N.-facing rocky slope. It is mainly a montane species elsewhere in Europe with most records from amongst basic rocks, but it is also known from walls and from damp soil in flushes.

The species grows as perennial patches. It is dioicous and capsules are unknown in Ireland (very rare in Britain). Tubers occur rarely on the rhizoids (in British material); other gemmae are unknown. Propagation and dispersal of the species is most likely to occur from shoot or leaf fragments.

World distribution

The species is widespread in N. and C. Europe from Iceland and arctic Scandinavia southwards in the mountains to SE Spain, Sardinia, the Balkans and Caucasus, but is listed as *Vulnerable* in Luxembourg, *Data Deficient* in Germany and 'very rare' in Estonia. Elsewhere, it is reported from N. Africa, Asia (Ural Mountains; Turkey; Afghanistan; Mongolia: Tsegmed 2001; Inner Mongolia: Zhao *et al.* 2006; Kamchatka: Czernyadjeva 2005; W. Taimyr: Zolotov 2006) and apparently also N. America (listed by Anderson *et al.* 1990 as *B. capillare* var. *ferchelii* and as *B. stirtonii*). In Europe, it has been assigned to a European Boreal-montane phytogeographical element (Hill *et al.* 2007), but this does not take account of records from N. and C.

Asia published in recent years or of its probable occurrence in N. America; these would imply a Circumpolar Boreal-montane designation might be appropriate.

Threats

No immediate threats are apparent. Occurrence of *B. elegans* among rocks and on small ledges may imply that it is at lower risk than some other montane bryophytes from the intensive grazing and erosion caused by overstocking with sheep in recent years.

Conservation

All of the Irish sites are on protected land.

Protected sites with recent records: Ben Bulben, Gleniff and Glenade Complex SAC; **Unprotected sites with recent records:** none.

Cloontyprughlish, Co. Leitrim.

Bryum moravicum Podp.

Syed's Thread-moss

syn. *B. flaccidum* auct. non Brid., *B. laevifilum* Syed, *B. subelegans* auct. non Kindb., *Rosulabryum laevifilum* (Syed) Ochyra
Status in Ireland: Critically Endangered (B1a, bii, iv, B2a, bii, iv); **Status in Europe:** Least Concern

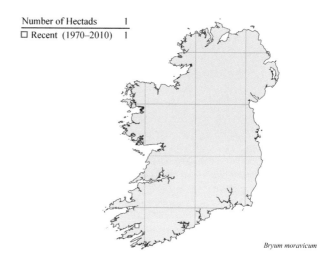

Number of Hectads	1
☐ Recent (1970–2010)	1

Bryum moravicum

Identification

An acrocarpous moss that grows in loose, light green tufts 5–40 mm high. It resembles several other species of *Bryum* in having leaves bordered with several rows of long narrow cells, hexagonal cells in mid-leaf and a costa varying from evanescent to excurrent as an awn. The resemblance to the very common *Bryum capillare* is particularly close, as they share a leaf shape that is ovate or ovate-lanceolate to obovate, the leaf being widest around the middle or just above the middle of the leaf. The main differences from *B. capillare* are the presence in *B. moravicum* of filiform gemmae in the axils of the lower leaves, frequent presence of decurrent leaf bases, and little or no tendency for the leaves to be spirally imbricate when dry. Sporophytes are unknown in Ireland or Britain; the capsule is cylindrical, cernuous and exserted on a long seta.

Distribution in Ireland

The only record is based on a specimen collected in S. Kerry at Uragh Wood near the SW shore of Inchiquin Lough by H.M.H. van Melick in 1979. The species was not refound when the area was searched for it in 2006, although the precise locality of the original find was not recorded. This occurrence is widely disjunct, but the voucher specimen (**BBSUK**) is correctly identified.

Ecology and biology

The single Irish specimen was from a 'tree trunk in native oak woodland'. In England, it is characteristically an epiphyte on the bark of trees and bushes (especially Elder, Ash, Sycamore and maple), occurring more rarely on stumps, rotten logs, rocks or soil. In continental Europe, it is common on rocks and soil in some regions.

The plants are short-lived perennials and their protonemata are also long-persistent (Pressel *et al.* 2007). The species is dioicous and capsules are unknown in Ireland and Britain, although at least occasional in continental Europe (e.g. in Pyrenees). Besides the plentiful axillary gemmae, foliar gemmae are sometimes produced and protonemal gemmae occur (Pressel *et al.* 2007); rhizoidal tubers are also often present.

World distribution

This species is widespread in Europe from N. Iceland and N. Fennoscandia southwards to S. Spain, Italy, Serbia and the Caucasus. It is assigned to a Circumpolar Temperate floristic element in Europe (Hill *et al.* 2007), but this inadequately represents its occurrence in the far north (Circumpolar Wide-boreal might be more apt). Elsewhere, the species is known in N. Africa, N., C., E. and SW Asia and N. America. Reports from the West Indies and S. America need checking.

Threats

As the only record in Ireland has not been refound, there is little information on threats. However, the oakwood at Uragh Wood is a nature reserve and plenty of 'tree trunks in native oak woodland' are found there, which suggests suitable habitat for *B. moravicum* is still available.

Conservation

Although widespread in E. Scotland, E. Wales and much of England, the species is extremely rare along the western seaboard of Britain (see map in Hill *et al.* 1992), with isolated records in Wigtownshire and E. Cornwall perhaps representing only casual and impermanent occurrences in regions that may be climatically unsuitable. It is uncertain if *B. moravicum* still survives at the locality in S. Kerry, which is even more widely separated from the main area of distribution and perhaps therefore also likely to represent only a temporary occurrence.

Protected sites with recent records: Cloonee and Inchiquin Loughs, Uragh Wood SAC; Uragh Wood Nature Reserve; **Unprotected sites with recent records:** none.

Bryum torquescens Bruch & Schimp.   Twisting Thread-moss

syn. *B. capillare* subsp. *torquescens* (Bruch & Schimp.) Kindb., *B. capillare* var. *torquescens* (Bruch & Schimp.) Husn., *B. obconicum* auct. non Hornsch. ex Bruch & Schimp., *Rosulabryum torquescens* (Bruch & Schimp.) J.R.Spence
Status in Ireland: Vulnerable (B2a, bi, ii, iv); **Status in Europe:** Least Concern

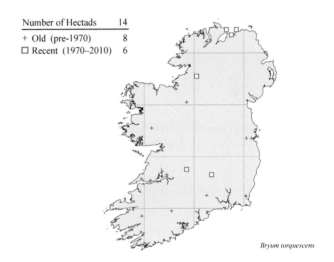

Number of Hectads	14
+ Old (pre-1970)	8
☐ Recent (1970–2010)	6

Bryum torquescens

Identification

This is an acrocarpous moss that grows as loose or dense tufts, or forms low turfs. The plants are usually 10–25 mm high, green or sometimes reddish tinged, with pendent capsules. *B. torquescens* is very similar to the much more common *B. capillare* in having bordered leaves widest at or above middle and the costa excurrent in a cuspidate or mucronate point. It differs from *B. capillare* in usually being synoicous (rarely dioicous as in *B. capillare*, or autoicous), in often (not invariably) having red rather than red-brown rhizoidal tubers, and in having the tip of the apical cell of synoicous and male paraphyses pointed rather than rounded. It is often not distinguishable in the field from *B. capillare*, but spiral twisting of dried upper leaves is much less tight and regular than in many forms of that species, and the habitat and range are more restricted in that *B. torquescens* usually grows on calcareous soil rather than rocks or trees.

Distribution in Ireland

Recent records are from six localities in six vice-counties: N. Tipperary (Garryard West, 2008); Kilkenny (Spahill, 2010); E. Donegal (substantial population at Kinnagoe Bay, 2002); Fermanagh (Monawilkin, 2008); Antrim (White Rocks, 2008) and Londonderry (The Umbra, 2003). At least eight older records appear to be correct: S. Kerry (Muckross, 1861 to 1899); E. Cork (Mallow, 1885); S. Tipperary (near Clonmel, 1858); Clare (Shannon, undated in 19th century); W. Galway (near Cong, 1871); Dublin (near Sheep Hill, 1863; Finglas Bridge, 1879) and Roscommon (near Boyle, 1940). Old records from seven other localities are known to be errors, likely to be errors, or at best unconfirmed: W. Galway (Galway, 1871; Lough Muck, Killary, 1957); Dublin (Abbotstown, 1855–1871; Ashton, 1859); Longford (near Lanesborough, 1957); E. Donegal (Bundoran, 1937) and Antrim (Ballymacash, as *B. obconicum*, leg.

Davies: Megaw 1938). Although this species can be overlooked as the more common *B. capillare*, the preponderance of old over recent records and failure to refind it at any of the old sites implies that it has declined in Ireland. It is therefore remarkable that four of the five modern records of this declining species, which has a predominantly southern range in Europe, are among the most northerly localities ever reported.

Ecology and biology

Three of the recent records from Ireland are from unshaded coastal sites: at Kinnagoe Bay on loose sand on a sparsely vegetated foredune slope above the beach, among sparse *Festuca rubra*; at The Umbra among low herbs on a S.-facing bank at landward edge of sand dunes; at White Rocks on chalky soil exposed on a bank in an old quarry. At Garryard West, it occurred on partly bare soil among shaly rocks at the base of a N.-facing slope in an old water-filled quarry at c. 105 m altitude. At Spahill, it was found in soil gaps in a small area of limestone pavement at c. 300 m altitude. At Monawilkin it was found on thin unshaded dry soil among sparse low grasses and herbs on a SE-facing slope, c. 150 m altitude. Three of the older records noted that the specimens were collected from walls. In Britain and further south in Europe, it typically grows on calcareous soil in open sunny places, especially on free-draining substrates, on banks, in open patches in grassland, on roadsides, about old quarries, and on thin soil overlying rocks, especially limestone but also hard metamorphic rocks and concrete.

The species is a short-lived perennial. Plants are usually synoicous and produce capsules in abundance, with spores maturing in spring. Tubers are usually plentiful on the rhizoids.

World distribution

B. torquescens is widespread and common in much of S. Europe, becoming more scarce northwards and reaching northern limits in Scotland (E. Ross), Sweden (Gotland) and the Czech Republic. Frahm & Klaus (2001) found that recent and historic records of it in Germany were mainly associated with warm years, perhaps implying they represented impersistent populations that had rapidly colonised during warmer than usual climatic conditions. It is listed as *Extinct* in Sweden, *Endangered* in the Netherlands, *Vulnerable* in Bulgaria, *Data Deficient* in the Czech Republic and 'presumably threatened' in Germany. It is assigned to an Oceanic Mediterranean-Atlantic floristic element in Europe. Elsewhere, it is known in Macaronesia, Africa (including Sudan, Kenya and S. Africa), Asia (including Middle East, Pakistan and Nepal), Australia, New Zealand, N. America, C. America (Mexico) and S. America (southwards to Chile).

Threats

Reasons for its apparent decline in Ireland are uncertain, although some populations may have been lost as the practice of capping walls with soil ceased. Although it is possible that some Irish records only represented casual colonists, its apparent persistence around Muckross from 1861 to 1899 implies that it was well established in at least one area.

Conservation

Most of the sites are on protected land. At The Umbra it grows on protected land of an ASSI (Magilligan) that is managed as a nature reserve. *B. torquescens* is listed as a Northern Ireland Priority Species.

Protected sites with recent records: Magilligan ASSI; Magilligan SAC; Monawilkin ASSI; Monawilkin SAC; North Inishowen Coast SAC; Spahill and Clomantagh Hill SAC; White Rocks ASSI; **Unprotected sites with recent records:** Garryard West.

Bryum creberrimum Taylor   Tight-tufted Thread-moss

syn. *B. affine* F.Schultz (non Gmelin ex Broth.), *B. cuspidatum* (Bruch & Schimp.) Schimp., *B. lisae* De Not., *Plagiobryum lisae* (De Not.) N.Pedersen

Status in Ireland: Data Deficient; **Status in Europe:** Least Concern

Identification

An acrocarpous moss that forms tight tufts, green above, reddish-brown and matted with rhizoids below, 10–40 mm high. *B. creberrimum* is very similar to several other *Bryum* species and reliably distinguished only by using microscopic characters of the peristome and spores.

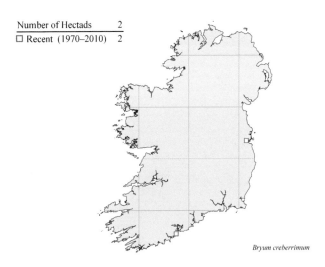

Number of Hectads 2
☐ Recent (1970–2010) 2

Bryum creberrimum

Bryum pallescens is closest to *B. creberrimum*, and best distinguished by its larger spores (> 18 μm cf. 14–16 μm, although plants with spores of intermediate size occur occasionally: Smith 1978) and narrower perforations in the endostome processes. *B. pallescens* can be autoicous or synoicous, whereas *B. creberrimum* is only known to be synoicous. *B. pallescens* often has wider ± ovate leaves which are shortly pointed but forms also occur with narrower ovate-lanceolate leaves indistinguishable from those of *B. creberrimum*. *B. pseudotriquetrum* var. *bimum* resembles *B. creberrimum* in being synoicous, but is usually distinguishable by its more shortly acuminate leaves with (typically, but not always) more shortly excurrent costa. Well-grown plants of *bimum* also differ in the equidistant rather than rosulate leaf arrangement and sometimes more decurrent leaf bases but these characters become unclear on shorter plants.

Distribution in Ireland

B. creberrimum is known from two localities in Ireland: a single specimen, collected close to the Quarry Lake in Phoenix Park, Dublin in 1988 by D.L. Kelly (the species has apparently not persisted there) and from the Sacred Heart Catholic church, Minane Bridge, Mid Cork, collected by C.D. Preston during the BBS field meeting in 2009. Two older collections from Ireland that were assigned to this species are known to have been misidentified: N. Kerry (Muckross, 1872) and N. Tipperary (Loughnaminch, 1949).

Ecology and biology

The Phoenix Park record was from an unshaded rotten log with *Oxyrrhynchium hians*. The Minane Bridge record was from a flowerpot in a churchyard. British and other European records are from unshaded to lightly shaded basic soil in waste places, on banks, on dunes, by roadsides and in crevices of rocks and walls.

Tufts of the species appear to behave as short-lived perennials, although individual stems probably only live for one or two years. The plants are synoicous and frequently produce capsules which mature in summer. Tubers and gemmae are unknown.

World distribution

Widespread in Europe from Iceland and Spitsbergen southwards to the Mediterranean and east to the Caucasus, but scarce to rare in many countries (including Britain, where there are few recent records), and listed as *Near Threatened* in Switzerland and *Data Deficient* in Bulgaria, the Czech Republic, Germany and Serbia and Montenegro. In Europe, it is assigned to a Circumpolar Boreo-temperate floristic element. Elsewhere, it is recorded in the Azores, Morocco, Asia, N. America, Argentina, Australia and New Zealand.

Threats

The only extant population of *B. creberrimum* in Ireland is in an inherently temporal habitat and is not likely to persist there.

Conservation

The temporary nature of the Irish occurrences imply that the species should be a low conservation priority.

Protected sites with recent records: none; **Unprotected sites with recent records:** Quarry Lake in Phoenix Park, Dublin; Sacred Heart Catholic church, Minane Bridge.

Bryum pallescens Schleich. ex Schwägr.

Tall-clustered Thread-moss

syn. *B. lonchocaulon* Müll.Hal., *B. obconicum* Hornsch. ex Bruch & Schimp.
Status in Ireland: Least Concern; **Status in Europe:** Least Concern

An acrocarpous moss that grows in a varied range of open, basic habitats, including walls, banks and sand dunes. It was included in the Provisional Red List (Holyoak 2006b). However, recent fieldwork in Ireland has shown that it is widespread in sites with high zinc levels that result from rainwater running off galvanised-iron roofs and fences and roadside crash barriers. It has been reported from 28 vice-counties, with records from 44 hectads (4 old, 40 recent) and it is doubtless still under-recorded.

Bryum caespiticium L. ex Hedw.

Tufted Thread-moss

syn. *Bryum badium* (Brid.) Schimp., *B. comense* Schimp., *B. imbricatulum* Müll.Hal.,
Ptychostomum badium (Brid.) J.R.Spence, *Ptychostomum imbricatulum* (Müll.Hal.) Holyoak & N.Pedersen
Status in Ireland: Vulnerable (D2); **Status in Europe:** Least Concern

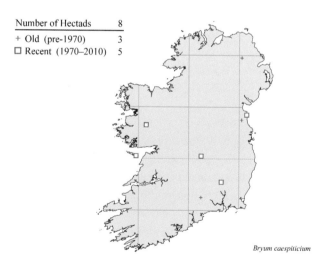

Number of Hectads	8
+ Old (pre-1970)	3
□ Recent (1970–2010)	5

Bryum caespiticium

Identification

An acrocarpous moss that forms rather dense dull green tufts or low turfs, with stems to 10 mm high (occasionally 20 mm) and pendent capsules. Reliable separation from other species of *Bryum* depends on detailed microscopic study. Small plants of *B. caespiticium* can show a strong superficial similarity to *B. dichotomum*, *B. rubens* or *B.*

radiculosum, larger plants can be superficially similar to *B. archangelicum*, *B. algovicum* and several other species. Good fertile material should therefore be identified by a careful assessment of at least most of the following characters: plants often growing in dense tufts, leaves rosulate, imbricate and only slightly twisted when dry, flat or only slightly concave, widest below middle, weakly bordered, margin recurved, leaf red at base, mid-leaf cells narrow (12–16 *μ*m); costa long excurrent in upper leaves; plants dioicous; cilia appendiculate; spores 10–14 *μ*m. Small plants of *B. caespiticium* are easily confused with *B. dichotomum* even with good fertile material, as both are variable and almost all of the characters of their gametophytes and sporophytes overlap (Holyoak & Pedersen 2007). Characters of *B. caespiticium* alone include the red leaf base and longer capsule; numerous well-developed axillary bulbils (rather than buds) occur only in *B. dichotomum*, but these are not always present.

Distribution in Ireland

Recent accepted records are from five localities: Clare (Inishmore, Aran Islands, 2008); Kilkenny (Catholic church at Goresbridge, 2006); Offaly (Cadamstown, 2009); E. Mayo (NW of Keel Bridge, 2003) and Louth (Clogher Head, 2007). Two older records have been confirmed as correct: Louth (Mellifont Abbey, 1964) and Antrim (near Mossvale, 1939), and a third is likely to be correct: S. Tipperary (Clonmel, 1879, **BM**). Known errors include reidentified herbarium specimens from Clare, Wexford, Dublin, Roscommon, W. Mayo, Sligo, Fermanagh, E. Donegal, Armagh, Down, Antrim and Londonderry. Voucher specimens for some other vice-counties have not been re-examined (e.g. S. Kerry, W. Cork, S. Tipperary, Limerick) but even if the specimens can be located it seems unlikely that many of them will prove to be correctly identified.

Ecology and biology

Little information is available because there are few correctly identified records of the species. In Kilkenny, it grew on peat soil in a pot on a grave; in Offaly, it grew on an old sandstone shed; in E. Mayo, it grew with other mosses and low grasses and herbs in a small unshaded crevice in limestone pavement. Two records from Louth were from 'between stones' and as a weed on a heap of disturbed soil near the coast. In Antrim it grew on a wall. In Britain and elsewhere in Europe, the species typically grows on unshaded basic soil in rather dry, open places on hillsides, above cliffs, among rocks, in quarries, on sand dunes, at roadsides or on top of walls.

The plants are perennial. They are dioicous and frequently produce capsules, in which the spores mature in summer. Reports of tubers (e.g. A.C. Crundwell in Hill *et al.* 1994) appear to be based on misidentifications.

World distribution

B. caespiticium is widespread in Europe from Iceland and Scandinavia southwards to the Mediterranean and often very common in S. Europe, but often misidentified and scarcer than the literature would imply in some countries. It is assigned to a Circumpolar Boreo-temperate floristic element in Europe. Elsewhere, it has a very wide range in Asia, Africa, Australasia, N. America, C. America, S. America and some oceanic islands.

Threats

The status of *B. caespiticium* in Ireland is unclear because of misidentifications. At least some of its records are from disturbed soil, where it may be a temporary colonist and behave as a weed, disappearing as taller plants shade the ground. Elsewhere, it may become established for longer on walls or in crevices of limestone pavement.

Conservation

This species is so abundant in other European countries that protection of small populations in Ireland seems a low priority, especially if their occurrences are partly as weeds of disturbed ground.

Protected sites with recent records: Inishmore Island SAC; Lough Carra/Mask Complex SAC; **Unprotected sites with recent records:** Cadamstown; Catholic church at Goresbridge; Clogher Head (possibly within Clogher Head SAC).

North-west of Keel Bridge, Lough Carra, Co. Mayo.

Bryum gemmiferum R.Wilczek & Demaret

Small-bud Bryum

Status in Ireland: Least Concern; **Status in Europe:** Least Concern

A small acrocarpous moss with conspicuous clusters of yellowish-green, orange or red axillary bulbils. It grows on exposed, periodically wet but well-drained sandy, loamy or gravelly soil on banks, stream sides, arable fields, dune slacks, margins of reservoirs and other open sites. It was included in the Provisional Red List (Holyoak 2006b), but has been recorded from 18 vice-counties and 25 hectads (all recent, 19 hectads in the last decade) and is probably still under-recorded.

Bryum dyffrynense Holyoak

Dyffryn Bryum

Status in Ireland: Near Threatened; **Status in Europe:** Not Evaluated

A small acrocarpous moss that colonises damp coastal sand. It was first described from British coasts by Holyoak (2003b) and has now been recorded also from Belgium (De Beer & Martens 2007) and NW France (D.T. Holyoak unpublished). Recent molecular data place it as part of the *B. dichotomum* group (Holyoak & Pedersen 2007, Pedersen *et al.* 2007), although it is distinct from the '*B. bicolor* phenotype' in morphology. It has been reported in Ireland from four vice-counties, with records made between 2002 and 2004 in six hectads, including some strong populations. However, it may still be somewhat under-recorded so that treatment as *Near Threatened* rather than *Vulnerable* seems appropriate. This plant is endemic to Europe, as far as is currently known.

Bryum violaceum Crundw. & Nyholm

Status in Ireland: Least Concern; **Status in Europe:** Least Concern

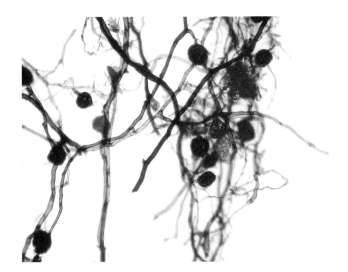

A small acrocarpous moss, with dull mauve to violet-coloured rhizoids and small purplish-red tubers, that grows on bare soil, especially in arable (tillage) fields. It was placed on the Provisional Red List (Holyoak 2006b) because there were few records up to 1998. However, subsequent fieldwork has resulted in many more so that there are now records from 21 vice-counties and 31 hectads (4 old, 28 recent). *Bryum violaceum* has large populations in some stubble fields.

Bryum tenuisetum Limpr.

syn. *Gemmabryum tenuisetum* (Limpr.) J.R.Spence & H.P.Ramsay
Status in Ireland: Data Deficient; **Status in Europe:** Insufficiently Known

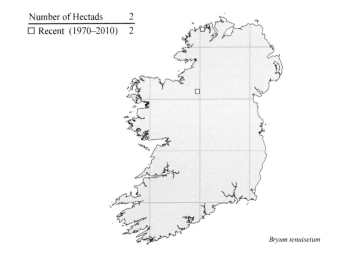

Number of Hectads	2
☐ Recent (1970–2010)	2

Bryum tenuisetum

Identification

A small acrocarpous moss that grows as loose green to dull dark green or reddish tufts or sparse low turfs, 3–10 mm high, sometimes with pendent capsules resembling those of other species of *Bryum*. *B. tenuisetum* is one of several small species of the genus with rhizoidal tubers, but it differs from most of these in having yellow tubers. However, it is only safely identifiable using microscopic characters since yellow tubers also occur in *B. dichotomum*

and (rarely) in *B. subapiculatum* and *B. rubens*. Characters diagnostic for *B. tenuisetum* are presence, in combination, of narrow leaf cells along with bright yellow to orange-brown subspherical tubers occurring singly on side branches of long yellow to brown rhizoids, the tubers being mainly 100–200 μm long and composed of large somewhat bulging cells. Atypical plants of *B. subapiculatum* with yellow (or orange) tubers are distinct from *B. tenuisetum* mainly in their larger tuber

491

size (> 200 μm) and their less protuberant tuber cells. Occasional British gatherings with small-celled dull yellow to brown tubers mainly > 200 μm long (sometimes > 300 μm) are apparently referable to *B. dichotomum*.

Distribution in Ireland

There are two confirmed records from Ireland: Leitrim (E. shore of Lough Allen, W. of Cleighran More, 2001) and W. Donegal (E. bank of Lackagh River near Lackagh Bridge, 2002). The report from W. Cork (near League Point, 1979) is based on specimens that have been reidentified as *B. subapiculatum* bearing yellow rhizoidal tubers. *B. tenuisetum* is almost certainly under-recorded because it is a small and inconspicuous moss that is only identifiable from microscopic study.

Ecology and biology

In Ireland, it has been recorded on unshaded damp sand of disturbed ground by a lake shore (Leitrim) and on unshaded, thin soil in a crevice of damp horizontal rocks among *Schoenus nigricans* tussocks beside a tidal estuary and just above the highest tide levels (W. Donegal). In Britain and continental Europe, it is a calcifuge, found in open places on damp soils, sand, peat, mud and sandy shale. Many records are from moist ground and from edges of ponds and reservoirs, sometimes within their inundation zones. Other reports are from disturbed ground in a rough pasture, a boggy flush, on heathland or more rarely in arable fields or damp ground on coastal dunes (Crundwell & Nyholm 1964, During 1973, Smith 1978, Whitehouse in Hill *et al.* 1994, Whitehouse 2001).

The plants are probably short-lived in many sites. They are dioicous with occasional synoicous inflorescences and frequently produce capsules with spores maturing in summer. Rhizoidal tubers are plentiful; linear gemmae occur on the protonema (Arts 1992, Duckett & Ligrone 1992).

World distribution

The species is widely but rather sparsely distributed in N. and C. Europe, from Iceland and Fennoscandia southwards to NE Spain, Italy and the Ukraine. It is listed as *Vulnerable* in Luxembourg and Spain, *Data Deficient* in the Czech Republic, 'presumably threatened' in Germany and 'declining' in Norway. In Europe, it is assigned to a European Boreo-temperate floristic element. Elsewhere, it is known only in Macaronesia (Azores: Crundwell *et al.* 1994, Sjögren 2001; Tenerife: Koppe & Düll 1982, Dirkse *et al.* 1993) and locally in N. America (e.g. Quebec: Whitehouse 2001).

Threats

Potential threats to the species are poorly understood, but may include drainage, alteration of flooding or grazing regimes, shading and eutrophication. The site in Leitrim could be at risk from changes on the lake shore, including building of jetties or boathouses.

Conservation

The site in W. Donegal is on protected land.

Protected sites with recent records: Cloghernagore Bog and Glenveagh National Park SAC; **Unprotected sites with recent records:** E. shore of Lough Allen.

Lackagh River, Co. Donegal.

Bryum bornholmense Wink. & R.Ruthe

Potato Bryum

syn. *Ptychostomum bornholmense* (Wink. & R.Ruthe) Holyoak & N.Pedersen
Status in Ireland: Near Threatened; **Status in Europe:** Least Concern

A small acrocarpous moss of slightly acidic soil, usually on peat, where it is a colonist of open ground, often where burnt. It has been reported from six vice-counties, with records from seven hectads (1 old, 6 recent). Crundwell & Whitehouse (2001) have shown that there has been considerable confusion of *B. bornholmense* with the more common *B. rubens*, so that earlier accounts of the differences between them are partly incorrect and older determinations therefore need checking. Although some records of this taxonomically critical species have been shown to be erroneous, it is still under-recorded (five of its seven acceptable records were made in the last decade).

Bryum riparium I.Hagen

River Thread-moss

syn. *Bryum alpinum* subsp. *riparium* (I.Hagen) Podp., *B. mildeanum* auct. non Jur.
Status in Ireland: Endangered (B2a, bii, iv); **Status in Europe:** Rare

Number of Hectads	9
+ Old (pre-1970)	6
☐ Recent (1970–2010)	4

Bryum riparium

Identification

An acrocarpous moss that grows in tufts or as low turfs that are pale green or yellowish-green above, blackish below and 10–30 mm high. It is easily overlooked as a small form of *Bryum pseudotriquetrum*, although the equidistant leaves are more closely imbricate than in that species. Detailed study reveals closely placed, rather narrow leaves concealing the brown (not reddish) stem, a distinct leaf border and green or brownish costa. More importantly, *B. riparium* differs from all other European species of *Bryum* in having distinctive red tubers that are flattened and serrate or lobed apically. The very long, narrow cells (c. 80 × 10 μm) forming the decurrent leaf base provide another useful microscopic character for a species of Bryaceae that at first sight seems to lack distinctive features.

Distribution in Ireland

There are recent records from four localities in two vice-counties: W. Galway (Maumtrasna, 1957 and 2003) and W. Mayo (Corryloughaphuill, 1982; Mweelrea, 1987 and 2003; Slievemore, Achill Island, 2003; also poorly documented reports from two other localities on Achill Island in 1987). There are older records from a further six localities: S. Kerry (Lough Currane, 1951); Waterford (Sgilloge Loughs, 1966); W. Galway (Benchoona, 1957; SE valley of Maumtrasna, 1957); W. Mayo (Clare Island, 1909) and Down (Slievenabrock, 1885). It has not been refound at some of the old localities in recent years, but the species tends to grow in small patches and it can be rather inconspicuous, so there is no firm evidence of decline. Although collected in Ireland in 1885, and named from a Norwegian specimen in 1908, *B. riparium* was not generally recognised as distinct from *B. mildeanum* until the study by Whitehouse (1963).

Ecology and biology

It is mainly restricted to sediment banks of upland streams, rivers and ditches, and wet rocks (including gullies in montane crags and a sea cliff), growing on soil, sand, rocks and in rock crevices. Several records are from rocks that are poor in bases (sandstone, quartzite, slate, schist and other metamorphic rocks). It has been recorded in Ireland at up to 472 m altitude. In Scotland, atypical records have been made in an arable field (amongst stubble) and on rotting wood.

The species appears to be a short-lived perennial. It is evidently dioicous as only female plants are known (Whitehouse 1963), so capsules are of course unknown. Tubers are abundant on the rhizoids, including the short rhizoids that may form a tomentum on the stem amongst the lower leaves. Other gemmae are unknown.

World distribution

B. riparium is widespread but rather scarce in W. Britain from S. Wales to N. Scotland (Hill *et al.* 1994). The only confirmed records from Europe outside Ireland and Britain are from SW Norway (Whitehouse 1963, Nyholm 1993) (*Vulnerable*), but it has recently been reported from Austria (Carinthian Alps, *leg.* Michael Suanjak, *fide* H. Köckinger, pers. comm.). It is currently assigned to a Hyperoceanic Temperate floristic element in Europe by Hill *et al.* (2007), although confirmation of the record from Austria should lead to modification of this treatment. Outside Europe, it is known from NE Turkey (Çetin 1988, Frey & Kürschner 1991, Nyholm 1993; although Düll 1992 expressed doubts, the specimen at **S** has been confirmed by DTH) and North Carolina (single record given by A.C. Crundwell in Hill *et al.* 1994: 114; also accepted for N. American list by Anderson *et al.* 1990).

Threats

This species is potentially at risk from erosion and eutrophication in the uplands, although those localities on steep crags may be less susceptible to erosion caused by sheep. Some other sites are on earthy banks of gullies where some erosion may be beneficial in providing open sites for it to colonise.

Conservation

All of the Irish localities are on protected land.

Protected sites with recent records: Ballycroy National Park; Croaghaun/Slievemore SAC; Maumtrasna Mountain Complex pNHA; Mweelrea/Sheeffry/Erriff Complex SAC; Owenduff/Nephin Complex SAC; **Unprotected sites with recent records:** none.

Bryum gemmiparum De Not.

Welsh Thread-moss

syn. *Bryum alpinum* subsp. *gemmiparum* (De Not.) Kindb., *Imbribryum gemmiparum* (De Not.) J.R.Spence
Status in Ireland: Vulnerable (D2); **Status in Europe:** Least Concern

Identification

An acrocarpous moss that grows in dull dense tufts, greenish above, reddish below, up to 30 mm tall. It somewhat resembles wide-leaved forms of *Bryum alpinum*, but is clearly distinct from that species in the occurrence of large axillary bulbils. The shortly acute and often concave leaves of *B. gemmiparum* differ from the tapering leaves with flat apices normally found in

B. alpinum, but many specimens placed as *B. gemmiparum* in herbaria are nevertheless forms of *B. alpinum* with wide leaves. Robust plants of *B. dichotomum* have sometimes been confused with *B. gemmiparum*, but these have a weaker costa (rarely > 60 μm wide at leaf base, compared to > 80 μm in *B. gemmiparum*), relatively wider ± hexagonal mid-leaf cells, and the forms with costa evanescent or percurrent usually also differ in leaf shape.

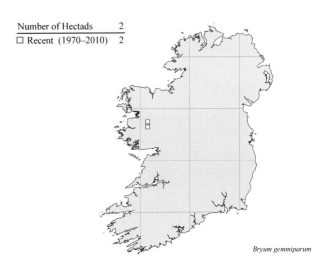

Bryum gemmiparum

Distribution in Ireland

This species has only recently been detected in Ireland, where it has been recorded from three localities in E. Mayo (E. shore of Lough Carra, 2003–2004; E. shore of Lough Mask, 2003; NW of Keel Bridge, 2003). It was found growing as small scattered patches at all three sites, but the areas of similar habitat are extensive so larger populations may be present.

Ecology and biology

Found only in unshaded, damp, calcareous sites with sparse vegetation. Two localities are on shores of base-rich lakes, within the inundation zones, but 10–80 cm above typical summer water levels, in crevices of horizontal limestone or on thin sandy soil on limestone boulders in the water near the lake shore. The third locality is on open limestone pavement where it grows in small damp crevices amongst other mosses. In Britain, this is a rare species of crevices in rocks by streams or rivers, e.g. found growing in small cushions on flat silted sandstone rocks above the mean water level but in the flood zone, with *Cinclidotus fontinaloides* and *Didymodon luridus* (Church *et al.* 2001). It is more common in S. Europe, and occupies a wider range of periodically wet habitats, e.g. in Almería Province (Spain) found on humiferous soils, accumulated soil at the bases of rocks, edges of riverbeds and leaking walls (García-Zamora *et al.* 1998).

The species is probably a short-lived perennial. It is dioicous and capsules are unknown in Ireland or Britain and rare in S. Europe. Caducous bulbils are frequent and doubtless function as propagules. Reports of rhizoidal 'gemmae' or tubers from Belgium and elsewhere (A.C. Crundwell in Hill *et al.* 1994, Preston 2004, Smith 2004, Hill *et al.* 2007) are probably all based on misidentification of forms of *B. alpinum*.

World distribution

The Irish populations are the most northerly known populations in the world. In Europe, it occurs at a very few localities in S. Wales and SW England and more widely from France and S. Germany (where it is listed as 'extremely rare') southwards to the Mediterranean and east to the Caucasus. It is listed as *Critically Endangered* in Switzerland, *Vulnerable* in Britain and *Vulnerable* in Bulgaria. In Europe, it is assigned to an Oceanic Mediterranean-Atlantic floristic element. Elsewhere, it is widespread in Macaronesia, N. Africa and the Near East, with reports also from Chad (Jelenc 1959, Ros *et al.* 1999). Records from Belgium, Holland, India and Yunnan are apparently errors; those from California (Kellman 2003) and elsewhere in N. America need confirmation.

Threats

Potentially vulnerable to changes to lake shores such as might result from increased amenity use, building jetties, shading (e.g. by trees), from changes in water-level regimes, or from eutrophication or other pollution of lake water.

Conservation

All of the Irish populations are on protected land. The rare *B. knowltonii* occurs close to it at some sites.

Protected sites with recent records: Lough Carra/Mask Complex SAC; **Unprotected sites with recent records:** none.

Rhodobryum roseum (Hedw.) Limpr.

Rose-moss

syn. *Bryum proliferum* Lindb. & Arn., *B. roseum* (Hedw.) P.Gaertn. *et al.*
Status in Ireland: Near Threatened; **Status in Europe:** Least Concern

A robust acrocarpous moss with large comal leaves that grows in short grassland, among rocks or on sand dunes. There are reports from 22 vice-counties, with records from 40 hectads (27 old, 11 recent, 2 undated). Fieldwork over the past decade has made no effort to refind the old localities, so the impression of decline may result from this lack of attention. Seven new records made from 2000 to 2010 include a very large population in E. Mayo.

Pohlia elongata Hedw. **var.** *elongata*

Long-fruited Thread-moss

syn. *Pohlia acuminata* Hoppe & Hornsch., *Webera acuminata* (Hoppe & Hornsch.) Schimp., *W. elongata* (Hedw.) Schwägr.
Status in Ireland: Near Threatened; **Status in Europe:** Least Concern

An acrocarpous moss with long-necked capsules that grows on soil of banks and ledges, mostly in the mountains. There are reports from 13 vice-counties, with records from 22 hectads (10 old, 13 recent, 2 undated). In the past decade, it has been found at more than 20 localities, but almost always as small populations, suggesting it is likely to be an impersistent colonist at most sites. Until recently, autoicous plants have been treated as a distinct species (*P. acuminata*) or as var. *acuminata*, with confirmed records from S. Kerry (in 1828), S. Tipperary (1966) and W. Galway (2004), and unconfirmed reports from four other vice-counties (Holyoak 2003a). However, Smith (2004) notes that, apart from the inflorescence, the characters separating them are not constant, so they were not considered worth maintaining even as a variety. This treatment was followed in Hill *et al.* (2006, 2008).

Pohlia elongata Hedw. **var.** *greenii* (Brid.) A.J.Shaw

Changeable Thread-moss

syn. *Pohlia elongata* var. *polymorpha* (Hornsch.) Nyholm, *P. elongata* subsp. *polymorpha* auct. (comb. inval.), *P. minor* Schwägr., *P. polymorpha* Hornsch., *Webera polymorpha* (Hornsch.) Schimp.

Status in Ireland: Endangered (B1a, bi, ii, iv, B2a, bi, ii, iv); **Status in Europe:** Least Concern

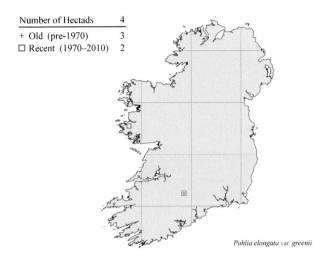

Number of Hectads	4
+ Old (pre-1970)	3
☐ Recent (1970–2010)	2

Pohlia elongata var. *greenii*

Identification

An acrocarpous moss that grows in green or yellowish-green tufts that are usually less than 10 mm high. The stem leaves are lanceolate, acuminate, with a stout percurrent or excurrent costa. The leaf margins are plane or recurved and denticulate above. The leaf cells are linear, measuring 8–12 μm wide and about 40 μm long in mid-leaf. Perichaetial bracts are crowded into a comal tuft, longer than the leaves (1.0–2.5 mm) and narrowly lanceolate to linear-lanceolate and acuminate. The capsules are exserted on a seta up to about 10 mm high, narrowly pyriform, cernuous, with neck shorter than theca and an endostome that has a very short basal membrane and lacks cilia. Distinct from other forms of *P. elongata* in the consistently paroicous (never autoicous) sexuality combined with mainly shorter perichaetial bracts, mainly shorter mid-leaf cells, capsule with neck shorter than theca and consistently reduced endostome. However, Nyholm (1993) does not recognise intraspecific taxa within the 'extremely variable' *P. elongata*.

Distribution in Ireland

There are two recent records: S. Tipperary (Lough Curra in Galty Mountains, 1966 and 2005) and W. Galway (Muckanaght, 1970). In addition, four old records appear to be correct: S. Kerry (Brandon Mountain, 1840; Connor Hill Pass, 1873) and S. Tipperary (Galtymore, 1855; Lough Diheen, 1943). A record from Armagh (Brackagh Bog, 1909) was based on misidentified *Philonotis*. Several other records are unconfirmed or dubious: S. Kerry (Tomies Mountain, 1965 and 1970); Dublin (Templeogue, 1853) and W. Mayo (Mweelrea, 1987).

Ecology and biology

Habitats of specimens collected in Ireland have been recorded as earthy cliff ledges, a rock ledge and 'cliffs', all of them being at moderate to high elevations in the mountains. In Britain, it grows on skeletal peaty or gritty soils on rock ledges, in crevices, on soil amongst boulders on mountain summits and occasionally on rocky stream banks, at 400–1050 m altitude (M.J. Wigginton in Hill *et al.* 1994).

The longevity of tufts of the plant is unknown. *P. elongata* var. *greenii* is paroicous and frequently produces capsules, which mature in late summer and autumn. Gemmae and tubers are unknown.

World distribution

It is widespread in N. Europe and the mountains of central Europe, from Iceland and Spitsbergen through Fennoscandia to Spain, Italy and the Caucasus. It is listed as *Data Deficient* in Switzerland and Germany. In Europe, it is assigned to a Circumpolar Boreal-montane

497

floristic element. Elsewhere, it is recorded from Turkey, Kashmir, the Himalaya, China, N. America and Greenland.

Threats
There is little information, but some populations are likely to be at risk from the overgrazing, erosion and eutrophication that result from excessive stocking levels of sheep in the mountains.

Conservation
All sites with confirmed records appear to be on protected land.

Protected sites with recent records: Galtee Mountains SAC; The Twelve Bens/Garraun Complex SAC; **Unprotected sites with recent records:** none.

Pohlia cruda (Hedw.) Lindb.
Opal Thread-moss

syn. *Webera cruda* (Hedw.) Bruch
Status in Ireland: Least Concern; **Status in Europe:** Least Concern

A glaucous-green acrocarpous moss with a metallic sheen that grows mainly in sheltered rock crevices in the mountains. It was included in the Provisional Red List (Holyoak 2006b), but numerous additional populations have been found during fieldwork over the past decade, including new vice-county records for Sligo (King's Mountain, 2003) and Waterford (Comeragh Mountains, 2007). It has now been reported from 17 vice-counties, with records from 22 hectads (8 old, 16 recent, 3 undated).

Pohlia drummondii (Müll.Hal.) A.L.Andrews
Drummond's Thread-moss

Status in Ireland: Least Concern; **Status in Europe:** Least Concern

A small acrocarpous moss with large reddish axillary bulbils that grows on open, acidic, sandy or gravelly substrata. It was included in the Provisional Red List (Holyoak 2006b), but additional records resulting from fieldwork during the past decade show that it was previously under-recorded. There are now reports from 11 vice-counties, with records from 20 hectads (5 old, 18 recent). It is likely that numerous other small populations exist, such as on gravelly track edges and in disused sandpits.

Pohlia filum (Schimp.) Mårtensson

syn. *Pohlia gracilis* (Bruch & Schimp.) Lindb., *P. schleicheri* H.A.Crum
Status in Ireland: Vulnerable (A3c, D1); **Status in Europe:** Least Concern

Number of Hectads	7
+ Old (pre-1970)	2
□ Recent (1970–2010)	5

Pohlia filum

Identification

An acrocarpous moss that grows as scattered plants or small, glossy, yellowish-green tufts, becoming brownish or blackish with age, from a few millimetres to 4 cm high. The leaves are appressed when dry, stiffly erect when moist, keeled, slightly concave, ovate-triangular to broadly lanceolate, with an acute apex. The leaf margin is plane, dentate above and broadly decurrent at the base; the costa is evanescent. Mid-leaf cells are elongate-hexagonal, 8–14 μm wide. Large yellowish to brownish bulbils occur singly in the leaf axils, these being 350–600 μm long, ovate, crowned at the apex with 3–5 very short triangular leaf-primordia that comprise less than 20% of the total length of the bulbil. Capsules (unknown in Ireland) are ovate to pyriform, pendulous, exserted on a tall yellowish-red to reddish-brown seta. *P. filum* is distinctive among the small bulbiliferous species of *Pohlia* in its erect leaves combined with solitary large yellowish bulbils bearing very small leaf primordia.

Distribution in Ireland

Recent records are accepted from (at least) eight localities in four vice-counties: W. Mayo (E. of Lough Doo, 1987–2003; c. 4 km E. of Keel, 2003; Pollranny Sweeny, 1987; E. of Pollranny, 2003 [probably same locality as the preceding]); W. Donegal (SE end of Lough Nacung Upper, 1991–2002); Tyrone (W. of Brackagh South, 2002) and Londonderry (above Whitewater Bridge,

2002; Crockandun Hills, 2002). Older accepted records are from Waterford (2 miles N. of Cappoquin, 1966) and Tyrone (Baronscourt, 1957).

Ecology and biology

P. filum is an acidophile that is restricted to moist unshaded substrata with very low nutrient levels and very low organic content, at low elevations (15–315 m altitude). Six of the eight recent Irish records are from in or beside active or disused sand and gravel pits, on damp sand or soil, usually with sparse low vegetation (e.g. of mosses, grasses and *Juncus bufonius*). Two older records are from the side of a stony path and a wet sandy track by a river. It occurs in similar habitats in Britain, with records from beside streams and rivers, on rocks, on sandy tracks and roadsides, on dunes and in sandpits, but it was found once on damp cindery soil.

The plants are annual to short-lived perennials. It is a dioicous species in which male and female plants grow intermixed; capsules are very rare in Britain (unknown in Ireland), maturing in late spring or early summer. The large caducous bulbils that are present on most of the plants doubtless function as propagules. Gemmae and tubers are absent.

World distribution

In Europe, *P. filum* is most common in the north, occurring from N. Iceland, Spitsbergen, N. Fennoscandia and arctic Russia southwards, but with records extending to N. Portugal, N. Spain (Guerra 2007), Italy, Hungary (Erzberger 2005) and the Caucasus. It is listed as *Vulnerable* in Germany, *Data Deficient* in the Czech Republic, Montenegro, Spain and Portugal. It is assigned to a Circumpolar Boreo-arctic montane floristic element in Europe. Elsewhere, it is known in SW Asia (Georgia and Armenia: Ignatov *et al.* 2007), N. and C. Asia (widespread from W. and S. Siberia to Yakutia and Russian Far East: Ignatov *et al.* 2007), N. Japan (Iwatsuki 1991), N. America (Shaw 1981) and Greenland.

Threats

All of the recent finds were in or beside sand and gravel pits, several of which are unlikely to remain open for long. Most of its populations are small and vulnerable to loss of habitat caused by shading as cover of vascular plants develops. As a colonist of mainly bare substrata, *P. filum* will depend on creation of a succession of new sites as excavation of sand and siliceous gravel continues in base-poor areas.

Conservation

None of the sites are on protected land. *P. filum* is listed as a Northern Ireland Priority Species.

Protected sites with recent records: none; **Unprotected sites with recent records:** above Whitewater Bridge; c. 4 km E. of Keel; Crockandun Hills; E. of Lough Doo; Pollranny Sweeny/E. of Pollranny; SE end of Lough Nacung Upper; W. of Brackagh South.

Pohlia andalusica (Höhn.) Broth.

Roth's Thread-moss

syn. *Pohlia rothii* (Correns) Broth.
Status in Ireland: Endangered (B1a, biii, B2a, biii); **Status in Europe:** Least Concern

Number of Hectads	4
+ Old (pre-1970)	2
☐ Recent (1970–2010)	4

Pohlia andalusica

Identification

An acrocarpous moss that grows in light green or red-tinged tufts or patches (short turfs) with stems usually 10–30 mm high. The leaves are lanceolate to ovate-lanceolate with an evanescent costa and plane margins that are denticulate above. Mid-leaf cells are narrowly rhomboidal and 6–10 μm wide. Distinctions from closely related species of *Pohlia* rely mainly on the occurrence and characters of bulbils in leaf axils. These first appear in upper leaf axils, usually three to six together in each axil. They are yellowish-green when young, soon becoming red-brown basally, with three to five erect green leaf primordia forming the upper third of the bulbil; these leaf primordia are broad, they partly overlap basally and all arise at approximately the same level. Capsules are obovoid, cernuous and exserted on a long seta. This species was often confused with other bulbiliferous *Pohlia* in Ireland or Britain prior to the study by Lewis & Smith (1978), who used the name *P. rothii* for it (cf. Shaw 1981, Smith 1978 and 2004). Older British records of *P. rothii* are mainly based on forms of the more common *P. annotina* with large bulbils.

Distribution in Ireland

Recent records are from five localities in two vice-counties: W. Cork (Allihies, 1968–2008; NE of Cappaghglass, 2006–2008; Dromore, 2009) and Waterford (E. of Bunmahon, 1966–2008; Knockmahon, 2008).

Ecology and biology

Known mainly from the vicinity of disused copper mines, on substrata that probably have high concentrations of copper and perhaps other metals. It grows unshaded or partly shaded, on damp silty, stony or gravelly soil that is partly bare of other plants or that has low carpets of *Cephaloziella*. It often occurs in or beside small hollows where water stands after rain and is recorded from flat and gently sloping mine spoil, in an old quarried area, near a lane edge and on open ground above a sea cliff. A recent record from Dromore was from a damp sandy track, with *Riccia subbifurca* and *Fossombronia caespitiformis* subsp. *multispira*. Most British records are from Cornwall and Devon where they are also closely associated with contaminated soils at old copper mines, but in W. Scotland it was found on soil at the foot of a cliff at 600 m altitude (M.J. Wigginton in Hill *et al.* 1994).

Individual plants are short-lived, surviving a year or two at most. The species is dioicous and sporophytes are rare (unrecorded in Ireland; one record from Cornwall: Holyoak 1997). Tubers are unrecorded; caducous axillary bulbils are plentiful and these apparently provide the principal means of propagation and dispersal.

World distribution

Widespread in Europe from Iceland, Jan Mayen and Fennoscandia southwards to S. Spain and eastwards to C. Europe, but listed as *Critically Endangered* in the Netherlands, *Near Threatened* in Britain and *Data Deficient* in the Czech Republic, Spain, Portugal and Andorra. It is assigned to a Suboceanic Boreal-montane floristic element in Europe. Elsewhere, it is recorded from the Azores, N. Asia and N. America.

Threats

P. andalusica is a colonist of open soils that disappears when taller plants become established and shade the ground, so it is dependent on disturbance to recreate open sites. Although vascular plants tend to be slow to colonise copper-contaminated soils they may cause deleterious shading after becoming established on ground close by that is less contaminated.

Parts of the locality NE of Cappaghglass are being used for house building and associated access roads and driveways, so that these developments and 'tidying' in the vicinity threaten the metallophyte bryophytes.

Conservation

The sites at Allihies and east of Bunmahon are on protected land.

Protected sites with recent records: Ballyvoyle Head to Tramore pNHA; Kenmare River SAC; **Unprotected sites with recent records:** Dromore; Knockmahon; NE of Cappaghglass.

Pohlia proligera (Kindb.) Lindb. ex Broth.

Bent-bud Thread-moss

Status in Ireland: Regionally Extinct; **Status in Europe:** Least Concern

Identification

A small acrocarpous moss that grows in green tufts, lax patches (short turfs) or as scattered plants among other bryophytes, with stems 5–15 mm high. The leaves are lanceolate to ovate-lanceolate, glossy when dry, acute, with evanescent costa and margins recurved below and denticulate above. Distinction from other small species of *Pohlia* depends on characters of the bulbils that are abundant in the axils of the upper leaves. These are vermicular, translucent, green when young becoming yellowish to reddish when old, 150–300 μm long and up to 60 μm wide, with one or two unicellular and often bent leaf primordia apically. Capsules are cernuous, narrowly pyriform and exserted on a long seta.

The name *P. proligera* was used in error for the more common *P. annotina* in the taxonomic review by Lewis & Smith (1978) and the *Flora* by Smith (1978) (cf. Shaw 1981, Smith 2004). There has been much confusion in recent literature regarding the authorship of the name, which follows Hill *et al.* (2006) here.

Distribution in Ireland

The only record is of a specimen collected by the Altalacky River at Mullaghmore near Dungiven in

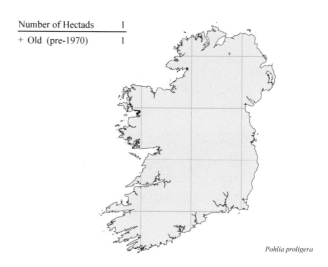

| Number of Hectads | 1 |
| + Old (pre-1970) | 1 |

Pohlia proligera

Londonderry in 1965 by R.D. Fitzgerald which was first identified as *P. proligera s.str.* by A.C. Crundwell in 1993. Attempts to refind the species at this site in 1999 were unsuccessful, but hindered by the rather imprecise locality information available.

Ecology and biology

The only specimen was from crumbling schist near a river. Information from Britain indicates that it grows in disturbed open habitats, in unshaded places on moist soils, that are moderately to slightly acidic (although more often on soils with pH above 6.0 than related species) and that it ascends to 800 m altitude (A.C. Crundwell in Hill *et al.* 1994, Hill *et al.* 2007).

The plants are apparently short-lived; they are dioicous and capsules are unknown in Ireland or Britain. Tubers are unknown but the abundant caducous axillary bulbils doubtless provide the principal means of propagation and dispersal.

World distribution

Widespread in Europe from Iceland, Spitsbergen, N. Fennoscandia and N. Russia (Kola Peninsula) southwards to Portugal, Spain and Italy, but listed as *Vulnerable* in Bulgaria and *Near Threatened* in Switzerland. In Europe, it is assigned to a European Boreal-montane floristic element. Elsewhere, it is recorded in China (Xinjiang and widely in C. and SE China: Zhang Da-cheng *et al.* in Li Xing-jiang *et al.* 2007), N. America (S. to Colorado) and Greenland.

Threats

No information; open habitat with *Pohlia annotina* was present along the banks of the Altalacky River at Mullaghmore in 1999.

Conservation

No action is proposed unless a population is found or refound in Ireland.

Protected sites with recent records: none; **Unprotected sites with recent records:** none.

Pohlia proligera, Lilla Dyngadalen, Bräcke, Jämtland, Sweden.

Pohlia lutescens (Limpr.) H.Lindb.

Status in Ireland: Least Concern; **Status in Europe:** Least Concern

A small yellowish-green acrocarpous moss that usually grows on rather acidic soil on banks. It was included in the Provisional Red List (Holyoak 2006b) but several additional populations have been found during fieldwork over the past decade. It has now been reported from 12 vice-counties, with records from 14 hectads (1 old, 13 recent) and is usually found as small populations. *P. lutescens* was added to the British list by Warburg (1965) and discovered in Ireland by J.A. Paton in 1966, but it was rarely recorded until the rhizoidal tubers were described by Whitehouse (1973). The species is doubtless still under-recorded since it is rather inconspicuous, it occupies a widespread and rather ordinary habitat (often amongst *Dicranella heteromalla*) and microscopic confirmation of identification is usually necessary from the tubers.

Pohlia lescuriana (Sull.) Ochi

syn. *Mniobryum pulchellum* (Hedw.) Loeske, *Pohlia pulchella* (Hedw.) Lindb.
Status in Ireland: Data Deficient; **Status in Europe:** Least Concern

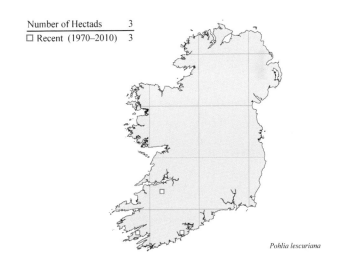

Number of Hectads	3
☐ Recent (1970–2010)	3

Pohlia lescuriana

Identification

A small acrocarpous moss that grows as scattered stems or small tufts or patches that are dull or pale green with stems up to 7 mm high, rarely taller. The leaves are spreading, ovate-lanceolate on the lower part of the stem, lanceolate on the upper stem, with acuminate apices. The leaf margin is plane or narrowly recurved below, denticulate or weakly toothed above; the costa is evanescent. Mid-leaf cells in upper leaves are narrowly rhomboidal to linear-rhomboidal and mainly 10–14 μm wide. Multicellular gemmae which are frequent on the longer rhizoids are pale brown, spherical to ellipsoid or shortly pyriform, 75–150 μm long. The perichaetial bracts are much longer than the upper leaves, narrowly lanceolate, with percurrent to excurrent costa. The capsule is ovoid with a short but distinct neck and yellow peristome teeth, pendulous and exserted on a seta 6–20 mm high. Separation of *P. lescuriana* from other small *Pohlia* species and from small *Bryum* species with rhizoidal tubers requires careful attention to leaf shape and size, and shape of both leaf cells and tubers.

Distribution in Ireland

There are three records from three vice-counties: W. Cork (by Glenbeg Lake, 1979); Mid Cork (9 km S. of Cork Airport, 1983) and Limerick (E. of Knock-animpaha, 1979). All three finds were made by George Bloom. This is an inconspicuous small moss that may often have been overlooked. It was added to the British list by Warburg (1965) but was rarely recorded until the tubers were described by Whitehouse (1973).

Ecology and biology

Habitats for the three Irish collections were recorded as a ride in woodland, top of a garden wall by a house and 'near road by stream'. In Britain, it is mainly a lowland plant of moisture-retentive, circumneutral to mildly acidic soils, especially clays, occurring on banks of streams and ditches, on open soil in fields, beside ponds and reservoirs, on rutted tracks and at path edges and on open soil in woodland rides. It normally occurs on open patches of substratum, often in association with other small acrocarpous mosses.

The plants are short-lived perennials or annual. It is a dioicous species (male plants usually being mixed with female plants) in which capsules are occasional to rare in Britain (unknown in Ireland), maturing from spring to autumn. Rhizoidal tubers are usually present on mature plants and these presumably function as propagules. Gemmae and bulbils are absent.

World distribution

This species is very widespread in Europe from N. Fennoscandia and arctic Russia southwards to N. Portugal, the Pyrenees, C. and S. Italy and the Ukraine, but listed as *Vulnerable* in Switzerland, *Data Deficient* in the Czech Republic, Germany, Spain and Portugal and 'very rare' in Estonia. It is assigned to a Temperate Eurosiberian floristic element in Europe. Elsewhere, it occurs in N. Asia (widespread from W. Siberia to Russian Far East: Ignatov *et al.* 2007), Japan and N. America. Reports from the Caucasus are apparently erroneous.

Threats

One population has probably been lost, from the top of a garden wall by Glenbeg Lake, since the habitats there appeared unsuitable by 2006. Localities recorded for the other two sites were insufficiently precise to offer much hope of refinding these inconspicuous plants, even if they still persist. However, the species is likely to be much under-recorded because it is so inconspicuous and troublesome to identify. In Britain, the species is often a colonist of open patches of damp soil and hence likely repeatedly to need new substrata to colonise.

Conservation

None of the sites are on protected land.

Protected sites with recent records: none; **Unprotected sites with recent records:** by Glenbeg Lake; E. of Knockanimpaha; 9 km S. of Cork Airport.

Pohlia wahlenbergii var. *glacialis* (Brid.) E.F.Warb.

Status in Ireland: Regionally Extinct; **Status in Europe:** Not Evaluated

A tall pale green acrocarpous moss that grows in wet places in the mountains. A single Irish record has been accepted: Sligo (Benbulbin, 1963). Although var. *glacialis* is recognised in recent lists (Hill *et al.* 2006, 2008), it appears to be merely a large, luxuriant, montane form of *P. wahlenbergii* with wider leaf cells. Smith (2004) comments that it is 'probably no more than a luxuriant habitat form'. Similarly, Nyholm (1993) noted that in Scandinavia the species 'varies gradually from small, almost filiform plants to the large swollen tufts of f. *glaciale* ... ; this inflated form is common in the mountains.' Several specimens from lowland localities in Ireland show characters intermediate between those of var. *glacialis* and var. *wahlenbergii*.

Pohlia wahlenbergii (F.Weber & D.Mohr) A.L.Andrews **var. *calcarea*** (Warnst.) E.F.Warb.

syn. *Webera calcarea* Warnst.
Status in Ireland: Data Deficient; **Status in Europe:** Not Evaluated

A small acrocarpous moss that grows on calcareous soil, differing from other forms of the common *P. wahlenbergii* in having narrower, lanceolate leaves with narrower cells. It has been reported from four vice-counties, with records from four hectads (2 old, 2 recent). Although it is recognised by Hill *et al.* (2006, 2008), the taxonomic standing of var. *calcarea* is obscure (Smith 2004). The taxon is easily overlooked in the field and almost certainly still under-recorded in Ireland and Britain. The two Irish records from the past decade may represent a small fraction of what might have been found if it were deliberately sought.

Epipterygium tozeri (Grev.) Lindb.

Tozer's Thread-moss

Status in Ireland: Least Concern; **Status in Europe:** Least Concern

A small acrocarpous moss that grows on exposed non-calcareous soil, often in humid, sheltered places. It was included in the Provisional Red List (Holyoak 2006b) because there were few records in 1998. However, recent fieldwork has found it to be much more frequent and there are now reports from 13 vice-counties, with records from 26 hectads (5 old, 19 recent, 2 undated). There is very little evidence of any decline (one site has been lost to development) and no doubt that it is still under-recorded.

Mnium thomsonii Schimp.

Short-beaked Thyme-moss

syn. *Mnium orthorhynchum* auct. non Brid.

Status in Ireland: Near Threatened; **Status in Europe:** Least Concern

An acrocarpous moss that grows in tufts amongst basic rocks, usually limestone. It has been reported from six vice-counties, with records from 10 hectads (5 old, 10 recent). In the last decade, it has been found in at least 20 localities, representing all of its historically known range in Ireland (from Clare to W. Donegal), with most records coming from its stronghold in the Dartry Mountains. There is no evidence that the species has declined.

Mnium marginatum (Dicks.) P.Beauv. var. *marginatum*

syn. *Mnium riparium* Mitt., *M. serratum* Schrad. ex Brid.
Status in Ireland: Least Concern; **Status in Europe:** Least Concern

An acrocarpous moss with bordered leaves that grows on soil and among basic rocks. It was included in the Provisional Red List (Holyoak 2006b) and has been reported from 13 vice-counties, with records from 24 hectads (15 old, 13 recent). Over the past decade the species has been found or refound at many localities in the limestone districts of Sligo, Leitrim and Fermanagh, so it is not threatened overall. Two varieties are recognised by Hill *et al.* (2006, 2008), but the dioicous var. *dioicum* has not been recorded in Ireland.

Cinclidium stygium Sw.

Status in Ireland: Vulnerable (B2a, biii); **Status in Europe:** Least Concern

Number of Hectads	7
+ Old (pre-1970)	4
□ Recent (1970–2010)	6

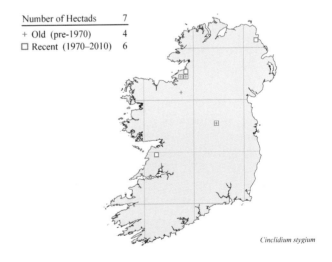

Cinclidium stygium

Identification

A robust acrocarpous moss that forms dense green or reddish tufts or patches, purplish to black below, that grows to 2–10 cm high. The relatively large leaves are broadly elliptical to orbicular or obovate, apiculate, with an entire, unistratose border of narrow cells, slightly decurrent leaf base and evanescent to percurrent costa. As in most Mniaceae, the leaf cells are relatively large, those of this species being rectangular-hexagonal in mid-leaf, arranged in radiating rows. The dense brownish tomentum on lower parts of the stem consists only of macronemata, which are distributed in rows along the stems. Distinctions from *Plagiomnium* and *Rhizomnium* species include the combination of an apiculate leaf apex, lack of teeth on the leaf margin, unistratose border, absence of micronemata, distribution of macronemata and synoicous inflorescences. Capsules are ovate, pendulous and exserted on a long seta. Spores are remarkably variable in size (25–60 μm) in the same capsule (Mogensen 1973).

Distribution in Ireland

Recent records are from eight localities in five vice-counties: Clare (E. of Carran, 2004); Westmeath (Scragh Bog, 1966–2009); Sligo (Benbulbin, 2003; Annacoona, Gleniff, 2003); Leitrim (above Glencar Waterfalls, 2000; SW of Aghavogil, 2000; W. of Glenade Lough, 2000, a record from 'Peakadaw' in 1969 perhaps being from same area) and Antrim (E. of Crockravar, 1999). There are two additional older records: Sligo (NE of Carrowkeel, 1963) and Leitrim (S. of Glencar Lough, 1965).

Ecology and biology

A rather scarce moss of weakly to strongly calcareous, nutrient-poor fens and flushes, which is absent from many habitats that appear suitable for it. Several populations in the hills are in flushes over limestone with very short, species-rich vegetation, at up to 335 m altitude. On the Garron Plateau of Antrim, it was found in a less strongly basic, peaty flush over basalt. In contrast, the large population at Scragh Bog is in a wet, calcareous, lowland fen, growing with larger pleurocarps such as *Campylium stellatum* and *Calliergon giganteum* and patchy tall vegetation including *Menyanthes trifoliata* and *Schoenus nigricans*. The record from Clare was from a shallow hollow in a lowland fen meadow by a turlough.

The plants are perennial and can be found in all months of the year. The species is synoicous; ripe capsules were plentiful at Scragh Bog in September 2007, but records from other localities are apparently of non-fertile plants. In Britain, capsules are described as rare or occasional, and ripe in summer, but sporophytes are common in Swedish Lappland (Mårtensson 1956).

World distribution

Mainly a northern species in Europe, widespread in the Arctic, in Iceland and common over much of Fennoscandia, occurring rather locally in N. Britain (perhaps now extinct in E. Anglia), and in continental Europe southwards to the Alps and Ukraine. It is considered *Extinct* in the Netherlands and *Endangered* in Germany. It is assigned to a Circumpolar Boreal-montane floristic element in Europe. Elsewhere, *C. stygium* is widespread in N. and C. Asia (from arctic Siberia southwards to S. Siberia [Ignatov *et al.* 2007] and Yunnan [Li Xing-jiang *et al.* 2007]), northern N. America (southwards to New York and British Columbia) and Greenland with an isolated record from Argentina (Tierra del Fuego).

Threats

There is little information, but survival of its populations presumably depends on the integrity of the vegetation, hydrology and water chemistry of the calcareous flushes and fens in which it occurs. Presence of strong populations in closely sheep-grazed flushes in Leitrim, but relatively tall fen vegetation in Westmeath, may imply that it is not especially vulnerable to changes in grazing pressure. However, its absence from any eutrophic site may point to eutrophication as a potential danger, since nutrient enrichment of fens by drainage from agricultural land apparently accounts for its marked declines in E. Anglia and on the N. German plain (Meinunger & Schröder 2007).

Conservation

Most populations are on protected land. *C. stygium* is listed as a Northern Ireland Priority Species.

Protected sites with recent records: Arroo Mountain SAC; Ben Bulben, Gleniff and Glenade Complex; SAC; East Burren Complex SAC; Garron Plateau SAC; Scragh Bog Nature Reserve; Scragh Bog SAC; Garron Plateau ASSI; **Unprotected sites with recent records:** W. of Glenade Lough.

Rhizomnium pseudopunctatum (Bruch & Schimp.) T.J.Kop.

Felted Thyme-moss

syn. *Mnium pseudopunctatum* Bruch & Schimp.
Status in Ireland: Near Threatened; **Status in Europe:** Least Concern

A handsome acrocarpous moss with large bordered leaves that grows mainly in calcareous flushes and fens. It was included in the Provisional Red List (Holyoak 2006b), but recent fieldwork has found additional populations. There are now reports from 21 vice-counties, with records from 29 hectads (15 old, 13 recent, 2 undated). It has undoubtedly been lost from some localities due to drainage, cessation of grazing, eutrophication or afforestation, but there are still numerous strong populations.

Plagiomnium cuspidatum (Hedw.) T.J.Kop.

Woodsy Thyme-moss

syn. *Mnium cuspidatum* Hedw., *M. silvaticum* auct., *M. sylvaticum* Lindb. *nom. illeg.*
Status in Ireland: Near Threatened; **Status in Europe:** Least Concern

An acrocarpous moss with bordered leaves that grows in varied damp habitats, including grassland, tree bases and shaded rock ledges. There are reports from 25 vice-counties, with records from 37 hectads (21 old, 14 recent, 3 undated). This impression of decline in Ireland is, however, likely to be very much exaggerated because the species was not deliberately sought during fieldwork over the past decade.

Aulacomnium androgynum (Hedw.) Schwägr.

Bud-headed Groove-moss

syn. *Orthopyxis androgyna* (Hedw.) P.Beauv.

Status in Ireland: Vulnerable (B2a, bii, iv); **Status in Europe:** Least Concern

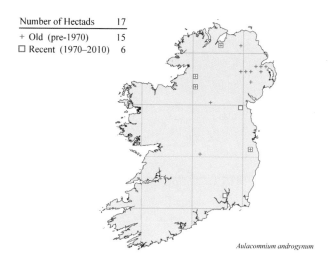

Number of Hectads	17
+ Old (pre-1970)	15
☐ Recent (1970–2010)	6

Aulacomnium androgynum

Identification

A tufted acrocarpous moss up to about 25 mm high, with ovate-lanceolate to narrowly lanceolate leaves, costa extending to the leaf apex and rounded-hexagonal, unipapillose mid-leaf cells. Even in the field, it is usually distinctive because many of the stems terminate in a pseudopodium bearing a club-shaped head of brownish, stalked, spherical to ovoid gemmae, suggesting a pin-head or miniature drumstick. *Aulacomnium palustre* occasionally also produces pseudopodia with gemmae, but it is normally a larger plant, with stems matted below with much more brown tomentum and distinct microscopically in the inflated leaf basal cells. Sporophytes (unknown in Ireland) have a narrowly ellipsoid capsule, ribbed when dry, suberect at first, becoming inclined to horizontal later, exserted on a rather long seta.

Distribution in Ireland

Recent records are from seven localities in six vice-counties: Kilkenny (The Pink Point, Bearstown, 2010); Wicklow (Powerscourt Waterfall, 2007); Cavan (Englishman's House, 1965–2000); Louth (Ardee Bog, 1978); Fermanagh (E. of Meenameen Lough, 1999; Braade Scarp, 1993–2005) and Londonderry (Ness Wood, 1971). There are rather numerous old records: Offaly (Clonbeale Bog [or Beg?], 1907); Wicklow (Lough Bray, 1915); Cavan (Tents Mountain, 1916);

Fermanagh (N. of Lough Navar, 1960); Armagh (Ardmore, 1883–1902); Down (Holywood, 1814; near Lenaderg, 1908); Antrim (Colin Glen, 1804; Cave Hill, 1809) and Londonderry (Ness Glen, 1936; near Kilrea, 1912–1938). Several other unconfirmed reports may have been correct as the species should be difficult to misidentify: Armagh (Montiaghs near Lurgan, leg. H.W. Lett [in Stewart & Corry 1888]; S. of Derrycrow, 1964) and Down (Purdysburn, 1835, but record doubtful according to Stewart & Corry 1888 and Megaw 1938).

Ecology and biology

Recent Irish records are mainly from N.-facing sandstone scarps, e.g. on thin humus on a boulder and in crevices, on unshaded overhang of a steep sandstone rock face, also from crevices in a siliceous estuarine cliff. Some of the populations at these sites appear to have persisted for many years. Other records were from acidic, humic substrata, including an old peat bank with *Mnium*, bog oak stumps, branch of a tree over a bog pool and a 'hedgebank', apparently from impersistent habitats. In Britain, it is usually found on decaying organic matter, especially rotting tree stumps, but also twigs, old grass tussocks, peat diggings and humic soil, as well as sandy banks and sandstone rocks.

The species is a short-lived perennial that can be found in all months of the year. It is dioicous and capsules (in Britain) are very rare, maturing in spring and summer.

Besides the abundant gemmae at stem apices, different gemmae are produced on the protonema in culture (Duckett & Ligrone 1992).

World distribution
Widespread in Europe from C. Norway, C. Sweden and S. Finland southwards to montane areas of Portugal and Spain. It is abundant over much of C. Europe, but described as rather rare in much of S. and E. Europe (although recorded in Ukraine). In England, it is common and known to have increased in frequency during the 20th century (Jones 1991, C.D. Preston in Hill *et al.* 1994), but it remains absent or very rare near the western seaboard in W. Wales and Cornwall. In Europe, it is assigned to a European Temperate floristic element. Elsewhere, it is recorded from the Canary Islands, N. Africa, Georgia, China (Li Xing-jiang *et al.* 2007), Korea, Japan, N. America and Argentina (Patagonia).

Threats
Populations on sandstone crags in Fermanagh and Cavan do not appear to face any immediate threats, although shading from adjacent conifer plantations might still be a problem at some locations in the Lough Navar Forest. The preponderance of old records noted above may not point to a real decline since there has been rather little bryological fieldwork in many parts of Northern Ireland for almost a century and the species might anyway be something of a short-lived colonist on at least its bared peat and dead wood habitats. The rarity of *A. androgynum* in Ireland compared to its abundance in C. England and much of Germany possibly relates to climatic factors.

Conservation
Conifers shading the sandstone scarp E. of Meenameen Lough have been removed to benefit the flora on the scarp. *A. androgynum* is listed as a Northern Ireland Priority Species and several sites are on protected land.

Protected sites with recent records: Boleybrack Mountain SAC; Braade ASSI; Lough Navar Scarps and Lakes ASSI (scheduled for declaration 2011); Ness Wood ASSI (within Ness Country Park); Powerscourt Waterfall pNHA; **Unprotected sites with recent records:** Ardee Bog (possibly within Ardee Cutaway Bog pNHA); The Pink Point, Bearstown (just outside River Barrow and River Nore SAC).

Orthodontium gracile (Wilson) Schwägr. ex Bruch & Schimp.   Slender Thread-moss

Status in Ireland: Critically Endangered (B2a, biii); **Status in Europe:** Vulnerable

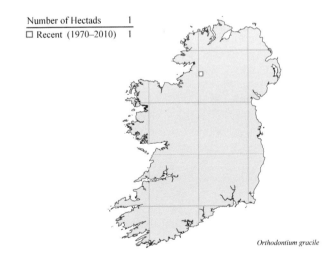

Number of Hectads	1
□ Recent (1970–2010)	1

Orthodontium gracile

Identification
This is a small bright green acrocarpous moss with long, narrow, linear to linear-lanceolate leaves. It forms tufts up to 1 cm tall. It is very similar to the common introduced species *O. lineare*, but has smooth (not papillose) exostome teeth and no stereids in the costa (seen in cross section). The capsules are also paler and less sulcate, and it is paroicous, not autoicous. It could also be mistaken for *Dicranella heteromalla*, but the leaves of that species are distinctly falcato-secund, whereas

511

those of *Orthodontium* tend to spread rather untidily, or are at the most, weakly secund. Furthermore, *Orthodontium* leaves have a rather distinctive 'jewelled' appearance, probably due to their large cells, that is lacking in *Dicranella*. *O. gracile* and *O. lineare* are fairly distinct in the field and can be distinguished vegetatively (Pierrot 1961, Porley 1998, Porley & Matcham 2003).

Distribution in Ireland

This species has been found only once in Ireland, when Cecilia Sérgio found it on a sandstone cliff face in Lough Navar Forest, Fermanagh, in 1993 (Hodgetts & Hallingbäck 1994), during a meeting of the European Committee for the Conservation of Bryophytes. It was initially thought to be *O. lineare*, which would have been a new county record, but on closer examination the specimen (which was very depauperate) was clearly paroicous, and was confirmed as *O. gracile*. Several prolonged searches of the same area in subsequent years have revealed only *O. lineare*.

Ecology and biology

O. gracile is a plant of damp sandstone rocks and, less often, gritstone and rotten standing tree trunks.

It is paroicous and capsules are frequent. Foliar gemmae are unknown, but protonemal gemmae are abundant (Duckett *et al.* 2001).

World distribution

A rare plant in Europe, *O. gracile* has been recorded only in Britain (where it is listed as *Vulnerable*) and north-western France. In Europe, it is assigned to an Oceanic Southern-temperate floristic element. Elsewhere, it is known from California and many tropical and subtropical areas.

Threats

The biggest threats are fire and encroaching conifers. Fire had clearly burned vegetation on the cliff face at the time of the plant's discovery, and a maturing conifer plantation was perilously close. While it appears that it is outcompeted by *O. lineare* (Smith 2004), in at least some localities in Britain, it has reached an equilibrium with the more common species.

Conservation

This plant has not been refound in Lough Navar Forest, in spite of searching, but might possibly occur somewhere in the area. *O. gracile* is listed as a Northern Ireland Priority Species and a UK Biodiversity Action Plan (UKBAP) species.

Protected sites with recent records: Braade ASSI; **Unprotected sites with recent records:** none.

Leptotheca gaudichaudii Schwägr. var. *gaudichaudii*   Gaudichaud's Slender-fruited Moss

Status in Ireland: Not Evaluated; **Status in Europe:** Not Evaluated

This is a tufted moss that grows in Ireland as an epiphyte on the 'trunks' of tree ferns (*Dicksonia* spp.). It is a native of Australia, New Zealand, S. Africa and southern S. America (Gilmore 2006) that was added to the European list following its discovery in the woodland garden at Derreen Garden (S. Kerry) in 1998 by Willem Labeij, where it was still well established in 2008. Another, larger population was found on tree ferns on Garinish Island (S. Kerry) in 2008 (Holyoak & Lockhart 2009b), and it has also been detected in Cornwall in SW England.

Calomnion complanatum (Hook.f. & Wilson) Lindb.

Status in Ireland: Not Evaluated; **Status in Europe:** Not Evaluated

This is an attractive moss with three-ranked leaves that grows as an epiphyte on the 'trunks' of tree ferns (*Dicksonia* spp.). The species is native only in E. Australia, Tasmania and New Zealand. It was added to the European list following its discovery in the woodland garden at Derreen Garden (S. Kerry) in 1998 by Willem Labeij, but had apparently become extinct there by 2006. In 2008, a larger population was found on tree ferns on Garinish Island (S. Kerry) (Holyoak & Lockhart 2009b). *C. complanatum* is listed as *Endangered* in Australia (Scott *et al.* 1997: 100, Catcheside & Bell in McCarthy 2006) so that its Irish populations may merit protection.

Calyptrochaeta apiculata (Hook.f. & Wilson) Vitt

syn. *Eriopus apiculatus* (Hook.f. & Wilson) Mitt.
Status in Ireland: Not Evaluated; **Status in Europe:** Not Evaluated

An attractive moss with oval, complanate leaves that usually grows on shaded soil. It is a native of the southern hemisphere in S. America (Chile, Tierra del Fuego), Australia, Tasmania and New Zealand. The species was discovered new to Europe at two localities in 1967, both in S. England, on the Isles of Scilly where it apparently arrived with horticultural plants (Paton 1968) and on the coast in E. Sussex where it may have arrived with shipping or smuggling (Wallace 1971, Stern 1991). It was discovered in Ireland in 2007 by F.H. O'Neill in wet woodland on Fota Island South, near Fota Island Arboretum (E. Cork) (Rothero 2008, O'Neill 2009), and seen there again in 2009 during the BBS summer field meeting.

Daltonia splachnoides (Sm.) Hook. & Taylor

syn. *Daltonia angustifolia* Dozy et Molk. var. *gemmiphylla* M.Fleisch., *D. novae-zelandiae* Mitt.,
D. pusilla Hook.f. & Wilson
Status in Ireland: Least Concern; **Status in Europe:** Near Threatened

Identification

An elegant moss that grows as small dark green tufts or, occasionally, larger patches (rough mats) 4–10 mm high, with procumbent stems. The keeled leaves are distinctive: linear lanceolate, acute or acuminate, with stout evanescent costa, a strong entire yellowish border of

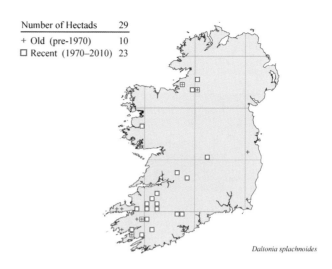

Number of Hectads	29
+ Old (pre-1970)	10
□ Recent (1970–2010)	23

Daltonia splachnoides

narrow cells and elongate-hexagonal cells in the upper part of the lamina. Capsules are ovoid, erect, exserted on a papillose deep red seta. The whitish calyptra is fringed and the operculum is rostrate.

Distribution in Ireland

There are recent records from 34 localities in 13 vice-counties: S. Kerry (Cahnicaun Wood, 1998; Derreen Garden, 2006, 2008; Rossdohan Island, 2008); N. Kerry (Barnanageehy Valley, Slieve Mish Mountains, 2009; NE of Leamydoody, 2009; NW of Knockatee, 2009; above Ardnagragh, Cordal, E. of Castleisland, 2009; Torc Cascade, 1829–2010; NW of Loo Bridge, 2005); W. Cork (Glengarriff Woods, 1979; Pass of Keimaneigh, 2009); Mid Cork (Meentinny, 2003; Tooreenmacauliffe, 2003; Glenamucklagh, 2009; Taurbeg, 2009; Gloun Dine Bridge, 2009; Cummery Connell, 2009); E. Cork (Gortroche Forest, 2009; Toorgarriff, 2009); Limerick (Knockanimpaha, 1994; Glengort, 2007); Clare (Slieve Bernagh, 2004); N. Tipperary (Keeper Hill, 2005); Laois (Gorteenameale, 2006); W. Mayo (Devil's Mother, 1987); Leitrim (Glencar Waterfalls, 1963–2005; ESE of Bronagh, 2000; near Dergvone, 2000); Cavan (S. of Englishman's House, 2001) and Fermanagh (Culcarrick Scarp, 2000; Meenameen Scarp, 2000; Bolusky Beg, 2000; Lough Achork, 2000; NE of Lough Navar, 2000). Older records are from a further 14 localities, including an additional vice-county (Dublin, the provenance of the type specimen of the species).

Ecology and biology

It grows in very humid, sheltered locations, most often in ravines, by waterfalls, or below N.-facing crags. It is probably most common as an epiphyte (preferring Rowan, Ash, Grey Willow and Hazel, often on pendent twigs, sometimes on exposed roots), but often also occurs on rocks (mainly by streams and in ravines, sometimes on boulders in woodland or scrub), occasionally on rotting wood. An unusual and possibly atypical record was from 10 m above the ground on the trunk of Sitka Spruce in a 32-year-old plantation in Mid Cork (leg. L. Coote, det. D.L. Kelly, in Rothero 2007), a habitat rarely searched by bryologists. Records are from the lowlands up to 460 m altitude.

Patches of the plant growing on small moribund twigs are unlikely to persist for more than a few years, and the prevalence of small patches on all substrata suggest it repeatedly recolonises. The species is autoicous and dioicous, commonly producing capsules which mature in summer.

At Derreen Garden in S. Kerry in 2006 and 2008, numerous small patches were found on the trunk of a large *Eucalyptus* tree, close to tree ferns with the epiphytic antipodean moss *Leptotheca gaudichaudii*. Study of the *Daltonia* specimens revealed foliar gemmae (Holyoak & Lockhart 2009b), which had not been reported for European *D. splachnoides* (although found by N.G. Hodgetts unpublished in a specimen from the Isle of Skye). However, although the gemmae match those of the antipodean *D. angustifolia* var. *gemmiphylla*, that taxon is now synonymised with *D. splachnoides* (Streimann 2000). Hence it seems more likely that 'native' *D. splachnoides* is involved rather than another Australasian adventive.

World distribution

Known in Europe only in W. Scotland and in Ireland and listed as *Vulnerable* in Britain. It is assigned to a

Hyperoceanic Southern-temperate floristic element in Europe. It has been correctly recorded elsewhere in Madeira, W. Africa (Bioko) and, following taxonomic revision by Streimann (2000), in E. Australia and New Zealand. Frequently cited reports from western N. America, Mexico and the West Indies all appear to be based on other species of the genus (cf. Delgadillo *et al.* 1995); those from the Azores are now known to be referable to *D. stenophylla* Mitt. (Hill *et al.* 2006: 240, note 322).

Threats

Not immediately threatened at many of the Irish sites. Potential threats could include removal of scrub or trees, especially from ravines or sheltered stream banks. Its occurrence in a spruce plantation (see above) suggests it might be either overlooked in that habitat, or have plenty of additional sites to colonise.

Conservation

The threat status is correctly regarded as of *Least Concern* in Ireland because there are numerous localities and there is little evidence of decline. Hence, its European threat

status may need revision. Nevertheless, it is included here because most of the European population occurs in W. Ireland, providing a special responsibility for conservation of the species. *D. splachnoides* is listed as a UK Biodiversity Action Plan (UKBAP) and a Priority Species in Northern Ireland.

Protected sites with recent records: Ben Bulben, Gleniff and Glenade Complex SAC; Boleybrack Mountain SAC; Cliffs of Magho ASSI; Glengarriff Harbour and Woodland SAC; Killarney National Park; Killarney National Park, Macgillycuddy's Reeks and Caragh River Catchment SAC; Lough Navar Scarps and Lakes ASSI (scheduled for declaration 2011); Maumtrasna Mountain Complex pNHA; Slieve Bernagh Bog SAC; Slieve Mish Mountains SAC; **Unprotected sites with recent records:** Ardnagragh, Cordal, E. of Castleisland; Cummery Connell; Dergvone; Derreen Garden; Glenamucklagh; Glengort; Gloun Dine Bridge; Gorteenameale; Gortroche Forest; Keeper Hill; Knockanimpaha; Lough Achork; Meentinny; NE of Leamydoody; NW of Knockatee; Pass of Keimaneigh; Rossdohan Island; Taurbeg; Tooreenmacauliffe; Toorgarriff.

Cyclodictyon laetevirens (Hook. & Taylor) Mitt.

Bright-green Cave-moss

syn. *Cyclodictyon laete-virens* (Hook. & Taylor) Mitt.
Status in Ireland: Near Threatened; **Status in Europe:** Rare

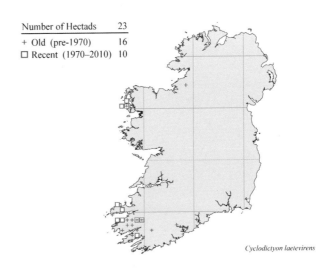

Number of Hectads	23
+ Old (pre-1970)	16
□ Recent (1970–2010)	10

Cyclodictyon laetevirens

Identification

A large, handsome, pleurocarpous moss that forms glossy bright green patches (rough mats). Its stems are up to

8 cm long, irregularly branched, with decumbent to pendent branches, bearing complanate leaves. The large leaves are highly distinctive, being broadly ovate with a

515

long apiculus, with a double costa extending to the upper part of the leaf and a distinct border of long narrow cells. The mid-leaf cells are rather large, hexagonal and thin-walled. The capsule is ovoid, horizontal and exserted on a rather stout, smooth seta.

Distribution in Ireland

Recent records in Ireland are from 13 localities in three vice-counties, mainly in the south-west: S. Kerry (Canglass Point, 1983; Gulls Rocks, 1983; Knockowen, 1983; Coomasaharn, 1983; Lough Gouragh, 1983–2009; O'Sullivan's Cascade, 1831–1983; Brandon Mountain, 2009; Loch an Duin, 2009); N. Kerry (Killarney, 1860–1988; Torc Cascade, 1831–2005) and W. Mayo (Lough Bunafreva West, 1987; Slievemore, 1962–1987; Doonty, 1987). Older records are from S. Kerry (Slea Head, 1961–1967; Finglas River, 1967; Lough Coomeathcun, 1951; Ballaghbeama Gap, 1967; Blackstones Bridge, 1961–1967; Inchiquin Lough, 1967; Uragh Wood, 1967; Cummeenduff Glen, 1967); N. Kerry (Upper Lake, undated); W. Cork (Adrigole, 1963; Lackawee, 1967; Pass of Keimaneigh, 1967); Mid Cork ('Cork', 1815–1900); Waterford (Glendine Wood, 1967) and Leitrim (Glenade, 1967). With strong populations in SW Ireland, it was not especially looked for during recent fieldwork.

Ecology and biology

Restricted to locations that are consistently very humid, often dripping with water, on acidic or slightly basic rocks in shaded recesses such as cave entrances, crevices in the spray zone beside waterfalls and amongst boulders in ravines and alongside cascades. The Killarney Fern (*Trichomanes speciosum*) often occurs near it, along with other notable associates that may include *Jubula hutchinsiae*, *Lejeunea eckloniana* and *Radula holtii*. Its few sites in Britain are all coastal, in a sea cave in Cornwall and caves along raised-beach platforms on Islay and Jura, but most Irish localities are inland (up to 330 m altitude above sea level).

The plants are perennial, with long-lived patches such as that at Lough Gouragh, which has persisted in the same cave for at least 26 years. The species is reported to be synoicous, autoicous or dioicous; its capsules may be less rare in Ireland and Britain than claimed in the literature, with spores maturing in late summer and autumn. Gemmae, bulbils and tubers are unknown, but detached leaf or stem fragments may serve as propagules.

World distribution

Restricted in Europe to the Atlantic seaboard of W. Scotland (Islay and Jura), Ireland, SW England (W. Cornwall, where one population is extant), NW Spain and NW Portugal (Minho, where recently regarded as extinct: Casas *et al.* 2006, cf. Sérgio & Carvalho 2003). It is listed as *Endangered* in Britain and *Vulnerable* in Spain and Portugal (Sérgio *et al.* 2006). It is assigned to a Hyperoceanic Southern-temperate floristic element in Europe. Elsewhere, it is known from the Azores, Madeira and tropical Africa.

Threats

Recent visits to several localities in Kerry revealed no immediate threats. The species doubtless depends on continued humidity and clean water at its sites, so potential threats could include water regulation (e.g. by reservoirs or for hydroelectric power developments) or eutrophication (e.g. from run-off from agricultural land).

Conservation

All sites are on protected land. Although not immediately threatened, *C. laetevirens* is undoubtedly a very uncommon and local plant in Ireland. Ireland has a special responsibility to protect the species because it has the majority of its European populations.

Protected sites with recent records: Caha Mountains SAC; Croaghaun/Slievemore SAC; Doulus Head to Cooncrome Harbour pNHA; Killarney National Park; Killarney National Park, Macgillycuddy's Reeks and Caragh River Catchment SAC; Mount Brandon SAC; **Unprotected sites with recent records:** none.

Crags with *Cyclodictyon laetevirens*, above Lough Gouragh, Co. Kerry.

Hypopterygium immigrans Lett

Status in Ireland: Not Evaluated; **Status in Europe:** Not Evaluated

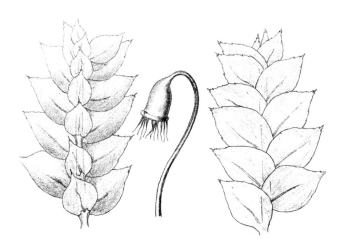

Lett (1915) reported this moss as being established for some years in a cold fern house at Easton Lodge, Monkstown, Dublin, as 'an immigrant'. He had named it new to science in 1904 (*Journal of Botany* **42**: 249–252; a reproduction of part of his Table 463 is shown to left). The provenance of the moss and its modern taxonomic identity remain uncertain. It was excluded from Hill *et al.* (2008) because of the 'indoor' habitat.

Fontinalis antipyretica Hedw. **var.** *gracilis* (Lindb.) Schimp.

Lesser Water-moss

syn. *Fontinalis antipyretica* subsp. *gracilis* (Lindb.) Kindb.
Status in Ireland: Near Threatened; **Status in Europe:** Not Evaluated

A robust aquatic moss up to 40 cm long, green, dark green or brownish, with trailing stems that are irregularly branched, found on submerged rocks in flowing water of streams and rivers, in insolated or lightly shaded places, from the lowlands to moderate elevations in the hills. In this variety, the leaves are narrower than in other forms. It has been reported from six vice-counties, with records from seven hectads (1 old, 6 recent) but there is no secure evidence that this taxon has declined in Ireland or much indication that any of its populations are currently threatened. Var. *gracilis* is accepted as a valid taxon in the monograph by Welch (1960) and much of the recent literature, despite occurrence of some plants intermediate with var. *antipyretica*. Frahm (2006) argues that *gracilis* is only a phenotypic modification, since narrow leaves and typical leaves can both develop on the same stem under different growth conditions. However, a fuller molecular and morphological study is desirable to assess whether genetic differences exist.

Fontinalis antipyretica Hedw. **var.** *cymbifolia* W.E.Nicholson   Boat-leaved Water-moss

Status in Ireland: Data Deficient; **Status in Europe:** Not Evaluated

A large pleurocarpous moss that grows in shallow, hard water. It differs from the common var. *antipyretica* in having leaves that are deeply channelled rather than sharply keeled. Its taxonomic status is uncertain so that it was not recognised by Hill *et al.* (2006), but it was reinstated by Hill *et al.* (2008) largely because recent gatherings from Ireland appear distinctive in having leaves that are consistently unkeeled. Recent fieldwork has produced records from four vice-counties (N. Kerry, Offaly, Westmeath and Longford) and five hectads. Some of these were found in large waterbodies (Lough Leane, River Shannon, Royal Canal, Lough Ree), implying that large populations probably exist, but var. *cymbifolia* almost certainly remains under-recorded in Ireland. There is also an older record from the River Fergus in Clare.

Campyliadelphus elodes (Lindb.) Kanda   Fine-leaved Marsh Feather-moss

syn. *Amblystegium elodes* Lindb., *Campylium elodes* (Lindb.) Kindb., *Hypnum elodes* Spruce *nom. illeg.*

Status in Ireland: Near Threatened; **Status in Europe:** Regionally Threatened

A small, slender and inconspicuous pleurocarpous moss that grows in loosely branched patches or as straggling shoots amongst other bryophytes in fens and marshes, dune slacks, turloughs and other calcareous wetlands. It is widely distributed in Ireland, with reports from 26 vice-counties and records from 48 hectads (33 old, 19 recent, 1 undated). It has undoubtedly been lost from some localities due to drainage or eutrophication, but the species is easily overlooked and hence still likely to be under-recorded.

Amblystegium confervoides (Brid.) Schimp.

Tiny Feather-moss

syn. *Amblystegiella confervoides* (Brid.) Loeske, *Platydictya confervoides* (Brid.) H.A.Crum, *Serpoleskea confervoides* (Brid.) Loeske

Status in Ireland: Near Threatened; **Status in Europe:** Least Concern

An extremely slender pleurocarpous moss, forming mainly small patches, with stiff stems and irregular branching. Its resemblance to a filamentous alga or mat of fine green hair is increased by the minute leaves being appressed when dry. This is a localised lowland calcicole of shaded places that grows on the surfaces of limestone rocks and several recent finds have been on stones or fragments of limestone on the floor of Hazel scrub or low woodland. It has been reported from six vice-counties, with records from 10 hectads (4 old, 6 recent) but the plants are tiny and mainly restricted to a special habitat, so there is little doubt they are still under-recorded and that failure to refind some old records in recent years need not point to local extinctions. Molecular studies (Vanderpoorten *et al.* 2002, Vanderpoorten & Hedenäs 2009) have established that this species should be removed from *Amblystegium* and placed in the monotypic genus *Serpoleskea*.

Hygroamblystegium fluviatile (Hedw.) Loeske

Brook-side Feather-moss

syn. *Amblystegium fluviatile* (Hedw.) Schimp.

Status in Ireland: Near Threatened; **Status in Europe:** Least Concern

A slender pleurocarpous moss that grows in and beside rivers, usually on rocks or exposed tree roots. It was included in the Provisional Red List (Holyoak 2006b), but was evidently under-recorded. There are now reports from 14 vice-counties, with records from 24 hectads (11 old, 12 recent, 1 undated), some involving large populations. Although the species is potentially vulnerable to eutrophication and other water pollution, there is no evidence of extensive decline. Recent research has demonstrated great morphological plasticity within *Hygroamblystegium* so that taxonomic separation of *H. fluviatile* and *H. tenax* from *H. varium* is unnecessary (Vanderpoorten 2004, Vanderpoorten & Hedenäs 2009).

Hygroamblystegium varium (Hedw.) Mönk. Willow Feather-moss

syn. *Amblystegium varium* (Hedw.) Lindb.
Status in Ireland: Near Threatened; **Status in Europe:** Least Concern

A slender pleurocarpous moss that grows in wet places, usually on lake shores or beside streams and rivers. There are reports from 23 vice-counties, with records from 37 hectads (22 old, 11 recent, 4 undated). The taxon may be somewhat under-recorded and there is little evidence that it has declined. Recent research has demonstrated great morphological plasticity within *Hygroamblystegium* so that taxonomic separation of *H. fluviatile* and *H. tenax* from *H. varium* is unnecessary (Vanderpoorten 2004, Vanderpoorten & Hedenäs 2009).

Hygroamblystegium humile (P.Beauv.) Vanderp. *et al.* Constricted Feather-moss

syn. *Amblystegium humile* (P.Beauv.) Crundw., *A. kochii* Schimp.,
Hygroamblystegium varium subsp. *varium* var. *humile* Vanderpoorten & Hedenäs, *Leptodictyum humile* (P.Beauv.) Ochyra
Status in Ireland: Endangered (B1a, bi, ii, iv, B2a, bi, ii, iv); **Status in Europe:** Least Concern

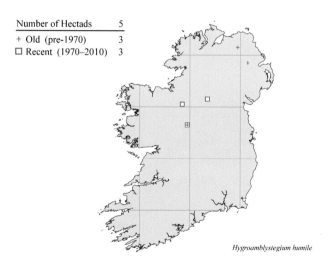

Number of Hectads	5
+ Old (pre-1970)	3
□ Recent (1970–2010)	3

Hygroamblystegium humile

Identification

A pleurocarpous moss that grows as dull green, straggling patches (rough mats) with shoots up to about 35 mm long. It is typically larger than the common *Amblystegium serpens* with longer mid-leaf cells (mainly 28–56 μm long, compared to 28–40 μm), but a smaller plant and shorter-celled than *Leptodictyum riparium*. However, these and other related species are rather variable and prone to develop atypical leaves on young branches, so careful study of microscopic characters is needed for reliable identification. Other important characters of *A. humile* are the lack of decurrent leaf bases, leaves markedly narrowed basally and the plane, entire leaf margins. Although *H. humile* is treated as a valid species in Hill *et al.* (2008), recent morphological and molecular studies have demonstrated great morphological plasticity within the genus *Hygroamblystegium* (Vanderpoorten 2004), leading Vanderpoorten & Hedenäs (2009) to treat *humile* as *H. varium* subsp. *varium* var. *humile*.

Distribution in Ireland
Confirmed recent records are from three localities in two vice-counties: Roscommon (Lough Ree, shore west of Lanesborough, 1968 and 2002; Lough Key, near Rockingham Demesne, 2002) and Cavan (Derrybrick Lough, 2009). Older accepted records are from Antrim (Lough Neagh at Loughshore Park, 1951) and London-derry (Kilea, leg. J.D. Houston, 1912–1940: Megaw 1938). A report from E. Donegal (Bundoran, 1937) was erroneous. It is probably still somewhat overlooked in Ireland because it is a rather unprepossessing pleurocarp that often grows intermixed with other plants in eutrophic lowland habitats that do not attract the attention of bryologists.

Ecology and biology
It has been recorded from lake shores, sides of pools, tall-herb swamp, marshy meadows, on the ground in a fen and from a 'swamp'. In Britain, it grows on mud, silty soil or over rocks beside lowland rivers and reservoirs, in damp pasture, in carr, on open marshy ground and on tree boles by streams and ponds. Its sites are generally well lit to lightly shaded, wet, basic and rich in nutrients.

The plants are perennial, autoicous and frequently fertile, with capsules maturing in summer. Tubers and gemmae are unknown. Propagation and dispersal are likely to occur both from shoot fragments and from spores.

World distribution
Widespread in Europe from Iceland and Fennoscandia south to Portugal, Spain, Italy and the Caucasus, but listed as *Critically Endangered* in Bulgaria, *Vulnerable* in Norway and Switzerland, *Near Threatened* in Finland, 'presumably threatened' in Germany and 'very rare' in Estonia. It is assigned to a Circumpolar Temperate floristic element in Europe. Elsewhere, the species has been reported from Asia (Turkey, Iran, Siberia, Himalaya), N. America (Newfoundland to British Columbia and throughout much of the United States: A.J. Sharp & H. Crum in Sharp *et al.* 1994), Mexico and New Guinea.

Threats
Potential threats to the species are poorly understood, although developments on lake shores, alteration of flooding regimes or water pollution would be harmful.

Conservation
Two sites are on protected land.

Protected sites with recent records: Lough Oughter and Associated Loughs SAC; Lough Ree SAC; **Unprotected sites with recent records:** Lough Key, near Rockingham Demesne.

Conardia compacta (Drumm. ex Müll.Hal.) H.Rob.　　　　Compact Feather-moss

syn. *Amblystegium compactum* (Drumm. ex Müll.Hal.) Austin, *Rhynchostegiella compacta* (Drumm. ex Müll.Hal.) Loeske
Status in Ireland: Regionally Extinct; **Status in Europe:** Least Concern

Identification
A very slender pleurocarpous moss that is irregularly branched and usually forms soft, dense, green or yellow-green mats. The leaves are lanceolate, gradually acuminate, somewhat decurrent, with percurrent costa and plane margins that are serrulate all around, but especially towards the base where the teeth are somewhat spreading to recurved. Mid-leaf cells are linear-rhomboidal, basal cells shorter and broader and the angular cells small and subquadrate. The rhizoids are warty-papillose, red-brown, strongly branched and often form a tomentum. Careful attention to microscopic details of leaf structure and rhizoids may be needed to confirm identification, although the frequent presence of filamentous gemmae growing from the dorsal surface of the costa near the leaf tip provides an obvious difference (when they are present) from most similar species. Capsules (unknown in Europe) are oblong-cylindric with a short neck, suberect to somewhat inclined, exserted on a seta 8–14 mm long.

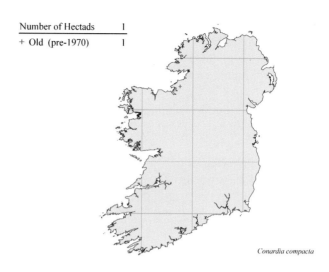

Number of Hectads	1
+ Old (pre-1970)	1

Conardia compacta

Distribution in Ireland

The only record from Ireland is based on a specimen collected in Gleniff in Sligo by J.B. Duncan during the British Bryological Society Meeting in 1928; the voucher specimen has not been located. The species has not been refound, although the rather imprecise locality prevents any effective attempts to relocate it. A later record (Sligo, Knocknarea Glen, 1965, **NMW**) is based on misidentified *Cratoneuron filicinum*.

Ecology and biology

Nothing was recorded of the habitat of the only Irish find of the species. In Britain, it is a lowland moss that grows on calcareous substrata in shade, including damp rocks and soil below calcareous crags, mostly on limestone, but also occasionally on slate or sandstone. In N. Europe it mostly grows on rocks and soil on sea shores (Hedenäs 2003), including open, damp sand at saltmarsh edges around the Gulf of Bothnia. In N. America it grows on damp cliffs (especially limestone) but also extends on to logs, stumps and humus, and bark at the base of trees in wooded swamps (Crum & Anderson 1981).

The plants are perennial, growing as dense mats that can be located in all months of the year. In Europe, the species is dioicous and capsules are unknown; in N. America it is autoicous and capsules are rare. Filamentous, multicellular, often branched gemmae commonly arise from the dorsal surface of the costa near the leaf apex and these doubtless serve as propagules.

World distribution

Widespread in Europe from Iceland and N. Norway southwards to Spain, Italy and Greece, but local and rare in many countries: *Critically Endangered* in the Czech Republic and Finland, *Vulnerable* in Luxembourg, *Near Threatened* in Spain, 'presumably threatened' in Germany, 'very rare' in Estonia and 'very rare and susceptible' in the Netherlands. Scattered records in Britain extend from N. Scotland to E. Cornwall and the Isle of Wight. In Europe as a whole, it is assigned to a Circumpolar Boreal-montane floristic element. Elsewhere, it is known in N. Africa, widely in SW Asia and Siberia (Ignatov *et al.* 2007), Kashmir, N. America (widespread), Greenland and C. America.

Threats

Lack of precise information on the location at which it was found in Sligo in 1928 prevents checking whether it is still present or, if not, ascertaining possible causes of disappearance. Since the species is inconspicuous and easily overlooked as a weak form of *Amblystegium serpens*, even when substantial patches are present, it might well be refound in Ireland.

Conservation

No action is proposed, although bryologists should remain vigilant for the continued presence of the species in Ireland, particularly in rocky limestone districts.

Protected sites with recent records: none; **Unprotected sites with recent records:** none.

Drepanocladus sendtneri (Schimp. ex H.Müll.) Warnst.

Chalk Hook-moss

syn. *Amblystegium sendtneri* (Schimp.) De Not., *A. sendtneri* var. *hamatum* (Schimp.) Braithw., *A. sendtneri* var. *wilsonii* (Schimp. ex Lorb.) Braithw., *Drepanocladus sendtneri* var. *wilsonii* (Schimp. ex Lorb.) Warnst., *Hypnum wilsonii* Schimp. ex Lorb.

Status in Ireland: Near Threatened; **Status in Europe:** Regionally Threatened

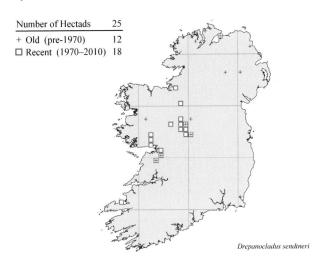

Number of Hectads	25
+ Old (pre-1970)	12
□ Recent (1970–2010)	18

Drepanocladus sendtneri

Identification

A medium-sized pleurocarpous moss, occasionally more robust, that forms green or brown patches or grows among other plants. The stems are pinnately or irregularly pinnately branched, up to about 20 cm long. Stem leaves are ovate to ovate-triangular, tapering to a long acumen, secund to falcato-secund, with entire margins and costa that is usually rather strong and ends in the acumen. Mid-leaf cells are linear; the alar cells are shorter, inflated, thin-walled to strongly incrassate and form well-defined groups extending 40–55% of the distance to mid-leaf along the leaf insertion. The relatively small groups of alar cells that are separated from the costa by a conspicuous gap provide the best distinction from *D. aduncus*; other characters used in British floras being unreliable. Capsules are cylindrical, curved, suberect and exserted on a long seta.

Distribution in Ireland

Recent records are from 21 localities in 10 vice-counties: S. Kerry (Magherabeg, 2003, 2006); Clare (Knockaunroe, 2004; Mullagh More, 1959–2004; Lough Bunny, 1945–2004); SE Galway (Tirneevan, 1966–2004; Caranavoodaun, 2004; W. Galway (S. of Carrowmoreknock, 2004; NW of Gortachalla Lough, 2004; NE Galway (E. of Glennamaddy, 2004); Westmeath (Killinure Lough, 1970); Roscommon (Fin Lough, near Lough Key, 2002;

Shad Lough, 2002; Ballinturly Turlough, 2002; Lisduff Turlough, 2002; Fin Lough, near Strokestown, 2002; Lough Funshinagh, 1981–2002; Portrunny Bay, Lough Ree, 1968–2002; Barry Beg, 1970); E. Mayo (Skealoghan Turlough, 2005); Sligo (Colgagh Lough, 2003) and Londonderry (Magilligan, 1904–2003). There are older records from a further nine localities and an additional five vice-counties. The species has undoubtedly been lost over the past forty years from numerous localities in Northern Ireland and the lowland districts of the Republic of Ireland.

Ecology and biology

A characteristic moss of unshaded calcareous lowland mires, occurring mainly in sites where water levels fluctuate such as dune slacks, lake margins and turloughs. It is apparently restricted to nutrient-poor sites and disappears when eutrophication occurs.

The plants are perennial and form long-lived patches. The species is dioicous and capsules are rare, maturing in summer. Bulbils, gemmae and tubers are unknown, but vegetative propagation probably occurs from leaf and stem fragments.

World distribution

Widespread in Europe from S. Iceland and N. Fennoscandia southwards to the Alps (including N.

Italy), Balkans and Caucasus (reports from Spain are no longer accepted). It is listed as *Critically Endangered* in the Czech Republic, the Netherlands and Switzerland, *Vulnerable* in Bulgaria and Serbia, *Near Threatened* in Finland, 'presumably threatened' in Germany and 'declining' in Norway. It is assigned to a Circumpolar Boreo-arctic montane floristic element in Europe. Elsewhere, it is known in SW, C. and N. Asia, N. America, Greenland and at Kerguelen Island.

Threats

D. sendtneri is categorised as *Near Threatened* because it has numerous localities in Ireland, but treated in detail here because there is clear evidence of ongoing decline. The drainage and eutrophication that appear to be responsible for the recorded losses are probably still increasing in extent. The species is declining for similar reasons in other European countries, e.g. Germany,

where many populations have been lost (Meinunger & Schröder 2007).

Conservation

Most extant localities are on protected land.

Protected sites with recent records: Ballinturly Turlough SAC; Ballymaclary Nature Reserve; Burren National Park; Castletaylor Complex SAC; Colgagh Lough pNHA; East Burren Complex SAC; Fin Lough (Roscommon) pNHA; Lisduff Turlough SAC; Lough Corrib SAC; Lough Funshinagh SAC; Lough Lurgeen Bog/Glenamaddy Turlough SAC; Lough Ree SAC; Magilligan ASSI; Magilligan SAC; Shad Lough pNHA; Skealoghan Turlough SAC; Tralee Bay and Magharees Peninsula, West to Cloghane SAC; **Unprotected sites with recent records:** Barry Beg (possibly within Lough Ree SAC); Fin Lough, near Strokestown; S. of Carrowmoreknock.

Tomentypnum nitens (Hedw.) Loeske

Woolly Feather-moss

syn. *Camptothecium nitens* (Hedw.) Schimp., *Homalothecium nitens* (Hedw.) H.Rob.
Status in Ireland: Vulnerable (A3c); **Status in Europe:** Least Concern

Number of Hectads	12
+ Old (pre-1970)	3
□ Recent (1970–2010)	11

Tomentypnum nitens

Identification

A handsome medium-sized to robust pleurocarpous moss that grows as green, yellowish or brownish patches (turfs), with pinnately branched stems up to 15 cm high that are densely tomentose below with brown rhizoids. The stem leaves are straight and erect, elongate-lanceolate to elongate-triangular, widest near the base, shortly or longly acuminate and strongly plicate. The leaf margin is plane or narrowly recurved, entire or sinuose; the costa extends

to about three-quarters of leaf-length. Mid-leaf cells are linear-vermicular; a few alar cells are enlarged, but not or hardly differentiated into auricles. The capsule is cylindrical, curved, with conical operculum, horizontal and exserted on a tall purplish seta.

Distribution in Ireland

Recorded from 18 sites in six vice-counties: Limerick (Grageen Fen, 1996–1998); W. Galway (Bunscannive,

1988); Kildare (Pollardstown Fen, 1957–2003); Westmeath (Scragh Bog, 1971–2010; Kilpatrick Bridge, 1993); W. Mayo (Bellacorick Bog, 1957–2003; Brackloon Lough, 1987–1988; Coolturk, 1999–2010; Dooleeg More Bog, 1957–1987; Cloonooragh, 1987; Formoyle, 1987–2010; NE of Lough Keeran, 1989; ESE of Lough Nambrackkeagh, 1987; NE of Maumykelly, 1987; Rathavisteen, 1987; Sheskin East, 1986; Srahmeen Bog, 1987) and W. Donegal (Meentygrannagh Bog, 1998–2010). Older records are from: W. Mayo (N. of Beltra, 1959) and Fermanagh (W. of Meenameen Lough, 1957). The series of records from W. Mayo in the 1980s resulted from widespread searching for the species and its habitats (Lockhart 1987, 1988, 1991).

Ecology and biology

This is a species of open calcareous mires and flushes, occurring at several large wet fens in the Irish lowlands but at more numerous and mainly smaller basic flushes in extensive blanket-bog regions, especially in W. Mayo, where it reaches 330 m altitude. It apparently tolerates slightly acidic conditions in some intermediate fens but requires wet sites with relatively stable water levels and is usually associated with species-rich vegetation (Lockhart 1987). Similarly, in Scandinavia it occurs at pH 5.7–8.0, with variable calcium levels (2.1–74 mg/l), sometimes tolerating somewhat nutrient-rich habitats (Hedenäs 2003).

The plants are perennial, typically growing in long-lived patches. It is a dioicous species in which capsules are occasional in some Irish populations, maturing in summer (capsules are very rare in Britain: Smith 1978, R.A. Finch in Hill *et al.* 1994). Gemmae, bulbils and tubers are absent, but vegetative propagation doubtless occurs from detached stem and leaf fragments.

World distribution

Widespread in N. and C. Europe, from Spitsbergen, N. Iceland, N. Fennoscandia and arctic Russia southwards to C. Spain, S. Italy, Bulgaria and the Caucasus; mainly montane in the southern part of this range. It is listed as *Critically Endangered* in Luxembourg and in the Netherlands, *Endangered* in Bulgaria, Germany and Serbia, *Vulnerable* in Spain and Portugal and *Near Threatened* in the Czech Republic. It is assigned to a Circumpolar Boreo-arctic montane floristic element in Europe. Elsewhere, it has a very wide range throughout arctic and boreal latitudes of the northern hemisphere (Schuster 1983: 514), from the High Arctic southwards

to Armenia and Kazakhstan (Ignatov *et al.* 2007), C. Asia, NE China and the southern USA (New Mexico).

Threats

T. nitens became extinct at its only locality in Northern Ireland (W. of Meenameen Lough) as a direct result of extensive afforestation with conifers. Several other Irish populations have been lost due to drainage or afforestation. It has apparently declined at Pollardstown Fen over the past decade as much of the fen vegetation has grown taller and *Phragmites* has spread. Drainage, eutrophication and shading by taller vegetation probably represent the main potential threats to surviving Irish populations.

In Britain, fossil records demonstrate a wider range 11,000 to 6,000 years ago than at present (Dickson 1973), with declines in the lowlands apparently due to changing land use and drainage and those in the uplands resulting from natural processes of soil acidification. These declines have greatly accelerated over the last two centuries; the species may now be extinct in E. Anglia as a result of eutrophication of the groundwater draining into fens from agricultural land. Drainage and eutrophication have also caused large declines in continental Europe, notably in Germany (Meinunger & Schröder 2007).

Conservation

Some populations are on protected land.

Protected sites with recent records: Ballycroy National Park; Bellacorick Bog Complex SAC; Connemara Bog Complex SAC; Glenamoy Bog Complex SAC; Grageen Fen and Bog NHA; Meentygrannagh Bog SAC; Owenduff/Nephin Complex SAC; Pollardstown Fen Nature Reserve; Pollardstown Fen SAC; Scragh Bog Nature Reserve; Scragh Bog SAC; **Unprotected sites with recent records:** Kilpatrick Bridge; NE of Lough Keeran; Sheskin East; Srahmeen Bog.

Hygrohypnum duriusculum (De Not.) Jamieson

Broad-leaved Brook-moss

syn. *Hygrohypnum dilatatum* (Wilson ex Schimp.) Loeske, *Hypnum dilatatum* Wilson ex Schimp.
Status in Ireland: Critically Endangered (B1a, bi, ii, iv, B2a, bi, ii, iv); **Status in Europe:** Least Concern

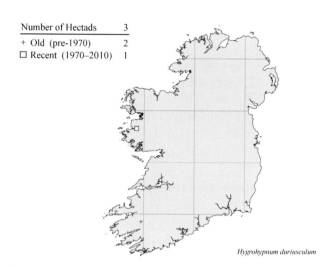

Number of Hectads	3
+ Old (pre-1970)	2
□ Recent (1970–2010)	1

Hygrohypnum duriusculum

Identification

An aquatic pleurocarpous moss that grows in green or yellowish-green tufts with rather stiff, uncrowded shoots 20–60 mm long. Leaves are subsecund, concave, ovate-orbicular, with plane margins that are entire or faintly denticulate and an obtuse to rounded apex. The costa is double and extends one-third to one-half of the length of the leaf. Cells in mid-leaf are linear, the alar cells enlarged and somewhat incrassate, often orange or brownish in older leaves, but not forming auricles. Capsules are inclined, ellipsoid, curved and exserted. The very broad leaves with a bluntly rounded apex attract attention, but distinction from other rare *Hygrohypnum* species with similar leaf shape depends on the subsecund leaves and characters of the costa and leaf margin.

Distribution in Ireland

The only recent record is from W. Mayo, on the slopes of Mweelrea, where it was discovered by D.G. Long in 2003. There are two old records, from S. Kerry (Connor Hill Pass, 1897) and N. Kerry (Torc Cascade, 1865).

Ecology and biology

In W. Mayo, it occurs on unshaded horizontal rock (Mweelrea Grit) in fast-flowing water at or just above water level in a base-poor stream at about 290 m altitude. In Britain, it also grows on rocks in fast-flowing streams and rivers, usually in montane areas but sometimes at low altitudes.

The plants are presumably perennial. The species is dioicous and capsules are very rare (unknown in Ireland). Gemmae and tubers are unknown, so propagation and dispersal is most likely to occur from shoot and leaf fragments.

World distribution

The species is widespread in N. and C. Europe, from Iceland and Fennoscandia southwards to N. Wales, the Pyrenees, Alps and Caucasus, being listed as *Vulnerable* in Germany and *Near Threatened* in Switzerland. It is assigned to a Circumpolar Boreo-arctic montane floristic element in Europe. Elsewhere, it is known from N. and C. Asia, Kashmir, China, Japan, Greenland and N. America.

Threats

Reasons for the apparent disappearance of the species from two localities in Kerry during the 19th century are unknown. However, bryophytes at Torc Cascade suffered heavily and repeatedly from specimen collecting and possibly it was destroyed at Connor Hill Pass by disturbance connected with road improvements. Potential threats to the population in Mayo could include diversion of the stream flow (e.g. for hydroelectric power generation or water storage) and eutrophication or other pollution that might result from the current overstocking of the hills with sheep.

Conservation

The site on Mweelrea is on protected land.

Protected sites with recent records: Mweelrea/Sheeffry/Erriff Complex SAC; **Unprotected sites with recent records:** none.

Pseudocalliergon lycopodioides (Brid.) Hedenäs

Large Hook-moss

syn. *Amblystegium lycopodioides* (Brid.) De Not., *Drepanocladus lycopodioides* (Brid.) Warnst., *Hypnum lycopodioides* Brid.
Status in Ireland: Vulnerable (A2c); **Status in Europe:** Regionally Threatened

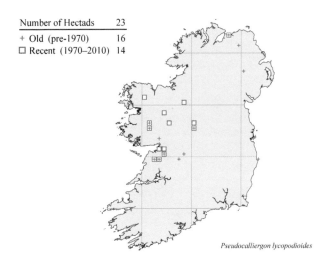

Number of Hectads	23
+ Old (pre-1970)	16
□ Recent (1970–2010)	14

Pseudocalliergon lycopodioides

Identification

A robust pleurocarpous moss that forms green, brownish or yellow-brown patches (wefts or rough mats) with slightly branched to irregularly pinnately branched shoots that are often somewhat turgid and up to 15 cm long, occasionally 25 cm. Stem leaves are erecto-patent to spreading, more or less strongly falcate, ovate to broadly ovate and gradually narrowed to an acuminate apex. The leaf margins are plane and entire or slightly denticulate; the costa is single, ending in the acumen. Cells in mid-leaf are linear, 5–7 μm wide and smooth. The alar cells are inflated, incrassate, rectangular or shortly rectangular and form an indistinctly delimited triangular group. Capsules (apparently unknown in Ireland) are cylindrical, curved, horizontal or almost so and exserted on a long seta. Hedenäs & Rosborg (2009) provide molecular data showing that *Pseudocalliergon lycopodioides* should be reinstated as a species of *Drepanocladus*.

Distribution in Ireland

Recent records are accepted from 16 localities in nine vice-counties: Clare (Rinnamona, 1970–2004; Lough George, 2004; Cooloorta Lough, 2004; Lough Bunny, 1945–2004); SE Galway (W. of Cloghballymore, 2004; Lough Managh, 2004; Caranavoodaun, 2004); NE Galway (S. of Coothagh, 2004); Westmeath (Muckahagh, 1979); Longford (S. of Lismacmannus, 2007); Roscommon (Fin Lough, near Lough Key, 2002); E. Mayo (SW of Inishard, 1966–2003; Inishcoog, 1966–2003; Island Lake, 2003); W. Mayo (Coolturk, 2003) and Londonderry (Ballymaclary, 1999). There are older records from another 15 localities and a further four vice-counties (Wicklow, W. Donegal, Armagh, and Antrim). A report from W. Galway is unconfirmed and that from Dublin (Howth, 1905) seems unlikely to be correct.

Ecology and biology

A rather local moss of strongly calcareous lowland wetlands, often where water levels fluctuate so that it is flooded in winter but at least intermittently dry in summer. Large populations occur in several turloughs and on lake margins, smaller populations in other basic fens, hollows in limestone pavement and a dune slack. It apparently favours infertile sites, avoiding those that are eutrophicated or heavily shaded by bushes or trees. Likewise in Sweden, it grows mainly in small strongly calcareous wetland habitats, in shallow depressions on flat limestone rocks, on sea and lake shores and in man-made hollows and ditches, the sites being circumneutral to basic (pH 6.0–8.2) with high calcium levels (c. 26–218 mg/l) (Hedenäs 2003).

527

The plants are perennial. It is a dioicous species in which capsules are very rare in Britain and in Fennoscandia (apparently unknown in Ireland). Gemmae, bulbils and tubers are absent, but vegetative propagation presumably occurs from detached leaf and stem fragments.

World distribution

P. lycopodioides is widespread in Europe from S. Iceland, N. Sweden and N. Finland southwards to France, N. and C. Italy, the Ukraine and the Caucasus. It is listed as *Critically Endangered* in the Netherlands, *Endangered* in Germany, *Vulnerable* in Finland and Switzerland, *Data Deficient* in the Czech Republic and 'declining' in Norway. It is assigned to a European Temperate floristic element in Europe. The species was treated as endemic to Europe in the European *Red Data Book* (ECCB 1995) but this is not strictly true since it has a range 'barely reaching east of the Ural Mts.' in W. Siberia (Hedenäs 2003, Ignatov *et al.* 2007).

Threats

Although there are numerous localities, this species has undoubtedly declined and will doubtless continue to decline due to drainage and eutrophication of its habitats.

Nearly half the Irish localities have records only from before 1970 and it has certainly been lost from some of these sites. In Northern Ireland, it has been lost from three sites and survives as a very small patch at the fourth (in one wheel rut in a dune slack at Ballymaclary Nature Reserve in Londonderry). There have also been marked declines in England (Hill *et al.* 1994), in agricultural areas of Scandinavia (Hedenäs 2003) and Germany (Meinunger & Schröder 2007), all of them mainly due to land drainage and eutrophication resulting from agriculture.

Conservation

All populations are on protected land. *P. lycopodioides* is listed as a Northern Ireland Priority Species.

Protected sites with recent records: Ballymaclary Nature Reserve; Bellacorick Bog Complex SAC; Burren National Park; Castletaylor Complex SAC; East Burren Complex SAC; Fin Lough (Roscommon) pNHA; Fortwilliam Turlough SAC; Lough Carra/Mask Complex SAC; Lough Fingall Complex SAC; Lough Ree SAC; Magilligan ASSI; Magilligan SAC; River Moy SAC; Williamstown Turloughs SAC; **Unprotected sites with recent records:** none.

Pseudocalliergon trifarium (F.Weber & D.Mohr) Loeske

Three-ranked Spear-moss

syn. *Acrocladium trifarium* (F.Weber & D.Mohr) P.W.Richards & E.C.Wallace, *Calliergon trifarium* (F.Weber & D.Mohr) Kindb., *Drepanocladus trifarius* (F.Weber & D.Mohr) Broth. ex Paris
Status in Ireland: Vulnerable (D2); **Status in Europe:** Least Concern

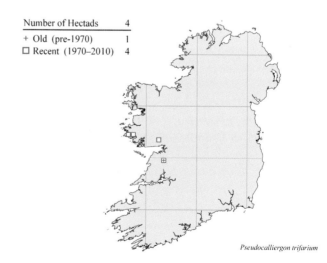

Number of Hectads	4
+ Old (pre-1970)	1
□ Recent (1970–2010)	4

Pseudocalliergon trifarium

Identification

A medium-sized pleurocarpous moss that grows as scattered procumbent to erect stems or forms tufts or patches (smooth or rough mats) that are green, brownish

or yellowish-brown, with stems somewhat turgid and slightly and irregularly branched, up to 10 cm long, rarely 15 cm. Stem leaves are imbricate, concave, broadly ovate with a broadly rounded apex. The leaf margin is entire and the costa is single, extending 60–90% of leaf length. Cells in mid-leaf are linear-vermicular, smooth, with rather incrassate cell walls. The alar cells are elongate-rectangular, inflated, incrassate with yellow cell walls when mature, forming an indistinctly delimited triangular group. The capsule (unknown in Ireland or Britain) is ellipsoid, curved, horizontal to inclined and exserted on a long seta. *P. trifarium* is easily identified with a hand lens by its unbranched or almost unbranched shoots with imbricate, broadly ovate leaves that have broadly rounded apices. Molecular data shows that *Pseudocalliergon trifarium* should be classified as a species of *Drepanocladus* (Hedenäs & Rosborg 2009).

Distribution in Ireland

There are recent records from eight localities in two vice-counties: Clare (Lough Cullaun, 1994; Mullagh More, 1953–2004; Cooloorta Lough, 2004; Travaun Lough, 2004) and W. Galway (S. side of Errisbeg, 1980; Derrylea Lough, 1986; near Lough Nalawney, 1987–2004; NW of Gortachalla Lough, 2004–2010). There are older records from a further two localities: Clare (Little Templebanagh Lough, 1959; Castle Lough, 1967).

Ecology and biology

This is an uncommon moss of open, base-rich, lowland fens, including intermediate fens that may have rather low calcium levels. It commonly grows among other fen mosses, sedges, etc. in rather wet sites with deep peat, but there is also a record from the dried floor of a turlough. Associates include *Carex laevigata*, *C. lepidocarpa*, *Eriophorum angustifolium*, *Schoenus nigricans* and (especially) *Scorpidium scorpioides*. In Sweden, it occurs in similar habitats, with pH recorded as 5.6–8.1 and low to rather high calcium levels (4–76 mg/l) (Hedenäs 2003).

The plants are perennial. It is a dioicous species in which capsules are rare (unknown in Ireland or Britain, but recorded in Fennoscandia). Gemmae, bulbils and tubers are absent, but vegetative propagation is likely to occur from detached leaves and stem fragments.

World distribution

P. trifarium is widespread in N., W. and C. Europe, from N. Iceland, Spitsbergen and N. Fennoscandia southwards to France, N. Italy (in Alps), the Balkans and Ukraine, but listed as *Critically Endangered* in the Czech Republic, *Endangered* in Germany, *Vulnerable* in Bulgaria, *Near Threatened* in Switzerland and 'very rare' in the Netherlands. It is assigned to a Circumpolar Boreo-arctic montane floristic element in Europe. Elsewhere, it occurs in SW and N. Asia (Armenia and Kazakhstan; widespread from W. Siberia and Yakutia to Russian Far East: Ignatov *et al.* 2007), C. Asia (Mongolia: Karczmarz 1971), N. America and Greenland. There are also isolated records in Haiti and Venezuela (Karczmarz 1971, Delgadillo *et al.* 1995).

Threats

Attempts to refind the species in the last decade have been unsuccessful at a few localities (e.g. Derrylea Lough), but strong populations persist elsewhere, especially NW of Gortachalla Lough. It does not appear to be under any immediate threat at the sites with recent records, although the species would be potentially vulnerable to drainage, eutrophication or shading from afforestation.

Conservation

Most sites are on protected land.

Protected sites with recent records: Burren National Park; Connemara Bog Complex SAC; East Burren Complex SAC; Lough Corrib SAC; **Unprotected sites with recent records:** Derrylea Lough (probably within Connemara Bog Complex SAC); S. side of Errisbeg (probably within Connemara Bog Complex SAC).

Hamatocaulis vernicosus (Mitt.) Hedenäs

syn. *Amblystegium vernicosum* (Lindb.) Lindb., *Drepanocladus vernicosus* (Mitt.) Warnst.
Status in Ireland: Near Threatened; **Status in Europe:** Vulnerable

Varnished Hook-moss
Shining Sickle Moss
Slender Green feather-moss

Identification

A medium-sized to rather robust pleurocarpous moss with pinnately branched, procumbent to ascending stems up to 12 cm long, that grows amongst other plants or forms green, dull green or brownish (rarely reddish) tufts or patches. Stem leaves are strongly falcato-secund (so the shoot apex is often hooked like a walking stick), ovate and tapering to an acuminate apex, with the base erect and the

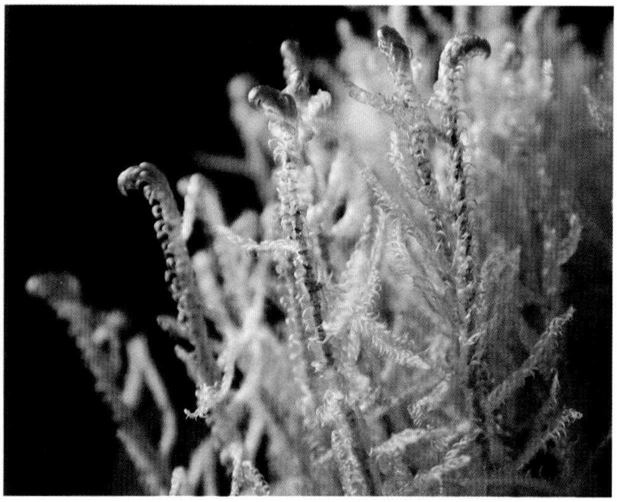

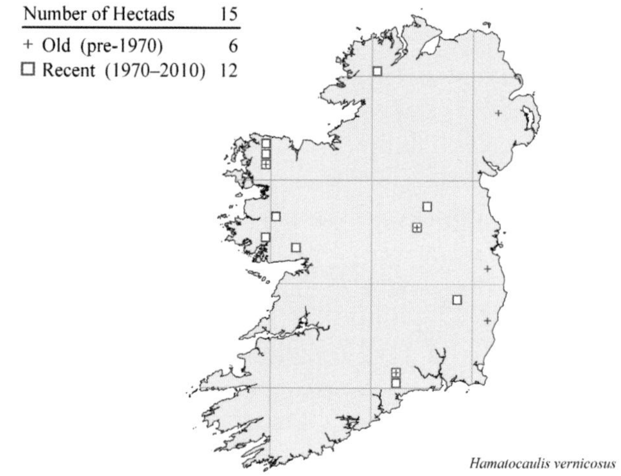

upper part of the leaf rather abruptly curved, the leaf base concave, usually strongly plicate and with a red colour often present in a transverse band. The leaf margins are plane and entire, the costa extends half to three-quarters of the way up the leaf, mid-leaf cells are linear and the alar cells are short but do not form differentiated auricles. Capsules are shortly cylindrical, curved and exserted on a long, smooth seta. *H. vernicosus* has often been misidentified in the past, but errors are easily avoided through careful attention to microscopic characters (including lack of stem hyalodermis, plicate leaves lacking differentiated alar cells) along with the characteristic erect leaf base and suddenly curved upper part of the leaf.

Distribution in Ireland

Records are accepted from 14 localities in seven vice-counties: Waterford (Sgilloge Loughs, 1966–2010; beside R. Nire in Comeragh Mountains, 1963–2010; Coumtay, 2007); W. Galway (W. side of Lough Mask, 1983–2010; Maam Cross, 1987; NW of Gortachalla Lough, 2004–2010); Wicklow (E. of Yellowford Cross Roads, 1975); Meath (between Lough Bane and Drumone, 1978); Westmeath (Scragh Bog, 1946–2010); W. Mayo (ESE of Lough Nambrackkeagh, 1987; Largan More, 1999–2010; Rathavisteen, 1999; Uggool, 1999) and W. Donegal (Meentygrannagh, 1999–2010). Older records are from Wexford (Pallis Bridge, 1969); W. Mayo (between Bellacorick and Dooleeg, 1958) and Down (by River Lagan above Lisburn, 1901). In addition there are numerous known errors of identification and reports unsupported by specimens, including all reports from 12 additional vice-counties (S. Kerry, N. Kerry, Clare, NE Galway, Kildare, Longford, Roscommon, Sligo, Leitrim, E. Donegal, Antrim and Londonderry).

Ecology and biology

Its typical habitats are in intermediate fens which are usually influenced by springs, often mineral-rich (but usually not rich in calcium) and often slightly nutrient-enriched, from the lowlands to at least 310 m altitude. It avoids shade, habitats that dry out and eutrophicated places. In Ireland, it has been found in upland flushes, lowland fens and on seasonally flooded lake margins. Species present close by at different Irish sites include *Calliergon giganteum*, *Pseudocalliergon trifarium*, *Campylium stellatum*, *Cinclidium stygium* and *Sphagnum contortum*, as well as *Saxifraga hirculus*, sedges and other herbs. Its habitats are very similar elsewhere in Europe (cf. Hedenäs & Kooijman 1996, Hedenäs 1999, Bosanquet *et al.* 2006, Štechová & Kučera 2007, Štechová *et al.* 2008).

The plants are perennial. It is a dioicous species and capsules are rare (perhaps unknown in Ireland), maturing in summer. Gemmae, bulbils and tubers are absent, but vegetative propagation doubtless occurs from detached leaf and stem fragments.

World distribution

Widespread in N. Europe from N. Sweden, N. Finland and arctic Russia southwards; much more local in S. Europe, where known southwards to WC Spain, the SE Alps and the Caucasus. It is listed as *Extinct* in Luxembourg, *Critically Endangered* in the Netherlands, *Endangered* in Germany and Spain, *Vulnerable* in Bulgaria, the Czech Republic and Finland, *Near Threatened* in Sweden and Switzerland and 'declining' in Norway. It is assigned to a Circumpolar Boreal-montane floristic element in Europe. Elsewhere, it is known in SW, C. and N. Asia, Japan, N. America, Greenland, Dominican

Republic and mountains of S. America (Peru). *H. vernicosus* comprises two cryptic species (see below).

Threats

Six of the eleven Irish populations that were known before 1990 (55%) had apparently been lost by 2007, one due to large-scale peat extraction, another to afforestation and the remaining four to various combinations of drainage and eutrophication. Similar factors underlie widespread declines in N. and C. Germany (Meinunger & Schröder 2007). Its extinction in E. England (E. Anglia) over the past few decades is attributed largely to eutrophication from adjoining agricultural land (Holyoak 1999). Current threats to Irish populations are probably similar to the causes of loss in the past, with eutrophication of groundwater potentially threatening even some fens on protected land.

Conservation

H. vernicosus is listed on Appendix 1 of the Bern Convention, protected under the EU Habitats Directive and covered by the Flora (Protection) Order, 1999 in the Republic of Ireland. A majority of the extant Irish populations are on protected land. In the last decade, new surveys have revealed many previously overlooked populations in some regions of Europe (e.g. C. and S.

Wales: Bosanquet *et al.* 2006) and large populations are known in the boreal zone of Fennoscandia, suggesting that despite losses of many regional populations it is not threatened in Europe as a whole. However, Hedenäs & Eldenäs (2007) have recently demonstrated that *H. vernicosus* comprises two cryptic species, one clade widespread in Europe and also occurring in the USA, the other known only south of the boreal zone in Europe but also in Peru and NE Asia. Three British samples are all referable to the latter clade; no molecular studies have been carried out on Irish plants. Štechová & Kučera (2007) analyse effects of habitat management intended to benefit the species in the Czech Republic, finding that it was positively influenced by mowing only at a site with high vascular plant cover, and that gap cutting was only beneficial at sites with a low water table.

Protected sites with recent records: Ballycroy National Park; Carrowmore Lake Complex SAC; Comeragh Mountains SAC; Connemara Bog Complex SAC; Glenamoy Bog Complex SAC; Holdenstown Bog SAC; Lough Carra/Mask Complex SAC; Lough Corrib SAC; Meentygrannagh Bog SAC; Owenduff/Nephin Complex SAC; Scragh Bog Nature Reserve; Scragh Bog SAC; **Unprotected sites with recent records:** between Lough Bane and Drumone.

Abietinella abietina (Hedw.) M.Fleisch. **var.** *abietina*   Fir Tamarisk-moss

syn. *Thuidium abietinum* (Hedw.) Schimp. subsp. *abietinum*
Status in Ireland: Endangered (B2a, biii, iv); **Status in Europe:** Least Concern

Number of Hectads	3
+ Old (pre-1970)	3
☐ Recent (1970–2010)	2

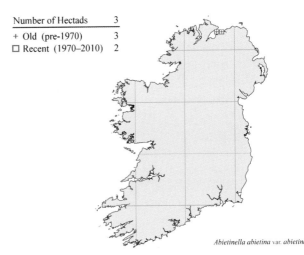

Abietinella abietina var. *abietina*

Identification

A. abietina is a distinctive pleurocarpous moss with arcuate to erect stems 2–8 cm high (rarely 12 cm) from

which branches arise in four ranks. Its rather sparse branches often spread at wide angles, giving the impression of a miniature conifer. It differs from the closely related *Thuidium* species in having only a simply pinnate rather than two- or three-pinnate (and complanate) arrangement of branches, but shares their strong costa extending to above mid-leaf and almost isodiametric, unipapillose upper leaf cells. Stem leaves are patent, broadly ovate, plicate at the base and taper to a long acuminate apex. Branch leaves are more concave, broadly ovate to lanceolate, with a shorter apex. The main distinctions between var. *abietina* and var. *hystricosa* are that the former has shorter, ovate branch leaves which are appressed when dry, whereas the latter has longer, ovate to lanceolate branch leaves some of which are secund when dry, so that dry branches of var. *abietina* are terete and neatly cylindrical, whereas those of var. *hystricosa* are not terete and appear rough due to projecting leaf apices. A detailed study by Düll-Hermanns (1981) reviewed the taxonomy of *A. abietina* and showed that plants which are intermediate between var. *abietina* and var. *hystricosa* occur widely throughout the range of var. *abietina* outside the range of var. *hystricosa*, so that their current treatment as varieties rather than separate species is appropriate.

Distribution in Ireland

A review of herbarium specimens by N.G. Hodgetts (unpublished) has revealed that numerous Irish records of the species are of var. *hystricosa*, although they have been uncritically referred to var. *abietina*. Confirmed records of var. *abietina* are only from Dublin (Malahide 1861–1902, probably also 1912; Portmarnock 1825–1860, perhaps 1915), where it may now be extinct, and Londonderry (Magilligan area 1926–2008 to Castlerock 1926–1938; refound at Ballymaclary in 1999 and 2008, with strong populations in one slack).

Ecology and biology

It is only recorded in Ireland on calcareous sand in coastal dunes. At Ballymaclary Nature Reserve it grows in short vegetation of moss carpets on dry edges of a dune slack, often near to *Rhytidium rugosum*, *Hylocomium splendens* and sparse *Salix repens*. In Britain, it occurs mainly in short-grazed chalk grassland, but with strong populations locally in dune slacks (Upton Towans in W. Cornwall) and a few records from basic montane rock ledges, screes and *Dryas*-heath.

The plants are dioicous and capsules are unknown in Ireland (rare in Britain). No gemmae, tubers or other propagules have been recorded, so dispersal probably occurs by stem and leaf fragments. The plants appear to be short-lived perennials that can be found in all months of the year, but details are lacking.

World distribution

Var. *abietina* is the widespread form of the species. In Europe, it ranges from the Arctic in Iceland, Spitsbergen and N. Fennoscandia south to N. Spain and the Caucasus. *A. abietina s.l.* is listed as *Critically Endangered* in the Netherlands and 'declining' in Germany. Although rather local and uncommon in Britain, it is common with large populations elsewhere, e.g. in limestone regions of Germany (Meinunger & Schröder 2007). It is assigned to a Circumpolar Boreo-arctic montane floristic element in Europe. Elsewhere, it is known in SW Asia, Kashmir, China (widespread: Wu *et al.* 2002), Japan, N. America (southwards to Colorado and Virginia) and Greenland, with an isolated southern hemisphere report from Lesotho.

Threats

The apparent extinction of populations in Dublin is due mainly to coastal development in the Malahide and Portmarnock areas, where houses, other buildings and golf courses have replaced the former dune grassland and slacks. In Londonderry, habitat has probably also been lost to the extensive golf course development at Castlerock, while protected dune areas at The Umbra and elsewhere now have much tall undergrazed vegetation that is unsuitable for the species. Where var. *abietina* persists at Ballymaclary the short, open vegetation at edges of dune slacks is maintained by intense rabbit grazing. *A. abietina* would be vulnerable to any reduction in this grazing pressure. Other potential threats could include damage to the thin vegetation cover by military vehicles that use the area, or changes in hydrology.

Conservation

At Ballymaclary, the land is used for military training as part of the Magilligan Ministry of Defence camp, so care is needed to ensure that conservation needs of *A. abietina* and other biota are included in management agreements ensuring sustainable use of the land. Surveys are needed to ascertain if other populations still exist elsewhere at Magilligan. *A. abietina* is listed as a Northern Ireland Priority Species.

Protected sites with recent records: Ballymaclary Nature Reserve; Magilligan ASSI; Magilligan SAC; **Unprotected sites with recent records:** none.

Abietinella abietina (Hedw.) M.Fleisch. **var. *hystricosa*** (Mitt.) Sakurai

Prickly Tamarisk-moss

syn. *Thuidium abietinum* (Hedw.) Schimp. subsp. *hystricosum* (Mitt.) Kindb.
Status in Ireland: Near Threatened; **Status in Europe:** Least Concern

Much the more frequent of the two varieties of *A. abietina* in Ireland, var. *hystricosa* is frequent on calcareous sand dunes in the north-west, with reports from five vice-counties and records from 18 hectads (10 old, 17 recent). Although originally included in the Provisional Red List (Holyoak 2006b), it was not particularly sought during recent fieldwork when found to be under-recorded in Ireland. There is no evidence of decline but as the populations are usually small and the habitat restricted and threatened, a status of *Near Threatened* is considered appropriate.

Thuidium recognitum (Hedw.) Lindb.

Lesser Tamarisk-moss

Status in Ireland: Vulnerable (B2a, bii, iv); **Status in Europe:** Least Concern

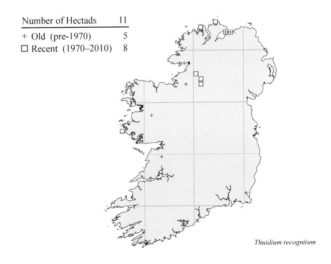

Number of Hectads	11
+ Old (pre-1970)	5
□ Recent (1970–2010)	8

Thuidium recognitum

Identification

An elegant pleurocarpous moss that grows as yellowish-green wefts or rough mats, often among other low plants, with stems up to 90 mm long that are 3-pinnately branched. The stem leaves are ovate-lanceolate tapering to a long acuminate, filiform acumen, the leaf apex being reflexed or recurved when dry. Leaf margins are crenulate-denticulate and narrowly recurved below; the costa extends almost to the apex of the acumen. The mid-

leaf cells are shortly rectangular and unipapillose, but cells at the leaf tip beyond the end of the costa are elongate. Branch leaves are much smaller than stem leaves; the apical cell of leaves at branch tips is crowned with 2–3 papillae. The stems are clothed with branched uniseriate paraphyllia on which the prominent papillae occur only on the end walls of the cells. Capsules (unknown in Ireland or Britain) are cylindrical, curved, inclined and exserted on a long seta. In the field, *T. recognitum* looks much like *T. delicatulum* and *T. assimile*, with a branching pattern less neatly complanate than that of the common *T. tamariscinum*; identification then needs to be confirmed by microscopic study of the branch leaf apical cells, the stem leaves and paraphyllia.

Distribution in Ireland

Recent records are accepted from 10 localities in five vice-counties: W. Galway (Truska Machair, 1999); Fermanagh (Pollawaddy and Owenbrean, 2005, at two adjacent sites; Monawilkin, 2005; Belmore Mountain, 2005); E. Donegal (Doagh Isle, 2002); W. Donegal (N. of Lough Nagreany, 2002) and Londonderry (Magilligan, 1954–1990; records there from 1999 were from two localities, near Magilligan Point and in Ballymaclary N.R.; The Umbra, 1913–2008). Older records are accepted from Clare (N. of Lough Trabaun, 1959); E. Mayo (E. shore of Lough Carra, 1953) and Leitrim (Boggaun, 1963). Numerous specimens labelled as *T. recognitum* have been reidentified as other *Thuidium* species. These and reports without voucher specimens originate from eight additional vice-counties: S. Kerry, W. Cork, Kildare, Meath, Roscommon, Sligo, Louth and Down.

Ecology and biology

T. recognitum is a calcicole of open or lightly shaded habitats on free-draining substrata in the lowlands or on low hills. Its Irish habitats are of two different types, among limestone rocks inland and on calcareous coastal sand. Inland, it is recorded from limestone pavements, ledges of crags and a low rocky ridge above a lake, usually growing with other plants on thin soil and rock fragments, in grassland, open scrub or at woodland edges. The coastal sites are in dune slacks, on dune slopes or ridges, or on machair, growing amongst other mosses, low phanerogams, or both, on dry to damp sand. In Britain, it is recorded mainly from inland limestone areas, including montane rock ledges at up to 950 m altitude, with only very rare records from sand dunes (M.J. Wigginton in Hill *et al.* 1994).

The plants are perennial. It is a dioicous species in which sporophytes are unknown in Ireland or Britain (capsules have been found in Austria). Gemmae, bulbils and tubers are lacking, but vegetative propagation is likely to occur from detached leaf and stem fragments.

World distribution

It has a wide range in Europe from NW Iceland, C. Norway, N. Sweden, N. Finland and arctic Russia southwards to N. Spain, S. Italy, the Crimea and the Caucasus, but is listed as *Endangered* in the Netherlands and 'declining' in Germany. It is assigned to a Circumpolar Temperate floristic element in Europe. Elsewhere, it occurs in Algeria, SW and N. Asia (Azerbaijan and Georgia to Kazakhstan; S. and W. Siberia to Yakutia and Russian Far East: Ignatov *et al.* 2007), N. America (Alaska to Newfoundland and southwards to Georgia) and Greenland. Reports from Japan are referable to *T. delicatulum* (Iwatsuki 1991) and its occurrence in China needs confirmation (Wu Pengcheng *et al.* 2002).

Threats

There is only scanty evidence that the species has declined in Ireland and it is probably still somewhat under-recorded because of the similarity to more common *Thuidium* species. Nevertheless, most of its populations are potentially vulnerable to loss from shading if scrub develops on dunes or limestone slopes and pavements. Potential threats from overstocking and erosion are probably less because it can persist in short open vegetation.

Conservation

Several localities are on protected land. *T. recognitum* is listed as a Northern Ireland Priority Species.

Protected sites with recent records: Ballymaclary Nature Reserve; Lough Nagreany Dunes SAC; Magilligan ASSI; Magilligan SAC; Monawilkin ASSI; Monawilkin SAC; North Inishowen Coast SAC; Slyne Head Peninsula SAC; **Unprotected sites with recent records:** Belmore Mountain; Pollawaddy and Owenbrean.

Plasteurhynchium striatulum (Spruce) M.Fleisch.　　Lesser Striated Feather-moss

syn. *Eurhynchium striatulum* (Spruce) Schimp., *Hypnum striatulum* Spruce, *Isothecium striatulum* (Spruce) Kindb.
Status in Ireland: Near Threatened; **Status in Europe:** Least Concern

A pleurocarpous moss that grows in mats on dry limestone rocks or less often on walls or tree bases. It has been reported from 12 vice-counties, with records from 17 hectads (12 old, 7 recent). It was not included in the Provisional Red List (Holyoak 2006b), and therefore not deliberately sought during recent fieldwork, but there is no reason to believe that it has declined. Strong populations persist around Lough Gill in Leitrim.

Platyhypnidium lusitanicum (Schimp.) Ochyra & Bednarek-Ochyra　　Portuguese Feather-moss

syn. *Eurhynchium alopecuroides* (Brid.) P.W.Richards & E.C.Wallace, *E. alopecurum* auct.,
E. riparioides var. *alopecuroides* auct., *Hypnum rusciforme* var. *alopecuroides* Brid.,
Platyhypnidium alopecuroides (Brid.) A.J.E.Sm., *Rhynchostegium alopecuroides* (Brid.) A.J.E.Sm.,
R. lusitanicum (Schimp.) A.J.E.Sm. *nom. illeg.*
Status in Ireland: Near Threatened; **Status in Europe:** Least Concern

A calcifuge pleurocarpous moss with julaceous shoots of imbricate leaves, forming green or brownish patches, at or below water level, in fast-flowing streams and rivers. It has a scattered distribution in Ireland, found mostly at lower altitudes in upland areas and has been reported from 10 vice-counties, with records from 17 hectads (6 old, 12 recent). It was not included in the Provisional Red List (Holyoak 2006b), and therefore not deliberately sought during recent fieldwork, but there is no reason to believe it has declined.

Rhynchostegium megapolitanum
(Blandow ex F.Weber & D.Mohr) Schimp.

Megapolitan Feather-moss

syn. *Brachythecium cardotii* H.Winter, *Eurhynchium megapolitanum* (F.Weber & D.Mohr) Milde,
Hypnum megapolitanum Bland. ex F.Weber & D.Mohr
Status in Ireland: Near Threatened; **Status in Europe:** Least Concern

A medium-sized, pale green pleurocarpous moss that grows in straggling patches on sandy soils. It has a mainly southern and eastern distribution in Ireland, found mostly on coastal sand dunes, but with a few localities inland, including on roadside gravel at Lower Lough Macnean, Co. Fermanagh; its only known site in Northern Ireland. It was included in the Provisional Red List (Holyoak 2006b) but fieldwork over the past decade has located additional populations. There are reports from seven vice-counties, with records from 12 hectads (5 old, 10 recent). There is little or no evidence of any decline.

Rhynchostegiella curviseta (Brid.) Limpr.

Curve-stalked Feather-moss

syn. *Eurhynchium curvisetum* (Brid.) Delogne, *Rhynchostegium curvisetum* (Brid.) Husn.
Status in Ireland: Regionally Extinct; **Status in Europe:** Least Concern

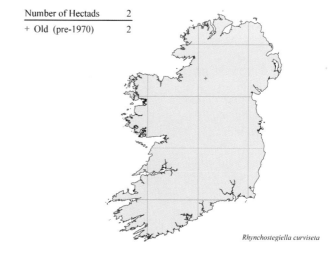

Number of Hectads	2
+ Old (pre-1970)	2

Rhynchostegiella curviseta

Identification

This is a slender pleurocarpous moss that grows in small dense yellowish-green or green smooth mats, with stems up to 30 mm long. Leaves are lanceolate to oblong-lanceolate, three to five times as long as wide, with costa extending to mid-leaf or just above and plane margins that are faintly denticulate above. Cells in mid-leaf are narrowly rhomboidal to linear-rhomboidal. The capsules are ovoid, horizontal, exserted on a strongly papillose seta and have a lid with a subulate beak. *R. curviseta* usually differs from *R. teneriffae* in its short costa and longer mid-leaf cells (40–72 μm and mainly 8–10 times as long

536

as wide, compared to 32–48 μm and mainly 5–7 times as long as wide), but intermediate plants occur in S. England. A molecular study has recently disclosed that *R. curviseta*, some *R. teneriffae* and *R. litorea* form a single clade, with no evidence that three distinct species can be resolved (Aigoin *et al.* 2009).

Distribution in Ireland

Only two records appear to be correct, from Fermanagh (by Cladagh River near Marble Arch, 1965; not refound on several recent visits) and Antrim (White Rocks E. of Portrush, 1885; not refound in 2008). Three other records are based on misidentified specimens, from S. Kerry (Dingle, 1935), W. Mayo (N. side of Menawn on Achill Island, 1962) and Leitrim (N. end of Glencar Lough, 1928).

Ecology and biology

In Ireland, it has been recorded from wet boulders (presumably of limestone) by the Cladagh River and rocks and stones near water at White Rocks. In Britain, it mainly grows on damp basic to neutral stones (especially limestone and sandstone) and tree roots on wooded stream banks, but also occurs on bridge supports and retaining walls close to water and on the banks of shaded lanes.

Patches of the species live for at least several years. It is autoicous and capsules are frequent, maturing in winter and spring. Tubers and gemmae are unknown.

World distribution

It occurs in S. and W. Europe from Belgium, Germany and Romania south to the Mediterranean, and is listed as *Critically Endangered* in Switzerland and 'rare' in the Netherlands. In Europe, it is assigned to an Oceanic Mediterranean-Atlantic floristic element. Elsewhere, it is recorded from N. Africa, Cyprus, Turkey, Lebanon, Israel, Jordan and Iraq (Herrnstadt & Heyn 2004). Although reported from the Azores, Madeira and Canary Islands (Eggers 1982, Sjögren 2001) these records are questioned by Düll (1986) and Dirkse & Bouman (1996), and Hedenäs (1992) does not accept it for Madeira.

Threats

It has not been refound at Marble Arch or White Rocks, although *R. teneriffae* was plentiful at the former locality and the habitat there still appears suitable for both species.

Conservation

The locality near Marble Arch is on protected land. No action is proposed unless a population is found or refound in Ireland.

Protected sites with recent records: none; **Unprotected sites with recent records:** none.

Oxyrrhynchium schleicheri (R.Hedw.) Röll.　　　Twist-tip Feather-moss

syn. *Eurhynchium schleicheri* (R.Hedw.) Milde
Status in Ireland: Critically Endangered (B2a, biii); **Status in Europe:** Least Concern

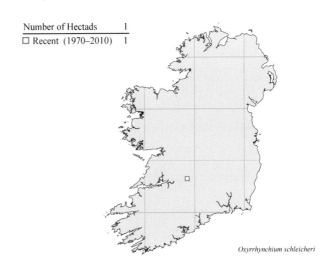

Number of Hectads	1
☐ Recent (1970–2010)	1

Oxyrrhynchium schleicheri

Identification

A medium-sized pleurocarpous moss that forms yellowish-green tufts or patches (rough mats or wefts) with creeping stems up to about 60 mm long giving rise to erect or ascending branches. Stem leaves are patent to spreading, rounded-triangular to ovate-triangular, gradually narrowed to an acuminate apex which is usually twisted through 180°. The leaves are concave and not or only slightly plicate, with plane, denticulate margins. The costa is single and ends in the lower part of the acumen where it forms a short, obtuse spine on the dorsal surface of the leaf. Mid-leaf cells are linear, slightly flexuose and mainly 4–5.5 μm wide; the alar cells are rectangular, slightly inflated, forming an indistinctly delimited transversely-triangular group that is slightly decurrent. Branch leaves are shorter and more triangular than stem leaves, often complanate, with coarsely denticulate margins. Capsules are ellipsoid to shortly cylindrical, inclined to horizontal, with a long subulate beak, exserted on a papillose seta. *O. schleicheri* is distinct from other Brachytheciaceae in the combination of creeping (stoloniferous) primary stems and leaf characters that include the twisted apex and narrow cells in the middle of the stem leaves.

Distribution in Ireland

There is a single record from N. Tipperary (Keeper Hill, 1979, leg. H. van Melick). Reports from N. Kerry (near Ross Castle, 1983) and Leitrim (SE of Glencar Lough, 1928) are based on misidentified specimens.

Ecology and biology

The only Irish collection was made by H. van Melick 'on loamy soil in a dark wet forest on an east slope with *Salix*, *Betula pubescens* and *Fraxinus*'. In Britain, it grows on friable, well-drained, basic or slightly acidic soil on shaded banks in woodland and by roads and sunken lanes, occasionally on stream sides and riverbanks (C.D. Preston in Hill *et al.* 1994).

The plants are perennial. It is a dioicous species; capsules are infrequent in Britain, maturing from December to March. Gemmae, bulbils and tubers are unknown, but vegetative propagation is likely to occur from detached leaf and stem fragments.

World distribution

The species is widespread in Europe from N. England, S. Norway, S. Sweden and Latvia southwards to Portugal, SE Spain, Italy and the Caucasus, but listed as *Critically Endangered* in Bulgaria, *Near Threatened* in Sweden, *Data Deficient* in Germany and 'rare' in the Netherlands. It is assigned to a Suboceanic Mediterranean-Atlantic floristic element in Europe. Elsewhere, it occurs in Madeira, Canary Islands and SW Asia from Turkey and Armenia to Iran. Reports from the Russian Far East are unconfirmed (Ignatov *et al.* 2007).

Threats

O. schleicheri has only been found once in Ireland, in 1979. It was not refound in 2005, but the original record was not accurately localised. Although there has been much planting of conifers in the area, it may still persist somewhere.

Conservation

No action is proposed.

Protected sites with recent records: none; **Unprotected sites with recent records:** Keeper Hill (possibly within Keeper Hill SAC).

Keeper Hill, Co. Tipperary.

Oxyrrhynchium speciosum (Brid.) Warnst.

Showy Feather-moss

syn. *Eurhynchium speciosum* (Brid.) Jur., *Hypnum speciosum* Brid.
Status in Ireland: Near Threatened; **Status in Europe:** Least Concern

A trailing pleurocarpous moss that grows in moist shaded sites. It was included in the Provisional Red List (Holyoak 2006b), but several additional finds over the past decade suggest it is somewhat under-recorded and unlikely to be seriously threatened. There are reports from 18 vice-counties, with records from 24 hectads (15 old, 8 recent, 2 undated). During the fieldwork over the past decade, little effort was made to refind old records of this species, so there is no real evidence that it has declined.

Scleropodium cespitans (Wilson ex Müll.Hal.) L.F.Koch

Tufted Feather-moss

syn. *Brachythecium appleyardiae* McAdam & A.J.E.Sm., *B. caespitosum* (Wilson) Dixon, *Scleropodium caespitosum* (Wilson) Schimp.
Status in Ireland: Near Threatened; **Status in Europe:** Least Concern

A pleurocarpous moss that grows in patches in two main types of habitat, on rocks and trees of the inundation zone beside rivers and lakes, and in rather dry places at the base of large limestone crags. The plants from limestone crags tend to be smaller and more slender and these were regarded as *Brachythecium appleyardiae* until Blockeel *et al.* (2005b) demonstrated from a combined morphological and molecular study that they are merely a small form of *S. cespitans*. There are reports from 13 vice-counties, with records from 24 hectads (10 old, 14 recent). There is no evidence of decline.

Scleropodium touretii (Brid.) L.F.Koch

Glass-wort Feather-moss

syn. *Hypnum illecebrum* Hedw., *Scleropodium illecebrum* auct., *S. tourettii* auct.

Status in Ireland: Endangered (B1a, bi, ii, iii, iv, B2a, bi, ii, iii, iv); **Status in Europe:** Least Concern

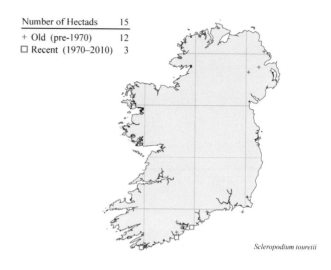

Number of Hectads	15
+ Old (pre-1970)	12
□ Recent (1970–2010)	3

Scleropodium touretii

Identification

A medium-sized pleurocarpous moss that grows as green, yellowish or brownish patches (rough or smooth mats) with irregularly branched stems up to 50 mm long, giving rise to somewhat turgid branches that are characteristically curved when dry. The stem leaves are erect and imbricate to erecto-patent, very concave, ovate-oblong to rounded-triangular, narrowed to an acuminate or shortly acute apex. The leaf margin is plane, entire below and denticulate in the upper part of the leaf; the costa is single and extends for 50–80% of leaf length. Mid-leaf cells are smooth, linear-vermicular, 3.5–7 μm wide; angular cells are rectangular or shortly rectangular. Branch leaves are smaller, imbricate, ovate and acute to obtuse. Capsules (apparently unknown in Ireland) are ovate-ellipsoid with a rostrate operculum, inclined to horizontal, exserted on a long, coarsely papillose, red seta. The short curved branches with ovate, imbricate leaves are a good field character of typical forms of this species, but shaded plants are more slender and much less distinctive.

Distribution in Ireland

Recent records are accepted from three localities in three vice-counties: W. Cork (by S. Harbour, Clear Island, 2008); Mid Cork (Charles Fort, Kinsale, 2006) and E. Cork (Ballycotton, 2006). Older accepted records are from 13 localities in eight vice-counties: W. Cork (Sherkin Island, 1934); Mid Cork (Passage, 1865; Cork, 1876; Kinsale, 1865); E. Cork (Queenstown, 1872–1880; Youghal, 1951); Waterford (near Old Pike Bridge near Dungarvan, 1956); Wexford (Great Saltee Island, 1913); Dublin (Howth, 1872; Killiney, 1872); Armagh (Ardmore Glebe, 1885) and Antrim (Black Mountain, 1804; Sallagh Braes, 1884). Unconfirmed or discounted records include all those from S. Kerry, N. Kerry (Muckross, 1905–1912) and S. Tipperary (Clonmel, 1872) and another from Dublin (Ballinascorney Gap, 1872).

Ecology and biology

In Ireland, as in Britain, this is a moss of open, sunny situations in short trampled or heavily grazed grassland, growing on free-draining basic or mildly acidic soil or thin soil over edges of low rocks, commonly on or by paths, most often on tops of sea cliffs, but sometimes also inland on hedge banks or near crags. In Britain, it sometimes also grows on banks in woodland. It is much more common in parts of S. Europe and Macaronesia, where it also occurs inside woodland and scrub, on walls and tree bases as well as on soil.

The plants are perennial. It is a dioicous species in which sporophytes are rare in Britain. Gemmae, bulbils and tubers are absent, but vegetative propagation presumably occurs from detached leaf and stem fragments.

World distribution

S. touretii occurs in W. and S. Europe, from Ireland, S. Scotland, NE and C. Germany, Denmark, Belgium and Luxembourg southwards through France to Spain, Portugal and much of the Mediterranean region. It is listed as *Endangered* in Bulgaria and Germany. It is assigned to an Oceanic Mediterranean-Atlantic floristic element in Europe. Elsewhere, the range includes the Azores, Madeira, Canary Islands, N. Africa, Turkey (Uyar & Çetin 2004) and western N. America.

Threats

Populations have not been refound at some of the old localities, although most were poorly localised. At Old Pike Bridge (near Dungarvan) the hedge bank on which it occurred has probably been destroyed by widening of the road. The species has declined inland over the past century in S. and C. England (Hill *et al.* 1994) and Germany (Meinunger & Schröder 2007). Little information is available on current threats to the species, but its persistence at some coastal sites apparently depends on open conditions being maintained by various combinations of trampling by people and grazing by sheep or rabbits.

Conservation

Only a few populations are on protected land.

Protected sites with recent records: Roaringwater Bay and Islands SAC; **Unprotected sites with recent records:** Ballycotton; Charles Fort, Kinsale.

Eurhynchiastrum pulchellum

Elegant Feather-moss

(Hedw.) Ignatov & Huttunen **var. *diversifolium*** (Schimp.) Ochyra & Żarnowiec

syn. *Eurhynchium pulchellum* (Hedw.) Jenn., *Eurhynchium pulchellum* var. *diversifolium* (Schimp.) C.E.O.Jensen
Status in Ireland: Regionally Extinct; **Status in Europe:** Least Concern

Number of Hectads	1
+ Old (pre-1970)	1

Eurhynchiastrum pulchellum var. *diversifolium*

Identification

This is a small pleurocarpous moss that forms low patches (rough mats) that are somewhat glossy and green, yellowish or brownish. The procumbent female stems are up to 30 mm long, closely and often subpinnately branched, the branches being short, obtuse, erect and straight. Stem leaves are cordate-triangular to triangular, acuminate, crowded and slightly complanate. The leaf margin is plane and denticulate, the costa slender, extending about three-quarters of the way up leaf. Mid-leaf cells are linear to linear-rhomboidal, 5–7 μm wide and about 8–12 times as long as wide; angular cells are enlarged, oval to rounded-quadrate, with thicker cell walls. Branch leaves are smaller, acute to obtuse and imbricate. Capsules (unknown in Ireland or Britain) are oval, inclined, curved, the operculum with a subulate beak, exserted on a smooth seta. Male plants are minute and bud-like, growing epiphytically on female plants. Hill *et al.* (2006) recognise three varieties in Europe; the Irish and British plants were all referred to var. *diversifolium* by Hill (1993).

Distribution in Ireland

Known only from high on Benbradagh (Londonderry) where it was discovered in 1964 (Fitzgerald & Fitzgerald 1966a) and collected again in 1966. It was not refound during searches in 1999 or 2007.

Ecology and biology

The only Irish collections were from 'exposed decomposing basalt c. 1400 feet' (elevation c. 430 m). Associated plants were recorded as *Myurella julacea*, *Anomobryum concinnatum* and *Plagiobryum zieri* (Fitzgerald & Fitzgerald 1966a), so the site was evidently on the small outcrops of gently sloping, crumbling basalt exposed on the north-facing slope of Benbradagh. In Fennoscandia, where the species is widespread, it grows on soil, rocks, rotting tree stumps or roots of trees in shaded habitats, chiefly in calcareous districts from the lowlands to the low-alpine belt of the mountains; var. *diversifolium* tends to be the montane form (Nyholm 1954–1969).

The plants are perennial and can be seen in all months of the year. The species is dioicous and capsules are unknown in Ireland or Britain, but recorded in Fennoscandia where they mature in winter. Gemmae, bulbils and tubers are absent, but vegetative propagation may occur from detached leaves or stem fragments.

World distribution

The species as a whole is widespread in Europe from Spitsbergen, Iceland and N. Fennoscandia southwards in mountains to Portugal, Spain, the Alps, Macedonia and the Caucasus, with var. *diversifolium* occurring widely in this range. It is listed as *Endangered* in Britain. *E. pulchellum s.l.* is listed as *Vulnerable* in Luxembourg and *Data Deficient* in the Czech Republic. The species is assigned to a Circumpolar Boreo-arctic montane floristic element in Europe. Elsewhere, it occurs in the Canary Islands, Algeria, SW, C., N. and E. Asia, N. America, Greenland, Mexico, Guatemala and Ecuador.

Threats

Prolonged searches failed to refind it on Benbradagh in 1999, when the habitat had suffered overgrazing and erosion due to sheep. A briefer search in 2007 was also unsuccessful, but the habitat was in much better condition with only moderate grazing pressure. It is therefore uncertain whether the species was collected to extinction in the 1960s, exterminated later by overstocking, or whether some tiny patch may still await rediscovery.

Conservation

The only locality is within an ASSI. The current light grazing pressure should be maintained because it benefits important bryophyte and phanerogam species that are still present. Additional searches may yet prove successful. *E. pulchellum* is listed as a Northern Ireland Priority Species and a UK Biodiversity Action Plan (UKBAP) species.

Protected sites with recent records: none; **Unprotected sites with recent records:** none.

Brachytheciastrum velutinum (Hedw.) Ignatov & Huttunen

Velvet Feather-moss

syn. *Brachythecium velutinum* (Hedw.) Schimp., *Chamberlainia velutina* (Hedw.) H.Rob.
Status in Ireland: Endangered (B2a, bi, ii, iv); **Status in Europe:** Least Concern

Identification

This is a slender pleurocarpous moss that grows as green or yellowish-green patches (rough mats) with stems up to about 50 mm long and irregular to subpinnate branching. Stem leaves are lanceolate-triangular, tapering from near base to a long slender acumen and with costa extending somewhat above mid-leaf. The inclined capsules are exserted on a papillose seta and have a conical operculum. Reliable identification probably requires capsules because leafy stems of the common *Rhynchostegium confertum* can be rather similar, although it normally has wider leaves. *Sciuro-hypnum populeum* is more similar to *B. velutinum* in leaf shape and capsule characters, but it has the costa extending into the leaf apex.

Distribution in Ireland

Recent records confirmed as correctly identified are from four localities: Clare (Ballyvaughan, Lough Rask, 2004); Offaly (W. of Clonmacnoise, 2007), Wicklow

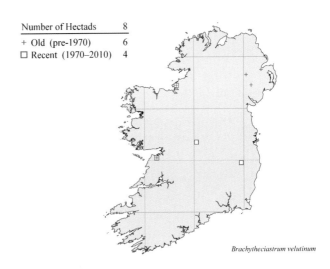

Brachytheciastrum velutinum

(Ballinabarney Bridge, 2010) and Sligo (Lissadell Wood, 1963 and 2003). Old records confirmed as correct are from four other localities: Dublin (Howth, 1850 and 1854); Armagh (Ardmore, 1884); Down (Aghaderg Glebe, 1886) and Antrim (Cave Hill, 1878). There is an erroneous recent record from W. Mayo and additional unconfirmed recent records from Wicklow, W. Mayo and Sligo. There are numerous old records for which the voucher specimens are known to be misidentified (N. Kerry, Wicklow at two sites, Dublin, Westmeath, Roscommon, W. Mayo at five sites, Tyrone, Down at four sites, Antrim at three sites and Londonderry) and many others that remain unconfirmed (S. Kerry, N. Kerry, E. Cork, Waterford, Wexford, Carlow, W. Galway, Dublin, Meath, Longford, E. Mayo, Cavan, Monaghan, Fermanagh, W. Donegal, Tyrone and Armagh at two sites). Evidence that the species has declined in Ireland is weak because so many specimens are known to have been misidentified.

Ecology and biology

Habitat notes with correctly identified specimens record that it was on an Ash tree by a ruin in swampy woodland near a lake, on a limestone block and a concrete wall in open grassland beside the River Shannon, a patch on top of the wall of a shaded bridge in a wooded valley and on wood of a footbridge in coastal woodland. In Britain, it is a relatively common species of well-drained, shaded to exposed, basic to mildly acidic habitats that occurs on tree bases, stumps and logs in woodland, but also on banks, rocks and soil beside lanes, hedges, streams and tracks, and on walls, stones and brickwork.

The species is perennial. It is autoicous and capsules are common, maturing from winter to spring. Gemmae and tubers have not been reported.

World distribution

B. velutinum is widespread in Europe, from Iceland and Fennoscandia southwards to the Mediterranean and Caucasus. In Europe, it is assigned to a Circumpolar Temperate floristic element. Elsewhere, it is recorded from Macaronesia, N. Africa, Cyprus, Iran, N. and C. Asia, Japan, northern USA (Oregon, New England), New Zealand and Campbell Island.

Threats

The species has apparently always been rare in Ireland, as it is also in parts of westernmost Britain such as Cornwall, although numerous erroneous records give a misleading impression that it is less rare. Threats to the Irish populations are poorly understood, although some patches are on impermanent substrata such as tree bark.

Conservation

At least one of the Irish populations is on protected land.

Protected sites with recent records: River Shannon Callows SAC; **Unprotected sites with recent records:** Ballyvaughan, Lough Rask; Lissadell Wood; Ballina-barney Bridge.

Taxiphyllum wissgrillii (Garov.) Wijk & Margad.

Depressed Feather-moss

syn. *Isopterygium depressum* (Brid.) Mitt., *Plagiothecium depressum* (Brid.) Spruce
Status in Ireland: Least Concern; **Status in Europe:** Least Concern

A pleurocarpous moss that grows on basic soil, rocks or tree bases in shaded places, often on wooded slopes with exposed limestone rock. It was included in the Provisional Red List (Holyoak 2006b) but fieldwork over the past decade has shown that it was under-recorded. There are now reports from 14 vice-counties, with records from 21 hectads (13 old, 12 recent). In the past decade, it has been found or refound at four localities in Leitrim and two in Fermanagh and it is very likely that other populations remain undiscovered in the limestone districts of these counties.

Hypnum uncinulatum Jur.

Hooked Plait-moss

syn. *Stereodon canariensis* Mitt., *S. circinalis* sensu Lett (1915)
Status in Ireland: Near Threatened; **Status in Europe:** Regionally Threatened

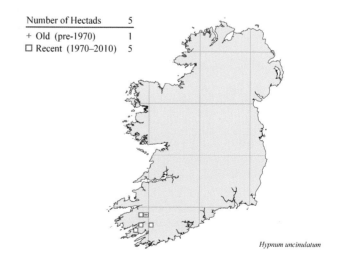

Number of Hectads	5
+ Old (pre-1970)	1
□ Recent (1970–2010)	5

Hypnum uncinulatum

Identification

A small to medium-sized pleurocarpous moss that forms slightly glossy, green, pale green to brownish-green patches (rough mats), with irregularly or more or less regularly pinnately branched stems up to at least 40 mm long. Stem leaves are erecto-patent to patent, more or less falcate, narrowly triangular to ovate triangular and gradually narrowed to an acuminate apex. The leaf margin is plane or slightly reflexed near the base, denticulate throughout or only in upper half; the costa is short and double or indistinct. Mid-leaf cells are mainly 48–117 μm long and 4.5–7 μm wide, straight or slightly flexuose. Alar cells form conspicuously excavated (pouch-like) groups of irregularly subquadrate thick-walled cells that are often brownish. The base of each leaf margin has 5–8 rectangular cells. Capsules are ovoid to obloid, often somewhat swollen, with a shortly rostrate operculum, exserted on a long seta. *H. uncinulatum* is easily overlooked among the more common *H. andoi* in Ireland, although the capsule of the former may be shorter and more swollen (but not always: Ando 1986) and the operculum is shortly rostrate rather than mamillate. Non-fertile plants are best separated by the deeply excavate alar cells of *H. uncinulatum* and its fewer rectangular cells on the leaf margin (5–8, cf. 7–15 in *H. andoi*). Contrary to the account by Smith (1997), alar cells in *H. andoi* are often brownish.

Distribution in Ireland

Confirmed recent records are from 11 localities in three vice-counties: S. Kerry (S. of Lough Beg, 2006; near Galway's Bridge, 2005; NW of Upper Lake, 2006; below O'Sullivan's Cascade, 2006; NW edge of Uragh Wood, 2006; below Lauragh Bridge, 2006; NW part of Derreen Garden, 2006); N. Kerry (Muckross, Killarney, 1973; E. of Galway's Bridge, 2005; E. of Brickeen, 2005) and W. Cork (E. of Coomroe, 2006). There is one older confirmed record from N. Kerry ('Turk Mt., Killarney' [= Torc], 1829). There are also unconfirmed old records for other sites in N. Kerry (Cromaglan, 1900–1906; under Torc near Muckross, 1896; Muckross, 1896–1900). Specimens collected from 'Turk Mt., Killarney' by W. Wilson in 1829 were included among the type material of *Stereodon canariensis* Mitten and the species was treated in the *Flora* by Dixon (1924). However, *H. uncinulatum* was erroneously omitted from the standard moss *Flora* by Smith (1978), as pointed out by Ando & Townsend (1980), and the species was subsequently assumed to be extinct or at least lost in Ireland. Intensive searching during 2005 and 2006 has revealed that it is in fact very locally frequent in SW Ireland.

Ecology and biology

H. uncinulatum grows in humid, lowland, woodlands; mainly in native *Quercus-Ilex* woodland, but also a coniferous plantation (Sitka Spruce and Lodgepole Pine) and a woodland garden with many large trees, in shade or partial shade. It occurs over a similar range of acidic substrata to the more common *H. andoi*, but it perhaps does not extend so far up trees (no gathering was from more than about one metre above ground level). The most common substrata were low sandstone rocks, but it was also found on bases of tree trunks (oak, Alder and Holly) and tree stumps (deciduous and conifer), with single collections from exposed roots of a dead tree and

decorticated wood lying on the ground. In Macaronesia, it occurs up to 1600 m elevation; it also grows as an epiphyte and has occasionally been collected from soil (Ando 1986, Hedenäs 1992); on Madeira and in the Azores it is even known as an epiphyll, growing on living leaves of shrubs and trees and fronds of ferns (Sjögren 1975, 1978).

The plants are perennial. It is a dioicous species in which capsules are frequent, maturing in late autumn or winter. Gemmae, bulbils and tubers are absent, but vegetative propagation probably occurs from dispersed fragments of leafy stems.

World distribution

Restricted to SW Ireland, C. Portugal (Mata do Bussaco), S. Spain (hills near Algeciras in Prov. Cádiz), Azores, Madeira and the Canary Islands (Ando 1986, Hedenäs 1992, Ruiz *et al.* 2006, Casas *et al.* 2006). It is listed as *Endangered* in Spain and Portugal. It is assigned to a Hyperoceanic Southern-temperate floristic element in Europe. Reports of the species from N. America, Turkey and Iran are almost certainly erroneous (cf. Ando 1986, Frey & Kürschner 1991).

Threats

H. uncinulatum is not immediately threatened at any of its sites in SW Ireland. The greatest risk to it is probably from excessive shading if Rhododendron colonises larger areas of native woodland understorey, but infestations of that species are now being reduced within the Killarney National Park. *H. uncinulatum* apparently needs shady, humid conditions so clear-felling should be avoided where it occurs.

Conservation

Most Irish populations are on protected land.

Protected sites with recent records: Cloonee and Inchiquin Loughs, Uragh Wood SAC; Derrycunihy Wood Nature Reserve; Killarney National Park; Killarney National Park, Macgillycuddy's Reeks and Caragh River Catchment SAC; Uragh Wood Nature Reserve; **Unprotected sites with recent records:** E. of Coomroe; NW part of Derreen Garden.

Hypnum callichroum Brid.   Downy Plait-moss

syn. *Stereodon callichrous* (Brid.) Braithw.
Status in Ireland: Near Threatened; **Status in Europe:** Least Concern

An attractive pleurocarpous moss with circinate-secund leaves that usually grows in sheltered places among rocks. It has been reported from eight vice-counties, with records from 21 hectads (15 old, 8 recent, 1 undated). It was not included in the Provisional Red List (Holyoak 2006b), so was not deliberately sought during fieldwork over the past decade, but there is no reason to believe it has declined.

Ptilium crista-castrensis (Hedw.) De Not.   Ostrich-plume Feather-moss

Status in Ireland: Critically Endangered (B2a, biii, D); **Status in Europe:** Least Concern

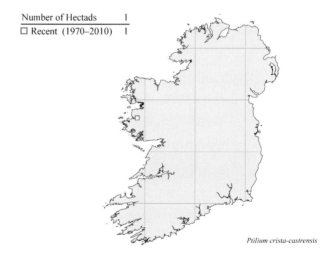

Number of Hectads	1
☐ Recent (1970–2010)	1

Ptilium crista-castrensis

Identification

An elegant medium-sized pleurocarpous moss that grows as lax green or yellowish-green wefts with shoots 5–8 cm long (rarely 20 cm), with striking complanate, closely pinnate branching and long parallel branches that are all of similar length except near the stem apex. The stem leaves are circinate-secund, ovate or ovate-lanceolate, longitudinally plicate and tapering to a long filiform acumen. The leaf margin is plane and entire, the costa short and double or lacking. Mid-leaf cells are linear-vermicular and narrow. The basal cells are inflated and hyaline, forming small, distinctly decurrent auricles. Capsules (unknown in Ireland) are ovoid to obloid, curved, horizontal and exserted on a long seta.

Distribution in Ireland

The only record that is accepted is from the W. side of the N. corrie of Mweelrea (W. Mayo) where it was discovered by D. Synnott and others during the British Bryological Society Meeting in 1987. A report from Antrim (Colin Glen, 1847, leg. D. Orr) was dismissed as an error of locality by Lett (1915).

Ecology and biology

The record from Mweelrea was from steep grass-covered scree on a N.-facing montane slope in a corrie at c. 410 m altitude (not 2000 feet as published). In Scotland, its typical habitats are on humus-rich soil in shaded places on the ground or boulders in coniferous and deciduous woodlands. Less frequently, it occurs under heather on steep N.- to E.-facing rocky slopes, shaded recesses in block screes or in low-lying wooded ravines (H.J.B. Birks in Hill *et al.* 1994). The Irish locality is thus remarkable in being from an unusually open montane habitat as well as in the strongly oceanic climatic region that the species tends to avoid in W. Scotland.

The plants are perennial. It is a dioicous species in which capsules are very rare in Britain (unknown in Ireland), maturing in autumn. Gemmae, bulbils and tubers are absent, but vegetative propagation is likely to occur from detached leaves or branches. Teleganova & Ignatov (2008) describe the reproductive biology of the species in its boreal habitat.

World distribution

The species is widespread in the boreal-forest zone of N. Europe from N. Fennoscandia southwards, but much more local and only in the mountains towards its southern range limits in the Pyrenees, S. Italy and Caucasus. It is listed as *Extinct* in Luxembourg, *Endangered* in Bulgaria, *Vulnerable* in Spain, 'rare' in the Netherlands and 'declining' in Germany. In Britain, it is widespread in Scotland, local in N. England and NW Wales and known from an isolated locality in Suffolk where it was probably introduced with conifers. It is assigned to a Circumpolar Boreal-montane floristic element in Europe. The range elsewhere includes SW and N. Asia (Georgia to Kazakhstan, W. Siberia to Yakutia and Russian Far East: Ignatov *et al.* 2007), Sikkim, Yunnan, N. America (southwards to Oregon and North Carolina) and Greenland.

Threats

Close searching in 2008 failed to refind *P. crista-castrensis* at its locality on Mweelrea. If it persists there, the population must be very small. Overgrazing resulting from excessive sheep numbers has become a problem on Mweelrea and many other Irish mountains over the past decade, but in 2008, the grassed-over scree locality had retained an intact vegetation cover including various pleurocarpous mosses. The locality is, however, close to a path used to climb the mountain and hence potentially vulnerable to erosion by climbers if mountain walking activity increases.

Conservation

The locality on Mweelrea is within a protected area.

Protected sites with recent records: Mweelrea/Sheeffry/ Erriff Complex SAC; **Unprotected sites with recent records:** none.

Ctenidium molluscum (Hedw.) Mitt. **var. *robustum*** Boulay   Vinous Comb-moss

syn. *Ctenidium molluscum* var. *croceum* Braithw.
Status in Ireland: Regionally Extinct; **Status in Europe:** Not Evaluated

Identification

This is a striking, robust, pleurocarpous moss that grows as deep, glossy, golden-brown tufts, frequently with a deep vinous red tinge. Shoots may reach 10 cm in length, with creeping primary stem, erect secondary stems, which in turn are distantly and irregularly branched into rather long, erect branches. All leaves are ecostate, strongly plicate, falcato-secund, with plane, denticulate margins and well-defined patches of enlarged alar cells. The stem leaves are up to 3 mm long, ovate-cordate with a long filiform acumen and mid-leaf cells 72–150 μm long. Branch leaves are shorter, ovate-lanceolate, more strongly falcate and more gradually tapering. Distinction of var. *robustum* from other forms of this variable species relies on its large size, irregular branching pattern, long stem leaves (> 2 mm) and their long mid-leaf cells (> 80 μm). However, Dixon (1924) noted that it passes into var. *condensatum* (which is smaller and more regularly branched) 'by intergrading forms'. Capsules in the species as a whole are ellipsoid, inclined and exserted on a rather long seta.

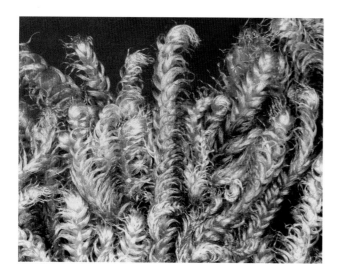

| Number of Hectads | 1 |
| + Old (pre-1970) | 1 |

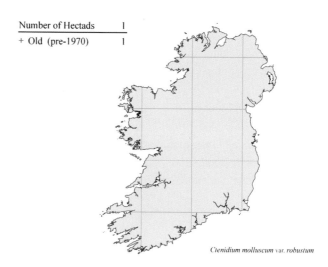

Ctenidium molluscum var. robustum

Distribution in Ireland

The only accepted records are from the Mourne Mountains in Down (Slieve Donard, 1905, by Rev. C.H. Waddell; Black Stairs, Thomas's Mountain, 1917, by Rev. Waddell & J. Glover). It was not refound on two recent visits to the Black Stairs. Other reports from four vice-counties are dubious or unconfirmed (N. and S. Kerry, Waterford and Antrim), although Megaw (1938) accepted a record from Antrim (White Mountain, by J.H. Davies).

Ecology and biology

The only comment on the habitat in Ireland is that Megaw (1938) attributed the Mourne Mountains records to mountain rocks. Likewise, in Britain, it is a rare plant of damp, basic montane rocks.

Little is known of var. *robustum*, but the species as a whole is perennial and dioicous. Capsules are rather rarely produced but they may be locally abundant, maturing in spring. Bulbils, gemmae and tubers are unknown in the species, although vegetative reproduction is likely to occur from stem and leaf fragments.

World distribution

Var. *robustum* is known mainly from Britain, in the mountains from Caernarvonshire and Mid-west Yorkshire northwards to Argyll, W. Ross and W. Sutherland. Although listed for 'Europe' by Smith (1978) and treated as a European Boreo-temperate floristic element by Hill *et al.* (2007), it is not one of the numerous forms of *C. molluscum* recognised in the principal European floras (e.g. Limpricht 1890–1895, Nyholm 1954–1969; 'v. *robustum* Mol.' of Roth 1905 is not the same taxon). In the latest list of European mosses,

Hill *et al.* (2006) point out that *C. molluscum* is a very variable species in which the genetic basis of the variation requires further elucidation. There are no reports of the taxon from outside Europe, although the species as a whole extends to N. Africa, Asia and north-western N. America.

Threats

No information.

Conservation

The localities in the Mourne Mountains are probably on protected land. Detailed surveys may yet reveal this striking moss is still present since there has been little modern bryological study of the Mourne Mountains.

Protected sites with recent records: none; **Unprotected sites with recent records:** none.

Slievelamagan, Mourne Mountains, Co. Down.

Heterocladium wulfsbergii I.Hagen
Wulfsberg's Tamarisk-moss

syn. *Heterocladium heteropterum* auct. pro parte, non (Bruch ex Schwägr.) Schimp.,
H. heteropterum subsp. *wulfsbergii* (I.Hagen) C.E.O.Jensen & Perss.
Status in Ireland: Near Threatened; **Status in Europe:** 'apparently threatened but presenting taxonomic problems'

A slender pleurocarpous moss that grows on rocks in the inundation zone of rivers. *H. wulfsbergii* was not generally recognised as distinct until the studies by A.C. Crundwell beginning in 1995 (see Crundwell & Smith 2000). Hedenäs & Isoviita (2008) have recently reinforced evidence that it is a distinct species from *H. heteropterum* by pointing out differences in their capsules. It is undoubtedly still somewhat under-recorded in Ireland, but has been reported from 13 vice-counties, with records from 21 hectads (9 old, 13 recent), including some large populations.

Pterigynandrum filiforme Hedw.
Capillary Wing-moss

syn. *Pterigynandrum filiforme* var. *heteropterum* Bruch & Schimp., *Pterigynandrum filiforme* var. *majus* (De Not.) De Not.
Status in Ireland: Regionally Extinct; **Status in Europe:** Least Concern

Number of Hectads	4
+ Old (pre-1970)	4

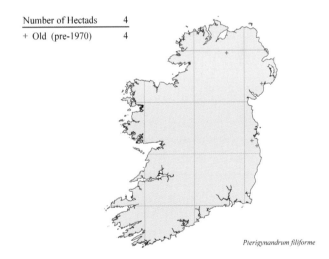

Pterigynandrum filiforme

Identification
A small and slender pleurocarpous moss that grows in neat yellow-green, green or brown mats with creeping stems up to 50 mm long from which erect branches arise. The leaves are imbricate to erecto-patent, sometimes subsecund, concave, and ovate to broadly ovate with an acute to obtuse apex that is sometimes apiculate. The leaf margin is plane or inflexed above and denticulate; the costa is single or forked above, weak and ends at or below the middle of the leaf. Cells in mid-leaf are shortly linear, arranged in rows radiating from the costa and smooth to unipapillose, with a large distal papilla on the dorsal surface. Alar cells are shorter, forming a distinct group extending far up along the leaf margin. Capsules

(unknown in Ireland) are cylindrical, erect and exserted on a reddish seta. Smith (2004) and Hill *et al.* (2006) recognised var. *majus* as a valid taxon, differing in its stouter, blunter branches that have more strongly curved tips, although intermediates occur. However, G.P. Rothero (in Hill *et al.* 1994) pointed out that var. *majus* is probably only a habitat modification and Hill *et al.* (2008) therefore treated it as a synonym. In Ireland, var. *majus* has been reported only from the Shimna River (Down).

Distribution in Ireland

Records, all old, are accepted from four localities in four vice-counties: Wicklow (Dargle, leg. Templeton in 1875); Dublin (Killakee Glen, leg. D. Moore in 1878); Down (Shimna River, Tollymore Park in 1829 and 1926; a record made before 1862 from the Mourne Mountains, leg. Mackay may be from the same locality) and Londonderry (Sawel Mountain, leg. Templeton in 1825). Another report from Wicklow (Glen of the Downs, 1858, leg. D. Orr) is based on a specimen (**DBN**) that was reidentified by H.N. Dixon in 1908 as *Anomodon rostratus* with a fragment of *Heterocladium dimorphum*. Neither of those species is known in Ireland, so this material provides part of the evidence that some of Orr's locality details are fraudulent.

Ecology and biology

Nothing is recorded for Irish plants other than 'by the Shimna River', since the 'rocks and trees on mntns.' in Megaw (1938) seems to be derived from Dixon's (1924) *Student's Handbook*. In Scotland, it grows in open sites that are mainly in the mountains (at 10–1100 m altitude), on basic rocks and, rarely, branches and roots of trees. Often it occurs on the larger boulders on the margins of montane lakes (G.P. Rothero in Hill *et al.* 1994).

The plants are perennial. It is a dioicous species in which capsules are rare in Britain (unknown in Ireland), maturing in summer. Uniseriate gemmae 2–5 cells long are often present on the stems. Occurrence of caducous branchlets has been reported from Norway and Switzerland (Bergamini 2006), but not from Ireland or Britain. Bulbils and tubers are unknown.

World distribution

It is widespread in Europe, although mainly restricted to mountains in the south, occurring from Spitsbergen, N. Iceland, N. Fennoscandia and arctic Russia southwards to Portugal, S. Spain, Sicily and the Caucasus. It is listed as *Vulnerable* in Germany and Luxembourg and 'very rare and susceptible' in the Netherlands. It is assigned to a Circumpolar Boreal-montane floristic element in Europe. The range elsewhere includes Madeira, Canary Islands, Algeria, SW and N. Asia (Georgia to Kazakhstan; Siberia, Yakutia and Russian Far East: Ignatov *et al.* 2007), Kashmir, Punjab, Indo-China, Korea, Japan, N. America, Greenland and Mexico.

Threats

P. filiforme was last recorded in Ireland in 1926 at the Shimna River. Searches there in 2002 were unsuccessful and many stretches of the river were found to be rather heavily shaded by trees, but details of the original locality are unknown. It may be significant that it appears to have decreased in England and Wales, where the few records are mainly old. There is also a possibility that some at least of these rather isolated records represented temporary colonists that did not become established.

Conservation

No action is proposed. The Shimna River at Tollymore Park is in a protected area.

Protected sites with recent records: none; **Unprotected sites with recent records:** none.

Rhytidiadelphus subpinnatus (Lindb.) T.J.Kop.

Scarce Turf-moss

syn. *R. calvescens* (Lindb.) Broth., *R. squarrosus* subsp. *calvescens* (Lindb.) Giacom., *R. squarrosus* var. *calvescens* (Lindb.) Warnst.
Status in Ireland: Regionally Extinct; **Status in Europe:** Least Concern

Identification

A robust pale green to yellowish-green pleurocarpous moss with red-brown stems that grows in coarse wefts with stems up to 120 mm long. Stem leaves are weakly squarrose, ovate or ovate-cordate and rather abruptly narrowed to an acuminate upper part, with short double costa and plane margins that are denticulate above. Cells in mid-leaf are linear-elliptic and smooth; the alar cells

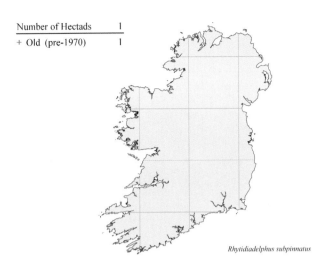

Number of Hectads	1
+ Old (pre-1970)	1

Rhytidiadelphus subpinnatus

are enlarged, forming a distinct hyaline or coloured group. Capsules are horizontal, ovoid, gibbous and exserted on a long seta. *R. subpinnatus* was often confused in the past with forms of the very common *R. squarrosus*, from which it differs in the erect, rather than sheathing, basal part of the stem leaves (so that much more of the stem is visible) and the leaf arrangement being not or hardly stellate at the shoot tips. Nevertheless, care is needed in making this distinction as shaded *R. squarrosus* somewhat resembles *R. subpinnatus*.

Distribution in Ireland

Known by a single specimen from Glendine Bridge, N. of Youghal (in Waterford), collected in 1966 by J. Appleyard. Prolonged efforts to refind the species in 2007 were unsuccessful. Although there was plenty of possible habitat extending for more than a kilometre near Glendine Bridge, the original locality may have been rather imprecise.

Ecology and biology

The only Irish specimen was labelled merely as from a 'wooded valley'. In Britain, it occurs on acidic soil and over rocks and well-rotted tree stumps on damp, lightly shaded banks, flat ground and grassy stream sides in open woodland. All of the Welsh colonies are in steep-sided, wooded river valleys in hilly districts (Bosanquet & Motley 2009).

The plants grow as perennial patches. The species is dioicous and sporophytes are unknown in Ireland and rare in Britain, maturing in winter or early spring (Bosanquet *et al.* 2005, Bosanquet & Motley 2009, cf. Holyoak 2001a). Tubers and gemmae are unknown. It is

likely that many populations in Britain are clones of plants of a single sex.

World distribution

It is widespread in N. and C. Europe from Iceland and Fennoscandia southwards to the Alps and Caucasus; plentiful in the boreal zone but scarcer and mainly in hill and mountain regions from S. Finland southwards (listed as *Endangered* in Britain and described as 'presumably threatened' in Germany). In Europe, it is assigned to a Circumpolar Boreal-montane floristic element. Elsewhere, the species is recorded in the Azores, Turkey, N. Asia, Japan and N. America.

Threats

No information. *R. subpinnatus* might still persist somewhere in the vicinity of Glendine Bridge. In Wales the main threats appear to be from livestock grazing and forestry works (Bosanquet & Motley 2009).

Conservation

The poorly localised site near Glendine Bridge may have been on protected land. No action is proposed unless the species is rediscovered in Ireland.

Protected sites with recent records: none; **Unprotected sites with recent records:** none.

Hylocomiastrum umbratum (Hedw.) M.Fleisch.

Shaded Wood-moss

syn. *Hylocomium umbratum* (Hedw.) Schimp.
Status in Ireland: Near Threatened; **Status in Europe:** Least Concern

An attractive, pinnately branched pleurocarpous moss that grows in sheltered, rocky places. It has been reported from eight vice-counties, with records from 28 hectads (21 old, 9 recent). It was not included in the Provisional Red List (Holyoak 2006b), so no effort was made to refind old records or to seek new ones during fieldwork over the past decade. This species is locally frequent in the west of Ireland and there is no reason to suspect a decline.

Rhytidium rugosum (Hedw.) Kindb.

Wrinkle-leaved Feather-moss

syn. *Hypnum rugosum* Hedw.
Status in Ireland: Vulnerable (D2); **Status in Europe:** Least Concern

Number of Hectads	2
+ Old (pre-1970)	2
☐ Recent (1970–2010)	2

Rhytidium rugosum

Identification

A handsome, robust, pleurocarpous moss that forms loose yellowish-green to golden-brown patches (wefts or rough mats), with trailing, irregularly pinnately branched stems up to 10 cm long and erect or spreading branches. The leaves are falcato-secund, concave, imbricate, ovate, tapering to an acuminate apex, up to 3.5–4 mm long, and conspicuously rugose, both longitudinally and transversely. The leaf margin is recurved and denticulate above; the single costa is often forked above and extends to above mid-leaf. Cells in mid-leaf are shortly linear to narrowly elliptical with papillae on the dorsal surface. Cells at the leaf base are quadrate or rhomboidal, extending up the leaf margin. The capsule (unknown in Ireland or Britain) is shortly cylindrical, curved, horizontal and exserted on a long red seta.

Distribution in Ireland

R. rugosum is known only at two localities in Londonderry. A large population occurs along several kilometres of dunes from the Magilligan Ministry of Defence range past Benone to the Umbra (many records from 1900–2008); a small population is known inland on Binevenagh (recorded 1913–1990).

Ecology and biology

The large coastal populations in Londonderry grow on slopes and low ridges of fixed sand dunes and at the edges of dune slacks, forming patches on unshaded calcareous sand in gaps among other plants, including *Ammophila arenaria*, sparse *Salix repens* and patches of other mosses including *Hylocomium splendens*. The habitat inland on Binevenagh was not described in detail, but it was presumably on rocky (basalt) slopes. In Britain, it is a calcicolous moss of dry sunny sites over limestone, calcareous sand, basic volcanic rocks and mica schist, with most records from short and rather open grasslands, but some from inland crags and quarries.

The plants are perennial. It is a dioicous species in which capsules are unknown in Ireland or Britain and very rare in Europe. Gemmae, bulbils and tubers are absent, but vegetative propagation presumably occurs from detached leaf and stem fragments.

World distribution

The species is widespread in Europe from Iceland and N. Fennoscandia southwards to N. Spain, S. Italy, the Crimea and the Caucasus. It is listed as *Vulnerable* in Germany and the Netherlands and 'very rare' in Estonia. It is assigned to a Circumpolar Boreo-arctic montane floristic element in Europe. Elsewhere, it occurs in Morocco, SW, C. and N. Asia, China, Japan, N. America, Greenland, Mexico, Guatemala and Bolivia.

Threats

No immediate threats to populations at Ballymaclary Nature Reserve, Benone or The Umbra were apparent in 1999. However, there is a potential threat on a longer timescale from shading as natural vegetation succession results in taller vegetation on the dunes, a process already well advanced on parts of Umbra Nature Reserve. Where grazing by rabbits is insufficient to maintain short, open vegetation, it is important that a combination of grazing by domestic stock and manual scrub clearance is used to ensure open conditions persist.

Conservation

Most of the localities where the species occurs are on protected land. *R. rugosum* is listed as a Northern Ireland Priority Species.

Protected sites with recent records: Ballymaclary Nature Reserve; Binevenagh ASSI; Binevenagh Nature Reserve; Binevenagh SAC; Magilligan ASSI; Magilligan Point Nature Reserve; Magilligan SAC; **Unprotected sites with recent records:** none.

Myurella julacea (Schwägr.) Schimp.

Small Mouse-tail Moss

syn. *Myurella julacea* var. *ciliata* (Chal.) Ochyra & Bednarek-Ochyra, *M. julacea* var. *scabrifolia* Lindb. ex Limpr.
Status in Ireland: Endangered (B2a, bii, iv); **Status in Europe:** Least Concern

Identification

A small slender pleurocarpous moss with cylindrical shoots that grows on basic montane rocks. It forms small patches (rough mats) or occurs as scattered shoots among other bryophytes. The shoots reach 10–15 mm long, the younger parts being bluish-green, the old parts red-brown. The leaves are closely imbricate, broadly ovate, very concave, with obtuse or rounded apex that is apiculate in some populations. The closely appressed concave leaves result in a cylindrical, catkin-like or worm-like shoot. The costa of the leaf is indistinct, short and double or single. The leaf margins vary from denticulate to sharply toothed. Mid-leaf cells are elliptical with papillae that vary from low and rounded to tall and conical. Capsules (unknown in Ireland) are erect to inclined, obovoid, held up on a curved seta. Although a pleurocarpous moss, the cylindrical stems with ovate, concave leaves give a strong superficial resemblance to the acrocarpous moss *Anomobryum julaceum*. However, *Anomobryum* differs in having a single long costa in each leaf, lack of papillae on the leaf cells, longer leaf cells and in many other details.

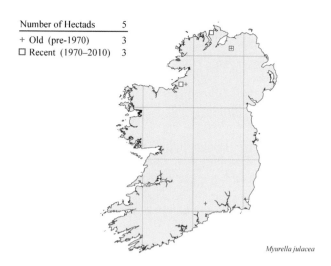

Number of Hectads	5
+ Old (pre-1970)	3
☐ Recent (1970–2010)	3

Myurella julacea

Plants of *Myurella julacea* with apiculate, strongly toothed leaves and tall conical papillae on the upper leaf cells were formerly separated as var. *scabrifolia* (e.g. Smith 1978, Blockeel & Long 1998) whereas var. *julacea* has no apiculus, less toothed leaves and lower papillae. The valid name for this form is now known to be var. *ciliata*. However, the differences are regarded as unimportant because the two phenotypes sometimes grow together and intergrade completely (Hill *et al.* 2006, note 401).

Distribution in Ireland

Recent confirmed records are from three localities in three vice-counties: Sligo (Gleniff, 2003); E. Donegal (Bulbin Mountain, 2002) and Londonderry (Benbradagh, 1964 and 1999). Two older records are accepted: Waterford (Bolagh Lough, 1902) and Leitrim (Glenade, 1963 and 1965). The report from 'Connemara' (Lett 1915) is rather vague and apparently unsupported by a specimen so it seems best discounted. In Ireland, the species has small populations that may be rather inconspicuous when they grow intermixed with other bryophytes, so that it might well still occur at the old localities.

Ecology and biology

It is restricted to a few basic sites in Ireland among montane rocks at 277–535 m altitude, on crags of limestone, shaly limestone, schist or basalt. It occurs in small amounts in moist to rather dry, sheltered or protected crevices or on small ledges, on N.-facing slopes that are largely unshaded other than as a result of their northerly aspect. Although it extends onto rock surfaces, it mainly grows on nutrient-poor, thin soil or humus layers with or among other bryophytes and small vascular plants, including other uncommon and rare montane species.

The plants are perennial and dioicous. Capsules are rare in Britain (maturing in autumn) and unrecorded in Ireland. The species is not known to produce gemmae or tubers, but asexual reproduction probably occurs from stem and leaf fragments.

World distribution

M. julacea has a wide range in Europe, from Iceland and N. Fennoscandia and in the mountains from Scotland to the Caucasus and southwards to the Pyrenees and Alps, with a southernmost outpost in the Sierra Nevada. The species is rather scarce in Scotland but locally common in Fennoscandia and the Alps, with little evidence of population decline from any of these regions (e.g. Meinunger & Schröder 2007). However, it is listed as *Endangered* in the Czech Republic and 'declining' in Germany. It is assigned to a Circumpolar Boreo-arctic montane floristic element. Elsewhere, it occurs in Asia, N. America, Greenland, with records also from Antarctica.

Threats

Some populations are on crags or rocky slopes that are too steep to be grazed by sheep, so they are not at much risk from the widespread overgrazing, erosion and eutrophication they have caused and which has damaged many montane bryophyte populations in recent decades. However, it grows on gently sloping rocks at Benbradagh where there is a serious threat of erosion and disturbance resulting from overstocking with sheep. Thoughtless and unnecessary collection of specimens would be potentially damaging to all populations. *M. julacea* is also one of the rare montane elements in the Irish flora that may be at risk from climate change over the next century.

Conservation

It is listed as a Northern Ireland Priority Species because the only population on Benbradagh is tiny (covering about 150 cm² in 1999) and vulnerable.

Protected sites with recent records: Ben Bulben, Gleniff and Glenade Complex SAC; Bulbin Mountain pNHA; **Unprotected sites with recent records:** Benbradagh (proposed ASSI).

Platydictya jungermannioides (Brid.) H.A.Crum

Spruce's Leskea

syn. *Amblystegiella sprucei* (Bruch) Loeske, *Amblystegium jungermannioides* (Brid.) A.J.E.Sm., *Amblystegium sprucei* (Bruch) Schimp.

Status in Ireland: Near Threatened; **Status in Europe:** Least Concern

A small and slender pleurocarpous moss that grows in sheltered basic sites, most often in crevices among limestone rocks. It has been reported from seven vice-counties, with records from eight hectads (4 old, 6 recent). Fieldwork during the past decade has discovered it at several new sites in both Leitrim and Fermanagh, including some strong populations (e.g. amongst scree at Glenade). A specimen collected in Clare in 2004 was probably this species but was too damaged by fungus to be certain and a site in W. Cork (Nowen Hill) was found during the BBS summer field meeting in 2009. It is likely that this species is still under-recorded in Ireland.

Orthothecium rufescens (Dicks. ex Brid.) Schimp.

Red Leskea

syn. *Stereodon rufescens* (Brid.) Mitt.

Status in Ireland: Near Threatened; **Status in Europe:** Least Concern

A large, handsome, red or pinkish pleurocarpous moss that grows mainly on periodically flushed limestone rocks. It has a restricted range in Ireland, with most populations in the Dartry Mountains of Sligo and Leitrim and a few in Clare, Fermanagh and W. Donegal. It has been reported from five vice-counties, with records from 11 hectads (8 old, 9 recent). Within the Dartry Mountains there are hundreds of strong populations, especially on Benbulbin and in Glenade. There is no evidence that the species has declined.

Plagiothecium latebricola Schimp.

Alder Silk-moss

Status in Ireland: Vulnerable (D2); **Status in Europe:** Least Concern

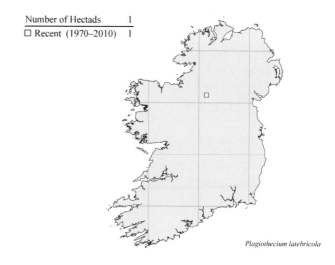

Number of Hectads — 1
☐ Recent (1970–2010) — 1

Plagiothecium latebricola

Identification

A small, slender pleurocarpous moss that grows as glossy bright green, pale or yellowish green patches (rough mats or wefts) with irregularly branched stems up to about 20 mm long. The leaves are only slightly complanate, 0.8–1.2 mm long, concave, symmetrical, ovate-lanceolate, and tapering to a rather long acuminate apex. The leaf margin is plane or narrowly recurved below, entire or faintly denticulate near the apex, decurrent on the stem in a single row of elongate rectangular cells. The costa is weak and extends less than a third of the way up the leaf. Mid-leaf cells are linear and 5–8 μm wide. The capsule is ellipsoid, erect to slightly inclined, with conical-rostellate operculum, exserted on a thin red seta. *P. latebricola* is the smallest species of *Plagiothecium* in Ireland and distinctive in its combination of narrow leaf cells, symmetrical leaves and decurrent leaf bases only one cell wide.

Distribution in Ireland

Known only from woodland N. of Garadice Lough in Leitrim, where it was first found by D.L. Kelly in 1974, and refound in two places in 2001.

Ecology and biology

It has been recorded only from rotting wood of low tree stumps in old mature woodland of oaks or of mixed deciduous trees, at c. 60 m altitude. One patch grew close to *Plagiothecium curvifolium*. In Britain, it mainly occurs on decomposing vegetable matter in damp shady places, particularly fern and tussock-sedge stools in shaded swampy woodland but also on decaying logs and less often on soil or living tree trunks.

The plants are perennial. It is a dioicous species in which capsules are rare in Britain (apparently unrecorded in Ireland), maturing in spring. Fusiform gemmae are frequently produced in leaf axils and on leaf tips and similar gemmae develop on the protonema of cultured plants (Whitehouse 1987). Vegetative propagation is also likely to occur from detached stem and leaf fragments. Bulbils and tubers are absent.

World distribution

The species is widespread in Europe from N. Fennoscandia and the northern Urals southwards (although rare in Fennoscandia north of S. Sweden and S. Finland) to the French Pyrenees, Alps and Ukraine. It is listed as *Extinct* in Luxembourg, *Vulnerable* in the Czech Republic and Finland, and 'declining' in Germany and Norway. It is assigned to a Circumpolar Temperate floristic element in Europe. Elsewhere, it is known in SW Asia (Turkey; Georgia and Kyrgyzstan: Ignatov *et al.* 2007), N. Asia (widespread from W. and S. Siberia to Russian Far East: Ignatov *et al.* 2007), N. Japan and eastern N. America (Nova Scotia to Minnesota and southwards to North Carolina).

Threats

No immediate threats were apparent at Garadice Lough in 2001, where its populations nevertheless appeared

556

rather small with limited availability of potentially suitable substrata. The species requires shaded, humid conditions with dead wood decaying on the ground, so the tree cover needs to be maintained at this locality and fallen dead wood should not be removed. *Plagiothecium curvifolium* (*q.v.*) occurs at the same locality and requires similar habitats.

Conservation
The old deciduous woodland at Garadice Lough is on protected land.

Protected sites with recent records: Garadice Lough Wood pNHA; **Unprotected sites with recent records:** none.

Plagiothecium denticulatum var. *obtusifolium* (Turner) Moore — Donnian Silk-moss

Status in Ireland: Near Threatened; **Status in Europe:** Not Evaluated

A pleurocarpous moss that grows among rocks in the mountains, distinct from the more common var. *denticulatum* mainly in the blunt rather than acute leaf apex. There are reports from seven vice-counties, with records from 12 hectads (7 old, 7 recent), with several new localities seen in 2005 in the Galty Mountains. There is no evidence that the taxon has declined or that it is currently much threatened.

Plagiothecium laetum Schimp. — Bright Silk-moss

Status in Ireland: Vulnerable (D2); **Status in Europe:** Least Concern

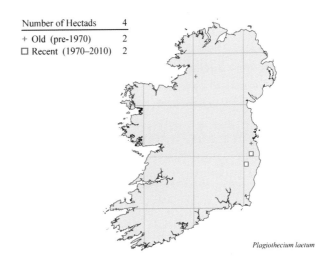

Number of Hectads	4
+ Old (pre-1970)	2
□ Recent (1970–2010)	2

Plagiothecium laetum

Identification
A small pleurocarpous moss that forms glossy pale green patches (smooth mats) with branched, prostrate stems up to about 23 mm long. The leaves are 1.0–2.0 mm long, strongly complanate, usually straight when moist, ovate-lanceolate but mostly asymmetrical with one straight

side, tapering to an acute or shortly acuminate apex. The leaf margin is plane and entire or slightly denticulate near the apex, the costa short, weak and double. Mid-leaf cells are linear-vermicular, mostly 6–8 μm wide; the angular cells are narrowly rectangular, decurrent in 1–3 rows, but not forming auricles. Capsules are narrowly ellipsoid, almost straight, held erect and exserted on a long seta. Differences from most other *Plagiothecium* species include the narrow mid-leaf cells, mainly asymmetrical leaves and form of the decurrent angular cells. However, *P. curvifolium* (*q.v.*) is very similar and it may be better treated as a variety of *P. laetum* rather than as a distinct species.

Distribution in Ireland

Two recent records are accepted: Wicklow (SW slopes of White Hill, N. of Roundwood, 2003; Ballycurragh, S. of Lugnaquilla, 2003). Two older records are also accepted: Dublin (N. slope of Killakee Mountain, 1969) and Fermanagh (near Carrick Lough, 1961). Another record from Wicklow (S. side of Seefingan Mountain, 2003) is probably of *P. laetum* rather than *P. curvifolium*.

Ecology and biology

The two oldest Irish records are probably from deciduous woodland, or at least beneath trees: on a shaded stream bank and on raw humus in a wood. Two more recent records (and a third probable record) are from Sitka Spruce plantations, on the southern sides of trunk bases, respectively in a glade in a 29-year-old plantation and in a 39-year-old plantation (L. Coote, *in litt.*). In Britain, it is a calcifuge found on tree bases, stumps, rotten logs and soil in broadleaved woodland, seldom under conifers, from lowlands up to 420 m altitude (N.G. Hodgetts in Hill *et al.* 1994). In N. America it is 'usually in coniferous woods' (Crum & Anderson 1981).

Patches of the plant are perennial. It is an autoicous species and capsules are common. Fusiform gemmae are occasionally or frequently produced in leaf axils and on leaf tips; bulbils and tubers are absent. Vegetative propagation might also occur from detached leaf and stem fragments.

World distribution

P. laetum is widespread in Europe from N. Fennoscandia and arctic Russia southwards to N. Portugal, N. Spain, S. Italy (Calabria) and the Caucasus. It is assigned to a Circumpolar Boreal-montane floristic element in Europe. Elsewhere, it occurs in SW Asia (Georgia to Kazakhstan and Kyrgyzstan: Ignatov *et al.* 2007), N. Asia (widespread from W. Siberia to Yakutia and the Russian Far East: Ignatov *et al.* 2007), N. America (Alaska and Newfoundland southwards to California, New Mexico and North Carolina) and Greenland; also reported from the subantarctic on Campbell Island (by D.H. Vitt, det. R.R. Ireland, in Crum & Anderson 1981).

Threats

Although *P. laetum* has not been refound at two localities with old records, neither of them was accurately localised so there is probably no real evidence of decline. The recent records from Sitka Spruce plantations suggest the species may be under-recorded in Ireland, since few bryologists spend much time searching tree bases in coniferous plantations. The spruce plantations involved will presumably be felled as part of the normal cycle of forestry operations, but there is much apparently similar habitat and replanting commonly occurs.

Conservation

It is uncertain whether the Carrick Lough site is (or was) on protected land since it was imprecisely localised. The coniferous plantations that have produced the recent records are not protected. No conservation action is proposed while doubt remains about the overall status of the species in Irish coniferous plantations.

Protected sites with recent records: none; **Unprotected sites with recent records:** Ballycurragh, S. of Lugnaquilla; SW slopes of White Hill, N. of Roundwood.

White Hill, Co. Wicklow.

Plagiothecium curvifolium Schlieph. ex Limpr.

Curved Silk-moss

syn. *P. laetum* var. *curvifolium* (Schlieph. ex Limpr.) Mastracci & M.Sauer,
P. laetum var. *secundum* (Lindb.) Frisvoll *et al.*

Status in Ireland: Vulnerable (D2); **Status in Europe:** Least Concern

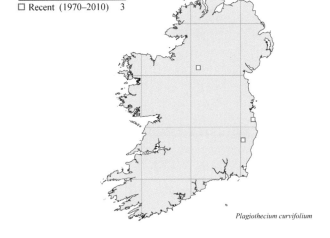

Number of Hectads	3
☐ Recent (1970–2010)	3

Plagiothecium curvifolium

Identification

A small pleurocarpous moss that forms glossy pale green patches (smooth mats) with stems up to about 33 mm long that give rise to prostrate branches. The leaves are 1.0–2.6 mm long, strongly complanate, downcurved when moist, lanceolate but mostly asymmetrical with one straight side, tapering to an acute or acuminate apex. The leaf margin is plane and entire or slightly denticulate near the apex, the costa short, weak and double. Mid-leaf cells are linear-vermicular, 6–8 μm wide; the angular cells are narrowly rectangular, decurrent in 1–4 rows, but not forming auricles. Capsules are cylindrical to narrowly ellipsoid, curved, and held inclined and exserted on a long seta. Differences from most other *Plagiothecium* species include the narrow mid-leaf cells, mainly asymmetrical leaves and form of the decurrent angular cells. However, *P. laetum* is very similar, differing only in its smaller leaves, lack of downcurving of moist leaf apices and erect capsules. Taxonomic separation of *P. curvifolium* as a species distinct from *P. laetum* is therefore questionable (cf. Ireland 1969) and varietal rank may be more appropriate.

Distribution in Ireland

Three records are accepted from two vice-counties: Wicklow (Bellvue Wood, Glen of the Downs, 1981–2008; Coolalug, 2010) and Leitrim (near N. shore of

Garadice Lough, 2000–2001). Another report from Leitrim (Dergvone, 1965) was based on a misidentified specimen as was a report from Fermanagh; a report from Antrim (Carnmoney Hill, 2000) is unconfirmed.

Ecology and biology

At Glen of the Downs, *P. curvifolium* formed extensive patches on bare soil in oak woodland; near Garadice Lough it grew on damp rotting wood of a fallen tree trunk and an old stump in old woodland dominated by oaks; and at Coolalug it was found as a small patch on a conifer stump. In Britain, it is a much more common species of lowland woodlands, growing on tree stumps, tree bases, exposed roots, fallen logs, litter and humus-rich soil; it often occurs luxuriantly in deep shade in coniferous plantations but also in more open deciduous woodlands.

The patches are perennial. It is an autoicous species on which capsules are common, maturing in late spring or early summer. Fusiform axillary gemmae are occasional or frequent. Bulbils and tubers are absent, but detached leaf and stem fragments can presumably function as propagules.

World distribution

P. curvifolium is widespread in Europe, from N. Norway, N. Sweden, C. Finland and Estonia southwards to N.

Spain (where it is montane), Hungary and Ukraine. In Britain, it is widespread from NE Scotland to S. England, but absent or very rare along the western seaboard (Hill *et al.* 1994). It is assigned to a European Temperate floristic element in Europe. Elsewhere, the range is somewhat uncertain because of varying taxonomic treatments, but *P. curvifolium* occurs in the Russian Far East (Ignatov *et al.* 2007), Japan and N. America (reported from Alaska to British Columbia, Montana and Minnesota).

Threats
No immediate threats were apparent at its Irish localities. The species occurs mainly in shaded places and probably depends on maintenance of low light levels and humidity beneath the tree canopy in woodland. Tree cover should therefore be maintained where it occurs. The rare *Plagiothecium latebricola* also occurs in the woodland N. of Garadice Lough, requiring similar habitat and conditions.

Conservation
Two localities are on protected land.

Protected sites with recent records: Garadice Lough Wood pNHA; Glen of the Downs Nature Reserve; Glen of The Downs SAC; **Unprotected sites with recent records:** Coolalug.

Plagiothecium platyphyllum Mönk.
Alpine Silk-moss

Status in Ireland: Vulnerable (D2); **Status in Europe:** Least Concern

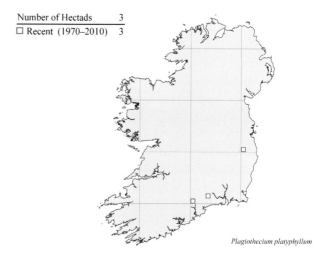

Number of Hectads	3
☐ Recent (1970–2010)	3

Plagiothecium platyphyllum

Identification
A rather large pleurocarpous moss that grows as glossy or dull patches (smooth mats) that are green, or pale or dark green, with branched stems up to 10 cm long. The leaves are complanate, sometimes subsecund, spreading, 2.0–2.5 mm long, symmetrical to slightly asymmetrical, ovate to ovate-lanceolate with a shortly acute apex. The leaf margin is plane, sharply denticulate near the apex and decurrent along the stem in 2–4 rows of rectangular cells that form auricles. The costa is branched, rather strong, ending below mid-leaf, sometimes bearing rhizoids on its dorsal surface. Mid-leaf cells are linear-rhomboidal, mainly 10–16 μm wide. Cells in a patch near the leaf apex have very thin walls that may be eroded and worn away, leaving a small 'window'. In Ireland and Britain, *P. platyphyllum* appears to be rather similar to the more common *P. nemorale* and *P. succulentum*, but it has narrower mid-leaf cells, more strongly denticulate leaf apices and often a distinctive 'window' near the leaf apex. *P. denticulatum* has more asymmetrical leaves with rounded angular cells. Recent British authors have regarded it as a valid species, albeit on the basis of specimens from rather few localities. However, Nyholm (1954–1969) regarded the species as 'variable, confusing and often difficult to interpret' in Fennoscandia. N. American authors regard it as part of a complex species treated under *P. cavifolium*.

Distribution in Ireland

Three records are accepted from three vice-counties: Waterford (Coumshingaun, 2007); S. Tipperary (Knockmealdown, 2007) and Wicklow (S. side of Lough Ouler, 1975). There are unconfirmed reports from Dublin and Down (Eagle Mountain, pre-1910).

Ecology and biology

This is a calcifuge montane species that has been recorded from three sites on flushed siliceous rocks of crags in high corries, at least one of them being on a N.-facing slope. The record from Knockmealdown was also in a corrie, but from a crevice among boulders on the shore of a small lake that was drying out. In Britain, it is a rare montane moss, recorded at up to 850 m altitude, growing in wet, shaded habitats in mountain flushes, crevices in crags and beside streams and waterfalls. In Fennoscandia, it also grows in woods (Nyholm 1954–1969).

The plants are perennial. It is an autoicous species in which capsules are frequent, maturing in summer. Gemmae, bulbils and tubers are unknown, but vegetative propagation might occur from detached leaves or stem fragments.

World distribution

It is widespread in Europe from N. Scotland, C. Norway, N. Sweden and N. Finland southwards in the mountains to N. Spain, N. Italy (in S. Alps), Bulgaria and Ukraine. It is listed as *Critically Endangered* in Luxembourg, *Vulnerable* in Bulgaria and Finland and 'declining' in Germany. It is assigned to a European Boreal-montane floristic element in Europe. Records from elsewhere are subject to taxonomic uncertainty (see above), although Turkey (e.g. Kürschner & Erdağ 2005) and Georgia (Ignatov *et al.* 2007) are reported. Nyholm (1954–1969) also gives Kamchatka (but Ignatov *et al.* 2007 regard records from Russian Far East as uncertain) and Alaska.

Threats

No immediate threats have been reported. However, the species might be vulnerable to erosion or eutrophication associated with high sheep-stocking levels in the hills.

Conservation

Two of the localities are on protected land.

Protected sites with recent records: Comeragh Mountains SAC; Wicklow Mountains National Park; Wicklow Mountains SAC; **Unprotected sites with recent records:** Knockmealdown.

Plagiothecium cavifolium (Brid.) Z.Iwats.

Round Silk-moss

syn. *P. roeseanum* Schimp.
Status in Ireland: Vulnerable (D2); **Status in Europe:** Least Concern

Identification

A creeping or trailing pleurocarpous moss that forms glossy yellowish-green patches (smooth mats) with shoots up to 50 mm long. The shoots are julaceous with leaves imbricate or sometimes subcomplanate. Leaves are ovate to broadly ovate, symmetrical, very concave, with apex acute and often reflexed, plane margins that are usually entire and a double costa extending to just above mid-leaf. Mid-leaf cells are linear-rhomboidal and 10–16 μm wide. The alar cells are enlarged, rectangular and decurrent down the stem in one to three rows. Capsules are cylindrical, straight or curved, erect to inclined and exserted. Forms with julaceous shoots are distinctive in the field, but identification of subcomplanate forms needs careful study of leaf shape, width of mid-leaf cells and the shape of the decurrent cells at the leaf base.

Distribution in Ireland

There are three recent records: S. Kerry (Brandon Mountain, 1946–2009); W. Mayo (Slievemore on Achill Island, 1987) and E. Donegal (Bulbin Mountain, 1907 and 2002).

Ecology and biology

Its Irish habitats have been described in detail only from Bulbin Mountain (E. Donegal), where it occurs in several places on N.- to NW-facing montane slopes among schist crags at 420–490 m altitude. The plants grow on

Plagiothecium cavifolium

thin damp soil in crevices or beneath overhangs, usually among other bryophytes. On Slievemore it was found in a NE-facing corrie. In Britain, it occurs on moist basic mountain rock ledges, where it may be associated with a wide variety of calcicoles, but less often it is on siliceous rock ledges at lower altitudes, sometimes where the basic influence is only slight. There are also a few recent British records from soil on banks or in woodland in the lowlands (E. Norfolk: Stevenson & Strauss 2001; E. and W. Cornwall) and it is well known in similar lowland sites in the Netherlands (Touw & Rubers 1989).

The plants are perennial and dioicous, sporophytes being rare (unknown in Ireland). Tubers are unknown, but fusiform axillary gemmae are occasionally present (in Britain) and these presumably function as propagules.

World distribution
Widespread in N. Europe and montane regions of C. and S. Europe, from Iceland, Jan Mayen and Fennoscandia southwards to Portugal, Spain and Italy, but described as 'rare' in the Netherlands. In Europe, it is assigned to a Circumpolar Boreal-montane floristic element. Elsewhere, it is reported from N. Asia, Japan, N. America, Greenland and the Falkland Islands.

Threats
Some populations in crevices or on ledges of montane rocks seem secure, but others may be at risk from overgrazing, erosion and eutrophication resulting from overstocking of the mountains with sheep. The populations are very small and may be at risk from thoughtless collection of specimens.

Conservation
All three of the recorded localities are on protected land.

Protected sites with recent records: Bulbin Mountain pNHA; Croaghaun/Slievemore SAC; Mount Brandon SAC; **Unprotected sites with recent records:** none.

Isopterygiopsis muelleriana (Schimp.) Z.Iwats.

Mueller's Silk-moss

syn. *Isopterygium muellerianum* (Schimp.) A.Jaeger, *Plagiothecium muellerianum* Schimp.
Status in Ireland: Vulnerable (D2); **Status in Europe:** Least Concern

Identification
A slender pleurocarpous moss that grows as glossy pale green or yellowish-green patches or as scattered shoots. Stems are rather sparsely branched, up to about 50 mm long, with large thin-walled epidermal cells of stem and branches. Leaves are complanate, directed forwards on the shoot, ovate to ovate-oblong, contracted to a narrow filiform acumen, with entire plane margins and the costa short and double or absent. Mid-leaf cells are linear. Capsules are inclined, cylindrical, curved and exserted. The complanate, sparsely branched shoots are noticeable in the field, but identification should be confirmed by microscopic study of the stem and branch exothecial cells and leaf structure.

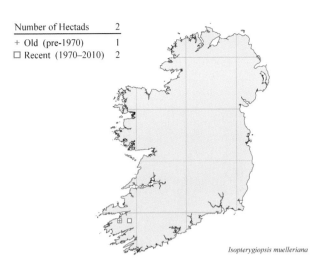

Isopterygiopsis muelleriana

Distribution in Ireland

Known only from three localities in S. Kerry, at Coomeeneragh Lake (1951 and 2006), S. of Coomacullen Lake (2006) and from cliffs above Lough Googh (2009).

Ecology and biology

At Coomeeneragh Lake and Coomacullen Lake, *I. muelleriana* grows with other bryophytes in damp, base-poor places. One is in a shaded hole at the base of a shallow gully in a N.-facing sandstone crag at 380 m altitude on a slope above a lake. The other is on a slightly overhanging, sheltered damp sandstone block on a slope at 315 m altitude. The site above Lough Googh is in a crevice in a species-rich calcareous rock outcrop at c. 700 m altitude. In Britain, the species is reported from similar very sheltered crevices in block scree or at the base of crags where there is either periodic irrigation or persistently high humidity; the substrate is usually at least mildly basic (G.P. Rothero in Hill *et al.* 1994).

The plants are perennial. The species is dioicous and capsules are rare (unknown in Ireland and Britain). Tubers are unknown, but clusters of axillary gemmae 60–100 μm long are occasionally present in British plants.

World distribution

Occurs in mountains of W., C. and E. Europe, from the Pyrenees and Alps north to Iceland and S. Norway and east to the Caucasus, and listed as *Critically Endangered* in the Czech Republic, *Vulnerable* in Bulgaria and 'declining' in Germany. It is assigned to a Suboceanic Boreal-montane floristic element in Europe. Elsewhere,

it is known in Turkey, Siberia, the Himalaya, China, Russian Far East, Japan, Greenland, N. America and New Zealand.

Threats

Potential threats to the small populations known in Ireland could arise from thoughtless collection of specimens, or erosion or eutrophication of the slopes resulting from overstocking with sheep.

Conservation

All sites are on protected land.

Protected sites with recent records: Killarney National Park, Macgillycuddy's Reeks and Caragh River Catchment SAC; **Unprotected sites with recent records:** none.

Isopterygiopsis muelleriana, Coomeeneragh Lake, Co. Kerry.

Hageniella micans (Mitt.) B.C.Tan & Y.Jia

Sparkling Signal-moss

syn. *Hygrohypnum micans* (Mitt.) Broth., *Sematophyllum micans* (Mitt.) Braithw., *S. novae-caesareae* (Austin) E.Britton
Status in Ireland: Near Threatened; **Status in Europe:** Regionally Threatened

A small pleurocarpous moss that grows in patches on periodically flushed rocks in sheltered, partly-shaded places. It has a hyperoceanic range, with reports from four vice-counties, and records from 20 hectads (15 old, 10 recent). Fieldwork during the past decade shows that strong populations still persist at least in Kerry. Some of them would be threatened if Rhododendron spreads even further into native oak woodland, but its scrub has recently been removed from large areas in Killarney National Park.

Sematophyllum demissum (Wilson) Mitt.

Prostrate Signal-moss

Status in Ireland: Near Threatened; **Status in Europe:** Rare

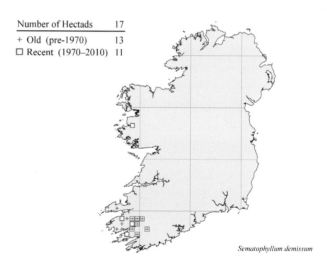

Number of Hectads	17
+ Old (pre-1970)	13
☐ Recent (1970–2010)	11

Sematophyllum demissum

Identification

A slender pleurocarpous moss that grows as glossy yellowish-green to golden patches (smooth mats), with stems up to c. 50 mm in length. The leaves are 1.0–1.2 mm long, lanceolate, narrowed at the base and tapered to an acuminate apex, with entire margins that are plane above and usually recurved below. The costa is short, single or double, or absent. Mid-leaf cells are linear rhomboidal, 7–16 times as long as wide, but shorter and sub-rectangular near the margin of the upper part of the leaf.

A distinctive character is provided by small auricles formed by a few inflated hyaline alar cells in a single row at the basal angles of the leaf. The capsules are narrowly ellipsoid, slightly curved, with a rostrate operculum, held inclined to horizontal and exserted on a reddish seta 8–12 mm long.

Distribution in Ireland

Mainly restricted to the south-west, with recent records from 16 localities in four vice-counties: S. Kerry (Drom East, Owbeg River, 1983; Lauragh Bridge, 2008; Uragh

Wood, 1979, 1981; Derrylea, E. of Owenreagh River, 1982; Looscaunagh Woods, 1973, 1983; O'Sullivan's Cascade, 1833–1983; below Galway's Bridge, 2005); N. Kerry (above Galway's Bridge, 1951–1983; Ullaun's Wood, 1975; Cromaglan, 1829–1972; Derrycunihy Wood, 1951–1973; Cahnicaun Wood, 1988; NW of Loo Bridge, 2005); W. Cork (Glengarriff Woods, 1829–1979; Pass of Keimaneigh, 1967, 2009) and W. Galway (Leenaun, 1982). There are older records from S. Kerry (Maghanaboe Glen, 1951; Lough Currane, 1967; Lough Coomeathcun, 1951; Coomalougha, 1961; Blackstones Bridge, 1951, 1967; Lough Caragh, 1951; Cummeenduff Glen, 1967; Kenmare, 1905); N. Kerry (Eagle's Nest, 1905–1938; 'Killarney', 1830–1878; Torc Mountain, 1831–1935; Cappagh River, 1963; Carrigawaddra, 1963) and W. Cork (Hungry Hill, 1963). The preponderance of old records from Kerry does not provide evidence of decline because the species was not sought during fieldwork over the past decade. Indeed, strong populations have recently been seen at several sites there.

Ecology and biology

It grows as low mats on boulders and other rocks in sheltered, humid sites. Most populations are in lightly or partly shaded places in natural deciduous woodlands on acidic or mildly basic rock (usually sandstone). It is mainly a lowland species, but recorded up to 330 m elevation. Typically, it grows on boulders or slabs of rock with sparse or patchy cover of other bryophytes, often in places intermittently flushed with water or near streams.

The patches of *S. demissum* are probably perennial, or at least persistent for several years. It is an autoicous species that commonly produces capsules, with spores maturing in summer or autumn. Specialised vegetative propagules are apparently lacking, but dispersal from detached leaves or shoot fragments is likely to occur.

World distribution

Discontinuously distributed in W. and C. Europe (see Schumacker & de Zuttere 1982 for map): in SW Ireland, NW Wales, Norway (one record: Frisvoll & Blom 1992), France, Belgium, Luxembourg (Werner 2003), W. and (mainly) SW Germany, Switzerland, Italy (mainly in north, but also reported for Toscana and Lazio: Cortini Pedrotti 2001) and N. Spain (Casas *et al.* 2006). It is assigned to a Temperate Oceanic floristic element in Europe. Elsewhere, the species occurs in Algeria (Ros *et al.* 1999), Turkey, Japan and eastern N. America (widespread from Nova Scotia southwards to Florida).

Threats

It does not currently appear to be threatened in Ireland, although potentially vulnerable if excessive shading develops from invasive Rhododendron scrub. Removal of native woodland could also be damaging by reducing humidity.

Conservation

Ireland supports much larger populations of *S. demissum* than occur in Britain (where it has five extant sites in NW Wales and is listed as *Endangered* by Church *et al.* 2001). Elsewhere in Europe, the species is known to be widespread in SW Germany (Meinunger & Schröder 2007), with strong populations in the Schwarzwald where it is not threatened (G. Philippi in Nebel & Philippi 2001). Most of the Irish populations are on protected land.

Protected sites with recent records: Cloonee and Inchiquin Loughs, Uragh Wood SAC; Dernasliggaun Wood pNHA; Derrycunihy Wood Nature Reserve; Glengarriff Harbour and Woodland SAC; Glengarriff Wood Nature Reserve; Killarney National Park; Killarney National Park, Macgillycuddy's Reeks and Caragh River Catchment SAC; Uragh Wood Nature Reserve; **Unprotected sites with recent records:** Lauragh Bridge; Pass of Keimaneigh.

Sematophyllum substrumulosum (Hampe) E.Britton   Bark Signal-moss

Status in Ireland: Vulnerable (D2); **Status in Europe:** Not Evaluated

Identification

A rather slender to medium-sized pleurocarpous moss that grows as loose, slightly glossy, yellowish-green mats (smooth mats or rough mats), with mainly creeping irregularly to subpinnately branched stems up to about 30 mm long. Stem leaves are erect on ventral side of the stem, erecto-patent on dorsal side of stem, concave, ovate-lanceolate to narrowly lanceolate with a distinctly

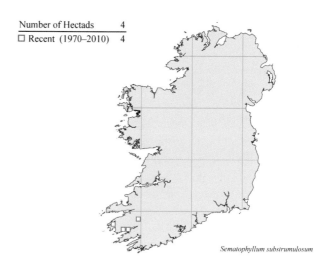

Number of Hectads	4
☐ Recent (1970–2010)	4

Sematophyllum substrumulosum

narrower base, tapering gradually to a flat, longly acuminate apex. The leaf margins are entire and narrowly recurved around the middle of most leaves; the costa is lacking or short and double. Mid-leaf cells are smooth, linear-vermicular, 4–6 μm wide; the lowest row of alar cells is inflated, rather thick-walled, forming well-defined auricles typically of 4–6 cells. The capsule is narrowly ellipsoid to shortly cylindrical, slightly curved, inclined, with a rostrate operculum and exserted on a smooth reddish seta 6–17 mm long. *S. substrumulosum* superficially resembles *Hypnum cupressiforme* var. *resupinatum*, differing in the inclined capsules and distinctive alar cells. *Rhynchostegium confertum* is also superficially similar, but it has wider costate leaves.

Distribution in Ireland

Records are from four localities in two vice-counties: S. Kerry (Glanleam, Valencia Island, 2006; Garinish Island, 2008; two sites on Rossdohan Island, 2008) and N. Kerry (Muckross, 2005).

Ecology and biology

The Irish records are all from partly shaded, humid, lowland sites in open woodland or woodland gardens near coasts and a lake shore. Three finds were on bark near the ground: at the base of a large living *Pinus sylvestris* tree, on the flat upper surface of a cut conifer trunk, and on the large trunk of a fallen tree. The other two records were from steep peaty soil of a path-side bank in a coniferous grove and steep, partly bare surfaces of a block of sandstone (growing with *Daltonia splachnoides*). Its habitats in Britain include bases of trunks and exposed roots of pines and other conifers, but also peaty soil and occurrence as an epiphyte on Gorse.

Elsewhere, it also grows mainly on acidic bark, including decaying branches and fallen logs in laurel forests in Macaronesia and bark of pines and olives in S. Europe.

The plants are perennial. It is an autoicous species in which capsules are abundant, maturing in autumn. Uniseriate protonemal gemmae have recently been reported in the wild in Britain and in cultivation (J.G. Duckett in Matcham *et al.* 2005). Bulbils and tubers are absent; vegetative propagation is also likely to occur from detached stem and leaf fragments.

World distribution

Until the 1970s, the European range of the species was apparently restricted to Portugal, N. and S. Spain and the Mediterranean basin from Mallorca to S. France, Italy, Sicily, the former Yugoslavia and N. Greece (De Beer & Arts 2000). In 1974, it was found at Isle d'Oléron on the Atlantic coast of France (Pierrot 1974), in 1995–96 at several localities on the Isles of Scilly off SW England (Holyoak 1996) and a 1964 gathering from Sussex was belatedly reported by Een (2004). The past decade has seen new records of the species in SW Ireland (see above), S. Britain (Pembrokeshire: Bosanquet 2006b; Isles of Scilly and mainland of both E. and W. Cornwall: Holyoak, unpublished; *Near Threatened* in Britain), Belgium (De Beer & Arts 2000) and the Netherlands (van Zanten 2003) ('very rare'). Contrary to the suggestion by Matcham *et al.* (2005) that it might have been overlooked in Britain, the evidence set out above seems to imply rapid colonisation of large areas of NW Europe over the past few decades. It has almost certainly spread recently in the well recorded areas of Cornwall and Isles of Scilly, even if previously it might have been present undetected in small amounts. The species is

566

(now) assigned to an Oceanic Southern-temperate floristic element in Europe. Elsewhere, it is known in Macaronesia (Azores, Madeira, Canary Islands) and NW Africa. Ignatova *et al.* (2009) give a convincing account of a remarkable disjunct record from E. Siberia (Zabaikalsky Territory), in a mountain tundra enviroment and c. 8000 km from its nearest localities in S. Europe.

Threats

Some Irish populations are small and potentially vulnerable, but at Rossdohan Island it was found along a seven-metre length of fallen tree trunk. As discussed above, the species appears to be rapidly increasing its range in NW Europe, apparently through natural colonisation. More Irish records are thus to be expected, particularly along southern and south-western coasts.

Conservation

The population at Muckross is on protected land. Others seem relatively safe in large woodland gardens. The species is likely to benefit from dead tree trunks and limbs being left to decay on the ground.

Protected sites with recent records: Killarney National Park; Killarney National Park, Macgillycuddy's Reeks and Caragh River Catchment SAC; **Unprotected sites with recent records:** Garinish Island; Glanleam, Valencia Island; Rossdohan Island.

Antitrichia curtipendula (Hedw.) Brid.
Pendulous Wing-moss

Status in Ireland: Near Threatened; **Status in Europe:** Least Concern

This is a large, handsome, pleurocarpous moss that forms dull or yellowish-green rough mats, or hangs as coarse wefts, with distinctive acuminate 'grapnel-like' apices to the leaves (having recurved spinose teeth that are visible with a hand lens). It is most often found on boulders and other rocks (including basalt, sandstone and metamorphic lithologies) on unshaded or lightly shaded hillsides, on lake edges or about crags and has a widespread distribution, with reports from 13 vice-counties and records from 23 hectads (18 old, 11 recent). Evidence for decline of this conspicuous moss is quite strong because it has not been refound at several of its former localities, but causes of its decline in Ireland are poorly understood. Molecular studies have revealed that in continental Europe, *A. curtipendula* consists of two cryptic species (Hedenäs 2008), which apparently cannot be discriminated from their morphology. It is uncertain whether one, or both of these occur in Ireland.

Leptodon smithii F.Weber & D.Mohr
Prince-of-Wales Feather-moss

Status in Ireland: Endangered (B1a, bi, ii, iv, B2a, bi, ii, iv); **Status in Europe:** Least Concern

Identification

A handsome pleurocarpous moss that forms bright green patches (fans). The primary stems are rhizomatous, with decumbent to ascending secondary stems up to about 25 mm long that are complanately 1–2 pinnately branched. The stems and branches are curved when moist, but

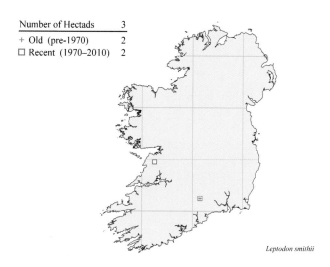

Number of Hectads	3
+ Old (pre-1970)	2
□ Recent (1970–2010)	2

Leptodon smithii

strongly inrolled when dry. Leaves are ovate with a rounded apex, one margin recurved, and a single faint costa in the lower half of the leaf. Mid-leaf cells are more or less hexagonal and smooth. The capsule is ellipsoid and shortly exserted on a seta 1.5–2 mm in length.

Distribution in Ireland

There are recent records from two localities: Waterford (near Knocklofty Bridge, 1956 and 2007) and Clare (Cathair Chomain, 2003–2005). It was also recorded in W. Cork (Bantry House grounds) in 1957 but not refound there in 2006.

Ecology and biology

Mainly known as an epiphyte on bark, reported recently from Ash and lime trees and formerly on Beech, elm, Spindle and Rhododendron, growing in rather open places and in shade. Patches were recorded as growing 0.6–2.1 m above ground and on the fallen part of a trunk that was originally > 4 m above the ground. Also found on limestone blocks in an old drystone wall of a hill fort. British records are likewise mainly from tree bark, infrequently from walls and basic rocks. The species is said to be notably tolerant of dry shade, and thus able to grow on the underside of leaning trees.

The plants grow as perennials in patches that persist for at least several years. The species is dioicous and sporophytes are occasional in Britain and more frequent in the Mediterranean region (but apparently unrecorded in Ireland), with capsules maturing in spring. Green (1958) suggested that production of sporophytes is limited by spatial separation of the sexes. Gemmae and tubers are unknown.

World distribution

Widespread in S. Europe, extending northwards up the Atlantic coasts to N. Wales (and formerly NW England) with outlying localities on the Black Sea coast and formerly in SW Germany. It is described as *Vulnerable* in Switzerland and 'very rare and susceptible' in the Netherlands. It is assigned to an Oceanic Mediterranean-Atlantic floristic element in Europe. Elsewhere, it is known from Macaronesia, N. Africa, Uganda, Tanzania, S. Africa, SW Asia, Chile, Australia and New Zealand (cf. Pócs 1960).

Threats

Beech and elm trees on which it grew in 1956 at the locality in Waterford had been lost by 2007 and a population on a large old lime tree was under threat because the upper part of the trunk had fallen. However, the species had become established on a young Ash tree nearby, giving reason to hope that it may still be successfully colonising new substrata.

Conservation

The population at Cathair Chomain is at the site of a protected ancient monument but care needs to be taken to ensure the stonework is not cleaned or exposed to herbicides.

Protected sites with recent records: Burren National Park; East Burren Complex SAC; Lower River Suir SAC; **Unprotected sites with recent records:** none.

568

Myurium hochstetteri (Schimp.) Kindb.

Hare-tail Moss

syn. *M. hebridarum* Schimp.
Status in Ireland: Regionally Extinct; **Status in Europe:** Least Concern

Number of Hectads	1
+ Old (pre-1970)	1

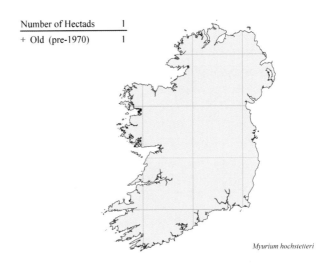

Myurium hochstetteri

Identification

A large and splendid pleurocarpous moss that forms dense golden-yellow or yellowish-green patches (rough mats). The primary stems are prostrate, with numerous crowded erect branches arising from them that are up to 60 mm long. The leaves are glossy, imbricate and strongly concave, rendering the branches julaceous when moist. Leaf shape is distinctive, being ovate-oblong and narrowed abruptly into a long apiculus. Leaf margins are plane below, inflexed above and denticulate; a costa is almost or quite absent. Leaf cells are linear with incrassate, porose cell walls. Capsules are exserted, horizontal, narrowly ellipsoid and curved.

Distribution in Ireland

Known in Ireland only from a small specimen (now in **DBN** Herbarium) collected in 1969 by G. Harmsen and labelled 'along rivulet, Roundstone' (W. Galway). Several bryologists have revisited the area to search for the species without success, but unfortunately the locality is rather imprecise.

Ecology and biology

Recorded only as 'along rivulet'. In Scotland, it grows mainly in damp crevices at the bases of sea cliffs and other coastal rocks, less often on humus amongst *Calluna* on steep wet N.-facing slopes or in open wet turf at the edge of exposed sea cliffs (H.J.B. Birks in Hill *et al.* 1994).

The species grows in perennial patches. It is dioicous and capsules have been found only in the Azores. Some Scottish plants produce shoots with deciduous leaves (Crundwell 1981), but gemmae and tubers are unknown.

World distribution

Endemic to Europe and Macaronesia, where known from W. Scotland (frequent in Outer Hebrides, occasional in Inner Hebrides, very rare in W. Sutherland and W. Inverness), Azores, Madeira and Tenerife. It is assigned to a Hyperoceanic Southern-temperate floristic element.

Threats

There is no information on the location of any population that might still persist in W. Galway or any threats it might face there.

Conservation

No action is proposed, unless some very lucky or very persistent bryologist succeeds in refinding the species in Galway or elsewhere.

Protected sites with recent records: none; **Unprotected sites with recent records:** none.

APPENDIX I. Notes on erroneously recorded or synonymised taxa

Liverworts

Jungermannia borealis Damsh. & Váňa

Northern Flapwort

syn. *Jungermannia karl-muelleri* auct. non Grolle, *J. oblongifolia* auct. non (Müll.Frib.) H.Buch, A.Evans & Verd., *Solenostoma oblongifolium* auct. non (Müll.Frib.) Müll.Frib.
Status in Ireland: Not Evaluated; **Status in Europe:** Least Concern

Recently listed for Ireland (Söderström *et al.* 2007) on the basis of a type specimen of *J. pumila* var. *nigricans* Hook. (J. Váňa, *in litt.*), but in error because its locality 'Breadalbane, Craigeallach' is in Scotland.

Lophozia longiflora (Nees) Schiffn.

Reddish Notchwort

syn. *Lophozia ventricosa* (Dicks.) Dumort. var. *longifolia* (Nees) Macoun
Status in Ireland: Not Evaluated; **Status in Europe:** Least Concern

Reports of this plant from Ireland are incorrect (Paton 1999).

Scapania uliginosa (Sw. ex Lindenb.) Dumort.

Marsh Earwort

syn. *Jungermannia uliginosa* Sw. ex Lindenb., *J. undulata* L. var. *uliginosa* Lindenb., *Scapania obliqua* (Arnell) Schiffn.
Status in Ireland: Not Evaluated; **Status in Europe:** Least Concern

All records of this plant from Ireland have proved to be erroneous (Long 1993).

Mosses

Bryum dunense A.J.E.Sm. & H.Whitehouse

syn. ? *Bryum excurrens* Lindb., ? *B. versicolor* A.Braun ex Bruch & Schimp.
Status in Ireland: Not Evaluated; **Status in Europe:** Not Evaluated

An acrocarpous moss that grows mainly in sandy coastal habitats, although similar plants occur in arable fields inland. It was included in the Provisional Red List (Holyoak 2006b), but it has been treated as part of *B. dichotomum* Hedw. in several recent studies, including the taxonomic review by Holyoak (2003b), because plants with intermediate morphology often connect it to '*B. bicolor* Dicks.'. Recent molecular data support the concept of a morphologically very variable *B. bicolor* (Holyoak & Pedersen 2007, Pedersen *et al.* 2007) but they also imply that some, but not all, plants showing characters of *B. dunense* from Britain may be a distinct taxon.

Bryum neodamense Itzigs.

Long-leaved Thread-moss

syn. *B. cavifolium* Wilson *nom. nud. in synon.*, *B. crispulum* Hampe ex Müll.Hal.,
*B. neodamens*e var. *ovatum* (Lange & C.E.O.Jensen) Lindb. & Arnell,
B. pseudotriquetrum subsp. *neodamense* (Itzigs.) J.J.Amann, *B. pseudotriquetrum* var. *cavifolium* Schimp.,
B. subneodamense Kindb.
Status in Ireland: Not Evaluated; **Status in Europe:** Not Evaluated

An acrocarpous moss that grows in open, damp or wet calcareous sites, mainly on the margins of calcareous lakes. Although apparently distinctive in its bluntly rounded leaves, intermediate plants connect it to the common *Bryum pseudotriquetrum* (Hedw.) P.Gaertn. *et al.* var. *pseudotriquetrum*, which occurs in a much wider range of open, damp habitats. A combination of morphological and molecular studies based partly on Irish plants has now shown *B. neodamense* is an invalid taxon since it is an inconstant phenotype produced by some populations of *B. pseudotriquetrum* when they are intermittently inundated (Holyoak & Hedenäs 2006).

Bryum weigelii Spreng.

Duval's Thread-moss

syn. *B. duvalii* Voit, *Ptychostomum weigelii* (Spreng.) J.R.Spence
Status in Ireland: Not Evaluated; **Status in Europe:** Least Concern

This species is known from two old specimens in the Glasnevin Herbarium (**DBN**), a scrap from one of them passed to the **BBSUK** herbarium and five old specimens pasted onto the same sheet at the herbarium of the Natural History Museum in London (**BM**). The specimens are variously annotated as from 'Waterford, Ireland' or 'near Waterford, 1852' with collector usually noted as E. Madden and provenance sometimes given as 'Com. J. Sadler Esq.' or 'J. Sadler, Edinb.' One of the **DBN** specimens is glued onto blue paper which is mounted alongside two Scottish specimens on the same blue paper labelled in the same handwriting.

All of these specimens might have been from a single large gathering and none of them appears to have any original label written by the collector. There is no doubt about their identification but grounds for concern exist over their geographical origin, with a possibility that Scottish material might have been mislabelled. Although there does not appear to be any Scottish locality called 'Waterford', the **DBN** specimens are associated with Scottish gatherings and E. Madden and J. Sadler are both otherwise unknown as collectors in the **DBN** herbarium (cf. Synnott 1980). The species was listed for Co. Waterford by Moore (1872) and Lett (1915) but deleted from the BBS *Census Catalogue* in 1981 because the record seemed 'dubious and almost certainly erroneous' (comm. A.J.E. Smith in Hill 1981). However, following rediscovery of the specimens at **DBN** it was reinstated (comm. D.M. Synnott) by Blockeel (1988). Although there are lots of flushes in the Comeragh Mountains in Co. Waterford that look potentially suitable for this plant, its full reinstatement on the Irish list should be based on firm evidence.

Campylophyllum calcareum (Crundw. & Nyholm) Hedenäs

Chalk Feather-moss

syn. *Campylium calcareum* Crundw. & Nyholm, *C. hispidulum* var. *sommerfeltii* auct., *C. sommerfeltii* auct. eur.
Status in Ireland: Not Evaluated; **Status in Europe:** Least Concern

A small and slender pleurocarpous moss that forms dense dull green or yellowish-green patches. Although *C. calcareum* is now classified in the Hypnaceae, identification requires careful separation from *Campyliadelphus chrysophyllus* and other small species of Amblystegiaceae, paying attention to the structure of the costa and presence of prorate upper leaf cells (cf. Hedenäs 1997). Re-examination of specimens from six Irish localities has revealed that they were all misidentified: Dublin (Portmarnock, 19th century); Westmeath; E. Mayo; W. Mayo (Bull's Mouth, 1987); Armagh (Middletown, 1885) and Antrim (Derriaghy, 1904).

There are old reports from five other localities in Ireland: W. Galway (Cong, 1872; Galway, 1872; Oughterard, 1872); Antrim (Glenballyemon, undated: Lett 1915) and Londonderry (Umbra Rocks, undated: Lett 1915). However, voucher specimens to support these records have not been located and populations have not been refound during recent fieldwork. In the absence of confirmed records, and given the serious doubts about the accuracy of identification, this species should be excluded from the Irish flora.

Ctenidium molluscum (Hedw.) Mitt. **var. *fastigiatum*** (Hobk.) Braithw. — Slender Comb-moss

syn. *Hypnum molluscum* var. *fastigiatum* Bosw. ex Hobk.
Status in Ireland: Not Evaluated; **Status in Europe:** Not Evaluated

A closely-branched pleurocarpous moss that grows on basic rocks. It has been reported from five vice-counties, with records from eight hectads (7 old, 2 recent). Although it was included in the Provisional Red List (Holyoak 2006b), var. *fastigiatum* is an infraspecific taxon of uncertain and probably rather dubious validity. Some gatherings appear distinctive, but others appear only to be small or stunted forms of var. *molluscum*. The latest list (Hill *et al.* 2008) therefore treats it as a synonym of var. *molluscum*.

Ephemerum stellatum H.Philib. — Starry Earth-moss

syn. *Ephemerum serratum* (Hedw.) Hampe *p.p.*
Status in Ireland: Not Evaluated; **Status in Europe:** Critically Endangered

A tiny acrocarpous moss that grows on exposed soil. A review of virtually every specimen from Ireland and Britain that has been assigned to this taxon has shown that all of them are forms of *E. serratum* or *E. minutissimum* with entire to denticulate leaves (Holyoak 2001b, 2010). The extent of toothing on the leaves commonly varies within a single population.

Fontinalis squamosa Hedw. **var. *dixonii*** (Cardot) A.J.E.Sm. — Dixon's Water-moss

Status in Ireland: Not Evaluated; **Status in Europe:** Not Evaluated

A large pleurocarpous moss that mainly grows submerged in soft-water rivers. It was included in the Provisional Red List (Holyoak 2006b), but specimens from the two Irish localities (Fermanagh: Cat's Hole and vicinity on Owenbrean River; W. Donegal: near Errigal) do not show the characters attributed to var. *dixonii* clearly (Rothero 2007). The taxon is regarded as a synonym of *F. squamosa* by Hill *et al.* (2008).

Homomallium incurvatum (Schrad. ex Brid.) Loeske — Incurved Feather-moss

Status in Ireland: Not Evaluated; **Status in Europe:** Least Concern

Re-examination of the voucher specimen (**BBSUK**) has established that a record from Marble Arch (Fermanagh) (Hodgetts & Hallingbäck 1994) is based on material lacking sporophytes that is probably a form of *Hypnum cupressiforme* var. *resupinatum* (Blockeel 1999).

Orthotrichum cupulatum Hoffm. ex Brid. **var. *riparium*** Huebener — Hooded Bristle-moss

syn. *O. cupulatum* var. *nudum* (Dicks.) Braithw.
Status in Ireland: Not Evaluated; **Status in Europe:** Not Evaluated

An acrocarpous moss that grows in tufts or patches, typically on surfaces of limestone rock or old concrete, *O. cupulatum* is relatively common in Ireland, but var. *riparium* is more local. However, although var. *riparium* was treated as a valid taxon in Hill *et al.* (2006: 215), information has continued to accumulate emphasising that the various characters used to separate this form from var. *cupulatum* vary independently of each other, so it is not recognised in the latest checklist (Hill *et al.* 2008).

Palustriella commutata (Hedw.) Ochyra **var. *virescens*** (Schimp.) Ochyra — Curled Hook-moss

syn. *Cratoneuron commutatum* (Hedw.) Roth var. *virescens* (Schimp.) P.W.Richards & E.C.Wallace
Status in Ireland: Not Evaluated; **Status in Europe:** Not Evaluated

This pleurocarpous moss grows submerged on basic rocks in streams, whereas most forms of *P. commutata* occur in fens, flushes or on flushed basic rocks. Var. *virescens* was recognised as a valid form in the past (Smith 1978, Holyoak 2003a), but it is treated as merely a synonym of *P. commutata* by Hedenäs in Hill *et al.* (2006) and by Hill *et al.* (2008).

Pylaisia polyantha (Hedw.) Schimp. — Many-flowered Leskea

syn. *Pylaisiella polyantha* (Hedw.) Grout
Status in Ireland: Not Evaluated; **Status in Europe:** Least Concern

A slender, glossy yellowish-green or green pleurocarpous moss that grows as an epiphyte in patches on trunks and branches of broadleaved trees and shrubs, in hedgerows and open woodland. Contrary to the literature (e.g. Holyoak 2003a, Hill *et al.* 2008), recent studies reveal that all well-localised Irish specimens labelled as *P. polyantha* in the principal herbaria appear to be misidentified *H. c.* var. *resupinatum*: S. Kerry (Glenbeigh, 1983); N. Kerry (Muckross, 1861 and 1935; Ballyseedy Wood, 1953; Slenageenty Wood, 1954); Down (Drumcro, 1882), as are several that are more poorly localised: 'Inishmakill', 1965, leg. J. Taylor; 'South of Ireland', 1806, leg. Mackay; no locality, leg. E. Hutchins (**BM**). A correctly identified specimen of *P. polyantha* in the **BM** has a printed label 'Dawson Turner. Irish Mosses. Presd by Council Linnean Society 1893', but there is no original label and the provenance of the specimen seems dubious since Turner (1804) gave no locality for his *Hypnum polyanthos* and material from his correspondent Ellen Hutchins is known to be misidentified. Five other Irish reports apparently lack voucher specimens: S. Kerry (Uragh Wood, 1967); N. Kerry (Muckross Demesne, 1872, etc.); E. Cork (Great Island, 1872); W. Mayo and W. Donegal. In the absence of any correctly identified voucher specimen, *P. polyantha* should be excluded from the Irish flora.

Timmia austriaca Hedw. — Sheathed Timmia

Status in Ireland: Not Evaluated; **Status in Europe:** Least Concern

Recorded for the first and only time on Benbulbin in 1970, critical examination of the specimens has shown that the record is a result of a misidentification of *T. norvegica* (Hodgetts 2004). *T. austriaca* has therefore not been correctly reported from Ireland.

Tortella fragilis (Hook. & Wilson) Limpr. — Brittle Crisp-moss

Status in Ireland: Not Evaluated; **Status in Europe:** Least Concern

Re-examination of the voucher specimen (**BBSUK**) has established that a record from Crossmurrin (Fermanagh) (Hodgetts & Hallingbäck 1994) was based on a form of *T. tortuosa* (Hedw.) Limpr. (cf. Holyoak 2003a, Rothero 2004, 2009). H33 was thus listed in error by Hill *et al.* (2008).

Scapania gymnostomophila, Keel Bridge, Lough Carra, Co. Mayo.

APPENDIX II. List of photographs and photographers
(h) = herbarium material

Page	Subject	Photographer	Year
iii	*Sphagnum skyense* and *Polytrichum commune*, Mweelrea, Co. Mayo.	Robert Thompson	2010
iv	Sruhauncullinmore River, Mweelrea, Co. Mayo.	Robert Thompson	2010
x	*Campylostelium saxicola*, Luke's Bridge, Benbulbin, Co. Sligo.	Robert Thompson	2011
xiv	Torc Waterfall, Co. Kerry.	Robert Thompson	2010
1	*Dumortiera hirsuta*, Killarney, Co. Kerry.	Robert Thompson	2010
2	Slievemore, Doogort, Achill Island, Co. Mayo.	Neil Lockhart	2010
3	Cloontyprughlish, Glenade, Co. Leitrim.	David Holyoak	2008
5	*Marchantia polymorpha* subsp. *polymorpha*, Achill Island, Co. Mayo.	Neil Lockhart	2005
6	*Lejeunea hibernica* habitat, Kylemore, Co. Galway.	Robert Thompson	2010
7	*Paludella squarrosa* and *Tomentypnum nitens*, north Co. Mayo.	Neil Lockhart	2010
8	Tree ferns (*Dicksonia* spp.), Garinish Island, Co. Kerry.	David Holyoak	2008
9	*Herbertus aduncus* and *Polytrichum commune*, Mweelrea, Co. Mayo.	Robert Thompson	2010
12 upper	Oak woodland, Torc Mountain, near Killarney, Co. Kerry.	David Holyoak	2005
12 lower	*Hypnum uncinulatum*, Brickeen, Co. Kerry.	David Holyoak	2005
13	Uragh Wood, Inchiquin Lough, Co. Kerry.	Neil Lockhart	2008
14	Hazel woodland, Poulacarra, The Burren, Co. Clare.	Robert Thompson	2008
15	Alluvial woodland, Glengarriff, Co. Cork.	Neil Lockhart	2008
16	Raven's Glen, Co. Wicklow.	Joanne Denyer	2010
17 upper	Kilcarren Bog, Co. Tipperary.	Nick Hodgetts	2005
17 lower	Tullycross, Co. Westmeath.	David Holyoak	2007
18	Garron Plateau, Co. Antrim.	Robert Thompson	2008
19 left	Oweninny peat-fuelled power station, Co. Mayo.	Neil Lockhart	2005
19 right	Rich fen vegetation, near Crossmolina, Co. Mayo.	Robert Thompson	2010
21	Lough Gealain, The Burren, Co. Clare.	Robert Thompson	2008
22	Sallagh Braes, Co. Antrim.	David Holyoak	2008
24	*Oedipodium griffithianum*, west of Lough Bellawaum, Mweelrea, Co. Mayo.	David Holyoak	2003
25	Lugnaquilla North Prison, Co. Wicklow.	Nick Hodgetts	2007
26 upper	The Blue Stack Mountains, Co. Donegal.	Robert Thompson	2011
26 lower	North crags of Carrignabinnia, Galty Mountains, Co. Limerick.	Nick Hodgetts	2005
27	Temple Hill, Galty Mountains, Co. Limerick.	Nick Hodgetts	2005
28	Sgilloge Loughs, Comeragh Mountains, Co. Waterford.	Nick Hodgetts	2007
29 upper	*Plagiochila carringtonii* and *Herbertus aduncus*, Mweelrea, Co. Mayo.	Robert Thompson	2010
29 lower	The Twelve Bens, Co. Galway.	David Holyoak	2004
30 upper	Lough Cruttia, below Brandon Mountain, Co. Kerry.	Nick Hodgetts	2006
30 lower	North-east slope of Bengower, Co. Galway.	David Holyoak	2004
31 upper left	North-east face of Carrauntoohil, Co. Kerry.	Neil Lockhart	2009
31 upper right	David Long, en route to Brandon Mountain during BBS field meeting, 2009.	Neil Lockhart	2009
31 lower right	*Grimmia muehlenbeckii* on knife-edge slab, Brandon Mountain, Co. Kerry.	Nick Hodgetts	2008
32 upper	Northern Atlantic hepatic mat vegetation, Muckish Mountain, Co. Donegal.	David Holyoak	2002
32 lower	Bulbin Mountain, Co. Donegal.	David Holyoak	2002
33	Northern Atlantic hepatic mat vegetation, Mweelrea, Co. Mayo.	Robert Thompson	2010
34	Benbradagh, Co. Londonderry.	David Holyoak	2008
35 upper	South side of Benbulbin, Co. Sligo.	Neil Lockhart	2008
35 lower	Cliffs of Annacoona, Gleniff, Co. Sligo.	Nick Hodgetts	2003
36	Soil erosion at Lettereeragh, Co. Mayo.	Neil Lockhart	2008
37	Coastguard Hill, Co. Donegal.	David Holyoak	2002
38 upper	Maritime turf near Ballycotton, Co. Cork.	Nick Hodgetts	2006
38 lower	Machair at Dooaghtry, Co. Mayo.	Neil Lockhart	2008
39 upper	Magilligan Point, Co. Londonderry.	Robert Thompson	2009
39 lower	Dune heath at Murlough, Co. Down.	Robert Thompson	2009
40	David Holyoak, Christina Campbell, Deirdre Lynn and Noeleen Smyth, North Bull, Co. Dublin.	Neil Lockhart	2008

Page	Subject	Photographer	Year
41 upper	Garter Hill, Co. Mayo.	Neil Lockhart	2009
41 lower	Dune slacks at Inch, Co. Kerry.	Neil Lockhart	2009
42	Golf course on machair at Keel, Achill Island, Co. Mayo.	Neil Lockhart	2007
43	*Hygrohypnum duriusculum*, south-east of Lough Bellawaum, Mweelrea, Co. Mayo.	David Holyoak	2003
44 left	Cloon River, Co. Mayo.	David Holyoak	2003
44 right	Garryland Turlough, Co. Galway.	David Holyoak	2004
45 upper	Spring vegetation, Glenamoy, Co. Mayo.	Neil Lockhart	2003
45 lower	Annaghmore Lough, Co. Roscommon.	David Holyoak	2002
46	Car Moss, Toberroe, Co. Galway.	Neil Lockhart	2005
47	*Cephaloziella nicholsonii*, Mountain Mine, Allihies, Co. Cork.	Neil Lockhart	2006
48	Sand pit, near Pollranny, Co. Mayo.	David Holyoak	2003
49	*Scapania ornithopodioides*, Mweelrea, Co. Mayo.	Robert Thompson	2010
50	Walter Wade.	Charles Nelson	
51 left	*Jubula hutchinsiae*, Kylemore, Co. Galway.	Robert Thompson	2010
51 right	Isaac Carroll.	National Botanic Gardens, Glasnevin	
52 left	Thomas Taylor.	British Bryological Society	
52 right	David Moore.	National Botanic Gardens, Glasnevin	
53	Samuel Alexander Stewart.	National Museums Northern Ireland	
54 upper	Cosslett Herbert Waddell.	National Museums Northern Ireland	
54 lower	Henry William Lett.	National Museums Northern Ireland	
55 upper	Clare Island, Co. Mayo.	Robert Thompson	2011
55 lower	William Rutledge Megaw.	National Museums Northern Ireland	
56 upper	BBS 1928 meeting, Belfast.	British Bryological Society	1928
56 lower	BBS 1935 meeting, Killarney.	British Bryological Society	1935
57 upper	BBS 1937 meeting, Bundoran.	British Bryological Society	1937
57 lower	Jane Smithson Thomson (1943).	British Bryological Society	1943
58 upper	BBS 1951 meeting, Kerry.	British Bryological Society	1951
58 lower left	A.L.Kathleen King.	National Botanic Gardens, Glasnevin	
58 lower right	Bob Fitzgerald (1962).	British Bryological Society	1962
59 upper	Jean Fitzgerald (1963).	British Bryological Society	1963
59 lower	Evelyn Lobley (1942).	British Bryological Society	1942
60 left	Roy Perry (with Jean Paton, 1974).	British Bryological Society	1974
60 right	Donal Synnott, Bull Island, Co. Dublin.	Neil Lockhart	2008
61 left	Jean Paton (1972).	British Bryological Society	1972
61 right	BBS 1979 meeting, Glengarriff.	British Bryological Society	1979
62	BBS 1983 meeting, Kerry.	David Long	1983
63	BBS 1994 meeting, Clare Island.	British Bryological Society	1994
65	*Grimmia anomala*, Easky Lough, Co.Sligo.	Robert Thompson	2011
66 upper left	David Holyoak and Nick Hodgetts, Killarney, Co. Kerry.	Neil Lockhart	2006
66 upper right	BBS 2009 meeting, Brandon, Co. Kerry.	Caroline Pannell	2009
66 lower	Dublin Naturalists' Field Club outing to Skerries, Co. Dublin.	Joanne Denyer	2010
71 upper	David Holyoak, Daniel Kelly, Christina Campbell and Noeleen Smyth, Avoca, Co. Wicklow.	Neil Lockhart	2009
71 lower	*Petalophyllum ralfsii* with sporophytes, Truska Machair, Co. Galway.	David Holyoak	2004
73	*Leiocolea rutheana* var. *rutheana*, near Crossmolina, Co. Mayo.	Robert Thompson	2010
97	North-east slope of Bengower, Co. Galway.	David Holyoak	2004
98 upper	Bellacorick Iron Flush, Co. Mayo.	Neil Lockhart	2001
98 lower	Murlough Dunes, Co. Down.	Robert Thompson	2008
103 upper	Tomacurry, Co. Wexford.	David Holyoak	2008
103 lower	Christina Campbell, Teagasc Laboratory, Kinsealy, Co. Dublin.	Neil Lockhart	2010
107	Glenveagh, Co. Donegal.	Robert Thompson	2008
112	*Amphidium mougeotii* and *Saccogyna viticulosa*, Killarney, Co. Kerry.	Robert Thompson	2010
114	Horn Head, Co. Donegal.	Robert Thompson	2008
115	Malin Head, Co. Donegal.	Robert Thompson	2009
116	Bulbin Mountain, just north-west of summit, Co. Donegal.	David Holyoak	2002
117	North-facing cliffs of Binevenagh, Co. Londonderry.	Robert Thompson	2008

Page	Subject	Photographer	Year
118	Coastal cliffs at Fair Head, Co. Antrim.	Robert Thompson	2009
119	Errigal Mountain and Dunlewy Lough, Co. Donegal.	Robert Thompson	2009
120	Meentygrannagh Bog, Co. Donegal.	Neil Lockhart	2011
121	Benbradagh Mountain, Co. Londonderry.	Robert Thompson	2009
122	Glenariff and Antrim Glens, Co. Antrim.	Robert Thompson	2008
123	Loughros Beg Bay, Co. Donegal.	Robert Thompson	2009
124	Lough Nabrackboy and Lough Asgarha, Blue Stack Mountains, Co. Donegal.	Robert Thompson	2009
125	Slieve League, Co. Donegal.	Robert Thompson	2008
126	South Woodburn Reservoir, Co. Antrim.	David Holyoak	1999
127	Cliffs of Magho, Lough Navar, Co. Fermanagh.	Robert Thompson	2008
128	Cloontyprughlish, Glenade, Co. Leitrim.	Robert Thompson	2010
129	Gleniff, Co. Sligo.	Robert Thompson	2011
130	Cuilcagh Mountain, Cos Cavan and Fermanagh.	Robert Thompson	2009
131	Lough Oughter, Co. Cavan.	Robert Thompson	2011
132	Silent Valley, Mourne Mountains, Co. Down.	Robert Thompson	2007
133	Carlingford Mountain, Co. Louth.	David Holyoak	2008
134	Knockmoyle, Co. Mayo.	Robert Thompson	2011
135	Croagh Patrick, Co. Mayo.	Robert Thompson	2011
136	Shingle beach, Trawmore, south of Dookinelly, Achill Island, Co. Mayo.	Robert Thompson	2010
137	Keel Lough, Achill Island, Co. Mayo.	Robert Thompson	2011
138	Inishard, Lough Mask, Co. Mayo.	Robert Thompson	2006
139	Mannin Lakes, Co. Mayo	Robert Thompson	2011
140	Carrowbehy/Caher Bog, Co. Roscommon.	Robert Thompson	2011
141	Bellanagare Bog, Co. Roscommon.	Robert Thompson	2011
142	Lough Rinn, Co. Leitrim.	Robert Thompson	2011
143	Truska Machair, Slyne Head, Co. Galway.	Robert Thompson	2010
144	North corrie, Mweelrea, Co. Mayo.	Robert Thompson	2010
145	Pollacappul Lough, Kylemore, Co. Galway.	David Holyoak	2004
146	Lough Ree, Co. Longford.	David Holyoak	2007
147	Scragh Bog, Co. Westmeath.	Robert Thompson	2011
148	Clara Bog, Co. Offaly.	Neil Lockhart	2011
149	Bull Island, Co. Dublin.	Robert Thompson	2011
150	Scarr Mountain, with Djouce Mountain behind, Co. Wicklow.	Robert Thompson	2010
151	Glenmacnass Valley, Wicklow Mountains, Co. Wicklow.	Robert Thompson	2010
152	The Burren, near Black Head, Co. Clare.	Robert Thompson	2010
153	Keeper Hill, Co. Tipperary.	Robert Thompson	2010
154	Grageen Fen, Cos Limerick and Tipperary.	Neil Lockhart	2011
155	River Nore, south of Thomastown, Co. Kilkenny.	Robert Thompson	2010
156	Mount Leinster, Blackstairs Mountains, Cos Carlow and Wexford.	Robert Thompson	2010
157	Galty Mountains, Cos Limerick and Tipperary.	Robert Thompson	2010
158	View from Cloghane towards Brandon, Co. Kerry.	Robert Thompson	2008
159	Faha Ridge, below Brandon, Co. Kerry.	Robert Thompson	2008
160	Torc Mountain from Newfoundland Bay, Killarney, Co. Kerry.	Robert Thompson	2010
161	Lough Erhogh, Co. Kerry.	David Holyoak	2005
161 inset	Carrauntoohil summit, with Beenkeragh behind, Co. Kerry.	David Holyoak	2006
162	Magannagan Loughs, Caha Mountains, Co. Cork.	Robert Thompson	2006
163	Lough Inchiquin and Uragh Wood, Co. Kerry.	Neil Lockhart	2008
164	Mountain Mine, Allihies, Co. Cork.	Robert Thompson	2010
165	Knockmealdown Mountains, Cos Cork and Waterford.	Robert Thompson	2010
166	Ballycotton Cliffs, Co. Cork.	Neil Lockhart	2009
167	Coumshingaun, Co. Waterford.	Nick Hodgetts	2007
168	Coumaknock Loughs, below Brandon Mountain, Co. Kerry.	Robert Thompson	2008
169	*Sphagnum pulchrum* and *Sphagnum magellanicum*, Roundstone Bog, Co. Galway.	Robert Thompson	2010
170	Robert Thompson (centre), Neil Lockhart (left) and Nick Hodgetts (right), Mweelrea, Co. Mayo.	Neil Lockhart	2010
173	*Anthoceros agrestis*, Säter, Dalarna province, Sweden.	Tomas Hallingbäck	2003

Page	Subject	Photographer	Year
174	*Marchantia polymorpha* subsp. *montivagans*, Glas Maol, Scotland.	John Birks	1966
175	*Riccia cavernosa*, Lough Rinn, Co. Leitrim.	David Holyoak	2005
176	*Riccia huebeneriana*, Angelzarke Reservoir, England.	Des Callaghan	2006
177 upper	*Riccia rhenana*, Madingby, England.	John Birks	1966
177 lower	*Riccia subbifurca*, Quigley's Point, Co. Donegal.	David Holyoak	2002
178	*Riccia crozalsii*, Tresco, Isles of Scilly, England.	David Holyoak	2003
179 upper	*Ricciocarpos natans*, east of Baronstown Demesne, Co. Westmeath.	David Holyoak	2007
179 lower	*Targionia hypophylla*, Stanner Rocks, Radnorshire, Wales.	David Holyoak	2003
180	*Dumortiera hirsuta*, Killarney, Co. Kerry.	Robert Thompson	2010
182	*Petalophyllum ralfsii*, Truska, Co. Galway.	Robert Thompson	2010
183	*Petalophyllum ralfsii*, Truska, Co. Galway.	Robert Thompson	2010
184	*Fossombronia foveolata*, Cargenwen Reservoir, West Cornwall, England.	David Holyoak	2005
185	*Fossombronia caespitiformis* subsp. *multispira*, Glanleam, Co. Kerry.	David Holyoak	2006
186	*Fossombronia maritima*, Trawmore, Achill Island, Co. Mayo.	Robert Thompson	2010
187	*Fossombronia fimbriata*, Preseli, Wales.	Sam Bosanquet	2003
188	*Moerckia hibernica*, Easter Ross, Coire Gorm, Am Faochagach, Scotland.	David Long	2008
189	*Pallavicinia lyellii*, Foulshaw Moss, Cumbria, England.	Des Callaghan	2010
190	*Metzgeria leptoneura*, Dundonnell, Scotland.	Gordon Rothero	2008
191	*Metzgeria pubescens*, Straidkilly, Co. Antrim.	David Holyoak	2008
192	*Aneura mirabilis*, north-east of Five Mile Bridge, Co. Kerry.	David Holyoak	2005
193	Great Sugar Loaf, Co. Wicklow.	Robert Thompson	2010
194 upper	*Porella cordaeana*, Lempäälä, S-SE Tampere, Iso-Riutta Lake, Finland.	Michael Lüth	2007
194 lower	*Porella pinnata*, River Barle, Somerset, England.	Des Callaghan	2010
195 upper	*Radula lindenbergiana*, Bla Bheinn (Blaven), Isle of Skye, Scotland.	Nick Hodgetts	2010
195 lower	*Radula voluta*, Kylemore, Co. Galway.	Robert Thompson	2010
196	*Radula holtii*, Lough Currane, Co. Kerry.	John Birks	1967
197	*Radula carringtonii*, Brickeen, Co. Kerry.	David Holyoak	2006
198	*Cololejeunea rossettiana*, Killarney, Co. Kerry.	Neil Lockhart	2011
199	*Lejeunea flava* subsp. *moorei*, Brandon, Co. Kerry.	John Birks	1967
200	*Lejeunea hibernica*, Kylemore, Co. Galway.	Robert Thompson	2010
201	*Lejeunea eckloniana*, Pollymounty River, Co. Carlow.	Alan Orange	1999 (h)
202	*Lejeunea mandonii*, Kynance Cove, Cornwall, England.	Des Callaghan	2010
203	*Ptilidium ciliare*, south of Duleek, Co. Meath.	David Holyoak	2007
204	*Ptilidium pulcherrimum*, Vosges Mountains, France.	Jan-Peter Frahm	2005
205	*Mastigophora woodsii*, south of Derrymore Lough, Co. Kerry.	David Holyoak	2005
206	*Bazzania pearsonii*, north corrie, Mweelrea, Co. Mayo.	Robert Thompson	2010
207	*Kurzia sylvatica*, Ben Farm, Killary Harbour, Co. Mayo.	Alan Orange	1970 (h)
208	*Telaranea europaea*, Kylemore, Co. Galway.	Robert Thompson	2010
209	Photographing *Telaranea europaea*, Kylemore, Co. Galway.	Neil Lockhart	2010
210 upper	*Lophocolea bispinosa*, Tresco, Isles of Scilly, England.	David Holyoak	2003
210 lower	*Lophocolea semiteres*, Tresco, Isles of Scilly, England.	David Holyoak	2003
211 upper	*Heteroscyphus fissistipus*, Garinish Island, Co. Kerry.	David Holyoak	2008
211 lower	*Plagiochila carringtonii*, north-east corrie, Mweelrea, Co. Mayo.	David Holyoak	2003
212	*Plagiochila britannica*, Castern Wood, England.	Des Callaghan	2006
213	*Plagiochila heterophylla*, Ariundle, Argyll, Scotland.	Nick Hodgetts	2005
214	*Adelanthus lindenbergianus*, north slope of Bengower, Connemara, Co. Galway.	David Long	2007
215	*Cephalozia macrostachya* var. *macrostachya*, Gwaun Valley, Pembrokeshire, Wales.	Alan Orange	1965 (h)
216	*Cephalozia macrostachya* var. *spiniflora*, Matley Bog, Hampshire, England.	Des Callaghan	2010
217	*Cephalozia pleniceps*, Keel Harbour, Achill Island, Co. Mayo.	Robert Thompson	2010
219	*Cephalozia loitlesbergeri*, Grey Hill, Ayrshire, Scotland.	Des Callaghan	2010
220	*Cephalozia crassifolia*, O'Sullivan's Cascade, Co. Kerry.	David Holyoak	2006
221	*Cladopodiella francisci*, Edergole, Lough Eske, Co. Donegal.	Neil Lockhart	2008
222	*Cladopodiella francisci*, Edergole, Lough Eske, Co. Donegal.	Robert Thompson	2011
223	*Odontoschisma elongatum*, Loch Druim a' Chliabhain, Scotland.	Des Callaghan	2006
224	*Cephaloziella spinigera*, Woahink Lake, Oregon, USA.	David Wagner	1980
225	*Cephaloziella elachista*, Cliburn Moss, Westmorland, England.	Alan Orange	1982 (h)
226	*Cephaloziella rubella*, Schwarzwald, Germany.	Michael Lüth	2003

Page	Subject	Photographer	Year
227	Tullaher Bog, Co. Clare.	Nick Hodgetts	2004
228 upper	*Cephaloziella stellulifera*, Allihies, Co. Cork.	Neil Lockhart	2009
228 lower	*Cephaloziella massalongi*, Allihies, Co. Cork.	Robert Thompson	2010
229	*Cephaloziella massalongi*, Allihies, Co. Cork.	Robert Thompson	2010
230	*Cephaloziella nicholsonii*, Knockmahon, Co. Waterford.	Neil Lockhart	2009
231	*Cephaloziella turneri*, Glen of the Downs, Co. Wicklow.	Neil Lockhart	2008
232	*Cephaloziella integerrima*, Porkellis Moor, Cornwall, England.	Des Callaghan	2010
234	*Barbilophozia kunzeana*, Nant y Twyn, Monmouthshire, Wales.	David Long	2011
235	*Barbilophozia atlantica*, Beckside Farm, Cumbria, England.	Nick Hodgetts	2004
236	*Barbilophozia barbata*, Freiburg, Kappel, Erzwäscherei, Germany.	Michael Lüth	2007
237	*Sphenolobopsis pearsonii*, Ben More, Mull, Scotland.	Sam Bosanquet	2007
238	*Anastrophyllum hellerianum*, Lammi, Evo area, Kotinen Nature Reserve, Finland.	Michael Lüth	2007
239	*Tritomaria exsecta*, Bozen, Mt. Segeda, Italy.	Michael Lüth	2002
240	O'Sullivan's Cascade, Co. Kerry.	Robert Thompson	2007
241 upper	*Lophozia wenzelii*, Grimselpass, Sidelhorn, Switzerland.	Michael Lüth	2006
241 lower	*Lophozia sudetica*, Mynydd Preseli, Pembrokeshire, Wales.	Sam Bosanquet	2004
242	*Lophozia opacifolia*, north slope of Muckish Mountain, Co. Donegal.	David Holyoak	2002
243 upper	*Diplophyllum obtusifolium*, Ballycorus, Co. Dublin.	Neil Lockhart	2009
243 lower	*Douinia ovata*, Ben Hee, Scotland.	Des Callaghan	2006
244	*Scapania gymnostomophila*, Keel Bridge, Lough Carra, Co. Mayo.	Neil Lockhart	2011
245	*Scapania cuspiduligera*, Lough Doo, Achill Island, Co. Mayo.	Neil Lockhart	2009
246	*Scapania curta*, east of Keel, Achill Island, Co. Mayo.	Robert Thompson	2010
247	*Scapania lingulata*, Picws Du, Carmarthenshire, Wales.	Des Callaghan	2010
248	*Scapania subalpina*, Tullyconor Bridge, Co. Galway.	Neil Lockhart	2010
250	*Scapania ornithopodioides*, north-east corrie, Mweelrea, Co. Mayo.	Robert Thompson	2010
251	*Scapania nimbosa*, Mount Brandon, Co. Kerry.	Rory Hodd	2010
252	*Acrobolbus wilsonii*, east of Coastguard Hill, Co. Donegal.	David Holyoak	2002
253	Devil's Mother, ravine on north-west slope, Co. Mayo.	David Holyoak	2003
254	*Southbya tophacea*, Gear Sands, West Cornwall, England.	David Holyoak	2003
255	Knocknarea Glen, Co. Sligo.	Robert Thompson	2011
256	*Calypogeia integristipula*, Lough Navar, Co. Fermanagh.	Neil Lockhart	2005
257	*Calypogeia suecica*, Vänge, Uppland province, Sweden.	Tomas Hallingbäck	1995
258	*Leiocolea rutheana* var. *rutheana*, west of Crossmolina, Co. Mayo.	David Holyoak	2003
259	*Leiocolea gillmanii*, Lough Doo, Achill Island, Co. Mayo.	Robert Thompson	2010
260	*Leiocolea gillmanii*, Lough Doo, Achill Island, Co. Mayo.	Robert Thompson	2010
261	Lough Doo, Achill Island, Co. Mayo.	Neil Lockhart	2009
262 upper	*Leiocolea bantriensis*, Klausenpass, Switzerland.	Michael Lüth	2006
262 lower	*Leiocolea fitzgeraldiae*, Gleniff, Co. Sligo.	Robert Thompson	2011
263	*Leiocolea heterocolpos*, Ben Griam Beag, Scotland.	Des Callaghan	2007
264 upper	*Eremonotus myriocarpus*, Muckanaght, Co. Galway.	Alan Orange	1968 (h)
264 lower	*Jungermannia exsertifolia* subsp. *cordifolia*, Beinn Dhorain, Scotland.	Des Callaghan	2006
265 upper	*Nardia geoscyphus*, east of Keel, Achill Island, Co. Mayo.	Robert Thompson	2010
265 lower	*Solenostoma sphaerocarpum*, Schwarzwald, Tennenbach, Germany.	Michael Lüth	2003
266	*Solenostoma paroicum*, Angelzarke Reservoir, England.	Des Callaghan	2010
267	*Solenostoma subellipticum*, Fintragh Bridge, Co. Donegal.	Neil Lockhart	2011
268	Lough Nakeeroge (east), Achill Island, Co. Mayo.	Neil Lockhart	2011
269	*Geocalyx graveolens*, Argyll, Scotland.	Ron Porley	2002
270 upper	*Anthelia juratzkana*, west slope of Croaghaun, Co. Mayo.	David Holyoak	2003
270 lower	*Gymnomitrion concinnatum*, Blue Stack Mountains, Co. Donegal.	Robert Thompson	2011
271	*Gymnomitrion obtusum*, Coum Iarthar, Co. Waterford.	Nick Hodgetts	2007
272	*Gymnomitrion corallioides*, Bulbin Mountain, Co. Donegal.	David Holyoak	2002
273	*Marsupella sphacelata*, Blue Stack Mountains, Co. Donegal.	Neil Lockhart	2001
274	*Marsupella funckii*, Schwarzwald, Feldberg, Germany.	Michael Lüth	2006
275	*Marsupella sprucei*, north-east corrie, Mweelrea, Co. Mayo.	David Holyoak	2003

Page	Subject	Photographer	Year
276	*Marsupella adusta*, north-east slope of Slieve Snaght, Co. Donegal.	David Holyoak	2002
277	*Sphagnum affine*, Ballinafad, Co. Galway.	David Holyoak	2004
278 upper	*Sphagnum teres*, Buxton Heath, East Norfolk, England.	David Holyoak	2004
278 lower	*Sphagnum girgensohnii*, Dergvone, Co. Leitrim.	David Holyoak	2000
279 upper	*Sphagnum russowii*, Estonia.	Michael Lüth	2003
279 lower	*Sphagnum warnstorfii*, Coolturk, Co. Mayo.	David Holyoak	2010
280	*Sphagnum capillifolium* subsp. *capillifolium*, Glen Cassley, Scotland.	Des Callaghan	2006
281 upper	*Sphagnum subnitens* var. *ferrugineum*, Coolturk, Co. Mayo.	Neil Lockhart	2010
281 lower	*Sphagnum skyense*, near Coumshingaun Lough, Co. Waterford.	David Holyoak	2008
282	*Sphagnum strictum*, Glen Cassley, Scotland.	Des Callaghan	2006
283	Cashel Hill, Roundstone Bog, Connemara, Co. Galway.	Robert Thompson	2010
284 upper	*Sphagnum subsecundum*, Meentygrannagh, Co. Donegal.	Neil Lockhart	2003
284 lower	*Sphagnum platyphyllum*, west of Lough Nalawney, Co. Galway.	David Holyoak	2004
285	*Sphagnum flexuosum*, Rushup Edge, England.	Des Callaghan	2006
286 upper	*Sphagnum angustifolium*, Cannock Chase, England.	Des Callaghan	2006
286 lower	*Andreaea megistospora*, Lough Gouragh, Co. Kerry.	David Holyoak	2006
287	Lough Gouragh, Co. Kerry.	David Holyoak	2006
288	*Oedipodium griffithianum*, above Lough Bellawaum, Mweelrea, Co. Mayo.	David Holyoak	2003
289 upper	*Atrichum crispum*, Bronagh, Co. Leitrim.	David Holyoak	2000
289 lower	*Atrichum tenellum*, Goss Moor, East Cornwall, England.	David Holyoak	2002
290	*Atrichum angustatum*, West Sussex, England.	Ron Porley	2000
291	*Pogonatum nanum*, near Lough Brawn, Co. Mayo.	David Holyoak	2008
292	*Polytrichum commune* var. *perigoniale*, Scarcewater, East Cornwall, England.	David Holyoak	2008
293 upper	*Tetrodontium brownianum*, Schwarzwald, Tennenbach, Germany.	Michael Lüth	2003
293 lower	*Buxbaumia aphylla*, Hangman's Hill, Worcestershire, England.	David Holyoak	2004
294	*Timmia norvegica*, Klausenpass, Chammli, Switzerland.	Michael Lüth	2006
295	*Timmia norvegica*, Gleniff, Co. Sligo.	Robert Thompson	2011
296	Gleniff, Co. Sligo.	Neil Lockhart	2011
297	*Encalypta alpina*, Hohe Tauern Nationalpark, Austria.	Michael Lüth	2005
298	*Encalypta rhaptocarpa*, Benbradagh, Co. Londonderry.	David Holyoak	2008
299 upper	*Encalypta vulgaris*, Crete, Greece.	Michael Lüth	2007
299 lower	*Encalypta ciliata*, Ben Vrackie, East Perthshire, Scotland.	Jonathan Sleath	2003
300	*Entosthodon muhlenbergii*, Topolia, Koutsamados, Crete, Greece.	Michael Lüth	2007
301	*Entosthodon muhlenbergii*, Humphrey Head, Cumbria, England.	Des Callaghan	2010
302 upper	*Entosthodon fascicularis*, south-east of Tomacurry, Co. Wexford.	David Holyoak	2008
302 lower	*Physcomitrium sphaericum*, Damflask Reservoir, Yorkshire, England.	Nick Hodgetts	2003
303	*Physcomitrium sphaericum*, Earnsdale Reservoir, Lancashire, England.	Des Callaghan	2010
304 upper	*Aphanorrhegma patens*, Cashel Turlough, Co. Mayo.	David Holyoak	2003
304 lower	*Discelium nudum*, Bellavally Gap, Co. Cavan.	David Holyoak	2002
305	Altscraghy, Cuilcagh, Co. Fermanagh.	Robert Thompson	2008
306	*Schistidium platyphyllum*, Ardtully Bridge, Co. Kerry.	Neil Lockhart	2011
307	*Schistidium platyphyllum*, Ardtully Bridge, east of Cloontoo, Co. Kerry.	David Holyoak	2008
308	*Schistidium agassizii*, Lackagh River, Glen Lough, Co. Donegal.	David Holyoak	2002
309	*Schistidium trichodon*, Schwarzwald, Windgfällweiher, Germany.	Michael Lüth	2006
311	*Schistidium pruinosum*, Camas Beag, Skye, Scotland.	Nick Hodgetts	2009
312 upper	*Schistidium strictum*, Lough Gouragh, Co. Kerry.	David Holyoak	2006
312 lower	*Schistidium robustum*, Ofenpass, Switzerland.	Michael Lüth	2006
314	*Schistidium confertum*, Sardinia, Italy.	Jan-Peter Frahm	2008
315	*Schistidium elegantulum* subsp. *elegantulum*, Savoie, Haute-Maurienne, France.	Michael Lüth	2005
316	*Schistidium elegantulum* subsp. *wilsonii*, Giffoni Valle Piana, Italy.	Des Callaghan	2006
317	*Grimmia crinita*, Oberrheinebene, Biengen, Germany.	Michael Lüth	2003
318	*Grimmia laevigata*, near Barragem de Póvoa, Alto Alentejo, Portugal.	David Holyoak	2007
319	*Grimmia donniana*, Lough Bellawaum, Mweelrea, Co. Mayo.	David Holyoak	2003
320	*Grimmia longirostris*, Skye, Scotland.	Ron Porley	2006
321	*Grimmia atrata*, east ridge of Aghla More, Co. Donegal.	David Holyoak	2002
322	*Grimmia orbicularis*, Leswidden, West Cornwall, England.	David Holyoak	2003
323	*Grimmia torquata*, Lough Muskry, Co. Tipperary.	Nick Hodgetts	2005

Page	Subject	Photographer	Year
324 upper	*Grimmia funalis*, Coomnacronia Lake, Co. Kerry.	David Holyoak	2006
324 lower	*Grimmia lisae*, Derrynane Gardens, Co. Kerry.	David Holyoak	2006
325	*Grimmia funalis*, Errisbeg, Co. Galway.	Robert Thompson	2010
326	*Grimmia dissimulata*, Caranavoodaun, Co. Galway.	David Holyoak	2004
327	*Grimmia muehlenbeckii*, Benbradagh, Co. Londonderry.	David Holyoak	2008
328	*Grimmia hartmanii*, Lough Cullin, Co. Mayo.	David Holyoak	2003
329	*Grimmia anomala*, Easky Lough, Co. Sligo.	Robert Thompson	2011
330	*Grimmia decipiens*, Black Stairs, Co. Down.	David Holyoak	2002
331 upper	*Grimmia ramondii*, Glen Nevis, Scotland.	Gordon Rothero	2004
331 lower	*Racomitrium macounii* subsp. *alpinum*, Engelberg, Ober Stäfeli, Switzerland.	Michael Lüth	2006
332	Lough Bellawaum, Co. Mayo.	David Holyoak	2003
333 upper	*Racomitrium sudeticum*, Mackoght, Co. Donegal.	David Holyoak	2002
333 lower	*Racomitrium affine*, Lough Ouler, Co. Wicklow.	Nick Hodgetts	2007
334	*Racomitrium elongatum*, Glendalough, Co. Wicklow.	Nick Hodgetts	2007
335	*Racomitrium canescens*, Murlough National Nature Reserve, Co. Down.	David Holyoak	2002
337	*Campylostelium saxicola*, Vosges Mountains, France.	Jan-Peter Frahm	2009
338	*Brachydontium trichodes*, near Carclaze, East Cornwall, England.	David Holyoak	2009
339 upper	River Liffey, south-west of Sally Gap, Co. Wicklow.	Neil Lockhart	2011
339 lower	*Seligeria pusilla*, Coaley Peak, England.	Des Callaghan	2005
340 upper	*Seligeria acutifolia*, Provence, France.	Michael Lüth	2006
340 lower	*Seligeria calycina*, Wiltshire, England.	Ron Porley	2005
341	*Seligeria calcarea*, Coaley Peak, England.	Des Callaghan	2005
342	*Seligeria donniana*, Bulgaria.	Michael Lüth	2005
343 upper	*Seligeria patula*, Cloontyprughlish, Glenade, Co. Leitrim.	David Holyoak	2008
343 lower	*Seligeria oelandica*, north of Glencreawan Lough, Co. Fermanagh.	David Holyoak	2000
344	Gleniff, Co. Sligo.	Robert Thompson	2011
345	*Fissidens crispus*, Cadgwith, Cornwall, England.	Des Callaghan	2010
346 upper	*Fissidens gracilifolius*, Knocknarea Glen, Co. Sligo.	Robert Thompson	2011
346 lower	*Fissidens incurvus*, Painswick Beacon, England.	Des Callaghan	2005
347	*Fissidens rivularis*, south of Ross Castle, Co. Kerry.	David Holyoak	2005
348	*Fissidens monguillonii*, Manch Bridge, Co. Cork.	Neil Lockhart	2010
349	*Fissidens rufulus*, Ederamone, Ballyshannon, Co. Donegal.	Robert Thompson	2011
350	*Fissidens rufulus*, Ederamone, Ballyshannon, Co. Donegal.	Robert Thompson	2011
352 upper	*Fissidens exilis*, near Penryn, West Cornwall, England.	David Holyoak	2003
352 lower	Spahill, Co. Kilkenny.	Neil Lockhart	2011
353	*Fissidens curvatus*, Talland Barton Farm, Cornwall, England.	Des Callaghan	2010
354	*Fissidens serrulatus*, Lauragh, Co. Kerry.	Neil Lockhart	2008
355	*Fissidens polyphyllus*, Glengarriff, Co. Cork.	Neil Lockhart	2008
356	*Fissidens fontanus*, Bridgewater Canal, Manchester, England.	Des Callaghan	2010
357	*Pleuridium subulatum*, Roadford Reservoir, North Devon, England.	David Holyoak	2004
358	*Ditrichum pusillum*, Tomasjorddalen, Balsfjord, Troms, Norway.	Tomas Hallingbäck	2004
359	*Ditrichum cornubicum*, Crow's Nest, East Cornwall, England.	David Holyoak	2004
360	*Ditrichum lineare*, Coire Lagan, Scotland.	John Birks	1966
361	*Ditrichum plumbicola*, West Chyverton, West Cornwall, England.	David Holyoak	2004
362	Vale of Glendasan, Co. Wicklow.	Neil Lockhart	2011
363	*Ditrichum zonatum*, Moylenanav, Co. Donegal.	David Holyoak	2002
364	*Ditrichum flexicaule*, Craig Leek, Scotland.	Gordon Rothero	2009
365	*Distichium inclinatum*, Garter Hill, Co. Mayo.	David Holyoak	2003
366	*Amphidium lapponicum*, Island NBS, Iceland.	Michael Lüth	2009
367	*Rhabdoweisia fugax*, Blue Stack Mountains, Co. Donegal.	Robert Thompson	2011
368 upper	*Rhabdoweisia crispata*, Germany.	Michael Lüth	2005
368 lower	*Cynodontium bruntonii*, Glendalough, Co. Wicklow.	Nick Hodgetts	2007
369	*Cynodontium jenneri*, Meenaguse, Co. Donegal.	Robert Thompson	2011
370 upper	*Dichodontium flavescens*, Gleniff, Co. Sligo.	Robert Thompson	2011
370 lower	*Arctoa fulvella*, south-east slope of Benchoona, Co. Galway.	David Holyoak	2004
371	*Kiaeria falcata*, Ben Alder, Scotland.	Gordon Rothero	2004
372	*Kiaeria blyttii*, Galtymore, Co. Tipperary.	Nick Hodgetts	2005

Page	Subject	Photographer	Year
373 upper	*Glyphomitrium daviesii*, Errisbeg, Co. Galway.	David Holyoak	2004
373 lower	*Aongstroemia longipes*, east of Pollranny, Co. Mayo.	David Holyoak	2003
374	*Dicranella grevilleana*, Gleniff, Co. Sligo.	Robert Thompson	2011
375	*Dicranella crispa*, Rinneen, Co. Kerry.	David Holyoak	2006
376	*Dicranella subulata*, Shaughnessy's Bridge, Maum, Co. Galway.	David Holyoak	2004
377 upper	*Dicranella cerviculata*, west of Carn Park, Co. Westmeath.	David Holyoak	2007
377 lower	*Dicranum undulatum*, Cumbria, England.	Ron Porley	2002
378	*Dicranoloma menziesii*, Garinish Island, Co. Kerry.	David Holyoak	2008
379	*Dicranodontium uncinatum*, north-east corrie, Mweelrea, Co. Mayo.	Robert Thompson	2010
380	*Dicranodontium asperulum*, Germany.	Michael Lüth	2005
381	*Campylopus subulatus*, Blackpool China Clay Works, East Cornwall, England.	David Holyoak	2009
382	*Campylopus schimperi*, Zirmsee-Alter Pocher, Kleines Fleisstal, Austria.	Tomas Hallingbäck	2004
384 upper	*Campylopus shawii*, Cloonaghlin Lough, Co. Kerry.	David Holyoak	2006
384 lower	Knockowen, Co. Cork.	David Holyoak	2006
385 upper	*Campylopus atrovirens* var. *falcatus*, Benchoona, Co. Galway.	David Holyoak	2004
385 lower	*Leucobryum juniperoideum*, Tollymore Forest Park, Co. Down.	David Holyoak	2002
386	*Scopelophila cataractae*, Caim, Co. Wexford.	Neil Lockhart	2009
387 upper	*Weissia controversa* var. *crispata*, Stackpole, Wales.	Sam Bosanquet	2005
387 lower	Kilcommon Bridge, Tinahely, Co. Wicklow, site for *Weissia controversa* var. *crispata*.	Neil Lockhart	2011
388 upper	*Weissia controversa* var. *densifolia*, Dunree Head, Co. Donegal.	David Holyoak	2002
388 lower	*Weissia perssonii*, Keel Harbour, Achill Island, Co. Mayo.	Robert Thompson	2010
389	*Weissia rutilans*, east of Portreath, West Cornwall, England.	Tomas Hallingbäck	2003
390	*Weissia condensa*, Butser Hill, Sussex, England.	Nick Hodgetts	2009
391	*Weissia brachycarpa* var. *brachycarpa*, Tomacurry, Co. Wexford.	Neil Lockhart	2008 (h)
392	*Weissia rostellata*, Darwell Reservoir, East Sussex, England.	David Holyoak	2005
393	*Weissia longifolia* var. *angustifolia*, Selsley Common, England.	Des Callaghan	2005
394	*Tortella bambergeri*, Brandon Mt, Com na Cailli, Co. Kerry.	Nick Hodgetts	2008
395 upper	*Tortella densa*, Ailwee, Co. Clare.	Nick Hodgetts	2004
395 lower	*Tortella inclinata*, Murlough National Nature Reserve, Co. Down.	David Holyoak	2008
396	*Pleurochaete squarrosa*, near South Bull, Co. Meath.	David Holyoak	2007
397	*Hymenostylium recurvirostrum* var. *insigne*, Cloontyprughlish, Co. Leitrim.	David Holyoak	2008
398	*Gymnostomum viridulum*, Fermoy, Co. Cork.	Neil Lockhart	2011
399 upper	*Molendoa warburgii*, south of Knockacorraun Lough, Co. Mayo.	David Holyoak	2003
399 lower	*Molendoa warburgii*, south of Knockacorraun Lough, Co. Mayo.	David Holyoak	2003
400	*Leptobarbula berica*, St Ives, West Cornwall, England.	David Holyoak	2004
401	*Ephemerum recurvifolium*, Castle Frome, Herefordshire, England.	Alan Orange	2004 (h)
402	*Ephemerum crassinervium* subsp. *sessile*, Powdermill Reservoir, East Sussex, England.	David Holyoak	2005
404	*Ephemerum crassinervium* subsp. *rutheanum*, Cloon River, Partry, Co. Mayo.	David Holyoak	2003
405	*Ephemerum cohaerens*, Reuss Valley, Aargau, Switzerland.	Norbert Schnyder	2003
407	*Ephemerum spinulosum*, Northrhine-Westphalia, Germany.	Jan-Peter Frahm	2008
408	*Paraleptodontium recurvifolium*, north-east corrie, Mweelrea, Co. Mayo.	Neil Lockhart	2010
409	*Leptodontium flexifolium*, Freshfield, England.	Des Callaghan	2005
410	*Didymodon acutus*, east of Baltray, Co. Louth.	David Holyoak	2008
411	*Didymodon icmadophilus*, Skye, Scotland.	Ron Porley	2006
412	*Didymodon nicholsonii*, Marazion, West Cornwall, England.	David Holyoak	2003
413	*Didymodon umbrosus*, Barcelona, Spain.	Michael Lüth	2006
414	*Didymodon tomaculosus*, south-west of Philleigh, East Cornwall, England.	David Holyoak	2004
416	*Didymodon maximus*, Gleniff, Co. Sligo.	Neil Lockhart	2001
417	*Pterygoneurum ovatum*, Kaiserstuhl, Germany.	Michael Lüth	2003
418	*Pterygoneurum lamellatum*, Kaiserstuhl, Germany.	Michael Lüth	2004
419	*Aloina rigida*, Silk Hill, Wiltshire, England.	Des Callaghan	2010
420	*Aloina ambigua*, Zypern, Germany.	Michael Lüth	2009
421	*Tortula cuneifolia*, Talland, East Cornwall, England.	David Holyoak	2009
422	*Tortula marginata*, Shropshire Union Canal, England.	Des Callaghan	2006
423	*Tortula vahliana*, Kaiserstuhl, Germany.	Michael Lüth	2003

Page	Subject	Photographer	Year
424	*Tortula canescens*, Ballycotton, Co. Cork.	Neil Lockhart	2009
425	*Tortula atrovirens*, Saunton, North Devon, England.	David Holyoak	2005
426	*Tortula lanceola*, Malvern Wells, Worcestershire, England.	David Holyoak	2004
427	*Tortula wilsonii*, Kynance Cliff, West Cornwall, England.	Des Callaghan	2010
428 upper	*Tortula viridifolia*, Ballyrobin, Co. Cork.	Nick Hodgetts	2006
428 lower	*Tortula modica*, Wiltshire, England.	Ron Porley	2005
430	*Tortula protobryoides*, Selsley Common, England.	Des Callaghan	2004
431 upper	*Phascum cuspidatum* var. *piliferum*, Tacumshin Lake, Co. Wexford.	David Holyoak	2006
431 lower	Brackish lagoon, Tacumshin Lake, Co. Wexford.	David Holyoak	2006
432	*Phascum cuspidatum* var. *papillosum*, Brightwell, East Sussex, England.	Alan Orange	1922 (h)
433	*Microbryum starckeanum*, Minera Lead Mine, Wales.	Des Callaghan	2008
434 upper	*Microbryum rectum*, Selsley Common, England.	Des Callaghan	2004
434 lower	*Microbryum curvicollum*, Selsley Common, England.	Des Callaghan	2004
435	*Hennediella stanfordensis*, Slimbridge, Gloucestershire, England.	Des Callaghan	2010
436 upper	*Hennediella heimii*, west of Dunfanaghy, Co. Donegal.	David Holyoak	2002
436 lower	*Acaulon muticum*, west of Pim Hill, Shropshire, England.	David Holyoak	2004
438	*Syntrichia princeps*, Germany.	Michael Lüth	2008
439	*Syntrichia virescens*, Freiburg, Germany.	Michael Lüth	2002
440 upper	*Syntrichia latifolia*, River Barrow at Borness Bridge, Co. Laois.	David Holyoak	2005
440 lower	*Cinclidotus riparius*, Stanford Bridge, England.	Richard Lansdown	2006
441	*Tayloria tenuis*, Schwarzwald, Germany.	Michael Lüth	2002
443	*Tetraplodon angustatus*, Vorarlberg, Freiburger Hütte, Austria.	Michael Lüth	2002
444	*Paludella squarrosa*, west of Crossmolina, Co. Mayo.	Neil Lockhart	2010
445	*Meesia uliginosa*, south-east of Rosepenna, Co. Donegal.	David Holyoak	2002
446	*Meesia triquetra*, Estonia.	Michael Lüth	2003
447	*Amblyodon dealbatus*, Truska, Co. Galway.	David Holyoak	2004
448 upper	*Zygodon rupestris*, near Upper Lake, Killarney, Co. Kerry.	David Holyoak	2006
448 lower	*Orthotrichum rivulare*, west of Steps Bridge, South Devon, England.	David Holyoak	2002
449	*Orthotrichum sprucei*, Cine vadisi, Turkey.	Michael Lüth	2007
450	*Orthotrichum stramineum*, Culbone, South Somerset, England.	David Holyoak	2007
452	*Orthotrichum pallens*, Weardale, Durham, England.	Nick Hodgetts	2004
453	*Ulota coarctata*, north-west of Loo Bridge, Co. Kerry.	David Holyoak	2005
454	*Ulota drummondii*, north Troendelag, Steinkjer, Norway.	Michael Lüth	2004
456	*Hedwigia ciliata* var. *ciliata*, Sgilloge Loughs, Co. Waterford.	Nick Hodgetts	2007
457	*Hedwigia integrifolia*, Glengarriff, Co. Cork.	David Holyoak	2006
458	*Catoscopium nigritum*, Lough Doo, Achill Island, Co. Mayo.	Robert Thompson	2010
460	*Plagiopus oederianus*, Penyghent Gill, England.	John Birks	1965
461	*Bartramia halleriana*, Ness Glen, Ayrshire, Scotland.	Des Callaghan	2010
462	*Bartramia ithyphylla*, Lough Muskry, Co. Tipperary.	Nick Hodgetts	2005
463	*Philonotis rigida*, Porthmeor Cove, West Cornwall, England.	David Holyoak	2003
465	*Philonotis arnellii*, Övertorneå, Norrbotten, Sweden.	Tomas Hallingbäck	2003
466 upper	*Philonotis caespitosa*, Whitewater Bridge, Co. Londonderry.	David Holyoak	2002
466 lower	*Philonotis tomentella*, Bulbin Mountain, Co. Donegal.	David Holyoak	2004
468	*Philonotis cernua*, Lough Coomasaharn, Co. Kerry.	Alan Orange	1951 (h)
469 upper	*Plagiobryum zieri*, Muckanaght, Co. Galway.	David Holyoak	2004
469 lower	*Anomobryum concinnatum*, Knocknarea, Co. Sligo.	Robert Thompson	2011
470	*Bryum marratii*, south of Mallaranny, Co. Mayo.	David Holyoak	2003
472	*Bryum warneum*, north of Fahan, Co. Donegal.	David Holyoak	2002
473	*Bryum calophyllum*, Dooaghtry, Co. Mayo.	David Holyoak	2003
475	*Bryum uliginosum*, east edge of Island Lake, Co. Mayo.	David Holyoak	2003
476	*Bryum turbinatum*, Vorarlberg, Freiburger Hütte, Austria.	Michael Lüth	2002
477	Lough Gall, Valley, Achill Island, Co. Mayo.	Neil Lockhart	2011
478	*Bryum salinum*, Iceland NBS, Iceland.	Michael Lüth	2009
479	*Bryum knowltonii*, Burnham Overy Staithe, West Norfolk, England.	David Holyoak	2003
481	*Bryum intermedium*, Whitebay Point, Co. Antrim.	David Holyoak	2008
482	*Bryum donianum*, Knockmahon, Co. Waterford.	David Holyoak	2008
483 upper	*Bryum elegans*, Worsaw Hill, Lancashire, England.	Des Callaghan	2010

Page	Subject	Photographer	Year
483 lower	Cloontyprughlish, Co. Leitrim.	David Holyoak	2008
484	*Bryum moravicum*, Bunge, Gotland, Sweden.	Tomas Hallingbäck	2002
485	*Bryum torquescens*, Ghajn Tuffieha, Malta.	David Holyoak	2005
487	*Bryum creberrimum*, Lillvallen, Suljätten, Jämtland, Sweden.	Tomas Hallingbäck	2002
488 upper	*Bryum pallescens*, south-west of Doonbeakin, Co. Sligo.	David Holyoak	2002
488 lower	*Bryum caespiticium*, east of Easton, Isle of Portland, Dorset, England.	David Holyoak	2003
489	North-west of Keel Bridge, Lough Carra, Co. Mayo.	Neil Lockhart	2011
490 upper	*Bryum gemmiferum*, Annaghmore Lough, Co. Roscommon.	David Holyoak	2002
490 lower	*Bryum dyffrynense*, north of Lough Nagreany, Co. Donegal.	David Holyoak	2002
491 upper	*Bryum violaceum*, Weston Underwood, Buckinghamshire, England.	David Holyoak	2003
491 lower	*Bryum tenuisetum*, Germany.	Michael Lüth	2007
492	Lackagh River, Co. Donegal.	David Holyoak	2002
493 upper	*Bryum bornholmense*, Lizard downs, West Cornwall, England.	Tomas Hallingbäck	2003
493 lower	*Bryum riparium*, north-east corrie, Mweelrea, Co. Mayo.	David Holyoak	2003
495	*Bryum gemmiparum*, north-west of Keel Bridge, Lough Carra, Co. Mayo.	David Holyoak	2003
496 upper	*Rhodobryum roseum*, east of Cong, Co. Mayo.	David Holyoak	2003
496 lower	*Pohlia elongata* var. *elongata*, Bulbin Mountain, Co. Donegal.	David Holyoak	2002
497	*Pohlia elongata* var. *greenii*, Lough Curra, Galty Mountains, Co. Tipperary.	Nick Hodgetts	2005
498 upper	*Pohlia cruda*, Bulbin Mountain, Co. Donegal.	David Holyoak	2002
498 lower	*Pohlia drummondii*, Bulbin Mountain, Co. Donegal.	David Holyoak	2002
499	*Pohlia filum*, Whitewater Bridge, Co. Londonderry.	David Holyoak	2002
500	*Pohlia andalusica*, south of Lower Ashton, South Devon, England.	David Holyoak	2002
502 upper	*Pohlia proligera*, Lilla Dyngdalen, Bräcke, Jämtland, Sweden.	Tomas Hallingbäck	2001
502 lower	*Pohlia proligera*, Lilla Dyngdalen, Bräcke, Jämtland, Sweden.	Tomas Hallingbäck	2001
503 upper	*Pohlia lutescens*, Gosford Forest Park, Co. Armagh.	David Holyoak	2002
503 lower	*Pohlia lescuriana*, Northrhine-Westphalia, Germany.	Jan-Peter Frahm	2007
505 upper	*Pohlia wahlenbergii* var. *glacialis*, South Troendelag, Dovrefjell, Norway.	Michael Lüth	2004
505 lower	*Pohlia wahlenbergii* var. *calcarea* Soldier's Hill, Malin, Co. Donegal.	Neil Lockhart	2002 (h)
506 upper	*Epipterygium tozeri*, St Mary's, Isles of Scilly, England.	David Holyoak	2003
506 lower	*Mnium thomsonii*, Cloontyprughlish, Glenade, Co. Leitrim.	David Holyoak	2008
507 upper	*Mnium marginatum* var. *marginatum*, Cloontyprughlish, Glenade, Co. Leitrim.	Neil Lockhart	2001
507 lower	*Cinclidium stygium*, Scragh Bog, Co. Westmeath.	Neil Lockhart	2004
509 upper	*Rhizomnium pseudopunctatum*, Coolturk, Co. Mayo.	Robert Thompson	2010
509 lower	*Plagiomnium cuspidatum*, Schwarzwald, Germany.	Michael Lüth	2003
510	*Aulacomnium androgynum*, Lindow Common, Cheshire, England.	Des Callaghan	2006
511	*Orthodontium gracile*, Penns Rocks, England.	John Birks	1967
512	*Leptotheca gaudichaudii* var. *gaudichaudii*, Garinish Island, Co. Kerry.	David Holyoak	2008
513 upper	*Calomnion complanatum*, Garinish Island, Co. Kerry.	David Holyoak	2008
513 lower	*Calyptrochaeta apiculata*, Tresco, Isles of Scilly, England.	David Holyoak	2003
514	*Daltonia splachnoides*, Killarney, Co. Kerry.	Robert Thompson	2010
515	*Cyclodictyon laetevirens*, Lough Gouragh, Co. Kerry.	Neil Lockhart	2009
516	Crags with *Cyclodictyon laetevirens*, above Lough Gouragh, Co. Kerry.	Neil Lockhart	2009
517 upper	*Hypopterygium immigrans*, Plate 463, Journal of Botany, 42 (1904).	Neil Lockhart	2010
517 lower	*Fontinalis antipyretica* var. *gracilis*, Dozmary Pool, East Cornwall, England.	David Holyoak	2009
518 upper	*Fontinalis antipyretica* var. *cymbifolia*, Lough Ree, Co. Longford.	David Holyoak	2007
518 lower	*Campyliadelphus elodes*, Ainsdale Dunes, Merseyside, England.	Des Callaghan	2010
519 upper	*Amblystegium confervoides*, Monawilkin, Co. Fermanagh.	David Holyoak	2008
519 lower	*Hygroamblystegium fluviatile*, near Hillsford Bridge, North Devon, England.	David Holyoak	2009
520 upper	*Hygroamblystegium varium*, Oberrheinebene, Blankenloch, Germany.	Michael Lüth	2009
520 lower	*Hygroamblystegium humile*, Keel, Co. Roscommon.	Nick Hodgetts	2002
522	*Conardia compacta*, Rocky Valley, East Cornwall, England.	Des Callaghan	2010
523	*Drepanocladus sendtneri*, Västergötland, Österplana, Sweden.	Michael Lüth	2009
524	*Tomentypnum nitens*, Coolturk, Co. Mayo.	Robert Thompson	2010
526	*Hygrohypnum duriusculum*, south-east of Lough Bellawaum, Mweelrea, Co. Mayo.	David Holyoak	2003
527	*Pseudocalliergon lycopodioides*, Inishcoog, Co. Mayo.	David Holyoak	2003
528	*Pseudocalliergon trifarium*, north-west of Gortachalla Lough, Co. Galway.	David Holyoak	2004

Page	Subject	Photographer	Year
530	*Hamatocaulis vernicosus*, Lough Mask, Co. Galway.	Neil Lockhart	2002
531	*Abietinella abietina* var. *abietina*, Ballymaclary, Co. Londonderry.	David Holyoak	2008
533 upper	*Abietinella abietina* var. *hystricosa*, Ballymaclary, Co. Londonderry.	David Holyoak	2008
533 lower	*Thuidium recognitum*, The Umbra, Co. Londonderry.	David Holyoak	2008
535 upper	*Plasteurhynchium striatulum*, Alpi Apuanae, Italy.	Michael Lüth	2004
535 lower	*Platyhypnidium lusitanicum*, above Porthmeor Cove, West Cornwall.	David Holyoak	2003
536 upper	*Rhynchostegium megapolitanum*, North Bull, Co. Dublin.	David Holyoak	2004
536 lower	*Rhynchostegiella curviseta*, Alpi Apuanae, Italy.	Michael Lüth	2004
537	*Oxyrrhynchium schleicheri*, Luxembourg.	Michael Lüth	2003
538	Keeper Hill, Co. Tipperary.	Robert Thompson	2010
539 upper	*Oxyrrhynchium speciosum*, Formby Dunes, England.	Des Callaghan	2005
539 lower	*Scleropodium cespitans*, Lough Fern, Co. Donegal.	David Holyoak	2002
540	*Scleropodium touretii*, near Botallack, West Cornwall, England.	David Holyoak	2003
541	*Eurhynchiastrum pulchellum* var. *diversifolium*, The Storr, Skye, Scotland.	Nick Hodgetts	2004
543	*Brachytheciastrum velutinum*, Schwarzwald, Ruine Falkenstein, Germany.	Michael Lüth	2005
544 upper	*Taxiphyllum wissgrillii*, Knocknarea Glen, Co. Sligo.	Robert Thompson	2011
544 lower	*Hypnum uncinulatum*, Killarney, Co. Kerry.	Robert Thompson	2010
546 upper	*Hypnum callichroum*, Kärnten, Nassfeld, Austria.	Michael Lüth	2007
546 lower	*Ptilium crista-castrensis*, Kindrogan, Scotland.	Gordon Rothero	2003
548 upper	*Ctenidium molluscum* var. *robustum*, Mourne Mountains, Co. Down.	Alan Orange	1917 (h)
548 lower	Slievelamagan, Mourne Mountains, Co. Down.	Robert Thompson	2007
549 upper	*Heterocladium wulfsbergii*, Draynes Wood, Cornwall, England.	Des Callaghan	2010
549 lower	*Pterigynandrum filiforme*, Suffolk, England.	Ron Porley	2005
551	*Rhytidiadelphus subpinnatus*, Nedd Fechan valley, Breconshire, Wales.	Graham Motley	2005
552 upper	*Hylocomiastrum umbratum*, Ben Hee, Scotland.	Des Callaghan	2006
552 lower	*Rhytidium rugosum*, The Umbra, Co. Londonderry.	David Holyoak	2008
554	*Myurella julacea*, Stilfser Joch, Mt. Scorrluzzo, Italy.	Michael Lüth	2006
555 upper	*Platydictya jungermannioides*, Cloontyprughlish, Glenade, Co. Leitrim.	David Holyoak	2008
555 lower	*Orthothecium rufescens*, south of Aghadunvane, Co. Leitrim.	David Holyoak	2005
556	*Plagiothecium latebricola*, Freiburg, Mooswald, Germany.	Michael Lüth	2002
557 upper	*Plagiothecium denticulatum* var. *obtusifolium*, Curraheen River, Co. Kerry.	Nick Hodgetts	2006
557 lower	*Plagiothecium laetum*, Jura, Doubs, Switzerland.	Michael Lüth	2009
558	White Hill, Co. Wicklow.	Neil Lockhart	2011
559	*Plagiothecium curvifolium*, Glen of the Downs, Co. Wicklow.	Neil Lockhart	2008
560	*Plagiothecium platyphyllum*, Ben Hee, Scotland.	Des Callaghan	2006
562	*Plagiothecium cavifolium*, Bulbin Mountain, Co. Donegal.	David Holyoak	2002
563 upper	*Isopterygiopsis muelleriana*, Ben Hee, Scotland.	Des Callaghan	2006
563 lower	*Isopterygiopsis muelleriana*, Coomeeneragh Lake, Co. Kerry.	David Holyoak	2006
564 upper	*Hageniella micans*, Torc Cascade, Co. Kerry.	David Holyoak	2005
564 lower	*Sematophyllum demissum*, near Lauragh Bridge, Co. Kerry.	David Holyoak	2008
566	*Sematophyllum substrumulosum*, Rossdohan Island, Co. Kerry.	David Holyoak	2008
567	*Antitrichia curtipendula*, Coumshingaun Lough, Co. Waterford.	David Holyoak	2008
568	*Leptodon smithii*, west of Godolphin House, West Cornwall, England.	David Holyoak	2008
569	*Myurium hochstetteri*, Loch Coruisk, Skye, Scotland.	Nick Hodgetts	2010
574	*Scapania gymnostomophila*, Keel Bridge, Lough Carra, Co. Mayo.	Robert Thompson	2011
596	*Southbya tophacea*, found by NL at Island Lake, Co. Mayo, whilst this book was in press.	Robert Thompson	2011

APPENDIX III. Protected areas

Note: Protected areas with different designations often have overlapping boundaries, so the same bryophyte population can appear more than once in this list.

Arroo Mountain SAC (IE0001403): *Cinclidium stygium* (VU); *Didymodon maximus* (NT); *Hymenostylium recurvirostrum* var. *insigne* (NT); *Schistidium robustum* (DD); *Schistidium trichodon* (VU); *Seligeria oelandica* (VU); *Timmia norvegica* (VU)

Ballinskelligs Bay and Inny Estuary SAC (IE0000335): *Petalophyllum ralfsii* (LC)

Ballinturly Turlough SAC (IE0000588): *Drepanocladus sendtneri* (NT)

Ballyness Bay SAC (IE0001090): *Bryum marratii* (LC)

Bellacorick Bog Complex SAC (IE0001922): *Cephalozia pleniceps* (VU); *Leiocolea rutheana* var. *rutheana* (EN); *Paludella squarrosa* (CR); *Pseudocalliergon lycopodioides* (VU); *Sphagnum warnstorfii* (VU); *Tomentypnum nitens* (VU)

Bellacorick Iron Flush SAC (IE0000466): *Tomentypnum nitens* (VU)

Ben Bulben, Gleniff and Glenade Complex SAC (IE0000623): *Bryum elegans* (VU); *Cinclidium stygium* (VU); *Daltonia splachnoides* (LC); *Didymodon maximus* (NT); *Dumortiera hirsuta* (NT); *Encalypta alpina* (VU); *Hymenostylium recurvirostrum* var. *insigne* (NT); *Lejeunea mandonii* (EN); *Marchantia polymorpha* subsp. *montivagans* (EN); *Myurella julacea* (EN); *Scapania cuspuligera* (VU); *Schistidium robustum* (DD); *Seligeria oelandica* (VU); *Timmia norvegica* (VU)

Binevenagh SAC (UK0030089): *Bartramia ithyphylla* (VU); *Rhytidium rugosum* (VU)

Black Head-Poulsallagh Complex SAC (IE0000020): *Didymodon acutus* (EN); *Petalophyllum ralfsii* (LC)

Blackwater River (Cork/Waterford) SAC (IE0002170): *Dumortiera hirsuta* (NT); *Fissidens fontanus* (VU); *Orthotrichum sprucei* (VU); *Schistidium elegantulum* subsp. *elegantulum* (DD); *Telaranea europaea* (NT)

Blackwater River (Kerry) SAC (IE0002173): *Dumortiera hirsuta* (NT); *Philonotis rigida* (VU)

Boleybrack Mountain SAC (IE0002032): *Aulacomnium androgynum* (VU); *Daltonia splachnoides* (LC); *Dicranodontium asperulum* (VU)

Broadhaven Bay SAC (IE0000472): *Catoscopium nigritum* (NT)

Bunduff Lough and Machair/Trawalua/Mullaghmore SAC (IE0000625): *Petalophyllum ralfsii* (LC)

Caha Mountains SAC (IE0000093): *Campylopus shawii* (NT); *Cyclodictyon laetevirens* (NT)

Carlingford Mountain SAC (IE0000453): *Campylopus subulatus* (VU); *Grimmia decipiens* (NT); *Grimmia ramondii* (NT); *Hedwigia integrifolia* (VU); *Leiocolea bantriensis* (NT); *Marsupella funckii* (NT); *Pogonatum nanum* (EN)

Carrowbehy/Caher Bog SAC (IE0000597): *Cephalozia pleniceps* (VU); *Sphagnum flexuosum* (VU); *Sphagnum subsecundum* (NT); *Sphagnum teres* (NT); *Sphagnum warnstorfii* (VU)

Carrowmore Lake Complex SAC (IE0000476): *Hamatocaulis vernicosus* (NT)

Castlemaine Harbour SAC (IE0000343): *Bryum marratii* (LC); *Petalophyllum ralfsii* (LC)

Castletaylor Complex SAC (IE0000242): *Drepanocladus sendtneri* (NT); *Grimmia dissimulata* (VU); *Pseudocalliergon lycopodioides* (VU)

Castletownshend SAC (IE0001547): *Cephalozia crassifolia* (EN); *Cephaloziella turneri* (VU)

Clara Bog SAC (IE0000572): *Cephalozia loitlesbergeri* (VU); *Tetraplodon angustatus* (DD)

Clare Glen SAC (IE0000930): *Dumortiera hirsuta* (NT)

Clew Bay Complex SAC (IE0001482): *Bryum marratii* (LC)

Clogher Head SAC (IE0001459): *Tortula modica* (VU)

Cloghernagore Bog and Glenveagh National Park SAC (IE0002047): *Adelanthus lindenbergianus* (VU); *Aneura mirabilis* (VU); *Bazzania pearsonii* (VU); *Bryum tenuisetum* (DD); *Ditrichum zonatum* (EN); *Grimmia atrata* (EN); *Marsupella sprucei* (VU); *Scapania ornithopodioides* (VU); *Schistidium agassizii* (VU); *Telaranea europaea* (NT)

Cloonee and Inchiquin Loughs, Uragh Wood SAC (IE0001342): *Aneura mirabilis* (VU); *Bryum moravicum* (CR); *Campylopus shawii* (NT); *Hypnum uncinulatum* (NT); *Lejeunea flava* subsp. *moorei* (VU); *Sematophyllum demissum* (NT)

Comeragh Mountains SAC (IE0001952): *Andreaea megistospora* (VU); *Antitrichia curtipendula* (NT); *Barbilophozia atlantica* (EN); *Bartramia ithyphylla* (VU); *Grimmia muehlenbeckii* (DD); *Hamatocaulis vernicosus* (NT); *Hedwigia ciliata* var. *ciliata* (VU); *Hedwigia integrifolia* (VU); *Marsupella sphacelata* (VU); *Plagiothecium platyphyllum* (VU); *Solenostoma paroicum* (NT); *Sphagnum skyense* (DD)

Connemara Bog Complex SAC (IE0002034): *Hamatocaulis vernicosus* (NT); *Pseudocalliergon trifarium* (VU); *Sphagnum flexuosum* (VU); *Sphagnum strictum* (DD); *Sphagnum warnstorfii* (VU); *Tomentypnum nitens* (VU)

Coolrain Bog SAC (IE0002332): *Cephalozia loitlesbergeri* (VU)

Corraun Plateau SAC (IE0000485): *Adelanthus lindenbergianus* (VU); *Dicranodontium uncinatum* (VU); *Molendoa warburgii* (VU)

Croaghaun/Slievemore SAC (IE0001955): *Adelanthus lindenbergianus* (VU); *Bazzania pearsonii* (VU); *Bryum riparium* (EN); *Cyclodictyon laetevirens* (NT); *Dicranodontium uncinatum* (VU); *Geocalyx graveolens* (EN); *Marsupella funckii* (NT); *Marsupella sprucei* (VU); *Mastigophora woodsii* (NT); *Plagiothecium cavifolium* (VU); *Scapania lingulata* (DD); *Scapania ornithopodioides* (VU); *Telaranea europaea* (NT); *Tritomaria exsecta* (VU)

Cuilcagh Mountain SAC (UK0016603): *Dicranodontium asperulum* (VU); *Sphenolobopsis pearsonii* (NT)

Cuilcagh-Anierin Uplands SAC (IE0000584): *Dicranodontium asperulum* (VU); *Discelium nudum* (NT); *Philonotis arnellii* (EN)

Cummeen Strand/Drumcliff Bay (Sligo Bay) SAC (IE0000627): *Didymodon acutus* (EN)

Derryclogher (Knockboy) Bog SAC (IE0001873): *Grimmia anomala* (EN); *Racomitrium macounii* subsp. *alpinum* (VU)

Doogort Machair/Lough Doo SAC (IE0001497): *Bryum calophyllum* (EN); *Bryum dyffrynense* (NT); *Catoscopium nigritum* (NT); *Leiocolea gillmanii* (VU); *Petalophyllum ralfsii* (LC); *Scapania cuspiduligera* (VU)

East Burren Complex SAC (IE0001926): *Cephalozia pleniceps* (VU); *Cephaloziella spinigera* (DD); *Cephaloziella stellulifera* (NT); *Cinclidium stygium* (VU); *Drepanocladus sendtneri* (NT); *Grimmia dissimulata* (VU); *Leptodon smithii* (EN); *Pseudocalliergon lycopodioides* (VU); *Pseudocalliergon trifarium* (VU)

Eastern Mournes SAC (UK0016615): *Cladopodiella francisci* (VU); *Marsupella sprucei* (VU)

Fortwilliam Turlough SAC (IE0000448): *Ephemerum cohaerens* (VU); *Pseudocalliergon lycopodioides* (VU)

Galtee Mountains SAC (IE0000646): *Bartramia ithyphylla* (VU); *Pohlia elongata* var. *greenii* (EN); *Sphenolobopsis pearsonii* (NT)

Garron Plateau SAC (UK0016606): *Cinclidium stygium* (VU)

Glanmore Bog SAC (IE0001879): *Dumortiera hirsuta* (NT); *Lejeunea hibernica* (NT); *Paraleptodontium recurvifolium* (NT); *Radula holtii* (NT); *Telaranea europaea* (NT)

Glen of The Downs SAC (IE0000719): *Cephaloziella turneri* (VU); *Plagiothecium curvifolium* (VU)

Glenamoy Bog Complex SAC (IE0000500): *Bryum marratii* (LC); *Bryum warneum* (EN); *Catoscopium nigritum* (NT); *Hamatocaulis vernicosus* (NT); *Petalophyllum ralfsii* (LC); *Tomentypnum nitens* (VU)

Glendine Wood SAC (IE0002324): *Dumortiera hirsuta* (NT); *Fissidens rivularis* (VU)

Glengarriff Harbour and Woodland SAC (IE0000090): *Daltonia splachnoides* (LC); *Fissidens polyphyllus* (VU); *Hedwigia integrifolia* (VU); *Lejeunea flava* subsp. *moorei* (VU); *Sematophyllum demissum* (NT); *Sphagnum flexuosum* (VU); *Telaranea europaea* (NT); *Tritomaria exsecta* (VU)

Gweedore Bay and Islands SAC (IE0001141): *Bryum marratii* (LC); *Catoscopium nigritum* (NT); *Petalophyllum ralfsii* (LC)

Holdenstown Bog SAC (IE0001757): *Hamatocaulis vernicosus* (NT)

Horn Head and Rinclevan SAC (IE0000147): *Acrobolbus wilsonii* (VU); *Catoscopium nigritum* (NT); *Geocalyx graveolens* (EN); *Petalophyllum ralfsii* (LC); *Scapania cuspiduligera* (VU)

Inishkea Islands SAC (IE0000507): *Petalophyllum ralfsii* (LC)

Inishmore Island SAC (IE0000213): *Bryum caespiticium* (VU)

Keel Machair/Menaun Cliffs SAC (IE0001513): *Bryum calophyllum* (EN); *Bryum marratii* (LC); *Catoscopium nigritum* (NT); *Fossombronia fimbriata* (VU); *Petalophyllum ralfsii* (LC); *Philonotis rigida* (VU); *Rhodobryum roseum* (NT); *Tortella inclinata* (EN); *Tortula modica* (VU)

Kenmare River SAC (IE0002158): *Cephaloziella integerrima* (VU); *Cephaloziella massalongi* (VU); *Cephaloziella nicholsonii* (VU); *Cephaloziella stellulifera* (NT); *Ditrichum cornubicum* (CR); *Ditrichum lineare* (CR); *Pohlia andalusica* (EN); *Scopelophila cataractae* (VU)

Kilcarren-Firville Bog SAC (IE0000647): *Cephaloziella spinigera* (DD)

Killarney National Park, Macgillycuddy's Reeks and Caragh River Catchment SAC (IE0000365): *Acrobolbus wilsonii* (VU); *Amphidium lapponicum* (VU); *Andreaea megistospora* (VU); *Aneura mirabilis* (VU); *Arctoa fulvella* (VU); *Bazzania pearsonii* (VU); *Campylopus shawii* (NT); *Campylostelium saxicola* (EN); *Cephalozia crassifolia* (EN); *Cephaloziella massalongi* (VU); *Cephaloziella stellulifera* (NT); *Cyclodictyon laetevirens* (NT); *Daltonia splachnoides* (LC); *Dumortiera hirsuta* (NT); *Fissidens crispus* (DD); *Fissidens fontanus* (VU); *Fissidens polyphyllus* (VU); *Fissidens rivularis* (VU); *Hypnum uncinulatum* (NT); *Isopterygiopsis muelleriana* (VU); *Lejeunea flava* subsp. *moorei* (VU); *Lejeunea hibernica* (NT); *Marsupella sprucei* (VU); *Mastigophora woodsii* (NT); *Moerckia hibernica* (DD); *Paraleptodontium recurvifolium* (NT); *Plagiochila heterophylla* (EN); *Radula carringtonii* (NT); *Radula holtii* (NT); *Scapania nimbosa* (DD); *Scapania ornithopodioides* (VU); *Sematophyllum demissum* (NT); *Sematophyllum substrumulosum* (VU); *Sphagnum affine* (VU); *Sphagnum strictum* (DD); *Sphenolobopsis pearsonii* (NT); *Telaranea europaea* (NT); *Tritomaria exsecta* (VU); *Ulota coarctata* (CR)

Knocksink Wood SAC (IE0000725): *Fissidens rufulus* (EN)

Largalinny SAC (UK0030045): *Calypogeia integristipula* (EN)

Leannan River SAC (IE0002176): *Schistidium agassizii* (VU)

Lisduff Turlough SAC (IE0000609): *Drepanocladus sendtneri* (NT)

Lough Carra/Mask Complex SAC (IE0001774): *Bryum caespiticium* (VU); *Bryum gemmiparum* (VU); *Bryum knowltonii* (EN); *Ephemerum crassinervium* subsp. *rutheanum* (NT); *Ephemerum crassinervium* subsp. *sessile* (NT); *Ephemerum spinulosum* (EN); *Hamatocaulis vernicosus* (NT); *Pseudocalliergon lycopodioides* (VU); *Scapania gymnostomophila* (VU); *Weissia rostellata* (NT)

Lough Corrib SAC (IE0000297): *Drepanocladus sendtneri* (NT); *Grimmia decipiens* (NT); *Hamatocaulis vernicosus* (NT); *Pseudocalliergon trifarium* (VU)

Lough Fingall Complex SAC (IE0000606): *Pseudocalliergon lycopodioides* (VU)

Lough Funshinagh SAC (IE0000611): *Drepanocladus sendtneri* (NT)

Lough Gill SAC (IE0001976): *Fissidens monguillonii* (NT); *Orthotrichum sprucei* (VU)

Lough Hyne Nature Reserve and environs SAC (IE0000097): *Riccia crozalsii* (EN)

Lough Lurgeen Bog/Glenamaddy Turlough SAC (IE0000301): *Drepanocladus sendtneri* (NT); *Ephemerum cohaerens* (VU)

Lough Nagreany Dunes SAC (IE0000164): *Bryum marratii* (LC); *Catoscopium nigritum* (NT); *Thuidium recognitum* (VU)

Lough Oughter and Associated Loughs SAC (IE0000007): *Ephemerum crassinervium* subsp. *rutheanum* (NT); *Fissidens monguillonii* (NT); *Hygroamblystegium humile* (EN); *Weissia rostellata* (NT)

Lough Ree SAC (IE0000440): *Drepanocladus sendtneri* (NT); *Hygroamblystegium humile* (EN); *Pseudocalliergon lycopodioides* (VU)

Lough Swilly SAC (IE0002287): *Bryum warneum* (EN)

Lower River Shannon SAC (IE0002165): *Schistidium platyphyllum* (VU)

Lower River Suir SAC (IE0002137): *Leptodon smithii* (EN)

Magilligan SAC (UK0016613): *Abietinella abietina* var. *abietina* (EN); *Bryum torquescens* (VU); *Drepanocladus sendtneri* (NT); *Petalophyllum ralfsii* (LC); *Pseudocalliergon lycopodioides* (VU); *Rhytidium rugosum* (VU); *Thuidium recognitum* (VU)

Malahide Estuary SAC (IE0000205): *Racomitrium canescens* (VU)

Meenaguse Scragh SAC (IE0001880): *Gymnomitrion concinnatum* (EN); *Marsupella sphacelata* (VU); *Marsupella sprucei* (VU); *Philonotis tomentella* (VU)

Meentygrannagh Bog SAC (IE0000173): *Hamatocaulis vernicosus* (NT); *Sphagnum subsecundum* (NT); *Sphagnum teres* (NT); *Sphagnum warnstorfii* (VU); *Tomentypnum nitens* (VU)

Monawilkin SAC (UK0016619): *Bryum torquescens* (VU); *Schistidium elegantulum* subsp. *elegantulum* (DD); *Thuidium recognitum* (VU)

Mount Brandon SAC (IE0000375): *Acrobolbus wilsonii* (VU); *Adelanthus lindenbergianus* (VU); *Amphidium lapponicum* (VU); *Bazzania pearsonii* (VU); *Campylopus shawii* (NT); *Cyclodictyon laetevirens* (NT); *Dumortiera hirsuta* (NT); *Grimmia muehlenbeckii* (DD); *Lejeunea flava* subsp. *moorei* (VU); *Lejeunea hibernica* (NT); *Lejeunea mandonii* (EN); *Mastigophora woodsii* (NT); *Paraleptodontium recurvifolium* (NT); *Plagiothecium cavifolium* (VU); *Radula carringtonii* (NT); *Radula holtii* (NT); *Scapania gymnostomophila* (VU); *Scapania nimbosa* (DD); *Scapania ornithopodioides* (VU); *Sphenolobopsis pearsonii* (NT); *Tritomaria exsecta* (VU)

Muckish Mountain SAC (IE0001179): *Adelanthus lindenbergianus* (VU); *Bazzania pearsonii* (VU); *Brachydontium trichodes* (EN); *Lophozia opacifolia* (VU); *Scapania ornithopodioides* (VU)

Mullet/Blacksod Bay Complex SAC (IE0000470): *Bryum marratii* (LC); *Petalophyllum ralfsii* (LC)

Murlough SAC (UK0016612): *Racomitrium canescens* (VU); *Tortella inclinata* (EN)

Murvey Machair SAC (IE0002129): *Petalophyllum ralfsii* (LC)

Mweelrea/Sheeffry/Erriff Complex SAC (IE0001932): *Amphidium lapponicum* (VU); *Bazzania pearsonii* (VU); *Bryum calophyllum* (EN); *Bryum marratii* (LC); *Bryum riparium* (EN); *Catoscopium nigritum* (NT); *Dicranodontium uncinatum* (VU); *Ditrichum zonatum* (EN); *Fissidens serrulatus* (VU); *Fossombronia caespitiformis* subsp. *multispira* (DD); *Hygrohypnum duriusculum* (CR); *Lejeunea flava* subsp. *moorei* (VU); *Lejeunea hibernica* (NT); *Lophozia opacifolia* (VU); *Marsupella sprucei* (VU); *Mastigophora woodsii* (NT); *Oedipodium griffithianum* (CR); *Paraleptodontium recurvifolium* (NT); *Petalophyllum ralfsii* (LC); *Philonotis cernua* (CR); *Philonotis rigida* (VU); *Philonotis tomentella* (VU); *Plagiochila carringtonii* (EN); *Pogonatum nanum* (EN); *Ptilium crista-castrensis* (CR); *Racomitrium macounii* subsp. *alpinum* (VU); *Radula holtii* (NT); *Scapania nimbosa* (DD); *Scapania ornithopodioides* (VU); *Scapania subalpina* (DD); *Solenostoma paroicum* (NT); *Sphagnum skyense* (DD); *Telaranea europaea* (NT)

Newport River SAC (IE0002144): *Ephemerum crassinervium* subsp. *sessile* (NT)

North Antrim Coast SAC (UK0030224): *Seligeria calcarea* (VU)

North Dublin Bay SAC (IE0000206): *Bryum intermedium* (EN); *Bryum marratii* (LC); *Bryum uliginosum* (EN); *Bryum warneum* (EN); *Didymodon umbrosus* (VU); *Petalophyllum ralfsii* (LC); *Rhynchostegium megapolitanum* (NT)

North Inishowen Coast SAC (IE0002012): *Bryum marratii* (LC); *Bryum torquescens* (VU); *Bryum uliginosum* (EN); *Sphagnum strictum* (DD); *Thuidium recognitum* (VU)

Omey Island Machair SAC (IE0001309): *Petalophyllum ralfsii* (LC)

Owenduff/Nephin Complex SAC (IE0000534): *Bryum riparium* (EN); *Dicranodontium uncinatum* (VU); *Hamatocaulis vernicosus* (NT); *Paraleptodontium recurvifolium* (NT); *Tomentypnum nitens* (VU)

Ox Mountains Bogs SAC (IE0002006): *Grimmia anomala* (EN); *Sphagnum strictum* (DD)

Pollardstown Fen SAC (IE0000396): *Tomentypnum nitens* (VU)

Raheenmore Bog SAC (IE0000582): *Cephalozia loitlesbergeri* (VU)

River Barrow and River Nore SAC (IE0002162): *Cephaloziella turneri* (VU); *Didymodon umbrosus* (VU); *Fissidens exilis* (VU); *Grimmia orbicularis* (VU)

River Boyne and River Blackwater SAC (IE0002299): *Tortula lanceola* (CR)

River Faughan and Tributaries SAC (UK0030361): *Fissidens monguillonii* (NT)

River Finn SAC (IE0002301): *Andreaea megistospora* (VU)

River Foyle and Tributaries SAC (UK0030320): *Orthotrichum sprucei* (VU)

River Moy SAC (IE0002298): *Bryum intermedium* (EN); *Bryum uliginosum* (EN); *Pseudocalliergon lycopodioides* (VU)

River Shannon Callows SAC (IE0000216): *Brachytheciastrum velutinum* (EN); *Ephemerum crassinervium* subsp. *rutheanum* (NT); *Fissidens monguillonii* (NT)

Roaringwater Bay and Islands SAC (IE0000101): *Cephaloziella stellulifera* (NT); *Riccia crozalsii* (EN); *Scleropodium touretii* (EN)

Scragh Bog SAC (IE0000692): *Cinclidium stygium* (VU); *Hamatocaulis vernicosus* (NT); *Ricciocarpos natans* (NT); *Tomentypnum nitens* (VU)

Sheephaven SAC (IE0001190): *Bryum marratii* (LC); *Catoscopium nigritum* (NT); *Cephaloziella turneri* (VU); *Leiocolea gillmanii* (VU); *Meesia uliginosa* (EN); *Petalophyllum ralfsii* (LC)

Skealoghan Turlough SAC (IE0000541): *Drepanocladus sendtneri* (NT)

Slaney River Valley SAC (IE0000781): *Grimmia orbicularis* (VU); *Orthotrichum sprucei* (VU); *Weissia brachycarpa* var. *brachycarpa* (DD)

Slieve Bernagh Bog SAC (IE0002312): *Daltonia splachnoides* (LC)

Slieve Bloom Mountains SAC (IE0000412): *Campylopus subulatus* (VU)

Slieve League SAC (IE0000189): *Arctoa fulvella* (VU); *Campylopus subulatus* (VU); *Ditrichum zonatum* (EN); *Gymnomitrion concinnatum* (EN); *Marsupella sphacelata* (VU); *Philonotis rigida* (VU); *Scapania gymnostomophila* (VU)

Slieve Mish Mountains SAC (IE0002185): *Bazzania pearsonii* (VU); *Daltonia splachnoides* (LC); *Dumortiera hirsuta* (NT); *Mastigophora woodsii* (NT); *Moerckia hibernica* (DD); *Paraleptodontium recurvifolium* (NT); *Radula carringtonii* (NT); *Scapania ornithopodioides* (VU)

Slieve Tooey/Tormore Island/Loughros Beg Bay SAC (IE0000190): *Lophozia opacifolia* (VU); *Scapania cuspiduligera* (VU)

Slyne Head Peninsula SAC (IE0002074): *Bryum calophyllum* (EN); *Catoscopium nigritum* (NT); *Petalophyllum ralfsii* (LC); *Thuidium recognitum* (VU)

Spahill and Clomantagh Hill SAC (IE0000849): *Bryum torquescens* (VU); *Fissidens exilis* (VU)

Strangford Lough SAC (UK0016618): *Bryum intermedium* (EN)

Tacumshin Lake SAC (IE0000709): *Phascum cuspidatum* var. *piliferum* (DD)

The Twelve Bens/Garraun Complex SAC (IE0002031): *Acrobolbus wilsonii* (VU); *Adelanthus lindenbergianus* (VU); *Arctoa fulvella* (VU); *Bazzania pearsonii* (VU); *Cephalozia crassifolia* (EN); *Dicranodontium uncinatum* (VU); *Fossombronia caespitiformis* subsp. *multispira* (DD); *Lejeunea hibernica* (NT); *Lophozia opacifolia* (VU); *Marsupella funckii* (NT); *Marsupella sprucei* (VU); *Plagiochila carringtonii* (EN); *Pohlia elongata* var. *greenii* (EN); *Scapania ornithopodioides* (VU); *Solenostoma paroicum* (NT); *Sphagnum affine* (VU); *Sphenolobopsis pearsonii* (NT); *Telaranea europaea* (NT)

Tralee Bay and Magharees Peninsula, West to Cloghane SAC (IE0002070): *Drepanocladus sendtneri* (NT); *Petalophyllum ralfsii* (LC)

Tranarossan and Melmore Lough SAC (IE0000194): *Bryum marratii* (LC); *Petalophyllum ralfsii* (LC)

Tullaher Lough and Bog SAC (IE0002343): *Cephaloziella rubella* (VU); *Ephemerum crassinervium* subsp. *rutheanum* (NT)

Upper Lough Erne SAC (UK0016614): *Weissia brachycarpa* var. *brachycarpa* (DD)

West of Ardara/Maas Road SAC (IE0000197): *Bryum marratii* (LC); *Petalophyllum ralfsii* (LC)

Wicklow Mountains SAC (IE0002122): *Aneura mirabilis* (VU); *Barbilophozia barbata* (CR); *Brachydontium trichodes* (EN); *Cephaloziella massalongi* (VU); *Cephaloziella nicholsonii* (VU); *Cephaloziella stellulifera* (NT); *Ditrichum plumbicola* (EN); *Ditrichum zonatum* (EN); *Hedwigia integrifolia* (VU); *Marsupella sphacelata* (VU); *Marsupella sprucei* (VU); *Plagiothecium platyphyllum* (VU); *Racomitrium elongatum* (VU); *Rhabdoweisia fugax* (VU)

Williamstown Turloughs SAC (IE0002296): *Pseudocalliergon lycopodioides* (VU)

Ballynagrenia and Ballinderry Bog NHA (000674): *Cephaloziella spinigera* (DD)

Clonreher Bog NHA (002357): *Cephalozia loitlesbergeri* (VU)

Crockauns/Keelogyboy Bogs NHA (002435): *Didymodon maximus* (NT); *Hymenostylium recurvirostrum* var. *insigne* (NT); *Timmia norvegica* (VU)

Dough/Thur Mountains NHA (002384): *Brachydontium trichodes* (EN); *Discelium nudum* (NT); *Solenostoma paroicum* (NT)

Grageen Fen and Bog NHA (002186): *Tomentypnum nitens* (VU)

Ballyvergan Marsh pNHA (000078): *Aloina ambigua* (EN)

Ballyvoyle Head to Tramore pNHA (001693): *Cephaloziella massalongi* (VU); *Cephaloziella stellulifera* (NT); *Pohlia andalusica* (EN)

Bulbin Mountain pNHA (000120): *Gymnomitrion corallioides* (CR); *Myurella julacea* (EN); *Philonotis tomentella* (VU); *Plagiothecium cavifolium* (VU)

Carrickaport Lough pNHA (001920): *Fissidens fontanus* (VU); *Weissia rostellata* (NT)

Clare Island pNHA (000477): *Marsupella funckii* (NT); *Radula carringtonii* (NT)

Colgagh Lough pNHA (001658): *Drepanocladus sendtneri* (NT)

Croagh Patrick pNHA (000483): *Adelanthus lindenbergianus* (VU); *Andreaea megistospora* (VU); *Bazzania pearsonii* (VU); *Dicranodontium uncinatum* (VU); *Scapania ornithopodioides* (VU)

Dargle River Valley pNHA (001754): *Fissidens rufulus* (EN)

Dernasliggaun Wood pNHA (001253): *Sematophyllum demissum* (NT)

Doulus Head to Cooncrome Harbour pNHA (001350): *Cyclodictyon laetevirens* (NT)

Fin Lough (Roscommon) pNHA (001636): *Drepanocladus sendtneri* (NT); *Pseudocalliergon lycopodioides* (VU)

Garadice Lough Wood pNHA (001413): *Plagiothecium curvifolium* (VU); *Plagiothecium latebricola* (VU)

Glasshouse Lake pNHA (000983): *Ephemerum crassinervium* subsp. *sessile* (NT); *Fissidens monguillonii* (NT)

Great Sugar Loaf pNHA (001769): *Aneura mirabilis* (VU)

Lough Allua pNHA (001065): *Schistidium platyphyllum* (VU)

Lough Gowna pNHA (000992): *Ephemerum cohaerens* (VU); *Ephemerum crassinervium* subsp. *sessile* (NT)

Lough Rinn pNHA (001417): *Ephemerum cohaerens* (VU); *Ephemerum crassinervium* subsp. *rutheanum* (NT); *Fissidens monguillonii* (NT)

Maumtrasna Mountain Complex pNHA (000735): *Acrobolbus wilsonii* (VU); *Andreaea megistospora* (VU); *Bryum riparium* (EN); *Daltonia splachnoides* (LC); *Philonotis rigida* (VU); *Radula holtii* (NT)

Powerscourt Waterfall pNHA (001767): *Aulacomnium androgynum* (VU); *Orthotrichum stramineum* (VU); *Rhabdoweisia fugax* (VU)

Ravensdale Plantation pNHA (001805): *Orthotrichum stramineum* (VU)

Rostellan Lough, Aghada Shore and Poulnabibe Inlet pNHA (001076): *Grimmia orbicularis* (VU)

Roughty River Estuary pNHA (002092): *Solenostoma paroicum* (NT)

Shad Lough pNHA (001648): *Drepanocladus sendtneri* (NT)

Vartry Reservoir pNHA (001771): *Riccia huebeneriana* (DD)

Binevenagh ASSI (ASSI212): *Bartramia ithyphylla* (VU); *Rhytidium rugosum* (VU)

Braade ASSI (ASSI108): *Aulacomnium androgynum* (VU); *Orthodontium gracile* (CR)

Cliffs of Magho ASSI (ASSI191): *Daltonia splachnoides* (LC); *Schistidium trichodon* (VU); *Seligeria oelandica* (VU)

Copeland Reservoir ASSI (ASSI345): *Ephemerum crassinervium* subsp. *sessile* (NT); *Physcomitrium sphaericum* (VU); *Weissia rostellata* (NT)

Cuilcagh Mountain ASSI (ASSI069): *Dicranodontium asperulum* (VU); *Sphenolobopsis pearsonii* (NT)

Downhill ASSI (ASSI068): *Metzgeria pubescens* (VU)

Eastern Mournes ASSI (ASSI095): *Cladopodiella francisci* (VU); *Marsupella sprucei* (VU)

Fair Head and Murlough Bay ASSI (ASSI330): *Hedwigia integrifolia* (VU); *Marsupella sprucei* (VU)

Garron Plateau ASSI (ASSI067): *Cinclidium stygium* (VU)

Glenariff Glen ASSI (ASSI335): *Leiocolea heterocolpos* (CR); *Philonotis rigida* (VU)

Inner Belfast Lough ASSI (ASSI029): *Racomitrium canescens* (VU)

Largalinny ASSI (ASSI111): *Calypogeia integristipula* (EN)

Little Deer Park ASSI (ASSI323): *Bryum intermedium* (EN); *Seligeria calcarea* (VU)

Lough Navar Scarps and Lakes ASSI: *Aulacomnium androgynum* (VU); *Calypogeia integristipula* (EN); *Daltonia splachnoides* (LC); *Geocalyx graveolens* (EN)

Magilligan ASSI (ASSI068): *Abietinella abietina* var. *abietina* (EN); *Bryum torquescens* (VU); *Drepanocladus sendtneri* (NT); *Petalophyllum ralfsii* (LC); *Pseudocalliergon lycopodioides* (VU); *Rhytidium rugosum* (VU); *Thuidium recognitum* (VU)

Monawilkin ASSI (ASSI013): *Bryum torquescens* (VU); *Schistidium elegantulum* subsp. *elegantulum* (DD); *Thuidium recognitum* (VU)

Murlough ASSI (ASSI089): *Racomitrium canescens* (VU); *Tortella inclinata* (EN)

Ness Wood ASSI (ASSI060): *Aulacomnium androgynum* (VU)

North Woodburn Reservoir ASSI (ASSI343): *Physcomitrium sphaericum* (VU); *Ephemerum spinulosum* (EN); *Weissia rostellata* (NT)

River Faughan and Tributaries ASSI (ASSI296): *Fissidens monguillonii* (NT)

Scrabo ASSI (ASSI091): *Brachydontium trichodes* (EN)

South Woodburn Reservoir ASSI (ASSI344): *Ephemerum crassinervium* subsp. *sessile* (NT); *Weissia rostellata* (NT)

Straidkilly ASSI (ASSI161): *Metzgeria pubescens* (VU)

Strangford Lough Part 3 ASSI (ASSI034): *Bryum intermedium* (EN)

Upper Lough Erne Trannish ASSI (ASSI094): *Weissia brachycarpa* var. *brachycarpa* (DD)

White Park Bay ASSI (ASSI107): *Seligeria calcarea* (VU)

White Rocks ASSI (ASSI174): *Bryum torquescens* (VU); *Seligeria calcarea* (VU)

Ballymaclary Nature Reserve: *Abietinella abietina* var. *abietina* (EN); *Drepanocladus sendtneri* (NT); *Petalophyllum ralfsii* (LC); *Pseudocalliergon lycopodioides* (VU); *Rhytidium rugosum* (VU); *Thuidium recognitum* (VU)

Binevenagh Nature Reserve: *Bartramia ithyphylla* (VU); *Rhytidium rugosum* (VU)

Bull Island Nature Reserve: *Bryum intermedium* (EN); *Bryum marratii* (LC); *Bryum uliginosum* (EN); *Bryum warneum* (EN); *Petalophyllum ralfsii* (LC); *Rhynchostegium megapolitanum* (NT)

Clara Bog Nature Reserve: *Cephalozia loitlesbergeri* (VU); *Tetraplodon angustatus* (DD)

Correl Glen Forest Nature Reserve: *Calypogeia integristipula* (EN)

Derrycunihy Wood Nature Reserve: *Hypnum uncinulatum* (NT); *Lejeunea flava* subsp. *moorei* (VU); *Sematophyllum demissum* (NT); *Telaranea europaea* (NT)

Glen of the Downs Nature Reserve: *Cephaloziella turneri* (VU); *Plagiothecium curvifolium* (VU)

Glenariff Nature Reserve: *Leiocolea heterocolpos* (CR); *Philonotis rigida* (VU)

Glendalough Nature Reserve: *Rhabdoweisia fugax* (VU)

Glenealo Valley Nature Reserve: *Barbilophozia barbata* (CR); *Cephaloziella massalongi* (VU); *Cephaloziella nicholsonii* (VU); *Cephaloziella stellulifera* (NT); *Ditrichum plumbicola* (EN); *Hedwigia integrifolia* (VU); *Racomitrium elongatum* (VU); *Rhabdoweisia fugax* (VU)

Glengarriff Wood Nature Reserve: *Fissidens polyphyllus* (VU); *Hedwigia integrifolia* (VU); *Lejeunea flava* subsp. *moorei* (VU); *Sematophyllum demissum* (NT); *Sphagnum flexuosum* (VU); *Telaranea europaea* (NT); *Tritomaria exsecta* (VU)

Knockomagh Wood Nature Reserve: *Riccia crozalsii* (EN)

Knocksink Wood Nature Reserve: *Fissidens rufulus* (EN)

Kyleadohir Nature Reserve: *Fissidens exilis* (VU)

Magilligan Point Nature Reserve: *Rhytidium rugosum* (VU)

Murlough Nature Reserve: *Racomitrium canescens* (VU); *Tortella inclinata* (EN)

Owenboy, Nephin Mor Forest Nature Reserve: *Cephalozia pleniceps* (VU)

Pollardstown Fen Nature Reserve: *Tomentypnum nitens* (VU)

Raheenmore Bog Nature Reserve: *Cephalozia loitlesbergeri* (VU)

Scragh Bog Nature Reserve: *Cinclidium stygium* (VU); *Hamatocaulis vernicosus* (NT); *Ricciocarpos natans* (NT); *Tomentypnum nitens* (VU)

Straidkilly Nature Reserve: *Metzgeria pubescens* (VU)

Uragh Wood Nature Reserve: *Aneura mirabilis* (VU); *Bryum moravicum* (CR); *Hypnum uncinulatum* (NT); *Lejeunea flava* subsp. *moorei* (VU); *Sematophyllum demissum* (NT)

Ballycroy National Park: *Bryum riparium* (EN); *Dicranodontium uncinatum* (VU); *Hamatocaulis vernicosus* (NT); *Paraleptodontium recurvifolium* (NT); *Tomentypnum nitens* (VU)

Burren National Park: *Drepanocladus sendtneri* (NT); *Grimmia dissimulata* (VU); *Leptodon smithii* (EN); *Pseudocalliergon lycopodioides* (VU); *Pseudocalliergon trifarium* (VU)

Connemara National Park: *Marsupella sprucei* (VU); *Sphenolobopsis pearsonii* (NT)

Glenveagh National Park: *Adelanthus lindenbergianus* (VU); *Aneura mirabilis* (VU); *Ditrichum zonatum* (EN); *Telaranea europaea* (NT)

Killarney National Park: *Acrobolbus wilsonii* (VU); *Aneura mirabilis* (VU); *Cephalozia crassifolia* (EN); *Cephaloziella massalongi* (VU); *Cephaloziella stellulifera* (NT); *Cyclodictyon laetevirens* (NT); *Daltonia splachnoides* (LC); *Dumortiera hirsuta* (NT); *Fissidens crispus* (DD); *Fissidens polyphyllus* (VU); *Fissidens rivularis* (VU); *Hypnum uncinulatum* (NT); *Lejeunea flava* subsp. *moorei* (VU); *Lejeunea hibernica* (NT); *Plagiochila heterophylla* (EN); *Radula carringtonii* (NT); *Radula holtii* (NT); *Sematophyllum demissum* (NT); *Sematophyllum substrumulosum* (VU); *Sphagnum affine* (VU); *Sphagnum strictum* (DD); *Telaranea europaea* (NT); *Tritomaria exsecta* (VU)

Wicklow Mountains National Park: *Barbilophozia barbata* (CR); *Cephaloziella massalongi* (VU); *Cephaloziella nicholsonii* (VU); *Cephaloziella stellulifera* (NT); *Ditrichum plumbicola* (EN); *Hedwigia integrifolia* (VU); *Marsupella sphacelata* (VU); *Marsupella sprucei* (VU); *Plagiothecium platyphyllum* (VU); *Racomitrium elongatum* (VU); *Rhabdoweisia fugax* (VU)

GLOSSARY

Terms defined here are those used in a specialised sense or those not in ordinary dictionaries. Cross references to other terms are underlined below where one definition refers to another.

For a detailed illustrated account of the terminology used to describe mosses and liverworts see Malcolm & Malcolm (2006).

abaxial   Side of leaf away from the axis; underside of leaf.

acrocarpous   Mosses in which sporophytes are usually produced at stem apex.

acumen   Tapering apex of leaf.

acuminate   Leaf apex that gradually tapers to point.

adaxial   Side of leaf towards axis; upperside of leaf.

alar cells   Cells at basal angle of leaf.

androecia   Male inflorescences.

angular cells   Cells at basal angle of leaf.

antheridia   Organ containing male gametes.

apiculate   With short abrupt point.

apiculus   Short abrupt point to leaf.

apophysis   Enlarged sterile basal part of capsule.

appendiculate   With short branches on cilia.

archegonia   Organ containing female gametes.

areolae   Geometric shapes on the upper surface of the thallus in some thallose liverworts.

areolation   The pattern or form of arrangement of leaf cells.

asexual reproduction   Reproduction other than from spores, e.g. from bulbils or gemmae.

attenuate   Gradually diminishing in width below the apex.

auricle   Well-defined group of enlarged or otherwise differentiated cells at basal angle of leaf.

autoicous   With male and female inflorescences borne on different branches of same plant.

awn   Hair-like point extending from leaf apex; 'hair-point'.

bilobed   Divided into two lobes.

bistratose   Two cells thick.

bract   Modified leaf associated with male or female inflorescence.

bryophytes   Mosses, liverworts and hornworts.

bulbil   Bulb-like or bud-like vegetative propagule, often with rudimentary leaves.

caducous   Falling off readily.

calciphile   Plants of basic habitats rich in calcium.

calyptra   Structure covering at least the apex of a developing capsule.

capsule   Spore-bearing structure of the sporophyte.

cernuous   Drooping at an angle between horizontal and vertically downwards.

cilia   Uniseriate hair-like structures between processes of endostome.

ciliate   With hair-like projections, e.g. on edge of a leaf.

circumneutral   Close to neutral in reaction (i.e. neither acidic nor basic).

clavate   Club-shaped.

clade   Evolutionary lineage.

cleistocarpous   Of capsules that do not dehisce, spores being liberated by decay of capsule wall.

clonal   Of plants that form a genetically uniform population.

columella   Central column of sterile tissue inside a moss capsule.

comal tuft   Rosette of leaves (usually enlarged) at shoot tip.

complanate   Of leaves or branches arranged in one plane.

confervoid   Fine and wispy, like filamentous green algae.

connate   Similar organs fused together although distinct in origin.

cortex   Outer layer of thin-walled cells around cells of central strand (in *Sphagnum*) or surrounding the medulla (in liverworts).

cortical   Of the cortex.

costa   'Nerve' of leaf.

cryptic species   Species differing from related species in chemical make-up including DNA and believed to be reproductively isolated, but not or only slightly different in morphology.

cucullate Of calyptrae, hood-shaped and split down one side; of leaves, hooded at apex by incurving of the margins.

cuspidate Of shoot with pointed, spear-like apex formed by imbricate concave leaves.

cygneous Strongly curved like a swan's neck.

deciduous Falling off at maturity.

dendroid Tree-like in habit or mode of branching.

denticulate Finely toothed.

dioicous Sexes on different plants.

distal Portion furthest from base or point of origin (cf. proximal).

dorsal Undersurface of leaf; abaxial surface.

ecostate Lacking a costa.

edentate Lacking teeth on the margin.

endostome Inner peristome.

endostome processes Principal teeth of inner peristome.

epidermal Of stem, the outermost cell layer(s).

epiphragm Of capsule, a thin membrane closing the mouth.

epiphyte A plant growing on another plant (but not parasitizing it).

epixylic Growing on dead wood.

equidistant Of leaves evenly spaced along stem (cf. rosulate).

erecto-patent Pointing upwards at angle of 20–45 degrees to stem.

eutrophication Enrichment or pollution with nutrients, especially nitrogen.

evanescent Of costa ending below leaf apex.

excurrent Of leaf costa, projecting beyond the end of the lamina.

exostome Outer peristome.

exostome teeth Outer ring of teeth of a double peristome.

exothecial cells Outer wall of cells of capsules.

exserted Of capsules, carried well clear of the leaves because of the length of the seta.

falcate Curved like a sickle.

falcato-secund Curved and pointing in one direction.

filamentous Long and slender, often of a single chain of cells.

filiform Fine or thread-like.

flagella Slender branches with or without leaves, bearing rhizoids.

flagelliform Long, tapering; whip-like.

flexuose Wavy.

foliar gemmae Gemmae borne on the leaves.

fugacious Falling or fading early.

fusiform Club-shaped.

gametangia Structures containing gametes, i.e. antheridia (male) or archegonia (female).

gametophyte Haploid sexual phase of bryophyte life cycle (the leafy or thallose plant).

gemmae Vegetative propagule, single-celled or larger, borne on various parts of plant (but not bulbils or tubers).

gibbous Leaf sinus rather strongly convex below its base on the adaxial side.

gymnostomous Of capsule lacking a peristome.

heteroicous With male and female inflorescences showing various arrangements in a single species.

homomallous Pointing in one direction.

hyaline Colourless and transparent when moist, often whitish when dry.

hyalocyst Large empty water-storage cell in *Sphagnum* leaf.

imbricate Of leaves that are overlapping and closely appressed.

incrassate Of cells with thick walls.

inflorescence The structure composed of male or female gametangia and associated bracts.

inner peristome Inner ring of teeth of a double peristome (= endostome).

innovation A new branch, usually arising below an inflorescence.

julaceous Swollen and catkin-like, with imbricate leaves.

laciniate   Margin irregularly divided into lobes bearing cilia and teeth.

lamellae   Flat plates of unistratose cells.

lamina   Blade of leaf, as distinct from costa.

leafy liverwort   Liverwort with leaves, as distinct from a thallose liverwort.

ligulate   Strap-shaped, narrow and parallel-sided.

linear   Very narrow, almost parallel-sided.

lingulate   Tongue-shaped.

macronemata   Rhizoids borne around the dormant buds in the leaf axils (usually large and profusely branched; cf. micronemata).

mamillate   Convex or hemispherical with a short point.

medulla   Internal cells of a stem surrounded by the cortex (in liverworts).

metapopulation   Regional population comprising short-lived local populations that frequently become extinct while colonists found new local populations elsewhere.

micron   Unit of measurement in microscopy; one micron = $^1/_{1000}$ millimetre.

micronemata   Rhizoids borne on initials at any part of the stem (cf. macronemata, which are usually larger and more profusely branched).

mitrate, mitriform   Of calyptra, conical, radially symmetrical, and without splits when young.

monophyletic   A single evolutionary lineage.

mucro   Short and abrupt point.

muticous   Leaf apex lacking hair-point (awn).

mycelia   Microscopic hyphae of fungi.

neck   The sterile portion of a moss capsule between the spore-bearing theca and the top of the seta.

nodulose   With minutely knobbed cilia (cf. appendiculate).

oblanceolate   Lanceolate, but widest above middle.

oblate   Wider than long.

papillae   Microscopic, solid projections, e.g. from surface of a cell.

papillose-crenulate   Of leaf margin, microscopically indented because of papillae on leaf cells.

paraphyllia   Minute hair-like or leaf-like structures inserted on stems of some pleurocarpous mosses between the leaves.

paraphyses   Uniseriate, hair-like structures amongst antheridia or archegonia of mosses.

paroicous   With antheridia in the axils of bracts (modified leaves) immediately below a female inflorescence.

patent   Of leaves pointing upwards at an angle to the stem of about 45 degrees.

pendent, pendulous   Of capsules, hanging more or less vertically downwards.

percurrent   Of costa ending at the leaf apex.

perianth   Bracts or tubular structure surrounding archegonia of a liverwort.

perichaetia   Male inflorescences, comprising antheridia and the surrounding perichaetial bracts.

perichaetial bract   Leaf-like structure surrounding antheridia in male inflorescence.

peristome   Single or double ring of teeth commonly surrounding mouth of moss capsule, visible after lid falls off.

phorophyte   The plant on which an epiphyte grows.

pinnate   Branches produced more or less regularly on each side of stem; simply-pinnate = divided once, twice-pinnate = branches again divided, thrice-pinnate = branches again divided then further subdivided.

pleurocarp, pleurocarpous   Mosses with all inflorescences produced on short lateral branches.

plicae   Longitudinal folds.

pluripapillose   With several papillae.

pores   In thallose liverworts, small openings on the upper surface of the thallus.

porose   With microscopic pores in walls of leaf cells.

primordia   Early growth stages.

pro parte   In part.

procumbent   Prostrate.

prorate   With surface roughened due to projecting ends of cells.

protonema, protonemata   In mosses, filamentous structure (resembling algal mat) from which leafy stems grow up; persistent in some genera.

protonemal gemmae   Gemmae growing from filaments of protonema.

proximal   At or near the base (cf. distal).

pseudoperianth   Hyaline, unistratose, beaked sheath around a sporophyte and calyptra in Marchantiaceae.

pseudopodium   Leafless prolongation of stem bearing gemmae.

pyriform   Pear-shaped.

receptacle   Compound sporophyte of some thallose liverworts (Marchantiopsida).

retuse   Broad apex with shallow notch and rounded sinus.

rhizoids   Uniseriate structures, usually arising from stems, often anchoring plant to substratum [analogous to roots of higher plants].

rostellate   With a short beak.

rostrate   With a long beak.

rosulate   Of leaves arranged in a rosette (cf. equidistant).

rugose   With irregular undulations.

rupestral   Growing on rock.

secund   Turned to one side.

sessile   Lacking a stalk.

seta   The stalk of a sporophyte, bearing capsule at apex.

shuttle species   Species with local populations that regularly reappear from spores, tubers or gemmae.

sinuose   Of leaf margins, wavy with curved indentations; of cells, with wavy walls.

sinus   Indentation between two lobes.

spathulate   Spatula or spoon-shaped (narrow below and broad above).

spores   Mainly microscopic and mainly unicellular propagules produced by sexual reproduction and liberated from capsule at dehiscence.

sporophyte   Diploid phase of bryophyte life cycle that produces spores; consisting of foot embedded in gametophyte (stem) along with seta and capsule.

squarrose   Strongly curved away from stem.

stellate   Star-shaped.

stereids, stereid cells   Long, slender, thick-walled cells in the costa of some mosses.

stipitate   Short, stalk-like base of a thallus with little or no lamina.

striae   Longitudinal lines or ridges.

striate   With longitudinal lines or ridges.

subsecund   Turned weakly to one side.

subula   Long slender point.

subulate   Bristle-like (i.e. very narrow).

sulcate   Furrowed or grooved.

synoicous   With antheridia and archegonia mixed together in same inflorescence.

taxa   Named taxonomic units, including species, subspecies, varieties, genera.

terete   Rounded in transverse section (more or less cylindrical).

thallose   With main axis a thallus.

thallus, thalli   Dorsi-ventrally flattened gametophyte, often forming a more or less horizontal axis, without well-defined leaves.

theca   The spore-bearing part of the capsule.

tomentum   Felt-like covering of rhizoids, occurring in some mosses.

trabeculae   Lamellae on inside of exostome teeth.

tubers   Gemmae occurring on rhizoids.

turbinate   Top-shaped; widest at apex.

underleaves   Third row of leaves often present on underside of stem of leafy liverworts, commonly smaller than leaves in the other rows.

uniseriate   Cells in a single row.

unistratose   One cell thick.

vaginula   The ring or sheath enveloping the base of the seta in mosses.

vegetative dispersal   Dispersal of gemmae, tubers, deciduous leaves or other propagules (but not spores).

vegetative reproduction   Growth of new plants from gemmae, tubers, deciduous leaves or other propagules (but not spores).

ventral   Upper surface of leaf (adaxial surface).

vermicular   Long and sinuose (shaped like a worm).

verruculose   Delicately or minutely roughened.

weft   A life form of loosely interwoven shoots.

Southbya tophacea, found by NL at Island Lake, Co. Mayo, whilst this book was in press.

BIBLIOGRAPHY

Aigoin, D.A., Huttunen, S., Ignatov, M.S., Dirkse, G.M. & Vanderpoorten, A. 2009. *Rhynchostegiella* (Brachytheciaceae): molecular re-circumscription of a convenient taxonomic repository. *Journal of Bryology* **31**: 213–221.

Akhani, H. & Kürschner, H. 2004. An annotated and updated checklist of the Iranian bryoflora. *Cryptogamie, Bryologie* **25**: 315–347.

Aleffi, M. 2005. New checklist of the Hepaticae and Anthocerotae of Italy. *Flora Mediterranea* **15**: 486–566.

Alpert, P. 1988. Survival of a desiccation tolerant moss, *Grimmia laevigata*, beyond its observed micro-distributional limits. *Journal of Bryology* **15**: 219–227.

Anderson, L.E., Crum, H.A. & Buck, W.R. 1990. List of the mosses of North America north of Mexico. *Bryologist* **93**: 448–499.

Anderson, S. 2002. *Identifying Important Plant Areas.* London: Plantlife International.

Anderson, S., Kušík, T., & Radford, E. (eds) 2005. *Important Plant Areas in Central and Eastern Europe.* Salisbury: Plantlife International.

Ando, H. 1986. Studies on the genus *Hypnum* Hedw. (IV). *Hikobia* **9**: 467–484.

Ando, H. & Townsend, C.C. 1980. *Hypnum uncinulatum* Jur. reinstated as an Irish species. *Journal of Bryology* **11**: 185–189.

Andriessen, L., Nagels, C., Arts, T., Sotiaux, A. & Vanderpoorten, A. 2002. Taxonomic assessment, distribution and ecology of *Tortula vahliana* var. *minor* (Pottiaceae, Bryopsida). *Journal of Bryology* **24**: 254–256.

Anon. 1899. Extracts from MEC notebook for 1898. *The Third Annual Report of the Moss Exchange Club (MEC Reports)* **1**: 16–19.

Appleyard, J. 1971. The Summer Meeting 1970. *Transactions of the British Bryological Society* **6**: 387–390.

Appleyard, J., Hill, M.O. & Whitehouse, H.L.K. 1985. *Leptobarbula berica* (De Not.) Schimp. in Britain. *Journal of Bryology* **13**: 461–470.

Armitage, E.[A]. 1938. Report of the Annual Meeting, 1937. *The British Bryological Society Report for 1937* **4**: 9–14.

Armitage, E.A. 1944. *A short account of the Moss Exchange Club and the British Bryological Society.* Privately published.

Armitage, E.A. 1956. *A short account of the Moss Exchange Club and the British Bryological Society.* 2nd ed. Privately published. 24 pp.

Arts, T. 1988. Rhizoidal tubers and protonemal gemmae in *Pseudocrossidium revolutum* (Brid.) Zander var. *revolutum* and *Scopelophila cataractae* (Mitt.) Broth. *Lindbergia* **14**: 59–62.

Arts, T. 1992. *Bryum demaretianum* sp. nov., a new species of the *B. erythrocarpum* complex from Belgium. *Journal of Bryology* **17**: 263–267.

Arts, T. 1994. Rhizoidal tubers and protonemal gemmae in European *Ditrichum* species. *Journal of Bryology* **18**: 43–61.

Arts, T. & Yamada, K. 1998. Four *Radula* (Radulaceae, Hepaticae) new to Réunion. *Botanical Research (Korea)* **7**: 178–180.

Atherton, I., Bosanquet, S. & Lawley, M. (eds) 2009. *British mosses and liverworts, a field guide.* Plymouth: British Bryological Society.

Augier, J. 1966. *Flore des Bryophytes. Morphologie, anatomie, biologie, ecologie, distribution géographique.* Paris: Paul Lechevalier.

Averis, A.B.G. 1991. A survey of the bryophytes of 448 woods in the Scottish Highlands. *Scottish Field Unit Survey Report No. 54.* Edinburgh: Nature Conservancy Council.

Babington, C.C. 1859. Hints towards a Cybele Hibernica. *Proceedings of Dublin University Zoological and Botanical Association* **1**: 246–250, and *Natural History Review* **6** (Proceedings): 533–537.

Bakalin, V.A. 2004. Notes on *Lophozia* V. Comments on Sect. *Sudeticae, Longidentatae* and *Saviczae. Arctoa* **13**: 229–240.

Bardat, J. & Hauguel, J.-C. 2002. Synopsis bryosociologique pour la France. *Cryptogamie, Bryologie* **23**: 279–343.

Barker, [T.], Ingham, W., Jones, D.A., Meldrum, R.H., Waddell, C.H., Lett, M.A. & Marquand, E.D. 1907. *A Census Catalogue of British Mosses with Lists of the Botanical Vice Counties and their boundaries, and Lists of Sources of Records, compiled under the Direction of the Moss Exchange Club.* York: Coultas & Volans, for M.E.C.

Barry, T.A. & Synnott, D.M. 1970. Recent Quaternary bryophyte records. *Irish Naturalists' Journal* **16**: 351–352.

Barry, T.A. & Synnott, D.M. 1973. Subfossil *Meesia longiseta* Hedw. in Ireland. *Irish Naturalists' Journal* **17**: 318.

Barry, T.A. & Synnott, D.M. 1984. Bryophytic succession in woody-fen and other peat types in two Hochmoore in Central Ireland. *Proceedings: 7th International Peat Congress, Dublin, Ireland* **1**: 1–26.

Barry, T.A. & Synnott, D.M. 1987. Further studies into bryophyte occurrence and succession in the Hochmoore peat types of Ireland. *Glasra* **10**: 1–21.

Bates, J.W. & Hodgetts, N.G. 1995. New and interesting bryophyte records from Brittany including *Cryptothallus mirabilis, Ulota calvescens* and *Weissia persssonii* new to France. *Cryptogamie, Bryologie, Lichénologie* **16**: 191–211.

Bączkiewicz, A. & Buczkowska, K. 2005. Genetic variability of the *Aneura pinguis* complex (Hepaticae) in central and western Europe. *Biological Letters* **42**: 61–72.

Bączkiewicz, A., Sawicki, J., Buczkowska, K. & Zielinski, R. 2008. Application of different DNA markers in studies on cryptic species of *Aneura pinguis* (Jungermanniopsida, Metzgeriales). *Cryptogamie, Bryologie* **29**: 3–21.

Belikovich, A.V., Galanin, A.V., Afonina, O.M. & Makarova, I.I. 2006. *Vegetation of Chukotka protected areas.* Wladiwostok: BSI DWO RAN, 260 pp.

Bell, G.H. 2006. *Bartramia*. In: *Flora of Australia* **51**: 249–256. Canberra: Government Printing Office.

Bellamy, D. & Bellamy, R. 1966. An ecological approach to the classification of lowland mires in Ireland. *Proceedings of the Royal Irish Academy* **65B**: 237–251.

Bergamini, A. 2006. Caducous branchlets in *Pterigynandrum filiforme* (Bryopsida: Pterigynandraceae). *Journal of Bryology* **28**: 149–151.

Biodiversity Reporting and Information Group 2007. *Report on the Species and Habitats Review.* Report to the UK Biodiversity Partnership.

Birks, H.H., Birks, H.J.B. & Ratcliffe, D.A. 1969. *Geocalyx graveolens* (Schrad.) Nees in Kerry, a hepatic new to Ireland. *Irish Naturalists' Journal* **16**: 204–205.

Birks, H.J.B., Birks, H.H. & Ratcliffe, D.A. 1969. Mountain plants on Slieve League, Co. Donegal. *Irish Naturalists' Journal* **16**: 203.

Bisang, I. 1996. Quantitative analysis of the diaspore banks of bryophytes and ferns in cultivated fields in Switzerland. *Lindbergia* **21**: 9–20.

Blackstock, T.H. 2000. New vice-county records and amendments to the *Census Catalogue*. Hepaticae. *Bulletin of the British Bryological Society* **75**: 40–45.

Blackstock, T.H. 2001. New vice-county records and amendments to the *Census Catalogue*. Hepaticae. *Bulletin of the British Bryological Society* **77**: 33–37.

Blackstock, T.H. 2002. New vice-county records and amendments to the *Census Catalogue*. Hepaticae. *Bulletin of the British Bryological Society* **79**: 38–42.

Blackstock, T.H. 2003. New vice-county records and amendments to the *Census Catalogue*. Hepaticae. *Bulletin of the British Bryological Society* **81**: 39–46.

Blackstock, T.H. 2004. New vice-county records and amendments to the *Census Catalogue*. Hepaticae. *Field Bryology* **83**: 32–35.

Blackstock, T.H. 2005. New vice-county records and amendments to the *Census Catalogue*. Hepaticae. *Field Bryology* **86**: 24–28.

Blackstock, T.H. 2009. New vice-county records. Hepaticae. *Field Bryology* **98**: 67–69.

Blackstock, T.H. & Long, D.G. 2002. *Heteroscyphus fissistipus* (Hook.f. & Taylor) Schiffn. established in south-west Ireland, new to the Northern Hemisphere. *Journal of Bryology* **24**: 147–150.

Bleasdale, A. 1995. *The vegetation and ecology of the Connemara uplands, with particular reference to sheep grazing.* Unpublished PhD thesis, National University of Ireland, Galway, 229 pp.

Blockeel, T.L. 1981. *Barbula tomaculosa*, a new species from arable fields in Yorkshire. *Journal of Bryology* **11**: 583–589.

Blockeel, T.L. 1988. New vice-county records and amendments to the Census Catalogue. Musci. *Bulletin of the British Bryological Society* **52**: 33–40.

Blockeel, T.L. 1991a. The Summer Meeting, 1990, Ireland. *Bulletin of the British Bryological Society* **57**: 5–11.

Blockeel, T.L. 1991b. The *Racomitrium heterostichum* group in the British Isles. *Bulletin of the British Bryological Society* **58**: 29–35.

Blockeel, T.[L.] 1995a. Summer Field Meeting, 1994, Second week, Clifden. *Bulletin of the British Bryological Society* **65**: 12–18.

Blockeel, T.L. 1995b. A note on *Phascum cuspidatum* subsp. *papillosum* in the British Isles. *Bulletin of the British Bryological Society* **65**: 59–60.

Blockeel, T.L. 1998. *Cinclidotus riparius* reinstated as a British and Irish moss. *Journal of Bryology* **20**: 109–119.

Blockeel, T.L. 1999. Musci, pp. 1–25 in Blockeel, T.L. & Long, D.G. The New Census Catalogue: supplementary lists of deleted, recent and replacement records. *Bulletin of the British Bryological Society* **73**: Supplement: 1–28.

Blockeel, T.L. & Long, D.G. 1998. *A Check-list and Census Catalogue of British and Irish Bryophytes.* Cardiff: British Bryological Society.

Blockeel, T.L., Bednarek-Ochyra, H., Ochyra, R., Garcia, C., Matcham, H.W., Sérgio, C., Sim-Sim, M., Stebel, A., Townsend, C.C. & Váňa, J. 2005a. New national and regional bryophyte records, 11. *Scopelophila cataractae* (Mitt.) Broth. *Journal of Bryology* **27**: 163–168 [note by C.C. Townsend on p. 167].

Blockeel, T.L., Ochyra, R. & Gos, L. 2000. *Seligeria campylopoda* Kindb. in the British Isles. *Journal of Bryology* **22**: 29–33.

Blockeel, T.L., Vanderpoorten, A., Sotiaux, A. & Goffinet, B. 2005b. The status of the mid-western European endemic moss *Brachythecium appleyardiae*. *Journal of Bryology* **27**: 137–141.

Blom, H.H. 1996. A revision of the *Schistidium apocarpum* complex in Norway and Sweden. *Bryophytorum Bibliotheca* **49**: 1–333.

Boros, Á. 1968. *Bryogeographie und Bryoflora Ungarns.* Budapest: Akadémiai Kiadó.

Bosanquet, S.D.S. 2006a. *Tortella bambergeri* (Schimp.) Broth. in the British Isles. *Journal of Bryology* **28**: 5–10.

Bosanquet, S.D.S. 2006b. Wildlife reports: Bryophytes. *British Wildlife* **17**: 211–212.

Bosanquet, S.D.S. 2009. *Orthotrichum* – Britain's bristle-mosses. *British Wildlife* **20**: 187–194.

Bosanquet, S.D.S. & Motley, G.S. 2009. *Rhytidiadelphus subpinnatus* in Wales. *Field Bryology* **98**: 8–13.

Bosanquet, S. & Preston, C. 2010. BBS Summer Meeting: Co. Cork and Co. Kerry, 27 June–11 July 2009. *Field Bryology* **100**: 47–63.

Bosanquet, S.D.S., Graham, J. & Motley, G. 2005. *The mosses and liverworts of Carmarthenshire.* Pontypool: published by the authors.

Bosanquet, S.D.S., Hale, A.D., Motley, G.S. & Woods, R.G. 2006. Recent work on *Hamatocaulis vernicosus* in mid and south Wales. *Field Bryology* **90**: 2–8.

Braun-Blanquet, J. & Tüxen, R. 1952. Irische Pflanzengesellschaften. *Veröffentlichung der Geobotanischen Institutes Rübel, Zürich* **25**: 224–421.

Brodie, J., John, D.M., Tittley, I., Holmes, M.J. & Williamson, D.B. 2007. *Important Plant Areas for algae: a provisional review of sites and areas of importance for algae in the United Kingdom.* Salisbury: Plantlife International.

Brummitt, R.K. & Powell, C.E. 1992. *Authors of plant names.* Kew: Royal Botanic Gardens.

Buczkowska, K., Adamczyk, M. Bączkiewicz, A. 2006. Morphological and anatomical differentiation within the *Aneura pinguis* complex (Metzgeriales, Hepaticae). *Biological Letters* **43**: 51–68.

Buryová, B. 2004. Genetic variation in two closely related species of *Philonotis* based on isozymes. *Bryologist* **107**: 316–327.

Buryová, B. & Shaw, A.J. 2005. Phenotypic plasticity in *Philonotis fontana* (Bryopsida: Bartramiaceae). *Journal of Bryology* **27**: 13–22.

Byfield, A.J. & Wilson, P.J. 2005. *Important Arable Plant Areas: identifying priority sites for arable plant conservation in the United Kingdom.* Salisbury: Plantlife International.

Cano, M.J. & Gallego, M.T. 2008. The genus *Tortula* (Pottiaceae, Bryophyta) in South America. *Botanical Journal of the Linnean Society* **156**: 173–220.

Cano, M.J., Ros, R.M., Gallego, M.T., Jiménez, J.A. & Guerra, J. 2002. Contribution to the bryophyte flora of Morocco: the Anti-Atlas catalogue. *Cryptogamie, Bryologie* **23**: 249–262.

Cano, M.J., Werner, O. & Guerra, J. 2005. A morphometric and molecular study in *Tortula subulata* complex (Pottiaceae, Bryophyta). *Botanical Journal of the Linnean Society* **149**: 333–350.

Casas, C., Brugués, M., Cros, R.M. & Sérgio, C. 2006. *Handbook of mosses of the Iberian Peninsula and the Balearic Islands. Illustrated keys to genera and species.* Barcelona: Institut d'Estudis Catalans.

Casas, C., Brugués, M., Cros, R.M., Ruiz, E. & Barrón, A. 2009. Checklist of mosses of the Spanish central Pyrenees. *Cryptogamie, Bryologie* **30**: 33–65.

Catcheside, D.G. & Bell, G.H. 2006. Calomniaceae. In: McCarthy, P. (ed.) *Flora of Australia.* **51** (Mosses 1). Canberra & Melbourne: ABRS and CSIRO Publishing, 367–368.

Caulfield, S., O'Donnell, R.G. & Mitchell, P.I. 1998. 14C dating of a Neolithic field system at Céide fields, County Mayo, Ireland. *Radiocarbon* **40**: 629–640.

Çetin, B. 1988. Checklist of the mosses of Turkey. *Lindbergia* **14**: 15–23.

C.[hase], C.D. 1954. William Rutledge Megaw, 1885–1953. *Irish Naturalists' Journal* **11**: 181–183.

Church, J.M., Hodgetts, N.G., Preston, C.D. & Stewart, N.F. 2001. *British Red Data Books: mosses and liverworts.* Peterborough: Joint Nature Conservation Committee.

Clausen, E. 1964. The tolerance of hepatics to desiccation and temperature. *Bryologist* **67**: 411–417.

Colgan, N. & Scully, R.W. 1898. *Contributions towards a Cybele Hibernica, being outlines of the geographical distribution of plants in Ireland.* 2nd ed. Dublin: Edward Ponsonby & London: Gurney & Jackson.

Corley, M.F.V. & Hill, M.O. 1981. *Distribution of bryophytes in the British Isles. A census catalogue of their occurrence in vice-counties.* Cardiff: British Bryological Society.

Corley, M.F.V. & Perry, A.R. 1985. *Scopelophila cataractae* (Mitt.) Broth. in South Wales, new to Europe. *Journal of Bryology* **13**: 323–328.

Cortini Pedrotti, C. 2001. New check-list of the mosses of Italy. *Flora Mediterranea* **11**: 23–107.

Cox, J. 1999. The nature conservation importance of dung. *British Wildlife* **11**: 28–36.

Coxon, P. 2008. Landscapes and environments of the last glacial-interglacial transition: a time of amazingly rapid change in Ireland. *Irish Naturalists' Journal, Special Supplement* pp. 45–62.

Crandall-Stotler, B.J. & Stotler, R.E. 2007. On the identity of *Moerckia hibernica* (Hook.) Gottsche (Moerckiaceae fam. nov., Marchantiophyta). *Nova Hedwigia* **131**: 41–59.

Crandall-Stotler, B.J., Stotler, R.E. & Ford, C.H. 2002. Contributions toward a Monograph of *Petalophyllum* (Marchantiophyta). *Novon* **12**: 334–337.

Cridland, A.A. 1958. An outline of the bryophytes of County Laois (Queen's County). *Transactions of the British Bryological Society* **3**: 339–417.

Cross, J.R. 1992. The distribution, character and conservation of woodlands on esker ridges in Ireland. *Proceedings of the Royal Irish Academy* **92B**: 1–19.

Cross, J.R. 2006. The potential natural vegetation of Ireland. *Biology and Environment, Proceedings of the Royal Irish Academy* **106B**: 65–116.

Cross, J.R. & Kelly, D.L. 2003. Wet Woodland. In: Otte, M. (ed.) *The Wetlands of Ireland.* University College Dublin Press, pp. 160–172.

Cruickshank, M.M. & Tomlinson, R.W. 1988. *Northern Ireland peatland survey.* Department of the Environment for Northern Ireland (Countryside and Wildlife Branch), Belfast.

Crum, H. 1988. *A focus on peatlands and peat mosses.* Ann Arbor: The University of Michigan Press.

Crum, H. 1992. *A focus on peatlands and peat mosses.* Paperback ed. Ann Arbor: The University of Michigan Press.

Crum, H. 2001. *Structural diversity of bryophytes.* Ann Arbor: The University of Michigan Herbarium.

Crum, H.A. 2007. *Dicranella.* In: FNA (eds) *Flora of North America, North of Mexico.* **27**. *Bryophyta, part 1.* New York & Oxford: Oxford University Press, pp. 386–393.

Crum, H.A. & Anderson, L.E. 1981. *Mosses of Eastern North America.* Vols. **1 & 2**. New York: Columbia University Press.

Crundwell, A.C. 1952. Some bryophytes from the Dingle Peninsula. *Irish Naturalists' Journal* **10**: 309–311.

Crundwell, A.C. 1959. Some bryophytes from Counties Cavan and Fermanagh. *Irish Naturalists' Journal* **13**: 36–39.

Crundwell, A.C. 1980. The Irish Meeting, August 1979. *Bulletin of the British Bryological Society* **36**: 9–11.

Crundwell, A.C. 1981. Reproduction in *Myurium hochstetteri*. *Journal of Bryology* **11**: 715–717.

Crundwell, A.C. 1995. *Hedwigia stellata* and *H. ciliata* in the British Isles. *Journal of Bryology* **18**: 807–810.

Crundwell, A.C. & Hill, M.O. 1977. *Anoectangium warburgii*, a new species of moss from the British Isles. *Journal of Bryology* **9**: 435–440.

Crundwell, A.C. & Nyholm, E. 1964. The European species of the *Bryum erythrocarpum* complex. *Transactions of the British Bryological Society* **4**: 597–637.

Crundwell, A.C. & Smith, A.J.E. 2000. *Heterocladium wulfsbergii* I. Hagen in the British Isles. *Journal of Bryology* **22**: 43–47.

Crundwell, A.C. & Whitehouse, H.L.K. 2001. A revision of *Bryum bornholmense* Wink. & R.Ruthe. *Journal of Bryology* **23**: 171–176 (prepared for publication by C.D. Preston; illustrated by J.A. Paton).

Crundwell, A.C., Greven, H.C. & Stern, R.C. 1994. Some additions to the bryophyte flora of the Azores. *Journal of Bryology* **18**: 329–337.

Crushell, P.H., Schouten, M.G.C., Smolders, A.J.P., Roelofs, J.G.M. & Giller, P.S. 2006. Restoration of minerotrophic vegetation within an Irish raised bog soak system. *Biology and Environment, Proceedings of the Royal Irish Academy* **106B**: 371–385.

Czernyadjeva, I.V. 2005. A check-list of the mosses of Kamchatka Peninsula (Far East). *Arctoa* **14**: 13–34.

DAHGI 2002. *National biodiversity action plan*. Department of Arts, Heritage, Gaeltacht and the Islands, Dublin, 49 pp.

Damsholt, K. 2002. *Illustrated flora of the Nordic liverworts and hornworts*. Lund, Sweden: Nordic Bryological Society.

Daniels, R.E. & Eddy, A. 1990. *Handbook of European Sphagna*. 2nd impression with additions. Swindon: Natural Environment Research Council.

Davenport, J.L., Sleeman, D.P. & Woodman, P.C. 2008. Mind the gap: postglacial colonization of Ireland. *Irish Naturalists' Journal, Special Supplement* pp. 138.

De Beer, D. & Arts, T. 2000. *Sematophyllum substrumulosum* (Musci, Sematophyllaceae) nieuw voor de Belgische flora. *Belgian Journal of Botany* **133**: 15–20.

De Beer, D. & Martens, C. 2007. *Bryum dyffrynense* in Zweebrugge en Zwijndrecht, nieuw voor België. *Dumortiera* **91**: 25–26.

Delgadillo M.C., Bello, B. & Cárdenas S.A. 1995. Latmoss. A catalogue of neotropical mosses. *Monographs in Systematic Botany from the Missouri Botanical Garden* **56**: 1–191.

Desmond, R. 1994. *Dictionary of British and Irish Botanists and Horticulturists: Including Plant Collectors, Flower Painters, and Garden Designers*. London: Taylor and Francis and the Natural History Museum.

Devoy, R.J.N. 1985. The problems of a Late Quaternary land-bridge between Britain and Ireland. *Quaternary Science Reviews* **4**: 43–58.

Dickson, J.H. 1973. *Bryophytes of the Pleistocene. The British record and its chorological and ecological implications*. Cambridge: Cambridge University Press.

Dierssen, K. 1982. *Die Wichtigsten Pflanzengesellschaften der Moore NW Europas*. Geneve: Conservatoire et Jardin Botaniques.

Dierssen, K. 2001. Distribution, ecological amplitude and phytosociological characterization of European bryophytes. *Bryophytorum Bibliotheca* **56**: 1–289.

Dines, T.D., Pearman, D.A. & Preston, C.D. 2002. Chapter 3. Scope of the New Atlas Project. In: Preston, C.D., Pearman, D.A. & Dines, T.D. *New atlas of the British & Irish flora. An atlas of the vascular plants of Britain, Ireland, the Isle of Man and the Channel Islands*. Oxford: Oxford University Press, pp. 9–11.

Direktoratet for naturforvalning. 1999. Nasjonal rødliste for truete arter 1998 [Norwegian Red List 1998] - *DN-rapport 1999-3*: 1–161.

Dirkse, G.M. & Bouman, A.C. 1996. A revision of *Rhynchostegiella* (Musci, Brachytheciaceae) in the Canary Islands. *Lindbergia* **20**: 109–121.

Dirkse, G.M., Bouman, A.C. & Losada-Lima, A. 1993. Bryophytes of the Canary Islands, an annotated checklist. *Cryptogamie, Bryologie Lichénologie* **14**: 1–47.

Dixon, H.N. 1924. *The student's handbook of British mosses*. 3rd ed. Eastbourne: Sumfield & Day Ltd., London: Wheldon & Wesley Ltd.

Douglas, C. 1987. The distribution and ecology of *Sphagnum pulchrum* (Braithw.) Warnst. in Ireland. *Glasra* **10**: 75–81.

Douglas, C., Fernandez, F. & Ryan, J. 2008. Peatland habitat conservation in Ireland. *Proceedings of the 13th International Peat Congress, Tullamore, Ireland*. pp. 681–685.

Douin, M. 1907. Étude sur l'*Ephemerum stellatum* Philibert et remarques sur les *Ephemerum* européens. *Bulletin de la Société Botanique de France* **54**: 242–251, 306–326.

Doyle, G.J. 1982. The vegetation, ecology and productivity of Atlantic blanket bog in Mayo and Galway, western Ireland. *Journal of Life Sciences of the Royal Dublin Society* **3**: 147–164.

Doyle, J. & Moore, J.J. 1980. Western blanket bog (*Pleurozio purpureae-Ericetorum tetralicis* in Ireland and Great Britain. *Colloques Phytosociologiques* **7**: 213–223.

Draper, I., Lara, F., Albertos, B., Garilleti, R. & Mazimpaka, V. 2006. Epiphytic bryoflora of the Atlas and Antiatlas Mountains, including a synthesis of the distribution of epiphytic bryophytes in Morocco. *Journal of Bryology* **28**: 312–330.

Duckett, J.G. & Ligrone, R. 1992. A survey of diaspore liberation mechanisms and germination patterns in mosses. *Journal of Bryology* **17**: 335–354.

Duckett, J.G. & Pressel, S. 2003. Studies of protonemal morphogenesis in mosses. IX. *Discelium nudum*: exquisite pioneer of unstable clay banks. *Journal of Bryology* **25**: 241–245.

Duckett, J.G., Goode, J.A. & Matcham, H.W. 2001. Studies of protonemal morphogenesis in mosses, VIII. The gemmiferous protonemata of *Orthodontium* and *Dicranoweisia*. *Journal of Bryology* **23**: 181–193.

Duckett, J.G., Pressel, S. & Ligrone, R. 2006. Cornish bryophytes in the Atlantic Arc: cell biology, culturing, conservation and climate change. In: Leach, S.J. *et al.* (eds) *Botanical links in the Atlantic Arc*. Botanical Society of the British Isles, Conference Report **24**: 165–176.

Düll, R. 1985. Distribution of the European Mosses, Part II. *Bryologische Beitraege* **5**: 110–232.

Düll, R. 1986. Revision of *Rhynchostegiella* and closely related taxa in Macaronesia with reference to their occurrence in Europe. *Bryologische Beitraege* **6**: 91–105.

Düll, R. 1992. Distribution of the European and Macaronesian mosses (Bryophytina), annotations and progress. *Bryologische Beitraege* **8/9**: 1–223.

Düll, R. 1994. *Deutschlands Moose*. 2. Teil. Bad Münstereifel - Olerath: IDH-Verlag.

Düll-Hermanns, I. 1981. Spezielle Untersuchungen zur modernen Taxonomie von *Thuidium abietinum* und der Varietät *hystricosum*. *Journal of Bryology* **11**: 467–488.

Duncan, J.B. 1926. *A Census Catalogue of British Mosses with Lists of the Botanical Vice Counties and their boundaries, and Lists of Sources of Records (2nd Edition), compiled for The British Bryological Society (Formerly The Moss Exchange Club) ...* Berwick-on-Tweed, Martin's Printing Works, for BBS.

Duncan, J.B. 1928. British Bryological Society. Annual Meeting and Excursion. Belfast, 25th to 31st August, 1928. *Irish Naturalists' Journal* **2**: 112–119.

Duncan, J.B. 1929a. Report of the Annual Meeting, 1928. *The British Bryological Society Report for 1928*, **2**: 128.

D.[uncan], J.B. 1929b. *British Bryological Society. Census Catalogue of British Mosses (2nd Edition, 1926), Supplement*. Berwick-on-Tweed: Martin's Printing Works, for BBS.

D.[uncan], J.B. 1935. British Bryological Society. Census Catalogue of British Mosses (2nd Edition, 1926) [Supplement], 6 pp. in *The British Bryological Society. Supplements to Census Catalogue of British Mosses (2nd Edition), and Census Catalogue of British Hepatics (3rd Edition)*. Berwick-on-Tweed: Martin's Printing Works, for BBS.

During, H.J. 1973. Some bryological aspects of pioneer vegetation in moist dune valleys in Denmark, the Netherlands and France. *Lindbergia* **1**: 99–104.

During, H.J. 1992. Ecological classifications of bryophytes and lichens. In: Bates, J.W., Farmer, A.M., (eds) *Bryophytes and lichens in a changing environment*. Oxford: Clarendon Press.

During, H.J. 1997. Bryophyte diaspore banks. *Advances in Bryology* **6**: 103-134.

Dyachenko, A.P. 1999. *Flora of the leafy mosses of the Urals*. Vol. **2**. Ekaterinburg: Izd-vo Uralsk. Univ. [in Russian].

Eckel, P.M. 1986. *Didymodon australasiae* var. *umbrosus* New to Eastern North America. *The Bryologist* **89**: 70–72.

Edwards, R. & Brooks, A. 2008. The island of Ireland: drowning the myth of an Irish land-bridge. *Irish Naturalists' Journal, Special Supplement* pp. 19–34.

Edwards, S.R. 2003. *English names for British bryophytes*. 3rd ed. Loughton, Essex: British Bryological Society Special Vol. **5**.

Een, G. 2004. *Sematophyllum substrumulosum* new to mainland Britain. *Field Bryology* **84**: 6–7.

Eggers, J. 1982. Artenliste der Moose Makaronesiens. *Cryptogamie, Bryologie, Lichénologie* **3**: 283–335.

EHS 2002. *Northern Ireland Biodiversity Strategy*. Belfast: Environment and Heritage Service, 22 pp.

Engel, J.J. & Merrill, G.L.S. 2004. Austral Hepaticae. 35. A taxonomic and phylogenetic study of *Telaranea* (Lepidoziaceae), with a monograph of the genus in temperate Australasia and commentary on extra-Australasian taxa. *Fieldiana, Botany*, N.S. **44**: 1–265.

Erdağ, A. & Kürschner, H. 2000. *Orthotrichum sprucei* Mont. (Orthotrichaceae, Musci), new to the moss flora of Turkey. *Nova Hedwigia* **71**: 145–150.

Erzberger, P. 2003. The number of stomata per sporophyte and its variability in the species of the *Ulota crispa* complex and *Ulota drummondii* (Musci, Orthotrichaceae). *Lindbergia* **28**: 14–22.

Erzberger, P. 2005. The bulbilliferous species of *Pohlia* (Bryaceae, Musci) in Hungary. *Studia Botanica Hungarica* **36**: 67–75.

Erzberger, P. & Papp, B. 2000. *Orthotrichum sprucei* discovered in continental central Europe. *Herzogia* **14**: 213–215.

Erzberger, P. & Papp, B. 2004. Annotated checklist of Hungarian bryophytes. *Studia Botanica Hungarica* **35**: 91–149.

European Committee for the Conservation of Bryophytes (ed.) 1995. *Red Data Book of European bryophytes*. Trondheim: European Committee for the Conservation of Bryophytes.

Farrell, C.A. 2008. The biodiversity value and future management of degraded peatland habitats in Ireland. *Proceedings of the 13th International Peat Congress, Tullamore, Ireland*. pp. 686–689.

Fedosov, V.E. 2009 ('2008'). *Tortula cuneifolia* (Dicks.) Turner (Pottiaceae, Musci) in Russia. *Arctoa* **17**: 85–90.

Feehan, J. 1997. The heritage of the rocks. In: Foster, J.W. (ed.) *Nature in Ireland, a scientific and cultural history*. Dublin: The Lilliput Press. pp. 3–22.

Feeser, I. & O'Connell, M. 2009. Fresh insights into long-term changes in flora, vegetation, land use and soil erosion in the karstic environment of the Burren, western Ireland. *Journal of Ecology* **97**: 1083–1100.

Fernandez, C.C., Shevock, J.R., Glazer, A.N. & Thompson, J.N. 2006. Cryptic species within the cosmopolitan desiccation-tolerant moss *Grimmia laevigata*. *Proceedings of the National Academy of Sciences, U.S.A.* **103**: 637–642.

Ferriss, S.E., Inskipp, T.P., Kloda, J. & Sinovas, P. 2007. *Wildlife trade in Ireland – a review*. Confidential report to the National Parks and Wildlife Service, Ireland. UNEP World Conservation Monitoring Centre, Cambridge. 85 pp.

Fitzgerald, J.W. 1950. Some Irish liverwort records. *Irish Naturalists' Journal* 10: 107.

Fitzgerald, J.W. 1951. Some Irish liverwort records: II. *Irish Naturalists' Journal* 10: 214.

Fitzgerald, J.W. 1958. *Eucalyx paroicus* (Schiffn.) Macv. new to Ireland. *Irish Naturalists' Journal* 12: 247.

Fitzgerald, J.W. 1960. *Calypogeia suecica* (Arn. & Pers.) K. Müll. and the epixylic bryophyte communities at Sheskinawaddy. *Irish Naturalists' Journal* 13: 129–133.

Fitzgerald, J.W. 1962. *Calypogeia suecica* (Arn. & Pers.) K. Müll. growing on peat. *Irish Naturalists' Journal* 14: 18.

Fitzgerald, J.W. 1969. Two hepatics new to Ireland. *Irish Naturalists' Journal* 16: 241.

Fitzgerald, J.W. & Fitzgerald, R.D. 1960a. Bryophytes found in Counties Tyrone, Londonderry and Fermanagh, including some new to the Irish list. *Irish Naturalists' Journal* 13: 174–177.

Fitzgerald, J.W. & Fitzgerald, R.D. 1960b. A bryophyte flora of Co. Tyrone. *Transactions of the British Bryological Society* 3: 653–687.

Fitzgerald, J.W. & Fitzgerald, R.D. 1961. Gleanings among the Waddell MSS. *Irish Naturalists' Journal* 13: 227–231.

Fitzgerald, J.W. & Fitzgerald, R.D. 1966a. Bryophytes new to the Irish list. *Irish Naturalists' Journal* 15: 178–180.

Fitzgerald, J.W. & Fitzgerald, R.D. 1966b. Bryophyte additions to *A Flora of the North-east of Ireland*. *Irish Naturalists' Journal* 15: 180–182.

Fitzgerald, J.W. & Fitzgerald, R.D. 1967. Bryophytes of County Armagh. *Irish Naturalists' Journal* 15: 324–326.

Fitzgerald, J.W. & Fitzgerald, R.D. 1968a. Bryophyte additions to *A Flora of the North-east of Ireland*. *Irish Naturalists' Journal* 16: 77.

Fitzgerald, J.W. & Fitzgerald, R.D. 1968b. *Calypogeia suecica* (Arn. & Pers.) K. Müll. in Kerry. *Irish Naturalists' Journal* 16: 79–80.

Fitzgerald, J.W. & Fitzgerald, R.D. 1969. Bryophyte additions to *A Flora of the North-east of Ireland*. *Irish Naturalists' Journal* 16: 240–241.

Fitzgerald, J.W. & Perry, A.R. 1964. *Herberta* in Ireland, and its occur[r]ence at Fair Head, County Antrim. *Irish Naturalists' Journal* 14: 229–232.

Fitzgerald, R.D. 1950. Some Irish moss records. *Irish Naturalists' Journal* 10: 108.

Fitzgerald, R.D. 1952a. Report of the Autumn Meeting in Ireland, 1951. *Transactions of the British Bryological Society* 2: 125–128.

Fitzgerald, R.D. 1952b. *Brachythecium rivulare* (Bruch) B. & S. var. *latifolium* Husn. new to Ireland. *Irish Naturalists' Journal* 10: 249.

Fitzgerald, R.D. 1952c. Some Irish moss records: II. *Irish Naturalists' Journal* 10: 250.

Fitzgerald, R.D. 1952d. Some Irish moss records: III. *Irish Naturalists' Journal* 10: 320.

Fitzgerald, R.D. & Fitzgerald, J.W. 1952. British Bryological Society excursion to Glenbeigh and

Waterville, Co. Kerry, 1st to 14th Sept. 1951. *Revue Bryologique et Lichénologique* 21: 179–182.

Flatberg, K.I. 1988. *Sphagnum skyense* sp. nov. *Journal of Bryology* 15: 101–107.

Fletcher, M.V. 1993. Coarse *Scopelophila* growing. *Bulletin of the British Bryological Society* 61: 44.

FNA = Flora of North America Editorial Committee. 2007. *Flora of North America, North of Mexico*. **27**. *Bryophyta, part 1*. New York & Oxford: Oxford University Press.

Forest Service 2007. *National Forest Inventory. Republic of Ireland – Results*. Unpublished Report, Forest Service, Department of Agriculture, Fisheries and Food, Wexford. 256 pp.

Forrest, L.L., Davis, E.C., Long, D.G., Crandall-Stotler, B.J., Clark, A. & Hollingsworth, M.L. 2006. Unraveling the evolutionary history of the liverworts (Marchantiophyta): multiple taxa, genomes and analysis. *Bryologist* 109: 303–334.

Fossitt, J.A. 2000. *A guide to habitats in Ireland*. Dublin: The Heritage Council.

Fox, H., Blockeel, T.[L.] & Perry, A.R. 2001. Summer field meeting, Dungarvan and New Ross, Ireland, 1999. *Bulletin of the British Bryological Society* 76: 3–10.

Frahm, J.-P. 2006. *Fontinalis antipyretica* 'var. *gracilis*' ist nur eine Modifikation. Notulae Bryologicae Rhenanae 4. *Archive for Bryology* 9: 1–4.

Frahm, J.-P. & Klaus, D. 2001. Bryophytes as indicators of recent climate fluctuations in Central Europe. *Lindbergia* 26: 97–104.

Frahm, J.-P. & Lüth, M. 2008. The bryophyte flora of the Maltese islands. Archive for Bryology 29: 1–10.

Frahm, J.-P., Lüth, M. & van Melick, H. 2008a. Kommentierte Artenliste der Moose von Sardinien. Archive for Bryology 31: 1–13.

Frahm, J.-P., Sabovljević, M. & Nokhbehsaim, M. 2008b. New data on the taxonomic status of *Ditrichum plumbicola* Crundw. (Bryophyta) and its relation to *D. lineare* (Sw.) Kindb. based on the *trn*L-F region of the cpDNA. *International Journal of Botany* 4: 113–116.

Fransén, S. 2004a. A taxonomic revision of extra-Neotropical *Bartramia* section *Vaginella* C.Müll. *Lindbergia* 29: 73–107.

Fransén, S. 2004b. A taxonomic revision of *Bartramia* Hedw. section *Bartramia*. *Lindbergia* 29: 113–122.

Frey, W. & Kürschner, H. 1991. Conspectus Bryophytorum Orientalum et Arabicorum. *Bryophytorum Bibliotheca* 39: 1–181.

Frey, W., Frahm, J.-P., Fischer, E. & Lobin, W. 2006. *The liverworts, mosses and ferns of Europe*. Colchester: Harley Books. English edition revised and edited by T.L. Blockeel.

Frisvoll, A.A. 1978. The genus *Tetraplodon* in Norway. A taxonomic revision. *Lindbergia* 4: 225–246.

Frisvoll, A.A. 1983. A taxonomic revision of the *Racomitrium canescens* group (Bryophyta, Grimmiales). *Gunneria* **41**: 1–181.

Frisvoll, A.A. 1985. Lectotypifications including nomenclatural and taxonomical notes on *Ditrichum flexicaule* sensu lato. *Bryologist* **88**: 31–40.

Frisvoll, A.A. 1988. A taxonomic revision of the *Racomitrium heterostichum* group (Bryophyta, Grimmiales) in N. and C. America, N. Africa, Europe and Asia. *Gunneria* **59**: 1–289.

Frisvoll, A.A. & Blom, H.H. 1992. Trua moser i Norge med Svalbarde; raud liste. *NINA Utredning* **42**: 1–55.

Fulford, M.H. 1968. Manual of the leafy Hepaticae of Latin America. III. *Memoirs of the New York Botanical Garden* **11**: 275–392.

Furness, S.B. & Hall, R.H. 1981. An explanation of the intermittent occurrence of *Physcomitrium sphaericum* (Hedw.) Brid. *Journal of Bryology* **11**: 733–742.

Gabriel, R., Sjögren, E., Schumacker, R., Sérgio, C., Frahm, J.-P. & Sousa, E. 2005. List of bryophytes In: *A list of the terrestrial fauna (Mollusca and Arthropoda) and flora (Bryophyta, Pteridophyta and Spermatophyta) from the Azores* (eds Borges, P.A.V., Cunha, R., Gabriel, R., Martins, A.M.F., Silva, L. & Vieira, V.). Direcção Regional de Ambiente e do Mar dos Açores and Universidade dos Açores, Horta, Angra do Heroísmo and Ponta Delgada.

Gao Chien, Crosby, M.R. & Si He. 1999. *Moss flora of China. English version. Vol. 1. Sphagnaceae–Leucobryaceae.* Beijing & New York: Science Press, St Louis: Missouri Botanical Garden.

Gao Chien, Crosby, M.R. & Si He. 2003. *Moss flora of China. English version. Vol. 3. Grimmiaceae–Tetraphidaceae.* Beijing & New York: Science Press, St Louis: Missouri Botanical Garden.

García-Zamora, P., Ros, R.M. & Guerra, J. 1998. Bryophyte flora of the Sierras de Filabres, Cabrera, Alhamilla and Cabo de Gata (Almería, S.E. Spain). *Journal of Bryology* **20**: 461–493.

Gärdenfors, U. 2005. *Rödlistade arter i Sverige 2005.* Uppsala: ArtDatabanken.

Gaynor, K. 2006. The vegetation of Irish machair. *Biology and Environment, Proceedings of the Royal Irish Academy* **106B**: 311–321.

Gaynor, K. 2008. *The Phytosociology and Conservation Value of Irish Sand Dunes.* Unpublished PhD thesis, National University of Ireland, Dublin, 361 pp.

Gilmore, S.R. 2006. Rhizogoniaceae. In: McCarthy, P. (ed.) *Flora of Australia.* **51** (Mosses 1). Canberra & Melbourne: ABRS and CSIRO Publishing, 354–366.

Gilpin, M. & Hanski, I. (eds) 1991. Metapopulation dynamics: empirical and theoretical investigations. *Biological Journal of the Linnean Society* **42**: 1-336.

Godwin, H. 1975. *History of the British flora.* 2nd ed. Cambridge: Cambridge University Press.

Goffinet, B. 2002. *Orthotrichum sprucei* Mont. (Musci), a European endemic discovered in Kazakhstan. *Arctoa* **11**: 27–30.

Goffinet, B. & Shaw, A.J. 2009. *Bryophyte Biology.* 2nd ed. Cambridge: Cambridge University Press.

Goffinet, B., Hollowell, V. & Magill, R. (eds) 2004. *Molecular systematics of bryophytes.* St Louis: Monographs in Systematic Botany from the Missouri Botanical Garden **98**.

Goffinet, B, Shaw, A.J. & Cox, C.J. 2004. Phylogenetic inferences in the dung-moss family Splachnaceae from analyses of cpDNA sequence data and implications for the evolution of entomophily. *American Journal of Botany* **91**: 748–759.

Gos, L. & Ochyra, R. 1994. New or otherwise interesting distributional data for species of *Seligeria* (Musci, Seligeriaceae) for Eurasia. *Fragmenta Floristica Geobotanica* **39**: 383–389.

Gradstein, S.R. & van Melick, H.M.H. 1996. *De Nederlandse levermossen en hauwmossen. Flora en verspreidingsatlas van de Nederlandse Hepaticae en Anthocerotae.* Utrecht: Stichting Uitgeverij van de Koninklijke Nederlandse Natuurhistorische Vereniging.

Greene, S.W. 1958. *Leptodon smithii* (Hedw.) Mohr in Ireland. *Transactions of the British Bryological Society* **3**: 392–398.

Greven, H. 1995. Grimmia *Hedw. (Grimmiaceae, Musci) in Europe.* Leiden: Backhuys Publishers.

Greven, H. 2003. *Grimmias of the world.* Leiden: Backhuys Publishers.

Grolle, R. 1995. The Hepaticae and Anthocerotae of the East African Islands. An Annotated Catalogue. *Bryophytorum Bibliotheca* **48**: 1–178.

Grolle, R. & Long, D.G. 2000. An annotated check-list of the Hepaticae and Anthocerotae of Europe and Macaronesia. *Journal of Bryology* **22**: 103–140.

Guerra, J. 2007. *Pohlia* section *Cacodon* (Mielichhoferiaceae, Bryophyta) with axillary bulbils in the Iberian Peninsula. *Anales del Jardin Botánico de Madrid* **64**: 55–62.

Guerra, J., Cano, M.J. & Ros, R.M. (eds) 2006. *Flora Briofítica Ibérica.* **3**. Murcia: Universidad de Murcia & Vitoria: Sociedad Española de Briología.

Guerra, J., Jimenez, M.N., Ros, R.M. & Carrion, J.S. 1991. El genero *Phascum* (Pottiaceae) en la Peninsula Ibérica. *Cryptogamie, Bryologie, Lichénologie* **12**: 379–423.

Hallingbäck, T., Hodgetts, N.G. & Urmi, E. 1995. How to apply the new IUCN Red List categories to bryophytes. *Species* **24**: 37–41.

Hallingbäck, T., Lönnell, N. & Weibull, H. 2008. *Nationalnyckeln till Sveriges flora och fauna. Bladmossor: Kompaktmossor-kapmossor. Bryophyta:* Anoectangium – Orthodontium. Uppsala: ArtDatabanken, SLU.

Hallingbäck, T., Lönnell, N., Weibull, H., Hedenäs, L. & von Knorring, P. 2006. *Nationalnyckeln till Sveriges flora och fauna. Bladmossor: Sköldmossor-blåmossor. Bryophyta:* Buxbaumia – Leucobryum. Uppsala: ArtDatabanken, SLU.

He, S. 1998. A checklist of the mosses of Chile. *Journal of the Hattori Botanical Laboratory* **85**: 103–189.

Hedenäs, L. 1992. Flora of Madeiran pleurocarpous mosses (Isobryales, Hypnobryales, Hookeriales). *Bryophytorum Bibliotheca* **44**: 1–165.

Hedenäs, L. 1994. The *Hedwigia ciliata* complex in Sweden, with notes on the occurrence of the taxa in Fennoscandia. *Journal of Bryology* **18**: 139–157.

Hedenäs, L. 1997. A partial generic revision of *Campylium* (Musci). *The Bryologist* **100**: 65–88.

Hedenäs, L. 1999. Altitudinal distribution in relation to latitude; with examples among wetland mosses in the Amblystegiaceae. *Bryobrothera* **5**: 99–115.

Hedenäs, L. 2003. The European species of the *Calliergon-Scorpidium-Drepanocladus* complex, including some related or similar species. *Meylania* **28**: 1–116.

Hedenäs, L. 2008. Molecular variation and speciation in *Antitrichia curtipendula s.l.* (Leucodontaceae, Bryophyta). *Botanical Journal of the Linnean Society* **156**: 341–354.

Hedenäs, L. & Eldenäs, P. 2007. Cryptic speciation, habitat differentiation and geography in *Hamatocaulis vernicosus* (Calliergonaceae, Bryophyta). *Plant Systematics and Evolution* **268**: 131–145.

Hedenäs, L. & Isoviita, P. 2008. A contribution to the understanding of *Heterocladium heteropterum* and its relationship with *H. wulfsbergii*: Nomenclatural issues and lectotypifications. *Journal of Bryology* **30**: 170–173.

Hedenäs, L. & Kooijman, A.M. 1996. Phylogeny and habitat adaptations within a monophyletic group of wetland moss genera (Amblystegiaceae). *Plant Systematics and Evolution* **199**: 33–52.

Hedenäs, L. & Rosborg, C. 2009 ['2008']. *Pseudocalliergon* is nested within *Drepanocladus* (Bryophyta: Amblystegiaceae). *Lindbergia* **33**: 67–74.

Hedenäs, L., Herben, T., Rydin, H. & Söderström, L. 1989. Ecology of the invading moss species *Orthodontium lineare* in Sweden: substrate preference and interactions with other species. *Journal of Bryology* **15**: 565–581.

Heinrichs, J. 2002. A taxonomic revision of *Plagiochila* sect. *Hylacoetes*, sect. *Adianthoideae* and sect. *Fuscoluteae* in the Neotropics with a preliminary subdivision of Neotropical Plagiochilaceae into nine lineages. *Bryophytorum Bibliotheca* **58**: 1–184.

He-Nygren, X., Juslén, A., Ahonen, I., Glenny, D. & Piippo, S. 2006. Illuminating the evolutionary history of liverworts (Marchantiophyta) – towards a natural classification. *Cladistics* **22**: 1–31.

Herrnstadt, I. & Heyn, C.C. 2004. Bryopsida (Mosses). In: Heyn, C.C. & Herrnstadt, I. (eds) *The bryophyte flora of Israel and adjacent regions.* Jerusalem: The Israel Academy of Sciences and Humanities.

Herzog, Th. 1926. *Geographie der Moose.* Jena: Verlag von Gustav Fischer (Reprint, 1974, Amsterdam: A. Asher & Co.).

Hill, M.O. 1981. New vice-county records and amendments to the Census Catalogues. Musci. *Bulletin of the British Bryological Society* **38**: 21–37.

Hill, M.O. 1984. *Racomitrium elongatum* Frisvoll in Britain and Ireland. *Bulletin of the British Bryological Society* **43**: 21–25.

Hill, M.O. 1988. A bryophyte flora of North Wales. *Journal of Bryology* **15**: 377–491.

Hill, M.O. 1993. *Eurhynchium pulchellum* (Hedw.) Jenn. in Britain and Ireland. *Journal of Bryology* **17**: 683–684.

Hill, M.O. & Preston, C.D. 1998. The geographical relationships of British and Irish bryophytes. *Journal of Bryology* **20**: 127–226.

Hill, M.O., Bell, N., Bruggeman-Nannenga, M.A., Brugués, M., Cano, M.J., Enroth, J., Flatberg, K.I., Frahm, J.-P., Gallego, M.T., Garilleti, R., Guerra, J., Hedenäs, L., Holyoak, D.T., Hyvönen, J., Ignatov, M.S., Lara, F., Mazimpaka, V., Muñoz, J. & Söderström, L. 2006. An annotated checklist of the mosses of Europe and Macaronesia. *Journal of Bryology* **28**: 198–267.

Hill, M.O., Blackstock, T.H., Long, D.G. & Rothero, G.P. 2008. *A checklist and census catalogue of British and Irish bryophytes updated 2008.* Middlewich, Cheshire: British Bryological Society.

Hill, M.O., Preston, C.D., Bosanquet, S.D.S. & Roy, D.B. 2007. *BRYOATT. Attributes of British and Irish mosses, liverworts and hornworts.* NERC Centre for Ecology and Hydrology & Countryside Council for Wales.

Hill, M.O., Preston, C.D. & Smith, A.J.E. 1991. *Atlas of the bryophytes of Britain and Ireland. 1. Liverworts (Hepaticae and Anthocerotae).* Colchester: Harley Books.

Hill, M.O., Preston, C.D. & Smith, A.J.E. 1992. *Atlas of the bryophytes of Britain and Ireland. 2. Mosses (except Diplolepideae).* Colchester: Harley Books.

Hill, M.O., Preston, C.D. & Smith, A.J.E. 1994. *Atlas of the bryophytes of Britain and Ireland. 3. Mosses (Diplolepideae).* Colchester: Harley Books.

Hodd, R.L. & Sheehy Skeffington, M.J. 2011. Climate change and oceanic montane vegetation: a case study of the montane heath and associated plant communities in western Irish mountains. In: Hodkinson, T.R. *et al.* (eds) *Climate Change, Ecology and Systematics.* Cambridge: Cambridge University Press pp. 490–515.

Hodgetts, N.G. 2003. *The status of pale bristle-moss* Orthotrichum pallens *in Britain.* Report No. **221**. Peterborough: English Nature, Salisbury: Plantlife.

Hodgetts, N.G. 2004. *Timmia austriaca* Hedw. deleted from the Irish list. *Irish Naturalists' Journal* **27**: 443–444.

Hodgetts, N.G. & Hallingbäck, T. 1994. Some bryophytes new to Ireland. *Irish Naturalists' Journal* **24**: 517–518.

Holland, C.H. (ed.) 1981. *A geology of Ireland.* Edinburgh: Scottish Academic Press.

Holyoak, D.T. 1996. *Sematophyllum substrumulosum* (Hampe) Broth. in the Isles of Scilly: a moss new to Britain. *Journal of Bryology* **19**: 341–345.

Holyoak, D.T. 1997. Mosses (Musci). In: Spalding, A. (ed.) *Red Data Book for Cornwall and the Isles of Scilly.* Camborne, Cornwall: Croceago Press, pp. 37–78.

Holyoak, D.T. 1999. *Status, ecology and conservation of the moss* Hamatocaulis vernicosus *in England and Wales.* Countryside Council for Wales & English Nature Science Report.

Holyoak, D.T. 2001a. A hybrid sporophyte on *Rhytidiadelphus subpinnatus* (Lindb.) T.J.Kop. (Hypnaceae). *Bulletin of the British Bryological Society* **76**: 56–58.

Holyoak, D.T. 2001b. Starry earth-moss *Ephemerum stellatum*. Report to Plantlife on work carried out during 2000. *Plantlife Report* No. **180**: 1–37.

Holyoak, D.T. 2002a. Coastal mosses of the Genus *Bryum*. Report to Plantlife on work carried out in Wales during 2001. *Plantlife Report* No. **203**, p. 49.

Holyoak, D.T. 2002b. Coastal mosses of the Genus *Bryum*. Report to Plantlife on work carried out in England during 2001. *Plantlife Report* No. **206**, p. 43.

Holyoak, D.T. 2003a. *The distribution of bryophytes in Ireland.* Dinas Powys, Vale of Glamorgan: Broadleaf Books.

Holyoak, D.T. 2003b. A taxonomic review of some British coastal species of the *Bryum bicolor* complex, with a description of *Bryum dyffrynense* sp. nov. *Journal of Bryology* **25**: 107–113.

Holyoak, D.T. 2003c. *Acaulon muticum* var. *mediterraneum* in Britain. *Bulletin of the British Bryological Society* **80**: 59–63.

Holyoak, D.T. 2004. Taxonomic notes on some European species of *Bryum* (Bryopsida: Bryaceae). *Journal of Bryology* **26**: 247–264.

Holyoak, D.T. 2006a. Summer field meeting 2005, Co. Fermanagh, Co. Leitrim and Co. Cavan, Ireland. *Field Bryology* **88**: 12–17.

Holyoak, D.T. 2006b. Progress towards a species inventory for conservation of bryophytes in Ireland. *Biology and Environment, Proceedings of the Royal Irish Academy* **106B**: 225–236.

Holyoak, D.T. 2009. Bryophytes: liverworts (Marchantiophyta), hornworts (Anthocerotophyta) and mosses (Bryophyta). In: Bennallick, I. *et al. Red data book for Cornwall and the Isles of Scilly.* 2nd ed. Praze-an-Beeble, Cornwall: Croceago Press, pp. 72–104.Holyoak, D.T. 2010. Notes on taxonomy and identification of European species of *Ephemerum* (Bryopsida: Pottiaceae). *Journal of Bryology* **32**: 122–132.

Holyoak, D.T. & Bryan, V.S. 2005. *Ephemerum hibernicum* sp. nov. (Bryopsida: Ephemeraceae) from Ireland. *Journal of Bryology* **27**: 89–95.

Holyoak, D.T. & Hedenäs, L. 2006. Morphological, ecological and molecular studies of the intergrading taxa *Bryum neodamense* and *B. pseudotriquetrum* (Bryopsida: Bryaceae). *Journal of Bryology* **28**: 299–311.

Holyoak, D.T. & Lockhart, N. 2009a. Notes on some rare and newly recorded bryophytes of metalliferous mine sites in Ireland. *Journal of Bryology* **31**: 267–282.

Holyoak, D.T. & Lockhart, N. 2009b. Australasian bryophytes introduced to South Kerry with tree ferns. *Field Bryology* **98**: 3–7.

Holyoak, D.T. & Long, D.G. 2005. Notable records of mosses (Bryopsida) from Co. Mayo, including four species new to Ireland. *Irish Naturalists' Journal* **28**: 7–10.

Holyoak, D.T. & Pedersen, N. 2007. Conflicting molecular and morphological evidence of evolution within the Bryaceae (Bryopsida) and its implications for generic taxonomy. *Journal of Bryology* **29**: 111–124.

Holyoak, D.T., Clements, R., Coleman, M.R.J. & MacPherson, K.S. 2000. Appendix 2. Notes on the status and ecology of *Ditrichum cornubicum. English Nature Research Reports* No. **328**: 40–50.

Hugonnot, V., Boudier, P. & Chavoutier, J. 2007. *Ephemerum cohaerens* (Hedw.) Hampe, répartition et écologie en France. *Cryptogamie, Bryologie* **28**: 267–279.

Ignatov, M.S., Afonina, O.M. & Ignatova, E.A. (eds) 2007 ['2006']. Check-list of mosses of east Europe and north Asia. *Arctoa* **15**: 1–130.

Ignatova, E.A., Tan, B.C., Afonina, O.M. & Ignatov, M.S. 2009. *Sematophyllum* (Sematophyllaceae, Bryophyta), a new genus and family for Russia. *Arctoa* **18**: 213–216.

Infante, M. & Heras, P. 2005. *Ephemerum cohaerens* (Hedw.) Hampe and *E. spinulosum* Bruch & Schimp. (Ephemeraceae, Bryopsida), new to the Iberian Peninsula. *Cryptogamie, Bryologie* **26**: 327–333.

Ingerpuu, N. 1998. Sammaltaimed, Bryophyta. In: Lillelecht V. (ed.), *Eesti punane raamat.* Tartu: Eesti Teaduste Akad. Lood., pp. 37–49.

Ingham, W. 1913. *A Census Catalogue of British Hepatics, with List of the Botanical Vice-Counties and their boundaries and lists of Sources of Records. Compiled for the Moss Ex-change Club,* 2nd ed. Darwen: W. H. Western, for MEC.

Ireland, R.R. 1969. A taxonomic revision of the genus *Plagiothecium* for North America, north of Mexico. *National Museum of Canada, Publications in Botany* **1**: 1–118.

IUCN 1978. *The IUCN Plant Red Data Book.* Richmond: International Union for the Conservation of Nature.

IUCN 2001. *IUCN Red List Categories and Criteria. Version 3.1.* Gland: International Union for the Conservation of Nature.

IUCN 2003. *Guidelines for Application of IUCN Red List Criteria at Regional Levels. Version 3.0.* Gland: International Union for the Conservation of Nature.

IUCN 2006. *Guidelines for using the IUCN Red List Categories and Criteria. Version 6.2 (December 2006).* Gland: International Union for the Conservation of Nature.

IUCN 2008. *Guidelines for using the IUCN Red List Categories and Criteria. Version 7.0 (August 2008).* Gland: International Union for the Conservation of Nature.

IUCN 2010. *Guidelines for using the IUCN Red List Categories and Criteria. Version 8.1 (August 2010).* Gland: International Union for the Conservation of Nature.

Ivimey-Cook, R.B. & Proctor, M.C.F. 1966. The plant communities of the Burren, Co. Clare. *Proceedings of the Royal Irish Academy* **64B**: 211–301.

Iwatsuki, Z. 1991. *Catalog of the mosses of Japan*. Nichinan, Miyazaki: Hattori Botanical Laboratory.

Jelenc, F. 1955. Muscinées de l'Afrique du Nord (Algérie, Tunisie, Maroc, Sahara). *Société de Géographie et d'Archéologie de la Province d'Oran* **72–76**: 1–152.

Jelenc, F. 1959. Contribution à l'étude de la Flore bryologique du Tibesti (2e fascicule). *Bulletin de la Société d'Histoire Naturelle de l'Afrique du Nord* **50**: 262–269.

Jessen, K. 1949. Studies in Late Quaternary deposits and flora-history in Ireland. *Proceedings of the Royal Irish Academy* **52**: 85–290.

Jiménez, J.A. 2006a. Taxonomic revision of the genus *Didymodon* Hedw. (Pottiaceae, Bryophyta) in Europe, north Africa and southwest and central Asia. *Journal of the Hattori Botanical Laboratory* **100**: 211–292.

Jiménez, J.A. 2006b. *Didymodon* Hedw. In: J. Guerra *et al.* (eds) *Flora Briofítica Ibérica*. Vol. **III**. Murcia: Sociedad Española de Briología. pp. 217–244.

Jiménez, J.A., Ros, R.M., Cano, M.J. & Guerra, J. 2005a. A new evaluation of the genus *Trichostomopsis* (Pottiaceae, Bryophyta). *Botanical Journal of the Linnean Society* **147**: 117–127.

Jiménez, J.A., Ros, R.M., Cano, M.J. & Guerra, J. 2005b. A revision of *Didymodon* Section *Fallaces* (Musci, Pottiaceae) in Europe, North Africa, Macaronesia, and southwest and central Asia. *Annals of the Missouri Botanical Garden* **92**: 225–247.

Jones, E.W. 1954. Bryophytes seen in north-eastern Ireland, 1952. *Irish Naturalists' Journal* **11**: 115–120.

Jones, E.W. 1991. The changing bryophyte flora of Oxfordshire. *Journal of Bryology* **16**: 513–549.

Jones, E.W. & Rose, F. 1975. *Plagiochila atlantica* F.Rose, sp. nov. – *P. ambagiosa* auct. *Journal of Bryology* **8**: 417–422.

Karczmarz, K. 1971. A monograph of the genus *Calliergon* (Sull.) Kindb. *Monographiae Botanicae*, Warszawa **34**: 1–209, pls I–XX.

Keever, C. 1957. Establishment of *Grimmia laevigata* on bare granite. *Ecology* **38**: 422–429.

Kellman, K. 2003. A report from the Seventh Annual SO BE FREE Outing. *Evansia* **20**: 22–30.

Kelly, D.L. 1975. *Native woodland in Western Ireland, with especial reference to the region of Killarney*. Unpublished PhD thesis, University of Dublin, Trinity College, 337 pp.

Kelly, D.L. 1981. The native forest vegetation of Killarney, south-west Ireland: an ecological account. *Journal of Ecology* **69**: 437–472.

Kelly, D.L. 1984. The summer meeting, 1983, Kerry. First week: Killorglin, 21–23 July. *Bulletin of the British Bryological Society* **43**: 5–6.

Kelly, D.L. & Iremonger, S.F. 1997. Irish wetlands woods: the plant communities and their ecology. *Proceedings of the Royal Irish Academy* **97B**: 1–32.

Kelly, D.L. & Kirby, E.N. 1982. Irish native woodlands over limestone. *Journal of Life Sciences of the Royal Dublin Society* **3**: 181–198.

Kelly, D.[L.] & Moore, J.J. 1975. A preliminary sketch of the Irish acidophilous oakwoods. In: Géhu, J.-M. (ed.) *Colloques Phytosociologiques III: La végétation des forêts caducifoliées acidiphiles. Lille – 1974*. Kramer, Vaduz, pp. 375–387.

Kelly, D.L. & Synnott, D.M. 1993. Bryophytes of the Phoenix Park, Dublin. *Glasra* N.S., **2**: 73–81.

Kertland, M.P.H. 1991. Obituary. Jean Wilgar Fitzgerald 1908–1988. Robert Desmond Fitzgerald 1914–1990. *Irish Naturalists' Journal* **23**: 345–346.

King, A.L.K. 1950. *Brachythecium caespitosum* Dixon in Co. Cavan. *Irish Naturalists' Journal* **10**: 21.

King, A.L.K. 1953a. Bryophyte records from the Athlone district. *Irish Naturalists' Journal* **11**: 50–51.

King, A.L.K. 1953b. Bryophyte records made on one-day excursions from Dublin during 1952. *Irish Naturalists' Journal* **11**: 98–99.

King, A.L.K. 1954a. The hepatic *Ptilidium pulcherrimum* (Web.) Hampe new to Ireland. *Irish Naturalists' Journal* **11**: 205.

King, A.L.K. 1954b. New records of bryophytes found during a botanical tour in June, 1952. *Irish Naturalists' Journal* **11**: 230–231.

King, A.L.K. 1956. Some interesting bryophytes. *Irish Naturalists' Journal* **12**: 70.

King, A.L.K. 1958. *Meesia tristicha* Bruch & Schimp. in Ireland. *Irish Naturalists' Journal* **12**: 332.

King, A.L.K. 1966a. Some interesting bryophytes: 1. Hepatics. *Irish Naturalists' Journal* **15**: 207–208.

King, A.L.K. 1966b. Some interesting bryophytes: 2. Mosses. *Irish Naturalists' Journal* **15**: 234–236.

King, A.L.K. 1967a. Some interesting bryophytes: Mosses. *Irish Naturalists' Journal* **15**: 304–305.

King, A.L.K. 1967b. *Cinclidium stygium* Sw. in Co. Westmeath. *Irish Naturalists' Journal* **15**: 331.

King, A.L.K. 1970. Recent additions to the Irish bryophyte census lists. *Irish Naturalists' Journal* **16**: 350–351.

King, A.L.K. & Scannell, M. 1960. Notes on the vegetation of a mineral flush in Co. Mayo. *Irish Naturalists' Journal* **13**: 137–140.

King, E.L., Haflidason, H., Sejrup, H. P., Austin, W.E.N., Duffey, M., Helland, H., Klitgaard-Kristensen, D. & Scourse, J.D. 1998. End moraines on the northwest Irish continental shelf. *3rd ENAM II Workshop, Edinburgh, 1998. Abstract Volume*.

Kirby, N., Lockhart, N.D. & Synnott, D.M. 1980. Observations on the bryology at Gleniff, Co. Sligo (H28). *Bulletin of the Irish Biogeographical Society* **4**: 30–32.

Kirkpatrick, A.H. 1988. *A vegetation survey of heath and moorland in Northern Ireland and Co. Donegal*. Unpublished DPhil thesis, Faculty of Science of the University of Ulster.

Köckinger, H., Werner, O. & Ros, R.M. 2010. A new taxonomic approach to the genus *Oxystegus* (Pottiaceae, Bryophyta) in Europe based on molecular data. *Nova Hedwigia* **138**: 31–49.

Konstantinova, N.A. & Bakalin, V.A. 2009. Checklist of liverworts (Marchantiophyta) of Russia. *Arctoa* **18**: 1–64.

Konstantinova, N.A. & Potemkin, A.D. 1996. Liverworts of the Russian Arctic: an annotated check-list and bibliography. *Arctoa* **6**: 125–150.

Kooijman, A.M. 1993. Causes of the replacement of *Scorpidium scorpioides* by *Calliergonella cuspidata* in eutrophicated rich fens 1. Field Studies. *Lindbergia* **18**: 78–84.

Koponen, A. 1990. Entomophily in the Splachnaceae. *Botanical Journal of the Linnean Society* **104**: 115–127.

Koppe, F. & Düll, R. 1982. Beiträge zur Bryologie und Bryogeographie von Tenerife. *Bryologische Beitraege* **1**: 37–107.

Krisai, R. 1999. Zur Gefährdungssituation von Moosen in Österreich. In: Rote Listen Gefährdeter Pflanzen Österreichs, ed. 2. *Grüne Reihe* **10**: 153–186. Bundesministerium für Umwelt, Jugend und Familie.

Kučera, J. 2000. Illustrierter Bestimmungsschlüssel zu den mitteleuropäischen Arten der Gattung *Didymodon*. *Meylania* **19**: 1–49.

Kučera, J. & Váňa, J. 2003. Check- and Red List of bryophytes of the Czech Republic (2003). *Preslia, Praha* **75**: 193–222.

Kürschner, H. 1996. Additions to the bryophyte flora of Yemen. New records from the Taizz and Jiblah areas. Studies in Arabian bryophytes 21. *Nova Hedwigia* **62**: 233–247.

Kürschner, H. 2000. Bryophyte flora of the Arabian Peninsula and Socotra. *Bryophytorum Bibliotheca* **55**: 1–131.

Kürschner, H. & Erdağ, A. 2005. Bryophytes of Turkey: an annotated reference list of the species with synonyms from the recent literature and an annotated list of Turkish bryological literature. *Turkish Journal of Botany* **29**: 95–154.

Laaka-Lindberg, S., Hedderson, T. & Longton, R.E. 2000. Rarity and reproductive characters in the British hepatic flora. *Lindbergia* **25**: 78–84.

Lara, F., Mazimpaka, V. & Garilleti, R. 2000. *Orthotrichum sprucei* Mont. in the Mediterranean area of the Iberian peninsula. *Cryptogamie, Bryologie* **21**: 267–271.

Lazarenko, A.S. 1955. *Identification book for Leafy mosses of Ukraine*. Kiev. [in Russian].

Leach S. J. & Corbett, P. McM. 1987. A preliminary survey of raised bogs in Northern Ireland. *Glasra* **10**: 57–73.

Lett, H.W. 1912. Clare Island Survey. Parts 11–12. Musci and Hepaticae. *Proceedings of the Royal Irish Academy* **31**: Nos. 11–12: 1–18.

Lett, H.W. 1915. Census report on the mosses of Ireland. *Proceedings of the Royal Irish Academy* **32**, Section **B**, No. **7**: 65–166.

Lewinsky-Haapasaari, J. 1995. Illustrierter Bestimmungsschlüssel zu den Europäischen *Orthotrichum*-Arten. *Meylania* **9**: 3–56.

Lewis, K. 1991. The Summer Meeting, 1990, Ireland. *Bulletin of the British Bryological Society* **57**: 5–8.

Lewis, K. & Smith, A.J.E. 1978. Studies on some bulbiliferous species of *Pohlia* section *Pohliella*. II. Taxonomy. *Journal of Bryology* **10**: 9–27.

Li Xing-jiang, Crosby, M.R. & Si He. 2001. *Moss flora of China. English version. Vol. 2. Fissidentaceae–Ptychomitriaceae*. Beijing & New York: Science Press & St Louis: Missouri Botanical Garden.

Li Xing-jiang, Crosby, M.R. & Si He. (eds) 2007. *Moss flora of China. English version. Vol. 4. Bryaceae–Timmiaceae*. Beijing & New York: Science Press & St Louis: Missouri Botanical Garden.

Ligrone, R., Pocock, K. & Duckett, J.G. 1993. A comparative ultrastructural study of endophytic basidiomycetes in *Cryptothallus mirabilis* and *Aneura pinguis* (Metzgeriales). *Canadian Journal of Botany* **71**: 666–679.

Limpricht, K.G. 1890–1895. Die Laubmoose Deutschlands, Oesterreichs und der Schweiz. Leipzig: Eduard Kummer. In: Rabenhorst, L. *Kryptogamen-Flora von Deutschland, Oesterreich und der Schweiz*, 2 edn, Band 4.

Little, E.R.B. 1967. *Fissidens celticus* Paton, new to Ireland. *Irish Naturalists' Journal* **15**: 271.

Lobley, E.M. 1954. Notes on Sphagna and other bryophytes from the north of Ireland. *Irish Naturalists' Journal* **11**: 197–198.

Lobley, E.M. 1955. Some Irish bryophyte records and localities. *Irish Naturalists' Journal* **11**: 253.

Lobley, E.M. 1958. The meeting of the British Bryological Society in Co. Galway, 1957. *Irish Naturalists' Journal* **12**: 285–290.

Lobley, E.M. 1962. Some records for bryophytes. *Irish Naturalists' Journal* **14**: 43–44.

Lobley, E.M. 1963. Bryophyte records for County Armagh. *Irish Naturalists' Journal* **14**: 98–99.

Lobley, E.M. & Fitzgerald, J.W. 1970. A revision of the genus *Sphagnum* L. in *A Flora of the North-east of Ireland*. *Irish Naturalists' Journal* **16**: 357–365.

Lockhart, N.[D.] 1984. The summer meeting, 1983, Kerry. First week: Killorglin, 24–26 July. *Bulletin of the British Bryological Society* **43**: 7–8.

Lockhart, N.D. 1987. The occurrence of *Homalothecium nitens* (Hedw.) Robins. in Ireland. *Journal of Bryology* **14**: 511–517.

Lockhart, N.D. 1988. Further records for *Homalothecium nitens* (Hedw.) Robins. in north County Mayo, Ireland. *Journal of Bryology* **15**: 234–235.

Lockhart, N.D. 1989a. Three new localities for *Saxifraga hirculus* L. in Ireland. *Irish Naturalists' Journal* **23**: 65–69.

Lockhart, N.D. 1989b. *Leiocolea rutheana* (Limpr.) K. Muell. new to Ireland. *Journal of Bryology* **15**: 525–529.

Lockhart, N.D. 1991. *Phytosociological and ecological studies of lowland blanket bog flushes in west Galway and north Mayo*. Unpublished PhD thesis, National University of Ireland, Galway, 301 pp.

Lockhart, N.D. 1999. *Paludella squarrosa* (Hedw.) Brid., a Boreal relic moss new to Ireland. *Journal of Bryology* **21**: 305–308.

Lohammar, G. 1954. The distribution and ecology of *Fissidens julianus* in northern Europe. *Svensk Botanisk Ttidskrift* **48**: 162–173.

Long, D.G. 1984a. The moss *Fissidens rivularis* (Spruce) B.S.G. in Kerry, new to Ireland. *Irish Naturalists' Journal* **21**: 347–348.

Long, D.G. 1984b. Bryophytes and lichens from Skellig Michael, Co. Kerry. *Irish Naturalists' Journal* **21**: 368.

Long, D.G. 1990. The bryophytes of Achill Island – Hepaticae. *Glasra* N.S., **1**: 47–64.

Long, D.G. 1993. *Scapania uliginosa* (Sw. ex Lindenb.) Dum. erroneously recorded in Ireland. *Bulletin of the British Bryological Society* **61**: 43.

Long, D.G. 2008. *Grimmia* updates. *Field Bryology* **95**: 16–20.

Long, D.G. 2010. The tragedy of the Twelve Bens of Connemara: is there a future for *Adelanthus lindenbergianus*? *Field Bryology* **100**: 2–8.

Longton, R.E. 1992. Reproduction and rarity in British mosses. *Biological Conservation* **59**: 89–98.

Longton, R.E. 1994. Reproductive biology in bryophytes. The challenge and the opportunities. *Journal of the Hattori Botanical Laboratory* **76**: 159–172.

Longton, R.E. 1997. Reproductive biology and life history strategies. *Advances in Bryology* **6**: 65–101.

Longton, R.E. & Schuster, R.M. 1983. Reproductive biology. In: R.M. Schuster (ed.) *New Manual of Bryology*, Vol. **1**. Nichinan: Hattori Botanical Laboratory, pp. 386–462.

Ludwig, G., Düll, R., Philippi, G., Ahrens, M., Caspari, S., Koperski, M., Lütt, S., Schulz, F. & Schwab, G. 1996. Rote Liste der Moose (Anthocerophyta et Bryophyta) Deutschlands. *Schriftenreihe für Vegetationskde* **28**: 189–306.

Macvicar, S.M. 1905. *Moss Exchange Club. Census Catalogue of British Hepatics*. York: Coultas & Volans for MEC.

Macvicar, S.M. 1926. *The student's handbook of British hepatics*. 2nd ed. Eastbourne: Sumfield & Day.

Maier, E. 2002. *Grimmia dissimulata* E. Maier sp. nova, and the taxonomic position of *Grimmia trichophylla* var. *meridionalis* Müll. Hal. (Musci, Grimmiaceae). *Candollea* **56**: 281–300.

Maksimov, A., Hokkanen, T., Potemkin, A. & Maksimova, T. 2001. Bryophyte diversity of mature spruce forests in North Karelia Biosphere Reserve (Finland). *The Finnish Environment* **485**: 160–163.

Malcolm, B. & Malcolm, N. 2006. *Mosses and other bryophytes: an illustrated glossary*. 2nd ed. Nelson, New Zealand: Micro-Optics Press.

Margadant, W.D. & Meijer, W. 1950. Preliminary remarks on *Orthodontium* in Europe. *Transactions of the British Bryological Society* **1**: 266–274.

Marino, P.C. 1991. Dispersal and coexistence of mosses (Splachnaceae) in patchy habitats. *Journal of Ecology* **79**: 1047–1060.

Marino, P.C. 1997. Competition, dispersal and coexistence of Splachnaceae in patchy habitats. *Advances in Bryology* **6**: 241–263.

Marstaller, R. 1993. Synsystematische Übersicht über die Moosgesellschaften Zentraleuropas. *Herzogia* **9**: 513–541.

Mårtensson, O. 1955–1956. Bryophytes of the Torneträsk Area, northern Swedish Lappland, I. II and III. *Kungliga Svenska Vetenskapsakademiens Avhandligar i Naturskyddsärenden* **12**: 1–107, **14**: 1–321, **15**: 1–94.

Matcham, H.W., Porley, R.D. & O'Shea, B.J. 2005. *Sematophyllum substrumulosum* – an overlooked native? *Field Bryology* **87**: 5–8.

McArdle, D. 1904. A list of Irish Hepaticae. *Proceedings of the Royal Irish Academy* **24B**: 387–502.

McCabe, A.M. 1987. Quaternary deposits and glacial stratigraphy in Ireland. *Quaternary Science Reviews* **6**: 259–299.

McKee, A.M. 2000. *A phytosociological study and detailed vegetation map of the heathlands of the western Twelve Bens Mountains, Connemara, Western Ireland*. Unpublished PhD thesis, National University of Ireland, Galway, 279 pp.

M.[egaw], W.R. 1925. James Glover, 1844–1925. *The British Bryological Society Report for 1925* **1**: 183.

Megaw, W.R. 1926a. Irish moss records. *Irish Naturalists' Journal* **1**: 77.

Megaw, W.R. 1926b. Irish moss records. *Irish Naturalists' Journal* **1**: 158.

Megaw, W.R. 1929a. Report on recent additions to the Irish fauna and flora: Musci and Hepaticae. *Proceedings of the Royal Irish Academy* **39 B**: 78–91.

Megaw, W.R. 1929b. Further Irish moss records. *Irish Naturalists' Journal* **2**: 186–187.

Megaw, W.R. 1929c. Corrections and additions. *Irish Naturalists' Journal* **2**: 187.

Megaw, W.R. 1930. Irish bryological records. *Irish Naturalists' Journal* **3**: 130.

Megaw, W.R. 1936. Two new Irish mosses. *Irish Naturalists' Journal* **6**: 149–150.

Megaw, W.R. 1937. Irish moss records. *Irish Naturalists' Journal* **6**: 196.

Megaw, W.R. 1938. Part II. Mosses and liverworts, pp. 325–430, in: Stewart, S.A. & Corry, T.H. *A flora of the North-east of Ireland*. 2nd ed. Belfast: The Quota Press.

Meinunger, L. & Schröder, W. 2007. *Verbreitungsatlas der Moose Deutschlands*. **1–3**. Regensburg: Herausgegeben von U. Dürhammer für die Regensburgische Botanische Gesellschaft.

Mhic Daeid, C. 1976. *A phytosociological and ecological study of the vegetation of peatlands and heaths in the Killarney Valley*. Unpublished PhD thesis, University of Dublin, Trinity College, 233 pp.

Miles, C.J. & Longton, R.E. 1987. Life history of the moss, *Atrichum undulatum* (Hedw.) P.Beauv. *Symposia Biologica Hungarica* **35**: 193–207.

Mitchell, F. 1976. *The Irish landscape.* London: Collins.

Mitchell, F.J.G. 2006. Where did Ireland's trees come from? *Biology and Environment, Proceedings of the Royal Irish Academy* **106B**: 251–259.

Mitchell, F.J.G. & Averis, A.B.G. 1988. *Atlantic bryophytes of three Killarney woods.* Unpublished Report, Royal Irish Academy, Dublin.

Mitchell, M.E. (ed.) 1999. Early observations on the flora of southwest Ireland. Selected letters of Ellen Hutchins and Dawson Turner 1807–1814. *National Botanic Gardens, Glasnevin, Dublin, Occasional Papers* **12**: 1–124.

Mogensen, G.S. 1973. A revision of the moss genus *Cinclidium* Sw. (Mniaceae Mitt.). *Lindbergia* **2**: 49–80.

Moore, D. 1872. A synopsis of the mosses of Ireland. *Proceedings of the Royal Irish Academy.* Science, Vol. **1**: 329–474.

Moore, D. 1878a. List of the mosses of the counties of Dublin and Wicklow, with their principal localities. *The Scientific Proceedings of the Royal Dublin Society* **1**: 228–249.

Moore, D. 1878b. List of the hepaticae which are found in the counties of Dublin and Wicklow, with their principal localities. *The Scientific Proceedings of the Royal Dublin Society* **1**: 250–258.

Moore, J.J. 1955. The distribution and ecology of *Scheuchzeria palustris* on a raised bog in Offaly. *Irish Naturalists' Journal* **11**: 321–329.

Moore, J.J. 1959. Botanical note (*Scheuchzeria palustris…* transplanted). *Irish Naturalists' Journal* **13**: 102.

Moore, J.J. 1968. A classification of the bogs and wet heaths of northern Europe (Oxycocco-Sphagnetea Br.-Bl. et Tx. 1943). In: Tüxen, R. (ed.) *Pflanzensoziologische Systematik: Bericht über das Internationalen Symposium in Stolzenau/Weser 1964.* Den Haag: Junk. pp. 306–320.

The Moss Group, Dublin Naturalists' Field Club. 1951. Bryological records. *Irish Naturalists' Journal* **10**: 186–188.

Müller, F. 2009. New and remarkable bryophyte records from Mongolia. *Cryptogamie, Bryologie* **30**: 281–288.

Müller, K. 1909. Die Lebermoose Deutschlands, Oesterreichs und der Schweiz. Leipzig: Eduard Kummer. In: Rabenhorst, L. *Kryptogamen-Flora von Deutschland, Oesterreich und der Schweiz*, 2 edn, Band 6 (7): 385–448.

Muñoz, J., Felicísimo, Á.M., Cabezas, F., Burgaz, A.R. & Martínez, I. 2004. Wind as a long-distance dispersal vehicle in the Southern Hemisphere. Science, New York **304** (no. 5674): 1144–1147.

Muñoz, J. & Pando, F. 2000. A world synopsis of the genus *Grimmia. Monographs in Systematic Botany from the Missouri Botanical Garden* **83**: 1–133.

Murray, B.M. 1987. *Andreaea schofieldiana* and *A. megistospora*, species novae, and taxonomic criteria for sect. *Nerviae* (Andreaeopsida). *Bryologist* **90**: 15–26.

Murray, B.M. 1988. The genus *Andreaea* in Britain and Ireland. *Journal of Bryology* **15**: 17–82.

Natcheva, R., Ganeva, A. & Spiridonov, G. 2006. Red list of the bryophytes in Bulgaria. *Phytologia Balcanica* **12**: 55–62.

Nebel, M. & Philippi, G. (eds) 2001. *Die Moose Baden-Württembergs.* Bd **2**. Stuttgart (Hohenheim): Ulmer.

Nelson, E.C. 1998. 'A willing Cicerone': Professor Robert Scott (c. 1757–1808) of Trinity College, Dublin, Fermanagh's first botanist. *Glasra*, **3**: 115–143.

Nelson, E.C. & McCracken, E.M. 1987. *The Brightest Jewel. A history of the National Botanic Gardens, Glasnevin, Dublin.* Kilkenny: Boethius Press.

Noguchi, A. 1988. *Illustrated moss flora of Japan.* **2**. Nichinan-shi: Hattori Botanical Laboratory.

Nyholm, E. 1954–1969. *Illustrated Moss Flora of Fennoscandia. II. Musci.* Lund: Gleerup. (Reprinted 1981, Kungälv: Swedish Natural Science Research Council).

Nyholm, E. 1971. Studies in the genus *Atrichum* P. Beauv. A short survey of the genus and species. *Lindbergia* **1**: 1–33.

Nyholm, E. 1993. *Illustrated Flora of Nordic Mosses. Fasc. 3. Bryaceae*, etc. Copenhagen & Lund: Nordic Bryological Society.

Nyholm, E. 1998. *Illustrated Flora of Nordic Mosses. Fasc. 4. Aulacomniaceae*, etc. Copenhagen & Lund: Nordic Bryological Society.

Nyholm, E. & Crundwell, A.C. 1958. *Bryum salinum* Hagen ex Limpr. in Britain and in America. *Transactions of the British Bryological Society* **3**: 375–377.

Ochi, H. 1972. A revision of African Bryoidea, Musci (First Part). *Journal of the Faculty of Education Tottori University, Natural Science* **23**: 1–126.

Ochyra, R. 1991. *Seligeria oelandica*, a phytogeographically interesting moss newly recorded from Central Europe. *Folia Geobotanica et Phytotaxonomica* **26**: 181–191.

Oesau, A. 2008. Ein salztoleranter Ökotyp von *Phascum cuspidatum* var. *piliferum* (Hedw.) Hook. & Taylor an den Salinen von Bad Kreuznach und Bad Münster a.St. *Archive for Bryology* **33**: 1–7.

Olsson, S., Rumsey, F., Grundmann, M., Russell, S., Enroth, J. & Quandt, D. 2009. The origin of British and Macaronesian endemic *Thamnobryum* species. *Journal of Bryology* **31**: 1–10.

Orange, A. 1995. Riparian taxa of *Schistidium* in the British Isles. *Bulletin of the British Bryological Society* **65**: 51–58.

Ordóñez, A. 2007. *Philonotis* Brid. In: Guerra, J. & Cros, R.M. *Flora Briofítica Ibérica.* Bartramiaceae. Murcia: Sociedad Española de Briología. pp. 13–27.

Ordóñez, M.C.F. & Prieto, M.A.C. 2003. *Briófitos de la Reserva Natural Integral de Muniellos, Asturias.* Oviedo: KRK Ediciones.

Osvald, H. 1949. Notes on the vegetation of British and Irish mosses. *Acta Phytogeographica Suecica* **26**: 1–62.

Overland, A. & O'Connell, M. 2008. Fine-spatial paleoecological investigations towards reconstructing late Holocene environmental change, landscape evolution and farming activity in Barrees, Beara Peninsula, southwestern Ireland. *Journal of the North Atlantic* **1**: 37–73.

Overland, A. & O'Connell, M. (in press). Pollen analytical investigations at Kilbegly 2, Co. Roscommon, on the route of the N6 Ballinasloe to Athlone: towards providing new insights into the environmental impact of local farming and technological developments in the medieval period. In: Jackman, N., Moore C. & Rynne, C. (eds) *The mill at Kilbegly and other archaeological excavations on the route of the N6 Ballinasloe to Athlone national road scheme.* NRA Monograph.

O'Connell, M. 1981. The phytosociology and ecology of Scragh Bog, Co. Westmeath. *New Phytologist* **87**: 139–187.

O'Connor, M. 2000. *A study of the phytosociology, vegetation distribution and ecology of the Roundstone Bog Complex, Connemara, Co. Galway.* Unpublished PhD thesis, National University of Ireland, Galway.

Ó Críodáin, C. & Doyle, G.J. 1994. An overview of Irish small-sedge vegetation: syntaxonomy and a key to the communities belonging to the Scheuchzerio-Caricetea nigrae (Nordh. 1936) Tx. 1937. *Biology and Environment, Proceedings of the Royal Irish Academy* **94B**: 127–144.

Ó Críodáin, C. & Doyle, G.J. 1997. Schoenetum nigricantis, the *Schoenus* fen and flush vegetation of Ireland. *Biology and Environment, Proceedings of the Royal Irish Academy* **97B**: 203–218.

O'Neill, F.H. 2009. Calyptrochaeta apiculata (Southern Hookeria): first Irish record confirmed in Co. Cork. *Field Bryology* **98**: 28–29.

O'Shea, B.J. 2006. Checklist of the mosses of sub-Saharan Africa. Version 5. *Tropical Bryology Research Reports* **6**: 1–253.

O'Sullivan, A.M. 1965. *A phytosociological survey of Irish lowland meadows and pastures.* Unpublished PhD thesis, National University of Ireland, Dublin.

Papp, B. 2005. Selection of Important Bryophyte Areas in Hungary. *Folia Cryptogamica Estonica* **44**: 101–111.

Papp, B. & Sabovljević, M. 2003. Contribution to the bryophyte flora of Turkish Thrace. *Studia Botanica Hungarica* **34**: 43–54.

Parker, R.E. 1958. The Summer Meeting in Ireland, 1957. *Transactions of the British Bryological Society* **3**: 493–498.

Parnell, J. 1982. Some remarks on the bryophyte herbarium of H.W. Lett in Trinity College Dublin. *Irish Naturalists' Journal* **20**: 489.

Paton, J.A. 1965. *Census catalogue of British hepatics (4th edition).* Ipswich: British Bryological Society.

Paton, J.A. 1968. Eriopus apiculatus (Hook. f. & Wils.) Mitt. established on Tresco. *Transactions of the British Bryological Society* **5**: 460–462.

Paton, J.A. 1969. Four hepatics new to Ireland. *Irish Naturalists' Journal* **16**: 171–173.

Paton, J.A. 1971. Three hepatics new to Ireland on Bulbin Mountain, Co. Donegal. *Irish Naturalists' Journal* **17**: 97–99.

Paton, J.A. 1972. Leiocolea heterocolpos (Thed.) Buch new to Ireland. *Irish Naturalists' Journal* **17**: 180.

Paton, J.A. 1974. *Fossombronia fimbriata* sp. nov. *Journal of Bryology* **8**: 1–4.

Paton, J.A. 1976. *Ditrichum cornubicum,* a new moss from Cornwall. *Journal of Bryology* **9**: 171–175.

Paton, J.A. 1979. *Plagiochila britannica,* a new species in the British Isles. *Journal of Bryology* **10**: 245–256.

Paton, J.A. 1999. *The liverwort flora of the British Isles.* Colchester: Harley Books.

Paton, J.A. & Perry, A.R. 1995. *Leiocolea fitzgeraldiae* sp. nov. in Britain and Ireland. *Journal of Bryology* **18**: 469–478.

Pearman, D.A. 2007. 'Far from any house' – assessing the status of doubtfully native species in the flora of the British Isles. *Watsonia* **26**: 271–290.

Pedersen, N., Holyoak, D.T. & Newton, A. 2007. Systematics and morphological evolution within the moss family Bryaceae: A comparison between parsimony and Bayesian methods for reconstruction of ancestral character states. *Molecular Phylogenetics and Evolution* **43**: 891–907.

Perold, S.M. 1998. Studies in the liverwort genus *Fossombronia* (Metzgeriales) from Southern Africa. 5. A new species from Northern and Western Cape. *Bothalia* **28**: 1–5.

Perrin, P.M., Martin, J.R., Barron, S.J. & Roche, J.R. 2006. A cluster analysis approach to classifying Irish native woodlands. *Biology and Environment, Proceedings of the Royal Irish Academy* **106B**: 261–275.

Perrin, P.[M.], Martin, J.[R.], Barron, S.[J.], O'Neill, F., McNutt, K. & Delaney, A. 2008. *National Survey of Native Woodlands – Volume 1 Main Report.* Unpublished Report to the National Parks & Wildlife Service, Dublin. 177 pp.

Perring, F.H. & Walters, S.M. 1962. *Atlas of the British Flora.* London & Edinburgh: BSBI & Thomas Nelson & Sons.

Perry, A.R. 1983. Mosses and liverworts. In: Webb, D.A. & Scannell, M.J.P. *Flora of Connemara and the Burren.* Cambridge: Royal Dublin Society & Cambridge University Press.

Perry, A.R. 1990. Obituaries. Jean Wilgar Fitzgerald BSc (1908–1988). *Journal of Bryology* **16**: 133–137.

Perry, A.R. 1991. Obituary. Robert Desmond Fitzgerald (1914–1990). *Journal of Bryology* **16**: 495–496.

Pierrot, R.B. 1961. Contribution à l'étude d'*Orthodontium pellucens* (Hook.) Br. et Schimp. *Revue Bryologique et Lichénologique* **30**: 113–116.

Pierrot, R.B. 1974. *Sematophyllum substrumulosum* (Hpe.) Broth. dans l'Ile de Oléron, muscinée nouvelle pour le littoral atlantique française. *Bulletin de la Société Botanique du Centre-Ouest,* N.S. **5**: 115.

Pocock, K. & Duckett, D.G. 1985. On the occurrence of branched and swollen rhizoids in British hepatics: their relationships with the substratum and associations with fungi. *New Phytologist* **99**: 281–304.

Pócs, T. 1960. Die Verbreitung von *Leptodon smithii* (Dicks.) Mohr und die Verhältnisse seines Vorkommens. *Annales Historico-Naturalis Musei Nationalis Hungarici, Pars botanica* **52**: 168–176.

Pohjamo, M. & Laaka-Lindberg, S. 2003. Reproductive modes in the epixylic hepatic *Anastrophyllum hellerianum*. *Perspectives in Plant Ecology, Evolution and Systematics* **6**: 159–168.

Porley, R.D. 1998. Using nerve sections to separate *Orthodontium gracile* Schwaegr. ex Br. Eur. and *O. lineare* Schwaegr. *Journal of Bryology* **20**: 500–501.

Porley, R.D. 2001. Mosses and liverworts of the sandstone scarps of the Lough Navar Forest region, Co. Fermanagh. *Irish Naturalists' Journal* **26**: 393–404.

Porley, R.D. 2004. *Grimmia dissimulata* E. Maier in Britain. *Field Bryology* **82**: 13–17.

Porley, R.D. 2008. *Arable bryophytes. A field guide to the mosses, liverworts and hornworts of cultivated land in Britain and Ireland.* Old Basing: WildGuides.

Porley, R. & Hodgetts, N. 2005. *Mosses and liverworts.* London: HarperCollins (The New Naturalist Library).

Porley, R.D. & Maier, E. 2007. *Grimmia muehlenbeckii* Schimp. in Britain and Ireland. *Journal of Bryology* **29**: 188–193.

Porley, R.D. & Matcham, H.W. 2003. The status of *Orthodontium gracile* in Britain and Ireland. *Journal of Bryology* **25**: 64–66.

Porley, R.D., Papp, B., Söderström, L. & Hallingbäck, T. 2008. European bryophyte conservation in the new millennium. In: Mohamed, H., Bakar, B., Boyce, A.N., Lee, P.K.Y., (eds) *Bryology in the New Millennium.* Kuala Lumpur: University of Malaya, pp. 459–485.

Praeger, R.Ll. 1901. Irish Topographical Botany. *Proceedings of the Royal Irish Academy* **23** (3rd series, 7): 1–410.

Pressel, S., Matcham, H.W. & Duckett, J.G. 2005. Studies of protonemal morphogenesis in mosses. X. Ephemeraceae revisited: new dimensions underground. *Journal of Bryology* **27**: 311–318.

Pressel, S., Matcham, H.W. & Duckett, J.G. 2007. Studies of protonemal morphogenesis in mosses. XI. *Bryum* and allied genera: a plethora of propagules. *Journal of Bryology* **29**: 241–258.

Preston, C.D. 2004. An updated list of British and Irish bryophytes from which tubers have been reported. *Field Bryology* **83**: 2–13.

Preston, C.D. 2006. A revised list of nationally scarce bryophytes. *Field Bryology* **90**: 22–31.

Preston, C.D. & Hill, M.O. 1999. The geographical relationships of the British and Irish flora: a comparison of pteridophytes, flowering plants, liverworts and mosses. *Journal of Biogeography* **26**: 629–642.

Preston, C.D., Pearman, D.A. & Hall, A.R. 2004. Archaeophytes in Britain. *Botanical Journal of the Linnean Society* **145**: 257–294.

Pursell, R.A. 1994a. Fissidentaceae. In: Allen, B., Moss Flora of Central America. *Monographs in Systematic Botany from the Missouri Botanical Garden* **49**: 40–80.

Pursell, R.A. 1994b. Fissidentaceae. In: Sharp, A. J., Crum, H. & Eckel, P.M. (eds) Moss Flora of Mexico. *Memoirs of the New York Botanical Garden* **69**: 31–81.

Radford, E.A. & Odé, B. (eds) 2009. *Conserving Important Plant Areas: investing in the green gold of south east Europe.* Salisbury: Plantlife International.

Raeymaekers, G. 1983. *Philonotis rigida* Brid. in Europe. *Lindbergia* **9**: 29–33.

Ratcliffe, D.A. 1962. The habitat of *Adelanthus unciformis* (Tayl.) Mitt. and *Jamesoniella carringtonii* (Balf.) Spr. in Ireland. *Irish Naturalists' Journal* **14**: 38–40.

Ratcliffe, D.A. 1968. An ecological account of Atlantic bryophytes in the British Isles. *New Phytologist* **67**: 365–439.

Ratcliffe, D.A., (ed.) 1977. *A nature conservation review.* Volumes 1 & 2. Cambridge: Cambridge University Press.

Renker, C., Heinrichs, J., Proschold, T., Groth, H. & Holz, I. 2002. ITS sequences of nuclear ribosomal DNA support the generic placement and the disjunct range of *Plagiochila* (*Adelanthus*) *carringtonii*. *Cryptogamie, Bryologie* **23**: 23–29.

Reynolds, S.C.P. 2002. *A catalogue of alien plants in Ireland. National Botanic Gardens, Glasnevin, Dublin. Occasional Papers* **14**: pp. 414.

Richards, P.W. 1938. The bryophyte communities of a Killarney oakwood. *Annales Bryologici* **11**: 108–130.

Richards, P.W. 1952. Meeting of the British Bryological Society in Southwestern Ireland, September 1951. *Revue Bryologique et Lichénologique* **21**: 177–179.

Richards, P.W. & Smith, A.J.E. 1975. A progress report on *Campylopus introflexus* (Hedw.) Brid. and *C. polytrichoides* De Not. in Britain and Ireland. *Journal of Bryology* **8**: 293–298.

Rodwell, J.S. (ed.) 1991–2000. *British Plant Communities. Volumes 1–5.* Cambridge: Cambridge University Press.

Rodwell, J.S. 2006. *National Vegetation Classification: Users' Handbook.* Peterborough: Joint Nature Conservation Committee.

Ros, R.M., Cano, M.J. & Guerra, J. 1999. Bryophyte checklist of Northern Africa. *Journal of Bryology* **21**: 207–244.

Ros, R.M., Mazimpaka, V., Abou-Salama, U., Aleffi, M., Blockeel, T.L., Brugués, M., Cano, M.J., Cros, R.M., Dia, M.G., Dirkse, G.M., El Saadawi, W., Erdağ, A., Ganeva, A., González-Mancebo, J.M., Herrnstadt, I., Khalil, K., Kürschner, H., Lanfranco, E., Losada-Lima, A., Refai, M.S., Rodíguez-Nuñez, S., Sabovljević, M., Sérgio, C., Shabbara, H., Sim-Sim, M. & Söderström, L. 2007. Hepatics and Anthocerotes of the Mediterranean, an annotated checklist. *Cryptogamie, Bryologie* **28**: 351–437.

Roth, G. 1903–1905. *Die europäischen Laubmoose. Beschrieben und gezeichnet von Georg Roth.* 2 Bände, xiii + 598 pp., xvi + 733 pp. Leipzig: Engelmann.

Rothero, G.P. 1984. The summer meeting, 1983, Kerry. Second Week: Kenmare, 27 July–3 August. *Bulletin of the British Bryological Society* **43**: 8–11.

Rothero, G.P. 1988. The summer meeting, 1987, Co. Mayo. Second week at Westport: 12–18 August. *Bulletin of the British Bryological Society* **51**: 10–15.

Rothero, G.P. 2000. New vice-county records and amendments to the *Census Catalogue*. Musci. *Bulletin of the British Bryological Society* **75**: 45–62.

Rothero, G.P. 2001. New vice-county records and amendments to the *Census Catalogue*. Musci. *Bulletin of the British Bryological Society* **77**: 37–48.

Rothero, G.P. 2002. New vice-county records and amendments to the *Census Catalogue*. Musci. *Bulletin of the British Bryological Society* **79**: 42–56.

Rothero, G.P. 2003. New vice-county records and amendments to the *Census Catalogue*. Musci. *Bulletin of the British Bryological Society* **81**: 46–63.

Rothero, G.P. 2004. New vice-county records and amendments to the *Census Catalogue*. Musci. *Field Bryology* **83**: 35–44.

Rothero, G.P. 2005. New vice-county records and amendments to the *Census Catalogue*. Musci. *Field Bryology* **86**: 29–43.

Rothero, G.P. 2006. New vice-county records and amendments to the *Census Catalogue*. Musci. *Field Bryology* **89**: 25–42.

Rothero, G.P. 2007. New vice-county records and amendments to the *Census Catalogue*. Musci. *Field Bryology* **93**: 32–46.

Rothero, G.P. 2008. New vice-county records. Musci. *Field Bryology* **95**: 52–67.

Rothero, G.P. 2009. New vice-county records. Musci. *Field Bryology* **98**: 69–79.

Rothero, G.P. & Synnott, D.[M.] 1988. The British Bryological Society in Ireland, August 1987. *Irish Naturalists' Journal* **22**: 495.

Rubers, W.V. 1975. Notes on some bryophytes from the Lough Ree area. *Irish Naturalists' Journal* **18**: 177–183.

Ruiz, E., Brugués, M. & Casas, C. 2006. *Hypnum uncinulatum* Jur. new to peninsular Spain. *Cryptogamie, Bryologie* **27**: 399–402.

Sabovljević, M. 2006. Checklist of mosses of Croatia. *Archives of Biological Sciences* **58**: 45–53.

Sabovljević, M., Cvetić, T. & Stevanović, V. 2004. Bryophyte Red List of Serbia and Montenegro. *Biodiversity and Conservation* **13**: 1781–1790.

Satake, K., Shibata, K., Nishikaw, M. & Fuwa, K. 1988. Copper accumulation and location in the moss *Scopelophila cataractae*. *Journal of Bryology* **15**: 353–376.

Savicz-Ljubitzkaja, L.I. & Smirnova, Z.N. 1970. *The Handbook of the Mosses of the U.S.S.R. The Mosses Acrocarpous.* Leningrad: Academy of Sciences of USSR & Komarov Botanical Institute.

Scannell, M.J.P. 1977. The bryophyte collection of Mrs A.L.K. King. *Irish Naturalists' Journal* **19**: 130.

Schill, D. & Long, D.G. 2002. *Anastrophyllum lignicola* (Lophoziaceae), a new species from the Sino-Himalayas, and *A. hellerianum* new to China. *Annales Botanici Fennici* **39**: 129–132.

Schnyder, N., Bergamini, A., Hofmann, H., Müller, N., Schubiger-Bossard, C. & Urmi, E. 2004. *Liste Rouge des espèces menacées en Suisse. Bryophytes.* Berne: Office fédéral de l'environnement, des forêts et du paysage.

Schofield, W.B. 1985. *Introduction to bryology.* New York: Macmillan Publishing Co. & London: Collier Macmillan Publishers.

Schouten, M.G.C. 1984. Some aspects of the ecogeographical gradient in the Irish ombrotrophic bogs. *Proceedings of the 7th International Peat Congress, Dublin, Ireland* **1**: 414–432.

Schouten, M.G.C. 1990. Problems of scale in the phytosociology of Irish bogs. In: Doyle, G.J. (ed.) *Ecology and conservation of Irish peatlands.* Royal Irish Academy, Dublin, pp. 91–107.

Schouten, M.G.C. (ed.) 2002. *Conservation and restoration of raised bogs; geological, hydrological and ecological studies.* Dúchas – The Heritage Service of the Department of the Environment and Local Government, Ireland; Staatsbosbeheer, the Netherlands; Geological Survey of Ireland.

Schriebl, A. 1991. Experimentelle Studien über die Laubmoosgattung *Polytrichum. Carinthia II* **181/101**: 461–506.

Schumacker, R. & Brugués, M. 1991. *Scopelophila cataractae* (Mitt.) Broth. (Pottiaceae, Bryophytina), new for Spain. *Journal of Bryology* **16**: 486–488.

Schumacker, R. & De Zuttere, P. 1982. *Sematophyllum demissum* (Wils.) Mitt. (Musci), espèce nouvelle pour la bryoflore belge. Étude critique de sa répartition en Europe. *Bulletin de la Société Royale de Botanique de Belgique* **115**: 14–22.

Schumacker, R. & Váňa, J. 2000. *Identification keys to the liverworts and hornworts of Europe and Macaronesia (distribution & status).* Documents de la Station scientifique des Hautes-Fagnes, Belgium.

Schumacker, R. & Váňa, J. 2005. *Identification keys to the liverworts and hornworts of Europe and Macaronesia.* 2nd revised ed. Poznań: Sorus.

Schuster, R.M. (ed.) 1983. *New manual of bryology.* **1**. Nichinan, Miyazaki, Japan: The Hattori Botanical Laboratory.

Schuster, R.M. (ed.) 1984. *New manual of bryology.* **2**. Nichinan, Miyazaki, Japan: The Hattori Botanical Laboratory.

Scott, G.A.M. & Pike, D.C. 1984. New species of *Fossombronia* from Australia. *Journal of the Hattori Botanical Laboratory* **56**: 339–349.

Scott, G.A.M. & Stone, I.G. 1976. *The mosses of southern Australia.* London, New York & San Francisco: Academic Press.

Scott, G.A.M., Entwisle, T.J., May, T.W. & Stevens, G.N. 1997. *A conservation overview of Australian non-marine lichens, bryophytes, algae and fungi.* Wildlife Australia. Canberra.

Séneca, A. & Söderström, L. 2009. Sphagnophyta of Europe and Macaronesia: a checklist with distribution data. *Journal of Bryology* **31**: 243–254.

Sérgio, C. & Carvalho, S. 2003. Annotated catalogue of Portuguese bryophytes. *Portugaliae Acta Biologica* **21**: 5–230.

Sérgio, C., Brugués, M., Cros, R.M., Casas, C. & Garcia, C. 2006. The 2006 Red List and an updated checklist of bryophytes of the Iberian Peninsula (Portugal, Spain and Andorra). *Lindbergia* **31**: 109–125.

Sharpe, A.J., Crum, H. & Eckel, P.M. (eds) 1994. *The Moss Flora of Mexico. Vols. 1–2.* New York: Memoirs of the New York Botanical Garden **69**.

Shaw, A.J. 1981. A taxonomic revision of the propaguliferous species of *Pohlia* (Musci) in North America. *Journal of the Hattori Botanical Laboratory* **50**: 1–81.

Shaw, [A.] J. 1987. Evolution of heavy metal tolerance in bryophytes. II. An ecological and experimental investigation of the 'copper moss' *Scopelophila cataractae* (Pottiaceae). *American Journal of Botany* **74**: 813–821.

Shaw, [A.] J. 1993. Population biology of the rare copper moss *Scopelophila cataractae*. *American Journal of Botany* **80**: 1034–1041.

Shaw, A.J. & Goffinet, B. (eds) 2000. *Bryophyte biology.* Cambridge: Cambridge University Press.

Shaw, A.J., Cox, C.J. & Boles, S.B. 2005. Phylogeny, species delimitation and recombination in *Sphagnum* Section *Acutifolia*. *Systematic Botany* **30**: 16–33.

Sherrin, W.R. 1937. *The British Bryological Society. Census Catalogue of British Sphagna. Compiled for the B.B.S. ...* [1st ed.] Berwick-on-Tweed: Martin's Printing Works, for BBS.

Sherrin, W.R. revised by Thompson, A. 1946. *The British Bryological Society. Census Catalogue of British Sphagna. Compiled for the B.B.S. ...* [2nd ed.] Berwick-on-Tweed: Martin's Printing Works, for BBS.

Siebel, H.N., Bijlsma, R.J. & Bal, D. 2006. *Toelichting op de Rode Lijst Mossen.* Ede: Ministry of Agriculture, Nature and food quality, report DK2006/034.

Sjögren, E. 1975. Epiphyllous bryophytes of Madeira. *Svensk Botanisk Tidskrift* **69**: 217–288.

Sjögren, E. 1978. Bryophyte vegetation in the Azores Islands. *Memorias de Sociedade Broteriana* **26**: 1–283, figs 1–7.

Sjögren, E. 2001. Distribution of Azorean bryophytes up to 1999, their island distribution and information on their presence elsewhere, including Madeira and the Canary Islands. *Boletim do Museu Municipal do Funchal (História Natural)*, Suplemento No. 7, pp. 89.

Smith, A.G. 1958. Pollen analytical investigations of the mire at Fallahogy Td., Co. Derry. *Proceedings of the Royal Irish Academy* **59**: 329–343.

Smith, A.J.E. 1978. *The Moss Flora of Britain and Ireland.* Cambridge, London, New York, Melbourne: Cambridge University Press.

Smith, A.J.E. 1990a. *The Liverworts of Britain and Ireland.* Cambridge, London, New York, Melbourne: Cambridge University Press.

Smith, A.J.E. 1990b. The bryophytes of Achill Island – Musci. *Glasra* N.S., **1**: 27–46.

Smith, A.J.E. 1993. *Ditrichum flexicaule* and *D. crispatissimum* in Great Britain and Ireland. *Bulletin of the British Bryological Society* **61**: 45–54.

Smith, A.J.E. 1997. The *Hypnum cupressiforme* complex in the British Isles. *Journal of Bryology* **19**: 751–774.

Smith, A.J.E. 2004. *The moss flora of Britain and Ireland.* 2nd ed. Cambridge: Cambridge University Press.

Söderström, L. (ed.) 1996. *Preliminary distribution maps of bryophytes in northwestern Europe. 2. Musci (A–I).* Trondheim: Mossornas Vänner.

Söderström, L. & During, H.J. 2005. Bryophyte rarity viewed from the perspectives of life history strategy and metapopulation dynamics. *Journal of Bryology* **27**: 261–268.

Söderström, L. & Herben, T. 1997. Dynamics of bryophyte metapopulations. *Advances in Bryology* **6**: 205–240.

Söderström, L. & Jonsson, B.G. 1989. Spatial pattern and dispersal in the leafy hepatic *Ptilidium pulcherrimum*. *Journal of Bryology* **15**: 793–802.

Söderström, L., Urmi, E. & Váňa, J. 2002. Distribution of Hepaticae and Anthocerotae in Europe and Macaronesia. *Lindbergia* **27**: 3–47.

Söderström, L., Urmi, E. & Váňa, J. 2007. The distribution of Hepaticae and Anthocerotae in Europe and Macaronesia – Update 1–427. *Cryptogamie, Bryologie* **28**: 299–350.

Solga, A. & Frahm, J.-P. 2002. Verbreitung und Ökologie von *Ditrichum plumbicola* Crundw. in Deutschland. *Limprichtia* **20**: 205–211.

Sotiaux, A., De Zuttere, P., Schumacker, R., Pierrot, R.B.P. & Ulrich, C. 1987. *Scopelophila cataractae* (Mitt.) Broth. (Pottiaceae, Musci), nouveau pour le continent européen en France, en Belgique, aux Pays-Bas et en République fédéral allemande. *Cryptogamie, Bryologie, Lichénologie* **8**: 95–108.

Sotiaux, A., Pioli, A., Royaud, A., Schumacker, R. & Vanderpoorten, A. 2007. A checklist of the bryophytes of Corsica (France): new records and a review of the literature. *Journal of Bryology* **29**: 41–53.

Sotiaux, A., Stieperaere, H., Sotiaux, O. & Pohl, H. 2009. *Fossombronia caespitiformis* De Not. *ex* Rabenh. subsp. *multispira* (Schiffn.) J.R. Bray *et* Cargill in Belgium, a remarkable extension of its European range. *Cryptogamie, Bryologie* **30**: 265–269.

Spence, J.R. & Ramsay, H.P. 2006. Bryaceae. In: *Flora of Australia* **51**: ii, 183, 274–313, 319–348, 400–403, 411–412. Canberra: Government Printing Office.

Spirina, U.N. & Zolotov, V.I. 2004. Mosses of the Orenburg State Nature Reserve (south-eastern European Russia). *Arctoa* **13**: 51–56.

Stace, C.A. 2010. *New flora of the British Isles.* 3rd ed. Cambridge: Cambridge University Press.

Štechová, T. & Kučera, J. 2007. The requirements of the rare moss, *Hamatocaulis vernicosus* (Calliergonaceae, Musci), in the Czech Republic, in relation to vegetation, water chemistry and management. *Biological Conservation* **135**: 443–449.

Štechová, T., Hájek, M., Hájková, P. & Navrátilová, J. 2008. Comparison of habitat requirements of the mosses *Hamatocaulis vernicosus*, *Scorpidium cossonii* and *Warnstorfia exannulata* in different parts of temperate Europe. *Preslia* **80**: 399–410.

Stern, R.C. 1991. *Tortula freibergii* and *Eriopus apiculatus* in East Sussex. *Journal of Bryology* **16**: 488–489.

Stevenson, C.R. & Strauss, D.F. 2001. *Plagiothecium cavifolium* in East Norfolk (VC 27). *Journal of Bryology* **23**: 141–142.

Stewart, N.F. 2004. *Important stonewort areas. An assessment of the best areas for stoneworts in the United Kingdom.* Salisbury: Plantlife International.

Stewart, S.A. & Corry, T.H. 1888. *A flora of the north-east of Ireland ...* Cambridge: Macmillan & Bowes, for The Belfast Naturalists' Field Club.

Stieperaere, H. 1994. *Lophocolea semiteres* (Lehm.) Mitt. in Belgium and the Netherlands. *Lindbergia* **19**: 29–36.

Stone, I.G. 1988. *Acaulon granulosum*, a new species in the *Acaulon muticum* complex: a comparison and key to Australian species. *Journal of Bryology* **15**: 257–268.

Störmer, P. 1969. *Mosses with a western and southern distribution in Norway.* Oslo, Bergen & Tromsö: Universitetsforlaget.

Stotler, R.E., Bray, J.R., Jr., Cargill, D.C., Krayeski, D. & Crandall-Stotler, B.J. 2003. Typifications in the genus *Fossombronia* (Marchantiophyta). *Bryologist* **106**: 130–142.

Streimann, H. 2000. Taxonomic studies on Australian Hookeriaceae (Musci). 3. The genera *Calyptrochaeta*, *Daltonia*, *Hookeriopsis* and *Sauloma*. *Journal of the Hattori Botanical Laboratory* **88**: 101–138.

Streimann, H. & Klazenga, N. 2002. Catalogue of Australian mosses. Canberra: *Flora of Australia Supplementary Series* **17**.

Suanjak, M. 1999. Rhizoidgemmen bei *Atrichum undulatum* (Hedw.) P. Beauv. und *A. angustatum* (Brid.) B. & S. *Abhandlungen der Zoologischen-Botanischen Gesellschaft in Österreich* **30**: 17–24.

Subhisha, S. & Subramoniam, A. 2005. Antifungal activities of a steroid from *Pallavicinia lyellii*, a liverwort. *Indian Journal of Pharmacology* **37**: 304–308.

Syed, H. & Crundwell, A.C. 1973. *Barbula maxima*, nom. nov., an endemic Irish moss. *Journal of Bryology* **7**: 527–529.

Synnott, D.M. 1964. Contributions to the bryophyte census of Counties Meath and Louth. *Irish Naturalists' Journal* **14**: 210.

Synnott, D.[M.] 1967a. The summer meeting, 1966. *Transactions of the British Bryological Society* **5**: 428–431.

Synnott, D.M. 1967b. Contributions to the bryophyte census of Counties Meath and Louth: II. *Irish Naturalists' Journal* **15**: 293–296.

Synnott, D.M. 1967c. The summer meeting of the British Bryological Society in Ireland, 1966. *Irish Naturalists' Journal* **15**: 306–307.

Synnott, D.[M.] 1976a. The summer meeting, 1975. *Bulletin of the British Bryological Society* **27**: 5–9.

Synnott, D.[M.] 1976b. The British Bryological Society in Ireland, August1975. *Irish Naturalists' Journal* **18**: 366.

Synnott, D.M. [1977]. Progress in Irish Bryology: Hepaticae. Unpublished typescript, 66 pp.

Synnott, D.M. 1978. The bryophyte herbarium of Henry William Lett in the Herbarium, National Botanic Gardens, Glasnevin. *Glasra* **2**: 43–48.

Synnott, D.[M.] 1979. Bryophytes. pp. 146–148. In: Booth, E.M. *The Flora of County Carlow*. Dublin: Royal Dublin Society.

Synnott, D.M. 1980. A catalogue of collectors in the bryophyte herbarium, National Botanic Gardens, Glasnevin (DBN). *Glasra* **4**: 17–30.

Synnott, D.[M.] 1982. An outline of the bryophytes of Meath and Westmeath. *Glasra* **6**: 1–71.

Synnott, D.[M]. 1983a. *Anoectangium warburgii* – a new Irish moss. *Irish Naturalists' Journal* **21**: 91–92.

Synnott, D.[M]. 1983b. *Barbula icmadophila* Schimp. ex C. Muell. – a delayed addition to the Irish moss flora. *Irish Naturalists' Journal* **21**: 177–178.

Synnott, D.[M]. 1984. The bryological collection of Arnold Patrick Fanning (1905–1980). *Irish Naturalists' Journal* **21**: 233–235.

Synnott, D.[M.] 1988. The summer meeting, 1987, Co. Mayo. First week in Achill Island: 5–12 August. *Bulletin of the British Bryological Society* **51**: 7–10.

Synnott, D.M. 1990a. The bryophytes of Achill Island – a preliminary note. *Glasra* N.S., **1**: 21–26.

Synnott, D.M. 1990b. The bryophytes of Lambay Island. *Glasra* N.S., **1**: 65–81.

Synnott, D.M. & Robinson, D.W. 1989. The moss *Trichostomopsis umbrosa* (C.Müll.) Robins. in Ireland. *Irish Naturalists' Journal* **23**: 113–114.

Synnott, D.M. & Robinson, D.W. 1990. The moss *Trichostomopsis umbrosa* (C.Mueller) H.Robinson in Ireland. *Glasra* **1**: 15–19.

Teleganova, V.V. & Ignatov, M.S. 2008. ['2007']. On the reproductive biology of *Ptilium crista-castrensis* (Pylaisiaceae, Bryophyta). *Arctoa* **16**: 87–98.

Thiers, B. 2010. *Index Herbariorum: A global directory of public herbaria and associated staff.* New York Botanical Garden's Virtual Herbarium. http://sweetgum.nybg.org/ih/

Thingsgaard, K. 2003. New national and regional bryophyte records, 8. *Journal of Bryology* **25**: 219.

Threlkeld, C. 1726. *Synopsis Stirpium Hibernicarum.* Dublin. (Reproduced with introduction by E.C. Nelson, Kilkenny: Boethius Press, 1988).

Touw, A. & Rubers, W.V. 1989. *De Nederlandse bladmossen.* Utrecht: Stichting Uitgeverij van de Koninklijke Nederlandse Natuurhistorische Vereniging.

Tsegmed, Ts. 2001. Checklist and distribution of mosses in Mongolia. *Arctoa* **10**: 1–18.

Turner, D. 1804. *Muscologiae Hibernicae Spicilegium.* Great Yarmouth & London. Facsimile reprint (ed. J.L. De Sloover), Namur, Belgium: Presses Universitaires de Namur.

Uyar, G. & Çetin, B. 2004. A new check-list of the mosses of Turkey. *Journal of Bryology* **26**: 203–220.

van der Velde, M. & Bijlsma, R. 2000. Amount and structure of intra- and interspecific genetic variation in the moss genus *Polytrichum. Heredity* **85**: 328–337.

van Groenendael, J.M., Hochstenbach, S.M.H., van Mansfeld, M.J.M. & Roozen, A.J.M. 1979. *The Influence of the sea and of parent material on wetlands and blanket bog in West Connemara, Ireland.* Unpublished MSc thesis, Department of Geobotany, Catholic University, Nijmegen, 180 pp.

van Melick, H. 1986. *Scopelophila cataractae* (Mitt.) Broth. ook in Nederland. *Lindbergia* **12**: 163–165.

van Zanten, B.O., 2003. *Sematophyllum substrumulosum* (Hampe) Britt. nieuw voor Nederland en eerste vondst van *Lophocolea semiteres* in Drenthe. *Buxbaumiella* **63**: 7–13.

van Zanten, B.O. & Pócs, T. 1981. Distribution and dispersal of bryophytes. *Advances in Bryology* **1**: 479–562.

Váňa, J. 1988. *Cephalozia* (Dum.) Dum. in Africa, with notes on the genus. *Beiheft zur Nova Hedwigia* **90**: 179–198.

Vanderpoorten, A. 2004. A simple taxonomic treatment for a complicated evolutionary story: the genus *Hygroamblystegium* (Hypnales, Amblystegiaceae). *Monographs in Systematic Botany from the Missouri Botanical Garden* **98**: 320–327.

Vanderpoorten, A. & Hedenäs, L. 2009. New combinations in the Amblystegiaceae. *Journal of Bryology* **31**: 129–132.

Vanderpoorten, A., Hedenäs, L., Cox, C.J. & Shaw, A.J. 2002. Circumscription, phylogenetic relationships and taxonomy of Amblystegiaceae inferred from nr and cpDNA sequence data and morphology. *Taxon* **51**: 115–122.

Vitt, D.H. 1973. A revision of the genus *Orthotrichum* in North America, north of Mexico. *Bryophytorum Bibliotheca* **1**: 1–208 + 59 pl.

Wade, W. 1804. Plantae rariores in Hibernia inventae. *Transactions Dublin Society* **4**: i–xiv, 1–214.

Wallace, E.C. 1952. The British Bryological Society's Field Meeting in Co. Kerry, 1951. *Irish Naturalists' Journal* **10**: 259–263.

Wallace, E.C. 1963. The Summer Meeting in Ireland, 1962. *Transactions of the British Bryological Society* **4**: 531–534.

Wallace, E.C. 1971. An *Eriopus* in Sussex. *Transactions of the British Bryological Society* **6**: 327–328.

Walsh, L. 2001. *Heavy metal concentrations in the soil substrates associated with rare bryophytes at former metalliferous mining sites in East Cornwall.* Research project report submitted as part requirement for the degree of BSc in Environmental Studies, University of Hertfordshire. (62 pp., unpublished).

Warburg, E.F. 1958a. *Meesia tristicha* Bruch & Schimp. in the British Isles. *Transactions of the British Bryological Society* **3**: 378–381.

Warburg, E.F. 1958b. New vice-county records, Musci. *Transactions of the British Bryological Society* **3**: 471–490.

Warburg, E.F. 1963a. *Census catalogue of British mosses (3rd edition).* Ipswich: British Bryological Society.

Warburg, E.F. 1963b. Notes on the bryophytes of Achill Island. *Irish Naturalists' Journal* **14**: 139–145.

Warburg, E.F. 1965. *Pohlia pulchella* in Britain. *Transactions of the British Bryological Society* **4**: 760–762.

Watson, E.V. 1971. *The structure and life of bryophytes.* 3rd ed. London: Hutchinson University Library.

Watson, H.C. 1852. *Cybele Britannica.* Vol. 3. London.

Watson, H.C. 1883. *Topographical Botany.* 2nd ed. London: Bernard Quaritch.

Watson, W. 1936. Report of the Annual Meeting, 1935. *The British Bryological Society Report for 1935* **3**: 263–265.

Watson, W. 1937. British Bryological Society at Killarney, 1935. List of records. *Irish Naturalists' Journal* **6**: 161–165.

Watts, W.A. 1984. Contemporary accounts of the Killarney woods 1580–1870. *Irish Geography* **17**: 1–13.

Welch, W.H. 1960. *A monograph of the Fontinalaceae.* The Hague: Martinus Nijhoff.

Werner, J. 2002. A comparison of *Dichodontium flavescens* (Dicks.) Lindb. and *D. pellucidum* (Hedw.) Lindb. (Bryopsida). *Journal of Bryology* **24**: 215–221.

Werner, J. 2003. Liste rouge des bryophytes du Luxembourg. *Ferrantia* **35**:1–71.

Werner, O., Patiño, J., González-Mancebo, J.M., Almeida Gabriel, R.M. de & Ros, R.M. 2009. The taxonomic status and the geographical relationships of the Macaronesian endemic moss *Fissidens luisieri* (Fissidentaceae) based on DNA sequence data. *Bryologist* **112**: 315–324.

Werner, O., Ros, R.M. & Grundmann, M. 2005. Molecular phylogeny of Trichostomoideae (Pottiaceae, Bryophyta) based on nrITS data. *Taxon* **54**: 361–368.

Werner, O., Ros, R.M., Guerra, J. & Cano, M.J. 2004. Inter-Simple Sequence Repeat (ISSR) markers support the species status of *Weissia wimmeriana* (Sendtn.) Bruch & Schimp. (Pottiaceae, Bryopsida). *Cryptogamie, Bryologie* **25**: 137–146.

West, R.G. 2000. *Plant life of the Quaternary cold stages.* Cambridge: Cambridge University Press.

White, J. 1982. A history of Irish vegetation studies. *Journal of Life Sciences of the Royal Dublin Society* **3**: 15–42.

White, J. 1985. The Gearagh Woodland, Co. Cork. *Irish Naturalists' Journal* **21**: 391–396.

White, J. & Doyle, G.J. 1982. The vegetation of Ireland: a catalogue raisonné. *Journal of Life Sciences of the Royal Dublin Society* **3**: 289–368.

Whitehouse, H.L.K. 1963. *Bryum riparium* Hagen in the British Isles. *Transactions of the British Bryological Society* **4**: 389–403.

Whitehouse, H.L.K. 1973. The occurrence of tubers in *Pohlia pulchella* (Hedw.) Lindb. and *Pohlia lutescens* (Limpr.) Lindb. fil. *Journal of Bryology* **7**: 533–540.

Whitehouse, H.L.K. 1976. *Ditrichum pusillum* (Hedw.) Brit. in arable fields. *Journal of Bryology* **9**: 7–11.

Whitehouse, H.L.K. 1987. Protoncma-gemmae in European mosses. *Symposia Biologica Hungarica* **35**: 227–231.

Whitehouse, H.[L.K.] 1995. Summer Field Meeting, 1994, First week, The Burren. *Bulletin of the British Bryological Society* **65**: 8–12.

Whitehouse, H.L.K. 2001. Bryophytes of arable fields in Québec and Slovakia, including new records of *Bryum demaretianum* Arts. *Lindbergia* **26**: 29–32.

Whitehouse, H.L.K. & Crundwell, A.C. 1991. *Gymnostomum calcareum* Nees & Hornsch. and allied plants in Europe, North Africa and the Middle East. *Journal of Bryology* **16**: 561–579.

Whitehouse, H.L.K. & Crundwell, A.C. 1992. *Gymnostomum calcareum* Nees & Hornsch. and *G. viridulum* Brid. in Europe, North Africa and the Middle East. *Bulletin of the British Bryological Society* **59**: 35–50.

Whitehouse, H.L.K. & During, H.J. 1987. *Leptobarbula berica* (De Not.) Schimp. in Belgium and the Netherlands. *Lindbergia* **12**: 135–138.

Wickett, N.J. & Goffinet, B. 2008. Origin and relationships of the myco-heterotrophic liverwort *Cryptothallus mirabilis* Malmb. (Metzgeriales, Marchantiophyta). *Botanical Journal of the Linnean Society* **156**: 1–12.

Wigginton, M.J. & Grolle, R. 1996. Catalogue of the Hepaticae and Anthocerotae of sub-Saharan Africa. *Bryophytorum Bibliotheca* **48**: 1–267.

Williams, R.S. 1913. Dicranaceae. In: N.L. Britton *et al.* (eds) *North American Flora.* New York. **15**: 77–158.

Wilson, A. 1930. *A Census Catalogue of British Hepatics, with List of the Botanical Vice-Counties and their boundaries and lists of Sources of Records. Compiled for the British Bryological Society (Formerly The Moss Exchange Club) …* 3rd ed. Berwick-on-Tweed: Martin's Printing Works, for BBS.

W.[ilson], A. 1935. British Bryological Society. Census Catalogue of British Hepatics (3rd Edition, 1930) [supplementary records], 3 pp. in *The British Bryological Society. Supplements to Census Catalogue of British Mosses (2nd Edition), and Census Catalogue of British Hepatics (3rd Edition).* Berwick-on-Tweed: Martin's Printing Works, for BBS.

Wilson, W. 1855. *Bryologia Brittanica; containing the mosses of Great Britain and Ireland, …* London: Longman, Brown, Green, and Longmans.

Wiltshire, E. 1995. The mosses and liverworts of Foynes Island and adjacent mainland, Co. Limerick (H8). *Irish Naturalists' Journal* **25**: 123–128.

World Conservation Union. 1994. *IUCN Red List categories.* Gland: International Union for the Conservation of Nature. Wu Peng-cheng, Crosby, M.R. & Si He 2002. *Moss flora of China. English version. Vol. 6. Hookeriaceae–Thuidiaceae.* Beijing & New York: Science Press, St Louis: Missouri Botanical Garden Press.

Yamada, K. 1995. *Radula carringtonii* (Hepaticae, Radulaceae) new to the New World. *Fragmenta Floristica et Geobotanica* **40**: 123–126.

Zander, R.H. 1993. Genera of the Pottiaceae: mosses of harsh environments. *Bulletin of the Buffalo Society of Natural Sciences* **32**: 1–378.

Zhao, Dong-Ping; Bai, Xue-Liang; Wang, Li-Hong and Zhao, Na. 2009. *Microbryum* (Pottiaceae) in mainland China. *Bryologist* **112**: 337–341.

Zhao, Dong-Ping; Bai, Xue-Liang; Wang, Xian-Dao & Jing, Hui-Min. 2006. Bryophyte flora of Helan Mountain in China. *Arctoa* **15**: 219–235.

Zolotov, V.I. 2006. On systematics and distribution of some species of *Bryum* (Bryaceae, Bryophyta) in Russia. *Arctoa* **15**: 155–162.

TAXON INDEX

Page numbers are in bold type for the main account of each taxon treated in detail, including those with short accounts and taxa in Appendix I. Trees and shrubs are indexed under English names, other vascular plants under their scientific names.

GENERAL INDEX (people, places and topics)

Locality and other place names are given separately for names of Important Bryophyte Areas (IBrA) and those of official Protected Areas (ASSI, NHA, pNHA, SAC, Nature Reserves)

Aasleagh 208, 463, 464
Abbotstown 481, 485
Achill Island ix, 2, 3, 40, 42, 56, 59, 60, 62, 136, 137, 182, 187, 189, 208, 209, 220, 221, 240, 246, 247, 248, 260, 261, 268, 381, 382, 396, 429, 458, 463, 470, 473, 477, 494, 537, 561
Achill Island and Corraun Plateau IBrA 112, 113, 136, 137, 144
acidophile bryophytes 22
Adare 410
Addroon Bridge 152
Adrigole 457, 516
afforestation, as threat 36, 40
Aghaderg Glebe 543
Aghadunvane 34, 296, 310, 313, 344, 397, 416
Aghahoorin 257
Aghavogil 508
Agher Bog 219
Aghla More 321
Agnew's Hill 299
agricultural restructuring, as threat 42
Ahoghill 55
Aillebrack 182, 458
Albert, Duke of Saxony 50
alien bryophytes 7
alien plants, invasive (see also under Rhododendron) 45
Allihies 47, 164, 185, 229, 230, 233, 359, 360, 361, 386, 387, 501
Allihies IBrA 112, 113, 164
Allison, G.H. 477
Allorge, V. 58
Altalacky River 501, 502
Altidore Glen 181
Altscraghy 305
An Loch Dubh 31, 181, 196, 200, 236
An Loch Geal 200
An Loch Iochtarach 328
Annacoona 34, 35, 96, 296, 297, 344, 397, 483, 508
Annageeragh Bridge 307, 308
Annaghmore Lough 45, 475
Annamoe 454
anthropogenic habitats 7, 46
Antrim Glens 122
Antrim Hills and Glens IBrA 112, 113, 122
Antrim Reservoirs IBrA 112, 113, 126
Appleyard, Joan viii, 551
aquatic habitats, threats 45
arable land, see tillage
Aran Islands 20, 396, 489
Archies Bridge 316, 317
Ardagh 266
Ardaloo 429
Ardara 458, 459
Ardee Bog 510, 511
Ardee Cutaway Bog pNHA 511
Ardmore 54, 510, 543
Ardmore Glebe 540
Ardnagragh 514, 515
Ardnamona 210

Ards Peninsula 422
Ardtully 160, 307, 308
Ardtully Bridge 306
Argent, George viii
Argory, The 449, 450
Arklow 61, 379
Armitage, Eleonora 53, 57
Arroo Mountain SAC 128, 296, 310, 313, 344, 398, 416, 508, 586
Ashton 485
Assaroe Lake 307, 308
Athlone 61
Athy 419
Atlantic bryophytes 2
atlas recording 63–64
Aughaloge Bridge 389
Aughrim 50
Aughrim Lough 326
Averis, Ben 213
Bacon, A.S. 56
Bagenalstown 415, 429
Baker's Bridge 404
Baldoyle 451
Balgriffin 419
Ballaghbeama Gap 181, 196, 197, 201, 205, 237, 253, 409, 461, 516
Ballaghdacker Lough 177
Ballard 429
Ballinabarney Bridge 542, 543
Ballinaboy 144
Ballinascorney Gap 540
Ballinderry 224, 392
Ballindooly Castle Fen 68
Ballinhassig Glen 181, 291, 461
Ballinlig 344
Ballinrobe 429
Ballinskelligs Bay and Inny Estuary SAC 184, 586
Ballintober 138, 451, 452
Ballintoy 218
Ballinturly Turlough 523
Ballinturly Turlough SAC 524, 586
Ballsbridge 413, 414
Ballyarr Wood SAC 119
Ballybarney Bridge 150
Ballycastle 363
Ballyconneelly 40, 473
Ballycorey Bridge 152
Ballycorus 150, 229, 362
Ballycotton Cliffs 38, 166, 424, 425, 540, 541
Ballycotton Cliffs IBrA 112, 113, 166
Ballycoyle 150, 217, 218
Ballycroy National Park 134, 380, 409, 494, 525, 531, 591
Ballycurragh 150, 558
Ballydonohoe House 351
Ballyduff 181
Ballyfin 422
Ballyfinnane Bridge 198
Ballygalley Head 457
Ballyglass turlough 406

Ballykeenan 155, 451, 452
Ballyknockan 429
Ballylickey 51
Ballymacart Bridge 348
Ballymacart River 348
Ballymacash 392, 485
Ballymaclary 182, 527, 528, 532, 534
Ballymaclary Nature Reserve 184, 524, 528, 532, 534, 553, 590
Ballymaghan 481
Ballymore Eustace 307, 308, 394
Ballynagrenia and Ballinderry Bog NHA 225, 589
Ballynahone Bog 17
Ballynerroon East 449
Ballyness Bay SAC 114, 471, 586
Ballyogan Bridge 152, 315, 316
Ballyreagh Wood 150
Ballyseedy Wood 573
Ballyshannon 307, 308, 350, 351
Ballysitteragh 196, 250
Ballysmuttan 280
Ballyteigelia Bridge 322
Ballyvaughan 542, 543
Ballyvergan Marsh pNHA 421, 589
Ballyvoyle Head to Tramore pNHA 229, 501, 589
Ballywaltrim Lane 401, 402
Balmoral 53
Baltray 410, 411
Banagher 377
Banagher Glen 238, 266, 337
Bann Estuary 470, 481
Banna 182
Bantry 51, 189, 213, 221, 232, 254, 457, 464
Bantry House Grounds 568
Barnanageehy Valley 514
Barnesmore Bog NHA 287
Barnesmore Gap 287
Barnynagappul Strand 473
Baronscourt 499
Barrigone 351, 352
Barry Beg 523, 524
Barry, T. A. viii
BBS 49, 53, 54–64
BBS atlas recording 63–64
BBS Census Catalogues 63–64
BBS Field Meetings in Ireland 55–63, 66
BBSUK herbarium 61, 70, 387, 484, 571, 572, 573
Beara Peninsula 164
Bearstown 155, 231, 510, 511
Beenkeragh 161, 206, 237, 250, 251, 371
Beennaman 328
BEL herbarium 59, 70
Belcoo 59
Belfast 51, 52, 53, 55, 56, 58, 191, 227, 291, 305, 311, 314, 342, 358, 382, 432, 437, 449, 481
Belfast Deerpark 301
Belfast Harbour 335, 336
Belfast Mountains 367